THE OXFORD HISTORY OF THE BRITISH EMPIRE

THE OXFORD HISTORY OF THE BRITISH EMPIRE

Volume I. *The Origins of Empire*
EDITED BY Nicholas Canny

Volume II. *The Eighteenth Century*
EDITED BY P. J. Marshall

Volume III. *The Nineteenth Century*
EDITED BY Andrew Porter

Volume IV. *The Twentieth Century*
EDITED BY Judith M. Brown and Wm. Roger Louis

Volume V. *Historiography*
EDITED BY Robin W. Winks

THE OXFORD HISTORY OF THE BRITISH EMPIRE

Wm. Roger Louis, CBE, D.Litt., FBA

Kerr Professor of English History and Culture, University of Texas, Austin and Honorary Fellow of St Antony's College, Oxford

EDITOR-IN-CHIEF

VOLUME V

Historiography

Robin W. Winks, Ph.D.

Townsend Professor of History, Yale University

EDITOR

Alaine Low, D.Phil.

ASSOCIATE EDITOR

OXFORD UNIVERSITY PRESS

OXFORD
UNIVERSITY PRESS

Great Clarendon Street, Oxford OX2 6DP

Oxford University Press is a department of the University of Oxford.
It furthers the University's objective of excellence in research, scholarship,
and education by publishing worldwide in

Oxford New York

Athens Auckland Bangkok Bogotá Buenos Aires Cape Town
Chennai Dar es Salaam Delhi Florence Hong Kong Istanbul Karachi
Kolkata Kuala Lumpur Madrid Melbourne Mexico City Mumbai Nairobi
Paris São Paulo Shanghai Singapore Taipei Tokyo Toronto Warsaw

with associated companies in Berlin Ibadan

Oxford is a registered trade mark of Oxford University Press
in the UK and in certain other countries

Published in the United States
by Oxford University Press Inc., New York

First published 1999
First published in paperback 2001

British Library Cataloguing in Publication Data
Data available

Library of Congress Cataloging in Publication Data
Data applied for

ISBN 0-19-820566-X (V. 5) Hbk

ISBN 0-19-924680-7 (V. 5) Pbk

1 3 5 7 9 10 8 6 4 2

Typeset in Minion
by Cambrian Typesetters, Frimley, Surrey
Printed in Great Britain
on acid-free paper by
Bookcraft Ltd
Midsomer Norton, Somerset

The Editor-in-Chief and Editors of the *Oxford History of the British Empire* acknowledge with gratitude support from

The Rhodes Trust

The National Endowment for Humanities, Washington, DC

St Antony's College, Oxford

The University of Texas at Austin

FOREWORD

From the founding of the colonies in North America and the West Indies in the seventeenth century to the reversion of Hong Kong to China at the end of the twentieth, British imperialism was a catalyst for far-reaching change. British domination of indigenous peoples in North America, Asia, and Africa can now be seen more clearly as part of the larger and dynamic interaction of European and non-Western societies. Though the subject remains ideologically charged, the passions aroused by British imperialism have so lessened that we are now better placed than ever before to see the course of the Empire steadily and to see it whole. At this distance in time the Empire's legacy from earlier centuries can be assessed, in ethics and economics as well as politics, with greater discrimination. At the close of the twentieth century, the interpretation of the dissolution of the Empire can benefit from evolving perspectives on, for example, the end of the cold war. In still larger sweep, the *Oxford History of the British Empire* as a comprehensive study helps to understand the end of the Empire in relation to its beginning, the meaning of British imperialism for the ruled as well as the rulers, and the significance of the British Empire as a theme in world history.

It is nearly half a century since the last volume in the large-scale *Cambridge History of the British Empire* was completed. In the meantime the British Empire has been dismantled and only fragments such as Gibraltar and the Falklands, Bermuda and Pitcairn, remain of an Empire that once stretched over a quarter of the earth's surface. The general understanding of the British imperial experience has been substantially widened in recent decades by the work of historians of Asia and Africa as well as Britain. Earlier histories, though by no means all, tended to trace the Empire's evolution and to concentrate on how it was governed. To many late-Victorian historians the story of the Empire meant the rise of worldwide dominion and Imperial rule, above all in India. Historians in the first half of the twentieth century tended to emphasize constitutional developments and the culmination of the Empire in the free association of the Commonwealth. The *Oxford History of the British Empire* takes a wider approach. It does not depict the history of the Empire as one of purposeful progress through four hundred years, nor does it concentrate narrowly on metropolitan authority and rule. It does attempt to explain how varying conditions in Britain interacted with those in many other parts of the world to create both a constantly changing territorial Empire and ever-shifting patterns of social and economic relations. The *Oxford History of the British Empire* thus deals with the impact of British imperialism on dependent peoples in a broader sense than was usually attempted in earlier historical writings while it also takes into account the significance of the Empire for the Irish, the Scots, and the Welsh as well as the English.

The volume on historiography deals with the evolving or changing interpretations of history of the British Empire, with the legacy of historical writing, and with today's perspectives on previous scholarship. It is concerned with the ways the history of British imperialism has been written from one generation of historians to the next. The volume is especially dedicated to the period in which British Imperial history developed as an academic discipline. It thus addresses itself mainly to how historians in the past one hundred years or so have dealt with the subject, though individual chapters take into account early works on British expansion and colonization. Historians from the eighteenth century generally took pride in the Empire. They believed, as is clear from their writings on British settlements spreading across the world, that Britain had a destiny to be a 'Greater Britain' beyond the seas and a duty, particularly in India, to govern 'less fortunate peoples'. The academic historians—notably those in Cambridge, Oxford, and London who created the *English Historical Review* in 1886—rebelled against the romantic view of the Empire held by earlier writers, but these late-Victorian historians also believed in progress and the moral validity of British rule no less than their predecessors. Whatever its assumptions, professional history emerged in the decades before the First World War in a form recognizable today with such themes as migration, commercial regulation, and defence, and with footnotes citing sources at the Public Record Office. By 1914, for example, a clear concept had taken shape of the commercial system of the 'First British Empire' in North America, the West Indies, and Ireland. How long the system lasted, and at what point it gave way to that of a 'Second British Empire' in India and the East remained a subject of ongoing historical research and controversy.

If historiography is, in a sense, the art of explaining why historians wrote as they did at certain times, it is useful to bear in mind that all history reflects the period in which it was written. In the decades before the First World War, British historians wrote against the background of economic and military competition among the European powers. They tended to project back into earlier periods the subjects of contemporary debate such as free trade versus the proposal for economic protection known as Imperial Preference. The South African or Boer War at the turn of the century caused journalists, and eventually historians, to ponder the economic causes of war. At about this time the idea of 'colonial nationalism' in the colonies of white settlement and India began prominently to emerge in historical writing. The two themes of economic imperialism and nationalism help in turn to explain the economic and constitutional preoccupations of historians in the inter-war period. According to the main current of historical interpretation, which flowed in the same direction as Sir Frederick Lugard's *The Dual Mandate* published in 1922, the indigenous inhabitants would be protected against economic exploitation, and those administering the colonies would be held accountable to Parliament. Historians such as Sir Reginald Coupland, who perhaps as much as anyone represented the trends in British historial writing in the era before the Second World War, believed that nationalist aspirations could be fulfilled within the constitutional structure of the Empire.

In still another sense historiography is the art of depicting historical controversy. From the late nineteenth century, historians clashed on whether or not the system of self-government in the colonies of white settlement could be reconciled with 'despotism' in India and more generally with British rule in Asia and Africa. Other broad areas of controversy included the nature of what is now called the colonial state, and the responsibilities of the British government. Could nationalist demands in India, or for that matter in Australia, be reconciled with the aspiration to unite and federate the Empire? To what extent did historical research demonstrate the need for state intervention in local economies to promote economic development and welfare, as argued for example in W. M. Macmillan's *Warning from the West Indies* published in 1936? Macmillan pursued a line of analysis not incompatible with Marxist thought, and he inspired dissent from the assumptions of Coupland and others who believed that the British Empire had the moral capacity to shape a better world and to help dependent peoples advance towards self-government. There was thus a divide between historians affirming the benevolent purpose of the Empire and those denouncing, both implicitly and explicitly, British imperialism as exploitative and ruthless. Even radical historians, however, usually did not want so much to abolish the Empire as to reform it and make it more accountable. The acrimony among historians supporting or attacking the Empire before the Second World War was as acute as that between Imperial historians and Africanists, and historians representing other area studies, in the generation of the 1960s.

Historiography may also be regarded as the way certain historians have left a mark on the subject. As may be inferred from the number of references to the articles of John Gallagher and Ronald Robinson, and to their book, *Africa and the Victorians*, published in 1961, it is no exaggeration to say that these two historians brought about a conceptual revolution. They did so essentially in three ways. They presented an argument that denied the sharp breaks in the chronological periods upheld by most previous historians (who had emphasized substantial changes of attitude, for example, between the mid- and late-Victorian periods), and they insisted on a continuity of the forces of imperialism throughout the nineteenth century and indeed the twentieth. Next, by putting forward an interpretation of 'informal empire' of trade and commerce and degrees of informal political control in such places as China, the Middle East, and Latin America, they gave expanded meaning and coherence to the concept of a worldwide British 'Imperial system'. Last, they attempted to destroy the traditional historiographical assumption that the springs of European expansion lay wholly within Europe. From Robinson and Gallagher onwards, the history of British imperialism would be the history of the interaction between the British and indigenous peoples. In the last point lies the significance of the historiographical revolution of the 1950s and 1960s.

Finally, historiography may be viewed as the study of trends in interpretation. It would appear that historians from the 1970s onwards have been no less swayed by contemporary affairs than historians of previous generations and no less inclined to project the problems of the present into earlier eras. In the last three decades, historians of the Empire have demonstrated an interest in globalization and national cultures that reflects general intellectual preoccupations of the latter part of the twentieth century. Post-colonial historians often assume, for example, that there is a continuing colonial hegemony, cultural as well as economic, over Asia, Africa, and other parts of the world that must be broken if former colonial subjects are truly to be liberated. Such assumptions are just as teleological as any in the past, but in any event historians and other scholars with such interests have invigorated the general field of the history of the British Empire. Looking at the subject over a period of centuries, it is clear that there is no danger that interest in the history of British imperialism is waning, and no crisis in the historiography. The field can only benefit from areas studies, literary criticism, and cultural studies. As this volume makes clear, the historiography of the British Empire is as diverse and rich as ever before as it approaches the next millennium.

A special feature of the series is the Select Bibliography of key works at the end of each chapter. They are not intended to be comprehensive bibliographical or historiographical guides but rather they list useful and informative works on the themes of each chapter.

The Editor-in-Chief and Editors acknowledge, with immense gratitude, support from the Rhodes Trust, the National Endowment for the Humanities in Washington, DC, St Antony's College, Oxford, and the University of Texas at Austin. We have received further specific support from Lord Dahrendorf, former Warden of St Antony's College, Oxford; Sheldon Ekland-Olson, former Dean of Liberal Arts, now Provost, at the University of Texas; and, for the preparation of maps, the University Cooperative Society. Mr Iain Sproat helped to inspire the project and provided financial assistance for the initial organizational conference.

It is also a true pleasure to thank our patrons Mr and Mrs Alan Spencer of Hatfield Regis Grange, Mr and Mrs Sam Jamot Brown of Durango, Colorado, and Mr and Mrs Baine Kerr of Houston, Texas. Our last word of gratitude is to Dr Alaine Low, the Associate Editor, whose dedication to the project has been characterized by indefatigable efficiency and meticulous care.

Wm. Roger Louis

PREFACE

History is, minimally, three things: what happened in the past, what people believe happened in the past, and what historians say happened in the past. Historiography is largely about the second and third of these definitions of history. It is in this sense an adventure in the history of ideas, the study of how a subject has been written about, how trends and interests in research have changed, how public events, world affairs, and so simple a matter as the opening of an archive shapes the way in which writers explore the past. Historiography is also about how and why a people have come to comprehend themselves in a certain way. Historiography is thus more than the record of what has been written. It is also the examination of why a body of writing has taken the shape it has.

Historians seek patterns in the events of the past, historiographers, patterns in the interpretation of historical writing. One of the most illuminating aspects of historiography is its application to subjects that are historically contentious: subjects in which outlines of debate have been altered substantially or redefined. Some fields of study have seen great shifts in popular and scholarly perceptions of the subject and its significance. In the study of imperialism as well as in the related fields of race relations and slavery, developments have been far-reaching because of interdisciplinary debate.

Few aspects of modern history have grown so rapidly in sheer bulk of literature, or have encountered so many changes in interpretation, as the history of the British Empire and Commonwealth. Originally viewed as related dimensions of constitutional, economic, and military history, the study of imperialism and of empires expanded so greatly as a coherent subject that by the 1960s it seemed to break into its component parts. This fragmentation was due in part to the specialization in 'area studies' devoted to Asia, Africa and elsewhere, and also to the influence of methodologies from other fields. Disciplines such as literary criticism and cultural studies have contributed in recent decades to a greater understanding of the Empire's history. The expansion of the subject itself into many disciplines should not deter the historiographer from charting its controversial course. The British Empire-Commonwealth historian has an obligation to bridge these gaps. The historian stands central to the growth of interdisciplinary and comparative studies.

The study of the British Empire fell into decline in the 1960s and 1970s. In an era of political activism, the traditional subject of Imperial history, at least to much of the scholarly world, seemed to be associated with outdated notions and antiquated ideals. In the late nineteenth century many besides Cecil Rhodes could declare that they were proud to be called Imperialists; but few would claim such pride by the 1960s. Today, half the population of the United Kingdom has been born after the collapse of the British Empire and their impressions have been shaped in part by the fact and fiction derived from the popular press, film, and contemporary world-views. We now can place these developments in historiographical perspective. The focus of scholarly study shifted from the metropolitan centre to the periphery. When area studies in Asia and Africa seemed to overtake Imperial studies in the 1960s, there was a flowering of scholarship by historians based in universities in India and Africa. At the end of the twentieth century colonial and Imperial studies are once again of central concern for British historiography as well as that of Asia and Africa. The numerous post-colonial assessments of the British Empire attest to the renewed interest in colonial rule and in the Empire's origins and consequences. The ongoing historiographical debate is vigorous.

This volume comprises forty-one chapters, each by an authority in his or her field. There will be readers whose main interest is bibliography. The bibliographies that accompany the chapters are intended to provide a guide to significant books in each field of specialization. The chronology is intended to chart the most important events in the historiography and to place them in the historical context.

The organization of the volume is chronological, thematic, and regional. The opening chapters survey the historiography of the Empire from its origins through the period of the American revolution and the founding of the British Raj in India. Thematic chapters in this part of the volume include those dealing with exploration and empire, science and medicine, gender, slavery and the slave trade, and missions and empire. Further themes are developed in the chapters on the Scramble for Africa, the Royal Navy and the Empire, and issues of defence and the origins of the two world wars. Throughout the volume runs the theme of the Commonwealth as the successor to the Empire. The dimension of the Dominions is represented in separate chapters on Ireland, Canada, Australia, New Zealand, and, in the context of southern Africa, South Africa.

The regional chapters include separate accounts of the historiography of the West Indies, the Pacific Islands, and particular attention is devoted in several chapters to the problems of India, Pakistan, and Ceylon. South-East Asia is dealt with in the comparative perspective of the other major colonial powers in the region, France, the Netherlands, and Japan. The theme 'informal empire' emerges especially in the chapters on the Middle East, China, and Latin America. The historiography of British colonial rule in Africa is dealt with in a survey chapter and in individual chapters on western, eastern, and southern Africa. The issues of decolonization are drawn together in a separate chapter. The chapters towards the end of the volume emphasize such themes as art and architecture. Issues such as colonial discourse theory as well as economic development are here given specific attention. The last chapters include a reflection on the fundamental issues in the historiography of the Empire and on where we stand today.

R. W. W.

CONTENTS

List of Contributors

1. Introduction *Wm. Roger Louis* 1
2. The First British Empire *P. J. Marshall* 43
3. The Second British Empire *C. A. Bayly* 54
4. British North America in the Seventeenth and Eighteenth Centuries *Stephen Foster* 73
5. The American Revolution *Doron Ben-Atar* 94
6. Ireland *David Harkness* 114
7. The British West Indies *B. W. Higman* 134
8. Canada and the Empire *D. R. Owram* 146
9. Australia and the Empire *Stuart Macintyre* 163
10. Colonization and History in New Zealand *James Belich* 182
11. India to 1858 *Robert E. Frykenberg* 194
12. India, 1858 to the 1930s *Tapan Raychaudhuri* 214
13. India in the 1940s *Robin J. Moore* 231
14. Ceylon (Sri Lanka) *K. M. de Silva* 243
15. Pakistan's Emergence *Ian Talbot* 253
16. Science, Medicine, and the British Empire *Richard Drayton* 264
17. Disease, Diet, and Gender: Late Twentieth-Century Perspectives on Empire *Diana Wylie* 277
18. Exploration and Empire *Robert A. Stafford* 290
19. Missions and Empire *Norman Etherington* 303
20. Slavery, the Slave Trade, and Abolition *Gad Heuman* 315
21. The Royal Navy and the British Empire *Barry M. Gough* 327
22. Imperial Defence *David Killingray* 342
23. The Empire-Commonwealth and the Two World Wars *Ritchie Ovendale* 354

24. Imperial Flotsam? The British in the Pacific Islands
Bronwen Douglas 366

25. Formal and Informal Empire in East Asia *C. M. Turnbull* 379

26. The British Empire in South-East Asia *Nicholas Tarling* 403

27. Formal and Informal Empire in the Middle East *Peter Sluglett* 416

28. Informal Empire in Latin America *Rory Miller* 437

29. Britain and the Scramble for Africa *John E. Flint* 450

30. The British Empire in Tropical Africa: A Review of the Literature to the 1960s *A. D. Roberts* 463

31. West Africa *Toyin Falola* 486

32. East Africa: Metropolitan Action and Local Initiative
Charles Ambler 500

33. Southern and Central Africa *William H. Worger* 513

34. Decolonization and the End of Empire *John Darwin* 541

35. The Commonwealth *W. David McIntyre* 558

36. Art and Empire *Jeffrey Auerbach* 571

37. Architecture in the British Empire *Thomas R. Metcalf* 584

38. Orients and Occidents: Colonial Discourse Theory and the Historiography of the British Empire *D. A. Washbrook* 596

39. The Shaping of Imperial History *A. P. Thornton* 612

40. Development and the Utopian Ideal, 1960–1999 *A. G. Hopkins* 635

41. The Future of Imperial History *Robin W. Winks* 653

Chronology 669

Index 701

LIST OF CONTRIBUTORS

CHARLES AMBLER (Ph.D., Yale) is Professor of History and Associate Vice-President for Graduate Studies at the University of Texas at El Paso. He is author of *Kenyan Communities in the Age of Imperialism*, and Editor, with Jonathan Crush, of *Liquor and Labor in Southern Africa*.

JEFFREY AUERBACH (Ph.D., Yale) is Lecturer and Humanities Fellow at Stanford University. He is the author of *The Great Exhibition of 1851: A Nation on Display* (forthcoming).

C. A. BAYLY (Litt.D., Cambridge) FBA is Vere Harmsworth Professor of Imperial and Naval History at Cambridge University. His books include *Rulers, Townsmen and Bazaars: North Indian Society in the Age of British Expansion, 1770–1870*; *Imperial Meridian: The British Empire and the World, 1780–1830*; and *Empire and Information: Intelligence Gathering and Social Communication in India, 1780–1870*.

JAMES BELICH (D.Phil., Oxford) is Professor of History at the University of Auckland. His books include *The New Zealand Wars and the Victorian Interpretation of Racial Conflict*, which won the Trevor Reese Memorial Prize; *I Shall Not Die: Titokowaru's War*; and *Making Peoples: A History of the New Zealanders, from Polynesian Settlement to the End of the Nineteenth Century*.

DORON BEN-ATAR (Ph.D., Columbia) is Associate Professor of History at Fordham University. He is the author of *The Origins of Jeffersonian Commercial Policy and Diplomacy*, and Editor, together with Barbara Oberg, of *Federalists Reconsidered*.

JOHN DARWIN (D.Phil., Oxford) is Beit Lecturer in the History of the British Commonwealth, Oxford University, and Fellow of Nuffield College. His books include *Britain, Egypt, and the Middle East: Imperial Policy in the Aftermath of War, 1918–1922*; and *Britain and Decolonisation: The Retreat from Empire in the Post-War World*.

BRONWEN DOUGLAS (Ph.D., Australian National University) is a Fellow in Pacific and Asian History, Australian National University. She is the author of *Across the Great Divide: Journeys in History and Anthropology*, and has published numerous articles on Oceania, with a particular focus on New Caledonia and

Vanuatu. She is writing a book on post-colonial histories in the South-West Pacific.

RICHARD DRAYTON (Ph.D., Yale) is Associate Professor of Modern British History at the University of Virgina. He is author of *Nature's Government: Kew Gardens, Science, and Imperial Britain, 1772–1903* (forthcoming). He is a contributor to Volume II of this series.

NORMAN ETHERINGTON (Ph.D., Yale) is Professor of History at the University of Western Australia and a Fellow of the Academy of the Social Sciences in Australia. His books include *Preachers, Peasants, and Politics in Southeast Africa*; *Theories of Imperialism: War, Conquest and Capital; Rider Haggard*; and *Peace, Politics, and Violence in the New South Africa.*

TOYIN FALOLA (Ph.D., Ife) is Professor of African History at the University of Texas at Austin. He is the author of *Yoruba Historiography*; and *Nigeria in the Twentieth Century* as well as articles in the *Journal of African History.* He has served as Editor of the *Journal of West African Studies* and is currently Joint Editor of *African Economic History.*

JOHN E. FLINT (Ph.D., London) is Professor Emeritus of History at Dalhousie University. He is the author of *Sir George Goldie and the Making of Nigeria*; *Nigeria and Ghana*; and *Cecil Rhodes.* He edited Volume V of *The Cambridge History of Africa.*

STEPHEN FOSTER (Ph.D., Yale) is Distinguished Research Professor at Northern Illinois University. He is the author of *Their Solitary Way: The Puritan Social Ethic in the First Century of Settlement in New England; The Long Argument: English Puritanism and the Shaping of New England Culture*; and *Notes from the Caroline Underground.*

ROBERT E. FRYKENBERG (Ph.D., London) is Professor of History at the University of Wisconsin. He is the author of *Guntur District, 1788–1848: A History of Local Influence and Central Authority in South India.* His edited books include *Land Control and Social Structure in Indian History; Land Tenure and Peasant in Asia;* and *Delhi Through the Ages.*

BARRY M. GOUGH (D.Lit., London) is Professor of History and University Research Professor, Wilfrid Laurier University, and Archives Fellow of Churchill

College, Cambridge. He has written extensively on the age of the Pax Britannica and on Canadian and international history. His books include *The Royal Navy and the Northwest Coast of North America*; and *Gunboat Frontier*.

W. TRAVIS HANES III (Ph.D., Texas), author of the chronology of this volume, is a Research Associate at the Center for Middle Eastern Studies, University of Texas at Austin. His publications include *Imperial Diplomacy in the Era of Decolonization: The Sudan and Anglo-Egyptian Relations, 1945–56*; and *World History: Continuity and Change*.

DAVID HARKNESS (Ph.D., Trinity College, Dublin) OBE is Emeritus Professor of Irish History at Queen's University Belfast. His books include *The Restless Dominion: The Irish Free State and the Commonwealth, 1921–1931*; *The Post-War World*; *Northern Ireland Since 1920; Ireland in the Twentieth Century: Divided Island*; and as Joint Editor, *The Town in Ireland*.

GAD HEUMAN (Ph.D., Yale) is Reader in the Department of History at the University of Warwick. His publications include *Between Black and White*, and a study of the Morant Bay rebellion in Jamaica, *The Killing Time*. He has edited books on slave resistance and on labour, and is Co-Editor of the journal *Slavery and Abolition*.

B. W. HIGMAN (Ph.D. in History, University of the West Indies, and Ph.D. in Geography, University of Liverpool) is Professor of History at the Australian National University. He is author of *Slave Population and Economy in Jamaica, 1807–1834; Slave Populations of the British Caribbean, 1807–1834*; and *Jamaica Surveyed*.

A. G. HOPKINS (Ph.D., London) FBA is Smuts Professor of Commonwealth History at the University of Cambridge and Fellow of Pembroke College. He is author of *An Economic History of West Africa* and, with P. J. Cain, of *British Imperialism: Innovation and Expansion, 1688–1914*; and *British Imperialism: Crisis and Deconstruction, 1914–1990*.

DAVID KILLINGRAY (Ph.D., London) is Professor of Modern History, Goldsmiths College, University of London. He is the co-author of *Khaki and Blue: Military and Police in British Colonial Africa*, and Co-Editor of *Policing the Empire, 1830–1940*, *Policing and Decolonisation*, 1917–65, and *Guardian of Empire*. He is Co-Editor of *African Affairs*.

WM. ROGER LOUIS (D.Litt., Oxford) FBA is Kerr Professor of English History and Culture and Distinguished Teaching Professor at the University of Texas at Austin, and Fellow of St Antony's College, Oxford. His books include *Imperialism at Bay*; and *The British Empire in the Middle East.* He is Editor-in-Chief of the *Oxford History of the British Empire.*

STUART MACINTYRE (Ph.D., Cambridge) is Ernest Scott Professor of History at the University of Melbourne. His publications include Volume IV of *The Oxford History of Australia*; *A Colonial Liberalism: The Lost World of Three Victorian Visionaries*; and *A History for a Nation.* With Graeme Davison and John Hirst he edited the *Oxford Companion to Australian History* .

W. DAVID MCINTYRE (Ph.D., London) OBE is Emeritus Professor of History at the University of Canterbury, Christchurch, New Zealand. His books include *Colonies into Commonwealth*; *The Imperial Frontier in the Tropics*; *The Rise and Fall of the Singapore Naval Base*; *The Significance of the Commonwealth*; and *Background to the Anzus Pact.*

P. J. MARSHALL (D.Phil., Oxford) FBA is Emeritus Professor of Imperial History at King's College, London. He has been Editor of the *Journal of Imperial and Commonwealth History* and is Associate Editor of *The Writings and Speeches of Edmund Burke.* His books include *The Impeachment of Warren Hastings*; and *Bengal: The British Bridgehead.* He is Editor of Volume III of the *Oxford History of the British Empire.*

THOMAS R. METCALF (Ph.D., Harvard) is Professor of History of India and the British Empire at the University of California, Berkeley. He is the author of *The Aftermath of Revolt: India, 1857–1870*; *An Imperial Vision: Architecture and Britain's Raj*; *Land, Landlords, and the British Raj*; and *Ideologies of the Raj.*

RORY MILLER (Ph.D., Cambridge) is Senior Lecturer in the Economic and Social History of Latin America at the University of Liverpool. He is the author of *Britain and Latin America in the Nineteenth and Twentieth Centuries*, and has co-edited, with Carlos Dávila, *Business History in Latin America: The Experience of Seven Countries.*

ROBIN J. MOORE (D.Lit., London) FAHA is Professor of History at The Flinders University of South Australia. His books include *Liberalism and Indian Politics, 1872–1922*; *The Crisis of Indian Unity, 1917–1940*; *Churchill, Cripps and India, 1939–1945; Escape from Empire*; *Making the New Commonwealth*; and *Paul Scott's Raj.*

RITCHIE OVENDALE (D.Phil., Oxford) is former Professor in International Politics at the University of Wales, Aberystwyth. His books include *'Appeasement' and the English-Speaking World*; and *The English-Speaking Alliance: Britain, the United States, the Dominions and the Cold War 1945–51*.

D. R. OWRAM (Ph.D., Toronto) FRSC is Professor of History at the University of Alberta. His areas of specialization are Canadian intellectual and social history. His books include *Promise of Eden*, a study of Canadian expansion into the West, and *The Government Generation*, a study of the rise of social and economic planning in the Canadian government.

TAPAN RAYCHAUDHURI (D.Litt., Oxford) is former Professor of Indian History and Civilization, University of Oxford and Emeritus Fellow, St Antony's College, Oxford. His books include *Europe Reconsidered: Perceptions of the West in Nineteenth-Century Bengal*. He was General Editor, with D. Kumar, of the *Cambridge Economic History of India*.

A. D. ROBERTS (Ph.D., Wisconsin) is Emeritus Professor of the History of Africa in the University of London. He edited the *Cambridge History of Africa*, Volume VII. His books include *A History of Zambia*. He was an Editor of the *Journal of African History* from 1974 to 1990.

K. M. DE SILVA (D.Lit., London) was formerly Professor of Sri Lankan History, University of Peradeniya. His publications include *A History of Sri Lanka*; and *Managing Ethnic Tensions in Multi-Ethnic Societies: Sri Lanka*. He is the Editor of the volume on Ceylon in the British Documents on the End of Empire Project series.

PETER SLUGLETT (D.Phil., Oxford) is Professor of History and Director of the Center for Middle Eastern Studies at the University of Utah. His books include *Britain in Iraq, 1914–1932* and, with Marion Farouk-Sluglett, *Iraq Since 1958: From Revolution to Dictatorship*.

ROBERT A. STAFFORD (D.Phil., Oxford) is an Honorary Fellow, History and Philosophy of Science Department, University of Melbourne. He is the author of *Scientist of Empire: Sir Roderick Murchison, Scientific Exploration, and Victorian Imperialism*. He is a contributor to Volume III of this series.

IAN TALBOT (Ph.D., London) is Reader in South Asian Studies at Coventry University. He is author of *Provincial Politics and the Pakistan Movement*;

Freedom's Cry: The Popular Dimension in the Pakistan Movement; *Partition Experience in North-West India*; and Co-Editor of the *International Journal of Punjab Studies*.

NICHOLAS TARLING (Litt.D., Cambridge) MNZM, formerly Professor of History at the University of Auckland, is a Fellow of the New Zealand Asia Institute. He is the Editor of *The Cambridge History of Southeast Asia* and author of fourteen books on South-East Asia, the latest being *Britain, Southeast Asia and the Onset of the Cold War*.

A. P. THORNTON (D.Phil., Oxford) FRSC is Professor Emeritus of History at the University of Toronto. His books include *The Imperial Idea and Its Enemies*; *Doctrines of Imperialism*; *For the File on Empire*; and *Imperialism in the Twentieth Century*. He is now completing *Rights: A Political Anatomy*.

C. M. TURNBULL (Ph.D., London) is formerly Professor of History at the University of Hong Kong. Her books include *The Straits Settlements, 1826–67*; *A History of Singapore, 1819–1988*; *A History of Malaysia, Singapore and Brunei*; and *Dateline Singapore: 150 Years of the Straits Times*.

D. A. WASHBROOK (Ph.D., Cambridge) is Reader in Modern South Asian History and Fellow of St Antony's College, Oxford. He is author of *The Emergence of Provincial Politics: Madras Presidency, 1870–1920*, and many articles on modern Indian history. He has taught at the Universities of Cambridge, Warwick, Harvard, and Pennsylvania.

ROBIN W. WINKS (Ph.D., Johns Hopkins) is Townsend Professor of History at Yale University. In 1992–93 he was Eastman Professor and Fellow of Balliol College, Oxford. His publications include *Canada and the United States*; *The Historiography of the British Empire-Commonwealth*; *The Blacks in Canada*; and works on New Zealand and Malaysia.

WILLIAM H. WORGER (Ph.D., Yale) is Associate Professor of History at the University of California at Los Angeles. He has taught African History at the Universities of Michigan and Stanford. His works include *South Africa's City of Diamonds: Mine Workers and Monopoly Capitalism in Kimberley, 1870–1895*.

DIANA WYLIE (Ph.D., Yale) is Associate Professor, Boston University. She is author of *A Little God: The Twilight of Patriarchy in a Southern African Chiefdom*; and *Starving on a Full Stomach: Hunger and the Triumph of Cultural Racism in South Africa* (forthcoming).

1

Introduction

WM. ROGER LOUIS

In this volume the word 'historiography' is used in the sense of the evolving or changing interpretations of the history of the British Empire. The term thus means the history of the Empire's history. It represents the effort to portray the *Zeitgeist* or the spirit of the time in which historians wrote and the influences on them. In another sense it deals with the art of writing Imperial history and the development or professionalization of the discipline. The volume is therefore concerned with the ways historians have responded to the problems of the British Empire. How did historians of the Empire go about their tasks and what were their assumptions? How were their accounts influenced by the political and cultural climate of their age? Above all, which of the historians of the Empire had the strength of intellect and personality to write works that have stood the test of time? This introductory chapter addresses itself to those questions through the historiographical revolution of the early 1960s.[1] The subsequent chapters then examine in detail the full sweep of the historiography of the Empire, including area studies. The last two chapters pick up the general theme of changing perspectives where the introductory chapter leaves off, from 1960 onwards.

In tracing the antecedents of British Imperial history, the era of the Enlightenment is critical. Historians since Herodotus had grappled with the problem of how to write history, but modern historiography had its birth in the Enlightenment's axiom that historical truth could be ascertained through the exercise of reason and, in the case of Edward Gibbon, by fidelity to written evidence. Reaching its zenith of optimism in the nineteenth century, the idea developed that history might be perfected as a science whereby events would be recorded not only as they actually happened but in a true and universal account. Yet at the same time history continued to be used for political purposes. Though few historians of quality have betrayed themselves as propagandists, many have

[1] There are certain themes and topics that I have not been able to deal with in the limited scope of this chapter, except in passing. These include the historiography of colonial America and the American Revolution, the question of Ireland, and what might be called the Hakluyt tradition of exploration. These subjects are dealt with in specific chapters in the volume.

been caught up, consciously or unconsciously, in the ideological struggles of their times. Most historians today probably recognize that there is an element of subjectivity in virtually all historical accounts. Those who have the good fortune of being able to pursue their calling according to their own lights face the same perplexities as the academic historians who created the modern profession in the nineteenth century. From then onwards the aim of professional historians has been to interpret events and analyse institutions and traditions as accurately and as free from overt bias as possible. This volume reveals the dilemmas of historians who have attempted to explain 'imperialism', sometimes at the risk of public condemnation. It conveys not only the dominant intellectual passions as they carried over from one generation to the next, but also the way in which preoccupation with national and world affairs influenced historical writing on the British Empire.

Leopold von Ranke was the father of the modern historical profession, British as well as German. Founding one of the first scholarly seminars in the mid-nineteenth century in Berlin, he played a major part in the historical revolution that trained students to examine documents systematically and to write history in a spirit of detachment and precision. The great English historians during most of the nineteenth century, like many historians of the British Empire to the present, were fairly oblivious to German historical scholarship. But by the last two decades of the century British historians had taken steps towards the creation of the modern discipline as it is known today. The founding in 1886 of the *English Historical Review* (*EHR*) at the initiative of James Bryce may be taken as a symbolic date.[2] 'The object of history', proclaimed the anonymous preface penned by Bryce in the first issue, 'is to discover and set forth facts.' After noting that English historical scholarship was 'as thorough in quality as that even of the Germans', he stated the aim of the new journal in a way that bears remarkable similarity to that of the *Oxford History of the British Empire*: the *EHR* would be devoted 'to the person called the "general reader" ', as well as to scholars, and would present historical essays 'which an educated man, not specially conversant with history, may read with pleasure and profit'.[3] The hope met with disappointment. The *EHR* failed to arouse the interest of the general public, but it did mark the arrival of

[2] The *Historische Zeitschrift* had been founded in 1859; the *Revue Historique* in 1876; and the *Rivista storica italiana* in 1884. The first issue of the *American Historical Review* appeared in 1895. (Lord) Bryce had a long-standing interest in America, later publishing *The American Commonwealth* in 1888 and serving as Ambassador in Washington 1907–13. He hoped that the *EHR* would provide a common forum for American as well as British historians and would be a historical journal for 'the whole race'.

[3] 'Prefatory Note', *EHR*, I (Jan. 1886), pp. 1–6.

the academic or professional historian in Britain, and it set the standard of excellence in the field.[4]

Among the greatest works by past masters in British history—Lord Clarendon, David Hume, Edward Gibbon, Thomas Carlyle, Thomas Babington Macaulay, and J. R. Seeley—there are three that are especially significant for the background of the volume. They are Gibbon's *Decline and Fall of the Roman Empire* (1776–88), Macaulay's *History of England* (1849–55), and Seeley's *Expansion of England* (1883). The three works have a central bearing on the interpretation of the Empire's end, its purpose as well as its beginning, and they all continue to inspire debate.

Gibbon set a high standard of accuracy, he had a perspective that extended over centuries, and he possessed an incomparable literary style. His *Decline and Fall* casts a long shadow that falls even on the *Oxford History of the British Empire*. Readers expect to know whether Gibbon helps us to understand not only the end but the course of the British Empire. He wrote in the era of the American Revolution. But he was austere in not projecting the lessons of the past into the present. He did not necessarily think that the loss of the American colonies was the beginning of the end for the British Empire in the Roman sense.[5] Nevertheless, there is a key question that has captivated the historian's imagination: was there an undeviating line of decline that characterized the British Empire? The question is significant because it has haunted generations. Was there in the British Empire a period of tolerant and benevolent rule comparable to Gibbon's golden age in Antonine Rome? Did Britain as the first industrialized nation, with the greatest navy and a worldwide Empire, decline because of moral weakness at the centre and a failure of the will to resist the onslaught at the periphery? Gibbon might or might not have agreed with the trajectory of descent as portrayed by recent historians such as Correlli Barnett, who believe that, with greater determination, British statecraft after 1945 might have modernized Britain's industry and reversed

[4] See Philippa Levine, *The Amateur and the Professional: Antiquarians, Historians and Archaeologists in Victorian England, 1838–1886* (Cambridge, 1986), chap. 7. See also esp. Rosemary Jann, 'From Amateur to Professional: The Case of the Oxbridge Historians', *Journal of British Studies*, XXII, 2 (Spring 1983), pp. 122–47, and Doris S. Goldstein, 'The Origins and Early Years of the English Historical Review', *EHR*, CI, 398 (Jan. 1986), pp. 6–19. Llewellyn Woodward makes the essential point that in the latter part of the nineteenth century college tutors rather than professors in Oxford and Cambridge controlled the curriculum, which was designed more as a preparation for competitive examinations for entry into the Home and Indian Civil Service examination than for the advancement of knowledge. Oxford established a research degree of B.Litt. requiring a thesis in 1895, but not the more advanced degree of Doctor of Philosophy until 1917. Llewellyn Woodward, 'The Rise of the Professional Historian in England', in K. Bourne and D. C. Watt, eds., *Studies in International History* (London, 1967), pp. 16–34.

[5] See J. G. A. Pocock, 'Between Machiavelli and Hume: Gibbon as Civic Humanist and Philosophical Historian', in G. W. Bowersock, John Clive, and Stephen R. Graubard, eds., *Edward Gibbon and the Decline and Fall of the Roman Empire* (Cambridge, Mass., 1977), pp. 103–19.

the process of economic decline.[6] On the question of the Empire's collapse—of determining whether or not there was infirmity of will in the metropole as well as insurgency in the provinces—Gibbon continues to provoke thought.

The issue of economic decline has been the specific Gibbonian theme applied to the history of the Empire. On this point Adam Smith provides a clue to the complexity of the problem, because he held that the loss of the colonies would not endanger Britain's long-term economic prospects.[7] Smith was probably more right than Gibbon, because empires revive as well as fall, and Britain's long-term economic prosperity was not necessarily dependent on the Empire.[8] In view of natural resources, the size of population, and the geographical extent of the British Isles, what seems surprising in retrospect is that the British maintained the Empire as long as they did. One significant point in assessing Gibbon is that those living at the time did not believe that the Empire, and Britain's place in the world, were doomed to inevitable decline. Gibbon's interpretation would have left the British people with little choice other than to be defeatist. It would have denied them any significant voice in their own fate. The emotional and creative energy of the post-Second World War period can only be explained by the determination to halt the decline and collapse of the economy, and to prevent Britain from sinking into the status of 'a second-class European power'. Contrary to Gibbon, decline is a relative concept. Barry Supple, one of the foremost authorities on British economic performance, points out that the national decline and degradation, if it can be so described, was replaced with something else. He quotes a concluding passage in A. J. P. Taylor's *English History:*

> [In the Second World War] the British people came of age . . . Imperial greatness was on the way out; the welfare state was on the way in. The British empire declined; the condition of the people improved. Few now sang "Land of Hope and Glory". Few even sang "England Arise". England had risen all the same.[9]

What would Gibbon have made of that? He had a habit of ignoring criticism, but he might have been jolted by John Gallagher's argument in the Ford Lectures in Oxford in 1974 that in history, at least in the history of the British Empire, there is no 'unbroken movement' in the same direction:

> Edward Gibbon said of the Roman empire that 'the causes of destruction multiplied with the extent of conquest; and, as soon as time and accident had removed the artificial supports, the

[6] See esp. Correlli Barnett, *The Lost Victory: British Dreams, British Realities, 1945–1950* (London, 1995).

[7] For Smith in the context of the British Empire see esp. Donald Winch, *Classical Political Economy and Colonies* (London, 1965), chap. 2.

[8] See Vol. IV, chap. by D. K. Fieldhouse.

[9] Supple quoting Taylor in Peter Clarke and Clive Trebilcock, eds., *Understanding Decline: Perceptions and Realities of British Economic Performance* (Cambridge, 1997), p. 16. On the theme of economic decline, this is the key work that connects with the history of the Empire.

> stupendous fabric yielded to the pressure of its own weight.' 'Time and accident'. We might look at the fall of the British empire in a briskly functionalist way, and conclude that it was simply the damage of the Second World War which brought the British empire down. But . . . a result of the Second World War was (temporarily) to reintegrate the system, reversing the trend and turning it back from influence towards empire before the downfall.[10]

Empires can revive as well as die, and the British Empire attempted to resurrect itself in the form of the Commonwealth. The themes of decline and fall, revival and collapse, and the nature of the post-colonial era recur in the historiography of the subject. Paul Kennedy's *The Rise and Fall of the Great Powers: Economic Change and Military Conflict from 1500 to 2000* is a case in point, since it is a major work of synthesis. The inspiration, however, derives explicitly from von Ranke's empirical treatment of the rise and decline of nations and implicitly rejects Gibbon's unwavering line of descent.[11]

Thomas Macaulay holds a place of unique importance in the history of the British Empire, not least because of the way he linked the Empire's purpose with that of progress. Macaulay was the pre-eminent historian in nineteenth-century England. Indelibly associated with the Whig interpretation of history, he is also famous as the man who served in India, devising the Indian penal code and penning the famous Minute on Education. Seminal ideas—for example, 'informal empire'—can be traced to his work. Macaulay held arrogant but representative views on England's cultural ascendancy in the world and on what he believed to be the benevolent impact of British rule in India and elsewhere. The controversial Minute on Education, written in India in 1835, managed to reconcile British *realpolitik* and idealism in a way that left a lasting mark on subsequent interpretations of British rule: 'It is impossible for us, with our limited means, to attempt to educate the body of the people. We must at present do our best to form a class who may be interpreters between us and the millions whom we govern; a class of persons, Indian in blood and colour, but English in taste, in opinions, in morals, and in intellect.'[12] On another occasion Macaulay proclaimed the progress of India towards order and rationality, and said of the Indian desire for British institutions: 'never will I attempt to avert or to retard it. Whenever it comes, it will be the proudest day in English history. To have found a great people sunk in the lowest depths

[10] John Gallagher, *The Decline, Revival and Fall of the British Empire*, ed. Anil Seal (Cambridge, 1982), p. 73. R. G. Collingwood makes the same point in assessing the work of Arnold Toynbee: 'There are no mere phenomena of decay: every decline is also a rise': R. G. Collingwood, *The Idea of History* (Oxford, 1946), p. 164. Collingwood was a philosopher as well as historian, and his book remains the indispensable general work on historiography.

[11] New York, 1987, p. xxiv.

[12] See John Clive, *Macaulay: The Shaping of the Historian* (New York, 1973), chap. 12; and the chap. by Robert E. Frykenberg, p. 210, for the relationship of the Minute to broader and later themes of historiographical controversy.

of slavery and superstition, to have so ruled them as to have made them desirous and capable of all the privileges of citizens, would indeed be a title to glory all our own.'[13] In advance of most others of his time, but with his characteristic streak of arrogance, Macaulay anticipated eventual Indian independence, believing that it would come as a result of beneficent collaboration, and specifically the use of English education to transform Indian society.[14] Eric Stokes, Smuts Professor of the History of the British Commonwealth at Cambridge, 1970–81, once wrote that Macaulay's writing 'with its shrewd blend of altruism and self-interest . . . represented the permanent political instinct of British colonial policy'.[15]

Macaulay was an unabashed supporter of the Whig cause, claiming throughout his life that the party of reform had saved England from revolution. He held that the Whigs championed principles of English liberty, toleration, and improvement. In short, he believed in progress. A distinction must be made, however, between Macaulay as a Whig historian and the Whig school of history. Whig history is history reflecting the anxieties and preoccupations of the present and emphasizing the evolution of certain principles, as if, for example, English history should be read as the unfolding triumph of liberty.[16] Macaulay's writings embodied all of those things, and he certainly would have defended the celebration of liberty. But he cannot be held responsible for the reductionist interpretations perpetuated by subsequent historians.[17] Macaulay remains in a class by himself.[18]

[13] Quoted in Ronald Hyam, *Britain's Imperial Century, 1815–1914: A Study of Empire and Expansion* (London, 1976), p. 220; see also esp. Thomas R. Metcalf, *Ideologies of the Raj* (Cambridge, 1994), pp. 39–40.

[14] Though he was in advance of his time, he was not alone. James Mill also anticipated that self-government might eventually be achieved, but on the basis of good government, just law, and 'scientific' taxation. For Macaulay in relation to James Mill and John Stuart Mill, see Hyam, *Britain's Imperial Century*, e.g. p. 55.

[15] Eric Stokes, 'Macaulay: The Indian Years, 1834–38', *Review of English Literature*, I, 4 (Oct. 1960), pp. 41–50 and *The English Utilitarians and India* (Oxford, 1959), pp. 46–47.

[16] See Herbert Butterfield, *The Whig Interpretation of History* (London, 1931); his much more substantial work is *Man on His Past: The Study of the History of Historical Scholarship* (Cambridge, 1955). For a fair assessment that has implications for Imperial history, see G. R. Elton, 'Herbert Butterfield and the Study of History', *Historical Journal*, XXVII, 3 (1984), pp. 729–43. In the 1960s Elton generally opposed the expansion of the Cambridge curriculum into 'Third World' studies or, as he put it, 'bits of history' from 'Mexico to Malawi'.

[17] For example Robert Mackenzie, *The Nineteenth Century* (London, 1880), caricatured by Collingwood as a work 'depicting that century as a time of progress from a state of barbarism, ignorance and bestiality which can hardly be exaggerated to a reign of science, enlightenment, and democracy . . . everybody was rapidly getting happier and happier until a culmination of joy was reached in the dazzling victories of the Crimea. But the victories of peace were no less dazzling; they included the splendours of the cotton trade, the magnificent conception of steam locomotion, which awakened the dormant love of travel and taught people in distant parts of the earth to love one another instead of hating one another as before . . .' Collingwood, *Idea of History*, p. 145.

[18] As may be gathered from Lord Acton, the Regius Professor of Modern History at Cambridge,

The Whig interpretation of history has a direct bearing on Imperial history, in which it forms a respected tradition. Even in the time of Adam Smith and the era of the American Revolution, historical works reflected the belief of progress in the Empire. Historians in the nineteenth century generally held that British rule brought to indigenous peoples the benefits of civilization. British colonies would advance towards self-governing status, or what was later called Dominionhood. In the early twentieth century the same idea was applied to India. Ramsay MacDonald of the Independent Labour Party, among others, advocated Dominion Status for India before the First World War. The cause was later championed by historians, above all by Lionel Curtis, Reginald Coupland, and W. K. Hancock. The Empire would justify itself by the end result: equal nations freely associating in the British Commonwealth. The tradition reached its apogee after the Second World War in the works of Nicholas Mansergh, who accepted the progress of the Commonwealth as an article of faith and achieved the highest level of scholarly accuracy and balanced treatment.[19] The idealism of Mansergh and others is far removed from the crude Whig interpretation of the nineteenth century.[20] But there is a teleology in much of the historical writing on the Empire, whether Whig or, eventually, Marxist.[21]

1895–1902, recounting conversations with William Stubbs, the foremost English historian of his time, and Mandell Creighton, the first Editor of the *EHR*; and later with two equally distinguished German historians:

> I was once with two eminent men, the late Bishop of Oxford [William Stubbs] and the present Bishop of London [Mandell Creighton]. On another occasion I was with two far more eminent men, the two most learned men in the world. I need hardly tell you their names—they were [Theodore] Mommsen and [Adolf von] Harnack. On each occasion the question arose: who was the greatest historian the world had ever produced? On each occasion the name first mentioned, and on each occasion the name finally agreed upon, was that of Macaulay. (James Westfall Thompson, *A History of Historical Writing*, 2 vols. New York, 1942, II, p. 300.)

Who among the historians of the British Empire would hold the comparable place of honour? There is obviously an element of subjectivity in any such judgment, but, on the basis of the formal and informal discussions among historians of the *OHBE* and on the assessments in the volume, it is Sir Keith Hancock. See below, p. 30.

[19] See esp. Nicholas Mansergh, *The Commonwealth Experience* (London, 1969). Constitutional progress to Mansergh was a cardinal principle, but he saw a tension between empire and liberty. For him the Colonial Empire did not inevitably give way to Commonwealth. Liberty and equality had to be fought for and won. The Commonwealth, in Mansergh's view, should be regarded as the achievement of anti-Imperial nationalists such as Smuts of South Africa, Mackenzie King of Canada, de Valera of Ireland, and Nehru of India.

[20] See also the works by D. A. Low, esp. *Eclipse of Empire* (London, 1991), for 'the profound sense of positive achievement' and 'positive sense of direction [that] lasted right through to the end of empire and beyond' (p. xiii). 'The last of the great Whig historians!', according to Sarvepalli Gopal, the historian of British rule in India, only half in jest describing Low. OHBE Archives.

[21] For an important reassessment of the idea of progress in a Marxist context see Barrington Moore, Jr., 'On the Notion of Progress, Revolution, and Freedom', *Ethics*, LXXII, 2 (Jan. 1962), pp. 106–19. For general Marxist interpretation of the Empire, see esp. V. G. Kiernan, *Marxism and Imperialism* (London, 1974).

The founders of the *English Historical Review* in the 1880s objected to Macaulay not because he was a Whig historian, but because he championed the cause of the Whig party in his history. They criticized Gibbon not because he had portrayed Rome falling before the forces of barbarism and religion, but because of his bias in favour of pagan Rome.[22] This was the era of the rise of the academic historians, of William Stubbs and Frederic Maitland, Lord Acton and Seeley. Seeley was especially severe and referred to Macaulay as a 'charlatan'. He warmly and pointedly despised Macaulay's romanticism. Of the historians associated with the creation of the *EHR*, all of whom were more or less in open rebellion against Macaulay, Seeley is of particular interest because he has a fair claim to be regarded as the founder of the field of Imperial history, though he would not have described himself as having such a purpose.[23] His *Expansion of England* published in 1883 provided inspiration for men of affairs as well as historians. He spoke for his generation when he stated that lessons or morals could be drawn from the study of history to instruct politicians and statesmen, not least servants of the Empire.

Seeley was not a historian of the same rank as Gibbon or Macaulay, but his work had a comparable intellectual rigour, and the *Expansion of England* did remain in print until the year of the Suez crisis in 1956.[24] It was the first systematic account of the eighteenth-century Empire. Regius Professor of Modern History at Cambridge from 1869 until his death at the age of 61 in 1895, Seeley passionately believed in empirical method, reasoned argument, and impartiality. In the spirit of the new scholarship, he conducted research at the Public Record Office, and was an admirer of von Ranke's accuracy and rigorous use of evidence. He was a student of German as well as British history, and had a general grasp of the history of Europe since antiquity as well as an impressive command of the history of the European colonial empires. He disliked the phrase 'British Empire', preferring 'Greater Britain' to convey the idea that the colonies of white settlement were an extension of England overseas. In that sense he believed the British Empire to be organic: whether in Britain or abroad, everyone 'British' belonged to a single Imperial nation. The British Empire was thus an empire of kith and kin in which India formed a perplexing and alien part. Like other writers since the 1860s, including Charles Dilke and J. A. Froude, Seeley held that Imperial federation might be England's destiny, depending in part on whether or not the

22 See Collingwood, *Idea of History*, pp. 146–47.

23 See Peter Burroughs, 'John Robert Seeley and British Imperial History', *Journal of Imperial and Commonwealth History* (hereafter *JICH*), I, 2 (Jan. 1973), pp. 191–211. On Seeley's life and career, Deborah Wormell, *Sir John Seeley and the Uses of History* (Cambridge, 1980).

24 It was republished in 1971 by the University of Chicago Press, with a useful introduction by John Gross.

British were prepared to see themselves as a world power rather than merely as part of Europe:

> If the United States and Russia hold together for another half century, they will at the end of that time completely dwarf such old European States as France and Germany and depress them into a second class. They will do the same to England, if at the end of that time England still thinks of herself as simply a European State . . .[25]

He did not commit himself to federation. He merely debated it vigorously, just as he inquired into whether India might be too large a defence commitment for the British government. What if a Russian invasion of India were to spark another mutiny? One of the reasons for the continued success of his book was his ability to ask provocative questions and to appeal for imaginative answers. Seeley was a publicist. He believed that the British government had a responsibility honestly to answer difficult questions and to acknowledge that the state itself had ethical responsibilities, and his work thus had a moral as well as a clear intellectual thrust that appealed to Cecil Rhodes and others committed to British expansion.

There were many ways in which Seeley's work had a lasting historiographical influence. One is quite simple: his famous phrase that the British seemed 'to have conquered and peopled half the world in a fit of absence of mind' caused historians as well as the general public to reflect on the origins of the Empire. Perhaps no other single phrase in the Empire's history is so famous or has had such a stimulating effect in the classroom. As is clear from his general style, Seeley intended it as a provocative remark on the dynamics of British expansion. He was drawing attention to the unconscious acceptance by the English public of the burdens of Empire, particularly in India. Economic history was not Seeley's strength, but he clearly grasped the commercial principles of 'the old colonial system' and by using that phrase lent his academic authority to a lasting and useful concept.[26] Although he lamented the American Revolution, he took heart that the United States had inherited 'the language and traditions of England', and that the British had learned the lesson not to regard colonies as mere estates 'out of which the mother-country is to make a pecuniary profit'. There had gradually developed, he believed, 'a better system' whereby colonies could over time achieve 'emancipation'. Despite his repudiation of Macaulay, Seeley was still

[25] *Expansion of England* (Chicago edn.), p. 62. For Dilke, see *Greater Britain* (London, 1868); for Froude, *Oceana* (London, 1885). For Dilke, Froude, and other nineteenth-century writers who provided the antecedents of such concepts as the 'special relationship' with the United States, and the 'informal empire' of British influence beyond the Empire, see Hyam, *Britain's Imperial Century.*

[26] See chap. by P. J. Marshall. See also esp. John S. Galbraith, 'The Empire since 1783', in Robin W. Winks, ed., *The Historiography of the British Empire-Commonwealth: Trends, Interpretations, and Resources* (Durham, NC, 1966), pp. 46–68.

enough of a Whig historian to see progress over the course of the nineteenth century. But he did not believe that human progress was inevitable. It required statesmanship and determination. Thus again there was the moral ring to his work, especially in the passages in the *Expansion of England* concerning liberty.

The concept of liberty is another reason why Seeley's work has a permanent historiographical significance. He drew inspiration from John Stuart Mill's idea that democracy and despotism are incompatible. Seeley faced squarely the central contradiction of the British Empire: how could the British reconcile the despotism of the Indian Empire with the democracy enjoyed by the colonies of white settlers? The famous passage reads:

> How can the same nation pursue two lines of policy so radically different without bewilderment, be despotic in Asia and democratic in Australia, be in the East at once the greatest Musulman Power in the world . . . and at the same time in the West be the foremost champion of free thought and spiritual religions, stand out as a great military Imperialism to resist the march of Russia in Central Asia at the same time that it fills Queensland and Manitoba with free settlers?[27]

By posing so clearly the conjunction of liberty and despotism, Seeley's work continued to engage subsequent generations of readers.

Seeley's successor in Cambridge was Lord Acton, whose achievement at the beginning of the twentieth century, the *Cambridge Modern History* (*CMH*), was a culmination of nineteenth-century historical thought. In time it inspired other Cambridge series, including the *Cambridge History of the British Empire* (*CHBE*). Acton himself was a man of vast erudition, dignity, and epigrammatic style. With the rigour of German background and training tempered by his association with the *English Historical Review*, he seemed to be the best possible editor for a series that would set the standard for the next century. He believed, or at least hoped, that the *CMH* would be definitive. He took as a premise that the opening of the archives in the nineteenth century made possible the revelation of his historical truth—in the words of the preface to the first volume, composed by his successors but with him in mind: 'the long conspiracy against the revelation of truth has gradually given way.'[28] It seemed obvious to Acton and his colleagues that it lay beyond the grasp of any single individual to write the history of the modern world.[29] He

[27] *Expansion of England* (Chicago edn.), p. 141.

[28] For the beginning of the project see esp. G. N. Clark, 'The Origins of the Cambridge Modern History', *Cambridge Historical Journal*, VIII, 2 (1945), pp. 57–64.

[29] The assumption did not command universal agreement either at the time or later. In 1949 Max Beloff commented that the planning and execution of the *Cambridge Modern History* marked the beginning of 'the decadence of English historical writing'. Quoted in Gertrude Himmelfarb, *Lord Acton: A Study in Conscience and Politics* (Chicago, 1952), p. 228.

recruited 160 authors, mainly British but also prominent European and American historians, including Woodrow Wilson, then President of Princeton University. The planning of the series and preliminary editing was a heavy responsibility, and when Acton died in 1902 it was still two years before the publication of the first instalment. The *CMH* appeared in thirteen volumes from 1904 to 1912; one of the assistant editors, E. A. Benians, Master of St John's College and Vice-Chancellor of Cambridge University, became one of the three editors of the *Cambridge History of the British Empire*.

The first volume of the *Cambridge History of the British Empire*, published in 1929, opened by quoting Macaulay on the greatness of England and commenting on the forty-five years that had elapsed since Seeley's *Expansion of England*.[30] Benians and his two fellow-editors, J. Holland Rose (Vere Harmsworth Professor of Imperial and Naval History at Cambridge) and A. P. Newton (Rhodes Professor of Imperial History in London), planned the series on the Acton model.[31] Appearing in nine volumes, the last instalment was not published until 1959.[32] None of the original editors lived to see its completion. Though some of the chapters by younger scholars in Volume III, on the Empire-Commonwealth, reflected the changing mood after 1945, the *CHBE* in its entirety was essentially a work of the inter-war years. Its planning and ideas reflected the era of the aftermath of the Great War, the international Depression, and the drift towards war in the 1930s. Though not quite so confident in tone as that of the generation of Acton, it does have a ring of certainty, especially on the nature of the British Empire–Commonwealth as a benevolent and progressive force in human history. Some of the chapters in the present volume conclude that the ethos of the *CHBE* as a collective work tended to muffle dissent and to encourage consensus on what was believed to be the underlying, essentially noble, purpose of the Empire.[33] The general commitment of the contributors in the inter-war years is well brought out in a comment by Benians on Holland Rose, who seemed to epitomize the generation of *CHBE* historians: he was 'intensely loyal to the British

[30] The *CHBE* followed chronologically from the *Cambridge History of India*, 6 vols. (Cambridge, 1922–32). Two of the *CHI* vols., Vol. V, *British India, 1497–1858* and Vol. VI, *The Indian Empire, 1858–1918*, served as the two Indian vols. in the *CHBE*. For the landmarks in the Indian historiography such as Vincent A. Smith. *The Oxford History of India: From the Earliest Times to the End of 1911* (Oxford, 1919) and H. Dodwell, *A Sketch of the History of India from 1858 to 1919* (London, 1925), see chap. by Tapan Raychaudhuri, p. 214.

[31] Much of the detailed planning was done by Newton, who had begun his career as a physicist and whose 'scientific method' is reflected in the project. In the inter-war period Newton also took the lead in the supervision of research students. See chap. by A. D. Roberts, p. 475, n. 90.

[32] For the controversy over the number of vols. in the *CHBE*, see below, Select Bibliography.

[33] See esp. the chap. by Stuart Macintyre, p. 171: 'If some [of the Australian contributors] were critical of British policy in the colonial period, they minimized points of strain in the recent past.'

Empire, and [had] . . . a strong faith in its historical and future significance to mankind.'[34]

The focus of the present volume is principally on the work of professional historians since the 1880s. Gibbon and Macaulay, and Seeley help to provide the background and context, but the critical point in the historiography is the changing interpretation over the last one hundred years. Having established the *Cambridge History of the British Empire* as a landmark, these introductory comments will now draw from the *OHBE* chapters various antecedent and subsequent themes that help in understanding, in turn, the historiographical revolution of the 1960s and its aftermath to the present.

In assessing the historiography up to 1914, it is useful to note significant works that capture the spirit of the times as well as the issues of substance, including, for example, the problem of imperialism as a cause of war. The ideological battle-lines on the Empire had long been drawn by those upholding the idealism of the Empire and those who attacked the system of European imperialism. How did the academic historians of the late nineteenth century respond to shifting public moods as they studied earlier periods in the Empire's history? How did they begin to re-evaluate 'the old colonial system' up to the American Revolution and the 'second British Empire' in the century thereafter, 1783–1879?[35]

Hugh Egerton was the pioneer in the field after Seeley, publishing *A Short History of British Colonial Policy* in 1897 (London) and becoming the first Beit Professor of Colonial History in Oxford in 1905. His book, which reached a twelfth edition in 1950, is a clear and systematic narrative dealing with such major issues as the commercial system of the first British Empire, the rise of British power in India, the abolition of slavery, the influence of Gibbon Wakefield's colonization schemes in New Zealand,[36] the beginnings of constitutional government in Australia, and the attainment of Canadian self-government.[37] Egerton's history reflected the preoccupations

[34] E. A. Benians in the *Dictionary of National Biography, 1941–1950*. R. E. Robinson—Beit Professor of Commonwealth History at Oxford 1971–1987 and himself a contributor to the *CHBE*—has written: 'These tomes stand as the classic historiographical monument to the Seeleyan unity of organic empire . . . Their standpoint was anglocentric and their values Anglo-Saxon, although there was much of value in their pioneer narrative': Ronald Robinson, 'Oxford in Imperial Historiography', in Frederick Madden and D. K. Fieldhouse, eds., *Oxford and the Idea of Commonwealth: Essays Presented to Sir Edgar Williams* (London, 1982), p. 33.

[35] These are the conventional dates, but for a discussion of the chronological boundaries see P. J. Marshall, p.p 43–44; for the second British Empire see chap. by C. A. Bayly, p. 54. See also Vol. I, chap. by P. J. Marshall, for a discussion of the origins and changing meaning of the phrase 'British Empire'.

[36] For the historiography of New Zealand, see chap. by James Belich.

[37] Egerton wrote also with a certain historiographical purpose: for example, in commenting on Thomas Carlyle, Egerton believed his interest in the Empire to have been more negligible than commonly assumed, and that he was 'most unfair' in his comment on certain personalities: *British Colonial Policy*, p. 307, n. 3.

of the time. A cautious federationist, his ideas in many ways were an extension of Seeley's. According to *The Times*: 'The publication of Seeley's "Expansion of England" in 1883 had made a deep impression on public opinion in this country: and Egerton was one of those who accepted Seeley's dictum that the maintenance of the unity of the British Empire was the great question of the age.'[38] But there was already a shift in the background. While Seeley had emphasized Britain's historic antagonism towards Russia and France, Egerton wrote in the era of naval rivalry with Germany and the extension of colonial control into Africa.[39]

During Egerton's career as an historian, powerful books by politicians called for unity of the Empire and the fulfilment of Britain's Imperial destiny. They included Alfred Milner's *England in Egypt* (London, 1893), George N. Curzon's *Problems of the Far East* (London, 1894), and in the next decade, the Earl of Cromer's *Modern Egypt*, 2 vols. (London, 1908). For the evolving historiography, Milner is the critical figure. Many held him responsible for the war in South Africa at the turn of the century that had split British society. Egerton wrote of him in the 1907 edition of *British Colonial Policy*:

> The time has not yet come to form the final judgment on the great Governor, who, after eight years of arduous labour retired in 1905 from South Africa. His doings are still involved in the smoke of controversy. But if, in the fullness of time British South Africa works out its own salvation, and Dutch racial patriotism takes a more sentimental form, compatible with political patriotism to a common Empire, it will largely be due to the determination and courage, which shirked no difficulty, and looked squarely in the face even the horrors of war, rather than that South Africa should remain an exception to the general history of British development, along the lines of progress and freedom.[40]

In 1905 Milner had served as one of Egerton's electors to the Beit Professorship, but without enthusiasm: he was exceedingly sceptical about whether academic historians could rise to the occasion by producing history worthy of the Empire, in other words, history of high quality with a political purpose. He did not doubt Egerton's enthusiasm but the quality of his intellect.[41]

With a vision combining 'race patriotism' and Empire idealism, Milner inspired a younger generation of British Imperialists known, in the aftermath of the South African War or Boer War, as the Kindergarten.[42] In 1909 they created the

[38] *The Times* obituary of Egerton, 23 May 1927.

[39] For the connection between colonial expansion and sea power, see chap. by Barry M. Gough, for the British army, see chap. by David Killingray.

[40] Egerton, *British Colonial Policy*, p. 501. Quotation from 1908 edn.

[41] See Colin Newbury, 'Cecil Rhodes and the South African Connection: "A Great Imperial University"?'; and Madden, 'The Commonwealth', in *Oxford and the Idea of Commonwealth*.

[42] Milner used the word 'Imperialist' and 'Imperialism' in a positive sense. See, for example, his speech 'The Imperialist Creed', in Lord Milner, *The Nation and the Empire* (London, 1913). For the

Round Table movement, with a quarterly of the same name, dedicated to the strengthening and eventual unification of the Empire. Among the most able of Milner's disciples, and the most dynamic in the new movement, was Lionel Curtis, who held the Beit Lectureship in Oxford from 1912 and from 1921 a Fellowship at All Souls College. Curtis stands in the historiography as the central figure who believed—to his everlasting credit—that India and other dependencies should eventually achieve the same status of equality as the old Dominions. In that sense he clearly envisaged the British Commonwealth of Nations.[43] From Curtis's arrival in Oxford can also be dated the birth of Imperial history as it is known today, with the seminar, the visitors, and the camaraderie. He had a vigorous intellect and a compelling force of personality: Egerton complained that Curtis made him feel 'like a country rector with the Prophet Isaiah as his curate'.[44] Among Curtis's recruits were historians of such diverse background and personality as Lewis Namier, whose research was sponsored by the Round Table and the Rhodes Trust,[45] Frank Underhill, who became one of the leading Canadian historians,[46] and George Louis Beer, one of the outstanding American historians of the British colonial system before the American Revolution.[47] The historiographical influence of Curtis, the Round Table, and Oxford was considerable. But the response to Curtis's political commitment was ambiguous. Far more than Milner, Curtis

negative as well as the positive use of the words, and for an important historiographical investigation, Richard Koebner and Helmut Dan Schmidt, *Imperialism: The Story and Significance of a Political Word, 1840–1960* (Cambridge, 1964).

43 See esp. *The Commonwealth of Nations* (London, 1916) and *Dyarchy* (London, 1920).

44 Deborah Lavin, *From Empire to International Commonwealth: A Biography of Lionel Curtis* (Oxford, 1995), p. 119. On the debate among historians on the Round Table movement see esp. John E. Kendle, *The Round Table Movement and Imperial Union* (Toronto, 1975); Leonie Foster, *High Hopes: The Men and Motives of the Australian Round Table* (Melbourne, 1986); and Alexander C. May, 'The Round Table, 1910–66', unpublished D.Phil. thesis, Oxford, 1995.

45 Namier won a Beit Prize in 1913 and received further assistance from the Rhodes Trust that enabled him eventually to publish *The Structure of Politics at the Accession of George III*, 2 vols. (London, 1929) and *England in the Age of the American Revolution* (London, 1930), the two works that placed him in the front rank of British historians. Vehemently anti-ideological, Namier demonstrated none of the commitment to the sense of progress of the British Empire that characterized many other historians of his era, and later opposed, like Geoffrey Elton, the development of the fields of Asian and African history. He gave the general impression, according to his obituary in *The Times* (22 Aug. 1960), 'of combining his Jewish character with a sturdy British Imperialism'.

46 Underhill's aim, like others of his generation, was not 'the breaking of the tie with Great Britain but the changing of its nature to that of a free association of equals'. For this theme and the development of Canadian historiography, see chap. by D. R. Owram. For Underhill's own ideas, see Frank H. Underhill, *The British Commonwealth: An Experiment in Co-operation among Nations* (Durham, NC, 1956).

47 Beer's books include *The Origins of the British Colonial System, 1578–1660* (New York, 1908). For Beer in relation to other American historians, and for the North American colonies as an autonomous unit in the historiography, see chaps. by Stephen Foster, and Doron Ben-Atar.

held that the Empire must unite or disintegrate. This view had implications for historical studies, both for historians in Britain and those in the Dominions. C. P. Lucas, one of the Round Table stalwarts and a Colonial Office official as well as the editor of a three-volume edition of Lord Durham's Report on Canada, resented Canadian historians, for example, who described 'the development of Canada from a dependency to a nation as something which was wrung by clear-sighted, freedom-loving Canadians from purblind politicians in a repressive Mother Country'.[48]

Curtis's dogmatism on the need to 'unite or bust' divided the members of the Round Table, some of whom, notably Leopold Amery, believed development of Dominion nationalism to be compatible with Empire nationalism. 'Britannic' nationalism would emerge as a common bond if the British encouraged the leaders of Canada, Australia, New Zealand, and South Africa, and eventually India, to develop their own sense of identity and allowed them to retain control over tariffs, defence, and external affairs.[49] Amery formed his ideas over the course of a long career that began as a correspondent for *The Times* during the Boer War and came to a climax as Churchill's Secretary of State for India, 1940–45. He championed the protectionist principles expressed by Joseph Chamberlain while Secretary of State for the Colonies, 1895–1903, but above all saw himself as carrying forward the work of Lord Milner.[50] Amery rendered 'signal service to the cause of sovereign equality and national freedom in the Dominions and India'.[51] He thus holds a particular place in the historiography; and his own view on accounts of the Empire before 1914 is acute. He acknowledged inspiration from the work of Richard Jebb, the author of *Studies in Colonial Nationalism* published in 1905.[52] Jebb had originally popularized the idea of Britannic nationalism. Travelling in Australia, New Zealand, Canada, and later South Africa, he recognized earlier than most that the 'White Dominions' would develop their own sense of identity and would expect to retain control over internal affairs and defence, not relinquish it in a federation such as proposed by Curtis. Jebb did not believe that the self-governing colonies wished to break with Britain, but that

[48] Quoted in Carl Berger, *The Writing of Canadian History: Aspects of English-Canadian Historical Writing, 1900–1970* (Toronto, 1976), p. 45. C. P. Lucas, ed., *Lord Durham's Report on the Affairs of British North America*, 3 vols. (Oxford, 1912).

[49] For the theme of Britannic nationalism, see Vol. IV, chap. by John Darwin.

[50] See Wm. Roger Louis, *In the Name of God, Go! Leo Amery and the British Empire in the Age of Churchill* (New York, 1992). For Amery's own thought, see esp. L. S. Amery, *The Forward View* (London, 1935).

[51] W. K. Hancock, *Smuts: The Sanguine Years, 1870–1919* (Cambridge, 1962) and *Smuts: The Fields of Force, 1919–1950* (Cambridge, 1968); quotation from *Sanguine Years*, p. 459.

[52] For Jebb see J. D. B. Miller, *Richard Jebb and the Problem of Empire* (London, 1956), and esp. John Eddy and Deryck Schreuder, eds., *The Rise of Colonial Nationalism: Australia, New Zealand, Canada and South Africa First Assert Their Nationalities, 1880–1914* (Sydney, 1988).

they would if confronted with the stark choice between federation or separatism. He advocated a partnership or alliance between Britain and the Dominions, believing, for example, that the separate Dominion navies would willingly co-operate with the Royal Navy. Like Amery, he stood for tariff reform as a means of unity. In measuring Jebb's historiographical influence, it is useful to bear in mind that the developments after 1914 took place along the lines he had anticipated a decade earlier. The vision of Jebb and Amery, not Curtis, proved to be closer to the reality of the emerging Commonwealth.

In the turbulent years before the First World War, British radicals began to attack the system of European imperialism and to offer theories that have an influence on historical interpretation to the present day. Drawing inspiration from William Cobbett, John Bright, and Richard Cobden—names 'redolent of our English past'[53]—the economist J. A. Hobson in 1902 wrote *Imperialism: A Study*, a book that overshadows in popular influence all other works on the British Empire in the twentieth century. In 1935 William L. Langer of Harvard wrote: 'Hobson was the ablest critical writer on the subject in his time, and his *Imperialism* is perhaps the best book yet written on the subject. The most divergent theories can be traced back to his writings.'[54] Hobson's shadow fell on Lenin as well as on the economist Joseph Schumpeter, whose sociological interpretation offers the principal alternative to Marxist theory.[55] In his attack on imperialism, Hobson unwittingly laid the eventual ideological basis for Soviet foreign policy. Above all, he popularized the idea that the causes of war—the Boer War in particular—originated in the conspiracy of financiers who profited from investments and the arms industry.

Ironically, at least until recently, Hobson has been a somewhat discredited figure in the historiography of the Empire because of D. K. Fieldhouse's effective exploding of his theory in southern and tropical Africa.[56] Many assumed that if Hobson stood convicted as wrong on investment in tropical Africa and misleading on the flow of capital to Latin America and the Dominions, then not only his authority but that of all economic explanations had been undermined. Hobson's theory on the Boer War, however, must be seen against a half-century of prolific writing until his death in 1940. Hobson refined his views, continued to challenge

[53] A. J. P. Taylor, *The Trouble Makers: Dissent over Foreign Policy, 1792–1939* (London, 1957), p. 14.

[54] William L. Langer, *The Diplomacy of Imperialism*, 2 vols. (New York, 1935; 2nd edn. with supplementary bibliographies, 1950); quotation from 2nd edn., p. 97.

[55] Joseph Schumpeter, 'Zur Soziologie der Imperialismen', *Archiv für Sozialwissenschaft und Sozialpolitik*, XLVII (1918–19), pp. 1–39, 275–310; translated as *Imperialism and Social Classes* (Cambridge, Mass., 1951).

[56] D. K. Fieldhouse, ' "Imperialism": An Historiographical Revision', *Economic History Review* (hereafter *EcHR*), Second Series., XIV (Dec. 1961), pp. 187–209; see also D. K. Fieldhouse, ed., *The Theory of Capitalist Imperialism* (London, 1967).

orthodox economic thought, and acquired the reputation of a saint of rationalism. *Imperialism* remains his most important work. It reads as well at the end of the century as it did at the beginning, if it is regarded not as a social science theory but as an ethical and intellectual inquiry into the nature, in his famous phrase, of 'The Economic Taproot of Imperialism'. One of the virtues of P. J. Cain and A. G. Hopkins's recent *British Imperialism* is that they demonstrate the continuing vitality of Hobson's ideas. Along with resuscitating him, they have produced an assessment of the British Empire on the eve of the First World War with which Hobson would have agreed: 'despite her many problems, Britain was still formidably strong when war broke out.'[57]

In catching the spirit of the frenzied nationalism before 1914, it is the British radical writers on imperialism rather than the historians of the Empire who provide the historiographical landmarks.[58] Norman Angell in *The Great Illusion* in 1910 (London) and H. N. Brailsford in *The War of Steel and Gold* in 1914 (London) both agreed with Hobson's argument that wars were essentially irrational and were exploited by those making financial profit from munitions and armaments. It was an illusion to believe that wars for overseas empire would benefit the aggressor. In an era when the German navy and German colonial ambitions seemed to threaten the British Empire, the arguments of Hobson, Angell, and Brailsford were unpopular and misunderstood. They were not pacifists, nor were they opposed to the Empire in the sense of wanting to liquidate it. They were courageous writers who wished to reform the Empire and to make it humane, believing that rational men could arrive at rational solutions, even for Ireland. In the Home Rule crisis in the two years before 1914 there were still grounds for optimism on Ireland, though it was left to a later writer, George Dangerfield in *The Strange Death of Liberal England* (New York, 1935), to pose the unanswerable question: would Britain have plunged into civil war over Ireland had it not been for the outbreak of the First World War?[59]

The outbreak of the First World War marked the beginning of a new phase in the historiography of the Empire, in part because historians began to undermine the

[57] P. J. Cain and A. G. Hopkins, *British Imperialism: Innovation and Expansion, 1688–1914* and *British Imperialism: Crisis and Deconstruction, 1914–1990* (London, 1993); quotation from *Innovation and Expansion*, p. 464.

[58] For the British radicals see Vol. IV, chap. by Nicholas Owen. See also esp. Bernard Porter, *Critics of Empire: British Radical Attitudes to Colonialism in Africa, 1895–1914* (London, 1968) and Norman Etherington, *Theories of Imperialism: War, Conquest and Capital* (London, 1984).

[59] Two of the key works on Ireland in this period are Erskine Childers, powerfully putting forward the Irish case in *The Framework of Home Rule* (London, 1911), and F. S. Oliver, a respected and influential member of the Round Table, *The Alternatives to Civil War* (London, 1913). See chap. by David Harkness on the historiography of Ireland and the Empire, p. 122.

popular view that British rule had entered a golden age. They and other writers dissented from the myth of the Pax Britannica establishing peace and harmony in India and Africa, though their work did not find full expression until the inter-war period. Both in this and the pre-war period, it is necessary to bear in mind the work not only of historians but of writers such as Lytton Strachey[60] and T. E. Lawrence[61] who influenced historical interpretation. It is useful also to note the two novelists who most contributed to the anti-Empire spirit of the times: E. M. Forster, in *A Passage to India* (London, 1924), and George Orwell, in *Burmese Days* (London, 1935). Scholarly interest in the inter-war years ranged over the chronological and geographical extent of the Empire, though in the public debate on 'imperialism'—the word now commonly used by radicals but not yet accepted by most British historians—there were certain preoccupations. In the 1920s Africa emerged in the public eye as a problem almost of the same magnitude as India. In the realm of international affairs historians began to study economic imperialism as a cause of war on the basis of previously inaccessible documents.[62] In the 1930s the Great Depression generated debate on the possibility of shoring up the Empire by devising measures of economic protection that eventually became known as the Ottawa System. Throughout the entire period the problem of the constitutional future of the Empire stirred the historical imagination.

Most historians during the First World War found the wartime experience too overwhelming and too distracting to be able to continue with their own work, still

[60] Strachey's *Eminent Victorians* (London, 1918) placed him in the forefront of the reaction against the Victorian age with its debunking of such heroes as General Charles Gordon. His book was an anti-imperialist as well as an anti-Victorian work, but it was also written with such quirkiness, occasional stylistic brilliance, and irony that it was read with interest by Lord Curzon and others of the Lloyd George government.

[61] *Revolt in the Desert* (London, 1926) and *Seven Pillars of Wisdom: A Triumph* (London, 1935). Lawrence's aim, apart from writing a literary masterpiece, was to establish his place in history as the leader of the Arab uprising against the Turks and also to lament the lost opportunity of securing a place in the Empire or Commonwealth for 'our brown [Arab] brothers'. For a critical view, see esp. Albert Hourani, 'The Myth of T. E. Lawrence', in Wm. Roger Louis, ed., *Adventures with Britannia* (London, 1995), pp. 9–24. The best general study is by John E. Mack, *A Prince of Our Disorder: The Life of T. E. Lawrence* (London, 1976), a work that probably comes as close as any other to applying successfully the methods of clinical psychiatry to history.

[62] Responding to Allied propaganda that Germany had caused the First World War, the German government in 1922 began publishing documents from the German archives: Johannes Lepsius, Albrecht Mendelssohn-Bartholdy, and Friedrich Thimme, eds., *Die Große Politik der Europäischen Kabinette, 1871–1914*, 40 vols. (Berlin, 1922–27). The German series marked a revolution in access to recent documentary evidence. The British began a comparable series in 1927: G. P. Gooch and Harold Temperley, eds., *British Documents on the Origins of the War, 1898–1914*, 11 vols. (London, 1927–38). For other series see the bibliography in A. J. P. Taylor, *The Struggle for Mastery in Europe, 1848–1918* (Oxford, 1954). For the theme of the Empire and the origins of the two world wars, see chap. by Ritchie Ovendale.

less to assess the conflict's long-term significance.[63] During the war itself patriotism prevailed over reason, though Hobson, Brailsford, Angell, and other radicals held their own against champions of the British colonial mission such as Sir Harry Johnston.[64] To most British writers, Germany virtually overnight had become a barbaric power forfeiting the right to rule over indigenous peoples in Africa and the Pacific.[65] Public revulsion against the Turks, though slower to crystallize, led irrevocably to the same conclusion: the former Ottoman territories could not be returned. Here was an opportunity not merely to secure lines of British communication but to create a national home for the Jewish people in Palestine.[66] The war was being fought for a purpose, the Imperial aims of which were complex. At one level the purpose could be summed up in the phrase 'security of the Empire'. At another level it found expression in the insistence by the Dominions on equal status, a demand that eventually culminated in the Statute of Westminster of 1931.[67]

Above all, the wartime debate on colonial issues centred on the question of accountability. Should the conquered territories be placed under the supervision of an international body to be known as the League of Nations, or should national trusteeship prevail? On the whole the consensus in Britain held British rule to be superior to that of others, and Parliament to be the highest authority. At least obliquely, much of the historiography of the inter-war years reflects such concerns. The British were accountable to themselves, with little significant nationalist dissent except in India and Egypt, and without much fear of international interference either by the League of Nations or by rival powers, at least until the challenges by Japan, Italy, and Germany in the 1930s. After 1929 economic turbulence shook assumptions about the Empire's commercial viability; defence commitments placed the armed forces as well as the economy under further strain, especially after

[63] C. P. Lucas is an exception, a transitional figure from the pre-war period. During the war he wrote *The Beginnings of English Overseas Enterprise* (London, 1917), and afterwards *The Partition and the Colonization of Africa* (Oxford, 1922). He also edited with great and subtle skill the major work begun during the war *The Empire at War*, 5 vols. (London, 1921–26).

[64] A Proconsul during the Scramble for Africa, Johnston wrote a knowledgeable, encyclopaedic, and lucid but entirely Eurocentric book ('superior races' is a representative phrase) that survived into the post-Second World War era in Nigerian schools: Sir Harry H. Johnston, *A History of the Colonization of Africa by Alien Races* (Cambridge, 1899). See chap. by Toyin Falola, pp. 489–90. On Johnston as polymath as well as Proconsul, see Roland Oliver, *Sir Harry Johnston and the Scramble for Africa* (London, 1957).

[65] See Wm. Roger Louis, *Great Britain and Germany's Lost Colonies, 1914–1919* (Oxford, 1967).

[66] For the Middle Eastern issues, see chap. by Peter Sluglett. See also esp. John Darwin, *Britain, Egypt and the Middle East: Imperial Policy in the Aftermath of War, 1918–1922* (London, 1981). More generally the key work in the historiography is Elizabeth Monroe, *Britain's Moment in the Middle East, 1914–1956* (London, 1963: 2nd edn. 1981 with a comment on the consequences of the Suez crisis of 1956).

[67] See chap. by W. David McIntyre on the Commonwealth.

the British began seriously to plan for a possible war in the eastern as well as in the western hemisphere; and the potential of major unrest in India preoccupied British officials throughout the entire period. Nevertheless, the British Empire in 1939 remained intact. It appeared to many as a permanent institution in British public life. Churchill, in a famous speech rallying morale against a possible German invasion in 1940, expressed the hope that the Empire would last for a thousand years. Subsequent historical interpretation had to take into account the buoyancy of hope for the Empire's future as well as the deep strain of pessimism on the possibility of resolving the economic and military predicaments of the Imperial system.

Leonard Woolf's *Empire and Commerce in Africa* (London, 1920) sustained the radical argument that the League of Nations should supervise colonial administration. His book is significant because of the rigour of the analysis as well as the thesis that international supervision would assist in reforming the colonial system and perhaps help to root out economic imperialism as a cause of war.[68] Woolf had a powerful intellect informed by his service as 'a renegade former Colonial Officer' in Ceylon.[69] But his major historiographical significance is that, along with his wife Virginia Woolf, he founded the Hogarth Press, whose publications on colonial issues included three books by Norman Leys attacking the colonial administration in Kenya;[70] four books by Sydney Olivier, including *Anatomy of African Misery* (London, 1927);[71] Leonard Barnes's *The New Boer War* (London, 1932);

[68] Historians in America picked up on the same themes. Parker Thomas Moon's *Imperialism in World Politics* (New York, 1926) is an outstanding example, serving as a standard college text and running to its 20th edition in 1964. Other significant books by American writers pursuing the economic theme include Leland Hamilton Jenks, *The Migration of British Capital to 1875* (New York, 1927), and Herbert Feis, *Europe the World's Banker, 1870–1914: An Account of European Foreign Investment and the Connection of World Finance with Diplomacy before the War* (New Haven, 1930); J. Fred Rippy, who began his career in the inter-war years, eventually published *British Investment in Latin America, 1822–1949: A Case Study in the Operations of Private Enterprise in Retarded Regions* (Minneapolis, 1959).

One American historian in the 1930s set the standard for detachment as well as comprehensive analysis and stands in a class by himself in the attempt to take account of economic developments, military calculations, national sentiment, and individual leadership: William L. Langer, *The Diplomacy of Imperialism* (cited above). Chap. 3, 'The Triumph of Imperialism', is perhaps the single most brilliant essay on the subject.

[69] The phrase is John E. Flint's, see below, p. 453. For the historiography of Ceylon, see chap. by K. M. de Silva.

[70] Norman Leys, *Kenya* (London, 1924), *A Last Chance in Kenya* (London, 1931), and *The Colour Bar in Africa* (London, 1941). On Leys, see John W. Cell, *By Kenya Possessed: The Correspondence of Norman Leys and J. H. Oldham, 1918–1926* (Chicago, 1976).

[71] The others were *The Empire Builder* (London, 1927), *White Capital and Coloured Labour* (London, 1929, a revision of an earlier work published in 1906), and *The Myth of Governor Eyre* (London, 1933), an account of Eyre's suppression of the 1865 rebellion in Jamaica. Olivier had served in the Colonial Office and as Governor of Jamaica but was an outspoken critic on economic and racial issues. See Francis Lee, *Fabianism and Colonialism: The Life and Political Thought of Lord Sydney Olivie*r (London, 1988).

C. R. Buxton's *Race Problem in Africa* (London, 1931); Horace Samuel's pro-Zionist indictment of the British administration in Palestine;[72] and three books critical of British rule in India.[73] At the Hogarth Press, Woolf himself published *Imperialism and Civilization* (London, 1928) and *The League and Abyssinia* (London, 1936). Many other books and pamphlets could be listed.[74] The anti-imperialist outlook of the Hogarth Press and of the group of Bloomsbury writers associated with Leonard and Virginia Woolf represented a major dimension of British intellectual and literary life in the inter-war period.

The First World War, like the Second, witnessed a revival of the British colonial mission. The affirmation of moral purpose found full expression in the writings of Sir Frederick (Lord) Lugard (1858–1945) and his disciple (Dame) Margery Perham (1895–1982). Lugard was the Proconsul whose name is indelibly associated with the creation of British Nigeria and the system of colonial administration known as Indirect Rule.[75] Margery Perham was an Oxford don and eventually the first woman Fellow of Nuffield College.[76] Regarded in Oxford, and indeed throughout the world, as a formidable intellect, she had close connections with British colonial officials throughout the Empire. Working together and individually in the 1930s, both Lugard and Perham emphasized the duties and responsibilities of colonial administration. The earlier publication of Lugard's *Dual Mandate in Tropical Africa* (Edinburgh, 1922) can be taken as a critical point in the development of the cult of the British District Officer, who was idealized as almost single-handedly managing to preside with fairness and justice over vast regions in the tropics. The District Officer, like the British nation, had a dual duty to protect indigenous subjects and to promote economic development for the benefit of the world at large.[77]

[72] Horace Barnett Samuel, *Beneath the Whitewash: A Critical Analysis of the Report of the Commission on the Palestine Disturbances of August, 1929* (London, 1930).

[73] Edward Thompson, *Other Side of the Medal* (London, 1925); Graham Pole, *India in Transition* (London, 1932); and K. M. Panikhar, *Caste and Democracy* (London, 1933).

[74] See J. H. Willis, Jr., *Leonard and Virginia Woolf As Publishers: The Hogarth Press, 1917–41* (Charlottesville, Va., 1992), esp. chap. 6.

[75] See Vol. IV, chap. by John W. Cell.

[76] On her place in the historiography, see Anthony Kirk-Greene, 'Margery Perham and Colonial Administration: A Direct Influence on Indirect Rule', in Madden and Fieldhouse, *Oxford and the Idea of Commonwealth.* See also esp. Alison Smith and Mary Bull, eds., *Margery Perham and Colonial Rule in Africa* (London, 1991).

[77] Lugard wrote *The Dual Mandate* to serve among other things as a handbook for District Officers. It can thus be read as a systematic attempt to place problems of local administration within the context of the worldwide British Imperial system. In that sense it bears contrast with the work of the American political scientist Raymond Leslie Buell, *The Native Problem in Africa*, 2 vols. (New York, 1928), a remarkable pioneering survey that remains indispensable to the present day. For assessment of it, and for tropical Africa generally in the historiography of the Empire, see chap. by A. D. Roberts, p. 472.

Then as now the doctrine of the Dual Mandate drew fierce criticism.[78] But it also gained wide acceptance, in part because it had an ethical as well as a patriotic appeal to the British as a nation to act as wards for less fortunate peoples. According to Lugard, Africans would be ruled best through their own institutions, thus preserving tradition and drawing on the African genius for adaptation. The high tide of Indirect Rule may be marked by the publication in 1937 of Perham's *Native Administration in Nigeria* (London), which among other things reveals the collaborative basis of British rule. In their own time both Lugard and Perham were immensely influential figures, suspicious of rapid change yet champions of gradual reform. Part of their aim in the slow pace was to forestall the advent of 'hot-headed' Indian-type nationalism in Africa. To a later age they seemed to be nothing less than agents of British imperialism striving to perpetuate the Empire indefinitely by propping up traditional rulers and frustrating African nationalists; but to many contemporaries they were colonial reformers locked in combat with the Colonial Office.[79] There is a certain irony that Lugard, the champion of national trusteeship yet endlessly at odds with the Colonial Office, served from 1922 to 1936 as the British representative on the Mandates Commission of the League of Nations.[80] Margery Perham became the foremost authority on Africa of

[78] The contemporary criticism by Leonard Barnes (like Leonard Woolf a former colonial official) is representative:

> To rob and exploit the 'lesser breeds' too weak for self-defence against machine guns and high explosives, to disintegrate their distinctive cultures, to pull down their traditional livelihoods, to conscript them as protesting and bewildered auxiliaries of industrialism—all this was seen not as a chaotic fury of looting (which is what it in fact was), but as a beneficent process of tidying up a disorderly world, of spreading the salt of civilization more easily over the earth and of sweeping the scum of barbarism away from inconspicuous corners.

Leonard Barnes, *The Duty of Empire* (London, 1935), p. 87. See also the same author's *Soviet Light on the Colonies* (London, 1944), which expressed admiration for the achievement of Soviet rule in the former Tsarist empire. For the scholarly deconstruction of Indirect Rule, see I. F. Nicolson, *The Administration of Nigeria, 1900–1960: Men, Methods, and Myths* (Oxford, 1969).

[79] Though both were closely associated with the Colonial Office, there was no love lost on the bureaucracy. *The Dual Mandate* can be read in a sense as an extended complaint by Lugard on the trammelling of local administration by an ignorant and arbitrary Colonial Office. Perham believed that the government in London (especially the Foreign Office in relation to the Sudan) sacrificed Imperial obligations to larger issues of foreign policy. Her scepticism of Colonial Office motives perhaps reached a culmination when, after examining the evidence in R. E. Robinson's unpublished Ph.D. thesis ('The Trust in British Central African Policy, 1889–1939', Cambridge, 1951), she commented: 'I'll never again trust the Colonial Office.' (Information from R. E. Robinson.)

[80] In fact Lugard and Perham as colonial reformers had much in common with the British radicals. They all thought that uncontrolled capital enterprise would damage the political economy of indigenous societies. But Hobson held that exploitation was the aim of Empire, whereas Lugard believed that the Empire needed to protect Africans and others from capitalist exploitation. Norman Etherington has written, 'the difference between Hobson and Lugard is in fact no more than a sheet of paper' (Etherington, *Theories of Imperialism*, p. 75). This is a shrewd insight. But it was a pretty thick piece of paper.

her generation. She explicated the theory of Indirect Rule,[81] and wrote a two-volume biography of Lugard;[82] but her most effective writing found expression in letters to *The Times*.[83] In the aftermath of the fall of Singapore in 1942 she called for a renewal of Britain's Imperial mission. As a preliminary step, she urged the abolition of the 'Colour Bar', a phrase officially denied but which expressed a reality in the British colonial world.[84] In late life she demonstrated great courage by travelling to Nigeria in 1968 in an attempt to end the Nigerian civil war. She was in many respects the embodiment of the British colonial conscience.

The inter-war years can be described not merely as the age of Lugard and Perham but also as the Coupland era in Imperial history. (Sir) Reginald Coupland succeeded Egerton in 1920 as Beit Professor in Oxford. Coupland's electors deliberately chose 'a first-class mind' to raise the level of scholarship above that of Egerton, whom they regarded as too much of a specialist. Coupland had a distinguished career, but in the end it was clouded by the attack on him by Eric Williams, who in 1938 became the first student from the West Indies to receive an Oxford D.Phil. and who later became Prime Minister of Trinidad and Tobago. No one could have worked harder than Coupland to bring 'colonial history' up to the standard of Stubbs and Maitland and others who had founded the *English Historical Review*.[85] A Fellow of All Souls, he contributed to the college's reputation as a place where important decisions were made on the Empire as well as on national and world affairs; and by sponsoring the Ralegh Club (an undergraduate society that debated colonial issues on Sunday evenings at Rhodes House), he attempted to recruit outstanding Oxford students into service of the Empire. He was, however, a Proconsul *manqué*. He did his best work in a semi-official capacity as a member of the Peel Commission on Palestine, drafting its report with such historical sweep and exactitude of detail that it stands as one of the great state papers of modern times. He conducted research at the Public Record Office, and his two major works on East Africa remain as solid if unimaginative accounts based on archival records and private papers.[86] One of Coupland's lasting contributions to

81 See esp. her introduction to the 1965 edn. of *The Dual Mandate*.

82 *Lugard: The Years of Adventure, 1858–1898* (London, 1956) and *Lugard: The Years of Authority, 1898–1945* (London, 1960).

83 See Margery Perham, *Colonial Sequence, 1930 to 1949: A Chronological Commentary Upon British Colonial Policy Especially in Africa* (London, 1967).

84 See Wm. Roger Louis, *Imperialism at Bay, 1941–1945: The United States and the Decolonization of the British Empire* (Oxford, 1977), pp. 135–38.

85 'Under Coupland, colonial history came of age and took its place beside the older historical studies': *The Times*, 7 Nov. 1952, obituary of Coupland.

86 *East Africa and its Invaders: From the Earliest Times to the Death of Seyyid Said in 1856* (Oxford, 1938) and *The Exploitation of East Africa, 1856–1890: The Slave Trade and the Scramble* (London, 1939). Coupland's accounts of missionary activity left subsequent historians in his debt. See esp. Roland Oliver, *The Missionary Factor in East Africa* (London, 1952). Oliver can be seen in the tradition of Coupland but, in A. D. Roberts's phrase, Coupland 'leavened by irony': see chap. by Roberts, p. 477.

historical scholarship was his study of the interaction between the British and the Arab empire extending from Oman to Zanzibar and the East African coast. In his last book, published posthumously, *Welsh and Scottish Nationalism: A Study* (London, 1954), he began to explore tensions within British society that reflected his knowledge of multinational identities in Palestine, India, South Africa, and Canada.

Coupland was an idealist. He believed in the moral capacity of the British Empire to shape a better world and to help dependent peoples to advance towards self-government. He was almost, but not quite, as unabashed as Macaulay in believing in the history of the Empire as the story of unfolding liberty. In his work on India he was the first writer to make clear to the general public the significance of the Pakistan movement.[87] He also wrote more generally on humanitarian issues such as Wilberforce and the abolition of the slave trade. It was his latter-day championing of the British humanitarian mission that brought him into collision with Eric Williams. In 1944 Williams published a revised version of his D.Phil. thesis, *Capitalism and Slavery*, which challenged the primacy of the humanitarian motive by arguing that the end of the slave trade came about essentially for economic reasons: sugar was no longer profitable. In mounting the attack against Coupland, Williams included charges of 'poetic sentimentality', a deliberate effort 'to present a distorted view of the abolitionist movement', and a 'deplorable tendency' to confuse supposed humanitarian aims with veiled economic motives.[88] The problem, however, was not the attack itself but that Williams had much the better part of the argument, or so it appeared to many at the time.[89] The confrontation was not entirely personal—it represented a clash between generations as well as between Oxford Imperial history and the beginning of what became known as area studies.[90]

The development of area studies in relation to Imperial history can be traced

[87] See his *The Indian Problem: Report on the Constitutional Problem in India*, 3 vols. (Oxford, 1942–43), and *India: A Re-Statement* (London, 1945). For Pakistan in the historiography, see chap. by Ian Talbot. For India in the 1940s see chap. by Robin J. Moore.

[88] Eric Williams, *Capitalism and Slavery* (Chapel Hill, NC, 1944), pp. 45, 178, 211. Coupland's Oxford colleagues thought the comments to be entirely unjustified and indeed scandalous. According to Frederick Madden, Coupland's relations with 'Rhodes Scholars, Indians, and the few Africans around were easy and friendly: the more bitterly did he feel Eric William's personal attack on him' (Madden, 'The Commonwealth, Commonwealth History, and Oxford', p. 13). For the historiography of the Empire and the slave trade see chap. by Gad Heuman.

[89] Williams's economic argument in turn received substantial criticism. In the context of the Empire see esp. Roger Anstey, *The Atlantic Slave Trade and British Abolition, 1760–1810* (Cambridge, 1975).

[90] Williams defined his own purpose as a contribution to 'West Indian and Negro history' as well as economic history. It is significant that he dedicated his book to Lowell Joseph Ragatz, the author of *The Fall of the Planter Class in the British Caribbean, 1763–1833: A Study in Social and Economic History* (New York, 1928), which was a pioneer work in the field. For the historiography of the West Indies and the Empire see chap. by B. W. Higman.

to the 1930s. Parts of the *Cambridge History of the British Empire* anticipated later regional specialization, for example, the work by Cornelius de Kiewiet.[91] Above all, the books by W. M. Macmillan are significant for his coherent general interpretation and specifically because of his radical line of class analysis on such issues as the 'industrial colour bar'.[92] His work inspired a later generation of historians of southern Africa.[93] In *The Cape Colour Question: A Historical Survey* (London, 1927), and in *Bantu, Boer, and Britain: The Making of the South African Native Problem* (London, 1929), Macmillan tenaciously pursued social and economic research—with Marxist overtones, or at least with a line of analysis not incompatible with Marxism that made him unwelcome in many British academic circles, as well as in South Africa. In 1936, in *Warning from the West Indies: A Tract for Africa and the Empire*, he challenged Lugard's idea of static trusteeship and minimal colonial government, demanding that the Colonial Office accept responsibility for educational as well as economic and social development. Macmillan's work, like A. P. Newton's before him, represents a historiographical connection between Africa and the West Indies.[94]

In other regions historians in the 1930s began to deal with non-European nationalism in a manner that marked the beginning of a new era. George Antonius's *The Arab Awakening: The Story of the Arab National Movement* (London, 1938) provided the first sympathetic account in English of the development of Arab nationalism, challenging the optimistic assumption of the Balfour Declaration and thus the basis of British rule in Palestine: 'the logic of facts is inexorable. It shows that no room can be made in Palestine for a second nation except by dislodging or exterminating the nation in possession.'[95] On India, Edward Thompson and G. T. Garratt's *Rise and Fulfilment of British Rule in India*

[91] See his chaps. in *CHBE*, VIII, esp. chap. 30, 'Social and Economic Developments in Native Tribal Life': 'The significance of the nineteenth century in native history is that it produced a black proletariat' (p. 828). See also esp. C. W. de Kiewiet, *A History of South Africa: Social and Economic* (Oxford, 1941).

Though the South African vol. in the *CHBE* did foreshadow later regional research, it should also be said that this was an exception in the series. With the further exception of some of the younger authors in Vol. III, notably Frederick Madden, most of the contributors to the *CHBE* had little to say about such areas as Africa or the Pacific. What did emerge from the *CHBE* in relation to other scholarship on the Empire in the 1930s was the outstanding regional work on Canada, Australia, New Zealand, and South Africa.

[92] For Macmillan and generally for the historiography of Southern Africa see chap. by William H. Worger.

[93] See Hugh Macmillan and Shula Marks, eds., *Africa and Empire: W. M. Macmillan, Historian and Social Critic* (London, 1989).

[94] Newton's books included *The European Nations in the West Indies, 1493–1688* (London, 1933).

[95] p. 412. For historiographical assessment of Antonius see esp. Albert Hourani, 'The Arab Awakening Forty Years After', in Albert Hourani, *The Emergence of the Modern Middle East* (London, 1981).

(London, 1934) was the first major British attempt to understand the Indian nationalist movement on its own terms.[96] The authors also occasionally drew historical parallels: in the early twentieth century 'most Englishmen began to understand that there was an Indian "problem", just as there was an Irish "problem", and that, as in the case of Ireland, it was based on a national movement'.[97] On South-East Asia, from a radically different perspective, Rupert Emerson of Harvard in 1937 wrote *Malaysia: A Study in Direct and Indirect Rule* (New York, 1937), the scope of which included the Netherlands East Indies as will as British Malaya.[98] Emerson, like W. M. Macmillan, later inspired a new generation of scholars pursuing questions of nationalism and independence.[99] In dealing with the political economy of South-East Asia, he rigorously challenged the assumptions of the colonial administration in Malaya on such issues as monopolies in tin-mining and rubber production, as well as favouritism shown to 'European and Chinese land seekers'.[100] The 1930s also witnessed the publication of some of the most original work of J. S. Furnivall, an administrator-scholar in Burma, for example, *An Introduction to the Political Economy of Burma* (Rangoon, 1931). His later book, *Colonial Policy and Practice: A Comparative Study of Burma and Netherlands India* (Cambridge, 1948), lent academic credibility to the voguish but exceedingly useful phrase 'plural society', which conveyed the meaning of separate peoples with different purposes that were determined in large part by the economic functions of

[96] See chap. by Tapan Raychaudhuri, for the historiography of nationalism in India as well as India generally since 1857.

[97] p. 550. On the 'problem' of Indian and Irish nationalism, Nicholas Mansergh later became the acknowledged authority. In 1967 he became Editor-in-Chief of *Constitutional Relations Between Britain and India: The Transfer of Power, 1942–7*, 12 vols. (London, 1970–83). Though he is remembered above all for the Transfer of Power series and his work on the Commonwealth, from the 1930s he had written on Ireland and he stands as 'one of the finest historians of Ireland'. David Harkness, 'Philip Nicholas Seton Mansergh, 1910–1991', *Proceedings of the British Academy*, LXXXII (London, 1993). See esp. Nicholas Mansergh, *The Unresolved Question: The Anglo-Irish Settlement and Its Undoing, 1912–72* (New Haven, 1991). See also *Nationalism and Independence: Selected Irish Papers by Nicholas Mansergh*, ed. Diana Mansergh (Cork, 1997).

[98] For South-East Asia, see chap. by Nicholas Tarling.

[99] See, for example, Crawford Young, *The African Colonial State in Comparative Perspective* (New Haven, 1994), which is the key work on the idea of the colonial state. For example, on Lugard and the assumptions of European colonial administration: 'As a Platonic guardian class, colonial officialdom represented itself as the disinterested servant of the subject population, basking as philosopher-king in the full sunlight of wisdom, ruling firmly but justly over those still enclosed in the cave of ignorance, who could see only distorted shadows of their true interests flickering on the darkened walls' (p. 165).

[100] Emerson used deft quotations to let British administrators speak for themselves, sometimes with unwitting irony. For example, on the appointment of Malays to the Malayan Civil Service: 'the new High Commissioner, Sir Shenton Thomas, replied [in 1936] in language worthy of precise analysis: "This is the sixth country in which I have served, and I do not know of any country in which what I may call a foreigner—that is to say, a person not a native of the country or an Englishman—has ever been appointed to an administrative post." ' *Malaysia*, p. 515.

the colonial state.[101] Many other authors might be mentioned. The decade of the 1930s, in short, was a seminal period for comparative studies and for works more favourably disposed to emergent nationalism.

The new trends in the historiography of the 1930s by no means represented the inter-war period as a whole. If one single vein of interpretation predominated, it was the constitutional. In this field there looms in the historiography a giant whose erudition matches that of any other: the Sanskrit scholar and constitutional lawyer (Sir) Arthur Berriedale Keith. The historian with whom he should be compared is (Sir) Kenneth Wheare, whose books on the constitutional history of the Empire will probably continue to be read more widely than Keith's. The third scholar to bear in mind is Frederick Madden, whose work continues to the present. In this specialized and now neglected field it is useful to ask: why did constitutional history figure so largely in the history of the Empire in the inter-war years? The short answer is that it was the dominant mode of study in British schools and universities, but beyond that, people generally believed that constitutional solutions could be found to problems of such magnitude as Ireland, India, and Palestine. Like their Victorian predecessors—above all, Stubbs and Maitland—historians such as Curtis, Coupland, and Perham, along with Keith, continued to view Imperial history from the perspective of British constitutions and administration. They generally 'read back into the imperial past the gradual but inevitable triumph of Commonwealth institutions and ethics'.[102] It might require time, perhaps even centuries, but even the African dependencies could be launched on the course of self-government and eventual democracy. Disillusionment with the ideals of the Empire and Commonwealth—or at least with common British ethical and constitutional assumptions on the colonies—is essentially a post-Imperial phenomenon. Historians of the inter-war years, with varying degrees of scepticism, continued to affirm the Whig idea of progress. It would do them an injustice to measure them against the *Zeitgeist* of a later age.

In 1914 Keith was appointed Regius Professor of Sanskrit and Comparative Philology at the University of Edinburgh. His recondite knowledge and scholarly works on Sanskrit were already legendary, but in the previous decade he had also worked as a civil servant in the Dominions Department at the Colonial Office, where he began systematically to study the constitutional law of the Empire. His greatest work in this field was his first: *Responsible Government in the Dominions*

[101] Furnivall anticipated the idea of the colonial state by using the concept of the 'Leviathan': J. S. Furnivall, *The Fashioning of Leviathan: The Beginnings of British Rule in Burma* (Canberra, 1991), reprinted from *Journal of Burma Research Society*, XXIV (1939), pp. 3–137. See Vol. IV, chap. by Ronald Hyam.

[102] Ronald Robinson, 'Oxford in Imperial Historiography', p. 37. For the Commonwealth theme see chap. by W. David McIntyre.

(London, 1909), which he expanded in subsequent editions until its final two-volume version in 1928. Like Antonio Vivaldi, Keith continued to reshape the same themes in many different works. Among his outstanding publications are a constitutional history of the Empire from the beginning to the time of the loss of the American colonies, *Constitutional History of the First British Empire* (London, 1930), and *A Constitutional History of India, 1600–1935* (London, 1936). Yielding to no other perspective, he wrote with a legal insistence that sometimes approached belligerence, and with such density of style and crabbed exposition of obscure evidence that his work was read mainly by other learned scholars. Like Margery Perham, some of his most effective writing for a general audience found expression in letters to *The Times*, to which in Keith's case should be added *The Scotsman*.[103] He had no rival to the time of his death in 1942, though Wheare's first book, *The Statute of Westminster, 1931*, appeared in 1933 and his second, *The Statute of Westminster and Dominion Status*, in 1938. Wheare was the Gladstone Professor of Government and Public Administration at Oxford (1944–57) and a Fellow of All Souls. He placed the subject of the British constitution in much broader perspective than Keith by studying political as well as constitutional traditions. By taking into account the world of politics and administration he raised the field of the constitutional history of the Empire 'to its highest intellectual level'.[104] He was also a stylist, who wrote concisely and elegantly.[105] His most stimulating work, *Government By Committee: An Essay on the British Constitution* (Oxford, 1955), remains mandatory reading. As a genre, the constitutional history of the Empire has perhaps quietly reached its apex in the ongoing series by Frederick Madden, assisted by D. K. Fieldhouse and John Darwin, *Select Documents on the Constitutional History of the British Empire and Commonwealth*.[106] In scholarly detail and insight, the series sustains in every sense the tradition of Keith and Wheare.

In the late 1930s the work of W. K. (Sir Keith) Hancock transformed the subject of Imperial history by integrating its component parts—especially the constitutional, economic, demographic, and religious—into a single, coherent and comprehensive interpretation. More than that of any other historian of the British Empire, his historiographical influence bridged the period of the 1930s

[103] See, for example, Arthur Berriedale Keith, *Letters on Imperial Relations, Indian Reform, Constitutional and International Law, 1916–1935* (Oxford, 1935).

[104] David Fieldhouse, in *Oxford and the Idea of Commonwealth*, p. 159.

[105] He was also, in Max Beloff's words, 'the model of a true Oxford don': *Dictionary of National Biography, 1971–1980*.

[106] Seven vols. to date, Greenwood Press, Westport, Conn., 1985–1994. This is a labour of love representing decades of dedication to the subject by Frederick Madden. The last volume in the series, Vol. VIII, will deal with the final stage of decolonization from 1948.

to the 1950s and beyond. Hancock had arrived in Oxford at Balliol as a Rhodes Scholar, and in 1924 became the first Australian to be elected a Fellow of All Souls College. At All Souls Lionel Curtis influenced him but failed to convert him to the belief that the Empire must federate or disintegrate. Hancock from early on developed the view that dominion nationalism must be respected as much as Imperial patriotism. In *Australia* (London, 1930) he not only attempted to reconcile *imperium et libertas* by writing that 'it is not impossible for Australians . . . to be in love with two soils'; he also developed the three resounding themes of mastering a continent, framing a polity, and forging an identity. These grand ideas reflected his wide reading in American as well as European and specifically Italian history.[107] After holding the post of Professor of Modern History in Adelaide, he accepted a chair in Birmingham in 1934 with the explicit purpose in mind of coming to grips with the economic history of the Empire. This was his most creative period. At the invitation of Arnold Toynbee he wrote the *Survey of British Commonwealth Affairs*,[108] and in the Second World War undertook the editing of the civil series in the official war histories, which were eventually published in twenty-eight volumes.[109] Hancock returned to Oxford as Chichele Professor of Economic History at All Souls (1944–49), then became the first Director of the Institute of Commonwealth Studies at the University of London (1949–56), finally returning to Australia to be the Director of the Research School of Social Sciences at the Australian National University (1957–61). In the latter part of his career he published his two-volume biography of J. C. Smuts, ultimately a flawed work in that it stops short of exploring the African dimension of the subject, but nevertheless one of the great biographies of the twentieth century.[110]

[107] His first book had been *Ricasoli and the Risorgimento in Tuscany* (London, 1926).

[108] Published by the Oxford University Press for the Royal Institute of International Affairs (Chatham House) in 2 vols., 1937–42. The 1st vol. (1937) carried the subtitle *Problems of Nationality, 1918–1936*; the second volume was published in two parts (1940–42), both with the subtitle *Problems of Economic Policy, 1918–1939*. Hancock viewed publication by the RIIA as an opportunity to influence policy not only of the British government but also of the Dominions, an ambition that distinguished him from virtually all other historians then and later. The connection with Toynbee is significant. Hugh Trevor-Roper's attack on Toynbee in the 1950s has obscured the esteem and gratitude felt by those such as Albert Hourani and Hancock who worked with Toynbee at Chatham House in the 1930s. See the biography by William H. McNeill, *Arnold J. Toynbee: A Life* (New York, 1989), esp. p. 239 for the attack by Trevor-Roper (later Lord Dacre).

[109] The full title of the series is *History of the Second World War: United Kingdom Civil Series*. With M. M. Gowing, Hancock in the series wrote *British War Economy* (London, 1949). The standard of the series was exceptionally high. Unlike Acton and the editors of the *Cambridge History of the British Empire*, Hancock did not die before his editorial duties were complete, but his experience appears to have resembled that of the *OHBE* editors, emerging with 'white hair and . . . exhaustion'. K. S. Inglis quoting Margaret Gowing in the *Dictionary of National Biography, 1986–1990*.

[110] Cited above, no. 51.

Unlike most of his predecessors, Hancock mastered the art of the case study. Following Acton's maxim that one should study problems, not subjects, in the *Survey* Hancock began immediately with Ireland and progressed to Palestine. In his analysis of the settler colonies of Kenya and Rhodesia he brought into sharp focus the part played by missionaries[111] and (in the case of Kenya) the immigrant community of Indians, as well as the land policies of the colonial governments.[112] With a capacious knowledge of the breadth and scope of the Empire's history, he used case studies to draw conclusions on universal issues, including those of the world economy. Partly on the basis of his own understanding of the Australian economy, but largely because of the power of his intellect, he was able brilliantly to assess the protectionist policies of the 1930s.[113] In short, he established the interaction of what are now called the centre and the periphery, reminding the reader constantly of the historian's virtues of attachment (empathy with the subject), justice, and span.[114] Yet for all his reach there are two aspects of his work that are unsatisfactory. In spite of his efforts to see the Empire as a worldwide system, the Indian dimension of his work is curiously limited. He never assimilated India into his general analysis in the way that he did Palestine or West Africa.[115] As to the second aspect, although his West African case study is a *tour de force* it is flawed by the same blind spot that mars his masterpiece on Smuts: Hancock never quite got the African side of the problem into focus or saw the full force of the initiative of the Africans themselves in shaping their own history. In the biography Africans are conspicuous by their absence.[116] Yet despite these shortcomings Hancock remains, like Macaulay, in a class by himself. As has already been mentioned, there would probably be a consensus among the historians involved in the *Oxford History of the British Empire* that he was far and away the greatest historian of the Empire and Commonwealth.

[111] For this theme see chap. by Norman Etherington.

[112] For the historiography of East Africa see chap. by Charles Ambler.

[113] Hancock's treatment of the Ottawa System remained for decades the most incisive analysis and still must be read along with Ian M. Drummond's *Imperial Economic Policy, 1917–1939: Studies in Expansion and Protection* (London, 1974). The single best comment on Hancock as an economic historian is by David Fieldhouse, 'Keith Hancock and Imperial Economic History', in *Oxford and the Idea of Commonwealth.*

[114] 'Attachment, justice, and span' were the words Hancock used to describe the work of Mary Kingsley, but they could well be used to characterize his own work. Mary H. Kingsley was the author of *Travels in West Africa: Congo Français, Corisco and Cameroons* (London, 1897), and to her he attributed part of his intellectual heritage. See *Problems of Economic Policy*, pt. 2, Appendix A. Kingsley was a pioneer in the field of anthropology and she advanced scientific knowledge in such areas as disease, diet, and malnutrition. For these themes see chap. by Diana Wylie.

[115] In part perhaps because he intended to move on to India as one of his future case studies. For the historiography of West Africa see chap. by Toyin Falola.

[116] See the review by Roland Oliver in the *Journal of African History*, 'Blinkered Genius', IX, 3 (1968), pp. 491–94.

On the eve of the Second World War Lord Hailey's *An African Survey* was published.[117] This massive account, written in effect by a team of experts, immediately became a classic. It provided a full discussion of the colonial policies of France, Belgium, and Portugal as well as of Britain; and it also covered such topics as law and education as well as such technical subjects as soil-erosion, crops, and mining. It helped to define what later became known as the field of African studies. Above all, it had a historiographical significance—in the words of Hailey's biographer: 'It was a pivotal work, looking both ways.' Looking forward, it argued for 'constructive' trusteeship rather than the static system of minimal government and non-intervention. It anticipated the colonial reforms of the wartime era and even 'the postwar transfer of power'. Looking backward, it distilled the discussion by the inter-war generation of such African problems as 'race, culture, primitiveness, and what would later be called colonial dependence'.[118] Hailey believed it inevitable that Africans at some distant point would master their own destinies. He regarded 'Indirect Rule' as a temporary stage in the process of political evolution. Indirect Rule had already, in his view, become an anachronism except as a form of local government.[119] He came to these conclusions after dispassionate deliberation. During a distinguished career in the Indian Civil Service, Hailey rose to the rank of Governor of the Punjab and subsequently of the United Provinces. In retirement he became Lugard's successor as British representative on the Permanent Mandates Commission, 1936–39.

Hailey possessed a rare ability to synthesize great amounts of material and, like Margery Perham, a capacity to present general views on controversial subjects in a persuasive manner, proving especially effective with American audiences. He emerged during the war, along with Perham, as one of the most influential speakers on the future of the British Empire. In late 1942 a Colonial Office report well expressed the consensus on Hailey's public stature and caught the mood of British sensitivity to American criticism of the Empire. The report dealt with a conference convened in Canada to debate 'the colonial issue', which in a phrase summed up a major point of wartime tension between the British and the Americans that is reflected in much of the historiography:

117 With the subtitle *A Study of Problems Arising in Africa South of the Sahara* (London, 1938); Hailey made extensive changes for its revised edn. published in 1957 when he was 86 years old. In this edition he referred to emergent African nationalism as 'Africanism' to suggest that it was a 'racial' idea rather than one reflecting the concept of the nation state. The revised edn. of the *Survey* appeared in the year after the historiographical landmark, Thomas Hodgkin, *Nationalism in Colonial Africa* (London, 1956), which argued persuasively that African nationalism possessed the same 'universal' attributes of nationalism elsewhere.

118 John W. Cell, *Hailey: A Study in British Imperialism, 1872–1969* (Cambridge, 1992), p. 217.

119 According to John Flint, 'an elaboration of indirect rule institutions could, at most, have led to "self-administration" of small units . . . The concept had a good deal in common with that of the "Bantustans" in South Africa today.' John Flint, 'Planned Decolonization and Its Failure in British Africa', *African Affairs*, LXXXII, 328 (1983), pp. 389–411.

> Hailey throughout was truly superb . . . [and] without a trace of condescension. I was lost in admiration at the whole ten-day performance and many times as I watched him cross swords with the American 'Professors' and gracefully prick one balloon after another, I thought what a stupid tragedy it would be to take the management of great affairs from men like Hailey and give them over to the [American] boys with thick-lensed glasses, long hair and longer words nasally intoned.[120]

Margery Perham and others identified Hailey as the moving spirit behind the colonial reforms in progress during the war despite, in the contemporary view, intolerable official delay and incompetence. Hailey, however, moved at a stately pace. He had little personal warmth and, though he spoke cogently and convincingly, did not convey the sincerity of Perham's dedication to the cause. If any single person can be said to represent the revival of Britain's colonial mission during the war, it would be Margery Perham. But the two of them stood out in the public eye as superintendents of the British Empire.

The Second World War distracted historians from their research and writing, but more works of substance appeared than during the First World War.[121] It is illuminating to note briefly the wartime experiences of a few historians and future historians of the British Empire, for some of whom the war was merely an impediment to scholarly work, while for others it became a formative experience. A few, such as J. C. Beaglehole in New Zealand, managed to persevere: a 'casually dressed scholar, somewhat resembling E. M. Forster',[122] Beaglehole continued to work on the editions of the *Journals of Captain James Cook* later published by the Hakluyt Society. Many prominent historians were drawn by the war into the vortex of the bureaucracy in London. Vincent Harlow worked in the Ministry of Information; Richard Pares, who had produced *War and Trade in the West Indies* in 1936, spent the war at the Board of Trade, as did Lucy Sutherland, already acknowledged as an authority on the East India Company; the young Jack Gallagher served in the Royal Tank Regiment in North Africa. Rather like a latter-day T. E. Lawrence (who chose in the 1920s to enlist in the ranks in the Royal Air Force), Gallagher refused to be commissioned as an officer. He later said that he wanted his epitaph to read simply 'Tank Soldier and Historian'. The young Ronald Robinson served in the RAF and won the Distinguished Flying Cross. At war's end he was inspired—to his later embarrassment—by a book by Eric A. Walker, *The British Empire: Its*

[120] Report by D. M. MacDougall (Colonial Office), 22 Dec. 1942, quoted in *Imperialism at Bay*, p. 13.

[121] In addition to books already mentioned by C. W. de Kiewiet and Eric Williams, these works included Arthur J. Marder, *The Anatomy of British Sea Power: A History of British Naval Policy in the Pre-Dreadnought Era, 1880–1905* (New York, 1940); S. E. Crowe, *The Berlin West African Conference, 1884–1885* (London, 1942); and John Bartlet Brebner, *North Atlantic Triangle: The Interplay of Canada, the United States and Great Britain* (New York, 1945).

[122] E. H. McCormick in the *Dictionary of National Biography, 1971–1980*.

Structure and Spirit, a book that seemed to imply that during the war God had stood on the side of the Empire.[123]

Keith Hancock took enough time from his job supervising the beginning of the civil histories to write *Argument of Empire* (published in 1943 as a 'Penguin Special'), a didactic book of some interest because of its teleology, because of its distillation of some of the more controversial elements in the *Survey of British Commonwealth Affairs*, and also because of its clarity on the regeneration of Britain's colonial purpose. Hancock wanted Americans to reflect on the ideals of the British Empire and Commonwealth. In that sense the book was propagandistic. In powerful words, he defined the purpose of the Empire to be the guardian of liberty: 'Freedom is something which unites men. In our own history it has united English and Scots and Welsh, French-Canadians and British-Canadians, Dutch-South-Africans and British-South-Africans, white New Zealanders and Maoris.'[124] To Americans it might appear that the British were fighting to preserve the Empire, perhaps even to add to it, but the reality, according to Hancock, was that the Empire represented the most extensive system of freedom that had ever existed in human history.[125] 'Monarchy grows into democracy, empire grows into commonwealth, the tradition of a splendid past is carried forward into an adventurous future.'[126] The Empire's history as the unfolding story of liberty continued to be the dominant mode of interpretation by Imperial historians. The major shift in the teleology did not occur until ten years later, emblazoned in the historiography by the publication of Gallagher and Robinson's article, 'The Imperialism of Free Trade', in 1953.[127]

At the end of the Second World War there was a resurgence of interest in the Pacific as well as Africa. In the historiography of the Pacific the name of J. C. Beaglehole is writ large, but it is useful to consider briefly the works of J. W.

[123] The Empire's 'Faith, hope and charity were justified in the long run.' (p. 236, 1947 edn.) The book was first published in 1943, went through its 4th impression in 1947, and was republished in extended form in 1953. It was perhaps the best text on the Empire of its time. Walker was the Vere Harmsworth Professor of Naval and Imperial History at Cambridge. He was a major contributor to the vol. on South Africa (Vol. VIII) in the *Cambridge History of the British Empire* (Cambridge, 1936). For an assessment of his work, and generally for the historiography of Southern and Central Africa, see chap. by William Worger, p. 518–18.

[124] *Argument of Empire*, p. 137. The key to Hancock's argument on India was that Canada, Australia, New Zealand, and South Africa had all achieved national unity. In India there was still no national consensus. 'The future of India rests upon Indian decision' (p. 38). This was a representative British view during the wartime period.

[125] Hancock's thought already bore a remarkable similarity to that of J. C. Smuts, who had given a famous interview to *Life* magazine in Dec. 1942 along those lines.

[126] *Argument of Empire*, p. 12.

[127] *EcHR*, Second Series, VI, 1 (1953), pp. 1–15. 'They sought to rescue the subject from teleology,' see below, A. D. Roberts, p. 477.

Davidson along with Beaglehole's. Davidson in 1942 had completed his Cambridge Ph.D. thesis, 'The European Penetration of the South Pacific, 1779–1842'. About a decade earlier Beaglehole had decided to write a biography of Captain James Cook, including a full account of Cook's voyages and exploration of the Pacific. As a prelude, in a task that would take well over a quarter of a century, he began editing Cook's *Journals*, the first of which was published in 1955 and the last in 1967. His editing was a model of scholarly exactitude. The biography appeared posthumously in 1974.[128] Beaglehole wrote with a style that sometimes had a poetic ring to it, and, in his own words describing the early explorers, with 'a passion to see and to report truly'.[129] Devoted to the history of exploration in the Pacific, he stands as one of the principal historians of the eighteenth century. In a sense J. W. Davidson's work reflected the intellectual interests of the next generation. He attempted to shift the focus from the Europeans to the islanders and, rather like Hancock, used the method of the case study to achieve his aims. Western Samoa became the microcosm. Davidson argued that Samoan resentment at the European intrusion had existed from early on, and that the presence of missionaries, traders, and colonial administrators[130] galvanized and shaped the Samoan national movement. Davidson has a fair claim to be described as the founder of Pacific Studies that emerged in the 1960s along with African Studies. In 1949 he was appointed Professor of Pacific History at the Australian National University and in 1967 he published *Samoa mo Samoa*, the pioneer work on nationalism in the Pacific.[131]

Of the historians of the 1950s, Richard Pares and Lucy Sutherland are exceptional because of the quality of their work. Both were concerned with the major issues of the Empire in the eighteenth century, and each in different ways wove the politics of the era into the fabric of economy and society in a manner that few historians have achieved before or since. But they were slightly removed from the mainstream of Imperial history. Both were what might be called *EHR* historians, from whom a line could be drawn back to Bryce, Stubbs, and others

[128] J. C. Beaglehole, *The Life of Captain James Cook* (London, 1974). The vol. appeared as Vol. IV in *The Journals of Captain James Cook on His Voyages of Discovery*, Hakluyt Society Extra Series, No. XXXVII. For the themes of exploration and science, see chaps. by Robert A. Stafford and Richard Drayton.

[129] J. C. Beaglehole, *The Exploration of the Pacific* (London, 1934), p. 3. His other books include *The Discovery of New Zealand* (Wellington, 1939).

[130] For this theme see chap. by Norman Etherington.

[131] J. W. Davidson, *Samoa mo Samoa: The Emergence of the Independent State of Western Samoa* (Melbourne, 1967). Davidson's work generally built on the accounts of earlier historians such as Ralph S. Kuykendall, *The Hawaiian Kingdom, 1778–1854: Foundation and Transformation* (Honolulu, 1938), and Harold Whitman Bradley, *The American Frontier in Hawaii: The Pioneers, 1789–1843* (New York, 1942). In the more strictly British context see W. P. Morrell, *Britain in the Pacific Islands* (Oxford, 1960). For the historiography of the Pacific see chap. by Bronwen Douglas.

who created the journal. The point is significant because until the 1960s—before the proliferation of the area journals—historians of the Empire continued to measure their own work against the standard set by the *EHR*. Pares was in fact its editor from 1939 to the time of his death in 1958. He had begun his career as an historian as a Fellow of All Souls, 1928–45. Thereafter he was Professor of History at the University of Edinburgh until 1954, when he returned to All Souls because of ill health (he was progressively crippled by paralysis). His 1936 book *War and Trade in the West Indies, 1739–1763* pursued thematic issues of finance and trade based on private business papers as well as official archives. His work had both a Caribbean and a European focus, but he made no attempt at a conventional synthesis of the subject. 'It is much to be regretted', complained A. P. Newton, that Pares 'flinched' from the historian's duty to provide a general history.[132] Pares's method indeed pointed to the economic and social history of future decades.[133] Lucy Sutherland's approach to history had a complementary but quite different thrust. Born in Australia but raised in South Africa, she had studied under W. M. Macmillan. At Oxford she was a Fellow of Somerville, 1928–45, and then Principal of Lady Margaret Hall, 1945–1971. Macmillan's influence can be traced in her work, but it was to Namier that she owed her inspiration. Her significance for Imperial history is that she used Namier's conceptual framework to analyse the finances and politics of the East India Company.[134] At once an economic and social as well as an administrative history, *The East India Company in Eighteenth-Century Politics* (Oxford, 1952) established the relationships of pressure-groups both in Parliament and in the Company from London to Calcutta.[135] Her work, like that of Pares, had an uncompromising academic integrity.

The leading Imperial historian of the 1950s was Vincent T. Harlow, and it was Pares who provided the most searching critique of his work. Harlow was pre-eminently a Public Record Office historian. No one of his era better mastered the records of the various departments, including the Board of Trade and the Admiralty and above all the Colonial Office, but his reliance on official records was at once his

[132] *EHR*, LIII (Jan. 1938), p. 143. Pares's other books include *A West-India Fortune* (London, 1950) and *Yankees and Creoles: The Trade Between North America and the West Indies Before the American Revolution* (London, 1956), and *Merchants and Planters* (Cambridge, 1960). See also esp. 'The Economic Factors in the History of the Empire', *EcHR*, VII (1937), pp. 119–44.

[133] In intellectual rigour he stood unsurpassed and was an inspiration to his fellow historians. 'He was the best and most admirable man I have ever known': Isaiah Berlin, *Personal Impressions* (London, 1949). Quotation from 1981 New York edn., p. 95.

[134] Like Pares, Sutherland was a disciple of Namier, though she far more consciously than Pares followed Namier's method. She was not, however, uncritical. See Lucy S. Sutherland, 'Sir Lewis Namier, 1888–1960', *Proceedings of the British Academy, 1962* (London, 1963), pp. 371–85.

[135] For the historiography of the East India Company, and for India generally to mid-nineteenth century, see chap. by Robert E. Frykenberg.

weakness as well as his strength. One does not gain from *The Founding of the Second British Empire*, as one does from Hancock's work, a sense of the impact of demography and emigration or religion and the work of missionaries. One does find a keen mastery of the official documents and a grasp of the full geographical scope of the Empire. Harlow was among the first to study the element of continuity in the minds of the policy-makers and to define the nature of the Empire at specific times. He followed the thinking of British statesmen through the linked crises of imperialism and nationalism in Ireland, North America, and India, thus dealing with the interconnected emergencies in the Empire as a whole. His scholarly and original interpretation set the level of debate for subsequent historians.[136]

There are two general problems in Harlow's historical interpretation, one of which was clearly identified by Pares. Harlow powerfully argued that a transition was already in progress, even before the American Revolution, from colonization to trade—a transition summed up in the phrase: 'We prefer trade to dominion.' In short, the thesis holds that the British renounced formal control in favour of trade, bases, and influence—informal rather than formal Empire—with an emphasis on the East rather than the West. The argument rested on the assumption of Britain's industrial supremacy and her competitive power. With a certainty of touch confirmed by later historians, Pares challenged Harlow's thesis by questioning the extent of Britain's lead in the industrial revolution and the confidence of British businessmen and traders. The second problem is that Harlow was seduced by the power of his own argument on the dynamism of the shift to the East with trade replacing dominion. The old Empire resting on conquest and subjugation seemed to be giving way to a more enlightened yet 'authoritative' rule.[137] His work does not take satisfactorily into account the plantation economies in the Caribbean based on slavery, still less the slave trade itself. The West Indies and the slave trade do not fit easily into his general scheme. Force continued to play an important part in sustaining the Empire. But let there be no doubt that *The Founding of the Second British Empire* is one of the great works in the literature. Pares described the first volume as 'not only a *magnum opus* but also, in certain respects, a masterpiece'.[138]

[136] See esp. the comprehensive assessment of Harlow's work by Ronald Hyam, 'British Imperial Expansion in the Late Eighteenth Century', *Historical Journal*, X, 1 (1967), pp. 113–31.

[137] For Harlow's use of this term, see C. A. Bayly, *Imperial Meridian: The British Empire and the World, 1780–1830* (London, 1989), which comments (p. 8) on the 'curious paradox' of Harlow drawing a conclusion at variance with the evidence presented. Harlow concludes that there was a steady growth of order and justice within the colonial system under a structure of 'authoritative' rule. But Bayly argues that 'Harlow could not bring himself to say "authoritarian" ' for what was really a systematic attempt to centralize power. In my own view, Harlow may have used the word 'authoritative' to mean 'legitimate' in the sense of the rule of law prevailing over authoritarian force but refrained from saying so explicitly. The idea that imperial rule could be 'legitimate' was already unpopular by the 1950s.

[138] Pares in the *EHR*, LXVIII, 267 (April 1953), pp. 282–85. I am much indebted to P. J. Marshall for an exchange of views on Harlow.

The 1950s give the impression of being a claustrophobic decade paradoxically bursting with new ideas. Its confined dimension is well represented by Harlow, who presided over the Imperial History Seminar in Oxford with an almost 'suffocating' sense of moral purpose.[139] He was a learned scholar and a master in his field, but he was also a martinet who wanted his followers to march in the traditional and, ultimately, narrow lines of the subject that would be shaped by a study of documents and would still be, essentially, Anglocentric.[140] Anthony Low, for example, studied under Harlow in the 1950s for his D.Phil. thesis, 'The British in Uganda, 1862–1900' (1957). Low wanted to place his Imperial subject in the context of African history, but Harlow resisted the new trends, deploring the development of area studies. Low went on to bridge the fields of African and Indian history, to become Hancock's spiritual successor in Canberra, and later, as Smuts Professor in Cambridge (1983–87), to hold the balance between Imperial history and area studies.[141]

In the decade of the 1950s dozens of historians were pushing the subject of Imperial history beyond its traditional boundaries. A good example can be found in the work of Gerald Graham and the historians in the Imperial History Seminar in the Institute of Historical Research at London University.[142] Graham was a Canadian who combined the history of the Empire with that of sea power.[143] He took a prominent part in the new direction of research in the 1950s, including the supervision of Africans working towards the Ph.D.[144] The London historians

[139] According to Frederick Madden, Harlow's seminar's were 'more than a little serious and morally earnest . . . week after week it could be school-masterly and suffocating': 'The Commonwealth, Commonwealth History, and Oxford', pp. 19–20.

[140] Pares picked up on this point. Like C. P. Lucas before him, Harlow resisted the initiatives taken on what is now called the periphery. According to Pares, Harlow demonstrated 'a courage . . . unusual among imperial historians. Many of them write as if there were no such place as the mother-country': *EHR*, review cited above n. 138, p. 283.

[141] See esp. D. A. Low, *Lion Rampant: Essays in the Study of British Imperialism* (London, 1973), *Congress and the Raj: Facets of the Indian Struggle, 1917–45* (London, 1977), *Britain and Indian Nationalism: The Imprint of Ambiguity, 1929–1942* (Cambridge, 1997), and *Eclipse of Empire* (cited above n. 20). Low played a critical part in the launching of the British Documents on the End of Empire Project, which began publication in 1992.

[142] Another equally good example would be the seminar at the Institute for Commonwealth Studies, where Kenneth Robinson had succeeded Hancock as Director (1957–65). Robinson wrote one of the most useful and concise analytical works on the Empire: *The Dilemmas of Trusteeship: Aspects of British Colonial Policy Between the Wars* (London, 1965).

[143] See esp. Gerald S. Graham, *Empire of the North Atlantic: The Maritime Struggle for North America* (Toronto, 1950) and *Great Britain in the Indian Ocean: A Study of Maritime Enterprise, 1810–1850* (Oxford, 1967). See also esp. *The China Station: War and Diplomacy, 1830–1860* (Oxford, 1978).

[144] The Africans included J. F. A. Ajayi, who later published *Christian Missions in Nigeria, 1841–1891: The Making of a New Elite* (London, 1965).

included John Flint,[145] Glyndwr Williams,[146] and later P. J. Marshall.[147] Merely to list some of the work coming to completion in the late 1950s and early 1960s gives an indication of the continuing vitality in the field. In Cambridge, Gallagher and Robinson stimulated new research in area as well as Imperial history,[148] and Anil Seal later wrote his creative and influential work on Indian nationalism.[149] In Oxford, David Fieldhouse had already become famous as the economic historian of the Empire,[150] and Colin Newbury had conducted extensive research on comparative studies in emigration, land, and labour in French as well as British archives.[151] In Canada, A. P. Thornton completed his inquiry into the reasons for the decline of British power.[152] In New Zealand, Keith Sinclair wrote on the Maori wars.[153] In Australia, J. D. B. Miller pursued the international politics of the Commonwealth.[154] In South Africa, Leonard Thompson studied the consequences of the Boer War.[155] In Southern Rhodesia, Eric Stokes brought to conclusion his book on the Utilitarians and India.[156] In South-East Asia, Cyril Parkinson traced the absorption of the Malay States into the Empire.[157] John Hargreaves had begun research in Africa and France as well as Britain that would make him one of the principal historians of the Partition of Africa.[158] Not least, in the 1950s John Fage and Roland Oliver prepared the field of African history and successfully countered the attacks by the Regius Professor of History at Oxford, Hugh Trevor-Roper, who declared with a Gibbonian ring that Africa had no history other than that of the unrewarding gyrations of barbarous tribes. The launching of the *Journal of African History* by Oliver and Fage in 1960 symbolically marked the

[145] John E. Flint, *Sir George Goldie and the Making of Nigeria* (London, 1960).

[146] Glyndwr Williams, *The British Search for the Northwest Passage in the Eighteenth Century* (London, 1962).

[147] P. J. Marshall, *The Impeachment of Warren Hastings* (Oxford, 1965).

[148] For example, Thomas R. Metcalf, *The Aftermath of Revolt: India, 1857–1870* (Princeton, 1964).

[149] Anil Seal, *The Emergence of Indian Nationalism: Competition and Collaboration in the Later Nineteenth Century* (Cambridge, 1968).

[150] See esp. Fieldhouse's later work, *Economics and Empire, 1830–1914* (Ithaca, NY, 1973).

[151] For example, C. W. Newbury, *The Western Slave Coast and its Rulers: European Trade and Administration Among the Yoruba and Adja-Speaking Peoples of South-Western Nigeria, Southern Dahomey, and Togo* (Oxford, 1961).

[152] A. P. Thornton, *The Imperial Idea and its Enemies: A Study in British Power* (London, 1959).

[153] Keith Sinclair, *The Origins of the Maori Wars* (Wellington, 1957).

[154] J. D. B. Miller, *The Commonwealth in the World* (London, 1958). Miller had actually completed this book at the University of Leicester before returning to Australia to become Professor of International Relations at the Australian National University.

[155] L. M. Thompson, *The Unification of South Africa, 1902–1910* (Oxford, 1960).

[156] Stokes, *The English Utilitarians and India*, cited above n. 15.

[157] C. Northcote Parkinson, *British Intervention in Malaya, 1867–1877* (Singapore, 1960); see also esp. C. D. Cowan, *Nineteenth-Century Malaya: The Origins of British Political Control* (London, 1961).

[158] John D. Hargreaves, *Prelude to the Partition of West Africa* (London, 1963).

coming of age of area studies. But above all the 1950s will be remembered in Imperial history because of the revolution in the historiography brought about by Robinson and Gallagher.

There were two parts to the revolution: one was the article published in 1953, 'The Imperialism of Free Trade'; the other their book, *Africa and the Victorians* in 1961.[159] As will be apparent from references in the chapters in this volume, 'The Imperialism of Free Trade' is far and away the most frequently cited article in the historiography. It is a model of its kind in stating a clear yet complex and sophisticated thesis, which essentially has two parts. First is the argument of 'informal empire',[160] and second that of continuity. Both these ideas had already been expressed by Harlow, to whom, among others, Robinson and Gallagher acknowledged their debt; but no previous author had written so sharply or so lucidly, or with such unforgettable metaphors as that of the Empire as an 'iceberg'. The iceberg represented, below the waterline, the empire of informal trade and influence and, above the waterline, the formal Empire obvious to everyone because it was painted red on the map. Robinson and Gallagher denied the conventional, sharp, chronological divisions of mid- and late-Victorian imperialism, thereby affirming the continuity of the forces of imperialism throughout the century and indeed to the present. The theory thus helps one to understand the era of decolonization as well as the nineteenth century, and, perhaps, American as well as British imperialism.[161] All of this was a lasting as well as a controversial achievement.

The circumstances of the creation of both the article and the book help to explain the thrust of their thought as well as the ongoing controversy. The essay was very much the product of its time. The two young authors were committed British socialists, wary of both the red sickle and hammer of Soviet communism and the red claw of American capitalism. They wrote at a time when both feared the consequences of American economic assistance to Europe, the Marshall Plan, and the attempt, in their view, by the United States to reduce Britain to the status of an economic satellite. A similar anxiety can be detected in their masterpiece *Africa and the Victorians*, written mainly in the aftermath of the Suez crisis of 1956. Arabi Pasha became the forerunner of Gamal Abdel Nasser, and proto-nationalism

[159] 'Imperialism of Free Trade' cited above n. 127. Ronald Robinson and John Gallagher with Alice Denny, *African and the Victorians: The Official Mind of Imperialism* (London, 1961). The American edn. had a more dramatic but less revealing subtitle: *The Climax of Imperialism in the Dark Continent.*

[160] For the concept of informal empire in Latin America see chap. by Rory Miller. For China and Asia generally, see chap. by C. M. Turnbull. Robinson and Gallagher's most persistent critic was the economic historian D. C. M. Platt. See 'The Imperialism of Free Trade: Some Reservations', *EcHR*, Second Series, XXI, 2 (Aug. 1968), and 'Further Objections to an "Imperialism of Free Trade," 1830–60', *EcHR*, Second Series, XXVI, 1 (Feb. 1973).

[161] For decolonization see chap. by John Darwin.

in Egypt the antecedent of full-blown Egyptian nationalism of the 1950s. Was it anachronistic to relate so emphatically though implicitly the problems of the 1950s to those of the 1880s? The arguments and themes remain as provocative today as when conceived, and they are discussed in many of the chapters in this volume. The historiographical significance of both the article and the book lies in the brilliance of the writing as well as the boldness of the ideas. What *Africa and the Victorians* accomplished once and forever was to destroy the European notion of causation—that the springs of British action, for example, lay in Britain alone. Africa and the world at large can no longer be seen as a blank map on which Europeans freely wrote their will. Robinson and Gallagher overturned the traditional historiographical assumption that European expansion originated wholly within Europe. From Robinson and Gallagher onwards, the history of British imperialism would be the history of the interaction between the British and indigenous peoples.[162]

In 1948 Robinson had married Alice Denny, an American with radical determination to uphold civic virtues and an unwavering faith in the constitutional principles of the United States government. Without her persistence and accuracy—and typing skills—*Africa and the Victorians* might never have seen the light of day. Both authors were responsible in equal measure for the shaping of the book, though in Robinson's methodical reasoning can be found the connecting links in the argument that the response by British imperialism to the two crises in Egypt and in Southern Africa set off a tertiary crisis in tropical Africa. From Gallagher came the wit of Jonathan Swift and the deft pen-portraits of Salisbury, Chamberlain, Rhodes, and other 'fabulous artificers' who galvanized the African continent in the same way that their predecessors had dealt with America, Australia, and Asia.[163]

In 1963 Gallagher became Harlow's successor as the Beit Professor in Oxford. Gallagher was a beloved figure. One of his former students provided a Falstaffian dedication to 'sweet Jack, kind Jack, true Jack, valiant Jack'.[164] When he returned to Cambridge in 1971 to hold the Vere Harmsworth Chair until his death in 1980, Robinson succeeded him as Beit Professor, 1971–87. Robinson's colleagues and former students throughout the world attested to his uncompromising intellectual standards and diligence as a supervisor.[165] Each continued to exert immense

[162] Comments on Robinson and Gallagher run throughout the volume, but for the themes of *Africa and the Victorians* see esp. chap. by John E. Flint. For full discussion see Wm. Roger Louis, *Imperialism: The Robinson and Gallagher Controversy* (New York, 1976).

[163] *Africa and the Victorians*, p. 472.

[164] D. M. Schreuder, *Gladstone and Kruger: Liberal Government and Colonial 'Home Rule', 1880–85* (London, 1969), p. xvi.

[165] See the Festschrift in the *Journal of Commonwealth and Imperial History*, XVI, 3 (May 1988): 'Theory and Practice in the History of European Expansion Overseas: Essays in Honour of Ronald Robinson'.

influence, Gallagher concentrating especially on the study of the history of Indian nationalism,[166] Robinson making a seminal contribution on collaboration as the basis of British rule.[167] Both, of course, are famous in their own right, but in the historiography they are, in Frederick Madden's phrase, as inseparable as the pantomime horse.

We live today in the shadow of the reshaping of Imperial history by Robinson and Gallagher and others in the 1950s and 1960s. Despite this creative effort, there was great foreboding that, with the end of the Empire, the history of British imperialism might become a dead subject. Beyond that anxiety, and much more significantly, Imperial history appeared to be cracking up because of the emergence of area studies in India, Africa, and elsewhere. Looking at the subject over the long haul, however, it is clear that there was no crisis in the historiography. Area studies naturally developed when the consequences as well as the causes of Empire began systematically to be studied. What seemed to be the supremacy of area studies in recent decades can now be viewed as part of a much longer history of the British and other European empires as well as the emergence of fields of concentration in their own right. Imperial history can only benefit from the wider perspectives offered by area studies, literary criticism, and cultural studies.[168] Whatever the changes in academic fashion, there will always be an interest in the history of the British Empire simply because of human curiosity to know more about the domination of one people or nation over others, and the interaction of peoples and cultures. As this volume makes clear, the historiography of the Empire, as it enters a new century, is as rich and diverse as ever before.

[166] See *The Decline, Revival and Fall of the British Empire* cited above n. 10.

[167] Ronald Robinson, 'Non-European Foundations of European Imperialism: Sketch for a Theory of Collaboration', in Roger Owen and Bob Sutcliffe, eds., *Studies in the Theory of Imperialism* (London, 1972). For Robinson's more recent work see esp. 'The Conference in Berlin and the Future of Africa, 1884–1885', in Stig Förster, Wolfgang J. Mommsen, and Ronald Robinson, eds., *Bismarck, Europe and Africa: The Berlin Africa Conference, 1884–1885, and the Onset of Partition* (Oxford, 1988); and 'Railways and Informal Empire', in Clarence B. Davis and Kenneth E. Wilburn, Jr., with Ronald E. Robinson, eds., *Railway Imperialism* (Westport, Conn., 1991).

[168] See chaps. by D. A. Washbrook, Thomas R. Metcalf, and Jeffrey Auerbach. These topics lie beyond the scope of this chapter and are dealt with by A. G. Hopkins and Robin W. Winks in chaps. 40 and 41.

Select Bibliography

J. C. BEAGLEHOLE, *The Life of Captain James Cook* (London, 1974) (Vol. IV, *Journals of Captain James Cook on His Voyages of Discovery*, Hakluyt Society Extra Series, No. XXXVII).

E. A. BENIANS and others, eds., *The Cambridge History of the British Empire*, 9 vols. (Cambridge, 1929–59). It is debatable whether the *CHBE* appeared in 8 or 9 vols., depending on Vol. VIII, in two parts, Australia and New Zealand, being counted as single or separate units. The *OHBE* refers to 9 vols., thus restoring to New Zealand a separate identity.

P. J. CAIN and A. G. HOPKINS, *British Imperialism*, 2 vols. (London, 1993): Vol. I, *Innovation and Expansion, 1688–1914*; Vol. II, *Crisis and Deconstruction, 1914–1990*.

R. G. COLLINGWOOD, *The Idea of History* (Oxford, 1946).

D. K. FIELDHOUSE, ' "Imperialism": An Historiographical Revision', *Economic History Review*, Second Series, XIV (Dec. 1961), pp. 187–209.

JOHN GALLAGHER and RONALD ROBINSON, 'The Imperialism of Free Trade', *Economic History Review*, Second Series, VI, 1 (1953), pp. 1–15.

W. K. HANCOCK, *Survey of Commonwealth Affairs*, 2 vols. (London, 1937–42): Vol. I, *Problems of Nationality, 1918–1936* (1937); Vol. II, in two parts, *Problems of Economic Policy, 1918–1939* (1940–42).

VINCENT T. HARLOW, *The Founding of the Second British Empire, 1763–1793*, 2 vols. (London, 1952–64): Vol. I, *Discovery and Revolution* (1952); Vol. II, *New Continents and Changing Values*, published posthumously (1964).

J. A. HOBSON, *Imperialism: A Study* (London, 1902).

WILLIAM L. LANGER, *The Diplomacy of Imperialism*, 2 vols. (New York, 1935; 2nd edn. with supplementary bibliographies, 1950).

WM. ROGER LOUIS, ed., *Imperialism: The Robinson and Gallagher Controversy* (New York, 1976).

F. D. LUGARD, *The Dual Mandate* (Edinburgh, 1922; see esp. the 1965 edn. with an introduction by Margery Perham).

FREDERICK MADDEN and D. K. FIELDHOUSE, eds., *Oxford and the Idea of Commonwealth: Essays Presented to Sir Edgar Williams* (London, 1982).

NICHOLAS MANSERGH, *The Commonwealth Experience* (London, 1969).

ELIZABETH MONROE, *Britain's Moment in the Middle East, 1914–1956* (London, 1963; 2nd edn. 1981 with her reflections on the Suez crisis).

MARGERY PERHAM, *Native Administration in Africa* (London, 1937).

RONALD ROBINSON and JOHN GALLAGHER with ALICE DENNY, *Africa and the Victorians: The Official Mind of Imperialism* (London, 1961) (US edn. with subtitle *The Climax of Imperialism in the Dark Continent*).

J. R. SEELEY, *Expansion of England* (London, 1883; see esp. the Chicago edn. 1971 with introduction by John Gross).

ERIC WILLIAMS, *Capitalism and Slavery* (Chapel Hill, NC, 1944).

ROBIN W. WINKS, ed., *The Historiography of the British Empire-Commonwealth: Trends, Interpretations, and Resources* (Durham, NC, 1966).

2

The First British Empire

P. J. MARSHALL

The first volume of the *Cambridge History of the British Empire*, published in 1929, was entitled *The Old Empire from the Beginnings to 1783*. By 1929 the tradition that British Imperial history could be divided into phases, with an 'old' or 'first' Empire separate from what was to follow, was long established. It was a tradition that went back into the first half of the nineteenth century. Commentators on Imperial affairs in the 1840s, such as George Cornewall Lewis[1] or Herman Merivale,[2] made comparisons between what they usually called the 'old system' and the pattern of relations between Britain and her dependencies that had evolved in their own time. For J. R. Seeley, in his *Expansion of England* of 1883, it was clear that there had been two Empires and that the first had been based on an 'old colonial system'.[3] In the early twentieth century scholarly studies were made of that 'old colonial system', beginning with those of George Louis Beer.[4] Since then concepts of an 'old' or 'first Empire' have held their ground in historians' usage without serious challenge. A collection of documents illustrating *The Classical Period of the First British Empire, 1689–1783* was published in 1985.[5]

Throughout its long usage there has been a rough consensus as to what is meant by the term 'first British Empire', even if some points have been contested. There has never been any doubt about the geographical extent of the first Empire. It was an Atlantic Empire, based on North America and the West Indies. The spread of British dominion into Asia, Africa, and Australasia was one of the indications that the first Empire was giving way to a second one. There is general agreement too that the first Empire was based on a system of commercial regulation. Indeed the

[1] *An Essay on the Government of Dependencies* (London, 1841).

[2] *Lectures on Colonization and Colonies Delivered before the University of Oxford in 1839, 1840, and 1841* (London, 1861).

[3] *The Expansion of England: Two Courses of Lectures* (London, 1883), pp. 14, 65.

[4] *The Origins of the British Colonial System, 1578–1660* (New York, 1908) and *The Old Colonial System, 1660–1754*, Part I, *The Establishment of the System, 1660–1688*, 2 vols. (New York, 1912).

[5] Frederick Madden with David Fieldhouse, eds., *Select Documents on the Constitutional History of the British Empire and Commonwealth*, Vol. II, *The Classical Period of the First British Empire, 1689 to 1783: The Foundations of a Colonial System of Government* (Westport, Conn., 1985).

terms first Empire and 'commercial Empire' are often taken to be synonymous. The first Empire has also been depicted as primarily an Empire of British settlement overseas. From this it has generally followed that the first Empire was based on constitutional arrangements which involved a high level of local autonomy with extensive participation by the white population, subject to supervision from London. Interpretations differ about the chronological span of the first Empire. When did conscious Empire-building begin? To the Victorians a British Empire began with the Tudor seamen. Others see little in British activities overseas worth calling an Empire until at least the mid-seventeenth century. If the loss of the American colonies in 1783 seemed to be the terminal crisis of the first Empire, the birth of a second Empire is less easy to date. For some historians it did not come into existence until 1815 or even later; others see a second Empire overlapping the first from 1763.

Scholars from the United States writing in the early twentieth century, who have come to be identified as an 'Imperial School', played a commanding role in the historiography of the first Empire. As an inevitable consequence, the thirteen colonies that rebelled in 1776 have tended to dominate that historiography. A huge body of writing has been devoted to colonial America's place in the first Empire.[6]

By contrast, the West Indies have attracted rather less attention, even if their pivotal role in the first Empire has never been in doubt. Earlier generations of British Imperial historians, such as A. P. Newton or Vincent T. Harlow, studied the origins of settlement in the West Indies,[7] while A. P. Thornton published his first book on the West Indies under the restored monarchy after 1660.[8] There is now a vigorous school of Caribbean historians.[9] Nevertheless, attempts to relate the history of the West Indian colonies to that of the first Empire as a whole have not been very numerous.

Recent scholarship has gone some way to remedy this deficiency. Slavery in the British Atlantic has been put into a comparative perspective by important studies that link the West Indies and the northern colonies. Such work reveals, among other major differences, strikingly contrasting demographic histories. Comparative studies, such as those of Richard S. Dunn, examine conditions on West Indian estates that produced death rates among slaves far exceeding birth rates until well into the nineteenth century, while slave populations on the mainland, especially in Virginia

[6] See below, pp. 74–82.

[7] V. T. Harlow, ed., *Colonizing Expeditions to the West Indies and Guiana, 1623–1667* (London, 1925); Arthur Percival Newton, *The Colonising Activities of the English Puritans: The Last Phase of the Elizabethan Struggle with Spain* (London, 1914).

[8] *West-India Policy under the Restoration* (Oxford, 1956).

[9] See chap. by B. W. Higman.

and Maryland, became self-sustaining much earlier.[10] White migration to the New World is also now studied in a framework that embraces both the mainland colonies and the islands. Movements of indentured servants have been explained by the developing needs of the West Indies and North America. For the earlier seventeenth century the Caribbean, especially Barbados, was the main destination for servants from the British Isles. From mid-century West Indian sugar plantations began to take black rather than white labour, but the displacement of white servants by slaves for the tobacco of the Chesapeake was both a slower and a less complete process.[11]

The planter élite of the British West Indies, with their close links to Britain—whence most of them wished to retire to live the life of an English gentleman supported by an income from sugar—once seemed to be far removed from the élite of the thirteen colonies, where an increasing sense of American identity found its ultimate expression in the creation of the new republic. This stark contrast has, however, been called into question. Caribbean whites are now depicted not merely as producers of sugar, but as a politically conscious society whose ideals were not very different from those of the continental colonies and who, for all their self-conscious sense of Britishness, also identified themselves closely with their islands.[12]

For Imperial historians at any time, Ireland straddles awkwardly between metropolitan Britain and the Empire. Ireland hardly featured at all in the earlier historiography of the first Empire. Appropriately, it has been Irish historians in the main who in recent years have fitted Ireland into an Imperial context. Strong similarities have been revealed between the 'planting' of Ireland and of America. D. B. Quinn showed how sixteenth and early seventeenth-century American colonizing ventures grew out of much more powerful Irish ones.[13] In the eighteenth century an Irish Protestant 'colonial nationalism' developed that was not unlike that in the American colonies. In spite of being formally excluded from certain sectors of colonial trade, it is now clear that the Irish were vigorous participants in the British Atlantic economy of the eighteenth century.[14]

[10] 'A Tale of Two Plantations: Slave Life at Mesopotamia in Jamaica and Mount Airy in Virginia, 1799 to 1828', *William and Mary Quarterly*, Third Series, XXXIV (1977), pp. 32–65.

[11] For a sample of a huge literature, see David W. Galenson, *White Servitude in Colonial America: An Economic Analysis* (Cambridge, 1981); Peter Clark and David Souden, eds., *Migration and Society in Early Modern England* (London, 1987); Nicholas Canny, ed., *Europeans on the Move: Studies on European Migration, 1500–1800* (Oxford, 1994), pt. II.

[12] See, for instance, Jack P. Greene, 'Changing Identity in the British Caribbean: Barbados as a Case Study', in Nicholas Canny and Anthony Pagden, eds., *Colonial Identity in the Atlantic World, 1500 to 1800* (Princeton, 1987), pp. 213–66; Michael Craton, 'Reluctant Creoles: The Planters' World in the British West Indies', in Bernard Bailyn and Philip D. Morgan, eds., *Strangers within the Realm: Cultural Margins of the First British Empire* (Chapel Hill, NC, 1991), pp. 314–62.

[13] David B. Quinn, *The Elizabethans and the Irish* (Ithaca, NY, 1966), chap. 9.

[14] Nicholas Canny, *Kingdom and Colony: Ireland in the Atlantic World, 1560–1800* (Baltimore, 1988); Thomas Bartlett, *The Fall and Rise of the Irish Nation: The Catholic Question, 1690–1830* (Dublin, 1992), chaps. 3–5.

Historians of the first Empire, though sometimes reluctantly, have conceded the importance of slave labour to the development of British America, and therefore have included the West African slave trade in accounts of the workings of the Empire. K. G. Davies's *Royal African Company* of 1957 is, for instance, an authoritative account of the trade in its Imperial framework in the late seventeenth century. Accounts of the first Empire, however, rarely move beyond the Atlantic to Asia. For the editors of the *Cambridge History of the British Empire*, India was not fully part of British Imperial history as they understood it, but something separate to be dealt with in its own volumes. Until recently it has proved almost impossible for historians not to see British activities in Asia in the period of the first Empire as a prelude to the British Raj in India, which was the centrepiece of an entirely different Imperial phase. Current approaches, as exemplified in the title of K. N. Chaudhuri's *The Trading World of Asia and the English East India Company, 1660–1760*,[15] now treat the East India Company not as the founder of later British dominion in India, but as a trading body operating in an Asian environment, which it in no sense dominated. This trading world was largely separate from the Atlantic world, but Asian commodities, which constituted a major component of Britain's non-European imports, were obtained with American silver and in some cases, such as tea to North America or cotton cloth to West Africa, were extensively re-exported around the Atlantic.

In ringing phrases Adam Smith described in 1776 how: 'A great empire has been established with the sole purpose of raising up a nation of customers who should be obliged to buy from the shops of our different producers, all the goods with which these could supply them.' At another point in *The Wealth of Nations* he wrote: 'The maintenance of this monopoly has hitherto been the principal, or more properly perhaps the sole end and purpose of the dominion which Great Britain assumes over her colonies.' Colonial rule, in short, was one of the 'mean and malignant expedients of the mercantile system'.[16] This identification of the old Empire with a set of commercial regulations has been extremely influential. In 1841 Merivale adopted Smith's analysis without question.[17] For Beer early in the twentieth century, 'the underlying principles of English colonial policy' were expressed by 'the laws of trade and navigation'.[18]

For those who have followed Adam Smith in seeing the first British Empire as defined by a system of commercial regulations, the lifespan of the Empire was determined by the famous Navigation Acts or Laws of Trade. Thus, the first

[15] Cambridge, 1978.

[16] R. H. Campbell, A. S. Skinner, and W. B. Todd, eds., *Adam Smith: An Inquiry into the Nature and the Causes of the Wealth of Nations*, 2 vols. (Oxford, 1976), II, pp. 610, 661.

[17] *Lectures*, pp. 73–74.

[18] *Origins*, p. v.

Empire was often said to have come into existence during the Interregnum, since an act passed in 1651 was usually taken as the prototype for the later Laws of Trade, and to have lasted until the Navigation Acts began to be modified and dismantled in the early nineteenth century.

The proposition that British colonial policy for most of the seventeenth and eighteenth centuries was based on a set of commercial regulations is an uncontroversial one. Few historians have, however, been content to leave matters there. They have sought for the specific influences behind policy-making and for the more precise objectives embodied in the acts. For Adam Smith the answers to both were simple. The mercantile system was a contrivance of merchants for their own profit. Later historians have rarely agreed with him. Colonial commercial regulations, with the possible exception of the 1651 Act,[19] have been seen as the policy of governments, even if governments might have been influenced by commercial pressure groups. Governments have been presumed to have had more complex and ambitious objectives than the enrichment of merchants.

From late in the nineteenth century it has been assumed that these objectives were inspired by doctrines which historians came to call 'mercantilism'.[20] There was no precise agreement as to what these doctrines might be. The chapter by J. F. Rees in the first volume of the *Cambridge History of the British Empire* described mercantilism as 'the economic expression' of English or of British 'nationalism'; 'Its exponents assumed that it was the business of the State to promote the economic interests of the country.'[21] This meant that state action should be taken to ensure that colonies contributed to Britain's interests. The Navigation Acts and other legislation were analysed in a vast literature to show how colonial trade was regulated. A wide variety of objectives has been detected behind these regulations: the encouragement of British shipping or of British manufacturers; reducing British dependence on foreign imports, especially of strategic commodities, and promoting re-exports; stimulating employment, and generating public revenue through customs. Interpretations have emphasized one objective over another. The tendency in more recent writing is, however, to stress that governments tended to pursue limited objectives, above all, the enhancement of the public revenue, or to respond to the demands of particular pressure groups, rather than to follow elaborate mercantilist programmes. The Navigation Acts remained a talisman throughout the eighteenth century, but the system was flexible enough to allow many

[19] J. E. Farnell, 'The Navigation Act of 1651, the First Dutch War, and the London Merchant Community', *Economic History Review*, Second Series, XVI (1964), pp. 439–54.

[20] D. C. Coleman, 'Eli Heckscher and the Idea of Mercantilism', in D. C. Coleman, ed., *Revisions in Mercantilism* (London, 1969), pp. 94–96.

[21] 'Mercantilism and the Colonies', J. Holland Rose, A. P. Newton, and E. A. Benians, eds., *The Old Empire from the Beginnings to 1783* (Cambridge, 1929), p. 561.

concessions and exceptions.[22] Mercantilism survives as a term signifying attempts by the state to regulate economic activity, but it is now rarely used to imply that colonial policy was shaped to a model based on an agreed set of mercantilist principles.

For those who saw the first Empire as dominated by the enforcement of commercial regulations, its constitutional or political history was a secondary issue. The assumption was that authority at home had little interest in how overseas communities conducted their affairs so long as they obeyed the Navigation Acts. Even when governments took an interest in what was happening across the Atlantic, they lacked the capacity to impose their will on distant communities. Except for periods of what was taken to be mistaken ambition, such as the last years of Charles II or the reign of James II, colonies were left alone. The result was the rise of local representative government, enjoying a wide measure of autonomy. To Cornewall Lewis it seemed that the colonies of the first Empire 'were generally placed under subordinate governments resting upon a completely democratic basis'.[23]

The scholarship of the 'Imperial School' in the United States and of their successors extending beyond the Second World War gave flesh to this outline. The British machinery for enforcing the Navigation Acts and therefore for exercising supervision over the colonies was exhaustively studied. The lack of any single authority with the power to devise and enforce a coherent colonial policy was much stressed, as was the weakness of the agents of metropolitan authority in the colonies. The opposite side of the coin, the rise of American self-government through the Colonial Assemblies, has also been minutely examined.[24] The great bulk of this work was focused on the North American colonies, but some studies were also made of the West Indies.[25]

Seeley was one of many historians who pointed out the inherent instability of the first Empire: the British claimed absolute authority over their colonies but allowed local autonomies to grow to the point where any exercise of control, however limited its objectives, would be resisted, especially by peoples nurtured in traditions of English liberty.[26] For him and for many others this was the history of the American Revolution in a nutshell. But most interpretations of the Revolution went further and accepted an argument propounded in 1774 by Edmund Burke,[27] that Britain had hastened the demise of the first Empire by shifting its objectives from the purely commercial to an imperialism of rule over territory and people.

22 D. C. Coleman, 'Mercantilism Revisited', *Historical Journal*, XXIII (1980), pp. 773–91.

23 *Essay*, ed. C. P. Lucas (1891 edn.), p. 158.

24 See the discussion on pp. 77–78, 81.

25 e.g. George Metcalf, *Royal Government and Political Conflict in Jamaica, 1729–83* (London, 1965).

26 *Expansion of England*, p. 69.

27 'Speech on American Taxation', in Paul Langford, ed., *The Writings and Speeches of Edmund Burke*, Vol. II, *Party, Parliament, and the American Crisis, 1766–1774* (Oxford, 1981), pp. 430–31.

One scholar, Stephen Saunders Webb, now questions the priority of commercial concerns in colonial governance at any time from the later seventeenth century.[28] Earlier work, such as that of Lawrence Henry Gipson or Charles M. Andrews,[29] suggested that a commercial Empire began to change its character as a result of its success in the eighteenth-century wars against France. Gipson found change beginning in 1748, when he detected an increasing stress on 'certain aspects of what can be called "modern imperialism", meaning the effective control of both distant lands and foreign peoples comprehended within the territorial possessions of the expanding state'.[30] Andrews saw in the huge acquisitions of territory after 1763 an indication that 'To the old and well tried colonial policy of mercantilism was now to be added a new and untried policy of imperialism,' concerned with 'extent of territory and the exercise of authority'.[31] A recent essay by Daniel A. Baugh puts the case for mid-century change in new light. A stricter policy of commercial regulation, he argues, was being backed by a new willingness to deploy naval and military force from the 1750s.[32] Continuity is, however, still the dominant interpretation. An authoritative survey of the coming of the Revolution by the Anglo-American team of Ian R. Christie and Benjamin W. Labaree concluded that British theories of empire in the 1760s were those of the seventeenth century, based on the assumption that colonies were intended 'to contribute to the economic well-being and so to the power of the metropolitan state'.[33]

Debates about metropolitan policy and colonial self-assertion treated Britain and the colonies as separate entities. The appearance in 1970 of a volume of essays on *Anglo-American Political Relations* was evidence of new interests in an Atlantic world that was integrated in a political sense. The work of Alison Gilbert Olson in particular has shown how connections of many different kinds, including political alliances, spanned the Atlantic. The Imperial system was not simply one of command on the British side and compliance or disobedience from the colonies; it was also one of influence and manipulation that went both ways. Colonies were becoming members of an extended British polity.[34] Assertions of metropolitan authority and the counter-claims of colonial autonomy underlay the political life

[28] See below, pp. 84–85. [29] See below, pp. 74–80.

[30] *The British Empire Before the American Revolution*, Vol. XIII, *The Triumphant Empire: The Empire Beyond the Storm, 1770–1776* (New York, 1967), p. 182.

[31] *The Colonial Background of the American Revolution: Four Essays in American Colonial History* (New Haven, 1924), p. 125.

[32] 'Maritime Strength and Atlantic Commerce: The Uses of a "Grand Marine Empire" ', in Lawrence Stone, ed., *An Imperial State at War: Britain from 1689 to 1815* (London, 1994), pp. 203–14.

[33] *Empire or Independence, 1760–1776* (London, 1976), pp. 20–21.

[34] Alison Gilbert Olson and Richard Maxwell Brown, eds., *Anglo-American Political Relations, 1675–1775* (New Brunswick, NJ, 1970); see also Olson, *Anglo-American Politics, 1660–1775: The Relationship Between Parties in England and Colonial America* (Oxford, 1973) and the discussion by Stephen Foster, pp. 85–87.

of the first Empire, but for long periods conflict was masked by compromises brought about by the effective workings of transatlantic politics of give and take by both sides.

For British historians of the late nineteenth and early twentieth centuries, overseas expansion seemed to be a process which over a long period slowly but surely took the British people towards the worldwide Empire that was their national destiny. The Empire therefore had deep roots, going back at least to the Tudors, who played so prominent a part in the Victorian sense of English national identity. Like courses in Imperial history at London University until the 1980s, the first volume of the *Cambridge History of the British Empire* began with John Cabot's voyages at the end of the fifteenth century. Sir Charles Lucas explained that these were 'the immediate prelude to the empire'. From the sixteenth century 'A kindly destiny led our people to concentrate on developing their island nationhood and building up their sea-power.'[35] The American G. L. Beer had been even more explicit: the British Empire began with Henry VII's grant to Cabot and was taken forward by the Elizabethans.[36] Since the Second World War knowledge of English sixteenth-century maritime activity has been greatly enhanced, above all by the work of David B. Quinn and his disciples. From their writings a more sceptical view has emerged, both of the achievements of the seamen and the purposes of those who promoted the voyages. In a book that sums up much recent scholarship, K. R. Andrews stresses 'failures and disasters', although he concedes that between 1550 and 1630 'the path of English history did turn in the direction of seaborne empire', leading 'to the effective beginnings of the British Empire' in the reign of James I. Even so, he contests the arguments of Beer and Charles M. Andrews that a state policy of mercantilist regulation was beginning to shape an empire in James's reign. He sees no state policy of any kind, beyond participation in any profits that might be realized.[37] The case for seeking the origins of a first British Empire in terms of state involvement rather than private ventures in the Interregnum, in the Restoration, or even later remains a strong one.

The case for ending the first Empire in 1783 with the loss of America is less clear-cut. Changes in the features that had characterized the first Empire occurred at different times between the mid-eighteenth and the early nineteenth century. This has led to a variety of attempts to find a point of demarcation between the first and second Empires.

The British Empire of the nineteenth century was overwhelmingly an eastern,

[35] 'Introduction', *The Old Empire*, pp. 3–5. [36] *Origins*, pp. 4–5.

[37] *Trade, Plunder and Settlement: Maritime Enterprise and the Genesis of the British Empire, 1480–1630* (Cambridge, 1984), pp. 1–2, 13.

not an Atlantic one. Vincent Harlow detected a 'change of outlook on the part of British merchants and politicians [which] effected a diversion of interest and enterprise from the Western World to the potentialities of Africa and Asia' in the later eighteenth century.[38] He called this the 'swing to the east'. While the growth of Britain's involvement in Asia in this period is undeniable, Harlow's critics have pointed out that it was not at the expense of the Atlantic. British exports continued to go predominantly to the west, especially to the new United States, and the West Indies remained of the utmost importance, both economically and in terms of military priorities, well into the nineteenth century.[39]

The commercial regulations that are so often seen as the dominant characteristic of the first Empire were not significantly modified until the 1820s. Changes in methods of governing the Empire began, however, even before the loss of the American colonies. With the acquisition of the *diwani* of Bengal in 1765 by the East India Company, a huge non-European population came under British rule for the first time. They presented completely new problems of governance for which the experience of the Atlantic Empire, with the devolution of authority to colonists of British origin seemed to have no relevance. The conquest of French Quebec in 1760 also brought a new problem of rule: a population of non-British Europeans for whom local self-government was at first deemed inappropriate. During the French Revolutionary and Napoleonic Wars more territory in India and additional colonies populated either by other Europeans or by non-European peoples were acquired by the British.

By the end of the eighteenth century self-governing Anglo-Saxon communities no longer predominated in the British Empire. British officials were exercising autocratic authority over huge non-British populations. To Lucas, in the first volume of the *Cambridge History*, 'the capacity to rule, which is among the Englishman's best qualities' and 'the sense of trusteeship for coloured races' were at last being called into play.[40] C. A. Bayly has recently applied a very different interpretation to these developments: 'colonial despotisms . . . characterised by a form of aristocratic military government supporting a viceregal autocracy', and emphasizing 'hierarchy and racial subordination', reflected conservative values at home.[41] With its emphasis on the ideological assumptions embodied in Empire, his book has established new criteria for demarcating the phases of British imperialism: the Whig libertarian ideas of the white populations of the first Empire were being replaced by a more authoritarian conservative nationalism that shaped the second Empire.

[38] *The Founding of the Second British Empire, 1763–1793*, 2 vols. (London, 1952–64), I, p. 62.

[39] e.g. Peter Marshall, 'The First and Second British Empires: A Question of Demarcation', *History*, XLIX (1964), pp. 13–23.

[40] 'Introduction', *The Old Empire*, p. 10.

[41] *Imperial Meridian: The British Empire and the World, 1780–1830* (London, 1989), pp. 8–9.

The uneven way in which an old Imperial order, based on the Atlantic, on colonies of white settlement, and on commercial regulation, gave way to a new order with different characteristics has left historians with a wide range of choices for the dates at which to terminate the first Empire. The earliest date with the most carefully worked out theory of transition is that initially put forward by Harlow and recently restated by Frederick Madden. Harlow argued for a 'Second Empire' of trade and bases, rather than settlement and rule, beginning 'to develop alongside the old colonial system' after 1763.[42] Madden sees the second Empire as characterized by 'colonial self-government and trusteeship', while reiterating its overlap with the first Empire.[43] In 1930 Reginald Coupland chose 1783 as the date for the emergence of a 'new and better Empire from the ruins of the old'.[44] Many still find 1783 a convenient date. For Bayly, for instance, the 1780s mark the beginning of a second Empire that was to last until the 1860s.[45] Others put that beginning later. Although the first volume of the *Cambridge History of the British Empire* ended in 1783, the preface to the second volume argued that the second Empire did not take shape until after 1815.[46]

For all its lack of precision, the concept of a first British Empire has proved to be a useful and even an indispensable one for some 150 years. While the chronological volumes of the *Oxford History of the British Empire* do not explicitly use the terms first or second Empire, the divide between the second and the third volumes is the traditional watershed—the turn of the eighteenth and nineteenth centuries. Yet if much of the history of British Imperial expansion can still be encompassed within the commonly accepted phases of Empire, the chronological volumes also show that much else which has become the preoccupation of Imperial history fits less easily into them. Historians of the first Empire from Beer to Harlow were mainly concerned with what mattered to policy-makers in Britain, that is, with defence, government, and trade. They had less to say about other aspects of British expansion, such as the great movements of peoples and the shaping of new societies that followed these movements, the diffusion of Christianity, the adaption of British cultural models in cities as varied as Philadelphia and Calcutta, or the increasing self-confidence with which knowledge of the world was gathered and circulated throughout Britain. Such activities developed a dynamism of their own that was largely independent of official attempts to impose order on the British Empire.

42 *Second British Empire*, I, p. 4.

43 *Classical Period of First Empire*, p. xxxi.

44 *The American Revolution and the British Empire* (London, 1930), p. 45.

45 See the following chap. and Bayly, *Imperial Meridian*.

46 J. Holland Rose, A. P. Newton, and E. A. Benians, eds., *The Cambridge History of the British Empire*, Vol. II, *The Growth of the New Empire, 1783–1870* (Cambridge, 1940), p. v.

Select Bibliography

Charles M. Andrews, *The Colonial Period of American History*, 4 vols. (New Haven, 1934–38).

Kenneth R. Andrews, *Trade, Plunder and Settlement: Maritime Enterprise and the Genesis of the British Empire, 1480–1630* (Cambridge, 1984).

C. A. Bayly, *Imperial Meridian: The British Empire and the World, 1780–1830* (London, 1989).

George L. Beer, *The Origins of the British Colonial System, 1578–1660* (New York, 1908).

—— *The Old Colonial System, 1660–1754*, Part I, *The Establishment of the System, 1660–1688*, 2 vols. (New York, 1912).

K. G. Davies, *The Royal African Company* (London, 1957).

Richard S. Dunn, *Sugar and Slaves: The Rise of the Planter Class in the English West Indies, 1624–1713* (Chapel Hill, NC, 1972).

Lawrence Henry Gipson, *The British Empire Before the American Revolution*, 15 vols. (Caldwell, Id., and New York, 1936–70).

Jack P. Greene and J. R. Pole, eds., *Colonial British America: Essays in the New History of the Early Modern Era* (Baltimore, 1984).

Vincent T. Harlow, *The Founding of the Second British Empire, 1763–1793*, 2 vols. (London, 1952–64).

Sir Lewis Namier, *England in the Age of the American Revolution* (1930; London, 1961).

Richard Pares, *War and Trade in the West Indies, 1739–1763* (Oxford, 1936).

J. Holland Rose, A. P. Newton, and E. A. Benians, eds., *The Cambridge History of the British Empire*, Vol. I, *The Old Empire from the Beginnings to 1783* (Cambridge, 1929).

J. R. Seeley, *The Expansion of England: Two Courses of Lectures* (London, 1883).

L. S. Sutherland, *The East India Company in Eighteenth-Century Politics* (Oxford, 1952).

Stephen Saunders Webb, *The Governors-General: The English Army and the Definition of Empire, 1569–1681* (Chapel Hill, NC, 1979).

Eric Williams, *Capitalism and Slavery* (1944; London, 1964).

3

The Second British Empire

C. A. BAYLY

The writing of history can never be divorced from the making of history. In the eighteenth and early nineteenth centuries, learned historical writing was itself part of a much wider debate which was conducted in newspapers, travelogues, and memoirs. In this sense, the historiography of the second British Empire of the period 1783–1860 was already in vigorous debate at the very time when that Empire was being established. From the American Revolution onwards, writers of histories began to take up a number of broad positions on this phase of British territorial expansion that set the terms of debate for the next century.

Historiographical Traditions

One broad band of opinion, which included writers as diverse as G. F. Leckie and Mountstuart Elphinstone,[1] ranged from conservative Whigs of the late eighteenth century through to early Victorian Tories. These writers argued that Britain's territorial Empire in Asia, the Americas, and even the Mediterranean world, being the natural result of the expansion of human enlightenment and industry, was heartily to be welcomed. This vision of Empire as moral improvement became a dominant sentiment during the Napoleonic Wars, uniting conservatives and many liberals and radicals. It received support from an evangelical Christian public, alerted by massive new sources of printed information, which saw Empire as part of God's work.[2] It also drew on an emerging official tradition of political economy, buttressed now by Utilitarians who argued that government should bring the greatest good to the greatest number. This held that though Empire had been managed badly in the past, good government would bring economic advantages to the

[1] G. F. Leckie, *An Historical Survey of the Foreign Affairs of Great Britain with a View to Explaining the Causes and Disasters of the Late and Present Wars* (London, 1808); Mountstuart Elphinstone (posthumously edited by Sir E. Colebrooke), *The Rise of the British Power in the East* (London, 1887); Thomas Southey, *A Chronological History of the West Indies*, 3 vols. (London, 1827).

[2] e.g. Claudius Buchanan, *Colonial Ecclesiastical Establishment: Being a Brief View of the State of the Colonies of Great Britain, and of her Asiatic Empires, in Respect of Religious Instruction* (London, 1813); J. W. Kaye, *Christianity in India: An Historical Narrative* (London, 1859).

metropolis from both tropical and temperate colonies.[3] Historical biography played a leading role in promoting this resolute Imperial vision. Beginning about 1830, writers such as Montgomery Martin,[4] John Malcolm,[5] and John Kaye[6] had produced favourable assessments of the lives of earlier Imperial Proconsuls, including Clive, Warren Hastings, Cornwallis, Wellesley, and Raffles,[7] whose achievements had often been disparaged by both conservatives and radicals during their careers.

A second strand of historical writing emphasized the ancient rights and liberties of settler communities of British subjects overseas. These writers, acutely aware of the American precedent, deplored the repeated intervention of the Imperial executive and legislature in the management of the colonies, especially in the matter of the settlers' land and indigenous labour. Typical of this position was Bryan Edwards's *The History, Civil and Commercial of the British Colonies in the West Indies* (1793),[8] which depicted the tyranny of the British Parliament as a threat to the liberty of the English gentlemen of Jamaica. By the middle of the nineteenth century patriotic histories in this tradition had emerged in the Australasian, South African, and Canadian colonies.[9] In the 1840s and 1850s, when Imperial garrisons were being recalled, it was natural that the efforts of pioneer settlers rather than the policies of Imperial statesmen should attract approbation in these works. Their authors' suspicion of metropolitan motives was to be echoed by the first generation of truly nationalist historians of the Dominions.

Two other broad strands of opinion were altogether more sceptical of the consequences of territorial Empire. Radicals and free-trade liberal publicists wrote

[3] P. Colquhoun, *A Treatise on the Wealth, Power and Resources of the British Empire in Every Quarter of the World, Including the East Indies*, 2nd edn. (London, 1815). This work contained long historical sections, bemoaning previous colonial misgovernment and foolish acquisitions, such as that of Australia.

[4] Montgomery Martin, ed., *The Despatches, Minutes and Correspondence of the Marquess Wellesley, K.G. during the Administration in India*, 5 vols. (London, 1836–37), began the rehabilitation of this once-spurned Empire-builder.

[5] Sir John Malcolm, *The Life of Robert Lord Clive*, 3 vols. (London, 1836).

[6] Sir John Kaye, *Lives of the Indian Officers Illustrative of the History of the Civil and Military Services of India*, 2 vols. (London, 1867).

[7] Sophia, Lady Raffles, *Memorials and Public Services of Sir Thomas Stamford Raffles* (London, 1830).

[8] Bryan Edwards, *The History, Civil and Commercial, of the British Colonies in the West Indies*, 2 vols. (London, 1793); John McGregor, *British America*, 2 vols. (London, 1832); this genre persisted, see e.g. J. A. Froude, *The English in the West Indies: Or the Bow of Ulysses* (London, 1888), which compared the betrayal of the West Indian planters to that of the Anglo-Irish landowners; cf. Edward Brathwaite, *The Development of Creole Society in Jamaica* (Oxford, 1971).

[9] e.g. John Duncan Lang, *Freedom and Independence for the Golden Lands of Australia: The Right of the Colonies, and the Interest of Britain and of the World* (London, 1852) and his *An Historical and Statistical Account of New South Wales* (London, 1837, 1852, and 1875).

histories drawing on eighteenth-century critics who argued that overseas territorial dominion would pollute the British constitution with 'vice and luxury' and suffocate economic growth with monopolies.[10] Writers such as Henry Brougham,[11] James Silk Buckingham,[12] and J. A. Roebuck[13] were not necessarily hostile to the overseas settlement of British people or to colonies of trade in themselves, but they implied that these had in the past, and would in the future, naturally separate themselves from the metropolis to create self-governing communities. The radicals criticized war and territorial dominion, especially in Asia, on grounds that it had swelled the power of the executive, endangered English liberties, and snuffed out the independence of free peoples.

We must also remember that there already existed in parts of Asia and North Africa distinct indigenous traditions which viewed the expansion of the British Empire with a jaundiced eye. The Persian chroniclers of late-eighteenth-century India, many of whom served British masters, wrote histories of 'the Moderns' or the contemporary era which they distinguished from the earlier history of Islam and the Muslim emperors. They held that the Mughal, Persian, and Ottoman empires had declined because of the corruption of public office. But they attacked with equal vigour the British greed and violence which had replaced these failed polities. Writers such as Gholam Hossain-Khan Tabatabai[14] were already denouncing the 'drain of wealth' from India almost a century before the foundation of the Indian National Congress. Indigenous annals and tracts on statecraft which chart the rise of British power in East and South-East Asia and in North Africa[15] give a similar picture of division and corruption among local rulers as an explanation of the collapse of the old order. But they also expatiate on the pollution, vices, and bad conduct of the Europeans. To some degree, popular legends,

[10] Anthony Pagden, *Lords of All the World: Ideologies of Empire in Spain, Britain and France, c.1500–c.1850* (New Haven, 1995).

[11] Henry Brougham, *An Inquiry into the Colonial Policy of the European Powers*, 2 vols. (Edinburgh, 1803); cf. Miles Taylor, '*Imperium et Libertas*? Rethinking the Radical Critique of Imperialism during the Nineteenth Century', *Journal of Imperial and Commonwealth History*, XIX (1991), pp. 1–23.

[12] James Silk Buckingham, *History of the Public Proceedings on the Monopoly Question of the East India Company during the Past Year* (London, 1830); Herman Merivale, *Lectures on Colonization and Colonies Delivered before the University of Oxford in 1829, 1840, and 1841*, 2 vols. (London, 1841–42).

[13] John Arthur Roebuck, *The Colonies of England: A Plan for the Government of Some Portion of our Colonial Possessions* (London, 1849).

[14] Seid Gholam Hossain-Khan Tabatabai, *A Translation of the Seir Mutaqherin or View of Modern Times*, trans. Nota-Manus (Calcutta, 1789; repr. 3 vols., Lahore, 1975, New Delhi, 1986), which supported Warren Hastings, and attacked other Britons.

[15] e.g. Peter Carey, ed., *The British in Java, 1811–1816: A Javanese Account* (Oxford, 1992); James M. Polachek, *The Inner Opium War* (Cambridge, Mass., 1992); J. K. Leonard, *Wei Yuan and China's Rediscovery of the Maritime World* (Cambridge, Mass., 1994); S. Boustany, ed., *The Journals of Bonaparte in Egypt, 1798–1801*, 10 vols. (Cairo, 1966–72).

ballads, and dramatic performance also kept alive memories of patriotic resistance to Europeans. Indigenous anti-colonial histories in the non-white Empire could trace a much longer pedigree than has been commonly realized. These literary and symbolic resources were, after the 1880s, drawn upon by the first generation of nationalist writers.

These overlapping traditions in writing on the British Empire persisted into the later nineteenth century, but a distinct set of themes began to emerge from about 1880 and held sway until the First World War. Historians of the late Victorian and Edwardian Age—imperialists, liberals, and early nationalists—were all influenced by a growing awareness of the challenges posed to British hegemony by the rise of the continental powers, the United States, and Japan. Several writers also dimly recognized the stirrings of Dominions' nationalism and anti-colonial sentiment in the dependent Empire. These premonitions of coming struggles were projected back into the past and influenced the contemporary understanding of the 'old colonial system' before 1860. Writers of different political hues began to give particular prominence to themes of race and racial destiny which were colouring contemporary scientific and anthropological ventures.[16] Sir John Seeley's *The Expansion of England* (1883) gave the genre an intellectual impetus. 'The whole future of the planet', he wrote, depended on the racial amity between Britain and America.[17] 'Nationality problems' had riven Canada in the 1840s and had simultaneously reached a crescendo in South Africa at the time of the Great Trek.[18] A federal form of Imperial government could alone avert repeat performances of 1776 and allow Greater Britain to attain 'a higher form of organisation'.[19] Even in India, the localism and religious division which underpinned colonial rule might eventually succumb to a broader national mobilization. Seeley's unease led him to challenge the accepted view of the Empire's past. England should remember that she had never really 'conquered' India; British expansion in the later eighteenth century was 'an internal revolution within Indian society',[20] an insight which has been fully developed by historians writing after 1960.

The two Anglo-Boer conflicts, increasing international tension, and the development of eugenicist theories further emphasized the theme of Empire as

[16] Susan Bayly, ' "Caste" and "Race" in the Colonial Ethnography of India', in Peter Robb, ed., *The Concept of Race in South Asia* (New Delhi, 1995), pp. 165–218.

[17] J. R. Seeley, *The Expansion of England*, ed. with an Introduction by John Gross (London, 1971), p. 120.

[18] Ibid., pp. 41–43. On the Great Trek see Vol. III, chap. by Christopher Saunders and Iain R. Smith.

[19] Seeley, *Expansion of England*, p. 120.

[20] Ibid., p. 167; the optimistic, conservative view of the Indian Empire was maintained by Sir Alfred Lyall, *The Rise and Expansion of the British Dominion in India*, 3rd edn. (London, 1894), see Seeley, *Expansion of England*, 'Introduction', p. xiv.

race-triumph and race-conflict. This was particularly true in southern Africa, where rising Afrikaner consciousness rediscovered and elaborated the Dutch separatism of the 1840s and 1850s and lauded the Calvinist pioneers' mission to civilize the 'Bantu'.[21] In the context of the South African War, G. M. Theal, for the British side, published a justificatory narrative of the expansion of Britain's commerce and government into southern Africa after 1796.[22] The sense of race also influenced history in North America. André Siegfried's *The Race Problem in Canada* popularized a number of French Canadian historians who rejoiced in the 'old French island still afloat on the Anglo-Saxon flood', despite the bitter half-century of conflict which led to the constitutional settlement of 1867. Siegfried predicted the coming triumph of the yet more vigorous American 'blood'.[23] Racial nationalism also permeated the dependent Empire. Hindu cultural nationalists, active in the years 1905–10, began to elaborate the theme of the manifest destiny of the Indian branch of the great Aryan race whose glories had only been extinguished temporarily by Muslim tyranny and British conquest because Hindus had failed to unite.[24]

If, up to 1914, the racialist and nationalist tide was running strongly, the effect of the two world wars was to bring some historians back to a more favourable view of wider Imperial bonds and a consequent revaluation of the history of the second British Empire. It is pertinent that more than half of the Dominions' troops enlisted during the first year of the First World War were British-born.[25] Post-1919 Canadian histories of the 'winning of popular government' in the early nineteenth century tended to re-emphasize the positive features of the British connection,[26] even though Lord Durham's 'assimilationist' vision of the absorption of the French into an Anglo-Canada was rejected. Both 'races' had served the Empire in its hour of need, 'representing two civilizations in one body'.[27] In South Africa the fragile inter-war Anglo-Boer coalition under J. C. Smuts's leadership also helped to keep alive a vision of Anglo-Boer condominium there, even while a more vigorous nationalist school developed at Afrikaner universities.

[21] The first major historical work in this genre was Revd Mr. du Toit, C. P. Hoogenhout, and Gideon Malherbe, *Die Geskiedenis van ons Land in die Taal van ons Volk* (The History of our Land in the Language of our People) (1877); see F. A. van Jaarsveld, *The Awakening of Afrikaaner Nationalism, 1868–1881* (Cape Town, 1961), pp. 118 ff.

[22] G. M. Theal, *The History of South Africa since September 1795*, 5 vols. (London, 1908). See also chap. by William H. Worger.

[23] André Siegfried, *The Race Question in Canada* (London, 1907), p. 326.

[24] e.g. V. D. Savarkar, *Six Glorious Epochs of India History*, trans. S. T. Godbole (Delhi, 1971); Savarkar, *The Indian War of Independence of 1857* (first written *c.*1912), 8th edn. (Delhi, 1970).

[25] Gerald S. Graham, in Sir R. Coupland, *British Empire History* (London, 1950), p. 166. See Vol. IV, chap. by Robert Holland.

[26] See e.g. G. M. Wrong and H. H. Langton, eds., *The Chronicles of Canada*, 32 vols. (Toronto, 1920).

[27] Graham, in Coupland, ed., *British Empire History*, p. 9; cf. p. 112.

This castigated the early-nineteenth-century British liberals for their hypocritical attitude to the 'Bantu question'.[28]

Seeley's *Expansion of England*, then, proposed many of the themes for Imperial history through to the point after the Second World War when schools of professional historians of Empire began to emerge. Of course conservative, even reactionary histories continued to appear which treated the second British Empire as a providential expansion of civilization, stressing the depravity of pre-colonial societies in Africa and Asia. But increasing numbers of liberal histories were written, and these mirrored in the past the nationalist pressures and ethnic revivals of their contemporary world. For example, Edward Thompson and G. T. Garratt excoriated the East India Company for its unjust annexations of a century earlier.[29] J. S. Marais, following W. M. Macmillan, traced the origin of the subservience of the Cape 'coloured people' to British policies of the early nineteenth century, while castigating the 'Nazi-like' understandings of race which had infected the South Africa of the 1930s.[30] Meanwhile, independent traditions of nationalist historiography in India, Burma, Malaya, and the Caribbean were given great impetus by the social tensions and political programmes of the Great Depression era. These replaced earlier histories of progress with a picture of vital indigenous societies and economies devastated by the intrusion of British manufactures and settlers in the early nineteenth century.

During the onrush of decolonization after the Second World War, liberal imperialist histories of the earlier Empire on the theme of British 'progress' and 'benevolence' continued to be written. At the same time, the conflicts of professional academic history, which drew on methodological trends in British and European studies, began to give the field an internal dynamic. The pattern of revision and counter-revision between generations of scholars effected profound changes. Imperial history had not, and has not even today, become a coherent sub-discipline within history. But academic interest in Marxism combined with the new history of international relations after 1950 to give rise to a debate about 'theories of imperialism'. This debate influenced the following generation of historians of the regions who had incorporated into their work the methods of British economic history, the French Annales School, and American cultural anthropology. Journals devoted to Imperial history and the history of European expansion were

[28] T. Dunbar Moodie, *The Rise of Afrikanerdom: Power, Apartheid and the Afrikaner Civil Religion* (Berkeley, 1975), pp. 146–207; Ken Smith, *The Changing Past: Trends in South African Historical Writing* (Johannesburg, 1988).

[29] Edward Thompson and G. T. Garratt, *The Rise and Fulfilment of British Rule in India* (London, 1934).

[30] J. S. Marais, *The Cape Coloured People, 1652–1937* (London, 1939), p. 282; for a similar treatment see his *The Colonisation of New Zealand* (London, 1927).

founded. New chairs were established in Imperial history in many Commonwealth and some American universities, and by 1960 undergraduates were able to leaven a diet of European history with courses on Empire and nationalism.

Historical Interpretations, 1950–1980

Over the last generation the new breed of professional historians of Empire have concentrated much effort on two related issues: first, is it possible to periodize major changes in the Empire as a whole? Secondly, what were the critical forces in Britain's overseas expansion in the late-eighteenth and early-nineteenth centuries?

PERIODIZING THE BRITISH EMPIRES

The question of timing is to some extent semantic,[31] but the debates over whether there was a distinct 'second British Empire' after 1783 or an 'age of imperial reform' after 1830 have also helped to uncover some major differences of method and perspective among Imperial historians.

Debates about the date at which a first Empire gave way to a second one are discussed in the previous chapter. Many contemporaries believed that the governance of the Empire had changed after the Peace of Paris of 1783. They believed stronger executive power and parliamentary scrutiny had avoided any repetition of the sort of settler revolt which had sundered the American colonies from Britain. Later historians in the heyday of Empire agreed that a new balance between an invigorated Crown and settler rights had paved the way for the devolution of power to the 'white colonies' after 1838. It was Vincent T. Harlow, however, who did most to shape the thesis of the second British Empire.[32] He argued that the American débâcle finally convinced ministers that an Empire of expanding trade was better than one of settlement or territorial control, and that the East was a fair field for such expansion. This policy was reinforced by Britain's expanding American markets after 1783 and European ones during the Napoleonic continental blockade. To Harlow, 1783 was not a particularly dramatic turning-point, for he traced the origin of his second British Empire to the policies which successive ministries had pursued since 1763.

As part of a much wider scholarly reaction against 'Whiggism', many of the next generation of historians argued for absolute continuity across the boundary

[31] Frederick Madden with David Fieldhouse, *Select Documents on the Constitutional History of the British Empire and Commonwealth*, Vol. III, *Imperial Reconstruction, 1763–1840: The Evolution of Alternative Systems of Colonial Government* (Westport, Conn., 1987), pp. xxvi–xxvii.

[32] Vincent T. Harlow, *The Founding of the Second British Empire, 1763–93*, 2 vols. (1952; Oxford, 1964).

date of 1783, abandoning even Harlow's nuanced discussion of continuities and change. Whether in Bengal or the eastern seas, they argued, everything that came after 1783 was implicit before it; the illusion of a new Empire was created by the particular conditions of the French Revolutionary and Napoleonic Wars, and America apart, the pattern set in the mid-eighteenth century was resumed again after 1815 when Britain's Imperial ambitions retreated to their more usual courses.[33]

This argument depended above all on discovering consistencies in intention and policy between the 'first' and 'second' Empires. Here the 1960s revisionists scored some points. Policies designed to stabilize Imperial boundaries or establish monopolies of tropical trade did, of course, remain fairly firm over the supposed divide of 1783. For instance, the search for revenue to support the Company's Indian Army—the main motive force in Britain's conquest of India—remained constant from Clive's assumption of the land-revenue management of Bengal in 1765 through to the subsidiary alliances constructed by Wellesley after 1798.

By contrast, more-recent historians have argued for change and assert that the Empire was a different animal in 1800 from what it had been in 1783. They put more emphasis on issues of ideology, governmental apparatus, and international economic integration than on surface continuities of policy. Territorial Empire became a more acceptable ideology for the state and the élites after 1783; Britain could be both a 'free' and a 'conquering' people.[34] Philosophical writers and political economists apart, the political nation became less fearful that Empire would corrupt the body politic than its predecessors had been. The organization of the Imperial state became more integrated after 1783, and later a small Colonial Office came into being. Imperial governments became more concerned with science and statistics and a kind of Imperial science policy developed under Sir Joseph Banks.[35] The role of the colonial Governor was strengthened in different contexts, and their despotic powers continued for some years after the end of European war with the satrapies of Somerset in the Cape, Maitland in the Mediterranean, and Lords Hastings and Amherst in the East.[36] Most striking, after their intervention in Egypt in 1801, the Indian armed forces increasingly took up a role outside the Subcontinent which was not to be abandoned until after independence in 1947.

33 Ronald Hyam and Ged Martin, *Reappraisals in British Imperial History* (London, 1975), chap. 1, epitomizes this line of thought.

34 P. J. Marshall, 'A Free Though Conquering People: Britain and Asia in the Eighteenth Century', Inaugural Lecture, Kings College, London, 1981; Linda Colley, *Britons: Forging the Nation, 1707–1837* (London, 1992).

35 John Gascoigne, *Joseph Banks and the English Enlightenment: Useful Knowledge and Polite Culture* (Cambridge, 1994).

36 See C. A. Bayly, *Imperial Meridian: The British Empire and the World, 1780–1830* (London, 1989), pp. 193–209.

Harlow had argued for a 'swing to the East' after 1783, and had conceived this new Empire as an Empire of monopoly supplemented by a rising Empire of free trade. It was equally important that, over the course of the wars of 1783–1826, Britain became an Asian military power and secured her naval dominance in every sector of the globe except American waters.

Arguments about continuity and change are generally semantic and often populated with straw men, but they do help to isolate convergences and trends over large areas of historiography. This is equally true of the debate over the 'Age of Reform' of the 1830s. To contemporaries and Imperial historians of the heyday of Empire the changes were palpable and represented by constitutional initiatives. The abolition of slavery, the reform of the electorate at home, greater press freedom in the colonies, and the beginnings of 'responsible government' in the Durham Report (1839) signalled a new era. Once again the generation of the 1960s and 1970s gloried in discovering, on the basis of archival materials, that 'nothing happened', something which appeared characteristic of the British historical profession more generally. The slave trade was simply transformed into 'a new system of slavery' represented by indentured labour;[37] in colonies such as the Cape or Jamaica, pass-laws and provisions against vagrancy tied former slave populations to their former owners. Just as British historians were arguing that the reformed electorates actually perpetuated the power of the landed oligarchs, so in India Lord William Bentinck's overhaul of East India Company administration was said to have come to nothing because the reforming part of his agenda was neutralized by his government's refusal to spend money on anything.[38] Historians have also pointed out that, in the supposed age of free-trade imperialism and disdain for territorial annexation, large tracts of South Asia were annexed and the basis for territorial Empire was laid in South-East Asia and the lands north of the Cape. Thus, according to revisionists, the 'Age of Reform' proved only a hiccough in the piecemeal progress of territorial expansion connived at by the 'men on the spot'. Even in North America, Lord Durham's Report, far from being a blueprint for a new Empire for free peoples, was depicted as the consequence of a series of blunders by a vain and superficial statesman.[39] If anything brought about the new age of settler Dominions, according to this view, it was expansion by white settlers on the periphery and continuing apprehension about the rivalry of the United States in North America and a resurgent France in the Pacific. But this was nothing new.

The scepticism of the 1960s generation was salutary, yet the wrangler's art may

[37] Hugh Tinker, *A New System of Slavery: The Export of Indian Labour Overseas, 1830–1920* (London, 1974).

[38] Eric Stokes, *The Peasant and the Raj: Studies in Agrarian Society and Peasant Rebellion in Colonial India* (Cambridge, 1978), chap. 2; cf. his earlier *The English Utilitarians and India* (Oxford, 1959).

[39] Hyam and Martin, eds., *Reappraisals*, pp. 75–88.

again have restricted the historians purview overmuch. If we look, as more recent commentators have done, at the context of institutions and debate in which government functioned, at the public representation of power, at ideology, and at indigenous context, more changed in the 1830s than the most sceptical have been prepared to admit. Christian evangelization, for instance, which the historians of the 1960s tended to write off, had subtle effects both on which settler communities and on indigenous peoples during the 1830s and 1840s.[40] Late-twentieth-century Imperial historians began once again to take religion seriously, a reflection perhaps of what was called the 'revival of faith' by contemporaries. Recent historians have also become more aware of the complex consequences of the freeing of trade, perhaps in response to contemporary economic nostrums. Free trade may actually have increased economic dependency by making it easier for European goods to pass into the interior. Even in the sphere of government, the impact of 'economical reform' and Peelite rational government was, perhaps, underplayed by sceptics of the 1960s generation. The military fiefdoms and 'old corruption' of the period of the Napoleonic Wars certainly gave way to new styles of government which stressed the importance of statistics, public instruction, and public probity. Most important, the rapid expansion of printing and of the newspaper faced colonial governments with more vigorous opposition not only from white settler communities, but in India, Ceylon, and the South-East Asian bastions, from the first generation of non-European publicists.[41] Current controversies about communications, political surveillance, and the media alerted historians after 1980 to the importance of these issues.

The 1850s and 1860s are the final era of change around which historical debates have flourished. Contemporaries and many historians emphasized the technical changes of the period: the steamship, the telegraph, the railway, and developments in tropical medicine, all of which brought colony and metropolis closer together and drove the effects of the world economy deeper into the periphery. Robert Livingston Schuyler described the 1850s and 1860s as an age of equipoise.[42] The delayed consequences of the move to free trade and responsible government, alongside the withdrawal of Imperial garrisons from the colonies of white settlement, marked the final decline of the 'old colonial system'. The American Civil War also caused Britain to review her policy in Canada and elsewhere. The years 1861–67

[40] G. A. Oddie, ed., *Religion in South Asia: Religious Conversion and Revival Movements in Medieval and Modern Times* (London, 1977); or, more recently, Jean Comaroff, *Body of Power, Spirit of Resistance: The Culture and History of a South African People* (Chicago, 1985).

[41] S. Natarajan, *A History of the Press in India* (Bombay, 1962), chap. 1; A. Fauteux, *Les Patriotes de 1837–8* (Montreal, 1950); van Jaarsveld, *Awakening*.

[42] Robert Livingstone Schuyler, *The Fall of the Old Colonial System: A Study in British Free Trade, 1770–1870* (London, 1945); cf. C. A. Bodelsen, *Studies in Mid-Victorian Imperialism* (London, 1924). See Vol. III, chap. by Robert Kubicek.

were, consequently, 'the critical period in British imperial history'.[43] Liberal allies of the Manchester School were effectively arguing for the dismemberment of the Empire, at least the white Empire. By the early 1870s, however, there was a growing consensus in Britain that Empire was a buffer against a resurgent Russia and Germany, while 'crisis in the periphery' over the invasion of native land had convinced some colonists of the need for Imperial defence. Here, then, was a break in the continuity of Imperial aims and methods.

Ronald Hyam, writing in the 1970s, saw another pan-Imperial disjunction at this period in the rash of uprisings that faced Imperial authorities.[44] Alongside the New Zealand wars, historians have pointed to the concurrence of a final round of Xhosa wars, the Indian Rebellion of 1857, and sundry tribal explosions, revolt in Jamaica, and even, in a sense, the Taiping Rebellion, which transformed the relations between the British government and China. Historians remained uncertain about the reasons why these uprisings clustered in the later 1850s and 1860s. To some they were testimony to the delayed consequences of the severe pressures put on the Imperial system by the effects of the 'Age of Reform'. Others asserted that the vigour of indigenous resistance resulted from the transfer of military organization and technology across the boundary between colonizer and colonized. The rebel sepoy army of 1857 was, after all, a modern army trained by the British. Likewise, Taipings, Maoris, and Zulus had all become more formidable because they had gained access to rifles, gunpowder, and metallurgical techniques. Most writers agreed that the uprisings of this period definitely inaugurated a new era in Imperial history. In the case of India and Jamaica, the demise of planter government and the East India Company finally spelled the end of major actors which had characterized the second British Empire.

The debate about continuity and change remains fierce, but the proponents of the idea that the Empire changed significantly in the 1780s, the 1830s, and again in the 1860s have certainly scored some points by moving the focus of argument from the intentions and policies of Colonial Secretaries and Governors to a consideration of ideology, public representations of power, and indigenous politics.

THE MOTIVE FORCE OF BRITISH EXPANSION

Underlying these historians' wars of continuity and change was a deeper concern about the reasons for Imperial expansion and the move from 'informal' to 'formal': that is, the shift from a position where Britain dominated peripheral territories through her relations with indigenous intermediaries to direct territorial

[43] Schuyler, *Fall of the Old Colonial System*, p. v.

[44] Ronald Hyam, *Britain's Imperial Century, 1815–1914: A Study of Empire and Expansion* (London, 1976).

Empire. These arguments represented the backwash from the fierce debates that have grown up around the partition of Africa and the supposed 'New Imperialism' after 1880. The ebb and flow of discussion on the period to 1860 has been a pale reflection of that classic historiographical encounter. As in the case of the African partition, contemporaries and most historians of the heyday of Empire explained territorial expansion between 1780 and 1860 in terms of strategic initiatives and foreign threats. France was the main 'threat' to the British Empire between 1780 and 1815. The conquest of inland India, the early Imperial ventures in Egypt, the taking of the Cape, and the expansion towards the South-East Asian seas were all seen as attempts to counterbalance the power of France or her Dutch surrogate. That line of argument still attracts support from historians who approach Imperial history from the perspective of international relations.

Until the 1960s it was only orthodox Marxists who gave prime place to economic factors in the expansion of Britain between 1783 and 1860.[45] They encountered the logical difficulty that the economic effects of industrial revolution—the search for markets and raw materials—came after the groundwork for this new expansion had been laid, not before it. Harlow pushed the debate about economic imperialism back two generations by arguing for a free-trade imperialism as early as the administration of Lord Shelburne in the 1780s. By the mid-1960s several historians were writing not of metropolitan initiatives, but of the independent interests of free-traders and other European agencies in the periphery. Echoing revisions in the historiography of Africa and Latin America in the later nineteenth century, Pamela Nightingale, for instance, asserted that the occupation of western India between 1780 and 1808 resulted from the influence exerted on East India Company officials by private British traders in raw cotton and spices.[46] Writers on other Imperial territories also tilted towards an argument for this so-called economic sub-imperialism. Historians have argued that sugar planters in the West Indies during the French Wars wished to seize the enemy islands to eliminate competition from slave-trading competitors. Canadians moved west to keep the Americans from the fur and timber trades. Commercial motives are also said to have determined the reoccupation of the Cape after 1806, the taking of Aden, and the beginnings of Empire in South-East Asia.

Until recently few historians have doubted the importance of local sub-imperialism, especially in an era when metropolitan control was so distant from the scene of colonial expansion. The debate has focused instead on the motives of these local agents. In the Indian case, for instance, and by extension on all the

[45] e.g. Maurice Dobb, *Studies in the Development of Capitalism* (London, 1947); Rudrangshu Mukherjee tried to revive the idea of an economic motive for Indian annexation, 'Trade and Empire in Awadh, 1765–1804', *Past and Present*, XCIV (1982), pp. 85–102.

[46] Pamela Nightingale, *Trade and Empire in Western India, 1783–1806* (Cambridge, 1970).

peripheries of the emerging British Indian Empire, historians have urged that it was the military and fiscal needs of the Company, and not trade, corporate or private, which was really the impetus for expansion. The prize, it is argued, was India's territorial revenues, not her raw materials or artisan manufactures. Scholars have also attributed early-nineteenth-century expansion of formal Empire in the Pacific Ocean and New Zealand to local agencies; the issue has been whether economic, strategic, or humanitarian motives were critical. Indigenous resistance has also been brought firmly back into the picture, in part as an intellectual consequence of the end of Empire. The argument goes that it was native enemies as diverse as Tipu Sultan, the emir of Afghanistan, the Xhosa, the sultan of Naning in Malaya, or the Canadian Indians who pulled the British ever onward in a desperate attempt to settle the 'turbulent frontier'.[47]

The indigenous enemies need not even have been great kings and magnates. There are many examples of territorial expansion designed to suppress peasant rebels, 'thugs', nomadic 'banditti', runaway slaves or, later, slave-traders. Historians argue that it was not only the extent, but the form of Empire which was determined by the degree and depth of indigenous resistance. In some places, tribal and peasant revolt caused the British to make deals with important native intermediaries; in others, revolt by notables caused them to level society down to the 'sturdy' village leaders.

Broadly speaking, non-economic arguments for British territorial expansion have had a field day since the mid-1970s, partly because of the declining esteem for economic history generally. The imperialism of sexual adventure[48] and missionary imperialism have all taken their places beside the imperialism of the military 'man on the spot'. At the same time, Roger Anstey restated the importance of moral and political imperatives in the abolition of the slave trade,[49] an enactment which had profound consequences for Imperial policy in all parts of the globe.

As in the case of the later nineteenth century, economic imperialism has recently been given a shot in the arm with the appearance of P. J. Cain and A. G. Hopkins, *British Imperialism*.[50] These authors have powerfully asserted both the argument for continuity and the argument for metropolitan economic imperialism. In some respects their position is quite apposite for the first forty years of the period. East India Company bonds, shipping, insurance, official and military salaries—the stuff of 'gentlemanly capitalism'—were powerful incentives for

[47] John S. Galbraith, *Reluctant Empire: British Policy on the South African Frontier, 1834–54* (Berkeley, 1963).

[48] Ronald Hyam, *Empire and Sexuality: The British Experience* (Manchester, 1990).

[49] Roger Anstey, *The Atlantic Slave Trade and British Abolition, 1760–1810* (London, 1975).

[50] P. J. Cain and A. G. Hopkins, *British Imperialism*, 2 vols. (London, 1993): Vol. I, *Innovation and Expansion, 1688–1914*; Vol. II, *Crisis and Deconstruction, 1914–1990*.

Imperial expansion in all parts of the world, and at the end of the period to 1860 the export of capital through railway loans or the funding of indigenous rulers seems to have been more characteristic of British imperialism than the search for markets of raw materials. The Asian empire was definitely 'gentlemanly-capitalist', though one might add, also military. Gentlemen also began to seek land, office, and bishoprics in the Cape, Canada, and later Australasia. Industrial and trading interests definitely played second fiddle over much of the Empire.

As a description of the Weberian 'spirit' animating it, Cain and Hopkins's characterization of the Imperial enterprise feels right for many periods and many regions. Yet commentators have pointed up some problems in the heavy emphasis they place on metropolitan influences. What R. E. Robinson called the 'excentric' historiography of the 1960s (the emphasis on crises in the periphery) had evidently gone too far, but the relative autonomy of forces for expansion on the frontiers of Empire was still attested to by many regional studies written during the 1970s and 1980s. Metropolitan economic motives for British attacks on Kandy (1818), Nepal (1814–16), and Burma (1824–26 and 1852) are quite difficult to discern. In southern Africa, the logic of the 'turbulent frontier', which argues that local resistance drew the British on to further conquests, seems equally difficult to refute. Even in the case of the Opium and Arrow wars against China (1840–42 and 1856–57), the dependence of the finances of the East India Company—a local agent—on the opium trade was of the first importance as a cause of war,[51] domestic gentlemanly capitalists certainly justified and supported such aggressions, but they were driven initially by the uneven growth of trade in the periphery.

Historical Interpretations in the 1980s and 1990s

The debates over the phases and timing of British Imperial expansion during the post-1945 development of higher education were largely determined by the dynamics of scholarly revisionism. The younger generation of the 1960s pulled scholarship in the direction of fashionable regional studies and anthropologically informed history. But contemporary politics did exercise a subtle influence. Robinson and Gallagher argued that the 'official mind' in London countenanced intervention in Africa because it perceived 'crisis in the periphery' of the British informal Empire. They made an explicit reference to the 1956 Suez crisis in their work and may also have been thinking of contemporary security problems in Cyprus, Aden, and Egypt. At the height of the cold war, the radical right and the radical left both disavowed the simple Marxism which had driven earlier diagnoses of economic imperialism.

[51] John Y. Wong, *Deadly Dreams: Opium and the Arrow War (1856–1860) in China* (Cambridge, 1998).

Similarly, P. J. Cain and A. G. Hopkins's emphasis on the City of London may well have been influenced by the debate during the 1970s on the City's role in Britain's long-term decline. As memories of the Second World War receded and the Vietnam conflict radicalized the intelligentsia, Dominions' nationalism also took on a new lease of life. The apartheid era in South Africa brought renewed emphasis on the racial and religious significance of the Great Trek among Afrikaners. In Australia, Manning Clark anticipated much of the anachronistic academic radicalism of the 1980s and 1990s. As early as 1973 he denounced the 'cult of respectability' in early-nineteenth-century Australia, pillorying one of her bishops for 'xenophobia, racism, an abominable attitude to the aborigine, [and] absence of romantic love for women'.[52]

Since 1980 the overt politicization of Imperial history and its regional components has become much more evident once again; so has the influence of international academic fashion. Regional historians have led the way in the turn towards 'subaltern' studies, gender studies, considerations of ecology, and a broader move to the study of texts and European images and misinterpretations of other societies. The political context of these trends is clear. The collapse of communism, the decline of organized labour movements in Europe and North America, and the triumph of the 'market' both within and outside academia forced the intellectual left to de-link itself from classic materialism and the vision of class struggle through the ages which had structured earlier histories.

The graduate students of the 1980s sought to understand the struggles of subordinated colonial peoples not in the context of broad economic conjunctures, but of principles of power and culture which they derived from post-Marxist writers such as Michel Foucault and Antonio Gramsci. The grand narratives of improvement and capitalist expansion were abandoned; instead, the new historians recorded the 'decentred narratives' of particular groups of 'natives', peasants, tribals, slaves, and women, sometimes oblivious to the distortions which their own agendas of anti-colonialism imposed on them. Influenced by 'post-modernist' theory and cultural studies, a yet more radical group of historians seemed to insist that it was almost impossible to recover anything of the lives of the Imperial subject, and insisted that the main academic task was the analysis and deconstruction of the topological, anthropological, and travel literature of the white intruders.[53]

Since Imperial historians, in contrast to historians of regions within the former British Empire, have necessarily worked with broad, comparative narratives and

[52] C. Manning Clark, *History of Australia*, Vol. III, *The Beginnings of Australian Civilisation, 1824–51* (Carlton, Victoria, 1973), p. 277.

[53] See, e.g. Stuart B. Schwartz, ed., *Implicit Understandings: Observing, Reporting and Reflections on the Encounters between Europeans and Other Peoples in the Early Modern Era* (New York, 1994), introduction.

have emphasized to one degree or another the importance of 'the centre', these developments have been perplexing.[54] They have, nevertheless, been influential. Ideas have flowed along the old Imperial routeways even for historians who formally disavow Imperial history. The Indian Subaltern Studies 'collective'[55] derived much of their intellectual impetus from the work of E. P. Thompson and Eric Hobsbawm, despite more recent obeisances to French theory. In turn, their influence has been felt directly or indirectly among southern African, Latin American, and South-East Asian historians working on the experience of resistance. In North America and the Caribbean, the new 'history from below' which concentrates on lived experience has revivified the study of slavery, especially of women slaves.

There are some fields where the political influences of the 1980s have enlivened fields of true Imperial history, in the sense that they concern substantive economic or intellectual links between parts of the Empire. One such area is the study of the ecological impact of British expansion, including famine, which had attracted the concern of experts in the first half of the nineteenth century.[56] It is now becoming possible to see how the demand for timber for naval ships during the Anglo-French wars, for merchant ships during the great trade expansion of 1820–40, and the initial demand for railway sleepers changed the Empire's relations with its forests and 'tribal' peoples. Even before 1860 much of the forest land of north-western Australia, the Indian west coast, or seaboard Canada had been heavily exploited. In all these regions, armed conflicts between Imperial troops and local peoples had followed struggles over land and timber. Before 1860, too, administrators and scientists operating at an Imperial level had begun to foretell the danger of environmental 'dessication' and to establish protected forest areas, the scenes of severe conflict in the later Empire. As cattle- and sheep-farming expanded across South Africa and the Australian colonies after 1840, colonial administrators began to face similar problems of exploitation and control. Here, then, the environmental politics of the 1980s helped create a new branch of Imperial history.[57]

There are other fields in which present concerns have reopened issues which are properly studied at an Imperial level. Studies of emigrants, both convicts and

[54] For a robust assault on these trends, see John M. MacKenzie, *Orientalism: History, Theory and the Arts* (Manchester, 1995).

[55] Ranajit Guha and others, eds., *Subaltern Studies: Writings on South Asian History and Society*, 9 vols. (New Delhi, 1982–96).

[56] Alfred W. Crosby, *Ecological Imperialism: The Biological Expansion of Europe, 900–1900* (London, 1986); William Beinart, ed., *Putting a Plough to the Land: Accumulation and Dispossession in Rural South Africa, 1850–1930* (Johannesburg, 1986); Ramachandra Guha, *Writing Environmental History in India* (Delhi, 1993); Amartya Sen, *Poverty and Famines: An Essay on Entitlement and Deprivation* (Oxford, 1981); John M. MacKenzie, ed., *Imperialism and the Natural World* (Manchester, 1990).

[57] Richard H. Grove, *Green Imperialism: Colonial Expansion, Tropical Island Edens and the Origins of Environmentalism, 1600–1860* (Cambridge, 1995).

free, from the British Isles and their experience in the colonies of settlement have taken on a new lease of life.[58] In part this has reflected the influence of Bernard Bailyn's *Voyages to the West: A Passage in the Peopling of America on the Eve of the American Revolution* (New York, 1986). But new urgency has been imparted to these studies by the interest in histories of resistance by the poor and, in particular, studies of women of the lower class. Investigations of other labour migrations around the Empire, such as the diaspora of Indian indentured labour to Mauritius, Ceylon, and the Caribbean, have been given a similar boost. The enlightened patronage of the Wellcome Institute of London in the field of medical history has also rediscovered the early history of colonial medical and psychiatric services, and the history of the encounter between western and native medical practices in the context of epidemic disease.[59]

The most fashionable development of the 1980s and 1990s has, however, been the fierce debate about Edward W. Said's *Orientalism*.[60] Historians of the Empire have inevitably been alerted to this not only because Said indicted imperialism in general, but because the debate has implications for the epistemological basis of Imperial history. Said and his disciples claimed that almost all European knowledge of other peoples was generated simply by the needs of conquest, and hence was false. Specialists in the history of northern Africa, India, and southern Africa quickly began to discern a link between concepts they were wont to use and the 'project' of Imperial domination. Marrying Said to Eric Hobsbawm and Terence Ranger's influential *The Invention of Tradition* (Cambridge, 1983), historians began to argue that Indian caste, African tribe, 'Islam', or 'native polity'—the basic building-blocks of the subject—were inventions of the colonial power in the early nineteenth century.

Some of this work was retrogressive. The faddishness of 'post-colonial' theorizing in the last two decades of the twentieth century caused many commentators to overlook the great body of work in British intellectual history which relates to the question of orientalism and Imperial ideas. They saw only the tendency to create the Other, rather than the reverberations of long-standing debates among Europeans about commerce, virtue, and polity. Other histories in this vein tended to deny Asians, Africans, or Polynesians 'agency' in their own histories more thoroughly than had the nineteenth-century Imperial writers. Some even espoused the view that history could only represent the view of the white conqueror; we can never know the mind of the 'native'.

[58] P. C. Emmer and M. Mörner, eds., *European Expansion and Migration: Essays on the Intercontinental Migration from Africa and Europe* (New York, 1992).

[59] Gerald W. Hartwig and K. David Patterson, eds., *Disease in African History: An Introductory Survey and Case Studies* (Durham, NC, 1978); David Arnold, ed., *Imperial Medicine and Indigenous Societies* (Manchester, 1988).

[60] Edward W. Said, *Orientalism* (London, 1978) and *Culture and Imperialism* (New York, 1993).

Recently there are signs that historians have regrouped and are subjecting the idea of colonial discourse to sophisticated analyses which are restoring it to its political and social context. These writers have begun to draw attention to the role of indigenous informants and debates in the construction of stereotypes about non-western societies.[61] They discern the varied and unstable features of the ideologies of the second British Empire, their complex functions in relation to different interest groups, and even in some cases, to their scholarly and heuristic status, divorced from any immediate imperative of domination. Perhaps the most positive outcome of the debate on 'colonial discourse' has been the spark of interest it has aroused among a few historians of Britain and Ireland. Now that the periphery, or its intellectual proxies, are intervening in the debates of the centre in Europe and North America, the obverse is greatly to be desired. The Imperial history of the future will have to take seriously the question of how far, and in what ways, the Imperial experience contributed to the making of national identity and regional identities in the British Isles itself. Linda Colley, for instance, has studied the role of the Empire in the forging of the British nation between 1763 and 1830.[62]

Some Imperial historians, especially in Britain, have deplored what they see as the politicization of Imperial history by issues of gender, race, and 'post-coloniality'. While the naiveté of some of this work deserves their disparagement, this chapter has argued that Imperial history has always been intensely political.

[61] e.g. Eugene F. Irschick, *Dialogue and History: Constructing South India, 1795–1895* (Berkeley, 1994).

[62] Linda Colley, *Britons: Forging the Nation.*

Select Bibliography

TARASANKAR BANNERJEA, *Indian Historical Research Since Independence* (Calcutta, 1987).

JAMES BELICH, *The New Zealand Wars and the Victorian Interpretation of Racial Conflict* (Auckland, 1986).

PAUL W. BENNETT, *Emerging Identities: Selected Problems and Interpretations in Canadian History* (Scarborough, Ontario, 1986).

CARL BERGER, *The Writing of Canadian History: Aspects of English-Canadian Historical Writing: 1900–1970* (Toronto, 1976).

P. J. CAIN and A. G. HOPKINS, *British Imperialism*, 2 vols. (London, 1993): Vol. I, *Innovation and Expansion, 1688–1914*; Vol. II, *Crisis and Deconstruction, 1914–1990.*

RANAJIT GUHA, *An Indian Historiography of India: A Nineteenth-Century Agenda and Its Implications* (Calcutta, 1988).

VINCENT T. HARLOW, *The Founding of the Second British Empire, 1763–93*, 2 vols. (Oxford, 1952–64).

STEPHEN HOLT, *Manning Clark and Australian History, 1915–63* (St Lucia, Queensland, 1982).

Ronald Hyam and Ged Martin, *Reappraisals in British Imperial History* (London, 1975).

Ronald Hyam, *Britain's Imperial Century, 1815–1914: A Study of Empire and Expansion* (New York, 1976; new edn., Basingstoke, 1993).

John M. MacKenzie, *Orientalism: History, Theory and the Arts* (Manchester, 1995).

Rosalind O'Hanlon, 'Recovering the Subject: Subaltern Studies and the History of Resistance in South Asia', *Modern Asian Studies*, XXII, 1 (1988), pp. 189–224.

Anthony Pagden, *Lords of All the World: Ideologies of Empire in Spain, Britain and France, c.1500–c.1850* (London, 1995).

Ronald Robinson and John Gallagher with Alice Denny, *Africa and the Victorians: The Official Mind of Imperialism* (London, 1961).

Edward W. Said, *Orientalism* (London, 1978).

C. C. Saunders, *The Making of the South African Past: Major Historians on Race and Class* (Totowa, NJ, 1988).

J. R. Seeley, *The Expansion of England*, ed. with an Introduction by John Gross (Chicago, 1971).

Ken Smith, *The Changing Past: Trends in South African Historical Writing* (Johannesburg, 1988).

Miles Taylor, '*Imperium et Libertas*? Rethinking the Radical Critique of Imperialism During the Nineteenth Century', *Journal of Imperial and Commonwealth History*, XIX, 1 (1991), pp. 1–23.

4

British North America in the Seventeenth and Eighteenth Centuries

STEPHEN FOSTER

Map-makers just after the Second World War still took as their charge the representation not just of magnitude and proximity but of possession. In consequence, the author of this chapter belongs to the last generation of schoolchildren to have stood before the massive world maps then dominating grade-school classrooms and asked the once ubiquitous question, why was so much of the land-mass of the globe a rosy red? As Americans, we ourselves lived in an orange or purple polity to be found in the centre of the map in question, but at only a slightly more advanced stage of our education came historical maps and the additional discovery that the East Coast too had once borne the same rose hue currently assigned to British Guiana and Fiji. Successive historical maps, especially when placed in conjunction with something laying out the conquests of Alexander or the extent of the Roman Empire in the reign of Trajan, made abundantly clear a few basic, even primitive propositions about American history and History more generally: that for most peoples in recent centuries it was very much the story of a struggle, first to obtain their own unique colour and then to propagate it.

These maps both incarnated and inculcated the preoccupations of their makers: the dialectic between the presumptively motor forces of territorial expansion and state-making, and, more particularly for American historiography, the interaction between the spread of English colonial power to the New World and the creation of an American nationality on the same site. Such concerns virtually defined the very field of early American historiography at its inception a century ago. And for the time being they still define the boundaries, temporal and spatial, within which this discipline is currently pursued by the bulk of its practitioners.[1] In a fundamental sense its central questions have always assumed some sense of the possibility of empire and of the British Empire in particular, and have

The author wishes to thank P. J. Marshall and Edmund S. Morgan for their help and encouragement.

[1] Jack P. Greene, 'Interpretive Frameworks: The Quest for Intellectual Order in Early American History', *William and Mary Quarterly* (hereafter *WMQ*), Third Series, XLVIII (1991), pp. 515–30.

remained in broadest outline closely akin to the same ones that concern an historian of Canada or Australia or New Zealand. Inevitably, one must wonder if this situation can long withstand the coming of generations for whom a representation of the extent of the British Empire carries the same significance as a display of the areas under the hegemony of the Golden Horde, and for whom the very notion of Great Britain as 'Top Nation' is surreal. The end of this chapter will ponder that matter; its bulk, however, must be taken up with the founders of colonial history and then with the ways their successors have built upon or reworked the original framework.

The maps that laid out the evolution of America from colony to an imperial power in its own right were mostly the work of the Harvard scholar-entrepreneur A. B. Hart, often denominated the creator of American history as an academic subject.[2] Of all Hart's assorted ventures in curriculum-building, however, the one with the most enduring influence has been the American Nation series, twenty-eight volumes, each by a different author, that has dictated the subsequent arrangement of the American history syllabus by topic and chronology. For volume five, *Colonial Self-Government, 1652–1689* (New York, 1904), Hart secured the services of the great Charles M. Andrews, by far the most gifted and influential of the emerging 'Imperial School'. And Andrews, far more than any other individual, has given us the notion of a specifically *colonial period* in American history.[3]

The term *Imperial School* has come to designate, first, the triptych of Andrews and his near contemporaries, Herbert Osgood and George Louis Beer,[4] then the students of Andrews and Osgood who practised early American history (Beer never entered academic life), and finally some individuals who were the students of other scholars but who also chose to spend their time extending or substantiating the propositions one or another of the three masters had laid down. Of this composite second generation, the leading member was Lawrence Henry Gipson,

[2] *Dictionary of American Biography*, Supplement Three (New York, 1973), under 'Hart, Albert Bushnell'. I owe my knowledge of Hart's influence on American historical map-making to John Long of the Newberry Library's Atlas of Historical County Boundaries Project.

[3] Richard R. Johnson, 'Charles McLean Andrews and the Invention of American Colonial History', *WMQ*, Third Series, XLIII (1986), pp. 528–31.

[4] Biographical entries for all three men can be found in *Dictionary of American Biography* and in Clyde N. Wilson, ed., *Twentieth-Century American Historians, Dictionary of Literary Biography*, Vol. XVII (Detroit, 1983), under 'Andrews, Charles M.', and Clyde N. Wilson, ed., *American Historians, 1866–1912 Dictionary of Literary Biography*, Vol. XLVII (Detroit, 1986), under 'Beer, George Louis', 'Osgood, Herbert'. Osgood's main works are *The American Colonies in the Seventeenth Century* (New York, 1904–07) and *The American Colonies in the Eighteenth Century* (New York, 1924). Beer's most important work is *British Colonial Policy, 1754–1765* (New York, 1907). Also important, however, are *The Origins of the British Colonial System, 1578–1660* (New York, 1908) and *The Old Colonial System, 1660–1754*, Part I, *The Establishment of the System, 1660–1688* (New York, 1912).

who remained active almost to his death in 1971, age 90, producing and revising the fifteen volumes of his *The British Empire before the American Revolution* (New York, 1936–70).[5]

Osgood, Andrews, and Beer were of the first generation of professional academic historians in America, exposed directly or indirectly to the full force of German 'scientific' history as it descended from Ranke. All three, additionally, were well grounded in English medieval history as then practised and had grown up in the age of modern European state-creation. Unsurprisingly, the experience of working in the Public Record Office, a great shrine to centralizing power, came as a revelation to them, not least for its voluminous documentation of the links that made the New World an annexe of the old. Traditional attempts to find a unifying theme in American history from the earliest settlements to the late nineteenth century, particularly if that theme was the growth of democracy, were accordingly dismissed for their lack of scientific method and wilful ignorance of the proper British archives.

Ironically, the School's scorn was reserved particularly for Edward Channing, Hart's collaborator, and even more especially for the German-trained George Bancroft, whose epic *A History of the United States. From the Discovery of the American Continent* took the greatest and most regular beating item-by-item from the point of its inception, the creation of the elected House of Burgesses in Virginia in 1619, that he credited with 'having auspicated liberty in America'.[6] In contrast with these false trails laid by an uncritical nationalism, the Imperial School held that the successful retention of the initiative by the Jamaican Assembly in 1678 was more significant for the constitutional development of English-speaking polities than anything accomplished by the putative auspicators of liberty in seventeenth-century Virginia, who, in fact, caved in to Imperial demands for colonial Poynings' laws.[7]

Andrews (ordinarily a non-combatant on principle) came to see the survival of

[5] There are biographical entries for Gipson in the sources cited above, n. 4. The most useful interpretation is John Shy, 'The Empire Remembered: Lawrence Henry Gipson, Historian', in Shy, *A People Numerous and Armed: Reflections on the Military Struggle for American Independence* (New York, 1976), pp. 109–31.

[6] George Bancroft, *History of the United States from the Discovery of the American Continent*, 23rd edn. (Boston, 1866–75), I, p. 158. The creation of the Massachusetts General Court receives a similar encomium at I, p. 367.

[7] Cf. Andrews, *Our Earliest Colonial Settlements: Their Diversities of Origin and Later Characteristics* (New York, 1933), p. 44; Leonard Woods Labaree, *Royal Government in America: A Study of the British Colonial System Before 1783* (New Haven, 1930), pp. 219–22. For the anomalous position of the West Indies in colonial historiography see Michael Watson, 'The British West Indian Legislatures in the Seventeenth and Eighteenth Centuries: An Historiographical Introduction', in Philip Lawson, ed. *Parliament and the Atlantic Empire* (Edinburgh, 1995), pp. 89–98, and for the development of British West Indian historiography more generally see the chap. by B. W. Higman.

various Bancroftian 'perversities' about the continuous course of American history from colonies to nation as akin to the Fundamentalist rejection of Darwinism. His own work, he insists, 'brings the mother country into the forefront of the picture as the central figure, the authoritative and guiding force, the influence of which did more than anything else to shape the course of colonial achievement'. The mainland colonies prior to 1776 have to be understood as in the first instance colonial, that is, as thirteen among the thirty-odd units in an Empire that centred on Westminster. Or, as Lawrence Henry Gipson wrote of his teacher, using the highest compliment he knew, 'he is concerned with English history, not merely the setting for later United States history'.[8]

Long considered standard fare in any historiographic survey of this period, the work of the Imperial School will soon be wholly unfamiliar. The arguments *in extenso* of Osgood and Beer, the monographs on central issues, by O. M. Dickerson and Viola Barnes, even the multi-volume effusion of the inexhaustible Gipson, are out of print, their authors, like the slow learners of 'The Fury of Aerial Bombardment', names on a list. Andrews alone has been something more. If his magnum opus, *The Colonial Period of American History*, has been relegated to the second-hand book stores, two shorter, summary works have remained continuously in *paperback* for decades: *Our Earliest Colonial Settlements* (originally published in 1933) and the all but perennial *The Colonial Background of the American Revolution* (originally published in 1924, revised edition in 1931), which finally sank into the oblivion of out-of-print status shortly before the publication of this volume.

One can hardly avoid the question of what has made for this unique instance—why have historians remained interested in the late thoughts of a man born a few months before the Battle of Gettysburg? Andrews is, to be sure, far more acceptable to contemporary sensibilities than any of his rivals. An elderly man writing in the 1930s was safely distanced from such grotesquerie as Beer's call for an alliance of English-speaking peoples or Osgood's Teutonic obsession with the taxonomy of corporate forms in colonial America. Those political sympathies that do peek through his magisterial pronouncements (his endorsement of women's suffrage, his distaste for Fundamentalism, imperialism, and the anti-syndicalist legislation of his day) betoken a generous soul likely to earn and keep the trust of readers of a later era. Andrews is less dated, as well, in the way he says what he has to say. Osgood seems to have written dull books from unavoidable necessity, Beer to have embraced dullness as a matter of choice—he also wrote high-toned but

[8] Charles M. Andrews, *The Colonial Background of the American Revolution: Four Essays in American Colonial History*, 2nd edn. (New Haven, 1931), p. 217; and *The Colonial Period of American History* (New Haven, 1934–38), I, p. xi; Lawrence Henry Gipson, *Charles McLean Andrews and the Reorientation of the Study of American Colonial History*, Lehigh University Publications, Studies in the Humanities, XVII (Lehigh, Pa., 1935), p. 8.

effective political journalism—in order to demonstrate his scholarly bona fides. Andrews, despite growing deafness, retained a fine sense of the cadence of words on the page and a shameless willingness to use all the standard rhetorical tropes. In similar fashion, his scope is broader, his interests and sympathies more balanced than either of his peers or any of their immediate successors. Osgood regards metropolitan impositions of power as interference with a beneficent natural process of domestic growth. Beer, on the other hand, has no real use for the locals, who mainly get in the way of the various administrative initiatives emanating from the Mother Country that are the object of his study. It was left to Andrews to bring what he calls 'a duality of interest' to the subject, and write of the interaction of Mother Country and colonist in settling North America, creating some kind of overall colonial system, however minimally systematic, and in the end undoing in short order this particular great work of time. A summary of Andrews begins to sound very much like a standard undergraduate lecture, precisely because he laid down the argument in broad outline that subsequent scholarship, even after so many years, has failed to replace.

Andrews always begins with the circumstance that England's overseas expansion was almost entirely the work of private enterprise. Colonizers created colonies for reasons of their own, and as these reasons were many so were the kinds of colonies. England's attempts to co-ordinate the various colonial economies for its own benefit began in earnest relatively late, in the 1650s and 1660s with the passage of the Navigation Acts. Defence of these Acts against colonial intransigence required increasingly ambitious attempts at centralized control culminating in a panoply of administrative devices worked out in the 1690s or just afterwards: the Board of Trade, the colonial customs service and courts of vice-admiralty, above all, 'royal government' (the gradual resumption by the Crown in colony after colony of the right to name and give binding orders to all members of the colonial executive).[9]

Andrews's contrapuntal theme to Imperial centralization is colonial self-government. From the time of the Crown takeover of the Virginia colony from the Virginia Company, some kind of body representative of local opinion was held to be necessary in each colony in order to induce migration and to ensure that the colonists would live together with their Governors and each other in a more-or-less peaceful manner. These lower houses of Assembly were merely the overseas extensions of the governing bodies of English boroughs and chartered companies, and were drawn from an equally narrow and narrow-minded social base. (Andrews assumes, incorrectly, that the colonial franchise laws were severely restrictive.) Gradually, however, out of self-interest and ambition the Assembly

[9] Andrews, *Colonial Background*, pp. 7–28.

leadership assumed the trappings and pretensions to authority of the House of Commons.[10] Conventionally denominated 'the Rise of the Assembly', this process of legislative encroachment on executive power in the Royal colonies might more pointedly be called by the title subsequently used by Jack P. Greene, self-consciously following Andrews's lead: *The Quest for Power*.[11]

At times Andrews writes as if the events of the period between 1763 and 1776 can be reduced to the moment when the irresistible force of Assembly aggression finally makes full contact with the immovable obduracy of Imperial bureaucrats and short-sighted politicians still convinced that they were dealing with an American situation little changed since the Peace of Utrecht.[12] Most often, however, the Revolution just seems to happen because it has to.[13] The Imperial School had given so much time to understanding why the British did what they did and put so much effort into the contention that the Navigation Acts and mercantilist policy *per se* were *not* inherently objectionable to the colonists, that there was no mental energy left over to explain what then did make Americans angry and why. Andrews was considerably more respectful towards American protest than, say, Beer or Gipson, but he could not believe that either 'certain philosophical declarations regarding the inherent rights of man' or 'the reasoned arguments and vigorous utterances of contemporary writers of a legal and meditative turn of mind' could be anything other than 'of interest chiefly to intellectual circles'.[14]

Andrews, nevertheless, still feels the need to explain 1776. The frustration of even the most distinguished and able member of the Imperial School when faced with the Revolution can be measured by the sheer number of different causal explanations that he manages to offer in just two chapters of the short book in which he confronts the problem. Andrews employs two different time schemes, one long-term and determinist, the other centred on the choices of the moment. 'For a hundred years before that event the colonies and the mother country were moving in exactly opposite directions, each in obedience to historical tendencies that could not be resisted', yet the situation hung in the balance as late as 1773 because colonial leadership was still in the hands of 'temperate' men averse to

[10] Ibid., pp. 30–40. Cf. the literature on the extent of the colonial franchise summarized in Jack P. Greene, 'Changing Interpretations of Early American Politics', in Ray Allen Billington, ed., *The Reinterpretation of Early American History: Essays in Honor of John Edwin Pomfret* (San Marino, Calif., 1966), pp. 151–184.

[11] Cf. Andrews's plan for a projected sixth volume of *The Colonial Period* in his 'On the Writing of Colonial History', *WMQ*, Third Series, I (1944), pp. 38–41; Jack P. Greene, *The Quest for Power: The Lower Houses of Assembly in the Southern Royal Colonies, 1689–1776* (Chapel Hill, NC, 1963), pp. viii–ix, ix n.

[12] Andrews, *Colonial Background*, pp. 40–44.

[13] Andrews tackled the origins of the Revolution explicitly only twice: in the third chapter of *Colonial Background* (pp. 121–69) and in his description of how he would have written the projected seventh, final volume of *The Colonial Period* in 'On the Writing of Colonial History', pp. 41–48.

[14] Andrews, *Colonial Background*, pp. 135–37; cf. pp. 201–03.

provocation and fundamentally loyal to the Crown. The British in their turn threw away this opportunity because they continued to operate by out-of-date rules, still looking on the colonies as little more than sources of profit, but it is also the case that they were led into a new and disastrous policy after 1763 because, in the course of the Seven Years War, traditional 'mercantilism', rational if myopic, had been replaced by a dangerously adventurist 'Imperialism', a quest for territory and grandeur without sufficient regard to the balance-sheet.[15] Structure and contingency are not necessarily irreconcilable; Andrews, however, apparently was too perplexed by the whole phenomenon to take on the responsibility of weaving his two themes together into a coherent whole.

Other than Andrews, only his student Gipson was willing to deal in its entirety with the subject of the dissolution of the first British Empire. Gipson sharply separates the war in Europe from the Anglo-French conflict elsewhere, which he renames the Great War for the Empire and designates 'perhaps the most momentous event in the life of the English-speaking people in the New World'.[16] That premise justifies nine volumes before the earliest stages of the Imperial crisis (1763–66) can be reached, and reduces what comes afterwards to a simple reflex of what came before. Of and in itself there is little to object to in the proposition that the American Revolution was an 'aftermath' of the Seven Years War (and much recent scholarship has attempted to develop precisely how this came to be).[17] But even four volumes should surely have been enough for Gipson to get beyond this semi-commonplace.

When one comes down to it, the Revolution, for the Imperial School in general, is not an event but a hiatus. Andrews was the most cautious and nuanced of the lot (meaning, really, the cagiest), but for all his biological metaphors he, no less than his pupils and his peers, wrote as if 1776 was the year of the Flood. Nothing before that date, God and Noah excepted, really has much to do with anything after it. The very success of the Imperial School rendered their chosen field of endeavour nugatory. If the Revolution had few domestic causes and the colonial period no significant effects, if American democracy 'would have come had the

[15] Ibid., pp. 122–29, 152–56, 183.

[16] Lawrence Henry Gipson, 'The American Revolution as an Aftermath of the Great War for the Empire, 1754–1763', *Political Science Quarterly*, LXV (1950), p. 87.

[17] Cf. William Pencak, 'Warfare and Political Change in Mid-Eighteenth-Century Massachusetts', *Journal of Imperial and Commonwealth History* (hereafter *JICH*), VIII (1979–80), pp. 51–73; Jack P. Greene, 'The Seven Years' War and the American Revolution: The Causal Relationship Reconsidered', ibid., pp. 85–105; Fred Anderson, *A People's Army: Massachusetts Soldiers and Society in the Seven Years' War* (Chapel Hill, NC, 1984); T. H. Breen, 'Narrative of Commercial Life: Consumption, Ideology and Community on the Eve of the American Revolution', *WMQ*, Third Series, L (1993), pp. 471–501; see chap. by Doron Ben-Atar.

colonies remained attached to Great Britain',[18] then sooner or later someone—chairs of departments and deans of colleges, to name two possibilities—was going to wonder why anyone should have to study early American history.

After Andrews, and despite the prolific Gipson, scholarship on the colonial period mostly petered out for a time. Even college survey texts during the last decade before the Second World War paid an oblique tribute to the Imperial School by beginning only in 1763.[19] Surveying 'The Neglected First Half of American History' for the American Historical Association in 1947, Carl Bridenbaugh had an unmentioned but obvious enough candidate to take the blame. Lamenting, in very un-Andrewsish terms, the decline of interest in 'a period in which present institutions took their origin and in which the existing way of life in this country germinated and received its character and direction', he then warned that students 'prefer social and cultural history to the so-called arid narrative of political happenings'.[20] Social history would presumably discover what the Imperial School could not, the colonial roots of the Revolution and, by implication, American identity. Just three years after Andrews's death the recovery of early American history as an academic discipline was, in effect, held to depend on Bancroft by other means.

Where exceptions are to be found to the immediate post-Andrews drought, the enthusiasm in question was most frequently sustained by special circumstances external to the discipline of history as practised in American universities. Studies of American Puritanism, for example, well launched at Harvard in the 1920s and 1930s by Samuel Eliot Morison and Kenneth B. Murdock, flourished in the works of Perry Miller and a little later Edmund S. Morgan. But this was a discipline closely allied (through the programme in American Civilization) with kindred interests in English literature and not suffering from any excessive delicacy when it came to using early America to link Elizabethan origins with nineteenth-century American denouements.[21] Similarly, beginning in 1927 with *New*

[18] Andrews, *Colonial Background*, p. 203.

[19] Carl Bridenbaugh, 'The Neglected First Half of American History', *American Historical Review*, LIII (1947–48), pp. 506–09.

[20] Ibid., pp. 506, 513.

[21] The earlier, heroic phase of American Puritan studies is reviewed in Edmund S. Morgan, 'The Historians of Early New England', in Billington, ed., *Reinterpretation of Early American History*, pp. 41–63. For later developments see Michael McGiffert, 'American Puritan Studies in the 1960's', *WMQ*, Third Series, XXVII (1970), pp. 36–67; David D. Hall, 'On Common Ground: The Coherence of American Puritan Studies', *WMQ*, Third Series, XLIV (1987), pp. 193–229. The most recent work is, if anything, yet more transatlantic in orientation: David D. Hall, *Worlds of Wonder, Days of Judgement: Popular Religious Belief in Early New England* (New York: 1989); Stephen Foster, *The Long Argument: English Puritanism and the Shaping of New England Culture, 1570–1700* (Chapel Hill, NC, 1991); Francis J. Bremer, ed., *Puritanism: Transatlantic Perspectives on a Seventeenth-Century Anglo-American Faith*, Massachusetts Historical Society Studies in American History and Culture, III (Boston, 1993); Janice Knight, *Orthodoxies in Massachusetts: Rereading American Puritanism* (Cambridge, Mass., 1994).

England's Outpost, John Bartlett Brebner at Columbia University made colonial history a little more Imperial by bringing the Maritimes into the study of the subject. They have retained a toehold there ever since, if only because Nova Scotia remains a useful counter-example when explaining why the other thirteen colonies chose revolution.[22] Brebner, however, was Canadian by birth and earlier education, as for the most part have been those who succeeded to his interests.[23]

Some progress was also made along familiar lines, despite Morison's prediction that 'industrious young workers in the Public Record Office will find it pretty dry gleaning after Andrews'.[24] Royal Governors, on close examination, generally turned out to have been honestly intentioned, hard-working types doing the best they could under the difficult circumstances created for them by the colonial Assemblies.[25] The Assemblies, in their turn, continued to rise, but in more detail and in more interesting ways that integrated their politics into the histories of the societies they purported to represent.[26] Whitehall, on the whole, got the kinds of

[22] John Bartlett Brebner, *New England's Outpost: Acadia before the Conquest of Canada*, Columbia University Studies in History, Economics, and Public Law, CCXCIII (New York, 1927); John Bartlett Brebner, *The Neutral Yankees of Nova Scotia: A Marginal Colony During the Revolutionary Years* (New York, 1937). Alternative accounts of the lack of revolutionary sentiment can be found in J. M. Bumsted, *Henry Alline, 1748–1784* (Toronto, 1971) and Gordon Stewart and George Rawlyk, *A People Highly Favoured of God: The Nova Scotia Yankees and the American Revolution* (Toronto, 1972). Other studies that place Nova Scotia in context include George A. Rawlyk, *Nova Scotia's Massachusetts: A Study of Massachusetts–Nova Scotia Relations, 1630–1784* (Montreal, 1973) and John C. Reid, *Acadia, Maine, and New Scotland: Marginal Colonies in the Seventeenth Century* (Toronto, 1981).

[23] In general, the points of contact between early Canadian and colonial American historiography are few. See Philip Buckner, 'Britain and British North America Before Confederation', in D. A. Muise, ed., *A Reader's Guide to Canadian History*, Vol. I, *Beginnings to Confederation* (Toronto, 1982), pp. 193–213, and in this volume the chap. by D. R. Owram. For the scholarship dealing with the general question of the remaining British Empire in the aftermath of the Revolution see the chap. by P. J. Marshall.

[24] *New England Quarterly*, VII (1934), p. 732.

[25] The most important work was done by John A. Schutz: *Thomas Pownall, British Defender of American Liberty: A Study of Anglo-American Relations in the Eighteenth Century* (Glendale, Calif., 1951) and *William Shirley: King's Governor of Massachusetts* (Chapel Hill, NC, 1961). See, in general, the list of biographical studies in Jack P. Greene, comp., *The American Colonies in the Eighteenth Century, 1689–1763*, Goldentree Bibliographies in American History (New York, 1969), pp. 35–37.

[26] See, in particular, in addition to Green's *Quest for Power* (cited above, n. 11), Charles S. Sydnor, *Gentlemen Freeholders: Political Practices in Washington's Virginia* (Chapel Hill, NC, 1952), which is better known under its reprint title of *American Revolutionaries in the Making*; Lucille B. Griffith, *The Virginia House of Burgesses, 1750–1774*, revised edn. (University, Ala. 1970); Patricia U. Bonomi, *A Factious People: Politics and Society in Colonial New York* (New York, 1971); Robert Zemsky, *Merchants, Farmers, and River Gods: An Essay on Eighteenth-Century American Politics* (Boston, 1971). For pre-Revolutionary politics more generally, see the historiographic summaries by Greene (cited above, n. 9) and John Murrin, 'Political Development', in Jack P. Greene and J. R. Pole, eds., *Colonial British America: Essays in the New History of the Early Modern Era* (Baltimore, 1984), pp. 408–56. An important recent work that argues for a distinctive American political culture developing precisely because the colonists operated within, and gradually adapted to, imperial constraints is Allan Tully, *Forming American Politics: Ideas, Interests, and Institutions in Colonial New York and Pennsylvania* (Baltimore, 1994).

low marks that Andrews himself would have awarded.[27] The reputation of the politicians at the apex of the pyramid underwent a kind of levelling: cutting the few surviving heroes down to size had the effect of improving the standing of the architects of colonial taxation.[28] Overall, the picture of Imperial governance in North America remained for a quarter-century and more after the end of the Second World War pretty much as Andrews had painted it in the 1930s—for the good reason that relatively few new people took on his enterprise.

As early American history revived in the rapidly expanding academy of the 1950s and 1960s, the most significant scholarship was produced by Edmund S. Morgan and Bernard Bailyn, Harvard-trained scholars who had written their first books on aspects of seventeenth-century New England, and who now chose to address the intellectual content of the American protest leading up to the Revolution, a pursuit that required no special interest in the mass of paper generated at Whitehall. Often described as a straightforward riposte to the earlier dismissal of Revolutionary ideas as derivative and cynically opportunistic 'window-dressing', the turn towards intellectual history was intended as a far more ambitious undertaking: an attempt to make good the Bancroftian claim that American history began well before 1776 or 1787.[29] Apart from their attempt to demonstrate the consistency, complexity, and tough-mindedness of the colonial protest against British policy, Morgan and Bailyn (and their students subsequently) have insisted on the lasting importance of the late-colonial material they resurrected. Bailyn writes at length of its transformative power in creating a post-Revolutionary republican ideology. Edmund Morgan justifies the whole preoccupation with

[27] Ella Lonn, *The Colonial Agents of the Southern Colonies* (Chapel Hill, NC, 1945); Oliver M. Dickerson, *The Navigation Acts and the American Revolution* (Philadelphia, 1951); Dora Mae Clark, *The Rise of the British Treasury: Colonial Administration in the Eighteenth Century* (New Haven, 1960); John Shy, *Toward Lexington: The Role of the British Army in the Coming of the American Revolution* (Princeton, 1965); Franklin B. Wickwire, *British Subministers and Colonial America, 1763–1783* (Princeton, 1966); Thomas C. Barrow, *Trade and Empire: The British Customs Service in Colonial America, 1660–1775* (Cambridge, Mass., 1967); Michael G. Kammen: *A Rope of Sand: The Colonial Agents, British Politics, and the American Revolution* (Ithaca, NY, 1968); Ian K. Steele, *The Politics of Colonial Policy: The Board of Trade in Colonial Administration, 1696–1720* (Oxford, 1968); James A. Henretta, *'Salutary Neglect': Colonial Administration under the Duke of Newcastle* (Princeton, 1972).

[28] Jack M. Sosin, *Whitehall and the Wilderness: The Middle West in British Colonial Policy, 1760–1775* (Lincoln, Nebr., 1961); P. D. G. Thomas, *British Policy and the Stamp Act Crisis: The First Phase of the American Revolution, 1763–1767* (Oxford, 1975) and *The Townsend Duties Crisis: The Second Phase of the American Revolution, 1767–1773* (Oxford, 1987); John L. Bullion, *A Great and Necessary Measure: George Grenville and the Genesis of the Stamp Act, 1763–1765* (Columbia, Mo., 1982). Even the Duke of Newcastle is rehabilitated (up to a point) in Reed Browning, *The Duke of Newcastle* (New Haven, 1975) and in Richard Middleton, *The Bells of Victory: The Pitt–Newcastle Ministry and the Conduct of the Seven Years' War, 1757–1762* (Cambridge, 1985).

[29] The manifesto is Edmund S. Morgan, 'The American Revolution: Revisions in Need of Revising', *WMQ*, Third Series, XIV (1957), pp. 3–15.

two-century-old tracts and manifestoes on the grounds that the ideas contained in them were crucial 'for a collection of human beings to be or become a people'.[30]

Social history, on which Bridenbaugh had pinned his hopes, took a little longer to come on the scene, and arrived in a form that had not been anticipated. Advocates of the New Social History dispensed with the usual preliminary obeisance or repudiation of the work of their predecessors, on the straightforward grounds that earlier generations would have found their methods and goals as unfathomable as quantum mechanics would have been to an alchemist. Heavily influenced by the social sciences, and especially sociology and demography, the new departure favoured the application of theoretical models, concentration on local studies, and, as its trademark, ruthless quantification which, much like Beer's syntax in an earlier era, established one's right to be taken seriously. Since the focus of the early work was New England again, this time in the form of town studies, it could also be assumed somehow that the topic was literally self-contained. Politics, war, commerce (all topics at least partly dependent on what happened on the other side of the Atlantic) simply had no effect on an autochthonous narrative of—strange to say it—the establishment and decay of demographic regimes, fluctuations in economic opportunity and the distribution of wealth, and the travail of a traditional, corporatist 'mentality' slowly yielding to the forces of individualism.[31] A subsequent shift in the centre of gravity of local studies to the Chesapeake compelled a degree of recognition of the importance to the plantation economy of developments at its market centre. However, the distinctive nature of the raw source material, where there are more account books and court records to be counted than diaries and election sermons to be read, made for a positive distaste for Imperial themes of an overtly political or cultural nature.[32]

[30] The two most persuasive statements are Bernard Bailyn, *The Ideological Origins of the American Revolution* (Cambridge, Mass., 1967) and Edmund S. and Helen Morgan, *The Stamp Act Crisis: Prologue to Revolution*, 3rd edn. (Chapel Hill, NC, 1995), originally published in 1953. The quotation (from the new preface of the latter work) is found at p. viii.

[31] Despite significant work at a slightly earlier date by Darrett B. Rutman and Richard L. Bushman, the New Social History was thought of as a coherent movement because of the simultaneous publication of four New England local studies: John Demos, *A Little Commonwealth: Family Life in Plymouth Colony* (New York, 1970); Philip J. Greven, Jr., *Four Generations: Population, Land, and Family in Colonial Andover, Massachusetts* (New York, 1970); Kenneth A. Lockridge, *A New England Town, the First Hundred Years: Dedham, Massachusetts, 1636–1736* (New York, 1970); and Michael Zuckerman, *Peaceable Kingdoms: New England Towns in the Eighteenth Century* (New York, 1970). Inevitably, the four were the subject of a number of essay reviews, of which the most influential has been John M. Murrin, 'Review Essay', *History and Theory*, XI (1972), pp. 226–75.

[32] Most of this literature in its most positivist phase appeared as articles. A good summary of work up until the time of its publication is Thad W. Tate, 'The Seventeenth-Century Chesapeake and its Modern Historians', in Thad W. Tate and David L. Ammerman, eds., *The Chesapeake in the Seventeenth Century: Essays on Anglo-American History* (Chapel Hill, NC, 1979), pp. 3–50. Later developments are reviewed in Lois Green Carr and others, eds., *Colonial Chesapeake Society* (Chapel Hill, NC, 1988), pp. 1–46.

The book that finally endowed the resultant aggregations with some kind of mental life, Edmund S. Morgan's *American Slavery, American Freedom: The Ordeal of Colonial Virginia* (New York, 1975), was not a product of the New Social History at all but the work of a senior scholar venturing away from his Puritans and Revolutionaries for just long enough to bring England back into the story of its first colony in America, and also to attempt to explain how the political upheavals of Virginia from Bacon's Rebellion through the recall of Governor Nicholson in 1705 were logically correlated with the colony's switch-over to slavery in the same three decades.

One can take 1975 or, anyway, the mid-1970s as a moment of pause when older aversions had spent themselves and newer enthusiasms began to be tempered by a sense of the limitations that accompanied their achievements. If the Revolution had been endowed with a degree of dignity and intellectual purpose, one still did not know much about the recent past, personal and institutional, of the revolutionaries: the years between the Glorious Revolution and the French and Indian War (Seven Years War) continued to suffer from 'shameful neglect' (Andrews's phrase). And, if demos had been recovered at least in part from his quantifiable traces, and if he (when he had the good fortune to be white and a he) had been endowed with economic aspirations, the right to vote, and perhaps the right and fact of bearing arms, then there remained no good account of why pre-Revolutionary society was so obsessed with hierarchy in public when it was so blatantly under-stratified in fact. In different ways, both problems led back to the nature and situation of colonial élites and the unremarkable discovery that they, more obviously than their more ordinary contemporaries, were enmeshed in the business of Empire.

The most radical assault on the problems raised during this latest revival of interest in Imperial history is Stephen Saunders Webb's *The Governors General: The English Army and the Definition of Empire, 1569–1681* (Chapel Hill, NC, 1979). Webb points out that colonization was necessarily a military operation as much as a species of commercial expansion and, like Andrews, finds the commercial mentality of the Imperial era short-sighted and intermittent in its attention to colonial governance. But most colonial Governors had military experience, and the military mind was systematic, authoritarian, and, really, rather honest and efficient. In consequence, the expansion of the power of the colonial executive in the course of 'garrison government' (Webb's coinage, now much used) was not necessarily unwelcome to the bulk of the colonial population, because it offered protection against exploitation at the hands of legislatures dominated (again, as in Andrews) by self-serving local oligarchies. The Assemblies did get around to rising, but only in the atypical, if fatal, Newcastle era when a slack mercantilism temporarily superseded a vigilant Imperialism.

In a period when transatlantic approaches are again in vogue, Webb has the distinction of bringing the creation of the European standing army into prominence in an account of colonial history. The difficulties in such an argument, however, are considerable.[33] Allowing for the importance of the exercise of government by military men in certain places at certain times in the seventeenth century, the English army was still never a continuing entity, professionally and institutionally, at any point before 1702.[34] Nor was the military in the colonies quite the austere affair Webb makes it out to be: the supply and financing of English or British armies in America created opportunities for political and personal corruption on a scale quite impossible to conceive of when there was only the local boodle to misappropriate.[35] All told, one would like to see Webb's argument extended past 1681, and to have a view of the military in politics that goes beyond the impact of individual soldier-governors on the power of the executive.[36]

Webb's thesis stands out for its boldness, but it is only one of a number of studies seeking to reintegrate early American history within the overall development of the Mother Country.[37] Significant as this newer work is for what it illuminates, especially when not deviating into a more-than-Osgoodian dryness, it is more significant for what it implies about the ligaments between the hard

[33] The most extended discussion of Webb's argument can be found in Richard R. Johnson, 'The Imperial Webb: The Thesis of Garrison Government in Early America Considered', *WMQ*, Third Series, XLIII (1986), pp. 408–30. Webb responds in ibid., pp. 431–59. The alleged conflict between mercantilist and imperialist motifs, central to the arguments of *both* Andrews and Webb, is critically evaluated in W. A. Speck, 'The International and Imperial Context', in Greene and Pole, eds., *Colonial British America*, pp. 384–407, and endorsed in Daniel A. Baugh, 'Maritime Strength and Atlantic Commerce: The Uses of "a Grand Marine Empire" ', in Lawrence Stone, ed., *An Imperial State at War: Britain from 1689 to 1815* (London, 1994), pp. 185–223. The claim for a connection between political reform, imperialism, and middle-class self-assertion is also relevant: see Kathleen Wilson, *The Sense of the People: Politics, Culture and Imperialism in England, 1715–1785* (Cambridge, 1995).

[34] John Childs, *The British Army of William III, 1689–1702* (Manchester, 1987), pp. 147–52, 184–208, 259–64.

[35] For the amounts involved, see Julian Gwyn, 'British Government Spending and the North American Colonies, 1740–1775', *JICH*, VIII, 1 (Jan. 1980), pp. 74–84. For some of the consequences to those at the receiving-end of this largesse, see William T. Baxter, *The House of Hancock: Business in Boston, 1724–1775* (Cambridge, Mass., 1945), pp. 95–110, 118–23, 129–46, 150–56; Byron Fairchild, *Messrs. William Pepperrell: Merchants at Piscataqua* (Ithaca, NY, 1954), p. 184; Schutz, *William Shirley*, pp. 67–68, 106–07, 135–36, 146–48, 233–34.

[36] Webb's next work after *The Governors-General* is *1676: The End of American Independence* (New York, 1984), which still deals with the seventeenth century. He has linked his argument with eighteenth-century developments only briefly in both books and in 'Army and Empire: English Garrison Government in Britain and America, 1569 to 1763', *WMQ*, Third Series, XXXIV (1977), pp. 1–31.

[37] David S. Lovejoy, *The Glorious Revolution in America* (New York, 1972); Alison G. Olson, *Anglo-American Politics, 1660–1775: The Relationship Between Parties in England and Colonial America* (New York, 1973); Jack M. Sosin, *English America and the Revolution of 1688: Royal Administration and the Structure of Provincial Government* (Lincoln, Nebr., 1982); Robert M. Bliss, *Revolution and Empire: English Politics and the American Colonies in the Seventeenth Century* (Manchester, 1990).

skeletal structure of formal Imperial institutions. These implications, however, have been drawn in full just twice: in a broad survey of quotidian Imperial politicking by Alison G. Olson, and in a detailed study by Richard R. Johnson of the New England colonies as they passed from resistance and insurgency into routine resentment of an Imperial connection that had come to seem a familiar and unquestioned part of the landscape.[38] Together, the two books go far towards explaining how the legitimization of Empire in the eighteenth century and the growth of internal stability within the colonies were interlinked processes.

From Osgood onwards to much more recent work by Jack M. Sosin, examination of the formal workings of the Imperial system generally begins by pointing to the period from roughly 1680 to 1720 as the time when the Empire developed a lasting institutional apparatus, only to finish by stressing that by the latter date opportunities for any further extension of central control had been hopelessly squandered.[39] Olson and Johnson, in parallel ways, suggest otherwise. The Imperial institutions in question (the Board of Trade, the royalized executives, the customs service) may have been the playthings of patronage-mongers at home and they may have been easily defeated by adroit wire-pullers in the colonies. But they served their functions by the mere fact of being, for they became the focal points around which existing transatlantic connections—religious, commercial, familial—all coalesced. Johnson, in addition, building on a much-studied, often-cited, never-published dissertation by John M. Murrin, has spelled out the ways in which political integration into the Empire forced the pace of social differentiation within the colonies.[40] Colonial élites came to enjoy their élite status in part because they were colonial: their somewhat more visible and deliberately imitative Englishness in manner and material display warranted their status as advocates for the domestic population in matters Imperial, and also as potential instruments for Imperial designs, mostly military, when it came to mobilizing the recalcitrant locals.[41]

[38] Alison Olson, *Making the Empire Work: London and American Interest Groups, 1690–1790* (Cambridge, Mass., 1992); Richard R. Johnson, *Adjustment to Empire: The New England Colonies, 1675–1715* (New Brunswick, NJ, 1981).

[39] In addition to Jack M. Sosin, *English America and Imperial Inconstancy: The Rise of Provincial Autonomy, 1696–1715* (Lincoln, Nebr., 1985), see the studies by Steele and Henretta cited above, n. 27.

[40] Johnson, *Adjustment to Empire*, pp. 413–21; John M. Murrin, 'Anglicizing an American Colony: The Transformation of Provincial Massachusetts', unpublished Ph.D. dissertation, Yale 1966. Stanley N. Katz, *Newcastle's New York: Anglo-American Politics, 1732–1753* (Cambridge, Mass., 1968), pioneered the exploration of the importance for colonial politics of having a British 'connection'.

[41] This literature is summarized (along with much else) in Ian K. Steele, 'The Empire and the Provincial Elites: An Interpretation of Some Recent Writings on the English Atlantic', *JICH*, VIII, 1 (Jan. 1980), pp. 2–19. The mores and material basis of American gentry culture are explored in Richard L. Bushman, 'American High-Style and Vernacular Cultures', in Greene and Pole, eds., *Colonial British America*, pp. 345–83; Richard L. Bushman, *The Refinement of America: Persons, Houses, Cities* (New

An expanded sense of the nature and substance of *imperium* has led to a new respect for the transplantation of British culture and for its periodic renewal and reinforcement.[42] An earlier breed of study took its England whole, deploying topical survey of assorted aspects of a more-or-less homogenous culture as it stood on tiptoe at some putative moment, ready to pass the American strand.[43] More recent scholarship concentrates on the ways that the differing British regional origins and social experiences of first-generation colonists shaped their subsequent colonial careers. (The most ambitious of these works are David H. Fischer, *Albion's Seed: Four British Folkways in America* (New York, 1989), which explains the most significant differences between the various mainland colonies as a perpetuation of variations within Great Britain, and Bernard Bailyn, *Voyagers to the West: A Passage in the Peopling of America on the Eve of the Revolution* (New York, 1986), a massive and intensive study of ten thousand English and Scottish migrants on the very eve of the Revolution.)[44] And where the earlier work would have bleached imported habits and institutions out of colonial society by the second generation, if not earlier, the newer literature is more concerned with the regular renewal of British ways through continued migration and improvements in transportation and communication.[45] In particular, a steady rise in British imports per capita suggests that the colonies

York, 1992), pp. 30–203; Cary Carson and others, eds., *Of Consuming Interests: The Style of Life in the Eighteenth Century* (Charlottesville, Va., 1994). The Virginia gentry in particular always seem to receive the greatest attention on this score. Cf. Carl Bridenbaugh, *Myths and Realities: Societies of the Colonial South* (Baton Rouge, La., 1952); Carole Shammas, 'English Born and Creole Elites in Turn-of-the-Century Virginia', in Tate and Ammerman, eds., *The Chesapeake in the Seventeenth Century*, pp. 274–96; T. H. Breen, *Tobacco Culture: The Mentality of the Great Tidewater Planters on the Eve of the Revolution* (Princeton, 1985).

42 Ian K. Steele provides a (somewhat triumphalist) survey of 'Empire of Migrants and Consumers: Some Current Atlantic Approaches to the History of Colonial Virginia', *Virginia Magazine of History and Biography*, XCIX (1991), pp. 489–512. This broad-ranging survey is in no way restricted to Virginia in its scope.

43 The classic statement is Wallace Notestein, *The English People on the Eve of Colonization, 1603–30* (New York, 1954). However, Carl Bridenbaugh, *Vexed and Troubled Englishmen, 1590–1642* (New York, 1968), is already sensitive to regional and temporal variations.

44 There is an extended, critical 'symposium' on Fischer's work in *WMQ*, Third Series, XLVIII (1991), pp. 223–308, while Bailyn has provided a prolegomenon to his projected multi-volume study of migration in *The Peopling of British North America: An Introduction* (New York, 1986). In addition to the Fischer and Bailyn titles, see (among other recent works) David Grayson Allen, *In English Ways: The Movement of Societies and the Transferal of English Local Law and Custom to Massachusetts Bay in the Seventeenth Century* (Chapel Hill, NC, 1981); Ned C. Landsman, *Scotland and its First American Colony, 1683–1765* (Princeton, 1985); James P. P. Horn, *Adapting to the New World: English Society in the Seventeenth-Century Chesapeake* (Chapel Hill, NC, 1994).

45 See especially Ian K. Steele, *The English Atlantic, 1675–1740: An Exploration of Communication and Community* (New York, 1986); David Hancock, *Citizens of the World: London Merchants and the Integration of the British Atlantic Community, 1735–1785* (Cambridge, 1995). The tendency to see the colonies as Anglicizing while retaining a sense of difference has led to various kinds of comparisons with Scotland. Cf. John Clive and Bernard Bailyn, 'England's Cultural Provinces: Scotland and

gradually came to participate in the same qualitative shift in the availability of consumer goods that is supposed to have overtaken the metropolis, and supports the claim that the built environment of America and its material culture became increasingly English.[46] Even the seismic shock of the Great Awakening, the pervasive religious revival of the 1740s that was once seen as the American 'national baptism', can be reinterpreted as a single phenomenon uniting its proponents in England, Scotland, Ireland, and the colonies in a self-conscious, common crusade.[47]

For the first time since the unjustly neglected work of Michael Kraus, the transformative land has yielded to the sustenant sea: a first, silent American Revolution, preparatory to the visible and noisy one, has been abandoned for a maturing Atlantic Civilization.[48] Current scholarship seems bent on rediscovering what might be called the Problem of Gipson: how do we account for events from 1763 onwards in a more telling and profound way than as post-war political twitch? A venerable line of historical theodicy, of which the benchmark is probably J. R. Pole, *Political Representation in England and the Origins of the American Republic* (London, 1966), traces an ultimately fatal divergence between England and the colonies growing over time out of a once-common political and constitutional tradition. But only four book-length studies can be said to confront the thrust of much recent historiography by explaining the Revolution as an American invention built out of mainly contemporary British materials.[49]

America', *WMQ*, Third Series, XI (1954), pp. 200–13; Nicholas Phillipson, 'Culture and Society in the Eighteenth-Century Province: The Case of Edinburgh and the Scottish Enlightenment', in Lawrence Stone, ed., *The University in Society* (Princeton, 1974), II, pp. 407–48; Ned C. Landsman, 'The Provinces and the Empire: Scotland, the American Colonies and the Development of British Provincial Identity', in Stone, ed., *An Imperial State at War*, pp. 258–87. Other ways of thinking about the development of a colonial sense of provinciality include Jack P. Greene, 'Search for Identity: An Interpretation of the Meaning of Selected Patterns of Social Response in Eighteenth-Century America', *Journal of Social History*, III (1969–70), pp. 189–224; Michael Zuckerman, 'Identity in British America: Unease in Eden', in Nicholas Canny and Anthony Pagden, eds., *Colonial Identity in the Atlantic World, 1500–1800* (Princeton, 1987), pp. 115–57; Jack P. Greene, 'Changing Identity in the British Caribbean: Barbados as a Case Study', in ibid., pp. 213–66.

46 In addition to the sources in n. 41 above, see T. H. Breen, 'An Empire of Goods: The Anglicization of Colonial America, 1690–1776', *Journal of British Studies* (hereafter *JBS*), XXV (1986), pp. 467–99; and, ' "Baubles of Britain": The American and Consumer Revolutions of the Eighteenth Century', *Past and Present*, CXIX (May, 1988), pp. 73–104.

47 Marilyn J. Westerkamp, *Triumph of the Laity: Scots-Irish Piety and the Great Awakening, 1625–1760* (New York, 1988); Leigh Eric Schmidt, *Holy Fairs: Scottish Communions and American Revivals in the Early Modern Period* (Princeton, 1989); Michael J. Crawford, *Seasons of Grace: Colonial New England's Revival Tradition in Its British Context* (New York, 1991); Frank Lambert, *'Pedlar in Divinity': George Whitefield and the Transatlantic Revivals, 1737–1770* (Princeton, 1994).

48 The reference is to Michael Kraus, *Intercolonial Aspects of American Culture on the Eve of the Revolution, with Special Reference to the Northern Towns*, Columbia University Studies in History, Economics and Public Law, XXXII (New York: 1928) and *The Atlantic Civilization: Eighteenth-Century Origins* (Ithaca, NY, 1949).

49 In addition to the discussion here, see chap. by Doron Ben-Atar.

Bernard Bailyn's *The Origins of American Politics* (New York, 1968) argues that the common Anglo-American façade of authority, when coupled with a radical divergence in the actual distribution of political power, led American political writers in the course of the eighteenth century to adopt English radical Commonwealthmen ideology as their gospel. The executive in both Mother Country and colonies was held to be perpetually in danger of degenerating into a tyranny over hapless subjects too easily robbed of their precious liberties. When the British 'reform' programme mushroomed in 1764 and afterwards, it could be interpreted only in one way and in consequence met in only one way. In a parallel argument, contained in his *Peripheries and Center: Constitutional Development in the Extended Polities of the British Empire and the United States, 1607–1788* (Athens, Ga., 1986), Jack P. Greene, who was an early critic of Bailyn, begins with the multiple centre of authority to be found in British constitutionalism and suggests that customary considerations, based on local practice, hypertrophied in America at the same time that they were rendered otiose in Britain by what were until 1764 largely theoretical assertions of parliamentary sovereignty. Attempts by the Grenville ministry and its various successors to put abstract British principle into practice in the colonies met the adamantine opposition of British practice rendered into colonial principle by long, largely uncontested usage. Edmund S. Morgan tackles a similar theme in a somewhat similar way in *Inventing the People: The Rise of Popular Sovereignty in England and America* (New York, 1988), recounting the uses to which the legal and constitutional fiction of the popular origins of government were put. Essentially, the fiction in question was less troubled in the colonies than in Great Britain either by competing fictions or by some sort of Humean brute realism, and so came to seem less factitious there. Popular sovereignty, taken as a description of how governments were actually created, also became the accepted prescription on how to re-create them and not merely a partisan and retroactive justification of what had already taken place willy-nilly. And most recently, J. C. D. Clark has built on his own earlier work arguing for the centrality of the Anglican church to an English 'confessional state'. Seizing on the far greater numerical strength of Dissent in the colonies, he has attempted to substantiate a conviction of the High-flyers—that heterodoxy, by natural proclivity and deliberate choice alike, sooner or later veers into sedition and republicanism.[50]

[50] Cf. J. C. D. Clark, *English Society, 1688–1832: Ideology, Social Structure, and Political Practice during the Ancien Régime* (Cambridge, 1985) and *The Language of Liberty, 1660–1832: Political Discourse and Social Dynamics in the Anglo-American World* (Cambridge, 1994). The most detailed discussion of English Dissent and 'the American Crisis' can be found in James E. Bradley, *Religion, Revolution, and English Radicalism: Nonconformity in Eighteenth-Century Politics and Society* (Cambridge, 1990).

All four arguments possess the cardinal virtue of explaining how an Anglo-American colonial period could issue in a more distinctively American national one, yet it is surely fair to say that none of them has been taken as entirely successful in explaining the conundrum of the Revolution. One may suggest, a little gloomily, that the general lack of satisfaction here is in part a symptom of a fading of interest in the question being addressed. Another turn of the wheel is apparently in progress, a particularly dramatic one.

In 1970 the nearly simultaneous appearance of four studies of colonial New England towns heralded the rise to pre-eminence of the New Social History. Another clutch of four titles between 1989 and 1992, all deservedly well received, suggests we may be about to see a comparable triumph for ethnohistory.[51] The latter is usually referred to simply as 'Indian history' or 'Native American history', but its partisans, like their predecessors of the 1970s, would insist that they do not study a subject; they practise a newer, truer (because more comprehensive) way to look at history.[52] Both earlier and later reformations are primarily but not exclusively the work of younger scholars trained in new methodologies not easily accessible to more traditional types. Both assert an affinity between history and the social sciences, though the preference for positivist, quantitative methods has been replaced by the cultural relativism of the anthropologists. Both movements, however, can lay claim to an imperative moral justification in taking as their object the recovery of the history of the neglected majority, whose deeds are recorded in unusual ways requiring unusual tactics to decipher them.

[51] James H. Merrell, *The Indians' New World: Catawbas and Their Neighbors from European Contact through the Era of Removal* (Chapel Hill, NC, 1989); Richard White, *The Middle Ground: Indians, Empires, and Republics in the Great Lakes Region, 1650–1815* (New York, 1991); Daniel K. Richter, *The Ordeal of the Longhouse: The Peoples of the Iroquois League in the Era of European Colonization* (Chapel Hill, NC, 1992); Daniel H. Usner, Jr., *Indians, Settlers, and Slaves in a Frontier Exchange Economy: The Lower Mississippi Valley before 1783* (Chapel Hill, NC, 1992). As in the case of the New Social History, the near simultaneous appearance of a group of significant studies in ethnohistory gives a deceptive impression of the sudden emergence of an historiographical revolution. There had been a good deal of earlier important work, including a number of books by, among others, White himself, James Axtell, and Francis Jennings. (This material is summarized in the three articles cited below, n. 52, and in James H. Merrell, ' "The Customes of Our Countrey": Indians and Colonists in Early America', in Bernard Bailyn and Philip D. Morgan, eds., *Strangers within the Realm: Cultural Margins of the First British Empire* (Chapel Hill, NC, 1991), pp. 117–56.

[52] Cf. James Axtell, 'The Ethnohistory of Early America: A Review Essay', *WMQ*, Third Series, XXXV (1978), pp. 110–44; James H. Merrell, 'Some Thoughts on Colonial Historians and American Indians', *WMQ*, XLVI (1989), pp. 94–119; Daniel K. Richter, 'Whose Indian History?', *WMQ*, L (1993), pp. 379–93. Oddly, the claims for the *reciprocal* nature of the Indian–European cultural interaction have enjoyed a more favourable reception than the comparable contentions for cultural fusions between Europeans and Africans. For this latter argument, see especially Mechal Sobel, *The World They Made Together: Black and White Values in Eighteenth-Century Virginia* (Princeton, 1987).

The earlier new historiography delivered a fair share of the substantive gains it promised; less obvious but no less significant losses became apparent only in retrospect. The current turn, it may be suggested, is likely to follow a similar trajectory. In the proposed grand ethnohistorical narrative, the pasts of the contending parties are a secondary matter compared to their respective states at the points and periods of close intersection. If each of two or three groups (European, Native American, and sometimes African American) must be discussed under comparable headings, then one can talk about the varying roles of religion, for example, or of political leadership, or whatever, as they influence the ongoing racial interaction, but there can be little or nothing to say about major formative events of the specifically British past, such as the Reformation or the constitutional crises—and the passions, momentums, and unfulfilled aspirations they generated that were carried over the Atlantic. Not to put too fine a point on it, whatever weight is given to the Europeans in this story, their sponsoring powers, the respective empires, are of interest primarily as archival repositories or sometimes as late-coming wreckers of a dynamic equilibrium among the contending parties. Albany and Quebec perhaps, but rarely Westminster and Versailles, let alone Geneva and Rome.[53]

Ethnohistory encapsulates a mood as well as a methodology. Considerable as its recent achievements and future potential may be, they entail the neglect of certain kinds of activity fundamental to Western history, in particular, the habit of creating formal, durable organizations to effect collective undertakings over substantial periods of time. Thus, for example, the tendency to attribute the survival of Jamestown to chance and Powhattan inadvertence, without regard for the joint-stock company that produced enough capital for the misguided adventurers who ran it to come back for more until one of their improbable projects, tobacco, took hold.[54] Or the attribution of the administrative failings that precipitated Pontiac's Rebellion in 1763 to a distinctively British cultural myopia, when the main problem, arguably, was fiscal: the marvellous money machine that paid for the victories of the Seven Years War was held to be overextended, requiring some kind of overall retrenchment in America, not to mention new forms of revenue by

[53] In fairness it must be noted that Richter, *Ordeal of the Longhouse*, is at least a partial exception to this stricture, as is Richard I. Melvoin, *New England Outpost: War and Society in Colonial Deerfield* (New York, 1989).

[54] Theodore K. Rabb, *Enterprise and Empire: Merchant and Gentry Investment in the Expansion of England, 1575–1630* (Cambridge, Mass., 1967), pp. 58–61; Carole Shammas, 'English Commercial Development and American Colonization, 1560–1620', in K. R. Andrews and others, eds., *The Westward Enterprise: English Activities in Ireland, the Atlantic, and America, 1480–1650* (Liverpool, 1978), pp. 151–74; Kenneth R. Andrews, *Trade, Plunder, Settlement: Maritime Enterprise and the Genesis of the British Empire, 1480–1630* (Cambridge, 1984), pp. 318–19, 321–22. Rabb's apportionment of the company's stock between mercantile and gentry investors has been severely criticized, but the relative size of the overall amount (much larger than other colonizing ventures) is not in dispute.

way of the Sugar and Stamp Acts.[55] The explanatory gaps here are no worse than in any other approach, but the positive distaste for institutional history, the lack of interest in progression over time, the notion that 'power' has little to do with politics and is less a matter of economic wherewithal than cultural 'hegemony'—all this suggests a far more pervasive and deeply rooted mindset than anything that can be deduced solely from the changing whims of American academic fashion. As a way of looking at the world it is oddly consonant with the latest *National Geographic Atlas* (1992), in which the United States, Norway, Brazil, Germany, and (more appropriately) Ireland are indiscriminately an ecological green, Canada is a burnt sienna, and the rose glimmers fitfully only in Bermuda, South Georgia, and the Falklands.

For good reason, prophecy is not a customary feature of chapters in Oxford histories. Whatever directions early American historiography may subsequently lurch along, nothing suggests that it is permanently moribund. Indeed, when—some five decades after his death—the work of Charles M. Andrews still has something to say to us, we profit even from his faith in the intermittent but inevitable progress of humanity, which was forged in the unlikely crucible of the Gilded Age and remained steadfast despite the First World War. We are the better placed to ignore the failings and faddishness of much of twentieth-century historiography and, by taking comfort in its real successes, to rest content with the assumption that our successors will know more and better than we do and will do so in part because their achievements will incorporate our own.

[55] John Shy, *Toward Lexington*, pp. 89–125, attributes much of the blame for Pontiac's Rebellion to the admittedly unlovely personality of Jeffrey Amherst, the Commander-in-Chief in America, but also details the way his resources were spread thin and under orders to be spread thinner. Later research, in turn, has revealed the political and financial constraints that created this situation: John Bullion, *A Great and Necessary Measure*, pp. 15–21; Patrick K. O'Brien, 'The Political Economy of British Taxation, 1660–1815', *Economic History Review*, Second Series, XLI (1988), pp. 1–32; Philip Harling and Peter Mandler, 'From "Fiscal-Military" State to Laissez-faire State, 1760–1850', *JBS*, XXXII (1993), pp. 44–70.

Select Bibliography

DAVID L. AMMERMAN and PHILIP D. MORGAN, compilers, *Books about Early America: 2001 Titles* (Williamsburg, Va., 1989).

RAY ALLEN BILLINGTON, ed., *The Reinterpretation of Early American History: Essays in Honor of John Edwin Pomfret* (San Marino, Calif., 1966).

LESTER J. CAPPON and others, eds., *Atlas of Early American History: The Revolutionary Era, 1760–1790* (Princeton, 1976).

PETER GAY, *A Loss of Mastery: Puritan Historians in Colonial America* (Berkeley, 1966).

LAWRENCE HENRY GIPSON, *A Bibliographical Guide to the History of the British Empire, 1748–1776*, Vol. XIV of *The British Empire Before the American Revolution* (New York, 1968).

—— *A Guide to Manuscripts Relating to the History of the British Empire, 1748–1776*, Vol. XV of *The British Empire Before the American Revolution* (New York, 1970).

JACK P. GREENE, compiler, *The American Colonies in the Eighteenth Century, 1689–1763*, Goldentree Bibliographies in American History (New York, 1969).

—— 'Colonial North America', in Mary Beth Norton and Pamela Gerard, eds., *The American Historical Association Guide to Historical Literature* (New York, 1995), Vol. II, pp. 1239–79.

—— and J. R. POLE, eds., *Colonial British America: Essays in the New History of the Early Modern Era* (Baltimore, 1984).

R. COLE HARRIS and GEOFFREY J. MATTHEWS, eds., *Historical Atlas of Canada*, Vol. I, *The Beginning to 1800* (Toronto, 1987).

LAWRENCE H. LEDER, ed., *The Colonial Legacy*, 4 vols. (New York, 1973).

DAVID LEVIN, *History as Romantic Art: Bancroft, Prescott, Motley, and Parkman* (Stanford, Calif., 1959).

JOHN J. MCCUSKER, 'New Guides to Primary Sources on the History of Early British America', *William and Mary Quarterly*, Third Series, XLI (1984), pp. 277–95.

—— and RUSSELL R. MENARD, *The Economy of British America, 1607–1789: Needs and Opportunities for Study* (pbk. edn. with supplementary bibliography, Chapel Hill, NC, 1991).

D. A. MUISE, ed., *A Reader's Guide to Canadian History*, Vol. I, *Beginnings to Confederation* (Toronto, 1982).

JOHN SHY, compiler, *The American Revolution*, Goldentree Bibliographies in American History (Northbrook, Ill., 1973).

ALDEN T. VAUGHAN, compiler, *The American Colonies in the Seventeenth Century*, Goldentree Bibliographies in American History (New York, 1971).

CLYDE N. WILSON, ed., *American Historians, 1607–1865, Dictionary of Literary Biography*, Vol. XXX (Detroit, 1984).

5

The American Revolution

DORON BEN-ATAR

How did the British Empire in America unravel less than two decades after its zenith? Why did the North American colonists sever their ties to the Mother Country in the name of the 'rights of Englishmen'? The national American narrative tells of loyal subjects driven to revolt by the British decision to tighten Imperial controls and raise revenues in the New World in the aftermath of the French and Indian War (the Seven Years War). Students of the Empire, however, point out that London's infringements on colonial autonomy were not exclusive to the post-1763 era. Throughout the period of 'salutary neglect', when the metropolis supposedly left the affairs of the peripheries more or less in the hands of local élites, the Walpole and Pelham ministries frequently challenged provincial self-rule. Moreover, had Parliament successfully asserted its supremacy and collected the taxes it sought, Americans still would have remained the freest, most prosperous, and least taxed citizens in the Western world. In other words, the ministerial provocations of the 1760s and 1770s were neither new nor harsh.

Loyalist historians were the first to question the motives and justifications of the patriots. In their judgement the rebels sacrificed 'real and substantial happiness, in the hope of obtaining that which, after all, is but imaginary'. Revolutionary leaders used the fact that the public was 'little versed in matters of state' to 'incite the ignorant' to sever a beneficial connection 'without subjecting themselves to any Controul'.[1] Loyalist insistence on the merits of Anglo-American connection, its obvious political motive aside, is on the mark. Imperial forces protected the colonists from their French and Indian enemies. The Navigation system, which supposedly limited the colonists' freedom to trade, simultaneously

[1] Jonathan Boucher, *A View of the Causes and Consequences of the American Revolution in Thirteen Discourses*, 2nd edn. (London, 1797; New York, 1967), p. xxvii; Daniel Leonard, *The Origins of the American Contest with Great-Britain* (New York, 1775), p. 24; Joseph Galloway, *Historical and Political Reflections on the Rise and Progress of the American Rebellion* (London, 1780), p. 59; Douglass Adair and John A. Schutz, eds., *Peter Oliver's Origin and Progress of the American Rebellion* (Stanford, Calif., 1961), p. 11. The best works on loyalist ideology are Bernard Bailyn, *The Ordeal of Thomas Hutchinson* (Cambridge, Mass., 1974) and Janice Potter, *The Liberty We Seek: Loyalist Ideology in Colonial New York and Massachusetts* (Cambridge, Mass., 1993).

guaranteed a market for North American agricultural exports. Indeed, the colonies prospered under British rule—so much so that when access to the Empire was checked following independence, they plunged into a severe economic depression. Americans also delighted in their connection to Britain. The political culture of pre-Stamp Act Massachusetts, for example, was defined by loyalty to the King and Empire.[2] As John Shy put it, 'Americans were never more British than in 1763'.[3] Yet, within a dozen years, these same British subjects renounced both their interest and history and embarked on the uncertain road of independence and republican government.

This chapter examines the last thirty years of revolutionary historiography. The vast literature is divided into three approaches: first, the Atlantic interpretations, by which is meant studies of the 'big picture'—the internal and external workings of the Empire: secondly, the New Social History and its efforts to locate the origins of the Revolution in colonial structures and processes; thirdly, the heated historiographical debate over the ideological interpretation which emphasizes the role of the republican tradition. The sequence of the discussion does not suggest any linear progression. Categorizing historians under one approach or another is a matter of emphasis. Most of the historians discussed here considered the Revolution's Imperial, its socio-economic, and its ideological contexts. Scholars such as Jack P. Greene, Edmund S. Morgan, and Bernard Bailyn have made significant contributions to all three approaches. This chapter challenges exclusive monocausal interpretations of the Revolution, and suggests that the event is best explained by effective integration of all three approaches.

Lawrence Henry Gipson towers over the Atlantic approach. His fifteen-volume study of *The British Empire Before the American Revolution* remains unmatched in both scope and depth. Gipson has argued that the overwhelming British victory in the Seven Years War (French and Indian War) and the elimination of the Gallic peril led to the break-up of the Empire. As long as France ruled Canada the colonists understood that challenging British rule risked inviting the Catholic enemy. British control of Canada removed the necessity for protection. Thereafter, Americans could boldly refuse to finance British debts incurred in a war supposedly fought on their behalf. Remaining within the Empire seemed neither essential nor advantageous in the aftermath of the 1763 Treaty of Paris. Where the French threat remained, for example, in the West Indies, the colonists dared not to challenge Imperial rule and even submitted to the Stamp Act.[4]

[2] Richard Bushman, *King and People in Provincial Massachusetts* (Chapel Hill, NC, 1985).

[3] See Vol. II, chap. by John Shy, p. 308.

[4] Lawrence Henry Gipson, *The British Empire Before the American Revolution*, 15 vols. (New York, 1936–70). Gipson provided a more succinct statement of his thesis in *The Coming of the Revolution*,

There are, however, limits to what the lifting of the French peril may explain. Though Gipson has insisted that the French threat discouraged resistance to British rule, strife between the metropolis and provinces was widespread for much of the eighteenth century. In fact, while France controlled Canada, Americans earned a reputation for being unruly and disrespectful to their Imperial administrators. French expansionism in the years preceding the war, as John M. Murrin points out, did not prevent deep political crises from developing in New York, New Hampshire, New Jersey, and North Carolina. On the other hand, Virginia, geographically immune to the Gallic peril before 1750, experienced three decades of political calm from 1723 to 1753. The colonists rebelled in spite of their anxiety that they might be inviting the hated French back.[5]

How, then, did the British victory trigger the loss of the American colonies? Jack P. Greene explains that the elimination of France from North America 'sent the postwar expectations of men on opposite sides of the Atlantic veering off in opposite directions'. The war confirmed the centrality and importance of the colonies to the Empire. In its aftermath, Americans expected 'a more equal and secure future'. The peace, meanwhile, persuaded the British government that it had 'a much freer hand to proceed with its program of colonial reform'. Greene believes that for all of their conflicting expectations, the Atlantic connection could have lasted longer had British leaders not launched 'a fundamental attack' on the *status quo*.[6]

Why did London insist on such a destructive policy? In popular consciousness, epitomized by Barbara W. Tuchman's *March of Folly: From Troy to Vietnam*, the metropolis foolishly squandered the Empire. Given that the road to Lexington was, by and large, a series of responses to Imperial measures by hitherto faithful subjects, 'the story of the loss of the American colonies', writes Ian R. Christie, 'is a story of the misjudgments and inadequacy of British politicians'. Parliament,

1763–1775 (New York, 1954) and 'The American Revolution as an Aftermath of the Great War for the Empire, 1754–1763', *Political Science Quarterly*, LXV (1950), pp. 86–104. Gipson, together with Charles M. Andrews, Herbert Osgood, and George Louis Beer, are the most prominent historians of the 'Imperial School'. For a discussion of the Imperial School see above, chap. by Stephen Foster, and Robert L. Middlekauf, 'The American Continental Colonies in the Empire', in Robin W. Winks, ed., *The Historiography of the British Empire-Commonwealth: Trends Interpretations, and Resources* (Durham, NC, 1966), pp. 23–45. For a discussion of pre-1965 historiography see Middlekauf's excellent essay and Jack P. Greene, ed., *The Reinterpretation of the American Revolution, 1763–1789* (New York, 1968), pp. 2–74.

[5] Bernard Bailyn, *The Origins of American Politics* (New York, 1967); John M. Murrin, 'The French and Indian War, the American Revolution, and the Counterfactual Hypothesis: Reflections on Lawrence Henry Gipson and John Shy', *Reviews in American History*, I (1973), pp. 307–18.

[6] Jack P. Greene, 'The Seven Years War and the American Revolution: The Casual Relationship Reconsidered', in Peter Marshall and Glyn Williams, eds., *The British Atlantic Empire Before the American Revolution* (London, 1980), p. 100, p. 94.

ministries, and George III fought zealously to enforce collection of taxes of negligible financial value. As Shy demonstrates, the victory in the French and Indian War generated much sympathy towards Britain and her troops. The army was overwhelmingly popular before the occupation of Boston in 1768; a surprising number of colonists sought to enlist in it and local Assemblies routinely funded its supplies. Yet policy-makers in London needlessly forced a show-down by passing irritating measures and using the army to enforce them. As Edmund and Helen Morgan dramatically put it, the Crown forced Americans to decide 'whether they would be men and not English or whether they would be English and not men'. In the power-struggle that ensued, the British ministry squandered the goodwill of the colonists and sacrificed the fruits of the great victory over France.[7]

P. D. G. Thomas's three-volume study of British Imperial policy suggests that it sprang from diverse and not necessarily related origins. The Proclamation of 1763, for example, originated in commitments incurred during the French and Indian War. The Bute ministry decided to maintain a larger standing army in the colonies to allow timely and effective response in case troubles arose from either the 20,000 French troops in the West Indies or the 90,000 former French subjects in Canada. The decision to tax the colonists to finance the new Imperial commitments stemmed from the ministry's assumption that Parliament would refuse to finance this peacetime military expenditure. Colonial reaction to the Stamp Act forced its repeal while concurrently demonstrating the need to assert Parliamentary authority throughout the Empire. True, most British leaders never doubted the need to bring North American settlers into line with the rest of the Empire. The measures of the post-1763 era, however, seemed a coherent programme only to the subjects in America.[8]

[7] Barbara W. Tuchman, *The March of Folly: From Troy to Vietnam* (New York, 1984), pp. 127–231; Ian R. Christie, *Crisis of Empire: Great Britain and the American Colonies, 1754–1783* (New York, 1966), p. 111; Edmund S. Morgan and Helen M. Morgan, *The Stamp Act Crisis: Prologue to Revolution* (Chapel Hill, NC, 1953), p. 152; John Shy, *Toward Lexington: The Role of the British Army in the Coming of the American Revolution* (Princeton, 1965); Christie and Benjamin W. Labaree, *Empire or Independence, 1760–1776* (New York, 1976); Robert Middlekauf, *The Glorious Cause: The American Revolution, 1763–1789* (New York, 1982); Paul David Nelson, 'British Conduct of the American Revolutionary War: A Review of Interpretations', *Journal of American History* (hereafter *JAH*), LXV (1978), pp. 623–53. Ironically, the separation from the colonies reinvigorated British shipbuilding, while British merchants continued to dominate the North American trade. See Charles R. Ritcheson, *Aftermath of Revolution: British Policy Toward the United States, 1783–1795* (New York, 1969).

[8] P. D. G. Thomas, *British Politics and the Stamp Act Crisis: The First Phase of the American Revolution, 1763–1767* (Oxford, 1975), *The Townshend Duties Crisis: The Second Phase of the American Revolution, 1767–1773* (Oxford, 1987), and *Tea Party and Independence: The Third Phase of the American Revolution* (Oxford, 1991). See also J. L. Bullion, *A Great and Necessary Measure: George Grenville and the Genesis of the Stamp Act, 1763–1765* (Princeton 1982); Bernard Knollenberg, *Origins of the American Revolution, 1759–1765* (New York, 1966); Morgan, *The Stamp Act Crisis.*

Historians who focus on the personalities, intrigues, and blunders of William Pitt, George Grenville, and George III risk overlooking political and constitutional developments of the second half of the eighteenth century which fundamentally transformed the Anglo-American world. John Brewer has shown how the conflict-ridden popular political culture challenged the power of élites and forced a reconfiguration of the relation between the Crown, Parliament, and the public. Colonial resistance followed patterns of other eighteenth-century politically excluded groups who used pamphlets, clubs, and crowds to articulate their concerns. 'By 1770 an alternative structure of politics was as much an enduring feature of the English political scene as the House of Commons itself.'[9]

British leaders consistently failed to grasp the political expectations of the peripheries. Greene, the pre-eminent authority on the dysfunctional relations between Britain and the American colonies, has shown that London began its crackdown on colonial autonomy in the late 1740s. Imperial leaders recognized that the rapid demographic and economic growth of the colonies had dramatically altered power relations between the metropolis and the peripheries and worried that the possible loss of the colonies would undermine British strategic and economic welfare. In response to reports of unruly colonists from Bermuda to Nova Scotia, the Board of Trade, under the leadership of the Earl of Halifax, undertook to reassert Imperial control particularly through instructing Royal Governors to curb the power of colonial Assemblies. These efforts provoked hostile opposition by politicians who had grown accustomed to a great degree of autonomy in running local affairs. In 1757 the discord drew the House of Commons into intervening in colonial affairs when it censured the Jamaican Assembly for resisting instructions from London. The resumption of battles between local Assemblies and local Governors in the aftermath of the French and Indian War persuaded the colonists that the metropolis was seeking to enhance its prerogative in the colonies. As Bailyn put it, 'swollen claims and shrunken powers' created 'troubled', 'contentious', and ultimately 'explosive' Imperial politics.[10]

The American Revolution, then, must be understood in the contexts of the structure of Imperial politics and its constitutional framework. Both colonists and metropolis, explains John Phillip Reid, based their claims on legitimate, though

[9] John Brewer, *Party Ideology and Popular Politics at the Accession of George III* (New York, 1976), p. 269.

[10] Jack P. Greene, 'An Uneasy Connection: An Analysis of the Preconditions of the American Revolution', in Stephen G. Kurtz and James H. Hutson, eds., *Essays on the American Revolution* (New York, 1973), pp. 32-80, *The Quest for Power: The Lower Houses of Assembly in Southern Royal Colonies, 1689–1776* (New York, 1963), and 'Political Mimesis: A Consideration of the Historical and Cultural Roots of Legislative Behavior in the British Colonies in the Eighteenth Century', *American Historical Review* (hereafter *AHR*), LXXV (1969), pp. 337–60; Bailyn, *The Origin of American Politics*, pp. 96, 105.

competing, constitutional doctrines. Imperial measures were in line with the principle of 'arbitrary Parliamentary supremacy' which allowed Parliament to change customary legal practices. Colonial resistance, on the other hand, was justified by seventeenth-century constitutional doctrine of 'customary powers'. From 1765 to 1775, as Greene explains, 'the metropolis simply could not secure colonial consent to its emerging view of the constitutional structure of the empire' without resorting to military repression.[11]

Because Colonial Governors and royal agents did not have access to coercive powers capable of enforcing parliamentary supremacy, they did not contest colonial adherence to customary powers. Community consensus and public consent were essential to Imperial rule. Before 1763 local juries and community practices effectively constructed the substance of common law in the colonies. As Jack N. Rakove writes, it was 'precisely because colonial common law courts had frustrated Imperial officials . . . that the Revenue and Stamp Acts of 1764–65 provided for enforcement in vice-admiralty courts where juries did not hold sway'.[12] The colonists, in turn, resisted in a variety of crowd actions which, under the doctrine of customary powers, were considered a legitimate constitutional response to illegal acts of the state. When Parliament responded swiftly and harshly to the Tea Party, Americans realized they had 'encountered the fundamental finality of the new constitution, the sovereignty of Parliament', and appealed to the Crown 'to revive the prerogatives of the old seventeenth-century balanced constitution'.[13]

The only alternative, then, that could have appeased Americans involved equalizing the power of their Assemblies with that of Parliament so that they became equal legislative bodies under a common monarch. Such a reform, as Robert W. Tucker and David C. Hendrickson explain, was unacceptable, for it would have 'signaled the complete unraveling' of the British political system. Both Parliament and colonial Legislatures viewed challenges to their authority as a direct assault on

[11] John Phillip Reid, *Constitutional History of the American Revolution*, Vol. I, *The Authority of Rights* (Madison, 1986), p. 229; Jack P. Greene, *Negotiated Authorities: Essays in Colonial Political and Constitutional History* (Charlottesville, Va., 1994), p. 41.

[12] Jack N. Rakove, *Original Meanings: Politics and Ideas in the Making of the Constitution* (New York, 1996), p. 301.

[13] John Phillip Reid, *Constitutional History of the American Revolution*, Vol. IV, *The Authority of Law* (Madison, 1993), p. 162. See also, Reid, *Constitutional History of the American Revolution*, Vol. II, *The Authority to Tax* (Madison, 1987); *Constitutional History of the American Revolution*, Vol. III, *The Authority to Legislate* (Madison, 1991); Jack P. Greene, *Peripheries and Center: Constitutional Development in the Extended Polities of the British Empire and the United States* (Athens, Ga., 1986); Michael Zuckerman, *Peaceable Kingdoms: New England Towns in the Eighteenth Century* (New York, 1970); William Nelson, *Americanization of the Common Law: The Impact of Legal Change on Massachusetts Society, 1760–1830* (Cambridge, Mass., 1975); Pauline Maier, 'Popular Uprisings and Civil Authority in Eighteenth-Century America', *William and Mary Quarterly* (hereafter *WMQ*), Third Series, XXVII (1970), pp. 3–35.

traditional constitutional liberties. According to Richard R. Johnson, the Imperial conflict originated in 'the collision of legislative bodies each at the peak of its game and each convinced that it could not—must not—retreat'. The Revolution, writes Theodore Draper, was in essence a power struggle between Imperial and provincial élites over who would be in charge of colonial policy decisions. The Empire crumbled because neither side could have been satisfied with anything short of complete control.[14]

The Atlantic approach examines the Revolution in the context of a metropolis with the dependent colonies. In focusing on how the bonds of the Empire were loosened it treats the Revolution as a problem of Imperial administration. Atlantic studies naturally centre on London and North American élites. The Imperial perspective, however, denies the agency of the British subjects who, at great personal risk, turned against their rulers and history. As historians over the last three decades rejected 'history from the top down' and turned to the life of ordinary men and women, the Atlantic approach lost favour. In contrast, social and ideological studies of the Revolution mushroomed.[15]

Writing earlier in the century, Progressive historians proposed that the Revolution's causes were 'economic rather than political'. Northerners who wanted to throw off the shackles of the Imperial trade regulations were joined by southern planters seeking to repudiate their large debts to British merchants. According to Louis M. Hacker, 'the economic breakdown of the Mercantile System

[14] Robert W. Tucker and David C. Hendrickson, *The Fall of the First British Empire: Origins of the War of American Independence* (Baltimore, 1982), p. 410; Richard R. Johnson, ' "Parliamentary Egotism": The Clash of Legislatures in the Making of the American Revolution', *JAH*, LXXIV (1987), p. 359; Theodore Draper, *A Struggle for Power: The American Revolution* (New York, 1996).

[15] Much of the best work on the Revolutionary era of the last three decades studies the problems of race, gender and Native Americans. These are not discussed here because they do not focus on the Revolution in its Imperial context. For a taste of that vast literature see Sylvia Frey, *Water from the Rock: Black Resistance in a Revolutionary Age* (Princeton, 1991); David Brion Davis, *The Problem of Slavery in Western Culture* (Ithaca, NY, 1966), *The Problem of Slavery in the Age of Revolution, 1770–1823* (Ithaca, NY, 1975), and *Slavery and Human Progress* (New York, 1987); Edmund S. Morgan, *American Slavery, American Freedom: The Ordeal of Colonial Virginia* (New York, 1975); Mary Beth Norton, *Liberty Daughters; The Revolutionary Experience of American Women, 1750–1800* (Boston, 1980); Linda K. Kerber, *Women of the Republic: Intellect and Ideology in Revolutionary America* (Chapel Hill, NC, 1980); Elaine F. Crane, 'Dependence in the Era of Independence: The Role of Women in a Republican Society', in Jack P. Greene ed., *The American Revolution: Its Character and Limits* (New York, 1987), pp. 253–75; Colin G. Calloway, *The American Revolution in Indian Country: Crisis and Diversity in Native American Communities* (New York, 1995); Richard White, *The Middle Ground: Indians, Empires and Republics in the Great Lakes Region, 1650–1815* (New York, 1991); Dorothy V. Jones, *License for Empire: Colonialism by Treaty in Early America* (Chicago, 1982); Barbara Graymount, *The Iroquois in the American Revolution* (Syracuse, NY, 1972); Anthony F. C. Wallace, *The Death and Rebirth of the Seneca* (New York, 1969).

. . . was the basic reason for' the collapse of the Empire.[16] The Progressive interpretation was later cast aside because of the overwhelming evidence that the colonies prospered within the Empire. Colonial population nearly doubled from 1750 to 1775, and the Navigation Acts provided the colonists with a protected market for their exports of staple products, of cattle, pig-iron, and shipbuilding.[17]

One strand of the new social historians returned to the economic context of the Revolution, focusing on how the eighteenth-century market economy, for all the prosperity that it brought, destabilized colonial class relations. Neo-Progressives Joseph A. Ernst and Marc Egnal argue that the Revolution was led by a coalition of planters and merchants who feared that their control over their economic autonomy and social position was slipping. In the second half of the eighteenth century merchants in the New England and mid-Atlantic colonies watched hopelessly as British mercantile houses bypassed them and marketed dry goods directly to colonial consumers. Non-importation, the most popular colonial response to Parliamentary measures, had less to do with constitutional notions of representation than with the accumulation of dry goods on the shelves of American businesses. By 1770, when inventories ran low, merchants abandoned non-importation. Similarly, planters grew more and more dependent on credit provided by Glasgow tobacco houses. When credit collapsed in 1772, Scottish mercantile houses demanded payment. The financially squeezed planter class opted to sever colonial ties to prevent its imminent collapse.

Egnal's (1988) *A Mighty Empire: The Origins of the American Revolution*, further develops the neo-Progressive argument. The Revolution, he explains, was led by an expansionist colonial upper class and its 'belief in America's potential for greatness' defined by economic development and territorial growth. The Proclamation of 1763, for example, which forbade expansion west of the Appalachian turned land-speculators such as George Washington against Imperial policy. The resurgence of Benjamin Franklin's expansionist views in the late 1760s 'firmly committed him to resistance'. Expansionist and pro-development élites concluded in the aftermath of the Boston Port Act of 1774 that the 'growth of America must take place outside the confines of the British Empire'.

[16] Carl Becker, *The History of Political Parties in the Province of New York, 1760–1776* (Madison, 1909), p. 26; Louis M. Hacker, 'Economic and Social Origins of the American Revolution', in John C. Whalke, ed., *The Causes of the American Revolution*, revised edn. (Boston, 1962), p. 10. See also Arthur Meier Schlesinger, *The Colonial Merchants and the American Revolution* (New York, 1918) and 'The American Revolution Reconsidered', *Political Science Quarterly*, XXXIV (1919), pp. 61–78; Charles A. and Mary R. Beard, *The Rise of American Civilization*, Vol. I (New York, 1927); Hacker, 'The First American Revolution', *Columbia University Quarterly*, XXVII (1935), pp. 259–95.

[17] See in particular O. M. Dickerson, *The Navigation Acts and the American Revolution* (London, 1951) and Stanley L. Engerman and Robert F. Gallman, eds., *The Cambridge Economic History of the United States*, Vol. I, *The Colonial Era* (New York, 1996).

In their struggle against the non-expansionist Tories, 'wealthy patriots mobilized the common people in the towns and countryside, transforming the dynamics of the revolt'.[18]

The neo-Progressives have failed to carry the day, however. Merchants' grievances against their British competitors notwithstanding, their livelihood was utterly dependent on trade within the Empire. Indeed, provincial élites were economically and socially far more secure under British rule than in the revolutionary camp. True, planters were increasingly alarmed by their mounting indebtedness. But the road from debt to rebellion is hardly straight and narrow. Increasing indebtedness among the Chesapeake gentry undermined their hegemony, heightened tensions among competing élites, and exposed the social and cultural vulnerability of a society bound to staple agriculture and slave labour. Indebtedness, explains Timothy Breen, 'provided a psychological ground from which a spirit of rebellion could grow'. Yet planters did not opt for independence to repudiate their financial obligations before 1775. As late as 1780 a substantial group, including James Madison, favoured full and immediate payment of pre-war debts. The credit crisis of 1772, as Bruce A. Ragsdale writes, persuaded small tobacco producers, gentry, planters, and resident merchants of the need to 'establish some degree of economic independence from Great Britain'.[19] As for the Proclamation of 1763, previous prohibitions on grabbing Indian land never produced a Revolution and land-speculators could reasonably assume that the Empire would again fail to honour its agreement with the Indians. Finally, the notion that territorial and economic expansion were incongruent with existence within the Empire ignores the phenomenal growth and expansion of the colonies in the little more than a century-and-a-half of British colonization.[20]

In explaining popular support for the Revolution, neo-Progressives paint a picture of innocent masses duped by a highly co-ordinated, conspiratorial,

[18] Marc Egnal, *A Mighty Empire: The Origins of the American Revolution* (Ithaca, NY, 1988), pp. 6, 207, 271, 272. Marc Egnal and Joseph Albert Ernst, 'An Economic Interpretation of the American Revolution', *WMQ*, Third Series, XXIX (1972), pp. 3–32; Other noted neo-Progressive studies include Ernst, *Money and Politics in America, 1755–1775; A Study in the Currency Act of 1764 and the Political Economy of Revolution* (Chapel Hill, NC, 1973); Jackson Turner Main, *The Social Structure of Revolutionary America* (Princeton, 1965); Merrill Jensen, *The Founding of A Nation: A History of the American Revolution, 1763–1776* (New York, 1968); James Kirby Martin, *Men in Rebellion: Higher Governmental Leaders and the Coming of the American Revolution* (New Brunswick, NJ, 1973).

[19] Timothy H. Breen, *Tobacco Culture: The Mentality of the Great Tidewater Planters on the Eve of the Revolution* (Princeton, 1985), p. 203; Bruce A. Ragsdale, *A Planters' Republic: The Search for Economic Independence in Revolutionary Virginia* (Madison, 1996), p. 172. See also Doron S. Ben-Atar, *The Origins of Jeffersonian Commercial Policy and Diplomacy* (London, 1993), pp. 18–29; Jacob M. Price, *Capital and Credit in British Overseas Trade: The View from the Chesapeake, 1770–1776* (Cambridge, Mass., 1980); Allan Kulikoff, *Tobacco and Slaves: The Development of Southern Cultures in the Chesapeake, 1680–1800* (Chapel Hill, NC, 1986); Herbert E. Sloan, *Principle and Interest: Thomas Jefferson and the Problem of Debt* (New York, 1995).

[20] Jack P. Greene, 'The Madness of King George', *The Times Literary Supplement*, 17 May 1996, p. 5.

trans-colonial élite. In contrast, social historians have sought to demonstrate the agency of ordinary colonists in the revolutionary movement. The renewed focus on the socio-economic evolution originates in the Atlantic tradition. To a degree, social historians merely elaborate on Charles M. Andrews's old claim that colonial society grew apart from the metropolis from the early days of settlement. Employing social-science jargon and methodology, social historians search for the seeds of the break-up within the daily existence of the colonial experience. They see the Revolution as primarily a civil war in which common women and men chose to replace their abstract loyalty to the Crown with an intercolonial American continental allegiance. Eighteenth-century social and economic change fuelled the drive for independence.

James A. Henretta, Bruce H. Mann, and Kenneth Lockridge show how eighteenth-century demographic and economic evolution eroded social cohesion. Obligation and interdependence which characterized early settlement communities gave way to impersonal, structured, social arrangements and institutions. While men spoke as if they lived in a pre-capitalist community, their actions conformed to the new market-driven reality. Land shortages in the established communities, decline in the average size of individual farms, increasing social stratification, and greater concentration of wealth in the hands of the upper class frustrated people who expected ever-growing prosperity and opportunity. Americans saw the Imperial measures of the 1760s as representative of an order that progressively limited their economic opportunities and took to the streets.[21] At the same time, the transformation from an authoritarian patriarchical family model to an affectionate parental ideal prepared the colonists for the 'psychologically painful enterprise of overthrowing the father figure of George III and breaking the historical connection' with the Empire. The Revolution replaced the 'unnatural father' who tyrannized his children with the caring, benevolent 'Father of his Country', George Washington.[22]

[21] James A. Henretta, *The Evolution of American Society, 1700–1815: An Interdisciplinary Analysis* (Lexington, Mass., 1973); Bruce H. Mann, *Neighbors and Strangers: Law and Community in Early Connecticut* (Chapel Hill, NC, 1987); Kenneth A. Lockridge, 'Land, Population and the Evolution of New England Society, 1630–1790', *Past and Present*, XXXIX (1968), pp. 62–80 and 'Social Change and the Meaning of the American Revolution', *Journal of Social History*, VI (1973), pp. 403–39. Other classic formulations of this thesis are Main, *Social Structure of Revolutionary America*; Richard Bushman, *From Puritan to Yankee: Character and the Social Order in Connecticut, 1690–1765* (Cambridge, Mass., 1967).

[22] Kenneth Lynn, *A Divided People* (Westport, Conn., 1977), p. 68; Paul K. Longmore, *The Invention of George Washington* (Berkeley, 1988), pp. 204–05. See also Edwin B. Burrows and Michael Wallace. 'The American Revolution: The Ideology and Psychology of National Liberation', *Perspectives in American History*, VI (1972), 167–306; Daniel Blake Smith, *Inside the Great House: Planter Family Life in Eighteenth-Century Chesapeake Society* (Ithaca, NY, 1980); Jay Fliegelman, *Prodigals and Pilgrims: The American Revolution Against Patriarchal Authority, 1750–1800* (Cambridge, Mass., 1982).

By its very nature, social history has not provided an overarching synthesis, but many local studies on how individual communities chose the revolutionary path. Among the many outstanding monographs on colonial New England towns, Robert Gross's *The Minutemen and Their World* is unique for its effort to connect long-term social developments to the American uprising. Gross sets out to explain how Concord, which paid little attention to the outside world in the 1760s, became the centre of revolutionary sentiment. He argues that in the decades preceding the Revolution Concordians saw their town's fortunes declining with falling property values, worn-out soil, rising poverty, and mass exodus of the town's youth. They revolted, he concludes, less against the Empire than against the 'deepening social and economic malaise' in their midst.[23]

Radical social historians have searched for working-class consciousness and empowerment in the revolutionary legacy, primarily in the urban mid-Atlantic colonies. In 1967 Alfred F. Young concluded, somewhat disappointedly, that consensus historians were right: bourgeois liberals—lawyers, merchants, and businessmen, not working-class radicals—were the true revolutionary movers and shakers in New York. But the younger generation of 'New Left' historians re-examined the rank and file of the movement and found much that they liked. Gary B. Nash argues that the advance of commercial capitalism in Boston, New York, and Philadelphia brought about social and economic polarization and led to the development of urban class antagonisms. In the 1760s and 1770s, Nash explains, with the standard of living declining and opportunities diminishing, urban workers turned revolutionaries and 'shattered the equilibrium of the old system of social relations'. Edward Countryman points to the rising number of riots, ranging from attacks on brothels to protests against the Stamp Act, and concludes that the awakening of working-class consciousness brought about the Revolution in New York.[24]

Was the Revolution a class conflict? The second part of the eighteenth century saw the top 10 per cent of urban property-owners amass an increasing proportion of the wealth, while spending on poor relief in New York, Boston, and Philadelphia more than doubled from 1740 to 1770. Yet, less than 5 per cent of the

[23] Robert A. Gross *The Minutemen and Their World* (New York, 1976), p. 105. David Hackett Fischer has taken the interpretive social history model down to the choices of 'individual actors with the context of large cultural processes': *Paul Revere's Ride* (New York, 1994), p. xv.

[24] Alfred F. Young, *The Democratic Republicans of New York: The Origins, 1763–1797* (Chapel Hill, NC, 1967); Edward Countryman, *A People in Revolution: The American Revolution and Political Society in New York, 1760–1790* (Baltimore, 1981), p. 184; Gary B. Nash, *The Urban Crucible: Social Change, Political Consciousness and the Origins of the American Revolution* (Cambridge, Mass., 1979), p. 283. Eric Foner tried to finesse the political orientation of radicals such as Tom Paine by suggesting that republicanism was the language of class antagonism. See *Tom Paine and Revolutionary America* (New York, 1976).

colonial population resided in cities. Moreover, it is difficult to argue convincingly that the 'best poor man's country', with its dramatic commercial expansion and abundance of rich and cheap land, was an economically distressed society.[25] Pauline Maier and Paul A. Gilje show that colonial élites often orchestrated, controlled, and contained revolutionary mob actions. The crowd actions of the 1760s and 1770s challenged traditional political leadership in New York, where élite revolutionary leaders worked to recruit the urban poor. But the oligarchy held on to power through the crisis precisely because residents were accustomed to conflict politics. The long history of contentious politics in the mid-Atlantic colonies, as Alan Tully demonstrates, made their systems capable of containing the dissent, and their residents were at ease with interest-based politics. Thus, the revolutionary movement flourished in Virginia and New England, while 'New York and Pennsylvania trailed in the rear'. When the Revolution reached the mid-Atlantic colonies it transcended class and ethnicity.[26]

The central monograph of revolutionary Chesapeake is Rhys Isaac's *The Transformation of Virginia, 1740–1790*. According to Isaac, the planter class, for all its power and wealth, was anxious about losing control of Virginia. Compounding the damage to its status caused by dependence on British creditors, the gentry's cultural hegemony was being challenged by religious revivalists who created an 'evangelical counterculture'. Revivalist preachers challenged the fundamental tenets of élite culture, from the dress code to the privileged position of the Church of England. Some meetings, as Mechal Sobel shows, crossed the racial line and some preachers even questioned the morality of slavery. The gentry turned to the republican ideology, Isaac explains, because its doctrines of community promised to revitalize 'traditional structures of local authority'. Slave-holding planters became revolutionaries 'as a defensive response to the open rejection of deference that was increasingly manifested in the spread of evangelicalism'.[27]

Social historians who see the Revolution as a social conflict fail, however, to

[25] Elaine Forman Crane, *A Dependent People: Newport, Rhode Island in the Revolutionary Era* (New York, 1985), p. 162; James T. Lemon, *The Best Poor Man's Country* (Baltimore, 1972); Alice Hanson Jones, *Wealth of a Nation To Be* (New York, 1980); John J. McCusker and Russell R. Menard, *The Economy of British America* (Chapel Hill, NC, 1985).

[26] Pauline Maier, *From Resistance to Revolution: Colonial Radicals and the Development of American Opposition to Britain, 1763–1776* (New York, 1972); Paul A. Gilje, *The Road to Mobocracy: Popular Disorder in New York City, 1763–1834* (Chapel Hill, NC, 1987); Alan Tully, *Forming American Politics: Ideals, Interests, and Institutions in Colonial New York and Pennsylvania* (Baltimore, 1994), p. 425. See also J. R. Pole, 'Historians and the Problem of Early American Democracy', *AHR*, LXVIII (1962), pp. 626–46; Richard Buel, Jr., 'Democracy and the American Revolution: A Frame of Reference', *WMQ*, Third Series, XXI (1964), pp. 165–90.

[27] Rhys Isaac, *The Transformation of Virginia, 1740–1790* (Chapel Hill, NC, 1982), p. 164, p. 265; Mechal Sobel, *The World They Made Together: Black and White Values in Eighteenth-Century Virginia* (Princeton, 1987).

establish the connection between social structure, processes, and the specific revolutionary step. Gross, for example, admits that the 'social and economic changes did not "cause" the townspeople rebellion'. Isaac concedes that his 'interpretation of collective psychology is . . . speculative'.[28] Further, colonial society and economy were united primarily through their connection to the Empire. Focusing on the specific socio-economic conditions which led to local revolts overlooks the basic nature of the Revolution—collective political action that transcended provincial concerns.

The New Social History accepted the consensus premise that colonial and revolutionary America were shaped by Lockean, bourgeois, individualistic ideology. Historians, however, have pointed out that, in revolting, the colonists spurned the supposedly Lockean traditions that hitherto defined them. Borrowing from Clifford Geertz's cultural anthropology and Thomas Kuhn's paradigm of scientific development, historians searched for the structured consciousness of the movement. They see the Revolution as first and foremost an ideological turning-point, a paradigm shift in which some Englishmen ceased to think of themselves in Imperial terms and constructed a distinct American identity. As John Adams wrote, 'The Revolution was in the Minds of the People, and this was affected, from 1760 to 1775, in the course of fifteen Years before a drop of blood was drawn at Lexington.'[29]

Consensus readings of eighteenth-century North America assumed that the rebels embraced Lockean individualism and the sanctity of private property because they reflected their actual experience. In the words of Louis Hartz, John Locke 'is a massive national cliché.'[30] Historians of ideology study the language used to mobilize the North American rebels and conclude that the Lockean influence was grossly overstated. Douglass G. Adair's 1943 Yale dissertation was the first to point out that the revolutionaries drew more from David Hume and the Scottish Enlightenment than from John Locke. In 1959 Caroline Robbins articulated the case for the influence of the English country-party opposition ideology.[31]

[28] Gross, *Minutemen*, p. 107; Isaac, *Transformation*, p. 266.

[29] John Adams to Thomas Jefferson, 24 Aug. 1815, in Lester J. Cappon, ed., *The Adams–Jefferson Letters* (Chapel Hill, NC, 1959), p. 455.

[30] Louis Hartz, *The Liberal Tradition in America: An Interpretation of American Political Thought Since the Revolution* (New York, 1955), p. 140. Other studies emphasizing the Lockean tradition include Carl L. Becker, *The Declaration of Independence: A Study in the History of Political Ideas* (New York, 1922); Daniel Boorstin, *The Lost World of Thomas Jefferson* (New York, 1948), *The Genius of American Politics* (Chicago, 1953), and *The Americans: The Colonial Experience* (New York, 1958).

[31] Douglass G. Adair, 'The Intellectual Origins of Jeffersonian Democracy: Republicanism, the Class Struggle, and the Virtuous Farmer', unpublished Ph.D. dissertation, Yale, 1943; Caroline Robbins, *The Eighteenth-Century Commonwealth* (Cambridge, 1959). For a similar emphasis on the Scottish Enlightenment see Garry Wills, *Inventing America: Jefferson's Declaration of Independence* (New York, 1978).

The republican synthesis came to centre stage when it was embraced by Bernard Bailyn, the most distinguished historian of early America. In a 1965 introduction to a collection of revolutionary pamphlets, and a few years later in *The Ideological Origins of the American Revolution*, Bailyn argued that the revolutionaries understood their conflict with the Empire in terms of the Tory and country-party critique of the Walpole ministry. Gordon Wood, following in his mentor's footsteps, has documented the republican vocabulary used by the rebels to describe their anxiety over both Imperial measures and the rise of commercial capitalism. Finally, J. G. A. Pocock has demonstrated the hold of the Renaissance civic humanist tradition on the Atlantic world, suggesting that the Empire was dissolved in the name of these ideas. The American Revolution, he writes, was 'the last great act of the Renaissance'.[32]

American pamphleteers continually described the colonies as innocent victims of ministerial aggression. Yet, how could white male colonists who ruthlessly seized land from the Indians, owned over half-a-million African slaves, treated women as property, and lived under the freest government in the European world see themselves as victims of English tyranny? Eighteenth-century Americans, historians explain, interpreted their reality through the republican prism—an ideology riddled with paranoid fears of ministerial conspiracy against the liberty of the people. Americans were, writes Wood, 'prone to fears of subversion', and the Revolution is best understood as a 'psychological phenomenon'.[33]

Bailyn, Wood, and Pocock acknowledge that North American economy and society underwent dramatic changes as the pre-capitalist order gave way to a market-oriented economy. Little in America resembled an ideal, virtuous, self-sufficient republican community. Prosperity depended on the Atlantic economy. Rather than adjust their values to the new order, however, fear generated by colonial dependence on the Imperial market triggered calls for adherence to the idealized world left behind in England and for the rustic beginnings of the colonial era. In that sense, the Great Awakening and the Revolution expressed

[32] Bernard Bailyn, ed., *Pamphlets of the American Revolution* (Cambridge, Mass., 1965) and *The Ideological Origins of the American Revolution* (Cambridge, Mass., 1967); Gordon S. Wood, *The Creation of the American Republic, 1776–1787* (Chapel Hill, NC, 1969); J. G. A. Pocock, *The Machiavellian Moment: Florentine Political Thought and the Atlantic Republican Tradition* (Princeton, 1975) and 'Virtue and Commerce in the Eighteenth Century', *Journal of Interdisciplinary History*, III (1972), p. 120. Morgan and Morgan's *The Stamp Act Crisis* is equally concerned with revolutionary rhetoric and its appeals to the principles of a republican past.

[33] Wood, 'Conspiracy and the Paranoid Style: Causality and Deceit in the Eighteenth Century', *WMQ*, Third Series, XXXIX (1982), pp. 404–05, 401; James H. Hutson, 'The Origins of the Paranoid Style in American Politics: Public Jealousy from the Age of Walpole to the Age of Jackson', in David D. Hall, John M. Murrin, and Thad W. Tate, eds., *Saints and Revolutionaries: Essays on Early American History* (New York, 1984), pp. 332–72. See also Richard Hofstadter, *The Paranoid Style in American Politics and Other Essays* (New York, 1965), pp. 3–40.

similar longings for a mythic past.[34] Anxious about their slipping control over their economy and society, eighteenth-century Americans resorted to religious and political jeremiads and yearned for the moral economy of their forefathers.[35] Earthquakes, fires, economic recessions, military defeats, and the post-1763 Imperial measures were interpreted as deserved punishment for the sin of selling out to commercialism and consumerism. The Crown's demand that Americans help pay for the wars that preserved the Empire highlighted the colonists' concerns about their own moral and cultural bankruptcy. They projected these anxieties on to Great Britain and rebelled in order to protect their supposed republican world from political and moral degeneracy.[36]

The rebels believed that republics could exist only if their citizens were free, independent, and civic-minded. There was an antagonism between commercial ethics and civic-minded virtue. The ideal republican citizen was independent of the impersonal market forces. Republics, explains Drew R. McCoy, 'had to be rather rude, simple, pre-commercial societies free from any taint of corruption'. This model hardly resembled the colonies whose livelihood depended on active trade. All the same, Americans opted for the republican ideal as 'a final attempt to come to terms with the emergent individualistic society that threatened to destroy once and for all' the civic-minded community of their imagination.[37]

The republican synthesis never enjoyed overwhelming scholarly acceptance. In fact, the paradigm 'was reified and popularized less by its formulators than by its

[34] For studies emphasizing this dimension of the Great Awakening and its connection to the Revolution see Bushman, *Puritan to Yankee*; Alan Heimert, *Religion and the American Mind, From the Great Awakening to the Revolution* (Cambridge, Mass., 1966); Edmund S. Morgan, 'The Puritan Ethic and the American Revolution', *WMQ*, Third Series, XXIV (1967), pp. 3–41; Harry S. Stout, 'Religion, Communications, and the Ideological Origins of the American Revolution', *WMQ*, Third Series, XXXII (1975), pp. 519–41. For a critique see Jon Butler, 'Enthusiasm Described and Decried: The Great Awakening as Interpretive Fiction', *JAH*, LXIX (1982–83), pp. 305–25.

[35] Historians examining similar data disagree whether the moral pre-capitalist economy ever existed. Christopher Clark has found a century-long transition from the moral economy to agrarian capitalism. See *The Roots of Rural Capitalism: Western Massachusetts, 1780–1860* (Ithaca, NY, 1990). Winfred Barr Rothenberg, on the other hand, finds no moral economy in Massachusetts rural towns in the middle of the eighteenth century: *From Market-Places to a Market Economy: The Transformation of Rural Massachusetts, 1750–1850* (Chicago, 1992). For the republican synthesis, however, it does not really matter because it focuses not on the commercial reality, but on the colonial perception of a 'lost world'.

[36] Bailyn, *Ideological Origins*, pp. 22–66, 94–95; Pocock, *Machiavellian Moment*, pp. 526–27; Wood, *Creation of the Republic*, pp. 7–45, 49.

[37] Drew R. McCoy, *The Elusive Republic: Political Economy in Jeffersonian America* (Chapel Hill, NC, 1980), p. 120; Wood, *Creation of the Republic*, p. 419; John M. Murrin, 'The Great Inversion, or Court versus Country: A Comparison of the Revolutionary Settlement in England (1688–1721) and America (1776–1816)', in J. G. A. Pocock, ed., *Three British Revolutions: 1641, 1688, 1776* (Princeton, 1980), pp. 368–453.

antagonists'.[38] Soon after Bailyn, Wood, and Pocock made their case, critical evaluations appeared, and in 1976 Alfred F. Young edited a collection of challenges.[39] Chief critics of the synthesis are Isaac Kramnick, John Patrick Diggins, and Joyce Appleby. Kramnick demonstrates the lasting influence of John Locke and suggests that 'liberal individualism was fast pushing aside' the old republican paradigm. Diggins explains that republican ideology was not the cause of the Revolution, but merely its justification. And Appleby, the synthesis's sharpest critic, argues that common men and women understood that participation in the market extended economic opportunities and elevated their social and political status. The gentry who sought to emulate the values of landed British aristocracy may have spoken ambivalently about it, using republican language. 'But what struck the colonial gentry as a lamentable human failing was hailed by their inferiors as an extension of individual freedom.'[40]

In his celebrated synthesis *The Radicalism of the American Revolution*, Gordon Wood continues to focus on the tensions between the reality of everyday colonial life and the aspirations and anxieties of the colonists. Colonial society was initially a patriarchical order held together by a complex network of personal obligations and kinship. Democratization of consumption, demographic explosion, and geographical mobility in the second half of the century undermined the authority of both local gentry and British rule, creating a 'society in tension, torn between contradictory' forces. The colonists clung to the paternalistic model, with George III as father and Britain as Mother Country, as long as the parents did not force the colonies to integrate further in the Atlantic market. Alarmed by the Imperial measures, the colonists fell back on pre-capitalist republican traditions. They imagined their community and hierarchy could be restored if only the connection to the source of their social instability, the commercial British Empire, was severed.[41]

Both proponents and critics of the republican synthesis, as Peter Onuf and Cathy Matson write, make persuasive arguments. Neither liberalism nor republicanism 'should be accorded a decisive, determinative role in the American founding'. Republican or liberal, revolutionary rhetoric engaged the changed material condition of the eighteenth-century colonial world. Recent historians actually

[38] Daniel T. Rodgers, 'Republicanism: The Career of a Concept', *JAH*, LXXIX (1992), p. 23.

[39] Alfred F. Young, ed., *The American Revolution: Explorations in the History of American Radicalism* (Dekalb, Ill., 1976).

[40] Isaac Kramnick, 'Republicanism Revisionism Revisited', *AHR*, LXXXVII (1982), p. 664; John Patrick Diggins, *The Lost Soul of American Politics: Virtue, Self Interest, and the Foundations of Liberalism* (New York, 1984), p. 23; Joyce Appleby, *Liberalism and Republicanism in the Historical Imagination* (Cambridge, Mass., 1992), p. 182.

[41] Wood, *The Radicalism of the American Revolution* (New York, 1992), p. 124.

observe the coexistence of the two competing ideologies. Eighteenth-century Americans ignored their contradictory nature. Sometimes they panicked over the loss of the 'old world'. At other times they celebrated the prosperity and freedom of the new market economy. Robert Shalhope explains that 'Lockean liberalism and classical republicanism provided the essential underpinning' of the revolutionary credo.[42] Timothy Breen suggests that the sharp rise in colonial consumption of English manufactured goods redefined Imperial relations. Consumption allowed common women and men to assert their equality with the gentry. The standardized goods themselves created a common colonial vocabulary. And yet, many were alarmed by the acquisitiveness, selfishness, and cruelty of the new order. Parliamentary measures which targeted consumption politicized the public. The favourite colonial weapon—the boycott of British goods—fostered a coalition that transcended regional and class differences.[43] Further, historians increasingly appreciate the religiosity of the colonial world. Protestant theology was, after all, more central to colonial society and culture than either liberalism or republicanism. As James T. Kloppenberg explains, the two 'blended and functioned together within the context of religious faith'. And J. C. D. Clark goes further, suggesting that Protestant dissident denominations in North America launched a Revolution in order to defend themselves against the rising tide of Anglicanism.[44]

The foundations of the ideological approach are being challenged. First, as the ideological interpretation of the Revolution became more nuanced, it lost its coherence. A paradigm containing contradictory beliefs about the motives and meaning of the Revolution is of questionable explanatory value. Secondly, republican synthesis historians analyse the Revolution as psychological phenomena of paranoia and projection. The applicability, however, of psychotherapeutic theories

[42] Peter Onuf and Cathy Matson, *A Union of Interests: Political and Economic Thought in Revolutionary America* (Lawrence, Kan., 1990), p. 5; Robert E. Shalhope, *The Roots of Democracy: American Thought and Culture, 1760–1800* (Boston, 1990), p. 158.

[43] Timothy Breen, ' "Baubles of Britain": The American and Consumer Revolutions of the Eighteenth Century', *Past and Present*, CXIX (1988), pp. 73–104. See also, Gary Carson, Ronald Hoffman, and Peter J. Albert, eds., *Of Consuming Interests: The Style of Life in the Eighteenth Century* (Charlottesville, Va., 1994).

[44] James T. Kloppenberg, 'Republicanism in American History and Historiography', *The Tocqueville Review*, XII (1992), p. 125, and 'The Virtues of Liberalism: Christianity, Republicanism, and Ethics in Early American Political Discourse', *JAH*, LXXIV (1987), pp. 9–33; J. C. D. Clark, *The Language of Liberty, 1660–1832: Political Discourse and Social Dynamics in the Anglo American World* (Cambridge, 1994), *Revolution and Rebellion: State and Society in England in the Seventeenth and Eighteenth Centuries* (Cambridge, 1986), and *English Society, 1688–1832: Ideology, Social Structure and Political Practice during the Ancien Régime* (Cambridge, 1985). Jon Butler, on the other hand, has argued that 'at its heart, the Revolution was a profoundly secular event': *Awash in a Sea of Faith: Christianizing the American People* (Cambridge, Mass., 1990), p. 195.

to the conduct of a large and diverse colonial society remains controversial. Finally, the straightforward manner in which historians read revolutionary rhetoric is challenged. Recent deconstructions of the revolutionary world instruct us to examine the symbols, pamphlets, and speeches of the founders in the context of the eighteenth-century 'revolution in self-expression'. Republican language 'ought more properly to be considered self-conscious performances intended to create beautiful tableaux' rather than representations of private–public reality.[45] As Michael Zuckerman explains, republicanism is best understood as a 'reactionary ethic' which received popular acclaim precisely because 'the reality in which that ideology was rooted slipped steadily away'.[46]

In sum, the three basic approaches of modern historiography seek to explain how and why seemingly manageable political and constitutional disagreements between the colonists and the British government shattered the Empire. Social and ideological historians contend that the advance of impersonal commercial capitalism destabilized the Empire, while Atlantic historians focus on Imperial politics in the aftermath of the great victory in the French and Indian War. Both social and ideological historians focus on the Revolution as a critical event of modern capitalism. Yet both approaches are plagued by parochial self-centredness. Social history is in principle devoted to the provincial perspective, and some historians have recast the claim for American exceptionalism by portraying the colonists as paranoid provincials unable to come to terms with their changing surroundings. Both read the existence of American otherness back to the 1760s. Current scholarship has began to question these provincial assumptions, moving back to the larger perspective of the Atlantic approach. Historians are increasingly urging that greater attention be paid to the international and cosmopolitan nature of the Revolution.[47] Others point to the widespread use of hand-bills and

[45] Jay Fliegelman, *Declaring Independence: Jefferson, Natural Language, and the Culture of Performance* (Stanford, Calif., 1993), p. 196; Nell Irvin Painter, 'Soul Murder and Slavery: Toward a Fully Loaded Cost Accounting', in Linda K. Kerber, Alice Kessler-Harris, and Kathryn Kish Sklar, *U.S. History as Women's History: New Feminist Essays* (Chapel Hill, NC, 1995), p. 146; Richard R. Beeman, 'Deference, Republicanism, and the Emergence of Popular Politics in Eighteenth-Century America', *WMQ*, Third Series, XLIX (1992), pp. 401–30. Modern critical analysis of the founders' rhetoric acknowledges their sincerity, unlike Progressive historians who considered the talk of rights and virtue merely a hypocritical exercise in the service of economic self-interest.

[46] Michael Zuckerman, 'A Different Thermidor: The Revolution Beyond the American Revolution', in James A. Henretta, Michael Kammen, and Stanley Katz, eds., *The Transformation of Early American History: Society, Authority and Ideology* (New York, 1991), p. 181.

[47] The classic work on the Revolution in its international context is Robert R. Palmer, *The Age of the Democratic Revolution*, 2 vols. (Princeton, 1959, 1964). In 1993 Peter and Nicholas Onuf explained that patriot leaders believed their colonies were states and that Imperial measures violated their sovereignty. Relying on international law, the rebels sought not to establish a separate American entity, but to reintegrate as equals in the international state system. See *Federal Union, Modern World: The*

the popularity of English novels in the eighteenth century, suggesting that the mass mobilization of the Revolution originates in the transformation of Anglo-American political print culture.[48] The collapse of Soviet communism inspires a more critical look at the relationship between commercial capitalism and the Revolution. The apparent erosion of the nineteenth-century order of nation states has triggered a reconsideration of the meaning of American nationalism and a renewed interest in issues of political rights and identity.[49] The task ahead is to integrate the Atlantic, social, and ideological approaches, and to restore the American Revolution to its context in the international age of revolutions while paying close attention to the social and ideological nuances advanced by modern historiography.

Law of Nations in the Age of Revolutions, 1776–1814 (Madison, 1993). See also Edward Countryman, 'Indians, the Colonial Order, and the Social Significance of the American Revolution', *WMQ*, Third Series, LIII (1996), pp. 342–62, and *Americans: A Collision of Histories* (New York, 1996), pp. 45–85.

[48] Michael Warner, *The Letters of the Republic: Publication and the Public Sphere in Eighteenth-Century America* (Cambridge, Mass., 1990); Fliegelman, *Prodigals and Pilgrims*; David D. Hall, 'Books and Reading in Eighteenth-Century America', in Carson, Hoffman, and Albert, *Of Consuming Interests*, pp. 354–72.

[49] For studies of political culture, ritual, and national identity in revolutionary America see Peter Shaw, *American Patriots and the Rituals of Revolution* (Cambridge, Mass., 1981); Edmund S. Morgan, *Inventing the People: The Rise of Popular Sovereignty in England and America* (New York, 1988); Ann Fairfax Withington, *Toward a More Perfect Union: Virtue and the Formation of American Republics* (New York, 1991); David Waldstreicher, *In the Midst of Perpetual Fetes: The Making of American Nationalism, 1776–1820* (Chapel Hill, NC, 1997). Two influential comparative studies of the origins of modern nationalism are Benedict Anderson, *Imagined Communities: Reflections on the Origin and Spread of Nationalism* (London, 1983) and Eric J. Hobsbawm, *Nations and Nationalism Since 1789; Programme, Myth, Reality* (Cambridge, 1990).

Select Bibliography

JOYCE O. APPLEBY, *Liberalism and Republicanism in the Historical Imagination* (Cambridge, Mass., 1992).

BERNARD BAILYN, *The Ideological Origins of the American Revolution* (Cambridge, Mass., 1967).

—— *The Ordeal of Thomas Hutchinson* (Cambridge, Mass., 1974).

T. H. BREEN, '"Baubles of Britain": The American and Consumer Revolution of the Eighteenth Century', *Past and Present*, CXIX (1988), pp. 73–104.

JAY FLIEGELMAN, *Prodigals and Pilgrims: The American Revolution Against Patriarchal Authority, 1750–1800* (Cambridge, Mass., 1982).

LAWRENCE HENRY GIPSON, 'The American Revolution as an Aftermath of the Great War for the Empire, 1754–1763', *Political Science Quarterly*, LXV (1950), pp. 86–104.

JACK P. GREENE, *The Quest for Power: The Lower Houses of Assembly in Southern Royal Colonies, 1689–1776* (New York, 1963).

Robert A. Gross, *The Minutemen and Their World* (New York, 1976).

Alan Heimert, *Religion and the American Mind: From the Great Awakening to the Revolution* (Cambridge, Mass., 1966).

Rhys Isaac, *The Transformation of Virginia, 1740–1790* (Chapel Hill, NC, 1982).

Pauline Maier, *From Resistance to Revolution: Colonial Radicals and the Development of American Opposition to Britain, 1763–1776* (New York, 1972).

Jackson Turner Main, *The Social Structure of Revolutionary America* (Princeton, 1965).

Edmund S. Morgan and Helen M. Morgan, *The Stamp Act Crisis: Prologue to Revolution* (Chapel Hill, NC, 1953).

Gary B. Nash, *The Urban Crucible: Social Change, Political Consciousness, and the Origins of the American Revolution* (Cambridge, Mass., 1979).

Peter Onuf and Nicholas Onuf, *Federal Union, Modern World: The Law of Nations in the Age of Revolutions, 1776–1814* (Madison, 1993).

John Phillip Reid, *Constitutional History of the American Revolution*, 4 vols. (Madison, 1986–93).

Daniel T. Rodgers, 'Republicanism: The Career of a Concept', *Journal of American History*, LXXIX (1992), pp. 11–38.

John Shy, *Toward Lexington: The Role of the British Army in the Coming of the American Revolution* (Princeton, 1965).

P. D. G. Thomas, *British Politics and the Stamp Act Crisis: The First Phase of the American Revolution* (Oxford, 1975).

Gordon S. Wood, *The Radicalism of the American Revolution* (New York, 1992).

6

Ireland

DAVID HARKNESS

'What is it but a secondary kingdom? An inferior member of a great Empire without any movement or orbit of its own . . . A suburb of England we are sunk in her shade.'[1] Thus in 1790 Sir Lawrence Parsons regretted the position of Ireland, in a debate in its long-established House of Commons. His country was soon to lose its Parliament, when the Act of Union of 1800 merged it with the Imperial Parliament at Westminster and absorbed this 'secondary kingdom' into the United Kingdom of Great Britain and Ireland. The former colony, model for expansion and settlement across oceans far wider than St George's Channel, the 'secondary kingdom', so recently an aspirant to constitutional equality with its more powerful neighbour, had been put firmly in its place. Now it would be a region of the Imperial motherland, with its own contribution to the process of Empire-building, to be sure, from the provision of pioneer farmers, footsoldiers, and domestic servants to the more dashing supply of generals, Consuls, Governors, and, in time, assertive politicians, but it would no longer be entitled to aspire to nationhood of its own.

Daniel O'Connell would challenge this restriction powerfully in the early decades of the nineteenth century, when he sought to return his country to the status of a 'great nation' from its humiliating present position as a 'pitiful province',[2] and it is with the nineteenth- and twentieth-century outworkings of this ambition that the present chapter will be concerned. It is worth reflecting, however, that the contribution of Ireland to the British Empire, begun long before the nineteenth century, is not to be found solely in the annals of Ireland itself. The Irish in Ireland and the colonial citizens of Irish origin who flooded into the settlement colonies, or who helped to win, to administer, and to hold other colonial territories, were themselves often the source of nationalist inspiration where they settled or where their home struggles were observed as suitable for emulation.

[1] W. E. H. Lecky, *A History of Ireland in the Eighteenth Century*, 3 vols. (London, 1892), III, p. 7.

[2] Daniel O'Connell, 'Second Letter to the People of Ireland' (12 April 1833). See M. F. Cusack, ed., *The Speeches and Public Letters of the Liberator* (Dublin, 1875), p. 394. This is just one of numerous such statements.

Ireland's role in the Empire-Commonwealth throughout its evolution, from expansion to decline, was Janus-like. The evidence of this two-facedness, however, is not contained in an easily identifiable array of monographs spaced neatly across the centuries. Rather, it lies in the statistics of population transfer, the innumerable tales of individual lives, and in such varied sources as the accumulated records of emigration and immigration, the debates of representative Parliaments, and the memoirs of officials: sources often buried in the narrow histories of individual territories, as well as subsumed in those sweeping general accounts of the 'expansion of England', of Imperial aggrandizement, or of the end of Empire.

There are indeed many references to Ireland and Irishmen throughout the volumes of this history: Ireland, the temporary domicile of wandering Scots who would proceed to North America; Ireland, the practice-ground of settlement; Ireland, the source of convicted transportees, famine victims, get-up-and-go adventurers, priests, merchants, doctors, or of the general building-blocks of emerging colonial city populations. As a colonized island (England's oldest colony), as an 'internal colony',[3] as a 'peripheral region' of those islands that constituted the motherland of Empire, Ireland features in separate chapters, where its chronological contribution is witnessed. There was a heady moment at the end of the eighteenth century when Ireland almost attained equality of status with Great Britain, a 'constitutional experiment of association between equals', but this was soon 'abandoned'.[4] The 'experiment' drew forth perceptive analyses from British statesmen of what was needed if a second British Empire was to grow and be sustained. As Vincent T. Harlow has pointed out, Wellesley was able to observe to Pitt in 1792 that it was the absence of genuinely responsible government that constituted Ireland's problem: 'Parliamentary self-government without ministerial responsibility was a fantastic anomaly and a parody of the parent constitution.' Pitt failed to reconcile Westminster control of Imperial affairs with Irish autonomy, and Union was forced as the alternative solution. Thus Ireland 'disappeared from the imperial scene in 1800 and did not emerge again until the twentieth century'.[5] Well, not quite: there were numerous points of impact and reference during the nineteenth century, and it is in this century that this chapter begins. It will concentrate on those aspects of Ireland that stimulated national consciousness within the modern Empire: a story that developed in the nineteenth century and grew in effectiveness and momentum into the twentieth.

O'Connell provided the focus for Irish dissatisfaction with the Union. He

[3] See Michael Hechter, *Internal Colonialism: The Celtic Fringe in British National Development, 1536–1966* (London, 1975).

[4] See Vincent T. Harlow:,'The New Imperial System', in E. A. Benians and others, eds., *Cambridge History of the British Empire* (hereafter *CHBE*), 9 vols., II (London, 1940), p. 132.

[5] Ibid., p. 135.

sought justice for his country, in equality of treatment or, failing that, repeal of the Union and the restoration of the Irish Parliament. He remained loyal to the Crown, however, and provided inspiration to many later Irish nationalists who continued to see advantage in the Imperial connection, in the retention of opportunities which the Empire offered to a people who had done so much to make that Empire what it was.[6] His was not the only perspective, however, and even in his own time more radical elements desiring to break the link with Britain appeared, articulated their views, and in some cases asserted their convictions in arms. The impact upon the Empire of Young Ireland[7] in the 1840s, and of the Fenians a generation later, requires consideration, while the repercussions of the Great Famine in Ireland, 1845–49, particularly in regard to emigration, can hardly be overemphasized in terms both of settlement and of attitudes. This latter phenomenon has been described as having 'led to the most revolutionary change in nineteenth century imperial history. Alike in dramatic quality and far-reaching political consequences, the Irish exodus occupies the central place in the history of nineteenth century emigration.'[8] Furthermore, it was the judgement of W. E. H. Lecky in 1861 that the impact of 'the great clearances and the vast un-aided emigrations, that followed the famine' constituted 'the true source of the savage hatred of England that animates the great bodies of Irishmen on either side of the Atlantic'.[9] Modern scholarship continues to emphasize the internationalization of the demand for Irish freedom and the unquantifiable degree of bitterness that has flowed down the years since.[10] As for the presence of Irish immigrants in the settlement colonies, there are innumerable studies, from the narrowest local to the colony-wide survey, as well as studies of the process of emigration itself.[11] It is in the midst

[6] See Maurice O'Connell, *The Correspondence of Daniel O'Connell*, 8 vols. (Dublin, 1972–80); M. F. Cusack, *Speeches;* Fergus O'Ferrall, *Daniel O'Connell* (Dublin, 1981); Oliver MacDonagh, *O'Connell: The Life of Daniel O'Connell, 1775–1847* (London, 1991).

[7] For a discussion of this movement see Richard Davis, *The Young Ireland Movement* (Dublin, 1987); but see also the works of Sir Charles Gavan Duffy, as listed in n. 24 below.

[8] J. L. Morrison, 'Problems of Settlement, ii, Emigration and Land Policy', in *CHBE*, II, pp. 452–54.

[9] W. E. H. Lecky, *Leaders of Public Opinion in Ireland*, 2 vols. (1st edn., Dublin, 1861); see 1903 edn., 2 vols., (London), II, p. 177.

[10] See, for example, Robert Kee, *The Green Flag* (London, 1972) and his somewhat less scholarly chap. 5 in the *Famine in Ireland: A History* (London, 1981); and D. G. Boyce, *Nationalism in Ireland* (London, 1982).

[11] For the process of emigration see D. Fitzpatrick, *Irish Emigration, 1801–1921* (Dundalk, 1984), the first volume in 'Studies in Irish Economic and Social History', published for the Irish Economic and Social History Society. For settlement in individual colonies the following are examples: Bruce S. Elliott, *Irish Migrants in the Canadas: A New Approach* (Kingston, 1988); Robert J. Grace, *The Irish in Quebec: An Introduction to the Historiography* (Quebec, 1993); Donald Harman Akenson, *The Irish in Ontario: A Study in Rural History* (Kingston, 1984), *The Irish in New Zealand, 1860–1950* (Wellington, 1990), and *The Irish Diaspora: A Primer* (Toronto, 1993); Con Costello, *Botany Bay: The Story of the Convicts Transported from Ireland to Australia, 1791–1853* (Cork, 1987); Patrick James O'Farrell, *The Irish in Australia* (Kensington, NSW, 1987); Donal P. McCracken, ed., *The Irish in South Africa, 1795–1910* (Durban, 1992) and his 'Irish Settlement and Identity in South Africa before 1910', *Irish Historical Studies*, XXVIII, 110, pp. 134–49.

of this phenomenon that the best accounts of Irishwomen's place in the expansion of Empire lie, with emigrant female orphans one notable example.[12] The role of Irish educators, female as well as male, often missionaries but by no means exclusively so, is one of the unsung contributions of Ireland to the Dominion and colonial worlds alike.[13]

Those indefatigable analysts of evolving capitalism, Marx and Engels, should also be noted as they monitored Ireland's contribution to England's greatness, charting the relentless exploitation of Irish land and people, and urging Irish self-determination and the economic liberation of the colony from the metropolis, in letters, books, and pamphlets, from the early 1840s onwards.[14] Their perspective was to retain its appeal and win adherents, from James Connolly and Lenin to silent thousands who would accept the role and position of Ireland along with their acceptance of the Marxist analysis of society. The writings of Marx and Engels, and those of the main protagonists of the nationalist movements, constitute the most immediate of our sources, but the accounts of more recent historians can serve both to put these into context and to draw attention to individual works. Mention has already been made of O'Connell and Young Ireland. The writings of Thomas Davis were the most persuasive to later generations,[15] but John Mitchel's *Jail Journal* (New York, 1854), also influential through its vivid denunciation of English exploitation, was constantly reprinted throughout the century. The Fenians too were active publicists, from the romantic novel, *Knocknagow*,[16] of Charles Kickham, to the journalistic propaganda of the *Irish People*,[17] but recent studies by R. V. Comerford[18] and the essays edited by T. W. Moody[19] should be

[12] See Trevor McLaughlin, *Barefoot and Pregnant? Irish Famine Orphans in Australia* (Melbourne, 1991); Australia is the best-reported area, but see for the broader picture, Patrick O'Sullivan, ed., *Irish Women and Irish Migration* (London, 1995).

[13] T. J. Walsh, *Nano Nagle and the Presentation Sisters* (Dublin, 1959); R. Burke Savage, *Catherine McAuley: First Sister of Mercy* (Dublin, 1949); W. Hutch, *Mrs Ball: Foundress of the Institute of the Blessed Virgin Mary in Ireland and the British Colonies* (Dublin, 1879); D. Rushe, *Edmund Rice: The Man and his Times* (Dublin, 1981); and J. Towey, *The Irish De La Salle Brothers in Christian Education* (Dublin, 1980) will serve to illustrate the astonishing outpouring of Irish men and women to Africa, India, North America, Australia, New Zealand, West Indies, Papua New Guinea, Mauritius, Fiji, and Gibraltar from the early nineteenth century onwards.

[14] Although their writings can be extracted from contemporary papers, or from their collected works published subsequently, the handiest source is Marx and Engels, *Ireland and the Irish Question*, ed. L. I. Goldman (London, 1971). But see also Nicholas Mansergh, *The Irish Question, 1840–1921* (London, 1965), esp. chap. 3 'The Communist International and the Irish Question'.

[15] See Thomas Davis, *Essays and Poems, With a Centenary Memoir* (Dublin, 1945), also Richard Davis, *The Young Ireland Movement* (Dublin, 1987).

[16] Charles Kickham, *Knocknagow, or The Homes of Tipperary* (Dublin, 1879).

[17] The newspaper of the Fenian movement, established by James Stephens in 1863, and edited by John O'Leary.

[18] R. V. Comerford, *Charles J. Kickham: A Study in Irish Nationalism and Literature* (Dublin, 1979) and *The Fenians in Context: Irish Politics and Society, 1848–82* (Dublin, 1985).

[19] T. W. Moody, ed., *The Fenian Movement* (Cork, 1968).

consulted. Of their activities abroad, Hereward Senior, *The Fenians and Canada* (Toronto, 1978) and Keith Amos, *The Fenians in Australia, 1865–80* (Kensington, NSW, 1988) will serve as examples.

Contemporaneously with the founders of communism, Charles Gavan Duffy, a survivor of Young Ireland, an Imperial statesman, and a link with the next phase of nationalist demand in Ireland, was adding Australian distinction to his credentials as an advocate of Irish self-government. Duffy made his political contribution as MP (1856–80), Prime Minister (1871–72), and Speaker (1876–80) in Victoria (where the 40,000 Irish-born of the mid-1850s, when he arrived, had grown to over 100,000 well before his departure).[20] He returned to Europe in 1880 and until his death in 1903 remained concerned to further Irish self-government within the context of a new cause, Imperial Federation. His career, along with that of Thomas D'Arcy McGee in Canada (perhaps the only other comparable contributor, but one whose career was cut short at the moment of Canadian Confederation),[21] illustrates another area of Irish Imperial contribution: the settler politician. His reflective historical works have been referred to above. His interventions in later nineteenth-century debate follow shortly, for his return coincided with a new phase in Ireland's demand: Home Rule. This innovation, firmly launched by Isaac Butt between 1870 and 1876, was given momentum by Charles Stewart Parnell from 1880. Once its specifically Irish aims had become associated with concepts of devolution and federalism in the United Kingdom, and of Imperial Federation on a wider canvas, however, Ireland found itself thrust again to the leading edge of Imperial argument.

Discussion of the considerable literature on Ireland's Home Rule movement, and its impact upon both the Mother Country and the Empire as a whole, should properly begin with the work of Isaac Butt himself, but reference must also be made to the pioneering contribution of W. Sharman Crawford, Ulster landlord and champion of tenant right, who flirted with both Repeal and Federalism in the 1830s and 1840s and whose fullest exposition of Federalism (heavily reliant on the recent Canada Act) was set out in public letters in the *Northern Whig*, citing many colonial precedents, in November 1844. In these articles and in other pamphlets of the time lie the genesis of future Home Rule schemes.[22]

[20] See N. Coughlan, 'The Coming of the Irish to Victoria', *Historical Studies, Australia and New Zealand*, XXII (1965), pp. 68–86.

[21] The writings of D'Arcy McGee include: *A History of the Irish Settlers in North America from the Earliest Period to 1850* (Boston, 1852); *Notes on Federal Governments Past and Present* (Montreal, 1865); *Two Speeches on the Union of the Provinces* [of Canada] (Quebec, 1865); and *The Irish Position in British and in Republican North America* (Montreal, 1866).

[22] See, for example, J. G. V. Porter, *Ireland* (London, 1844). For reference to this and for an account of Crawford's ideas see B. A. Kennedy, 'Sharman Crawford's Federal Scheme for Ireland', in H. A. Cronne, T. W. Moody, and D. B. Quinn, eds., *Essays in British and Irish History in Honour of James Eadie Todd* (London, 1949), pp. 235–54.

Butt's tempestuous career, brilliant and flawed as it was, had taken him from opposition to O'Connell and Repeal, to the legal defence of Young Irelanders (in the early months of 1848), which helped to convince him that Federalism offered the best solution to the Irish problem. This solution he took up actively after his first Parliamentary career had closed and he found himself back in the Irish courts, this time defending Fenian prisoners in 1865. In an effort to wrest the initiative from the physical force movement, he proposed the founding of a political party to win a sufficient measure of self-government for Ireland within the Empire, to enable the Irish to manage their own affairs according to their own lights (and better, by far, than the Westminster Parliament seemed capable of doing): in other words, a devolved Irish Parliament, in Dublin, which would be subordinate in Imperial matters to the Parliament in London. His ideas were spelled out in *Home Government for Ireland, Irish Federalism: Its Meaning, Its Objects, and Its Hopes* (Dublin, 1870).

Butt's 'Federal Home Rule was no mere tactical second-best; it was at once the thought-out expression of his own emotional view of the relationship between the two islands, and an offer of partnership to Irish Protestantism'; it was a 'framework for suggestion and deliberation'; and it envisaged England and Scotland embracing similar devolved legislatures, with the Imperial Parliament remaining as the great Council of Empire.[23] The scheme gained significance only after Charles Stewart Parnell[24] had made his impact upon the Westminster Parliament in general and upon the Liberals and Gladstone in particular. But the 1870s and 1880s did witness an increasing debate on the need to restructure the governance of both the United Kingdom and the Empire at large. House of Commons Home Rule debates in 1874 and 1876,[25] and the increasing realism of the Irish demand in the 1880s, generated a plethora of articles and books. The most formidable critic of Home Rule, then and for many years to come, was Albert Venn Dicey, Vinerian Professor of Law at Oxford, who made his first foray in 1882.[26] He argued that Home Rule, or Federalism as he categorized it, would undermine the Parliamentary sovereignty that lay at the centre of the United Kingdom's power at home and abroad and gave strength and elasticity to its constitutional arrangements. It would damage

[23] Quoted from D. Thornley's excellent *Isaac Butt and Home Rule* (London, 1964), which has a full discussion of the context.

[24] See F. S. L. Lyons, *Charles Stewart Parnell* (London, 1977).

[25] 30 June 1874, *Parliamentary Debates* (Commons), CC, cols. 700–92; 2 July, cols. 874–969; 30 June 1876 (Commons), CCXXX, cols. 738–822; and see, for example, Freeman, 'Federalism and Home Rule', *Fortnightly Review*, XXII (1874), pp. 204–15. J. E. Kendle, *Ireland and the Federal Solution: The Debate over the United Kingdom Constitution, 1870–1921* (Kingston, 1989), argues that the American Civil War and the British North America Act, 1867, stimulated thought on Federalism, and he goes on to cite many of the contemporary articles submitted in these decades.

[26] A. V. Dicey, 'Home Rule From an English Point of View', *Contemporary Review* (July 1882), pp. 66–86.

Westminster and fail to satisfy Ireland. Dicey further elaborated his views on Federalism in his classic *Law of the Constitution* (London, 1885: see in particular Lecture IV, 'Parliamentary Sovereignty and Federalism'), and he returned to the specific problem presented by Ireland with *England's Case against Home Rule* (London, 1886), after the failure of Gladstone's first Home Rule Bill. He insisted on preserving the 'unity of the state which is essential to the authority of England and to the maintenance of the Empire' (p. 283). Meanwhile, the returned Sir Charles Gavan Duffy had committed himself to a federal future for the Empire and elaborated his views in major articles from 1884 to 1886 in *Nineteenth Century*, the *National Review*, and the *Contemporary Review*.[27] As J. E. Kendle pointed out in his definitive *Ireland and the Federal Solution: The Debate over the United Kingdom Constitution, 1870–1922* (Kingston and Montreal, 1989), other important contributions were made at this time by Justin McCarthy, Goldwin Smith, and Joseph Chamberlain, while Gladstone himself made a formidable impact, not only by embracing Home Rule and committing his party to legislation, but with a series of pamphlets and articles.[28] The second attempt to implement Home Rule, in 1893, generated further alarms of 'The Empire in Danger', and further literature, including Dicey once more.[29] It should also be observed that it was in these turbulent years that first J. A. Froude (1881) and then W. E. H. Lecky (1892) produced their massive histories of Ireland in the eighteenth century: works as much influenced by their determined views on the necessity of Union at the close of the nineteenth century as by their concern with the affairs of Ireland in the eighteenth.[30]

The debate on Home Rule subsided somewhat with Gladstone's second defeat,

[27] Duffy hoped to see Ireland reconciled to Empire, contributing from its position as a self-governing unit, in equality with others in an Imperial Federation. For a discussion of his views see Helen F. Mulvey, 'Sir Charles Gavan Duffy: Young Irelander and Imperial Statesman', *Canadian Historical Review*, XXX, 4 (1952), pp. 369–86. See also the books he wrote in these years to record for posterity the earlier events of which he had been a part: *Young Ireland, 1840–50*, 2 vols. (London, 1880–83); *Thomas Davis: The Memoirs of an Irish Patriot, 1840–46* (London, 1890); *My Life in Two Hemispheres* (London, 1898).

[28] See, for example, W. E. Gladstone, *Special Aspects of the Irish Question: A Series of Reflections in and Since 1886: Collected from Various Sources and Reprinted* (London, 1892). For this and other writings see James Loughlin, *Gladstone, Home Rule and the Ulster Question, 1882–93* (Dublin, 1986). The classic on Gladstone and Ireland is J. L. Hammond, *Gladstone and the Irish Nation* (London, 1938), but see also John Morley, *The Life of William Ewart Gladstone*, 3 vols. (London, 1903).

[29] A. V. Dicey, *A Leap in the Dark, or Our New Constitution* (London, 1893).

[30] James Anthony Froude, *The English in Ireland in the Eighteenth Century*, 3 vols. (London, 1881); for Lecky see n. 1 above. Froude expressed himself in unrelentingly hostile terms to all things Irish, and was certain that Ireland was unfit for self-government; Lecky, more scholarly, of Irish origin, and deeply sympathetic to the landed Protestant class but critical of the impact of British influence over the centuries, hostile to the Roman Catholic Church, and by no means a supporter of democracy (rule by 'the most ignorant and the most disaffected': IV, p. 2), came to a similar conclusion about the unfitness of the majority of the Irish to rule themselves. Union was necessary alike for the good of Ireland and of England and the Empire. For an interesting analysis of their views see Anne Wyatt, 'Froude, Lecky and the "Humblest Irishman"', *Irish Historical Studies*, XIX, 75 (March 1975), pp. 261–85.

in 1893, though discussion on Imperial Federation continued, and the two came together again with a vengeance when a Third Home Rule Bill was proposed amid the volatile circumstances of the major constitutional crisis in 1909–10. Before reaching those exciting years and the actual introduction of the Bill in 1912, it is worth glancing at another aspect of Ireland's Imperial impact: the lesson it provided for interested spectators in the non-settlement arena.

It was, after all, in the last two decades of the nineteenth century that Indians began to organize to obtain a greater degree of self-government, and while their theoretical inspiration came from European continental and American sources, it has been argued that 'the immediate lessons of a country struggling to free itself from the British "colonial" yoke were essentially provided by Ireland'.[31] Irish Home Rule MPs informed themselves of the range of Imperial problems around the world,[32] but were particularly sympathetic towards India and actively encouraged the growth of Indian national awareness from the mid-1870s. The Indian press followed events in Ireland closely, once Parnell took charge, and the strong belief of many Indian commentators that Home Rule for Ireland would lead to Home Rule for India was reflected in the corresponding fears of British statesmen and Indian Governors (not least those of Irish stock, such as Dufferin).[33]

Ireland's nineteenth-century economic development, more of internal than Imperial significance, centred upon the land, and especially landlord–tenant relations. It has a considerable historiography of its own, but W. E. Vaughan's exploratory essay, *Landlords and Tenants in Ireland, 1848–1904* (Dublin, 1984), provides a helpful start, while Barbara L. Solow's *The Land Question and the Irish Economy, 1870–1903* (Cambridge, Mass., 1971) surveys the transforming legislation. If the steamship galvanized Imperial communications, tying Ireland, according to some, ever closer to its dominant neighbour, it is worth noting a westward-looking O'Connell's observation in 1841 that 'the steamships, which John Bull says

[31] Howard Brasted, 'Indian Nationalist Development and the Influence of Irish Home Rule, 1870–1886', *Modern Asian Studies*, XIV, 1 (1980), pp. 37–63. The same author has taken the Irish influence on Indian nationalism further in 'Irish Models and the Indian Nationalist Congress, 1870–1922', *South Asia*, VIII, 1–2 (1985), pp. 24–45; while Scott B. Cook has written a number of articles, as well as his book. *Imperial Affinities: Nineteenth-Century Analogies and Exchanges Between India and Ireland* (New Delhi, 1993). For evidence of an earlier connection, see R. D. Collison Black, 'Economic Policy in Ireland and India in the time of J. S. Mill', *Economic History Review*, Second Series, XXI (1968), pp. 321–36. 'Those Englishmen who know something of India, are even now those who understand Ireland best', wrote Mill, in 1868, and as Black points out; also Isaac Butt, in *The Irish People and the Irish Land* (Dublin, 1867), is seen to lament that while the British seemed able to treat India on its own merits they all too readily assumed that Ireland was a kind of inferior England, and could be treated accordingly.

[32] See Alan O'Day, *The English Face of Irish Nationalism* (Dublin, 1977), esp. chap. 10, 'Overseas Affairs and Parnellite Imperialism'.

[33] The Victorian version of the 'domino theory' is often expressed in these years, as it was to be throughout the first three decades of the twentieth century, in relation to Ireland. See, for example, Lord Salisbury, 'Disintegration', *Quarterly Review*, CLVI (Oct. 1883), pp. 559–95.

unite us to England, can come from America in ten days'.[34] Railways opened up markets to British goods, not least in Ireland, from their steady expansion from 1834 (Kingstown to Dublin) onwards. As the century advanced they facilitated the departing emigrant in a contrary direction.

The most intense debate on Ireland and the Empire centred on the events following Lloyd George's 'Peoples Budget' of 1909, and the subsequent showdown between Commons and Lords. Prime Minister H. H. Asquith, anxious to mobilize both the Irish vote in Britain and the support of the Irish Parliamentary Party, led since 1900 by John Redmond, reaffirmed the Liberal commitment to give Ireland 'a system of self-government in regard to purely Irish affairs'.[35] Once the power of the Lords had been curbed by the Parliament Act, 1911, there seemed to be no bar to the implementation of Home Rule. Objections were still forthcoming, however, and the outraged opponents of the measure were careful to ensure that fears of 'The Empire in Danger' were again voiced.

A contribution in 1910 by F. S. Oliver, under the *nom de plume* 'Pacificus', in reaction to the failed attempt of Conservative and Liberal leaders to reach a compromise in the constitutional crisis, recommended Conservatives to support a measure of devolution for Ireland, followed by Home Rule all round and the pursuit of Imperial Federation as the best answer to the Irish problem in a deteriorating world situation. The case was unfolded in seven letters to *The Times* in October and November 1910, and was speedily turned into a book.[36] It was followed in 1911 by *The Framework of Home Rule*, the first of many books on the subject published over the next few years. This closely argued submission by Erskine Childers was perhaps the best of those supporting the Irish demand.[37] It was filled with analyses of the Irish past, the Irish in relation to each of the Dominions, and

[34] Quoted by French Consul in Dublin, to Paris, 21 Aug. 1841. See Archives, Quai d'Orsay, Paris, 'Correspondence Politique de l'origine a 1871, 3^{e} Partie', *Correspondence de Consuls, 1826–70, Angleterre*, XIII (1841–44).

[35] Denis Gwynn, *The Life of John Redmond* (London, 1932), p. 169; but see also Ronan Fanning, 'The Irish Policy of Asquith's Government and the Cabinet Crisis of 1910', in Art Cosgrove and Donal McCartney, eds., *Studies in Irish History Presented to R. Dudley Edwards* (Dublin, 1979).

[36] Pacificus, *Federalism and Home Rule* (London, 1910). The author is identified by H. Montgomery Hyde, *Carson* (London, 1953), p. 278. See also his *Alexander Hamilton: An Essay in American Union* (London, 1906), described by J. E. Kendle as 'a brilliant federal tract disguised as a biography of Alexander Hamilton' (John Kendle 'Federalism and the Irish Problem in 1918', *History*, LVI, 187 (June 1971), p. 209); *The Alternatives to Civil War* (London, 1913); and *What Federalism is Not* (London, 1914). A fascinating further discussion of Oliver and his co-operative ventures with Lord Selborne is: D. G. Boyce and J. O. Stubbs, 'F. S. Oliver, Lord Selborne and Federalism', *Journal of Imperial and Commonwealth History* (hereafter JICH), V, 1 (Oct. 1976). J. E. Kendle, 'The Round Table Movement and Home Rule All Round', *Historical Journal*, XI, 2 (July 1968), pp. 332–53, adds further detail, while John Conway, 'The Round Table: A Study in Liberal Imperialism', unpublished Ph.D. dissertation, Harvard, 1951, contains two chaps. on Ireland. *The Round Table*, the quarterly journal of the movement, also provides a running commentary in these years.

[37] Erskine Childers, *The Framework of Home Rule* (London, 1911).

'the analogy' (chapter 8), which led to the logical conclusion, after an Irish Constitution had been drafted (chapter 15), that Home Rule was inevitable and must be achieved soon to ensure that Ireland would remain within the Empire. Childers argued both from the liberal principle of representative government and also from the necessity of relieving Westminster's burdens. He evoked swift responses.

One came from L. S. Amery, who directed an essay specifically against Childers entitled 'Home Rule and the Colonial Analogy'. In this he reduced his opponent's argument to 'analogy, and little else', regretted that even men such as Cecil Rhodes should have been seduced by the Home Rule idea, and then proceeded to assert that 'there is no such analogy bearing on the question which, here and now, is at issue'. Confusion alone could argue otherwise, for the whole trend of the colonial experience was towards union ('the fulfillment of colonial experience'), not away from it. In short, 'the material, social and moral interests, alike of Ireland and of Great Britain, demand that they should remain members of one effective, undivided legislature and administrative organization'.

Amery's was one of twenty essays by leading politicians and lawyers which together constituted *Against Home Rule: The Case for the Union*,[38] a book which appeared just before the introduction of the Home Rule Bill in April 1912. A book which appeared just after that introduction was J. H. Morgan, ed., *The New Irish Constitution* (London, 1912), which reasserted the case for Home Rule, and countered Dicey's *A Leap in the Dark* (London, 1911) by denying that Home Rule was 'at bottom Federalism' (rather, it was a case of devolution, a delegation of authority, not a diminution of it). It then explained the many aspects of the new arrangements, financial, judicial, historical, calling on Mrs J. R. Greene, R. Barry O'Brien, and Lord Dunraven, amongst others, and including 'Colonial Forms of Home Rule' by Sir Alfred Mond, in which he drew conclusions diametrically opposite to those of Amery. What was now being offered to Parliament, asserted Mond, was in 'harmony with the true process of evolution' (p. 414).

If the crisis of 1912–14 made the Empire tremble, and almost led to civil war in the United Kingdom, only to be subsumed in a mightier and more widespread conflict, Ireland did continue to affect (and be affected by) Imperial development during the Great War. The attempt to assert Irish nationality at Easter 1916 echoed round the colonial world. It was even noted at the time by Lenin.[39] The Easter

[38] R. Rosenbaum, ed., *Against Home Rule: The Case for the Union* (London, 1912). With an introduction by Edward Carson, a preface by Bonar Law, and contributions from Balfour, Salisbury, Long, A. Chamberlain, Wyndham, Londonderry, and some lesser political lights from both Ireland and England, it was a heavyweight contribution.

[39] V. I. Lenin, *Collected Works* (London, 1964), XXII, 'The Discussion on Self-Determination Summed Up' (July 1916): see section 6 'The Irish Rebellion of 1916', pp. 353–58.

Rising and the events that followed in the next five years exposed the weakness of the British Empire to its subject races and, eventually, even to diehard Imperialists themselves, according to Charles Duff's *Six Days To Shake an Empire*.[40]

The Irish Convention was summoned in 1917 to find in wartime a solution to the now exacerbated Irish problem. It was inspired by the South African precedent, so often seductive to British statesmen. In this instance it was used more realistically as a diversionary tactic to relieve Westminster from having actually to do something, and was another example of Empire–Ireland interaction. The Convention brought F. S. Oliver's pen back into action,[41] and when it was on the brink of failure in 1918, inspired a wider debate at the top, once more, on the federal solution to the intractable Irish and Ulster dilemma.[42]

As the Irish republican and separatist Sinn Fein Party advanced in popular support, wiping out the Parliamentary Party in the post-war 1918 elections, so the debate on United Kingdom and Empire management seemed of increasing irrelevance to Ireland. It was not to work out quite like that, however, and in a rearguard action the indefatigable Chairman of the abortive Irish Convention, Sir Horace Plunkett, represented a straw in the wind when he founded his Irish Dominion League in June 1919. The *Irish Statesman*, founded to publicize the new party, offered its manifesto in its first issue,[43] and carried the flag until it was wound up a year later in June 1920 (it was to be revived in 1923 and to continue, in its second series, until 1930). Here was an enthusiasm for an Irish Dominion solution that would keep Ireland united and within the emerging British Commonwealth. That perspective was not widely shared, however, and the actual creation of an Irish Dominion, in 1922, after truce and 'Treaty' in 1921, was a compromise that represented the relativities of brute force at the time, even though, as a solution, it turned out to have more to recommend it than was generally realized: more, that is, for Ireland. Whether this would be true also for the emerging but unconsulted Commonwealth association would become a matter of judgement.

It remains significant that the practical compromise reached between Imperial Britain and Nationalist Ireland, the creation of an Irish Dominion (the Irish Free State) for twenty-six of the thirty-two Irish counties, leaving the remaining six as part of the United Kingdom of Great Britain and Northern Ireland, introduced a

[40] Charles Duff, *Six Days to Shake an Empire* (London, 1966). See his epilogue in particular.

[41] Earl of Selborne and F. S. Oliver, *A Method of Constitutional Co-operation: Suggestions For the Better Government of the United Kingdom* (London, 1917).

[42] See John Kendle, 'Federalism and the Irish Problem in 1918'. For an account of the Convention itself, see R. B. McDowell, *The Irish Convention, 1917–18* (London, 1970).

[43] *Irish Statesman*, Dublin, 28 June 1919; see also its supplement (8 Nov.) for 'Irish Misgovernment and the Essentials of a Settlement'; and, for a discussion of this phase, T. T. West, *Horace Plunkett, Co-operation and Politics* (Gerards Cross, 1968), chap. 10.

radical and self-conscious new member into the Commonwealth at a sensitive time in its evolution. Partition, already achieved *de facto* by the Government of Ireland Act 1920, set an ambiguous precedent for later decolonization, as may be observed, for example, in T. G. Fraser's *Partition in Ireland, India and Palestine: Theory and Practice* (London, 1984) and R. J. Moore's *Escape from Empire: The Attlee Government and the Indian Problem* (Oxford, 1983).

The Irish, determined to achieve full sovereignty, as a Dominion or otherwise, could only have influence in one direction. Those favouring Dominion equality with the Mother Country, a definition of a several as opposed to a unitary monarchy, and an association linked by mutual interest, not bonds of loyalty or fealty, had from now on a thrusting new partner. From 1922 until its departure in 1949, the Irish Dominion would at last make its own, direct contribution to the Empire-Commonwealth as an independent player.

It was in the Treaty itself that the term 'British Commonwealth of Nations' was first used in an official document,[44] and during the course of its realization a good deal of newspaper and other print had been directed at the Irish plenipotentiaries in order to persuade them of the virtues of the club which they were being asked to join. One of the most influential was probably the young Duncan Hall's *The British Commonwealth of Nations: A Study of its Past and Future Development* (London, 1920),[45] but there was much to add from the recently concluded Imperial Conference, and no less a figure than J. C. Smuts had joined the persuaders, meeting secretly with the Irish 'President', de Valera, and contributing to the determination of the King himself to bring about a peaceful settlement. Ironically, one of their most difficult opponents was the now disillusioned Childers, secretary to the Irish negotiating team, who had lost faith that a Dominion solution would be honoured by a neighbour so near and so powerful as Britain. This would be the case especially after an agreement which permitted Britain naval and military rights that would compromise Ireland's freedom to declare its own policies on peace and war.

Those who signed the Treaty as the best deal they could get assured themselves of the direction of Dominion evolution, and they were satisfied of their power to control their own constitution, to appoint a Governor-General of their own choosing, and to begin the process of establishing their own diplomatic

[44] Articles of Agreement for a Treaty between Great Britain and Ireland, signed 6 Dec. 1921 (12 Geo. V, c. 4). This is included in R. M. Dawson's classic, *The Development of Dominion Status* (London, 1937), pp. 230–33, and is discussed in D. W. Harkness, *The Restless Dominion: The Irish Free State and the British Commonwealth of Nations, 1921–31* (London, 1969).

[45] This has been reflected upon in tranquillity in later times: see H. Duncan Hall, *Commonwealth* (London, 1971).

representation.[46] Once they had accepted Commonwealth membership, weathered the civil war that it provoked, and attended their first Imperial Conference in 1923, some Irish Ministers gained an insight into the advantages of an association jealous of its privileges, in which all members would be alert to the intimidation of any, and which afforded a measure of security in a post-war world of turbulence and uncertainty. But the voting public did not share these insights, and the government was committed in any event to the establishment of an Irish state and to its 'exaltation amongst the nations'[47] of the world, as soon as possible. Hence the push for equality, for full sovereignty, and for recognition; the development of a role at the League of Nations; the registration of the Treaty there in 1924, despite British objections regarding inter-Imperial agreements; the despatch of an Irish Minister to Washington, also in 1924; and a strong insistence at the Imperial Conference of 1926 that the anachronistic trappings of a former Empire, which contradicted or concealed the newly declared equality of Dominions, must be cleared away.[48]

Like the Treaty, itself an unprecedented midwife for the birth of a new Dominion 'freely associated' with the existing group, the Constitution of the Irish Free State contributed to the advance to sovereignty of these emerging states, helping to inspire 'the redefinition of Imperial Relations by the Imperial Conferences of 1926 and 1931'.[49] The oath of allegiance of Members of Parliament, the origins of authority, and the ambiguous finality of the Irish Courts were among the matters stretched towards Dominion autonomy, obscured somewhat by the requirement that the articles of the Constitution comply with the Treaty provisions.[50] What was to follow in the 1920s and 1930s, as Canada, South Africa,

[46] There is a discussion of this, and of the state of Dominion evolution, in David Harkness, 'Britain and the Independence of the Dominions: The 1921 Crossroads', in T. W. Moody, *Nationality and the Pursuit of National Independence* (Belfast, 1978), pp. 141–59.

[47] Proclamation of the Irish Republic, 1916; see Dorothy McArdle, *The Irish Republic* (London, 1937), p. 168.

[48] These points are discussed in Harkness, *Restless Dominion*, and pursued into the 1930s in D. Harkness, 'Mr de Valera's Dominion: Irish Relations with Britain and the Commonwealth, 1932–1938', *Journal of Commonwealth Political Studies*, VIII, 3 (1970), pp. 206–28. Something of the remaining period of Irish Commonwealth involvement is covered in David Harkness, 'Patrick McGilligan: Man of Commonwealth', *JICH*, VIII, 1 (Oct. 1979), pp. 117–35. This Number was published separately as Norman Hillmer and Philip Wigley, eds., *The First British Commonwealth: Essays in Honour of Nicholas Mansergh* (London, 1980).

[49] See Leo Kohn, *The Constitution of the Irish Free State* (London, 1932), p. 16. The second of these two Imperial Conferences was, of course, in 1930, but no doubt the author wished to emphasize the resulting 1931 Statute of Westminster.

[50] Kevin O'Higgins, the Minister charged with putting the Constitution through the Dail, explained the limitations on Irish action in a letter to the leader of the Labour Opposition, in the *Irish Times*, 23 Sept. 1922, but see also the opinions of Hugh Kennedy, Attorney-General at the time and soon to be made Chief Justice, in 'The Character and Sources of the Constitution of the Irish Free State', *Journal of the American Bar Association*, XIV (New York, Sept. 1928), pp. 437–45, and 'The Association of Canada with the Constitution of the Irish Free State', *Canadian Bar Review*, VI (Dec. 1928), pp. 747–58.

and the Irish Free State pushed determinedly to equate Dominionhood with complete independence, was a period dense with constitutional argument, innovation, and advance. Britain remained mindful of the colonial, non-settlement world, where in places its own authority was facing serious challenge, while Australia and New Zealand, more aware of exposure to danger on the rim of Asia, sought to slow down the pace of evolution. This scenario is most brilliantly described and analysed in the successive Commonwealth Surveys, first by W. K. Hancock,[51] and later by Nicholas Mansergh,[52] while the books and collections of documents of Arthur Berriedale Keith also include material of Irish interest.[53] In this context too, it is well worth consulting A. G. Donaldson's *Some Aspects of Irish Law* (Durham, NC, 1957), where the contribution of Ireland to the events of these two decades is assessed as 'considerable'.[54] K. C. Wheare's *The Statute of Westminster and Dominion Status* (Oxford, 1938) was an immediate authority at the time and remains of value.

Part of Ireland's concern was to avoid any return to the *status quo ante* the Treaty, and this led it to emphasize its role at the League of Nations, which it joined in 1923 as a 'fully self-governing state',[55] and it strove throughout these years to ensure prominence at what was an alternative international forum to the gatherings of Commonwealth members. In the process it won a certain reputation for speaking out on behalf of the small states of the world, and it achieved a position on the League Council in 1930 rather earlier than a new state might have had a right to expect.[56]

The Commonwealth was not neglected, however, for here too was a stage upon which the Irish could proclaim their sovereign rights. In 1926, led by Kevin

51 W. K. Hancock, *Survey of British Commonwealth Affairs*, Vol. I, *Problems of Nationality, 1918–1936* (London, 1937); Vol. II, *Problems of Economic Policy, 1918–39*, which appeared in two parts: Part 1 (London, 1940); Part 2 (London, 1942), should also be noted.

52 Nicholas Mansergh, *Survey of British Commonwealth Affairs: Problems of External Policy, 1931–39* (London, 1952). Mansergh continued the series with a second magisterial volume, *Problems of Wartime Co-operation and Post-War Change, 1939–1952* (London, 1958).

53 Arthur Berriedale Keith, *The Sovereignty of the British Dominions* (London, 1929); *Speeches and Documents on the British Dominions, 1918–31: From Self-Government to Sovereignty* (London, 1932); *Letters on Imperial Relations, Indian Reform, Constitutional and International Law, 1916–35* (London, 1935), and *The King, the Constitution, and the Empire and Foreign Affairs* (London, 1938), should all be noted.

54 For a discussion of these works see Helen F. Mulvey, 'Ireland's Commonwealth Years, 1922–49' in Robin W. Winks, ed., *The Historiography of the British Empire-Commonwealth: Trends, Interpretations and Resources* (Durham, NC, 1966).

55 Harkness, *Restless Dominion*, p. 36.

56 There has been an increase in interest in Ireland's international role in recent years. See Patrick Keatinge, *The Formulation of Irish Foreign Policy* (Dublin, 1973) and *A Place Amongst the Nations: Issues of Irish Foreign Policy* (Dublin, 1978); Dermot Keogh, *The Vatican, the Bishops and Irish Politics* (Cambridge, 1986), *Ireland and Europe, 1918–48* (Dublin, 1988), and *Ireland and the Vatican: The Policy and Diplomacy of Church–State Relations, 1922–60* (Cork, 1995); and Michael Kennedy, *Ireland and the League of Nations* (Dublin, 1996).

O'Higgins,[57] the Irish delegation backed South African Premier J. B. M. Hertzog in his call for a declaration of Dominion equality, but expressed itself more interested in demonstrating that equality before the world by having removed the vestiges of a previous Imperial order. Its request led eventually to the 1929 Conference on Dominion Legislation where, as the delegation longest in office of those present, the Irish perhaps wielded more authority than might otherwise have been the case. The recommendations of that Conference, accepted in the 1930 Imperial Conference, were translated into legislation as the Statute of Westminster, 1931. Other spheres too were being explored and initiatives taken, with the expansion of Irish diplomatic representation, the signing of treaties (authenticated by an Irish Seal, on the advice of Irish Ministers), and the flouting of British *inter se* doctrines of Commonwealth practice.

The process did not end with the replacement of Cosgrave's Cumman na nGaedheal regime by de Valera's Fianna Fail government in 1932. A more strident tone entered into Anglo-Irish relations, and de Valera adopted a unilateral stance in dealing with London, whereas his predecessor had endeavoured to effect change through bilateral agreement. But the direction of Irish policy remained the same: the establishment of that 'ultimate freedom that all nations aspire and develop to'.[58] The work of Sir Keith Hancock first highlighted the impact of 'the only conscript member of the British Commonwealth of Nations' (the phrase is John M. Ward's),[59] but the bulk of scholarship illumining these years is that of Nicholas Mansergh, who succeeded him as author in the *Survey* series but who had already written substantial accounts of both parts of Ireland even before the first *Survey* volume was published.[60] My own *Restless Dominion* has dealt with Ireland's actions up to 1931, and Deirdre McMahon's excellent *Republicans and Imperialists: Anglo-Irish Relations in the 1930s* (New Haven, 1984) covers de Valera's first years, when controversies over the oath of allegiance, the appeal to the Judicial Committee of the Privy Council, separate Irish Nationality, the elimination of the Crown from domestic matters, and the practical implementation of the right of neutrality were bones of contention. Brendan Sexton's scholarly and exhaustive *Ireland and the Crown, 1922–36* (Blackrock, Co. Dublin, 1989) has treated the specific matter of the Governor-General at fuller and more satisfying length

[57] A full study of this outstanding Irishman has still to be written, but see Terence de Vere White, *Kevin O'Higgins* (London, 1948), which pays tribute to his role in Commonwealth affairs.

[58] Michael Collins, speaking in Dail Eireann. See *Official Report: Debate on the Treaty Between Great Britain and Ireland Signed in London on 6 Dec. 1921* (Dublin, n.d.), p. 32, See also p. 33 for an appreciation of the protection afforded by Commonwealth membership.

[59] John M. Ward, 'The Historiography of the British Commonwealth', *Historical Studies Australia and New Zealand*, XII (April 1967), p. 560.

[60] The present author has attempted an overall assessment of Mansergh's immense contribution. See David Harkness, 'Philip Nicholas Seton Mansergh, 1910–91', *Proceedings of the British Academy* (1992, Lectures and Memoirs), LXXXII (1993), pp. 415–30.

than either of the foregoing. But Nicholas Mansergh, as historian of Ireland and of the Commonwealth, was an analyst as well as a contributor to unfolding events as they happened, and a scholar of the sources when they and the passage of time permitted more reflective comment. His *Irish Free State: Its Government and Politics* (London, 1934) and *The Government of Northern Ireland: A Study in Devolution* (London, 1936) had put the two Irish experiments under close scrutiny, and were drawn upon by Hancock.

Anglo-Irish relations deteriorated sharply in 1932, when constitutional differences were exacerbated by a quarrel over the payment of Land Annuity moneys that soon degenerated into an 'economic war', embracing disputed financial agreements and resulting in trade sanctions. This was to last from July 1932 to April 1938. Tied closely to these differences were personality clashes, and the de Valera government's determination to dispense with the much-resented remaining articles of the Treaty. The Abdication crisis enabled the Irish Premier to remove the King from Ireland's domestic legislative processes in December 1936, while a new Constitution in 1937 further reduced the attachment of Ireland (now styled Eire) to the Crown. At this point it was seriously questioned whether Ireland was still a Dominion, but the Westminster government chose to keep stretching its definition of Dominionhood to keep the Irish in, and as the international situation deteriorated, so further concessions were made in the interests of Commonwealth solidarity. Good pointers to these events are to be found in Henry Harrison, *Ireland and the British Empire, 1937: Conflict or Collaboration?* (London, 1937), a contribution from a reconciler, but much of the contemporary record has been wisely assessed by McMahon and Mansergh (in his first *Survey*, available of course to McMahon). This is also the case, so far as Mansergh is concerned, with Ireland's neutrality in the Second World War (in his second *Survey*). Here again Henry Harrison, *The Neutrality of Ireland: Why It Was Inevitable* (London, 1942), gives a contemporary flavour and points to past British policy to explain the Irish stance. Irish neutrality has generated a historiography of its own in recent years, but the war experience and some of the wider Imperial implications can be gleaned from Robert Fisk, *In Time of War* (London, 1983), while the extent of undisclosed Anglo-Irish collaboration is neatly summarized in Ronan Fanning, *Independent Ireland* (Dublin, 1983), especially pp. 124–25, where a list of Irish contraventions of neutrality in Britain's favour, drawn up by Dominions Secretary Cranborne, is quoted.

The departure of the Republic of Ireland from the Commonwealth showed further, as neutrality had illustrated already, that a Dominion could now take unfettered action, even, in this latter case, to the extent of seceding from the Association. The events leading up to that secession, the disappointments of the major anti-partition campaign which preceded it, and the controversy surrounding the announcement of intent, made in Canada, are dealt with in Ian McCabe, *A Diplomatic History of Ireland, 1948–49: The Republic, the Commonwealth and Nato* (Blackrock, Co. Dublin, 1991), which opens with a survey of Anglo-Irish constitutional developments since 1932 and a fuller account of events from 1945 to 1948. A number of scholarly articles help to fill out the role of Dominion leaders in these events, including Fred McEvoy, 'Canada, Ireland and the Commonwealth: The Declaration of the Irish Republic, 1948–9', *Irish Historical Studies*, XXIV, 96 (Nov. 1985), pp. 506–27; John B. O'Brien, 'Ireland's Departure from the British Commonwealth', *Round Table*, CCCVI (April 1988), pp. 179–94; and two articles in *International Affairs*: Sean McBride, 'Anglo-Irish Relations', XXV (July 1949), pp. 257–73 and Robert F. V. Heuston, 'British Nationality and Irish Citizenship', XXVI (Jan. 1950), pp. 77–90.[61] The speech by Taoiseach John A. Costello in Canada, which lay at the start of these events, 'Ireland in International Affairs', appeared in the *Canadian Bar Review*, XXVI (Oct. 1948), pp. 1195–211. Which brings us back to the breadth and depth of Nicholas Mansergh's discussion of these events.[62]

In two chapters on Ireland in *The Commonwealth and the Nations* (London, 1948), Mansergh brought the reader almost to the point of its departure from the Association, and assessed the significance of its then situation. This latter assessment may count as one of those occasions when a historian has been permitted to contribute to political decision-making, for it was first delivered as an address to an influential Chatham House audience on 25 November 1947, entitled 'The Implications of Eire's Relationship with the British Commonwealth of Nations'. Mansergh stressed the necessity of reconciling the sovereign needs of ex-colonial nations with continued association with Britain and the Commonwealth, and pointed out Ireland's long struggle for 'external association' and the relevance of the concept at that time to the Indian subcontinent and in the future to other parts of Asia and to Africa. The address was published in *International Affairs*, XXIV, 1 (Jan. 1948), and was then reprinted as chapter 8 of his book.[63] Ireland's wartime role as a neutral, the Commonwealth's failure to accommodate Ireland in republican form, while at the same time managing to come to terms satisfactory to India, and the negotiation of Ireland's departure, engineered in 1948 and completed at Easter, 1949, are fully described in his 1958 *Survey*,[64] but analysed at the time in his 'Ireland: The Republic Outside the Commonwealth', *International Affairs*, XXVIII (July 1952), pp. 277–91.

[61] See also Harkness, 'Patrick McGilligan'.

[62] See, for example, *Britain and Ireland* (London, 1942), in Longman's 'Pamphlets on the British Commonwealth' series, and *The Commonwealth Experience* (London, 1969). Heavily revised in a new edition in 1982, the latter contains two major sections on Ireland.

[63] See also Nicholas Mansergh, *The Unresolved Question: The Anglo-Irish Settlement and Its Undoing, 1912–72* (New Haven, 1991), App., p. 372.

[64] Nicholas Mansergh, *Documents and Speeches on British Commonwealth Affairs, 1931–52*, 2 vols. (London, 1953), should also be noted in the context of the two *Surveys*.

In the final work of his career, posthumously published as *The Unresolved Question* (see note 63), Mansergh returned to the first of his interests and proffered a comprehensive overview of Ireland's twentieth-century experience, not least its experience of Commonwealth membership. The very fact that the imperfect attempt in 1921 to resolve the Irish Question involved a Dominion solution renders Mansergh's final study relevant to students of the Empire-Commonwealth. Extraordinarily well informed, from the archival side, and also with a wealth of secondary sources upon which to draw, he reflects on the conflict of nationalism with imperialism, on the inconsistencies of the 1921 settlement, and on the subsequent phases of readjustment and rejection. In the joining, in the belonging, and in the leaving, the Irish Dominion had made its mark.[65]

Perhaps, as a conclusion to this chapter, fleeting reference should be made to the contribution of Ireland to Britishnesss itself, through the long interrelationship of the two islands, the constant traffic of their peoples, and the long sojourn of so many Irish on the larger island. Keith Robbins, in his 1986–87 Ford Lectures, published as *Nineteenth-Century Britain: England, Scotland and Wales, The Making of a Nation* (Oxford, 1989), remarked early that he was formally excluding the 'Irish dimension' from his treatment of Britain, but felt that the ' "integration/non-integration" of Ireland requires a book in itself'. In 1989 Hugh Kearney published *The British Isles: A History of Four Nations* (Cambridge), determined to include Ireland's contribution to the common evolution, and stressed an inclusive 'Britannic' approach. Linda Colley, in her much shorter-spanned but none the less illuminating study *Britons: Forging the Nation, 1707–1837* (New Haven, 1992), again opted to leave out Ireland, though she did take proper note of the impact of the Union and of Catholic Emancipation. The great flood of Irish famine immigrants into Britain lay still ahead of her period, of course, but in any case none of these refreshing books set out to record, let alone assess fully, the cultural contribution of Irish people to what we think of as British (or even English, for that matter). A beginning can be provided by two books edited by Roger Swift and Sheridan Gilley,[66] and M. A. G. O'Tuathaigh's 'The Irish in Nineteenth-Century Britain: Problems of Integration' (*Transactions of the Royal Historical Society*, Fifth Series, XXXI, pp. 149–73), but this broader subject too requires a study of its own.

Mention should be made also of two other sources for the pursuit of enlightenment, one general and sweeping, the other more precise but nevertheless wide-ranging in its field: the Royal Historical Society's bibliography on CD-ROM: *The*

[65] For a useful assessment of the relevance of Ireland's long constitutional impact on Imperial evolution see Alan Ward, *Irish Constitutional Tradition: Responsible Government and Modern Ireland, 1782–1992* (Dublin, 1994).

[66] Roger Swift and Sheridan Gilley, eds., *The Irish in the Victorian City* (London, 1985) and *The Irish in Britain, 1815–1939* (London, 1989).

History of Britain, Ireland and the British Overseas; and the series of Australian-Irish Conference publications and bicentenary volumes, not all mentioned above. The Royal Historical Society project, under the general editorship of John Morrill, with the relevant Volume VII edited by Andrew Porter, will produce both a comprehensive computer data-bank and a shorter, hard copy, printed version. When completed, this should offer an invaluable source for researchers. At the more particular level, it seems that the Irish contribution to the development of Australia has been better recorded than to other countries thanks to the regular series of conferences, started by Oliver MacDonagh and Bill Mandle in Canberra in 1980.[67] Supplemented by two collections, edited by Colm Kiernan to anticipate the celebration of the bicentenary of modern Australia,[68] these contributions cover a wide range of topics—cultural, demographic, political, economic, and social—and should not be overlooked.

Finally, one further book should be mentioned, and not just because of its title. It is Keith Jeffery, ed., *'An Irish Empire'? Aspects of Ireland and the British Empire* (Manchester, 1996). It makes no proprietorial claim, in fact, but opens with an excellent summary of Ireland's modern contribution to the Empire, especially the decolonizing process, adds essays on film, sport, military traditions, and business, as well as aspects of the relationship with India, the tradition of Irish Unionists and the Empire, the celebration of Empire Day in Ireland, and 'Ulster resistance and loyalist rebellion in the empire'. It would seem to confirm that, while the bulk of Ireland is no longer a player in the game of Empire or Commonwealth, consideration of its contribution to both rightly continues.

[67] These Conferences were begun in Canberra in 1980, followed up in 1985, and by the time of the third to be held in that city (1988), two others had been held in Ireland. Since then two further Conferences have been held elsewhere in Australia, in Melbourne, 1991, and Hobart, 1995. Papers from the three Canberra Conferences have been published as: *Irish Culture and Nationalism* (Dublin, 1983), eds. Oliver MacDonagh, W. F. Mandle, and Pauric Travers; *Ireland and Irish Australia* (London, 1986), eds. Oliver MacDonagh and W. F. Mandle; and, with the same editors, *Irish-Australian Studies* (Canberra, 1989).

[68] Colm Kiernan, ed., *Australia and Ireland, 1788–1988: Bicentenary Essays* (Dublin, 1986), the fruit of an Irish-Australian Conference in Ireland in 1983; and Colm Kiernan, ed., *Ireland and Australia* (Dublin, 1984), the publication of the 1983 Radio Eireann Thomas Davis Lectures. See also n. 11 above, where the breadth of Donald Harman Akenson's contribution is acknowledged.

Select Bibliography

ISAAC BUTT, *Home Government for Ireland, Irish Federalism: Its Meaning, Its Objects and Its Hopes* (Dublin, 1870).

W. SHARMAN CRAWFORD, 'Federalism', 4 parts, *Freeman's Journal* (Dublin), 9, 13, 15 and 16 Nov. 1844, and *Northern Whig* (Belfast), 12, 14, 16 and 19 Nov. 1844.

ERSKINE CHILDERS, *The Framework of Home Rule* (London, 1911).

A. V. DICEY, 'Home Rule from an English Point of View' (July 1882), in *Law of the Constitution* (London, 1885), pp. 66–86.

CHARLES GAVAN DUFFY, *My Life in Two Hemispheres* (London, 1898).

JAMES ANTHONY FROUDE, *The English in Ireland in the Eighteenth Century*, 3 vols. (London, 1881).

W. E. GLADSTONE, *Special Aspects of the Irish Question: A Series of Reflections In and Since 1886, Collected from Various Sources and Reprinted* (London, 1892).

H. DUNCAN HALL, *The British Commonwealth of Nations: A Study of its Past and Future Development* (London, 1920).

W. K. HANCOCK, *Survey of British Commonwealth Affairs*, Vol. I, *Problems of Nationality, 1918–36* (London, 1937).

D. W. HARKNESS, *The Restless Dominion: The Irish Free State and the British Commonwealth of Nations, 1921–31* (London, 1969).

ARTHUR BERRIEDALE KEITH, *The Sovereignty of the British Dominions* (London, 1929).

J. E. KENDLE, *Ireland and the Federal Solution: The Debate Over the United Kingdom Constitution, 1870–1922* (Kingston, 1989).

W. E. H. LECKY, *A History of Ireland in the Eighteenth Century*, 3 vols. (London, 1892).

DEIRDRE MCMAHON, *Republicans and Imperialists: Anglo-Irish Relations in the 1930s* (New Haven, 1984).

NICHOLAS MANSERGH, 'The Implications of Eire's Relationship with the British Commonwealth of Nations', *International Affairs*, XXIV, 1 (Jan. 1948), pp. 1–18.

—— *Survey of British Commonwealth Affairs: Problems of External Policy, 1931–39* (London, 1952).

—— *Problems of Wartime Co-operation and Change, 1939–1952* (London, 1958).

—— *The Unresolved Question: The Anglo-Irish Settlement and Its Undoing, 1912–72* (New Haven, 1991).

F. S. OLIVER (Pacificus), *Federalism and Home Rule* (London, 1910).

Lord SALISBURY, 'Disintegration', *Quarterly Review*, CLVI (Oct. 1883), pp. 559–95.

BRENDAN SEXTON, *Ireland and the Crown, 1922–36: The Governor-Generalship of the Irish Free State* (Blackrock, Co. Dublin, 1989).

K. C. WHEARE, *The Statute of Westminster and Dominion Status* (Oxford, 1938).

7

The British West Indies

B. W. HIGMAN

British imperialism had an extended history in the Caribbean. The majority of the sixteen modern Caribbean territories which were part of the British Empire obtained their political independence only in recent years, beginning in 1962 with Jamaica, and Trinidad and Tobago; a number of them appear destined to remain colonies of Britain into the twenty-first century (Montserrat, Anguilla, Turks and Caicos, the Cayman Islands, and the British Virgin Islands, for example). Several of the territories were central elements of the first British Empire, being taken by the British in the early seventeenth century (Barbados, St Kitts, Nevis, Antigua, Montserrat, and the Bahamas) or in the second half of that century (Jamaica, Anguilla, Barbuda, and the Virgin Islands). All of these had British colonial histories extending over 300 years, substantially longer than the experience of the typical British colony. Even Caribbean territories such as Dominica, St Lucia, St Vincent, Grenada, Tobago, Trinidad, and Guiana, which did not enter the British Empire until the late eighteenth century, remained a part of it longer than, for example, Virginia, New South Wales, or the Gold Coast.

In spite of the longevity of the British colonial experience in the Caribbean, and the importance of those colonies in the economy of the first British Empire, the historiography of the West Indies has proved a persistently underdeveloped field. Indeed, as the chapters of P. J. Marshall and Stephen Foster in this volume make clear, twentieth-century histories of the first British Empire and of the American colonies have often slighted the West Indies, and the same is true of British economic histories of the seventeenth and eighteenth centuries. At the same time, the West Indies have been more likely to appear in general accounts of British Imperial policy and administration than in accounts of the internal histories of the territories themselves. This tendency can be seen as more or less coterminous with the trajectory of imperialism in the region and the granting of political independence in the 1960s.

In an essay published in 1966, D. A. G. Waddell identified three phases in the

The author thanks Stephen Foster and Howard Johnson for their comments on a draft of this chapter.

historiography of the British West Indies. The first phase, according to Waddell, extended from the beginnings of British colonization to the early twentieth century, and was dominated by British sojourners whose histories were centred on local knowledge and events, as seen through the eyes of the Imperial white male insider. Most of the works written in this phase were portmanteau descriptions of the colonies, few of them paying particular attention to questions of historical interpretation, and even fewer taking advantage of documentary sources available in local record-keeping institutions. The second phase, effectively covering the first half of the twentieth century, saw professional historians enter the field, most of them working from British or United States universities, making extensive use of documentary materials located in metropolitan archives but rarely spending much time in the colonies. The perspective of most of this work was that of the Imperial outsider. Waddell contended that the third phase in the historiography began in the early 1950s and, when he wrote, was 'as yet in its early stages'. This phase, he predicted, 'may be expected to be dominated by the West Indian professional historian'.[1] All three of these phases in the development of West Indian historiography present fruitful opportunities for analysis. The present chapter, however, will concentrate on the third of Waddell's phases.

It is perhaps significant that in the periods before Waddell's third phase there was no attempt to study the history of the writing of West Indian history. The first substantial work was Elsa V. Goveia's *A Study on the Historiography of the British West Indies to the End of the Nineteenth Century*, published in 1956. Goveia, born in British Guiana in 1925, studied at the University of London, where she obtained her doctorate. In 1950 she joined the newly founded Department of History at the University College of the West Indies (a college of the University of London) at Mona, Jamaica, and went on to become the first Professor of West Indian History at that University in 1961. Her work on historiography, published before the appearance of her substantial contributions to the history of the West Indies, was focused very clearly on the period before 1900, though she believed her findings 'not irrelevant to the discussion that is still unfinished'. Changes in the interpretation of British West Indian history, she contended, were not simply to be defined by chronological periods. Rather, to appreciate properly such change it was necessary 'to seek, beyond the narrative of events, wider understanding of the thoughts, habits, and institutions of a whole society'. At the same time, Goveia asserted that 'humanism is as necessary an element of objective historical writing as is detachment'.[2] The interpretation of race, and the role of racism in defining

[1] D. A. G. Waddell, 'The British West Indies', in Robin W. Winks, ed., *The Historiography of the British Empire-Commonwealth: Trends, Interpretations, Resources* (Durham, NC, 1966), p. 344.

[2] Elsa V. Goveia, *A Study on the Historiography of the British West Indies to the End of the Nineteenth Century* (Mexico City, 1956), pp. 170, 176–77.

the assumptions of the early historians of the West Indies, were central to Goveia's reading of their narratives.

Race and racism were similarly prominent themes in the second major work on the historiography of the territories, Eric Williams's *British Historians and the West Indies* (London), published in 1966. Born in Trinidad, Williams won an island scholarship and travelled to study at Oxford, where he received his D.Phil. in 1938. After a period in the United States, he returned home to lead the people of Trinidad and Tobago to independence and become the nation's first Prime Minister. Although he did not continue in the guild of professional historians, and in fact largely isolated himself from the development of the discipline in the academy, Williams wrote and published a great deal. He sometimes called history-writing his hobby, and proudly told his readers how he had completed books during the brief holiday periods of Christmas and Carnival while the people of Trinidad and Tobago engaged in bacchanal. *British Historians and the West Indies* was no exception, but Williams argued that ultimately 'it is the heart that matters more than the head', and explained that his aim was 'principally to emancipate his compatriots whom the historical writings that he analyses sought to depreciate and to imprison for all time in the inferior status to which these writings sought to condemn them'. In fact the British historians selected for analysis were a somewhat eclectic group, with the significant omission of Vincent T. Harlow, Williams's Oxford mentor, whose racial assumptions as expressed in his *History of Barbados, 1625–1685* (Oxford, 1926) were equally deserving of criticism. Williams sought to identify the historical field as 'the battleground on which imperialist politics struggle against nationalist politics', and history-writing as a weapon in the fight against the return of imperialism in new forms. Williams argued vehemently that 'the West Indian historian of the future has a crucial role to play in the education of the West Indian people in their own history and in the merciless exposure of the shams, the inconsistencies, the prejudices of metropolitan historians'.[3]

These two pioneer works of Goveia and Williams have not been followed by the substantial historiographical monographs that might have been expected. West Indian historians of the last thirty years have shown no great taste for historiographical reflection or discussion of issues in the philosophy of history. Perhaps the passion to expose the false assumptions of colonialist historians, a passion born in the labour disturbances of the 1930s and during the movement to federation and independence, has lessened in the post-colonial world of the West Indies.

3 Eric Williams, *British Historians and the British West Indies* (London, 1966), pp. 12, 234. Vincent T. Harlow, *A History of Barbados* (Oxford, 1926); Eric Williams, *Inward Hunger: The Education of a Prime Minister* (London, 1969); Elsa V. Goveia, 'New Shibboleths for Old', *Caribbean Quarterly*, X (1964), pp. 48–54; Paul Sutton, 'The Historian as Politician: Eric Williams and Walter Rodney', in Alistair Hennessy, ed., *Intellectuals in the Twentieth-Century Caribbean*, 2 vols. (London, 1992), I, pp. 98–114.

Energies have been directed to rewriting the history and effectively extracting it from the history of the British Empire, rather than concentrating much on the theory, method, and technique underlying that rewriting. Only a handful of historiographical essays have been produced since the books of Goveia and Williams, most of them in bibliographical or review article mode.[4] The UNESCO *General History of the Caribbean*, which has been in the making for a decade, is to include a volume completely devoted to method and historiography, but this history considers the Caribbean at large and does not respect the territorial boundaries imposed by European imperialism.

An important general feature of history-writing in the West Indies since 1950 has been an effort to think of the British colonies as part of a larger region and a larger world to subvert the fragmentation rooted in the geophysical history of the archipelago and exploited by European imperialism. This means that historians no longer attempt to write general histories of the British West Indies, but always seek to include the British colonies within the scope of the entire Caribbean mosaic, however the limits of the region may be defined. The effort has not been completely successful, because of the very history of imperialism that has inserted the fundamental difficulties of language and communication. Knowledge, including historical knowledge, remains confined within old Imperial geographies to a significant extent. The modern Anglophone Caribbean is not coterminous with the former British West Indies, but educational, trade, sport, and communication systems continue to tie the former colonies together through formal institutions and sentimental attachments. Higher levels of loyalty generally go beyond the region, to Africa, Asia, and parts of Europe. In this setting, the University of the West Indies (which ceased to be a college of the University of London in 1962) has played a vital role as a truly regional institution, with contributing territories spread throughout the former British colonial sites, with the exception of Guyana which has its own university. The University of the West Indies has three interdependent Departments of History, based at the major campuses in Jamaica, Trinidad, and Barbados, and these are closely linked through curricula and assessment to the College of the Bahamas. Links outside the University of the West Indies system, to territories descended from the Spanish, French, and Dutch

[4] Woodville K. Marshall, 'A Review of Historical Writing on the Commonwealth Caribbean since *c*.1940', *Social and Economic Studies*, XXIV (1975), pp. 271–307; O. Nigel Bolland, 'Creolization and Creole Societies: A Cultural Nationalist View of Caribbean Social History', in Hennessy, *Intellectuals*, I, pp. 50–79; William A. Green, 'The Creolization of Caribbean History: The Emancipation Era and a Critique of Dialectical Analysis', *Journal of Imperial and Commonwealth History*, XIV (1986), pp. 149–69; B. W. Higman, 'Theory, Method and Technique in Caribbean Social History', *Journal of Caribbean History*, XX (1985–86), pp. 1–29; and 'Small Islands, Large Questions: Post-Emancipation Historiography of the Leeward Islands', in Karen Fog Olwig, ed., *Small Islands, Large Questions: Society, Culture and Resistance in the Post-Emancipation Caribbean* (London, 1995).

empires, remain tenuous, with little exchange of staff and students, though courses offered increasingly include specialized periods in the history of Haiti, Cuba, and Puerto Rico, for example, and interchange occurs within the conferences of the global Association of Caribbean Historians founded in 1968.

Thus the writing and teaching of Caribbean history has developed in two distinct directions. On the one hand, regional histories have increasingly aspired to a pan-Caribbean coverage, while separate histories of the British West Indies as a unit have largely disappeared. On the other, specialized monographs have rarely ventured beyond the old Imperial boundaries, and most remain focused on single territories or the groupings defined by Empire. General histories of the British colonies in the Caribbean were common in the eighteenth and nineteenth centuries but petered out with the coming of independence. The last major example appears to be Sir Alan Burns's *History of the British West Indies*, 2nd edn. (London, 1965), first published in 1954 with federation in the air; a revised edition, bringing the narrative beyond independence to the end of 1964, appeared with an unchanged title. In spite of his title, Burns in fact included a good deal of material on territories outside the British system, particularly when he reached the twentieth century.

Looking to the new markets for West Indian history in high schools and universities, a number of texts were produced to conform to the rapidly changing definitions of the boundaries of the region's history. In 1956 John Parry, the first Professor of History at the University College, and Philip Sherlock published *A Short History of the West Indies*, which tackled the entire Caribbean but was 'particularly addressed to readers in the British Caribbean'. Another joint product of the newly established University College was *The Making of the West Indies*, published in 1961. Its scope was similar to that of Parry and Sherlock, admitting to an increasingly strong focus on the British colonies 'when the British West Indies were finally determined' in the early nineteenth century. It was directed at the requirements of the syllabuses of the Oxford and Cambridge Examination Board and of the Cambridge Syndicate. The more recent establishment of the Caribbean Examinations Council provided an internal alternative to metropolitan assessment of high-school students in the Anglophone Caribbean and generated a new round of texts. Once again, however, there was conflict between a desire to comprehend the entire Caribbean and a continuing bias towards the experience of the British territories. Outside the high-school textbook market, writers of general histories published in English since 1960 have preferred Caribbean to West Indies in their titles, and have been successful to varying degrees in achieving a regional objective. But almost all of these general histories in English, like most of the teaching of West Indian history in the Anglophone territories, maintain a lingering attachment to the region as defined by Empire, including the mainland countries of Belize

(British Honduras) and Guyana (British Guiana), and making the occasional glance towards Suriname (Dutch Guiana) and Cayenne (French Guiana), but excluding almost all of the Hispanic mainland from analysis of most periods.[5]

Specialized monographs treating particular periods or themes with an exclusive focus on the British colonies as a unit began to appear in the second phase of the historiography, the first half of the twentieth century. Examples include Frank Pitman's *The Development of the British West Indies, 1700–1763* (New Haven, 1917), Lowell Ragatz's *The Fall of the Planter Class in the British Caribbean, 1763–1833: A Study in Social and Economic History* (New York, 1928), William Law Mathieson's *British Slave Emancipation, 1838-1849* (London, 1932), and W. L. Burn's *Emancipation and Apprenticeship in the British West Indies* (London, 1937), all of which gave substantial attention to the Imperial framework. To this group must be added the seminal work of Eric Williams, *Capitalism and Slavery* (Chapel Hill, 1944), the first significant book to be published on British West Indian history by a West Indian academic historian. *Capitalism and Slavery* is not a piece of British West Indian history seen from a peculiarly West Indian perspective, but rather it reaches for the significant issues in Atlantic and British history. In a sense, then, it is truly Imperial history, through a modern globalized lens, taking off from the work of the Americans Pitman and Ragatz.

In the third phase, since 1950, there has been a continuing flow of work based on the British West Indies as a unit of analysis, often recognizing the possibilities for comparison provided by the diversity of experience within the system. A large proportion of these more recent studies are concerned with slavery and emancipation, an area which has a well-established comparative method.[6] Slavery has also provided the focus for a number of works which purport to study the institution throughout the British Empire, but in fact have a relatively heavy emphasis on the West Indies.[7] Political and constitutional history has also been written from

[5] J. H. Parry and P. M. Sherlock, *A Short History of the West Indies* (London, 1956; 2nd edn., 1963; 3rd edn., 1971), p. v; F. R. Augier, S. C. Gordon, D. G. Hall, and M. Reckord, *The Making of the West Indies* (London, 1960), p. x; Franklin W. Knight, *The Caribbean: The Genesis of a Fragmented Nationalism* (New York, 1978; 2nd edn., 1990). Jan Rogozinski, *A Brief History of the Caribbean: From the Arawak and the Carib to the Present* (New York, 1992), is unusual in concentrating exclusively on the islands.

[6] Richard S. Dunn, *Sugar and Slaves: The Rise of the Planter Class in the English West Indies, 1624–1713* (Chapel Hill, NC, 1972); Richard S. Sheridan, *Sugar and Slavery: An Economic History of the British West Indies, 1623–1775* (Baltimore, 1974); William A. Green, *British Slave Emancipation: The Sugar Colonies and the Great Experiment, 1830–1865* (London, 1976); Michael Craton, *Testing the Chains: Resistance to Slavery in the British West Indies* (Ithaca, NY, 1982); B. W. Higman, *Slave Populations of the British Caribbean, 1807–1834* (Baltimore, 1984); J. R. Ward, *British West Indian Slavery, 1750–1834: The Process of Amelioration* (Oxford, 1988).

[7] Michael Craton, *Sinews of Empire: A Short History of British Slavery* (New York, 1974); James Walvin, *Black Ivory: A History of British Slavery* (London, 1993).

the viewpoint of the British West Indies as a whole, but these topics became relatively unpopular after about 1970.[8] The Imperial, British aspect of the subject has generally proved central in all of these works. War and trade have also been studied at the British West Indian level, most often with some further unifying thread employed.[9] Cricket, which along with the University is one of the few truly regional institutions initially defined by the British Empire, has also found its historians, and these have increasingly come from the academy.[10]

Monographs concerned with the history of individual colonies and territories have been much more common in the production of professional historians than regional narratives, and these 'local' works rarely concern themselves with questions of 'Britishness' or Empire. These are the works most readily written from a West Indian perspective, whether the authors be West Indian or outsiders. The genre has also proved popular because of the advantages offered in archives and continuity of setting. These advantages do not exist for every territory, of course, as several of them were passed back and forth by the British, French, and Dutch, creating language challenges for the historian. Parochialism creates its own problems, West Indian historians tending to write the histories of their own particular territories.

In the monographic as well as the regional literature, certain themes have dominated the historiography of the modern phase. Some of these themes and issues equally concerned historians from the earlier phases, but others have emerged in response to West Indian nationalisms and the broader pattern of change in the production of histories in the academy globally. Professionalization has meant an increasing insertion of West Indian historical scholarship into the international system, and exposure to ideological tendencies beyond those rooted in the region.

The long period of British colonialism in the Caribbean is broadly divided at 1838, the year marking the formal abolition of slavery. Slavery was a central feature of British West Indian economy and society from its very beginning, with only a few colonies maintaining significant free, white populations beyond their initial decades of settlement. In looking at slavery in the British West

[8] Frederick G. Spurdle, *Early West Indian Government* (Palmerston North, New Zealand, n.d. [1964]); D. J. Murray, *The West Indies and the Development of Colonial Government, 1801–1834* (Oxford, 1965); H. A. Will, *Constitutional Change in the British West Indies, 1880–1903* (Oxford, 1970).

[9] Frances Armytage, *The Free Port System in the British West Indies: A Study in Commercial Policy, 1766–1822* (London, 1953); Stephen Alexander Fortune, *Merchants and Jews: The Struggle for British West Indian Commerce, 1650–1750* (Gainsville, Fla., 1984); Selwyn H. H. Carrington, *The British West Indies During the American Revolution* (Dordrecht, 1988).

[10] C. L. R. James, *Beyond a Boundary* (London, 1963); Michael Manley, *A History of West Indies Cricket* (London, 1988); Hilary McD. Beckles and Brian Stoddart, eds., *Liberation Cricket* (Kingston, 1995).

Indies, scholars have largely been concerned with questions that apply to slave societies generally, and the methods and approaches they have employed have much in common with the historiography of slave societies throughout the Americas. This is not meant to suggest that West Indian historians have been mere borrowers; in many cases they have been creators, particularly on the conceptual level. Probably the most influential work in this area has been that centred on competing models of social organization. Goveia employed a slave society model, in which force is the ultimate source of social power. Her model drew heavily on the ideas of the Jamaican anthropologist M. G. Smith, who in turn derived his plural society theory from J. S. Furnivall's studies of tropical Asia. Smith applied the plural society model to British West Indian slavery in a paper published in 1953.[11] In the 1960s Orlando Patterson, a Jamaican sociologist, produced a full-scale study of slavery in Jamaica with an even greater emphasis on anomie. Kamau (Edward) Brathwaite, from Barbados, almost simultaneously produced a very different picture of Jamaica during slavery, stressing the creative aspects of what he termed a creole society. Brathwaite's expansion of the concept of creolization from language to a broad range of cultural interaction has stimulated much debate, and has been particularly influential in the development of a more nuanced portrayal of slavery in the West Indies and elsewhere.[12]

These competing models of West Indian society during slavery have proved focal in discussion of more specialized aspects of the history. For example, they inform analysis of the internal marketing system, in which slaves in several of the British West Indian colonies were allocated provision grounds for the cultivation of their own food, but quickly came to produce a surplus and so inserted their commodities into the wider system of exchange. The system has sometimes been characterized as an arrangement imposed from above, a creation of the plantation as total institution, but increasingly the slaves have been attributed an active role and a degree of independence, so that the whole system may be viewed as evidence of creolization. Allied to this more recent conceptualization of the internal marketing system has been a characterization of West Indian slaves as labour negotiators, actively seeking to determine the conditions of their existence rather than being mere objects whose living conditions depended on the master's treatment of

[11] Elsa V. Goveia, *Slave Society in the British Leeward Islands at the End of the Eighteenth Century* (New Haven, 1965); M. G. Smith, 'Some Aspects of Social Structure in the British Caribbean about 1820', *Social and Economic Studies*, I (1953), pp. 55–79.

[12] Orlando Patterson, *The Sociology of Slavery: An Analysis of the Origins, Development, and Structure of Negro Slave Society in Jamaica* (London, 1967); Edward Brathwaite, *The Development of Creole Society in Jamaica, 1770–1820* (Oxford, 1971).

them in law and custom.[13] This more complex vision can also be identified in discussion of slave 'resistance'. Rather than seeing resistance as confined to the more obvious acts of rebellion, sabotage, and 'running away', historians have come to understand it as a part of a whole range of ambiguous behaviours.[14] Arguably, these more complex readings of the period of slavery parallel changing interpretations of West Indian independence and the post-colonial world.

Another aspect of West Indian slavery that has received considerable attention is its demographic history. Extending beyond the British West Indian colonies, there has been a growing interest in the Atlantic slave trade, particularly in terms of the biological and cultural history of Caribbean populations. Some of this work has been part of the numbers game, building on the baseline estimates of Philip D. Curtin in *The Atlantic Slave Trade: A Census* (Madison, 1969), but with an increasing concern for the components of the trade in terms of African ethnic origins, gender, and language. A continuing debate surrounds the causes of natural decrease in the slave population of the British West Indies. Quantitative studies have encouraged closer attention to the diversity of the slave experience in the British West Indies, pushing analysis beyond the sugar plantation to other crops (such as coffee and cotton), other economic activities (livestock production, timber getting, fishing), and other contexts (especially urban). It has become clear that the demographic experience of slaves in these varied contexts was often strongly contrasted. This scholarly enterprise has also led to a fruitful analysis of the 'marginal' territories of the British Caribbean, such as the Bahamas and Belize, which never produced sugar and were only slightly touched by the plantation system.[15]

An important theoretical issue linking the history of slavery to the history of the post-emancipation period is the question of the causes of slavery and coerced

[13] Sidney W. Mintz and Douglas Hall, *The Origins of the Jamaican Internal Marketing System* (New Haven, 1960); Robert Dirks, *The Black Saturnalia: Conflict and its Ritual Expression on British West Indian Slave Plantations* (Gainsville, Fla., 1987); Roderick A McDonald, *The Economy and Material Culture of Slaves: Goods and Chattels on the Sugar Plantations of Jamaica and Louisiana* (Baton Rouge, La., 1993).

[14] Craton, *Testing the Chains*; Hilary Beckles, *Black Rebellion in Barbados: The Struggle Against Slavery, 1627–1838* (Bridgetown, Barbados, 1984); David Barry Gaspar, *Bondmen and Rebels: A Study of Master–Slave Relations in Antigua, With Implications for Colonial British America* (Baltimore, 1985); E. Kofi Agorsah, ed., *Maroon Heritage: Archaeological, Ethnographic and Historical Perspectives* (Mona, Jamaica, 1994).

[15] Kenneth F. Kiple, *The Caribbean Slave: A Biological History* (Cambridge, 1984); B. W. Higman, *Slave Population and Economy in Jamaica, 1807–1834* (Cambridge, 1976); Richard B. Sheridan, *Doctors and Slaves: A Medical and Demographic History of Slavery in the British West Indies, 1680–1834* (Cambridge, 1985); Michael Craton and Gail Saunders, *Islanders in the Stream: A History of the Bahamian People*, Vol. I (Athens, Ga., 1992); O. Nigel Bolland, *The Formation of a Colonial Society: Belize, from Conquest to Crown Colony* (Baltimore, 1977).

labour systems generally. One of the leading explanations is based on the ratio of labour to land. In its simple form, this theory can be traced back to the seminal ideas of Herman Merivale as expounded in his *Lectures on Colonization and Colonies*, first delivered in 1839–41 at Oxford where he was Professor of Political Economy.[16] These ideas were later taken up by Eric Williams and Elsa Goveia to explain both the establishment of slavery and its overthrow. For the post-emancipation period, the ratio has been used to explain why some of the British West Indian colonies imported large numbers of indentured labourers whereas other, thickly populated, colonies came to export labour after 1838. The theory held sway until a debate between Nigel Bolland and William Green made it appear a little too simple and in need of a complexity that, Bolland argued, might be supplied by a dialectical approach.[17]

The post-emancipation world of the British West Indies has been a period of fascination, beginning with the Imperial historians Mathieson and Burn before 1940. Most territories now boast one or more narratives. Apart from the questions of labour and immigration, these works have had a strong political focus, often with conflicting interpretations of individual colonies. On the other hand, the demographic and social history of the period 1838–65 remains relatively impoverished compared to the overall richness of the work on the period of slavery.[18]

Histories of the hundred years from 1865 to decolonization have emerged slowly and spottily. Detailed work on economic and demographic change has been achieved only partially for some of the larger territories. Migration from Jamaica and Barbados to work on the Panama Canal has attracted a series of historians, but other aspects of the modern diaspora are less well understood. The history of tourism, another defining feature of the twentieth-century Caribbean, has been written only for Jamaica. Political and constitutional developments have been better served, perhaps reflecting interest in the new arrangements required by independence and the general failure of movements towards closer association between the West Indian territories. Radical political ideas, as expressed particularly by Garveyism and Rastafarianism, have been given a lot of attention, perhaps because of their international significance. Popular culture, on the other hand, has

[16] Herman Merivale, *Lectures on Colonization and Colonies Delivered before the University of Oxford in 1839, 1840, and 1841* (London, 1861).

[17] O. Nigel Bolland, 'Systems of Domination after Slavery: The Control of Land and Labour in the British West Indies after 1838', *Comparative Studies in Society and History* (hereafter *CSSH*), XXIII (1981), pp. 591–619; William A. Green, 'The Perils of Comparative History: Belize and the British Sugar Colonies after Slavery', *CSSH*, XXVI (1986), pp. 112–19; Bolland, 'Reply', ibid., pp. 120–25.

[18] Philip D. Curtin, *Two Jamaicas: The Role of Ideas in a Tropical Colony, 1830–1865* (Cambridge, Mass., 1955); Douglas Hall, *Free Jamaica, 1838–1865: An Economic History* (New Haven, 1959); Brian L. Moore, *Race, Power and Social Segmentation in Colonial Society: Guyana after Slavery, 1838–91* (New York, 1987).

been largely neglected, in spite of the importance of music and dance for contemporary West Indian and world cultures.[19]

Efforts to rethink the history of the territories which once formed the British West Indies and to rewrite that history from a West Indian point of view have been only partially successful. Having rejected the Imperial or metropolitan focus, historians have still been faced with the problem of choosing between a (British) West Indian perspective, a broader Caribbean perspective, an Atlantic or diasporic perspective, and a local or island-level perspective. The fragmented nationalisms of the modern Caribbean reflect the Imperial realities of the past, and some questions can be conceptualized efficiently only by restoring to the narrative the organizing principles of Empire. The tension between the search for a truly creole vision of the Caribbean past and the necessity of understanding the visible ruins of colonialism cannot easily be resolved. What is emerging is a much more complex picture, in which the diversity of environments and contexts of life within the Caribbean are seen to contribute to the growth of a vital creole culture ambiguously rooted in Empire.

19 Bonham C. Richardson, *Panama Money in Barbados, 1900–1920* (Knoxville, Tenn., 1985); Frank Fonda Taylor, *To Hell with Paradise: A History of the Jamaican Tourist Industry* (Pittsburgh, Pa., 1993); Rupert Lewis and Patrick Bryan, eds., *Garvey: His Life and Impact* (Mona, Jamaica, 1988); Errol Hill, *The Jamaican Stage, 1655–1900: Profile of a Colonial Theatre* (Amherst, Mass., 1992).

Select Bibliography

O. Nigel Bolland, 'Creolization and Creole Societies: A Cultural Nationalist View of Caribbean Social History', in Alistair Hennessy, ed., *Intellectuals in the Twentieth-Century Caribbean*, 2 vols. (London, 1992), Vol. I, pp. 50–79.

Elsa V. Goveia, *A Study on the Historiography of the British West Indies to the End of the Nineteenth Century* (Mexico City, 1956).

William A. Green, 'The Creolization of Caribbean History: The Emancipation Era and a Critique of Dialectical Analysis', *Journal of Imperial and Commonwealth History*, XIV (1986), pp. 149–69.

B. W. Higman, 'Theory, Method and Technique in Caribbean Social History', *Journal of Caribbean History*, XX (1985–86), pp. 1–29.

—— 'Small Islands, Large Questions: Post-Emancipation Historiography of the Leeward Islands', in Karen Fog Olwig, ed., *Small Islands, Large Questions: Society, Culture and Resistance in the Post-Emancipation Caribbean* (London, 1995).

Woodville K. Marshall, 'A Review of Historical Writing on the Commonwealth Caribbean Since c.1940', *Social and Economic Studies*, XXIV (1975), pp. 271–307.

Paul Sutton, 'The Historian as Politician: Eric Williams and Walter Rodney', in Alistair Hennessy, ed., *Intellectuals in the Twentieth-Century Caribbean*, 2 vols. (London, 1992), Vol. I.

D. A. G. Waddell, 'The British West Indies', in Robin W. Winks, ed., *The Historiography of the British-Empire Commonwealth: Trends, Interpretations, and Resources* (Durham, NC, 1966).

Eric Williams, *Capitalism and Slavery* (Chapel Hill, NC, 1944).

—— *British Historians and the West Indies* (London, 1966).

8

Canada and the Empire

D. R. OWRAM

In 1929 the University of Toronto historian, Chester Martin, wrote a work with the ambitious title of *Empire and Commonwealth*. It was nothing less than an attempt to chronicle and explain the evolution of the British Empire in North America, from the fall of Quebec to the recent Imperial Conference of 1926. There was no bibliography because, as Martin said 'bibliographies of these studies would amount to a bibliography of Canadian, to say nothing of early American history'.[1] He then proceeded to centre the story of the evolution of the Empire around one event—the 'transition from governance to self-government in British North America'.[2]

Martin's work was a major contribution to Canadian historical writing, reflecting the cumulative efforts of the first generation of professional Canadian historians. His belief that all Canadian history was tied to the evolution of Imperial relations was thus significant. For before 1960 Canadian writing about the Empire was characterized by two major tendencies. First, the course and significance of the Empire has been seen through a Canadian prism. In Canadian historiography, as in many other former colonies, Imperial history has really been interpreted as the bilateral study of Canadian–British events. In Canada's case, though, this means more than a Canadian perspective on international events. Canadian historians have tended to interpret the Empire and Commonwealth almost as a Canadian invention.

Secondly, as Carl Berger put it in 1970, in at least English Canada 'Imperialism was one form of nationalism'.[3] Canada's sense of its own identity was closely connected to its British ties. Few Canadian historians have seen the link to the Empire as anything but voluntary and, for the most part, as protection for a small nation

[1] Chester Martin, *Empire and Commonwealth: Studies in Governance and Self-Government in Canada* (Oxford, 1929), p. viii. For a discussion of early American and British North American history see Vol. II, chap. by Peter Marshall and Vol. III, chap. by Ged Martin.

[2] Martin, *Empire and Commonwealth*, p. xiv.

[3] Carl Berger, *Sense of Power: Studies in the Idea of Canadian Imperialism, 1867–1914* (Toronto, 1970), p. 259.

in a large and potentially hostile world. Even in French Canada, where Imperial sentiment has been understandably less pronounced, the blame for colonialism has tended to be put on local zealots rather than on the British government. Not all Canadian historians were as enthusiastic as University of Toronto historian George M. Wrong. 'Britain controls today', Wrong wrote in 1909, 'the destinies of some 350,000,000 alien people, unable as yet to govern themselves, and easy victims to rapine and injustice, unless a strong arm guards them. She is giving them a rule that has its faults, no doubt, but such, I would make bold to affirm, as no conquering state ever before gave to a dependent people.'[4] The tenor, if not the excessive rhetoric of Wrong, was common among early Canadian historians. In more subdued form it shaped the interpretation of Canadian history into the latter part of the twentieth century.

The place of the Empire in Canadian historiography is closely connected to defining national myths. In the nineteenth century British North American colonial identity was linked to two key Imperial events. The first was the conquest of New France in 1763. From the beginning, Anglophone historians had tended to see the conquest as a providential event. Thus, to give one rather extravagant example, an 1818 writer commented that 'how happy, then, ought the Canadians to be, that God in his providence, has severed them from the ancient stock to which they belonged'.[5] The interpretive framework behind such sentiments, however, was not established until the American Francis Parkman wrote during the late nineteenth century. In works such as *A Half Century of Conflict* Parkman wrote of the romantic, backward, and doomed *ancien régime* of New France in its contest against the rising British Empire.[6] The moral was unequivocal. The course of progress lay in the spread of the British Empire, its constitution, and commerce. A later generation of academic historians would modify and eventually repudiate Parkman's teleological approach. For many decades, though, his interpretations were echoed in popular histories and even by those who claimed to be revising him. Chester Martin (1914) and George Wrong (1928) both looked to Parkman for their understanding of the conquest of New France.[7]

Not surprisingly, French Canadian interpretations of the conquest were somewhat different. Even for many of them, however, the moral in the separation from

[4] Carl Berger, *The Writing of Canadian History: Aspects of Canadian Historical Writing in English-Speaking Canada*, 2nd edn. (Toronto, 1986), p. 11.

[5] Michel Brunet, 'The British Conquest and the Canadiens', in *Canadian Historical Readings: Approaches to Canadian History* (Toronto, 1967), pp. 84–98, 86.

[6] Francis Parkman, *The Old Regime in Canada* (Boston, 1874); *A Half Century of Conflict* (Boston, 1910); *Montcalm and Wolfe* (Boston, 1910).

[7] Chester Martin, *The Fall of Canada: A Chapter in the History of the Seven Years War* (Oxford, 1914); George M. Wrong, *The Rise and Fall of New France* (Toronto, 1928).

France was ambivalent. The surrender of their homeland to a foreign and Protestant Empire was hardly something to be celebrated. Nor were they likely to accept Parkman's implication that progress had triumphed over reaction.[8] Yet the tragedy of the conquest was inseparable from the French Revolution less than a generation later. For many conservative and clerical nineteenth-century historians there was a degree of 'providentialism' about the conquest.[9] Secularism and terror had gripped the former motherland, while the British Empire had at least tolerated the continuance of a conservative Catholicism. This led some to praise the English monarchy as a natural substitute for the *ancien régime*. Others remained suspicious of this Anglophone nation with its spirit of unbridled commercialism. Even for them, however, the conquest may have been a fortuitous event, protecting New France from the horrors of 1789.

The second key event in the development of a Canadian mythology of Empire was the rupture of that Empire during the American Revolution and, most importantly, the decision of some to resist the rupture. These were the 'Loyalists'. They fought for the Crown in the dreadful years of 1776–83 and, when they lost, exiled themselves to new lands in British North America. Two new colonies were formed as a result, Upper Canada (Ontario) and New Brunswick. More importantly, the mythology of sacrifice became the British North American means of giving their new set of colonies an identity distinct from the former colonies to the south. Over the decades the myth of the Loyalists was reinforced by the continued threat of American encroachment. The War of 1812 was especially important in this regard and served, in the words of one historian, to turn 'prejudice into a cult'.[10] By the later nineteenth century the notion of Canadian loyalty to the Empire and of Imperial membership as a bulwark against American 'manifest destiny' was well entrenched as an expression of the Canadian national consciousness.[11]

During the high Imperial era pre-dating the First World War the idea of loyalty and Empire was automatically a part of any English Canadian historical work. A 1914 piece by Duncan McArthur summed up the standard perspective: 'The declaration of independence of the United States was likewise the assertion of the individuality of the Canadian nation within the British Empire.'[12] Similar themes were expressed in works like John George Bourinot's *Canada Under British Rule, 1760–1905* (1909) and William Kingsford's massive, ten-volume *History of*

[8] For a twentieth-century commentary on Parkman, see Brunet, 'The British Conquest and the Canadiens', pp. 84–98.

[9] Serge Gagnon, *Quebec and its Historians, 1840 to 1920* (Montreal, 1982), p. 64.

[10] Fred Landon, *Western Ontario and the American Frontier* (Toronto, 1967), p. 23.

[11] S. F. Wise and R. C. Brown, *Canada Views the United States* (Toronto, 1967), pp. 109–10.

[12] Duncan McArthur, 'Canada Under the Quebec Act', in Adam Shortt and Arthur Doughty, eds., *Canada and Its Provinces*, Vol. III, *British Dominion* (Toronto, 1914), p. 117.

Canada.[13] As military tensions increased in Europe, English Canadian writing became all the more fervent. Even 'disappointments' such as the British handling of the Alaska Boundary dispute could not shake the fundamental faith in the 'greatest Empire the world had ever seen'.

The same trends that promoted English Canadian enthusiasm were making the Empire more problematic for French Canadians. An accord of sorts still continued between the Roman Catholic Church and the voices of the Crown and Empire. A succession of events, however, from the Boer (South African) War onward, began to raise concerns that loyalty to the British Empire might mean commitment in money and lives to overseas concerns. All the French Canadian fears seemed to come true when the terrible slaughter of First World War led in 1917 to conscription and electoral division along linguistic lines. Given such divisions, the enthusiasm for Empire ranged from muted to hostile. Thus, when *Le Devoir* editor Henri Bourassa assessed the real meaning of the American Revolution from a perspective of the early twentieth century, he commented sardonically that the Quebecois had little enthusiasm for either the English or the Americans. Ultimately, however, the English were further away and the French Canadian hated them less.

Yet it would be wrong to overstate the differences between French Canadian and English Canadian writings. Even in the pre-war English Canadian patriotic writings there existed the germ of a second major school of interpretation. English Canadian historians interpreted local events as fundamental to the creation of the modern Empire and, eventually, the Commonwealth. The argument went as follows. The British North American colonies were a laboratory in the period between the fall of the first British Empire and the rise of the second. Britain had learned from the American defeat that colonial government required a measure of colonial autonomy and a degree of flexibility. Canadians were the ones who reminded them. They reminded the Empire of its duty in the War of 1812, during the rebellions of 1837, and most of all, in the political battles surrounding the granting of local autonomy (responsible government) in 1846. Finally, in 1867 the British North American colonies federated into a new political structure, the Dominion. Subsequent Canadian historians and statesmen prided themselves that Canada was 'the senior Dominion' which, as such, demanded pride of place in the story of the evolving British Empire.

Responsible government, granted in 1846, became the central event of this

[13] Sir John George Bourinot, *Canada Under British Rule, 1760–1900* (Cambridge, 1900); William Kingsford, *History of Canada*, 10 vols. (Toronto, 1887–98). On Kingsford's *History* see M. Brook Taylor, *Promoters, Patriots and Partisans: Historiography in Nineteenth-Century English Canada* (Toronto, 1989), pp. 261–65

school of interpretation. George Wrong, often described as Canada's first academic historian, wrote a major biography of the Earl of Elgin which revolved around the issue.[14] George Lucas's 1912 edition of Lord Durham's report pointed towards the same event.[15] The *Canada and Its Provinces* series, published in 1914, devoted more than 130 pages to the arrival of responsible government. In all of these works the forces for progress were thought to be on the side of responsible government.[16] Never mind that much of the political manœuvering involved control of patronage. Never mind that partisanship and power as much as principle were involved. It was, to Canadian minds, an event central to both British Imperial development and even constitutional liberty itself. 'Lord Durham's report', wrote Edward Kylie in 1914, 'may be taken, therefore, as in many ways parallel with the constitutional documents of the English revolution [of 1688].'[17] For French Canadian Benjamin Sulte, the real significance of responsible government was the proof it gave of Canada's central role in the Empire. 'Have we not been the pioneers of political ideas, not only in Canada but in all English colonies?'[18]

Responsible government has mystified generations of Canadian students. Yet it endured for so long because it held a powerful attraction for a young nation asserting its place in the world and worried about unity at home. Here was a series of events where Canada truly was at the centre of a major British constitutional decision. Here too was a step in the direction of national autonomy and a precursor to Confederation in 1867. There was one other piece of important symbolism. Responsible government was achieved in part because the majority French Canadian political grouping, led by Louis Lafontaine, allied itself with English reformers under Robert Baldwin during the 1840s. The message was the same as twenty years later, when John A. Macdonald and George E. Cartier built the first administration of the new Dominion of Canada. Canada achieved its goals when French and English co-operated. There was little drama and certainly no adventure in responsible government, but there was a close link between national aspirations and historical myth.

This emphasis on responsible government was peculiar to Canadian writings. With some exceptions, British Imperial historians of the early twentieth century

[14] George Wrong, *The Earl of Elgin* (London, 1905).

[15] C. P. Lucas, ed., *Lord Durham's Report on the Affairs of British North America*, 3 vols. (Oxford, 1912).

[16] Shortt and Doughty, eds., *Canada and Its Provinces*, Vol. V, *United Canada* (Toronto, 1914), pp. 12–146.

[17] Edward Kylie, 'Constitutional Development, 1840–1867', in ibid., pp. 105–06.

[18] Benjamin Sulte, *Histoire des canadiens français, 1608–1880*, 7 vols. (Montreal, 1883), III, p. 94. Cited in Gagnon, *Quebec and its Historians*, p. 75.

barely noticed the event.[19] In 1930, however, the *Cambridge History of the British Empire* turned for the most part to Canadian historians for the volume on Canada. Many of the same people who had participated in *Canada and Its Provinces* a quarter-century earlier now presented their interpretation for this semi-official record of Imperial history. J. L. Morison fully accepted the Canadian interpretation of responsible government and Canada's role in the transformation of the Empire. 'The fourteen years from the proclamation of the union between Upper and Lower Canada are the most important in Canadian political history, for they witnessed the decisive stages in the constitutional experiment which determined the future, not only of Canada, but of all self-governing colonies of the Empire.'[20]

The question in the pre-war years was: where had the lessons of responsible government led? Would, as some Imperial enthusiasts argued, a new form of governance arise which would allow Dominions and Mother Country to govern the vast Empire jointly? Yet there were English Canadians who were acutely aware of growing French Canadian discomfort with the military overtones of the Empire, or who believed that a new Imperial Federation would be a backward and impractical step. When the First World War nearly tore the nation apart, English Canadian nationalism turned in new directions, looking for autonomy rather than interdependence.

The stresses of the war shaped subsequent historiography. Even among those identified with Imperial causes, the vision of autonomy won out over that of a closer federation. In 1921 former Prime Minister Sir Robert Borden gave the Marfleet Lectures at the University of Toronto. In these talks Borden sketched out an interpretation of Canadian history within the Empire that, true to form, started with the fall of New France and proceeded through the American Revolution, responsible government, and Confederation. Borden did not stop there, however, but traced the evolution of Canadian constitutional relations within the Empire through the recent war. The war, said Borden, was the final demonstration that the traditional Empire had changed. Dominion participation in the war effort and Dominion insistence on recognition in London promoted the final constitutional step. By 1917 the British government had recognized the equality of nationhood between the Dominions and the Mother Country. The Dominions, and Canada in particular, had thus brought about 'the final stages in the evolution of constitutional relations within the British Commonwealth'.[21]

[19] See, for example, A. Wyatt Tilby, *British North America, 1763–1867* (London, 1911). Tilby does not even mention responsible government.

[20] J. L. Morison, 'Canada Under Responsible Government, 1840–1854', *Cambridge History of the British Empire*, Vol. II, *Canada* (Cambridge, 1930), p. 308.

[21] Sir Robert Borden, *The Marfleet Lectures: University of Toronto, October 1921* (Toronto, 1922), p. 104.

Borden's interpretation, which echoed both academic and popular sentiment at the time, added the final dimension to an interpretation of Imperial history in which the Dominions in general and Canada in particular transformed the Empire. Borden's use of the term 'Commonwealth' was significant and was continued by Chester Martin's 1929 study, *Empire and Commonwealth*. George Wrong,[22] R. M. Dawson,[23] W. S. Wallace,[24] and others wrote along the same lines. The emphasis on the Empire-Commonwealth and on the rise of the Canadian nation was the natural response of those who had lived through the co-operation of the First World War, the growing autonomy of the Dominions at Versailles, the various post-war Commonwealth Conferences, and the attempt at international co-operation expressed in the League of Nations. 'For Canadian internationalists Canada's historic part in transforming the Empire and in the League of Nations were more than matters of status. These complementary roles were the grand and fitting outcome of its whole development.'[25]

The Empire-to-Commonwealth school provided a bridge between Imperialist and nationalist interpretations of Canada in the Empire. Much of Canada's adherence to the Imperial vision had come from fear of United States's expansionism. By the 1920s, though, the Americans seemed an unlikely enemy, having fought, if belatedly, beside the Empire in the war. Economically and culturally Canadians also found themselves more and more linked to the North American world of Ford automobiles, Hollywood movies, and the new American radio programmes that flooded across the border. Some lamented this 'Americanization of Canada', but the average Canadian found it increasingly difficult to think of the United States as a dark and foreign threat. As Chester Martin wrote in 1937, the post-war generation was the first 'for whom the spectre of annexation to the United States has never risen above the horizon'.[26]

Indeed, for some nationalists the war had demonstrated that the real danger to Canada came from excessive attachment to Imperial issues. Given these changes, the same historical events—responsible government, Confederation, the First World War—could be employed to promote a vision of national autonomy. This 'colony to nation school'[27] celebrated the triumphs of local autonomy over the resistance of short-sighted British politicians, or, more usually, even

[22] George M. Wrong, 'Canada's Problem of Equality with Great Britain', Empire Club of Canada, *Addresses*, 1926 (Toronto, 1927), pp. 262–70; 'Nationalism in Canada', *Journal of the Royal Institute of International Affairs*, V (July, 1926), pp. 177–94.

[23] R. M. Dawson, *The Development of Dominion Status, 1900–1936* (Toronto, 1937).

[24] W. S. Wallace, 'Notes and Comments', *Canadian Historical Review*, I (Dec. 1920), p. 344.

[25] Berger, *Writing of Canadian History*, p. 40.

[26] Ibid., p. 140.

[27] The name of the school is retrospective, drawn from A. R. M. Lower's text, *Colony to Nation: A History of Canada* (Toronto, 1946).

more short-sighted Canadians. In the 1920s and 1930s a new generation, including prominent individuals such as O. D. Skelton, Frank Underhill, and J. W. Dafoe, began to emphasize the drive to Canadian autonomy and the distinct nature of Canadian identity.[28]

Strictly speaking, these were not Imperial historians, because for them the Empire was less relevant than Canada's place in North America. The enthusiasm of George Wrong's generation was replaced by a new scepticism towards the relevance of the Empire and its worth to Canada. This view, it must be stressed, did not rest on the harsh anti-colonial rhetoric seen in some nationalist historiography elsewhere in the Empire. The writings took pride in Canada's peaceful evolution, and portrayed any problems as a combination of reactionary local élites and British ignorance of Canada. As Toronto historian Frank Underhill claimed, 'what liberals in Canada have sought throughout has not been the breaking of the tie with Great Britain but the changing of its nature to that of a free association of equals'.[29] The real division, in the minds of these writers, was between those who understood the future and those who would cling to the past.

The colony-to-nation school did not develop unopposed. A number of historians between the wars continued to emphasize the traditional notion that Canada was inherently British, that the real enemy was the United States, and that the colony-to-nation school was ignoring the lessons of history. The work of the great Canadian historian Donald Grant Creighton perhaps best exemplifies the survival of pro-Imperial interpretation into mid-century. In his *The Commercial Empire of the St. Lawrence, 1760–1850* (Toronto, 1937) and two-volume biography of Canada's first Prime Minister, *John A. Macdonald* (Vol. I: *The Young Politician*, Toronto, 1952 and Vol. II: *The Old Chieftan*, Toronto, 1955), Creighton charts a history that celebrates the rise of Canada as a British nation, distinct from the United States and tied by webs of loyalty and trade to the Mother Country. *Empire of the St. Lawrence*, for example, studies the relationship between the Montreal business community, the St Lawrence–Great Lakes system, and politics from the time of the fall of New France to the mid-nineteenth century. Two themes predominate. First, the geographical circumstances of the St Lawrence valley determined that Canada would develop an east–west trade system of Imperial scope. At the one end was London and at the other the vast resources of the interior of North America. This east–west trade axis, moreover, exemplified Canada's historical destiny. It was an extension of Empire, distinct from the United States.

[28] J. W. Dafoe, *Canada: An American Nation* (New York, 1935); O. D. Skelton, *The Life and Letters of Sir Wilfrid Laurier*, 2 vols. (Toronto, 1921).

[29] Frank Underhill, Preface to 'Some Aspects of Upper Canadian Radical Opinion in the Decade Before Confederation', in his *In Search of Canadian Liberalism* (Toronto, 1960).

Secondly, Creighton made his moral judgements on the basis of Imperial destiny. Those who, like the French Canadians, resisted the pull of the Imperial system and Canada's destiny were criticized. Those who comprehended the significance of the river were on the winning side of history and thus far-sighted. Yet the story of the river and its trade system cannot be termed a celebration. There are too many defeats: the artificial boundary of 1783, the division of Quebec into Upper and Lower Canada in 1791. The future remained uncertain, as short-sighted or self-serving groups ignored destiny. Only later, when John A. Macdonald combined an understanding of the Empire and a vision of the Canadian national future, does near-tragedy translate into triumph.

There was a partial fusion of the Imperial and national schools of Canadian history. Between the wars there were a growing series of connections between Canadian and American scholars. Oxford was still the university of choice for advanced degrees but others, such as Harvard, Chicago, and Columbia, attracted a greater percentage of Canadians studying abroad. Even more significantly, American bodies, such as the Carnegie Foundation, supported Canadian historians while, at the same time, they promoted the view that North American history was the story of partnership emerging from confrontation. The real story, it turned out, was not just the existence of Canada as a separate and British state but also the growing alliance between the English-speaking peoples.[30]

Works such as J. B. Munro's *American Influences on Canadian Government* (1929), Hansen and Brebner's *The Mingling of the Canadian and American Peoples* (1940), and A. L. Burt, *Canada, the United States and Great Britain* (Toronto, 1940), attached a new importance to the influence of the United States.[31] The Second World War cemented the trend, at least after the United States joined the war in 1941. As Percy Corbett, Canadian lawyer, internationalist, and scholar, put it in 1942, 'it may be that the British peoples suffered enough by war to be willing to give up their cherished and somewhat haughty separateness'.[32] This was a theme expressed in many works, but it was John Bartlett Brebner who perhaps stands as the best example of the new sense of partnership. Educated at Toronto, Oxford, and Columbia, Brebner's personal experience mirrored his belief in the transatlantic community. His *The North Atlantic Triangle*, published at the end of the

[30] Carl Berger, 'Internationalism, Continentalism, and the Writing of History: Comments on the Carnegie Series on the Relations of Canada and the United States', in Richard Preston, ed., *The Influence of the United States on Canadian Development* (Durham, NC, 1972), pp. 32–54.

[31] M. L. Hansen and J. B. Brebner, *The Mingling of the Canadian and American Peoples* (New Haven, 1940); W. B. Munro, *American Influences on Canadian Government* (Toronto, 1929); A. L. Burt, *The United States, Great Britain and British North America from the Revolution to the Establishment of Peace after the War of 1812* (New Haven, 1940).

[32] P. E. Corbett, *Post-War Worlds* (New York, 1942), pp. 92–93.

war, synthesized the work of the past fifteen years to describe the linked destiny of the three English-speaking nations of that triangle.[33]

Brebner's work was perhaps the best expression of a North Atlantic perspective on Canada. Recounting the well-known struggles for control of North America, the rupture of the American Revolution, and the hostilities of the War of 1812, Brebner was well aware of the conflict that had marked the North American continent. His real theme, though, was the growing interdependence of a North Atlantic community tied by trade, language, and history. His final sentence pointed the way to a complex but ongoing special relationship. 'Americans, Britons and Canadians may heartily share in the aspiration which was voiced in "Let it roll on full flood, inexorable, irresistible," but they also know from the record of the past that they must share in hard work if they are to make real the rest of Mr. Churchill's sentence—"benignant, to broader lands and better days" '.[34]

Brebner's interpretation was extremely influential. For one thing, it was hard to deny the historic importance of the North Atlantic triangle in the history of Canada. For another, the sense of common purpose arising from the war accentuated that importance. The three North Atlantic English-speaking nations were now linked in a common cause. After the war many works, such as that by George Glazebrook, continued to emphasize the importance of the North Atlantic triangle rather than of the Empire as such.[35]

Yet the very emphasis on the triangle in the Empire pointed to a serious concern among other post-war writers. The growing power of the United States challenged both the older faith in the Empire and the more recent belief that Canada could survive as a distinct nation by looking to two powerful allies. If Canada were the product of this balance of forces, however, the question arose as to what the future might bring.[36] Within a few years of Brebner's work the fading power of the British Empire left open the possibility that the influence in future would come almost exclusively from south of the border.

In the post-war years several incidents brought home to Canadians the shifting relationships within the North Atlantic triangle. The North Atlantic Treaty Organization (formed 1949) was an American-led anti-communist alliance. It also

[33] J. B. Brebner, *The North Atlantic Triangle: The Interplay of Canada, the United States and Great Britain* (New Haven, 1945).

[34] Ibid., p. 336.

[35] G. T. de P. Glazebrook, *A History of Canadian External Relations* (Toronto, 1950). On the North Atlantic Triangle see Vol. IV, chap. by David Mackenzie.

[36] One of the first post-war expressions of this concern came in a Royal Commission headed by former High Commissioner to Great Britain, Vincent Massey. See *Canada: Report of Royal Commission on National Development in the Arts, Letters and Sciences* (Ottawa, 1952).

confirmed the linkage between the three members of the triangle. In the Suez crisis of 1956 Canada sided with the United States against Britain, though not without considerable anguish. In 1957 Canada joined the North American Air Defence Command (NORAD), a purely bilateral Canadian–American defence arrangement. For the first time in history Canadian–American military ties were closer than Anglo-Canadian ones.[37] For those who saw the Imperial-Commonwealth connection as fundamental to Canadian survival, these were disturbing events indeed.

Three post-war musings on the subject of rising American and declining British influence have become classics in Canadian historiography. The first in time was a speech given by University of Toronto political economist Harold Innis at the University of Nottingham in 1948. Innis had always been a nationalist, and the integration of the Second World War had only deepened his alarm. At Nottingham he restated the need for 'the old world to redress the balance of the new', and went on to coin his already mentioned colony-to-nation-to-colony rejoinder to nationalist historians.[38] By failing to understand the significance of the Imperial connection, Innis warned, Canadians had left themselves vulnerable to cultural and economic absorption into American hegemony.

In 1965 one of Canada's best-known philosophers, George Parkin Grant, restated the theme raised by Innis. Writing in the wake of the fall of the mildly anti-American and pro-British Conservative government, Grant lamented the end of Canada as a distinct national culture. Conservatism, Grant argued, had been an essential counter to American progressivism. Echoing philosophers such as Jacques Ellul, Grant concluded that in the modern world technology dominated spirit, and that the United States, as the home of technology, was an unstoppable culture.[39] Finally, an elderly Donald Creighton wrote a survey to mark Canada's centennial. *Canada's First Century*, published in 1970, however, was far from a celebration. Instead, it was the story of the betrayal of the nation by continentalist politicians and an expansionist American empire. 'Canada had become an autonomous nation during the First World War; she reverted to the position of a dependent colony during the Second.'[40]

The writings of Manitoba historian W. L. Morton reinforced the dark picture set out by Innis, Grant, and Creighton. Though less iconoclastic than the others,

[37] On the diplomatic side of these events see John Holmes, *The Shaping of Peace: Canada and the Search for World Order, 1948–1957*, 2 vols. (Toronto, 1979, 1982).

[38] Harold Innis, 'Great Britain, the United States and Canada', 21st Cust Foundation Lecture, delivered at the University of Nottingham, 21 May, 1948, in M. Q. Innis, ed., *Essays in Canadian Economic History* (Toronto, 1956), pp. 394–412, 405.

[39] George P. Grant, *Lament for a Nation: The Defeat of Canadian Nationalism* (Toronto, 1965).

[40] Creighton, *Canada's First Century* (Toronto, 1970), p. 245. See also his final book, *Canada 1939–1957: The Forked Road* (Toronto, 1976).

Morton shared many of their values. He was a conservative in an age dominated by a succession of Liberal governments. He was a nationalist in a time when American influence seemed to grow ever stronger. He was a staunch monarchist in a time when the monarchy, like the other trappings of the Empire-Commonwealth, seemed to be fading in the minds of Canadians. In 1963 he synthesized his views in a widely read text, *The Kingdom of Canada*. The title summed up the argument that Canada's distinctiveness rested on its historical connection to the Empire.[41] The fact that Canada had led the evolution of that Empire into the new form of the Commonwealth, 'an association founded on principles universally valid', strengthened rather than diminished the importance of the British tie.[42]

The writings of Innis, Grant, Creighton, and Morton were the retrospective views of an older generation that watched as their pro-Imperial enthusiasms were swamped by American culture, American materialism, and American foreign policy. They were also, in the radical days of the 1960s, to rally to their cause a younger generation who feared the overwhelming presence of the United States. The revival, however, was more apparent than real. The real focus of the new nationalists was not the British Empire but the American. The British Empire was useful historically because it reminded Canadians they were different from the United States. No one seriously believed, however, that the Empire or its modern variation, the Commonwealth, would compensate for the overwhelming presence of the United States. If anything, Britain and Canada were operating at the same level, subordinate to American technology, American foreign policy, and American international corporations.

The unavoidable fact was that the Empire-Commonwealth was moving from the mainstream to the margins of Canadian life. In parallel, Canadian historiography relegated its treatment of Imperial history to the same fate. By the 1960s the study of Canada and the Empire had became a specialized field rather than, as Chester Martin had concluded forty years earlier, the basis of most Canadian historical writing.

There were secondary reasons for the decline of interest in Imperial issues. In Canada in the 1960s and after, as in many other countries, political and diplomatic history was replaced by social history as the predominant choice of graduate students and academics. In Canada this was compounded at the end of the 1960s by the rise of what became known as the 'limited identities' school of history.[43] In the midst of ascendant Quebec nationalism, and new concerns with ethnicity and

41 W. L. Morton, *The Kingdom of Canada* (Toronto, 1963).

42 W. L. Morton, *The Canadian Identity* (Toronto, 1961), p. 55.

43 J. M. S. Careless, ' "Limited Identities" in Canada', *Canadian Historical Review*, L (March 1969), pp. 1–10.

with social reform, this view asserted that there might not be any single Canadian history. Instead, history in Canada might best be understood through a series of regional, provincial, and other sub-groupings. Without even a national history, it became ever more difficult to envisage an historical record that encompassed an Imperial vision.

The historical interests of the newer generation mirrored personal experience. Born during or after the Second World War, this generation of historians had never known a time when the Empire or, for that matter, Britain, was central to their own culture. The cold war and the vast hegemonic North American culture framed their respective political and personal experiences, which reinforced the notion of the marginal role of the Empire. As Canadian graduate schools expanded, it became increasingly unlikely that a prospective Canadian historian would make the trek to Oxford or Cambridge. The personal links that had made the Empire seem real were becoming more tenuous. The historiography of the Empire was increasingly a specialized sub-discipline in the study of Canadian history.

These changes in the profession have brought about a significant redefinition of historical writing on Canada and the Empire over the last thirty years. Of course some strong works continue to assess the major themes of Canadian–Imperial relations. Helen Taft Manning, Ged Martin, Philip G. Wigley, Peter Burroughs, and Richard Preston have all added insight and information to the understanding to aspects of Canada within the British Empire.[44] They, as well as various historians of the Empire rather than of Canada, have revisited Canadian events to argue that they must be viewed in an Imperial context.[45] Yet, important though some of these works are, they are not dominant in shaping the modern view of Canada. Nor are they central to the study of Canadian history. Indeed, it is revealing that many of the foremost historians of Canada and the Empire are not Canadian by birth, many actually making their living outside of Canada. In recent years the real focus of historians who studied and teach in Canada has been the broader field of international relations rather than Commonwealth or Imperial studies.

An influential group of historians, including C. P. Stacey, Robert Bothwell, and J. L. Granatstein, have glanced at Canada and the Empire-Commonwealth, yet

[44] Helen Taft Manning, *British Colonial Government after the American Revolution* (Hamden, Conn., 1966); Ged Martin, *The Durham Report and British Policy: A Critical Essay* (Cambridge, 1972); Philip G. Wigley, *Canada and the Transition to Commonwealth: British–Canadian Relations, 1917–1926* (Cambridge, 1977); Peter Burroughs, *The Colonial Reformers and Canada, 1830–1849* (Toronto, 1969); Richard Preston, *Canada and 'Imperial Defense': A Study of the Origins of the British Commonwealth's Defense Organizations, 1867–1919* (Durham, NC, 1967).

[45] Philip Lawson, *The Imperial Challenge: Quebec and Britain in the Age of the American Revolution* (Montreal, 1989).

none of them would be thought of as Imperial historians.[46] Their tradition, perhaps, derives from the concept of the North Atlantic triangle. The United States is as important to their work—both in archival research and subject-matter—as is Britain. The Empire and Commonwealth are viewed in mildly nationalistic terms. Canada's story is that of increasing autonomy. For these writers the study of Canada and the Empire has been incorporated within the broader study of Canadian foreign policy. The Empire was, like the United States, a somewhat earlier and admittedly special aspect of the study of Canada's relations abroad. The notion of Imperialism itself became, not a matter taken for granted, but a study of a peculiar Canadian historical era.[47] If anything this school tends to downplay the importance of Empire, because it cannot help but foreshadow the eventual rise of the United States to a position of pre-eminence.

The real emphasis on the Empire in recent decades has been driven by a different historical perspective. With the rise of social history from the 1960s, peoples rather than constitutions have been the focus of writing. This is as true of Imperial issues as of others. The treatment of 'natives' has formed one locus of attention. Older images of the British as a benevolent ruling society have tended to give way to darker pictures of indigenous peoples displaced. Even in works more favourably disposed to British intentions, the emphasis has been on the dislocation brought to indigenous societies by European rule. Another favoured topic has been immigration. The question of how the British adjusted, or failed to adjust, to their new homeland has played an important role in these studies.[48] In both instances the theme has been the interplay of different cultures and circumstances in a new land. How did rivalries across the Atlantic become transplanted or transformed on Canadian soil? The Irish have been of particular interest, though many other issues have been discussed.[49] How did the New World and Old World cultures treat each other?[50]

[46] C. P. Stacey, *Canada and the Age of Conflict: A History of Canadian External Policies, 1867–1948*, 2 vols. (Toronto, 1977, 1981); Robert Bothwell, *Loring Christie and the Failure of Bureaucratic Imperialism* (New York, 1988); J. L. Granatstein, *How Britain's Weakness Forced Canada into the Arms of the United States* (Toronto, 1989).

[47] This was a popular field of study in the 1960s and 1970s. See, for example, Norman Penlington, *Canada and Imperialism, 1896–1899* (Toronto, 1965); Robert J. D. Page, ed., *Imperialism and Canada, 1895–1903* (Toronto, 1972).

[48] Donald H. Akenson, *The Irish in Ontario: A Study in Rural History* (Montreal, 1984); Joy Parr, *Labouring Children: British Immigrant Apprentices to Canada, 1869–1924*, 2nd edn. (Toronto, 1994).

[49] Hereward Senior, *Orangeism: The Canadian Phase* (Toronto, 1972); Cecil Houston, *The Sash Canada Wore: A Historical Geography of the Orange Order in Canada* (Toronto, 1980); Cecil Houston, *Irish Emigration and Canadian Settlement* (Toronto, 1990).

[50] Robin Fisher, *Contact and Conflict: Indian–European Relations in British Columbia, 1774–1890*, 2nd edn. (Vancouver, BC, 1992); Jim Miller, *Skyscrapers Hide the Heavens: A History of Indian–White Relations in Canada* (Toronto, 1991).

The second theme is best encapsulated in the previously mentioned statement of Carl Berger that 'Imperialism was one form of Canadian nationalism'. A new generation, more detached from the loyalties and divisions of pre-war years, has nevertheless recognized that Britain was the focus of crucial debates over generations. Beginning with the work of S. F. Wise in the 1960s, a new perspective has appeared on the role of the Empire in Canadian history.[51] The notion of 'Britain' and 'British' was, several writers have concluded, an essential part of the formation of the Canadian identity. Being part of a great Empire was a source of pride, protection, and sometimes, delusion, for generations of Canadians. Those in the past who talked of British culture and British loyalty were simultaneously capable of ridiculing British snobbery and ignorant Colonial Office administrators. Thus George T. Denison, the quintessential Victorian imperialist, could complain of British snobbery towards the colonials.[52] Conversely, early twentieth-century nationalists such as O. D. Skelton could apply for entry into the Indian Civil Service.

Being British was, for generations of Canadians, something different from what it was in, say, the United Kingdom or Australia. Being British was also, from the American Revolution to the 1950s, a formative ingredient in Canadian national identity. These facts have provided a rich basis for reinterpretation of traditional events. Carl Berger's ground-breaking work on the idea of imperialism in Victorian Canada made clear the differences between a Canadian imperialist and the British version. Jane Errington's work on the Loyalists and David Mills's study of the concept of loyalty in Upper Canada have, in effect, revisited the enthusiasms of earlier generations for the Empire, and asked why they thought the way they did.[53]

A particular fertile ground for exploring this sense of Britishness lies in the Canadian West. Throughout the nineteenth century, Canadians were continually searching for reasons why immigrants should come to Canada to settle. Climate was a challenge. So too was the affluence south of the border. American lawlessness and mistreatment of natives provided clear contrasts with a more orderly Canadian expansion.

To contemporary propagandists and subsequent historians, however, the contrast was no accident. It was another example of the British counterpoint to American republicanism. The export of particularly British traditions to the 'frontier' distinguished Canada from the United States in the nineteenth-century mind. Canada, according to the original myth, was more orderly and peaceful in

[51] S. F. Wise, 'Upper Canada and the Conservative Tradition', in Edith Firth, ed., *Profiles of a Province* (Toronto, 1967).

[52] Berger, *Sense of Power*, p. 52.

[53] Jane Errington, *The Lion, The Eagle, and Upper Canada: A Developing Colonial Ideology* (Kingston, Ontario, 1987); David Mills, *The Idea of Loyalty in Upper Canada* (Montreal, 1988).

its movement westward because it took with it British concepts of rule by law and a sympathy for those over whom it governed. The North West Mounted Police, appointed from Ottawa and headed by the sons of well-to-do British families, was a particularly potent symbol of the Imperial connection in the West. Recent literature has not discounted the reality behind the myth of orderly Western development entirely, but it has emphasized the purposes of such self-congratulation to a young nation trying to carve out a distinct place in North America.[54] It also recognizes that, at a very specific level, the presence of Imperial institutions such as the Hudson's Bay Company, had a profound impact upon the evolution of the region.

As we approach the end of the century, many of the forces that shaped Canada's view of its place in the Empire have changed. In the two world wars Canada gained control over foreign policy. Subsequently, Canada and Britain both became subordinate in economic and political terms to the superpower of the United States.[55] The Commonwealth is still, on the whole, a pleasant and useful association, but does not play a central role in Canadian foreign policy. Britain is much more oriented towards Europe than towards her former colonies. Canada's population has become much more multicultural over the past thirty years. British roots and British connections are less relevant than they once were. The 'Pacific rim' draws more and more attention as the trading region of the future. There is little likelihood, therefore, that the earlier view that Canadian history is inseparable from Imperial history is likely to return. Yet neither is work on the Empire-Commonwealth going to cease. For two centuries English Canadians (and many French Canadians) defined themselves as British. Canadian institutions derive directly from Westminster, and Canadian education from British (often Scottish) inspiration. The 'Empire', therefore, will seem more remote to generations of the late twentieth or early twenty-first centuries. It will, however, remain one of the great forces that shaped the Canadian past and will thus continue to be a subject of at least some historical interest.

In all the changes there is also one constant theme. The notion of 'empire' has always been bilateral in Canadian writing. It found its focus on Canada and Britain, though the notion of a vast Empire lay in the background. That remains the case today. With few exceptions, the real theme has been the origin of Canada, whether in terms of the constitution, society, identity, people, or character. That has implied reaching across the Atlantic rather than around the globe.

[54] Keith Walden, *Visions of Order: The Canadian Mounties as Symbol and Myth* (Toronto, 1982); R. G. Moyles and Doug Owram, *Imperial Dreams and Colonial Realities: British Views of Canada, 1880–1914* (Toronto, 1988), chaps. 2, 5, 7; Dick Harrison, *Unnamed Country: The Struggle for a Canadian Prairie Fiction* (Edmonton, 1977).

[55] Granatstein, *How Britain's Weakness . . .*, chap. 3.

The historiography of Empire in Canada, therefore, is in reality only partly about the Empire. It is instead the story of Canada and her main link to the wider world.

Select Bibliography

CARL BERGER, *The Sense of Power: Studies in the Ideas of Canadian Imperialism, 1867–1914* (Toronto, 1970).

—— *The Writing of Canadian History: Aspects of English-Canadian Historical Writing: 1900–1970* (Toronto, 1976).

KENNETH BOURNE, *Britain and the Balance of Power in North America, 1815–1908* (Berkeley, 1967).

J. B. BREBNER, *The North Atlantic Triangle: The Interplay of Canada, the United States and Great Britain* (New Haven, 1945).

A. L. BURT, *The Evolution of the British Empire and the Commonwealth From the American Revolution* (Boston, 1956).

J. M. S. CARELESS, 'Limited Identities in Canada', *Canadian Historical Review*, L (March, 1969).

D. G. CREIGHTON, *Empire of the St Lawrence* (first published as *The Commercial Empire of the St Lawrence, 1760–1850*, 1937) (Boston, 1958).

—— *Canada's First Century, 1867–1967* (Toronto, 1970).

JANE ERRINGTON, *The Lion, the Eagle, and Upper Canada: A Developing Colonial Ideology* (Kingston, Ontario, 1987).

J. L. GRANATSTEIN, *How Britain's Weakness Forced Canada into the Arms of the United States* (Toronto, 1989).

M. L. HANSEN and J. B. BREBNER, *The Mingling of the Canadian and American Peoples* (New Haven, 1940).

HAROLD INNIS, 'Great Britain, the United States and Canada', in M. Q. Innis, ed., *Essays in Canadian Economic History* (Toronto, 1956).

PHILIP LAWSON, *The Imperial Challenge: Quebec and Britain in the Age of the American Revolution* (Montreal, 1989).

CHESTER MARTIN, *Empire and Commonwealth: Studies in Governance and Self-Government in Canada* (Oxford, 1929).

GED MARTIN, *The Durham Report and British Policy: A Critical Essay* (Cambridge, 1972).

C. P. STACEY, *Canada and the Age of Conflict: A History of Canadian External Policies*, Vol. I, *1867–1921*; Vol. II, *1921–1948* (Toronto, 1977; 1981).

REGINALD TROTTER, *The British Empire-Commonwealth: A Study in Political Evolution* (New York, 1932).

PHILIP G. WIGLEY, *Canada and the Transition to Commonwealth: British–Canadian Relations, 1917–1926* (Cambridge, 1977).

S. F. WISE and R. C. BROWN, *Canada Views the United States* (Toronto, 1967).

9

Australia and the Empire

STUART MACINTYRE

Colonial Australians complained repeatedly of Imperial neglect. Hoping to press their concerns upon decision-makers in London, anxious to win the approval of the arbiters of taste and accomplishment in the old country, they made the long journey back to a place with which they already felt such imaginative affinity, only to find it utterly different, preoccupied, heedless of their presence. In the words of Rudyard Kipling's republican Australian, this was an Empire 'that don't care what you do'.[1] Time brings its revenge. A later generation of post-colonial Australians have so completely expunged the Imperial connection that its historical traces are now almost unintelligible. The links that earlier historians took for granted are now broken, and the Imperial dimension of Australian history lies in neglected, often unrecognized fragments.

The earlier historians produced a colonial and later a national story within an Imperial framework. Australian civilization was the product of a transfer of people, institutions, technology, and culture from the metropolitan centre to a new setting; whether the preference was for faithful imitation of the original or for improvement upon it, the experiment was judged against received standards. Imperial history was thus the indispensable counterpoint of colonial history, for it traced the determination of the policies and administrative practices that had called forth the colonial response. The Governors who directed the initial process of British settlement constituted 'Lilliputian sovereigns', as an incisive commentator on this historiography put it, in a local version of kings-and-queens history.[2] Then came limited self-government, with local parliaments and responsible ministers operating within a framework of Imperial control, followed by Federation and eventually full national autonomy. This was a Whiggish history of filial

[1] J. D. B. Miller, ' "An Empire that Don't Care What You Do . . ." ', in A. F. Madden and W. H. Morris-Jones, eds., *Australia and Britain: Studies in a Changing Relationship* (Sydney, 1980), p. 97.

[2] R. M. Crawford, 'History', in A. G. Price, ed., *The Humanities in Australia: A Survey with Special Reference to the Universities* (Sydney, 1959), p. 149. Here and afterwards I draw on Stuart Macintyre, 'The Writing of Australian History', in D. H. Borchardt and Victor Crittenden, eds., *Australians: A Guide to Sources* (Broadway, NSW, 1987), pp. 1–29.

growth directed by sometimes erratic but ultimately prudent statesmanship towards final maturity.

Current historical writing has long since abandoned such a framework. The process of settlement is now regarded as a violent invasion of a rich and subtle indigenous culture, the colonists' material practices as destructive of a fragile environment, their aesthetic response to it blinkered and prejudiced, the cultivation of British forms timid and unresponsive. The earlier historiographical emphasis on constitutional, political, and administrative progress has yielded to the concerns of social history with popular experience structured by class, gender, and ethnicity, and after the linguistic point of departure, to a multiplicity of post-colonial identities.

A survey of the British Empire in Australian historiography must, therefore, work from an earlier literature that was explicitly occupied with Imperial and colonial relations to a later and far more diffuse literature in which Imperial issues are barely recognized. Elsewhere the study of Empire has itself taken on the new historiographical methods: much recent work has shifted from high politics to the presence of Imperial effects in metropolitan culture, from networks of powerful men to the differentiated experience of imperialism among women and children, and from material practices to the inscription of the colonial condition in discourse. Some of this work has been carried out in Australia, but little of it has been taken up by Australian historians. There is something in Australia's present disposition, it would seem, that resists the Imperial past. Any examination of how the British Empire has figured in Australian historiography must seek to account for this outcome. This one does by turning back to the earlier ways of writing Imperial history to show both the supersession and lingering effects.

The first phase of Australian historiography began in 1788 with the arrival of the First Fleet. Governor Arthur Phillip and several of his officers kept journals that they subsequently reworked and published for a British readership curious to learn of the strange antipodean land of contrarities. These narratives of the British settlement of Australia were followed by memoirs, records of exploration and travel, descriptive and scientific reports, emigrant manuals, and company prospectuses, all of which typically incorporated a historical sketch. Such communications, as well as the official despatches, both recorded and anticipated a process of Imperial expansion within familiar literary conventions. In his *Account of a Voyage to Establish a Colony at Port Phillip*, the naval officer J. H. Tuckey recalled how he had watched a team of convicts yoked to a cart, the wheels of which were sunk up to the axles in sand. As he witnessed their exertions on this unpromising shore he had a vision of 'a second Rome, rising from a coalition of

Banditti . . . superlative in arms and in arts, looking down with proud superiority upon the barbarous nations of the northern hemisphere'.[3]

The trope was a familiar one long before Macaulay described a future New Zealander standing on a broken arch of London Bridge, and it enabled colonial writers to overcome the apparent absence of history in the primordial wilderness. 'Anticipation is to a young country what antiquity is to an old', wrote Barron Field, the judge of the Supreme Court of New South Wales, in 1819.[4] Just as the sound of axes breaking the timeless solitude of the virgin forest served many of these chroniclers as a metaphor of Imperial conquest, so the creation of a local historical record was one of the ways settlers negotiated their colonial condition.

In the period of direct rule from London, which lasted until the 1850s, a series of more ambitious histories were produced with the purpose of influencing Imperial policy. Of these the most notable were William Wentworth, *A Statistical, Historical and Political Description of the Colony of New South Wales and Its Dependent Settlements* (London, 1819), John Dunmore Lang, *An Historical and Statistical Account of New South Wales: Both as a Penal Settlement and a British Colony* (London, 1834), and James Macarthur, *New South Wales: Its Present State and Future Prospects: Being a Statement with Documentary Evidence* (London, 1837). All three writers were closely involved in colonial politics, the native-born Wentworth as champion of the emancipated convicts and their children, the Presbyterian minister Lang as the leading advocate of free immigration, and Macarthur, son of the founders of the Australian wool industry, as spokesman for the exclusivist landowners (though his work was ghosted by an English author). All three employed the literary narrative mode for polemical effect and all three published in London to persuade the Colonial Office, Parliament, and the governing class of their version of the lessons of the past.

For Wentworth, the history of the colony showed the disastrous effects of the penal regime. His vision, expressed in a poem written three years later in Cambridge, was of 'A new Britannia in another world', and his purpose was to raise the colony 'from the abject state of poverty, slavery and degradation to which she is so fast sinking, and to present her with a constitution which may gradually conduct her to freedom, prosperity and happiness'.[5] For Lang, too, the mistaken policies of the Crown had stifled progress, first by the encouragement of convicts and then by the promotion of pastoralism at the expense of 'a numerous, industrious and virtuous agricultural population'.[6] He would harden his opposition to the

[3] (London, 1805), pp. 185–90, quoted in H. M. Green, *History of Australian Literature: Pure and Applied*, 2 vols. (Sydney, 1961), I, p. 17.

[4] *First Fruits of Australian Poetry* (Sydney, 1819).

[5] Wentworth, quoted in Douglas Pike, ed., *Australian Dictionary of Biography*, 14 vols. to date (Melbourne, 1966–), II, p. 584.

[6] J. D. Lang, *An Historical and Statistical Account of New South Wales*, 2 vols. (London, 1834), I, p. 24. See D. W. Baker, *Days of Wrath: A Life of John Dunmore Lang* (Carlton, Victoria, 1985).

Colonial Office in subsequent publications of repetitive prolixity until by 1852, in *Freedom and Independence for the Golden Lands of Australia*, he advocated a republican United States of Australia. Macarthur, on the other hand, sought to warn the British government of the ruinous consequences of laxity, arguing that 'if wise measures are now adopted, the false steps of the past may soon be retrieved'.[7]

John West's *History of Tasmania* (Launceston, Tasmania, 1852) is at once the culmination of this form of historical literature and its point of transition. West, a Congregational minister and journalist, was prominent in the movement to abolish convict transportation. He began his history in 1847, as that movement took on major dimensions in eastern Australia with the threat of continued transportation to the island colony of Van Diemen's Land (Tasmania), and he completed it on the eve of the British decision to abandon the practice (except under restricted conditions in Western Australia). More than two hundred pages of West's superb polemic are given to an account of the penal system, and the entire work is permeated by his abhorrence of its penicious effects. Significantly, the arguments are addressed to an Australian audience. The book itself was published in Launceston and offered by the author to the rising generation of native Tasmanians—he preferred that term to the older Van Diemen's Land, with the connotations of 'bondage and guilt'—in the hope that it would 'gratify their curiosity, and offer to their view the instructive and inspiriting events of the past'.[8]

With the abandonment of the convict system and the granting of self-government to the five colonies of New South Wales, Victoria, South Australia, Tasmania, and Queensland in the 1850s, it was no longer necessary to address such arguments to Westminster, or to embed them within the elaborate historical comparisons whereby British legislators could appreciate the error of their policies. A page had been turned. The dominant theme of the historical literature produced in the second half of the nineteenth century was the triumph of local initiative. The gold rush of the 1850s brought an influx of new settlers. The weight of numbers quickly democratized the colonial legislatures, and liberal ministries set about meeting popular expectations. The colonies commanded plentiful natural resources, they enjoyed buoyant British markets for their primary products, cheap British capital underwrote their extensive public works, and in the heyday of Imperial prosperity they achieved rapid growth and high living standards. Most historical writing of the period was restricted in its preoccupations, measuring achievement in flocks and crops, bricks and mortar, and the amenities of civilization these riches

[7] James Macarthur, *New South Wales: Its Present State and Future Prospects* (London, 1837), p. 170. See John Manning Ward, *James Macarthur: Colonial Conservative, 1798–1867* (Sydney, 1981).

[8] John West, *History of Tasmania*, 2 vols. (Launceston, Tasmania, 1852), I, pp. 2–3.

made possible. Such colonial historiography remained Imperial in its assumptions, marking the successful application of British values and energies to new circumstances, though with room for local innovations the Scottish merchant William Westgarth celebrated *Half a Century of Australasian Progress: A Personal Retrospect* (London, 1889) just as the New South Wales statistician and later Agent-General in London, Sir Timothy Coghlan and T. T. Ewing, recorded *The Progress of Australasia in the Nineteenth Century* (Toronto, 1903). It was left for visiting Englishmen such as Charles Dilke, Anthony Trollope, and J. A. Froude to discern the distinctive patterns of Australian development and validate the colonial achievement.[9] Trollope sounded a cautionary note: 'Don't blow.'

This era of growth ended during the 1890s in economic depression, industrial conflict, and political reconstruction that called the Imperial relationship into question. Two of its principal defenders were G. W. Rusden, a public servant whose three-volume *History of Australia* (Melbourne, 1883) was an extended critique of all departures from Imperial verities: 'The most successful colonization is that which founds abroad a society similar to that of the parent society.'[10] In similar tone, the banker Henry Gyles Turner wrote *A History of the Colony of Victoria: From Its Discovery to Its Absorption in the Commonwealth of Australia* (London, 1904) in two volumes and then *The First Decade of the Australian Commonwealth: A Chronicle of Contemporary Politics, 1901–1910* (Melbourne, 1911) to lament the colonists' failure to make good their British heritage, because of mischievous innovations that had turned local government into a 'mere reflex of the popular will'.[11] For these critics, an appreciation of the lessons of the past was a necessary condition of wise government, and the Imperial connection a providential safeguard against rash experiment.

In opposition to this conservative Imperial history there was a new temper of radical nationalism, associated especially with the creative writers who contributed to the popular weekly *Bulletin*. Its avowed purpose was to define and express an Australian sentiment that it found in the local experience. Republican and stridently anti-Imperial, the *Bulletin* celebrated a lineage of martyred convict rebels, egalitarian gold-diggers, bush selectors, and rural workers. The past it evoked in poems and fiction was not so much history as counter-history. Against the official record of the Governors and the plutocracy, it asserted a popular memory of resistance to authority, endurance, and mateship. But history in the sense

[9] Charles Wentworth Dilke, *Greater Britain: A Record of Travel in English-Speaking Countries during 1866 and 1867*, 2 vols. (London, 1868); Anthony Trollope, *Australia and New Zealand*, 2 vols. (London, 1873), II, p. 387; J. A. Froude, *Oceania, or England and Her Colonies* (London, 1886).

[10] G. W. Rusden, *History of Australia*, 3 vols. (London, 1883), I, p. viii.

[11] Henry Gyles Turner, *A History of the Colony of Victoria: From Its Discovery to Its Absorption in the Commonwealth of Australia*, 2 vols. (London, 1904), I, p. viii.

that these nationalists understood it, as a record of real achievement, had yet to be made, and this was the special opportunity of the new world. 'If we are not History's legatees,' explained the *Bulletin*'s literary editor, 'it is because we have the chance to be History's founders and establishers.'[12]

As so often in Australia, the middle way prevailed. The men who led the process of Federation, drafted the constitution of the new Commonwealth during the 1890s, and then directed its early activities in the new century were Imperial nationalists, liberal in their sympathies, Australian in sentiment, and firm in their attachment to the Empire. Alfred Deakin, who with Edmund Barton was the outstanding figure in this group, combined a religious fervour for the national cause with an exalted loyalty to the British connection. His inner history of Federation, which remains an indispensable source, discloses the strength of this now almost incomprehensible combination, and his subsequent contributions as the anonymous correspondent of a London newspaper, when he was active in federal politics and often in dispute with the Imperial government, show an appreciation of its ambiguities.[13] From his insistence to Lord Salisbury at the Colonial Conference of 1887 that Britain serve Australian ambitions in the Pacific to the equally unwelcome advocacy of trade preference at the Imperial Conference of 1887, and from his persistence in negotiations with Joseph Chamberlain over the British enactment of Commonwealth Constitution in 1900 to many subsequent disputes with the Colonial Office while Prime Minister, Deakin sought to augment Australian influence within a strengthened Empire.

This distinctive allegiance of the 'Independent Australian Britons' (as Deakin characterized them) was served by various historical initiatives. The period marks the formation of state historical societies, though that of New South Wales not atypically arrogated to itself the title of the Australian Historical Society.[14] The formation of the federal Commonwealth (the title chosen for the new national government) did not erase the separate identities of its far-flung component states. Indeed, it probably stimulated a compensatory desire to protect them, but there was no antagonism to the burgeoning national sentiment; rather, the ire of the historical societies was directed towards those radical nationalists of the *Bulletin* variety who wanted to sweep away the colonial legacy. Composed for the most part of professional men of standing, typically enjoying viceregal patronage,

12 A. G. Stephens, *Bulletin*, 9 Dec. 1897.

13 Stuart Macintyre, ed., *'And Be One People': Alfred Deakin's Federal Story* (Carlton South, Victoria, 1995); J. A. La Nauze, ed., *Federated Australia: Selections from Letters to the Morning Post, 1900–1910* (Carlton, Victoria, 1968).

14 K. R. Cramp, 'The Australian Historical Society: The Story of its Foundation', *Australian Historical Society: Journal and Proceedings*, IV (1917–18), pp. 1–14; Brian H. Fletcher, *Australian History in New South Wales* (Kensington, NSW, 1993), chap. 3.

these societies collected records, published proceedings, and fostered reverence for the first-comers. In 1906 the government of New South Wales also accepted the offer of a major collection of manuscripts and printed Australiana assembled by David Scott Mitchell, an obsessive bibliophile.[15] Following the earlier transcription of early colonial records in London along the lines of a Canadian scheme, the Commonwealth commissioned Dr Frederick Watson, an irascible surgeon and antiquarian, to edit the *Historical Records of Australia*. He described the thirty-one volumes he completed by 1925, based mainly on official despatches, as 'the birth certificates of a nation'.[16]

The influential Australian Natives Association (the term then meant Australian-born whites rather than the original inhabitants) and other patriotic organizations joined with the historical societies to raise statues of illustrious colonial figures and built cairns to mark the trails of explorers. In Victoria from 1911 schools marked Exploration Day on 19 April, when Cook had first sighted Australia in 1770, just as they already marked Empire Day. Exploration offered a rich lode for Imperial nationalism, joining as it did the epic deeds of mostly British heroes to the destiny of the island-continent, and works such as Ernest Favenc, *The History of Australian Exploration from 1788 to 1888* (Sydney, 1888) and Louis Becke and Walter Jeffery, *The Naval Pioneers of Australia* (London, 1899) worked the lode. Even the deeds of other maritime powers could be used to affirm Australia's good fortune in its founders. Thus, the journalist Ernest Scott's 1910 account of the voyage of the Frenchman Baudin rejoiced in the providential conclusion that the French had no designs on Australia and hence the way had been kept clear for 'unimpeded development, on British constitutional lines, of a group of flourishing states forming "one continent-isle" whose bounds are "the girdling seas alone" '.[17] Scott's later *Life of Matthew Flinders, R.N.* (Sydney, 1914) made much of 'the great denominator's' naming of the continent he circumnavigated as Australia, and he was present in 1912 when Alfred Deakin announced that a new Australian naval base would in turn be named after Flinders before he pulled away a Union Jack to reveal a plaque set on the peak the Englishman had climbed during a landfall in 1802.[18]

In schools there was a growing emphasis on Australian history to supplement

[15] H. J. Gibbney, 'Prehistory of an Archives', *Archives and Manuscripts*, IV, 6 (Feb. 1972), pp. 2–7; Fletcher, *Australian History*, chap. 4.

[16] Graeme Powell, 'The Origins of the Australian Joint Copying Project', *Archives and Manuscripts*, IV, 5 (Nov. 1971), pp. 9–24; Ann Mosley Mitchell, 'Dr Frederick Watson and *Historical Records of Australia*', *Historical Studies*, XX (1982–83), pp. 171–97.

[17] Ernest Scott, *Terre Napoléon: A History of French Explorations and Projects in Australia* (London, 1910), p. 281.

[18] Stuart Macintyre, *A History for a Nation: Ernest Scott and the Making of Australian History* (Carlton, Victoria, 1994), chap. 3.

the established curriculum of British and Imperial history. Edward Jenks wrote his textbook *History of the Australasian Colonies (From Their Foundation in the Year 1893)* (Cambridge, 1895) while Professor of Law at the University of Melbourne, and presented that history as a fulfilment of the British inheritance. Arthur W. Jose, another Englishman, taught in Australia and followed *The Growth of Empire: A Handbook to the History of Greater Britain* (London, 1897) with *A Short History of Australasia* (Sydney, 1899); after serving in South Africa as war correspondent and lecturing in England for the Imperial Tariff League, he returned to Australia as correspondent for *The Times*. The Melbourne headmaster W. H. Fitchett complemented his exhortatory *Deeds That Won the Empire* (London, 1898) with *The New World of the South: The Romance of Australian History* (London, 1913). So too Ernest Scott, also an English immigrant, who had reported the federal conventions in the 1890s and then worked as *Hansard* reporter in the Commonwealth Parliament, published his *Short History of Australia* (London, 1916) to show his Australian readers that 'British history is their history, with its failings to be guarded against and its glories to be emulated'.[19]

In the universities Imperial nationalist history took on new momentum. Until the early part of the twentieth century history was a minor part of the academic curriculum, taught from standard texts to familiarize those training for the liberal professions with the lessons of the past. A new emphasis on history as a research-based discipline bore fruit, first in the universities of Sydney and Melbourne, and then in the remaining four Australian universities in which graduates of the two older foundations took up appointments. At Sydney, George Arnold Wood, a high-minded English nonconformist who had trained at Balliol, stressed European and English history as a source of moral elevation, though advanced students undertook research on the early colonial period.[20] At Melbourne, where the degreeless Ernest Scott was appointed to the chair in 1913 on the strength of his exploration studies, there was a closer relationship between the study of history, economics, and politics. Scott put greater emphasis on Australian history, which he taught systematically and comparatively as an integral part of British and European imperial history. His teaching, based on student essays embodying original research, fostered an impressive list of future historians including Sir Keith Hancock, Sir Stephen Roberts, and Fred Alexander.

By the inter-war years the basis of an academic historical profession was apparent.[21] Wood and Scott were now the only non-Australians to occupy a chair of history. Typically, the younger academic historians followed a first Australian

[19] Ernest Scott, *A Short History of Australia* (London, 1916), p. 336.

[20] R. M. Crawford, *'A Bit of a Rebel': The Life and Work of George Arnold Wood* (Sydney, 1975).

[21] Stuart Macintyre and Julian Thomas, eds., *The Discovery of Australian History* (Carlton, Victoria, 1995).

degree by proceeding to England for further study—a second undergraduate degree at Oxford in most cases, a postgraduate research degree at London for a growing minority. Their education initiated them into a particular milieu: as members of the professional élite they moved easily among the political and administrative decision-makers. Since they taught a significant proportion of the diplomats and public servants who would assume direction of Australian foreign policy from the Second World War, these connections enabled the academics to induct their charges into positions of influence. They were men of affairs, often contributing commentary on national or international issues to the press, frequently members of the Round Table and later the Royal Institute of International Affairs, sometimes gathering in overseas as well as domestic assemblies on contemporary issues though seldom in academic conferences. The Institute of Pacific Relations was an important forum as the Australian intelligentsia, sensing an eastward shift of power, became more engaged with their region. Yet they were also scholars, and despite the limited research facilities and restricted outlets for publication—there was still no academic journal and but one university press—they produced an impressive body of work, mostly but by no means exclusively Australian in subject, increasingly Australian in perspective. Monographs on such subjects as French colonial policy and contemporary foreign affairs accompanied pioneer accounts of Australian constitutional and economic development, land policy, and immigration.[22]

The Australian volume of the *Cambridge History of the British Empire* (Cambridge, 1933) marks the apogee of this form of Australian historical scholarship. The team assembled by Scott comprised seven academic historians supplemented by lawyers, geographers, economists, and politicians. Eleven of its sixteen Australian contributors were members of the imperial brotherhood of the Round Table. If some were critical of British policy in the colonial period, they minimized points of strain in the recent past. The English editors of the *Cambridge History* prefaced the Australian and New Zealand volumes with the understanding that 'The history of both Dominions takes a special character from this comparatively free development of English life transplanted to coasts and islands on the other side of the world.' With some reservations, the

[22] S. H. Roberts, *History of French Colonial Policy (1870–1925)* (London, 1929); F. Alexander, *From Paris to Locarno and After: The League of Nations and the Search for Security, 1919–1928* (London, 1929); A. C. V. Melbourne, *Early Constitutional Development in Australia* (Oxford, 1934); Stephen H. Roberts, *History of Australian Land Settlement, 1788–1920* (Melbourne, 1924); E. O. G. Shann, *An Economic History of Australia* (Cambridge, 1930); Richard Charles Mills, *The Colonization of Australia (1929–1842)* (London, 1915); R. B. Madgwick, *Immigration into Eastern Australia, 1788–1851* (London, 1937); Myra Willard, *History of the White Australia Policy to 1920* (Melbourne, 1923).

Australians agreed that their compatriots were coming to appreciate 'the responsibilities as well as the privileges which nationhood involves'.[23]

Scott expressed the expectation that the *Cambridge History of the British Empire* would 'probably be used all over the world for a century to come'.[24] In fact it was superseded within less than a quarter of a century by a new compendium, edited by Gordon Greenwood, *Australia: A Social and Political History* (Sydney, 1955). Greenwood's textbook was aimed at the vastly augmented number of students of Australian history as a result of the post-war expansion of the educational system; it also drew on a far richer scholarly literature made possible by the concomitant expansion of the profession and the scholarly infrastructure. Beyond these altered disciplinary conditions, it spoke to new circumstances. Between the pre-war and post-war publications there had been a fight for national survival in which Australia had discovered the limits of the Imperial capacity. The war in the Pacific and then the new post-war international order had altered the nation's strategic and economic orientation. The Labor government that mobilized the nation in arms and planned the post-war reconstruction fostered an increased measure of autonomy. A nationalism that was no longer synonymous with imperialism required a new kind of national history. Where Scott's work had appeared in an Imperial series, Greenwood's was sponsored by the committee that organized the celebration of the fiftieth anniversary of the Australian Commonwealth.

Signs of this challenge to the established historiographical orientation had been apparent in a dismissive allusion to the *Cambridge History of the British Empire* written in 1939 by H. V. Evatt, then a judge of the High Court, later an aggressively internationalist Minister for External Affairs in the Labor ministries from 1941 to 1949. He had derided the book's complacent affirmation of the perspective of the educated Anglophile élite, and suggested that a reader 'would suppose that every important event in our history must, in some mysterious way, have revealed its true importance to a Melbourne coterie exclusively'.[25] Evatt identified himself with the dissident, progressive intelligentsia whose sympathy for a revived radical nationalism was strengthened during the war against fascism and the preparation for a new social order. A principal figure in this circle was Brian Fitzpatrick, a student of Scott who had turned to journalism and was a founder of the Australian Council of Civil Liberties. In his two studies of economic history, *British Imperialism in Australia, 1788–1833: An Economic History of Australasia*

[23] J. Holland Rose and others, eds., *Cambridge History of the British Empire*, 9 vols. (Cambridge, 1929–59), VII, Part 1, pp. v, 624.

[24] Ernest to Emily Scott, 11 Sept. 1926, Scott Papers, National Library of Australia, MSS 703/10/293–9.

[25] H. V. Evatt, preface to Francis Clancy, *They Built a Nation* (Sydney, 1939), p. vi.

(London, 1939) and *The British Empire in Australia: An Economic History* (Melbourne, 1941), Fitzpatrick discerned a pattern of exploitation of the Australian people by British capital and its Australian servants.[26] While Fitzpatrick was denied a university post, a younger generation of left-wing historians took advantage of the opportunities for study offered to returned service personnel to embark on academic careers. Most began as members of the Communist Party, though few remained communists after 1956. One of them, Robin Gollan, contributed a substantial chapter to Greenwood's volume. Another, Russel Ward, produced the influential *The Australian Legend* (Melbourne, 1958), which traced a demotic tradition of egalitarian mateship as the basis of the national self-image.

That was one line of assault on the older historical dispensation. The other came from the opposite direction and again it was expressed in criticism of Scott and his school. Scott had hoped that Keith Hancock, his most distinguished student, would succeed him in the Melbourne chair. Upon Scott's retirement in 1936, however, Hancock made it clear he would not leave England, and he advised the selection committee that a new approach was needed at Melbourne: 'Colonial history is quite important but not important enough to be central in a history school . . . The soil is too narrow for growing minds to take root in it and draw strong nourishment from it.'[27] This summary dismissal of Scott's curriculum, which was in fact Imperial as much as it was colonial, is surely surprising. Hancock had contributed a chapter to the Australian volume of the *Cambridge History*; while professor at Adelaide he had written *Australia* (1930), an extended historical essay mordant in its diagnosis of the patterns of national excess and yet expressive of deep emotional ties to his homeland. Hancock has explained his inability to return to Australia at this juncture as a predicament of *Country and Calling* (London), the stimulation and opportunity of the metropolis winning out over the limitations of the province, and at this time he was engaged on his magisterial *Survey of British Commonwealth Affairs* (London, 1937–42), which could not have been pursued in Australia.[28] Beyond this, however, was his conviction that both the subject-matter and the scholarly literature of Australian history lacked intellectual nourishment, that it was too narrow and cramped. The incompatibility of country and calling was here a disciplinary deficiency and one that Scott's successor, R. M. Crawford, shared. Crawford, originally a student of Wood at Sydney who had proceeded to Balliol, reshaped the history curriculum at Melbourne by reducing the emphasis on both Imperial and Australian history,

[26] Don Watson, *Brian Fitzpatrick: A Radical Life* (Sydney, 1978).

[27] Hancock to the Acting Vice-Chancellor, 28 Aug. 1936, University of Melbourne Registry Files, 1936/201.

[28] W. K. Hancock, *Country and Calling* (London, 1954), p. 126.

and consequently on original research, and by extending the range and depth of a liberal education in a disciplinary mode.[29] Crawford's school became the seminary for a new generation of historians in the Australian universities, while the later return of Hancock to take up the chair of history in the Research School at the new Australian National University strengthened the orientation.

Neither the radical nationalists nor the cosmopolitan internationalists carried the day. The onset of the cold war blunted the radical edge of nationalism, while both Crawford and Hancock were drawn into the rapid post-war expansion of Australian history, Crawford guiding the creation in 1940 of the first professional journal, *Historical Studies: Australia and New Zealand*, Hancock initiating the *Australian Dictionary of Biography* (1966–). Indeed, both camps felt the strong undertow of their institutional setting within the universities. There was a proliferation of postgraduate research and publication, now the requisite steps of professional advancement. A trickle of theses, articles, and books on Australian topics became a flood, blocking in the details of a national history and the channelling into increasingly specialized fields of political, economic, religious, social, and labour history, all of which in turn established their own journals, literature, and conventions.[30] This unbroken expansion of the profession, which lasted until the 1970s, was by no means restricted to Australian specialists: British as well as continental European, American, and Asian history all flourished. It was the older Imperial dimension that dwindled.

It used to be said of a course in Australian history delivered at one Australian university that the lecturer did well if he got the First Fleet out of Portsmouth Harbour before the end of the final term. By the 1970s it was a rare teacher who lingered on the British origins. The shift of perspective is apparent in the work of C. M. H. Clark, the most influential and accomplished of these national historians.[31] Clark's training at Melbourne under Scott and Crawford was followed by study at Balliol and then a thesis on Tocqueville. At Melbourne immediately after the war he embarked on Australian history, firing a generation of distinguished future historians with his conviction that this was a subject of depth and substance in which a drama of inherited religious and secular faiths was played out. Moving to the chair of history at Canberra, he embarked on a large-scale *History*

[29] Robert Dare, 'Max Crawford and the Study of History', in Macintyre and Thomas, eds., *The Discovery of Australian History*, pp. 174–91.

[30] Geoffrey Serle, 'The State of the Profession', *Historical Studies*, XV (1972–73), pp. 686–702.

[31] Clark's biographical writing includes *The Puzzles of Childhood* (Ringwood, Victoria, 1989), *The Quest for Grace* (Ringwood, Victoria, 1990), and *A Historian's Apprenticeship* (Carlton, Victoria, 1992). The extensive literature on him includes Stephen Holt, *Manning Clark and Australian History, 1915–1963* (St Lucia, Queensland, 1982) and Carl Bridge, ed., *Manning Clark: Essays on His Place in History* (Carlton, Victoria, 1994).

of Australia in six volumes (Carlton, Victoria, 1962–87). At first he told a familiar story in terms of epic tragedy, a history in which the explorers, Governors, improvers, and perturbators vainly endeavoured to impose their received schemes of redemption on an alien, intractable setting; gradually, as the *History* unfolded, it expanded to take in those on whom these men of agency and vision acted, Aborigines, convicts, rural selectors, urban battlers, women. By the final volumes Australia had ceased to be a marginal output of European civilization; its story was now a story of discovery as its people threw off the encumbering, derivative culture they had brought with them in order to grasp the wisdom of what was distinctively Australian.

Clark's prophetic stance, charged prose, and disdain for academic pedantry had a greater influence on artists, writers, and opinion-makers than on his professional colleagues. In book and film, museum and art gallery, the newly diagnosed 'cultural cringe' was discarded and an assertive nationalism came to prevail.[32] Not that the historical profession resisted the altered cultural climate. On the contrary, as the strategic significance of the British Commonwealth declined, as patterns of trade and investment changed, and such institutions as the courts and the church moved to full autonomy, so the nation's textbooks registered growing separation from the Mother Country. Where Hancock's *Australia* (London, 1930) had traced what independent Australian Britons made of their patrimony, a series of post-war short histories—R. M. Crawford, *Australia* (London, 1952), A. G. L. Shaw, *The Story of Australia* (London, 1955), Douglas Pike, *Australia: The Quiet Continent* (London, 1962), C. M. H. Clark, *A Short History of Australia* (London, 1963), and finally the collection edited by Frank Crowley, *A New History of Australia* (Melbourne, 1974)—became increasingly autochthonous in coverage and treatment. In studies of the convicts the comparative perspective of A. G. L. Shaw, whose *Convicts and the Colonies* (London, 1966) was subtitled *A Study of Penal Transportation from Great Britain and Ireland to Australia and Other Parts of the British Empire*, yielded to the national approach suggested by the title of L. L. Robson's *The Convict Settlers of Australia* (Carlton, Victoria, 1955). His reorientation came to prevail. In *Convict Society and Its Enemies* (1983) J. B. Hirst traced the unlikely origins of a free society, while Portia Robinson's *The Women of Botany Bay* (Macquarie, 1988) and Stephen Nicholas, ed., *Convict Workers: Reinterpreting Australia's Past* (Cambridge, 1988), edited by Stephen Nicholas, construed the felons as respectively the mothers and labour force of a future nation. Conversely, another revisionist school challenged the accepted explanation of the reasons for settlement of Australia with the claim

[32] The phrase was coined by the literary critic A. A. Phillips, *The Australian Tradition* (Melbourne, 1958).

that the strategic significance of new British naval bases and sources of naval supplies outweighed the desire, after the loss of the American colonies, to find a new place of exile for felons. Yet this apparent rejoining of early Australian history to its larger Imperial context did not disturb the insularity of Australian historiography; rather, the re-engagement served to reinforce national self-esteem with the discovery of more auspicious national origins.[33]

In economic history the earlier battle between Edward Shann and Brian Fitzpatrick over the beneficent or maleficent effects of imperialism yielded to the formidable quantitative analyses of endogenous factors in Australian growth conducted by Noel Butlin and his school.[34] In cultural history the early work of George Nadel, *Australia's Colonial Culture: Ideas, Men and Institutions in Nineteenth-Century Eastern Australia* (Melbourne, 1957), showed the adaptation of derivative models, whereas A. G. Serle, in *From Deserts the Prophets Come: The Creative Spirit in Australia, 1788–1972* (Melbourne, 1973), celebrated the realization of distinctively Australian styles. In military history the official war historian C. E. W. Bean, born in Australia, educated at Clifton College and Oxford, wrote six volumes on the Australians in the Great War and edited eight more (Sydney, 1922–42). His Imperial nationalism validated the deeds and character of the Australian Imperial Force and his first two volumes on the Gallipoli campaign, *The Story of Anzac* (Sydney, 1922–24), ended with a declaration that 'it was on the 25th of April 1915, that the consciousness of Australian nationhood was born'.[35] When interest in military history revived as K. S. Inglis reconsidered 'The Australians at Gallipoli' (1970) and L. L. Robson took up the *The First A.I.F.: A Study of Its Recruitment, 1914–1918* (Carlton, Victoria, 1970), there was a new emphasis on the antagonism between the Australian soldiers and the British high command and the deep domestic divisions engendered by the Australian commitment.[36] Subsequently the affirmative official history of the Second World War in twenty-two volumes edited by Gavin Long (Canberra, 1952–77) was challenged

[33] Ged Martin, ed., *The Founding of Australia: The Argument about Australia's Origins* (Sydney, 1978), is an anthology of the first stage of the debate. The revisionist argument has been extended by Alan Frost, *Convicts and Empire: A Naval Question, 1776–1811* (Melbourne, 1980), *Arthur Phillip, 1738–1814: His Voyaging* (Melbourne, 1987), and *Botany Bay Mirages: Illusions of Australia's Convict Beginnings* (Carlton, Victoria, 1994).

[34] Principally N. G. Butlin, *Australian Domestic Product, Investment and Foreign Borrowing, 1861–1938/9* (Cambridge, 1962), *Investment in Australian Economic Development, 1861–1900* (Cambridge, 1964), and *Forming a Colonial Economy: Australia, 1810–1850* (Melbourne, 1994).

[35] C. E. W. Bean, *The Story of Anzac from the Outbreak of War to the End of the First Phase of the Gallipoli Campaign, May 4, 1915* (Sydney, 1921) and *The Story of Anzac from 4 May, 1915 to the Evacuation of the Gallipoli Peninsula* (Sydney, 1924), p. 910.

[36] K. S. Inglis, 'The Australians at Gallipoli', Parts I and II, *Historical Studies*, XIV (1969–71), pp. 219–30, 361–75.

even more stridently by critics alleging Britain's neglect of Australian security interests.[37]

These examples are necessarily summary and selective. Not all Australian historians abandoned Imperial interests. They benefited from the more generous provision of research support and cheaper air-travel, and they were assisted by Phyllis Mander-Jones's extensive bibliography of *Manuscripts in the British Isles Relating to Australia, New Zealand and the Pacific* (Canberra, 1972), as well as the Australian Joint Copying Project, which systematically microfilmed material relevant to Australia held in British archives. J. M. Ward published extensively on British colonial policy in Australia and the Pacific, and others made closer studies of particular colonial topics, while K. S. Inglis's path-breaking social history of *The Australian Colonists: An Exploration of Social History, 1788–1870* (Carlton, Victoria, 1974) was acutely sensitive to the interplay of what was brought and what was made.[38] The era of colonial nationalism was served by Gavin Souter's wide-ranging study of exchanges between *The Lion and the Kangeroo: Australia, 1901–1919: The Rise of a Nation* (Sydney, 1976) in the early Commonwealth period, and Chris Cunneen in *Kings' Men: Australia's Governors-General from Hopetown to Isaacs* (Sydney, 1983) suggested how the early Governors-General had mediated the exchanges. Other scholars of Australian foreign relations and defence history continued to explore the Imperial–colonial relationship.[39] Distinguished biographies traced the careers of the statesmen—Deakin, Hughes, Menzies, Casey—who mediated the transition from Empire to Commonwealth.[40] Even so, the growing strength of national boundaries was unmistakable: for most historians of Australia, the Empire was of interest insofar as it bore on evolution of the colonies towards independent nationhood and no further. G. C. Bolton and

[37] D. M. Horner, *High Command: Australia and Allied Strategy, 1939–1945* (North Sydney, 1982); David Day, *Menzies and Churchill at War* (Sydney, 1986) and *Reluctant Nation: Australia and the Allied Defeat of Japan, 1942–45* (Melbourne, 1992).

[38] J. M. Ward, *British Policy in the South Pacific, 1786–1893: A Study of British Policy in the South Pacific Islands Prior to the Establishment of Governments by the Great Powers* (Sydney, 1948), *Earl Grey and the Australian Colonies, 1864–1857: A Study of Self-Government and Self-Interest* (Melbourne, 1958), *Empire in the Antipodes: The British in Australia* (London, 1966), and *James Macarthur* (full citation n. 7); J. J. Eddy, *Britain and the Australian Colonies, 1818–1831* (Oxford, 1969); John Ritchie, *Punishment and Profit* (Melbourne, 1970).

[39] See T. B. Millar, *Australia in Peace and War: External Relations, 1788–1977* (Canberra, 1978); Neville Meaney, *Australia and the World: A Documentary History from the 1870s to the 1970s* (Melbourne, 1985); Geoffrey Grey, *A Military History of Australia* (Melbourne, 1990); Michael McKernan and Michael Browne, eds., *Australia: Two Centuries of Peace and War* (Canberra, 1988).

[40] J. A. La Nauze, *Alfred Deakin: A Biography*, 2 vols. (Carlton, Victoria, 1965); L. F. Fitzhardinge, *A Political Biography of William Morris Hughes*, 2 vols. (Sydney, 1964–79); A. W. Martin, *Robert Menzies: A Life*, Vol. I, 1893–1943 (Carlton, Victoria, 1993); W. J. Hudson, *Casey* (Melbourne, 1986).

J. D. B. Miller were rare exceptions in their Hancockian combination of Australian and wider interests.[41]

From the late 1960s a series of challenges were issued to this triumphal nationalism. Younger Australians fired by the iconoclastic enthusiasms of the New Left accompanied radical protest against the domestic and international order with a vigorous critical reappraisal of their country's past: they dwelt on the less attractive aspects of the national character, the reliance upon great and powerful friends to allay regional insecurity, the authoritarianism and ready recourse to violence, the xenophobia, and racial discrimination. The New Left scholar and activist Humphrey McQueen took William Wentworth's phrase as the title of his influential tract, *A New Britannia: Social Origins of Australian Radicalism and Socialism* (Harmondsworth, 1970), to indict the Australian labour movement for its complicity in capitalism and imperialism. Feminist historians who contested the overwhelmingly masculine character of Australian historiography presented the oppression of women as intrinsic to the national story.[42] A forgotten history of genocidal expropriation of Aboriginal Australians was rediscovered.[43] New studies of migration emphasized its exploitative and discriminatory effects.[44] These attacks on the established order at once employed the framework of national history and contested it. Initially the dissidents sought to redefine the national identity; unlike the earlier radical nationalists, however, they did not romanticize the history of their homeland in order to discern its dormant potential but rather arraigned the Australian past in order to break with it. As that millenarian ambition faded, the cumulative effect of their multiple assaults was to fragment the structures that had given national history its unit and coherence, and ultimately to call the very category of the nation into question. This outcome was by no means unique to Australian historiography, of course, for elsewhere as well the post-structural incursion into the discipline dissolved the nation into an ideological effect, a contested site of meaning. In this spirit, Richard White's influential *Inventing Australia: Images and Identity, 1688–1980* (Sydney, 1981) surveyed the

[41] Bolton's non-Australian writing included *The Passing of the Irish Act of Union: A Study in Parliamentary Politics* (London, 1966) and *Britain's Legacy Overseas* (London, 1973), while Miller wrote *Britain and the Old Dominions* (London, 1966) and *Survey of Commonwealth Affairs: Problems of Expansion and Attrition, 1953–1969* (London, 1974).

[42] Miriam Dixson, *The Real Matilda: Women and Identity in Australia, 1788 to the Present* (Ringwood, Victoria, 1975); Anne Summers, *Damned Whores and God's Police: The Colonization of Women in Australia* (Ringwood, Victoria, 1975).

[43] C. D. Rowley, *The Destruction of Aboriginal Society* (Canberra, 1970); Henry Reynolds, *Aborigines and Settlers: The Australian Experience, 1788–1939* (North Melbourne, 1972).

[44] Jean Martin, *The Migrant Presence: Australian Response, 1947–1977: Research Report for the National Population Inquiry* (Sydney, 1978).

changing self-images pursued in literature and art, and by government and advertising agencies, as a constantly unfolding process of disputation.

As if mocking its detractors, the nation reinvented itself anew. The reform programme of the federal Labor government returning to office in 1983 combined economic reconstruction aimed at integrating Australian industry into the world economy, closer engagement with the country's regional neighbours, and in social and cultural policy, the cultivation of a more inclusive, confident, and enterprising citizenship. Multiculturalism, affirmative action for women, land rights and reconciliation of Aborigines, which were all institutionalized in state agencies, both accepted and accommodated diversity as a national asset. The promotion of Australian studies in schools and universities was a product of the same impulse, though the planting of Australian studies centres abroad had a nice twist in London where the centre was located in the Institute for Commonwealth Studies and subsequently named after Sir Robert Menzies.

Historians were prominent in the articulation of the new Australia. Paul Keating, Prime Minister from 1991 to 1996, drew heavily on Australian history for the substance and symbolism of a nationhood that now prefigured the future republic as a proper recognition of what was best in national tradition. (His speechwriter, Don Watson, was the biographer of the radical nationalist exemplar, Brian Fitzpatrick.) Particular speeches delivered by Keating, such as on the fall of Singapore and the burden of white responsibility for Aboriginal deaths, as well as his allusions to a 'postcolonial' Australia, drew accusations of 'Pom bashing' and—in the epithet of Geoffrey Blainey, who was at once a distinguished historian and prominent critic of multiculturalism and Aboriginal land rights—a 'black armband' view of the country's past.[45] This was to confuse the populist rhetoric of a ferocious polemicist with his profoundly affirmative patriotism, which he skilfully reworked to embrace new circumstances.

'Post-colonial' in its hyphenated form conventionally refers to the aftermath of Empire. 'Postcolonialism', as theorized more recently by its circle of adherents, refers to the circumstances, both before and after formal independence, whereby colonized peoples seek to take their place as historical subjects.[46] In countries such as Australia where the nation had its origins in colonial settlement, postcolonialism involves a dual process: first, the final emancipation of the settler society from the extended consequences of its subordination to the Empire, and second, the struggle to be heard of those who were silenced during that initial transition from colony to nation. Postcolonialism poses a sharp challenge to a settler society because it repositions the

[45] Mark Ryan, ed., *Advancing Australia: The Speeches of Paul Keating, Prime Minister* (Sydney, 1995); Geoffrey Blainey, *All for Australia* (North Ryde, NSW, 1984) and *Eye on Australia: Speeches and Essays of Geoffrey Blainey* (Melbourne, 1991).

[46] Elleke Boehmer, *Colonial and Postcolonial Literature: Migrant Metaphors* (Oxford, 1995), p. 3.

colonists as colonizers, complicit in the imperial project of domination. So it is that the British settlement of Australia is now construed as an invasion, and much recent writing on Aboriginal history seeks to listen to the voices of the invaded people. So, too, other Australians of non-British ethnic origins assert their distinctive identities. The public commemoration in 1988 of the bicentenary of the arrival of the First Fleet negotiated these sensitivities by turning Australian history into a journey in which all participated and by which all can live together.[47]

Where does this leave the Imperial dimension of Australian history? It is present, most obviously, in the debate on the republic. The need to explain how the removal of the last lingering traces of the Crown from the Australian system of government would effect a final deliverance calls for Talmudic powers of constitutional exegesis that few Australian republicans possess. Alternatively, the contention of the anti-republicans that Australia already possesses full independence requires them to identify when and how that release from Imperial tutelage occurred. Historians have been active in both endeavours.[48] In its more popular usage, the republic signifies a final break with the fetters of the past, a sweeping away of the last symbols and habits of deference in order to attach loyalties more securely to the new national order.[49] The Empire here is a powerful signifier but conspicuously vague and imprecise, for appreciation of its history has long since fallen into neglect. If the transition from colonial to independent nation was accompanied by an Imperial amnesia, the advent of postcolonial nationalism seems to have resulted in a double displacement of the Imperial past that is only now reviving as the reconstituted nation bends back to settle accounts with its origins. Conspicuous here is the discovery in British law that the Aboriginal inhabitants were indeed a sovereign people, and the appreciation of the Colonial Office that the Australian colonists could not extinguish their rights. The arguments of the historian Henry Reynolds on these matters were a direct influence on the High Court of Australia when it handed down its decision in the Mabo case and recognized native title.[50]

Thus the Imperial past is reworked to meet present needs. The reworking, however, remains selective and incomplete. As treated in contemporary Australian historical scholarship, the Empire is a solipsism. The interlocking perspective that joined an earlier generation of colonial nationalist historians to their colleagues in

[47] Susan Janson and Stuart Macintyre, eds., *Making the Bicentenary* [Australian] *Historical Studies* (special issue, Parkville, Victoria), XXIII, 91 (Oct. 1988); Tony Bennett and others, eds., *Celebrating the Nation: A Critical Study of Australia's Bicentenary* (St Leonards, NSW, 1992).

[48] David Headon and others, eds., *Crown or Country: The Traditions of Australian Republicanism* (St Leonards, NSW, 1994); Alan Atkinson, *The Muddle-Headed Republic* (Melbourne, 1993); John Hirst, *A Republican Manifesto* (Melbourne, 1994); W. J. Hudson and M. P. Sharp, *Australian Independence: Colony to Reluctant Kingdom* (Melbourne, 1988).

[49] Tom Keneally, *Our Republic* (Port Melbourne, Victoria, 1993).

[50] Henry Reynolds, *The Law of the Land* (Ringwood, Victoria, 1987).

other parts of the Empire, a perspective that saw the Empire holistically as a reciprocal movement of energies and comparatively as part of a broader regional and global pattern, has yielded to national preoccupations. The responsibility for this shrinkage is not solely local. British Imperial historians have drawn back from the study of the White Dominions, and the insights that a Jebb or Bryce could bring to Australian developments have yielded to the incomprehension of a visiting professor from Cambridge.[51] Periodically, an overseas scholar rejoins Australia to a larger historical pattern.[52] Periodically, an Australian scholar seeks to break down the isolation of Australian history.[53] Occasionally, an effort is made to revive awareness of the time when colonialism and nationalism coexisted.[54] But not until the lingering effects of the colonial condition are finally expunged to Australian satisfaction is the Empire likely to find acceptance in its future historiography.

[51] Charles Wilson, *Australia, 1788–1988: The Creation of a Nation* (London, 1987).

[52] Mancur Olson, 'Australia in the Perspective of the Rise and Decline of Nations', *Australian Economic Review*, LXVII (1984), pp. 7–17; Avner Offer, *The First World War: An Agrarian Interpretation* (Oxford, 1989).

[53] J. B. Hirst, 'Keeping Colonial History Colonial', *Historical Studies*, XXI (1984–85), pp. 85–104; Donald Denoon, *Settler Capitalism: The Dynamics of Dependent Development in the Southern Hemisphere* (Oxford, 1983) and 'The Isolation of Australian History', *Historical Studies*, XXII (1986–87), pp. 252–60.

[54] John Eddy, Deryck Schreuder, and others, eds., *The Rise of Colonial Nationalism: Australia, New Zealand, Canada, and South Africa First Assert Their Nationalities, 1880–1914* (Sydney, 1988).

Select Bibliography

D. H. BORCHARDT and VICTOR CRITTENDEN, eds., *Australians: A Guide to Sources* (Broadway, NSW, 1987).

CARL BRIDGE, ed., *Manning Clark: Essays on His Place in History* (Carlton, Victoria, 1994).

MANNING CLARK, *Occasional Writings and Speeches* (Sydney, 1980).

R. M. CRAWFORD, MANNING CLARK, and GEOFFREY BLAINEY, *Making History* (Fitzroy, Victoria, 1985).

GRAEME DAVISON, JOHN HIRST, and STUART MACINTYRE, eds., *The Oxford Companion to Australian History* (Melbourne, 1998).

FRANK FARRELL, *Themes in Australian History: Questions, Issues and Interpretations in Evolving Historiography* (Kensington, NSW, 1990).

BRIAN H. FLETCHER, *Australian History in New South Wales, 1888–1938* (Kensington, NSW, 1993).

W. K. HANCOCK, *Country and Calling* (London, 1954).

STUART MACINTYRE, *A History for a Nation: Ernest Scott and the Making of Australian History* (Carlton, Victoria, 1994).

—— and JULIAN THOMAS, eds., *The Discovery of Australian History, 1890–1939* (Carlton, Victoria, 1995).

J. A. MOSES, ed., *Historical Disciplines and Culture in Australasia: An Assessment* (St Lucia, Queensland, 1979).

ROB PASCOE, *The Manufacture of Australian History* (Carlton, Victoria, 1979).

10

Colonization and History in New Zealand

JAMES BELICH

British expansion was accompanied by a great human diaspora, in which 18 million migrants sought to create better Britains on three continents. Historical literature was among their tools, shaping and reshaping the past for the purpose of the present and future. One of these neo-Britains was New Zealand, where substantial European settlement began in the 1830s. A traumatic but dynamic era of colonization, in which settlers attempted the mass conversion of nature and natives, lasted until the 1880s. The succeeding era, from the 1880s to the 1940s, was characterized by 're-colonization'. A multifaceted phenomenon not widely recognized by historians to this day, re-colonization can be explained as a tightening of links with the metropolis, against the grain of expectations about the steady development of national maturity and independence. Decolonization emerged erratically and incompletely between the 1940s and 1980s. Clean cuts are rare in history, and the three phases overlapped. But they do usefully divide both New Zealand's past and the representation of it.

From the 1830s, the organizers of New Zealand colonization, Edward Gibbon Wakefield and Company, became the first organizers of New Zealand historiography. They specialized in propaganda, and their crusade for progressive colonization needs to be respected as well as suspected. It extended far beyond the colonizing companies; it converted authors as well as victims, and it laid the foundations of both Pakeha (New Zealand Europeans) and their historiography. Books merging history with propaganda and prophecy flowered as early as the 1850s. Charles Hursthouse's copywriting classic *New Zealand or Zealandia: The Britain of the South*, 2 vols. (London, 1857) was obvious advertising, yet it shared basic axioms with more substantial works, notably army surgeon Arthur Saunders's *Thomson's Story of New Zealand*, 2 vols. (London, 1859). This was the first important general history, selectively mined as well as underestimated by posterity.

Another major historiographical influence was that of George Grey (Governor 1845–53 and 1861–67), who attempted to make sure he was not underestimated by his posterity. His despatches doubled as drafts of his own epitaph, and he co-authored the first major exercise in publishing Maori tradition. Between 1849 and

1854, Grey employed the Arawa chief Wiremu Maihi Te Rangikaheke, New Zealand's first professional historian, at a salary of £36 per annum plus accommodation. Together, they produced *Polynesian Mythology* (London, 1855), published under Grey's name alone—the foundation text in a long Pakeha–Maori reinvention of traditional Maori history. This mutated and homogenized a rich and tribally diverse oral literature, but also helped preserve it. The fruitful 1850s also produced Thomas Chomondeley's *Ultima Thule* (London, 1984), which concluded a wide-ranging mix of Spencerian philosophy, gentle emigration propaganda, and prophecy with a plea for the preservation of historical records:

> All these will be read with avidity and invested with importance by the New Zealander of the year 2000; little as they command attention now . . . In the history of 'beginnings', especially, are minute accounts and descriptions valued for instruction, and powerful to awaken passions. So dear are they to the nations, that, if wanting, their place must be supplied by legends and mythical stories.[1]

The central theme of colonial historiography was rapid progress towards a great future, with young New Zealand, an 'infant Hercules' strangling serpents that reared in her path: short-sighted Colonial Office policies, autocratic Governors, and intransigent Maori. 'Select stock', the best of the British; an environment peculiarly suited to bring out the best in Britons, and vice versa; and the racial Anglo-Saxon genius packed conveniently in settlers' genes featured large. The achievement of self-government (1853–56) and narrow victory over the Maori in the New Zealand Wars (1860–72) were benchmarks. Britishness did not preclude colonial collective identity, expectations of independence, or pride in a distinctive history. The alleged edge of colonial over British troops, for example, was thought to demonstrate the superiority of Better Britons over Worse Britons, foreshadowing ANZAC legends.[2] Colonial historians did not deprecate the brevity of their subject; they celebrated it. It corroborated the presumed trajectory of the future: onwards and upwards.

Re-colonization began in the 1880s, established itself fully by the 1920s, persisted strongly to the 1940s, and has residues in the present. It reshaped links with Britain, tightened New Zealand society, and narrowed its prospects and retrospects. New Zealand became London's town supply district; London became New Zealand's cultural capital; refrigerated meatships bridged the gap as if with interisland ferries of a single entity. Expectations shifted from a qualitative and quantitative replication of Britain, which in its New Zealand form would ultimately be great and independent, to a close, permanent, and junior partnership, whose superiority to the original was qualitative alone. This shift from American to Scots

[1] pp. 329–30, 326–27.

[2] e.g. William Fox, *The War in New Zealand* (London, 1866).

models, as it were, meant less dynamism and more subordination, but the latter was by no means static. The favourite child traded prolonged adolescence for special access to Mother's ear, purse, and markets, and for higher living standards—almost an inversion of conventional colonial exploitation.

Re-colonization consolidated some colonial myth-history, such as 'select stock' and 'racial harmony'—both used to distinguish New Zealand from Australia—but also transformed it. Rapid, ruthless colonial progress, led by schemes, camps, instant towns, and extraction, was retrospectively replaced by slow, steady, and virtuous farm-led progress. Australia and America, important influences on colonial New Zealand, were written out; Britain and the Maori were written further in. Like colonization, re-colonization overcame its enemies in benchmark battles. Economic stagnation was beaten by the pragmatic 'state socialism' of Liberal and Labour governments (1891–1912 and 1935–49), and 'enemies of the people', from militant unionists to gentry, also succumbed to state power, notably in the industrial struggle of 1912–13. National independence was earned through loyalty to Britain, especially in war. There was even greater emphasis on ethnic homogeneity: '98.5 per cent British' was a common slogan. This unique New Zealand definition of 'British' incorporated both Irish and Maori.

The co-option of the Maori developed the missionary motif of the 'whitening Maori'—exceptional savages, perfect prospects for conversion and civilization—which fought a long battle with Fatal Impact's 'dying Maori' stereotype before triumphing around 1900. The key texts emerged between the 1880s and the 1920s,[3] with Stephenson Percy Smith prominent among their producers. They argued that the Maori were descended from proto-European Aryans, and that this helped explain their excellence and assimilability relative to other native peoples. Because New Zealand used the Maori and allegedly good Maori–Pakeha relations to symbolize herself, overtly bad relations were undesirable, and the legend became to some extent self-actualizing. Maori scholars sometimes collaborated with this 'Smithing' of Maori history, perhaps to gain leverage with Pakeha state and society. One Maori-controlled product of collaboration was *Tikao Talks*, a book told by Ngai Tahu scholar Teone Taare Tikao to a Pakeha scribe over eleven days.[4]

The ideological shift from colonization to re-colonization can be traced in popular and scholarly histories. E. M. Bourke's *Little History of New Zealand* (Auckland, 1881), did not explain much, but it did emphasize rapid progress and the history of 'our own country' rather than the British heritage—in marked contrast to twentieth-century successors. F. J. Moss's transitional *School History of*

[3] Edward Tregear, *The Aryan Maori* (Wellington, 1885); John White, *The Ancient History of the Maori*, 6 vols. (Wellington, 1887–90); S. Percy Smith, *The Lore of the Whare-Wananga*, 2 vols. (Wellington, 1913–15); Elsdon Best, *The Maori*, 2 vols. (Wellington, 1924).

[4] Herries Beattie, ed., *Tikao Talks* (1939; repr. Auckland, 1990), p. 160.

New Zealand (Auckland, 1889) re-colonially whitened Maori to the point where their rats, which they ate, became 'a kind of small rabbit'. But he also spoke colonially of 'what we all hope will become a great and noble nation'.[5] *Our Nation's Story*, first published for senior primary-school children about 1928, illustrates the full development of re-colonization's ideology. 'Our Nation' was Britain; 'our country' was New Zealand. Select stock, Maori–Pakeha harmony and racial homogeneity were celebrated, and New British interpretations of Old British history, such as an emphasis on Anglo-Saxon influence in Scotland, were supplied. A. H. Reed's late re-colonial *Story of New Zealand* (Wellington, 1945) was a lively and immensely popular book. A 1974 'revised edition' noted that the pioneer settlers were 'a better class of people even than the average British town or village'; eulogized re-colonization's milestones and Great Men (the only Great Woman was refrigeration, a 'fairy godmother'); described the welfare state as 'a huge Friendly Society'; and glowingly recounted 'How New Zealand sprang to the side of the Mother Country' in two world wars. Reed also noted that the Maori were descended from a 'people called Aryans', as were 'our own Anglo-Saxon race'.[6]

Re-colonization's ideology blended with keen insight and fine prose in William Pember Reeves's influential general history, first published in 1898. A minister in the Liberal government of the 1890s and Director of the London School of Economics (1908–19), Reeves helped construct the history of New Zealand as an exemplary paradise, 'the world's social laboratory', in both myth and actuality. He noted vices as well as virtues in his 'Briton of the South', including a kind of voluntary totalitarianism—'the conventional became a tyranny; bright people tried humbly to seem dull'.[7] Mythology also featured in a fine 1930s crop of scholarly general histories: economic historian J. B. Condliffe's *New Zealand in the Making* (London, 1930), which claimed, defensibly, that farmers were currently the socio-economic backbone and, indefensibly, that they always had been; W. P. Morrell's *New Zealand* (London, 1935); and the collectively authored New Zealand volume of the *Cambridge History of the British Empire*.[8] Morrell's theme, the steady development of nationalism through loyalty to Britain culminating on the slopes of Gallipoli, was a touchstone. How independence is demonstrated by a disastrous attack on a place one has never heard of, occupied by people who have never heard of New Zealand, on the instructions of another country, has yet to be satisfactorily explained. A camouflaged note of dissent was sounded by J. C. Beaglehole, later renowned for his work on early exploration, in his *New Zealand: A Short History* (London, 1936). Except for the revisionism of H. D. Skinner on

[5] pp. 9, 52. [6] pp. 137, 269, 313, 297, 25–26.

[7] *The Long White Cloud: Ao Tea Roa*, 4th edn. (London, 1950), pp. 36, 302.

[8] Vol. VII, Part 2. James Hight, ed. (Cambridge, 1933).

Maori history, which was ignored, the *Cambridge History* was more typical of its era. It concluded that 'the Dominion thus is, and is likely to remain, more British even than Britain'. But it was a Britain without the mistakes, 'a revised edition of the Motherland'.[9]

Between the 1900s and the 1930s useful works emerged in bibliography, biography, and historical documents.[10] A. J. Harrop pioneered the sub-genre of the human photocopier masquerading as historian; T. Lindsay Buick and James Cowan skilfully wrote up iconic events.[11] These writers pursued a partly nationalist project, asserting the fascinations of New Zealand's own past to an unconvinced present. But they achieved wide acceptance when they endorsed and adumbrated cherished myths such as the co-option of Maori and the exclusion of Australia. New Zealand, wrote Cowan, 'has a history. Australia has none.'[12] He enshrined racial harmony, forged in heroic and chivalrous battle, as a symbol of the new nation, echoed by *Our Nation's Story* and by A. H. Reed in *Story of New Zealand*. There are intriguing analogies in the English co-option of Celtic resistance history, as with the Arthurian legend, and the 'invention' of Highland Scotland.

Since 1940 New Zealand historiography has profited from four developments: an international explosion in the scope of history; the growth of universities; great bursts of public history; and the slow and incomplete collapse of re-colonization. The state contributed the important 'centennial surveys' and associated works in 1940, and a handy fifty-volume *Official History of New Zealand in World War Two*, completed in 1986. The later was a gargantuan feat of energy and scholarship; quite a good history could be distilled solely from its pages. But it demonstrated that there are two ways to bury history: writing too little, and writing too much. Successor organizations to the War History Branch, housed like it in the Department of Internal Affairs, continue to produce important books.[13] An attempt to meet Maori claims for recompense under the Treaty of Waitangi, signed in 1840, has generated a mass of state-sponsored historical research. This

[9] John Macmillan Brown, 'Epilogue', in ibid., pp. 253–54.

[10] e.g. T. M. Hocken, *A Bibliography of the Literature Relating to New Zealand* (Wellington, 1909); J. R. Elder, ed., *The Letters and Journals of Samuel Marsden* (Dunedin, 1932); Robert McNab, ed., *Historical Records of New Zealand*, 2 vols. (Wellington, 1908–14).

[11] e.g. Harrop, *England and the Maori Wars* (London, 1937); Buick, *The Treaty of Waitangi* (1914; 3rd, substantially revised edn., New Plymouth, 1936); Cowan, *The New Zealand Wars and the Pioneering Period*, 2 vols. (Wellington, 1922–23).

[12] 'Domett and his Work Ranolf and Anohia', *New Zealand Illustrated Magazine*, V (1901), pp. 214–23.

[13] e.g. Richard Hill, *The History of Policing in New Zealand*, 3 vols. (Wellington, 1986–95); W. H. Oliver and Claudia Orange, eds., *The Dictionary of New Zealand Biography*, 2 vols. (Wellington, 1990–93).

claim-driven history has problems as well as great potential. It is prone to emphasize the particular over the general, and Maori as victim over Maori as agent. Historians sometimes find it difficult to combat legal insistence on advocacy. But knowledge of Maori land alienation has burgeoned. History appears to be the one area of state activity which has boomed since 1984: the future of the welfare state is in the past.

In general history, W. B. Sutch preached decolonization from 1941, denouncing colonialism radically and forcefully, if not always convincingly.[14] But his work tended to be sealed off from the mainstream; colleagues noted but did not engage with it, and it generated more the illusion than the substance of debate. The high standard of mainstream general histories was maintained by Keith Sinclair (*A History of New Zealand*, London, 1959) and W. H. Oliver (*The Story of New Zealand*, London 1960). Both broke with re-colonization to some extent, but without fully recognizing it. Sinclair's history in particular had great impact. He argued that a populist, rather than loyalist, independent nationhood had developed, almost as though he was seeking to boost it by claiming it had long existed.[15] Sinclair's total corpus warrants his status as the doyen of post-colonial historians, and his rank with Reeves in a very small pantheon. It is somehow symbolic that the biographies of both demigods were written by Sinclair himself.[16] A fresh crop of general histories, now collectively authored, emerged from 1981, of which the most important was the *Oxford History of New Zealand* edited by W. H. Oliver (Auckland, 1981)—a competent report on the state of scholarship which, with exceptions such as essays by John Owens, Ann Parsonson, and Peter Gibbons, might have been either more accessible or more challenging.

Biography, especially political biography, has also maintained productivity and high standards.[17] Here, as elsewhere in the historical literature, it is noticeable that the Left dominates the past, leaving the Right only the present and future. The study of Maori-Pakeha relations is another sphere of achievement—one in which Pakeha women historians are intriguingly prominent.[18] Led by Keith Sinclair's *Origins of the Maori Wars* (Wellington, 1957), a steady trickle of competent monographs has emerged, revisiting traditional approaches focusing on British policy

[14] e.g. *Poverty and Progress in New Zealand* (1941; Wellington, 1969).

[15] Also see *A Destiny Apart: New Zealand's Search for National Identity* (Wellington, 1986).

[16] *William Pember Reeves: New Zealand Fabian* (Auckland, 1965); *Halfway Round the Harbour: An Autobiography* (Auckland, 1993).

[17] e.g. Judith Bassett, *Sir Harry Atkinson, 1831–1892* (Auckland, 1975); Erik Olssen, *John A. Lee* (Dunedin, 1977); Raewyn Dalziel, *Julius Vogel: Business Politician* (Auckland, 1986).

[18] e.g. Ruth Ross, 'Te Tiriti of Waitangi: Texts and Translations', *New Zealand Journal of History* (hereafter *NZJH*), VI (1972), pp. 129–57; Judith Binney and others, *Mihaia: The Prophet Rua Kenena and his Community at Maungapohatu* (Wellington, 1979); Claudia Orange, *The Treaty of Waitangi* (Wellington, 1987).

in the 1960s, moving towards the study of the contact with the Maori and prophetic movements in the 1970s and 1980s, and culminating in 1990 in a rare cluster of studies of the Treaty of Waitangi—some good, some prone to iconize. The early Maori response to Christianity is one of the few issues on which substantive scholarly debate exists, thanks to a controversial but seminal 1959 study by the American scholar Harrison Wright.[19]

Much recent history has been written about the Maori; there is still not much by the Maori themselves. Reasons include the difficulties of adapting an oral art form which is not designed to be fair to more than one tribal group, and competing demands on a still-limited pool of Maori intellectuals. Notable exceptions are the work of Ranginui Walker,[20] Tipene O'Regan[21] and—most traditionally—the late Ruka Broughton.[22] The demand that Pakeha stay out of Maori history is occasionally heard. Maori essays into Pakeha history would be illuminating. A work which has yet to have the impact it deserves is M. P. K. Sorrenson's edition of letters between Apirana Ngata and Te Rangi Hiroa, arguably the leading intellectuals of their day, Maori or Pakeha.[23]

Good new work has emerged in old fields, such as economic and political history,[24] and—slowly—in several fields new to scholarly history in New Zealand such as the flavour of colonial society, the gold rushes, business history, and Pakeha ethnicity.[25] The nineteenth century is favoured over the twentieth; there tend to be only one or two historians in each field, but progress has been made. An important development is the unmasking of serious class conflict in 1912–13.[26] There are a couple of welcome exceptions to the rule that Australian and New Zealand historians should ignore each other,[27] and a few overseas historians have

[19] *New Zealand, 1769–1840: Early Years of Western Contact* (Cambridge, Mass.).

[20] *Ka Whawhai Tonu Matuou: Struggle Without End* (Auckland, 1990).

[21] e.g. 'Old Myths and New Politics: Some Contemporary Uses of Traditional History', *NZJH*, XXVI (1992), pp. 5–27.

[22] *Ngaa Mahi Whakaari a Tiitokowaru* (Wellington, 1993).

[23] *Na To Hoa Aroha—From Your Dear Friend: The Correspondence between Sir Apirana Ngata and Sir Peter Buck, 1925–50*, 3 vols. (Auckland, 1986–87).

[24] e.g. Gary Hawke, *The Making of New Zealand: An Economic History* (Cambridge, 1985); David Hamer, *The New Zealand Liberals: The Years of Power, 1891–1912* (Auckland, 1988).

[25] John Miller, *Early Victorian New Zealand: A Study of Racial Tensions and Social Attitudes, 1839–1852* (Wellington, 1958); Philip Ross May, *The West Coast Gold Rushes* (Christchurch, 1962); R. C. J. Stone, *Makers of Fortune: A Colonial Business Community and its Fall* (Auckland, 1973); Donald Harman Akenson, *Half the World from Home: Perspectives on the Irish in New Zealand, 1860–1950* (Wellington, 1990).

[26] Erik Olssen, *The Red Feds: Revolutionary Industrial Unionism and the NZ Federation of Labour, 1908–1913* (Auckland, 1988).

[27] H. R. Jackson, *Churches and People in Australia and New Zealand, 1860–1930* (Wellington, 1987); Patrick O'Farrell, *Vanished Kingdoms: The Irish in Australia and New Zealand* (Sydney, 1990).

made good use of the New Zealand laboratory.[28] Major steps have been taken in women's history,[29] but there is some tendency to accept the prevailing methodology of undirected empiricism and to trump Great Men with Great Women. This is no worse than in some other fields, but seems especially regrettable in an important new genre with the potential for fresh departures in which fruitful discussion of theory and method is taking place internationally.

Neighbouring disciplines are important contributors to New Zealand historiography. Anthropologists such as Anne Salmond have written interesting history, though it has been attacked by New Zealand's leading historical philosopher, Peter Munz, for post-modern relativism and the mere inversion of Eurocentrism.[30] In the early 1990s historical geographers, demographers, sociologists, and literary, art, and statistical historians produced indispensable history books.[31] The state of play in sport, military, religious, institutional, local, and regional history is less encouraging. The writing on these fields is immense; there are over 600 books on Rugby Union alone, but few if any historically analyse their subject. New Zealand should be to rugby as Bali is to cockfights; the game expressed otherwise sublimated collective identities, regional and national, and was the site of a long struggle between high-, middle-, and low-class cultures. Yet there is little scholarly history of New Zealand rugby, or sport in general. The situation is better in the other sub-genres, but not always by much, and there is still a reluctance to integrate specialist sub-disciplines with history as a whole. A difference between history and historiography is the superiority of the South Island to the more populous North in regional history. Otago and Canterbury each have two substantial histories published since 1948; Auckland and Wellington have nothing comparable.[32] Since

[28] e.g. Donald Denoon, *Settler Capitalism: The Dynamics of Dependent Development in the Southern Hemisphere* (Oxford, 1983); Alfred W. Crosby, *Ecological Imperialism: The Biological Expansion of Europe, 900–1900* (Cambridge, 1986).

[29] e.g. Raewyn Dalziel, 'The Colonial Helpmeet: Women's Role and the Vote in Nineteenth-Century New Zealand', *NZJH*, XI (1977), pp. 112–23; Sandra Coney, *Standing in the Sunshine: A History of New Zealand Women Since They Won the Vote* (Auckland, 1993).

[30] Anne Salmond, *Two Worlds: First Meetings Between Maori and Europeans, 1642–1772* (Auckland, 1991); Peter Munz, 'The Two Worlds of Anne Salmond in Postmodern Fancy-Dress', *NZJH*, XXVIII (1994), pp. 60–75. Also see Salmond's response, ibid., pp. 76–79.

[31] Rollo Arnold, *New Zealand's Burning: The Settlers World in the Mid-1880s* (Wellington, 1994); Ian Pool, *Te Iwi Maori: A New Zealand Population: Past, Present, and Projected* (Auckland, 1991); David Pearson, *A Dream Deferred: The Origins of Ethnic Conflict in New Zealand* (Wellington, 1990); Terry Sturm, ed., *The Oxford History of New Zealand Literature* (Auckland, 1991); Leonard Bell, *Colonial Constructs: European Images of Maori, 1840–1914* (Auckland, 1992); G. T. Bloomfield, *New Zealand: A Handbook of Historical Statistics* (Boston, 1991).

[32] A. H. McLintock, *The History of Otago: The Origins and Growth of a Wakefield Class Settlement* (Dunedin, 1949); Erik Olssen, *A History of Otago* (Dunedin, 1984); J. Hight, C. R. Straubel, and W. J. Gardner, eds., *A History of Canterbury*, 2 vols. (Christchurch, 1957–71); Stevan Eldred-Grigg, *A New History of Canterbury* (Dunedin, 1982).

1880 the South has had a lower rate of demographic change; Pakeha folklore—in the form of children's games, for example[33]—persists more strongly; and so does regionalism, as expressed in history.

If recent New Zealand historiography has a problem, simple lack of bulk is not it. Several hundred history books have been published since 1945, graduate theses now average twenty or more a year, and the *New Zealand Journal of History*, established in 1967, produces consistently useful articles supplemented by those in other journals. Quality is variable. Much work lacks the crucial element which digests and contextualizes good research into good narrative or analysis. But published research reports have their uses; other historiographies also have long tails; and the best work is excellent. The distinction is not academic. Important work has been produced outside state and university history departments.[34] Some might argue that the problem is the subject-matter, that New Zealand history is brief, mundane, and insignificant. It is true that, under re-colonization, New Zealand history was written and taught as a boring course in 'Better Britishness' and civic virtue. It is true that New Zealand's colonized past is short, but in history it is not the length that counts. The country is potentially a historian's paradise, if not a social one, a test-tube whose glass sides are a thousand miles thick. The great games of myth-making, class, race as well as gender; war, work, state formation, and collective identity were often played out here perhaps more discernibly than elsewhere. New Zealand is also the intersection of two of the most reproductive cultures of human history, British and Polynesian. Though not quite a human Galapagos, it is a good place to study the origin of peoples. The notion that New Zealand historians sit on a molehill, that real history happens overseas, is one of re-colonization's leading myths. In fact, they sit on a goldmine. The problem is that the occupational subculture prefers alluvial panning to pit-mining, and that it does not put much energy into seeking to pan in the optimal places.

An understandable but ultimately misguided reaction to cultural colonialism was to leave out the world, to mistake parochialism for historiographical maturity. A 'common criticism' of the first edition of the *Oxford History of New Zealand* 'was its virtual neglect of external relations'.[35] But the second edition's welcome new chapters in the 'external relations' tradition, focusing on the formal interaction of governments, are not the whole answer. Understanding New Zealand's relations with Britain, for example, is as much a matter of the social histories of technology, ideas, and economics. A global approach to New Zealand history requires an awareness of

33 See Brian Sutton-Smith, *A History of Children's Play: New Zealand, 1840–1950* (Philadelphia, 1981).

34 e.g. H. O. Roth, *Trade Unions in New Zealand, Past and Present* (Wellington, 1973); E. H. McCormick, *Alexander Turnbull: His Life, His Circle, His Collections* (Wellington, 1974); Stevan Eldred-Grigg, *A Southern Gentry: New Zealanders who Inherited the Earth* (Wellington, 1980); Michael King, *Moriori: A People Rediscovered* (Auckland, 1989).

35 Geoffrey W. Rice, ed., *The Oxford History of New Zealand*, 2nd edn. (Auckland, 1992), p. x.

such themes, and it need not be deferential. New Zealand historians have something to teach as well as something to learn. The baby of globalism should not be thrown out with the bathwater of the colonial cringe. On the other hand, definitions of the appropriate scope of research projects and of disciplinary demarcation tend to be uncritically imported. Rigid disciplinary distinctions, tendencies not to read each other's work or speak each other's tongue, seem unwise when a historian and a historical sociologist are the only two scholars in a field. Big volumes on small topics may be legitimate if sister studies exist; wider scope is desirable if they do not, if only because it permits linking-up with the work of colleagues and educates more guesses. The 'generation of pedants' which Sinclar called for in 1950[36] has produced fine trees, but few woods. Some trees cluster in twos and threes, but look past each other. Most trees are widely scattered, or to change the metaphor, islands of well-researched knowledge linked by bridges of inherited assumption, to which frequent repetition has lent the authority of fact. The scattering is rather random, and staggering lacunae persist. There is, for example, no modern study of the intertribal Musket Wars of 1818–35, the most lethal conflict in New Zealand history.

New Zealand historiography is strong at the top, in general history; and quite strong, in patches, at the bottom, in specialist monographs and theses; but weak in the middle—crucial to a young scholarly historiography—where major problems are pursued over substantial chunks of space and time. Between 1986 and 1991 several works appeared which were aimed at this 'neglected middle distance', and made and tested strong cases—at first sight an encouraging development.[37] All had flaws, such as the strong possibility of being wrong. But they were intended as one side of an argument about major historical issues, and their main problem was that the other side failed to show up. Substantive debate is rare, with most criticism taking the form of guerrilla sniping. There are a scant dozen historiographical essays, some quite trite. They seldom engage with each other, but emerge independently every five or ten years like some ritual act of expiation, or as helpful hints from neighbouring countries or disciplines to the disadvantaged.[38] Sinclair described debate as 'the wine of scholars'.[39] If so, New Zealand is still subject to six o'clock closing.

36 *The Maori Land League* (Auckland, 1950), p. 3.

37 James Belich, *The New Zealand Wars and the Victorian Interpretation of Racial Conflict* (Auckland, 1986); Jock Phillips, *A Man's Country? The Image of the Pakeha Male* (Auckland, 1987); Miles Fairburn, *The Ideal Society and its Enemies* (Auckland, 1989); David Thomson, *Selfish Generations? The Ageing of the New Zealand Welfare State* (Wellington, 1991).

38 The better examples include Keith Sinclair, 'History in New Zealand', in John A. Moses, ed., *Historical Disciplines and Culture in Australasia: An Assessment* (Brisbane, 1979); Graeme Wynn, 'Reflections on the Writing of New Zealand History', *NZJH*, XVIII (1984), pp. 104–116; Roy Shuker and Chris Wilkes, 'History from the High Wire: The Relationship between Sociology and History in New Zealand', *New Zealand Sociology*, II (1987), pp. 1–24.

39 'New Zealand', in Robin W. Winks, ed., *The Historiography of the British Empire-Commonwealth: Trends, Interpretations, and Resources* (Durham, NC, 1966), p. 182.

Behind this, perhaps, is the fear of theory, a well-known characteristic of New Zealand historiography, with deep roots in neo-British anti-intellectualism and the occupational culture of historians generally. As far as macro-theories of knowledge, method, or history are concerned, suspicion is not indefensible. Such theories are prone to generate exclusivity, rather like religious denominations—there is only one God and Gramsci, Popper, or Foucault is his prophet. It can be argued that methodological eclecticism is the historian's stock in trade, and that theory and empiricism, scholarship and accessibility, truth and relativism, subtext and context, myth and history, are best treated as rubber gloves for handling each other. But justifiable doubts about macro-theory do not justify extreme empiricism. They do not justify rejection of the obligation to use sparse resources to best effect by identifying and debating key issues to guide empirical probes, to posit generalizations which enhance understanding more than they risk inaccuracy, or to attempt coherently to explain major historical phenomena in one or more cases. There is an underlying fallacy that, because so much remains to be done, one need not bother too much about what it is. On the contrary, the larger the task, the sparser the resources, the greater the case for methodological self-awareness and strategic approaches. New Zealand historical scholarship at the end of the twentieth century has substantial achievements to its credit, but it has yet to realize its full potential.

Select Bibliography

J. C. BEAGLEHOLE, *New Zealand: A Short History* (London, 1936).

JUDITH BINNEY, *Redemption Songs: A Life of Te Kooti Arikirangi Te Turuki* (Auckland, 1995).

THOMAS CHOLMONDELEY, *Ultima Thule, or Thoughts Suggested by a Residence in New Zealand* (London, 1854).

JOHN BELL CONDLIFFE, *New Zealand in the Making: A Survey of Economic and Social Development* (London, 1930).

SANDRA CONEY, *Standing in the Sunshine: A History of New Zealand Women Since They Won the Vote* (Auckland, 1993).

MILES FAIRBURN, *The Ideal Society and its Enemies: The Foundations of Modern New Zealand Society, 1850–1900* (Auckland, 1989).

Sir JOHN ELDON GORST, *The Maori King: Or, the Story of Our Quarrel with the Natives of New Zealand* (London 1864).

WILLIAM HOSKING OLIVER, *The Story of New Zealand* (London, 1960).

ERIK OLSSEN, *A History of Otago* (Dunedin, 1984).

WILLIAM PEMBER REEVES, *The Long White Cloud: Ao Tea Roa* (1898; 4th edn., London, 1950).

GEOFFREY W. RICE, ed., *The Oxford History of New Zealand* (1981; 2nd edn., Auckland, 1992).

KEITH SINCLAIR, *The Origins of the Maori Wars* (Wellington, 1957).

—— *A History of New Zealand* (London, 1959).

M. P. K. SORRENSON, ed., *Na To Hoa Aroha—From Your Dear Friend: The Correspondence between Sir Apirana Ngata and Sir Peter Buck, 1925–50*, 3 vols. (Auckland, 1986–87).

WILLIAM BALL SUTCH, *Poverty and Progress in New Zealand: A Reassessment* (1941; 2nd edn., Wellington, 1969).

ARTHUR SAUNDERS THOMSON, *The Story of New Zealand: Past and Present—Savage and Civilized*, 2 vols. (London, 1859).

RANGINUI WALKER, *Ka Whawhai Tonu Matuou: Struggle Without End* (Auckland, 1990).

ALAN WARD, *A Show of Justice: Racial 'Amalgamation' in Nineteenth-Century New Zealand* (Toronto, 1974).

11

India to 1858

ROBERT E. FRYKENBERG

Historical understandings achieved during years of the East India Company's rise and during its subsequent rulership can be reduced, perhaps simplistically, into two main categories: explanation and exploration, or enlightenment.[1] The first was immediate and urgent. Its aim was to explain challenges and claims, initially for mere survival, but later for supremacy. The second, though differently interpreted in our own day, was culturally expansive and inquisitive. Its purpose was to satisfy curiosity and to acquire basic, often necessary, information. It eventually resulted in a systematic search for a deeper and broader understanding of India and of India's peoples. Both kinds of understanding were important and necessary for strengthening the Empire—for building an All-Indian union of peoples, territories, and cultures. Each activity held the potential of reinforcing the other.

Among the earliest attempts to explain Company triumphs, first in the Carnatic and then in Bengal, was Robert Orme's *A History of the Military Transactions of the British Nation in Indostan*, 2 vols. (London, 1763–78). Fifty years later more comprehensive and critical insights, based upon deeper investigations of Indian sources, began to appear. Mark Wilks, in *Historical Sketches of the South of India*, 3 vols. (London, 1810–14), used local sources to explain events since the fall of the Vijayanagar empire, and showed how concern over the 'balance of power' in India had gradually grown into a bid for imperial supremacy.[2] James Grant Duff, John Malcolm, and Mountstuart Elphinstone also relied upon Indian materials.[3] Meanwhile in London, James Mill gained direct access to Company

[1] William A. Green and John P. Deasy, Jr., 'Unifying Themes in the History of British India, 1757–1857: An Historiographical Analysis', *Albion*, XVII (Spring, 1985), pp. 15–45.

[2] What Wilks hinted in *Historical Sketches of the South of India in an Attempt to Trace the History of Mysoor . . .* was explicitly asserted in Henry T. Prinsep's *History of the Political and Military Transactions in India during the Administration of the Marquess of Hastings, 1813–1823* (London, 1825).

[3] James Grant Duff, *History of the Mahrattas*, 3 vols. (London, 1826); John Malcolm, *The Political History of India, from 1784 to 1823*, 2 vols. (London: 1826; expanding his *Sketch of the Political History of India*, 1811), and *A Memoir of Central India*, 2 vols. (London, 1832); Mountstuart Elphinstone, *The History of India*, 2 vols. (London, 1841), drew from the works of Ferishta, Seid Gholam Hossein-Khan Tabatabai, Khafi Khan, and the Peshwa Daftar in Pune.

records and wrote his massive, and controversial, three-volume work on *The History of British India* (London, 1817).[4]

Two traditions mark historical explanations produced during the Company period: a long-lasting tension, or partisan controversy, over policy positions, often cloaked in lofty 'principle'; and a heavy reliance upon indigenous sources, both European and Indian, to fuel arguments over policy. Both traditions continue to generate historical debates down to this day. The first tradition, long prevalent in British public life, became deeply rooted in India. From its earliest days, when monopoly was often at issue, down to struggles over corruption, jobbery, debt, education, expansion, customs, landholding, missionaries, or religious institutions, divisions were endemic. But divisions—between Whig and Tory, Anglicist and Orientalist, conservative and radical, liberal and autocratic—tended to look different in India than in Britain.[5] Alignments based on 'Native Authorities' also became a chronic feature of historiography. A line can be discerned, running from Clive to Cornwallis, from Burke to Bentham, and from Mill to Macaulay. Arguments 'for' and 'against—'Native' or 'European' elements, 'Hindu' or 'Christian' institutions, 'state control' or 'proprietary' holdings, 'conserving' or 'interfering' customs—continued from generation to generation.[6] Words, eloquent and furious, swirled and smoked—on whether or not to admit missionaries, whether or not to use English, whether or not modern education in vernacular languages was possible. The controversies lasted long after words over whether or not to send troops across the Sutlej were buried. Arguments remained on record, were picked up by later generations, and became part of the legacy of historical lore. The lore generated by each conflict, as reflected in manuscript and printed materials, was enormous. Its literary remains fuelled the writings of Burke and Macaulay, the 'pamphlet wars', and the 'Fifth Report' (of 1812). Information gathered by Ram Mohan Roy for the abolition of suttee (*sati*) remains as valuable

[4] Revised, expanded, and brought up to 1835, 6 vols. in 2nd and 3rd edns. (1858) by H. H. Wilson, Mill's work, like Gibbon, became a classic against which other works were measured—e.g. Edward Thornton, *The History of the British Empire in India*, 6 vols. (London, 1841–45) and J. C. Marshman, *The History of India from the Earliest Period to the Close of Lord Dalhousie's Administration*, 3 vols. (London, 1867); abridged version, introduced by William Thomas, ed., *The History of British India* (Chicago, 1975). Lynn Zastoupil, *John Stuart Mill and India* (Stanford, Calif., 1994), is definitive.

[5] What looked 'conservative' in England became 'radical' if applied in India: Burke, so conservative of British institutions, looked 'radical' in India; and Hastings, so conservative of Indian institutions, looked dangerously reactionary and 'despotic' in Britain.

[6] Each time the Company charter came up for renewal, new works appeared. John W. Kaye's, *The Administration of the East India Company: A History of Indian Progress* (London, 1853) was never superseded, even by B. B. Misra's *The Central Administration for the East India Company, 1773–1833* (Manchester, 1959). J. Dickinson, *India, Its Government Under a Bureaucracy* (London, 1853) and J. S. Mill's *Memorandum on Improvements in the Administration of India* (London, 1858) defended the Company from its critics.

as ever. Conflicts between Indian notables became just as acrimonious as those between their British contemporaries.[7]

What seems clear from early works produced during the Company period, is their reliance not just upon Company records, but upon sources upon which those records rested. Beneath surface documents lay a bedrock of data and thinking gathered by Indian employees and their contacts. Still deeper lay traditional Indian sources. Company officials were eager to buy, collect, translate, and publish whatever indigenous material they could find. Items of local history produced by non-British scholars, both Indian and European,[8] were avidly sought and bought. Ferishta's remarkable *History of the Rise of Mohomedan Power in India* (London, 1829, translated and published by John Briggs),[9] Seid Gholam Hossein-Khan's [Tabatabai] incomparable *A Translation of the Seir-ul Mutaqherin or View of Modern Times*, 4 vols. (1789; New Delhi, 1986), Ja'far Sharif's penetrating *Qanun-i-Islam: The Customs of the Musalmans* (translated by G. A. Herklots, *Islam in India*, Madras, 1832), or Sayyid Ahmad Khan's *Asar-us-Sanadid* (Delhi, 1847), and numerous regional or family or court histories, provided rich insights.[10] In each locality, works of this kind were, and are still acquired, translated, and published.[11]

Organized acquisition from Indian sources took two forms: official and non-official, or private. Official acquisition was formally begun by Warren Hastings. Inspired by the Enlightenment,[12] he fostered systematic explorations of all things

[7] Macaulay and Marx remain, not surprisingly, notable examples of rhetoric produced within this polarizing of tensions over events in India.

[8] Abbé J. A. Dubois's classic, *Hindu Manners, Customs, and Ceremonies* (London, 1818), even if plagiarized—as shown by Sylvia Murr, 'N. J. Desvaulx (1745–1825) veritable auteur des "moeurs, institutions et ceremonies des peuples de l'Inde" de l'Abbé Dubois', in *Purusartha: recherches de sciences sociales sur l'asie du sud*, III (Paris, 1977)—was one among a host of such acquisitions.

[9] While translation of Muhammad Kasim Hindu (Hindu Shah) Ferishta's, *History*, in 4 vols. took Briggs twenty years, his was not the first English version. Earlier translations were *The History of Hindostan* (London, 1767–72), in 3 vols., by Alexander Dow, and *History of the Dekkan* (London, 1794), in 2 vols., by Jonathan Scott.

[10] Also see *The History of India as Told By Its Own Historians*, 8 vols. (London, 1867–77), trans. and ed. by Henry Elliot and John Dowson; translations of the *Akbarnamah* or *Shahjahanamah*, and other residues of indigenous understandings which lay just below the surface. Notable for South India are V. Raghavan, ed., 'The Sarva-deva-vilâsa', *The Adyar Library Bulletin*, XXI (1957), pp. 315–414; XXII (1958), pp. 45–118; J. Frederick Price and T. Rangachari, trans. and eds., *The Private Diary of Ananda Ranga Pillai*, 12 vols. (Madras, 1904–28), and the more recently uncovered *Diary of Savariraya Pillai*, 3 vols. (1836–74), in Tamil, now being translated for publication. Also V. V. Gopal Row, ed., *The Life of Vennelacunty Soob Row* (Madras, 1873) (cited in note 69).

[11] Other examples of local narratives drawing heavily upon Indian materials: *Pandurang Hari: Memoirs of a Hindu*, trans. by W. B. Hockley (London, 1826); *Annals and Antiquities of Rajasthan*, by James Tod, 2 vols. (London, 1829–32); *Phansigars in India*, by W. H. Sleeman (Philadelphia, 1939); *Confessions of a Thug*, by Philip Meadows Taylor, 3 vols. (London, 1839); *Revelations of an Orderly*, by 'Panchkouree Khan' (Benares, 1848); and *Ras Mala: Hindoo Annals of the Province of Goozerat*, by Alexander Kinloch Forbes (London, 1856).

[12] Science, for Europeans and for Indians alike, had yet to become 'Western' or 'Eastern'.

Indian. The search for knowledge about India and Indian culture, later to become known as 'Orientalism', was never merely a 'colonialist' imposition upon a hapless India.[13] Orientalist enterprises provided careers for hundreds of Indian scholars throughout India. The scholarly tradition so founded continues down to this day. All-India surveys followed: archaeological, epigraphic, numismatic, and geographic.

The most impressive orientalist explorations were collaborative, unofficial, and voluntary. Among these, none matched the enormous privately funded venture by Colonel Colin MacKenzie. His teams of Maratha Brahman scholars begged, bought, or borrowed, and copied, from village leaders. Virtually every manuscript of value they could find they acquired. Collections so acquired, reflecting the civilization of South India, manuscripts in every language, became a lasting legacy—something still being explored.[14] Privately financed efforts by dedicated and enthusiastic gentry, European and Indian alike, multiplied. Collections of manuscripts in every part of India, such as those of C. P. Brown (Madras) and Walter Elliot (London), Saraswat Mahal (Thanjavur), Saiyidia Library (Madras and Hyderabad), Khuda Bhaksh (Patna), and Salar Jung (Hyderabad) and Inayat Jung (Aligarh), proliferated. Work done by the Asiatic Society of Bengal and by the Madras Literary Society, reflected in their journals, became a fashion. Neither the scorn of James Mill, nor that of Edward Said, has diminished the appeal of this tradition in India.

By and large, all forms of historical understanding and writing begun during Company Raj continued to develop and expand after Crown Raj took its place. India's history never seemed to enjoy the same degree of historical enthusiasm in Britain, however, at least not until British rule came to an end. To be sure, fresh research in select and specialized topics, often remarkable work focusing more closely upon one region or religion, continued. But overall efforts, while continuing, never matched what had been done during Company's times. District gazetteers, on the whole, were not as well done as district manuals. Handbooks of documents, required for day-to-day administration, were produced. Prodigious, multi-volume compilations, such as C. U. Aitchison's *Collection of Treaties, Engagements, and Sunnuds Relating to India and Neighbouring Countries*, 4th edn., 13 vols. (Calcutta, 1909) and B. H. Baden-Powell's *Manual of Land Revenue Systems and Land Tenures of British India* (Calcutta, 1882, and renamed *Land Systems of British India*, 3 vols. Oxford, 1892), appeared. But with few exceptions the age of creative and dynamic excitement seems to have subsided. Most work focusing on

[13] See below chap. by D. A. Washbrook.

[14] Ships loaded with privately acquired Mackenzie manuscripts were sent to London; the manuscripts were later returned to Madras, where they lie in the Oriental Manuscripts Library.

events in India before 1858 became more localized, occasional, mundane, or antiquarian in character. From the 1860s onwards few scholars attempted to produce comprehensive studies of the Company period, and even fewer were successful. Typical among these were synthetic works, such as Robert Sewell's *Analytical History of India, From the Earliest Times to the Abolition of the Honourable East India Company in 1858* (London, 1870), produced for use as a textbook in schools and colleges.[15] Certainly, the *Rulers of India* series, some twenty-five biographies published by the Clarendon Press at the turn of the century (1892 to 1926), made few, if any, fresh contributions to historical knowledge, though they did represent a synthesis of contemporary knowledge.

In the twentieth century, new histories about India before 1858, as about Indian history as a whole, did not increase until the third decade. The single best general work, sound in scholarship and restrained in judgement, was P. E. Roberts, *History of British India to the End of the East India Company* (Oxford, 1921).[16] Together with the first *Oxford History of India*, by V. A. Smith (Oxford, 1919),[17] the monumental, multi-volumed *The Cambridge History of India* (1922–32), along with H. H. Dodwell, *Cambridge Shorter History of India*, 3rd. edn. (Cambridge, 1934),[18] served to form the capstone of British understanding of India's past.

[15] J. Talboys Wheeler, like Sewell also Keeper of the Madras Record Office, produced a useful handbook describing perhaps the richest archival repository in Asia: *Madras in Olden Times, Being a History of the Presidency*, 3 vols. (Madras, 1861–62), *Early Records of British India* (London, 1878), and *A Short History of India* (London, 1880). W. W. Hunter's richly informative *Annals of Rural Bengal* (London, 1871) and his massive, if dull, *Imperial Gazetteer of India*, 1st edn., 9 vols. (London, 1881), 2nd edn. 14 vols. (London, 1885–87), was followed by *A Brief History of the Indian Peoples* (Oxford, 1895). H. G. Keene's *The Fall of the Moghal Empire* (London, 1876), *A Servant of 'John Company'* (London, 1897), and *History of India from the Earliest Times to the Present Day*, 2 vols. (London, 1893; Edinburgh, 1902) added little new light. More enlightening new works include H. E. Busteed's *Echoes of Old Calcutta*, 4th edn. (London, 1908); H. G. Keene's *Hindustan under Free Lances, 1770–1820; Sketches of Military Adventure* (Calcutta, 1901; London, 1907) and *A Handbook for Visitors to Delhi and its Neighbourhood* (Calcutta, 1862; 1876, 1882, 1888, and later edns.); and H. D. Love, *Vestiges of Old Madras*, 3 vols. (London, 1913).

[16] 3rd edn., expanded and renamed *History of British India Under Company and Crown*, by T. G. P. Spear (Oxford, 1952).

[17] This, competent and clearly 'colonial' and Imperial in tone, by an ex-ICS officer whose previous works had been on Ashoka, Akbar, and fine art in India and Ceylon, was later revised. Smith's modern section (3rd edn., Oxford, 1958), as rewritten by Percival Spear, was more Indocentric and nationalist.

[18] J. Allan, T. Wolseley Haig, and H. H. Dodwell, *The Cambridge Shorter History of India*, 3rd edn., ed. H. H. Dodwell (Cambridge, 1934), was expanded and edited by R. R. Seth (Delhi, 1962). H. H. Dodwell, another former Keeper of Madras Record Office, went to the London School of Oriental Studies (before it became the School of Oriental and African Studies), wrote *The Nabobs of Madras* (London, 1926), and edited vols. V and VI of the *Cambridge History of India*: Vol. V, *British India, 1497–1858*; Vol. VI, *The Indian Empire, 1858–1918*. Others who looked at Company Raj were H. G. Rawlinson, *The British Achievement in India: A Survey* (London, 1948), and Edward Thompson and

After the Second World War and Independence, especially during the early 1960s, when scholarly publications began to increase, new questions led to the uncovering of data long buried and forgotten. Once again, this new surge of historical interest exhibited a binary character: older, more traditional, 'top-down' history was increasingly mingled with, or supplanted by, more innovative, 'bottom-up' forms of history. This polarity has itself more recently been challenged, if perhaps only for a short time, as increasingly 'anti-historical' or 'nihilist' doctrines have become more and more pronounced, especially in circles where 'colonial discourse analysis' has captured attention.

As late as the 1960s, understandings of events in India before 1858 tended to be pursued mainly from the 'top down', concentrating narrowly upon concerns of government, and relating contexts and consequences of decision-making and public policy to Imperial development. Moreover, Imperial historians, preoccupied with how the British had first come, conquered, and then constructed a unified *Pax Indica*, had often forgotten to look at indigenous contributions to that development. Even works by nationalist historians, harking back to glorious ages, tended merely to describe how foreigners had come, conquered, and exploited their sacred land and its peoples. On the whole, Imperial and national writing remained, despite its rhetoric, a single form of historiography: a flipside of rulers-eye-view history, in various shades of black and white on obverse and reverse sides. Understandings merely varied in how much critical detachment or fresh data was blended into otherwise Imperial or national outlooks. In ideological and moral terms, these were all Whig interpretations of history, with appropriate adaptations to events in India.[19] For some, the benefits of constructing a *Pax Indica* always outweighed costs. For others, India had always existed and never needed any 'reconstructing': India's golden age—with centralized state structures, bureaucracies of élite officials (mandarins), and clear boundaries which defined territorial frontiers, social structures, administrative units, communication systems, legal proceedings, and other institutions—had been interrupted by foreign intrusion. The India discovered by national historians was, in short, just the mirror-image of the Empire described by Imperial historians. Moreover, top-down history tended to view the Subcontinent as a whole and its countries or regions (described as 'presidencies', 'provinces', 'princely states') as integral to that whole. Often Eurocentric in tone, such histories dealt with impacts of Indo-British personalities, perspectives, and policies. Commerce, conquest, or conversion had provoked Indian reactions; and

G. T. Garratt, *Rise and Fulfilment of British Rule in India* (London, 1934). Burning current issues evoked such specialized works as Courtenay Ilbert's *The Government of India, A Brief Historical Survey* (Oxford, 1922); A. B. Keith's *A Constitutional History of India, 1600–1935* (London, 1936); and L. S. S. O'Malley's *The Indian Civil Service, 1601–1930* (London, 1931).

[19] Ernst Haas, *Nationalism and Imperialism* (New York, 1955), explains this flip-sided identity.

Indians had tried to acquire a greater say in government. Indian life itself, ageless and eternal, remained a timeless *tabula rasa* upon which a small number of persons, whether Europeans or Indians, had been free to write their own story, something almost entirely free of other constraints.

But during the 1930s and especially after 1960, as historical research and writing began to increase, newer approaches also emerged. These stressed a more local, bottom-up, or Indocentric perspective. Research drawing upon freshly uncovered sources showed that, whatever British aims may have been, they had almost always been shaped by hard realities of events occurring on the ground. A recognition that *Indian realities*, not British or national purposes, had shaped the course of events, began to spread. Local conditions and circumstances, as reflected in local conflicts between social entities rooted in family, caste, and village, language and culture, or religion or culture, received closer attention. Indigenous institutions, rather than high Imperial policy or national aspiration, were examined more carefully. English-language materials, once ascendant, were no longer deemed sufficient. Local, vernacular-language materials again, as in Company times, received greater attention.[20]

No serious historical work perfectly reflects this simple set of stereotypes. One tendency or another becomes increasingly evident. Exactly how this polarity developed can be seen in more recent historical works. Events so treated fall into three categories: British expansion; control—central and local; and finally, cultural interaction. A fourth category of commercial and economic history should be borne in mind.

The central question of how India could ever have fallen under British rule continues to engage almost obsessive attention. How so few Britons, as servants of a private business enterprise, could have conquered so huge an area and so many people, so far away, has never ceased to amaze or embarrass. Neither British nor national historiography has proven satisfactory.[21] Old explanations of Mughal decline and disintegration, or of British prowess, no longer convince. Prior assumptions—of Mughal power as highly centralized or of Mughal disintegration

[20] Early among such newly insightful, and useful works were M. Ruthnaswamy's *Some Influences That Made the British Administrative System in India* (London, 1939) and K. N. V. Sastri's *The Administration of Mysore Under Sir Mark Cubbon, 1834–1861* (London, 1932). Ruthnaswamy, in particular, revealed long-forgotten, neglected indigenous elements undergirding the Raj, foreshadowing changes in perspective which would not come into vogue for another twenty years.

[21] C. H. Philips, ed., *Historians of India, Pakistan, and Ceylon* (London, 1961); S. P. Sen and R. C. Majumdar, eds., *Historians and Historiography in Modern India* (Calcutta, 1973). European and South Asian alike, such as K. K. Aziz, *The British in India: A Study in Imperialism* (Islamabad, 1976), tend towards caution.

as due to external or internal forces—are being disputed.[22] Similarly, whether global factors generated military forces sufficient to bring about the conquest of India is still being debated.[23] Two decades ago P. J. Marshall concluded that both internal and external factors, together, were important in bringing about this event.[24]

Clearly, resources for the conquest and construction of Empire lay *within* India. Exactly how resources were actually harnessed was not well explained. An enormous modern military machine was indeed put together out of materials within the Subcontinent. This machine required Indian money and Indian manpower. How attempts to protect Company holdings grew into a booming regiments-for-hire business, a self-perpetuating engine for British expansion, is a question still requiring further investigation. Over forty years ago Amiya Barat, in her *The Bengal Native Infantry: Its Organization and Discipline, 1796–1852* (Calcutta, 1962), described a chronic tendency toward historical amnesia which, when blended with incompetence, insensitivity, mismanagement, niggardliness, and snobbery, squandered accumulated reserves of loyalty. Loyalty, so crucial within Bengal regiments precariously built for a century, was often neglected; and this neglect left a legacy of unrest and mutiny within both European and Indian ranks. Philip Mason, in *A Matter of Honour: An Account of the Indian Army, Its Officers and Men* (London, 1974), looked at how the oath of loyalty was sworn by each sepoy. This ritual, customized to what was most sacred, was pivotal. The Imperial edifice, such works suggest, rested on structures of loyalty built into minds of Company servants, Indian and European alike. Permanence in recruitment was crucial. How this was accomplished calls for more bottom-up research.[25] To date, one of the better synthetic

[22] André Wink, *Land and Sovereignty in India: Agrarian Society and Politics Under the Eighteenth-Century Maratha Svarajya* (Cambridge, 1986), challenged the findings of Aligarh historians Irfan Habib, *The Agrarian History of Mughal India* (London, 1963); M. Athar Ali, *The Mughal Nobility under Aurangzeb* (Aligarh, 1966); Satish Chandra, *Parties and Politics at the Mughal Court, 1707–1740*, 2nd edn. (New Delhi, 1972). Views of Stewart Gordon, *The Marathas, 1600–1818* (Cambridge, 1993) and *Marathas, Marauders, and State Formation in Eighteenth-Century India* (Delhi, 1994), and J. C. Heesterman, *The Inner Conflict of Tradition: Essays in Indian Ritual, Kingship and Society* (Chicago, 1985), also support this 'bottom-up' approach and question the character and effectiveness of centralizing institutions.

[23] James W. Hoover, 'The Indian Saltpetre Trade and World Gunpowder Production during the Early Modern Military Revolution', Ph.D. dissertation, Madison (forthcoming), may yet overturn many previous understandings on this front.

[24] P. J. Marshall, 'British Expansion in India in the Eighteenth Century: A Historical Revision', *History* (1975), p. 39.

[25] Dirk H. A. Kolff, *Naukar, Rajput and Sepoy: The Ethno-History of the Military Labour Market in Hindustan, 1450–1850* (Cambridge, 1990), has made a start.

overviews is Penderel Moon's *The British Conquest and Dominion of India* (London, 1989).[26]

But, even as more is being learned of how the Company's sword was forged, new works are also showing how the Company exercised its power. Each generation traces the path of Imperial expansion differently. Fifty years ago C. C. Davies wrote about both frontier expansion, to the North-West, and internal expansion into Oudh.[27] Focus has ever shifted from the moving frontier[28] to the 'Great Game' beyond India.[29] The 1839 disaster in Afghanistan never ceases to fascinate.[30] All frontier histories, with their varying perspectives, fuel ongoing geopolitical debates over decision-making and diplomacy.[31] Yet, few if any studies of Imperial expansion have been bottom-up histories.

British control consisted of two components: central and local. Central decision-making has always fascinated historians. In 1940 C. H. Philips, in *The East India Company, 1784–1813* (Manchester), described internal operations of the Company as an English institution after it came under the Board of Control. L. S. Sutherland, *The East India Company and Eighteenth Century Politics* (Oxford, 1952), made a detailed, Namierite study of murky events leading to that control. Holden Furber, *John Company at Work* (Cambridge Mass., 1948), showed how the

[26] While self-described as 'an old fashioned, conventional history, concentrating on the deeds, motives and thoughts of British actors in the drama of events rather than on the almost unmoving background of the mass of populations against which they played their parts', this critic of British rule and friend of Gandhi cannot be lightly dismissed. His works on Gandhi and Hastings, and years of 'staying on' after Independence, gave special insight and perspective to his posthumously published final work.

[27] C. C. Davies, *Warren Hastings and Oudh* (Oxford, 1939).

[28] Also see 'top-down' works by Robert A. Huttenback, *British Relations with Sind, 1799–1843: An Anatomy of Imperialism* (Berkeley, 1962); H. T. Lambrick, *Sir Charles Napier and Sind* (Oxford, 1952); Khushwant Singh, *A History of the Sikhs*, 2 vols. (Princeton, 1966); Bikrama Jit Hasrat, *Anglo-Sikh Relations, 1799–1849: A Reappraisal of the Rise and Fall of the Sikhs* (Hoshiarpur, 1968) and *Punjab on the Eve of the Sikh War* (Hoshiarpur, 1956); Bawa Satinder Singh, *The Jammu Fox: A Biography of Maharaja Gulab Singh of Kashmir, 1792–1857* (Carbondale, Ill., 1974).

[29] Mountstuart Elphinstone, *Account of the Kingdom of Caubool*, 2 vols. (London, 1839) and J. W. Kaye, *History of the War in Afghanistan*, 2 vols., 1st edn. (London, 1851) provide the base. G. J. Alder, 'Britain and the Defence of India—The Origins of the Problem', *Journal of Asian History*, VI (1972), pp. 14–44; W. K. Fraser-Tytler, *Afghanistan: A Study of Political Developments in Central and Southern Asia* (London, 1950); G. S. Misra, *British Foreign Policy and Indian Affairs, 1783–1815* (New York, 1963); Edward Ingram, *The Beginning of the Great Game in Asia, 1828–1834* (Oxford, 1979); and M. E. Yapp, *Strategies of British India: Britain, Iran, and Afghanistan, 1798–1850* (Oxford, 1980), add superstructure.

[30] Kaye, *History of the War in Afghanistan*; P. Sykes, *History of Afghanistan*, 2 vols. (London, 1940); J. A. Norris, *The First Afghan War, 1838–1842* (Cambridge, 1967).

[31] Ainslie T. Embree, 'Frontiers into Boundaries', in Richard G. Fox, ed., *Realm and Region in Traditional India* (Durham, NC, 1977), pp. 255–80. Also see Benoy Kumar Sarkar, *The Politics of Boundaries* (Calcutta, 1926).

Company functioned overseas. Early concerns over India were comprehensively taken into account by P. J. Marshall, *Problems of Empire: Britain and India, 1757–1813* (London, 1968). Others have studied the control of Imperial affairs in India—under Clive, Hastings, Cornwallis, Bentinck, and others.[32]

For two centuries inquiries into the ideological foundations of policy have continued to engage the historians attention. This has been especially true of studies concerned with agrarian relations and land revenue. Eric Stokes, in *The English Utilitarians and India* (Oxford, 1959), showed how James Mill and others tried to impose a radical Benthamite agenda upon British India. Ranajit Guha found traces of French physiocratic influence behind the Permanent Settlement.[33] Both Timothy Beaglehole and Nilmani Mukherjee, questioning ideological factors as explaining Munro's *Ryotwari* Settlement in Madras, continued to examine British intentions rather than what was actually happening on the ground.[34] Dharma Kumar doubted whether landless labour was a result of British rule, arguing that caste and village institutions had effectively thwarted British policies.[35] All such debates have continuously swirled around whether or not, and in what measure, British rule did serious damage in India.[36] Overall, the increasing volume of debate over decisions at highest levels have signalled an increased interest in events which occurred under the Company Raj.

But understanding of control *within* the Indian Empire required a new and different approach. This was foreshadowed, first in Percival Spear's *The Nabobs: A Study of the Social Life of the English in Eighteenth-Century India* (Oxford, 1932),

[32] H. H. Dodwell, *Dupleix and Clive* (London, 1920); A. M. Davies, *Clive of Plassey* (London, 1939); T. G. Percival Spear, *Master of Bengal: Clive and his India* (London, 1975); and Nirad Chaudhuri, *Clive in India* (London, 1975). Sophia Weitzman, *Warren Hastings and Philip Francis* (Manchester, 1929); Keith Feiling, *Warren Hastings* (London, 1954); Penderel Moon, *Warren Hastings and British India* (London, 1954); and P. J. Marshall, *The Impeachment of Warren Hastings* (Oxford, 1965), a fine-grained and intricate study. Franklin and Mary Wickwire, *Cornwallis: The Imperial Years* (Chapel Hill, NC, 1980); John Rosselli, *Lord William Bentinck: The Making of a Liberal Imperialist, 1774–1839* (London, 1974).

[33] Ranajit Guha, *A Rule of Property for Bengal: An Essay in the Idea of the Permanent Settlement* (Paris, 1963); H. R. C. Wright, 'Some Aspects of the Permanent Settlement in Bengal', *Economic History Review* (hereafter *EcHR*), Second Series, VII (1954), pp. 217–19.

[34] T. H. Beaglehole, *Thomas Munro and the Development of Administrative Policy in Madras, 1792–1818* (Cambridge, 1966). Arguments over benefits of policy for people in India were carried forward by Nilmani Mukherjee, *The Ryotwari System of Madras, 1792–1827* (Calcutta, 1962); C. Gupta, *Agrarian Relations and Early British Rule* (Bombay, 1963); Neil Rabitoy, 'System vs. Expediency: The Reality of Land Revenue Administration in Bombay Presidency, 1812–1820', *Modern Asian Studies* (hereafter *MAS*), IX, 4 (Oct. 1975), pp. 529–46; Asiya Siddiqi, *Agrarian Change in a Northern Indian State: Uttar Pradesh, 1819–1833* (Oxford, 1973).

[35] Dharma Kumar, *Land and Caste in South India: Agricultural Labour in Madras Presidency During the Nineteenth Century* (Cambridge, 1965).

[36] Kenneth Ballhatchet, *Social Policy and Social Change in Western India, 1817–1830* (London, 1957).

and especially in his *Twilight of the Mughals: Studies in Late Mughul Delhi* (Cambridge, 1951). Events in India received every more attention when Robert Frykenberg, in *Guntur District, 1788–1848: A History of Local Influence on Central Authority* (Oxford, 1965), showed how *local* sources could describe *local* events. Indigenous forces, working silently, had successfully nullified elements of British control. The capacity of the Raj to control events within villages of the Subcontinent came into question.[37] The Raj itself, in its conquest, construction, and control of India, could not be understood without reference to indigenous power structures.[38] In day-to-day control, the Raj was an Indian institution.

Central to 'bottom-up' history was control *within* India. At each institutional and social level, from village lord to Governor-General in Council, actual control began to look more complex, and divided, than had been thought. Eric Stokes, reversing his earlier perspective,[39] no longer looked so much at how British rule had altered structures in India. He wondered whether the British had made any real impact upon village peoples. Each caste and village seemed to give a different answer. Local institutions survived even as relations of power changed, with battlefields moving into courts of law.[40] Thomas R. Metcalf saw such a reversal as too extreme. British rule might not have altered the fabric of agrarian relations during its early decades, especially at village levels, but disruption among the great lords in North India could not be denied.[41]

Clearly the degree of disruption was greater the higher the lord under consideration. Abdul Majed Khan revealed, in fine detail, how one noble of the Mughal ruling class had helped the Company to establish its rule and had striven for its continuance.[42] Other studies began to show that the Permanent (*Zamindari*, or Bengal) Settlement, far from being disruptive, had actually consolidated the

[37] R. E. Frykenberg, ed., *Land Control and Social Structure in Indian History* (Madison, 1969) and *Land Tenure and Peasant in South Asia* (Delhi, 1977).

[38] R. E. Frykenberg, ' "Company Circari" in Carnatic, *c.*1799–1859; The Inner Logic of Political Systems in India', in Richard G. Fox, ed., *Realm and Region in Traditional India* (Durham, NC, 1977).

[39] Eric Stokes, 'A New Approach to Indian History', *Historical Journal*, X, 4 (1967), pp. 460–62.

[40] Eric Stokes, *The Peasant and the Raj: Studies in Agrarian Society and Peasant Rebellion in Colonial India* (Cambridge, 1978).

[41] Thomas R. Metcalf, *Land, Landlords and the British Raj: Northern India in the Nineteenth Century* (Berkeley, 1979), concentrated upon the *taluqdars* of Oudh; and *The Aftermath of Revolt: India, 1857–1870* (Princeton, 1964); 'Rural Society and British Rule in Nineteenth-Century India', *Journal of Asian Studies* (hereafter *JAS*), XXXIV (1979), 111–19; and review in *Journal of Imperial and Commonwealth History*, XIII (1985), pp. 199–299.

[42] Abdul Majed Khan, *The Transition in Bengal, 1756–1775: A Study of Saiyid Muhammad Reza Khan* (Cambridge, 1969). In an earlier study Brijen K. Gupta, *Sirajuddaullah and the East India Company, 1756–1757: Background to the Foundation of British Power in India* (Leiden, 1962), had laid the groundwork for a fresh approach.

power of a rising Bengali gentry (*bhadralok*).[43] Differently textured descriptions by Nilmani Mukherjee and John R. McLane—one about a famous ancestor and another about Burdwan—made this outlook clearer.[44] Studies of princes by Michael Fischer and John Pemble examined the intricate relations between the Nawabi durbar and the British in Oudh, tracing an ever-tightening control, as demands for more tribute ultimately drove that princely state to extinction.[45] A closer look at one European adventurer within the Oudh durbar by R. Llewellyn-Jones, added another kind of bottom up history.[46]

Similar kinds of investigations were conducted in the south. Frank Conlon, Karen Leonard, and Henny Sender produced 'caste' histories, each revealing exactly how a particular élite community had prospered under the Raj.[47] Arun Bandhopadhyay applied such investigations to what actually happened within *ryotwari* districts of Madras.[48] Nicholas Dirks, in his ethnohistory, drew upon local sources to examine how Company rule appeared in the eyes of the Raja of Pudukottai.[49] David Ludden probed complexities of agrarian relations with special reference to peasants and village rulers in the adjacent district of Tirunelveli.[50] Most recently, Pamela G. Price has demonstrated how rivalries among royal families within the 'little kingdoms' of Ramnad and Sivaganga, combined with religious practices and symbols, have contributed to the development of new political ideologies and identities among peoples in southern Tamil country.[51]

The twin capstones upon the edifices of new historiography, combining bottom-up and top-down perspectives of British control in North India and South

43 As found in work done by Ratna Ray, 'Land Transfer and Social Change Under the Permanent Settlement', *IESHR*, XI (1974), pp. 1–45; Rajat and Ratna Ray, 'Zamindars and Jotedars: A Study of Rural Politics in Bengal', *MAS*, IX (1975), pp. 81–102.

44 Nilmani Mukherjee, *A Bengal Zamindar: Jaykrishna Mukherjee of Uttarpara and His Times, 1808–1888* (Calcutta, 1975); John R. McLane, *Land and Local Kingship in Eighteenth-Century Bengal* (Cambridge, 1993).

45 Michael Fisher, *A Clash of Cultures: Awadh, the British, and the Mughals* (Riverdale, Md., 1987), is enhanced by his more comprehensive *Indirect Rule in India: Residents and the Residency System, 1764–1857* (Delhi, 1991); J. Pemble, *The Raj, the Indian Mutiny, and the Kingdom of Oudh, 1801–1859* (Rutherford, NJ, 1977).

46 Rosie Llewellyn-Jones, *The Fatal Friendship: The Nawabs, the British, and the City of Lucknow* (Delhi, 1985) and *A Very Ingenious Man: Claude Martin in Early Colonial India* (Delhi, 1992).

47 Frank Conlon, *A Caste in a Changing World: The Chitrapur Saraswat Brahmans, 1700–1935* (Berkeley, 1977); Karen Leonard, *Social History of an Indian Caste: The Kayasthas of Hyderabad* (Berkeley, 1978); Henny Sender, *The Kashmiri Pandits: A Study of Cultural Choice in North India* (Delhi, 1988).

48 Arun Bandhopadhyay, *The Agrarian Economy of Tamilnadu, 1820–1855* (Calcutta, 1992).

49 Nicholas B. Dirks, *The Hollow Crown: Ethnohistory of an Indian Kingdom* (Cambridge, 1987).

50 David Ludden, *Peasant History in South India* (Princeton, 1985).

51 Pamela G. Price's recent work, *Kingship and Political Practice in Colonial India* (Cambridge, 1996), constitutes yet another important contribution to the European and Indian symbiosis in the historiography of the Raj.

India, were put in place by C. A. Bayly and Burton Stein. Reversing previous assumptions of decline, Bayly drew together a rich panoply of data urging that increasing prosperity in North India reinforced the expanding system of political alignments put together by the Company's Raj.[52] Burton Stein, looking at Madras Presidency as envisioned by its most famous British ruler, convincingly explained how British rule grew in South India.[53]

A third category of new historiography—beyond factors of control, influence, or loyalty—concerns cultural contact. Cultural interactions could strengthen or weaken support for the Raj among India's élites. Neither cultural integration nor cultural conflict within such highly segmented societies were matters which could be taken for granted. Thus, behind, if not beneath and beyond, studies of the ongoing impact of the Enlightenment in India, as manifest in Orientalism and Indology, have been studies of complex interactions both within and between religious and social institutions. Acute sensitivities within either of these kinds of closely interlinked institutions have brought, since the 1960s, an ever-widening stream of fresh historical research. Whenever such institutions in India, whether Hindu or Muslim, have been examined, the impacts of, and responses to, two other kinds of interconnected European cultural activity have also continued to attract scholarly interest. These are the modern missionary movement and the modern movement in education.

The impetus of this new interest was already clear when S. N. Mukherjee's *Sir William Jones: A Study in Eighteenth-Century British Attitudes to India* (Cambridge, 1968), David Kopf's *British Orientalism and the Bengal Renaissance: The Dynamics of Indian Modernization, 1773–1835* (Princeton, 1969),[54] and P. J. Marshall's *The British Discovery of Hinduism in the Eighteenth Century* (Cambridge, 1970) appeared.[55] Works on Muslin India by such historians as S. M. Ikram, I. H. Qureshi, Peter Hardy, Barbara Daly Metcalf, and Gregory Kozlowski served, in some measure, to balance outpourings of scholarship by Indologists

[52] C. A. Bayly, *Rulers, Townsmen and Bazaars: North Indian Society in the Age of British Expansion, 1770–1870* (Cambridge, 1989). Also useful in this connection is Anand A. Yang, *The Limited Raj: Agrarian Relations in Colonial India, Saran District, 1793–1920* (Berkeley, 1989).

[53] Burton Stein, *Thomas Munro: The Origins of the Colonial State and His Vision of Empire* (Delhi, 1989).

[54] See also David Kopf, *The Brahmo Samaj and the Shaping of the Modern Indian Mind* (Princeton, 1988) and Tapan Raychaudhuri, *Europe Reconsidered: Perceptions of the West in Nineteenth Century Bengal* (Oxford, 1988), and Killingley's, *Rammohun Roy in Hindu and Christian Tradition.*

[55] Marshall focused attention upon what British Orientalists had written from 1767 to 1800. Rosane Rocher, *Orientalism, Poetry, and the Millennium: The Checkered Life of Nathaniel Brassey Halhed, 1751–1830* (Calcutta, 1983), magnified this focus by examining one of these Orientalists.

and Sanskritists.[56] Such a spate of new works, rich in strength, was an event in itself. New research in oriental studies enhanced historical understandings as never before, especially in various fields of religion.

Not surprisingly, such enhancements brought about a sharp reaction. The entire tradition of Orientalist scholarship, from its very inception, has been under attack. Edward W. Said, in *Orientalism* (New York, 1978) and *Culture and Imperialism* (London, 1993), has used literary and Marxist theory as a tool for condemning such scholarship. Stigmatizing it as inherently 'colonialist', he saw Orientalism itself as having always been an instrument for the enslavement of non-Western peoples. The explosion of controversy which Said aroused has yet to subside. Applying his views to India were Ranajit Guha, Gayatri Spivak, Bernard S. Cohn, and various 'subalternist' disciples of Ranajit Guha.[57] In opposition, Kopf argued that Said's conclusions were anti-historical and deeply antithetical to responsible historical scholarship.[58] A host of others, especially Middle East scholars such as Ernst Gellner and Bernard Lewis, have also vigorously opposed Said's views.[59] Their argument has been that the entire corpus of anti-Orientalist 'colonial discourse analysis' is itself a form of neo-colonialist, Eurocentric nihilism—an ideological approach which hoists and impales itself upon its own petard. All in all, renewed excitement over various aspects of Orientalism has not been damaged nor diminished by the 'attack' led by Edward Said.

Christian missions and missionary history have never generated as much attention for India as for Africa, or even China.[60] The Company's Raj, ever dependent on Hindu resources and support as it most certainly was, never left relations between the Company and Christians, especially missionaries, anything but tense. Even after Parliament forced the Company to admit missionaries into British India, ambivalences remained. Prior to the Charter Renewal Act of 1813, official

56 S. M. Ikram, *Muslim Civilization in India*, ed. Ainslie T. Embree (New York, 1964); Ishtiaq Husain Qureshi, *The Muslim Community in the Indo-Pakistan Subcontinent* (610–1947) (S'Gravenhage, 1962); Peter Hardy, *The Muslims of British India* (Oxford, 1972); Barbara D. Metcalf, *Islamic Revival in British India: Deoband, 1860–1900* (Princeton, 1982); and Gregory C. Kozlowski, *Muslim Endowments and Society in British India* (Cambridge, 1985).

57 Edward W. Said, 'Foreword', *Selected Subaltern Studies* (New York, 1988), p. vi.; Ranajit Guha, 'A Note on the Terms "elite", "people", "subaltern" ', appended to 'Some Aspects of the Historiography of Colonial India', in ibid., p. 44—or any of at least six vols. in the series.

58 David Kopf, 'Hermeneutics versus History', *JAS*, XXXIX, 3 (May 1980), pp. 495–505.

59 For an essay on this controversy see R. E. Frykenberg, 'History as Rhetoric: A Disputed Discourse', in Frykenberg, *History and Belief: The Foundations of Historical Understanding* (Grand Rapids, 1996), pp. 263–88.

60 See works by John W. Kaye, *Christianity in India: A Historical Narrative* (London, 1855); Julius Richter, *A History of Protestant Missions in India*, trans. Sidney H. Moore (Edinburgh, 1908); and Stephen Neill, *A History of Christianity in India*, 2 vols. (Cambridge, 1984, 1985), the latter being somewhat 'neo-colonial' in its Anglicanism.

prohibition of missionary activity had occasionally been violated by Company governments in India, especially when a local need for scholars or teachers arose. But appeals against Hindu persecution fell upon deaf ears. Knowledge of Catholic and Syrian (Thomas) Christian activities remained largely hidden from view, either in India (e.g. Goa or Shambhaganur) or Europe (Lisbon and Rome). Similarly, details about Protestant activities remained buried within archives of the London-based Society for Promoting Christian Knowledge (SPCK) or, for the Danish Mission, mostly within the Franckesche Stiftungen in Halle.

Understandings of missions have tended to run on a parallel track, often separated from other events in India's history. In the 1790s, the Evangelical awakening generated missionary societies, pamphlets, and tracts. Collaboration between Charles Grant,[61] Charles Simeon, and William Wilberforce enabled them to 'bring a tiny group of missionary chaplains into Company stations in India'. William Carey and British Baptists in Serampore raised pubic consciousness. 'Pamphlet wars' erupted and political pressures mounted.[62] Hero accounts of various figures, such as Claudius Buchanan, Henry Martyn, and Reginald Heber proliferated.[63] H. N. Pearson's *Memoirs of the Life and Correspondence of the Revd Christian Frederick Swartz*, 2 vols. (London, 1834–) described the deeds of a German who had ended forty-nine years in India as the Raja-Guru of Thanjavur. James Hough's *History of Christianity in India*, 4 vols. (London, 1830) and John W. Kaye's *Christianity in India: An Historical Narrative* (London, 1859) set missionary activities within a broader context. But the Vellore Mutiny of 1806 and the Great Mutiny of 1857 seemed to bear out the worst fears and predictions of those who opposed missionary activity. Those concerned about the Indian Empire could hardly remain indifferent.

Yet writing about Christian missions in India has never ceased, despite the decline of missions after the end of Empire. Serious interest among professional historians, strengthened by the publication of Ainslie T. Embree's *Charles Grant and British Rule in India* (New York, 1962), E. Daniel Potts's *British Baptist*

[61] Charles Grant, *Observations on the State of Society among the Asiatic Subjects of Great Britain, Particularly with Respect to Morals and on the Means of Improving It Written Chiefly in the Year 1792, Parliamentary Papers*, 1813, IX, pp. 1–112, focused missionary attention upon India. It was followed by Claudius Buchanan's *Christian Researches in Asia* (London, 1811), a work which went into many printings.

[62] A study by Penelope S. E. Carson, 'Soldiers of Christ: Evangelicals and India, 1780–1833', unpublished Ph.D. thesis, London, 1988, explores political pressures in Britain.

[63] Hugh N. Pearson, *Memoirs of the Life and Writings of the Revd. Claudius Buchanan*, D.D., 2 vols. (London, 1817); John Sargent, *A Memoir of the Revd. Henry Martyn* (London, 1819) and Reginald Heber's posthumous *Narrative of a Journey Through the Upper Provinces of India from Calcutta to Bombay*, 2 vols. (London, 1828), are examples of this kind of writing.

Missionaries in India, 1793–1837: The History of Serampore and its Missions (Cambridge, 1967), and M. A. Laird's *Missionaries and Education in Bengal, 1793–1837* (Oxford, 1972), has increased. What began as a tendency towards Eurocentric or policy-oriented research has shifted toward bottom-up approaches, informed by exegetical and phenomenological excursions into intellectual or religious history.[64] This shift, partly ushered in by Frykenberg's research,[65] reached a new level in Susan Bayly's *Saints, Goddesses, and Kings: Muslims and Christians in South India* (Cambridge, 1989) and Avril Ann Powell's, *Muslims and Missionaries in Pre-Mutiny India* (London, 1993). In such works, emphasis upon the Indianness of Christianity in India, as an *Indian* phenomenon in its own right rather than as some sort of European or 'colonial' imposition, has increased. Recent work on relationships between missionaries and the Raj has brought a rediscovery of usages with special reference to the terms 'Hindu' and 'Hinduism'. As they first emerged during early years of the Company's rule, they tended to denote anything 'native' to India, rather than any one, reified system of religion.[66]

Modern education has had a contentious historiography.[67] If Christian missions are seen the handmaiden of colonialism, English education is also viewed as a colonial imposition. Neither 'Orientalists' nor 'Anglicists', in arguing against each other, showed awareness of Indian demands or of German contributions.[68] As early as 1727, when Benjamin Schultz established schools in Madras, children of native gentry flocked to learn 'sciences' in English. During the 1780s English schools teaching to Maratha Brahman youth in Thanjavur, Ramnad, and Shivaganga were run by Schwartz. When some in Madras, Calcutta, and Bombay

[64] See Richard Fox Young, *Resistant Hinduism: Sanskrit Sources on Anti-Christian Apologetics in Early Nineteenth Century India* (Vienna, 1981); and R. F. Young and S. Jebanesan, *The Bible Trembled: The Hindu–Christian Controversies of Nineteenth-Century Ceylon* (Vienna, 1995) can be compared and contrasted with Killingley, *Rammohun Roy.*

[65] R. E. Frykenberg, 'The Impact of Conversion and Social Reform Upon Society in South India During the Late Company Period: Questions Concerning Hindu–Christian Encounters', in C. H. Philips and M. D. Wainwright, eds., *Indian Society and the Beginnings of Modernization, c.1830–50* (London, 1976), pp. 187–243 and, 'Conversion and Crises of Conscience Under Company Raj in South India', in Marc Gaboreieau and Alice Thorner, eds., *Asie du Sud, traditions et changements* (Paris, 1979), pp. 311–321, and 'On Roads and Riots in Tinnevelly: Radical Change and Ideology in Madras Presidency during the 19th Century', *South Asia*, IV, 2 (Dec. 1982), pp. 34–52. These throw light upon the emergence of modern 'public' facilities, e.g. hotels, restaurants, transport.

[66] R. E. Frykenberg, 'The Emergence of Modern "Hinduism" as a Concept and as an Institution: A Reappraisal With Special Reference to South India', in Gunther Sontheimer and Hermann Kulke, eds., *Hinduism Reconsidered* (Heidelberg, 1989), pp. 1–29 and 'Constructions of Hinduism At the Nexus of History and Religion', *Journal of Interdisciplinary History*, XXIII, 3 (Winter 1993), pp. 523–50.

[67] R. E. Frykenberg, 'Modern Education in South India, 1784–1854: Its Roots and Its Role as a Vehicle of Integration under Company Raj', *American Historical Review*, XCI, 1 (Feb. 1986), pp. 37–65.

[68] Gerald and Natalie Robinson Sirkin, 'The Battle of Indian Education: Macaulay's Opening Salvo Newly Discovered', *Victorian Studies*, XIV (1970–71), pp. 407–28, show that this lack of awareness persists.

favoured vernacular-medium schools, the clamour for English increased.[69] Petitions by Indian notables received thousands of signatures—over 70,000 in Madras alone (1939). The 1835 decision of Lord Bentinck was, in short, largely a recognition of local Indian demands.[70]

The subsequent history of Macaulay's Minute would surely have pleased orientalists and vernacularists of his day. Its ritual demonization and parroting rhetoric are twentieth-century events, related more to polemical discourse than to critical investigations of India before 1858. Had someone other than Lord Macaulay used such language it might have vanished, instead of being republished so many times. Had not G. O. Trevelyan boasted about it, out of filial piety, its prominence might never have been so exaggerated. But its significance has been challenged, on different grounds, by Percival Spear (1938), Kenneth Ballhatchet (1951), and Robert Frykenberg (1988).[71] Meanwhile, much nationalist historiography has continued to demonstrate that the myth of colonialist imposition of English, like that of 'divide and rule', occupies an important place.[72] More chapters about English as *the* élitist language necessary for promoting nationalist interests, and about vernacular modern education as *the* tool essential for lifting the downtrodden, have yet to be written.[73]

One by-product of radical changes in religion and education was social reform. The history of such reform begins with English-educated Indians and their European allies, both official and non-official, along with views expressed by their opponents. Whatever the issue, whether female infanticide, widow burning, child marriage, widow remarriage, child labour, literacy, caste pollution (untouchability) or 'public facilities' (bridges, hotels, restaurants, streets, vehicles), controversy has focused upon the relative roles played by European (Christian) missionaries and enlightened (English-educated) Indians concerning the plight of the downtrodden (untouchables, women, and children). Some

[69] V. V. Gopal Row, ed., *The Life of Vennelacunty Soob Row* (Madras, 1873), describes this demand, and activities of the Madras School Book Society. Notables in Calcutta and Bombay gave parallel accounts.

[70] The text of the resolution is in C. H. Philips, ed., *The Correspondence of Lord William Cavendish Bentinck, Governor–General of India, 1828–1835*, 2 vols. (Oxford, 1977). Charles E. Trevelyan, *On the Education of the People of India* (London, 1838), reflects this. J. F. Hilliker, 'C. E. Trevelyan as an Educational Reformer in India, 1827–38', *Canadian Journal of History*, VI (1974), pp. 275–91.

[71] Percival Spear, 'Bentinck and Education', *Cambridge Historical Journal*, X (1938), pp. 77–101; Kenneth Ballhachet, 'The Home Government and Bentinck's Educational Policy', ibid. (1951), pp. 224–29; and R. E. Frykenberg, 'Macaulay's Minute and the Myth of English as a "Colonialist" Imposition upon India: A Reappraisal with Special Reference to South India', *Journal of the Royal Asiatic Society* (London, 1988), pp. 305–15.

[72] Syed Nurullah and J. P. Naik, *A History of Education in India* (*British Period*) (Calcutta, 1951).

[73] Chittabrata Palit, 'Vernacular Education and the Structure of Politics in Bengal (1835–1870)', *Quarterly Review of Historical Studies*, XV (1975–6), pp. 163–72.

works have brought enlightenment. Kenneth Ingham, *Reformers in India, 1793–1833: An Account of the Work of Christian Missionaries on Behalf of Social Reform* (Cambridge, 1956), while valuable, exaggerated 'progressive' elements in missionaries and minimized indigenous contributions. This bias is corrected in Bruce Carlisle Robertson, *Raja Rammohan Ray: The Father of Modern India* (Delhi, 1995), D. Killingley, *Rammohun Roy in Hindu and Christian Tradition* (Newcastle upon Tyne, 1993), N. G. Cassells, *Religion and the Pilgrim Tax Under the Company Raj* (Delhi, 1988), and V. N. Datta, *Sati: Widow Burning in India* (Delhi, 1988).

As far as methodology is concerned, approaches to historical understanding remain in many ways very similar. Whether or not any specific approach is top-down or bottom-up, the oscillating between such approaches continues. Both focus upon matters of limited scope and smaller framework. Both, whether Imperial or local, look at narrowed sets of specific events; and events, however looked at, are particular, and can never be anything but specific. Objects focused upon are fitted within frameworks. They are, of necessity, bounded and constrained by contexts of place or time, person, or process. Perceptions of an event, however imperfect, cannot be confused with timeless theory. If one history is more narrative- or personality-oriented, this cannot be from any essential scorn for empirical and scientific enquiry. If another history is somewhat more 'faceless' and positivistic, more oriented to impersonal processes and systems analysis, this does not necessarily reflect essential or necessary scorn for decisive 'turns' made by individuals, or for the intrinsic uniqueness of an event.

At least for the moment, some historians have been listening to the siren song of anti-historical literary criticism. Theory, in the names of current fashions, has become a cloak for dogma, for denial of empirical evidence, and for scorning real events in historical understandings. By whatever name such fashions parade, whether as 'colonial discourse analysis', 'deconstruction', or whatever else such nihilist impulses might be called, fulminations of this sort cannot be accepted as genuine historical understanding, certainly not by historians as such. Such views, as applied to India, damaged the otherwise brilliant historical work of Nicholas Dirks in *The Hollow Crown: Ethnohistory of an Indian Kingdom* (Cambridge, 1987).[74] They reached a high point of anti-historical dogma in the 'discourse' of Gauri Vishwanath, *Masks of Conquest: Literary Study and British Rule in India* (New York, 1980).[75] As a disciple of Edward Said, she represents an ironic twist—imposition of a Eurocentric, even 'neocolonial' doctrine upon 'hapless natives'

[74] Reviewed in *JAS*, XLIX, 1 (Feb. 1990), pp. 181–82, by R. E. Frykenberg.

[75] Reviewed in *The American Historical Review*, XCVII (1992), pp. 272–73, by R. E. Frykenberg.

from a Westernized Brahman at Columbia. The prevalence of this interpretation is evident in many of the chapters of *Orientalism and the Postcolonial Predicament: Perspectives on South Asia* (Philadelphia, 1993), edited by Carol A. Breckenridge and Peter Van der Veer. Ironically, all such diatribes are themselves, at the very least, Eurocentric and, by their own definition, 'Orientalist' constructions.[76]

Among Indianists,[77] aside from an earlier attack by David Kopf,[78] perhaps only Eugene Irschick has raised a somewhat lonely recent voice against this kind of 'anti-historical' history among historians of the Raj.[79] His argument, when all equivocations are removed, is simple: Indians have always been in the forefront of historical understandings of events in India. They were engaged in the production of such histories before 1858 and they have always remained so engaged. Ironies persist: some Indians, especially Marxists and those currently attacking constructions of Orientalism, are often Eurocentric in conceptual and theoretical frames of reference; and some Europeans, especially those who have depended upon local peoples of India for their understandings, are often more Indocentric in outlook. The argument of this chapter, to summarize, is that historical understandings of India, never wholly one or the other, always were and still are products of a dialectical process in which both Indians and Westerners have contributed to an evolving synthesis.

[76] See review by William A. Sax, in *JAS*, LIV, 2 (May 1995), pp. 591–92.

[77] Attacks upon Said's view by such scholars as Ernest Gellner, *Postmodernism, Reason, and Religion* (London, 1992) and 'The Mightier Pen? Edward Said and the Double Standards of Inside-Out Colonialism', *The Times Literary Supplement* (19 Feb. 1993), pp. 3–4, with Letters to the Editor (2 and 9 April, 1993); J. B. Kelly, 'Imperial Masquerade', *National Review* (26 April 1993), pp. 48–50.

[78] David Kopf, 'Hermeneutics versus History', *JAS*, XXXIX, 3 (May 1980), pp. 495–505.

[79] Eugene F. Irschick, *Dialogue and History: Constructing South India, 1795–1895* (Berkeley, 1994), reviewed by Pamela G. Price, *JAS*, LIV, 2 (May 1995), pp. 598–99.

Select Bibliography

SINNAPPAH ARASARATNAM, *Merchants, Companies and Commerce on the Coromandel Coast, 1650–1740* (Delhi, 1986).

AMIYA BARAT, *Bengal Native Infantry: Its Organisation and Discipline, 1796–1852* (Calcutta, 1962).

C. A. BAYLY, *Rulers, Townsmen and Bazaars: North Indian Society in the Age of British Expansion, 1770–1870* (Cambridge, 1983).

—— *Empire and Information: Intelligence-Gathering and Social Communication in India, 1780–1870* (Cambridge, 1996).

SUSAN BAYLY, *Saints, Goddesses and Kings: Muslims and Christians in South Indian Society, 1700–1900* (Cambridge, 1989).

MICHAEL FISHER, *Indirect Rule in India: Residents and the Residency System, 1764–1858* (Delhi, 1991).

R. E. FRYKENBERG, *Guntur District, 1788–1848: A History of Local Influence and Central Authority in South India* (Oxford, 1965).

ABDUL MAJED KHAN, *The Transition in Bengal, 1756–1775; A Study of Saiyid Muhammad Reza Khan* (Cambridge, 1969).

DIRK H. A. KOLFF, *Naukar, Rajput and Sepoy: The Ethno-History of the Military Labour Market in Hindustan, 1450–1850* (Cambridge, 1990).

P. J. MARSHALL, *East Indian Fortunes: The British in Bengal in the Eighteenth Century* (Oxford, 1976).

JOHN R. MCLANE, *Land and Local Kingship in Eighteenth-Century Bengal* (Cambridge, 1993).

SIR PENDEREL MOON, *The British Conquest and Dominion of India* (London, 1989).

AVRIL ANN POWELL, *Muslims and Missionaries in Pre-Mutiny India* (London, 1993).

PAMELA PRICE, *Kingship and Political Practice in Colonial India* (Cambridge, 1996).

TAPAN RAYCHAUDHURI, *Europe Reconsidered: Perceptions of the West in Nineteenth-Century Bengal* (Delhi, 1988).

PERCIVAL SPEAR, *Twilight of the Mughuls* (Cambridge, 1951).

BURTON STEIN, *Thomas Munro: The Origins of the Colonial State and His Vision of Empire* (Delhi, 1989).

ERIC STOKES, *The English Utilitarians and India* (Oxford, 1959).

ANDRÉ WINK, *Land and Sovereignty in India: Agrarian Society and Politics Under the Eighteenth-Century Maratha Svarajya* (Cambridge, 1986).

ROBERT FOX YOUNG, *Resistant Hinduism: Sanskrit Sources on Anti-Christian Apologetics in Early Nineteenth-Century India* (Vienna, 1981).

12

India, 1858 to the 1930s

TAPAN RAYCHAUDHURI

The concerns, methods, and findings of Indian historiography for the period of direct rule by Crown-in-Parliament have undergone fundamental changes since the Second World War, though there are marked continuities in perceptions in some areas of the enterprise. The sixth and final volume of the *Cambridge History of India* (Cambridge, 1932) typifies the older approach. The various chapters describe the evolution of the Imperial legislature and superior governments, district administration, governmental policies regarding matters such as famine, education, and finance, and the Indian government's relations with Central Asia. Sir Richard Burn contributed a brief, and not entirely dismissive, chapter on the Indian National Congress. It contains an illuminating statement on the venomous Anglo-Indian agitation against the Ilbert Bill, 1883, which sought to remove the racially discriminatory privilege enjoyed by the Queen's white subjects in India. (In the countryside, they could not be tried by judges of Indian origin.) The agitation, Burn commented, was led by the planters who were often the 'subject of groundless or exaggerated charges'. V. A. Smith, in his *Oxford History of India* (Oxford, 1919), agreed that the said planters' fears were not unfounded. A much more professional work, H. H. Dodwell's *A Sketch of the History of India from 1858 to 1918* (London, 1925), based on archival research, devoted 232 pages to British policy, including the reforms, and forty to 'political sentiment'. The emphasis in all these works is on the history of British rule, its needs and mistakes. For Dodwell the latter included 'the astonishing blunder of the Ilbert Bill'. Such surveys included one which was exceptionally liberal in spirit, *The Rise and Fulfilment of British Rule in India* (London, 1934) by Edward Thompson and G. T. Garratt. It gave a fair coverage to the nationalist movement and commented critically on 'the behaviour of responsible Englishmen' who evidently believed that Indians 'should be treated as an inferior race'. The comment was certainly not typical of pre-Second World War British historiography of the Raj.

The older tradition, with its emphasis on British policy, remains one of the strands in post-war historiography of the Raj but it acquired a much greater degree of professionalism. Simple narration and impressionistic comments gave place to a more analytical approach. Enquiries into the decision-making process were based on very detailed research into public and private archives. Monographs on Viceroys such as Minto, Ripon, Curzon, and Irwin, and surveys covering longer time-spans,[1] were now much more concerned with the encounter and interchanges between indigenous politics and Imperial policy and the pulls and pressures within the latter at various levels. Policy-making was no longer treated as the end products of Viceregal will, at most modified by the superior authority of Secretaries of State. One massive survey, Sir Penderel Moon's posthumously published *The British Conquest and Dominion of India* (London, 1989), does hark back to the practice of narrative and impressionistic comment but has a preoccupation with discovering where the British went wrong. It is distinctive in its concern for ethically correct judgements—not a feature of either the old or the new historiography of British India.

A new dimension to the study of the Raj was enquiry into the British administration, how Empire was made to work as opposed to how policy was made and conceived. A. P. Kaminsky concentrated on the London end of government in his *The India Office, 1880–1910* (London, 1986), and on a variety of lobby and interest groups which attempted to pressurize the home government in this period. Several studies focused on the men who were recruited into the Indian Civil Service, their backgrounds, their ideas, training, and work. Philip Mason, himself an ICS officer, wrote an almost hagiographical and anecdotal account of the service in two volumes in 1953–54, *The Men who Ruled India* (London, 1953–54), and the subtitle of the second volume, *The Guardians*, indicated his approach. A later analytical study by David Potter, *India's Political Administrators, 1919–1983* (Oxford, 1986), examined the shaping of the recruits, their conditions of service, and the intensely political work they did to anchor British rule securely in informal alliances with local Indian notables. It showed how the increasing Indianization of the service ultimately weakened it as a tool of British rule, but ironically made its influence powerful in the creation of independent India's administrative élite. Clive Dewey's study, *Anglo-Indian Attitudes: The Mind of the Indian Civil Service* (London, 1993), was a sympathetic interpretation of the education of ICS men at the close of the nineteenth century. On a similar theme of 'the mind of the Raj' and the significance of British understanding of India for Indians were Thomas R. Metcalf's *Ideologies of the Raj* (Cambridge, 1994) and David E. Omissi's work on the Indian Army, *The Sepoy and the Raj: The Indian Army, 1860–1940* (Basingstoke, 1994). The Indian

[1] See for example, M. N. Das, *India under Minto and Morley: Politics behind Revolution, Repression and Reforms* (London, 1964); S. Gopal, *The Viceroyalty of Lord Ripon, 1880–1884* (Oxford, 1953), *The Viceroyalty of Lord Irwin, 1926–1931* (Oxford, 1957), and *British Policy in India, 1858–1905* (Cambridge, 1965); R. J. Moore, *Crisis of Indian Unity, 1917–40* (Oxford, 1974).

police have also received scrutiny, particularly by David Arnold, *Police Power and Colonial Rule: Madras, 1859–1947* (Delhi, 1986).

If British governmental institutions and policy were the central historiographical themes before the Second World War, indigenous, especially nationalist, politics acquired a similar centrality in the post-war literature on Indian history since the 1857 rising. This new preoccupation is first traceable to an initiative of the Indian government, which appointed a commission for writing the history of the independence movement. The person originally in charge of the project, Ramesh C. Mazumdar, refused to accept the new official perception which saw the struggle for independence as a unified and heroic endeavour and all opposition to it as acts of betrayal encouraged by the imperialist ruler. He left the project, to produce his own version of the struggle in three volumes, *History of Freedom Movement in India* (Calcutta, 1962–63). It is a somewhat simplistic narrative with an overt Hindu nationalist, especially Bengali, bias that implicitly accepts the theory that the Muslims constituted a separate nation and criticizes the leadership for pro-Muslim and allegedly anti-Bengali policy. Mazumdar repeated the statement in a somewhat different format in the last two volumes of *The History and Culture of the Indian People*, which he edited.[2] At the centre of his argument is the nationalist perception that independence was wrested from a reluctant colonial regime which was forced to surrender power in stages. The main virtue of these volumes is the detailed information they provide, which is not easily accessible in any other secondary work. P. Sitaramayya's *History of the National Congress*, 2 vols. (Bombay, 1946–47), the official history of the organization, is an amateurish and unsatisfactory account by comparison. The official project eventually produced a four-volume work, Tara Chand's, *History of the Freedom Movement* (Delhi, 1961–72). It reflects on the one hand the nationalist perception, and on the other undertakes a rudimentary analysis of the class basis of the movement. In its latter aspect it drew heavily on Marxist writings such as R. Palme Dutt's *India To-day* (London, 1947) and A. R. Desai's *Social Background of Indian Nationalism* (Bombay, 1959), works which traced the origins of Indian nationalism to the aspirations and frustrations of the colonial middle class.

The earliest writings on modern Indian nationalism are, however, not of Indian origin. Under colonial rule, Indian writers generally avoided the topic. Pronouncements on the subject came mostly from people who had an unqualified faith in the permanence of Empire. The idea of an Indian nation was an absurdity to writers such as Sir John Strachey, Verney Lovett, and Sir Valentine

[2] R. C. Mazumdar, ed., *British Paramountcy and the Indian Renaissance* (Bombay, 1974) and *Struggle for Freedom* (Bombay, 1969).

Chirol.[3] According to them, it was a figment of imagination invented by a small group of self-serving, English-educated Indians. A society so divided by language, religion, and caste could never aspire to nationhood. Writing three years after the split between Moderates and Extremists in the Indian National Congress, Chirol predicted in 1910 the imminent demise of what he believed to be a seditious organization. There were other variants within the pro-imperialist perception of indigenous politics. Writing in the last decades of the Raj, Reginald Coupland, the Beit Professor of Colonial History at Oxford, did not deny the reality of Indian nationalism, but emphasized the divisiveness in indigenous politics, especially the Hindu–Muslin problem, and the unreasonable attitudes of the nationalists as the main factors which frustrated the government's policy of handing down power in graduated doses.[4]

The notion that nationalism was the concern of the unrepresentative few, and that consciousness of a wider identity transcending ethnic and parochial boundaries was never achieved, remains central to the arguments of an influential group of historians. Judith M. Brown, in her two monographs on Gandhi, estimated as miniscule the proportion of the population directly involved in the mass movements, and concluded that Gandhi's agenda was a failure because none of his stated goals was ever achieved.[5] As the title of her monumental biography, *Gandhi: Prisoner of Hope*, suggests, Gandhi lived and died a prisoner of unrealized (and unrealizable) hopes of unity. The support he secured was mediated by 'contractors' and 'sub-contractors' who found him useful for reasons of their own. Those reasons had little to do with either aspirations for political independence or resentment against perceived injustice, especially racism.

Racism as a factor in the colonial nexus has received inadequate attention from historians, although the autobiographies of Gandhi and Nehru, for example, point to it, as do novels such as E. M. Forster's *A Passage to India* (London, 1924). One monograph discusses how the official élite in India was drawn in the main from the British middle class, which sought to emulate the aristocracy and considered the preservation of social distance 'essential to the maintenance of structures of power and authority'.[6] This observation is borne out by widely differing works, dealing with topics such as the building of European bungalows and hill

[3] See John Strachey, *India* (London, 1888); Sir Valentine Chirol, *Indian Unrest* (London, 1910); Sir Verney Lovett, *A History of the Indian Nationalist Movement* (London, 1921).

[4] R. Coupland, *The Indian Problem, 1833–1935* (London, 1942); and *The Goal of British Rule in India* (London, 1948).

[5] Judith M. Brown, *Gandhi's Rise to Power: Indian Politics, 1915–1922* (Cambridge, 1972) and *Gandhi and Civil Disobedience: The Mahatma in Indian Politics, 1928–34* (Cambridge, 1977).

[6] See Kenneth Ballhatchet, *Race, Sex and Class under the Raj: Imperial Attitudes and Policies and their Critics, 1793–1905* (London, 1980); Nemai Sadhan Bose, *Racism, Struggle for Equity, and Indian Nationalism* (Calcutta, 1981); and Sumit Sarkar, *Modern India, 1885–1947* (India, 1983), pp. 22–235.

stations, where the ruling race could live their life apart and enjoy their own lifestyle, or the role of white women in policing the moral boundaries of British communities throughout India. Sumit Sarkar analysed the implications of this policy for the development of nationalist sentiment. Nirad Chaudhuri qualifies his great admiration for the British *imperium* in his discussion of the social apartheid in India, and concludes angrily that the British in India in the latter days of the Raj were 'the Nazis of their time'.[7]

As Brown points out in her survey of modern Indian history,[8] recent research has unravelled the complexities of nationalist politics partly by focusing on the provinces which, owing to the constitutional arrangements especially since 1919, were the chief arenas for indigenous political action. Aspiring regional élites formed networks of alliances which could put pressure on the provincial governments, the source of power and patronage, for realization of local goals. And the same logic of power politics led to country-wide networks which sought to pressurize the central authorities in the hope of achieving provincial aspirations. The studies of southern India by D. A. Washbrook and Christopher J. Baker explored the structures based on client–patron relationships between 'rural-local magnates' and people further down the socio-economic ladder.[9] If this was the structure of Indian politics, the dynamics of it derived from governmental initiatives towards constitutional reform, which were meant to secure support and acquiescence and lower the cost of governance. Each initiative accentuated the competition between rival networks, some of whom ended up as the 'haves' and the others as 'have nots' of power. At the prospect of each new initiative the 'have nots' organized agitations to see how far the government could be pushed, and to secure legitimacy in the eyes of the constituents. The ruling power made concessions, not to the agitators, but in order to confer credibility on their collaborators until a point was reached where further concession equalled decolonization. And throughout these see-saw movements the overriding concern of the rulers was the long-term interests of Britain in terms of power and resources. The limits to concessions were set by that overriding purpose.

[7] Nirad C. Chaudhuri, *Thy Hand, Great Anarch: India, 1921–1952* (London, 1987).

[8] Judith M. Brown, *Modern India: The Origins of an Asian Democracy* (Oxford, 1985; 2nd revised edn., Oxford, 1994).

[9] The thesis so summarized are developed through a large body of articles and monographs, including: John Gallagher, Gordon Johnson, and Anil Seal eds., *Locality, Province and Nation: Essays on Indian Politics* (Cambridge, 1977); Christopher Baker, Gordon Johnson, and Anil Seal eds., *Power, Profit and Politics: Essays on Imperialism, Nationalism and Change in Twentieth Century India* (Cambridge, 1981); C. A. Bayly, *Local Roots of Indian Politics: Allahabad, 1880–1920* (Oxford, 1975); D. A. Washbrook, *The Emergence of Provincial Politics: Madras Presidency, 1870–1920* (Cambridge, 1976); and Christopher J. Baker, *The Politics of South India, 1920–1927* (Cambridge, 1976).

The above summary of a highly sophisticated and gradually evolving interpretation inevitably distorts a complex set of arguments developed through a large number of monographs and articles which do not speak in the same voice. One can identify only what can be described as their common denominator. It includes the perception, not explored in any detail, that for Britain the Indian Empire was a source of power and profit, and policy was geared to the task of securing these in perpetuity. But the British were aided in the task by their Indian collaborators, 'sub-imperialists' who shared their gains as junior partners in the Imperial enterprise.

This line of argument has come in for expected criticism. It has been identified, not quite fairly, as a sophisticated restatement of the old colonial perception of Indian nationalism seen to be nothing but theatre and rhetoric covering up a cynical quest for material gain. Since the Indian Empire was no doubt based on extensive collaboration on the part of the indigenous élite and acquiescence on the part of the masses, the exploration of collaborative politics, their structure and dynamics, has certainly enriched understanding of the entire historical process. It is, however, difficult to accept the view that genuine opposition was no more than collaboration by other means, or that nationalism, a powerful force in many parts of the world since the nineteenth century, was a mere make-believe in the Indian case. Such analysis also pays inadequate attention to non-rational factors such as frustration, a pervasive feeling of humiliation, and the need for cultural self-assertion central to the historical experience of subject populations in Europe's Afro-Asian colonies.

Other explanations of Indian nationalism have also been attempted. The collections of essays edited by D. A. Low, *Soundings in Modern South Asian History* (London, 1969) and *Congress and the Raj: Facets of the Indian Struggle, 1917–47* (London, 1977), are based on a shared assumption that Indian nationalism was a real and powerful force in shaping the history of the period. The contributors explore the social bases of the movement in various parts of the Subcontinent—the patterns and circumstances of mobilization—on the basis of very detailed archival research. Low argued in an introductory essay that the conversion of the affluent peasant to the nationalist cause guaranteed its eventual victory. A somewhat different thesis on the class bases of Indian nationalism based on neo-Marxist analysis of Indian's 'colonial bourgeoisie' was projected by Soviet historians in V. V. Balabushevitch and A. M. Dayakov, eds., *A Contemporary History of India* (New Delhi, 1964).[10] The role of particular social groups or classes in indigenous politics—the merchants in Bombay, the upper caste *bhadralok* in Bengal—is the theme

[10] See also John McLane, *Indian Nationalism and the Early Congress* (Princeton, 1977), and esp. Anil Seal, *The Emergence of Indian Nationalism: Competition and Collaboration in the Later Nineteenth Century* (Cambridge, 1986).

of a number of monographs. Gyanendra Pandey questioned the received wisdom projecting a steady expansion in the social base of nationalist politics. He developed an alternative hypothesis: the Congress secured a strong and solid base among several social groups, including the majority of the Hindu population in United Provinces, but it lost or excluded others, the majority of the Muslims and the marginal peasants among them, who had at one time been its supporters and allies. Both the inclusion and the exclusion resulted from the developing politico-economic realities of colonial rule. The nationalist rituals, institutions, propaganda (often xenophobic in tone and content), and spectacular acts of martyrdom were important components of that reality.[11] A very different explanation is found in Sumit Sarkar's study of the *swadeshi* movement in Bengal. He underlined the very limited *bhadralok* base of the agitation, but suggested, in Gramscian terms, that this narrow social group sought to act as a 'substitute' for the absence of popular support.[12] The emphasis on the distinctive linguistic cultures of India has been carried farthest in the United States, where conferences on Punjab, Maharashtra, Bengal, and other zones act as channels for multidisciplinary studies, including history.

Biographies of Proconsuls and Imperial administrators were at one time the very stuff of Indian political history. Lord Ronaldshay's three-volume *Life of Lord Curzon* (London, 1928) is a classic example of this older approach to colonial history perceived as the arena for the unfolding of great lives. This tradition more or less died out after decolonization. There are, however, some highly interesting studies, such as Lord Beveridge's biography of his parents, *India Called Them* (London, 1947), or Martin Gilbert's *Servant of India: A Study of Imperial Rule as Told Through the Correspondence and Diaries of Sir James Dunlop Smith* (London, 1966); a collection of his own letters home by a young ICS man, W. H. Saumarez Smith *A Young Man's Country: Letters of a Subdivisional Officer in the Indian Civil Service, 1936–1937* (Salisbury, 1977); and John W. Cell's *Hailey: A Study in British Imperialism, 1872–1969* (Cambridge, 1992). Something like a collective biography is the study by Roland Hunt and John Harrison, *The District Officer in India, 1930–1947* (London, 1980), which quotes extensively from surviving ICS officers.

The interest in the history of Indian nationalism has generated a large number of biographical studies of major Indian politicians such as Gandhi, Gokhale, Tilak, and Jawaharal Nehru, as well as lesser luminaries. These works focus almost entirely on their political careers, and as such form part of the growing corpus on the indigenous politics of colonial India. There have also been valuable published

[11] Gyanendra Pandey, *The Ascendancy of the Congress in Uttar Pradesh, 1926–34: A Study in Imperfect Mobilisation* (Delhi, 1978).

[12] Sumit Sarkar, *Swadeshi Movement in Bengal, 1903–1908* (New Delhi, 1973).

collections of writings of several significant leaders, including ninety volumes of Gandhi's works and a continuing collection of those of Jawaharal Nehru.[13] The work and the ideals of the 'Moderates' and 'Liberal' politicians, central to British political calculations, have also received some attention from historians in recent years.[14] The Sahitya Akademi, the literary institute set up by the Government of India, has published a large number of short biographies of Indian writers which illuminate the cultural history of colonial India. Similar works in Indian languages are numerous.

A considerable gap in Indian historiography is serious study of the internal dynamics of the princely states which covered two-fifths of the Subcontinent's territory. Despite their image as glamorous, wealthy, powerful, and sometimes decadent, they varied greatly in size and structure as well as in the ethos of their ruling families, and some—at least in southern India—were laying the groundwork for modern welfare policies and more representative government. By the time of the Second World War, however, the autocratic princes, responsible to no one except their British protectors, had become an unsupportable anachronism. This was evident in the growth of political movements allied to Indian nationalism. At the moment of decolonization the British abandoned these subordinate allies without hesitation: they were advised to join one or other of the successor states.[15]

The study of Indian history, once dominated by political historians, has been increasingly opened wider by insights from other intellectual disciplines. In an important essay, which has not received adequate attention, Bernard S. Cohn in 1987 underlined the problem of speaking in terms of large social categories as he saw it from the standpoint of an anthropologist.[16] He argued that unless one studied 'behaviour on the ground' in the context of the total social system, such categories could often be misleading. 'Bhadralok', 'Non-Brahmins', and 'Muslims' are terms which cover a wide variety of people whose interests and roles can be

[13] e.g. B. R. Nanda, *The Nehrus: Motilal and Jawaharlal* (London, 1962) and *Gokhale: The Indian Moderates and the British Raj* (Delhi, 1977); see also S. Gopal's three-volumed biography *Jawaharal Nehru* (London, 1975–1984); Judith M. Brown, *Gandhi, Prisoner of Hope* (New Haven, 1989).

[14] D. A. Low has published several articles on the life of T. B. Sapru, a leading 'Moderate': for example, 'Sir Tej Bahadur Sapru and the First Round-Table Conference', in Low, ed., *Soundings in Modern Asian History* (London, 1968). Sapru is also a figure in several essays by Low in *Britain and Indian Nationalism: The Imprint of Ambiguity, 1929–1942* (Cambridge, 1997).

[15] Barbara N. Ramusack, *The Princes of India in the Twilight of Empire: Dissolution of a Patron–Client System, 1914–1939* (Columbus, Oh., 1978); Robin Jeffery, ed., *People, Princes and Paramount Power: Society and Politics in the Indian Princely States* (Delhi, 1978); Ian Copland, *The British Raj and the Indian Princes: Paramountcy in Western India, 1857–1930* (Bombay, 1982) and *The Princes of India in the Endgame of Empire, 1917–1947* (Cambridge, 1997).

[16] See his 'Is there a New Indian History? Society and Social Change under the Raj', in B. S. Cohn, *An Anthropologist among the Historians and Other Essays* (Delhi, 1987).

very different. The same institutions—the Indian durbar for instance—can perform different functions at different points in time. Only a small number of monographic studies on the history of India since 1858 meet the requirement posited in Cohn's essay. C. A. Bayly's study of client–patron relationships as the basis of indigenous politics in Allahabad is one of the best-known works to do so.[17]

To repeat, the plea for disaggregated studies as a prerequisite for aggregative statements covering large social categories has so far had limited impact. A number of papers published in the volumes entitled *Subaltern Studies*, and monographs by the historians who contribute to these, do focus on specific instances of 'behaviour on the ground' which flesh out their grand category of subaltern class, a paradigm covering very disparate elements. Susan Bayly's monograph on Muslims and Christians in southern India questions, on the basis of detailed studies of particular groups of Muslims and Christians, the generally held view that conversions were a means of escape from the inequities of Hindu society, or that the popular forms of religion were at odds with some imagined universal set of norms rooted in Brahminical scriptures. Her study of 'behaviour on the ground' unravels the interplay between 'pure worship' and 'demonic' forms of divinity, the close links between religion and politics of power, and shows how the Hinduism we know today is largely a modern construct.[18]

While the impact of anthropological method on modern Indian historiography has been limited, in the 1960s a number of historians, many based in American universities, introduced sociological perspectives in their work. J. H. Broomfield discussed the communal problem in Bengal in terms of élite conflict and identified the 'bhadralok' as a specific formation of élite status.[19] Eugene F. Irschick, in a study of non-Brahmin movements in South India, similarly tried to map a particular social category and their aspirations in the nineteenth century.[20] Paul Brass tried to explain both nationalism and communalism as concentric circles of politicized ethnicity.[21] In India, M. N. Srinivas's influential contribution to the study of Indian sociology, especially his concept of Sanskritization as a characteristically Indian variant of acculturization and upward social mobility, and the debate which developed around this concept, had their impact on historical writings of the period.[22] Historical studies also focused on the notions of tradition

[17] See note 9.

[18] Susan Bayly, *Saints, Goddesses and Kings: Muslims and Christians in South Indian Society, 1700–1900* (Cambridge, 1989).

[19] J. H. Broomfield, *Elite Conflict in a Plural Society: Twentieth Century Bengal* (Berkeley, 1968).

[20] Eugene F. Irschick, *Politics and Social Conflict in South India: The Non-Brahman Movement and Tamil Separatism, 1916–1929* (Berkeley, 1969).

[21] Paul R. Brass, *Language, Religion and Politics in North India* (London, 1974).

[22] Mysore Narasimhachar Srinivas, *Social Change in India* (Berkeley, 1966).

and modernity also identified the artificiality of boundaries between the two and discussed the modernizing role of tradition itself.[23]

Another human science which has had a limited but interesting impact on the study of Indian history is analytical psychology. Erik Erikson's monograph on 'Gandhi's truth'[24] was received as a remarkable *tour de force*, but it has had few followers. Only Ashish Nandy's essays on the mentality of the educated Indian, their ambivalence and contradictions in relation to the dominant western culture, and his biographical studies of Indian scientists, together with Sudhir Kakar's work on the Indian family and childhood, apply consistently the tools of psychology to historical studies.[25] Studies of childhood, which marked the real beginning of psycho-history as a discipline, are an underdeveloped area in Indian historiography. An interesting contribution is Judith Walsh's *Growing Up in British India* (New York, 1983), based on autobiographies written in English by men born in different parts of India between 1850 and 1920. The links between psychological development and the experience of political subjection are explored in a more recent monograph, Mrinalini Sinha's *Colonial Masculinity: The 'Manly' Englishman and the 'Effeminate' Bengali in the Late Nineteenth Century* (Manchester, 1995).

A number of works by political scientists such as Bhikhu Parekh[26] and Rajni Kothari[27] introduced another dimension to the study of India's recent past. Such works have brought to bear on Indian historical studies the evolving and varied approaches of a different discipline. Parekh has explored the indigenous cultural roots of Gandhian ideology, while Kothari identified the behavioural and institutional determinants of Indian politics. An early contribution to Indian historical studies from the discipline of political science was Francis G. Hutchins's *The Illusion of Permanence: British Imperialism in India* (Princeton, 1967), which made the important point that there was close interaction between the politics of Britain and that of her Indian dependency. Most studies of Imperial rule in India treat the subject as something self-contained or merely refer to the British background without exploring its relevance in any detail. Hutchins points out that India, ruled by Britain's 'middle-class aristocracy', was the transcendent hope of the British political right. Their idea of India's permanent subjection 'exerted a strong pressure on British life and thought'. R. J. Moore's studies of the last

[23] Lloyd I. Rudolph and Susanne Hoeber Rudolph, *The Modernity of Tradition: Political Development in India* (Chicago, 1967).

[24] Erik H. Erikson, *Gandhi's Truth: On the Origins of Militant Nonviolence* (New York, 1969).

[25] Ashish Nandy, *The Intimate Enemy, Loss and Recovery of Self under Colonialism* (Delhi, 1983); Sudhi Kakar, *Intimate Relations: Exploring Indian Sexuality* (Chicago, 1989) and *The Inner World: A Psycho-analytic Study of Childhood and Society in India* (Delhi, 1978).

[26] See Bhikhu C. Parekh, *Gandhi's Political Philosophy: A Critical Examination* (Basingstoke, 1989) and *Colonialism, Tradition and Reform: An Analysis of Gandhi's Political Discourse* (New Delhi, 1989).

[27] Rajni Kothari, ed., *Caste in Indian Politics* (New York, 1970).

decades of British rule in India confirms the truth of this insight. His *Crisis of Indian Unity, 1917–1940* (Oxford, 1974) shows how the only continuity in British policy towards India immediately prior to decolonization derived from the concern to stay on. Hence a series of *ad hoc* measures which did not even pretend to be mutually consistent.[28]

Perhaps the most influential movement in the field of modern Indian history in recent times is represented by the volumes entitled *Subaltern Studies* and the monographs written by the historians, anthropologists, and political scientists who have contributed to the movement. Its beginnings go back to Ranajit Guha's *Elementary Aspects of Peasant Insurgency in Colonial India* (Delhi, 1983), and his introductory statement in the first volume of the series published in 1982. The protagonists of this school include scholars from India, Britain, the United States, and Australia. Their monographic studies, articles, and papers are built around the core concept of a 'subaltern class' formulated by Antonio Gramsci: the notions of domination and subordination as key features of social-political relationships (and which bypass the Marxist analysis of relationship between classes, especially the emphasis on the means of production). They also draw on the post-modernist technique of deconstruction of texts in terms of the analysis of dominant discourses.[29] One object of *Subaltern Studies* is to move away from the preoccupation with the élite, both the colonial ruler and the privileged in Indian society. The underprivileged were to be studied not simply as passive mindless victims or camp-followers incapable of autonomous consciousness, but 'as the subject in their own history'.

Subaltern studies concentrate heavily on moments of rebellion, which help to gain perspective on the usual concern of the anthropologist with the structures such as family and kinship in everyday life, and focus also on 'the forms of domination belonging to the structures of modernity' such as western law, medicine, and bureaucracy. They also question the Weberian 'over-determination of man as a rational actor'.[30] One monograph, for example, analyses the history of popular agitation among the forest-dwellers of the Himalayan foothills, and sets out to construct a sociology of domination and resistance.[31] The sources for such

[28] See also Carl Bridge, *Holding India to the Empire: The British Conservative Party and the 1935 Constitution* (London, 1986).

[29] Here one can detect the influence of a literary scholar, Edward W. Said, and his seminal work *Orientalism* (London, 1978), though he has but a peripheral interest in India. See chap. by D. A. Washbrook.

[30] For an assessment of his school's specific contributions, see Veena Das, 'Subaltern as Perspective', in Ranajit Guha, ed., *Subaltern Studies: Writings on South Asian History and Society*, Vol. VI (Delhi, 1989).

[31] Ramachandra Guha, *The Unquiet Woods: Ecological Change and Peasant Resistance in the Himalaya* (Delhi, 1989).

studies include forest, medical, and judicial records. Conventional sources are analysed as 'texts' in the context of 'themes in the dominant discourse'. The end-products include a remarkable reconstruction of the way in which paradigms took shape in the official mind.[32] Shahid Amin's monograph on the Chauri Chaura incident—the massacre of policemen in a United Provinces village which led Gandhi to suspend his non-cooperation movement in 1922—explores the way in which the rural population interpreted the message of Gandhian non-cooperation.[33] The movement has also generated a considerable theoretical debate on the validity and limitations of its approach. The concern with the history of the underprivileged is not confined to the contributors to *Subaltern Studies*. Others have reconstructed non-literate consciousness through meticulous research into Indian-language material.[34]

The debates centring on *Subaltern Studies* and the post-modernist critique of western perceptions of Asia, allegedly determined by equations of power inherent in imperialism, have deflected attention from the controversy over the economic nexus between Britain as an Imperial power and her Indian dominion. That controversy goes back to the nineteenth century, when publicists such as Dadabhai Naoroji, and later Romesh C. Dutt, traced the roots of India's poverty to economic exploitation in the form of drainage of resources through undervalued exports, Home Charges, and the heavy cost of deploying the Indian Army for Imperial purposes.[35] This view was challenged by the defenders of the Imperial record, who posited the theory of a positive transformation of the Indian economy through infrastructural investments, development of modern industry, and the impact of international trade.[36] Estimates of national income, agricultural output, and trends in India's international trade in the 1950s and 1960s provided a quantitative basis for similar studies, but did not really terminate the controversy, which had strong ideological overtones.[37] The views that per capita income suffered a decline

[32] See the chap. entitled 'The Bigoted Julaha', in Gyanendra Pandey, *The Construction of Communalism in Colonial North India* (Delhi, 1990).

[33] Shahid Amin, *Event, Metaphor, Memory: Chauri Chaura, 1922–1992* (Berkeley, 1995).

[34] See Rosalind O'Hanlon, *Caste, Conflict and Ideology: Mahatama Jotirao Phule and Low Caste Protest in Nineteenth-Century Western India* (Cambridge, 1985); N. Gooptu, 'Caste and Labour: Untouchable Social Movements in Urban Uttar Pradesh in the Early Twentieth Century', in P. Robb, ed., *Dalit Movements and the Meaning of Labour in India* (Delhi, 1993), and 'The Urban Poor and Militant Hinduism in Early Twentieth-Century Uttar Pradesh', *Modern Asian Studies*, XXXI, 4 (Oct. 1997), pp. 879–918.

[35] Dadabhai Naoroji, *Poverty and Un-British Rule in India* (London, 1901); R. C. Dutt, *The Economic History of India*, 2 vols. (London, 1901, 1903).

[36] See L. C. A. Knowles, *The Economic Development of the British Overseas Empire*, 2 vols. (London, 1901); Vera Anstey, *Economic Development of India*, 3rd edn. (London, 1928).

[37] For estimates of national income see S. Sivasubrahmonian, 'National Income of India, 1900 to 1946/47' (mimeo, Delhi University, 1965); for agricultural output, George Blyn, *Agricultural Trends in*

or at least stagnated after 1921, and that the percentage of the workforce employed in agriculture remained unchanged over time, were questioned in estimates which raised serious doubts about the reliability of the statistics. Monographs on regional agriculture emphasized sustained growth in certain parts of the country. On the other hand, a study of private investment in India suggested that the differential rates of industrial growth in the different regions of India were causally linked to the differing patterns of colonial domination. Race was identified as a potent factor in determining the patterns of economic policy, which favoured the white over the native investor.[38] A recent study has explored the complex nature of the relationship between Indian entrepreneurs and their British counterparts: it subsumed collaboration and competition, just as the Indian entrepreneurs' relationship with the government had elements of resistance as well as co-operation.[39] The other side of the story consists of the economic concerns of Indian nationalism, far more radical than its political agenda in the early days, and the influential role of the Indian industrialists in the shaping of nationalist politics in the Gandhian era.[40]

An interesting development in modern Indian historiography is the concern with the history of modern Indian art. The two major contributions to the subject, both published in the 1990s, Partha Mitter's *Art and Nationalism in Colonial India, 1850–1922: Occidental Orientations* (Cambridge, 1994) and Tapati Guha-Thakurta's *The Making of a New 'Indian' Art: Artists, Aesthetics and Nationalism in Bengal, c.1850–1920* (Cambridge, 1992), go beyond the usual scope of art history and locate the development of modern Indian art firmly within the context of cultural development. The overarching importance of nationalist consciousness and the complex responses to western art are central to the argument of both studies. Guha-Thakurta concludes her account with a highly interesting development—the gradual deliverance from the cultural compulsions of nationalism, the movement towards expressions which ceased to be self-consciously 'Indian'.

India, 1891–1947: Output, Availability and Productivity (Philadelphia, 1966). For a critique of his views see Alan Heston 'National Income', chap. in Dharma Kumar, ed., with ed. assistance of Meghnad Desai, *The Cambridge Economic History of India*, Vol. II, *c.1757–c.1970*, (Cambridge, 1983). Neil Charlesworth was among the severest critics of the view which projected a negative picture of economic changes under the Raj: *British Rule and the Indian Economy, 1800–1914* (London, 1982). Also see B. R. Tomlinson, *The Economy of Modern India, 1860–1970* (Cambridge, 1993).

[38] See Amiya Kumar Bagchi, *Private Investment in India, 1900–1939* (Cambridge, 1972).

[39] Basudev Chatterji, *Trade, Tariffs and Empire: Lancashire and British Policy in India, 1919–1939* (Delhi, 1992).

[40] See Bipan Chandra, *The Rise and Growth of Economic Nationalism in India: Economic Policies of Indian National Leadership, 1880–1905* (New Delhi, 1966); Claude Markovits, *Indian Business and Nationalist Politics from 1931–1939; The Indian Capitalist Class and the Rise of the Congress Party* (Cambridge, 1985).

Architectural developments have also found their historian in Thomas R. Metcalf. His *An Imperial Vision: Indian Architecture and Britain's Raj* (London, 1989) is a highly original exploration of the subject.[41]

The cultural interaction with the West resulted, among other things, in a grand literary efflorescence in the Indian languages. A large body of work, partly in English, but mainly in the Indian languages, explores this development. Many of these are exercises in literary history and often explore the wider social context of creative writing. The histories of regional literatures, written in English, produced by the Sahitya Akademi, though uneven in quality, introduce the reader to this complex subject.

Closely related to these themes and the post-modernist analysis of discourse is the work of Edward W. Said, whose thesis informs a great deal of current discussion on colonial India. Its central argument concerning Europe's exploration of Asian cultures being linked to equations of power, and the consequent projection of these cultures as a homogeneity—one of Europe's several 'Others', quintessentially inferior to western civilization—has undoubted value as an explanatory paradigm of both popular stereotypes and many scholarly formulations. Its credibility has suffered because of the tendency to reject exceptions to and variations within the 'Orientalist' perception of Indian and other Asian cultures.

Current social and political concerns are expressed in a new genre of historical writings. Ecological changes, mostly of a negative character, are projected in these studies as a by-product of colonial policies. The imperialists' need for the products of the forest, nineteenth-century ideology which glorified the extermination of 'ferocious animals', and the insensitive intrusion into the primeval rights of the forest-dwellers generating their struggle for survival are central themes in these works.[42] Several earlier and pioneering works, however, had begun to touch on the impact of colonial rule on the environment, but through the medium of a more traditional economic history.[43]

Another worldwide historiographical trend has also found fertile ground in the study of Indian history—a realization of the importance of understandings of masculinity, and in particular a concern for women's history. In the Indian context it has shown how deeply gendered was the British view of themselves. The

[41] See chap. by Thomas R. Metcalf.

[42] See Richard H. Grove, *Green Imperialism, Colonial Expansion, Tropical Island Edens and the Origins of Environmentalism, 1600–1860* (Cambridge, 1994); Madhav Gadgil and Ramachandra Guha, *This Fissured Land: An Ecological History of India* (Delhi, 1992); and Mahesh Rangarajan, *Fencing the Forest: Conservation and Ecological Change in India's Central Provinces, 1860–1914* (New Delhi, 1996).

[43] Elizabeth Whitcombe, *Agrarian Conditions in Northern India*, Vol. I. *The United Provinces under British Rule, 1860–1900* (Berkeley, 1972); Ian Stone, *Canal Irrigation in British India: Perspectives on Technological Change in a Peasant Economy* (Cambridge, 1984).

role white women played in the structures and justification of Empire is examined in Antoinette Burton, *Burdens of History: British Feminists, Indian Women, and Imperial Culture, 1865–1915* (Chapel Hill, NC, 1994). Turning to the specific question of Indian women's status and experience, there has been a major flowering of scholarship in the attempt to recover the lives and voices of women, to investigate the development of social reform programmes, the patterns of patriarchy which informed the agenda for reforms affecting women, and the false idealization of perceptions concerning the position of women in ancient India, as well as to document change in the lives of women, particularly in relation to familial relations and access to education, and to discern the role of women protagonists as icons in the nationalist movement.[44]

Enquiry into family life takes the historian into the world of ideas and beliefs, and this has been another major area of recent scholarship. Some studies have taken the form of enquiry into the mental and emotional universe of élite groups who have left articulate accounts of their struggles in a changing world.[45] Others focus on aspects of religious reform and reconstruction, particularly in response to the presence of Christian missionaries and the ideological encounter with Christianity and its assumptions about the nature of 'religion'.[46]

The development of Muslim consciousness and identity, and the related theme of Hindu–Muslim conflict is covered to some extent in the chapters on partition and transfer of power.[47] Other significant areas of current research, such as the history of education and scientific developments, have reluctantly been omitted.

No study of historiography is adequate unless it relates the developments to the intellectual and cultural history of the relevant time-period. As C. A. Bayly notes

[44] e.g. Kumkum Sangari and Sudesh Vaid, eds. *Recasting Women: Essays in Colonial History* (Delhi, 1989); J. Krishnamurty, ed., *Women in Colonial India: Essays on Survival, Work and the State* (Delhi, 1989); Rosalind O'Hanlon, *A Comparison Between Women and Men: Tarabai Shinde and the Critique of Gender Relations in Colonial India* (Madras, 1994); Meredith Borthwick, *The Changing Role of Women in Bengal, 1849–1905* (Princeton, 1984); Gail Minault, *Secluded Scholars: Women's Education and Muslim Social Reform in Colonial India* (Delhi, 1998).

[45] e.g. R. K. Ray, ed., *Mind, Body and Society: Life and Mentality in Colonial Bengal* (Calcutta, 1995); Parekh, *Colonialism, Tradition and Reform*; Tapan Raychaudhuri, *Europe Reconsidered: Perceptions of the West in Nineteenth Century Bengal* (Delhi, 1988).

[46] Kenneth W. Jones, *Socio-Religious Reform Movements in British India* (Cambridge, 1989) and *Arya Dharm: Hindu Consciousness in 19th-Century Punjab* (Berkeley, 1976); Barbara D. Metcalf, *Islamic Revival in British India: Deoband, 1860–1900* (Princeton, 1982). Work on Christian missions is still in its infancy. Significant works include Henriette Bugge, *Mission and Tamil Society: Social and Religious Change in South India* (1840–1900) (Richmond, 1994); G. A. Oddie, *Social Protest in India: British Protestant Missionaries and Social Reform, 1850–1900* (New Delhi, 1979); Duncan B. Forrester, *Caste and Christianity: Attitudes and Policies on Caste of Anglo-Saxon Protestant Missions in India* (London, 1980); Gerald Studdert-Kennedy, *British Christians, Indian Nationalists and the Raj* (Delhi, 1991).

[47] See chaps. by Ian Talbot and Robin R. Moore, and in Volume IV, chap. by Judith M. Brown on India.

in his chapter, politics have been a major influence on the historiography of modern India. In some instances, such as the writings of the unabashed imperialists of an earlier epoch or the overtly nationalist writings of Mazumdar and others, the political concerns are obvious. The same is true of the *Subaltern Studies*, whose initiator sees his work as a contribution to the reversal of the relationship between the dispossessed and the dominant. The feminist contribution to Indian historical studies is also informed by an agenda for empowering women. At less obvious levels one encounters an impatience with the inheritance of Third World nationalism, a belief that the current fact of corruption has historical roots. This enhances inherited doubts regarding the bona fides of the Indian political élite shared by radicals and conservatives alike. There is also an extreme sensitivity regarding any critique of the Imperial record, which is more evident in reviews and seminars than in monographs or research papers. The other side of the picture is the tendency to label 'pro-imperialist' any positive statement concerning Britain's role in India. Assessments of the historiography of modern India which ignore such undertones would be less than adequate.

Select Bibliography

AMIYA KUMAR BAGCHI, *Private Investment in India, 1900–1939* (Cambridge, 1972).

C. BAKER, G. JOHNSON, and A. SEAL, eds., *Power, Profit and Politics: Essays on Imperialism, Nationalism and Change in Twentieth-Century Politics* (Cambridge, 1981).

JUDITH M. BROWN, *Gandhi: Prisoner of Hope* (New Haven, 1989).

Sir VALENTINE CHIROL, *Indian Unrest* (London, 1910).

R. COUPLAND, *The Indian Problem: Report on the Constitutional Problem in India, 1833–1935* (London, 1942).

H. H. DODWELL, ed., *Cambridge History of India*, Vol. VI, *The Indian Empire, 1858–1918* (Cambridge, 1932).

RAMESH C. DUTT, *The Economic History of India*, 2 vols.; Vol. I, *Under Early British Rule* (Calcutta, 1882).

R. PALME DUTT, *India To-day* (Bombay, 1947).

JOHN GALLAGHER, GORDON JOHNSON, and ANIL SEAL, eds., *Locality, Province and Nation, Essays on Indian Politics, 1870–1940* (Cambridge, 1973).

RANAJIT GUHA, ed., *Subaltern Studies*, Vol. I (New Delhi, 1982).

S. GOPAL, *Jawaharlal Nehru*, 3 vols. (London, 1975–84).

—— *British India, 1858–1905* (Cambridge, 1965).

L. C. A. KNOWLES, *Economic Development of the British Overseas Empire*, Vols. I–III (London, 1924).

Government of Maharashtra, *Source Materials for the History of the Freedom Movement in India* (Bombay, 1959).

RAMESH C. MAZUMDAR, *History of the Freedom of Movement in India*, 3 vols. (Calcutta, 1962–63).

DADABHAI NAOROJI, *Poverty and Un-British Rule in India* (London, 1901).

SUMIT SARKAR, *Modern India, 1885–1947* (Delhi, 1983).

VINCENT A. SMITH, *Oxford History of India* (Oxford, 1919).

JOHN STRACHEY, *India* (London, 1888).

EDWARD THOMPSON and G. T. GARRATT, *Rise and Fulfilment of British Rule in India* (London, 1934).

13

India in the 1940s

ROBIN J. MOORE

During the 1940s India crossed the bridge from colonialism to independence. Freedom was achieved by the division in August 1947 of the Subcontinent between two Dominions, truncated India and the Muslim state of Pakistan. The period has generally been rendered in terms of historic movements culminating in a climacteric, and its closing years as their aftermath. Such perspectives have been remarkably enduring, largely because historical writing was long dominated by the contributions of participants whose lives had been cast in imperialist or nationalist moulds. The historiography was unduly marked by national pride and prejudice, and the popular genre of biography by hagiography.

Historical writing on Indian politics under the later Raj has developed largely from the preparation of collective volumes. The pioneer emerged from an international conference at the School of Oriental and African Studies in August 1967: C. H. Philips and Mary Doreen Wainwright, eds., *The Partition of India: Policies and Perspectives* (London, 1970). The conference occurred in an historiographical context formed mainly by the writings and recollections of men in whose lives the 1940s were a critical period. It summed up historical writing to that stage. The volume's bibliography listed some 500 titles. The project also contributed to later scholarship by encouraging Her Majesty's Government to publish twelve volumes of documents drawn mainly from archives at the India Office: Nicholas Mansergh, E. W. R. Lumby, and E. P. Moon, eds., *The Transfer of Power, 1942–7* (London, 1970–83).[1] The roles of governments and administrations in Britain and India, of British parties and leaders, were exposed to reassessment against a received Whiggish historiography. Elsewhere in Britain a Cambridge School emerged in the late 1960s to question the nationalist pretensions of the Congress movement, which it characterized as élitist and self-serving: for example, John Gallagher, Gordon Johnson, and Anil Seal, eds., *Locality, Province and Nation: Essays on Indian Politics,*

[1] For full references of *Transfer of Power* vols. see chap. by Ian Talbot, note 12.

1870–1940 (Cambridge, 1973).[2] From the Australian National University there appeared a critique of Congress nationalism that represented the party's provincial electoral triumph of 1937 as the ascendancy of 'dominant peasants': D. A. Low, ed., *Congress and the Raj: Facets of the Indian Struggle, 1917–47* (London, 1977). A decade later the Nehru Memorial Museum and Library published a volume critical of the persistence of 'distinctive national viewpoints': Amit Kumar Gupta, ed., *Myth and Reality: The Struggle for Freedom in India, 1945–47* (New Delhi, 1987). In 1988 Hugh Tinker, a prolific contributor to the field, edited a special issue of the *Indo-British Review* that included several reinterpretations and a survey of over 150 publications during the previous twenty years: *The Partition of India* (Madras, 1988). Most recently, Mushirul Hasan has edited a collection of previously published readings, with an introduction and annotated bibliography: *India's Partition: Process, Strategy and Mobilization* (New Delhi, 1993). Among other things, it questions whether Jinnah and the Muslim League ever really intended to win freedom through a fully sovereign separate Pakistan nation.[3]

While the global context of the Second World War and the cold war has never been neglected in historical writing on the 1940s, its significance for Imperial policy and the freedom movements has only lately attracted due attention.[4] It is now being perceived that the intersection of the Indian and the international situations was important for the Subcontinent's development. Recent historiography sustains the view that from the first year of the Second World War the attention of British and Indian leaders became focused on the problem of India's international status. The unity of the decade may now be located in the stages by which an eventual solution to the problem was found in the emergence of the new Commonwealth in April 1949. This is to view the 1940s as the crisis of India's international identity rather than the climactic fulfilment of Imperial purposes and national aspirations.

The pre-eminent contemporary study of British policy for India was Sir Reginald Coupland's *Report on the Constitutional Problem in India*, 3 vols. (Oxford,

[2] For a trenchant attack on the School, see Tapan Raychaudhuri, 'Indian Nationalism as Animal Politics', *Historical Journal*, XXII, (1979), pp. 747–63. Ranajit Guha launched a sustained, multi-volumed critique of 'Elitist historiography' in the manifesto that introduces Subaltern Studies: *Writings on South Asian History and Society*, Vol. I (New Delhi, 1982).

[3] See also H. V. Brasted and Carl Bridge, 'The Transfer of Power in South Asia: An Historiographical Review', *South Asia*, XVII (1994), pp. 93–114.

[4] For a reworking of the 1942–47 period mainly in terms of the demands that the war imposed upon the Raj, see Indivar Kamteka, 'The End of the Colonial State in India, 1942–1947', unpublished Ph.D. thesis, Cambridge, 1988. See also Nicholas Owen, 'War and Britain's Political Crisis in India', in Brian Brivati and Harriet Jones, eds., *What Difference Did the War Make?* (London, 1993), pp. 106–29; Manzoor Ahmad, *Indian Response to the Second World War: A Political Study* (New Delhi, 1987); and Johannes H. Voigt, *India in the Second World War* (New Delhi, 1987).

1942–43). Coupland was conscious of the transformation of the British Empire's inter-war Indian problem into part of a worldwide crisis, and juxtaposed the principles of freedom and unity to elucidate it: 'It will be found that for a generation past the stress in Indian politics has been all on freedom, but that now, when the full attainment of freedom is in sight, the balance has swung over and unity has become again, as it was when British rule began, the major Indian problem.' Analysis of Coupland's Indian problem in the light of evidence that became available in the 1960s and 1970s has revealed, however, that Britain's main intention between the wars was not so much to advance Indian freedom as to underpin Imperial governance with Indian collaborative structures: R. J. Moore, *The Crisis of Indian Unity, 1917–40* (Oxford, 1974) and *Endgames of Empire: Studies of Britain's Indian Problem* (New Delhi, 1988). Both of the inter-war India Acts gave constitutional recognition, in electoral and provincial structures, to the separateness of the Muslims. Carl Bridge has found that the federal plan of the 1935 India Act was intended 'primarily to protect Britain's interests rather than hand over control', 'first and foremost as a means of stopping any chance of a Congress majority at the Centre': *Holding India to the Empire: The British Conservative Party and the 1935 Constitution* (New Delhi, 1986). S. R. Ashton, who has examined the possibility of the princes being brought into the federation prior to the Congress electoral victory of 1937 in *British Policy Towards the Indian States, 1905–1939* (London, 1982), shows that while the Viceroy, Lord Linlithgow, was eager to use carrot and stick to that end, the Cabinet, preoccupied with western Europe and unwilling to provoke 'diehard' opposition, was unimpressed by the seriousness of the emerging impasse. Ian Copland has recently clarified the constructive role of the princes in an authoritative study: *The Princes of India in the Endgame of Empire, 1917–1947* (Cambridge, 1997).

With the outbreak of war, the problem of achieving Indian unity was set aside. The wartime challenge to British Imperial statesmanship was to achieve the effective association of political India with the war effort: wartime collaboration in return for post-war freedom. Britain's wartime attempts to enlist Congress support coincided with the crisis of summer 1940 and the Japanese advance into Burma. The role of Linlithgow as quasi-Churchillian war leader has been loyally represented by his son. The title of John Glendevon's study, *The Viceroy at Bay: Lord Linlithgow in India, 1936–1943* (London, 1971), suggests Linlithgow's sense of embattlement. In September 1939 he announced India's automatic involvement in the war without consulting the parties. Congress questioned the implication of the war for India's freedom and sought a role in central government commensurate with its demonstrated importance in the provinces. The responses of Linlithgow, successive Secretaries of State, Churchill, and the Cabinet have been defended by Glendevon, but criticized for their divisive effects by historians generally: Gowher

Rizvi, *Linlithgow and India: A Study of British Policy and the Political Impasse in India, 1936–43* (London, 1978); Johannes H. Voigt, 'Co-operation or Confrontation? War and Congress Politics, 1939–42', in Low, ed., *Congress and the Raj*, pp. 349–74; Anita Inder Singh, *The Origins of the Partition of India, 1936–47* (New Delhi, 1987); and myself, in *Churchill, Cripps and India, 1939–1945* (Oxford, 1979). Linlithgow is revealed as reluctant to make concessions to Congress, either by acknowledging India's right of post-war self-determination or by associating the parties with the war effort on a participatory basis. He was only too ready to encourage the separatist tendencies of the anti-Congress Muslim League. He was supported by the Cabinet, which accepted with equanimity the resignation of the Congress provincial ministries in November 1939 and viewed the Congress–League conflict as the justification for consolidating Imperial rule. He was led, by Lord Zetland and Leopold Amery—the subject of a study by Wm. Roger Louis: *'In the Name of God, Go!' Leo Amery and the British Empire in the Age of Churchill* (New York, 1992)—to propose modest measures, but acquiesced readily in Churchill's emasculation of them in the 'August offer' (1940). He was disposed to marginalize Congress, indeed to 'crush' the organization as a whole and secure the support of the League, the minor parties, and the princes.

The first volume of the *Transfer of Power* documents, *The Cripps Mission*, reveals that the initiative to secure Congress collaboration was seized by the Labour members of the War Cabinet, who were mainly responsible for the Declaration that promised India full post-war Dominionhood and a constituent assembly. It shows how Cripps's attempt to bring the Indian leaders into a reformed central executive or 'national government' was undermined by Linlithgow and Churchill, both of whom underestimated Congress's representativeness and abilities. It also documents President Roosevelt's unsuccessful intervention, which was prompted by the extension of the war to the Pacific (see *Foreign Relations of the United States: Diplomatic Papers* (Washington D.C. ongoing series).[5] The second volume, *Quit India*, reveals the calamitous breakdown of Congress–Raj relations which precipitated the suspension of the political dialogue for almost three years.[6] Succeeding volumes, and Lord Wavell's diary—Penderel Moon, ed., *Wavell: The Viceroy's Journal* (Oxford, 1973)—document Wavell's concern at the deteriorating administrative situation and fears of an early post-war breakdown. He advocated a political initiative but was overruled by Churchill, for whom he was essentially a stopgap Viceroy.

[5] See also Christopher Thorne, *Allies of a Kind: The United States, Britain and the War Against Japan, 1941–1945* (Oxford, 1978) and Kenton J. Clymer, *Quest for Freedom: The United States and India's Independence* (New York, 1995).

[6] See also P. N. Chopra, ed., *Quit India Movement: British Secret Report* [by T. D. Wickenden] (Faridabad, 1976) and *Quit India Movement: British Secret Documents* (New Delhi, 1986).

Historical studies of India during the war show that the problem of unity was shelved, and insufficient inducement to Congress collaboration was offered. Meanwhile, the communal chasm was widened by the alienation of the Congress and the emergence of the League as a party of provincial government and the organ of a Muslim nation. Contrary to Coupland's thesis, while between the wars Indian freedom was scarcely the object of British policy, during the war unity can hardly be seen as an Imperial objective.

Though studies of the two-year interval between the end of the war and independence have continued to concentrate on communal and constitutional issues, there is a growing body of work on the ways that the war transformed the historical context in which they arose. Three broad aspects of the transformation may be discerned. First, conditions in the Subcontinent—military, economic, and administrative—changed profoundly and affected British–Indian bilateral relations. Secondly, at the metropolis Britain's own domestic problems bore upon Imperial questions at large, so that India's place in the Empire was at issue. Thirdly, the war revolutionized international relations, bringing in question Britain's future as a world power and her place among the new superpowers. Each set of developments bore upon the durability of the Raj. Each is illuminated to some extent in recent historical writing. Each will now be considered in turn.

The development of India's military potentialities during the war and its subsequent implications are the subject of A. Martin Wainwright's *Inheritance of Empire: Britain, India and the Balance of Power in Asia, 1938–55* (Westport, Conn., 1994). A volunteer army grew tenfold to over 2 million men, and the officer corps was Indianized. A massive problem of demobilization was created and at the same time India proved capable of its own defence. There were anxieties over the loyalty of the troops in the face of nationalist challenges to the Raj. There was the difficulty of dealing with the Indian National Army (INA), which had defected to Japan. In the course of a study of Britain's strategic purposes, Partha Sarathi Gupta observes the inadequacy of the published documents on the dent caused in the Imperial mind by the popular agitation over the INA trials ('Imperial Strategy and the Transfer of Power, 1939–51', in A. K. Gupta, ed., *Myth and Reality*, pp. 1–53).[7] Hugh Tinker, too, emphasizes the military impact upon the process of decolonization ('The Contraction of Empire in Asia, 1945–48', *Journal of Imperial and Commonwealth History* (hereafter, *JICH*), XVI (1988), pp. 218–33). Wainwright perceives a close correlation between the demise of the British Empire and the

[7] For the Indian National Army see Peter Ward Fay, *The Forgotten Army: India's Armed Struggle for Independence, 1942–1945* (Ann Arbor, 1993) and Leonard A. Gordon, *Brothers Against the Raj: A Biography of Indian Nationalists Sarat and Subhas Chandra Bose* (New York, 1990).

expansion of India's capabilities. He stresses the impetus given to industrial development by investment in munitions and capital equipment. B. R. Tomlinson has recognized the importance of the huge sterling balances that accrued to India during the war. They were a source of security for the future of British enterprise. Tomlinson has also traced the development of British and Indian business linkages: *The Political Economy of the Raj, 1914–47: The Economics of Decolonization in India* (London, 1979); 'Indo-British Relations in the Post-Colonial Era: The Sterling Balances Negotiations, 1947–49', *JICH*, XIII (1985), pp. 142–62. Again, by the end of the war Britain was excessively dependent upon the Indian element in the civil administration. D. C. Potter has revealed the inadequacy of the ageing and declining British administrative cadre to the purposes of Empire ('Manpower Shortage and the End of Colonialism: The Case of the Indian Civil Service', *Modern Asian Studies*, VII (1973), pp. 47–73).[8] Sucheta Mahajan has shown the decline of the civil cadre's prestige and morale in the face of popular agitation ('British Policy, Nationalist Strategy and Popular National Upsurge, 1945–46', in Gupta, *Myth and Reality*, pp. 54–98).[9]

In early post-war, debt-ridden Britain there was a need to focus on problems of manpower and production, of recovering prosperity at home and reducing Imperial commitments to affordable levels. Burdens in South-East Asia, the Middle East, the Mediterranean, and on the Continent weighed as heavily as that in India. Historical writings on India scarcely mention the metropolitan and wider Imperial contexts. There has been virtually no systematic study of what the Raj and its demise meant to the British public: of why, for example, there was no substantial debate on the future of India. Analyses of the press and public opinion are lacking. Wm. Roger Louis catches something of the grim mood of the country and explores the Imperial problem at large in *The British Empire in the Middle East, 1945–1951: Arab Nationalism, the United States and Postwar Imperialism* (Oxford, 1984). Further evidence can be found in such works as Kenneth O. Morgan, *Labour in Power, 1945–1951* (Oxford, 1984) and John Darwin, *Britain and Decolonization: The Retreat from Empire in the Postwar World* (London, 1988).

For the significance of India in Britain's wider geopolitical as well as Imperial strategic calculations, the most useful reference is now the volume edited by Ronald Hyam in the British Documents on the End of Empire Project series, *The*

[8] See also Potter, *India's Political Administrators, 1919–1983* (Oxford, 1986) and Simon Epstein, 'District Officers in Decline: The Erosion of British Authority in the Bombay Countryside, 1919 to 1947', *Modern Asian Studies*, XVI, (1982), pp. 493–518.

[9] A case for the importance of popular movements in precipitating the British withdrawal from India is argued in Sumit Sarkar, *Modern India, 1885–1947* (Delhi, 1983).

Labour Government and the End of Empire, 1945–1951, 4 vols. (London, 1992).[10] Fear of Russian intervention in the Subcontinent is an occasional theme in the *Transfer of Power* documents. The consequences of a disorderly British withdrawal were a nightmare for Attlee's government, as the international situation deteriorated. Such apprehensions go far to explain the determination to achieve an agreed solution to the constitutional conundrum and a devolution upon stable successor governments: see Singh, *Origins of Partition*, and my *Escape from Empire: The Attlee Government and the Indian Problem* (Oxford, 1983). The theme of India's place in Britain's cold war calculations is explored by Wm. Roger Louis and Ronald Robinson. They argue that, compared with the reinforcement of the Empire by an Anglo-American 'coalition' based on American wealth and power, 'the loss of India in the imperial Great Game seems almost derisory' ('The Imperialism of Decolonization', *JICH*, XXII (1994), pp. 462–511).

The recent historiography has, then, given increasing attention to the effects of historic forces unleashed by the war upon the timing and manner of Britain's departure.

In the historiography of the 1940s contention persists over responsibility for the duality of identity through which India achieved freedom. Jinnah apparently restated India's communal problem as an 'international' problem in his March 1940 presidential address to the Muslim League at Lahore. He drew upon the arguments of intellectuals from Lahore and Aligarh to vindicate a claim that Muslim India was a 'nation', with an inherent right to self-determination and independence apart from the non-Muslim majority provinces and states. Until separate nationhood was achieved Muslim India was entitled to a voice in central governance on the basis of equality or parity with non-Muslim India. As president of the League, Jinnah claimed for himself the exclusive right to speak for the Muslim nation. Mushirul Hasan has brought together several of the major contributions to the controversy over the significance of the Lahore resolution (in *India's Partition*). The resolution, the main new departure in Indian politics during the war, became the foundation of the League's position in all of the wartime and post-war negotiations for changes in governing structures. Jinnah observed that the word 'Pakistan' soon became synonymous with the resolution. It was 'a convenient and compendious method of discussing' it and he saw 'no objection to it'. Asim Roy has reviewed interpretations of 'the Pakistan demand' in 'The High Politics of India's Partition: The Revisionist Perspective', in Hasan, *India's Partition*, pp. 101–31. What is ultimately at issue is responsibility for the truncated or 'mutilated' form in which Pakistan emerged in 1947, and

[10] See also Alan Bullock, *Ernest Bevin: Foreign Secretary, 1945–1951* (London, 1983).

thus for the human tragedies that attended the partition and Pakistan's difficulties ever since.

There is no entirely satisfactory biography of Jinnah. Stanley Wolpert asserts that Jinnah 'no longer questioned the wisdom, viability, or aftermath impact of partition but had decided by the spring of 1940 that this was the only long-term resolution to India's foremost problem': *Jinnah of Pakistan* (New York, 1984), p. 182. At Lahore he 'lowered the final curtain on any prospects for a single united independent India'. Roy labels such assertions as the 'conventional' or 'orthodox' view of Jinnah, though paradoxically he compiles a substantial list of contemporaries and historians who interpreted the Pakistan demand as a bargaining-counter or, at least, questioned whether separate Muslim nationhood was intended. Roy agrees that his list diminishes the 'novelty' of the interpretation that he contrasts with that of the conventionalists, that is, Ayesha Jalal's 'revisionist' *The Sole Spokesman: Jinnah, the Muslim League and the Demand for Pakistan* (Cambridge, 1985). Nevertheless, Jalal's study merits the praise that Roy heaps upon it for elevating the interpretation from the realm of speculation to the level of academic credibility. Jalal argues that throughout his career Jinnah remained what he had certainly been between the wars, an 'ambassador of Indian unity'. He never sought nor favoured separate Muslim nationhood, but deployed the demand to place himself on a par with Congress spokesmen and so achieve equal status for Muslims in the governance of a united India.

In the saga of British negotiations with Indian leaders between 1940 and 1947 there is sufficient flexibility on Jinnah's part to invalidate Wolpert's 'final curtain' argument (see R. J. Moore, 'Jinnah and the Pakistan Demand', in *Endgames of Empire*, pp. 106–33). Jinnah shrank from defining 'Pakistan' in terms of either its national status or geographical extent. Why should he do so, in a context so fluid as that of the Raj in the Subcontinent from the abandonment of federation until independence? What he might successfully demand must eventually depend, first, upon what Britain would concede and support, and, second, upon how much power and influence Muslim India could secure to validate his claims. In the somewhat unreal politics of the war period, with Congress removed from the scene and the Raj in need of Muslim collaborators, there appeared prospects of all-India confederal structures in which Muslim India might enjoy parity with 'Congress India'. In this context the essential Pakistan demand might well be defined in terms, not of immediate realization of separate nationhood, but of the ultimate right to it. Jinnah, Conservative leaders, and Coupland doodled with drafts for such structures.

Coupland analysed Jinnah's position on the Pakistan demand:

(i) While claiming Dominion Status for Pakistan, Jinnah has more than once intimated that it need not be full Dominion Status and that he would like Foreign Affairs and Defence to remain, at least for the time being, in British hands; and

(ii) he has never asked that HMG should accept Pakistan, but only that it should not be ruled out of discussion nor the chance of its adoption prejudiced by the form of an interim constitutional system. Nevertheless, *Pakistanism might triumph as a counsel of despair.*[11]

Not prejudicing the eventual adoption of Pakistan meant, for Jinnah, the reflection of the two nations in the parity of representatives on a reformed central executive during the interim preceding constitution-making. The strength of the position accorded to Jinnah was tested at the Simla Conference of June–July 1945, when Wavell's attempt to reconstruct his executive broke down over his refusal to recognize the League's right to nominate all of the Muslim members, who would be equal in number to the Hindus. The premier Muslim province, the Punjab, did not have a Muslim League government. Jinnah could thus prevent an advance, but unless the League prevailed in the Muslim provinces he could not secure its parity with non-Muslim India. What ultimately mattered was the mobilization of Muslim communities by the League. Recent studies have added new depths and dimensions to the understanding of the League's successes and failures in the provinces: for example Hasan, *India's Partition*, and D. A. Low, ed., *The Political Inheritance of Pakistan* (London, 1991).[12]

A secure Conservative post-war government might have given Jinnah something very like what Ayesha Jalal believes he wanted: perhaps a full six-province Pakistan with subordinate Dominion Status, under a limited central authority reflecting the principle of parity and secured by British-commanded forces. Attlee's Cabinet Mission drafted a statement that came close to doing so, but recoiled under Congress's opposition. A national government and a constitutional assembly could scarcely be set up without Congress's co-operation. Ayesha Jalal's argument, which seems to assume the possibility of Jinnah realizing his vision of Indian unity, becomes less convincing as Britain's options shrank, especially once Labour decided that it could not impose and remain to enforce an award that Congress opposed.[13] Jinnah then had to choose between the limited sovereign Pakistan that he could win by popular support and a subordinate central status within a united India. At that time the Pakistan demand became useless as a bargaining-counter. It would either have to become the basis of a territorial

[11] Coupland's Diary, memorandum on 'Partition', 21 March 1942, pp. 269–70, Rhodes House, Oxford.

[12] See also David Gilmartin, *Empire and Islam: Punjab and the Making of Pakistan* (London, 1988); I. A. Talbot, *Provincial Politics and the Pakistan Movement: The Growth of the Muslim League in North-West and North-East India, 1937–47* (Karachi, 1988), and *Punjab and the Raj, 1849–1947* (Delhi, 1988); and Imran Ali, *The Punjab under Imperialism, 1885–1947* (Princeton, 1988).

[13] See Attlee to Bevin, 2 Jan. 1947, and to Smuts, 19 Feb. 1947, in Nicholas Mansergh, E. W. R Lumby, and E. P. Moon, eds., *The Transfer of Power, 1942–7* (London, 1970–83), IX, docs. 243 and 428; and Anita Inder Singh, 'Decolonization in India: The Statement of 20 February 1947', in *International History Review* (hereafter *IHR*), VI, (1984), pp. 191–208.

demand or vanish into history. From his representations to Wavell and British opposition leaders in late 1946 it seems that he was seeking a sovereign Pakistan Dominion of the largest achievable territorial extent. The logic of his Pakistan demand led, through the game of electoral self-determination that Labour monitored, to partition. The implication of the demand was that, at a level beyond the bargaining processes of politics, the Muslims, by dint of majority occupation, were entitled to a territorial 'homeland'. That is surely the measure of his achievement. Pakistan by partition can scarcely be regarded as the unintended consequence of the position that he adopted consciously in March 1940. As Coupland perceived in 1942, it was always on the cards. This is indeed to assume that the Congress held the trump: the power to insist upon an electorally or communally determined Pakistan. The provincial basis for that power and the timing and mode of its exercise still require further analysis.[14] The party's rehabilitation after the 1945 release of political prisoners and its performance at the 1945–46 elections require research. The effective strength of its hold upon the people during the volatile two years between war and independence is unclear. Recently, Joya Chatterji, in *Bengal Divided: Hindu Communalism and Partition, 1932–1947* (Cambridge, 1995), has clarified the Bengali influence upon the Congress High Command's determination for partition, with which Nehru's biographer associated him twenty years ago: Sarvepalli Gopal, *Jawaharlal Nehru: A Biography*, 3 vols. (London, 1975), I, pp. 343–44.[15]

The capacity of the last Viceroy, Lord Mountbatten, to influence the international identity of Britain's successors was more limited than is suggested either by his admirers or his latest detractor: by H. V. Hodson in his commissioned study, *The Great Divide: Britain, India, Pakistan* (London, 1969), and Philip Ziegler in his authorized biography, *Mountbatten: The Official Biography* (London, 1985) on the one hand, or by Andrew Roberts, 'Lord Mountbatten and the Perils of Adrenalin', in *Eminent Churchillians* (London, 1994), pp. 55–136, on the other. The principles espoused by Labour for a transfer of power were embodied in Attlee's statement of 20 February 1947 and became essential to Mountbatten's brief. His influence upon the terms of his appointment has been exaggerated and his enjoyment of 'plenipotentiary powers' misunderstood. He did enjoy freedom to negotiate, and he used it skilfully to facilitate the deal for dual Dominionhood.

From South Asian viewpoints, the unfinished business of August 1947 has usually been rendered as the aftermath of the accelerated transfer of power, on 15 August

[14] See Richard Sisson and Stanley Wolpert, eds., *Congress and Indian Nationalism: The Pre-Independence Phase* (Berkeley, 1988).

[15] For Gandhi's role in politics during the 1940s, see Judith M. Brown, 'The Mahatma in Old Age: Gandhi's Role in Indian Political Life, 1935–1942', in ibid., pp. 271–304.

1947, to the temporary Dominions of India and Pakistan. It is curious that the consequences of Lord Radcliffe's boundary awards and the integration of the Indian states have attracted little recent scholarship.[16] Of course, controversy still rages over Mountbatten's alleged interference to India's advantage with Radcliffe's demarcation in the Punjab, and the Maharaja of Kashmir's accession to India: see especially Roberts, 'Lord Mountbatten', pp. 93–132; S. Hashim Raza, ed., *Mountbatten and Pakistan* (Karachi, 1982); Alastair Lamb, *Kashmir: A Disputed Legacy, 1846–1990* (Hartingfordbery, 1991); and G. C. Rajiv Thomas, 'The Struggle for Kashmir: Alternative Interpretations and Solutions', *Contemporary South Asia*, II, 1993, pp. 199–215. Furthermore, historians of pre-independence South Asia have been pursuing continuities beyond the climacteric of 1947. Ayesha Jalal has done so for the internal development of Pakistan: *The State of Martial Rule: Pakistan's Political Economy of Defence* (Cambridge, 1990); Mushiril Hasan for communal relations in India: *Legacy of a Divided Nation: India's Muslims Since Independence* (London, 1997); Anita Inder Singh for international relations: *The Limits of British Influence: South Asia and the Anglo-American Relationship, 1947–56* (London, 1993); B. R. Tomlinson for India's economic development: *The Economy of Modern India, 1860–1970* (Cambridge, 1993); and myself for the Commonwealth dimension: *Making the New Commonwealth* (Oxford, 1987).[17]

From the Imperial and international viewpoints, Britain's main unfinished business in August 1947 was to settle relations with the new nations. The Great Game in Asia was being revived. The accumulating experience of the cold war reinforced the predilection of Attlee, Bevin, and Cripps for a new Commonwealth. Philip Ziegler believes that, but for Mountbatten, India would not have stayed in the Commonwealth. Certainly, he pursued her membership with skill, though it is arguable that the roles of Attlee and Cripps were more important.[18] But could they all have succeeded without Jinnah's insistence upon Pakistan's membership? It was difficult for India to leave an influential association to which Pakistan adhered. Could the new Commonwealth of April 1949 be represented as the unintended consequence of the Lahore resolution of March 1940? That would encapsulate with uncanny symmetry the unity of the decade for the historiographer.

[16] Ian Copland seeks to remedy some deficiencies in 'Lord Mountbatten and the Integration of the Indian States: A Reappraisal', *JICH*, XXI, (1993), pp. 385–408, and 'The Princely States, the Muslim League, and the Partition of India in 1947', *IHR*, XIII, (1991), pp. 38–69.

[17] For an analysis of the decade in terms of change and continuity in social and economic development, institutions, ideas, and leadership, see Judith M. Brown, *Modern India: The Origins of an Asian Democracy*, 2nd edn. (Oxford, 1994), chap. 6, 'India in the 1940s: A Great Divide?', pp. 317–62.

[18] Kenneth Harris writes enthusiastically of Attlee as the architect of Indian independence and the new Commonwealth: *Attlee* (London, 1982).

Select Bibliography

JOYA CHATTERJI, *Bengal Divided: Hindu Communalism and Partition, 1932–1947* (Cambridge, 1995).

IAN COPLAND, *The Princes of India in the Endgame of Empire, 1917–1947* (Cambridge, 1997).

KENTON J. CLYMER, *Quest for Freedom: The United States and India's Independence* (New York, 1995).

AMIT KUMAR GUPTA, ed., *Myth and Reality: The Struggle for Freedom in India, 1945–47* (New Delhi, 1987).

MUSHIRUL HASAN, ed., *India's Partition: Process, Strategy and Mobilization* (New Delhi, 1993).

H. V. HODSON, *The Great Divide: Britain, India, Pakistan* (London, 1969).

AYESHA JALAL, *The Sole Spokesman: Jinnah, the Muslim League and the Demand for Pakistan* (Cambridge, 1985).

D. A. LOW, ed., *Congress and the Raj: Facets of the Indian Struggle, 1917–47* (London, 1977).

—— ed., *The Political Inheritance of Pakistan* (London, 1991).

NICHOLAS MANSERGH, E. W. R. LUMBY, and E. P. MOON, eds., *The Transfer of Power, 1942–7*, 12 vols. (London, 1970–83).

PENDEREL MOON, ed., *Wavell: The Viceroy's Journal* (Oxford, 1973).

R. J. MOORE, *Churchill, Cripps and India, 1939–45* (Oxford, 1979).

—— *Escape From Empire: The Attlee Government and the Indian Problem* (Oxford, 1983).

—— *Making the New Commonwealth* (Oxford, 1987).

C. H. PHILIPS and MARY DOREEN WAINWRIGHT, eds., *The Partition of India: Policies and Perspectives, 1935–1947* (London, 1970).

GOWHER RIZVI, *Linlithgow and India: A Study of British Policy and the Political Impasse in India, 1936–43* (London, 1978).

PAUL SCOTT, *The Raj Quartet*, 4 vols. (London, 1966–75).

ANITA INDER SINGH, *The Origins of the Partition of India, 1936–47* (New Delhi, 1987).

IAN A. TALBOT, *Provincial Politics and the Pakistan Movement: The Growth of the Muslim League in North-West and North-East India, 1937–47* (Karachi, 1988).

B. R. TOMLINSON, *The Political Economy of the Raj, 1914–47: The Economics of Decolonization in India* (London, 1979).

14

Ceylon (Sri Lanka)

K. M. DE SILVA

The historiography of Ceylon (Sri Lanka) from the early nineteenth century to the 1830s was profoundly affected by the British conquest of the littoral districts in 1795–96, and the absorption in 1815–18 of the interior Kandyan kingdom, the last of a long line of Sinhalese kingdoms. The British thus achieved something that the Portuguese and the Dutch signally failed to do—to become effectively the rulers of the whole of Sri Lanka. Early studies of the island attempted by British civil servants, soldiers, and others involved in the conquest sought to provide some understanding of the significance of these events and of the history and the culture of the island as well as its value as a colonial territory. Among these was the first history of the island published in British times, *The History of Ceylon from the Earliest Period to the Year MDCCXV* by Reverend Robert Fellowes, using the pseudonym 'Philalethes'. This disjointed and fragmentary book incorporated the text of Robert Knox's celebrated *An Historical Relation of the Island Ceylon*, published in 1681 in London.

The 'rediscovery' of the interior of the island in the 1820s and 1830s, the heartland of the ancient irrigation system and what remained of its architectural splendours, led to a much greater awareness of the historical heritage of Ceylon, an awareness immeasurably enhanced by the publication of an English translation by a British civil servant, George Turnour, in 1837 of the *Mahavamsa*, the sixth-century Pali chronicle of the history of ancient Sri Lanka.[1] The influence of this translation on contemporary historical writings through a widening of the historian's vision and understanding was seen at once with the publication in 1845 of William Knighton's *The History of Ceylon from the Earliest Period to the Present Time* (London), superior in every way to the work of Robert Fellowes. Knighton's history was superseded, in turn, by two historical studies on Sri Lanka by a scholar-administrator, Sir James Emerson Tennent.

[1] George Turnour, 'Epitome of the History of Ceylon, with Explanatory Notes', *Ceylon Almanac*, 1833, pp. 224–85; subsequently he published *The Mahavamso* (sic) in Roman characters, Part I, with translation subjoined (Colombo, 1837).

Tennent's two-volume study *Ceylon* (London, 1859), a richly documented, superbly written work, went through five editions and lasted well into the twentieth century as a standard book on the island. Its success owed as much to conceptual boldness as to its masterly handling of disparate sets of source materials, for Tennent understood, as did few of his contemporaries, the revolutionary change in the economy of the island that had followed upon the successful cultivation of coffee in the 1830s. Tennent mastered the chronology of the history of ancient and medieval Sri Lanka, understood the processes of state-building under the Sinhalese kings, and above all was full of admiration for the technological skills demonstrated by ancient engineers in irrigation, urban planning, and construction of public buildings and monuments. *Ceylon* became a classic virtually from the time of first publication, and its enormous success seems to have had an overpowering, indeed intimidating, effect on all potential competitors into the new century.

Tennent's *Ceylon* had been preceded by his *Christianity in Ceylon* (London, 1853) which, in many ways, was an even more skilfully crafted work.[2] It still stands as the most sensitive and perceptive study by a nineteenth-century Western writer of the religious strand in colonial rule in the island from the time of the Portuguese intrusion to his own day. Nowhere else are the problems that confronted the Christian minority in nineteenth-century Sri Lanka, and the difficulties that missionary enterprise faced in its efforts to undermine the indigenous religions, Buddhism and Hinduism, analysed with such skill. No contemporary British author has shown greater discernment in this response to the island's indigenous religions, especially Buddhism, than Tennent.

The last quarter of the nineteenth century may be described as the second stage in the rediscovery of Sri Lanka's ancient past. It began with the publication of Eduard Muller's *Ancient Inscriptions of Ceylon*, 2 vols. (London, 1883), and the establishment of the Archaeological Survey of Ceylon, and reached maturity in the researches of men such as H. C. P. Bell, Archaeological Commissioner of Ceylon, 1890–1912.[3] Muller, Bell, and his Sri Lankan associates laid the foundation for later works on Ceylon's ancient history through their painstaking cataloguing of the hundreds of inscriptions carved on rocks scattered over many parts of the island and in the preservation of its archaeological heritage. By the end of the first decade of the twentieth century there were some specialized historical works being published on ancient Sri Lanka. Of these, the most significant was an

[2] For discussion of this see K. M. de Silva, *Social Policy and Missionary Organizations in Ceylon, 1840–1855* (London, 1965), pp. 102–37.

[3] See Bertha N. Bell and Heather M. Bell, *H. C. P. Bell: Archaeologist of Ceylon and the Maldives* (Denbigh, 1993).

English translation of a critical study of the *Mahavamsa* and *Dipavamsa* by the German Indologist Wilhelm Geiger, which appeared in 1908.[4]

Nevertheless, the most striking feature of historical scholarship in the island at that time was the comparative paucity of books and monographs. Perhaps the principal reason for this was the lack of a university which could have served as a nursery of talent and scholarship in history, as some of the Indian universities did. The first modern university college was established in Ceylon only in 1921, and even so the study of the history of the island was not an integral part of its syllabus until the early 1940s, the last decade of British rule. Thus, all that Sri Lanka had to set against the Indian achievement in historical studies was a school textbook written by a gifted schoolteacher, L. E. Blaze.[5] School texts, translations of ancient Pali chronicles, and the recording of inscriptions were not, of course, about the British Empire, but they provided the essential base for serious study of Sri Lanka's pre-European history.

Four scholars, three Sri Lankans and the other a British civil servant, established the focus on Sri Lanka within an Imperial context. They were Paulus (later Sir Paulus) Pieris,[6] Fr S. G. Perera,[7] H. W. Codrington,[8] and G. C. Mendis.[9] Of these scholars only one, Mendis, was a professional historian. All limited their range to the Portuguese period or, at most, to the early consolidation of British rule.

In Britain, Sri Lanka lay in the shadow of Indian history. In contrast to the wealth of studies in the latter field, there was not a single historical work on Sri Lanka produced by a British academic in any British university in the first half of the twentieth century, with the exception of L. D. Barnett's chapter in Volume I of the *Cambridge History of India* (1922). Indeed, the only Western scholar to have produced such a book was Lennox A. Mills, an American, whose *Ceylon Under British Rule, 1795–1932* (London, 1933) had neither Tennent's style nor his broad vision. Mills had never visited Sri Lanka, and his history, based on British sources, shows clear evidence that he had not made contact with Ceylonese historians. The

[4] Wilhelm Geiger, T*he Dipavamsa and Mahavamsa* (Colombo). Geiger's contribution to historical studies in Sri Lanka is reviewed in S. Kiribamune, 'Geiger and the History of Sri Lanka', in the *Ceylon Journal of Historical and Social Studies*, n.s., VII, 1 (1977), pp. 44–56.

[5] *A History of Ceylon for Schools* (Colombo, 1900).

[6] A distinguished civil servant and historian with a large number of books to his credit, of which the most notable is *Sinhala and the Patriots, 1815–1818* (Colombo, 1950).

[7] Apart from his *History of Ceylon for Schools, 1505–1911* (Colombo, 1932), Fr S. G. Perera's most significant contribution to historical studies is his translation of Fr Fernão de Queyroz, *The Temporal and Spiritual Conquest of Ceylon*, 3 vols. (Colombo, 1930).

[8] His best known work is *A History of Ceylon* (London, 1926). The study stops at 1833. As a senior civil servant he steered clear of any comments on the more recent periods of British rule in the island.

[9] On Mendis's contribution, see K. M. de Silva, 'History and Historians in Twentieth Century Sri Lanka', in *Sri Lankan Journal of Social Sciences*, II, 2 (1979), pp. 1–12.

reverse is also true. Even to the present time few Sri Lankan scholars are represented on the Advisory Boards of British scholarly journals, and the country itself generally is relegated to a few paragraphs in histories of the Indian Ocean, exploration, the Royal Navy east of Suez, or (on occasion) its current ethnic conflict. Sri Lanka has existed at the edge of British or Western historiographical awareness.

After the establishment of the University of Ceylon in 1942 historical study in Sri Lanka moved slowly from British and European to Indian history. G. C. Mendis, the university's first specialist teacher of Sri Lankan history, had contributed at two levels: the *Our Heritage* series for schools and more advanced works, such as his *Early History of Ceylon* (Calcutta, 1932) and *Ceylon Under the British* (Colombo, 1944), for university students. Now came a two-volume study which covered the early years of British rule with a thoroughness in the quest for documentation and mastery of research technique that no other historical work written by a Sri Lankan had displayed up to that time—Colvin R. de Silva's *Ceylon Under the British Occupation, 1795–1833* (Colombo, 1941–42).[10] With this book, historical writing in Sri Lanka came of age. Curiously there was very little evidence of Marxist thought in this volume written by one of Sri Lanka's most prominent Marxist politicians. It bears the unmistakable stamp of the British empiricist tradition in historiography. In 1950 came Sir Paulus Pieris's most substantial publication, *Sinhalé and the Patriots, 1817–1818* (Colombo), a stimulating study of the great Kandyan rebellion against the British. It was, equally unmistakably, a nationalist history of a momentous and tragic event in Sri Lanka's encounter with British colonialism.

In 1952–53 Sri Lankan history was moved to the core of the history syllabus at the university. At the honours level there were two courses, one specializing in the Ancient and Medieval History of the island, and the other in Modern History. This change, introduced through the initiative of H. C. Ray, Foundation Professor of History at the University of Ceylon, still survives at Peradeniya, the successor to the University of Ceylon, and through Peradeniya it has deeply influenced the organization of history courses at other universities on the island.

The project of a multi-volume history, initiated by Mendis, was completed nearly forty years later by others. The first volume, edited by S. Paranavitana in two parts, covered the ancient and medieval history of the island to the beginning of the sixteenth century and was published in Colombo in 1959–60 as The University of Ceylon, *History of Ceylon*, Volume I. This was as comprehensive a history as was possible at that time. In 1973 Volume III appeared (covering the

[10] The author, a founder member of the Trotskyist Lanka Sama Samaja Party, was in detention in Kandy for anti-war activities. Mendis arranged for and supervised the publication of the book.

period from the beginning of the eighteenth century to 1948). Volume II was expected to fill the gap between Volumes I and III; it took over twenty years to complete, appearing in 1995. Volumes II and III in the series were edited by K. M. de Silva; following Paranavitana's example in Volume I, each was meant to be 'an authoritative synthesis of material available in monographs, articles and unpublished works'.

During the thirty-five years in which these volumes were produced, a large number of monographs on virtually every phase of the island's historical evolution were published, mainly by teachers in the Department of History at the University of Ceylon (Peradeniya). The bulk of the research was conducted at British universities. Among the first of these monographs from the new generation of historians were K. W. Goonewardena's *Foundation of Dutch Power in Ceylon* (Amsterdam, 1958) and Sinnappah Arasaratnam's *Dutch Power in Ceylon* (Amsterdam, 1958), the former being a study of the expulsion of the Portuguese from Sri Lanka and the parallel events relating to the establishment of Dutch rule in the maritime regions of the island, and the latter a study of the consolidation of Dutch power in the islands' littoral regions in the second half of the seventeenth century. The focus shifted to the British connection with the publication of K. M. de Silva's *Social Policy and Missionary Organizations in Ceylon, 1840–1855* (London, 1965). T. B. H. Abeyasinghe's *Portuguese Rule in Ceylon, 1594–1612* (Colombo, 1966) and C. R. de Silva's *The Portuguese in Ceylon, 1617–1638* (Colombo, 1972) together provided a comprehensive study of the complexities of Portuguese rule in the island, while George Davison Winius, in his Harvard dissertation, published as *The Fatal History of Portuguese Ceylon: Transition to Dutch Rule* (Cambridge, Mass., 1971), brought the Portuguese imperial story to completion in 1658. L. S. Dewaraja's *The Kandyan Kingdom of Ceylon, 1707–1760* (Colombo, 1972) was an important contribution to the study of the history of the last Sinhalese kingdom.

Not all history is written by historians, of course, though other disciplines seldom have placed their questions in imperial contexts. The sociologist Ralph Pieris published his *Sinhalese Social Organisation: The Kandyan Period* (Colombo) in 1956. Kitsiri Malalgoda's excellent anthropological and historical study of the Buddhist revival of the eighteenth century in the Kandyan kingdom and its subsequent ramifications in other parts of the island, *Buddhism in Sinhalese Society, 1750–1900* (Berkeley, 1976), has had an important impact on Sri Lankan historiography. V. K. Jayawardena's *The Rise of the Labor Movement in Ceylon* (Durham, NC, 1972) may be mentioned as the first study to examine this important aspect of the island's recent history. Michael Roberts, historian turned anthropologist, published his *Caste Conflict and Élite Formation: The Rise of the Karava Élite in Sri Lanka, 1500–1931* (Cambridge) in 1982. Donald R. Snodgrass's *Ceylon: An Export*

Economy in Transition (Homewood, Ill., 1966), a path-breaking contribution to the island's recent economic history, is still to be superseded.

In the 1960s, in their retirement, two former teachers of the University of Ceylon published brief and idiosyncratic surveys of the island's history; both had considerable impact in the West. E. F. C. Ludowyk, former Professor of English at Peradeniya, wrote *Story of Sri Lank*a (London, 1963) and *The Modern History of Ceylon* (London, 1966), while S. A. Pakeman, an Englishman, the first Professor of History at University College, Colombo, published *Ceylon* (London, 1964). In 1981 K. M. de Silva published his *A History of Sri Lanka* (London), the first comprehensive history of the island by a single author published in the twentieth century, and the first such effort since the days of Sir James Emerson Tennent.

Pre-European, or at least pre-British, studies continued to dominate Sri Lankan scholarship. Even when authors wrote of the British rule, they had little to say about broad matters of Empire. The focus was inward, while scholars of South Asia, except for a few in the Netherlands, continued to look beyond Sri Lanka to India or Pakistan. Scholarship on the Raj, on gender, on Orientalism, grew apace in the West and in India, but hardly at all where Sri Lanka was concerned. It was only in the 1980s, when Sri Lanka was torn by internecine strife, that conferences and symposia on post-colonial destabilization or political violence began to include Sri Lanka. The most influential studies continued to look to the ancient past, as in Senake Bandaranaike's exciting survey of *Sinhalese Monastic Architecture: Viharas of Anuradhapura* (Leiden, 1974), which introduced the concept of Monsoon Asia to Sri Lankan studies and linked the development of architecture in ancient Sri Lanka to influences not merely from India (South Asia in general) and South-East Asia but from East Asia as well. An important study of the beginnings of Tamil settlements in Sri Lanka, K. Indrapala's 'Dravidian Settlements in Ceylon: The Beginnings of the Kingdom of Jaffna', a London University doctoral dissertation (1966), remains unpublished, leaving a significant gap in the study of ancient Sri Lanka. S. Pathmanathan published Part One of his monograph, *The Kingdom of Jaffna* (Colombo) in 1978.

One of the major gaps in Sri Lankan historiography is the paucity of collections of documents relating to the nineteenth and twentieth centuries, of which there have been several volumes on British India, by both Indian and Western scholars. G. C. Mendis made a beginning with his two-volume edition of the *Colebrooke–Cameron Papers* (Delhi, 1957), on the Commission of 1828–31. This was followed by Michael Roberts's *Documents of the Ceylon National Congress and Nationalist Politics in Ceylon, 1929–1950*, 4 vols. (Colombo, 1978); K. M. de Silva's *Sri Lanka* in two parts, in the British Documents on the End of Empire Project series published in 1997, is an extensive selection of primary materials illustrating the negotiations on the transfer of power in Ceylon covering the years 1939 to

1948.[11] While confirming Ceylon's status as an advanced colony, many of the documents reproduced here on the political divisions between the island's communities provide a telling counterpoint to the contemporary image, conveyed in public by the British, of a model colony.

The absence of compelling crises or dramas in the country's transition to independence is presumably a factor which explains why, in contrast to the Himalayan proportions of the literature on India and Pakistan, so little has been written about Ceylon during the same period. Prior to 1948 the British paraded Ceylon as their 'model colony', and Sir Charles Jeffries, a senior official in London who played a leading role in the independence negotiations, perpetuated this image in his *Ceylon: The Path to Independence* (London, 1962). Many historians have since endeavoured to challenge or qualify the image of a model colony, whether from political, social, or economic viewpoints. The emergence of political divisions in the island's pre-independence politics is reviewed in Jane Russell's *Communal Politics under the Donoughmore Constitution, 1931–1947* (Colombo, 1983), S. Nadesan's *A History of the Upcountry Tamil People* (Colombo, 1993), Karunanayake N. O. Dharmadasa's *Language, Religion and Ethnic Assertiveness: The Growth of Sinhalese Nationalism in Sri Lanka* (Ann Arbor, 1992), and K. M. de Silva's edited volume on *Universal Suffrage, 1931–1981: The Sri Lanka Experience* (Colombo, 1981). While some studies on the important question of Indian migration to the island have been published, Hugh Tinker's *Separate and Unequal: India and Indians in the British Commonwealth, 1920–1950* (London, 1976) and *The Banyan Tree: Overseas Emigrants from India, Pakistan and Bangladesh* (London, 1977) are still the standard accounts of the wider Imperial context of this movement of people from India to other British colonies. The later chapters (26–37) of K. M. de Silva's *A History of Sri Lanka* still remain the only significant study of twentieth-century Sri Lanka under British colonial government.[12]

Nor has the independence period in Sri Lanka's history been well served by political biography. D. S. Senanayake, the architect of the country's independence, still awaits comprehensive biographical treatment, and until this appears reliance must be placed on H. A. J. Hulugalle's rather inadequate *The Life and Times of Don Stephen Senanayake* (Colombo, 1975). On Senanayake's principal political rival, S. W. R. D. Bandaranaike, there is *The Expedient Utopian: Bandaranaike and Ceylon*, by James Manor, a Western political scientist (Cambridge, 1989). The contradiction in the main title conveys the central argument in this study of the leading

[11] For the period of Dutch rule there is one rather inadequate compilation, *Some Documents Relating to the Rise of the Dutch Power in Ceylon, 1602–1670, from the Translations at the India Office*, ed. P. E. Pieris (London, 1973).

[12] See K. M. de Silva, *A History of Sri Lanka* (London 1981), pp. 356–563.

exponent of Sinhala Buddhist nationalism from the mid-1930s. More than half the book is devoted to the pre-independence period, and while it grapples with the question of Sri Lankan ethnicity, it does so in a manner which has by no means been accepted by Sri Lankan scholars. In their study of *J. R. Jayewardene of Sri Lanka: A Political Biography*, Volume I, *The First Fifty Years* (London, 1988),[13] K. M. de Silva and Howard Wriggins have been fortunate in having had access to the only important and substantial collection of private papers accumulated by a Sri Lankan politician. J. R., as he was known, was Finance Minister at the time of independence, later becoming Prime Minister and then executive President. Among the more Indophile of Sri Lanka's politicians in the 1940s, he represented a radical alternative to the conservative leadership of D. S. Senanayake.

As with much of the British Empire, there are, of course, diaries, journals, and memoirs of colonial administrators, the occasional tea-planter, or the post-independence diplomat, but with a single exception these cannot be said to have influenced historiography, though they do comprise useful primary sources. That exception is the diaries of Leonard Woolf, which are rich on the social life and attitudes of the British. His *Diaries in Ceylon, 1908–1911* describe his life as an Assistant Government Agent in the Hambantota district; edited by Woolf, they appeared as a whole number in the *Ceylon Historical Journal*, IX (July 1959–April 1960). The patronizing tone and sometimes the candid substance of the diaries are at odds with Woolf's more guarded yet revealing and readable autobiographical writings, of which *Growing: An Autobiography of the Years, 1904–1911* (London, 1961) was particularly influential.[14]

Sri Lankan scholars continue to be preoccupied with prehistory and proto-history, the pre-European vitality of the great hydraulic states of Sri Lanka, with their legacy of archaeological inscriptions. Examples of these are R. A. L. H. Gunawardhana's *Robe and Plough: Monasticism and Economic Interest in Early Medieval Sri Lanka* (Tucson, Ariz., 1979) and S. U. Deraniyagala's *Pre-history of Sri Lanka: An Ecological Perspective*, 2 vols. (Colombo, 1992), a monumental pioneering study. Ananda Wickremeratne's *The Roots of Nationalism: Sri Lanka* (Colombo, 1996) surveys the history of the island in the last quarter of the nineteenth century, while the founding of a new journal, the *Ceylon Journal of Historical and Social Studies*, in 1959 helped to provide a more modern focus. When S. Arasaratnam surveyed 'Recent Trends in the Historiography of the Indian Ocean, 1500 to 1800',[15] that is, the pre-British period, he commented on

[13] See also K. M. de Silva and Howard Wriggins, *J. R. Jayewardene of Sri Lanka: A Political Biography*, Vol. II, *From 1956 to his Retirement* (London, 1994).

[14] On Woolf in Ceylon see T. J. Barron, 'Before the Deluge: Leonard Woolf in Ceylon', *Journal of Imperial and Commonwealth History* (hereafter *JICH*), VI (Oct. 1977), pp. 47–63.

[15] *Journal of World History*, I (Fall, 1990), pp. 225–48.

some forty titles published between 1952 and 1988, and despite being himself the author of a short history of *Ceylon* (Englewood Cliffs, NJ, 1964), Sri Lanka figured only modestly in the survey. Ceylon played no key role with respect to the theoretical constructions of K. N. Chaudhuri, Immanuel Wallerstein, or Janet Abu-Lughod on 'world systems' or indigenous trade in the Indian Ocean. Indeed, even Richard Hall, in *Empires of the Monsoon* (London, 1997), gave little attention to the island.

Clearly, students of certain products that entered into the world economy, notably tea, must write of Ceylon, and in an Imperial context, as Denys Forrest did in *Tea for the British* (London, 1973). T. J. Barron has essayed coffee in a more scholarly manner in 'Science and the Nineteenth-Century Ceylon Coffee Planters', a superb beginning to an unfinished story.[16] Equally clearly, there are themes of resurgent Imperial history for which Ceylon seems an ideal exemplar, as in Richard H. Grove's *Green Imperialism* (Delhi, 1995), the subtitle of which best reveals its contents: *Colonial Expansion, Tropical Island Edens and the Origins of Environmentalism, 1600–1860*. Scholars interested in issues of gender, colonial discourse theory, and to a lesser extent, the concept of the subaltern (derived from Indian historiography) would do well to look at Sri Lanka. Patrick Peebles's *Social Change in Nineteenth-Century Ceylon* (New Delhi, 1995), relies on almanacs, journals, the local press, and family genealogies in a way now commonplace in Britain and the United States but seldom seen in Sri Lanka. Known earlier in its dissertation form, submitted to the University of Chicago in 1973, this controversial work is critical of both nationalist and imperialist models of Sri Lankan historiography.

In his penetrating essays on the island's social and economic history, the French scholar Eric Meyer argues for the richness of Sri Lankan history in the period of British rule, and his insights provide clues for more research that is wed neither to ideology nor to the simple chronicling of the past. He is one of the very few scholars from outside Sri Lanka who has chosen to specialize on the island in the Imperial period—T. J. Barron, Patrick Peebles, and John Rogers are others—thus pressing far past the period so dominated by C. R. Boxer and other students of the seaborne empires. For Sri Lanka and the historiography of the British Empire, the easy cliché is, while easy, also true: much remains to be done, especially by those who would focus squarely on Ceylon-Sri Lanka rather than detect it from the corner of their eye while sailing to Malabar or to Chennai, or for the China Seas.

[16] *JICH*, XVI (Oct. 1987), pp. 5–23.

Select Bibliography

SINNAPPAH ARASARATNAM, *Dutch Power in Ceylon* (Amsterdam, 1958).

SENAKE BANDARANAIKE, *Sinhalese Monastic Architecture: The Viharas of Anuradhapura* (Leiden, 1974).

SIRAN DERANIYAGALA, *The Prehistory of Sri Lanka: An Ecological Perspective*, 2 vols. (Colombo, 1992).

KARUNANAYAKE DHARMADASA, *Language, Religion and Ethnic Assertiveness: The Growth of Sinhalese Nationalism in Sri Lanka* (Ann Arbor, 1995).

The University of Ceylon, *History of Ceylon*, 2 vols. to date, Vols. I and III (Colombo, 1959–60 and 1973).

The University of Peradeniya, *History of Sri Lanka*, Vol. II (Peradeniya, 1995).

KITSIRI MALALGODA, *Buddhism in Sinhalese Society, 1750–1900: A Study of Religious Revival and Change* (Berkeley, 1976).

LENNOX ALGERNON MILLS, *Ceylon Under British Rule, 1795–1932* (London, 1933).

PATRICK PEEBLES, *Social Change in Nineteenth-Century Ceylon* (New Delhi, 1995).

Sir PAULUS PIERIS, *Sinhalé and the Patriots, 1815–1818* (Colombo, 1950).

RALPH PIERIS, *Sinhalese Social Organization: The Kandyan Period* (Colombo, 1956).

COLVIN R. DE SILVA, *Ceylon Under the British Occupation, 1795–1833*, 2 vols. (Colombo, 1941–42).

K. M. DE SILVA, *A History of Sri Lanka* (London, 1981).

MICHAEL ROBERTS, *Caste Conflict and Élite Formation: The Rise of the Karava Élite in Sri Lanka, 1500–1931* (Cambridge, 1982).

Sir JAMES EMERSON TENNENT, *Ceylon*, 2nd edn., 2 vols. (London, 1859).

ANANDA WICKREMERATNE, *The Roots of Nationalism: Sri Lanka* (Colombo, 1996).

15

Pakistan's Emergence

IAN TALBOT

Historical writing on the partition of India and the emergence of Pakistan has been extensive and polemical, reflecting both the significance and the traumatic impact of the climacteric events of August 1947. The creation of Pakistan remains one of the major political achievements of modern Muslim history. It was not achieved, however, without immense sacrifice. At the most conservative estimate over 200,000 people were killed in the partition massacres. Millions more became refugees. Some 7 million people, one in ten of Pakistan's total population, were enumerated as of refugee origin in 1951.[1]

This chapter traces the development of historical writing on the creation of Pakistan from the 1940s to the present. The historical debate is overwhelmingly élitist in tone, with few concessions to the concerns of the so-called 'new history' of the subaltern groups and 'post-structuralist' distrust of universal narratives.

Historians have repeatedly addressed such questions as why did Mohammad Ali Jinnah traverse the path of Indian nationalism to Muslim separatism?[2] How did the Muslim League achieve Pakistan just a decade after its débâcle in the 1937

[1] Cited in K. R. Sipe, 'Karachi's Refugee Crisis: The Political, Economic and Social Consequences of Partition-Related Migration', unpublished Ph.D. dissertation, Duke University, 1976, p. 73.

[2] On the growth of 'communalism' see Gyanendra Pandey, *The Construction of Communalism in Colonial North West India* (Delhi, 1990); Sandria B. Freitag, *Collective Action and Community: Public Arenas and the Emergence of Communalism in North India* (Berkeley, 1989); Suranjan Das, *Communal Riots in Bengal* (Delhi, 1993); Richard G. Fox, *Lions of the Punjab: Culture in the Making* (Berkeley, 1985); Kenneth W. Jones, *Arya Dharm: Hindu Consciousness in Nineteenth-Century Punjab* (New Delhi, 1976). Major works on Muslims in politics are Farzana Shaikh, *Community and Consensus in Islam: Muslim Representation in Colonial India, 1860–1947* (Cambridge, 1989); Francis Robinson, *Separatism among Indian Muslims: The Politics of the United Provinces' Muslims, 1860–1923* (Cambridge, 1974); G. M. Minault, *The Khilafat Movement: Religious Symbolism and Political Mobilization in India* (New York, 1982); David Page, *Prelude to Partition: The Indian Muslims and the Imperial System of Control, 1920–1932* (Karachi, 1987); Mushirul Hasan, *Nationalism and Communal Politics in India, 1916–1928* (Delhi, 1979): Ayesha Jalal, T*he Sole Spokesman: Jinnah, the Muslim League and the Demand for Pakistan* (Cambridge, 1985); Ayesha Jalal and Anil Seal, 'Alternative to Partition: Muslim Politics between the Wars', in Christopher Baker, Gordon Johnson, and Anil Seal, eds., *Power, Profit and Politics: Essays on Imperialism, Nationalism and Change in Twentieth-Century India* (Cambridge, 1981).

provincial elections? Why did the Congress accept the partition of India after decades of championing its unity?[3] The responses have often generated more heat than light. Barren orthodoxies have been perpetuated by Pakistan's decades-long search for national identity and democratic stability. Moreover, it was not until the opening of government archives in the 1970s that fresh departures in scholarship were made possible.

Despite the sterility of much historical writing within Pakistan, there is intense interest at a popular level in the events surrounding partition. Popular works of fiction, autobiographies, and dramatizations continuously reproduce collective memories of these upheavals. While much of this material is ephemeral and crudely polemical, writers such as Saadat Hasan Manto, Intizar Husain, Krishan Chander, Khushwant Singh, and Rajinder Singh Bedi have produced modern masterpieces of South Asian literature on the partition theme.[4] They point to the sense of torn identities and uprootedness which was redeemed for some Muslims by the feeling they were involved in a true *hijrat*, with its opportunities for renewal and self-awareness.

Historians have focused on two separate but nevertheless interconnected sets of questions: first, what lay behind the raising of the Pakistan demand? Secondly, why was it successful? Muslim separatist demands have been variously depicted as deriving from the Islamic moral tradition, colonial institutions and policies, or from the cynical manipulation of Islamic symbols by self-interested élites. Explanations of the successful creation of Pakistan run the whole gamut from analyses based on concepts of 'historical inevitability' to those which stress the contingency of wartime developments. Mass struggle is posited alongside the 'great man of history'-type interpretations.

Two important historiographical developments have occurred since the 1970s. First, scholars have switched their focus from All-India to provincial politics. This has provided useful insights into the evolution of support for the Pakistan movement in the Muslim majority provinces. Many, although not all, of the puzzles surrounding the transformation in the Muslim League's fortunes have been solved. Secondly, there has been a revision of established views concerning the 'high politics' of the endgame of British rule. Jinnah's purposes in raising the Pakistan demand have been reinterpreted, as have the British and Congress motivations in accepting the partition plan.

The earliest works were part of the 'battle of words' between the Muslim

[3] See chap. by Robin J. Moore.

[4] For a useful introduction to fictional representations of the 1947 partition see John A. Hanson, 'Historical Perspectives in the Urdu Novel', in M. U. Memon, ed., *Studies in the Urdu Gazal and Prose Fiction* (Madison, 1979), pp. 257–84; M. U. Memon, 'Partition Literature: A Study of Intizar Husain', *Modern Asian Studies*, XIV, 3 (1980), pp. 377–410.

League and the Congress during the 1940s. Typical of such texts written in the heat of the moment are: Zia-ud-din Ahmad Suleri, *The Road to Peace and Pakistan Freedom* (Lahore, 1944); S. Rahman, *Why Pakistan?* (Calcutta, 1946); Ghulam Muhayyaddin Sufi, *Commonsense on Pakistan* (Bombay, 1946); and A. B. Rajput, *Punjab Crisis and Cure* (Lahore, 1947). These are works of propaganda rather than history. Historians can profit from them nevertheless, because they illuminate the construction of a 'communal' historical consciousness. F. K. Durrani's work, *The Meaning of Pakistan* (Lahore, 1944), is of particular interest in this respect. It represents a key text for understanding the emergence of Pakistan as an 'ideological state'.

Nationalist writers throughout the 1940s naturally adhered to the vision of a united India. Such authors as Rajendra Prasad, Humayan Kabir, and Asoka Mehta and Achyut Patwardhan imputed Muslim separatist demands to the Machiavellian intrigues of the Imperial authorities.[5] They also rejected the separatists' 'essentialization' of Muslim identity. They stressed rather the cross-cultural exchanges between Muslims and Hindus and the diversities present in Indian Islam. Although it is beyond the scope of this study, it is important to recognize that these arguments concerning the assimilationist and separatist tendencies in South Asian Islam persist in contemporary India.

Many of the participants in the transfer of power have penned their memoirs. Important accounts by British participants include: Alan Campbell-Johnson, *Mission with Mountbatten* (London, 1951; 3rd edn., 1985); H. V. Hodson, *The Great Divide: Britain-India-Pakistan* (London, 1969); Penderel Moon, *Divide and Quit* (London, 1961); Sir Francis Tuker, *While Memory Serves* (London, 1950); and Richard Symonds, *The Making of Pakistan* (London, 1950; 3rd edn., London, 1951; Karachi, 1976).

Campbell-Johnson and Hodson provide sympathetic accounts of the Mountbatten Viceroyalty. Moon, as befits his maverick reputation in the Punjab Commission, is far less complacent in his attitude towards the British responsibility for the upheaval of partition. His estimate of 200,000 fatalities in the massacres has formed a focus for historiographical debate. Moon also raises the issue of the Congress 'mistake' in the 1937 United Provinces' Coalition episode. The alienation arising from the Congress offer of 'absorption rather than partnership' following the provincial elections has subsequently become a central focus in the discourse on the Muslim League's growing legitimacy following its débâcle at the

[5] Rajendra Prasad, *India Divided* (Bombay, 1946); Humayun Kabir, *Muslim Politics, 1906–1942* (Calcutta, 1942); Asoka Mehta and Achyut Patwardhan, *The Communal Triangle in India* (Allahabad, 1942).

1937 polls.[6] Significantly, it was shortly after the experience of Congress 'majoritarian democracy' in the minority provinces that the Muslim League publicly espoused the Pakistan demand at its 1940 Lahore annual session.

Symonds, who worked with Quaker relief agencies at both the time of the 1942 Bengal famine and during the partition upheavals, reiterates the importance of the Congress's ill-advised rebuff to the United Provinces' Muslim League.[7] Tuker approaches the issues of identity formation and political mobilization from a purely law-and-order perspective. He sees communal strife as leaving the British with no option but to divide and quit. The insights he provides into the army's role in the aid of civil power should be read alongside the memoirs of Major-General Shahid Hamid, who acted as Field Marshall Sir Claude Auchinlek's private secretary: Shahid Hamid, *Disastrous Twilight: A Personal Record of the Partition of India* (London, 1986).

Well-known memoirs and reminiscences by Muslim figures include: Chaudhri Muhammad Ali, *The Emergence of Pakistan* (New York, 1967); Firoz Khan Noon, *From Memory* (Lahore, 1969); Choudhry Khaliquzzaman, *Pathway to Pakistan* (Lahore, 1961); Agha Khan, *The Memoirs of Agha Khan* (London, 1954); M. A. H. Ispahani, *Quaid-e-Azam Jinnah as I Knew Him* (Karachi, 1966); Jahan Ara Shahnawaz, *Father and Daughter* (Lahore, 1971); and M. A. K. Azad, *India Wins Freedom* (Calcutta, 1957). These works all contain much useful historical material, although this is sometimes accompanied by the repetition of contemporary polemics and the burnishing of myth. The final two texts are of particular interest. *Father and Daughter* provides tantalizing glimpses into the role played by élite Muslim women in the popularization of the Pakistan demand in the key Punjab region. Begum Shah Nawaz's daughter 'Tazi' (Mumtaz Shah Nawaz) explored this theme in fiction before her tragically early death in 1948.[8] A revised 'complete' version of Azad's work, containing thirty previously unpublished pages, created intense debate on its publication in 1988.[9] It reopened the issue of the Congress's 'betrayal' of the Muslim nationalists and its mishandling of the Muslim League's demands. Azad's role as the leading Muslim nationalist has made him the subject of a number of sympathetic Indian biographies.[10]

Professional historians and biographers produced many works on Pakistan's emergence during the fifteen or so years which followed the British transfer of

[6] See 'Introduction' in Mushirul Hasan, ed., *India's Partition: Process, Strategy and Mobilization* (Delhi, 1994), pp. 12–16.

[7] Richard Symonds, *Making of Pakistan* (Karachi, 1976), p. 58.

[8] Mumtaz Shah Nawaz, *The Heart Divided* (Lahore, 1957; 2nd edn., 1990).

[9] See Abul Kalam Azad, *India Wins Freedom: The Complete Version* (Delhi, 1988); Mushirul Hasan, ed., *Islam and Indian Nationalism: Reflections on Abul Kalam Azad* (Delhi, 1992).

[10] See, for example, V. N. Datta, *Maulana Azad* (Delhi, 1992).

power. Within Pakistan, the Muslim League's official two-nation theory or creed dominated the historical debate, until the emergence of Bangladesh in 1971 dealt it a grievous blow. At the heart of the two-nation theory was the belief that the Indian Muslims' identity was defined by religion rather than language or ethnicity. Islam had given birth to a distinctive social order which secured its 'natural' political expression in 1947. The doyen of this approach was Ishtiaq Husain Qureshi of Karachi University.[11] More sophisticated works within this framework were contributed during the 1960s by Pakistanis resident in the West.[12] C. A. Bayly's depiction of the distinct social formations in North India of the Muslim rural *qasbah* town and the Hindu market town (*ganj*), the former declining as a result of the impact of British rule, the latter flourishing, does provide some material substance, however, for the two-nation theory ideology.[13]

The most important works by western scholars produced during this period include: Hugh Tinker, *Experiment with Freedom: India and Pakistan, 1947* (London, 1967); Hector Bolitho, *Jinnah: Creator of Pakistan* (London, 1954); and Peter Hardy, *The Muslims of British India* (Cambridge, 1972). These studies provided a historical context and coherence which was lacking in many of the earlier, more personal interpretations. They were handicapped, however, by their lack of access to archival material. The New Zealander Bolitho, whose work had been commissioned by the Pakistan government, compensated for this in part by extensively interviewing Jinnah's former associates. Peter Hardy's work was significant, first because of its awareness of the competing political forces within the Muslim community and secondly, because he pointed to the impact of colonial policies and structures on identity formation and political mobilization. This was shortly to become a leading motif of the Cambridge School of Indian history.

Following the decision of the Wilson Labour Government, new sources became available under the thirty-year rule. The growing availability of private papers and party records in the Subcontinent further increased the sources at the historian's disposal. Easier access to documentary records also resulted from the publication of British official documents on the *Transfer of Power* in the monumental twelve-volume series (1970–83) edited by Nicholas Mansergh, Penderel Moon, and E. W. R. Lumby.[14]

[11] See, for example, his book, *The Muslim Community of the Indo-Pakistan Subcontinent* (The Hague, 1962).

[12] Note should be made of the following texts: Hafeez Malik, *Moslem Nationalism in India and Pakistan* (Washington, 1963); Khalid bin Sayeed, *Pakistan: The Formative Phase, 1857–1948* (Oxford, 1968).

[13] See C. A. Bayly, *Rulers, Townsmen and Bazaars: North Indian Society in the Age of British Expansion, 1770–1870* (Cambridge, 1983), pp. 449–57.

[14] The first four volumes were edited by Nicholas Mansergh and E. W. R. Lumby, the remainder by Mansergh and Penderel Moon: Vol. I, *The Cripps Mission, Jan.–April 1942* (London, 1970); Vol. II, *'Quit India', 30 April–21 Sept. 1942* (London, 1971); Vol. III, *Reassertion of Authority, Gandhi's Fast and the*

The availability of fresh source materials went hand in hand with a new interpretation of modern Indian history. The Cambridge School, as it became known, questioned conventional assumptions concerning the role of nationalism and of the western-educated élite in the freedom struggle.[15] Its chief representative work in the field of Muslim separatism is Francis Robinson's now-classic text, *Separatism Among Indian Muslims: The Politics of the United Provinces' Muslims, 1860–1923* (Cambridge, 1974). It moved the focus away from the All-India level and emphasized the importance of colonial rule for the establishment of a Muslim political identity.

Francis Robinson was in fact to shift his stance during the course of his debate[16] with the American political scientist Paul Brass, who argued that Muslim separatism had resulted from the manipulation of separatist symbols by élites. While Robinson strongly disagreed with this instrumentalist view of Islam, he differentiated himself from the earlier Cambridge position by claiming a 'dynamic relationship' between 'visions of the ideal Muslim life' and political activity. Farzana Shaikh further elaborated this idea in her work *Community and Consensus in Islam: Muslim Representation in Colonial India, 1860–1947* (Cambridge, 1989). The book powerfully questions the two widely held assumptions that Muslim separatism was inspired primarily by colonial definitions of Indian society and that the Pakistan demand was nothing more than a bid for power. In her view, the separatist platform was based on Islamically derived values of political consensus and legitimacy which increasingly conflicted with the liberal-democratic understanding as the British devolved power in India.[17]

Within Pakistan, the Islamization process of the Zia era (1977–88) inevitably encouraged a re-examination of Jinnah's career. A number of unconvincing attempts were made to depict him as wanting to establish an Islamic state. Typical

Succession to the Viceroyalty, 21 Sept. 1942–12 June 1943 (London, 1971); Vol. IV, *The Bengal Famine and the New Viceroyalty, 15 June 1943–31 Aug. 1944* (London, 1973); Vol. V, *The Simla Conference, Background and Proceedings, 1 Sept. 1944–28 July 1945* (London, 1974); Vol. VI, *The Post-War Phase: New Moves by the Labour Government, 1 Aug. 1945–22 March 1946* (London, 1976); Vol. VII, *The Cabinet Mission, 23 March–29 June 1946* (London, 1977); Vol. VIII, *The Interim Government, 3 July–1 Nov. 1946* (London, 1979); Vol. IX, *The Fixing of a Time Limit, 4 Nov. 1946–22 March 1947* (London, 1980); Vol. X, *The Mountbatten Viceroyalty, Formulation of a Plan, 22 March–30 May 1947* (London, 1981); Vol. XI, *The Mountbatten Viceroyalty, Announcement and Reception of the 3 June Plan, 31 May–7 July 1947* (London, 1982); Vol. XII, *The Mountbatten Viceroyalty: Princes, Partition and Independence, 8 July–15 Aug. 1947* (London, 1983).

[15] The Cambridge School approach was signalled in the now-classic collection: John Gallagher, Gordon Johnson and Anil Seal, eds., *Locality, Province and Nation: Essays on Indian Politics, 1870–1947* (Cambridge, 1973).

[16] See Paul Brass, 'Élite Groups, Symbol Manipulation and Ethnic Identity among the Muslims of South Asia', in David Taylor and Malcolm Yapp, eds., *Political Identity in South Asia* (London, 1979), pp. 35–77; Francis Robinson, 'Islam and Muslim Separatism', in ibid., pp. 78–112.

[17] Shaikh, *Community and Consensus.*

of this genre was Karam Hydri's work, *Millat ka pasban* (Karachi, 1981). The less suffocating atmosphere following the restoration of democracy has allowed for a more balanced assessment. This is illustrated by the most recent text, Saeed R. Khairi, *Jinnah Reinterpreted: The Journey from Indian Nationalism to Muslim Statehood*. It eschews arguments based on the two-nation theory and on the conception of Pakistan as a 'theocracy'. According to the author, Nehru not Jinnah destroyed the unity of India by his rejection of the 1946 Cabinet Mission proposals.[18]

Regional studies of the Pakistan movement were encouraged in part by the Cambridge School approach but also by the availability of new sources. The earliest works focused on the United Provinces, which were seen as the heartland of Muslim separatism. Attention subsequently shifted to the Muslim majority areas of Punjab, Bengal, the Frontier, and Sind. These provinces held the key to the successful creation of Pakistan, but were areas in which the Muslim League existed only on paper at the beginning of the pre-partition decade. The inter-communal Unionist Party for example had reduced it to a single seat in the 1937 Punjab elections.

The Muslim League's crucial breakthrough in the Punjab has been understood within a framework of élite factional realignment, the linking of Islamic appeals to social and economic grievances, and their transmission to the countryside where the bulk of the voters resided through the rural idiom of Sufi networks.[19] David Gilmartin has also effectively revealed the tensions during the Pakistan movement arising from the construction of a new ideological identity within the colonial state's structure of mediatory politics.[20]

Similar themes have emerged in the study of other provinces. The crucial importance of sufi pirs (spiritual guides) in Sindhi political developments during the period 1936–47 has been brought out in Sarah Ansari's work.[21] Erland Jansson, in his book *India, Pakistan or Pakhtunistan? The Nationalist Movements in the North-West Frontier Province, 1937–47* (Uppsala, 1981), echoed findings on the Punjab in his depiction of the Muslim League advance being linked to factional divisions. Moreover, he revealed that the Congress Government of the Khan brothers was ultimately as unsuccessful as the Punjab Unionists in countering the groundswell of opinion for the League following the communalization of politics elsewhere in India.[22]

[18] Saeed R. Khairi, *Jinnah Reinterpreted: The Journey from Indian Nationalism to Muslim Statehood* (Karachi, 1995), p. 455.

[19] See Ian Talbot, *Punjab and the Raj, 1849–1947* (New Delhi, 1988); and David Gilmartin, *Empire and Islam, Punjab and the Making of Pakistan* (Berkeley, 1988).

[20] Gilmartin, *Empire and Islam*, pp. 225–33.

[21] Sarah F. D. Ansari, *Sufi Saints and State Power: The Pirs of Sind, 1843–1947* (Cambridge, 1992).

[22] Erland Jansson, *India, Pakistan or Pakhtunistan? The Nationalist Movements in the North-West Frontier Province, 1937–47* (Uppsala, 1981), pp. 159–65.

Scholars have largely neglected Bengali Muslim politics during the pre-partition decade. Far more has been written about Muslims during the preceding era. Existing studies on the 1940s by Shila Sen, Humaira Momen, and Harun-or Rashid emphasize both the role of Dacca University students in popularizing the Pakistan message and the importance of the Muslim *jotedar* peasants' (tenure-holders) shift in allegiance from the rival Krishak Paraja Party of Fazlul Huq.[23]

Sugata Bose, in a brief but authoritative article, has reflected on the failure of the eleventh-hour United Bengal plan propounded by such Congress leaders as Sarat Chandra Bose and Husain Shahid Suhrawardy of the Muslim League. This was outlined in May 1947 in response to the fear that the creation of Pakistan would involve partition of the province. While Sugata Bose sees the veto of the Congress High Command as the main cause of its failure, he also draws attention to the existence of grass-roots divisions.[24] Joya Chatterji has recently examined these local pressures for partition.[25] She reveals that the Bengal Congress's Hindu élite ultimately argued for partition in order to regain the privileged position which had been eroded by political and economic developments from the 1932 Communal Award onwards.

Recent historical writing has also reconsidered the 'high politics' of the transfer of power. The work of R. J. Moore, *Escape from Empire: The Attlee Government and the Indian Problem* (Oxford, 1982) and Anita Inder Singh, *The Origins of the Partition of India, 1936–1947* (Delhi, 1987) revealed how the British came to accept the idea of partition as the only solution to the communal problem, which imperilled a speedy and smooth transfer of power. Moore provided the first authoritative examination of Labour Party strategies and policies towards the transfer of power, a theme on which he reflects in his chapter 'India in the 1940s' in this volume. Singh argued that the British short-term aims of encouraging the Muslim League as a counterweight to the non-cooperating Congress during the Second World War undermined their long-term commitment to a United India.

Jinnah's role in the partition has been radically revised by Ayesha Jalal in her seminal study *The Sole Spokesman: Jinnah, the Muslim League and the Demand for Pakistan* (Cambridge, 1985). She has controversially but authoritatively claimed that Jinnah's real political aim from 1940 onwards was for an equal say for Muslims in an All-India Union. Jinnah was, however, finally forced to accept the

[23] Shila Sen, *Muslim Politics in Bengal, 1937–47* (New Delhi, 1976); Humaira Momen, *Muslim Politics in Bengal: A Study of Krishak Praja Party and the Elections of 1937* (Dacca, 1972); Harun-or-Rashid, *The Foreshadowing of Bangladesh: Bengal Muslim League and Muslim Politics, 1936–1947* (Dhaka, 1987).

[24] Sugata Bose, 'A Doubtful Inheritance: The Partition of Bengal in 1947', in D. A. Low, ed., *The Political Inheritance of Pakistan* (London, 1991), p. 131.

[25] Joya Chatterji, *Bengal Divided: Hindu Communalism and Partition, 1932–1947* (Cambridge, 1994).

'moth-eaten' Pakistan of the 3 June Partition Plan, as it had become the only realistic option following the end of the Second World War and the acceleration of the British departure.[26] This bold reinterpretation of Jinnah's purpose has evoked considerable criticism for its disregard of the role of cultural and religious ideals in the Pakistan movement. Jalal's revisionist perspective has nevertheless had a lasting impact.

Akbar S. Ahmed, in his work *Jinnah, Pakistan and Islamic Identity: The Search for Saladin* (London, 1997), is the most recent scholar to grapple with Jalal's interpretation. He criticizes this for disconnecting Jinnah from his cultural community and portraying him as like a 'robot' who is 'programmed to play poker for high stakes' (p. 30). Ahmed, to the contrary, is at pains to present Jinnah with a 'human face'. Certainly our image of him can never quite be the same following Ahmed's discovery that his last act before leaving Bombay for the state he had helped to create was to visit the grave of his former Parsee wife, Rattanbhai Petit. Ahmed acknowledges the futility of projecting backwards contemporary understandings of secularism or fundamentalism in order to label Jinnah. He, rather, regards Jinnah as a blend of modernity and tradition who, in the closing period of his life, increasingly moored his concern for tolerance and the safeguarding of minority rights in his understanding of Islam. Hence Ahmed's claim that Jinnah provides a paradigm for Muslim identity and leadership in a modern world obsessed with Western media images of Islamic fanaticism and terrorism.

Traditional viewpoints on Mountbatten's Viceroyalty have also been questioned. Western scholars have increasingly supported Pakistani beliefs that Mountbatten favoured Indian interests during the transfer of power. Such actions, it has been claimed, jeopardized Pakistan's survival and help explain the cynical acceptance of partition by such members of the Congress High Command as Vallabhbhai Patel. Ian Stephens, in *Horned Moon: An Account of a Journey through Pakistan, Kashmir and Afghanistan* (London, 1966), initially queried Mountbatten's even-handedness concerning the contentious Kashmir issue.[27] Alastair Lamb has subsequently gone much further in questioning Mountbatten's 'detachment' regarding Kashmir.[28] He has also claimed that the deliberations of the Radcliffe Boundary Commission Award did not proceed in the total secrecy and isolation from politically interested parties which the Viceroy had always claimed.[29]

[26] Jalal, *The Sole Spokesman*, pp. 251–93.

[27] Stephens, *Horned Moon: An Account of a Journey Through Pakistan, Kashmir and Afghanistan*, pp. 106–13.

[28] Alastair Lamb, *Kashmir: A Disputed Legacy, 1946–1990* (Hertingfordbury, 1991), pp. 116–17, 139.

[29] Ibid., pp. 112–15.

Lamb's latter beliefs were based on circumstantial documentary evidence. They received fresh credibility from an unexpected source. Christopher Beaumont, Secretary to the Head of the Boundary Commission, circulated a private paper in 1989 entitled 'The Truth of the Partition of the Punjab in August 1947', in which he claimed that Mountbatten had manipulated the border in India's favour. Three years later he made public the revelation that Radcliffe was persuaded to change his mind about the award of the Ferozepore and Zira *tehsils* (subdivisions) to Pakistan at a lunch with Mountbatten from which he, Beaumont, had been 'deftly' excluded.[30] The fresh doubts which this cast over the Viceroy's impartiality were trumpeted by Andrew Roberts as part of his incandescent attack on Mountbatten's career in *Eminent Churchillians*.[31]

Many books were published to mark the golden jubilee of Pakistan's creation in 1997. Most of these celebrated achievements in various fields during the past fifty years, however, rather than examining afresh the background to independence. Typical of such works was the edition by Victoria Schofield entitled *Old Roads New Highways: Fifty Years of Pakistan* (Karachi, 1997).

As the Subcontinent enters the new century, it is likely that two themes which have recently emerged in scholarship will receive further encouragement. The first focuses on the colonial inheritance for contemporary Pakistan. This was initially addressed in the collection *The Political Inheritance of Pakistan*, edited by D. A. Low.[32] The second focuses on the participation of ordinary Muslims in the Pakistan movement and the impact of partition upon them. This theme is beginning to be explored.[33] It opens up a fresh perspective 'from below' to research and scholarship. Such an approach is certainly required if the 'inner' history of Pakistan's emergence is to be revealed.

30 *Daily Telegraph*, 24 Feb. 1992.

31 (London, 1994), pp. 55–137.

32 D. A. Low, ed., *The Political Inheritance of Pakistan* (London, 1991).

33 See Nighat Said Khan and others, eds., *Locating the Self: Perspectives on Women and Multiple Identities* (Lahore, 1994); Ian Talbot, *Freedom's Cry: The Popular Dimension in the Pakistan Movement and Partition Experience in North-West India* (Karachi, 1996).

Select Bibliography

JOYA CHATTERJI, *Bengal Divided: Hindu Communalism and Partition, 1932–1947* (Cambridge, 1994).

DAVID GILMARTIN, *Empire and Islam: Punjab and the Making of Pakistan* (Berkeley, 1988).

PETER HARDY, *The Muslims of British India* (Cambridge, 1972).

MUSHIRUL HASAN, ed., *India's Partition: Process, Strategy and Mobilization* (Delhi, 1993).

H. V. HODSON, *The Great Divide: Britain, India, Pakistan* (London, 1969).

AYESHA JALAL, *The Sole Spokesman: Jinnah, The Muslim League and the Demand for Pakistan* (Cambridge, 1985).

CHOUDHRY KHALIQUZZAMAN, *Pathway to Pakistan* (Lahore, 1961).

D. A. LOW, ed., *The Political Inheritance of Pakistan* (London, 1991).

R. J. MOORE, *Churchill, Cripps, and India, 1939–1945* (Oxford, 1979).

DAVID PAGE, *Prelude to Partition: The Indian Muslims and the Imperial System of Control, 1920–1932* (Delhi, 1982).

HARUN-OR-RASHID, *The Foreshadowing of Bangladesh: Bengal Muslim League and Muslim Politics, 1936–1947* (Dhaka, 1987).

FRANCIS ROBINSON, *Separatism Among Indian Muslims: The Politics of the United Provinces' Muslims, 1863–1923* (Cambridge, 1974).

KHALID BIN SAYEED, *Pakistan: The Formative Phase, 1857–1948* (Oxford, 1968).

FARZANA SHAIKH, *Community and Consensus in Islam: Muslim Representation in Colonial India, 1860–1947* (Cambridge, 1989).

ANITA INDER SINGH, *The Origins of the Partition of India, 1936–47* (New Delhi, 1987).

IAN TALBOT, *Punjab and the Raj, 1849–1947* (New Delhi, 1988).

—— *Freedom's Cry: The Popular Dimension in the Pakistan Movement and Partition Experience in North-West India* (Karachi, 1996).

STANLEY A. WOLPERT, *Jinnah of Pakistan* (New York, 1984).

MUKHTAR ZAMAN, *Students' Role in the Pakistan Movement* (Karachi, 1978).

16

Science, Medicine, and the British Empire

RICHARD DRAYTON

Science and medicine participated in British expansion from the age of Ralegh to that of Curzon and Nehru.[1] But the critical history of this involvement is hardly thirty years old.[2] The *Cambridge History of the British Empire* found a corner for literature but none for the research of nature. This new theatre of Imperial history is, in part, a consequence of that flowering of social enquiry which separates us from the world of the historians Hugh Egerton and Sir Reginald Coupland. It owes even more to that unravelling of assumptions which forms part of the unfinished cultural history of decolonization. Only the death of the imperial idea revealed the place of learning and healing in its plumage.

Science and medicine had furnished the means of navigation and war, and skills which allowed profitable intrusion into foreign environments. Intellectual curiosity spurred exploration and encouraged colonization from Elizabethan Virginia to the Victorian Zambezi. Merchants, missionaries, and modern major-generals such as Wellesley or Wolseley found inspiration in botany and geography. On the other hand, Europe's encounter with new lands and peoples shaped its intellectual ambitions. From Francis Bacon on, the growth of trade and colonies was expected to extend the empire of reason. Information and facts, human and natural curiosities, arrived from every ocean. By the late eighteenth century, moreover, the apparent utility of natural knowledge to Empire led to salaried posts being created at the frontier. Until perhaps as late as the Edwardian era, these colonial appointments provided vital opportunities for those participating in emerging disciplines.

What was happening, however, was an ideological symbiosis rather than a mere combination of scientific and imperial means and motives. The laws of mechanics and geometry, political arithmetic and anatomy, provided a perspective on Man's

[1] Themes raised below may also be pursued in the chaps. by Robert A. Stafford, and, in particular, Diana Wylie.

[2] Although see the failed historiographical bridgehead of Charles Forman, 'Science for Empire, 1895–1940', unpublished Ph.D. dissertation, Wisconsin, 1941.

place in nature which celebrated the power of informed authority to intervene. With Newton's laws, visible in the transit of cannonballs and stars, nature seemed to have shared her secrets with the British. By the era of Joseph Banks and Stamford Raffles, this universal knowledge appeared to equip Britain to undertake the cosmopolitan responsibility of 'improving' exotic lands and peoples. Science and technics came to supplement Christianity as justification for imperial outreach. By the late nineteenth century Comtean Positivism and Social Darwinism gave formal expression to older assumptions about Britain's rung on the ladder of Creation. Science was source and symbol of Progress, and Britain, as its mother and guardian, was entitled to her exalted position in the world. If the authority of St Peter had once empowered Pope Alexander VI to divide the world between the Iberian powers, an apostolic succession, which linked Newton to Kelvin, anointed new conquistadores with mission and prerogative. An alliance with the innocent cause of learning was thus as morally comforting as the gospel in the dark corners of the Earth. Scientific medicine similarly encouraged those who intervened in alien communities to think of themselves as bestowers of health as well as Christian light. Scientists and physicians, moreover, believed themselves to be bearers of precise and useful knowledge. Their faith in themselves as agents of rational improvement rested on the dramatic recent history of the sciences in the West. But this identity was also a precious tool used by scientists, such as Herschel and Huxley, when they campaigned for public and private funding, intellectual and social status. Indeed, Imperial service was itself used to strengthen claims by scientific professionals for support. The Proconsul and the savant thus had a common stake in a Positivist conception of the West's knowledge.

The terms of this alliance of science and Empire had historiographical consequences which endured well into the twentieth century. An emerging History of Science was tightly constrained by the idea of science as the progressive extinction of error. The subject depended on partisan pens, from which had flowed a Whig narrative of the good, usually mathematical, ideas of Great Men replacing ancient superstition. The importance of the medieval Arab world was recognized, but chiefly as a sterile incubator, preserving Greek learning until the West was ready to 'reclaim' it. This worldview positively discouraged research into imperial science or medicine. If Science was part of the cultural bounty which Europe delivered unto a wider world, then its historians could neglect its radiation into the periphery, thus to focus on the implicitly more important subject of its European rise and progress. By the same token, if Science sprang immaculate from Europe's brow, then it was not the concern of imperial historians. J. Holland Rose and his collaborators in the *Cambridge History of the British Empire*, in any event, like those of their contemporaries drawn to Copernicus or Kepler, would surely have reckoned the typical colonial surveyor, geologist, or plant collector to be a tradesman: an agent of civilization but not wholly worthy of the scholar's attention. Science, in the 1920s, was both too lofty and too common a matter to find its way into a Cambridge History of Empire.

Only the 'men on the spot' tended the shrine of Colonial Athena.[3] Governors and administrators were proud of the benevolent rule they had brought to barbarians. Colonial scientists similarly wanted to ensure that their contribution was not forgotten. Together they left behind vast, often still unmined, records of their work in the archives and publications of official departments and learned societies in every corner of the former Empire. But, until quite recently, historians did not consider these materials as significant. Europe's ignorance of the cultural achievements of a wider world extended to the activities of its own agents abroad. Imperial science and medicine were left to the nibbling curiosity of mice and antiquarians.

Their rescue after 1945 depended, first, on the rise of nationalist and 'peripheral' histories. These, initially, responded to the very cultural assumptions which had made the West's knowledge into the gold standard for civilization. Since by their measure a people without science was marked for subordination, those who rejected subordinacy were spurred to claim their part in its history. The Academy of Japan, for example, chose in 1941 to launch a great editorial project on the pre-Meiji history of Japanese science.[4] In the era of decolonization the 'Periphery', as discussed below, came to assert both its participation in the West's learning, and in some cases, the importance of its pre-colonial and indigenous knowledge or medicine. From the 1960s onwards this research of the imperial frontier was joined by attempts to explain peripheral poverty and 'dependency'. As historians came to question the Empire's connection to the work of civilization, they examined how science and medicine had participated in exploitation and subjugation. Some enquired into the colonial origins of the periphery's apparent scientific inferiority.

These examinations of the imperial role of learning and healing depended also

[3] See *inter alia*: C. A. Bruce, *The Broad Stone of Empire: Problems of Crown Colony Administration*, 2 vols. (London, 1910); Isaac Henry Burkill, *Chapters on the History of Botany in India* (Calcutta, 1965); Geoffrey B. Masefield, *A History of the Colonial Agricultural Service* (Oxford, 1972); L. Roger, *Happy Toil: Fifty-Five Years of Tropical Medicine* (London, 1950); Harold H. Scott, *A History of Tropical Medicine*, 2 vols. (Baltimore, 1939–42); George J. Snowball, ed., *Science and Medicine in Central Africa* (Oxford, 1965); W. T. Thistleton-Dyer, 'What Science has Done for the West Indies', *West Indies Bulletin*, XI (1911), pp. 249–51; E. Barton Worthington, *Science in Africa: A Review of Scientific Research Relating to Tropical and Southern Africa* (London, 1938).

[4] S. Yajima, 'Coup l'oeil sur l'histoire des sciences au Japon', *Japanese Studies in the History of Science*, I (1962), p. 4. See also the Fascist compilation of a history of Italian science: Gino Bargagli Petrucci, ed., *L'Italia e la Scienza: Studi* (Florence, 1932).

on a coincidental shift in conceptions of science within the West. Central to this was the rise of a social history and sociology of science and medicine, which paid attention to artisans, 'minor' scientists, and even non-European traditions, which had often been neglected amid the hero-worship of Galileo or Newton.[5] Marxists and Weberians pioneered research into the social construction and consequences of knowledge. Historians became more conscious of scientists and physicians prosecuting what Frank Turner acutely described as 'public science': a permanent campaign to secure resources, status, and influence within society.[6] Historians of science thus began to address the impact on intellectual life of politics, economics, cultural values, and disciplinary contexts. Interacting with this was a critique of the empiricist tradition which arose out of empiricism. Philosophers began to question whether science was a market-place where simple descriptions of nature competed, good ideas replacing bad ones.[7] Thomas Kuhn, for example, in his influential *The Structure of Scientific Revolutions* (1962), argued that participants in a discipline often have wholly irrational investments in those theories which have informed their training and professional achievements. If science and medicine were losing their aura of objectivity, after Auschwitz and Hiroshima they had lost their innocence. For the Frankfurt School and later Structuralists, they were implicated as often in the fabric of despotism as in the path to liberty and cosmopolitan progress.[8] By the 1960s, therefore, there were endogenous 'Western' reasons to study empire's impact on science and medicine and how these disciplines contributed to imperial domination.

These political and intellectual influences came together, first, in the United States. America, hospitable to immigrant scholars and ideas, was also a former colony. She shared the anxieties of all ex-colonies, and the particular ambivalence of the 'White Dominions'—a fascination, and perhaps a racial identification, with Britain's power and cultural authority. This sentimental colonization combined

[5] See, in particular, Richard H. Shryock, *The Development of Modern Medicine: An Interpretation of the Social and Scientific Factors Involved* (New York, 1947); Henry E. Sigerist, *A History of Medicine* (New York, 1951); John D. Bernal, *Science in History* (London, 1954); Robert King Merton, *Science, Technology and Society in Seventeenth-Century England* (Bruges, 1938); Joseph Needham, *Science and Civilisation in China*, 7 vols. (Cambridge, 1954). See also Steven Shapin, 'History of Science and its Sociological Reconstructions', *History of Science*, XX (1982), pp. 157–211.

[6] Frank M. Turner, 'Public Science in Britain, 1880–1919', *Isis*, LXXI (1980), pp. 589–608.

[7] For a guide to this diverse literature see John Losee, *A Historical Introduction to the Philosophy of Science*, 2nd edn. (Oxford, 1980), pp. 189–220; particularly important influences include: N. R. Hanson, *Patterns of Discovery: An Inquiry into the Conceptual Foundations of Science* (Cambridge, 1958); Willard van Orman Quine, 'Two Dogmas of Empiricism', in Quine, *From a Logical Point of View: Nine Logico-Philosophical Essays* (Cambridge, Mass., 1953); Ludwig Wittgenstein, *Philosophical Investigations* (Oxford, 1953).

[8] Max Horkheimer and Theodor W. Adorno, *Dialectic of Enlightenment*, trans. John Cumming (New York, 1972).

with a wish to assert the vitality and importance of their New World situation. Parallel to America's emergence as the dominant power in the West, the historians of her colonial period, as Stephen Foster discusses in this volume, began a revolt against conventional interpretation. Among the expressions of this initiative was the assertion that America, rather than being a derivative colony, had been a frontier of innovation. I. B. Cohen, in *Benjamin Franklin's Experiments* (1941), thus argued that it was precisely Franklin's distance from the restraining assumptions of the Royal Society which allowed his electrical discoveries.[9] The young Bernard Bailyn and John Clive asserted, similarly, that America's provinciality was its advantage, helping 'to shake the mind from the roots of habit and tradition'.[10] Daniel Boorstin gave this suggestion its 'end of ideology' apotheosis in *The Americans: The Colonial Experience* (1958), which celebrated how the practical American frontiersman had outflanked over-cultivated Europeans in science, medicine, and technology.[11]

This creole chest-beating might have stayed within the American tribe had it not sparked Donald Fleming in 1962 to offer a coded rebuttal to this intellectual twist on the frontier thesis via a comparison of American, Canadian, and Australian science.[12] Its romantic identification with pioneers seemed to Fleming an attempt to avoid the shame of a colonial past, to bypass the dishonourable 'psychology of abdication, of making over to Europeans the highest responsibilities in science'. These settler communities had consented to the intellectual 'absentee landlordship' of Europe. Linnaeus, Banks, and the Hookers turned Americans, Australians, and Canadians into subordinates supplying the specimens and data from which they confected a 'European' science and their own reputations. European scholars, he suggested, '*preferred* to have the Americans, Canadians, and Australians rehearse their repertory of exotic themes: the rattlesnakes . . . moose . . . [and] Stone Age Aboriginals'. Pointing out what would later be called the 'brain drain', Fleming argued that the best colonial minds, such as the New Zealand physicist Ernest Rutherford (who cracked the atom) and the Australian Howard Florey (pioneer in antibiotics), were drawn away into English and Scottish universities. He specifically blamed those scholarships which commemorated the 1851

9 A position from which Cohen himself admittedly retreated in *Franklin and Newton: An Inquiry into Speculative Newtonian Experimental Science and Franklin's Work in Electricity as an Example Thereof* (Philadelphia, 1956), and see his *Benjamin Franklin's Science* (Cambridge, Mass., 1990).

10 John Clive and Bernard Bailyn, 'England's Cultural Provinces: Scotland and America', *William and Mary Quarterly*, Third Series, XI (1954), pp. 200–13.

11 This patriotic line was supported by Brooke Hindle, *The Pursuit of Science in Revolutionary America, 1735–1789* (Chapel Hill, NC, 1956), and Raymond Phineas Stearns, *Science in the British Colonies of America* (Urbana, Ill., 1970), even in the wake of Cohen's hesitations.

12 Donald Fleming, 'Science in Australia, Canada, and the United States: Some Comparative Remarks', *Proceedings of the Tenth International Congress of the History of Science, Ithaca, 1962* (Paris, 1964), pp. 179–96.

Exhibition and Cecil Rhodes for this spiritual haemorrhage. This remarkable essay traced many outlines later filled in by Australian, Canadian, and 'Third World' historians of science.

More immediately influential, however, was an essay by George Bassala on 'The Spread of Western Science'.[13] Bassala, publishing in the principal American scientific journal, offered a model for the imperial history of science more congenial to those who saw Science as a field of cumulative advance, and Empire as no more than the diffusion of Europe into the world. In an argument which resembled, in its gait, W. W. Rostow's contemporaneous theory of economic growth, Bassala argued for a three-stage process: European reconnaissance, characterized by a peripatetic natural history managed from Europe, followed by an era of dependent 'colonial science', culminating in an autonomous national scientific tradition. Against Fleming, he argued that 'colonial science' should not pejoratively suggest that the non-European nation was suppressed or kept in a servile state by the imperial power. Bassala appeared untroubled that only his country, itself latterly an imperial power, provided an unqualified example of this intellectual 'take off'. His diffusionist approach, however, offered scaffolding against which arguments might lean, and attracted sympathy among those who aspired to be New World British.

The Bassala model, indeed, adequately described how scientists in the colonies of settlement had understood their own place as the partners of British science.[14] The problem of the boundary between 'colonial' and 'national' science, central to his essay, stimulated the beginnings of an Australian, Canadian, and New Zealand historiography of science.[15] Its pioneers often acted in spite of the

[13] George Bassala, 'The Spread of Western Science', *Science*, CLVI (1967), pp. 611–22.

[14] See, for example, Henry M. Tory, *A History of Science in Canada* (Toronto, 1939); E. Scott, 'The History of Australian Science', *Australian Journal of Science*, I (1939), pp. 105–16; Charles A. Fleming, *Science, Settlers, and Scholars: The Centennial History of the Royal Society of New Zealand* (Wellington, 1987); Alexander Claude Brown, *A History of Scientific Endeavour in South Africa: A Collection of Essays on the Occasion of the Centenary of the Royal Society of South Africa* (Cape Town, 1977).

[15] See, *inter alia*, for Australia: N. R. Barrett, 'The Contributions of Australians to Medical Knowledge', *Medical History*, XI (1967), pp. 321–33; Michael E. Hoare, 'Science and Scientific Associations in Eastern Australia, 1820–1890', unpublished Ph.D. dissertation, Australian National University, 1974; Roderick Weir Home, ed., *Australian Science in the Making* (Cambridge, 1988) and, with Sally Gregory Kohlstedt, eds., *International Science and National Scientific Identity: Australia Between Britain and America* (Dordrecht, 1991); Ann Mozley Moyal, *A Guide to the Manuscript Records of Australian Science* (Canberra, 1966); Roy M. MacLeod, ed., *The Commonwealth of Science, ANZAAS and the Scientific Enterprise in Australasia, 1888–1988* (Melbourne, 1988); for Canada: Richard A. Jarrell and Norman R. Ball, eds., *Science, Technology, and Canadian History* (Waterloo, Ont., 1980) and its 1983 and 1991 sequels; Suzanne Elizabeth Zeller, *Inventing Canada: Early Victorian Science and the Idea of a Transcontinental Nation* (Toronto, 1987); and for New Zealand: Michael Edward Hoare, *Reform in New Zealand Science, 1880–1926* (Melbourne, 1976) and *Beyond the 'Filial Piety': Science History in New Zealand: A Critical Review of the Art* (Melbourne, 1977); M. E. Hoare and L. G. Bell, eds., *In Search of New Zealand's Scientific Heritage: History of Science in New Zealand Conference* (Wellington, 1984).

self-doubt characteristic of the colonial, as the foreword to the papers of the first Canadian conference plaintively put it: 'In our efforts to follow the history of Canadian science and technology, we have to battle the notion that anything done here was, in any event, a pale imitation of more creative work done elsewhere.'[16]

Astute scholars noticed that the cultural insecurities had been shared by colonial scientists themselves. Roy MacLeod, in a seminal essay on the condition of 'White Dominion' science, enlarged Fleming's suggestion that intellectual dependency, not least in science, sustained, and was encouraged by, the colonial experience.[17] MacLeod and John Todd have argued that Australians, in the nineteenth and twentieth centuries, accepted a subordinate position in the intellectual world, supplying the needs of British men of science, while individually and in association they looked towards London and Oxford and Cambridge for guidance and approval.[18]

In independent India, both the 'modernizing' Nehru mainstream of the Congress Party and Marxists prized science as a cultural commodity. Between 1959 and 1963 the National Institute of Sciences thus constituted a National Commission for the Compilation of the History of Sciences of India and, in 1966, the *Indian Journal of the History of Science*. Under this Commission's influence, scholars attempted to prepare comprehensive histories.[19] The diffusion model had some appeal among them, with O. P. Jaggi, for example, presenting twentieth-century Indian science as the fruit of transplanted European learning.[20] But Indians, naturally, were less happy than Americans or Australians with a pre-conquest *tabula rasa*. Much effort thus went into the recovery of the wealth of ancient and medieval Indian science.[21] Deepak Kumar pointedly urged that the category

[16] B. Sinclair, 'Foreword', in Jarrell and Ball, eds., *Science, Technology, and Canadian History*, p. ix.

[17] R. M. MacLeod, 'On Visiting the "Moving Metropolis": Reflections on the Architecture of Imperial Science', *Historical Records of Australian Science*, V, 3 (1982), pp. 1–15.

[18] See John Todd, 'Transfer and Dependence: Aspects of Change in Australian Science and Technology, 1880–1918', unpublished Ph.D. dissertation, New South Wales, 1991; and 'Science at the Periphery: An Interpretation of Australian Scientific and Technological Dependency and Development Prior to 1914', *Annals of Science*, L (1993), pp. 33–58.

[19] O. P. Jaggi, *History of Science and Technology in India*, 15 vols. (New Delhi, 1969–); D. M. Bose, Samarendra Nath Sen, and B. V. Subarayappa, *A Concise History of Science in India* (New Delhi, 1971); K. Kumadamini and G. Kuppuram, eds., *History of Science and Technology in India*, 12 vols. (Delhi, 1990).

[20] See Jaggi, 'Preface' to *History of Science and Technology in India*, Vol. IX.

[21] Debiprasad Chattopadhyay, *Science and Society in Ancient India* (Calcutta, 1977); A. Rahman, *Bibliography of Source Material on History of Science and Technology in Medieval India: An Introduction* (New Delhi, 1975). See also the important contribution of David Edwin Pingree, *Census of the Exact Sciences in Sanskrit*, Series A (Philadelphia, 1970–81).

of 'pre-colonial science' should replace 'non-scientific society' in Bassala's model.[22] Kumar, Satpal Sangwan, and others have explored how this indigenous knowledge was appropriated, often without acknowledgement, by Europe, how Western science organized the administration and exploitation of India, how the colonial order led to the deprecation of local learning, and how Indians were long excluded from participation in 'modern' science.[23] They enlarged the suspicions of Flory, George Orwell's protagonist in *Burmese Days*, that Indian technology had been destroyed to give advantages to British industry. Some South Asians, such as Susantha Goonatilake, feared that Empire had produced a syndrome of 'aborted discovery', in which Indian practitioners of Western science and medicine were doomed both to look always to the West and to reproduce the unhappy social relations once imposed, from outside, on the East.[24]

Unlike South Asia, Africa, before or after colonial rule, had not enjoyed political or cultural unity, or a 'scientific tradition' which could easily be compared with European models.[25] Precisely, perhaps, because of this, historians of Africa pioneered studies in the 1960s of the role of science, technology, and medicine as imperial history. Philip D. Curtin showed how images of Africa as diseased and primitive, fit for slavery and (benevolent) conquest, were the obverse of Europe's modern identification with Enlightenment and progress.[26] From Curtin's exploration of the role of malaria, others examined how medicine, and the myth and reality of disease, had shaped the colonial experience.[27] The particular role of technology, in the form of firearms, attracted a volume of contributions to the *Journal of African History* in 1971. Others showed how anthropology, biology, and

[22] Deepak Kumar, 'Patterns of Colonial Science in India', *Indian Journal of the History of Science* (hereafter *IJHS*), XV (1980), p. 107.

[23] Matthew H. Edney, *Mapping an Empire: The Geographical Construction of British India, 1765–1843* (Chicago, 1997); Deepak Kumar, ed., *Science and Empire: Essays in Indian Context, 1700–1947* (Delhi, 1991); Satpal Sangwan, *Science, Technology and Colonisation: An Indian Experience, 1757–1857* (Delhi, 1991); S. K. Sen, 'The Character of the Introduction of Western Science in India During the Eighteenth and Nineteenth Centuries', *IJHS*, I (1966), pp. 112–22. More recently Faheer Baber, *Science of Empire: Scientific Knowledge, Civilization and Colonial Rule in India* (Albany, 1996).

[24] Susantha Goonatilake, *Aborted Discovery: Science and Creativity in the Third World* (London, 1984). See the comparable analysis of the intellectual consequences of slavery and the plantation system in the Caribbean in Richard Drayton, 'Sugar Cane Breeding in Barbados: Knowledge and Power in a Colonial Context', unpublished A.B. dissertation, Harvard, 1986

[25] Although see the provocative essay of Robin Horton, 'African Traditional Thought and Western Science', *Africa*, XXXVII (1967), pp. 51–71 and 155–87.

[26] Philip D. Curtin, *The Image of Africa: British Ideas and Actions, 1780–1850* (Madison, 1964).

[27] R. E. Dummett, 'The Campaign Against Malaria and the Expansion of Scientific, Medical and Sanitary Services in British West Africa, 1898–1910', *African Historical Studies*, I (1968); Leo Spitzer, 'The Mosquito and Segregation in Sierra Leone', *Canadian Journal of African Studies*, II (1968), pp. 49–61.

increasing technical prowess helped a 'scientific' racism to crystallize, which in turn gave confidence to the Victorians in Africa.[28]

This suggestion that modern science helped to construct the racial 'Other' was rapidly absorbed in the 1970s into the mainstream of imperial history.[29] At the same time, studies of the Dominions, India, and Africa interacted with more general explorations of science and technology's centrality to the imperial enterprise. Where Carlo Cipolla had suggested in 1965 that guns and ships were the original secret of Europe's predominance, Gerald Graham, Paul Kennedy, and Lucille Brockway examined the contribution of steam gunboats, submarine telegraphy, and economic botany to British expansion.[30] Daniel R. Headrick brought these threads together in two seminal studies which argued that territorial annexation in Asia and Africa and the consolidation of 'formal' Empire depended on nineteenth-century technological revolutions.[31] Both the regional and comparative work were stimulated by contemporary 'structuralist' analyses of the origins of modern inequality. Brockway, like Goonatilake, for example, took inspiration from Immanuel Wallerstein's 'world systems' approach, and sought to explain science's place in the imperial 'development of underdevelopment'.[32] The Gramscian concept of 'hegemony', refracted through Edward W. Said's *Orientalism*, similarly influenced Michael Adas's exploration of how science and technology as *ideas* gave confidence to Europeans and won submission from the colonized.[33]

By the early 1980s similar work began to emerge on colonial medicine.[34] This in part derived from metropolitan studies on the 'political economy of health'.[35]

[28] Christine Bolt, *Victorian Attitudes to Race* (London, 1971); T. O. Ranger, 'From Humanism to the Science of Man: Colonialism in Africa and the Understanding of Alien Societies', *Transactions of the Royal Historical Society*, XXVI (1976), pp. 115–41; Gloria Thomas-Emeagwali, ed., *Science and Technology in African History: With Case Studies from Nigeria, Sierra Leone, Zimbabwe, and Zambia* (Lewiston, NY, 1992).

[29] See Ronald Hyam, *Britain's Imperial Century, 1815–1915: A Study of Empire and Expansion* (new edn. London, 1976), and James Belich, *The New Zealand Wars and the Victorian Interpretation of Racial Conflict* (Auckland, 1988).

[30] Carlo Cippola, *European Culture and Overseas Expansion* (London, 1966); Gerald S. Graham, *Great Britain in the Indian Ocean: A Study of Maritime Enterprise, 1810–1850* (Oxford, 1968); Paul M. Kennedy, 'Imperial Cable Communications and Strategy, 1870–1914', *English Historical Review*, LXXXVI (1971), pp. 728–75; L. Brockway, *Science and Colonial Expansion: The Role of the British Botanic Gardens* (New York, 1979).

[31] Daniel R. Headrick, *Tools of Empire: Technology and European Imperialism in the Nineteenth Century* (New York, 1981) and *Tentacles of Progress: Technology Transfer in the Age of Imperialism, 1850–1940* (London, 1988).

[32] Immanuel Wallerstein, *The Modern World System* (New York, 1974).

[33] Edward W. Said, *Orientalism* (New York, 1978); Michael Adas, *Machines As the Measure of Men: Science, Technology, and Ideologies of Western Dominance* (Ithaca, NY, 1989).

[34] David J. Arnold, ed., *Imperial Medicine and Indigenous Societies* (Manchester, 1988); Roy M. MacLeod and Milton James Lewis, eds., *Disease, Medicine, and Empire: Perspectives on Western Medicine and the Experience of European Expansion* (London, 1988).

[35] Lesley Doyal, *The Political Economy of Health* (London, 1979).

Radhika Ramasubbin and Mark Harrison, for example, examined the colonial origins of the Indian public health system, and suggested that neither for the British nor Indian élites was the well-being of poor people a priority.[36] Roy MacLeod, Donald Denoon, and Randall Packard offered comparable studies for Tanzania, the Pacific, and South Africa.[37] Parallel to this, others investigated the 'social construction' of medical knowledge.[38] Under the coincident influence of Frantz Fanon and Michel Foucault, historians began to think of medicine as a set of discourses and practices through which control was exerted over non-Europeans.[39] Megan Vaughan and David Arnold, for example, showed that disease and healing shaped the colonial process by creating Western medical ideas of the 'African' and 'Indian' as through affecting mortality.[40]

The last frontier was the imperial centre itself. For if by the beginning of the 1980s many understood the contributions of science and medicine to expansion, almost none had asked how empire shaped science. A 'diffusionist' perspective, with which the age of high imperialism would have been comfortable still prevailed.[41] By its lights, while science in Africa or India might have been imbricated with colonial policy and circumstance, its history within Britain remained wholly separate. These old certainties have begun to disintegrate. Roy MacLeod and Michael Worboys began the process by showing how British science had responded to Imperial responsibilities it had undertaken in the age of Chamberlain.[42]

[36] R. Ramasubbin, *Public Health and Medical Research in India: Their Origins Under the Impact of British Colonial Policy* (Stockholm, 1982); Mark Harrison, *Public Health in British India: Anglo-Indian Preventive Medicine, 1859–1914* (Cambridge, 1994).

[37] Roy M. MacLeod and Donald Denoon, *Health and Healing in Tropical Australia and Papua New Guinea* (Townsville, 1981); Donald Denoon, *Public Health in Papua New Guinea, 1884–1984* (Cambridge, 1989); Randall Packard, *White Plague, Black Labour: Tuberculosis and the Political Economy of Health and Disease in South Africa* (Berkeley, 1989).

[38] See Peter Wright and Andrew Treacher, eds., *The Problem of Medical Knowledge: Examining the Social Construction of Medicine* (Edinburgh, 1982).

[39] Frantz Fanon, *Les Damnés de la terre* (Paris, 1961; *The Wretched of the Earth*), chap. 5; Michel Foucault, *Histoire de la Folie* (Paris, 1961) and *Naissance de la Clinique* (Paris, 1963; *The Birth of the Clinic: An Archaeology of Medical Perception*, London 1975).

[40] Megan Vaughan, *Curing Their Ills: Colonial Power and African Illness* (Stanford Calif., 1991), and David Wylie Arnold, *Colonizing the Body: State Medicine and Epidemic Disease in Nineteenth-Century India* (Berkeley, 1993). See chap. by Diana Wylie.

[41] See the trilogy by Lewis Pyenson, *Cultural Imperialism and the Exact Sciences: German Expansion Overseas, 1900–1930* (New York, 1985), *Empire of Reason: Exact Sciences in Indonesia, 1840–1940* (Leiden, 1989), and *Civilizing Mission: Exact Sciences and French Overseas Expansion, 1830–1940* (Baltimore, 1993). See also the critiques offered in Paulo Palladino and Michael Worboys, 'Science and Imperialism', *Isis*, LXXXIV (1993), pp. 91–102, and Richard Drayton, 'Science and the European Empires', *Journal of Imperial and Commonwealth History*, XXIII (1995), pp. 503–10.

[42] R. M. MacLeod, 'Scientific Advice for British India', *Modern Asian Studies*, IX (1975), pp. 343–84; Michael Worboys, 'Science and British Colonial Imperialism, 1895–1940', unpublished D.Phil. thesis, Sussex, 1980. See also Robert V. Kubicek, *The Administration of Imperialism: Joseph Chamberlain at the Colonial Office* (Durham, NC, 1972).

Later studies suggested that science and medicine, rather than merely profiting from the fashions of Edwardian policy, had enjoyed an old and fundamental connection to the Imperial enterprise. From the mid-1980s onwards, work by David Mackay on Sir Joseph Banks, Robert A. Stafford on geography and the Royal Geographical Society, Matthew Edney on surveying and geodesy, Crosbie Smith and Norton Wise on electrodynamics, Richard H. Grove on conservation, Richard Drayton on botany, and John Clark on entomology, has illustrated how Imperial outreach shaped the life of the sciences within Britain.[43] Much as P. J. Cain and A. G. Hopkins show, *mutatis mutandis*, the impact of the banking profession on imperialism, these scholars have suggested how scientists parasitized the apparatus of imperialism: fattening their disciplines on its opportunities, while pushing it to serve their purposes.[44] As Stafford has suggested, Victorian scientists were an important category of 'sub-imperialist', often leading rather than following the flag. The history of Imperial science, which once took encouragement from the post-1960 'regional' turn in Commonwealth history, is thus helping to refocus attention on British imperialism as a whole. Similarly, these historians are assisting in the discovery—being made, at the same time, by Linda Colley, Kathleen Wilson, and others—that the 'Mother Country' was as much the child of Empire as India, Nigeria, or Barbados.[45]

This inclusion of Britain (and Europe generally) into the space of Imperial history will have important consequences. In particular, by addressing how the 'indigenous' negotiated with the exotic, whether in Bombay or Bristol, we are now going beyond thinking of empire or science as crimes inflicted by Britain on its colonies. Michael Bravo and C. A. Bayly, for example, have shown, respectively, how Inuit and Indians entered into sophisticated dialogues with British geography, physic, and physics.[46] Their attempt to examine the surface of contact

43 David MacKay, *In the Wake of Cook: Exploration, Science, and Empire, 1780–1801* (London, 1985); Robert A. Stafford, *Scientist of Empire: Sir Roderick Murchison, Scientific Exploration, and Victorian Imperialism* (Cambridge, 1989); Edney, *Mapping and Empire*; Crosbie Smith and M. Norton Wise, *Energy and Empire: A Biographical Study of Lord Kelvin* (Cambridge, 1989); Richard H. Grove, *Green Imperialism: Colonial Expansion, Tropical Island Edens and the Origins of Environmentalism, 1600–1860* (Cambridge, 1995); Richard Drayton, *Nature's Government: Kew Gardens, Science, and Imperial Britain* (forthcoming); J. F. M. Clark, 'Science, Secularization and Social Change: The Metamorphosis of Entomology in Nineteenth-Century England', unpublished D.Phil. thesis, Oxford, 1994. See also John M. MacKenzie, ed., *Imperialism and the Natural World* (Manchester, 1990).

44 P. J. Cain and A. G. Hopkins, *British Imperialism*, 2 vols. (London, 1993). See in this context, S. Ravi Rajan, 'Imperial Environmentalism: The Agendas and Ideologies of Natural Resource Management in Colonial Forestry', unpublished D.Phil. thesis, Oxford, 1994.

45 Linda Colley, *Britons: Forging the Nation, 1707–1837* (London, 1992); Kathleen Wilson, *The Sense of the People: Politics, Culture, and Imperialism in England, 1715–1785* (Cambridge, 1995).

46 Michael T. Bravo, *The Accuracy of Ethnoscience: A Study of Inuit Cartography and Cross-Cultural Commensurability* (Manchester, 1996) and 'Science and Discovery in the Admiralty Voyages to the Arctic Regions in Search of a North-West Passage', unpublished Ph.D. thesis, Cambridge, 1992;

between the 'imperial' and the local illustrates two new and important trends. First, much notice is now being paid to how different knowledge systems, understood in their own terms, encounter both nature and each other at the many peripheries of empire. Secondly, there is philosophical interest in how science and medicine assimilate knowledge specific to particular places into universal categories.[47] The gloomy invocation of science's involvement in domination is giving way to research into how empire produced the creolization of different intellectual traditions. The story of riches lost in the horrors of invasion, expropriation, slavery, and the many variants of the 'Middle Passage', is thus being punctuated gradually by discoveries of persisting tradition, exchange, and trans-culturation. This happier theme will ultimately have more enlightening, and subversive, consequences than the old narrative of the once-heroic, and now demonic, West submitting the world to its manners, with the Bible in one hand and the *Novum Organum* in the other.

C. A Bayly, *Empire and Information Intelligence Gathering and Social Communication in India, 1780–1870* (Cambridge, 1996).

[47] For two attempts to address this problem see Bruno Latour, *Science in Action: How to Follow Scientists and Engineers through Society* (Milton Keynes, 1987), and in Volume II, chap. by Richard Drayton.

Select Bibliography

C. A. BAYLY, 'Knowing the Country: Empire and Information in India', *Modern Asian Studies*, XXVII (1993), pp. 3–43.

RICHARD D. BROWN, *Knowledge is Power: The Diffusion of Information in America, 1700–1865* (New York, 1989).

Sir ARCHIBALD DAY, *The Admiralty Hydrographic Service (1795–1919)* (London, 1967).

RICHARD DRAYTON, *Nature's Government: Kew Gardens, Science, and Imperial Britain* (London, forthcoming).

HOWARD T. FRY, *Alexander Dalrymple (1737–1808) and the Expansion of British Trade* (London, 1970).

JOHN GASCOIGNE, *Joseph Banks and the English Enlightenment: Useful Knowledge and Polite Culture* (Cambridge, 1994).

RICHARD H. GROVE, *Green Imperialism: Colonial Expansion, Tropical Island Edens and the Origins of Environmentalism, 1600–1860* (Cambridge, 1995).

O. P. KEJARIWAL, *The Asiatic Society of Bengal and the Discovery of India's Past, 1784–1838* (Delhi, 1988).

DAVID KOPF, *British Orientalism and the Bengal Renaissance: The Dynamics of Indian Modernization, 1773–1835* (London, 1969).

ARTHUR MACGREGOR, ed., *Sir Hans Sloane: Collector, Scientist, Antiquary, Founding Father of the British Museum* (London, 1994).

DAVID MACKAY, *In the Wake of Cook: Exploration, Science, and Empire, 1780–1801* (London, 1985).

P. J. MARSHALL, ed., *The British Discovery of Hinduism in the Eighteenth Century* (Cambridge, 1970).

—— and GLYNDWR WILLIAMS, *The Great Map of Mankind: British Perceptions of the World in the Age of Enlightenment* (London, 1982).

JAMES E. MCCLELLAN, *Science Reorganized: Scientific Societies in the Eighteenth Century* (New York, 1985).

—— *Colonialism and Science: Saint-Domingue in the Old Regime* (Baltimore, 1992).

DAVID PHILIP MILLER and PETER HANNS REILL, eds., *Visions of Empire: Voyages, Botany, and Representations of Nature* (Cambridge, 1996).

RAYMOND SCHWAB, *La Renaissance orientale* (Paris, 1950).

DIRK J. STRUIK, *Yankee Science in the Making* (Boston, 1948).

CHARLES WEBSTER, *The Great Instauration: Science, Medicine, and Reform, 1626–1660* (London, 1975).

HARRY WOOLF, *The Transits of Venus: A Study of Eighteenth-Century Science* (London, 1959).

17

Disease, Diet, and Gender: Late Twentieth-Century Perspectives on Empire

DIANA WYLIE

For nearly three-quarters of the twentieth century, historical writing on the British Empire concentrated on political and economic issues—on the way the Empire was administered, policy-making, the economic consequences of Imperial rule, and the emergence of political movements in opposition to British rule. Perhaps inevitably, in times when the Empire generated ideological controversy in Britain and on the periphery, historians tended to be either apologists for or opponents of Empire. But a more analytical and broadly encompassing genre of historical writing has now developed, partly with the emergence of scholars too young to have been personally involved in the colonial experience, and partly because of the influence on the history of the British Empire of wider trends in thinking and historical scholarship. These influences have included the seminal thought of the French philosopher Michel Foucault, the Italian socialist Antonio Gramsci, and literary theorists such as Edward W. Said.[1] Inspired by their writings, many historians of Empire have developed a far more subtle conceptualization of the nature and modes of power of British rule. In particular, historians have begun to examine how power was exercised through skills and disciplines which were once thought to be 'apolitical', such as medicine and other aspects of modern science; and how a range of social identities, such as race and gender, were constructed in the complex processes of British imperialism.

It is particularly striking how the human body has become a focus for historical enquiry in quite new ways. Discussions of the nature and meaning of tropical and colonial medicine have broken new ground. British rulers had, of course, sought to control disease and lower mortality, and many had pursued effective

[1] Michel Foucault, *The Birth of the Clinic: An Archaeology of Medical Perception* (Paris, 1963; English trans. London, 1975); Antonio Gramsci, *Selections from Prison Notebooks* (London, 1971). See esp. the comment by Perry Anderson in 'The Antimonies of Antonio Gramsci', *New Left Review*, C (1976–77), pp. 5–36; Edward W. Said, *Orientalism* (New York, 1978). On their influence see also the chap. by D. A. Washbrook.

and humane governance. Official attempts at promoting health were either supplemented by medical missionaries or, more usually, the missionaries assumed the lion's share of the medical burden. The earliest aim of colonial medicine was to eradicate major killer diseases. The eradication was celebrated as a colonial achievement. The British emphasized the power of Western medical intervention in treating tropical diseases, and assumed that Western doctors were benign and progressive. They paid little attention to the Imperial context in which Western medicine had come to operate, or to the ideas and activities of patients. A major example of this genre is the medical history written by Michael Gelfand, a physician practising in Southern Rhodesia. From the 1950s he produced over twenty books tracing the medical contribution of David Livingstone and other doctors in central Africa.[2] Such writers depicted colonial subjects as fortunate recipients of cures discovered in the medical laboratories of Britain. As Gwyn Prins has argued, British doctors in the Empire were more interested in changing the daily behaviour of indigenous people than in learning from it, or asking why their health problems occurred as they did: and the first histories of disease in a colonial context reflected this angle of vision.[3]

Reacting against this celebratory tone, some historians in the 1970s and 1980s criticized colonialism for having been responsible for disease in the first place. They blamed colonial intervention for introducing new patterns of disease by the encouraging development of plantations, industries, and irrigation schemes.[4] Others wrote on the spread of animal diseases which accompanied the increase of

[2] Michael Gelfand wrote *Livingstone the Doctor, His Life and Travels: A Study in Medical History* (Oxford, 1957) while the Central African Federation was being created, and the tone of his book reflects the hopes and values of that enterprise. Gelfand was also a highly respected authority on Shona medicine: see, for example, *The Traditional Medical Practitioner in Zimbabwe: His Principles of Practice and Pharmacopoeia* (Gweru, 1985), co-written with S. Mavi, R. B. Drummond, and B. Ndemera.

[3] In his review article 'But What Was the Disease? The Present State of Health and Healing in African Studies', *Past and Present* (hereafter *P&P*), CXXIV (1989), pp. 159–79, Gwyn Prins cites the following exemplars of this 'triumphalist and Whiggish literature': Paul F. Russell, *Man's Mastery of Malaria* (Oxford, 1955) and Harry F. Dowling, *Fighting Infection: Conquests of the Twentieth Century* (Cambridge, Mass., 1977).

[4] Meredeth Turshen, *The Political Ecology of Disease in Tanzania* (New Brunswick, NJ, 1984); Randall M. Packard, *White Plague, Black Labor: Tuberculosis and the Political Economy of Health and Disease in South Africa* (Berkeley, 1989); John Farley, *Bilharzia: A History of Imperial Tropical Medicine* (Cambridge, 1991); Steven Feierman, 'Struggles for Control: The Social Roots of Health and Healing in Modern Africa', *African Studies Review* (hereafter *ASR*) XXVIII, 2–3 (1985), pp. 73–147; G. W. Hartwig and K. D. Patterson, eds., *Disease in African History: An Introductory Survey and Case Studies* (Durham, NC, 1978). Landeg White incidentally made the same point when he discussed the deteriorating health of Africans living on a mission station founded by David Livingstone in *Magomero: Portrait of an African Village* (Cambridge, 1987).

trade and the establishment of international boundaries instead of frontier zones.[5] Their conclusions mirrored those of epidemiology scholars: Imperial rule caused local production to change in ways that had serious and demonstrable social costs, ones that earlier scholars had ignored.

In these histories of disease, historians followed the thematic lead of William McNeill and Alfred Crosby, who had written about disease as a powerful and often neglected cause of social change.[6] Philosophically, the new histories of disease were inspired, in part, by the work of René and Jean Dubos on tuberculosis, Thomas Kuhn on scientific research, and Thomas McKeown on nutrition.[7] All three authors underlined the limitations of scientific truth, and the fallibility of modern medicine. Dubos and McKeown demonstrated that tuberculosis had begun to decline in nineteenth-century Europe independently of medical intervention. Kuhn analysed the non-rational process of scientific research, noting that paradigms enjoyed moments of professional fashion unrelated to whether or not they were true. Together they provided scholars with a conceptual framework for rejecting some of the universal claims of modern science and for perceiving limits to the powers of modern medicine.

Scholars who left behind such a bipolar mode of studying the history of disease—either praising or condemning the medical acts of Empire—moved in two different directions in the 1980s. On the one hand, they engaged in cliometrics, counting the number of sick and dead in order to see how patterns of illness had changed over time and across the globe. On the other, they explored the theoretical perspectives of Gramsci or Foucault. The choice between more empirical and more theoretical perspectives entailed not only using different kinds of source material, but asking different kinds of questions. In *Death by Migration*, for example, Philip D. Curtin examined military records to measure the 'relocation costs', or comparative death rates, of European soldiers serving in the tropics as opposed to those staying in Europe between 1815 and 1914. He concluded that, during this period 'military doctors and their civilian colleagues . . . put an end to the vast majority of unnecessary deaths among the young', and so facilitated Imperial

[5] John Ford, *The Role of the Trypanosomiases in African Ecology: A Study of the Tsetse Fly Problem* (Oxford, 1971); Paul F. Cranefield, *Science and Empire: East Coast Fever in Rhodesia and the Transvaal* (Cambridge, 1991); Randall M. Packard, 'Maize, Cattle, and Mosquitoes: The Political Economy of Malaria Epidemics in Colonial Swaziland', *Journal of African History* (hereafter *JAH*), XXV, 2 (1984), pp. 189–212.

[6] William H. McNeill, *Plagues and Peoples* (New York, 1977); Alfred W. Crosby, *The Columbian Exchange: Biological and Cultural Consequences of 1492* (Westport, Conn., 1972).

[7] René J. and Jean Dubos, *The White Plague: Tuberculosis: Man and Society* (New Brunswick, 1952); Thomas S. Kuhn, *The Structure of Scientific Revolutions* (Chicago, 1962); Thomas McKeown, *The Modern Rise of Population* (New York, 1976).

expansion by lowering its human costs.[8] This kind of quantitative study can be done only on groups for which statistics were kept, such as on European soldiers.

The second, more theoretical, perspective on the history of disease presented a complex but rewarding analysis, since it focused on the interaction of the colonizer and colonized. David Arnold, writing in 1993 on epidemics in nineteenth-century India, for example, drew attention to the slow extension of British influence over the health of the colonized, and to the way in which Indians participated in this process.[9] Only when epidemics threatened popular welfare did the enclaves of British military medicine open to allow aggressive and coercive campaigns against Indian health-care practices. These secular assaults by the state initially provoked resistance—such as flight from smallpox vaccination—but as the century drew to an end, Indian élites selectively adopted elements of Western medicine, and after 1914 they made it part of their own claims to power in state and society. In this literature no Imperial 'victory' is one-sided or unambiguous. Rather, resistance by 'natives' to having their bodies 'colonized' by British doctors helped to produce a new 'system of medical thought and action' containing elements of both the Imperial and the local.[10]

Post-modern historians in the 1980s contributed insights derived from philosophers such as Foucault and literary critics such as Edward W. Said and Gayatri Spivak.[11] They saw biomedicine as a cultural system that turned 'natives' into objects of scrutiny and often identified indigenous traits as inherent in a 'race' or 'tribe'. These judgements, in turn, affected the experiences of the colonized, both the things that happened and the sense that people made of them. Megan Vaughan's *Curing their Ills: Colonial Power and African Illness* exemplifies this post-modern criticism of medicine.[12] Eschewing the cost–benefit analysis of Imperial medicine that predominated through the 1970s, she drew on the writings of Foucault to enquire more broadly and abstractly into the nature of colonial power by considering the body as a site where power relations are played out. From this perspective, not only scientific and medical knowledge but even epidemics could be seen as 'social constructs', or stories told by people wielding

[8] See Philip D. Curtin, *Death by Migration: Europe's Encounter with the Tropical World in the Nineteenth Century* (Cambridge, 1989), p. 159.

[9] David Arnold, *Colonizing the Body: State Medicine and Epidemic Disease in Nineteenth-Century India* (Berkeley, 1993).

[10] In his article 'Godly Medicine: The Ambiguities of Medical Mission in Southeastern Tanzania, 1900–45', Terence O. Ranger addressed the question whether African ideas about health had, in fact, been profoundly transformed during the colonial period. In Steven Feierman and John M. Janzen, eds., *The Social Basis of Health and Healing in Africa* (Berkeley, 1992), pp. 256–82.

[11] Said, *Orientalism*, and Gayatri Chakravorty Spivak, *In Other Worlds: Essays in Cultural Politics* (London, 1987).

[12] Megan Vaughan, *Curing their Ills: Colonial Power and African Illness* (Stanford, Calif., 1991).

power in a particular time and place.[13] Medicine thus lost its earlier status as purveying a certain kind of scientific and value-free 'truth'. Scholars criticized it both for making the human body into an object and for neglecting the social, political, and economic causes of disease. More broadly, environmental history began replacing the 'magic bullet' perspective of earlier years, and people accepted the multifaceted nature of disease and its 'cure'. Scholars had also become aware of the need to trace the interaction of politics, people, the environment, and pathogens over time.

Research on food consumed in the colonies, and its likely impact on health and population, began, like research on disease, for the purpose of informing colonial policy. While such research was not explicitly historical, it made assumptions about the nature of pre-colonial diet. An advisory body to the Privy Council, the Committee of Civil Research, first commissioned studies on diet in the 1920s, partly in reaction to a fear current at the time that the colonized would prove to be too weak to make a healthy journey into modernity and to meet the labour demands of modern industry. This concern had arisen first in Britain itself at the time of the South African War. It had become known that British soldiers were shorter and thinner than their predecessors who had served nearly fifty years earlier in the Crimean War. The nutritional health of the nation became a matter of official concern.[14]

If the industrial revolution had undermined the health of the British working class, there seemed to be no reason why the same process would not occur in the colonies. The degeneration of national stock might take the form of debility or of underpopulation. Research into these two subjects was first conducted among the Masai and the Kikuyu in Kenya by John Gilks and John Boyd Orr, who later became the first Director of the UN Food and Agriculture Organization.[15] In the 1930s the subject was of sufficient concern that the anthropologist Audrey Richards went to Northern Rhodesia to study the diet of the Bemba in relation to the changing nature of their work. She later chaired the Diet Committee of the International Institute of African Languages and Cultures. Richards structured her research around the expectation, based on medical investigation, that African people were malnourished. In the Bemba case, the cause was labour migration: it was destroying the productivity of local farming by taking away the men on whose

[13] Terence O. Ranger and Paul Slack, eds., *Epidemics and Ideas: Essays on the Historical Perception of Pestilence* (Cambridge, 1992).

[14] *Report of the Inter-Departmental Committee on Physical Deterioration, Parliamentary Papers*, XXXII, 1904, Cd. 2175.

[15] John Boyd Orr and John Langton Gilks, *Studies of Nutrition: The Physique and Health of Two African Tribes* (London, 1931).

tree-cutting labour its slash-and-burn agriculture depended.[16] The official concern that sent Boyd Orr to Kenya and Richards to Northern Rhodesia was further encouraged, during the inter-war years, by League of Nations reports that colonial populations were undernourished. Its main heritage was twofold: it fostered a static image of pre-colonial diet and the idea that, throughout the colonial period, the quality of life, as reflected in diet, had been declining.

Perhaps because there are few reliable sources for determining the nature and, more particularly, the effects of pre-colonial diets, and because the precise impact of certain diets on health anywhere in the world remains in dispute, the study of colonial nutrition moved away from simply charting the decline of indigenous cuisine and physiques.[17] With the exception of a study of Shona diet, written by Michael Gelfand in 1971,[18] historians did not confront these issues—the paucity of pre-colonial sources and the unclear effects of diet—until the 1980s, when three different approaches emerged.

First, and most prolificly, scholars in the 1980s addressed the political economy of famine. They built on a long scholarly tradition initiated by such critics of Empire as Ramesh C. Dutt, who had argued in 1900 that droughts in late-nineteenth-century India led to famines because British policies had impoverished Indian societies.[19] The debate continues on the issue whether more people died from famine in colonial or pre-colonial times. Did the commercialization of agriculture and the imposition of taxes destroy peasants' time-honoured strategies for coping with food shortages?[20] Did the cash nexus save people from starvation, while condemning the poor and landless to chronic hunger?[21] Influenced by the

[16] Audrey I. Richards, *Land, Labour and Diet in Northern Rhodesia: An Economic Study of the Bemba Tribe* (London, 1939). See also her preliminary study *Hunger and Work in a Savage Tribe: A Functional Study of Nutrition among the Southern Bantu* (London, 1932).

[17] Radiocarbon date lists with reference to food started to be published in the *JAH* by Brian Fagan in the 1960s; by the 1990s that journal was publishing food-related archaeological surveys with more sociological content. See, for example, Tim Maggs and Gavin Whitelaw, 'A Review of Recent Archaeological Research on Food-Producing Communities in Southern Africa', *JAH*, XXXII, 1 (1991), pp. 3–24.

[18] Michael Gelfand, *Diet and Tradition in an African Culture* (Edinburgh, 1971). This study covers the years from 1956 to 1971.

[19] Ramesh C. Dutt, *Open Letters to Lord Curzon on Famines and Land Assessments in India* (London, 1900); David Arnold, 'Social Crisis and Epidemic Disease in the Famines of Nineteenth Century India', *Social History of Medicine*, VI, 3 (1993), pp. 385–404.

[20] With reference to India, B. M. Bhatia, *Famines in India: A Study in Some Aspects of the Economic History of India (1860–1920)* (1963; 2nd edn., London, 1967); Paul R. Greenough, *Prosperity and Misery in Modern Bengal: The Famine of 1943–1944* (New York, 1982); and Hari Shanker Srivastava, *The History of Indian Famines and Development of Famine Policy (1858–1918)* (Agra, 1968) have argued in the affirmative.

[21] Michelle Burge McAlpin argues in *Subject to Famine: Food Crises and Economic Change in Western India, 1860–1920* (Princeton, 1983) that modern technology did, indeed, save Indian lives from starvation, except during the Bengal famine of 1943–44.

work of the economist Amartya Sen, scholars working on India and Africa have focused on 'entitlements', by asking which groups have been most vulnerable during famines and which have been socially entitled to eat the little food that was available.[22]

Others have followed Audrey Richards and investigated the impact of commercial farming on subsistence agriculture, and therefore diet.[23] This pairing of nutrition with agriculture, and not with public health and medicine, had characterized official research on colonial nutrition since 1936. In that year the Colonial Office first organized a survey of colonial nutrition.[24] Michael Worboys argued that such reports viewed nutritional deficiencies as technical problems rather than as signs of the flawed colonial economic structure.[25] Breaking away from narrowly defined conceptions of well-being, John Iliffe developed, in *The African Poor: A History*, a vision of the great transition of modern times: land-rich and labour-poor societies, threatened occasionally by famine, were becoming land-poor and labour-rich societies where large families were particularly susceptible to endemic malnutrition. Capitalist farming, as Iliffe argued in *Famine in Zimbabwe*, held famine at bay, but could not prevent the undernourishment of a growing population whose access to food was determined by scarce cash.[26]

A third approach derives, in part, from the lack of a reliable nutritional baseline even for the colonial period. (There are no quantitative data for most colonies on famine mortality or even live birth.) It focuses on ideas about gender, hunger, and poverty that the study of diet provokes. Henrietta Moore and Megan Vaughan, for example, set out in 1986 to write a sequel to Richards's study in what is now Zambia. Soon after revisiting the land of the Bemba, Moore and Vaughan discovered that the systems of agriculture and, therefore, local nutritional status were far more resilient and adaptable than Richards had predicted they would be. The scholarly 'anxiety to generalize' had, they believed, resulted in the creation of an overly rigid conception of slash-and-burn agriculture. Nor had there been a 'generalized breakdown in sharing mechanisms' due to the divisive effects of the

[22] Amartya Sen, *Poverty and Famines: An Essay on Entitlement and Deprivation* (Oxford, 1981); Megan Vaughan, *Story of an African Famine: Gender and Famine in Twentieth-Century Malawi* (Cambridge, 1987).

[23] Paul Richards, 'Ecological Change and the Politics of African Land Use', *ASR*, XXVI, 2 (1983), pp. 1–72; Michael Watts, *Silent Violence: Food, Famine and Peasantry in Northern Nigeria* (Berkeley, 1983).

[24] *Nutritional Policy in the Colonial Empire*, Colonial 121 (London, 1936).

[25] Michael Worboys, 'The Discovery of Colonial Malnutrition between the Wars', in David Arnold, ed., *Imperial Medicine and Indigenous Societies* (Manchester, 1988), pp. 208–25.

[26] John Iliffe, *The African Poor: A History* (Cambridge, 1987) and *Famine in Zimbabwe, 1890–1960* (Gweru, 1990); Diana Wylie, 'The Changing Face of Hunger in Southern African History, 1880–1980', *P&P*, CXXII (1989), pp. 159–99.

cash economy. Rather, cash and kinship were bound together in the rural economy because the new markets were too unevenly developed and unreliable to cause people to jettison the old ways.[27] Moore and Vaughan's work suggests that scholars of diet and nutrition within the British Empire will be obliged to focus more on ideas about hunger and food than to delineate their precise effects.

The significance of gender as a social construct is one of the most important new contributions to the history of Empire. It was not analysed during the Imperial zenith itself, largely because the Empire was assumed to be a naturally male domain. From the 1970s, however, historians have investigated assumptions about 'manliness' and femininity and their respective roles in the functioning of Empire. Some evidence may be found in the memoirs of colonial officials and their wives.[28] British attitudes towards gender are also richly documented in public crises that had some bearing on sexuality. In late-nineteenth-century India, the Ilbert Bill controversy on the age of consent is highly revealing of British and Indian assumptions. Protest against female circumcision in Kenya from 1929 to 1931 also revealed as much about British attitudes towards the proper roles and treatment of women as about those of the Kikuyu.[29] Historians now ask questions about the respective importance of gender, race, and class in determining identity and behaviour in the colonies. How did particular colonial situations influence gender and race ideologies and their relation to one another? To what extent did women collaborate in, or resist, the making of colonial hierarchies? And to what extent were assumptions about gender significant in British justifications of colonial rule?

At their most encompassing, studies of gender reflect the sense that the family, the state, and the economy are interconnected. The public and the private are both, emphatically and necessarily, involved in the 'unfolding history of global culture in the making' that formal empire aided so substantially.[30] Studies of women in particular provided a more full-bodied picture of the totality of an Imperial society, the nature of which would be incomprehensible if half the population were omitted. As Joan Wallach Scott noted: 'The realization of the radical potential of women's history comes in the writing of narratives that focus on

[27] Henrietta L. Moore and Megan Vaughan, *Cutting Down Trees: Gender, Nutrition, and Agricultural Change in the Northern Province of Zambia, 1890–1990* (London, 1994), esp. pp. 43, xvii, 72, 78.

[28] For example Joan Sharwood-Smith, *Diary of a Colonial Wife: An African Experience* (London, 1992).

[29] Ronald Hyam, *Empire and Sexuality: The British Experience* (Manchester, 1990), pp. 189–97.

[30] Karen Tranberg Hansen, review of Helen Callaway's *Gender, Culture and Empire: European Women in Colonial Nigeria* (London, 1987), in *Signs* (Summer 1989), p. 934.

women's experience *and* analyze the ways in which politics construct gender and gender constructs politics.'[31] In the 1980s and 1990s feminist scholars saw the work and identity of British women as fundamentally related to the purpose of British imperialism, even though women had been relegated to more private roles than men.

The first studies of gender within the context of the British Empire targeted the 'myth of the destructive female'. This 'myth' held that the arrival of white women in the colonies was responsible for the decay of Empire—specifically, for the drawing of increasingly rigid boundaries between colonizer and colonized. In the words of L. H. Gann and Peter Duignan: 'It was the cheap steamship ticket for women that put an end to racial integration.'[32] The champions of this view tend usually to be nameless, or non-academics such as film director David Lean or novelist Somerset Maugham. But as Ronald Hyam recognized in his controversial book *Empire and Sexuality*—despite his attack on 'humourless' feminist scholars 'fundamentally hostile to sex'—no credible historian could endorse the cruder versions of making the memsahib into a scapegoat: 'she did what she was told [by men], performed the role required of her.' The 'myth of the destructive female' provoked studies defending the welfare-and-development work carried out by white women in the colonies.[33] Some wrote in praise of the empathetic relationships women developed with the colonized.[34] While these studies may seem defensive, they demonstrate that white women did comply with colonial rule, although they sometimes resisted it, as did Annie Besant in her declared support for Indian home rule in 1917.[35] Western women did not destroy the Empire, contrary to Lean's and Maugham's implications.[36] Rather, many British women joined enthusiastically in the ideological work of maintaining it.[37] In much the same way, early nationalist studies of the heroic resistance were exposed. The view

[31] Joan Wallach Scott, 'Women in History: The Modern Period', *P&P*, CI (1983), pp. 141–57.

[32] L. H. Gann and Peter Duignan, *The Rulers of British Africa, 1870–1914* (Stanford, Calif., 1978), p. 242.

[33] Hyam, *Empire and Sexuality*, pp. 17–18, 208.

[34] Claudia Knapman, *White Women in Fiji, 1835–1930: The Ruin of Empire?* (Sydney, 1986); Janice Brownfoot, 'Sisters under the Skin: Imperialism and the Emancipation of Women in Malaya, c.1891–1941', in J. A. Mangan, ed., *Making Imperial Mentalities: Socialization and British Imperialism* (Manchester, 1900); Callaway, *Gender, Culture, and Empire*.

[35] Nancy L. Paxton, 'Complicity and Resistance in the Writings of Flora Annie Steel and Annie Besant', in Nupur Chaudhuri and Margaret Strobel, eds., *Western Women and Imperialism: Complicity and Resistance* (Bloomington, Ind., 1992).

[36] Margaret Strobel, *European Women and the Second British Empire* (Bloomington, Ind., 1991).

[37] Antoinette Burton, *Burdens of History: British Feminists, Indian Women, and Imperial Culture, 1865–1915* (Chapel Hill, NC, 1994), argues that British feminism was shaped by its Imperial context as British women claimed equality with British men by demonstrating their concern for 'the Indian woman'. For another aspect of the ideological significance of women and Empire, see Anna Davin, 'Imperialism and Motherhood', *History Workshop: A Journal of Socialist Historians*, V (1978), pp. 9–65.

that British feminists had unambiguously resisted Imperialist racism or their own subordination proved impossible to sustain.

A similar trajectory, from the defence of victims of historical amnesia to an assertion of their strengths, may be seen in studies of indigenous women under colonial rule. In the 1970s some scholars focused on the ways that the laws of the colonial state and the forces of foreign capitalism maintained or were partly responsible for the low status of native women. Subsequent studies have noted that their status had tended to be inferior even in pre-colonial patriarchies and that colonialism modified, rather than created, that status.[38] Others have written about the enthusiasm with which some colonized women, Nairobi prostitutes for example, embraced the opportunities for economic independence and gain that colonial rule provided.[39] The *Subaltern Studies* series, seeking to give voice to those excluded from more traditional history-writing, included women in its remit and drew attention to the role of Indian women in the development of Indian nationalism.[40] It was also noted that Indian nationalists depicted Indian women as symbols of India, and tried to defend them and their domestic sphere from British control, thereby continuing Indian patriarchy. The subaltern (a term drawn from Gramsci) perspective sometimes aimed to free the history of the former colonial world from a nationalist 'meta-narrative' constructed in élite and primarily masculine terms.[41] In so doing, authors also hoped to liberate the past of post-colonial peoples from the grip of regimes they were ceasing to regard as legitimate.

From the 1970s gender has joined class and race to complete the trio of strands that, in the lexicon of scholars, determine one's identity. In the context of Empire, the pattern woven with these three strands is particularly complex. As the Imperial enterprise developed, the boundaries of masculinity and femininity were drawn with greater rigidity and were often bitterly contested. Some historians have explained the increasingly ardent policing of appropriate Imperial male and female behaviour by emphasizing the malaise that was growing to plague the

[38] Claire Robertson and Iris Berger, eds., *Women and Class in Africa* (New York, 1986); Belinda Bozzoli, 'Marxism, Feminism and South African Studies', *Journal of Southern African Studies*, IX, 2 (1983), pp. 139–71; Elizabeth Schmidt, *Peasants, Traders and Wives: Shona Women in the History of Zimbabwe, 1870–1939* (London, 1992).

[39] Luise White, *The Comforts of Home: Prostitution in Colonial Nairobi* (Chicago, 1990).

[40] The series (OUP, Delhi) has been criticized for its neglect of gender, though one of its founding members, Partha Chatterjee, has an article ('The Nationalist Resolution of the Women's Question') on gender and Indian nationalism in Kumkum Sangari and Sudesh Vaid, eds., *Recasting Women: Essays in Indian Colonial History* (New Brunswick, NJ, 1990), pp. 233–53. See also his 'Colonialism, Nationalism and Colonialized Women: The Contest in India', *American Ethnologist*, XVI, 4 (1989), pp. 622–33.

[41] Frederick Cooper, 'Conflict and Connection: Rethinking Colonial African History', *American Historical Review*, LXLIX, 5 (1994), pp. 1516–45.

whole endeavour. One noted 'the correspondence between rationalized rule, bourgeois respectability and the custodial power of European women to protect their men seems strongest during the inter-war years, when Western scientific and technological achievements were then in question, and native nationalist and labor movements were hard pressing their demands'.[42] Others have depicted sexual jealousy between white and brown men as the force that transformed British class snobbery into racial attitudes.[43] Writers have generally assumed an intimate relationship between sex and racism. This pairing, for example, showed itself in the portrayal of some colonized men as feminine. This was a strong theme in British depictions of some Indian men, and the critique was often internalized by Indians: Gandhi observed in 1938, when discussing European doctors, 'we have become deprived of self-control and have become effeminate'.[44] Imperialism was, in short, so powerful that it could make some men feel as if colonized men had lost their gender.[45] Not surprisingly, male Imperial subjects began to reconstruct ideas of masculinity in response. Thus the significance and complexity of gender in the context of Empire has invited scholars to understand gender as a creation of social and political circumstances rather than as a biological given, and to see how critical it was in the interaction between colonized and colonizer.

By the mid-1990s studies of Empire were published by scholars who were not, strictly speaking, historians, but students of comparative literature or 'cultural studies'. Their sources included literary texts, the work of Kipling, for example, and even such talismans of popular culture as advertising. The questions often focused on the issue of identity or 'difference' within the Imperial context. What were the origins of people's feelings about their own gender, class, and race? Anne McClintock, in *Imperial Leather*, addressed this question by fusing psychoanalysis (especially Sigmund Freud's ideas on paranoia, anxiety, and fetish) with material

[42] Ann Laura Stoler, 'Making Empire Respectable: The Politics of Race and Sexual Morality in Twentieth-Century Colonial Cultures', *American Ethnologist*, XVI (1989), pp. 634–60, esp. p. 652; 'Rethinking Colonial Categories: European Communities and the Boundaries of Rule', *Comparative Studies in Society and History*, XIII, 1 (1989), pp. 134–61; and 'Carnal Knowledge and Imperial Power: Gender, Race and Morality in Colonial Asia', in Micaela di Leonardo, ed., *Gender at the Crossroads of Knowledge: Feminist Anthropology in a Postmodern Era* (Berkeley, 1991), pp. 51–101. See also Diana Jeater, *Marriage, Perversion, and Power: The Construction of Moral Discourse in Southern Rhodesia, 1894–1930* (Oxford, 1993).

[43] Kenneth Ballhatchet, *Race, Sex and Class under the Raj: Imperial Attitudes and their Critics, 1793–1905* (London, 1980), pp. 115, 121.

[44] Quoted in Arnold, *Colonizing the Body*, p. 287.

[45] Mrinalini Sinha, *Colonial Masculinity: The 'Manly Englishman' and the 'Effeminate Bengali' in the Late Nineteenth Century* (Manchester, 1995). See also David D. Gilmore, *Manhood in the Making: Cultural Concepts of Masculinity* (New Haven, 1990), and J. A. Mangan and James Walvin, eds., *Manliness and Morality: Middle-Class Masculinity in Britain and America, 1800–1940* (Manchester, 1987).

history in an explicit attempt to address the 'widespread epochal crisis in the idea of linear, historical progress'. Instead of joining what she terms 'the grand march of Western historicism and its entourage of binaries (self–other, metropolis–economy, center–periphery)' she chooses to examine the shifting but indissoluble relationships between gender, race, and class that shaped the Imperial endeavour.[46] Other scholars have criticized this focus on the politics of meaning: it pays, they argue, so little attention to policy issues and institutions that 'medium-term political change' and its impact on people's lives remain unexplained.[47] Post-modernists may also be faulted for refusing to 'privileg[e] one category over the others as the organizing trope' and, in the process, losing a grip on simple clarity.[48] By the late twentieth century scholars were disputing how much importance to give to gender as opposed to race and class as analytical categories.[49] The Empire offered fertile ground for waging this debate.

Historians of the 1990s note the ways that science and medicine were used by colonialists to define the identities of men and women as well as races. They observe the complexity of the justifications of hierarchies within the Empire. They have thus torn apart those categories to see how they were devised and what function they fulfilled, and have demonstrated the indirect and hidden way that power operates, especially in the guise of medical and scientific forms of knowledge, and in assertion of supposed 'natural' differences. In the process, Imperial history has become increasingly broader in its reach and linked with a range of worldwide intellectual interests which have greatly enriched it.

[46] Anne McClintock, *Imperial Leather: Race, Gender and Sexuality in the Colonial Contest* (New York, 1995), pp. 10–11.

[47] For example, Susan Pedersen, 'Women's History Meets the History of Empire: Some Problems of the Encounter', Plenary Lecture, 64th Anglo-American Conference of Historians, London, 28–30 June, 1995.

[48] McClintock, *Imperial Leather*, p. 8.

[49] Chandra Talpade Mohanty, Ann Russo, and Lourdes Torres, eds., *Third World Women and the Politics of Feminism* (Bloomington, Ind., 1991).

Select Bibliography

DAVID ARNOLD, ed., *Imperial Medicine and Indigenous Societies* (Manchester, 1988).

—— *Colonizing the Body: State Medicine and Epidemic Disease in Nineteenth-Century India* (Berkeley, 1993).

ANTOINETTE BURTON, *Burdens of History: British Feminists, Indian Women, and Imperial Culture, 1865–1915* (Chapel Hill, NC, 1994).

NUPUR CHAUDHURI and MARGARET STROBEL, eds., *Western Women and Imperialism: Complicity and Resistance* (Bloomington, Ind., 1992).

PHILIP D. CURTIN, *Death by Migration: Europe's Encounter with the Tropical World in the Nineteenth Century* (Cambridge, 1989).

TIM DYSON, ed., *India's Historical Demography: Studies in Famine, Disease and Society* (London, 1989).

STEVEN FEIERMAN and JOHN M. JANZEN, eds., *The Social Basis of Health and Healing in Africa* (Berkeley, 1992).

JOHN FORD, *The Role of the Trypanosomiases in African Ecology: A Study of the Tsetse Fly Problem* (Oxford, 1971).

DIANA JEATER, *Marriage, Perversion and Power: The Construction of Moral Discourse in Southern Rhodesia, 1894–1930* (Oxford, 1993).

MICHELLE BURGE MCALPIN, *Subject to Famine: Food Crises and Economic Change in Western India, 1860–1920* (Princeton, 1983).

ROY MACLEOD and MILTON LEWIS, eds., *Disease, Medicine, and Empire: Perspectives on Western Medicine and the Experience of European Expansion* (London, 1988).

HENRIETTA L. MOORE and MEGAN VAUGHAN, *Cutting down Trees: Gender, Nutrition, and Agricultural Change in the Northern Province of Zambia, 1890–1990* (London, 1994).

ROBERT I. ROTBERG, ed., *Imperialism, Colonialism and Hunger: East and Central Africa* (Lexington, Mass., 1983).

KUMKUM SANGARI and SUDESH VAID, *Recasting Women: Essays in Indian Colonial History* (New Brunswick, NJ, 1990).

MRINALINI SINHA, *Colonial Masculinity: The 'Manly Englishman' and the 'Effeminate Bengali' in the Late Nineteenth Century* (Manchester, 1995).

ANN LAURA STOLER, 'Making Empire Respectable: The Politics of Race and Sexual Morality in Twentieth-Century Colonial Cultures', *American Ethnologist*, XVI (1989), pp. 634–60.

MEGAN VAUGHAN, *The Story of an African Famine: Gender and Famine in Twentieth-Century Malawi* (Cambridge, 1987).

—— *Curing their Ills: Colonial Power and African Illness* (Stanford, Calif., 1991).

MICHAEL WATTS, *Silent Violence: Food, Famine and Peasantry in Northern Nigeria* (Berkeley, 1983).

18

Exploration and Empire

ROBERT A. STAFFORD

The historiography of British exploration began in 1589, with Richard Hakluyt's *Principal Navigations*.[1] This epic compendium constituted a paean to risk-taking in the national interest via overseas exploration, colonization, and trade. As the seminal effort from the age of Shakespeare and the King James Bible, it influenced all subsequent literature in the genre. The derivative Purchas's *Pilgrims*, for example, the only significant work of the seventeenth century, continued in the same vein.[2] Eighteenth-century works, reflecting the *philosophe's* encyclopaedic zeal for classification, chronicled further voyages, illustrating the behaviour of explorers as well as the maturation of cartography and long-distance sailing techniques.[3] Authors were not historians, but men such as the hydrographer Alexander Dalrymple, with a professional interest in what would coalesce into the discipline of geography. During this era the exploration narrative was established as an influential literary genre through first hand accounts such as those of Mungo Park and James Bruce. These works rendered histories irrelevant until explorers' deaths or attempts to extend their discoveries inspired secondary evaluation based on national interest as much as support for science.[4] Some popular works, such as William Desborough Cooley's, went further, disparaging French activities and advocating extensions of British colonization.[5] Cooley is the first major author of a history of exploration who can be described as a professional geographer; his support for Empire indicates the discipline's roots in Imperial affairs.

The nineteenth century also saw the development of a new genre of biography lauding England's early explorers.[6] The Hakluyt Society, an offshoot of the Royal

[1] Richard Hakluyt, *The Principal Navigations*, 8 vols. (London, 1589; repr. 1907).

[2] Samuel Purchas, *Purchas his Pilgrimes or Relations of the World and the Religions Observed in all Ages*, 4 vols. (London, 1625).

[3] e.g. Alexander Dalrymple, *An Historical Collection of the Several Voyages and Discoveries in the South Pacific Ocean*, 2 vols. (London, 1770–71, facs. edn., Amsterdam, 1967).

[4] F. B. Head, *The Life of Bruce, the African Traveller* (London, 1830; 3rd edn., 1838); John Barrow, *A Chronological History of the Voyages into the Arctic Regions* (London, 1818).

[5] W. D. Cooley, *The History of Maritime and Inland Discovery*, 3 vols. (London, 1831).

[6] e.g. Edward Edwards, *The Life of Sir Walter Raleigh*, 2 vols. (London, 1868).

Geographical Society (RGS) founded in 1846, extended this trend by publishing obscure accounts of early explorations that might contain valuable information or revive patriotic interest. Contemporary explorers who died on their quests, such as Sir John Franklin, inspired hagiographic works emphasizing the nation's exploring tradition.[7] Chronicles of exploration in specific colonies also began to appear. Such works were pro-development and based on published narratives and interviews with pioneers.[8] An interesting aspect of this trend towards colonials documenting their own exploratory efforts was explorers writing biographies of their predecessors in order to maintain momentum and public support.[9] On behalf of India, Clements Markham publicized the results of the various surveys carried out by the Raj. Geographer to the India Office and future President of the RGS, Markham emphasized how mapping bolstered British rule.[10]

As British exploration boomed during the 1850s and 1860s under the aegis of RGS President Sir Roderick Murchison, explorers' narratives (especially David Livingstone's) sold in unprecedented numbers. When Livingstone died, his published journals and semi-official biography sold nearly as well.[11] The message of these posthumous publications was to carry on Livingstone's work; some children's books explicitly connected his explorations and subsequent annexations.[12] Biographies of other explorers similarly suggested that their achievements should be emulated in the national interest.[13] In 1881 Markham wrote a patriotic and pro-Empire history of the RGS to commemorate its fiftieth year.[14] Contemporary popular histories of exploration by colonial authors lauded achievements, pointed out remaining work to be accomplished, and linked discovery to progress and prosperity.[15] In the 1890s imperial rivalry in Africa brought an increase not only in histories of the continent's exploration that beat the expansionist drum,[16] but also in geographical works that linked exploration to systematic plans for European development.[17] Some of these works, such as Sir John Scott Keltie's, were influenced by celebrities actively involved in furthering

7 Sherard Osborn, *The Career, Last Voyage, and Fate of Captain Sir John Franklin* (London, 1860).

8 William Howitt, *The History of Discovery in Australia, Tasmania, and New Zealand*, 2 vols. (London, 1865).

9 Hamilton Hume, *The Life of Edward John Eyre: Late Governor of Jamaica* (London, 1867).

10 Clements R. Markham, *Memoir on the Indian Surveys* (London, 1871).

11 Horace Waller, *The Last Journals of David Livingstone*, 2 vols. (London, 1874); William Blaikie, *The Life of David Livingstone* (London, 1880; 6th edn., 1910).

12 Vautier Golding, *The Story of David Livingstone* (London, n.d.).

13 e.g. Francis Hitchman, *Richard F. Burton*, 2 vols. (London, 1887).

14 Clements R. Markham, *The Fifty Years' Work of the Royal Geographical Society* (London, 1881).

15 George Grimm, *The Australian Explorers: Their Labours, Perils and Achievements* (Melbourne, 1888).

16 Robert Brown, *The Story of Africa and its Explorers*, 4 vols. (London, 1892).

17 Arthur Silva White, *The Development of Africa* (London, 1890).

British influence in Africa.[18] Geography was simultaneously emerging as a professional discipline: with primary exploration nearly completed, logic suggested that geographers could best demonstrate their utility during the Scramble for Africa by planning its exploitation.

The geographers also promoted their discipline through histories and biographies. Keltie co-edited a series that included contributions by Joseph Thomson on Mungo Park and Harry Johnston on Livingstone.[19] Here, made manifest, was the symbiotic relationship between exploration, Empire, and history (explorers who were agents of Empire writing studies of their predecessors' work in order to legitimize control through continuity, and to school the next generation to maintain commitment). Histories also began to emerge of English exploratory, trading, and diplomatic activity in other zones of imperial rivalry such as Persia. Again, these works were expansionist, often authored by men with a direct interest in the Indian Empire.[20] The 1890s also saw the emergence of a new school of 'scientific' history, first deployed to find authentic documents regarding early voyages and travels.[21] Other scholars used new archival sources to redefine early figures such as Drake in larger roles.[22] As imperialism peaked as a political, economic, and cultural phenomenon, it attracted a proportionate share of literary attention, much of which was expressed through popular history and biography that promoted exploration as one facet of national expansion. In Canada, an official history of the Hudson's Bay Company argued that the fur traders were the pioneers of civilization in the Far West.[23] The ubiquitous Keltie advised the author of the century's most comprehensive history of exploration[24] and edited the 'Story of Exploration' series. From India, the surveyor Thomas Holdich contributed several works on Himalayan exploration that argued for an aggressive forward policy.[25]

Antarctica now added a new element to this historiography. While not an imperial frontier, its exploration nevertheless exhibited all of the features of national competitiveness associated with zones of direct imperial rivalry. As reconnaissance of this last unknown continent accelerated toward the dramatic race for the South Pole that claimed Robert Scott's life in 1912, an increasing number of works appeared.[26] Reinterpretation of the great maritime explorers of the

[18] John Scott Keltie, *The Partition of Africa* (London, 1893; 2nd edn., 1895).

[19] Joseph Thomson, *Mungo Park and the Niger* (London, 1890); Harry H. Johnston, *Livingstone and the Exploration of Central Africa* (London, 1891).

[20] e.g. George N. Curzon, *Persia and the Persian Question*, 2 vols. (London, 1892).

[21] Henry Harrisse, *The Discovery of North America* (London, 1892; repr. Amsterdam, 1961).

[22] Julian S. Corbett, *Drake and the Tudor Navy*, 2 vols. (London, 1898).

[23] Beckles Willson, *The Great Company (1667–1871)*, 2 vols. (Toronto, 1900).

[24] C. G. D. Roberts, *Discoveries and Explorations in the Century* (Edinburgh, 1906).

[25] Thomas Holdich, *The Indian Borderland, 1880–1900* (London, 1901).

[26] e.g. H. R. Mill, *The Siege of the South Pole* (London, 1905).

past continued.[27] Canadian historians, like their American counterparts, began in this era to produce solid scholarship on westward exploration that nevertheless celebrated explorers as heroic harbingers of progress.[28] Australian historians too began an important new trend by examining the relationship between the work of Sir Joseph Banks as a metropolitan promoter of exploration and the colonization of Australia.[29] As the Great War began, Ernest Scott commenced his extended project of rewriting the history of Australian exploration with a biography of Matthew Flinders.[30] After the war G. Arnold Wood issued his classic survey *The Discovery of Australia*.[31] Meanwhile a general history of New Zealand's exploration aired new material culled from obscure sources.[32] In 1921, Clements Markham's posthumous study of polar exploration contributed a comprehensive account, despite its nationalism and melodrama.[33] The 1920s also brought revision of Victorian biographies of Elizabethans, and Hakluyt himself became the subject of a masterful biography.[34]

The history of African exploration also began to be reinterpreted as family papers became available, but the results were often still shot through with racism and ideas of progress.[35] The history of maritime exploration was advanced by bibliographical work on Cook, documents on early English voyages to North America, and the first biography of Vancouver.[36] Elizabeth Taylor's work on Tudor and Stuart geography defined the milieu in which early voyages were conceived and promoted.[37] Literature on Robert Scott now poured fourth: this generation too needed a champion. The dearth of unexplored lands made it perhaps appropriate that the bleakest of all should form the stage for the macabre final act of British exploratory drama. Here were duty and heroism wasted in an endeavour not worth the sacrifice (as if, in a prelude to the Great War, they had

[27] e.g. Arthur Kitson, *Captain James Cook, R.N., F.R.S., 'The Circumnavigator'* (London, 1907); Edward Heawood, *A History of Geographical Discovery in the Seventeenth and Eighteenth Centuries* (Cambridge, 1912; repr. New York, 1965).

[28] Lawrence J. Burpee, *The Search for the Western Sea* (London, 1908).

[29] J. H. Maiden, *Sir Joseph Banks: The 'Father of Australia'* (Sydney, 1909).

[30] Ernest Scott, *The Life of Captain Matthew Flinders, R.N.* (Sydney, 1914).

[31] G. Arnold Wood, *The Discovery of Australia* (London, 1922; revised edn., Melbourne, 1969).

[32] John Elder, *The Pioneer Explorers of New Zealand* (London, 1929).

[33] Clements R. Markham, *The Lands of Silence: A History of Arctic and Antarctic Exploration* (Cambridge, 1921).

[34] e.g. Henry Wagner, *Sir Francis Drake's Voyage Around the World* (San Francisco, 1926); George Bruner Parks, *Richard Hakluyt and the English Voyages* (New York, 1928; 2nd edn., 1961).

[35] R. Coupland, *Kirk on the Zambesi* (Oxford, 1928).

[36] Merle Beddie, ed., *Bibliography of Captain James Cook* (Sydney, 1928; 2nd edn., 1970); James A. Williamson, *The Voyages of the Cabots and English Discovery of North America Under Henry VII and Henry VIII* (London, 1929); George Godwin, *Vancouver, A Life, 1757–1798* (London, 1930).

[37] E. G. R. Taylor, *Tudor Geography, 1485–1583* (London, 1930) and *Late Tudor and Early Stuart Geography, 1583–1650* (New York, 1934; 2nd edn., 1968).

become dangerously outworn forms).[38] In 1930 Hugh Mill produced an authoritative centenary history of the RGS; in the following year J. N. L. Baker published the first comprehensive history of exploration (still the best overall survey).[39] Measured and objective, Baker also evinced pride in British accomplishments and satisfaction at the forestalling of imperial rivals. The following year women entered exploration historiography with the first biography of Mary Kingsley.[40] The year 1933 saw publication of the antipodean volume of the *Cambridge History of the British Empire*: J. A. Williamson discussed the probability of a pre-Cook Portuguese discovery of eastern Australia,[41] while Ernest Scott emphasized that geographical discovery destroyed the convict system and stockmen rivalled explorers in revealing the interior.[42]

Geographers, meanwhile, discussed exploration as an aspect of their discipline's historical development.[43] John Bartlet Brebner advanced the concept of continental design in rival imperial strategies of exploration in North America.[44] Sir Percy Sykes emphasized adventure and glorified British achievements in his general history.[45] J. C. Beaglehole examined British efforts in the Pacific in the context of other nation's contributions, and Rupert Gould's masterly short biography of Cook soon followed.[46] The best general history of Arctic exploration to date demonstrated that the 'decolonization' of exploration's history was beginning in the most marginal areas.[47] Exploration scholarship now deepened as well as broadened, examining the literary influence of explorers' narratives.[48] The inter-war years offered a curious mix, therefore, of works supporting the Imperial status quo and others opening up new perspectives that, deliberately or not, subverted it. This spectrum

[38] Stephen Gwynn, *Captain Scott* (London, 1929).

[39] H. R. Mill, *The Record of the Royal Geographical Society, 1830–1930* (London, 1930); J. N. L. Baker, *A History of Geographical Discovery and Exploration* (London, 1931; revised edn., New York, 1967).

[40] Stephen Gwynn, *The Life of Mary Kingsley* (London, 1932).

[41] J. A. Williamson, 'The Exploration of the Pacific', in E. A. Benians and others, eds., *The Cambridge History of the British Empire* (hereafter *CHBE*), Vol. VII, pt. I, *Australia* (Cambridge, 1933), pp. 25–53, at pp. 32–33, 49.

[42] Ernest Scott, 'The Extension of Settlement', in *CHBE*, VI, pp. 94–120; and 'The Exploration of Australia', ibid., pp. 121–145.

[43] R. E. Dickensen and O. J. R. Howarth, *The Making of Geography* (Oxford, 1933).

[44] John Bartlet Brebner, *The Explorers of North America, 1492–1806* (London, 1933; 2nd edn., 1964).

[45] Percy Sykes, *A History of Exploration from the Earliest Times to the Present Day* (New York, 1934; 4th edn., 1961).

[46] J. C. Beaglehole, *The Exploration of the Pacific* (Stanford, Calif., 1934; 3rd edn., 1966); Rupert T. Gould, *Captain Cook* (London, 1935; 2nd edn., 1978).

[47] Jeannette Mirsky, *To the Arctic! The Story of Northrn Exploration* (Chicago, 1934; 3rd edn., 1970).

[48] Willard Bonner, *Captain William Dampier: Buccaneer-Author* (Stanford, Calif., 1934); Robert Cawley, *The Voyagers and Elizabethan Drama* (London, 1938).

was further complicated by evolving colonial identities and aspirations. The first full history of Australia's Burke and Wills Expedition, for example, was undercut by its hero-worshipping tone and semi-novelized treatment.[49] In 1939 the New Zealand government began a series of 'Centennial Surveys', including brief studies by Beaglehole on maritime discovery and W. G. McClymont on terrestrial exploration.[50] Reginald Coupland, motivated beyond scholarship by desire to stop an East African giveaway in the name of appeasement, presented John Kirk, botanist to Livingstone's Zambezi Expedition and later Consul-General in Zanzibar, as a champion of British interests and the anti-slavery movement.[51] The third volume of the *Cambridge History of the British Empire* implied that Britain's exploration of the Niger, Nile, and Zambezi rivers justified subsequent annexation of their drainages.[52] During the Second World War J. P. R. Wallis wrote a biography of Thomas Baines, artist on the Zambezi Expedition and the previous North Australian Exploring Expedition.[53] Wallis here began the task of raising the status of second-rank explorers, and righting the wrongs done by Livingstone to his subordinates.

In post-war Australia maritime exploration and hydrographic charting received specialized treatment for the first time.[54] Histories of inland exploration continued to laud heroics and promote development.[55] Biographies of hitherto-untreated Australian explorers emphasized their contributions to nation-building.[56] The centenary of the Hakluyt Society inspired a study of the exploration genre in historical literature,[57] while George Seaver's *Scott of the Antarctic* broke new ground as a pseudo-psychological study.[58] New work on Joseph Banks extended knowledge of his central role in promoting exploration and empire.[59] Mountaineering also received treatment

49 Frank Clune, *Dig: The Burke and Wills Saga*, 3rd edn. (Sydney, 1937).

50 J. C. Beaglehole, *The Discovery of New Zealand* (Wellington, 1939; 2nd edn., London, 1961); W. G. McClymont, *The Exploration of New Zealand* (Wellington, 1940).

51 R. Coupland, *The Exploitation of East Africa, 1856–1890: The Slave Trade and the Scramble* (London, 1939; 2nd edn., Evanston, Ill., 1967).

52 Edward Heawood, 'The Exploration of Africa, 1783–1870', in J. Holland Rose and others, eds., *CHBE*, Vol. II, *The Growth of the New Empire, 1783–1870* (Cambridge, 1940), pp. 615–32.

53 J. P .R. Wallis, *Thomas Baines of King's Lynn: Explorer and Artist, 1820–1875* (London, 1941; repr. Cape Town, 1976).

54 Geoffrey C. Ingleton, *Charting a Continent* (Sydney, 1944).

55 Geoffrey Rawson, *Desert Journeys: An Account of the Arduous Exploration of the Interior of the Continent of Australia by Rival Expeditions in 1873–4* (London, 1948).

56 e.g. Keith Bowden, *George Bass, 1771–1803* (Melbourne, 1952).

57 Edward Lynam, ed., *Richard Hakluyt and his Successors* (London, 1946).

58 George Seaver, *Scott of the Antarctic: A Study in Character* (London, 1940).

59 Hector Cameron, *Sir Joseph Banks, K.B., P.R.S., the Autocrat of the Philosophers* (London, 1952); Warren Dawson, ed., *The Banks Letters* (London, 1958).

as a sub-genre of exploration,[60] while central Asian exploration was linked by popularizers with Imperial activity.[61] The mid-1950s marked the start of a long spate of scholarship on Livingstone, including publication of a new biography.[62] Historians of cartography illuminated the map as a heuristic tool, while atlases of exploration illustrated the shifting frontier between the known and unknown.[63] Andrew Sharp detailed the discoveries of exploring voyages in the Pacific; Beaglehole's edition of Banks's *Endeavour* journal demonstrated that a full biography of the great naturalist was required.[64] In the early 1960s analysis of the impact of African exploration appeared, as did studies on neglected explorers such as Barth.[65] Moorehead's histories of Nile exploration reawakened popular interest, and he soon performed a similar service for Australia.[66] New scholarship also supported a Bristol-based discovery of North America in the 1480s and illumined the quest for the North-west Passage.[67] Biographies of key explorers now divided between those attempting psychoanalysis and those hewing to traditional treatment.[68] Works examining the promotion of exploration continued to trickle forth, as did others analysing the achievements of subordinates such as Richard Thornton, the geologist on Livingstone's Zambezi Expedition.[69] J. H. Parry emphasized the connections between science, exploration, and trade in the activities of rival European nations.[70]

Dorothy Middleton pioneered work on women explorers in the 1960s,[71] and a valuable bibliography enriched Antarctic studies.[72] Australian explorers' biographies were divided between scholarly efforts, works of piety by descendants, and

[60] Ronald Clark, *The Victorian Mountaineers* (London, 1953).

[61] e.g. Kenneth Mason, *Abode of Snow: A History of Himalayan Exploration and Mountaineering* (London, 1955).

[62] George Seaver, *David Livingstone: His Life and Letters* (New York, 1957).

[63] R. A. Skelton, *Explorers' Maps* (London, 1958; 2nd edn. 1970); Frank Debenham, *Discovery and Exploration: An Atlas-History of Man's Wanderings* (New York, 1960).

[64] Andrew Sharp, *The Discovery of the Pacific Islands* (Oxford, 1960); J. C. Beaglehole, ed., *The Endeavour Journals of Joseph Banks, 1768–1771*, 2 vols. (Sydney, 1962).

[65] Richard Gray, *A History of the Southern Sudan, 1839–1889* (Oxford, 1961); A. H. M. Kirk-Greene, ed., *Barth's Travels in Nigeria* (London, 1962).

[66] Alan Moorehead, *The White Nile* (London, 1960), *The Blue Nile*, 1st edn. (London, 1962), and *Cooper's Creek* (Melbourne, 1963).

[67] James A. Williamson, *The Cabot Voyages and Bristol Discovery Under Henry VII* (Cambridge, 1962); Glyndwr Williams, *The British Search for the Northwest Passage in the Eighteenth Century* (London, 1962).

[68] Cf. Byron Farwell, *Burton* (London, 1963), and Fawn Brodie, *The Devil Drives: A Life of Sir Richard Burton* (New York, 1967).

[69] Robin Hallett, ed., *Records of the African Association for Promoting the Discovery of the Interior Parts of Africa, 1788–1831* (London, 1964); Edward Tabler, ed., *The Zambesi Papers of Richard Thornton*, 2 vols. (London, 1963).

[70] J. H. Parry, *The Age of Reconnaissance* (Berkeley, 1963; repr. 1981).

[71] Dorothy Middleton, *Victorian Lady Travellers* (London, 1965).

[72] S. A. Spence, *Antarctic Miscellany* (London, 1966; 2nd edn., 1980).

sycophantic books that praised explorers as national father figures.[73] Edward Eyre was at last examined objectively as a test case of an explorer reacting to an administrative emergency.[74] Again, the trend was toward psychological analysis, and deconstructing the myths that surrounded most explorers. Livingstone had escaped treatment in Lytton Strachey's *Eminent Victorians* because of his status as a martyr. Since then, he had only been examined tangentially, but as wholesale questioning of received values spread, decolonization proceeded, and the statues of imperialists were pulled down throughout newly liberated Africa, even Livingstone proved too tall an icon not to topple or tarnish. He was now interrogated objectively, if not critically, and his character judged.[75]

Revisionist Canadian historians began to break down the myth of a titanic imperial struggle for North America, dethroning explorers as agents of expansion in favour of traders.[76] Africa was the focus of the 1970s, however, as historians such as Robert I. Rotberg redefined explorers as precursors rather than progenitors of imperialism.[77] Popular historians of African exploration also helped smash monolithic stereotypes.[78] Peter Brent's re-examination of Mungo Park provided one of the best discussions of exploration as a cultural activity in print.[79] Yet the most startling feature of African exploration historiography in the 1970s was a direct attack on Livingstone. Tim Jeal's biography exploded the myth of the martyred saint, revealing Livingstone as a paradoxical character who failed in most of his endeavours but was influential as a prophet of annexation and theoretician of colonial policy.[80] Jeal's critical assessment was followed by Judith Listowel's more tendentious work on Livingstone's suppression of associates' work.[81] The first study of the role of Africans in exploration highlighted the dependence of Europeans on native knowledge.[82] The National Library of Scotland also produced a comprehensive catalogue of documents related to Livingstone.[83]

[73] James Mack, *Matthew Flinders, 1774–1814* (Melbourne, 1966); Adelaide Lubbock, *Owen Stanley, R.N., 1811–1850* (Melbourne, 1967); Michael Langley, *Sturt of the Murray* (London, 1969).

[74] Bernard Semmel, *The Governor Eyre Controversy* (London, 1962); Geoffrey Dutton, *The Hero as Murderer: The Life of Edward John Eyre, Australian Explorer and Governor of Jamaica, 1815–1901* (Sydney, 1967).

[75] George Martell, *Livingstone's River: A History of the Zambezi Expedition, 1858–1864* (New York, 1969).

[76] W. J. Eccles, *The Canadian Frontier, 1534–1760* (New York, 1969).

[77] Robert I. Rotberg, ed., *Africa and its Explorers: Motives, Methods and Impact* (Cambridge, Mass., 1970).

[78] e.g. Timothy Severin, *The African Adventure: A History of Africa's Explorers* (London, 1973).

[79] Peter Brent, *Black Nile: Mungo Park and the Search for the Niger* (London, 1977).

[80] Tim Jeal, *Livingstone* (New York, 1973).

[81] Judith Listowel, *The Other Livingstone* (Lewes, 1974).

[82] Donald Simpson, *Dark Companions* (London, 1975).

[83] G. W. Clendennen and I. C. Cunningham, *David Livingstone: A Catalogue of Documents* (Edinburgh, 1979).

Works on Asian exploration continued to emphasize trans-Himalayan work directed from India.[84] David B. Quinn capped a distinguished career's work with a survey of early English voyages to North America and *The Hakluyt Handbook*.[85] Beaglehole's magisterial biography of Cook completed another career's research, but Kenneth McIntyre claimed the Portuguese had secretly explored Australia's east coast 200 years earlier.[86] Antarctic works included Elspeth Huxley's portrait of Scott as a self-doubting hero attempting to conquer himself in the Pole, while David Thomson argued that Scott and his officers formed part of a marooned section of English society soon to be destroyed.[87] The effect, as with Livingstone, was the hero overthrown. Of all the explorers, Richard Burton (the most complex and rebellious) fared the best in transition to the age of counter-culture.

A new biography of Sir Francis Beaufort emphasized his leadership in transforming the Admiralty's Hydrographic Office into a premier maritime science centre and his key role, along with Sir John Barrow, as a promoter of scientific projects to the British government between the eras of Banks and Murchison.[88] In Canada, a history of the Geological Survey analysed the crucial role of geologists in exploring and mapping this colony (as many others) before a topographical survey department was established.[89] Australian historians of science, meanwhile, staked their claim to exploration, while Australian cartographic history also advanced.[90] In the late 1970s, however, Australian explorers were also pulled from their pedestals. By destroying Sturt's legend, Edgar Beale revealed the far more complex real man, a tragic, delusion-driven figure who, like Livingstone, was unfair to subordinates.[91] Australian historians subsequently pursued this line of research with a vigour bordering on ferocity, perhaps demonstrating, in the aftermath of the dismissal of Gough Whitlam, the Prime Minister, in 1975, the nation's

[84] e.g. Gerald Morgan, *Ney Elias: Explorer and Envoy Extraordinary in High Asia* (London, 1971); Indra Singh Rawat, *Indian Explorers of the Nineteenth Century* (New Delhi, 1973).

[85] David Beers Quinn, *England and the Discovery of America, 1481–1620* (New York, 1973); D. B. Quinn, ed., *The Hakluyt Handbook*, 2 vols. (London, 1974).

[86] J. C. Beaglehole, *The Life of Captain James Cook* (London, 1974); Kenneth MacIntyre, *The Secret Discovery of Australia* (Medindie, South Australia, 1977).

[87] Elspeth Huxley, *Scott of the Antarctic* (London, 1977); David Thomson, *Scott's Men* (London, 1977).

[88] Alfred Friendly, *Beaufort of the Admiralty: The Life of Sir Francis Beaufort, 1774–1857* (London, 1977).

[89] Morris Zaslow, *Reading the Rocks: The Story of the Geological Survey of Canada, 1842–1972* (Toronto, 1975).

[90] Peter Stansbury, ed., *100 Years of Australian Scientific Explorations* (Sydney, 1975); R. V. Tooley, *The Mapping of Australia* (London, 1979); Thomas Perry, *The Discovery of Australia: The Charts and Maps of the Navigators and Explorers* (Melbourne, 1982).

[91] Edgar Beale, *Sturt, the Chipped Idol* (Sydney, 1979).

need for independence from British sources of authority. In this climate of assertiveness, even Cook was reassessed.[92]

The 1980s opened with a derivative, illustrated history of the RGS celebrating its 150th year.[93] General histories and encyclopaedias of exploration offered narratives, biographies, and technical explanations.[94] Regional histories of exploration in particular colonies linked discovery with pioneer exploitation, tying environmental concern to a shared experience of the land over time, thereby demonstrating that white colonial cultures had matured to the point of incorporating concepts of stewardship.[95] Australian scholars continued to produce detailed biographies as well as specialized studies of particular expeditions.[96] Paul Carter challenged orthodox perspectives by examining landscape as explorers saw and imagined it, before horizons solidified under the imposition of European names and narratives.[97] The 1988 Australian Bicentennial triggered many new works, including a collection of essays on the evolution of speculative geographical theories about the southern continent and Ian McLaren's exhaustive bibliography of Australian exploration.[98] Works on Africa included a general survey,[99] while Antarctica received studies of the voyage of James Clark Ross and the British Antarctic Survey.[100] Scholars of Asia continued to focus on exploration as an aspect of the 'Great Game'.[101] Harold Carter contributed an authoritative biography of Banks, with a comprehensive companion bibliography,[102] and my study of Murchison highlighted the centrality of the successor to Banks and Barrow to the promotion of exploration.[103] Two works on the career of

[92] Robin Fisher and Hugh Johnston, eds., *Captain James Cook and His Times* (Canberra, 1979).

[93] Ian Cameron, *To the Farthest Ends of the Earth: The History of the Royal Geographical Society, 1830–1980* (London, 1980).

[94] Alan Reid, *Discovery and Exploration (A Concise History)* (London, 1980); Helen Delpar, ed., *The Discoverers: An Encyclopedia of Explorers and Exploration* (New York, 1980).

[95] e.g. C. J. Binks, *Explorers of Western Tasmania* (Devonport, Tasmania, 1989).

[96] Colin Roderick, *Leichhardt the Dauntless Explorer* (Sydney, 1988); Russell Braddon, *Thomas Baines and the North Australian Expedition* (Sydney, 1986).

[97] Paul Carter, *The Road to Botany Bay: An Essay in Spacial History* (London, 1987).

[98] Glyndwr Williams and Alan Frost, eds., *Terra Australis to Australia* (Melbourne, 1988); Ian McLaren, *Australian Explorers by Sea, Land and Air, 1788–1988*, 9 vols. (Melbourne, 1988).

[99] Christopher Hibbert, *Africa Explored: Europeans in the Dark Continent, 1769–1889* (London, 1982).

[100] M. J. Ross, *Ross in the Antarctic: The Voyages of James Clark Ross in H.M.S. Erebus and Terror, 1839–1843* (Whitby, Yorkshire, 1982); Vivian Fuchs, *Of Ice and Men: The Story of the British Antarctic Survey, 1943–73* (London, 1982).

[101] Gary Alder, *Beyond Bokhara: The Life of William Moorcroft* (London, 1985); Peter Hopkirk, *The Great Game* (London, 1990); Derek Waller, *The Pundits* (Louisville, Ky., 1990).

[102] Harold Carter, *Sir Joseph Banks (1743–1820): A Guide to Biographical and Bibliographical Sources* (London, 1987) and *Sir Joseph Banks, 1743–1820* (London, 1988).

[103] Robert A. Stafford, *Scientist of Empire: Sir Roderick Murchison, Scientific Exploration, and Victorian Imperialism* (Cambridge, 1989).

Halford Mackinder illustrated how this iconoclastic giant of geography shifted *fin de siècle* perceptions of the discipline from exploration to geopolitics and statecraft. An advocate of Imperial integration whose views remained marginalized in Britain despite the marked influence of his heartland theory abroad, Mackinder, with fitting irony, had previously been ignored by Imperial historians.[104] Valuable works on hitherto-neglected women explorers also appeared, and two new biographies examined Mary Kingsley.[105] James Casada's bibliographical study of Richard Burton set a new standard in evaluating source material on a particular explorer.[106]

The 1990s have seen both the continuation of established trends and new developments. In Australia, a pioneering study of Burke and Wills focused on the explorers' meaning in national culture, while a controversial re-examination of Leichhardt traced the slow development of bushcraft as essential to penetration of the interior.[107] More generally, Michael Jacobs offered an overview of the role of expeditionary artists in influencing European attitudes toward distant lands.[108] James Walvin's examination of the impact of exotic produce on British taste and consumption patterns, inspired by the new school of environmental history, emphasized the complex interrelationship between geography, Imperial conquest, and plantation-based exploitation of tropical crops.[109] Banks's central role as a power-broker between science, exploration, and imperialism was reinforced by scholarship based on his surviving papers.[110] An important study by both geographers and historians re-examined the relationship between geography and imperialism, suggesting fruitful new avenues of research.[111] Perhaps the most telling development of the decade was an outpouring of general works on the history of exploration.[112] It was almost as if the English-speaking world had to reformulate the subject in a popular, condensed form appropriate to the age of information.

[104] W. H. Parker, *Mackinder: Geography as an Aid to Statecraft* (Oxford, 1982); Brian W. Blouet, *Halford Mackinder: A Biography* (College Station, 1987); Wm. Roger Louis, *In the Name of God Go! Leopold Amery and the British Empire in the Age of Churchill* (New York, 1992).

[105] Jane Robinson, *Wayward Women: A Guide to Women Travellers* (Oxford, 1990); Robert Pearce, *Mary Kingsley: Light at the Heart of Darkness* (Oxford, 1990); Dea Birkett, *Mary Kingsley: Imperial Adventuress* (London, 1992).

[106] James A. Casada, *Sir Richard F. Burton: A Bibliographical Study* (London, 1990).

[107] Tim Bonyhady, *Burke and Wills: From Melbourne to Myth* (Balmain, NSW, 1991); Glen McLaren, *Beyond Leichardt: Bushcraft and the Exploration of Australia* (Freemantle, 1996).

[108] Michael Jacobs, *The Painted Voyage: Art, Travel and Exploration, 1564–1875* (London, 1995).

[109] James Walvin, *Fruits of Empire: Exotic Produce and British Taste, 1660–1800* (Basingstoke, 1997).

[110] R. E. R. Banks and others, eds., *Sir Joseph Banks: A Global Perspective* (Kew, 1994).

[111] Morag Bell and others, eds., *Geography and Imperialism, 1820–1940* (Manchester, 1995).

[112] Felipe Fernández-Armesto, *The Times Atlas of World Exploration* (London, 1991); John Keay, *The Royal Geographical Society History of World Exploration* (London, 1991); Robin Hanbury-Tenison, *The Oxford Book of Exploration* (Oxford, 1993).

Such works, usually by explorers themselves rather than historians, typically presented the explorer as a 'disinterested seeker after knowledge' whose work was 'manipulated' by the forces of imperialism.[113] While superficial and occasionally misleading, these works served once more to put the history of exploration before a new generation, and thus to keep it alive in general culture. Population growth and environmental degradation can only increase interest in what were once blank spots on the map and the process by which they were incorporated into Europe's economy and consciousness. Historians, therefore, will no doubt continue to work in the areas of study recently mapped out—regional, environmental, biographical, cultural, spatial, artistic, and organizational. Exploration has always been a complex cultural activity; its history remains so, influenced by changing trends, but continuously deepening our understanding of the motivations and consequences of those most unusual men and women compelled to go where others had not.

[113] Keay, *Royal Geographical Society History*, pp. 10–11.

Select Bibliography

J. N. L. BAKER, *A History of Geographical Discovery and Exploration* (London, 1931; revd edn., New York, 1967).

J. C. BEAGLEHOLE, *The Life of Captain James Cook* (London, 1974).

HAROLD B. CARTER, *Sir Joseph Banks, 1743–1820* (London, 1988).

PAUL CARTER, *The Road to Botany Bay: An Essay in Spacial History* (London, 1987).

W. D. COOLEY, *The History of Maritime and Inland Discovery*, 3 vols. (London, 1830).

ALFRED FRIENDLY, *Beaufort of the Admiralty: The Life of Sir Francis Beaufort, 1744–1857* (London, 1977).

ROBIN HALLETT, ed., *Records of the African Association for Promoting the Discovery of the Interior Parts of Africa, 1788–1831* (London, 1964).

RICHARD HAKLUYT (the younger), *The Principal Navigations* (London, 1589, repr. 8 vols., 1907).

TIM JEAL, *Livingstone* (New York, 1973).

JOHN SCOTT KELTIE, *The Partition of Africa* (London, 1893; 2nd edn., 1895).

CLEMENTS R. MARKHAM, *The Fifty Years' Work of the Royal Geographical Society* (London, 1881).

H. R. MILL, *The Record of the Royal Geographical Society, 1830–1930* (London, 1930).

JEANNETTE MIRSKY, *To the Arctic! The Story of Northern Exploration* (originally published as *Northern Conquest*) (Chicago, 1934; 3rd edn., 1970).

J. H. PARRY, *The Age of Reconnaissance* (Berkeley, 1963; repr. 1981).

DAVID B. QUINN, *The Hakluyt Handbook*, 2 vols. (London, 1974).

Sir Charles George Douglas Roberts, *Discoveries and Explorations in the Century* (London, 1903).

Jane Robinson, *Wayward Women: A Guide to Women Travelers* (New York, 1990).

Robert I. Rotberg, ed., *Africa and its Explorers: Motives, Methods and Impact* (Cambridge, Mass., 1970).

Robert A. Stafford, *Scientist of Empire: Sir Roderick Murchison, Scientific Exploration, and Victorian Imperialism* (Cambridge, 1989).

G. Arnold Wood, *The Discovery of Australia* (London, 1922; revd edn., Melbourne, 1969).

19

Missions and Empire

NORMAN ETHERINGTON

The study of Christian missions has not developed as a recognized and coherent branch of British Imperial and Commonwealth history. The most important reason is that the maps of the evangelical Christian world rarely coincided with the contours of formal empire. When the flag followed religion it was not always the national flag of the pioneer missionaries. In many places the advent of British missionaries preceded colonial annexations by decades. In other places missionaries could find themselves suddenly subjected to alien rule, as happened to British missionaries in Tahiti and to German missionaries after the First World War. When missionaries followed the flag, it was not always their own. Scandinavian, American, Austrian, and Swiss missions sheltered where they could under alien rulers. The important mission field of China remained almost entirely outside the penumbra of formal imperial power. Most of the larger British colonies became polyglot mission fields, generating enormous language difficulties for scholars who aspire to write comprehensive histories. In regions such as south-east Africa, south Asia, or China missionary records are written in Swedish, German, English, French, Norwegian, Dutch, and Portuguese.

Another problem is the ambiguity of the term 'mission'. The stereotype of missionaries as white Europeans labouring among the dark 'heathen' obscures a complex reality. In the eighteenth century the overriding objective of British missionary societies was to provide for white settlers overseas rather than to preach to the unconverted. Anglican, Presbyterian, and Methodist missions in the nineteenth century devoted a considerable portion of their income to providing for white settlers in British colonies. After the Reformation the Vatican treated all British territories as mission fields for the reclamation of apostates and heretics. Many parts of the Empire which began as mission fields later launched their own evangelical societies, notably Ireland, Canada, and the United States. Where Christian missions succeeded in displacing old religions, most of the work of conversion was done by local agents. They too were missionaries, though they never left home and seldom left written accounts of their achievements.

The story of missions is also a longer story than the chronicle of empire. Europe was once a mission field for Christians from the eastern Mediterranean. The church took root in North Africa centuries before it acquired footholds in northern Europe. Catholic missions under French, Spanish, and Portuguese patronage penetrated North America, south Asia, sub-Saharan Africa, and the Malay peninsula centuries before the advent of British rule. A facile analogy is sometimes made between the trajectories of empire and mission. First comes an invasion, then a period of arrogant hegemony, followed by retreat and the devolution of power. However, the aftermath of Christian missions in most parts of the Empire is very different from the post-colonial political relationship between new nations and their former masters. Christianity continues to make new converts in Africa and Asia. Most churches in the former colonies remain in full communion with the 'mother' denominations. While imperial overrule is an increasingly distant memory, mission history is absorbed into an ongoing church history. There are few ex-colonies where mission history can be neatly segregated from the history of religion in general. Christianity's centre of gravity has already shifted away from Europe and North America to Africa and Asia.[1] Some churches from those continents now despatch missionaries to the West.

Historiographically, missionaries ran well ahead of secular historians. Four decades before John Robert Seeley set out to explain to Cambridge students how Britain had absent-mindedly built an Empire, James Hough brought out a five-volume *History of Christianity in India* for the Church Missionary Society.[2] This was but one of many histories for immediate practical purposes: guiding evangelical strategies, arousing enthusiasm, raising funds. Their authors were often educated men who could hold their own in historical research and controversy with the best lay scholars of their day. In a nineteenth century obsessed by origins, inordinate attention was paid to pioneers and early martyrs. The lives of David Brainerd of New England, Johannes van der Kemp of South Africa, Bishop Patteson of Melanesia, William Carey, Henry Martyn, David Livingstone, and the 'St Andrew's Seven' of India were written and rewritten.

As missionary societies multiplied, so did historical sources. The societies' own voluminous tracts, biographies, and periodicals constitute a gigantic printed archive. Towards 1900, as numbers of Protestant societies began to celebrate the centenaries of their foundations, that archive was ransacked by the authors of multi-volume official histories still in use.[3] This first wave of missionary histories

[1] For annual projections on the global growth, see *International Bulletin of Missionary Research.*

[2] London, 1845.

[3] The most influential include: Eugene Stock, *The History of the Church Missionary Society* (London, 1899–1916); Richard Lovett, *The History of the London Missionary Society, 1795–1895* (London, 1898); C. F. Pascoe, *Two Hundred Years of the S.P.G.* (London, 1901); G. G. Findlay and

tended to emphasize the experience of individual organizations rather than the global enterprise of Christian evangelism. Societies with well-written histories and accessible archives in the English language probably commanded more than their fair share of scholarly interest.

The turn of the twentieth century approximates the high-water mark of Christian missionary prosperity and activity.[4] Throughout the British Empire, penny-pinching colonial administrations avoided welfare responsibilities by allowing missions to become the principal providers of educational and medical services to subject peoples. As economic change awakened appetites for education, millions of children took their first steps in literacy by reading Bible stories translated into their languages by missionaries. The missionary was often a more familiar figure in the countryside than the district officer. Thus, at the World Missionary Conference in Edinburgh in 1910 prospects seemed bright and the compelling slogan of the hour was 'the evangelization of the world in this generation'. The sense of shared effort transcending denominational and national boundaries inaugurated a new phase in the historiography of missions. The 'Continuation Committee' of the Conference launched the *International Review of Missions* in 1912, which developed into a bibliographical source of first importance to all scholars of missions. Subsequent world missionary conferences served as benchmarks of Christian advance. As delegations of Asian and African clergy swelled, their increasingly confident voices recalled something that had tended to be forgotten in the era of high imperialism—that only the creation of self-supporting indigenous churches could give the Christian advance a self-sustaining impulse. The non-European clergy also called attention to the enormous resentments caused by white racism and cultural arrogance.[5] The reflex effects of these messages were profound and pervasive in the inter-war years.

The ecumenical impulse and the need to build indigenous churches are central themes in Kenneth Scott Latourette's seven-volume *A History of the Expansion of Christianity* (London, 1938–47), which still stands alone as a global survey. Another consequence of the rising indigenous Christian churches was the slow but steady growth of a clerical revulsion against Eurocentric thinking about race and culture. Paradoxically, the roots of this reappraisal can be traced to the late-Victorian linguist Friedrich Max Müller and his linguistic theories of affinities

William W. Holdsworth, *The History of the Wesleyan Methodist Missionary Society* (London, 1921–24); and William E. Strong, *The Story of the American Board* (Boston, 1910).

[4] Andrew Porter, 'Religion and Empire: British Expansion in the Long Nineteenth Century, 1780–1914', *Journal of Imperial and Commonwealth History*, XX (1993), pp. 370–90; Torben Christensen and William R. Hutchison, *Missionary Ideologies in the Imperialist Era: 1880–1920* (Copenhagen, 1982).

[5] Powerfully evoked in Terence Ranger, 'Thompson Samkange: Tambaram and Beyond', *Journal of Religion in Africa* (hereafter *JRA*), XXIII (1993), pp. 318–46.

between 'Aryan' languages. Anglican missionaries working in India took up Max Müller's idea that Hinduism contained elements of spiritual truth which Christianity shared and 'fulfilled'.[6] In the first instance, this missionary strategy reflected a typically nineteenth-century European belief in a hierarchy of civilizations, but the reasoning could be extended to produce an opposite result. As in region after region missionaries began to discover previously unsuspected points of contact between Christian doctrine and traditional religion, the old overweening self-confidence ebbed.

This led to historical reappraisals. Missionaries in previous eras who had tried to adapt the Christian message to local circumstances were rediscovered and celebrated. Edwin William Smith provides a good example of the connection between the new spirit of cultural tolerance and revisionist history. In 1950 he edited a landmark collection of essays on *African Ideas of God: A Symposium* (London), just after the publication of his biography of the American missionary Daniel Lindley, whose work in nineteenth-century South Africa had shown some tolerance for Zulu customary practices.[7]

Political developments after the Second World War accelerated the trend towards missionary rapprochements with local cultures and religions. The reassertion of Islamic and Hindu values in the struggle for Indian independence cast a shadow over the prospects for further expansion of Christianity in South Asia. The triumph of revolutionary communism in China was an even bigger blow to missionary hopes. The World Council of Churches, which grew out of the old World Missionary Conference movement, emerged as a Christian analogue to the United Nations. Like the United Nations, it became a promoter of decolonization. In this new geopolitical climate, Africa, which had often been viewed in the nineteenth century as a dumping-ground for big-hearted missionaries of limited intellectual capacity, now seemed the best hope for future expansion. At the same time, it was clear that the churches must come to terms with insurgent nationalism. That meant coming to terms with their own historic relationship with colonialism.

Secular historians of Empire with sympathies for emergent nationalisms were likewise beginning to notice 'the missionary factor'. Pre-war Imperial historians had taken little interest in missions.[8] While recognizing links between the anti-slavery movement and the evangelical awakening of the late eighteenth century, historians concentrated on the political activities of churchmen rather than the

[6] Martin Maw, *Visions of India: Fulfilment Theology, the Aryan Race Theory and the Work of British Protestant Missionaries in Victorian India* (Frankfurt, 1990).

[7] Edwin W. Smith, *The Life and Times of Daniel Lindley* (London, 1949).

[8] Missions receive about fifty pages in the entire *Cambridge History of the British Empire*; most concern the nineteenth century in the Cape, New Zealand, and Central Africa.

ramifications of missionary activity *per se*. Reginald Coupland provided important studies of the Clapham Sect and anti-slavery.[9] W. M. Macmillan set about rehabilitating the reputation of the London Missionary Society and Dr John Philip, who had long been excoriated in South African histories for 'negrophile' politics.[10] Otherwise, missionaries are barely visible in the Imperial historiography of the 1930s and 1940s. A departure was Roland Oliver's *The Missionary Factor in East Africa*, which analysed the intricate interplay of religious and political forces leading up to annexation of Uganda and Kenya.[11]

Several studies of the 1960s carried this kind of historical analysis further. To a greater or lesser extent all of them castigated missionaries for promoting Imperial expansion, assuming racial superiority and inhibiting the development of indigenous clergy. Jacob F. Ade Ajaji's *Christian Missions in Nigeria, 1841–1891* and Emmanuel A. Ayandele's *The Missionary Impact on Modern Nigeria, 1842–1914* lent to this interpretation the growing reputations of two of West Africa's prominent historians.[12] A devastating aspect of their critique was the evidence they adduced to show that the attitudes of British missionaries had actually grown *more* racist, *more* colonialist, in the course of the nineteenth century. Robert I. Rotberg's study, *Christian Missions and the Creation of Northern Rhodesia, 1880–1924*, provided corroborating evidence of ecclesiastical high-handedness on the other side of the continent.[13] These three books, influentially published and widely reviewed, soon achieved the status of a new orthodoxy.

Missionaries who had already been agonizing over their origins and present utility displayed little overt hostility to such reappraisals. Stephen Neill, who had moved from active missionary work in India to the writing of church history, treated Rotberg's anti-missionary stance with considerable respect in *Colonialism and Christian Missions*.[14] The retreat of European power throughout the 'Third World' deprived missionaries of political support from the colonial state and home congregations. They had to reconcile themselves to nationalist governments which claimed a mandate to promote independence in every field, including religion.

At the level of theory, the very concept of foreign missions came under close scrutiny. Were they not essentially, inescapably 'Eurocentric'? Some churches made semantic changes to signal their new perception. The *International Review of Missions* dropped the 's' from its title to indicate that mission was a universal rather than an exclusively Western responsibility. At the level of practice, churches hurried

[9] *The British Anti-Slavery Movement* (London, 1933).

[10] *Bantu, Boer, and Briton: The Making of the South African Native Problem* (London, 1929).

[11] London, 1952.

[12] Jacob F. Ade Ajayi, *Christian Missions in Nigeria, 1841–1891: The Making of a New Elite* (London, 1965); Emmanuel A. Ayandele, *Missionary Impact* (London, 1966).

[13] Princeton, 1965. [14] London, 1966.

to install indigenous clergy at the heads of their national hierarchies, moves intentionally parallel to transfers of political power. While such self-effacing changes were more marked among missionary societies of the ecumenical tradition than among those of stridently evangelical purpose, a steady move towards devolution of authority could be detected almost everywhere after 1960.

The new climate of opinion sparked renewed interest in Henry Venn, Secretary of the Church Missionary Society from 1841 to 1872, and his American contemporary Rufus Anderson, who had advocated the speedy establishment of self-supporting 'national' churches.[15] While the output of conventional missionary hagiography withered, special attention continued to be paid to those rare individuals who had respected traditional religion and opposed the colonial state.[16]

And the movement did not stop there. As early as the 1850s the missionary Bishop of Natal had argued that the Zulu people acknowledged a God-creator. A century later the High God of African traditional religion was being rediscovered all over the continent. After a conference on the subject in Nigeria in 1964, clerical studies of traditional religion proliferated.[17] The word 'paganism' itself was shunned by progressive clergy. It now became important to know precisely where to draw the line between traditional beliefs which could and those which could not be accommodated to Christianity. Some clergy looked again at their scriptures and discovered approval for magic, divination, healing and other practices of traditional religion. Bibliographical listings on 'primal religions' in the *International Review of Mission* burgeoned.

The implications for missionary history were considerable. Perhaps the missionaries had done nothing for converts which the people could not have done for themselves. This subliminal message emerged even more clearly from studies of new religious movements. In the 1950s a number of sociological and anthropological studies had treated these movements as forms of resistance to European power in church and state—a concept encapsulated in the title of Vittorio Lanternari's book, *Religions of the Oppressed*.[18] This view began to change when clergy, who had once denounced breakaways as 'schismatic', 'syncretist' or 'neo-pagan', began to welcome them as authentic expression of Christianity in local idioms. The changed perspective is strikingly illustrated in alterations made by the Swedish missionary bishop, Bengt Sundkler, to the second edition of his highly influential *Bantu Prophets in South Africa* (London, 1948). The 1948 edition described 'the syncretistic sects' as

[15] C. Peter Williams, *The Ideal of the Self-Governing Church: A Study in Victorian Missionary Strategy* (Leiden, 1990).

[16] Good examples are Jeff Guy, *The Heretic: A Study of the Life of John William Colenso, 1814–1883* (Johannesburg, 1983), and Daniel O'Connor, *Gospel, Raj and Swaraj: The Missionary Years of C. F. Andrews, 1904–14* (Frankfurt, 1990).

[17] See esp. John S. Mbiti, *New Testament Eschatology in an African Background* (Oxford, 1971).

[18] London, 1963.

'bridges back to heathenism'. The second edition (London, 1961) accepted them as a creative and largely Christian response to the experiences of colonial subjugation and racial oppression. Religious innovators who had been feared as rebels now began to be counted among the ranks of the missionaries. A number of these figures have been the subject of intensive study, notably the Africans John Chilembwe, Simon Kimbangu, and William Wade Harris.[19] In the Pacific, scholars have begun to apply similar analysis to the 'Maasina Rule Movement' in the Solomon Islands and to nineteenth-century prophetic movements among the Maori of New Zealand.[20] Keeping track of new religious movements became a major scholarly enterprise after David Barrett published *Schism and Renewal in Africa*.[21]

As historians paid more attention to the way in which Christianity was acculturated and propagated by local agents, they modified their views of the role of missionaries in the colonial encounter. The old tendency to see missions as junior partners in the project of imperial overrule gave way to something like a new consensus. Phrased in different ways by different authors, it was that the missionaries, who aimed to replace indigenous cultures with European 'civilization' and who frequently allied themselves with colonial governments, nevertheless transmitted a religion which subjugated peoples turned to their own purposes: spiritual, economic, and political. Thus, Richard Gray argued that while 'there is much truth in . . . [the] critical analysis of the White missionaries' role in colonial Africa', it overlooks 'the complexities of the missionaries' relationships with colonialism'. The 'argument that Christianity in sub-Saharan Africa has been merely the ideological superstructure of Western capitalism ignores the fundamental contributions of African Christians and of African cosmologies'.[22] Jean Comaroff concluded that, while missions 'helped sow the state of colonialism on which the colonial state was founded', they simultaneously communicated 'a language for contesting the new modes of domination it had itself helped create'.[23] This perception shifted the spotlight away from missionaries and their projects of 'cultural imperialism' towards the communities who adopted and spread the new religion.

[19] Landmark studies include George Shepperson and Thomas Price, *Independent African: John Chilembwe and the Origins, Setting, and Significance of the Nyasaland Rising of 1915* (Edinburgh, 1958); Gordon M. Haliburton, *The Prophet Harris* (London, 1971); Marie-Louise Martin, *Kimbangu: An African Prophet and his Church* (Oxford, 1975).

[20] Hugh Laracy, *Pacific Protest: The Maasina Rule Movement: Solomon Islands, 1944–1952* (Suva, 1983); Bronwyn Elsmore, *Mana From Heaven: A Century of Maori Prophets in New Zealand* (Tauranga, NZ, 1989).

[21] London, 1968. Harold Turner established a Study Centre for New Religious Movements in Primal Societies at Selley Oak Colleges in Birmingham. See also Turner's 'Bibliography on NERMs', *Missiology: An International Journal*, XIII (1985), and occasional listings in the *JRA*.

[22] *Black Christians and White Missionaries*, pp. 60–61.

[23] Jean Comaroff, 'Missionaries and Mechanical Clocks: An Essay on Religion and History in South Africa', *JRA*, LXXI (1991), p. 7.

Focusing on local agents of Christian expansion stimulated interest on a number of fronts: what was conversion and why did it occur; what socio-political dynamics operated in newly converted Christian communities; and how did local agents participate in the process of conversion and acculturation? Because the development of mission studies differs greatly from region to region, these questions have been investigated along divergent lines and with varying degrees of sophistication in different parts of the Empire-Commonwealth.

Religious conversion is hard to measure. Churches in the evangelical Protestant tradition emphasize an interior transformation of the soul. Churches which put more stress on the sacramental and ritual aspects of religion are more likely to count baptisms, confirmations, and communicants. For a long time historians did not peer beyond the raw numbers. A breakthrough to a deeper discussion was opened by the controversial speculations of Robin Horton.[24]

He argued that the need for a closer relationship to the High God, acknowledged in most traditional African religions, was felt whenever economic and social change widened the boundaries of individual experience beyond the local arena which had been the principal sphere of action for lesser supernatural agencies. Thus, invading colonialism and capitalism, which created vital relationships with distant workplaces and centres of power, inclined people to listen to the Christian evangelists. In a later period, those who found the more austere missionary versions of Christianity irrelevant to their instrumental needs for 'explanation–prediction–control' were likely to turn to independent churches, especially those which stressed healing. Horton's thesis lacks historical specificity and is probably inherently unprovable using normal procedures of investigation and verification. None the less, scholars soon realized that it was capable of being applied to mission fields all over the world, and it became a continuing source of stimulation and controversy.[25]

An alternative and perennially popular approach to conversion has been to focus on the efficacy of particular missionaries and their methods. A spirited debate on personalities and strategies of early New Zealand missionaries was conducted in the 1970s.[26] Discussion of conversion in Melanesia has similarly stressed men and measures.[27] But reports from other fields have strongly suggested that circumstances mattered more than missionary capabilities.[28] Some of the most

[24] 'African Conversion', *Africa*, XLI (1971), pp. 85–108.

[25] Robert W. Hefner, ed., *Conversion to Christianity: Historical and Anthropological Perspectives on a Great Transformation* (Berkeley, 1993).

[26] Key issues are discussed in Robin Fisher, 'Henry Williams' Leadership of the CMS Mission to New Zealand', *New Zealand Journal of History*, IX (1975), pp. 142–53.

[27] David Hilliard, *God's Gentlemen: A History of the Melanesian Mission, 1849–1942* (Brisbane, 1978).

[28] Norman Etherington, *Preachers, Peasants and Politics in Southeast Africa* (London, 1978), pp. 24–46.

able and thoughtful European agents made few converts. Conversely, where predisposing conditions were favourable, feeble agents could do well.

Important studies have tried to pinpoint the conditions which favoured conversion. Social disruption promoted religious change. Sometimes, as in the island societies of the South Pacific and the inter-lake kingdoms of East Africa, the first onslaught of invading economic and ecological change caused significant chiefs to ally themselves to missionaries and their religion.[29] Disruption due to frontier wars has been singled out as an important factor stimulating religious speculation and change in South Africa.[30] James Axtell has suggested that a collective will to ethnic survival on the frontier of colonial New England was the pre-eminent reason why Indian communities formed 'praying towns'.[31] Thus, it was 'the Indians', not the missionaries, who decided the rate and timing of their conversion. Following a similar line of analysis in Australia, Peggy Brock has emphasized Aboriginal collective choices as determining factors in the development of mission communities.[32]

Missionaries almost everywhere began by aiming at top-down conversions, concentrating particular effort on rulers and social élites. Aside from the successes already noticed in the Pacific and East Africa, the results confounded expectations. Missionaries succeeded best among refugees, outcasts, and depressed social groupings.[33] This phenomenon has been particularly important in India, where recruits from 'pariahs' and others at the bottom of the hierarchy of caste eventually produced a Christian population numbering tens of millions of persons.[34] The enormous size of the whole population and the prominent role played by Hindu intellectuals in the achievement of independence has so far led to relative scholarly neglect of the social dynamics of Indian Christianity.[35] Elsewhere, paying attention to the origins of converts has shed light on broader aspects of social history. This is not only true of the black populations of the West Indies and North America, where the churches played well-known roles as social

[29] Parallels between the two examples are noted in Charles W. Forman, *The Island Churches of the South Pacific: Emergence in the Twentieth Century* (Maryknoll, NY, 1982), p. 2.

[30] See particularly Jeffrey B. Peires, *The Dead will Arise: Nongqawuse and the Great Xhosa Cattle-Killing Movement of 1956–7* (London, 1989).

[31] 'Some Thoughts on the Ethnohistory of Missions', *Ethnohistory*, XXIX (1982), pp. 35–39.

[32] *Outback Ghettos: A History of Aboriginal Institutionalisation and Survival* (Cambridge, 1993).

[33] For a contrary view, see Justin Willis, 'The Nature of Mission Community', *Past and Present*, CXL (1993), pp. 127–54.

[34] Hugald Grafe, *The History of Christianity in Tamilnadu from 1800 to 1975* (Bangalore, 1990), pp. 80, 167.

[35] A notable exception is G. A. Oddie, *Social Protest in India: British Protestant Missionaries and Social Reforms, 1850–1900* (New Delhi, 1979).

anchors under slavery and segregation.[36] Scattered studies have pointed to the importance of early converts in promoting economic change and developing ideas about nationalism and ethnicity.[37]

Despite recent emphasis on the significance of local agents, there have been disappointingly few studies of their work. This is particularly remarkable in the south-west Pacific, where the early Victorian missionary ideal of 'self-supporting, self-propagating' churches was most fully realized. Methodist Tongans were instrumental in carrying their religion to Fiji, and Fijians in their turn were pioneers of New Guinea missions. Yet we know little about their lives, works, and strategies.[38] Less work, too, has been done on agents of orthodox church missions in Africa than might have been expected.[39] Two factors help account for the void in the literature. Local agents left few records and rarely wrote for missionary periodicals. Published mission histories are generally weighted against the twentieth century, when most conversions were accomplished by indigenous agency.[40]

New directions for the study of local agency are suggested in the work of the West African theologian Lamin Sanneh. Denying that Christianity was an essentially European religion foisted upon other societies by missionaries in cahoots with colonialism, he none the less acknowledges that Christianity required acculturation.[41] The process by which that was accomplished he calls 'translation'. Just as signs were found to render the words of English Bibles into previously unwritten languages, so, eventually, ways were found to carry the underlying meaning of Christianity into multifarious cultures. Sanneh's suggestion that Christian missions should be studied as processes of cultural translation

[36] Porter, 'Religion and Empire', pp. 381–82; Robin W. Winks, *The Blacks of Canada* (New Haven, 1971), pp. 337–61, counts disadvantages as well as benefits.

[37] Terence Ranger, 'Missionaries, Migrants and the Manyika: The Invention of Ethnicity in Zimbabwe', and Shula Marks, 'Patriotism, Patriarchy and Purity: Natal and the Politics of Zulu Ethnic Consciousness', in Leroy Vail, ed., *The Creation of Tribalism in Southern Africa* (London, 1989), pp. 118–50, 215–40. On economic change, see Etherington 'African Economic Experiments in Colonial Natal', in William R. Guest, ed., *Enterprise and Exploitation in a Victorian Colony* (Pietermaritzburg, 1986), pp. 265–85, and Brock, *Outback Ghettos*, pp. 37–39, 142–48.

[38] See A. W. Thornley's review of A. Harold Wood, 'Overseas Missions of the Australian Methodist Church', *Journal of Pacific History*, XV (1980), pp. 247–48.

[39] Important contributions include Emmanuel A. Ayandele, *Holy Johnson: Pioneer of African Nationalism, 1836–1917* (London, 1970) and *A Visionary of the African Church: Mojola Agbebi, 1860–1917* (Nairobi, 1971); G. O. M. Tasie, 'Christian Awakening in West Africa, 1914–1918: A Study in the Significance of Native Agency', in Ogbu U. Kalu, ed., *The History of Christianity in West Africa* (London, 1980), pp. 293–308; M. Louise Pirouet, *Black Evangelists: The Spread of Christianity in Uganda, 1891–1914* (London, 1978); and A. D. Tom Tuma, *Building a Ugandan Church: African Participation in Church Growth and Expansion in Busoga, 1891–1940* (Nairobi, 1980).

[40] Grafe attributes the problem in *The History of Christianity in Tamilnadu*, p. 55, to 'missionary dominance of source preservation and history writing'.

[41] *Translating the Message: The Missionary Impact on Culture* (Maryknoll, NY, 1990).

reverberates sympathetically with other recent work, especially on the role of missions as makers of language and ethnicity. It helps to move historical studies of missions in the imperial era towards an understanding of 'the long conversation' between cultures whose legacy promises to be as long-lasting as that of the Christianity of late imperial Rome.[42]

To this point, the study of the religious aspects of Britain's Imperial experience has not featured prominently in mainstream secular journals, but there are indications of change in Africa and South Asia.[43] The renaissance of historical writing about American Indians and Native Canadians which began in the 1970s has invigorated the study of North American missions. In Malaysia, Australia, and New Zealand, on the other hand, missions barely figure in the principal journals of history. Mission history in the West Indies remains mostly the preserve of antiquarians, local churches, and retired clerics. On the positive side, missionary records have become more accessible through donation by the older societies to universities and other public repositories.

The last decades of the twentieth century have brought forth several regional surveys that transcend denominational boundaries. For Canada there is John W. Grant's *Moon of Wintertime: Missionaries and the Indians of Canada*.[44] For Australia, there is John W. Harris's *One Blood: Two Hundred Years of Aboriginal Encounter with Christianity*,[45] and an important anthology edited by Tony Swain and Deborah Bird Rose.[46] New surveys cover Africa and much of the South Pacific.[47] Most welcome of all are two general histories of Indian Christianity.[48]

[42] 'The long conversation' coined by John and Jean Comaroff in *Of Reason and Revolution: Christianity, Colonialism and Consciousness in South Africa* (Chicago, 1991).

[43] Norman Etherington, 'Missionaries and the Intellectual History of Africa: A Historical Survey', *Itinerario: Bulletin of the Leiden Centre for the History of European Expansion*, VII (1983), pp. 116–43, and 'Recent Trends in the Historiography of Christianity in Southern Africa', *Journal of Southern African Studies*, XXII (1996), pp. 201–19.

[44] Toronto, 1984.

[45] Sutherland, NSW, 1990.

[46] *Aboriginal Australians and Christian Missions: Ethnographic and Historical Studies* (Adelaide, 1988).

[47] Allen K. Davidson, *Christianity in Aotearoa: A History of Church and Society in New Zealand* (Wellington, 1991); John Garrett, *To Live Among the Stars* (Suva, 1982), and *Footsteps in the Sea: Christianity in Oceania to World War II* (Suva, 1992); Forman, *Island Churches of the South Pacific*; Elizabeth Isichei, *A History of Christianity in Africa from Antiquity to the Present* (London, 1995); Adrian Hastings, *The Church in Africa, 1450–1950* (Oxford, 1995), and *History of African Christianity, 1950–1975* (Cambridge, 1979); Richard Elphick and Rodney Davenport, eds., *Christianity in South Africa* (Oxford, 1997).

[48] Stephen Neill, *A History of Christianity in India: The Beginnings to 1707* (Cambridge, 1984) and *A History of Christianity in India, 1707–1858* (Cambridge, 1985). A separate series sponsored by the Church History Association of India is projected in six parts, several volumes of which have already appeared. The general plan is set out in the preface to Grafe, *History of Christianity in Tamilnadu*.

Select Bibliography

J. F. A. AJAYI, *Christian Missions in Nigeria, 1841–1891: The Making of a New Elite* (London, 1965).

OWEN CHADWICK, *Mackenzie's Grave* (London, 1959).

NORMAN ETHERINGTON, *Preachers, Peasants and Politics in Southeast Africa, 1835–1880* (London, 1978).

JOHN GARRETT, *To Live Among the Stars: Christian Origins in Oceania* (Geneva, 1982).

—— *Footsteps in the Sea: Christianity in Oceania to World War II* (Suva, 1992).

JOHN WEBSTER GRANT, *Moon of Wintertime: Missionaries and the Indians of Canada in Encounter since 1534* (Toronto, 1984).

RICHARD GRAY, *Black Christians and White Missionaries* (New Haven, 1990).

JEFF GUY, *The Heretic: A Study of the Life of John William Colenso, 1814–1883* (Johannesburg, 1983).

JOHN W. HARRIS, *One Blood: Two Hundred Years of Aboriginal Encounter With Christianity* (Sutherland, NSW, 1990).

ADRIAN HASTINGS, *A History of African Christianity, 1950–1975* (Cambridge, 1979).

—— *The Church in Africa, 1450–1950* (Oxford, 1994).

DAVID LOCKHART HILLIARD, *God's Gentlemen: A History of the Melanesian Mission, 1849–1942* (St Lucia, Queensland, 1978).

KENNETH SCOTT LATOURETTE, *A History of the Expansion of Christianity*, 7 vols. (1938–47).

STEPHEN NEILL, *A History of Christianity in India: The Beginnings to A.D. 1707* (Cambridge, 1984).

—— *A History of Christianity in India, 1707–1858* (Cambridge, 1985).

R. A. OLIVER, *The Missionary Factor in East Africa* (London, 1952).

ANDREW PORTER, 'Religion and Empire: British Expansion in the Long Nineteenth Century, 1780–1914', *Journal of Imperial and Commonwealth History*, XX (1993), pp. 370–90.

GEORGE SHEPPERSON and THOMAS PRICE, *Independent African: John Chilembwe and the Origins, Setting and Significance of the Nyasaland Rising of 1915* (Edinburgh, 1958).

C. PETER WILLIAMS, *The Ideal of the Self-Governing Church: A Study in Victorian Missionary Strategy* (Leiden, 1990).

Periodicals of special importance:

International Bulletin of Missionary Research
International Review of Missions
Journal of Religion in Africa

20

Slavery, The Slave Trade, and Abolition

GAD HEUMAN

The historiography of slavery has undergone a fundamental transformation, particularly since the 1960s. Initially, historians focused on the planter class and on slave-holders rather than on the slaves. At the same time, scholars writing earlier in the twentieth century reflected the racial attitudes of their time. Students of slavery in the last thirty years have not only attempted to correct these biases; they have also added materially to our understanding of slavery and paid more attention to the lives of slaves. In the process, there has been an explosion of literature on slavery in the Empire. Since most of this scholarship has focused on colonial America and the West Indies, this chapter will concentrate on these areas.[1]

There has also been a significant shift in studies of the slave trade. Earlier work tended to focus on the undoubted horrors of the trade but provided little analytical framework for understanding it. Other accounts of the trade stigmatized the Europeans as exploiters and regarded Africa as the victim of European greed.[2] However, recent scholarship has sought to answer more specific questions about

[1] For early work on the United States and the British West Indies, see Ulrich Bonnell Phillips, *American Negro Slavery: A Survey of the Supply, Employment and Control of Negro Labor as Determined by the Plantation Regime* (New York, 1918), and Lowell Joseph Ragatz, *The Fall of the Planter Class in the British Caribbean, 1763–1833* (New York, 1928). Some of the most important studies on the United States published in the 1970s focus more on the antebellum South than the colonial period; these include Eugene D. Genovese, *Roll, Jordon, Roll: The World the Slaves Made* (New York, 1972); John W. Blassingame, *The Slave Community: Plantation Life in the Antebellum South* (New York, 1972); and Robert William Fogel and Stanley L. Engerman, *Time on the Cross: The Economics of American Negro Slavery* (Boston, 1974). The published literature on slavery and the slave trade is listed annually in a bibliographical supplement in *Slavery and Abolition*, edited by Joseph Miller. Miller's single-volume bibliography is also invaluable: *Slavery and Slaving in World History: A Bibliography, 1900–1991* (Millwood, NY, 1993). Other forms of servitude, including debt bondage and forced labour, are discussed in W. Kloosterboer, *Involuntary Labour Since the Abolition of Slavery: A Survey of Compulsory Labour Throughout the World* (Leiden, 1960). An important recent study of slavery is Robin Blackburn, *The Making of New World Slavery: From the Baroque to the Modern, 1492–1800* (London, 1997).

[2] Daniel P. Mannix, with Malcolm Cowley, *Black Cargoes: A History of the Atlantic Slave Trade* (New York, 1962); Basil Davidson, *Black Mother: The Atlantic Slave Trade* (London, 1961).

the demography of the trade, the role of Africans in it, and the effect on the trade on Africa.

Central to any discussion of the demography of the slave trade is Philip D. Curtin's *The Atlantic Slave Trade.* Relying entirely on printed sources, Curtin substantially reduced the previous estimates of the number of African slaves in the trade to just under 10 million. Recent calculations have tended to raise this figure, but the importance of Curtin's analysis does not lie solely in the gross figures. Curtin tabulated the proportion of slaves imported into each part of the Americas and showed that the overwhelming number of Africans were sent to the Caribbean and Brazil. These figures have significant implications for the comparative study of slave societies.[3]

Other historians of the slave trade have concentrated on explaining the causes for slave mortality during the crossing. In *The Middle Passage: Comparative Studies in the Atlantic Slave Trade* (Princeton, 1978), Herbert S. Klein persuasively demolishes the traditional explanation that overcrowded conditions on board ship were the principal cause of mortality among the slaves. Instead, Klein cites several other potential causes: the length of the voyages, the incidence of highly communicable diseases *en route*, and the port of origin for the Africans. Klein also speculates on the conditions in Africa which could have accounted for the mortality on the crossing, pointing, for example, to local African disease patterns or food crises in specific regions.

Klein is not alone in suggesting that Africans themselves had a significant influence on another aspect of the trade—the gender and age of slaves. Although it is clear that slave-owners in the Americas preferred youths and young adults and males over females, David Eltis has shown that it was not planter preferences which determined the composition of the slaves. For Eltis, '. . . the major force shaping the age and sex of Africans entering the trade must be sought in Africa'.[4]

3 *The Atlantic Slave Trade: A Census* (Madison, 1969), pp. 268–69, xvii; Paul E. Lovejoy, 'The Volume of the Atlantic Slave Trade: A Synthesis', *Journal of African History* (hereafter *JAH*), XXIII (1982), pp. 473–501; David Richardson, 'Slave Exports from West and West-Central Africa, 1700–1810: New Estimates of Volume and Distribution', *JAH*, XXX (1989), pp. 1–22. For work on comparative slavery, see the pioneering study by Frank Tannenbaum, *Slave and Citizen* (New York, 1947), and a critique in Carl N. Degler, *Neither Black Nor White: Slave and Race Relations in Brazil and the United States* (New York, 1971). Important comparative studies of the United States and South Africa include George M. Fredrickson, *White Supremacy: A Comparative Study in American and South African History* (New York, 1981), and John W. Cell, *The Highest Stage of White Supremacy: The Origins of Segregation in South Africa and the American South* (Cambridge, 1982). There is also considerable research on slavery in South Africa; two significant examples are Robert C-H. Shell, *Children of Bondage: A Social History of the Slave Society at the Cape of Good Hope, 1652–1838* (Hanover, NH, 1994), and Nigel Worden and Clifton Crais, eds., *Breaking the Chains: Slavery and its Legacy in the Nineteenth-Century Cape Colony* (Johannesburg, 1994).

4 David Richardson, 'The British Slave Trade to Colonial South Carolina', *Slavery and Abolition*, XII (1981), pp. 125–72; David Eltis, 'Fluctuations in the Age and Sex Ratios of Slaves in the Nineteenth-Century Transatlantic Slave Traffic', *Slavery and Abolition*, VII (1986), p. 269.

There has also been a debate about the effects of the slave trade on Africa. Some, like Curtin, have speculated on its possible positive demographic consequences on population growth in Africa. In a highly measured treatment of the ending of the slave trade, Eltis questions the ultimate impact of the trade on African society, at least before the mid-nineteenth century. On the other hand, Joseph Inikori and Stanley Engerman maintain that the trade 'delayed the commercialization of economic activities and thus retarded capitalist development in sub-Saharan Africa'. While this controversy will undoubtedly continue, it is likely that the direction of future research on the slave trade will include work on African ethnicities in the New World and their specific effects in the West Indies and in colonial America.[5]

There has been related work on the origins of slavery in the early British American colonies. This is the principal issue which was raised in a series of articles by Oscar and Mary Handlin, Carl Degler, and Winthrop Jordan. Their differences centred largely around the question of whether slavery was the product of racism or whether racism emerged as a consequence of slavery. Winthrop Jordan had the most convincing answer to this perennial question when he concluded that racism and slavery were mutually reinforcing.[6] The experience of the seventeenth-century West Indies, and initially Barbados, was less complicated. There, according to Richard S. Dunn, planters quickly adopted slavery in 'an unthinking decision'.[7]

The transformation to a slave society in Virginia was more gradual. As Edmund S. Morgan has demonstrated, not all blacks in Virginia before 1660 were slaves. Indeed, T. H. Breen and Stephen Innes document the possibility of black mobility in mid-seventeenth-century Virginia. But in the last quarter of the century the situation of blacks deteriorated while that of whites improved. For Morgan, the white community became more unified at the expense of blacks.

[5] Curtin, *Atlantic Slave Trade*, pp. 269–71; David Eltis, *Economic Growth and the Ending of the Transatlantic Slave Trade* (New York, 1987), p. 68; Joseph Inikori and Stanley L. Engerman, 'Introduction: Gainers and Losers in the Atlantic Slave Trade', in Inikori and Engerman, eds., *The Atlantic Slave Trade: Effects on Economies, Societies, and Peoples in Africa, the Americas, and Europe* (Durham, NC, 1992), p. 7. On the direction of future research on the slave trade, see David Eltis and David Richardson, eds., 'Routes to Slavery: Direction, Ethnicity and Mortality in the Transatlantic Slave Trade', a special issue of *Slavery and Abolition*, XVIII, 1 (April, 1997).

[6] Oscar and Mary F. Handlin, 'The Origins of the Southern Labor System', *William and Mary Quarterly* (hereafter *WMQ*), Third Series, VII (1950), pp. 199–222; Carl N. Degler, 'Slavery and the Genesis of American Race Prejudice', *Comparative Studies in Society and History*, II (1959), pp. 49–66; Winthrop Jordan, 'Modern Tensions and the Origins of American Slavery', *Journal of Southern History*, XXVIII (1962), pp. 18–30.

[7] *Sugar and Slaves: The Rise of the Planter Class in the English West Indies, 1624–1713* (Chapel Hill, NC, 1972), p. 73. See also Carl and Roberta Bridenbaugh, *No Peace Beyond the Line: The English in the Caribbean, 1624–1690* (New York, 1972).

Demographic changes were also significant during the seventeenth century. Morgan calculated that the greater longevity of slaves meant that it made economic sense for settlers to switch from indentured labourers to slaves. It also helped, as Russell R. Menard has shown, that the price of indentured servants was rising and that of slaves was falling.[8]

The white labour force which preceded slavery has received increasing attention. For colonial America, this subject is ably treated by David W. Galenson. Galenson rightly emphasizes the importance of the indenture system; for him, it 'was greater than that of slavery in both the early settlement of British America and the development of its economy'.[9] Like Galenson, Richard Dunn and Carl and Roberta Bridenbaugh describe the composition of this labour force and also the transformation in the West Indies from a white to a largely slave population. Yet in the process, white indentured labourers and black African slaves often acted together. In a study of seventeenth-century Barbados, Hilary McD. Beckles traces the combined resistance of whites and blacks in a number of conspiracies and plots.[10]

The rapid growth of the black population in British America has led to a large literature on the nature of African culture in the New World. Views have diverged significantly over this issue. One model, proposed by the sociologist E. Franklin Frazier, contended that the slave trade and slavery destroyed African culture, especially in the United States. The anthropologist Melville Herskovits took an opposite stance and has documented a variety of African retentions in the Americas. A more sophisticated interpretation by Sidney W. Mintz and Richard Price argues for adaptation in African-American and Afro-Caribbean societies. Mintz and Price reject the direct formal continuities from Africa, but instead focus on '*process* in the development of African-American cultures'.[11]

Historians who have carefully examined colonial American and West Indian slave societies have found interesting evidence on this issue. For colonial South

[8] Edmund S. Morgan, *American Slavery, American Freedom: The Ordeal of Colonial Virginia* (New York, 1975); T. H. Breen and Stephen Innes, *'Myne Owne Ground': Race and Freedom on Virginia's Eastern Shore* (New York, 1980); and Russell R. Menard, 'From Servants to Slaves: The Transformation of the Chesapeake Labor System', *Southern Studies*, XVI (1977), pp. 355–90. For the changing racial composition of the Chesapeake at the end of the seventeenth century, see also Alan Kulikoff, *Tobacco and Slaves: The Development of Southern Culture in the Chesapeake, 1680–1800* (Chapel Hill, NC, 1986), pp. 40–41.

[9] *White Servitude in Colonial America: An Economic Analysis* (Cambridge, 1981), p. 4.

[10] Dunn, *Sugar and Slaves*; Bridenbaugh, *No Peace Beyond the Line*; Hilary McD. Beckles, *White Servitude and Black Slavery in Barbados, 1627–1715* (Knoxville, Tenn., 1989).

[11] E. Franklin Frazier, *The Negro Family in the United States* (Chicago, 1939); Melville J. Herskovits, *The Myth of the Negro Past* (Boston, 1941); Sidney W. Mintz and Richard Price, *An Anthropological Approach to the African-American Past* (Philadelphia, 1976), reissued with a new preface as *The Birth of African-American Culture: An Anthropological Perspective* (Boston, 1992), p. x.

Carolina, Peter Wood and Daniel Littlefield have discussed the African role in the development of the rice industry. In *Rice and Slaves*, Littlefield suggests that African slaves taught the English how to cultivate the crop.[12] Focusing on the history of All Saints Parish in South Carolina, Charles Joyner confirms the impact of Africa on colonial South Carolina. Yet Joyner also supports the concept of creolization, an argument put forward earlier by Edward Brathwaite in his study of Jamaica. Brathwaite convincingly demonstrates how Africa and Europe combined to produce a new culture and society in Jamaica. For Brathwaite, white and black influenced each other in the process of constructing a creatively creole society.[13]

Not all students of the British West Indies share this notion of creole culture. In *The Sociology of Slavery*, Orlando Patterson is more pessimistic about the nature of plantation society. For Patterson, there was very little cohesiveness in the society; instead, 'Jamaica is best seen as a collection of autonomous plantations'. Although not subscribing to this view, the West Indian historian Elsa Goveia none the less describes a highly stratified society in her account of the Leeward Islands. For Goveia, a sense of community existed in the Leeward Islands, but it was one based firmly on inequality and subordination.[14]

While scholars have debated the nature of creole West Indian societies, they are in agreement about the centrality of sugar and slavery. In *Sugar and Slavery: An Economic History of the British West Indies, 1623–1775* (Barbados, 1974), Richard B. Sheridan deals with the development of the sugar plantations and their economies up to the eve of the American Revolution. It was in the late eighteenth century that planters, under abolitionist pressure, began to be concerned about improving the condition of their slaves. However, J. R. Ward concludes that amelioration for the planters was 'a means to reinforce slavery', while the abolitionists regarded the policy as a first step toward freedom. In two highly significant books, B. W. Higman also finds sugar and slavery a central theme, but his focus is on the demography and the economy of the slave societies in the British Caribbean in the early nineteenth century. As Higman notes, sugar was associated with a high mortality rate

[12] Peter H. Wood, *Black Majority: Negroes in Colonial South Carolina From 1670 Through the Stono Rebellion* (New York, 1974); Daniel C. Littlefield, *Rice and Slaves: Ethnicity and the Slave Trade in Colonial South Carolina* (1981; repr. Urbana, Ill., 1991), pp. 113–14.

[13] Charles Joyner, *Down by the Riverside: A South Carolina Slave Community* (Urbana, Ill., 1984), p. xxii; Edward Brathwaite, *The Development of Creole Society in Jamaica, 1770–1820* (Oxford, 1971). For a similar view of colonial Virginia see Mechal Sobel, *The World They Made Together: Black and White Values in Eighteenth-Century Virginia* (Princeton, 1987), and for an important discussion of varying patterns of creolization in colonial African-American slave society see Ira Berlin, 'Time, Space, and the Evolution of Afro-American Society on British Mainland North America', *American Historical Review*, LXXXV (1980), pp. 44–78.

[14] *The Sociology of Slavery: An Analysis of the Origins, Development and Structure of Negro Slave Society in Jamaica* (London, 1967), p. 70; Elsa V. Goveia, *Slave Society in the British Leeward Islands at the End of the Eighteenth Century* (New Haven, 1965), pp. 318–19.

among slaves and a failure of the slave population to increase naturally. Higman also suggests that changes in the Jamaican slave population after the ending of the slave trade helped to account for the outbreak of the 1831 slave rebellion.[15]

Slave resistance, especially in the form of rebellions, is the focus of Eugene Genovese's *From Rebellion to Revolution: Afro-American Slave Revolts in the Making of The New World* (Baton Rouge, La., 1979). In his book, Genovese offers a typology of resistance. He characterizes seventeenth- and eighteenth-century revolts as led by Africans seeking to restore an African past, while the creole rebellions after the Saint-Domingue uprising were revolutionary in attempting to overthrow slavery as a social system. Although intriguing, Genovese's discussion of resistance is too schematic. For example, David Barry Gaspar's study of an Antigua conspiracy in 1736 demonstrates that African and creole slaves worked together to overthrow the system.[16]

The large number of rebellions in the West Indies has given rise to a significant literature on slave resistance. In *Testing the Chains: Resistance to Slavery in the British West Indies* (Ithaca, NY, 1982), Michael Craton has provided an overview of these outbreaks. There are also more specific studies of individual rebellions. The Demerara rebellion of 1823 is ably handled by Emilia Viotti da Costa, *Crowns of Glory, Tears of Blood: The Demerara Slave Rebellion of 1823* (New York, 1994), and the best account of the Christmas rebellion of 1831 in Jamaica is in Mary Turner's *Slaves and Missionaries: The Disintegration of Jamaican Slave Society, 1787–1834* (Urbana, Ill., 1982). There were far fewer outbreaks in colonial America, but Peter Wood's treatment of the Stono rebellion in South Carolina is excellent. The most recent discussion of this rebellion, Edward Pearson's 'A Countryside Full of Flames', includes an interesting gendered analysis of the outbreak.[17]

Slaves also resisted their own enslavement by running away, generally for short periods of time but sometimes permanently. Gerald W. Mullin makes good use of advertisements for runaway slaves in his book on resistance in eighteenth-century Virginia, *Flight and Rebellion: Slave Resistance in Eighteenth-Century Virginia* (New York, 1972). Gad Heuman's edited collection, *Out of the House of Bondage: Runaways, Resistance and Maroonage in Africa and the New World* (London, 1986), contains essays on runaways in Barbados and in colonial South

[15] J. R. Ward, *British West Indian Slavery, 1750–1834: The Process of Amelioration* (Oxford, 1988), p. 277; B. W. Higman, *Slave Population and Economy in Jamaica, 1807–1834* (Cambridge, 1976); B. W. Higman, *Slave Populations of the British Caribbean, 1807–1834* (Baltimore, 1984).

[16] *Bondmen and Rebels: A Study of Master–Slave Relations in Antigua* (Baltimore, 1985).

[17] Wood, *Black Majority*; '"A Countryside Full of Flames": A Reconsideration of the Stono Rebellion and Slave Rebelliousness in the Early Eighteenth Century South Carolina Low Country', *Slavery and Abolition*, XVII, (1996), pp. 22–50.

Carolina and North Carolina as well as on the Maroons in Jamaica, who established permanent communities in the interior of the island. The most recent study of the Jamaican Maroons is Mavis Campbell's *The Maroons of Jamaica, 1655–1796: A History of Resistance, Collaboration and Betrayal* (Trenton, NJ, 1990).

While many slaves sought to resist slavery, others worked to improve their lives within the institution of slavery. Masters generally ignored the personal lives of their slaves, and, as a result, slaves often had significant control over their economic, religious, and family lives. The literature on the slaves' economy has emphasized this point. For the Caribbean, Sidney Mintz and Douglas Hall pioneered the study of the slaves' own economy and, in particular, the use of their own provision grounds for self-subsistence. In an important collection, Ira Berlin and Philip D. Morgan bring together work in this area on the Caribbean and the United States. Roderick McDonald's comparative study of Jamaica and Louisiana usefully adds to this discussion; he is right to suggest that participation in the internal economy not only fostered slave initiative but also was 'at odds with the subservience characteristic of much of plantation life'.[18]

The slaves' religious lives were also often outside the control of the masters. Albert J. Raboteau discusses 'the invisible institution' of slave religion for the United States, while Mary Turner addresses the impact of European missionaries on Jamaican slave society. Turner's analysis is significant because she shows how slaves incorporated the missionaries' teaching in their own worldview. Similarly, the slave family was part of the private world of the slaves; its importance in the United States has been documented by Herbert Gutman and for the British West Indies by B. W. Higman and Michael Craton.[19]

In light of the increasing emphasis on gender, the role of slave women has received considerable attention in the past decade. Barbara Bush's *Slave Women in Caribbean Society, 1650–1838* (London, 1990) is an overview of the image of women as well as their role in Caribbean plantation society. Marietta Morrissey takes the argument further and explores the limited range of female occupations

[18] Sidney W. Mintz and Douglas Hall, 'The Origins of the Jamaican Internal Marketing System', *Yale University Publications in Anthropology*, LVII (New Haven, 1960), pp. 3–26; Sidney W. Mintz, *Caribbean Transformations* (Chicago, 1974); Ira Berlin and Philip D. Morgan, *The Slaves' Economy: Independent Production by Slaves in the Americas* (London, 1991); Roderick A. McDonald, *The Economy and Material Culture of Slaves: Goods and Chattels on the Sugar Plantations of Jamaica and Louisiana* (Baton Rouge, La., 1993), p. 169. See also the important article by Philip Morgan, 'Work and Culture: The Task System and the World of Lowcountry Blacks, 1700–1880', *WMQ*, Third Series (1982), pp. 563–99.

[19] Albert J. Raboteau, *Slave Religion: The 'Invisible Institution' in the Antebellum South* (Oxford, 1978); Turner, *Slaves and Missionaries*; Herbert G. Gutman, *The Black Family in Slavery and Freedom, 1750–1925* (New York, 1976); B. W. Higman, 'The Slave Family and Household in the British West Indies, 1800–1834', *Journal of Interdisciplinary History* (hereafter *JIH*) VI (1975), pp. 261–88; Michael Craton, 'Changing Patterns of Slave Families in the British West Indies', *JIH*, X (1979), pp. 1–36.

and the specific forms of female exploitation in Caribbean slave society. Women also resisted slavery, and as Hilary McD. Beckles points out in his study of slave women in Barbados, 'resistance . . . became a central part of their everyday behaviour and pervaded every known sphere of existence—work, sexual relations, leisure activity, and family life'.[20] Although most studies of slave women in the United States focus on the nineteenth century, Deborah Gray White includes a useful discussion of the colonial period in *Ar'n't I a Woman? Female Slaves in the Plantation South* (New York, 1985).

As slavery developed, an increasing proportion of slaves became free. However, in colonial America, the number of freed slaves remained small before the American Revolution. According to Ira Berlin, free blacks and free people of colour faced a series of legal limitations, including restrictions on holding public office, on voting, on testifying against whites, and on serving in the militia. Historians of the free coloureds in the British West Indies, including Edward Cox, Jerome S. Handler, and Gad Heuman, have also commented on the limited rights this group possessed, but have emphasized their rapid growth and their significance in these societies. In addition, some scholars have characterized the free people of colour as seeking to emphasize their affinity with whites. Yet other research, and especially that of Arnold Sio, has shown the important connections between the world of the free coloureds and that of the slaves. The free people of colour often had close connections with the abolitionists and some of them supported the campaign to abolish slavery. But the literature on the abolition of slavery as well as the slave trade has engendered a considerable debate which has gone far beyond the links with the free coloureds.[21]

Until the 1940s there was a general consensus among historians about the abolition of slavery in the Empire. For example, Reginald Coupland, Beit Professor of Colonial History at Oxford, maintained that the British abolished slavery largely because of the strength of religious feeling and humanitarianism. For Coupland, the abolitionists were able to mobilize public opinion in the campaign against

[20] Marietta Morrissey, *Slave Women in the New World: Gender Stratification in the Caribbean* (Lawrence, Ka., 1989); Hilary McD. Beckles, *Natural Rebels: A Social History of Enslaved Black Women in Barbados* (London, 1989), p. 177.

[21] Ira Berlin, *Slaves Without Masters: The Free Negro in the Antebellum South* (New York, 1974); Edward L. Cox, *Free Coloreds in the Slave Societies of St. Kitts and Grenada* (Knoxville, Tenn., 1984); Jerome S. Handler, *The Unappropriated People: Freedmen in the Slave Society of Barbados* (Baltimore, 1974); Gad J. Heuman, *Between Black and White: Race, Politics and the Free Coloreds in Jamaica, 1792–1865* (Westport, Conn., 1981); Arnold Sio, 'Marginality and Free Coloured Identity in Caribbean Slave Society', *Slavery and Abolition*, VIII (1987), pp. 166–82. For a discussion of the significant role of free coloureds in the slave society of Mauritius, see Richard B. Allen, 'Economic Marginality and the Rise of the Free Population of Colour in Mauritius, 1767–1830', *Slavery and Abolition*, X (1989), pp. 126–50.

slavery; in the end, they convinced Parliament to pay £20 million compensation to free the slaves.[22]

The work of the Trinidadian scholar and subsequent Prime Minister of Trinidad and Tobago, Eric Williams, sought to overturn this account of abolition. In Williams's view, slavery and the slave trade were abolished because they were no longer profitable. Williams used the argument developed by Lowell Ragatz in *The Fall of the Planter Class in the British Caribbean*, which sought to document the economic decline of the West Indies after the American Revolution. For Williams, the economic collapse of the West Indian plantations was linked to the success of the abolitionists; it was economic forces which explained the abolition of the slave trade and the emancipation of the slaves. There was another important element in Williams's argument: the role of the slave trade and slavery in underpinning the industrial revolution. Williams maintained that profits from these operations 'provided one of the main streams of that accumulation of capital in England which financed the Industrial Revolution'.[23]

Much like Coupland and the early historians of abolition, Williams's account in turn became the new orthodoxy. Since the 1960s, however, the Williams's thesis itself has been the subject of considerable controversy. The first significant critic of this argument, Roger Anstey, calculated that the profits from the slave trade were far less than Williams had suggested and insufficient to provide significant financing for the industrial revolution. Anstey also looked closely at the Parliamentary arithmetic for the abolition of the slave trade and found no evidence of Williams's economic forces in the vanguard of those supporting abolition.[24]

Although Anstey attacked elements of Williams's argument, it was the work of Seymour Drescher which aimed to undermine *Capitalism and Slavery*. In *Econocide*, a book devoted to the Williams's thesis, Drescher disputed the idea of West Indian economic decline at the end of the eighteenth and beginning of the nineteenth centuries. For Drescher, the abolitionists were attacking a system which was gaining in strength rather than faltering or on the verge of collapse. Contrary to Williams's position, the West Indies were expanding rather than declining, and continued to do so well after the abolition of the slave trade.[25]

Drescher is not alone in his criticism of Williams. David Eltis arrives at a similar conclusion, although he is concerned more specifically with the ending of the

[22] *The British Anti-Slavery Movement* (London, 1933).

[23] *Capitalism and Slavery* (1944; New York, 1966), p. 52.

[24] Roger Anstey, 'Capitalism and Slavery: A Critique', *Economic History Review* (hereafter *EcHR*), Second Series, XXI (1968), pp. 307–20; Roger Anstey, *The Atlantic Slave Trade and British Abolition, 1760–1810* (London, 1975).

[25] *Econocide: British Slavery in the Era of Abolition* (Pittsburgh, 1977).

Atlantic slave trade. Eltis is explicit in his view about the timing of the abolition of the trade: 'For the Atlantic region as for the British Empire, the slave trade did not expire naturally. Rather, it was killed when its significance to the Americas and to a lesser extent to Europe was greater than at any point in its history.' Others, such as J. R. Ward, have pointed to the continuing profitability of the West Indian plantation economies.[26]

In his recent work, Drescher has highlighted the role of popular pressure in the process of abolition. This is also the view of James Walvin, who regards anti-slavery as '*the* most popular political issue in these years [1787–1838]'.[27] Although Walvin is aware that women played an important role in the anti-slavery societies, Clare Midgley more fully explores the issue of gender and anti-slavery in *Women Against Slavery: The British Campaigns, 1780–1870* (London, 1992). In addition, Midgley emphasizes the independent role of women in their anti-slavery organizations.

Yet, in spite of the onslaught on Williams's work, his thesis still has its defenders; however, even they concede that Williams made significant errors. For example, in their introduction to a volume of conference essays, Barbara L. Solow and Stanley L. Engerman make it clear that the profits of the slave trade and slavery did not send a vast stream of capital to fund eighteenth-century technological changes in Britain. But, to many, the link between economies and abolition still seems persuasive. For example, Howard Temperley, while criticizing Williams, suggests that his work in this area 'is more important for the questions it raises than for the answers it gives'.[28] Another critic of Williams, David Brion Davis, who is the author of some of the most significant work on slavery and abolition, sees a subtle connection between new economic interests and the development of an anti-slavery ideology. For Davis, anti-slavery reflected 'the needs and values of the emerging capitalist order'. British

[26] Eltis, *Economic Growth*, p. 15; J. R. Ward, 'The Profitability of Sugar Planting in the British West Indies, 1650–1834', *EcHR*, Second Series, XXXI (1978), pp. 197–213. During much of the nineteenth century Britain also attempted to end the foreign slave trade, including the trade in Africa and the Middle East. For a discussion of Britain's role in the suppression of the trade see Suzanne Miers, *Britain and the Ending of the Slave Trade* (London, 1975).

[27] Seymour Drescher, 'Whose Abolition? Popular Pressure and the Ending of the British Slave Trade', *Past and Present*, CXLIII (1993), pp. 136–66; James Walvin, 'Freeing the Slaves: How Important Was Wilberforce?', in Jack Hayward, ed., *Out of Slavery: Abolition and After* (London, 1985), p. 35; James Walvin, *England, Slaves and Freedom, 1776–1838* (Jackson, Miss., 1986). Robin Blackburn also emphasizes the importance of popular mobilization in his overview of abolition, *The Overthrow of Colonial Slavery, 1776–1848* (London, 1988).

[28] Barbara L. Solow and Stanley L. Engerman, 'An Introduction', in Solow and Engerman, eds., *British Capitalism and Caribbean Slavery: The Legacy of Eric Williams* (Cambridge, 1987), p. 8; Howard Temperley, 'Eric Williams and Abolition: The Birth of a New Orthodoxy', in ibid., p. 254.

anti-slavery thus helped to ensure stability at a time of rapid political and economic change.[29]

The debate on the Williams thesis, is, therefore, far from over. This is also the case for a variety of issues dealing with slavery and the slave trade. As historians develop new techniques to explore the past and ask new questions of old material, they will continue to refine their knowledge of these often-contentious areas. In the process, it seems likely that the historiography of slavery and abolition will remain as vibrant in the future as it has in the past.

[29] David Brion Davis, *The Problem of Slavery in the Age of Revolution, 1770–1823* (Ithaca, NY, 1975), pp. 350, 384. For a further discussion on this point see Thomas Bender, ed., *The Antislavery Debate: Capitalism and Abolitionism as a Problem in Historical Interpretation* (Berkeley, 1992).

Select Bibliography

HILARY MCD.BECKLES, *White Servitude and Black Slavery in Barbados, 1627–1715* (Knoxville, Tenn., 1989).

IRA BERLIN and PHILIP D. MORGAN, *The Slaves' Economy: Independent Production By Slaves in the Americas* (London, 1991).

EDWARD BRATHWAITE, *The Development of Creole Society in Jamaica, 1770–1820* (Oxford, 1971).

PHILIP D. CURTIN, *The Atlantic Slave Trade: A Census* (Madison, 1969).

DAVID BRION DAVIS, *The Problem of Slavery in the Age of Revolution, 1770–1823* (Ithaca, NY, 1975).

CARL N. DEGLER, 'Slavery and the Genesis of American Race Prejudice', *Comparative Studies in Society and History*, Vol. II (1959), pp. 49–66.

SEYMOUR DRESCHER, *Econocide: British Slavery in the Era of Abolition* (Pittsburgh, 1977).

RICHARD S. DUNN, *Sugar and Slaves: The Rise of the Planter Class in the English West Indies, 1624–1713* (Chapel Hill, NC, 1972).

DAVID ELTIS, *Economic Growth and the Ending of the Transatlantic Slave Trade* (New York, 1987).

ELSA V. GOVEIA, *Slave Society in the British Leeward Islands at the End of the Eighteenth Century* (New Haven, 1965).

OSCAR and MARY F. HANDLIN, 'The Origins of the Southern Labor System', *William and Mary Quarterly*, Third Series, VII (1950), pp. 199–222.

B. W. HIGMAN, *Slave Population and Economy in Jamaica, 1807–1834* (Cambridge, 1976).

WINTHROP JORDAN, 'Modern Tensions and the Origins of American Slavery', *Journal of Southern History*, XXVIII (1962), pp. 18–30.

SIDNEY W. MINTZ and RICHARD PRICE, *An Anthropological Approach to the Afro–American Past: A Caribbean Perspective*) (Philadelphia, 1976), reissued with a new preface as *The Birth of African–American Culture: An Anthropological Perspective* (Boston, 1992).

EDMUND S. MORGAN, *American Slavery, American Freedom: The Ordeal of Colonial Virginia* (New York, 1975).

MARIETTA MORRISSEY, *Slave Women in the New World: Gender Stratification in the Caribbean* (Lawrence, Kan., 1989).

GERALD W. MULLIN, *Flight and Rebellion: Slave Resistance in Eighteenth-Century Virginia* (New York, 1972).

ORLANDO PATTERSON, *The Sociology of Slavery: An Analysis of the Origins, Development and Structure of Negro Slave Society in Jamaica* (London, 1967).

ERIC WILLIAMS, *Capitalism and Slavery* (1944; London, 1966).

PETER H. WOOD, *Black Majority: Negroes in Colonial South Carolina From 1670 Through the Stono Rebellion* (New York, 1974).

21

The Royal Navy and the British Empire

BARRY M. GOUGH

The eminent naval historian Alfred Thayer Mahan shall ever be remembered as the first to point to sea power, or control of the sea, as vital to the creation and maintenance of the British Empire. Much of the writing on British naval history during the early decades of the twentieth century produced studies designed to confirm Mahan's basic thesis. In volumes on the *Influence of Sea Power on History*, the first of which appeared in 1890, Mahan argued that Britain's national power, as shown in the rivalry between Britain and France from 1660 to 1815, rested on seaborne trade and communications protected by fleets and supported by bases and colonies spread throughout the world. Mahan advanced sophisticated arguments about Imperial geopolitics as well as stressing the strategic, operational, and tactical dimensions of sea power. This he did in numerous articles dealing with issues ranging from international rivalry in the Persian Gulf to Britain's position in the Boer (South African) War. To this day, Mahan's important, though often overlooked, *The Problem of Asia* remains a valuable analysis of the interactions between sea power and British imperialism on land. Mahan, however, was as much a publicist as a historian. His pitfall was that he wrote without the benefit of research in archival materials.[1] Beginning in the 1940s, Mahan's views were supplemented and broadened by professional historians such as Arthur Marder, writing on the anatomy of British naval power, and Gerald Graham, investigating the economic and strategic issues that underlay British maritime and Imperial supremacy. This broader approach culminated with the survey of British naval history in Paul M. Kennedy's *The Rise and Fall of British Naval Mastery* (New York, 1976).

[1] For a recent reassessment of Mahan see Jon Tetsuro Sumida, *Inventing Grand Strategy and Teaching Command: The Classic Works of Alfred Thayer Mahan Reconsidered* (Washington, 1997); and for the influences which informed Mahan's thought, John B. Hattendorf, ed., *The Influence of History on Mahan: The Proceedings of a Conference Marking the Centenary of Alfred Thayer Mahan's 'The Influence of Sea Power Upon History, 1660–1783'* (Newport, RI, 1991).

Until these changes, the corpus of writing on the subject of the interrelationship between naval and Imperial history was confined to two branches: one, dealing with heroes of Imperial daring such as Sir John Hawkins, Martin Frobisher, and Sir Francis Drake (largely for a popular audience); the other, a serious attempt by Julian (later Sir Julian) Corbett to link strategic requirements to Imperial expansion, undertaken in his study of combined, joint, and amphibious operations, *England in the Mediterranean: A Study of the Rise and Influence of British Power Within the Straits, 1603–1713* (London, 1904). Corbett may have been 'the pen behind the fleet'. His strategic theories had, it is true, some influence on British naval strategy.[2] However, Marder and Graham revolutionized, in their respective fields, the correlation of naval power and colonial empires in the nineteenth century.

It may be noted that a century ago, beginning in the 1890s, Mahan, Corbett, Professor Sir John Knox Laughton, Admiral P. H. Colomb, and Admiral Sir Cyprian Bridge championed the publication of books, articles, and documents on naval history. In the late nineteenth and early twentieth centuries British national security and well-being was predicated on naval strength and influence. At a time when colonial empires were prominent in world affairs and when fleets were being constructed or enlarged, naval affairs—and naval history—was much in vogue for popular audiences and was beginning to be a subject of serious concern in learned and strategic circles. In Britain, the founding of the Royal Colonial Institute (1868) drew attention to colonial issues in Imperial politics. Similarly, the Royal United Service Institution (1870) concerned itself with Imperial fortifications, small wars, and, increasingly, the protection of seaborne trade. The Navy Records Society (1893) published documents on British naval experiences, including personal accounts otherwise unavailable. At a time when public records were largely unavailable these societies encouraged study of naval and Imperial matters.

In spite of these developments, the study of the navy and its influence on the Empire and vice versa remained a largely untouched field of study. Little historical scholarship was undertaken until Marder and Graham made their appearance, and it may be suggested that 'navalism', seen as a cause of the First World War, was

[2] Julian Corbett's first notable book, which raised the accounts of English 'sea-dogs' above the normal class of such books, was *Drake and the Tudor Navy, With a History of the Rise of England as a Maritime Power* (London, 1898). Liam J. Cleaver, 'The Pen Behind the Fleet: The Influence of Sir Julian Stafford Corbett on British Naval Development, 1898–1918', *Comparative Strategy*, XIV, 1 (1995), pp. 45–57. For the navy and the first phase of colonization see Vol. 1, chap. by N. A. M. Rodger. See Corbett, *England and the Seven Years War*, 2 vols.: Vol. I, *1756–59*; Vol. II, *1759–63* (1907; London, 1922), and for a discussion of Corbett's influence see Vol. II, chap. by N. A. M. Rodger, esp. pp. 170–01. For the literature on the eighteenth century see Vol. II, chaps. and bibliographies by Rodger, Michael Duffy, and Bruce P. Lenman.

much in disrepute in academic circles. Perhaps more significantly, the inconclusive Battle of Jutland (1916) left a deep scar on the British psyche. The writing of the official history of the war at sea, undertaken by Corbett and Sir Henry Newbolt, was the subject of ongoing rancour and dispute. Their *Naval Operations*, 5 vols. (London, 1920–31) did not meet with Admiralty approval, and the portrayal of the navy as essentially passive or defensive was regarded as running counter to the traditions of the service and of Admiralty policy. Such a state of affairs did not encourage naval officers to write history. A rare exception to this was Captain (later Admiral Sir) Herbert Richmond, author of *The Navy in the War of 1739–48*, 3 vols. (Cambridge, 1923), a study of world-wide conflict based on a careful reading of many primary documents. Touching Imperial affairs, but emphasizing naval operations, Richmond also authored what remains the standard history of *The Navy in India, 1763–1783* (London, 1931). Richmond set high standards for the study of the navy as a useful tool for statesmen. His Ford Lectures, delivered at Oxford 1943 at a critical time in British and Imperial affairs, pursued his main argument over the course of modern British history, and were published after the war as *Statesmen and Sea Power* (Oxford, 1946).[3]

Contemporaries of Richmond who wrote on aspects of naval history that touched on imperial affairs were few. But here mention may be made of university-based scholarship that explored for the first time Admiralty and Colonial Office records: first, the pioneering study by Robert G. Albion that inquired into the material basis of British sea power entitled *Forests and Sea Power: The Timber Problem of the Royal Navy, 1652–1862* (Cambridge, Mass., 1926); secondly, a parallel study for British North America, undertaken as a thesis and not published until many years later: Arthur R. M. Lower, *Great Britain's Woodyard: British America and the Timber Trade, 1763–1867* (Montreal, 1973); and thirdly, a unique and important study of the navy's operations in the 'cockpit of empire': Ruth M. Bourne, *Queen Anne's Navy in the West Indies* (New Haven, 1939). These works explained linkages between colonial resources and naval power. Meanwhile, historians informed by their own service experience and connections continued to write 'operational' studies, of which the following are noteworthy: William R. James, *The British Navy in Adversity: A Study of the War of American Independence* (London, 1926), George A. Ballard, *Rulers of the Indian Ocean* (London, 1927), and John H. Owen, *War at Sea Under Queen Anne, 1702–1708* (Cambridge, 1938). The works of the 1920s and 1930s are broadly characterized by

[3] For recent assessments see James Goldrick and John B. Hattendorf, eds., *Mahan is Not Enough: The Proceedings of a Conference on the Works of Sir Julian Corbett and Admiral Sir Herbert Richmond* (Newport, RI, 1993).

the examination of external influences on maritime and Imperial policy, and of the search for an explanation of how, at an earlier time (principally the eighteenth century), British influence spread overseas and was retained (or in the case of the United States curtailed). No serious study of the era known as *Pax Britannica* (1815–1914) was undertaken until after the Second World War. To that date the only thorough history of the Royal Navy was that by Sir William Laird Clowes, *The Royal Navy: A History from the Earliest Times to the Present*, 7 vols. (Boston, 1897–1903).

Imperial matters were conspicuous in these histories by their common absence, save for discussion of 'small wars' of the nineteenth century. In 1905 Colonel C. E. Callwell, the army's well-known theorist of the Empire's 'small wars', published *Military Operations and Maritime Preponderance: Their Relations and Interdependence*. Examining a variety of Asian and North American cases from the eighteenth and nineteenth centuries, Callwell stressed the importance of co-operation between land and sea forces to the success of Imperial campaigns. Nearly a century later, in the aftermath of the cold war, Callwell has enjoyed a rediscovery among analysts of combined operations.[4] Corbett has similarly been revived in the 1990s as a pioneer in the study of amphibious campaigns.

Arthur J. Marder

Boston-born, Harvard-educated, Arthur Jacob Marder sought, in a doctoral thesis, to examine the workings of the British Admiralty to explain how statesmen, politicians, and public opinion worked in the United Kingdom to maintain Britain's naval pre-eminence. His *The Anatomy of British Sea Power: A History of British Naval Policy in the Pre-Dreadnought Era, 1880–1905* (New York, 1940) examined for the first time the workings of the Board of Admiralty, and used hitherto unexamined private and public collections. In those days Admiralty papers were embargoed, and Marder obtained special Admiralty permission to consult such papers, although he was prohibited from quoting from them. Notably persistent in leaving no stone unturned, he produced a massive study that became the prototype of sound naval historical study. The British edition, published in 1941, was a reminder to commentators of the time that Britain was again visited by a perilous challenge to her sea power. Marder, in noteworthy fashion, had shown that British naval history was not alone the purview of naval officers writing as historians. He brought academic rigour and broad historio-

[4] See especially Colin S. Gray's 'Introduction: Sir Charles E. Callwell, KCB—An "Able Theorist" of Joint Warfare', in C. E. Callwell, ed., *Military Operations and Maritime Preponderance: Their Relations and Interdependence* (Annapolis, Md., 1996), pp. xv–lxxiii.

graphical understanding to the problem of Britannia's diminishing authority. His work may now be seen as an aspect of international history, of great value to French, Russian, American, and German scholars. The book examined 'navalism' in all its guises, and linked naval and Imperial matters; indeed, Marder stressed that 'navalism' had its roots in imperialism.

From Marder's first book emerged a figure that delighted Marder's own reforming principles: Admiral Sir John Fisher, later Lord Fisher of Kilverstone. Marder saw Fisher as saviour of the navy, and called the era from the revolutionary battleship *Dreadnought* to the scuttling of the German High Seas Fleet at Scapa Flow 'the Fisher Era'. He also found in the progressive-minded Richmond another force for good. These became the focus of two works: *Portrait of an Admiral: The Life and Papers of Sir Herbert Richmond* (London, 1952) and *Fear God and Dread Nought: The Letters of Lord Fisher of Kilverstone*, 3 vols. (London, 1952–59). They led on to the inimitable *From the Dreadnought to Scapa Flow: The Royal Navy in the Fisher Era, 1904–19*, 5 vols. (London, 1961–70). Subsequent studies of the navy in the years after 1919 included several books and articles, the most important of which was *Old Friends, New Enemies*, 2 vols. (Oxford, 1981–90) on the relationship of the Royal Navy to the Imperial Japanese Navy, from 1936 to 1945.[5] Using Japanese, United States, and British sources, written and oral, Marder contributed mightily to the rising field of international military scholarship. The first volume took up a theme that attracted a spate of studies on naval disarmament and importance of the main fleet to Singapore strategy.[6] Marder explained the problem of British Imperial overstretch, and particularly the Admiralty's abundant worry that Singapore's defence prohibited freedom of action during the Abyssinian Crisis. Generally speaking, Marder gave wide latitude to the wisdom exhibited by Winston S. Churchill in the prosecution of the war, and it was this issue, among others, that led to his disagreement with naval historian Captain Stephen W. Roskill, RN.[7] All in all, Marder saw British naval power in a

[5] The second volume was completed by his former doctoral students John Horsfield and Mark Jacobsen.

[6] Wm. Roger Louis, *British Strategy in the Far East, 1919–39* (Oxford, 1970); Roger Dingman, *Power in the Pacific: The Origins of Naval Arms Limitation, 1914–22: The Origins of Arms Limitation* (Chicago, 1976); J. McCarthy, *Australia and Imperial Defence, 1918–39: A Study in Air and Sea Power* (St Lucia, 1976); W. David McIntyre, *The Rise and Fall of the Singapore Naval Base, 1919–42* (London, 1979); Paul Haggie, *Britannia at Bay: The Defence of the British Empire against Japan* (Oxford, 1981); Ian Hamill, *Strategic Illusion: The Singapore Strategy and the Defence of Australia and New Zealand* (Singapore, 1981); Ian McGibbon, *Blue-Water Rationale: The Naval Defence of New Zealand, 1919–42* (Wellington, 1981); James Neidpath, *The Singapore Naval Base and the Defence of Britain's Eastern Empire, 1919–1941* (Oxford, 1981); Malcolm Murfett, *Fool-Proof Relations: The Search for Anglo-American Naval Cooperation During the Chamberlain Years, 1937–40* (Singapore, 1984); Ian Cowman, *Dominion or Decline: Anglo-American Naval Relations in the Pacific, 1937–41* (Oxford, 1996).

[7] Appendix, 'A Historical Controversy', in Stephen Roskill, *Churchill and the Admirals* (New York, 1978).

global context.[8] He wrote about naval operations against Germany, France, and Japan, and his work spanned 1880–1945, arguably 'the modern era'.

Interrelated sub-themes of Marder's work were how personalities shape history and how systems confuse the implementation of policy. Subsequent historians have elaborated these issues. Richard Ollard has tackled the first of Marder's sub-themes in his *Fisher and Cunningham: A Study of Personalities of the Churchill Era* (London, 1991). Other historians reassessing the anatomy of British sea power in the early twentieth century have emphasized the interactions of money, engineering, and naval policy, as well as the pivotal bearing of personalities such as Lord Fisher. Jon Tetsuro Sumida's *In Defence of Naval Supremacy: Finance, Technology, and Naval Policy, 1889–1914* (Boston, 1989) represents an important contribution. Also significant are articles by Nicholas A. Lambert: 'British Naval Policy, 1913–1914: Financial Limitation and Strategic Revolution', *Journal of Modern History*, LXVII, 3 (Sept. 1995), pp. 595–626, and 'Admiral Sir John Fisher and the Concept of Flotilla Defence, 1904–1909', *Journal of Military History*, LIX, 4 (Oct. 1995), pp. 639–60. Sumida and Lambert have expanded the view of Fisher as reformer, presenting the inimitable First Sea Lord as a strategic radical who not only oversaw the introduction of the *Dreadnought* but also advocated alternative and more economical systems based on emerging technologies such as submarines and analog computers for gunfire control.

If Marder led the way in writing the history of the *Dreadnought* era, Stephen Roskill blazed a trail for historians working on the period from the end of the First World War through to the Second World War. While Roskill's *The War at Sea, 1939–1945*, 3 vols. (London, 1954–61) and *The White Ensign: The British Navy at War, 1939–1945* (Annapolis, Md., 1960) focused on operational history, much of his work emphasized, like Marder's, the wider context of British sea power. Roskill's *Naval Policy Between the Wars*, 2 vols. (London, 1962–76) laid bare the political and international problems, such as disarmament and relations with the United States and Japan, which confronted the inter-war navy. Imperial themes dominated Roskill's *Hankey: Man of Secrets*, 2 vols. (London, 1970–74). As the long-time Secretary to the Committee for Imperial Defence, Sir Maurice Hankey, a Royal Marines officer, was at the centre of Imperial grand strategy throughout much of the first half of the twentieth century.

Gerald S. Graham

Just as well known to international scholarship, and a giant in his field—and with more influence on doctoral students—was Gerald Sandford Graham, a Canadian

[8] For recent perspectives see Keith Neilson and Greg Kennedy, eds., *Far Flung Lines: Essays on Imperial Defence in Honour of Donald Mackenzie Schurman* (London, 1997).

and a graduate of Queen's University, Kingston, Ontario. He studied at Harvard and Cambridge (where he completed a thesis on Canada and mercantile policy to 1791), and was very much an initiator in a field which explored the maritime foundations of Imperial history. Like Harold Adams Innis and Donald Grant Creighton (fellow Canadians), Graham pursued the significance of staple trades in mercantile and thus Imperial policy and systems. After publishing several monographs on the influence of sea power on British North America, he wrote a major survey that used French as well as British and American sources: *Empire of the North Atlantic: The Maritime Struggle for North America* (Toronto, 1950; new edn., 1958). Other studies by Graham show a number of his interrelated themes about Britain's maritime pre-eminence and the Empire. He edited documents on Admiral Hovenden Walker's unsuccessful expedition to take Quebec in 1711; and he explained, that the ascendancy of the sailing ship continued long after the introduction of steam. Graham questioned customarily held assumptions. For example, his 'Fisheries and Sea Power', *Canadian Historical Association Annual Report for 1941* (Toronto, 1941), demonstrated that the Newfoundland fishery never fulfilled its function as a great 'nursery of seamen'. Newfoundland's value, he reasoned, was strategic, not economic. Graham taught a generation of post-graduate students the value of documentary analysis and of no-nonsense thinking free from liberal bias (which he thought 'a fraud'). But he will perhaps best be remembered for his attempt, an incomplete one, to explain the *Pax Britannia* in maritime terms.

Trying to bring his theories of history together, Graham most directly demonstrated his concept of the interrelationship between the navy and Empire in two books of lectures: *The Politics of Naval Supremacy: Studies in Maritime Ascendancy* (Cambridge, 1965) and *Tides of Empire: Discursions on the Expansion of Britain Overseas* (Montreal, 1972). Citing the theories propounded by the Edwardian geographer Sir Halford Mackinder, Graham concluded that the consolidation by the early twentieth century of great land-based empires—'continental colossuses', as he called Russia and the United States—signalled the eclipse of Britain's hundred-year ability to dominate world politics through the exercise of sea power. His argument set down a foundation on which other scholars have built. 'Mackinder versus Mahan', as prophets of Imperial destiny, subsequently emerged as a key theme in Kennedy's *The Rise and Fall of British Naval Mastery.* Making a case for the relative importance of land power in India over the Royal Navy as a foundation of Britain's status as a great power, Edward Ingram in *Commitment to Empire: Prophecies of the Great Game, 1797–1800* (Oxford, 1981), carried the Mackinderan explanation of Imperial decline emphasized by Graham and Kennedy back further still. Andrew D. Lambert, however, has gone in the other direction. In his recent examination of *The Crimean War: British Grand*

Strategy, 1853–56 (Manchester, 1990), he stresses the value of the navy to Britain in the 'Great Game' for Asia.

Graham dealt extensively with aspects of the 'Great Game' himself in two massive works: *Great Britain in the Indian Ocean: A Study of Maritime Enterprise, 1810–1850* (Oxford, 1967) and *The China Station: War and Diplomacy, 1830–1860* (Oxford, 1978), perhaps his best works. Graham's treatment of the Indian Ocean emphasized the crucial role played by British sea power in suppressing piracy and bolstering British India's 'Persian Shield'. Graham's emphasis on naval supremacy as a foundation of Empire along the Asian rim echoed the basic argument put forward by K. M. Panikkar, the well-known Indian historian more than twenty years earlier. As the British Raj in India entered its final phase, Panikkar had published a slender but incisive treatise on *India and the Indian Ocean: An Essay on the Influence of Sea Power on Indian History* (London, 1945). As it elaborated issues raised by Panikkar, Graham's work on sea power in the Indian Ocean complemented the contemporaneous appearance of another essential work dealing with British mastery in Middle Eastern waters: J. B. Kelly, *Britain and the Persian Gulf, 1795–1880* (Oxford, 1968). Like Graham and Panikkar, Kelly stressed the interconnected relationship between navy and Empire. 'Command of the sea,' he wrote in the opening sentence of his exhaustive study, 'is the prerequisite of power in the Persian Gulf.' Graham's work on the East Indies and China Stations similarly coincided with, and influenced, other scholarship. A number of studies were undertaken by his students, or associates who sooner or later sought his advice. For example, John Bach, an Australian, completed a Ph.D. thesis which became a book, *The Australia Station: A History of the Royal Navy in the South-West Pacific, 1821–1913* (Kensington, NSW, 1986); and H. A. Colgate had written earlier a notable MA thesis, 'Trincomalee and the East Indies Squadron, 1746–1844' (University of London, 1959).

Graham's themes were taken up by Barry Gough, also a Canadian, whose thesis, under Graham's direction, was a study of the Navy's Pacific Station. This was published, after extensive alteration, as *The Royal Navy and the Northwest Coast of North America, 1810–1914: A Study of British Maritime Ascendancy* (Vancouver, 1971). He argued that it was not solely North West Company and Hudson's Bay Company commercial influences that shaped British policy, but that state support for trade by the navy protected Canada's Pacific coast from Russia and the United States. Gough thus modified the mercantile theme as developed by John S. Galbraith in *The Hudson's Bay Company as an Imperial Factor, 1821–1869* (Berkeley, 1957). His work had demonstrated Imperial expansion at a time of apparent mid-century British Imperial indifference. The study integrated British Columbia defence and trans-Pacific aspirations into the larger questions of Imperial defence.

A renaissance in the study of Canadian native history in the 1970s shaped

Gough's thought, and suggested the role of policing forces in Imperial domains. Nineteenth-century naval records provide remarkable material on North American native reactions to imperialism and naval force. In *Distant Dominion* (Vancouver, 1980), he examined the relationship of trans-Pacific and global commerce to naval exploration.[9] Spain's responses to growing British authority provide a sub-theme. His study on nineteenth-century maritime power and the North-west coast American Indians, *Gunboat Frontier*, was published in 1984.[10]

J. C. Beaglehole and the Pacific

As a field for historical inquiry, oceanic discovery—and its influence in distant areas of Empire—had long interested the English, Scots, and Irish,[11] but it fell to a New Zealander, John Caut Beaglehole, the historian of Pacific exploration, to bring together all relevant documentation on Captain James Cook, RN. Under the patronage of the Hakluyt Society (founded 1846 in London to print accounts of English voyaging), Beaglehole compiled the definitive edition of Cook's journals and related texts. His massive biography of Cook was published posthumously in 1974, also by the Hakluyt Society.[12] His work documented British governmental interest in science and Empire overseas, particularly in a maritime and commercial Empire, the possibilities of which in scope and grandeur were dazzling. The 'Southern Continent'—both elusive and unknown—entered British scientific understanding, through Cook's achievements. Beaglehole's work marked the end of the first serious examination of British voyaging in the South Pacific, with all its international and British Imperial implications.

Scholarship begun in the late 1960s concentrated on the study of science, trade, and Imperial policy in regards to the Antipodes and the Pacific Ocean. David Mackay, another New Zealander, exploited scientific records bearing on British policy in his *In the Wake of Cook: Exploration, Science and Empire, 1780–1801* (New York, 1985). Meanwhile, Alan Frost had undertaken a more specific study on naval stores and their influence on the development of Australia. His book *Convicts and Empire: A Naval Question* (Melbourne, 1980), which was a contribution to the

[9] New edition entitled *The Northwest Coast: British Navigation, Trade and Discoveries to 1812* (Vancouver, 1992). See also Barry Gough, 'Pax Britannica: Peace, Force and World Power', *The Round Table*, CCCXIV (1990), pp. 167–88.

[10] Gough, *Gunboat Frontier: British Maritime Authority and Northwest Coast Indians, 1846–1890* (Vancouver, 1984).

[11] The first substantial work on this subject was undertaken by J. A. Williamson, an Oxford historian and biographer of Sir John Hawkins; a convenient summary of his work is *The Ocean in English History: Being the Ford Lectures* (Oxford, 1941).

[12] J. C. Beaglehole, ed., *The Journals of Captain Cook on his Voyages of Discovery*, Vols. I–III (London, 1955–67); Vol. IV, *The Life of Captain Cook* (London, 1974).

debate on Australia's convict foundation, argued that the material requirements of the British fleet underscored the British quest for places to transport convicts. In *The Voyage of the Endeavour: Captain Cook and the Discovery of the Pacific* (St Leonards, NSW, 1998), Frost emphasized the international and Imperial context of Cook's voyaging as well as the great navigator's contribution to science and the shaping of the modern imagination.[13]

Frost's line of argument was, in large measure, an extension of one theme of Vincent T. Harlow's *The Founding of the Second British Empire, 1763–1793*, 2 vols. (London, 1952, 1964). Frost's position did not go unchallenged by Mackay, but it supported an earlier theme of Antipodean historiography first developed by K. M. Dallas and extended by Howard T. Fry.[14] At a time when historians were to challenge once more the argument that the Australian colonies were a dumping-ground for British criminal classes, these studies pointed to the strategic and material, as well as the economic, scientific, and political needs of a widening network of trade routes and places of trade and settlement. Graham's work had so linked northern Australia to British Imperial interests in China and Japan, and Gough's did the same for the Canadian west coast's trans-Pacific relations. The navy provided a world-wide network of bases and influence. Rudy Bauss showed, too, how parts of the 'informal empire', such as Rio de Janeiro, could be employed by the British.[15]

The navy sailed all the seas, and historians and anthropologists realized that naval records and other documents for the study of maritime history offered fruitful opportunities for research. To be singled out in this context is Australian Greg Dening, anthropologist as well as historian. Dening first studied the impact of American mariners in the Marquesas. In the British Imperial context he produced noteworthy studies of HMS *Bounty* and of the social impact of Pacific islanders and circumstances on British mariners. In a reversal, possibly, of the argument of the 'fatal impact', Dening portrayed 'the beach' as a cross-cultural zone of influence. To him, the navy and the colonies were organic worlds in interchange, each susceptible to change by the other's influence. His work is best exemplified in his monographs *The Bounty: An Ethnographic History* (Melbourne, 1988) and *History's Anthropology: The Death of William Gooch*

[13] For these themes in relation to the earlier phase of British voyaging in the Pacific from Drake to Anson see Glyndwr Williams, *The Great South Sea: English Voyages and Encounters, 1570–1750* (New Haven, 1997).

[14] K. M. Dallas, *Trading Posts or Penal Colonies: The Commercial Significance of Cook's New Holland Route to the Pacific* (Hobart, 1969); Howard T. Fry, *Alexander Dalrymple (1737–1808) and the Expansion of British Trade* (London, 1970).

[15] Rudy Bauss, 'Rio de Janeiro, Strategic Base for Global Designs of the British Royal Navy, 1777–1815', in Craig L. Symonds and others, *New Aspects of Naval History* (Annapolis, Md., 1981), pp. 75–89.

(Lanham, Md., 1988).[16] Dening's work brought new ways of seeing to naval and Imperial history, and it points to possibilities for future scholarship.

It may be observed that Beaglehole not only opened the Pacific world to Mackay, Frost, Dening, and others, but he set new standards for the study of hydrography and marine surveying. Charts and sailing directions compiled by British naval surveyors may be the most lasting testament of the British Empire. The history of these achievements is still largely confined to institutional studies, which tend, understandably, to be self-serving. Building on a late-nineteenth-century study by Commander L. S. Dawson,[17] Vice-Admiral Sir Archibald Day (formerly hydrographer of the navy), using primary sources, produced *The Admiralty Hydrographic Service, 1795–1919* (London, 1967). Another hydrographer, Rear-Admiral George S. Ritchie, added to Day's survey by exploring certain themes on Australian, South American, North Pacific, and Arctic history in *The Admiralty Chart: British Naval Hydrography in the Nineteenth Century* (London, 1967). In his recent *Charts and Surveys in Peace and War: The History of the Royal Navy Hydrographic Service, 1919–1970* (London, 1995), Rear-Admiral Roger Morris—yet another former hydrographer of the navy—has carried the official story of British naval hydrography into the late twentieth century and the era of deep-ocean exploration.

This field, it may be here added, offers countless opportunities for research. Hugh Wallace, trained in the Graham school, pointed the way for others in his *The Navy, the Company, and Richard King: British Exploration in the Canadian Arctic, 1829–1860* (Montreal, 1980), based on Admiralty, Royal Geographical Society, and Hudson's Bay Company sources. Using Surgeon King as advocate for a means of discovering a North-west Passage that might have made Sir John Franklin's fatal expedition unnecessary, Wallace showed that King promoted the employment of lightweight equipment. The Admiralty never learned the lesson. In another context, Ruth McKenzie's edition of Henry Bayfield's surveying journals in eastern Canadian waters shows another legacy left by the navy to Empire and to safe navigation.[18]

Here it may be mentioned that the navy was guardian of seaborne commerce and was servant of official policy. Thus, after the British slave trade was abolished in 1807, it fell to the navy to try to eradicate the trade where diplomacy failed. The historiography of the navy and the slave trade is a branch of Imperial history, for

[16] Both these volumes appeared in enlarged or modified editions as, respectively, *Mr Bligh's Bad Language: Passion, Power, and Theatre on the Bounty* (Cambridge, 1992), and *The Death of William Gooch: A History's Anthropology* (Melbourne, 1995).

[17] Commander L. S. Dawson, *Memoirs of Hydrography* (Eastbourne, 1885).

[18] Ruth McKenzie, ed., *St Lawrence Survey Journals of Captain Henry Wolsey Bayfield, 1829–1853*, 2 vols. (Toronto, 1984 and 1986).

in order to promote and secure legitimate trade the navy assisted in Imperial expansion, for example, in Lagos. These themes were first explored, using Admiralty, Foreign Office, and other state documents printed in *Parliamentary Papers*, by Christopher Lloyd in his book *The Navy and the Slave Trade* (London, 1949). For many years this served as a model for popular accounts,[19] but it also offered fresh scope to Raymond Howell who, using Admiralty papers and embracing East as well as West Africa, wrote a detailed thesis, later published as *The Royal Navy and the Slave Trade* (London, 1987) on East Africa. Naval records remain a largely unexploited corpus of documentation for the study of the slave trade and counter-measures and of African and other participants.

The study of the navy in relation to the Empire has one major common theme—the study of bases, keys to authority, and naval influence in home and distant waters.[20] From the 1980s interest grew in administrative history and infrastructure in relation to operations. Of particular importance were the findings of Jonathan Coad in *The Royal Dockyards, 1690–1850: Architects and Engineering Works of the Sailing Navy* (Aldershot, 1989). He surveyed not only home bases but some overseas, providing full examinations of Gibraltar, Minorca, Malta, Antigua, and Bermuda. Coad concentrated on the age of sail, as did Daniel A. Baugh and N. A. M. Rodger in their earlier, ground-breaking work on naval administration and infrastructure.[21] Though much room for further research remains, Jon Tetsuro Sumida has made valuable preliminary examination of the transition of the navy and its bases to the machine age in his notable article on 'British Naval Operational Logistics, 1914–1918', *Journal of Military History*, LVII, 3 (July 1993), pp. 447–480. So too has G. A. H. Gordon, in his assessment of the industrial infrastructure behind the inter-war navy, *British Seapower and Procurement Between the Wars: A Reappraisal of Rearmament* (Annapolis, Md., 1988).

Unfinished Business

Led by J. R. Hill, ed., *The Oxford Illustrated History of the Royal Navy* (Oxford, 1995) and N. A. M. Rodger's *Safeguard of the Sea: A Naval History of Britain, 660–1649* (New York, 1997), several surveys of the navy's history have appeared in recent years. A sweeping collection of primary materials has been assembled in

[19] W. E. F. Ward, *The Royal Navy and the Slavers: The Suppression of the Atlantic Slave Trade* (London, 1969).

[20] For the eighteenth century the major contribution is that of Daniel A. Baugh.

[21] Daniel A. Baugh, *British Naval Administration in the Age of Walpole* (Princeton, 1965); N. A. M. Rodger, *The Wooden World: An Anatomy of the Georgian Navy* (London, 1986), and 'The Victualling of the Royal Navy during the Seven Years' War', *Bulletin du Centre d'Histoire des Espaces Atlantique* (Bordeaux, 1985).

John B. Hattendorf and others, eds., *British Naval Documents, 1204–1960* (London, 1993). It is also worth noting that Patrick O'Brian's beautifully written, acutely researched, and best-selling Aubrey-Maturin novels have done much to generate a wide, present-day interest in the sailing navy and its world. Similarly, the international commercial success of *One Hundred Days* (London, 1992), Admiral Sandy Woodward's compelling memoir of his experience as the task group commander in the Falklands campaign of 1982, can be seen as indicative of the level of interest that naval topics are capable of attracting. Though they deal with Imperial themes, the stories told by O'Brian and Woodward are, however, fundamentally accounts of the navy in action.

In fact, the history of the navy continues to be written mainly as one of operations in wartime. For instance, Correlli Barnett's *Engage the Enemy More Closely: The Royal Navy in the Second World War* (London, 1991), building on themes developed in Captain Stephen Roskill's massive official history *The War at Sea*, 3 vols. (London, 1954–61), is essentially an operational history. Yet it goes deeper—into ship's companies, policy formation, ship and armament design—and deeper still as an enquiry into the nature of British sea power in the modern era. Imperial themes, however, are not particularly conspicuous in writing about the navy in the Second World War. An important exception is David Stevens, ed., *The Royal Australian Navy in World War II* (St Leonards, NSW, 1996); for the most part, however, the Royal Navy's protection of Empire and trade during the Second World War, and Dominion co-operation with the navy in bases, equipment, and research, await their historians.

For the post-Second World War era new themes were partially exploited by Eric Grove's survey of British naval power: *Vanguard to Trident: British Naval Policy Since World War Two* (Annapolis, Md., 1987). The navy's relation to North Atlantic Treaty Organization (NATO) remains, however, largely untouched. British naval history is still very much a slice of national history, and neglects the study of the NATO alliance in which sea power is fundamental. The declining authority of the British Empire in the eastern waters offers notable scope for the historian. Pioneering work was done by Philip Darby in *British Defence Policy East of Suez, 1947–68* (London, 1973) and Malcolm Murfett in his *In Jeopardy: The Royal Navy and Far Eastern Defence Policy, 1945–1951* (Kuala Lumpur, 1995), which set forth models for the naval retreat from Imperial obligations after the end of the war. In his recent *Background to the ANZUS Pact: Strategy and Diplomacy, 1945–55* (New York, 1995), W. David McIntyre illuminates the Antipodean dimension of naval grand strategy in the post-war Pacific. Australia is the focus in Hector Donohue, *From Empire Defence to the Long Haul: Post-War Defence Policy and Its Impact on Naval Force Structure Planning, 1945–1955* (Canberra, 1996) and David Stevens, ed., *In Search of a Maritime Strategy: The Maritime Element in Australian*

Defence Planning Since 1901 (Canberra, 1997). An important article by Peter James Henshaw on 'The Transfer of Simonstown: Afrikaner Nationalism, South African Strategic Dependence, and British Global Power', *Journal of Imperial and Commonwealth History*, XX, 3 (Sept. 1992), pp. 419–44, brings South Africa into the picture of decolonization and the post-war navy. Much work remains to be done none the less—not least, as the archives open, on the decision of the Wilson government in the late 1960s to end the permanent presence of substantial British forces 'East of Suez'.

In retrospect, Marder, Graham, and Beaglehole advanced mightily the agenda for naval and Imperial historians. Marder analysed the workings of the Admiralty in relation to Parliament and the press, and also examined the documents, both contemporary and retrospective, of senior officers directly involved in policy-making operations. Graham integrated economic and trade matters into the general narrative of British maritime ascendancy, or enterprise—with focus on the navy. Beaglehole demonstrated the significance of maritime skill and technology in exploration and expansion in the most distant oceans. They did not, however, fully define the possibilities for the conjunction of naval and Imperial history.

The general linkage of navy to Empire continues to escape historians, perhaps because the task is such a daunting one. Case studies are needed: a survey of the role of British naval power and its relation to the *Pax Britannica*; a survey of overseas stations and bases; and a study of how the Royal Navy influenced the course of the early history of colonial and Commonwealth navies. Naval historians love to write about battles, but once they go beyond this they find unexplored subjects of equal excitement and value. Treating naval history as a branch of defence history or even strategic studies goes only part of the way towards integrating the study of the navy and the Empire. Far from being an old-fashioned field of inquiry, naval and Imperial themes are rich in possibilities for studying the interface of societies, systems, and states.

Select Bibliography

JOHN BACH, *The Australia Station: A History of the Royal Navy in the South West Pacific, 1821–1913* (Kensington, NSW, 1986).

CORRELLI BARNETT, *Engage the Enemy More Closely: The Royal Navy in the Second World War* (London, 1991).

JONATHAN G. COAD, *The Royal Dockyards, 1690–1850: Architecture and Engineering Works of the Sailing Navy* (Aldershot, 1989).

GRACE E. FOX, *British Admirals and Chinese Pirates, 1832–1869* (London, 1940).

ALAN FROST, *Convicts and Empire: A Naval Question, 1776–1811* (Melbourne, 1980).

BARRY M. GOUGH, *The Royal Navy and the Northwest Coast of North America, 1810–1914:*

A Study of British Maritime Ascendancy (Vancouver, 1971).

GERALD S. GRAHAM, *Empire of the North Atlantic: The Maritime Struggle for North America*, 2nd edn. (Toronto, 1958).

—— *Great Britain in the Indian Ocean: A Study of Maritime Enterprise, 1810–1850* (Oxford, 1967).

—— *The Politics of Naval Supremacy: Studies in British Maritime Ascendancy* (Cambridge, 1965).

ERIC GROVE, *Vanguard to Trident: British Naval Policy Since World War II* (Annapolis, Md., 1987).

PAUL M. KENNEDY, *The Rise and Fall of British Naval Mastery* (New York, 1976).

CHRISTOPHER LLOYD, *The Navy and the Slave Trade: The Suppression of the African Slave Trade in the Nineteenth Century* (London, 1949).

ARTHUR J. MARDER, *The Anatomy of British Sea Power: A History of British Naval Policy in the Pre-Dreadnought Era, 1880–1905* (New York, 1940). British edn.: *British Naval Policy, 1880–1905: The Anatomy of British Sea Power* (London, 1941).

—— *From the Dreadnought to Scapa Flow: The Royal Navy in the Fisher Era, 1904–1919*, 5 vols. (London, 1961–70).

MALCOLM H. MURFETT, *In Jeopardy: The Royal Navy and British Far Eastern Defence Policy, 1945–1951* (Kuala Lumpur, 1995).

EUGENE L. RASOR, *British Naval History Since 1815: A Guide to the Literature* (New York, 1990).

CAPTAIN S. W. [STEPHEN] ROSKILL, *The War at Sea, 1909–1945*, 3 vols. (London, 1954–61).

STEPHEN ROSKILL, *Naval Policy Between the Wars in the Period of Anglo-American Antagonism, 1912–1929* (New York, 1968).

—— Appendix: 'A Historical Controversy', in Roskill, *Churchill and the Admirals* (New York, 1977).

22

Imperial Defence

DAVID KILLINGRAY

Empires are gained by force and need to be maintained by force, and it was ever so with the British Empire. The term 'imperial defence' gained a specific meaning in the last decades of the nineteenth century when it came to be applied to an integrated system of defence for the home islands, the overseas territories whether formally or informally held, and the commercial and strategic links between them. The navy played a primary role in this system by protecting the waters around Britain and the expanding maritime trade routes vital to Britain's industrial economy. While warships helped to impose British informal authority on distant coasts, riverain peoples and polities, the army had the major role of securing and guarding the formal Empire against external aggression, protecting and securing unstable frontiers, and maintaining internal security. Garrisons, so called 'little-wars', and aid to the civil power were standard fare for the military guardians of Empire.

The official terminology of Imperial military activity needs to be viewed critically. Imperial 'defence' also included 'savage wars' of conquest and 'pacification' which, to the victims and opponents of British aggression, were wars of 'offence' and subjugation. This chapter is concerned principally with the historiography of the military and the schemes and strategies devised between the 1880s and 1960s to defend an Empire that was often overstretched, under threat from foreign powers, and where alien British rule was increasingly challenged by unwilling subjects.

In the late nineteenth century ideas on Imperial defence were discussed in service and other journals intended to influence ministers and service chiefs. Spenser Wilkinson, first holder of the Chichele Chair of Military History at Oxford, collaborated with Charles Dilke on a book entitled *Imperial Defence*, which argued the urgency of cohesion between colonies and metropole.[1] The urgency was due to the changed balance of power in Europe and Asia after the late 1870s and the perceived threat from Russia, which pushed against the North-West frontier of India and the other soft spots on the strategic route to the East. Leopold Amery,

[1] London, 1892.

in 1905, wrote of a possible future 'great war in Asia' and of the need 'first and foremost' of 'a supreme navy, and secondly an efficient army, capable of indefinite expansion, and available at the exposed frontiers of the Empire', to be paid for by the economic development of a united Empire having 'a common system of defence'.[2] By then it was clear also that Britain was likely to be faced with a military commitment in Europe while also having to safeguard worldwide Imperial interests. The dilemma of how to balance the requirements of metropolitan security with the need to uphold and maintain a greatly varied global Empire lay at the heart of Imperial defence schemes and their subsequent history.

The debate over Imperial defence was included in most of the general histories of British Imperial relations of the time, often by enthusiastic proponents of colonial ideology. Sir Charles Lucas's semi-official six-volume *The Empire at War* (London), published between 1921 and 1926, set out to demonstrate how the Empire had come to the aid of the Mother Country in time of war. A systematic, full scholarly survey of the history of Imperial defence did not appear until the *Cambridge History of the British Empire*, published over a thirty-year period from 1929, in which W. C. B. Tunstall's chapters were mainly a military history of Britain as a Great Power.[3] Much was ignored about relations with the colonies and Dominions, the legitimacy of Empire was not questioned, and although the third volume was about the Empire-Commonwealth, it stopped at the end of the First World War. Max Beloff's two-volume study plotting Britain's decline as an Imperial power also had a great deal to say on the twists and turns of Imperial defence, but for the most part from a metropolitan standpoint.[4]

Two outstanding accounts on the subject are both relatively brief: Michael Howard's Ford Lectures at Oxford in 1971,[5] and the final work of John Gallagher.[6] Howard takes a broad approach to British foreign and defence policies from the end of the nineteenth century to the end of the Second World War as he examines the conflict between Continental and Imperial strategies. Attempts by British politicians and military men to shelter within the fold of a united Empire and to

[2] L. S. Amery, 'Imperial Defence and National Policy', in Charles Sydney Goldman, ed., *The Empire and the Century: A Series of Imperial Problems and Possibilities by Various Writers* (London, 1905), pp. 174–96.

[3] E. A. Benians and others, eds., *Cambridge History of the British Empire*, 9 vols. (Cambridge, 1929–59), II, pp. 806–41, and III, pp. 230–54, 563–604.

[4] Max Beloff, *Imperial Sunset*, 2 vols. (London, 1969; Basingstoke, 1989).

[5] Michael Howard, *The Continental Commitment: The Dilemma of British Defence Policy in the Era of Two World Wars* (London, 1972).

[6] John Gallagher, 'The Decline, Revival and Fall of the British Empire', in Anil Seal, ed., *The Decline, Revival and Fall of the British Empire: The Ford Lectures and Other Essays* (Cambridge, 1982).

disregard or exploit the balance of power in Europe were unlikely to succeed except in the very short term. Empire was never strong enough or sufficiently cohesive to protect Britain from the changing realities of European politics that dragged the country into two Continental wars within thirty years. And the end of the story was a dependent alliance with the United States while Empire crumbled away. Not that Empire just slid neatly away, as might be implied from the title of Gallagher's brilliant essay. Indian security and control over oil supplies were the key objectives in securing an 'eastern arc of empire' during the First World War, a system of mainly informal control over a vast area of the Middle East that became subject to 'a British Monroe Doctrine'. This 'renewed search for the safety of the Raj', argues Gallagher, 'was building another empire in the Middle East' which 'was to leave the British desperately over-extended'. With a fragile Empire and domestic restraints on power, the Continental and Imperial dilemma took on new dimensions which most British politicians sought to resolve by keeping out of war. The path to appeasement, and the policy itself in the 1930s, made good sense in Imperial terms.

For a large part of the period under discussion the army's primary role was with the defence of Empire. Hew Strachan has argued that by the mid-nineteenth century the business of Imperial garrisoning, organization, and strategy was decisive in shaping the character and institutions of the British army.[7] By the 1860s the debate on colonial defence was twofold: how economically to secure overseas Empire, and how to encourage the colonies of white settlement to pay for their own defence. Domestic taxpayers were prepared to shoulder the strategic defence costs of the metropole but not internal policing and frontier wars in distant colonies.[8] Much scholarly attention has been directed at the various attempts to persuade colonies to pay for their own defence and how these colonies could be brought into a scheme of co-operative Imperial defence. N. H. Gibbs, in his inaugural lecture to the Chichele Chair at Oxford in 1955, focused on the origins of Imperial defence. Up to the 1870s, he argued, this was 'simply a series of separate colonial problems, mostly distasteful, wherein strategy was rarely treated on its merits and almost invariably ignored in favour of constitutional and financial arguments'.[9] Departmental differences and parsimonious colonial cautions were slowly overcome and crises in central Asia led to the creation, first of a Colonial Defence Committee and then, in 1902, of an advisory Committee of Imperial

7 Hew Strachan, *Wellington's Legacy: The Reform of the British Army, 1830–1850* (Manchester, 1984); see also Peter Burroughs, 'Imperial Defence and the Victorian Army', *Journal of Imperial and Commonwealth History* (hereafter *JICH*), XV (1986), pp. 53–72.

8 Bruce Knox, 'The Concept of Empire in the Mid-Nineteenth Century: Ideas in the Colonial Defence Inquiries of 1859–61', *JICH*, XV (1987), p. 248.

9 N. H. Gibbs, *The Origins of Imperial Defence* (Oxford, 1955), pp. 6–7.

Defence (CID) to the Cabinet charged with surveying what Balfour called 'the strategic military needs of the Empire'. The fifty-year rule closing official documents denied Gibbs the opportunity of taking his study further in the twentieth century. The same strictures applied to the American historian Franklyn Johnston, whose study of the CID was thus not always complete or accurate.[10]

As official documents and private papers became accessible, scholars could attempt more accurately to plumb the motives of the makers of Imperial defence policies in the twentieth century. Nicholas d'Ombrain's study, which benefited from the new rules of access, was largely concerned with the administration of British defence before the First World War. He concluded that before 1914 the CID was acting as 'an executive agency' and moving towards becoming a Department of National Defence.[11] A more recent study has looked at the Imperial defence policies of Prime Minister Balfour and the Conservative Party in advocating a blue-water strategy and a small regular army for colonial wars and home defence.[12] At the turn of the century Britain's diplomatic 'isolation' was marked by growing challenges from European rivals and compounded by the military weaknesses exposed in South Africa. This pushed London to think more radically about the organization of Imperial defence, to seek a regional alliance with Japan, negotiate an end to colonial confrontations with France, and also to maintain a territorial stand-off from Russia on the lengthy Asian borderlands. These crucial changes in British foreign policy at the beginning of the twentieth century, and subsequent debates, are reflected in the historiography of Imperial defence.[13]

In the early 1920s Paul Knaplund examined the attitudes of the white settler colonies towards intra-Imperial defence schemes during the late nineteenth century; he asked: 'why were the Dominions so reluctant to make binding defensive agreements?' His answer pointed to colonial reluctance to raise taxes, to use limited capital resources required for economic development, and to become engaged in defence schemes that might involve the colonies in wars for which there was no local popular consent or political control.[14] Metropolitan Imperial defence planners had to face the tricky business of balancing the broad sweeps of global strategy designed to uphold British power and prestige against local colonial external interests and a growing sense of colonial particularism. Geography

[10] Franklyn Arthur Johnston, *Defence by Committee: The British Committee of Imperial Defence, 1885–1959* (London, 1960).

[11] Nicholas d'Ombrain, *War Machinery and High Policy: Defence Administration in Peacetime Britain, 1902–1914* (Oxford, 1973).

[12] Rhodri Williams, *Defending the Empire: The Conservative Party and British Defence Policy, 1899–1915* (New Haven, 1991).

[13] G. W. Monger, *The End of Isolation: British Foreign Policy, 1900–1907* (London, 1963).

[14] Paul I. Knaplund, 'Intra-Imperial Aspects of Britain's Defence Question, 1870–1900', *Canadian Historical Review*, III (1922), pp. 120–42.

and resources largely dictated the territorial defence agendas of the Dominions. Sometimes these correlated with the broad global interests of Britain, but often they did not. Frontier defence, particularly in north-west India and the long border between Canada and the United States, preoccupied military men. Colonel C. P. Stacey, a major historian of Canadian defence, argued in 1950 that the border with the United States was not demilitarized and that the turning-point was the Treaty of Washington in 1871.[15] Bourne's study, some twenty years later, focused on the balance of power in North America and British plans for a possible war with the United States, modified after the 1870s when there was a 'decline in hostility rather than a rise of friendship'.[16] In the decade or so before the First World War, John Gooch has argued, Canadian defence was one of the most awkward issues faced by the CID. Considerable antipathy over strategy existed between the Admiralty and the War Office, 'and so strong the navalist sympathy among politicians, that resolution proved impossible'.[17] An overall view of the problems of Canadian security in relation to Imperial defence schemes was provided first by D. C. Gordon in 1965, but a more thoroughly documented study by Richard A. Preston appeared two years later.[18]

Britain's alliance with Japan, abandoned in 1921 in the interests of amity with the United States, was also a major concern for the Pacific Dominions. John McCarthy's pioneer study, *Australia and Imperial Defence, 1918–39: A Study in Air and Sea Power*, looked at British–Australian relations over questions of defence, and in particular the important matter of the Singapore naval base.[19] As D. C. Watt observed, in 1963, the paradox between an Imperial defence policy and an Imperial foreign policy was obvious before the First World War. The war changed that as the Dominions asserted their autonomy and became members of the League of Nations, and Britain ceased attempts to formulate a common Imperial foreign policy. Although Admiralty plans for a single Imperial navy were defeated, by the early 1930s, wrote Watt, 'the Commonwealth amounted for defence purposes virtually to a permanent alliance with armed forces, with a common centre of advice on defence both between the individual armed services and in the CID as a whole'.[20] British defence relations with the antipodean Dominions

[15] C. P. Stacey, 'The Myth of the Unguarded Frontier, 1815–1871', *American Historical Review*, LVI (1950), pp. 1–18.

[16] Kenneth Bourne, *Britain and the Balance of Power in North America, 1815–1908* (London, 1967).

[17] John Gooch, 'Great Britain and the Defence of Canada, 1896–1914', *JICH*, III (1975), p. 383.

[18] D. C. Gordon, *The Dominion Partnership in Imperial Defense, 1870–1914* (Baltimore, 1965); Richard A. Preston, *Canada and 'Imperial Defense': A Study of the Origin of the British Commonwealth Defense Organization, 1867–1919* (Toronto, 1967).

[19] St Lucia, Queensland, 1976.

[20] D. C. Watt, 'Imperial Defence Policy and Imperial Foreign Policy, 1911–1939: A Neglected Paradox', *Journal of Commonwealth Political Studies*, I (1963), p. 275.

were dominated by naval questions and, by the 1930s, the strategic deterrent value of Singapore. James Neidpath, in his 1981 study of the defence of Britain's eastern Empire, asked a fundamental question: whether the policy of building the Singapore naval base and sending a fleet to the East was inherently and fundamentally flawed. He argued that the strategy was right for the circumstances of the 1920s, but by the 1930s that calculated risk came undone when the United Kingdom was faced with the prospect of a one-ocean navy fighting a two-ocean war. And Singapore was not just a naval matter; it had also a military role, the defence of Malaya, and on both counts the British failed in 1941–42.[21]

The defence of India and the route via the Middle East was central to the strategic thinking of most British politicians from the eighteenth century onwards as they calculated how to maintain Britain's wealth, prestige, and status as a great Imperial power. It is thus a dominant theme in the historiography of Imperial defence, and consequently the literature on the subject is vast. It was given greater prominence by Ronald Robinson and John Gallagher's seminal *Africa and the Victorians: The Official Mind of Imperialism* (London, 1961), which was researched and written in the late 1950s, and no doubt influenced by the débâcle of Suez in 1956.[22] The book employed the inexact but stimulating term, 'the official mind', which was interpreted as the official consensus in the metropole of how Empire was to be extended, maintained, and defended. The British share in the carve-up of Africa starting from the 1880s, the authors maintained, was largely due to strategic considerations that arose from the need to protect the route to India via Suez and the Cape. 'British policy-makers', they stated in a well-known passage, 'moved into Africa, not to build a new African empire, but to protect the old empire in India. What decided when and where they would go forward was their traditional conception of world strategy' (p. 464). Local crises, in Egypt in 1882 and in South Africa in 1877–81, determined the timetable and process of expansion. The authors were criticized principally for their analysis of the partition of Africa, but the book was important in initiating a vigorous debate on the nature of imperialism.[23] Few, if any, critics questioned the British belief that the route to India had to be secured, although whether that required formal or informal control of territory certainly was a matter of debate.

Possession of India and the Empire was fundamental, and any abandonment of control was seen by all Imperial-minded British politicians, at least until the 1930s, as a negation of Britain's status as a great global power. The 'Great Game' in Asia pitched Britain into a long and largely inconclusive confrontation with

[21] James Neidpath, *The Singapore Naval Base and the Defence of Britain's Eastern Empire, 1919–1941* (Oxford, 1981), p. 215.

[22] London, 1961.

[23] See Wm. Roger Louis, *Imperialism: The Robinson and Gallagher Controversy* (New York, 1976).

Russia, although diplomacy, rather than war, averted all but one conflict. Russian–British relations, D. R. Gillard maintained, need to be looked at within a broad Eurasian context; it is still debatable whether either power sought hegemony in Asia and whether Russia really posed a threat to India.[24] The defence of the North-West frontier and the Middle Eastern route constantly exercised the minds of Imperial military strategists, although policy changed in response to European considerations. For example, John Gooch's study of the British General Staff in the first decade of this century looked at the vital shift in British military thinking from a concentration on Imperial problems to a continental strategy.[25] Nearly fifteen years later, Aaron Friedberg, in *The Weary Titan: Britain and the Experience of Relative Decline, 1895–1905*, covered similar ground, usefully dealing with the advance of the Russian railway system in central Asia and the impact that this had on British strategic thinking and diplomacy.[26] On the period of the inter-war years, J. O. Rawson's unpublished thesis looked at the place of India in Imperial defence schemes, a work which was used by Brian Bond to argue that from the 1920s onwards 'the notion grew steadily that India should contribute to the general defence of the Empire in a more coherent and systematic way than in the nineteenth century', although attempts at modernizing the Indian Army were too little and too late, so that 'it was weaker and less prepared for war in 1939 than in 1914'.[27]

Control of the Suez Canal, astride the route to the East, remained central to British Imperial strategic thinking from the 1880s to the crisis of 1956. 'War imperialism' in 1914–19 resulted in Britain becoming a great military land power in the Middle East. Oil supplies assumed strategic significance in a region where British formal and informal control was challenged by a rising tide of nationalism. Possession of this 'pseudo-empire', John Darwin argued in the early 1980s, raised new questions about methods and motives of Imperial policy, of how to reconcile the needs of domestic politics with the preservation of a global Empire.[28] Britain did not so much fear colonial nationalism as her imperial rivals who would exploit old tensions in an effort to extend their own control in the region. Three

[24] D. R. Gillard, *The Struggle for Asia, 1828–1914: A Study in British and Russian Relations* (London, 1977).

[25] John Gooch, *The Plans of War: The General Staff and British Military Strategy, c.1900–1916* (London, 1974).

[26] Princeton, 1988, chap. 5.

[27] J. O. Rawson, 'The Role of India in Imperial Defence Beyond Indian Frontiers and Home Waters, 1919–1939', unpublished D.Phil. thesis, Oxford, 1976. Brian Bond, *British Military Strategy Between the Two World Wars* (Oxford, 1980), pp. 102, 123. India's lack of preparedness for war in 1939 is challenged by Pradeep Barua, 'Strategies and Doctrines of Imperial Defence: Britain and India, 1919–45', *JICH*, XXV, 2 (1997), pp. 240–66.

[28] John Darwin, *Britain and Egypt in the Middle East: Imperial Policy in the Aftermath of War, 1918–1922* (London, 1981).

years later Keith Jeffery looked at how, in the post-war years, the army responded to the results of 'war imperialism', when military resources were stretched to their utmost in containing colonial unrest, establishing control over new areas of strategic interest, and there were fears of revolution in Britain.[29] Growing Indian nationalist sentiment meant that the Government of India now opposed supplying and paying for troops to be used as an Imperial fire brigade, while the Dominions were reluctant to get involved in Britain's adventures in the Middle East. Domestic war-weariness and the need for economic retrenchment heightened the dilemma. The solution to upholding British Imperial authority, wrote John Darwin, was found in pliant local collaborators, in acknowledging India's increasing political autonomy, and dealing as cheaply as possible with rebellion. The problems of Imperial defence became increasingly acute during the 1930s, but when war did break out in 1939 Britain was able to hold her position in the Middle East and successfully mobilize the largest Indian army ever to take the field. In the inter-war years, argues Anthony Clayton, Empire conferred Great Power status on Britain,[30] although by the 1930s that position was under severe challenge along a great arc of Empire from the Mediterranean to Singapore. Wartime survival of the 'gouty giant' was due more to the intervention of the United States than to any endowment conferred by the possession of an Empire.

Clayton details the many British colonial military campaigns in the inter-war years. Imperial defence schemes were invariably global or regional and shaped in London. But a major role for the army, and at times the other services, was in maintaining the internal security of the colonies. Indian security and the protection of the unstable North-West frontier figure prominently in the literature, but it is only more recently that systematic scholarly attention has been directed at local policies and the agents used in policing Empire. Philip Mason's study of the Indian Army largely addressed the internal economy and external roles of the force,[31] while two recent books look at how the army combated internal unrest.[32] British rule in India and the Middle East was severely challenged by colonial nationalists in the 1920s and 1930s, and substantial armed force was required to put down rebellion, especially in Iraq and Palestine, and to deal with the endemic violence that destabilized the North-West frontier. Elsewhere throughout the Empire, as indeed in India, the majority of military recruits were drawn from local peoples, mainly from the supposed 'martial races'. Colonial military forces in Asia

[29] Keith Jeffery, *The British Army and the Crisis of Empire, 1918–22* (Manchester, 1984).

[30] Anthony Clayton, *The British Empire as a Superpower, 1919–1939* (London, 1986).

[31] Philip Mason, *A Matter of Honour: An Account of the Indian Army, its Officers and Men* (London, 1974).

[32] T. A. Heathcote, *The Military in British India, 1600–1940* (London, 1993); David E. Omissi, *The Sepoy and the Raj: The Indian Army, 1860–1940* (Basingstoke, 1994).

and Africa became a subject of serious research only in the 1980s, with the focus on recruitment, the social impact of military service, Imperial roles, political responses, and internal security functions.[33]

Several studies in the 1980s looked at the controversial use of the Royal Air Force in policing large and inaccessible areas of Empire, particularly in the Middle East, north-east Africa, north-west India, and Africa. This policy was deemed both economical and practical, although 'bombing savages' gave rise to public disquiet in Britain.[34] The Royal Navy played a much smaller Imperial policing role, mostly in the Caribbean and the Pacific. The police, not the army, had the primary responsibility for maintaining colonial security. As with most colonial military forces, the police were recruited from local peoples and commanded by British officers. Colonial policing, long acknowledged as important by historians of Empire but largely ignored, has recently attracted growing interest.[35] Various studies have emphasized that in Malaya, Kenya, Cyprus, and Aden the end of Empire was anything but a peaceful process.

The loss of Empire, in Asia mainly in 1945–48 and in Africa between 1957 and 1964, helped fuel the debate about Britain's decline as a Great Power. The Imperial and military dimension has been comprehensively addressed by John Darwin in *Britain and Decolonisation: The Retreat from Empire in the Post-War World*.[36] His view is that British leaders after 1945 recognized Britain's economic and military weaknesses as a superpower role and hoped to prevent further erosion of power by pragmatic political responses to colonial nationalism. But, as Darwin writes, 'they were extremely reluctant to accept that even formal independence would end a relationship of special economic, political, and strategic intimacy' (p. 334). That global system of power was steadily eroded. In those cold war years Britain's defence policies were shaped not only by a nuclear strategy but also by a continued commitment to the defence of Europe as well as the defence of declining Imperial interests.[37] The attempt at the end of the Second World War to rebuild the British Empire as a global system, and to achieve a position of standing

[33] David Killingray, 'The Idea of a British Imperial African Army', *Journal of African History* (hereafter *JAH*), XX (1979), pp. 421–36.

[34] David E. Omissi, *Air Power and Colonial Control: The Royal Air Force, 1919–1939* (Manchester, 1990); David Killingray ' "A Swift Agent of Government": Air Power in British Colonial Africa, 1916–1939', *JAH*, XXV (1984), pp. 429–44.

[35] David Arnold, *Police Power and Colonial Rule: Madras, 1859–1947* (New Delhi, 1986); David M. Anderson and David Killingray, eds., *Policing the Empire: Government, Authority and Control, 1830–1940* (Manchester, 1991), and *Policing and Decolonisation: Nationalism, Politics and the Police, 1917–65* (Manchester, 1992).

[36] London, 1988

[37] John Baylis, *British Defence Policy: Striking the Right Balance* (London, 1989); C. J. Bartlett, *The Long Retreat: A Short History of British Defence Policy, 1945–1970* (London, 1972).

relative to the United States and the Soviet Union, argued John Kent, was focused on the Eastern Mediterranean and the Middle East, 'which formed the key imperial region and was the focus of Britain's military strategy'. The quest to regain Great Power status 'led imperial strategists to devise particular economic and military policies, rather than economic and military requirements dictating imperial strategy'.[38] The post-war policies to retain the Middle East as a British sphere of influence adhered to an Imperial defence strategy dating back to Napoleonic times; the paradoxical twists and turns can be followed in Wm. Roger Louis's magisterial *The British Empire in the Middle East*.[39] Refashioned, and to some extent strengthened, from the late 1940s to the 1960s as an 'East of Suez' policy, based on Aden and designed to resist Soviet ambitions in the region and to protect oil supplies, the policy was only abandoned due to a lack of resources.[40] Britain declined as a Great Power, but when did that process start? One view is that decline had set in before 1914 and had taken a firm grip by the early inter-war years, the outcome of economic and military rivalries and 'imperial overstretch'.[41] In 1991 four Canadian scholars questioned this analysis, particularly for the inter-war years. Britain, they argued, far from being weak and in decline, possessed substantial military and naval resources, held control over a global Empire, and had great prestige and confidence, all of which indicated Great Power status; indeed, said the concluding contributor, Britain was 'still pre-eminent in the world in September 1939'.[42]

The debate over Britain's decline from Imperial Great Power status seems set to continue as part of the broader debate on decolonization. A related debate concerns the balance sheet of the Empire and the costs of defending the Empire. It is an old question, considered by J. A. Hobson in his *Imperialism: A Study* (London, 1902), but given new impetus and direction by Lance E. Davis and Robert E. Huttenback's *Mammon and the Pursuit of Empire: The Political Economy of British Imperialism, 1860–1912*, in the mid-1980s.[43] In their cliometric analysis they argued that Empire was a fiscal burden to British taxpayers, diverting revenue and resources from more productive investment at home; in effect 'Britain actually maintained two defence establishments: one for the home islands and a second for the Empire' (p. 304). Their thesis on the costs of Imperial defence has been generally supported by

[38] John Kent, *British Imperial Strategy and the Origins of the Cold War, 1944–49* (Leicester, 1993), p. 212.

[39] Wm. Roger Louis, *The British Empire in the Middle East, 1945–1951: Arab Nationalism, the United States and Postwar Imperialism* (Oxford, 1984), particularly Part III.

[40] Philip Darby, *British Defence Policy East of Suez, 1947–1968* (London, 1973).

[41] Correlli Barnett, *The Collapse of British Power* (London, 1972) and Paul M. Kennedy, *The Rise and Fall of the Great Powers: Economic Change and Military Conflict from 1500 to 2000* (New York, 1987).

[42] Gordon Martel and others, in a special issue of the *International History Review*, XIII (1991), devoted to 'The Decline and Fall of Great Britain'.

[43] Cambridge, 1986.

Patrick K. O'Brien, who has argued that the vast expenditure devoted to militarily holding an Empire together at a time when the European balance of power needed to be addressed involved 'a gigantic misallocation of public money, disbursed over many years in pursuit of those conjoined chimeras: imperial defence and hegemony at sea'.[44] The riposte of more numerous critics is that the idea of a double defence establishment ignores Britain's global commercial role, that it was difficult to disentangle the 'British' from the 'Imperial' element in overall defence expenditure, and that Imperial defence expenditure was not a large proportion of the whole.[45] Another critic, Avner Offer, asserts that India was not a defence burden to Britain but an asset. Empire, particularly the Dominions, was a strategic asset to a beleaguered Britain in both world wars, with its huge contributions of raw material and manpower.[46]

In early 1942 Britain's loss of Singapore was a major step on the path towards the abandonment of Empire in Asia. Failure to defend that strategic and prized possession was largely due to the misfortunes of war in Europe and the Middle East. The United States was not then willing or able to assist Britain in protecting her Imperial possessions. Fourteen years later, in 1956, pressure from the United States forced the Conservative government to withdraw from its arrogant attempt to revive a past Imperial age. Another decade on, a Labour administration failed to deal firmly with a white settler rebellion in Rhodesia; African interests did not have a priority in Whitehall. It is ironic, then, that the last act of Imperial defence, the Falklands campaign of 1982, should not only be successful but take place in a post-Imperial age.

[44] Patrick K. O'Brien, 'The Costs and Benefits of British Imperialism, 1846–1914', *Past and Present*, CXX (1988), p. 199.

[45] Andrew Porter, 'The Balance Sheet of Empire, 1850–1914', *Historical Journal*, XXXI (1988), pp. 685–99; Paul Kennedy, 'Debate: The Costs and Benefits of British Imperialism, 1846–1914', *Past and Present*, CXXV (1989), pp. 186–92, and reply by O'Brien, pp. 192–99.

[46] Avner Offer, 'The British Empire, 1870–1914: A Waste of Money?', *Economic History Review*, XLVI (1993), pp. 215–38.

Select Bibliography

DAVID ANDERSON and DAVID KILLINGRAY, eds., *Policing the Empire: Government, Authority and Control, 1830–1940* (Manchester, 1991).

C. J. BARTLETT, *The Long Retreat: A Short History of British Defence Policy, 1945–1970* (London, 1972).

JOHN BAYLIS, *British Defence Policy: Striking the Right Balance* (Basingstoke, 1989).

MAX BELOFF, *Imperial Sunset*, 2 vols. (London, 1969 and Basingstoke, 1989): Vol. I, *Britain's Liberal Empire, 1897–1987*; Vol. II, *Dream of Commonwealth, 1921–42.*

E. A. BENIANS and others, eds., *The Cambridge History of the British Empire*, 9 vols. (Cambridge, 1929–59).

KENNETH BOURNE, *Britain and the Balance of Power in North America, 1815–1908* (London, 1967).

ANTHONY CLAYTON, *The British Empire as a Superpower, 1919–39* (Basingstoke, 1986).

PHILLIP DARBY, *British Defence Policy East of Suez, 1947–1968* (London, 1973).

JOHN DARWIN, *Britain, Egypt and the Middle East: Imperial Policy in the Aftermath of War, 1918–1922* (London, 1981).

Sir CHARLES WENTWORTH DILKE and SPENSER WILKINSON, *Imperial Defence* (London, 1892).

JOHN GALLAGHER, 'The Decline, Revival and Fall of the British Empire', in Anil Seal, ed., *The Decline, Revival and Fall of the British Empire: The Ford Lectures and Other Essays* (Cambridge, 1982).

N. H. GIBBS, *The Origins of Imperial Defence: An Inaugural Lecture Delivered Before the University of Oxford on 8 June, 1955* (Oxford, 1955).

MICHAEL HOWARD, *The Continental Commitment: The Dilemma of British Defence Policy in the Era of Two World Wars* (London, 1972).

KEITH JEFFERY, *The British Army and the Crisis of Empire, 1918–22* (Manchester, 1984).

FRANKLYN ARTHUR JOHNSTON, *Defence by Committee: The British Committee of Imperial Defence, 1885–1959* (London, 1960).

JOHN KENT, *British Imperial Strategy and the Origins of the Cold War, 1944–49* (Leicester, 1993).

WM. ROGER LOUIS, *The British Empire in the Middle East, 1945–1951: Arab Nationalism, the United States and Postwar Imperialism* (Oxford, 1984).

JOHN MCCARTHY, *Australia and Imperial Defence, 1918–1939: A Study in Air and Sea Power* (St Lucia, Queensland, 1976).

DAVID E. OMISSI, *The Sepoy and the Raj: The Indian Army, 1860–1940* (Basingstoke, 1994).

RONALD ROBINSON and JOHN GALLAGHER with ALICE DENNY, *Africa and the Victorians: The Official Mind of Imperialism* (London, 1961).

23

The Empire-Commonwealth and the Two World Wars

RITCHIE OVENDALE

The general histories of the two world wars and their origins, and in particular those of the second, until the 1960s, largely ignored the role of the Empire-Commonwealth. A possible explanation for this is that the reluctance of the Dominions to fight in September 1938 was cited as an explanation for Neville Chamberlain's policy at Munich by those who endorsed 'appeasement'. Political life in Britain, particularly in the 1950s, was dominated by men such as Winston Churchill, Anthony Eden, and Harold Macmillan, who had made their reputations denigrating Neville Chamberlain's policy of 'appeasement' in Europe and the Far East. The political climate changed in the 1960s. It was symbolized, perhaps, by the appointment of Chamberlain's private secretary, Alec Douglas-Home, as Prime Minister. The modification of the fifty-year closure rule to thirty years by Harold Wilson, and the subsequent opening of many of the documents in the Public Record Office in January 1968, followed by most of the 1939–45 material in 1972, enabled scholars to begin to assess the role of the Empire-Commonwealth more seriously.[1]

The writings in this field fall mainly into two categories. One school considers the Empire-Commonwealth in terms of the influence on British foreign policy. Another emphasizes the extent to which the events leading up to the wars, and the wars themselves, influenced developments within the countries, initially in relation to the growth of the British Commonwealth, and later on to the independence movements and decolonization.

The approach of much of the literature on the First World War and its origins is summed up by the editors, E. A. Benians, James Butler, and C. E. Carrington, of *The Cambridge History of the British Empire*, Volume III, *The Empire Commonwealth, 1870–1919* (Cambridge, 1959) in the preface: 'If the later chapters

[1] See Ritchie Ovendale, *'Appeasement' and the English Speaking World: Britain, the United States, the Dominions and the Policy of 'Appeasement', 1937–1939* (Cardiff, 1975), pp. 4–9 for a discussion of this literature.

on international relations and colonial policy seem to be in fact rather a history of British foreign policy, it may be urged that in this period colonial issues were so subordinate to other questions of foreign policy that they could not be kept, even in such a work as this, in the centre of the stage' (p. v). In the introductory chapter in Volume VIII, Benians argued the case that Britain followed her own policy, not one jointly conceived with the Dominions, and that the Dominions neither questioned it nor fully understood it.[2]

Max Beloff, in a work published ten years later, *Imperial Sunset*, Volume I, *Britain's Liberal Empire, 1897–1921* (London, 1969), pointed out that while Britain had an undoubted responsibility for defending the Imperial system, the principal constraint was 'the increasingly autonomous outlook of the self-governing dominions' (p. 15). In his treatment of the First World War, Beloff concentrates not only on the military contributions of the Empire and institutions devised for strengthening it, 'but also on the impact of Dominion policy-makers upon the conduct of the war and the definition of war aims' (p. 17). Similarly, almost another decade later, W. David McIntyre, in his contribution to the Minnesota series, 'Europe and the World in the Age of Expansion', *The Commonwealth of Nations: Origins and Impact, 1869–1971* (Minneapolis, 1977), emphasizes the importance of the Dominion war effort as 'an important factor in the growth of national feeling in the Dominions' (p. 175).[3]

Different authors have chosen to illuminate different facets of Empire policy during the first two decades of the twentieth century. Ronald Hyam, in *Britain's Imperial Century, 1815–1914: A Study of Empire and Expansion* (London, 1976), offered the central thesis that Britain's Imperial century came to an end, 'if not actually with the shots at Sarajevo in 1914, then in 1915 in the mud of Flanders' (p. 377). His work emphasizes the extent to which the pre-1914 Liberal government accepted the advice given by the Colonial Office, and argues that the Empire was more efficiently and humanely run. But Hyam points out that the Colonial Office was less worried about the threats of nationalist uprisings than by the fear that 'the white colonists would ultimately destroy the empire, not by wilful maliciousness, but by sheer stupidity, brutal insensitivity to the Non-European races, and by a parochial inability to see any problem either in its imperial perspective or within the realities of the international context' (p. 129). The relations between the various branches of government are also considered by R. B. Pugh. He mentions the increasing role the Foreign Office played in Colonial Office affairs, and points to the separation of Dominions work from

[2] E. A. Benians, 'The Empire in the New Age, 1870–1919', in E. A. Benians and others, eds., *The Cambridge History of the British Empire* (hereafter *CHBE*), 9 vols. (Cambridge, 1929–59), VIII, pp. 9–12.

[3] See also T. R. H. Davenport, 'The South African Rebellion, 1914', *English Historical Review*, LXXVIII (1963), pp. 73–94.

the management of the dependent Empire, leading to the creation of the Dominions Office in 1925.[4]

Authors analysing the military aspects have pointed to issues such as dissensions over the sharing of naval defence as sharpening Dominion self-consciousness,[5] and have discussed the extent to which Imperial military unity existed during the First World War and afterwards.[6] In this regard T. O. Lloyd, in *The British Empire, 1558–1983*, observes: 'Soldiers went out to fight because Britain was at war, but they fought as Canadians or as Australians.'[7]

Britain's Eastern policy during the First World War, and during the subsequent peace settlements, saw a vast addition to the British Empire in the Middle East. The division of the Middle East among the European powers resembled the Scramble for Africa in the 1890s. The powers, including Britain, pursued their own interests, at the expense of any ideas of self-determination.[8] The British role is criticized by David Fromkin in *A Peace to End All Peace: Creating the Modern Middle East, 1914–1922* (London, 1989). Fromkin argues that the 'crisis of political civilization that the Middle East endures today' is due to Britain's 'destruction of the old order in the region in 1918, and her decisions in 1922 about how it should be replaced' (p. 19).

Max Beloff, in *Imperial Sunset*, Volume II, *Dream of Commonwealth, 1921–42* (Basingstoke, 1989), published twenty years after the first part of his study, argued that a major line of division between policy-makers in London was between 'those who saw the maintenance of the Commonwealth as mainly a source of extra weight to Britain's own international diplomacy, and those who saw the maintenance of the Commonwealth itself and its evolution as the primary concern of British policy'. Beloff mentions the traditional separation between the study of foreign policy, and that of Commonwealth affairs, as the reason why the importance of the Commonwealth factor in the making of British policy has been difficult to assess. With a merging of the approaches 'it would seem that the imperial or Commonwealth factor was a more powerful one than has often been allowed' (p. 13).[9]

A similar observation had been made almost forty years previously by Nicholas Mansergh in his *Survey of British Commonwealth Affairs: Problems of*

[4] R. B. Pugh, 'The Colonial Office, 1801–1925', in *CHBE*, III, pp. 751–68; see also Charles Jeffries, *The Colonial Office* (London, 1956); Joe Garner, *The Commonwealth Office, 1925–1968* (London, 1978).

[5] Donald C. Gordon, *The Dominion Partnership in Imperial Defense, 1870–1914* (Baltimore, 1965), p. xiv.

[6] Keith Jeffery, *The British Army and the Crisis of Empire, 1918–22* (Manchester, 1984).

[7] T. O. Lloyd, *The British Empire, 1558–1995*, 2nd edn. (Oxford, 1996), p. 277.

[8] Ritchie Ovendale, *The Origins of the Arab-Israeli Wars*, 2nd edn. (London, 1992), pp. 17–63.

[9] But see R. A. C. Parker, *Chamberlain and Appeasement: British Policy and the Coming of the Second World War* (London, 1993), pp. 294–306.

External Policy, 1931–1939 (London, 1952), a work which not only examined developments within the Dominions, but also stressed that an understanding of their attitudes was essential to a proper appreciation of British policy before the Second World War. Mansergh lamented the curious indifference of 'the predominant school of contemporary English historians' to this (p. xviii).[10] A work published six years later, J. D. B. Miller's *The Commonwealth in the World* (London, 1958), suggested that reluctance of the Dominions to fight at Munich had become 'one of the stock arguments' in favour of Chamberlain's policy of 'appeasement' (p. 43); D. C. Watt, in *Personalities and Policies* (London, 1965), still argued that Dominion determination to keep out of Europe was a decisive factor in encouraging Chamberlain to pursue this policy (pp. 159–74).

When the fifty-year rule became the thirty-year rule, and the British documents opened up in January 1968, the primary sources were scrutinized in an attempt to answer the question of Dominion influence. Ritchie Ovendale's *'Appeasement' and the English Speaking World, Britain, the United States, the Dominions and the Policy of 'Appeasement', 1937–1939* (Cardiff, 1975) emphasizes that the Dominions were not bound by British policy decisions, and that they were informed rather than consulted. They were not responsible for the policy of appeasement: Dominion opinion only confirmed Chamberlain in a course of action on which he had already decided. Over Czechoslovakia, Chamberlain probably saw the reluctance of the Dominions to fight, and the consequent break-up of the Commonwealth as decisive. As the European situation became more serious with Hitler's occupation of Prague, Dominion influence diminished. E. M. Andrews, in *The Writing on the Wall: The British Commonwealth and Aggression in the East, 1931–1935* (Sydney, 1987), accuses Britain of muddle-mindedness, short-sightedness, and duplicity in its dealings with the Pacific Dominions. The subject of Dominion influence on British policy has also exercised a fascination for scholars writing in Germany.[11]

Even before the publication of the *Documents on Australian Foreign Policy, 1937–49*, Volumes I and II, edited by R. G. Neale (Canberra, 1975), on the origins of the Second World War, there was an impressive official history by Paul Hasluck, *The Government and the People*, Volume I, *1939–1941* (Canberra, 1952), and a study of Australian governmental and public opinion covering the period from the Abyssinian crisis to the outbreak of war in 1939: E. M. Andrews, *Isolationism and*

[10] See also P. N. S. Mansergh, *The Commonwealth Experience* (London, 1969), p. 282.

[11] See Rainer Tamchina, 'Commonwealth und Appeasement: Die Politik der britischen Dominions', *Neue Politische Literatur* (1972), pp. 471–89, and Rainer Tamchina, 'In Search of Common Causes: The Imperial Conference of 1937', *Journal of Imperial and Commonwealth History*, I (1972), pp. 79–105; J. C. Doherty, 'Die Dominions und die britische Aussenpolitik von München bis zum Kriegsausbruch 1939', *Vierteljahrshefte für Zeitgeschichte*, XX (1972), pp. 209–34.

Appeasement in Australia: Reactions to the European Crises, 1935–1939 (Canberra, 1970). Andrews argues that the Australian government strongly supported appeasement for its own reasons: fear of Japan in the Pacific; concern for the Mediterranean route; and the characteristics of its leaders (p. 214). Paul Twomey's 'Munich', in Carl Bridge, ed., *Munich to Vietnam: Australia's Relations with Britain and the United States Since the 1930s* (Carlton, Victoria, 1991), pp. 12–37, using archival material, argues that it was only with the 1939 invasion of Czechoslovakia that there was a consensus of Australian views, and that 'both because of their strong identification with Britain's predicament and their appreciation that the eclipsing of British power would be damaging to Australia's own security, the great majority of Australians in mid-1939 considered German domination of Europe unacceptable and agreed that it should be resisted by war if necessary (p. 37).

Much of the writing on Canada's international relations in the inter-war years focuses on the triangular relationship among Ottawa, Washington, and London. This work was aided by the publication of the *Documents on Canadian External Relations*, Volume V, *1931–1935* (Ottawa, 1973), and Volume VI, *1936–1939* (Ottawa, 1972). The official historian of the Canadian army, Colonel C. P. Stacey, in his two-volume study *Canada and the Age of Conflict: A History of Canadian External Problems* (Toronto, 1977 and 1981), insists that it was the political situation within Canada that dictated that country's reactions to external problems. Stacey's case is that the First World War was not a great turning-poïnt in the relations of Canada and the United States: indeed, for English Canada the wartime emotions strengthened the bond with Britain rather than friendship with the United States. But, he argues, it was the achievement of the Canadian army in France and Belgium which inspired Canadians with 'an impelling sense of nationhood never before experienced' (I, p. 239), and afterwards it was Canada that led the other Dominions to their place in the League of Nations. W. L. Mackenzie King, as Prime Minister, in Stacey's view, dominated Canadian external politics, and though Mackenzie King was convinced that it was easier for Canada to get what it wanted from the United States than from Britain, during the Second World War he became suspicious of Washington's long-term intentions towards Canada, and increasingly convinced that it was American policy to absorb Canada (II, p. 363). J. L. Granatstein and Robert Bothwell, in an article ' "A Self-Evident National Duty": Canadian Foreign Policy, 1935–1939', *Journal of Imperial and Commonwealth History*, III (1974–75), pp. 212–33, attempt to dispel the legend that Mackenzie King was isolationist and neutralist; they argue that he sought a close relationship with the United States in the hope that he could both influence American policy and bring Washington and London into a harmonious relationship.

The South African documents of the period are not published. In his biography of the South African Imperial and world statesman J. C. Smuts, *Smuts: The*

Sanguine Years, 1870–1919 (Cambridge, 1962) and *Smuts: The Fields of Force, 1919–1950* (Cambridge, 1968), W. K. Hancock suggests, perhaps mistakenly, that Smuts became disillusioned with Chamberlain's policy of appeasement.[12] Twenty years after the event, in his biography of the South African Prime Minister, *James Barry Munnik Hertzog* (Cape Town, 1958), Oswald Pirow, the Minister of Defence, wrote of the South African cabinet meeting of 3 September 1939 and South Africa's subsequent entry into the war, that it made it a certainty 'that when the political pendulum swung back again, as it was bound to do, D. F. Malan's extremists would take over and the English-speaking South Africans would become *bywoners* [aliens] in their own country' (p. 246).

Indeed, there is considerable debate about the effect on Afrikaner nationalism of South Africa's entry into the war in 1939, as well as the influence of National Socialism on Afrikaner leaders, some of whom dominated South African political life for four decades after the Nationalist government was elected in 1948, and implemented its apartheid policy. Some writers, such as William Henry Vatcher, Jr, and Brian Bunting, argue that Malan, who became Prime Minister in 1948, and many of his followers were orientated towards the Nazis, while another school of thought, led by D. W. Krüger, who held chairs at several South African Afrikaner universities and received his doctorate from the University of Berlin in 1937, argues that the Afrikaner nationalist movement split in 1941 and 1942 between followers of Pirow, who wanted a National Socialist republic, and those like Malan and another future Prime Minister, J. G. Strijdom, who declared for parliamentary democracy. A recent scholarly study by Patrick J. Furlong, *Between Crown and Swastika: The Impact of the Radical Right on the Afrikaner Nationalist Movement in the Fascist Era* (Hanover, NH, 1991), concludes that there was a complex pattern of links between the European radical right and a number of South Africa's leaders after 1948.[13]

The New Zealand government commissioned an official history, F. L. W. Wood's, *The New Zealand People at War: Political and External Affairs, Official History of New Zealand in the Second World War, 1939–45* (Wellington, 1958), which emphasizes throughout New Zealand's effort, as a small country, to be heard on the world stage, and argues the importance for New Zealand of the predominance of American power over that of Britain. This was the first in a fifty-volume series

[12] Ovendale, *'Appeasement' and the English Speaking World*, pp. 25–27.

[13] William Henry Vatcher Jr, *White Laager: The Rise of Afrikaner Nationalism* (London, 1965), pp. 58–88; Brian Bunting, *The Rise of the South African Reich* (Harmondsworth, 1964), pp. 54–68; Ivor Wilkins and Hans Strydom, *The Broederbond* (New York, 1979), pp. 53, 80; J. H. P. Serfontein, *Brotherhood of Power: An Exposé of the Secret Afrikaner Broederbond* (London, 1979), pp. 64, 81; D. W. Krüger, *The Making of a Nation: A History of the Union of South Africa, 1910–1961* (Johannesburg, 1969), pp. 206–23.

completed in 1986. The domestic front is covered in W. B. Sutch, *The Quest for Security in New Zealand, 1840 to 1966* (London, 1966), pp. 281–388, but his work reflects dissenting views and is not always considered balanced.

At the outset, Nicholas Mansergh, in his *Survey of British Commonwealth Affairs: Problems of Wartime Co-operation and Post-War Change, 1939–1952* (London, 1958), mentions that the theme of his coverage of the Second World War is 'the capacity of the Commonwealth system to sustain unity of purpose and effort among Commonwealth governments and peoples in war' (pp. xv, 26–27). Writing a decade later, J. D. B. Miller, in *Britain and the Old Dominions* (London, 1966), singles out two problems that complicated the relations between Britain and the Dominions during the Second World War, both being bound up with the character of Winston Churchill's leadership: first was the control of the forces which the Dominions committed to the fight; 'the second was how the Dominions were to influence decisions made about the war by Britain and the United States' (p. 130). The role of the Dominions is covered in the British official military history of the Second World War.[14]

In the late 1980s and the 1990s, at a time when Australian Labor governments raised the question of the severing of the links with the British Crown, the matter of the defence of Singapore and Britain's commitment to Australia's defence just before and during the early stages of the Second World War again became a live political issue which stimulated academic controversy. Two decades earlier, at the time of debates over Australian participation in the Vietnam war, Trevor R. Reese, in *Australia, New Zealand, and the United States: A Survey of International Relations, 1941–1968* (London, 1969), had examined the extent to which the Pacific Dominions moved out of a British orbit into an American one.

In 1991 Carl Bridge, in his introduction to Carl Bridge, ed., *Munich to Vietnam*, pointed out that the popularly received version of Britain ignominiously leaving the Australian scene with the fall of Singapore, never to return, and Australia and New Zealand moving into the United States's informal Pacific empire, is an exaggeration, and that the transition was 'not nearly so simple or absolute' (p. 2). He argues that 'Australians' perceptions of their country's relationship with Britain and the United States in the Second World War are hopelessly distorted by hindsight and by Labor patriotic myths'. The received version, widely disseminated in textbooks and on the television screen, points to the 'inexcusable betrayal' of the fall of Singapore in February 1942, and the case that while Britain was prepared to exploit Australia it was not prepared to defend it. The pro-British 'appeaser', Robert Menzies, had gone, and the 'heroic' and nationalist Labor leader, John

[14] N. H. Gibbs and others, *Grand Strategy*, 5 vols. (London, 1956–76); S. Woodburn Kirby, *The War Against Japan*, Vol. I, *The Loss of Singapore* (London, 1957).

Curtin, recalled Australian divisions from the Middle East, looked to the United States, and saved Australia in New Guinea and at the Battles of the Coral Sea and Midway. Bridge exposes these 'myths' as a 'travesty of the truth'.[15] Other Australian scholars have also challenged the myth that Australia switched her national allegiance from Britain to the United States during the Second World War.[16]

Another approach to the development of the Empire-Commonwealth during the Second World War is evidenced in the popular work by Colin Cross, *The Fall of the British Empire, 1918–1968* (London, 1968), which considers the war's importance for the emergence of independence movements, particularly the reverberations of the fall of Singapore in India and on British prestige throughout Asia as well as the experience for many black Africans of serving abroad and their subsequent role in independence movements.[17] R. D. Pearce, in his overall analysis of Britain's position in Africa, *The Turning Point in Africa: British Colonial Policy, 1938–48* (London, 1982), points to the inroads made into Indirect Rule during the Second World War: at the end of the war a relatively impoverished Britain was in debt to its African colonies as well as to India, a reversal of roles which eventually resulted in the granting of self-government (pp. 84–86).

Moves towards independence in the African colonies are specifically analysed in a number of texts. G. O. Olusanya, in *The Second World War and Politics in Nigeria, 1939–1953* (Lagos, 1973), demonstrates that, in response to the Allied propaganda which emphasized that the war was being fought to preserve democracy and ensure freedom, Nigerians came to expect that 'the freedom which was being fought for should be extended to them' (pp. 51–53). F. M. Bourret's study of the Gold Coast, *Ghana: The Road to Independence, 1919–1957* (London, 1960), also emphasizes the increased opportunities for technical and administrative training the Second World War afforded to Africans, 'which resulted in a deeper self-confidence and determination to take a more active part in the country's development' (p. 156).

Nicholas Owen, in his article 'War and Britain's Political Crisis in India', considers the position from the point of view of the metropolitan power and points

[15] Carl Bridge, 'Poland to Pearl Harbor', in Carl Bridge, ed., *Munich to Vietnam: Australia's Relations With Britain and the United States Since the 1930s* (Carlton, Victoria, 1991), pp. 38–51; see also G. St. J. Barclay, 'Australia Looks to America: The Wartime Relationship, 1939–1942', *Pacific Historical Review*, XLVI (1977), pp. 251–71.

[16] Roger J. Bell, *Unequal Allies: Australian–American Relations and the Pacific War* (Melbourne, 1977), p. 6. There are five series of official histories of Australia in the Second World War published by Australian War Memorial, Canberra. See also Paul Hasluck, *The Government and the People*, Vol. II, *1942–1945* (Canberra, 1970) and *Documents on Australian Foreign Policy*, Vols. III–VIII (Canberra, 1979–89).

[17] See also David Killingray and Richard Rathbone, eds., *Africa and the Second World War* (Basingstoke, 1986).

to the extent to which the British were 'deprived of the initiative and ability to control the events which was the vital underpinning of their plans to advance India to the status of a Dominion'.[18] India's role in the Second World War is treated in the literature from the strategic aspect of its contribution to the war effort,[19] the role played by the Indian National Army in the war and in the independence movement,[20] and the extent to which the Second World War and pressure from Washington ensured India's independence. The first five volumes of documents published as *The Transfer of Power, 1942–7*, under Nicholas Mansergh, as editor-in-chief (London, 1970–74), cover the moves towards independence in India during the Second World War. Developments in Burma are documented in Hugh Tinker, ed., *Burma: The Struggle for Independence, 1944–1948*, Volume I, *From Military Occupation to Civil Government, 1 January 1944 to 31 August 1946* (London, 1983).

Colonial issues, alongside those of League of Nations trusteeships and mandates, have attracted particular examination. These works show the divisions between the Foreign and Colonial Offices, as well as the importance of the United States in the equation. Wm. Roger Louis, in *Imperialism at Bay, 1941–1945: The United States and the Decolonization of the British Empire* (Oxford, 1977), considers American and British wartime planning for the future of the colonial world. He looks at the divisions between the Colonial and Foreign Offices, and the extent to which 'the Colonial Office regarded the trusteeship scheme, among other things, as a Foreign Office device to appease the Americans' (pp. vii, 66). Ritchie Ovendale, in *Britain, the United States, and the End of the Palestine Mandate, 1942–1948* (Woodbridge, Suffolk, 1989), examines the divisions between the Foreign and Colonial Offices during the Second World War as to whether Britain should pursue a policy of partition, which would mean the creation of a separate Zionist state, or trusteeship, which could safeguard British security interests in the Middle East, as well as the extent to which the United States attempted to dictate a policy to Britain for Palestine in the interests of its own domestic politics.[21]

In making an overall assessment of the significance of the Second World War for the Commonwealth-Empire some scholars have offered profit-and-loss

[18] Nicholas Owen, 'War and Britain's Political Crisis in India', in Harriet Jones and Brian Brivati, eds., *What Difference Did the War Make?* (Leicester, 1993), pp. 106–30 at p. 108.

[19] See Philip Mason, *A Matter of Honour: An Account of the Indian Army, Its Officers and Men* (London, 1974), pp. 412–527; Stephen P. Cohen, *The Indian Army: Its Contribution to the Development of a Nation* (Berkeley, 1971); B. Prasad, ed., *Official History of the Indian Armed Forces in the Second World War* (Delhi, 1956 *et seq.*).

[20] Milan Hauner, *India in Axis Strategy: Germany, Japan and Indian Nationalists in the Second World War* (Stuttgart, 1981).

[21] For a general account of developments in the Middle East during the Second World War see George Kirk, *Survey of International Affairs, 1939–1946: The Middle East in the War* (London, 1952).

accounts. Bernard Porter, for instance, points out that 'defence of the empire tied up more British troops than the war in Europe used colonial troops, so that the total military account of the empire was in debit'.[22]

John Gallagher, however, dismisses the idea of looking at the fall of the British Empire in 'a briskly functionalist way', concluding that it was the damage of the Second World War that brought it down. He suggests that the British world system had been showing signs of decay long before 1939, and that the Second World War reversed the trend, observable at the end of the First World War, of Britain moving from a system of formal rule towards a system of influence, back towards Empire. Gallagher argues that, in military terms, India exploited Britain during the Second World War. But Britain's decision to quit India was not intended to mark the end of Empire: 'Quitting India has to be seen in the light of the simultaneous decision to push British penetration deeper into tropical Africa and the Middle East.'[23]

A recent work which considers the economic relationship, also proposes the thesis that Britain's determination to retain her Empire and its informal influence was undiminished after both world wars: 'the idea that there was a "long retreat" from Empire fits ill with evidence not only of the revitalization of the colonial mission after the two world wars, but also of the firm grip which Britain retained in the areas of policy which mattered most'—the Dominions (except Canada), India, and the tropical colonies.[24] This substantiates the case made by R. F. Holland in *Britain and the Commonwealth Alliance, 1918–1939* (London, 1981), that 'the organisation of the Commonwealth was one way that the British state attempted to stem political and economic decline after 1918' (p. 24).

A. J. P. Taylor has argued that the Second World War was 'an Imperial war': 'It was fought by the British mainly in Imperial zones of the Mediterranean and the Far East. It was fought by Imperial armies serving in almost complete unity, and it ended in victory for every Imperial cause. The Commonwealth demonstrated its strength and spirit. The English-speaking peoples might have been expected to draw the moral that the Commonwealth alone provided the foundation for their greatness and security. This did not happen.' Taylor attributes this state of affairs to the mistaken idea that the British had of believing that there was a special relationship between Britain and the United States: the Commonwealth was thrown away to please the United States. Taylor also argues that the Second World War

[22] Bernard Porter, *A Short History of British Imperialism, 1850–1970* (London, 1975), p. 303.

[23] John Gallagher, 'The Decline, Revival and Fall of the British Empire', in Anil Seal, ed., *The Decline, Revival and Fall of the British Empire: The Ford Lectures and other Essays by John Gallagher* (Cambridge, 1982), pp. 73–153, esp. pp. 73, 139, 144.

[24] P. J. Cain and A. G. Hopkins, *British Imperialism: Crisis and Deconstruction, 1914–1950* (London, 1993), pp. 308–09.

produced a British obsession with Europe, and that it mistakenly came to be believed that Britain would only be secure if the entire European continent were secure and at peace. But most of all, Taylor argues, the Commonwealth perished from lack of faith: 'it was confused with the Empire of India and with the coloured colonies which the British once ruled in despotic fashion. When these countries achieved their freedom, it was imagined that there was nothing left.'[25]

Ernest Bevin, the Foreign Secretary of a Labour Government, chose the Anglo-American relationship as the cornerstone of British foreign policy: with the joining of the cold war even the combination of Europe and the United States was not thought strong enough to deter the Soviet Union. As part of cold war politics, India was allowed to become a member of the Commonwealth as a republic in 1949: the British Commonwealth became the Commonwealth, and Britain began to distinguish between the information it distributed to the old 'white' Dominions and the new members.[26]

[25] A. J. P. Taylor, 'Lament for a Commonwealth', in Winston Churchill, *History of the English Speaking Peoples: Based on the Text of 'A History of the English-Speaking Peoples' by Sir Winston Churchill* (published in 112 weekly parts, London, 1969), 4 vols. (London, 1971), I, pp. 12–13.

[26] See Ritchie Ovendale, *The English-Speaking Alliance: Britain, the United States, the Dominions, and the Cold War, 1945–51* (London, 1985); see also John Kent, *British Imperial Strategy and the Origins of the Cold War, 1944–49* (Leicester, 1993).

Select Bibliography

E. M. ANDREWS, *The Writing on the Wall: The British Commonwealth and Aggression in the East, 1931–1935* (London, 1987).

MAX BELOFF, *Imperial Sunset*, 2 vols., Vol. I: *Britain's Liberal Empire, 1897–1987* (London, 1969; 2nd edn., Basingstoke, 1987); Vol. II: *Dreams of Commonwealth* (Basingstoke, 1989).

E. A. BENIANS, JAMES BUTLER, and C. E. CARRINGTON, eds., *The Cambridge History of the British Empire*, Vol. III, *The Empire Commonwealth, 1870–1919* (Cambridge, 1959).

CARL BRIDGE, ed., *Munich to Vietnam: Australia's Relations With Britain and the United States Since the 1930s* (Carlton, Victoria, 1991).

COLIN CROSS, *The Fall of the British Empire, 1918–1968* (London, 1968).

JAMES EAYRS, I*n Defence of Canada*, Vol. II, *Appeasement and Rearmament* (Toronto, 1965).

DAVID FROMKIN, *A Peace to End All Peace: Creating the Modern Middle East, 1914–1922* (London, 1989).

DONALD C. GORDON, *The Dominion Partnership in Imperial Defense, 1870–1914* (Baltimore, 1965).

W. K. HANCOCK, *Smuts*, 2 vols. (Cambridge, 1962–1968).

R. F. HOLLAND, *Britain and the Commonwealth Alliance, 1918–1939* (London, 1981).

RONALD HYAM, *Britain's Imperial Century, 1815–1914: A Study of Empire and Expansion* (London, 1976).

T. O. Lloyd, *The British Empire, 1558–1995*, 2nd edn. (Oxford, 1996).

Wm. Roger Louis, *Imperialism at Bay: The United States and the Decolonization of the British Empire, 1941–1945* (Oxford, 1977).

Nicholas Mansergh, *Survey of British Commonwealth Affairs: Problems of External Policy, 1931–1939* (London, 1952).

—— *Survey of British Commonwealth Affairs: Problems of Wartime Co-operation and Post-War Change, 1939–1952* (London, 1958).

R. J. Moore, *Churchill, Cripps and India, 1939–1945* (Oxford, 1979).

Ritchie Ovendale, *'Appeasement' and the English Speaking World: Britain, the United States, the Dominions and the Policy of 'Appeasement', 1937–1939* (Cardiff, 1975).

—— *The English-Speaking Alliance: Britain, the United States, the Dominions and the Cold War, 1945–51* (London, 1985).

—— *Britain, the United States, and the End of the Palestine Mandate, 1942–1948* (Woodbridge, Suffolk, 1989).

F. L. W. Wood, *The New Zealand People at War: Political and External Affairs Official History of New Zealand in the Second World War, 1939–45* (Wellington, 1958).

24

Imperial Flotsam? The British in the Pacific Islands

BRONWEN DOUGLAS

European imperialism did not figure systematically in the major Pacific bibliographies, which focused on Islands and Islanders.[1] John M. Ward's 1966 historiography provided informed scholarly appraisal, but preceded a surge in publication of Pacific histories.[2] This chapter links contemporary British Imperial and colonial texts, produced in and about Oceania, to histories of British activities in the Pacific generally and in Britain's Pacific Empire, including its offshoots from Australia and New Zealand.[3] Contemporaneous, academic, and influential popular histories are considered, across O. H. K. Spate's 'two distinct . . . genera': 'Oceanic' and 'Insular'.[4] This chapter argues genealogically, tracing intellectual and political transitions and resemblances, without implying inevitable progression from one generation of historians to 'successors'.

Britain's 'Oceanic' presence and its historiography began in 1578–79 with Drake's circumnavigation, but his then conventional northern route permitted few 'Insular' encounters. James Burney, participant-historian of South Seas exploration, thought the first British 'Voyage of Discovery . . . undertaken expressly for the acquisition of knowledge' was Dampier's in the *Roebuck* in 1699–1700. Dampier's significance, however, was reckoned less in actual 'discoveries' than in

[1] C. R. H. Taylor, *A Pacific Bibliography* (Wellington, 1951; 2nd. edn., Oxford, 1965); *Journal of Pacific History Bibliography* (1966 *et seq.*).

[2] John M. Ward, 'The British Territories in the Pacific', in Robin W. Winks, ed., *The Historiography of the British Empire-Commonwealth: Trends, Interpretations, and Resources* (Durham, NC, 1966), pp. 197–211. For archival material see Phyllis Mander-Jones, ed., *Manuscripts in the British Isles Relating to Australia, New Zealand, and the Pacific* (Canberra, 1972).

[3] 'Contemporary' means contemporaneous to events described. 'Oceania' and 'the Pacific' refer to Polynesia, Micronesia, and Melanesia, including the island of New Guinea, but excluding the 'Pacific rim', Australia, and New Zealand (indigenously Polynesian; see chap. by James Belich).

[4] O. H. K. Spate, 'The Pacific as Artefact', in Niel Gunson, ed., *The Changing Pacific: Essays in Honour of H. E. Maude* (Melbourne, 1978), p. 32.

his popularity, the inspiration he provided for Defoe and Swift, and his 'natural genius' as the earliest 'scientific' voyager.[5]

This chapter traces only the contours of the plethora of contemporary Imperial and colonial texts. Always primitivist, their authors objectified and essentialized indigenous people as timeless savages, cannibals, or pagans, usually disparagingly, sometimes idealistically or romantically. Most found Polynesians and Fijians more appealing and civilized or civilizable than Melanesians, because of their apparently more attractive physical appearance, receptiveness to European commodities, hierarchical polities and pantheons, and the seemingly higher status of women. Prejudice shaped representation, so that writers on aristocratic societies such as eastern Fiji produced epic narratives familiarized by analogy—particularly with the Scottish Highlands—with chiefs personalized, whereas Melanesians were collectivized and rarely identified.

Contemporary European authors appropriated the 'primitive' to metropolitan and personal agenda. Explorers sought to discover unknown lands and peoples, and symbolically possessed them in conversations and contests with other imperialists. Scientists, artists, littérateurs, and ethnographers appropriated natives intellectually and symbolically in often revealingly empiricist representations. Traders, whalers, adventurers, and miners wrote sparingly of efforts to exploit natives for their natural products, labour, and sexuality: in the early 1930s the Australian prospector Michael Leahy filmed remarkable footage of first encounters with New Guinea Highlanders, which Bob Connolly and Robin Anderson included in their ethnographic film *First Contact* (Sydney, 1982). Settlers wrote utilitarian justifications for demands on native lands, complacently or regretfully endorsing evolutionist presumptions of the inevitable demise of inferior races. Evangelical missionaries, naval officers, and colonial rulers, yoking different motives and means to paternalistic ends—to save, transform, and protect natives—produced before-and-after narratives anticipating or lauding the triumph of grace or reason, blaming disappointments on Satan, savagery, unprincipled white men, or natural law. Down the chain of colonial command, young field officers, particularly in Australia's vast 'last unknown' of Papua New Guinea (PNG), contrived adventure epics of braving and taming savages at the coal-face of Empire. The few colonizing women to publish cast a different, often critical, light on colonial attitudes and race relations, even when endorsing or condoning prevailing values, because they were always structurally ambiguous: dominant by race and class, subordinate by gender.

[5] James Burney, *A Chronological History of the Voyages and Discoveries in the South Sea*, 5 vols. (London, 1816), IV, p. 388; J. C. Beaglehole, *The Exploration of the Pacific* (1934; 3rd edn. London, 1966), pp. 166, 177.

All these haphazard, partial, contested stories provided the archived debris of the past which historians call sources or texts, and from which ethnographic historians glean traces of long-past indigenous actions, contexts, and relationships. Colonial interests and ideologies were never unanimous or stable: ambivalence, discord, and dissonance within and between texts are key historical resources, while in practice rivalries between colonizers could deflect colonialism's impact, provide manœuvring space for the colonized, and eventually help undermine the colonial project.

Histories of British activities in the Pacific followed hard on circumnavigatory voyages. 'Oceanic' material featured in the great general compilations, starting with Hakluyt, while John Callander's plagiarized translation of Charles de Brosses inaugurated a specifically Oceanic mode, culminating in Hawkesworth's *Voyages*, with its harvest of popular success and critical outrage—it was the book most borrowed from the Bristol Library in 1773–84.[6] Mature reflections by protagonists included Burney's history and J. R. Forster's philosophy. Cook's three voyages inspired enduring metropolitan fascination with Pacific places, people, plants, and fauna, and with the explorer himself, apotheosized as hero in print, painting, and pantomime, in ironic counterpoint to his fatal identification by Hawaiians as a Polynesian god.[7] Then, as before and since, the Pacific's symbolic import in European science, art, literature, satire, fantasy, theatre, and eventually film was out of proportion to the islands' global material or Imperial significance: for example, the South Sea Bubble, the places Gulliver travelled, Omai, the *Ancient Mariner*, Darwin's intellectual odyssey, or the perennial lure of the *Bounty* narrative. With the decline of neo-classical relish for the primitive towards the end of the eighteenth century, evangelical disapproval and pity for the pagan, manifest in mission histories,[8] hagiographies, and humanitarian exhortations, began a long reign as the most prolific mode of British representation of Pacific Islanders. Some missionaries collaborated enthusiastically with pioneers of the fledgling sciences of geology, biology, and anthropology; a few wrote formal ethnographies.

The Pacific Islands were always insignificant in official British imperialism. Before the 1870s British governments sought to maintain order cheaply and

[6] John Callander, *Terra Australis Cognita*, 3 vols. (London, 1766–68); Charles de Brosses, *Histoire des navigations aux terres australes* (Paris, 1756); on Hakluyt see chap. by Robert A. Stafford. John Hawkesworth, *An Account of the Voyages Undertaken by the Order of His Present Majesty for Making Discoveries in the Southern Hemisphere and Successfully Performed . . .*, 3 vols. (London, 1773).

[7] Andrew Kippis, *The Life of Captain James Cook* (London, 1788); Bernard Smith, *European Vision and the South Pacific* (1960; 3rd edn., Melbourne, 1989), pp. 114–22; Marshall Sahlins, *Island of History* (Chicago, 1985), pp. 104–35.

[8] John Davies, *The History of the Tahitian Mission, 1799–1830*, ed. C. W. Newbury (Cambridge, 1961); Robert Steel, *The New Hebrides and Christian Missions* (London, 1880).

discourage European rivals, while placating humanitarian and Australasian demands for more energetic and permanent interventions. Aside from annexing New Zealand in 1840, British action was limited to appointment of Consuls in parts of Polynesia and Fiji, and largely ineffectual policing missions by Royal Navy vessels. Acceptance of the cession of Fiji in 1874 denoted revitalized Imperial spirit at home and more vigour on the Pacific periphery. Between 1884 and 1906, when European nations in collusive competition apportioned what remained of autonomous Oceania, Britain established Protectorates in south-eastern New Guinea (transferred to Australia in 1902), the Gilbert and Ellice Islands, the Solomons, and Tonga, and a joint administration with France in the New Hebrides (Vanuatu), while annexing the Cook Islands to New Zealand. In 1921 Australia and New Zealand gained Mandates over former German New Guinea, and Western Samoa, respectively and Nauru (together with the UK).

The historiography of the British in the Pacific until after 1950 was entirely 'Imperial', mostly accounts by or about participants in exploratory, exploitative, or paternalist enterprises. The first scholarly history was New Zealander Guy Scholefield's 1919 survey of Great Power policy, spanning the 'rim' as well as the islands.[9] The Pacific mattered little in the multi-volume works of Imperial historical synopsis which appeared from the end of the nineteenth century, and not until the 1920s was there a trickle of professional historical scholarship on the region.[10] Published works clustered about a handful of themes: the romance of 'discoveries', including J. C. Beaglehole's masterly general narrative; Imperial rivalries; Imperial policies, including implementation of Australian sub-imperialism in New Guinea.[11] G. C. Henderson, who held a chair in Adelaide from 1902–24 and taught Imperial history, became the first professional 'Insular' historian, doing detailed research on Fiji.[12] Of another order, anticipating the historiographic shift of the 1950s, was the American sociologist S. W. Reed's fine general history of culture contacts and acculturation in New Guinea, based on ethnographic fieldwork, library research, and wide travel.[13]

[9] Guy H. Scholefield, *The Pacific: Its Past and Future and the Policy of the Great Powers from the Eighteenth Century* (London, 1919).

[10] The best catalogue of theses on the Pacific, W. G. Coppell and S. Stratigos, *A Bibliography of Pacific Island Theses and Dissertations* (Honolulu, 1983), lists approximately fifty relevant research theses submitted to British, Australasian, or American universities before 1950, only eight for doctorates. At least a third were minor masters' dissertations based solely on published works.

[11] G. C. Henderson, *The Discoverers of the Fiji Islands* (London, 1933); J. C. Beaglehole, *Exploration of the Pacific* (London, 1934); Sylvia Masterman, *The Origins of International Rivalry in Samoa, 1845–1884* (London, 1934); Jean Ingram Brookes, *International Rivalry in the Pacific Islands, 1800–1875* (Berkeley, 1941); J. M. Ward, *British Policy in the South Pacific, 1786–1893* (Sydney, 1948); Lucy Mair, *Australia in New Guinea* (1948; 2nd edn., London, 1970).

[12] G. C. Henderson, ed., *The Journal of Thomas Williams: Missionary in Fiji* (Sydney, 1931); G. C. Henderson, *Fiji and the Fijians* (Sydney, 1931).

[13] S. W. Reed, T*he Making of Modern New Guinea* (Philadelphia, 1943).

'Imperial history' denotes a common focus on policies, interests, activities, and rivalries of Europeans. Islanders were stereotypical, ahistoric primitives: they were attributed the limited agency of reflex savagery, but otherwise constructed as passive objects or victims of European initiatives and influences; out of time, they entered history as actors only by undergoing religious or secular conversion to Christianity and civilization. Always ethnocentric, Imperial histories were also teleological, taking for granted European superiority and the reality of colonial control as an outcome assured at the moment of annexation. Decolonization was hardly conceivable. The Foreign Office Handbook *British Possessions in Oceania*, one of few scholarly histories of the Pacific before the 1930s, devoted half of its 126 pages to 'Economic Conditions', mentioning islanders only in passing: as victims of depopulation and labour traders; as actual or potential converts; as a labour force inadequate for economic development. Discriminations between islanders were routinely evolutionist: Polynesian Tonga was 'inhabited by a highly advanced native race who have accepted Christianity'; the Melanesian Solomon Islanders were 'naked savages scarcely beyond the head-hunting stage of development'.[14]

Wartime British defeats in South-East Asia, post-war collapse of European empires in Asia and Africa, and stirrings of local nationalism in the Pacific spurred an antipodean scholarly revolution in Pacific historiography in the 1950s and 1960s. The new way, usually labelled 'island-centred', paralleled emphasis on local 'initiative' or 'agency' in African history,[15] though Islanders' professional involvement lagged. Proponents stressed indigenous actions and experience over the policies and doings of the colonizers, and claimed to write from the Islanders' point of view, often using local oral histories. J. W. Davidson, appointed inaugural professor of Pacific History at the Australian National University in 1949, was acclaimed as founding father of an independent (sub)discipline.[16]

This myth of the origin of Pacific history is plausible, despite eliding scholarly genealogies rooted elsewhere in Australia and in New Zealand. As holder of the sole Pacific History chair, a research one, Davidson controlled most available doctoral scholarships: until recently, Pacific historians were usually Canberra-trained. His own work was path-breaking, especially his Cambridge thesis, for its local rather than Imperial focus, and his excellent general historical sections in the Admiralty Handbooks, *Pacific Islands*.[17] Davidson also wrote on island-centred

[14] Great Britain, Foreign Office, Historical Section, *British Possessions in Oceania* (London, 1920), p. 120.

[15] See chaps. by Charles Ambler and A. D. Roberts.

[16] H. E. Maude, 'Pacific History—Past, Present and Future', *Journal of Pacific History* (hereafter *JPH*), VI (1971), pp. 3–24; Niel Gunson, 'An Introduction to Pacific History', in Brij V. Lal, ed., *Pacific Islands History: Journeys and Transformations* (Canberra, 1992), pp. 1–13.

[17] J. W. Davidson, 'European Penetration of the South Pacific, 1779–1842', unpublished Ph.D. thesis, Cambridge, 1942; Great Britain, Admiralty, Naval Intelligence Division, *Pacific Islands*, 4 vols. (London, 1943–45).

history, and practised his precepts about historians' need for islands 'experience' and 'participation' by serving as consultant to emerging Pacific nations, starting with Western Samoa.[18] His outstanding recruit was H. E. Maude, an anthropologically trained, former British colonial official whose ethno-histories combined linguistic and cultural expertise, rigorous historical research, conceptual sophistication, and innovative method: he took oral traditions seriously as another culture's histories. His essays—especially those anthologized in *Of Islands and Men*—inspired Pacific specialists.[19]

The quarter-century after 1960 saw a Pacific history explosion, mainly Canberra-based, Island-centred, focusing on culture contacts, change, and decolonization, rather than colonial history. Historians depicted trade with Europeans as face-to-face encounters, often controlled and exploited by islanders for local reasons—notably Maude's seminal works on the Tahitian pork trade and beachcombers and castaways, and Dorothy Shineberg's elegant study of the south-west Pacific sandalwood trade.[20] Those writing about missionaries and missions acknowledged that indigenous conceptions of the sacred must inflect meanings made of Christianity: Niel Gunson produced a compelling, encyclopaedic general work.[21] Most concentrated on particular places or island groups: R. P. Gilson's history of nineteenth-century Samoa combined anthropological competence with obsessive detail; Peter France did write colonial history, anticipating recent interest in the invention of tradition by dissecting British official and Fijian élite connivance to construct an orthodoxy on indigenous land tenure; Barrie Macdonald sketched the transformation of the Gilbert and Ellice Islands into Kiribati and Tuvalu.[22] A few, notably K. L. Gillion, studied immigrant communities spawned by labour migration and the colonial diaspora.[23]

Some islanders wrote professional histories, mainly of their own societies, braving alien universities, limited publishing opportunities, and political, family, and community pressures. The Tongan Sione Latukefu was reproached for writing too much like a European. John Waiko, the first indigenous Professor of

[18] J. W. Davidson, 'Problems of Pacific History', *JPH*, I (1966), pp. 5–21; and 'Understanding Pacific History: The Participant as Historian', in Peter Munz, ed., *The Feel of Truth: Essays in New Zealand and Pacific History* (Wellington, 1969), pp. 27–40; J. W. Davidson, *Samoa mo Samoa: The Emergence of the Independent State of Western Samoa* (Melbourne, 1967).

[19] H. E. Maude, *Of Islands and Men: Studies in Pacific History* (Melbourne, 1968).

[20] Ibid., pp. 134–232; Dorothy Shineberg, *They Came for Sandalwood: A Study of the Sandalwood Trade in the South-West Pacific, 1830–1865* (Carlton, Victoria, 1967).

[21] Niel Gunson, *Messengers of Grace: Evangelical Missionaries in the South Seas, 1797–1860* (Melbourne, 1978).

[22] R. P. Gilson, *Samoa, 1830–1900*: *Towards a History of Kirabati and Tuvalu* (Melbourne, 1970); Peter France, *The Charter of the Land: Custom and Colonization in Fiji* (Melbourne, 1969); Barrie Macdonald, *Cinderellas of the Empire: The Politics of a Multi-Cultural Community* (Canberra, 1982).

[23] K. L. Gillion, *Fiji's Indian Migrants* (Melbourne, 1962) and *The Fiji Indians* (Canberra, 1970).

History at the University of Papua New Guinea, produced English and vernacular versions of his thesis and submitted it to local elders and academic examiners. Brij Lal traced the origins of Fiji's Indians, Malama Meleisea wrote about Samoa, 'Atu Emberson-Bain a social history of a Fijian gold-mine.[24]

Simultaneously, histories of imperialism shifted focus to the periphery. One of the best was by W. P. Morrell, who thought such a study 'should be centred . . . in the islands'.[25] Exploration retained its fascination, historical counterpart of the ethnological romance with Pacific voyaging. Davidson's biography of the trader-explorer Peter Dillon was completed posthumously by the geographer O. H. K. Spate, who personally contributed the trilogy *The Pacific Since Magellan*, a truly 'Oceanic' work, apologetically Eurocentric.[26] Beaglehole's Cook project straddled Imperial and Island-centred history, combining painstaking transcription and research in four massive volumes of text, biography, charts, and detailed textual, historical, and ethnological commentary.[27] Unusual then, but seminal, was art historian Bernard Smith's pioneer enquiry into the reciprocal impact of the Pacific in European art and ideas.[28] The Melbourne historians Greg Dening and Alan Frost also wrote on this theme,[29] largely the domain of literary critics and historians of ideas.[30] Island-centred historians were often disconcerted by the imperialist, idealist associations of Smith's work, though his Australian National University doctorate was in Pacific History, evidence of Davidson's intellectual generosity. Personalizing the theme, Davidson's successor, Gavan Daws, used psychohistory to explore the Islands' lure for narcissistic Euro-American writers and artists seeking self-discovery.[31]

[24] Sione Latukefu, *Church and State in Tonga* (Canberra, 1974); John D. Waiko, 'Be Jijimo: A History According to the Tradition of the Binandere People of Papua New Guinea', unpublished Ph.D. thesis, Australian National University, Canberra, 1982; Brij V. Lal, *Girmitiyas: The Origins of the Fiji Indians* (Canberra, 1983); Malama Meleisea, *The Making of Modern Samoa: Traditional Authority and Colonial Administration in the History of Western Samoa* (Suva, Fiji, 1987); 'Atu Emberson-Bain, *Labour and Gold in Fiji* (Melbourne, 1994).

[25] W. P. Morrell, *Britain in the Pacific Islands* (Oxford, 1960), p. vii.

[26] J. W. Davidson, *Peter Dillon of Vanikoro: Chevalier of the South Seas*, ed. O. H. K. Spate (Melbourne, 1975); O. H. K. Spate, *The Pacific Since Magellan*, 3 vols. (Canberra, 1979–88).

[27] J. C. Beaglehole, ed., *The Journals of Captain James Cook on his Voyages of Discovery*, 4 vols. (Cambridge, 1955–74).

[28] Smith, *European Vision;* Rüdiger Joppien and Bernard Smith, *The Art of Captain Cook's Voyages*, 3 vols. (Melbourne, 1985–87).

[29] Alan Frost, 'The Pacific Ocean: The Eighteenth Century's "New World" ', *Studies on Voltaire and the Eighteenth Century*, CLI–CLV (1976), pp. 779–822; Greg Dening, 'Possessing Tahiti', *Archaeology in Oceania*, XXI (1986), pp. 103–18.

[30] Walter Veit, ed., *Captain James Cook: Image and Impact*, 2 vols. (Melbourne, 1972–79); P. J. Marshall and Glyndyr Williams, *The Great Map of Mankind: British Perceptions of the World in the Age of the Enlightenment* (London, 1982).

[31] Gavan Daws, *A Dream of Islands: Voyages of Self-Discovery in the South Seas* (New York, 1980).

Still in Imperial mode, J. D. Legge looked narrowly at the British in Fiji, W. David McIntyre was broadly comparative, contrasting Pacific colonial policy with West Africa and Malaya, while in between was Deryck Scarr's regional history of the Western Pacific High Commission.[32] There were scholarly biographies of leading Proconsuls.[33] Legge dealt with Australian colonial policy, Angus Ross and Roger Thompson with New Zealand and Australian imperialism.[34] C. D. Rowley produced a penetrating study of Australian military administration in former German New Guinea.[35] Pacific campaigns during the Second World War were treated in Allied official histories, while John Lawrey wrote from experience of wartime Australian military and diplomatic involvement in New Caledonia.[36]

Economic history was patchy and Eurocentric, except for a few economic anthropologists, whose histories were sketchy.[37] Labour history lagged, but it inspired two excellent historiographical surveys.[38] Dependency theorists produced stringent anti-colonial critiques, but political economy was too broad a brush for most historians: its determinism discounted contingency and human agency, while a rigid Marxist class analysis distorted understandings of villagers' encounters with world systems, eliding other principles like gender, race, religion, and culture.[39] Peter Fitzpatrick provided a more effective, legal overview of the workings of colonialism in PNG, but historians usually preferred Rowley's bottom-up approach in *The New Guinea Villager*, an incisive, if pessimistic, investigation of colonialism's local impact.[40]

[32] J. D. Legge, *Britain in Fiji, 1858–1880* (London, 1958); W. David McIntyre, *The Imperial Frontier in the Tropics, 1865–75* (London, 1967); Deryck Scarr, *Fragments of Empire: A History of the Western Pacific High Commission, 1877–1914* (Canberra, 1967).

[33] Francis West, *Hubert Murray: The Australian Pro-Consul* (Melbourne, 1968); R. B. Joyce, *Sir William MacGregor* (Melbourne, 1971); Deryck Scarr, *The Majesty of Colour: A Life of Sir John Bates Thurston*, 2 vols. (Canberra, 1973–80).

[34] J. D. Legge, *Australian Colonial Policy* (Sydney, 1956); Angus Ross, *New Zealand Aspirations in the Pacific in the Nineteenth Century* (Oxford, 1964); Roger C. Thompson, *Australian Imperialism in the Pacific* (Carlton, Victoria, 1980).

[35] C. D. Rowley, *The Australians in German New Guinea, 1914–1921* (Carlton, Victoria, 1958).

[36] John Lawrey, *The Cross of Lorraine in the South Pacific: Australia and the Free French Movement* (Canberra, 1982).

[37] Margaret Steven, *Trade, Tactics and Territory: Britain in the Pacific, 1783–1823* (Melbourne, 1983); K. Buckley and K. Klugman, *The History of Burns Philp* ([Sydney], 1981) A. L. Epstein, *Matupit: Land, Politics and Change among the Tolai of New Britain* (Canberra, 1969); Richard F. Salisbury, *Vunamami: Economic Transformation in a Traditional Society* (Carlton, Victoria, 1970).

[38] Clive Moore, Doug Munro, and Jacqui Leckie, eds., *Labour in the South Pacific* (Townsville, Queensland, 1991); Jacqueline Leckie, 'The Long, Slow Haul: Issues in 20th Century Pacific Labour Historiography', in Lal, ed., *Pacific Islands History*, pp. 149–66; Clive Moore, 'Labour, Indenture and Historiography in the Pacific', in ibid., pp. 129–48.

[39] Azeem Amarshi, Kenneth Good, and Rex Mortimer, *Development and Dependency: The Political Economy of Papua New Guinea* (Melbourne, 1979); Michael C. Howard and Simione Duratalo, *The Political Economy of the South Pacific to 1945* (Townsville, Queensland, 1987).

[40] Peter Fitzpatrick, *Law and State in Papua New Guinea* (Sydney, 1980); C. D. Rowley, *The New Guinea Villager: A Retrospect from 1964* (Melbourne, 1965).

Island-centred historians were anti-colonial, empiricist, rationalist, and utilitarian towards anthropology: their signature concept of unfettered Islander initiative was liberating but naïve and ethnocentric. Anthropologists had theory, but the British and Australasian mainstream clung to essentialist, ahistoric functionalist or structuralist paradigms until the late 1970s. American cultural anthropologists and ethnographers of millenarianism and economic change adopted historical perspectives, but with peripheral interest in colonizers. Neither discipline impressed popular imaginings, in either 'the West' or the Islands. 'Westerners' persisted in elegiac objectification of timeless primitives in 'paradise' helplessly suffering the 'fatal impact' of European contact.[41] Hugh Laracy's remarkable edited collection of contemporary writings by Solomon Islanders during the anti-colonial Maasina Rule movement of the 1940s, and PNG villagers' recollections in the film *Angels of War*, showed the huge impact of the Second World War and its implications for colonial and post-colonial relations.[42] Indigenous 'people's histories' and edited autobiographies which began to appear in the late 1970s also revealed agendas different from those of academics: the indignities and inequities of recent colonialism, concerns about nationalism, development, 'custom', and religion.[43] Documentary films, which the Australian administration in PNG used for propaganda and education during the 1950s and 1960s, subsequently became a potent popular medium for anti-colonial and anti-modernist sentiments, though the nostalgic secular romanticism of some film-makers did not always coincide with the views of Christian, development-seeking Islanders for whom they claimed to speak.[44]

By the 1980s many anthropologists knew they needed to look beyond the ethnographic present, though historians found their archival and documentary skills wanting. Douglas Oliver appended a slim volume of history to his historical anthropology of Tahiti. His uneven narrative petered out, but this culturally

[41] e.g. Alan Moorehead, *The Fatal Impact: An Account of the Invasion of the South Pacific, 1767–1840* (London, 1966); Edward Wybergh Docker, *The Blackbirders: The Recruiting of South Seas Labour for Queensland, 1863-1907* (Sydney, 1970); David Howarth, *Tahiti: A Paradise Lost* (London, 1983); Julian Evans, *Transit of Venus: Travels in the Pacific* (London, 1992).

[42] Hugh Laracy, ed., *Pacific Protest: The Maasina Rule Movement, Solomon Islands, 1944–1952* (Suva, Fiji, 1983); Andrew Pike, Hank Nelson, and Gavan Daws, *Angels of War* (motion picture, Canberra, 1981).

[43] Alaima Talu and others, *Kiribati: Aspects of History* (Suva, Fiji, 1979); Hugh Laracy, ed., *Tuvalu: A History* (Suva, Fiji, 1983); Ongka, *Ongka: A Self-Account by a New Guinea Big-Man*, trans. Andrew Strathern (London, 1979); Jonathon Fifi'i, *From Pig-Theft to Parliament: My Life Between Two Worlds*, ed. Roger M. Keesing (Honiara, Solomon Islands, 1989).

[44] For informed reflections on film as history and its ambiguous roles in colonial and anti-colonial representations, see Rosaleen Smyth, 'Reel Pacific History: The Pacific Islands on Film, Video and Television', in Lal, ed., *Pacific Islands History*, pp. 203–24; Hank Nelson, 'Write History, Reel History', in ibid., pp. 184–202.

informed account of Tahitians' early encounters with mostly British Europeans was arguably equal to any by historians.[45] For fifteen years, Pacific historical anthropology has been dominated by Marshall Sahlins, whose writings on the dialectics of structure and action in Hawaii inspired emulation, hostility, and self-justification.[46] Roger Keesing wrote histories of the Kwaio of Malaita in the Solomon Islands, in collaboration with the historian Peter Corris and independently.[47] Ben Burt explored indigenization of Christianity elsewhere in Malaita.[48] Deborah Gewertz criticized Mead's Sepik ethnography for inadequate attention to colonial contingencies, while she and Frederick Errington combined field observation with oral and colonial texts to chart local encounters between tradition and modernity in PNG's Sepik region and East New Britain.[49] Historical anthropologists thus sought to extend their analytic gaze from natives to colonizers, and their mutual encounters.[50] As their expertise in location and critical evaluation of contemporary texts improved, so did their colonial histories gain cogency. The tendency to teleology—to reconfigure the past as cause of the ethnographic present of their own fieldwork—troubled historians, who properly challenged unreflective presentism.

The 1980s saw Pacific historical research and publication decentred from Canberra to elsewhere in Australia, Honolulu, Suva, and Auckland, and a blurring of generic as well as disciplinary boundaries: segregation of Imperial and Island-centred history seemed naïve and misguided, given the primacy of colonialism and modernity in shaping indigenous experience.[51] This final historiographic category, 'post-colonial' histories, refers to disparate deconstructionist approaches,

[45] Douglas L. Oliver, *Ancient Tahitian Society*, 3 vols. (Canberra, 1974), III.

[46] Marshall Sahlins, *Historical Metaphors and Mythical Realities: Structure in the Early History of the Sandwich Islands Kingdom* (Ann Arbor, 1981); Antony Hooper and Judith Huntsman, eds., *Transformations of Polynesian Culture* (Auckland, 1985); Gananath Obeyesekere, *The Apotheosis of Captain Cook: European Mythmaking in the Pacific* (Princeton, 1992); Marshall Sahlins, *How 'Natives' Think: About Captain Cook, For Example* (Chicago, 1995).

[47] Roger M. Keesing and Peter Corris, *Lightning Meets the West Wind: The Malaita Massacre* (Melbourne, 1980); Roger M. Keesing, *Custom and Confrontation: The Kwais Struggle for Cultural Autonomy* (Chicago, 1992).

[48] Ben Burt, *Tradition and Christianity: The Colonial Transformation of a Solomon Islands Society* (Chur, Switzerland, 1994).

[49] Deborah B. Gewertz, *Sepik River Societies: A Historical Ethnography of the Chambri and their Neighbours* (New Haven, 1983); Deborah B. Gewertz and Frederick K. Errington, *Twisted Histories, Altered Contexts: Representing the Chambri in a World System* (Cambridge, 1991); Frederick K. Errington and Deborah B. Gewertz, *Articulating Change in the 'Last Unknown'* (Boulder, Colo., 1995).

[50] Aletta Biersack, ed., *Clio in Oceania: Toward a Historical Anthropology* (Washington, 1991); James G. Carrier, ed., *History and Tradition in Melanesian Anthropology* (Berkeley, 1992).

[51] Bronwen Douglas, 'Doing Ethnographic History: Reflections on Practices and Practising', in Lal, ed., *Pacific Islands History*, pp. 92–106; Nicholas Thomas, 'Partial Texts: Representation, Colonialism and Agency in Pacific History', *JPH*, XXV (1990), pp. 139–58.

including feminist challenges to conventionally gendered histories,[52] and works by ethnographic historians who knew there could be no indigenous history free of colonial entanglements—particularly Greg Dening, whose *Mr Bligh's Bad Language* was justly celebrated within and beyond the academy.[53] The category is diverse in associations as well as content. Lineally, it recalls Bernard Smith's interest in how ideas and contexts are dialectically constituted in images and texts, but with explicit concern for power inequalities. Collaterally, it is related to eclectic recent interest—in anthropology, cultural studies, gender studies, and literary criticism—in radical critique of colonial texts and discourses, and in the politics of representation and narrative construction. There was widespread, disparate concern to eschew essentialism, expose ambiguities and fractures in dominant white male authority, emphasize variety and change in local experiences of colonialism, and locate the shadowy imprints of indigenous or female agency in structural and pragmatic contexts. Some probed the reciprocal significance of colonialism in shaping metropolitan identities and the disciplines of history and anthropology.[54]

Post-colonial Pacific histories have largely concentrated on the colonial period, though Keesing borrowed the 'Subaltern Studies' strategy of appropriating Marxist, post-modernist, and humanist elements to dissect national, as well as colonial power relations and abuses.[55] Other historical anthropologists acknowledged the bound-together relationship of colonized and colonizer: Margaret Jolly wrote on missionary and Vanuatu women; Martha Kaplan on negative colonial constructions of non-chiefly Fijian ritual politics; John D. Kelly on contested Hindu strategies of engagement with colonial authority in Fiji; Michael Young on the fractured colonial identities in Vanuatu of the adventurer-planter-novelist Robert Fletcher.[56] From the metropolitan direction, Christopher Herbert probed

[52] Claudia Knapman, *White Women in Fiji, 1835–1930: The Ruin of Empire?* (Sydney, 1986); Margaret Jolly and Martha Macintyre, eds., *Family and Gender in the Pacific: Domestic Contradictions and the Colonial Impact* (Cambridge, 1989).

[53] Greg Dening, *Islands and Beaches: Discourses on a Silent Land, Marquesas, 1774–1880* (Carlton, Victoria, 1980), *Mr Bligh's Bad Language: Passion, Power and Theatre on the Bounty* (Cambridge, 1992), *The Death of William Gooch: A History's Anthropology* (Carlton, Victoria, 1995), and *Performances* (Chicago, 1996).

[54] See generally Johannes Fabian, *Time and the Other* (New York, 1983); George W. Stocking, Jr., *Victorian Anthropology* (New York, 1987); Gayatri Chakravorty Spivak, *In Other Worlds: Essays in Cultural Politics* (New York, 1988); Sarah Mills, *Discourses of Difference: An Analysis of Women's Travel Writing and Colonialism* (London, 1991); Catherine Hall, *White, Male and Middle Class: Explorations in Feminism and History* (Cambridge, 1992); Edward W. Said, *Culture and Imperialism* (London, 1993).

[55] Keesing, *Custom and Confrontation*; Ranajit Guha, ed., *Subaltern Studies* (New Delhi, 1982 *et seq.*).

[56] Margaret Jolly, ' "To Save the Girls for Brighter and Better Lives": Presbyterian Missions and Women in the South of Vanuatu, 1848–1870', *JPH*, XXVI (1991), pp. 27–48; Martha Kaplan, *Neither Cargo nor Cult: Ritual Politics and the Colonial Imagination in Fiji* (Durham, NC, 1995); John D. Kelly, *A Politics of Virtue: Hinduism, Sexuality and Countercolonial Discourse in Fiji* (Chicago, 1991); Michael

links between evangelical and anthropological conceptions of nature and culture, but his work lacked ethnographic conviction.[57] Few historians of the British in the Pacific have published books in this vein, but Nicholas Thomas is a prolific exception: in *Entangled Objects* he looked at how objects were appropriated and given cultural and contextual meanings by both Islanders and Europeans; in *Colonialism's Culture* he examined the diverse, ambiguous, unstable values and interests which informed the attitude and actions of different categories of colonizers.[58] In an innovative work on the Tolai of New Britain, Klaus Neumann juxtaposed local stories and colonial accounts in an open-ended, reflexive narrative showing the constructed, contested nature of histories and the plurality and contingency of past realities.[59]

The first scholarly histories cited were general, perhaps because imperialism provided a focus, and an illusion of unity spurious in indigenous terms. For at least twenty years Island-centred historians have sporadically argued the need for general histories of Oceania and its island groups. A few wrote them, with worthy but unremarkable results.[60] Since the multiplicity of indigenous cultures and pre-colonial, colonial, and post-colonial experiences resists narrative control, it is comforting to import a synthesizing principle—waves of European invasion, or colonial (now post-colonial) geography—or shelter in the seeming consequence of formal policy and politics. Belying island-centred origins, general histories tend to be Eurocentric and élite-oriented. They no longer include works exclusively on 'The British in the Pacific'. Ironically, while British *colonialism* is a favourite theme for post-colonial histories, and whereas 'The United States' and 'France' in the Pacific have renewed scholarly credibility as organizing principles for imperial histories because of ongoing American and French colonial presence, 'The British in the Pacific Islands', once a dominant historiographic interest, is now *passé*.[61]

Young, 'Gone Native in the Isles of Illusion: In Search of Asterisk in Epi', in Carrier, ed., *History and Tradition in Melanesian Anthropology*, pp. 193–223.

[57] Christopher Herbert, *Culture and Anomie: Ethnographic Imagination in the Nineteenth Century* (Chicago, 1991).

[58] Nicholas Thomas, *Entangled Objects: Exchange, Material Culture, and Colonialism in the Pacific* (Cambridge, Mass., 1991) and *Colonialism's Culture: Anthropology, Travel and Government* (Cambridge, 1994).

[59] Klaus Neumann, *Not the Way it Really Was: Constructing the Tolai Past* (Honolulu, 1992).

[60] e.g. James Griffin, Hank Nelson, and Stewart Firth, *Papua New Guinea: A Political History* (Richmond, Victoria, 1979); K. R. Howe, *Where the Waves Fall: A New South Sea Islands History from First Settlement to Colonial Rule* (Honolulu, 1984); Deryck Scarr, *The History of the Pacific Islands: Kingdoms of the Reefs* (Melbourne, 1990); Brij V. Lal, *Broken Waves: A History of the Fiji Islands in the Twentieth Century* (Honolulu, 1992); John Dademo Waiko, *A Short History of Papua New Guinea* (Melbourne, 1993).

[61] Robert Aldrich, *The French Presence in the South Pacific, 1842–1940* (Sydney, 1990); John Dorrance, *The United States and the Pacific Islands* (Washington, 1992). But cf. Jane Samson, *Imperial Benevolence: Making British Authority in the Pacific Islands* (Honolulu, 1998).

Select Bibliography

J. C. BEAGLEHOLE, *The Exploration of the Pacific* (London, 1934; 3rd edn., 1966).

—— ed., *The Journals of Captain James Cook on His Voyages of Discovery*, 4 vols. (Cambridge, 1955–74).

JAMES G. CARRIER, ed., *History and Tradition in Melanesian Anthropology* (Berkeley, 1992).

BOB CONNOLLY and ROBIN ANDERSON, *First Contact* (motion picture, Sydney, 1982; New York, 1984).

Contemporary Pacific (Honolulu, 1989 *et seq.*).

J. W. DAVIDSON, *Samoa mo Samoa: The Emergence of the Independent State of Western Samoa* (Melbourne, 1967).

GREG DENING, *Mr Bligh's Bad Language: Passion, Power and Theatre on the Bounty* (Cambridge, 1992).

NIEL GUNSON, *Messengers of Grace: Evangelical Missionaries in the South Seas, 1797–1860* (Melbourne, 1978).

Journal of Pacific History (Canberra, 1966 *et seq.*).

MARTHA KAPLAN, *Neither Cargo Nor Cult: Ritual Politics and the Colonial Imagination in Fiji* (Durham, NC, 1995).

BRIJ V. LAL, ed., *Pacific Islands History: Journeys and Transformations* (Canberra, 1992).

H. E. MAUDE, *Of Islands and Men: Studies in Pacific History* (Melbourne, 1968).

MALAMA MELEISEA, *The Making of Modern Samoa: Traditional Authority and Colonial Administration in the History of Western Samoa* (Suva, 1987).

W. P. MORRELL, *Britain in the Pacific Islands* (Oxford, 1960).

KLAUS NEUMANN, *Not the Way it Really Was: Constructing the Tolai Past* (Honolulu, 1992).

MARSHALL SAHLINS, *Historical Metaphors and Mythical Realities: Structure in the Early History of the Sandwich Islands Kingdom* (Ann Arbor, 1981).

DOROTHY SHINEBERG, *They Came for Sandalwood: A Study of the Sandalwood Trade in the South-West Pacific, 1830–1865* (Carlton, Victoria, 1967).

BERNARD SMITH, *European Vision and the South Pacific* (Oxford, 1960; 3rd edn., Melbourne, 1989).

O. H. K. SPATE, *The Pacific Since Magellan*, 3 vols. (Canberra, 1979–88).

NICHOLAS THOMAS, *Colonialism's Culture: Anthropology, Travel and Government* (Cambridge, 1994).

25

Formal and Informal Empire in East Asia

C. M. TURNBULL

> The conduct of European Powers towards China will rank as the clearest revelation of the nature of Imperialism.
>
> (J. A. Hobson, *Imperialism*)

In the first systematic attempt to analyse the 'new' expansionist imperialism of the late nineteenth century, Hobson's *Imperialism: A Study* (London, 1902) cited China as the most crucial test of 'the spirit and methods of Western Imperialism' and the classic example of a drift from free trade and a civilizing mission to annexation and exploitation. His study was provoked by the late-nineteenth-century crises in South Africa and in China, where Britain's long pre-eminence was over, free trade was threatened, and the scramble for concessions brought Western nations to the brink of war. Hobson condemned late-Victorian imperialism as a perversion, driven by a small clique of private profit-mongers subordinating trade interests to those of finance capital and investment, breeding strife among rival empires, and stimulating resentful nationalism among victim peoples. Cynical about Britain's role as 'trustee for civilization', he saw missionaries as an *imperium in imperio*, standing outside Chinese law, supported by gunboats, and alienating people from their traditional beliefs. For Europe to rule Asia by force and justify this as civilizing 'will be adjudged by history, perhaps, to be the crowning wrong and folly of Imperialism'. Unless she roused herself quickly, China would break up under external pressure: 'Not till then shall we realize the full risks and folly of the most revolutionary enterprise history has known.'[1]

This was a far cry from the optimistic Canton-based missionary *Chinese Repository*[2] which, in the mid-nineteenth century, had challenged the long-accepted Jesuit-inspired view of a tranquil, stable, and changeless East Asia. The journal wanted Western traders and missionaries to sweep away the ignorance

[1] Hobson, *Imperialism* (London, 1902), p. 312.

[2] *The Chinese Repository*, 20 vols. (1832–51: Canton, 1832–39; Macau, 1839–44; Hong Kong, Oct. 1844–July 1845; Canton, 1845–51).

and oppression inflicted during 'tens of centuries of Old Custom'[3] by opening China, Japan, and Siam to free trade, modern knowledge, and Christianity.

While Hobson was an orthodox liberal free trader, he inspired diverse followers, ranging from Lenin and the neo-Marxists to the pioneering academic historian Arthur John Sargent, quaintly titled Appointed Teacher of Foreign Trade in the University of London, who endorsed Hobson's conclusions in *Anglo-Chinese Commerce and Diplomacy (Mainly in the Nineteenth Century)* (Oxford, 1907), and the distinguished diplomatic historian William L. Langer, who saluted Hobson's work more than thirty years later as probably the best book on imperialism.

By the early twentieth century an impressive body of Western-language sources was available to historians of Britain's involvement in East Asia: *Parliamentary Papers*, published collections of treaties, consular reports, and Imperial Maritime Customs publications, which Sargent commended as a 'mass of economic material such as is rarely available outside the circle of advanced industrial nations'. The Shanghai-based North China Branch of the Royal Asiatic Society, affiliated in 1858, published a scholarly journal and built up a splendid Oriental library,[4] which Henri Cordier used, along with French documents, for his *Relations de la Chine avec les puissances occidentales*, 3 vols. (Paris, 1901–02), a valuable source-book for the post-1860 period. The 'heroic' era was rich in journals recording the experiences of British diplomats who negotiated the opening up of China, Japan, and Siam;[5] in heavyweight biographies, such as Stanley Lane-Poole and F. V. Dickins, *The Life of Sir Harry Parkes: Sometime Her Majesty's Minister to China and Japan*, 2 vols. (London 1894); and in the type of 'memoire pour servir a l'histoire' by Sir Rutherford Alcock, the first British Minister to Japan, in *The Capital of the Tycoon* (London, 1863), which related experience without claiming the 'gravity and authority of history'. To Alcock, British motivation was clear: 'Commerce is with us, in Siam, China and Japan all equally . . . the one sole object.' But he contrasted the relative ease with which Western ambassadors obtained paper promises with the problem of Ministers trying to enforce treaties foisted on unwilling Asian peoples: to 'amalgamate two conflicting civilisations, and open new markets for our manufactures, without resort to force, or coercive means of any kind'.[6]

[3] *Chinese Repository*, I, 1 (May 1832), p. 1.

[4] Harold M. Otness, ' "The One Bright Spot in Shanghai": A History of the Library of the North China Branch of the Royal Asiatic Society', *Journal of the Hong Kong Branch of the Royal Asiatic Society*, XXVIII (1988), pp. 185–97.

[5] J. Bowring, *The Kingdom and People of Siam*, 2 vols. (London, 1856), *Autobiographical Recollections of Sir John Bowring, With a Brief Memoir by Lewis B. Bowring* (London, 1877); Laurence Oliphant, *Narrative of the Earl of Elgin's Mission to China and Japan in the Years 1857, '58, '59*, 2 vols. (Edinburgh, 1859).

[6] Sir Rutherford Alcock, *The Capital of the Tycoon: A Narrative of Three Years' Residence in Japan*, 2 vols., II, p. 352, quoted in D. C. M. Platt, *Finance, Trade and Politics in British Foreign Policy, 1815–1914* (Oxford, 1968), p. 265.

Chinese materials were less accessible. In the 1840s Westerners gave a cautious welcome to the writings of senior mandarins Wei Yuan and 'Confucian realist'[7] Hsü Chi-yu as indicating awakening Chinese interest in the outside world. Based largely on Western sources, Wei Yuan's *Hai-kuo t'u chih* or *Illustrated Treatise on the Sea Kingdoms* (Yangchou, 1844) and Hsü's *Ying-huan chih-lueh* or *Geography of the Surrounding Oceans* (Foochow, 1848) became texts for Ch'ing officials. But Wei Yuan and Hsü were deeply traditionalist mandarins, and there was no meeting of minds with the West. The Chinese saw the Nanking Treaty as a degradation dictated by force of arms. Attributing China's troubles to the disruption of world harmony by British barbarians breaking out of their Western Ocean to attack the Middle Kingdom, Wei Yuan advised mastering British military skills in order to repel them. Edward H. Parker translated a *Chinese Account of the Opium War* (Shanghai, 1888) from Wei Yuan's work, but *The Chinese Repository* remained the main source of official Chinese documents and was acknowledged by historians a hundred years later as 'a valuable treasure of information'.[8]

The most influential early historian of Western relations with China, Harvard-educated Hosea Ballou Morse, served for thirty-five years in the Imperial Maritime Customs Service in many parts of China, finishing as Statistical Secretary (in effect, research director). Retiring to England in 1908, Morse embarked on an equally distinguished second career as a historian and, over the next twenty years, published a series of monumental works. *The Trade and Administration of the Chinese Empire* (London, 1908; 3rd updated edn. 1921), portrayed late imperial China in historical context, while *The International Relations of the Chinese Empire*, 3 vols. (London, 1910–18) traced China's foreign relations from the end of the East India Company's monopoly to the collapse of the Ch'ing dynasty. *The Chronicles of the East India Company Trading to China, 1635–1834*, 4 vols. (Cambridge, Mass., 1926), with a fifth supplementary volume (Oxford, 1929), was an exhaustive compilation of facts, figures, and summaries of events derived from some 200 volumes of the Company's Canton records: a source-book rather than an analysis. 'From these records every fact has been extracted which could be of economic value to the student of the commercial history of the eighteenth and early nineteenth centuries', Morse claimed, surmising correctly that this would be the least controversial and most lasting of his works.

Reacting against nineteenth-century histories and biographies, which stressed picturesque highlights and portrayed characters in black and white, Morse set out, in the best tradition of the scholar-administrator, to tell the story dispassionately,

[7] Fred W. Drake, *China Charts the World: Hsü Chi-yu and His Geography of 1848* (Cambridge, Mass., 1975), p. 6.

[8] P. C. Kuo, *A Critical Study of the First Anglo-Chinese War, With Documents* (Shanghai, 1935).

the humdrum along with the colourful. He aimed to use history to understand the present, without passing moral judgement, but establishing a chronology and foundation of solid fact on which others could build. To his distress the Kuomintang government banned the one-volume condensation of his *International Relations*, published with Harley Farnsworth MacNair as *Far Eastern International Relations* (Shanghai, 1928 and Boston, 1931), and Chinese Marxist writers later condemned him as a chronicler of imperialist aggression. But for Western historians Morse's works established a model of accuracy and, until well into the second half of the twentieth century, were the essential foundation for the study of China's relations with the West.

As an Oxford Rhodes scholar, John King Fairbank met Morse in 1929 and later hailed him as the mentor and 'adopted grandfather' who launched him on a lifetime study of China, inspiring him with the same 'dedication to clarity, comprehensiveness and objectivity'. In his scholarly career at Harvard spanning six decades, Fairbank published scores of books and articles and established a base which nurtured generations of scholars. His unfinished biography and appraisal of Morse was subsequently completed by colleagues: John King Fairbank, Martha Henderson Coolidge, and Richard J. Smith, *H. B. Morse, Customs Commissioner and Historian of China* (Lexington, Mass., 1995). In an afterword, Smith commented, Morse's 'lasting contribution to Chinese studies was his own scholarship and Fairbank himself'.

The explosion of Chinese nationalism in the 1920s and Chinese demands to end the foreign privilege system attracted growing public and scholarly interest in the West. Men with long experience of China returned home to take up responsible posts, often in academia, while societies were formed to promote accurate information about East Asia: notably the Institute of Pacific Relations, an unofficial body founded in 1925, which sponsored research and held regular conferences in the region.

Westel W. Willoughby, Professor of Political Science at Johns Hopkins University and former legal adviser to the Chinese Republic, produced a comprehensive survey, *Foreign Rights and Interests in China* (Baltimore, 1920), which traced the growth of foreign encroachments since the Nanking Treaty. Nowhere else in the world, Willoughby pointed out, was there 'such a mixture of territorial rights with foreign privileges and understandings of purely political engagement with economic and financial concessions, of foreign interests conflicting with one another and with those of the nominally sovereign state'.

Former missionaries were more sanguine. *China and England* (London, 1928), by the Methodist, W. E. Soothill, who became Professor of Chinese at Oxford, was an affectionate interpretation of the Anglo-Chinese relationship: 'friendly intercourse with a friendly people, for mutual welfare, has been England's unwavering policy'. Using voluminous primary missionary sources, the former American Protestant missionary, Kenneth Scott Latourette, Professor of Missions and Oriental History at Yale University, produced the first authoritative general history, *A History of Christian Missions in China* (New York, 1929). He argued that, despite faults, missionaries were the one agency 'whose primary function was to bring China into contact with the best in the Occident and to make the expansion of the West a means of greater welfare of the Chinese people'. Latourette's standard history was still acknowledged half a century later as 'remarkably objective',[9] but he himself admitted that economic and political forces were more important than missionary influence in moulding the modern revolution in China, and it was these aspects which preoccupied later historians.

The vexed question of extraterritoriality was examined in Anatol M. Kotenev, *Shanghai, Its Mixed Court and Council* (Shanghai, 1925), and by G. W. Keeton, formerly Reader in Law and Politics at the University of Hong Kong, in *The Development of Extraterritoriality in China*, 2 vols. (London, 1928). The working of the Siamese consular courts was described by long-serving Consul W. A. R. Wood in a book first published in Bangkok in the 1930s and revised as *Consul in Paradise: Sixty Nine Years in Siam* (London, 1965). F. C. Jones's cogently argued *Extraterritoriality in Japan: And the Diplomatic Relations Resulting in Its Abolition, 1853–1899* (New Haven, 1931) showed how an age-old custom of mutual convenience was transformed in nineteenth-century East Asia into something imposed by unequal treaties, and in China by force.

No accurate nineteenth-century trade figures were obtainable, but in *Foreign Trade in China* (Shanghai, 1926) the American economist, Charles F. Remer, lecturer at St John's University, Shanghai, used more reliable twentieth-century statistics to substantiate the overall impression of disappointed expectations. Remer was then commissioned to research into foreign investment in China, returning to the United States to collate his material on the very day the Japanese invaded Manchuria in September 1931. In introducing a 1968 reprint of his *Foreign Investments in China* (New York, 1933), Remer commented that this coincidental end of an era gave his book 'a sort of footnote immortality'. In fact it remained an authoritative source of lasting value. Remer concluded: 'The study of China's international economic relations meant, until but yesterday [1933], the study of British trade, British shipping, the British business community, and British investments in China', but he disagreed with Chinese intellectuals portraying China as an innocent victim, whose troubles all stemmed from the unequal

9 Denis Twitchett and John Fairbank, general eds., *The Cambridge History of China* (hereafter *CHC*), 15 vols. (Cambridge, 1978–); Paul A. Cohen in John K. Fairbank, ed., Vol. X, *The Late Ch'ing, 1800–1911*, pt 1, (Cambridge, 1978), p. 611.

treaties: 'I resented the tyranny and over-simplification of the term "imperialism". '[10]

In the 1930s the renamed Chinese Maritime Customs Service centralized its archives in Shanghai and continued its publication programme, culminating in a comprehensive collection of post-1861 materials: *Documents Illustrative of the Origin, Development and Activities of the Chinese Customs Service*, 7 vols. (Shanghai, 1937–40). Commissioner Stanley F. Wright produced *The Collection and Disposal of the Maritime and Customs Revenue Since the Revolution of 1911* (Shanghai, 1925), and after his retirement published two tomes: *China's Struggle for Tariff Autonomy* (Shanghai, 1938) traced the story from the genesis of treaty tariff restrictions, with Wright himself admitting the detail was 'heavy going, a Sahara of facts, figures and opinions where the hapless reader may well founder and perish'; *Hart and the Chinese Customs* (Belfast, 1950) was a personal but meticulously referenced tribute to the public life of Sir Robert Hart, the most influential Briton in late-nineteenth-century East Asia and later described as 'one of those proconsuls of the Victorian age who built the empire—except that he did it in China'.[11] As Inspector-General from 1863 until his retirement in 1908, Hart moulded the Imperial Maritime Customs Service into a unique institution, responsible to the Chinese government, supporting the monarchy and encouraging reform, while enforcing the commercial provisions of the foreign treaties. Criticized by contemporary Western merchants for being too deferential towards the Chinese authorities, Hart's Service was subsequently denounced by nationalist Chinese scholars as a tool of Western imperialism. Only one slight contemporary biography was published, by an admiring niece,[12] but eventually Hart's own journals and letters became an invaluable source.[13]

The American academic, Earl H. Pritchard, was the first to make extensive use of Morse's *Chronicles*, which inspired him to trace the origin of the 'China question' to the Canton period in *Anglo-Chinese Relations During the Seventeenth and Eighteenth Centuries* (Urbana, Ill., 1929) and *The Crucial Years of Early Anglo-Chinese Relations, 1750–1800* (Washington, 1936). The Yale scholar, David Edward Owen, in *British Opium Policy in China and India* (New Haven, 1934), hailed

[10] Charles F. Remer, *Foreign Investments in China* (New York, 1933), Preface to 1968 reprint, pp. 406, xxvi.

[11] Katherine F. Brunner, John F. Fairbank, and Richard J. Smith (edited with narrative by), *Entering China's Service: Robert Hart's Journals, 1854–1863* (Cambridge, Mass., 1986), p. xi.

[12] Juliet Bredon, *Sir Robert Hart: The Romance of a Great Career* (London, 1909).

[13] John King Fairbank, Katherine Frost Brunner, and Elizabeth MacLeod Matheson, eds., *The I.G. in Peking: Letters of Robert Hart, Chinese Maritime Customs, 1868–1907*, 2 vols. (Cambridge, Mass., 1975); Brunner, Fairbank, and Smith, *Entering China's Service*; Richard J. Smith, John K. Fairbank, and Katherine F. Brunner, eds., *Robert Hart and China's Early Modernization: His Journals, 1863–1866* (Cambridge, Mass., 1991).

Morse's *Chronicles* as 'an admirable and reliable substitute for the manuscripts themselves' and acknowledged, 'I have not scrupled to follow his guidelines'. Other historians saw the most decisive period as the late nineteenth century when East Asia for the first time became central to European diplomacy. Neither official Western archives for the period nor those of China and Japan were open to scholars in the 1920s, but in *Foreign Diplomacy in China, 1894–1900: A Study in Political and Economic Relations with China* (London, 1928), Philip Joseph made careful use of British, French, German, and American published documents, memoirs, and contemporary newspapers, to examine what he termed the real factors behind the usual diplomatic incidents: law, finance, political geography, and trade. He saw 1894 as a turning-point, when China lost control over her own destiny and came to the brink of dissolution.

In 1935 William L. Langer published his monumental two-volume *The Diplomacy of Imperialism, 1890–1902*. Describing this era as the peak of 'that outburst of overseas expansion which we call *imperialism*', when competition for territory and influence dominated European international relations, Langer rated the East Asia crisis the most serious and complex issue at that time. He made much use of contemporary Western materials, including the new popular press, and for the first time investigated voluminous Russian sources. Langer inclined to the view expressed by J. R. Seeley in *The Expansion of England* (London, 1883), that Britain had conquered and peopled half the world 'in a fit of absence of mind', and agreed with C. A. Bodelsen, *Studies in Mid-Victorian Imperialism* (Copenhagen, 1924) that the 1840–70 period was the low point of imperialism in Britain, although ironically this included the era of the two Anglo-Chinese wars. Langer saw the 1870s and 1880s as a time of change, with the Empire becoming a matter of prestige. Endorsing the general view that British policy after the Sino-Japanese war still stood by the principle of Chinese integrity and British interests remained largely commercial, Langer represented Britain as bowing to the inevitable, finding herself isolated, with a vulnerable far-flung Empire. And he held that Britain miscalculated and faltered, deserting China but failing initially to align with Japan: the 1898 crisis 'was a calamity for the British who could not find a single power to stand by them. So they jumped from the frying pan into the fire.'[14]

The more conciliatory relationship between the British government and Chiang Kai-shek's Kuomintang administration in the 1930s stimulated interest among some British historians. G. F. Hudson, *The Far East in World Politics: A Study in Recent History* (Oxford, 1937), provided a lucid survey, and that same year the Oxford historian, W. C. Costin, who attended the Institute of Pacific Relations 1931 Hangchow Conference, published a Eurocentric study of *Great Britain and*

[14] William L. Langer, *The Diplomacy of Imperialism, 1890–1902*, 2nd edn. (New York, 1951), p. 480.

China, 1833–1860 (Oxford, 1937). Costin portrayed the British as bringing order and harmony, claiming that in 1858 'when they used force it was to meet the duplicity, evasion, cunning and cruelty of the Chinese officials'.[15]

The Cambridge Marxist historian Victor G. Kiernan, writing against the background of Japanese aggression in China in the late 1930s, was more pessimistic. His *British Diplomacy in China, 1880 to 1885* (Cambridge, 1939) studied in detail the latest years for which British official archives were then open, seeing the period as a prelude to the scramble of the late 1890s and condemning late-nineteenth-century British policy as 'confused rather than masterly'. For Kiernan, 'diplomacy and economics are two languages describing the same events'. Whereas Marx veiwed Western imperialism as a necessary catalyst for change and Kiernan recognized it brought some progress, in general he saw imperialism as 'deforming', breeding conflict in Europe and bolstering parasitic groups overseas. And he queried gloomily whether Western intervention had brought any good to China.

Costin, and even Morse, had been disparaging about the potential value of official Chinese sources, doubting if they would prove reliable or add much to Western accounts, whereas Kiernan recognized the limitations of English documents and described himself as writing 'in the obscurity of Western archives'. The publication by the Kuomintang government of voluminous official Ch'ing foreign-policy documents, notably *Ch'ou Pan Yi Wu Shih Mo (Reign of Tao-kuang): The Beginning and End of the Management of Barbarian Affairs* (Peking, 1930), enabled a new generation of scholars to present a more rounded view of Sino-Western relationships. Harvard-educated P. C. Kuo's *A Critical Study of the First Anglo-Chinese War with Documents* (Shanghai, 1935) was moderate and broad minded, concluding that opium merely precipitated the war, and the root cause went much further back. He claimed that, while opening the empire by force, Britain introduced China into the family of nations.

In China itself the 1930s were a time of intense Marxist historiographical debate. As early as 1900 Lenin had linked the Chinese with the Russian proletariat as victims of Western capitalism.[16] Developing Hobson's argument, Lenin's *Imperialism: The Highest Stage of Capitalism* (1916–17)[17] identified imperialism with monopoly capitalism, the British system of free trade having degenerated into parasitism, in which a few rich nations preyed on a large number of weak ones. China was cited as a typical example, and in his final pro-Communist days, Kuomintang leader Sun Yat-sen coined the term 'hypo-colony' to describe China's

[15] W. C. Costin, *Great Britain and China, 1833–1860* (Oxford, 1937), p. 344.

[16] V. I. Lenin, 'The War in China' (1900), reprinted in *The National Liberation Movement in the East* (Moscow, 1952), pp. 21–26.

[17] Extracts reprinted in Lenin, *National Liberation Movement*.

then subjection to a multiplicity of imperialist powers.[18] After their violent rift with the Kuomintang in 1927, Chinese communist intellectuals, engaging in a 'social history controversy', developed the theory of a 'semi-feudal, semi-colonial' society, in which foreign imperialism distorted the economy with the co-operation of indigenous reactionary collaborators: landlords, compradores, and officials.[19] This was to become the new orthodoxy after 1949.

The flow of publications about the Far East dried up during the Second World War, with a few important exceptions: F. C. Jones, *Shanghai and Tientsin with Special Reference to Foreign Interests* (London, 1940), was a report on the treaty port system commissioned before the war by the Institute of Pacific Relations; and *War and Politics in China* (London, 1943) by Sir John Pratt, a long-serving Consul and pre-war Adviser on Far Eastern Affairs at the Foreign Office, was later described as 'probably the most important book on Far Eastern policy written by a British official'.[20] Pratt admitted Britain 'was sometimes unjust and arbitrary . . . but that is a different thing to imperialism, which aims at domination and the destruction of political independence'. He argued that 'the main lines of British policy in the Far East have been immutably fixed by one governing consideration—the essential identity of interest between China and Great Britain . . . when China suffers British interests suffer, and when China prospers British interests also prosper'.[21]

The war brought fundamental changes in the Far East. In 1943 the unequal treaties were abandoned, ending the privilege system, and the establishment of the People's Republic of China in 1949 extinguished all but the last vestiges of imperialism. For the next thirty years China was virtually closed to all but sympathetic left-wing foreign scholars, while Chinese historians were isolated from the development of alternative indigenous approaches to history in liberated colonies. Hu Sheng expressed the official orthodoxy in his influential *Ti-kuo yu Chung-kuo ti cheng-chih* (Peking, 1952), translated as *Imperialism and Chinese Politics, 1840–1925* (Peking, 1955), which went into many editions. In a foreword to *The 1911 Revolution: A Retrospective after 70 Years* (Peking, 1983), co-editor Hu Sheng, then professor at Beijing University and deputy director of the Office of Documentation Research of the Central Committee of the Chinese Communist Party, claimed that from 1840 China had been steadily reduced to a semi-colonial and semi-feudal society, with the Ch'ing dynasty acting as the willing tools of the foreigners. While the 1911 revolution

[18] Sun Yat-sen, *San Min Chu I: The Three Principles of the People* (1924) trans. by Frank W. Price, ed. L. T. Chen, (Shanghai, 1930).

[19] Arif Dirlik, *Revolution and History: The Origins of Marxist Historiography in China, 1919–1937* (Berkeley, 1978).

[20] Wm. Roger Louis, *British Strategy in the Far East, 1919–1939* (Oxford, 1971).

[21] Sir John Pratt, *War and Politics in China* (London, 1943), pp. 37, 223–24.

toppled the monarchy, it left China still dominated by imperialism and feudalism under foreign-backed warlords and officials.

The Second World War delayed the publication of two important works for which research had been completed and which turned from diplomatic history to commerce: Nathan A. Pelcovits, *Old China Hands and the Foreign Office* (New York, 1948) and Michael Greenberg, *British Trade and the Opening of China, 1800–42* (Cambridge, 1951). Using Board of Trade documents, and the papers of Jardine Matheson, the Manchester Chamber of Commerce, and the China Association, Pelcovits set out to demolish the assumption made by Joseph and other diplomatic historians that, because Britain's sole interest in China was commercial, official policy throughout was dictated by British commercial interests. He argued that for half a century from 1860 official and mercantile attitudes clashed fundamentally: whereas the Foreign Office pursued a policy of 'benevolent non-interference', British merchants wanted their government to open up the whole of China, if necessary by force. Pelcovits concluded that the British government's refusal to go beyond limited commitments 'solves the historical riddle of why China never became another India'.

The archives of Jardine Matheson, the premier British firm on the China coast, which were discovered in a Hong Kong godown (warehouse) and lodged in Cambridge University Library during the 1930s, provided Greenberg's main source in arguing that private British merchants and the pressures of the expanding British economy were the decisive factors leading to the Opium War, 1840–42. Greenberg worked only with Western sources, but the publication of Commissioner Lin Tse-hsü's diary in 1955 led to the sinologist Arthur Waley's elegant *The Opium War Through Chinese Eyes* (London, 1958) and the more ponderous account by Chang Hsin-pao, *Commissioner Lin and the Opium War* (Cambridge, Mass., 1964).

On the British side, the most comprehensive Opium War narrative, which was by Lieutenant John Ouchterlony of the Madras Engineers, *The Chinese War: An Account of all the Operations of the British Forces from the Commencement to the Treaty of Nanking* (London, 1844), and combined personal experience with the published accounts of numerous British army and naval officer eyewitnesses, was reprinted in 1970, while Peter Ward Fay's lively narrative, *The Opium War, 1840–1842* (Chapel Hill, NC, 1975) put the opium trade in the context of its Indian origins and for the first time gave due weight to missionary influence. The Chinese-language archives of the British Embassy in Peking were lodged in the Public Record Office in London in 1959. J. Y. Wong classified the mid-nineteenth-century documents: *Anglo-Chinese Relations, 1839–1860: A Calendar of Chinese Documents in the British Foreign Office Records* (Oxford, 1983), and used them in his major study: *Deadly Dreams: Opium, Imperialism, and the Arrow War (1856–1860) in China* (Cambridge, 1998).

The expansion of higher education in the developed world after the Second World War bred a new generation of professional academic historians, eager to explore fresh approaches to the study of history. Diplomacy and the 'official mind' played a large part in British-based studies. W. G. Beasley, in *Great Britain and the Opening of Japan, 1834–1858* (London, 1951), insisted that imperialism lay outside his study, but inevitably it was an underlying factor. Beasley showed how the experience in China conditioned both Japanese and British attitudes: the Japanese being scared into submission, while for the British 'the China treaty pattern had become almost a habit of mind'.

The publication of a second, one-volume edition of Langer's *Diplomacy of Imperialism* (New York, 1951), with updated bibliography but unchanged text, coincided with the opening from the 1950s of twentieth-century Western official archives, which resulted in a wealth of publications. Many derived from doctoral dissertations based on meticulous research into a broad field of original documentation and often long years in gestation, such as Leonard K. Young's *British Policy in China, 1895–1902* (Oxford, 1970).

Up to this point historians had tended to treat undeveloped countries as passive objects of imperial ambitions and conflicts, but such Eurocentric views came under general challenge in the late 1950s. In a seminal work published in French in 1962 and in English translation in 1968,[22] French Marxist Jean Chesneaux took a new look at China in the 1920s in the light of the May Fourth Movement. He identified two basic anachronisms: the domination of the Treaty powers, and the continuing sway of the ruling class based on peasant exploitation. Chesneaux argued that, prior to 1919, only one had been tackled at a time: the Boxers attacked the foreigners, but the 1898 reformers were conciliatory to the West. Claiming the Chinese industrial working class had previously been neglected and 'trivialised', he portrayed a positive role for the Chinese labour movement in the 1919–27 period, both in the Chinese revolution and the broader twentieth-century Afro-Asian anti-capitalist and anti-imperialist struggle.

In a seminal article, 'The Imperialism of Free Trade', John Gallagher and Ronald Robinson challenged the prevailing view of mid-Victorian 'trade not rule' anti-imperialism. Instead they argued for continuity, with the British government steadily extending British interests by whatever means: 'trade with informal control if possible; trade with rule when necessary'.[23] Accordingly, 'the warships at Canton are as much part of the period as responsible government for Canada', together with forcing 'free trade and friendship' treaties on weaker states such as Siam and Japan, and backing stable governments as good investment links.

[22] Jean Chesneaux, *The Chinese Labor Movement, 1919–1927*, trans. H. M. Wright (Stanford, Calif., 1968).

[23] *Economic History Review* (hereafter *EcHR*), Second Series, VI (1953), pp. 1–15.

This appealing theory stimulated much interest, but it was fifteen years before it was challenged by D. C. M. Platt, who later described 'Imperialism of Free Trade' as a 'catchy phrase'.[24] In 'The Imperialism of Free Trade: Some Reservations',[25] and *Finance, Trade, and Politics in British Foreign Policy, 1815–1914* (Oxford, 1968) Platt advanced a different concept of continuity: he argued that in China, as in Latin America, the imperialism of free trade was limited to seeking 'a fair field and no favour' in opening world markets on equal terms to international trade, which occasionally led to violence but not to political control. The late-nineteenth-century change of approach was a defensive shift to protect existing trade, and Platt commented that the British government's January 1930 Memorandum on China, 'We have no territorial or imperialistic claims',[26] could apply to the whole period since 1834.

Covering a similar time-frame, D. K. Fieldhouse, in *Economics and Empire, 1830–1914* (London, 1973), portrayed British imperialism as 'a cumulative precautionary process', requiring decisions in the metropolis but reacting to conditions on the periphery rather than planning for Empire. In China he highlighted two typical features of mid-nineteenth-century imperialism: a purely economic interest, but use of force if necessary to achieve limited objectives, as in the two Opium Wars. Fieldhouse concluded this was the true 'imperialism of free trade', with economic rather than political objectives, and involving no annexation. The case of China showed that, 'where economic considerations were allowed to predominate and where an indigenous political structure could provide the essential framework of order, economic forces did not necessarily lead to formal empire'. Fieldhouse concluded that 'colonialism was not a preference but a last resort', with the imperial process 'a temporary expedient to bridge the time-gap between a "modernized" Europe and a pre-capitalist periphery'.[27]

While the fifty-year rule applied to opening British official archives, the tradition persisted that at least half a century was needed to give historical perspective. Many historians felt themselves on safe ground only in the pre-First World War period. But Nicholas R. Clifford, in a Harvard dissertation published as *Retreat from China: British Policy in the Far East, 1937–1941* (London, 1967), ventured into the 1930s and concluded that Britain was 'in full retreat from China', mainly concerned to protect existing British interests, which were trapped between Chinese nationalism and Japanese imperialism.

[24] D. C. M. Platt, 'Further Objections to the Imperialism of Free Trade, 1830–60', in Wm. Roger Louis, ed., *Imperialism: The Robinson and Gallagher Controversy* (New York, 1976), p. 159.

[25] *EcHR*, Second Series, XXI, (1968), pp. 296–306.

[26] Memorandum of 8 Jan. 1930, in R. Butler and J. P. T. Bury, eds., *Documents on British Foreign Policy, 1919–1939*, Second Series, VIII (London, 1960), p. 26.

[27] D. K. Fieldhouse, *Economics and Empire, 1830–1914* (London, 1973), pp. 476–77.

Clifford himself considered the 1930s still too recent to understand, but a year after his book appeared the official British archives moved to a thirty-year rule, bringing them closer to the twenty-five-year limit applicable in the United States and immediately releasing most inter-war documents. Three years later Wm. Roger Louis, in *British Strategy in the Far East, 1919-1939* (Oxford, 1971), provided a masterly analysis of the newly available documentation relating to East Asia. The picture that emerged confirmed Clifford's thesis. It demonstrated the British government in a dilemma over policy, the Foreign and Colonial Offices at odds in the face of China's civil war, with Hong Kong caught in the middle. Louis showed the retreat across China was intended to consolidate the hold on Shanghai, which was technically an International Settlement, but in Louis's words 'one of the glories of Britain's informal empire'. His overall impression was that the entire venture to bring China into the mainstream of the Western world had been futile: 'on the whole, a study of the British in the Far East during the inter-war years yields the impression that they felt themselves buffeted by Asian forces beyond their control.' Subsequently scholarly research confirmed and elaborated that view.

The thirty-year rule encouraged a focus on more modern times by shortening the period which historians were accustomed to regard as giving a respectable perspective—a focus already encouraged by the rapid changes in post-war East Asia—and fostering the use of oral history. Faced with such a sudden embarrassment of riches, the immediate reaction was to leapfrog the 1920s and examine highlights and crises, Imperial defence and the Pacific War. Such studies were much occupied with British policy, but increasingly historians turned to business history. Stephen Lyon Endicott, *Diplomacy and Enterprise: British China Policy, 1933–1937* (Manchester, 1975) extended research to commercial archives, including the Swire collection,[28] to show a different pattern of interaction between finance, trade, high politics, and diplomacy from the pre-1914 period studied by Pelcovits and Fieldhouse. Endicott concluded that 'imperialism in the era of capitalist ascendancy cannot be understood apart from capitalism'. E. W. Edwards, *British Diplomacy and Finance in China, 1895–1914* (Oxford, 1987), reverted to the turn-of-the-century period to study in detail the significant shift in British economic practice in favour of closer official involvement and support for British commercial interests.

Other historians published on a wide variety of Imperial aspects. Gerald S. Graham, Rhodes Emeritus Professor of Imperial History at the University of London, followed up his *Great Britain in the Indian Ocean, 1810–1850* (Oxford, 1967) with *The China Station: War and Diplomacy, 1830–1860* (Oxford, 1978),

[28] The archives of Butterfield and Swire, Ltd., the second large British agency and shipping firm on the China coast, housed in the School of Oriental and African Studies, London.

which saw no evidence of coherent colonial policy in the mid-nineteenth century but only pragmatism and a general desire to avoid being drawn into a 'second India' in China. P. D. Coates, in *The China Consuls: British Consular Officers, 1843–1943* (Hong Kong, 1988), insisted he was writing an account about a group of British officials, not an instrument of imperialism, but inevitably his study contributed to this impression. Lawyer Thomas B. Stephens's *Order and Discipline in China: The Shanghai Mixed Court, 1911–27* (Seattle, Washington, 1992) showed the West's failure from the earliest missionary days to understand the fundamental incompatibility of Western and Chinese systems of law and discipline.

Of the two areas of China which were leased to Britain in 1898—Wei-hai-wei and the New Territories of Hong Kong—ironically the documentation about sleepy Wei-hai-wei, 'the Cinderella of the British Empire',[29] provided the more complete source for historians. Whereas most official New Territories' documents perished in the Second World War, Wei-hai-wei's voluminous archives were transferred to London when it reverted to Chinese rule in 1930, and a successor British consulate reported on the new regime. The concession had already been vividly described by a district officer, Reginald F. Johnston, in *Lion and Dragon in Northern China* (London, 1910). Johnston, who went on to become Wei-hai-wei's second (and last Commissioner) and in 1931 Professor of Chinese at London University, pictured Wei-hai-wei as the meeting-place between the British and the Chinese, a surviving relic of 'Old China' and 'a little wilderness of research'.[30] Experienced ex-Hong Kong officials and Chinese scholars, both Johnston and his predecessor, James Haldane Stewart Lockhart, were content to administer justice as *fu-mu-kuan* (father and mother officials) in the best Confucian tradition, and Johnston concluded that British administration and its influence was by design very slight. He saw 'backward' Wei-hai-wei as a bulwark against extreme reform—slowing change and the inevitable collapse of Confucianism—and suspected the territory had most to fear from China's own revolutionary reformers and 'well-meaning but somewhat ignorant foreign friends'.[31]

This 'prediction' is discussed by Pamela Attwell, *British Mandarins and Chinese Reformers: The British Administration of Weihaiwei (1898–1930), and the Territory's Return to Chinese Rule* (Hong Kong, 1985). Using the official archives in London and Lockhart's papers in Edinburgh, Attwell contrasted the British, who pursued a 'minimalist' administration as traditional benign mandarins, with the unsettling successor Kuomintang regime, which swept away old customs in the attempt to modernize and create a sense of nationhood. Shiona M. Airlie, *Thistle and Bamboo: The Life and Times of Sir James Stewart Lockhart* (Hong Kong, 1989),

[29] R. F. Johnston, *Lion and Dragon in Northern China* (London, 1910), p. 2.

[30] Ibid., p. 5.

[31] Ibid., p. 449.

largely based on Lockhart's papers, portrayed him as 'a sharp Scottish thistle' transformed by Confucian principles into a 'pliant bamboo' and paternal mandarin in close contact with the people. The Colonial Office was not so admiring, describing Lockhart's time in Wei-hai-wei as a 'refuge in apathy'.[32]

By the outbreak of the Pacific War (1941) British imperialism in China had virtually run its course. Only Hong Kong remained. Like the colony itself, the history of Hong Kong excited little interest up to that time. *The Chinese Repository* had moved its office to Hong Kong in 1844 and in June 1845 published 'Notices of Hong Kong', detailing its brief history,[33] but the following month the journal reverted to Canton and carried little about the colony in its future issues. An Asiatic Society of China, formed in Hong Kong in 1847 with the Governor as president and senior officials on its council, was affiliated to the Royal Asiatic Society, but by 1859 it disintegrated in friction and went into abeyance for more than a century.

As *The Times* sneered in March 1859, 'Hong Kong is always connected with some fatal pestilence, some doubtful war, or some discreditable internal squabble'.[34] The most scandalous quarrels often centred on the judiciary and were brought vividly to life, with no pretence to impartiality, by the Registrar of the Supreme Court, James William Norton-Kyshe, in *History of the Laws and Courts of Hongkong*, 2 vols. (London, 1882 and 1898). E. J. Eitel, *Europe in China: The History of Hongkong from the Beginning to the Year 1882* (Hong Kong, 1885) provided the first history, much of it derived from sources which were later destroyed, and backed by over thirty years' eyewitness experience as a missionary and inspector of schools. Morse criticized Eitel's work as 'history written to support the utmost pretensions of the Hongkong residents',[35] but it remained the main source for the early period until well after the Second World War.

The Director of Education, Geoffrey Robley Sayer, published a modest *Hong Kong: Birth, Adolescence and Coming of Age* (London, 1937). In a foreword to a sequel, *Hong Kong, 1862–1919: Years of Discretion*, which fell victim to the war and was published in Hong Kong only in 1975, Sayer's son admitted, 'This work is not of great historical importance: indeed little of significance occurred during the period to excite the interest of anyone outside Hong Kong.' There were indeed no stirring events, no heroes of Empire.

The Second World War changed this dramatically. The fall of Hong Kong and the Japanese occupation inspired many books, some immediate, compelling, and autobiographical, such as that by the internee Jean Gittins, *I Was at Stanley* (Hong Kong, 1946) and Emily Hahn, *China To Me* (Philadelphia, 1949). More detailed

32 Airlie, *Thistle and Bamboo*, p. 194, quoting Colonial Office minute, 10 Aug. 1920.

33 *Chinese Repository*, XIV (June 1845), p. 291.

34 Quoted in G. B. Endacott, *A History of Hong Kong* (London, 1958), p. 87.

35 Morse, *International Relations*, I, p. 694.

accounts of the military campaign came later, such as Alan Birch and George B. Endacott, *Hong Kong Eclipse* (Hong Kong, 1978); Oliver Lindsay, *The Lasting Honour* (London, 1978) and *At the Going Down of the Sun* (London, 1981); and Edwin Ride, *BAAG: Hong Kong Resistance, 1942–1945* (Hong Kong, 1981).

The University of Hong Kong, founded in 1911 to offer a British-style curriculum to a well-to-do English-educated minority, expanded after the war, and in the 1960s three former China-based missionary colleges merged to form a Chinese University of Hong Kong. The Hong Kong Branch of the Royal Asiatic Society sprang to life again in 1960, and published an annual journal. Initially it was largely expatriate university staff who turned to Hong Kong history. George B. Endacott's *A History of Hong Kong* (London, 1958), using London-based official archives, established a framework, which from the outset seemed somewhat Eurocentric and old-fashioned, seen through the eyes of the Colonial Office and Government House. The political scientist Norman Miners' *The Government and Politics of Hong Kong*, first published in Hong Kong in 1977, became the standard work on government, to be followed by his *Hong Kong under Imperial Rule, 1912–1941* (Hong Kong, 1987), which showed that pre-war Governors enjoyed wide discretionary powers, despite pressure from the Colonial Office in such matters as labour reform legislation. A government official, James Hayes, revised his doctoral dissertation as *The Hong Kong Region, 1850–1911* (Hamden, Conn., 1977). The sociologist, James Henry Lethbridge, set *Hong Kong Stability and Change* (Hong Kong, 1978) in historical context. The lawyer Peter Wesley-Smith's *Unequal Treaty, 1898–1997: China, Great Britain and Hong Kong's New Territories* (Hong Kong, 1980) coincided with rising interest in the prospect of transfer of sovereignty to China.

With the opening of China in the 1970s and the dramatic expansion of secondary and tertiary education in the colony, a new generation of bilingual Western-trained Hong Kong graduates showed increasing enthusiasm for Asian history, but initially postgraduate studies focused on China itself or on Anglo-Chinese relations. The tense Anglo-Chinese negotiations, culminating in 1984 in the publication of Joint Declaration which confirmed the reversion of Hong Kong to Chinese rule in 1997, sparked intellectual debate and fostered a new awareness of Hong Kong identity. More local Chinese joined the Hong Kong Branch of the Royal Asiatic Society, which resolved to defy the fate of its Shanghai counterpart and continue its activities under its existing name after 1997. An upsurge of interest in the colony's past, as well as its present and future, led to important studies by bilingual local academics such as Steve Yui-sang Tsang, *Democracy Shelved: Great Britain, China and Attempts at Constitutional Reform in Hong Kong, 1945–1952* (Hong Kong, 1988), Chan Lau Kit-ching, *China, Britain and Hong Kong, 1895–1945* (Hong Kong, 1990), and Edmund S. K. Fung, *The Diplomacy of Imperial*

Retreat: Britain's South China Policy, 1924–1931 (Hong Kong, 1991), which showed Hong Kong's close connection with South China and the subordination of the colony's interests to wider concerns of Britain's China policy. Fung defined informal empire as 'imperialism without the desire to assume the responsibilities—administrative, financial, and military—of direct formal rule'. He portrayed an orderly retreat, a flexible, pragmatic policy, adapting gradually to Chinese nationalism: for the Foreign Office 'patient and liberal conciliation' or, in the words of John Gittings, 'ameliorative imperialism'.[36] James Tuck-hong Tang, *Britain's Encounter with Revolutionary China, 1949–54* (London, 1992), charted the final ending of British Imperial relations with the China mainland.

Various commercial institutions published their histories, most notably that by the historian, Frank H. H. King, *The History of the Hongkong and Shanghai Banking Corporation*, 4 vols. (Cambridge, 1987–91), which superseded the bank's readable but slender centenary history by Maurice Collis, *Wayfoong* (London, 1965). King's primary purpose was to write a business history about the evolution of a local Hong Kong and treaty port bank to become a multinational group, but for many years 'The Bank' was a major instrument of Britain's China policy.

The approach of 1997 prompted a spate of books about the recent history, current state, and future prospects of Hong Kong. Looking back over the whole colonial period, Frank Welsh's lively and well-researched *A History of Hong Kong* (London, 1993) provided the most complete general history, while attempting no overall analysis of British Imperial rule. A collection of essays, mainly by Hong Kong Chinese academics, Ming K. Chan, ed., *Precarious Balance: Hong Kong Between China and Britain, 1842–1992* (Hong Kong, 1994), queried the traditionally accepted view of Hong Kong playing a passive role throughout its history. In Judith M. Brown and Rosemary Foot, eds., *Hong Kong's Transitions, 1842–1997* (London, 1997), British-based historians saw Hong Kong as a link between formal and informal empire: a bridgehead to China between the two Opium Wars, a worthy backwater from 1860 to the 1940s, and a last surviving treaty port after 1949.

While most British-trained historians focused on Imperial policy, diplomacy, and the 'official mind', their North American counterparts usually had different priorities, concentrating on the indigenous society, using Chinese- and Japanese-language sources, and being more receptive to new social science methodology. In 1953 John K. Fairbank published his expanded and revised 1936 Oxford doctoral dissertation as *Trade and Diplomacy on the China Coast: The Opening of the Treaty Ports, 1842–1854*, 2 vols. (Cambridge, Mass., 1953), and the following year (with Teng Ssu-yü), *China's Response to the West: A Documentary Survey, 1839–1923*

[36] Fung, *The Diplomacy of Imperial Retreat*, p. 9, quoting John Gittings, *The World and China, 1922–1972* (New York, 1974).

(Cambridge, Mass., 1954). Fairbank dedicated *Trade and Diplomacy* to Morse's memory, but worked from a much broader base. After research in the British archives he studied Chinese in Peking, and his generation had access to the official Chinese-language sources, which became available in the 1930s, and the benefit of close association with western-educated Chinese scholars.

In China in the early 1930s Fairbank was much influenced by his tutor, T. F. Tsiang, who held the unusual view in that nationalist era that China was not merely a passive victim of foreign imperialism. Consequently, from the outset Fairbank appreciated the complexities of the Anglo-Chinese relationship: he did not moralize on the evils of foreign imperialism, but acknowledged that opium was 'the most powerful means to the inevitable end', and recognized that the role of foreign-led institutions implied joint rule, or 'synarchy'.[37] He interpreted the post-1860 treaty system as a 'Manchu-Chinese-western synarchy': a compromise in line with the Chinese tradition for absorbing foreigners. The synarchy concept, which Fairbank offered as a starting-point for understanding modern China and developed in 'Synarchy under the Treaties', in John K. Fairbank, ed., *Chinese Thought and Institutions* (Chicago, 1957), gained a widespread following.

In a foreword to Immanuel C. Y. Hsü, *China's Entrance into the Family of Nations: The Diplomatic Phase, 1858–1880* (Cambridge, Mass., 1960), William L. Langer paid tribute to the way in which Chinese scholars trained in the Western tradition had broadened the scope of diplomatic history to embrace cultural and sociological factors. Using Chinese and Japanese sources, Hsü explored the psychological resistance of the Chinese mandarinate to abandoning its traditional methods of barbarian management within a universal empire. He concluded that China's eventual move to what westerners saw as an 'incipient nation state' was made reluctantly out of expediency, not by choice, and queried whether the People's Republic of China had not re-created a universal state in modern form.

Some historians approached economic history as an aspect of Chinese nationalism rather than foreign imperialism. Sun E-tu Zen's *Chinese Railways and British Interests, 1898–1911* (New York, 1954), which was based on Chinese and British documents, stressed that the railway movement was only in part a protest against increased foreign domination. It was primarily part of China's adjustment to national modernization, in which the most crucial factors were the influence of traditional pre-industrial society and China's reaction to change. Albert Feuerwerker's pioneer study, *China's Early Industrialization: Sheng Hsuan-huai (1844–1916) and Mandarin Enterprise* (Cambridge, Mass., 1958), using Chinese- and Japanese-language materials and applying modern social science concepts,

[37] Paul M. Evans, *John Fairbank and the American Understanding of Modern China* (New York, 1988).

concluded that official corruption and the dead hand of Chinese tradition, rather than foreign pressures, impeded China's early industrialization.

There was considerable discussion about whether the Chinese economy profited or suffered from foreign attempts at modernization. Liu Kwang-ching, in *Anglo-American Steamship Rivalry in China, 1862–1874* (Cambridge, Mass., 1962), showed the benefits to Chinese commerce, with entrepreneurs able to bargain and play off foreign rivals. Hou Chi-ming, in *Foreign Investment and Economic Development in China, 1840–1937* (Cambridge, Mass., 1965), claimed foreigners introduced valuable modern technology and methods. But Singaporean Lee En-han argued that the foreigners' extraordinary economic privileges prevented China from achieving her economic nationalist goals until after 1949. Lee's *China's Quest for Railway Autonomy 1904–1911: A Study of the Chinese Railway-Rights Recovery Movement* (Singapore, 1977), which drew on extensive Chinese archives, including those held in Taipei, saw the railway rights recovery as '"defensive"-orientated nationalism' designed to annul the unequal treaties and raise China to Great Power status. Ralph William Huenemann, *The Dragon and the Iron Horse: The Economics of Railroads in China, 1876–1937* (Cambridge, Mass., 1984), also based on Chinese sources, endorsed the view that the real benefits of railway development only came to fruition after 1949.

Meanwhile Hao Yen-p'ing took up the comprador question, which had exercised Chinese Marxist intellectuals since the 1930s. His *The Comprador in 19th Century China: Bridge between East and West* (Cambridge, Mass., 1970) supported the concept of synarchy, showing that the comprador was not a Western creature but derived from the long-established Chinese institution of licensed broker. Convinced that China's economic relations with the West were more positive and vigorous than previous historians assumed, Hao went on to argue, in *The Commercial Revolution in 19th Century China: The Rise of Sino-Western Mercantile Capitalism* (Berkeley, 1986), that China's nineteenth-century trade with the West led to mercantile capitalism and a commercial revolution, which acted as a 'springboard for industrialization'. Hao highlighted a symbiotic relationship between Chinese and Western businessmen, in which the Chinese were not victims or pawns but played an active role in their own destiny. The idea of symbiotic penetration was also developed in S. A. M. Adshead, *The Modernization of the Chinese Salt Administration, 1900–1920* (Cambridge, Mass., 1970), and in Sherman Cochran, *Big Business in China: Sino-Foreign Rivalry in the Cigarette Industry, 1890–1930* (Cambridge, Mass., 1980), a case-study of the largest capitalist industry in China.

Other studies on a variety of subjects reinforced the concept of positive Chinese action, rather than mere response to Western initiative. In *China and the West, 1858–1861: The Origins of the Tsungli Yamen* (Cambridge, Mass., 1964),

Japanese academic Masataka Banno portrayed the founding of the Tsungli Yamen as a turning-point in ending the old inequality, but showed how Chinese officialdom continued to resist adapting to the modern state system. Richard J. Smith, *Mercenaries and Mandarins: The Ever-Victorious Army in Nineteenth-Century China* (Mullwood, NY, 1978), gave a rounded view of the interaction of General Gordon, the Chinese army, and the British and French. Paul Cohen, *China and Christianity: The Missionary Movement and the Growth of Chinese Anti-Foreignism, 1860–1870* (Cambridge, Mass., 1963), stressed the cultural incompatibility of Christianity and Confucianism. The American historian, Betty Wei Peh-T'i, in *Shanghai: Crucible of Modern China* (Hong Kong, 1987), challenged the general assumption that Shanghai was a foreign creation by showing that before 1949 this unique city comprised three Shanghais: the Shanghai of the foreigners, of the Chinese, and of the westernized Chinese, who played an increasing role in developing the metropolis into a modern financial, commercial, industrial, and cultural centre. In *To Change China: Western Advisers in China, 1620–1960* (Boston, 1969), Jonathan D. Spence argued that, unlike earlier barbarians whom China absorbed, the Westerners wanted to import their values and change China, but their influence was largely ephemeral.

While such studies touched only indirectly on the question of imperialism, cumulatively they threw light on its nature. Confucian historians did not believe in progress but in cycles of dynastic rise and fall: 'a series of circles, of returns, of repetitions.' But Frederic Wakeman, Jr., in *Strangers at the Gate: Social Disorder in South China, 1839–1861* (Berkeley, 1966), used Chinese and Japanese sources to show how the Western assault destroyed 'the very concept of a Confucian dynasty', dragging China into a global history not of her making. Edmund S. Wehrle, the first Western historian to apply the term informal imperialism, to China, described her in *Britain, China and the Anti-Missionary Riots, 1891–1900* (Minneapolis, 1960) as the 'classic example' of British informal empire which aimed to preserve economic dominance without creating a new Indian empire in the Yangtse valley. Britten Dean followed up his *China and Great Britain: The Diplomacy of Commercial Relations, 1860–1864* (Cambridge, Mass., 1974) by specifically addressing the question of imperialism in the 1860s in 'British Informal Empire: The Case of China', *Journal of Commonwealth and Comparative Politics*, XIV (1976), pp. 64–81. He argued that there was a superficial case for applying the term 'informal empire' because of Britain's considerable influence on the Chinese government through the treaty port system, the Tsungli Yamen, the Imperial Maritime Customs Service, and the legal system, but that influence and pressures for economic advantage did not amount to informal imperialism. Dean maintained 'effective subordination of the overseas country to the metropolitan country' was lacking and the proponents of informal empire ignored the long-established tradition of barbarian participation and synarchy in Chinese history.

Most contributors to Volumes X to XIII of the *Cambridge History of China*,[38] which encompassed the Imperial experience of the nineteenth and first half of the twentieth centuries, were American-trained sinologists, with Fairbank as editor or co-editor and a major contributor. He insisted on starting Volume X at 1800 rather than with the Opium War, stressing that foreign intrusion was merely one component in the troubles of a dynasty already in decline, and affected only a small part of the country. The preface to Volume XI predicted that preoccupation with foreign influence would decline as knowledge accumulated about China's indigenous experience, and by the time Volume XIII was published in 1986 the editors, Fairbank and Feuerwerker, commented on the vast increase of documents and research aids coming from the People's Republic of China, and of work by Japanese scholars. But younger American historians were already beginning to criticize the Western orientation of the *Cambridge History of China* and the Fairbank generation.[39]

The opening up of China in the 1980s broke down the decades-long physical isolation among scholars and to a degree facilitated research and exchange of ideas, although it did not soften the orthodox interpretation of imperialism among China's historians. There was a deep divide between the study of the metropolis and the periphery, between historians who treated China as the object of Great Power imperialism and those who concerned themselves with the indigenous scene; between left-wing scholars who denounced imperialism as oppression, others who saw foreign capital and technology as a regrettable necessity to modernize the Chinese economy, and yet others who dismissed Western influence as marginal. D. K. Fieldhouse's question, 'Can Humpty-Dumpty Be Put Together Again? Imperial History in the 1980s', could be applied particularly to China.[40] The proliferation of detailed research topics militated against grand theories of imperialism, and the terms 'informal empire' and 'semi-colonialism' were imprecise, embracing meanings ranging from a transition stage, or a permanent alternative to formal control, to simply the exercise of strong influence.

The need for an interpretative system attracted the scrutiny of German scholars, notably Jürgen Osterhammel. In *Britischer Imperialismus im Fernen Ost:*

[38] *CHC*, Vol. X, *The Late Ch'ing, 1800–1911*, Part 1 (Cambridge, 1978); John K. Fairbank and Kwang-ching Liu, eds., Vol. XI, *The Late Ch'ing*, Part 2 (Cambridge, 1980); John K. Fairbank, ed., Vol. XII, *Republican China, 1912–1949*, Part 1 (Cambridge, 1983); Fairbank and Albert Feuerwerker, eds., Vol. XIII, *Republican China*, Part 2 (Cambridge, 1986).

[39] e.g., Jane Kate Leonard, *Wei Yuan and China's Rediscovery of the Maritime World* (Cambridge, Mass., 1984).

[40] *Journal of Imperial and Commonwealth History* (hereafter *JICH*), XII, 2 (Jan. 1984), pp. 9–23.

Strukturen der Durchdringung und Einheimischer Widerstand auf dem Chinesischen Markt, 1932–1937 (Bochum, 1983) Osterhammel challenged the 'classic' theory that Britain was forced to relax her Imperial hold during the 1920s out of weakness. Rather, he saw a convergence of Chinese and British interests in the early 1930s, with active bilateral co-operation replacing servile compliance, and he examined British businesses, case by case in meticulous detail, to support this thesis. Developing the theme of co-operation in 'Imperialism in Transition: British Business and the Chinese Authorities, 1931–37'[41] and in *China und die Weltgesellschaft von 18 Jahrhundert bis in unsere Zeit* (Munich, 1989), Osterhammel linked China, Japan, and Siam (Thailand) in being intensively 'opened', but argued that even China's forced entry into the world economy was not simply a story of collision but of complex political and economic factors. In 'Semi-Colonialism and Informal Empire in Twentieth-Century China: Towards a Framework of Analysis', in Wolfgang J. Mommsen and Jürgen Osterhammel, eds., *Imperialism and After: Continuities and Discontinuities* (London, 1986), pp. 290–314, Osterhammel proposed a framework for the solid study still required about the foreign presence in China and its effects on the economy and society. He suggested the term 'informal empire' should be applied not to mere influence, dependence, or unequal development, but to particular ways in which superiority was exercised in asymmetrical relationships between societies and nations, whereby the stronger power exercised decision-making in foreign, domestic, and economic affairs.

As the twentieth century neared its close, Jonathan D. Spence, *In Search of Modern China* (London, 1990), and P. J. Cain and A. G. Hopkins, *British Imperialism*, 2 vols. (London, 1993), drew together various strands of scholarship of the last decades. While acknowledging the profound effect of imperialism, Spence put it in the wider context of post-1600 Chinese history, maintaining that outside the foreign enclaves penetration was slow and often almost invisible. Cain and Hopkins, setting China in the broad framework of British Imperial experience with strong emphasis on the metropolis, commented that little detailed research on China had been attempted yet by historians of European imperialism.

The historiography of British imperialism in the Far East stands at a crossroads, with a number of contrary paths beckoning. The return of Hong Kong to Chinese sovereignty in June 1997, finally severing the British connection, allowed historians to put Hong Kong's colonial experience, imperialism in East Asia, and the symbiotic relationship with the Overseas Chinese in true perspective. Under the influence of post-colonial theory and the criticism that the historiography of British imperialism has 'long been coloured by the political and methodological

[41] *China Quarterly*, XCVIII (June 1984), pp. 260–86.

conservatism of its practitioners',[42] historians might attempt to restore the balance between the centre and the periphery in order to trace the mutual interaction and effect on both parties. Alternatively, a new generation may dismiss British imperialism as a short, if at times traumatic, interlude in the long history of an ancient country.

[42] Dane Kennedy, 'Imperial History and Post-Colonial Theory', *JICH*, XXIV, 3 (Sept. 1996), pp. 345–63, esp. p. 345.

Select Bibliography (Chinese names follow the Harvard style.)

PAMELA ATTWELL, *British Mandarins and Chinese Reformers: The British Administration of Weihaiwei (1898–1930), and the Territory's Return to Chinese Rule* (Hong Kong, 1985).

CHAN LAU KIT-CHING, *China, Britain and Hong Kong, 1895–1945* (Hong Kong, 1990).

Chinese (formerly Imperial) Maritime Customs Service, *Documents Illustrative of the Origin, Development and Activities of the Chinese Customs Service*, 7 vols. (Shanghai, 1937–40).

NICHOLAS R. CLIFFORD, *Retreat from China: British Policy in the Far East, 1937–1941* (London, 1967).

BRITTEN DEAN, 'British Informal Empire: The Case of China', *Journal of Commonwealth and Comparative Politics*, XIV (1976), pp. 64–81.

JOHN KING FAIRBANK, *Trade and Diplomacy on the China Coast: The Opening of the Treaty Ports, 1842–1854*, 2 vols. (Cambridge, Mass., 1953).

—— with MARTHA HENDERSON COLLIDGE and RICHARD J. SMITH, *H. B. Morse, Customs Commissioner and Historian of China* (Lexington, Mass., 1995).

JOHN GALLAGHER and RONALD ROBINSON, 'The Imperialism of Free Trade', *Economic History Review*, Second Series, VI (1953), pp. 1–15.

HAO YEN-P'ING, *The Comprador in Nineteenth-Century China: Bridge between East and West* (Cambridge, Mass., 1970).

J. A. HOBSON, *Imperialism: A Study* (London, 1902).

IMMANUEL C. Y. HSÜ, *China's Entrance into the Family of Nations: The Diplomatic Phase, 1858–1880* (Cambridge, Mass., 1960).

F. C. JONES, *Extraterritoriality in Japan and the Diplomatic Relations Resulting in Its Abolition, 1853–1899* (New Haven, 1931).

P. C. KUO, *A Critical Study of the First Anglo-Chinese War, with Documents* (Shanghai, 1935).

WILLIAM L. LANGER, *The Diplomacy of Imperialism, 1890–1902* (New York, 1935; 2nd one-volume edn., New York, 1951).

V. I. LENIN, 'Imperialism: The Highest Stage of Capitalism' (1916–17), repr. in *The National Liberation Movement in the East* (Moscow, 1952), pp. 21–26.

HOSEA BALLOU MORSE, *The Chronicles of the East India Company Trading to China, 1635–1834*, 5 vols. (Cambridge, Mass., 1926; Oxford, 1929).

JÜRGEN OSTERHAMMEL, 'Semi-Colonialism and Informal Empire in Twentieth-Century

China: Towards a Framework of Analysis', in Wolfgang J. Mommsen and Jürgen Osterhammel, eds., *Imperialism and After: Continuities and Discontinuities* (London, 1986), pp. 290–314.

Steven Yui-sang Tsang, *Democracy Shelved: Great Britain, China, and Attempts at Constitutional Reform in Hong Kong, 1945–1952* (Hong Kong, 1988).

Frank Welsh, *A History of Hong Kong* (London, 1993).

Peter Wesley-Smith, *Unequal Treaty, 1898–1997: China, Great Britain and Hong Kong's New Territories* (Hong Kong, 1980; revd. edn. 1998).

26

The British Empire in South-East Asia

NICHOLAS TARLING

Much of the work on historiography of the British overseas has concentrated on the Americas, on India, on Africa. South-East Asia, however, offers examples of every type of Imperial relationship and of others that at first sight do not seem Imperial. Britain deeply affected the territories it did not rule: those of other colonial powers and of the Thais. Imperial historiography is enriched, but also enriches by the possibilities of comparison. Books on the Empire as a whole, and even more broadly on the nature of British interests overseas, are properly part of the historiography of South-East Asia.

Historiography does follow the flag, but it moves beyond it, too. Its main focus in South-East Asia has been British Burma and what came often to be called British Malaya and British Borneo, even though they were for the most part not formally British territory. South-East Asia displays diversity in many fields of activity, which include the relationship with the British. The 'unequal' treaties with Siam (Thailand) form part of the relationship, as do the British treaties with the Dutch and the Spaniards. The emphasis on Burma, Malaya, and Borneo is usefully seen in that context.

Comparison of other kinds is reflected in the historiography. Alongside British expansion in South-East Asia, competing and at times collaborating is the expansion of the Dutch and the French, of the Spaniards and later of the Americans, later still of the Japanese, and in some sense throughout, of the Chinese. Their interests and their approaches differed, but the juxtaposition is the more enlightening as a result. Britain's influence in South-East Asia in the nineteenth and twentieth centuries was encompassing. What others did was affected by what she did. To what extent have British activities in the area been treated as an extension of imperialism in India? Has the history of the region been neglected by Imperial historians?[1] What is the relationship between the historiography of South-East

[1] It is worth noting that it does not feature prominently in the recent work by P. J. Cain and A. G. Hopkins, *British Imperialism*, 2 vols. (London, 1993): Vol. I, *Innovations and Expansion, 1688–1914*; Vol. II, *Crisis and Deconstruction, 1914–1990*.

Asia and the history-writing of the wider Empire? These are questions not necessarily addressed in the historiography of the subject, but should be borne in mind in relation to the themes of the other chapters.

Although British power was built on commerce and finance, British authors wrote of travel, rule, and Empire. Many of them were administrators or ex-administrators, and their interests were reflected in their writings. The records they created, on which later historians were to draw, also reflected preoccupations. The other colonial powers had rather different concerns. Though the representatives of the Dutch East India Company had been keenly observant of all that might offer commercial opportunities, their nineteenth-century successors studied the role of *adat* (custom) and Islam. J. C. van Leur, who was the first to employ sociological methods in studying Indonesian history, did so as a civil servant, though also thus creating a trend in historiography.[2] Juxtaposing these different approaches highlights both gaps and opportunities in the historiography of South-East Asia, and also in that of British imperialism there. The records the British compiled can be explored with purposes in mind other than those for which they were compiled, and to some extent historians can draw on other disciplines.

Such are not the only arguments for a broadening in scope of the writings on imperialism. The word itself is susceptible of many interpretations, and the political and constitutional and territorial meanings have rarely seemed exhaustive. In the 1980s and 1990s it has seemed to some difficult to escape from an imperialist approach in any writing about Asia, and the relativism that historians have long recognized has led to questioning the validity of their whole enterprise. That seems a sterile conclusion, and in a sense illogical: certainly, the realization that total objectivity cannot be achieved is not an argument for subjectivity. Another trend seems in fact to be stronger. A broad definition of imperialism is accepted, and indeed it is associated with and revivified by the trend to 'globalism' of the 1980s and 1990s. To what extent have historians of the region employed the models familiar to historians of other parts of Empire, including that of informal empire? In reaction to globalism, the nationalism of the post-colonial period has been renewed and intensified. In the 1950s and 1960s the 'western element' was questioned and appraised by historians such as John Bastin, and a balance between the exogenous and indigenous had been sought.[3] Now again historians of the South-East Asian states are advocating national history, in part as a reaction to globalist trends. It might be argued that the historians of South-East Asia have tended to prefer the territorial or regional, European or international perspectives to the Imperial one.

[2] See his *Indonesian Trade and Society: Essays in Asian Social and Economic History* (The Hague, 1955).

[3] John Bastin, *The Western Element in Modern Southeast Asian History* (Singapore, 1960).

'Taken to the extreme, autonomous histories that push the colonizers or their élite collaborators into the shadows would produce the same distortions as do colonial histories that push the "natives" or subaltern groups into the shadows.'[4] In its extreme form, as advocated by some historians in Manila and Bangkok, the trend indeed raises many questions. Some are concerned with the politics of the states from which the historians come. Will their history now be written, and purveyed in national schools, in the language of the majority and in its interests? Will relationships not only within the states but among them be affected by an insistently national historiography that may undermine the acceptance of post-colonial frontiers or prejudice the peaceful settlement of inter-state disputes? Other questions are for the historian. It is not simply that the 'western element' is again in question—in question, indeed, in a stringent, even unanswerable form. The concept of South-East Asia as a region is also under challenge.

The historiography of British South-East Asia, because of the range of British approaches, offers opportunities for studying both the territories of South-East Asia and the region as a whole and considering the interrelationships. Though Britain's concerns were so often political and strategic, British officials produced records that offer wider insights into imperialism and into the societies with which the British were in contact. Few historians nowadays would concentrate merely on the history of the Empire, but that has proved and can, properly conceived, still prove, a way of tackling some of the complex problems that face the historian of South-East Asia.

'[P]eriods', Anthony Reid has written, 'are modes of dealing with specific questions and must change with the question.'[5] Periodization, the problem for every historian, particularly for those who write in short compass of large areas or long periods, is no less a problem for the analyst of historiography. In the case of the historiography of British South-East Asia, it might be thought desirable to treat the topic country by country, and borrow the periodization that country's history. That, however, would inhibit the region-wide approach which the breadth of British contacts suggests, and to which current controversies over national history must be related. It is better, perhaps, to risk periodizing the historiography itself following John Legge's masterly chapter in *The Cambridge History of South East Asia* (Cambridge, 1992), I, pp. 1–50. One phase is marked off from its successor by the emergence, mainly after 1945, of a number of professional historians, generally, but by no means exclusively, coming from outside South-East Asia. Before that the historiography is dominated by scholar-administrators, starting with

[4] Laurie J. Sears, *Autonomous Histories, Particular Truths: Essays in Honor of John Smail* (Madison, 1993), pp. 17–18.

[5] *Southeast Asia in the Age of Commerce, 1450–1860* (New Haven, 1993), II, p. xiv.

Stamford Raffles and John Crawfurd; thereafter they multiply.[6] A subsequent generation witnesses a number of changes: an expansion in historical writing, and in the range of its themes; a growing participation by local historians; a shift in perspective on their part and that of others. The 1990s may mark the opening of yet another phase, marked by what at first sight seems paradoxical, a sense of imperialism that is wider, yet a focus on nationalism that is still more intense.

A student of the British Empire in South-East Asia at the end of the Second World War would often have been reading works written by, or closely identified with, its makers, and some of them would reflect the new wave of imperialism associated with the end of the war and the desire to rebuild the Empire and make it better. The principal history of British Malaya was by the man who is said to have devised the term, Sir Frank Swettenham.[7] The history of the various Malay states, as related in the *Journal of the Malayan Branch of the Royal Asiatic Society (JMBRAS)*, was often the work of officers of the Malayan Civil Service, M. C. ff Sheppard and Walter Linehan, for example.[8] Sir Richard Winstedt wrote a history of Malaya as well as a history of Malay literature.[9] Not all wrote of the Malays. The service itself was indeed divided by training and attitude. Victor Purcell, a lecturer in Cambridge after a long period in the Chinese protectorate, published *The Chinese in Malaya* (London, 1948) and *The Chinese in South East Asia* (London, 1951).

Divergent views also came from outside the service. If, in Malaya, there was as yet no university where research might be based, the Canadian Lennox Mills had used the archives for 'British Malaya, 1924–67', *JMBRAS*, III, 2, (1925) and research had been published by the American Rupert Emerson, whose work *Malaysia* (New York, 1937), comparing Malaya and Indonesia, has become a classic. A French geographer, Charles Robequain, also placed Malaya in a different context in his *Le Monde Malais* (Paris, 1946). But the historiography of British Borneo was almost completely confined to writings of or about the Brookes and the semi-official history of Sarawak, written by S. Baring-Gould and a Sarawak official, C. A. Bampfylde, as part of Raja Charles's campaign against the establishment of the British Resident in Brunei in 1906.[10]

[6] e.g. Sir Thomas Stamford Raffles, *History of Java*, 3 vols. (London, 1817; 1830; new edn. with introduction by J. S. Bastin, Oxford in Asia Series Historical Reprints, 1965); John Crawfurd, *History of the Indian Archepelago*, 3 vols. (Edinburgh, 1820).

[7] Sir Frank Swettenham, *British Malaya: An Account of the Origin and Progress of British Influence in Malaya* (London, 1906; 1929; 1948).

[8] W. Linehan, 'A History of Pahang', *Journal of the Malayan Branch of the Royal Asiatic Society*, XIV, 2 (1936), pp. 1–256.

[9] Sir Richard Olaf Winstedt, *History of Malaya* (Singapore, 1935; rev. edn., 1962), *Malaya and its History* (London, 1948; 6th edn., 1962), and *The Malays: A Cultural History* (London, 1950).

[10] S. Baring-Gould and C. A. Bampfylde, *A History of Sarawak Under its Two White Rajahs, 1839–1908* (London, 1908, revised edn., Singapore, 1989).

The case of British Burma was different. There, too, scholar-officials had created a Western historiography, starting indeed with one of the founders of British Burma, Sir Arthur Phayre, and continuing with G. E. Harvey and B. R. Pearn.[11] There were divergent views, again, most notably in the case of J. S. Furnivall, [12] who compared the regime with that in Netherlands India in a way that seems in retrospect surprisingly to the advantage of the latter. The historiography of British Burma was, however, enriched even in the pre-war period, as a result of the founding of the University of Rangoon, itself, of course, also an essential source of Burman nationalism. Based there, the man who was to write the first history of South-East Asia, D. G. E. Hall, began his research career with an edition of the correspondence between Phayre and the Governor-General of India, Lord Dalhousie.[13] His later *History of Burma*,[14] perhaps affected too much by the experience of the war, was to attract the criticism of Emil Sarkisyanz in *Peacocks, Pagodas and Professor Hall* (Athens, Oh., 1972). But Hall's work on Burma in the nineteenth century, like his history, remains useful, as does that of his student, the Indian W. S. Desai, whose history of the Residency at Ava was published in Rangoon in 1939.[15] In his last work, *A Life of Henry Burney* (London, 1974), Hall reverted to the country of his deepest affection, and wrote of one of the most talented and sympathetic of the East India Company's servants in South-East Asia.

Desai's work was based on source material from the archives of the Company. The other writings were rarely based on similar research, not only because there was so limited a research tradition in South-East Asian history, but also because the public archives were open only to a limited extent. In the case of archives in London, the most accessible, a fifty-year rule applied, and it remained in force until 1967. Some documents had, by contrast, been published. The Thai government had published material relating to the Crawfurd and Burney missions to Bangkok in the 1820s, but no analysis of those missions had been published, nor any of Britain's subsequent relations with Thailand.

In the 1950s, 1960s, and early 1970s the writing on British imperialism in South-East Asia grew for a number of reasons. In the metropolitan country, South-East Asia attracted more attention. Initially, that was no doubt related to the increased

[11] Sir Arthur P. Phayre, *History of Burma* (London, 1883); G. E. Harvey, *History of Burma: From the Earliest Times to 10 March 1824: The Beginning of the English Conquest* (London, 1925) and *British Rule in Burma, 1824–1942* (London, 1946).

[12] Cf R. H. Taylor, 'Disaster or Release? J. S. Furnivall and the Bankruptcy of Burma', *Modern Asian Studies*, XXIX, 1 (1995), pp. 45–63; J. S. Furnivall, *Colonial Policy and Practice: A Comparative Study of Burma and Netherlands India* (Cambridge, 1948).

[13] D. G. E. Hall, ed., *The Dalhousie-Phayre Correspondence, 1852–56* (Calcutta, 1929).

[14] D. G. E. Hall, *Burma* (London, 1950).

[15] W. S. Desai, *History of the British Residency in Burma, 1826–40* (Rangoon, 1939).

interest in South-East Asia after the war, in particular in Malaya, source of tin and rubber, scene of constitutional experiment and emergency, and in Burma, which, becoming independent, did not join the emerging new Commonwealth.[16] The appointment of Hall to a chair of South-East Asian history at the London University School of Oriental and African Studies (SOAS) signified the interest in the past that accompanied these changes. At the same time, universities in other parts of the world became interested in South-East Asia, their personnel and their students often coming together at SOAS seminars. To some extent, again, political factors were involved in the interest evoked both in United States and in Australian universities. The University of Malaya itself, at first based in Singapore, then, in the early 1960s, in Kuala Lumpur also, became an active centre of historical research, in particular turning to account the records of the British administrators and the talents of Malayan students. While some of this material remained unpublished, new opportunities for publication were opened up. The *Journal of South East Asian History* (later *Journal of South East Asian Studies*), founded by K. G. Tregonning, was added to the long-standing *Journal of the Royal Asiatic Society Malayan* (previously *Straits*, later *Malaysian*) *Branch.* Oxford University Press became an enterprising publisher of monographs and reprints on South-East Asia.

Some of the work that was produced sought to establish the nature of British policy by reference, above all, to its original records, still for the most part relatively unexplored. C. D. Cowan built on initial work done in Malayan a well-argued thesis on the British intervention of the 1870s, later published as *Nineteenth-Century Malaya: The Origins of British Political Control* (London, 1961), while Nicholas Tarling threw a wider net in a Cambridge thesis, later published by *JMBRAS* as *British Policy in the Malay Peninsula and Archipelago, 1824–71* (Singapore, 1957). The map of Empire was also laid out by local scholars, such as Eunice Thio, *British Policy in the Malay Peninsula, 1880–1910* (Kuala Lumpur, 1969), Rollins Bonney, *Kedah, 1771–1821* (Kuala Lumpur, 1971), and Khoo Kay Kim, *The Western Malay States, 1850–1873* (Kuala Lumpur, 1972), while others studied its mode of operation, such as Emily Sadka, *The Protected Malay States* (Kuala Lumpur, 1968) and its commercial context. The Australian contribution included a pioneering study of intervention in Borneo, G. Irwin's *Nineteenth-Century Borneo: A Study in Diplomatic Rivalry* (The Hague, 1955), K. G. Tregonning, *A History of Modern Sabah* (Singapore, 1965), and John Ingleson's *Britain's Annexation of Labuan in 1846* (Perth, 1970). Though regrettably never completing the major biography of Sir Stamford Raffles that the historiography of the British in South-East Asia still lacks, John Bastin was a leading scholar in the field, both at Kuala Lumpur and later at SOAS.

16 See Vol. IV, chap. by A. J. Stockwell.

Bastin's inaugural lecture at Kuala Lumpur in 1960 helped to link research on the British Empire with the mainstream of studies on South-East Asia at the time. How could the western element in South-East Asian history be assessed? At the same time, not only scholars from Asian countries themselves, but other western scholars, such as Harry Benda[17] and John Smail, sought to identify ways of writing an indigenous history, the latter in a seminal article, 'On the Possibility of an Autonomous History of Modern Southeast Asia'.[18] Merely reversing the overemphasis on the West in the past, and driving the Europeans out of the history of South-East Asia, was not usually thought sufficient. Some of the work on Burmese history seemed not to advance much beyond that. In general, however, the new approach stimulated a re-examination of the evidence or a search for new evidence. Documents of the Imperial period could be read 'against the grain'.[19] Non-documentary evidence could be juxtaposed with it. South-East Asian historiography was indeed enriched by its use of other disciplines. The practice had in a sense been started by van Leur. It was an ex-official, John Gullick, who was to provide one of the first attempts to study the structure of the Malay states in his *Indigenous Political Systems of Western Malaya* (London, 1958).

The most thorough study of a Malay state was, however, by a professional anthropologist, using historical records. This was the American Donald E. Brown's *Brunei* (Brunei, 1970), to which, in some sense, Nicholas Tarling's diplomatic history *Britain, the Brookes and Brunei* (Kuala Lumpur, 1971) was a complement. In the latter, British records were so used that the work tended to become a biography of a heroic figure, Sultan Hashim. Most books on Borneo had tended to make heroes of the Brookes. Even Sir Steven Runciman's *The Three White Rajas: A History of Sarawak from 1841–1946* (Cambridge, 1960), commissioned by the successor colonial regime with an eye to the application of his Byzantine expertise, had adopted a dynastic approach, though it was not possible to see all the Rajas as heroic.

The way in which the study of British imperialism could lead in other directions was shown, too, by work on piracy. Pre-war accounts, such as Owen Rutter's *The Pirate Wind* (London, 1930), had been relatively uncomplicated successors to the works written in support of James Brooke's enterprise in Sarawak. But Victorian radicals had criticized that, and questioned the application of the term 'pirate' to what seemed merely enemies of Sir James. Legal questions had also

[17] Henry J. Benda, *The Crescent and the Rising Sun: Indonesian Islam under the Japanese Occupation, 1942–1945* (The Hague, 1958); 'The Structure of SouthEast Asian History: Some Preliminary Observations', *Journal of South east Asian History*, III, 1 (1962), pp. 106–38; and *Continuity and Change in Southeast Asia* (New Haven, 1972).

[18] *Journal of Southeast Asian History*, II, 2 (July 1961), pp. 72–102.

[19] See chap. by D. A. Washbrook.

been raised. Were the pirates in fact authorized by existing states? Were their rulers responsible? Re-examining these issues made it apparent, even before the days of 'deconstruction', that using the word 'piracy' might itself be a piece of imperialism, even as putting piracy down helped to establish a new Imperial order in maritime South-East Asia. Some of the issues were explored in Nicholas Tarling's *Piracy and Politics in the Malay World* (Melbourne, 1963). In the eyes of A. L. Reber, in a Cornell MA dissertation, 'The Sulu World in the Eighteenth and Early Nineteenth Centuries: A Historiographical Problem in British Writings on Malay Piracy', this seemed still too tied to a tradition of writing established by Stamford Raffles in the nineteenth century. The approach was taken further, however, in Carl Trocki's *Prince of Pirates* (Singapore, 1979) and, from a rather different perspective, in A. P. Rubin's *Piracy, Paramountcy and Protectorates* (Kuala Lumpur, 1974). The work of a Swedish anthropologist, Ulla Wagner, *Colonialism and Iban Warfare* (Stockholm, 1972), again undercut an older imperialist approach.

Much of this work concentrated on Malaya and Borneo, the main fields indeed of British colonial and what might be called, in order to cover Sarawak and North Borneo, informal colonial endeavour. The major role Britain had played elsewhere in South-East Asia in the Imperial period was, not surprisingly, less thoroughly covered. The break in Dutch relations with Indonesia in the 1950s in part accounted for that. The period did, however, see the publication of Nicholas Tarling's *Anglo-Dutch Rivalry in the Malay World, 1780–1824* (St Lucia, 1962), and of the first of several major works by another pupil of Victor Purcell's, the New Zealander Anthony Reid's *The Contest for North Sumatra* (Kuala Lumpur, 1969). Filipino historians still concentrated on the revolution of 1896. But the making of frontiers of the Philippines attracted the attention of an American historian, L. R. Wright, in *The Origins of British Borneo* (Hong Kong, 1970), and of Nicholas Tarling in *Sulu and Sabah* (Kuala Lumpur, 1978).

The historiography of British relations with the mainland states was enriched by the activities of a number of scholars in Thailand, including Thamsook Numnonda and Likhit Dhiravegin, while W. F. Vella's analysis of *Siam under Rama III* (Locust Valley, 1957) offered a sophisticated context. The struggles in Vietnam drew attention to the intervention of the French, rather than the British, though Alastair Lamb published accounts of British nineteenth-century diplomatic missions in *The Mandarin Road to Old Hué* (London, 1970).

What was written about Burma was also written mainly by outsiders. The origins of the Third Burma War, which culminated in the destruction of the monarchy, had been freshly examined in *The Annexation of Upper Burma* (Singapore, 1960), originally part of a thesis by the Indian historian D. P. Singhal at SOAS. His view, stressing commercial rather than strategic motives on the part of the British, was controverted in an important review by Hugh Tinker,[20] and also in C. L. Keeton's colourfully titled *King Thebaw and the Ecological Rape of Burma* (Delhi, 1974).

Many of these works were concerned with the delimitation of the nineteenth-century frontiers that were to be inherited by the post-colonial states of the 1940s and 1950s. Such works, and others, were, however, also deepening the understanding of what went on within those frontiers. The plural society of Malaya—the phrase 'plural society' was coined by Furnivall, but the concept seemed more relevant to the Peninsula—had attracted attention, naturally enough, from the scholar-administrators. Part of Victor Purcell's autobiography was published as *The Memoirs of a Malayan Official* (London, 1965), a counterpoint coming from Sheppard, more experienced on the Malay side of the service, only late in the following decade with his *Taman Budiman* (Kuala Lumpur, 1979). Others offered specialist knowledge, such as Leon Comber, *Chinese Secret Societies in Malaya* (Locust Valley, 1959), and Wilfred Blythe, *The Impact of Chinese Secret Societies in Malaya* (London, 1969). Scholars were now building on the administrators' histories, too, with pioneering works on the immigrants, for example, R. N. Jackson's *Immigrant Labour and the Development of Malaya* (Kuala Lumpur, 1961) and K. S. Sandhu's *Indians in Malaya: Some Aspects of their Immigration and Settlement (1786–1957)* (London, 1969).

Before the Second World War an American, Rupert Emerson, had offered what was in some ways the most perceptive study of Malaya. In 1970 another American, Robert M. Pringle, in *Rajahs and Rebels* (London, 1970), provided the most thorough-going analysis of the relationships between the rulers of Sarawak and the various communities that made up its population. Yet another American, with a long experience of Burma as a missionary and as an employee of the State Department, offered the best general history of that country.[21] A fourth, Robert H. Taylor, deepened the understanding of pre-war nationalism and British constitutional experiment in a Cornell doctoral dissertation, 'The Relationship Between Burmese Social Classes and British-Indian Policy on the Behavior of the Burmese Political Elite, 1937–1942'.[22]

The study of British imperialism in South-East Asia until the late 1960s had been constrained by the fifty-year rule. The change to a thirty-year rule by the Wilson government had a number of effects, short- and long-term. First of all it subjected both the opening of the Pacific War and its conclusion to archival study. The

[20] *Journal of Southeast Asian History*, I, 2 (Sept. 1960), pp. 105–08.

[21] John F. Cady, *A History of Modern Burma* (Ithaca, NY, 1958).

[22] Unpublished doctoral dissertation, Cornell University, 1974.

fall of Singapore had been covered in the official history by S. W. Kirby, also in his *Singapore: The Chain of Disaster* (London, 1971), as well as by a number of controversial books, such as Sir J. Smyth's *Percival and the Tragedy of Singapore* (London, 1971). New material, and the significance of the 'Yorktown' of the second Empire, led to the writing of several new works, such as W. David McIntyre's *The Rise and Fall of the Singapore Naval Base* (London, 1980), P. Haggie, *Britannia at Bay* (Oxford, 1981), and J. L. Neidpath, *The Singapore Naval Base and the Defence of Britain's Far Eastern Empire* (Oxford, 1981). The study of Britain in South-East Asia was also taken up by those who now restudied the Allied war effort, such as Wm. Roger Louis, *Imperialism at Bay: The United States and the Decolonization of the British Empire, 1941–1945* (Oxford, 1977) and Christopher Thorne, *Allies of a Kind: The United States, Britain, and the War Against Japan: 1941–1945* (London, 1978). Allied co-operation and competition also affected Britain's wartime planning, on which the newly opened archives were revealing.

That planning was, of course, interesting in itself, but it was also pertinent for the evolving historiographical dimension because of its continuities and discontinuities with the past, both in terms of particular territories and in terms of British imperialism as a whole. The planners themselves appraised the past, seeing the future as a chance for Britain to do better; and doing better was now associated with concepts of nation-building and partnership that displaced the more restricted objectives of earlier colonial enterprise. Studying them was a means to a critique of them but of the past, too. The fact that the plans were unrealistic, and in the event abandoned or drastically modified, gave their study a wider interest: it again reflected on the changing position of Britain in the world. The British had planned for decolonization, but not always in the way it came about.

The Malayan Union, its replacement by the Federation, and the subsequent Emergency, had already been the subject not only of contemporary controversy—in which the redoubtable Purcell took part—but also of a far-ranging historical study. J. de V. Allen published *The Malayan Union* (New Haven, 1967), and the New Zealander Michael Stenson, *Industrial Conflict in Malaya* (Kuala Lumpur, 1970). Now A. J. Stockwell's *British Policy and Malay Politics During the Malayan Union Experiment, 1942–1948* (Kuala Lumpur, 1979) and Albert Lau, *The Malayan Union Controversy* (Singapore, 1991) drew attention to new facets of the story, including Britain's concern about the impact of the Indonesian revolution. The Emergency itself, studied semi-officially by Anthony Short,[23] was restudied by Richard Stubbs, *Hearts and Minds in Guerrilla Warfare* (Singapore, 1989).

Documents on decolonization had been published by A. N. Porter and A. J. Stockwell in *British Imperial Policy and Decolonisation, 1938–64* (London, 1987),

[23] Anthony Short, *The Communist Insurrection in Malaya, 1948–1960* (London, 1975).

and the British Documents on the End of Empire Project must also be mentioned.[24] The documents on India, *The Transfer of Power*, had led the way.[25] The British government commissioned Hugh Tinker, another administrator-scholar, to prepare a parallel work on Burma, where the process and the outcome were very different. Two large volumes of documents, *Burma: The Struggle for Independence, 1944–1948*, appeared in 1983. At the same time Nicholas Tarling prepared his narrative, *The Fourth Anglo-Burmese War: Britain and the Independence of Burma* (Gaya, 1987), using much of the same material.

The British played a controversial role in other parts of post-war South-East Asia. That was studied, with the use of Foreign Office and State Department material, by Oey Hong Lee, *War and Diplomacy in Indonesia, 1945–50* (Townsville, 1981) and, with the use in particular of Dutch material, by Yong Mun Cheong, *H. J. van Mook and Indonesian Independence* (The Hague, 1982). D. B. Valentine prepared a dissertation on 'The British Facilitation of the French Re-entry into Vietnam',[26] while Peter Dunn engaged in what was rather an extensive apologia for General Douglas Gracey in his Ph.D. thesis (1979) and in *The First Vietnam War* (London, 1985).

Sarawak, too, was a centre of controversy once more. There, in contrast to Malaya, the British stuck to their planned policy. This story has been told by a man who combines journalistic flair with historical expertise, R. H. W. Reece, in *The Name of Brooke: The End of White Raja Rule in Sarawak* (Kuala Lumpur, 1982). The transformation of Sabah into a latter-day colony was less controversial, but it revivified the Philippines claim.

Work on this period was bound to put earlier periods into a new and longer-term context. Was Union or was Federation more in the tradition of Britain's policy in Malaya? How different were the pseudo-colonial and colonial regimes in Sarawak? How strong a hold did the British ever have in Burma? The work raised questions, too, that related the South-East Asian experience to that of the Empire in other parts of the world in ways that the historians of the latter had too often neglected. Theories of Britain's Imperial role, in particular the conceptualization of indirect rule by R. E. Robinson and John Gallagher,[27] might be exemplified. The priorities of Britain in this phase, but also in earlier phases, might be investigated.

[24] In the series see e.g. Ronald Hyam, ed., *The Labour Government and the End of Empire, 1945–1951*, British Documents on the End of Empire Project (BDEEP) 4 vols. (London, 1992); S. R. Ashton and S. E. Stockwell, eds., *Imperial Policy and Colonial Practice, 1925–1945*, BDEEP (London, 1996); A. J. Stockwell, ed., *Malaya, 1942–1957* (London, 1995).

[25] See chap. by Ian Talbot.

[26] Unpublished Ph.D. dissertation, UCLA, 1974.

[27] Cf. R. Robinson, 'Non-European Foundations of European Imperialism: Sketch for a Theory of Collaboration', in Roger Owen and Bob Sutcliffe, eds., *Studies in the Theory of Imperialism* (London, 1972), pp. 118–40

This Nicholas Tarling attempted in *The Fall of Imperial Britain in South East Asia* (Singapore, 1993).

At the same time, the historiography of South-East Asia was being enriched, not only by the extension of its purview, but by its deepening. The documents, properly used, were becoming the basis of new interpretations, even new kinds of writing, to which the longer-term perspectives were rather a support than a hindrance. The work, moreover, was done by local as well as foreign scholars. Histories of the Malay states were offered by younger scholars, such as Sharom Ahmat's *Kedah* (Kuala Lumpur, 1984), Sharahil Talib's *After its Own Image: The Trengganu Experience* (Singapore, 1984), and Aruna Gopinath's *Pahang* (Kuala Lumpur, 1991). New studies were undertaken of old topics, such as decentralization, by K. K. Ghosh, *Twentieth Century Malaysia* (Calcutta, 1977), and Yeo Kim Wah, *The Politics of Decentralisation* (Kuala Lumpur, 1982), and of new, such as John Butcher's social history of *The British in Malaya, 1880–1941* (Kuala Lumpur, 1979), Francis Loh Kok Wah's study of Kinta, *Beyond the Tin Mines* (Singapore, 1988), Heng Pek Koon's *Chinese Politics in Malaysia: A History of the Malaysian Chinese Association* (Singapore, 1988), and Daniel Chew's absorbing account of *Chinese Pioneers on the Sarawak Frontier* (Singapore, 1990). The history of Sabah attained a new level of sophistication with Ian Black's *A Gambling Style of Government* (Kuala Lumpur, 1983).

The emergence of a new state of Singapore was marked by new studies of the past, such as Ernest Chew and Edwin Lee, eds., *The History of Singapore* (Singapore, 1991) and C. F. Yong, *Chinese Leadership and Power in Colonial Singapore* (Singapore, 1991), amplifying the earlier work of Mary Turnbull, *The Straits Settlements* (London, 1972) and *A History of Singapore* (Kuala Lumpur, 1977). James Warren, who had earlier added a dimension to the work on the pirates by examining the statements of the prisoners liberated from them, in his *The Sulu Zone, 1768–1898* (Singapore, 1981), now used documents in Singapore, such as those of the coroners, to study the underside of its history. The result is a trilogy, the first two parts of which have been published, *Rickshaw Coolie* (Singapore, 1986) and *Ah Ku and Karayuki-san: Prostitution in Singapore, 1870–1940* (Singapore, 1993). The third book, on the way of death, is to follow. In a way they are the counterpart of a history of Singapore that sees it as a success story, the Imperial city followed and excelled by the city-state. In the meantime, too, Carl Trocki, in his *Opium and Empire: Chinese Society in Colonial Singapore, 1800–1910* (Ithaca, NY, 1990), has challengingly argued that opium was the essential source of Singapore's nineteenth-century success, and convincingly reinterpreted the shifting relationships among the Chinese communities and between them and the government.

The historiography of the British in South-East Asia has thus been transformed. Though there are many gaps, and perhaps surprisingly few biographies, it is far more mature than in the 1940s. New approaches, new documentation, the new participation of a range of local and other scholars, have had a cumulative effect on extending its perspectives and deepening its interpretation. The historiography of the Empire was readily susceptible to such a process because of the range of the activities of the British and of their recording of them. Britain's concern to build nations, more clearly expressed post-war, enforced the trend in historical research. Yet the endeavour was also international.

In the 1990s a new wave of nationalism penetrated the historical profession in South-East Asia. Strongest in the Philippines and Thailand, it is in some sense a reaction against the globalizing trends of the closing decade of the century. Asserting individuality, this nationalism may have political, and thus historical, effects both within and among the states of South-East Asia. Its effects on historiography will also be extensive. So far the historiography of South-East Asia, in part perhaps because it has grown out of studies of Imperial activities, has been enriched by an international approach in method, in authorship, and in publication.

Select Bibliography

M. ADAS, 'Imperialist Rhetoric and Modern Historiography: The Case of Lower Burma Before and After Conquest', *Journal Southeast Asian Studies*, III, 2 (1972), pp. 175–92.

C. D. COWAN and O. W. WOLTERS, eds., *Southeast Asian History and Historiography: Essays Presented to D. G. E. Hall* (Ithaca, NY, 1976).

J. D. LEGGE, 'The Writing of Southeast Asian History', in Nicholas Tarling, ed., *The Cambridge History of Southeast Asia* (Cambridge, 1992), I, pp. 1–50.

A. G. MILNER, 'Colonial Records History: British Malaya', *Modern Asian Studies*, XXI, 4 (1987), pp. 773–92.

E. SARKISYANZ, *Peacocks, Pagodas and Professor Hall* (Athens, Oh., 1972).

JOHN R. W. SMAIL, 'On the Possibility of an Autonomous History of Modern Southeast Asia', *Journal of Southeastern Asian History*, II, 2 (July, 1961), pp. 72–102.

YEO KIM WAH, 'The Milner Version of British Malayan History—A Rejoinder', *Kajian Malaysia*, v, 1 (1987), pp. 1–28.

27

Formal and Informal Empire in the Middle East

PETER SLUGLETT

This chapter deals with the historiography of the rise, consolidation, decline, and ending of British Imperial interests in the Middle East over some 200 years, from the late eighteenth to the late twentieth centuries. Naturally, during this long period the circumstances of, and the rationale for, Britain's acquisition of influence or territories in this extensive region varied substantially. In general terms, in the period before the First World War Britain was at pains to limit French and Russian influence in the region, and concern for the defence of India and later for the security of the Suez Canal, rather than more identifiably economic considerations, seems to have loomed most consistently large in the calculations of policy-makers, as well as providing those on the spot with the most appealing arguments for their expansionist aims.[1] In more recent times, the importance of oil and its discovery in Iran in 1908, Iraq in 1927, and in Bahrain, Kuwait, and Saudi Arabia in the 1930s, combined with the perceived threat of 'communism', inevitably changed the focus of British and other interests in the region.

Chronologically, then, this chapter starts with the development of Britain's interest in Iran and Afghanistan at the end of the eighteenth century, and ends in the third quarter of the twentieth century, with the independence of South Yemen (Aden) in 1967 and the creation of the United Arab Emirates in 1972. After this, apart from its continuing lease on the Dhekelia air base in Cyprus, Britain ceased to control any of the physical surface of the region.

A recurrent feature of the period before the end of the First World War, during which the Qajar and Ottoman empires still existed, was a continuous process in which British diplomats and administrators, acting on a combination of their own initiative—often the most potent ingredient—and of official backing from

I am grateful to Abbas Amanat, Glen Balfour-Paul, Roger Louis, Alaine Low, Roger Owen, and Peter von Sivers for their comments on earlier drafts of this chapter.

[1] See, for example, Edward Ingram, *Britain's Persian Connection: Prelude to the Great Game in Asia, 1798–1828* (Oxford, 1992), pp. 11–12: 'Expansion is always described as defence; remote as nearby, or immediate; and threats made as offers of help.' In the period before the First World War, of all Britain's Middle Eastern interests only Egypt could seriously be regarded as a 'profitable colonial venture'.

Bombay or London, attempted to bring British influence to bear on successive Iranian or Turkish governments. The main purpose of this pressure was to ensure that British political, strategic, or economic interests and claims—rather than those of other European powers, particularly France and Russia—would prevail in Tehran and Istanbul. However, from time to time this was accompanied, in the case of the Ottoman empire, by efforts to gain administrative control of quasi-autonomous or otherwise detachable Ottoman provinces if it was judged that Britain's interests could be best served in this way.

In the Ottoman empire the rivalries between the nineteenth-century European empires (Austria-Hungary, France, Great Britain, and Russia) resulted in a complex series of episodes known collectively as the Eastern Question. In addition to attempting to assert the right of passage of her vessels through the Straits (which the other European powers always contested), Russia began to claim (and eventually to annex) territories to the east of the Black Sea and in the Caucasus. These moves, together with Napoleon's invasion of Egypt in 1798, aroused concern in British government circles that the ultimate goal of the policies of France and Russia was to challenge British paramountcy in India. Further west, the Eastern Question took the form of national movements against Ottoman domination in the Balkans, in which the various powers intervened on behalf of their 'Christian' (Bulgarian, Greek, Romanian, Serb, etc.) protégés. This culminated in a major crisis in 1875–78, which substantially reduced the extent of Ottoman rule in Europe. Other aspects of the crisis underlined the connection between the vulnerability of the Ottomans and heightening Anglo-Russian rivalry further east.[2]

Britain's interests in Iran were almost entirely related to her interests in India. From about 1800 onwards, London considered that 'securing' the territories to the east, west, north-west, and north-east of India was a vital precondition for the defence of the Subcontinent. 'The Struggle for Asia' (in the words of one title) was essentially a struggle for ascendancy between Britain and Russia, in which Iranian (and Afghan) compliance was a constant British objective.[3] By 1873 Russia had

[2] M. S. Anderson's *The Eastern Question, 1774–1923* (London, 1966) is the classic account. There is a more up-to-date account in M. E. Yapp, *The Making of the Modern Near East, 1792–1923* (London, 1987), pp. 47–96, and the bibliographical survey on pp. 360–62. See also Marian Kent, ed., *The Great Powers and the End of the Ottoman Empire* (London, 1984).

[3] See M. E. Yapp, *Strategies of British India: Britain, Iran and Afghanistan, 1798–1850* (Oxford, 1980); Edward Ingram, *Commitment to Empire: Prophecies of the Great Game in Asia, 1797–1800* (Oxford, 1981); Edward Ingram, *In Defence of British India: Great Britain in the Middle East, 1797–1842* (London, 1984); and an earlier work, Rose L. Greaves, *Persia and the Defence of India, 1884–1892: A Study in the Foreign Policy of the Third Marquis of Salisbury* (London, 1959). For an overview of the strategic and diplomatic history see David Gillard, *The Struggle for Asia, 1828–1914: A Study in British and Russian Imperialism* (London, 1977); and Firuz Kazemzadeh, *Russia and Britain in Persia, 1864–1914: A Study in Imperialism* (New Haven, 1968).

absorbed Bukhara, Khiva, and Kokand; expansion into Persia (thus moving closer to the Gulf and British India) seemed the obvious next step. For most of the nineteenth century the economic stakes were not a high priority,[4] although this began to change with the Reuter concession in 1872 and more purposefully after the foundation of the (British) Imperial Bank of Persia in 1889.[5]

Thus, between 1800 and 1914, in addition to the annexation of Aden and the arrangements with the rulers of the smaller Persian Gulf sheikhdoms—the Trucial States—and Muscat and Oman (none of which was part of the Ottoman empire), Britain established unequal treaties with the rulers of Afghanistan, Bahrain, Iran, and Kuwait (and rather later with Qatar), invaded and occupied Egypt, established an Anglo-Egyptian 'Condominium' over the Sudan, took control of Cyprus, and entered into friendly relations with the ruler of Najd.[6] At the same time, Britain began to dominate the trade of the eastern Mediterranean, and to join in the scramble for railway concessions in the Ottoman empire.[7]

This process was continued, although in a different manner, as a result of military conquest and the defeat of the Ottoman empire in the First World War. Between 1918 and 1923 the Ottoman Arab provinces which had not already fallen under British, French, or Italian control between 1830 (Algeria) and 1911 (Libya) were divided (generally by the mutual agreement of the victors) between the principal allies, France acquiring Lebanon and Syria, and Britain acquiring Iraq, Palestine, and Transjordan, all as Mandates from the League of Nations. Perhaps the apogee of Britain's power in the region, or *Britain's Moment in the Middle East (1914–1971)*, to quote Elizabeth Monroe's felicitous title,[8] was between 1920

[4] 'A very modest market for Manchester cottons was created, but Persia's export trade lacked the dynamism to raise import-purchasing power substantially': P. J. Cain and A. G. Hopkins, *British Imperialism*: Vol. I, *Innovation and Expansion, 1688–1914* (London, 1993), p. 411. The total trade of the British Empire (i.e. India and Britain) with Persia amounted to £1m annually in the 1890s, and £5m in 1911. See David McLean, *Britain and Her Buffer State: The Collapse of the Persian Empire, 1890–1914* (London, 1979), p. 20.

[5] For British–Iranian economic relations, see Charles Issawi, *The Economic History of Iran, 1800–1914* (Chicago, 1971); Geoffrey Jones, *Banking and Empire in Iran: The History of the British Bank of the Middle East*, 2 vols. (Cambridge, 1986; 1987); and Frances Bostock and Geoffrey Jones, *British Businesses in Iran, 1860s–1960s* (London, 1989).

[6] For a readable general survey of these events, see Yapp, *Making of the Modern Near East*.

[7] In the last two decades of the nineteenth century British goods accounted for nearly half of the imports of the Ottoman ports of Beirut and Alexandretta: see Charles Issawi, *The Fertile Crescent, 1800–1914: A Documentary Economic History* (New York, 1988), pp. 127–57. However, in global terms the volume of trade was fairly small; the British share of imports into Alexandretta ranged from £0.8m to £1.3m between 1880 and 1900. See also Halil Inalçik, 'When and How British Cotton Goods Invaded the Levant markets', in Huri Islamoglu-Inan, ed., *The Ottoman Empire and the World-Economy* (Cambridge, 1987), pp. 374–83. For railways see Yagub N. Karkar, *Railway Development in the Ottoman Empire, 1856–1914* (New York, 1972).

[8] 2nd revd. edn. (London, 1981).

and 1939, when, by a variety of different instruments, Britain exerted effective control over Aden Colony, the Aden Protectorate, Bahrain, Cyprus, Egypt, Iraq, Kuwait, Palestine, Muscat and Oman, Qatar, Socotra, Somaliland, the Sudan, Transjordan, and the Trucial States, as well as having substantial influence over the ruler of the new kingdom of Saudi Arabia and, in spite of strenuous efforts on Lord Curzon's part to negotiate a pro-British treaty in 1919,[9] rather less influence over the newly established and avowedly nationalist Pahlavi monarchy in Iran.

During this period, as has been suggested already, new motives for British interest in the region emerged; oil, first and foremost, but also the Empire air route to India. The air route is the subject of much of David E. Omissi's *Air Power and Colonial Control: The Royal Air Force, 1919–1939* (Manchester, 1990). A line of military aerodromes (and later civil airports) was gradually constructed, making a 'red line' linking Gibraltar, Malta, Cyprus, Palestine, Iraq, Bahrain, Sharjah, Gwadar, and Karachi. On occasion, it was argued that a prime reason for not abandoning, say, Palestine or Cyprus, was the maintenance of this vital link. Aeroplanes gradually came to be used to counter civil disobedience and for 'pacification', particularly in South Arabia and Iraq.

Once oil began to be widely used by the world's navies around the turn of the twentieth century, it became a policy axiom that Britain, with the largest navy in the world, should be in a position to exert political influence in territories where oil was known, or equally important, thought likely, to exist. Just before the outbreak of the First World War, the British government made it its business to secure a majority share in the then Anglo-Persian Oil Company (eventually British Petroleum, BP). Concession hunting in the Ottoman empire had proceeded apace between 1900 and 1914, ending with the creation of the (Anglo-Dutch-German) Turkish Petroleum Company (TPC) in 1912. In 1913 Anglo-Persian and the TPC merged, which meant that the British government also came to acquire a controlling interest in the TPC.[10]

Much of the subsequent history of Britain's relations with the various states of the Arabian peninsula, Iran and Iraq—and of subsequent US interest in the region—was dictated by the perceived need to have access to oil, combined with a preference for having Middle Eastern oil exploited by British interests. A letter

[9] See William J. Olson, 'The Genesis of the Anglo-Persian Agreement of 1919', in Elie Kedourie and Sylvia Haim, eds., *Towards a Modern Iran: Studies in Thought, Politics and Society* (London, 1980), pp. 185–216. For the Reza Shah period see R. K. Ramazani, *The Foreign Policy of Iran, 1500–1941: A Developing Nation in World Affairs* (Charlottesville, Va., 1966), pp. 171–257. Curzon's interest in Iran was of long standing; see his *Persia and the Persian Question*, 2 vols. (London 1892; repr. 1966).

[10] For further details see Stephen Helmsley Longrigg, *Oil in the Middle East: Its Discovery and Development* (London, 1934; 2nd edn. London, 1954; 3rd edn. Oxford, 1969). Neither Libya nor the then Trucial States featured in a book on oil published in 1968.

from the Admiralty to the Foreign Office in December 1922, written a few days before the Lausanne Conference—at which it was thought likely that the fate of the oil-rich Mosul *wilayet* would be decided—states quite unequivocally that 'from a strategical point of view the essential thing is that Great Britain should control the territories on which the oil is situated'. Although Middle Eastern oil production amounted to only 5 per cent of world output in 1938, the tenacity with which Britain sought to retain influence in states where oil had been found or where its presence was strongly suspected—even where concessions had been awarded to the United States (as in Saudi Arabia and Bahrain) or shared with the United States and others (as in Iran, Iraq, and Kuwait)—indicates that this was always an especially high priority.[11]

The Middle East and the Mediterranean were vital theatres in the Second World War, largely because of their importance for both oil and communications. It was feared that the Germans might attack Iraq and, after the invasion of the Soviet Union, push through to Iran. Iraq was reoccupied in May 1941, and British (later also American and Soviet) forces occupied Iran, which became an important supply route for the Soviet Union. Earlier, Germany and Italy had occupied Greece and landed in North Africa, which presented a major threat to Egypt and the Suez Canal. Rommel was eventually halted at El Alamein in October 1942, and 'Egypt was secure for good'.[12] Shortly afterwards, Anglo-American troops landed in Algiers, a landmark in the history of the US presence in the Middle East.[13]

After the end of the Second World War financial, political, and other constraints, combined with growing pressures for change from nationalist and independence movements within the territories themselves, obliged Britain to relinquish her Empire in the Middle East within a few years, in spite of quite

[11] These events are described in Marian Jack [Kent], 'The Purchase of the British Government's Shares in the British Petroleum Company, 1912–1914', *Past and Present*, XXXIX (April, 1968), pp. 139–68; Marian Kent, *Oil and Empire: British Policy and Mesopotamian Oil, 1900–1920* (London, 1976), and *Moguls and Mandarins; Oil, Imperialism and the Middle East in British Foreign Policy, 1900–1940* (London, 1993). Two volumes of the history of BP have appeared so far: R. W. Ferrier, *The History of the British Petroleum Company*, Vol. I, *The Developing Years, 1901–1932* (Cambridge, 1982), and J. H. Bamberg, *The History of the British Petroleum Company*, Vol. II, *The Anglo-Iranian Years, 1928–1954* (Cambridge, 1994). For Iraq see Helmut Mejcher, 'Oil and British Policy Towards Mesopotamia, 1914–1918', *Middle Eastern Studies* (hereafter *MES*), VIII, 3 (Oct., 1972), pp. 377–91, and *Imperial Quest for Oil: Iraq, 1910–1928* (London, 1976).

[12] A. J. P. Taylor, *English History, 1914–1945* (Oxford, 1965), p. 559.

[13] For the Second World War in the Middle East and North Africa see the official history edited by I. S. O. Playfair, *The Mediterranean and Middle East*, 5 vols. (London, 1954–1973); George Kirk, *The Middle East in the War* (London, 1953); Geoffrey Warner, *Iraq and Syria in 1941* (London, 1974); A. B. Gaunson, *The Anglo-French Clash in Lebanon and Syria, 1940–1945* (New York, 1987); A. Roshwald, *Estranged Bedfellows: Britain and France in the Middle East During the Second World War* (Oxford, 1990).

strenuous efforts to prevent this happening on the part of both Labour and Conservative governments. By 1948 the determination of the Zionists, together with the general espousal of their cause by President Truman, obliged Britain to evacuate Palestine. Jordan became formally independent in 1946, and revolutions in Egypt in 1952 and Iraq in 1958 put a sudden and virtually complete end to British political influence in these two states. By 1954, when an international consortium replaced the Anglo-Iranian Oil Company, British influence in Iran had been almost entirely superseded by that of the United States.[14] The Italian and British parts of Somaliland, which the two countries had occupied since the end of the nineteenth century, were fused into an independent Somali Republic in July 1960.[15] The Sudan became independent at the beginning of 1956;[16] pressure from Greece, Turkey, and the indigenous nationalist movement led to the proclamation of a republic of Cyprus in 1960, although on somewhat precarious terms. British rule over Aden or southern Yemen, and the remaining treaty arrangements with the rulers of the Gulf states, had become too expensive, and too embarrassing, to uphold by 1967 and 1972 respectively. As far as the indirect influence once exerted over Saudi Arabia and Iran was concerned, Britain had been playing second fiddle to United States's interests in the region since the early 1940s, though the loss of indirect control had not occurred without a fair degree of acrimony on Britain's part.[17]

In general, the historiography reflects little work on the totality of this series of episodes, whose fragmentation and overall haphazardness were certainly exacerbated by the fact that relations between London and the various territories were

[14] See L. P. Elwell-Sutton, *Persian Oil: A Study in Power Politics* (London, 1955); James Bill and Wm. Roger Louis, eds., *Musaddiq, Iranian Nationalism and Oil* (London, 1988).

[15] After the construction of the Suez Canal in 1869 the Horn of Africa attracted the attention of Britain, France, and Italy, and the three states had established contiguous colonies in the area by 1897. Britain and Italy left in 1960; French Somaliland (Djibouti) became an independent (and separate) republic in 1977. See I. M. Lewis, *A Modern History of Somalia: Nation and State in the Horn of Africa* (1980; revd. edn., Boulder, Colo., 1988).

[16] For the end of British rule in the Sudan, see the memoirs of Sir James Robertson, *Transition in Africa: From Direct Rule to Independence* (London, 1974), and W. Travis Hanes III, *Imperial Diplomacy in the Era of Decolonization: The Sudan and Anglo-Egyptian Relations, 1945–1956* (Westport, Conn., 1995).

[17] The generally bipartisan nature of much of Britain's post-war colonial policy in the region, Ernest Bevin's strong sense of the importance of British influence and control in the Middle East, and the general reluctance of both Labour and Conservatives to yield to the United States are underscored in two books by Wm. Roger Louis: *Imperialism at Bay: The United States and the Decolonization of the British Empire, 1941–1945* (London, 1977) and *The British Empire in the Middle East, 1945–1951: Arab Nationalism, the United States and Post-War Imperialism* (Oxford, 1984), as well as in Ritchie Ovendale's edited collection, *The Foreign Policy of the British Labour Government, 1945–1951* (Leicester, 1984).

directed by three different departments of state, the Colonial, Foreign, and India Offices. Part of the explanation for this neglect may be that, with certain exceptions, historians of the Middle East see themselves primarily *as such* rather than as historians of part of the British Empire, even though their main sources of archival information are located in the Public Record Office and the India Office.[18] It is also the case that (perhaps because of the greater availability of materials for some areas than for others) historical writing on Britain in the Middle East has been distinctly patchy, with the Eastern Question, Egypt, and Palestine receiving the bulk of scholarly attention. Again, this is an area which has been surprisingly free of major intellectual, as opposed to political, controversy, and thus somewhat intellectually arid, with no major interpretative schools, apart perhaps from the apologists for and critics of Empire. There are few 'subaltern studies', few local histories, and with some notable exceptions, few major reinterpretations.[19]

Conversely, theoreticians and historians of Empire have tended to ignore the area, or to see its constituent units as parts of another whole—the Gulf as part of the wider history of British India, Egypt as part of the Scramble for Africa—or to subsume it under some generalized notion of 'the periphery'. This is particularly true of the period after 1918; while the first volume of Cain and Hopkins's magisterial two-volume study of the British Empire and British imperialism[20] has a chapter and a half on Egypt, Iran, and the Ottoman empire in the period before 1914, there are only the most perfunctory references to the area in the second volume on the period between 1915 and 1990, for much of which, as has been noted, Britain's Empire in the Middle East was at its largest extent. Only one author, Elizabeth Monroe in the work already mentioned, has attempted to deal with the 'Anglo-Arab' Middle East as a whole over a fairly long time-span, although there have been important studies of the formulation and

[18] There are important archival collections for the colonial period in the territories themselves and in India, although they vary greatly in accessibility and quality. The National Archives of India has extensive holdings on Aden, Muscat, the states of the Gulf, Iran, Afghanistan, and Iraq (the archive of the British High Commission in Baghdad—1918–32—was transferred to India more or less intact in 1941, and never returned to London). The Israel State Archives and the Central Zionist Archives, both in Jerusalem, are rich sources for the Palestinian and Transjordanian Mandates. The Sudan Government archives in Khartoum contain material on the Condominium. The National Archives of Egypt and of Iraq also have material on the 'British period'.

[19] The main exception here is Egypt, which has featured prominently, and (as will be mentioned below) in a rather misleading way, in the discussion of 'informal empire', and is also the subject of the only post-modernist study of any country in the region, Timothy Mitchell's *Colonising Egypt,* (1988; 2nd edn., Berkeley, 1991).

[20] P. J. Cain and A. G. Hopkins, *British Imperialism* (London, 1993): Vol. I, *Innovation and Expansion, 1688–1914*; Vol. II, *British Imperialism: Crisis and Deconstruction, 1914–1990.*

execution of British Middle Eastern policy before, during, and after the First[21] and Second World Wars.[22]

A few general points need to be made. First, unlike France's North African possessions, Britain had no colonies of settlement in the Middle East. Secondly, within this relatively confined geographical area, a wide variety of instruments regulated and to some extent defined Britain's relations with the various different territories: colonies, Mandates, Protectorates, a series of unequal treaties in which Britain was the dominant partner. Thirdly, there were substantial territories in the land mass occupied by the Arabian peninsula, Anatolia, the Fertile Crescent, and Iran where Britain had relatively sizeable economic interests (mostly in agriculture—cereals and cotton—banking, government bonds and public debts, public utilities and infrastructure, especially railways, and oil after its discovery in the 1900s) but, apart from Aden and Cyprus for all or part of the period under review, no actual Imperial presence.

The combination of the second and third of these points may have contributed to colouring Robinson and Gallagher's summary of the situation in the Empire as

[21] Two useful studies of the years leading up to 1914 are Stuart A. Cohen, *British Policy in Mesopotamia, 1903–1914* (London, 1976), and Rashid Ismail Khalidi, *British Policy Towards Syria and Palestine, 1906–1914* (London, 1980). See also Roger Adelson, *London and the Invention of the Middle East: Money, Power, and War, 1902–1922* (New Haven, 1995). For the First World War and its aftermath in the Middle East see Briton Cooper Busch, *Britain, India and the Arabs, 1914–1921* (Berkeley, 1971) and *Mudros to Lausanne: Britain's Frontier in West Asia, 1918–1923* (Albany, 1976); Michael Cohen and Martin Kolinsky, eds., *Britain and the Middle East in the 1930s* (London, 1992); John Darwin, *Britain, Egypt and the Middle East: Imperial Policy in the Aftermath of War, 1918–1922* (London, 1981); the chaps. on British policy in C. Ernest Dawn, *From Ottomanism to Arabism: Essays on the Origins of Arab Nationalism* (Urbana, Ill., 1973); Elie Kedourie, *England and the Middle East: The Destruction of the Ottoman Empire, 1914–1921* (London 1956; repr. 1978), *In the Anglo-Arab Labyrinth: The McMahon–Husayn Correspondence and Its Interpretations, 1914–1939* (Cambridge, 1976), and *Islam in the Modern World and Other Studies* (London, 1980); Aaron S. Klieman, *Foundations of British Policy in the Arab World: The Cairo Conference of 1921* (Baltimore, 1970); Helmut Mejcher, 'British Middle East Policy, 1917–1921: The Interdepartmental Level', *Journal of Contemporary History*, VIII, 4 (Oct. 1973), pp. 81–101; Jukka Nevakivi, *Britain, France and the Arab Middle East, 1914–1920* (London, 1969); Bruce Westrate, *The Arab Bureau: British Policy in the Middle East, 1916–1920* (University Park, Pa., 1992).

[22] Middle Eastern decolonization during and after the Second World War is covered especially well in the two studies by Wm. Roger Louis mentioned in note 17 above. Other studies of this period include Jacob Abadi, *Britain's Withdrawal From the Middle East, 1947–1971: The Economic and Strategic Imperatives* (Princeton, 1982); A. N. Porter and A. J. Stockwell, *British Imperial Policy and Decolonisation, 1938–1964*, Vol. I, *1938–1951*, British Documents on End of Empire Project (BDEEP) (London, 1987); Vol. II, *1951–1964* (London, 1989); Howard M. Sachar, *Europe Leaves the Middle East, 1936–1954* (New York, 1972). For wider-ranging studies see R. F. Holland, *European Decolonization, 1918–1981: An Introductory Survey* (New York, 1985), and John Darwin, *Britain and Decolonisation: The Retreat from Empire in the Post-War World* (Basingstoke, 1988). For economic policy during the war see Martin W. Wilmington, *The Middle East Supply Centre* (Albany, 1971); for British development assistance in the post-war period see Paul W. T. Kingston, *Britain and the Politics of Modernization in the Middle East, 1945–1958* (Cambridge, 1996).

a whole at the end of the nineteenth century: 'the late-Victorians were no more anti-imperialist than their predecessors even though they were driven to annex more often [in Africa]. British policy followed the principle of extending control informally if possible and formally if necessary.'[23] Recent scholarship has questioned the appropriateness of notions such as 'driven to annex' and the 'necessity' of extending control. Robinson and Gallagher's classic scenario in which the British found themselves invading and occupying Egypt almost by accident, and certainly not *primarily* for economic motives, has been challenged in the work of A. G. Hopkins, and by Alexander Schölch[24] and Juan Cole, both of whom suggest more businesslike objectives. In Cole's words: 'Britain invaded [Egypt] in order to ensure that a process of state formation did not succeed in creating a new sort of stable order that would end European privileges and threaten the security of European property and investments.'[25] In other words, Britain did so in order to maintain the kind of Imperial economic subordination which she had exercised since mid-century. It appears that the Canal was never seriously at risk from 'Urabi and his friends in 1882. The other pillar of earlier conventional wisdom, that the French would have occupied Egypt had the British not done so,[26] has also been shown to be without much foundation.[27]

It seems important to mention this, particularly in the case of Egypt, but also in the context of the expansion of the British Empire in the Middle East after 1918, where 'indirect rule,' as manifested in the Mandate system, was often upheld by contemporaries as a shining example of British disinterestedness. Some years before the First World War Lord Curzon had described Britain's role in the Persian Gulf in the nineteenth century as 'the most unselfish page in history'.[28] Similar sentiments can be found in the work of administrator-chroniclers of Iraq such as S. H. Longrigg's *Iraq, 1900 to 1950: A Political, Social and Economic History* (London, 1953) and Sir Arnold Wilson's *Loyalties: Mesopotamia: A Personal and Historical Record, 1914–1920*, 2 vols. (London, 1930–31), and of course in the writings of their more celebrated counterparts on Egypt in an earlier era: Auckland Colvin, *The*

[23] Ronald Robinson and John Gallagher with Alice Denny, *Africa and the Victorians: The Official Mind of Imperialism*. (1961; 2nd edn., London, 1981), p. xxi.

[24] A. G. Hopkins, 'The Victorians and Africa: A Reconsideration of the Occupation of Egypt, 1882', *Journal of African History*, XXVII (1986), pp. 363–91; Alexander Schölch, *Egypt for the Egyptians! The Socio-Political Crisis in Egypt, 1878–1882* (London, 1981).

[25] Juan R. I. Cole, *Colonialism and Revolution in the Middle East: Social and Cultural Origins of 'Urabi Movement* (Princeton, 1993), p. 17.

[26] As shown, for instance, in Robert L. Tignor, *Modernization and British Colonial Rule in Egypt, 1882–1914* (Princeton, 1966).

[27] Cain and Hopkins, *British Imperialism*, I, pp. 366–69.

[28] In the course of a speech in Muscat in 1903; *Lord Curzon in India: Being a Selection from his Speeches as Viceroy and Governor-General of India, 1898–1905* (London, 1906), p. 502.

Making of Modern Egypt, 2nd edn. (London, 1906), Lord Cromer, *Modern Egypt*, 2 vols. (London, 1908), and Alfred Milner, *England in Egypt* (London, 1893).

This sense of 'Imperial mission' is an important leitmotif in earlier writing on Egypt and Iraq, but, admittedly in a rather more nuanced and sophisticated form, it also pervades the work of relatively recent diplomatic histories, such as Elie Kedourie's *In the Anglo-Arab Labyrinth: The McMahon–Husayn Correspondence* (Cambridge, 1978) and J. B. Kelly's *Britain and the Persian Gulf, 1795–1880* (London, 1968). Edward W. Said's *Orientalism* (New York, 1978) and *Culture and Imperialism* (London, 1993) have tended to make such attitudes almost impossibly unfashionable, although Edward Ingram's fascinating studies of British and British Indian exploits in Iran and central Asia in the nineteenth century are unabashedly explicit in their fearless disregard of modern conventions of political correctness.[29]

Recent studies of the later period of British control and influence in the Middle East suggest that it may be difficult to make the formal–informal distinction in a meaningful manner. Thus, while Britain's ambitions for the post-Ottoman Middle East were at least partially blunted by the US entry into the war and the need to conciliate France, the Iraqi Mandate and the unequal Anglo-Iraqi Treaty of 1930 proved fairly effective instruments for Britain to control Iraq until the revolution of 1958. In much the same way, the Protectorate and the Anglo-Egyptian Treaty of 1936 enabled Britain to control Egypt until 1952. Sir John Shuckburgh minuted in 1919: 'It is generally agreed that we must not go through the official pantomime known as "declaring a protectorate", but it is not clear that this disability need limit to any practical extent the control we are able to exert over Mesopotamian affairs.'[30] To make the point again, although the Anglo-Iraqi and Anglo-Egyptian Treaties of 1930 and 1936 gave the two states seats at the League of Nations and a measure of independence, they were not free of British control until the revolutions of 1952 and 1958.

For most of the period until the 1940s, the arrangements Britain devised to maintain her presence, in systems of 'indirect rule', attracted eager collaborators[31]

[29] Edward Ingram, *The Beginning of the Great Game in Asia, 1828–1834* (Oxford, 1979), *Commitment to Empire: Prophecies of the Great Game in Asia, 1797–1800* (Oxford, 1981), *In Defence of British India: Great Britain in the Middle East, 1775–1842* (London, 1984), and *Britain's Persian Connection: Prelude to the Great Game in Asia, 1798–1829* (Oxford, 1992).

[30] Quoted in Peter Sluglett, *Britain in Iraq, 1914–1932* (London, 1976), p. 31.

[31] See Ronald Robinson, 'Non-European Foundations of European Imperialism: Sketch for a Theory of Collaboration', in Roger Owen and Bob Sutcliffe, eds., *Studies in the Theory of Imperialism* (London, 1972), pp. 117–42. The role of the minority communities in the Ottoman empire in this process is discussed by Marius Deeb, 'The Socioeconomic Role of the Local Foreign Minorities in Modern Egypt, 1805–1961', *International Journal of Middle East Studies*, IX (1978), pp. 11–22, and Charles Issawi, 'The Transformation of the Economic Position of the Millets in the Nineteenth Century', in Benjamin Braude and Bernard Lewis, eds., *Christians and Jews in the Ottoman Empire: The Functioning of a Plural Society*, 2 vols. (New York, 1982), Vol. I, *The Central Lands*, pp. 261–85.

throughout its Middle Eastern Empire—kings and their dependents in Egypt and Iraq, tribal leaders in various parts of the Arabian peninsula—so that it was indeed possible to have 'Empire on the cheap'. In such circumstances, Britain's contribution to the defence and internal security of Iraq could drop from £23m in 1921 to £0.48m in 1930.[32] In the same way—although the extraordinary prosperity of their fiefdoms helped the arrangements to last rather longer—the rulers of the Gulf sheikhdoms who signed the original treaties with Britain in the nineteenth century effectively created the 'sheikhships' for themselves and their descendants by doing so, since the pre-eminence of what are now the ruling families was only permanently established by their being recognized as such by Britain and the authorities in British India.[33]

In the 1920s and 1930s, the symbolism of Empire was, on the whole, effectively maintained in the Middle East. The Proconsuls and administrators who wrote about their experiences during this period seemed full of confidence in the general good sense and rightness of purpose with which they and their political masters carried out their tasks, combined, occasionally, with admonitions against 'giving in' to the demands of 'agitators'. The memoirs of Lord Lloyd, *Egypt since Cromer*, 2 vols. (London, 1933–34), Sir Alec Kirkbride in Transjordan, *A Crackle of Thorns* (London, 1956), and Sir John Bagot Glubb's account of his experiences in Iraq, *War in the Desert: An R.A.F. Frontier Campaign* (London, 1960), to pick almost at random from a very long list, can be seen as emblematic of this genre. There is some sense of betrayal in *Seven Pillars of Wisdom* (New York, 1926), but T. E. Lawrence's chief complaint was not against Britain's manifest destiny to rule the Arabs (who were to become 'our first brown Dominion') but against Britain's pusillanimity in sharing this destiny with the French. Lawrence's contemporary and rival, St John Philby, also launched broadsides at British policy in the Middle East after the First World War, but again, these attacks reflected his belief that Britain had backed the wrong horse in allowing the Hashimites to gain greater

[32] Sluglett, *Britain in Iraq*, pp. 270–71.

[33] Although it is not the author's main concern, the point emerges from Jill Crystal's *Oil and Politics in the Gulf: Rulers and Merchants in Kuwait and Qatar* (1990; 2nd edn., Cambridge, 1995). See also Rosemarie Said Zahlan, *The Origins of the United Arab Emirates: A Political and Social History of the Trucial States* (London, 1978) and *The Creation of Qatar* (London, 1979). For evidence of the vital nature of British support for the Saudi monarchy when its continued existence seemed to be threatened, see Peter Sluglett and Marion Farouk-Sluglett, 'The Precarious Monarchy: Britain, Abdul-Aziz ibn Saud, and the Establishment of the Kingdom of Hijaz, Najd and its Dependencies, 1925–1932', in Tim Niblock, ed., *State, Society and Economy in Saudi Arabia* (London, 1981), pp. 36–57, and Clive Leatherdale, *Britain and Saudi Arabia, 1925–1939: The Imperial Oasis* (London, 1983). See also Gary Troeller, *The Birth of Saudi Arabia: Britain and the Rise of the House of Sa'ud* (London, 1976), and Joseph Kostiner, *The Making of Saudi Arabia, 1916–1936: From Chieftaincy to Monarchical State* (New York, 1993).

power than the Saudis, rather than any aversion to colonial rule as such.[34] One of the few academic studies of contemporary events written during this period is Philip Willard Ireland's *Iraq: A Study in Political Development* (London, 1937), which combines critical distance with a scholarly examination of the source materials; Ireland, an American, who later served in the US Foreign Service, was given privileged access to documents in the Colonial, Foreign, and India Offices, and made good use of what he was shown.

For less fortunate scholars, the fifty-year rule, which was not relaxed until the late 1960s, meant that unpublished British sources for the post-First World War history of the British Empire in the Middle East were not available. Nevertheless, archive-based histories of earlier periods had already begun to be produced, occasionally based on a combination of European official and local, mostly Egyptian, archival collections. Among these were George Douin's *Histoire du règne du Khédive Ismaïl*, 2 vols. (Rome, 1936) and Angelo Sammarco's *Histoire de l'Egypte moderne dupuis Mohammad Ali jusqu'à l'occupation britannique*, 4 vols. (Rome, 1937). By this time young Egyptians were coming to England to do research in the Public Record Office; S. Ghorbal's MA thesis (London, 1924) was published as *The Beginnings of the Egyptian Question and the Rise of Mehemet Ali* in 1928, and remains a reliable guide to the diplomatic history of the period. In the 1950s John Marlowe, a journalist with many years' experience of the Middle East, began to produce a series of popular but partly archivally based histories of British activity in the Middle East, in a generally critical vein; perhaps the best known are *Anglo-Egyptian Relations, 1800–1953* (London, 1954), *Arab Nationalism and British Imperialism: A Study in Power Politics* (London, 1961), *Perfidious Albion: The Origins of Anglo-French Rivalry in the Levant* (London, 1971), and *Spoiling the Egyptians* (London, 1974).

In the course of the 1960s some of the present generation of established Middle Eastern historians had begun to publish their theses, or earliest books. Among these were E. R. J. Owen, *Cotton and the Egyptian Economy: A Study in Trade and Development, 1820–1914* (Oxford, 1969), and Afaf Lutfi al-Sayyid (Marsot), *Egypt and Cromer: A Study in Anglo-Egyptian Relations* (London, 1968). Owen's work comes under the general rubric of this chapter because of the intimate relationship between the Egyptian economy and the Lancashire cotton industry, and it remains a major contribution to Egyptian economic history. Marsot's work on diplomatic history was followed by research on the Egyptian political élite in the

[34] For Philby see the entertaining biography by Elizabeth Monroe, *Philby of Arabia* (London, 1973), which contains a bibliography of his writings. For an earlier example of a critical study of British imperialism, see Wilfrid Scawen Blunt, *The Secret History of the English Occupation of Egypt: Being a Personal Narrative of Events* (London, 1907).

1920s and 1930s, *Egypt's Liberal Experiment, 1922–1936* (Berkeley, 1977), a book on Muhammad 'Ali, *Egypt in the Reign of Muhammad 'Ali* (Cambridge, 1984), and a more general work on Egyptian history, *A Short History of Modern Egypt* (Cambridge, 1985). Owen's *The Middle East in the World Economy, 1800–1914* (London, 1981) is the standard work on this subject.

It is probably fair to say that the last twenty-five years have been the most productive in the historiography of the British Empire in the Middle East, although, increasingly, some of the best work has tended to treat the connection as secondary to some other narrative scheme. Thus, Afaf Lutfi al-Sayyid-Marsot's *Egypt's Liberal Experiment*, Eric Davis, *Challenging Colonialism: Bank Misr and Egyptian Industrialization, 1920–1941* (Princeton, 1983), Ellis Goldberg, *Tinker, Tailor, Textile Worker: Class and Politics in Egypt, 1930–1952* (Berkeley, 1986), and Joel Beinin and Zachary Lockman's *Workers on the Nile: Nationalism, Communism and the Egyptian Working Class, 1882–1954* (Princeton, 1987) all deal with roughly the same period of Egyptian history, when the British presence was very much felt, but the authors' concerns focus more on the effects of the relationship on Egyptian economy and society. The same is true of Hanna Batatu's path-breaking work, *The Old Social Classes and the Revolutionary Movements of Iraq: A Study of Iraq's Old Landed Classes and its Communists, Ba'thists, and Free Officers* (Princeton, 1978); in spite of the fact that well over half the book is concerned with the period before 1958, 'the English', as Batatu rather quaintly calls them, play a relatively minor and distant role.[35] The Sudan has been the object of rather more traditional historiography, though Martin Daly's penetrating studies of the Condominium are full of keen insights into the haphazard and accidental nature of what has often passed for 'British colonial policy-making'.[36]

There is a huge volume of literature on the history of the Palestine Mandate. Even an attempt to restrict one's scope fairly rigorously to the topic of British policy towards Palestine or British administrative policies in Palestine produces a very large number of titles,[37] and the list could be extended almost indefinitely to

[35] This point has been made by Roger Owen in 'Class and Class Politics in Iraq before 1958: The "Colonial and Post-Colonial State" ', in Robert A. Fernea and Wm. Roger Louis, eds., *The Iraqi Revolution of 1958: The Old Social Classes Revisited* (London, 1991), pp. 154–71.

[36] See Robert O. Collins, *Land Beyond the Rivers: The Southern Sudan, 1898–1916* (New Haven, 1971); Robert O. Collins and Francis M. Deng, eds., *The British in the Sudan, 1898–1956: The Sweetness and the Sorrow* (London, 1984); Gabriel Warburg, *The Sudan Under Wingate: Administration in the Anglo-Egyptian Sudan, 1899–1916* (London, 1971). M. W. Daly's two books on the Condominium are *Empire on the Nile: The Anglo-Egyptian Sudan, 1898–1934* (London, 1986) and *Imperial Sudan: The Anglo-Egyptian Condominium, 1934–1956* (London, 1991).

[37] Nicholas Bethell, *The Palestine Triangle: The Struggle between the British, the Jews, and the Arabs, 1935–1948* (London, 1979); David A. Charters, *The British Army and Jewish Insurgency in Palestine, 1945–1947* (New York, 1989); Michael J. Cohen, *Palestine: Retreat from the Mandate: The Making of*

include such topics as British influence on economic or land policy.[38] In general, most of what has been written has been based on careful use of British and Zionist archives, in spite of the fact that—especially for the latter years of the Mandate—many key British documents are still not available for consultation. It seems almost invidious to single out particular titles from this long list, but Louis and Stookey's *The End of the Palestine Mandate*, the careful discussions of British policy by Michael Cohen, Ritchie Ovendale, Gabriel Sheffer, and Bernard Wasserstein are particularly useful, as is the work of Ilan Pappé.

As has already been mentioned, there are surprisingly few local or regional studies of anywhere in the colonial Middle East in the nineteenth or twentieth centuries, in contrast to, for example, the kinds of research which has been undertaken on Indian provinces or cities in the British period, or on cities such as Damascus or Aleppo in the Ottoman period. In his recent *Le Caire* (Paris, 1993), which looks at the history of the city from the medieval period to the present, André Raymond devotes only eighty out of 370 pages of text to the history of the city since 1798. Again, apart from Robert Ilbert on Heliopolis and Alexandria, Michael J. Reimer on nineteenth-century Alexandria, and May Seikaly on Haifa under the Mandate—all, in an important sense, 'new towns'—there is remarkably little on the urban social history of any of the major towns of the region in the colonial period.[39]

British Policy, 1936–1945 (New York, 1978); Isaiah Friedman, *The Question of Palestine: British–Jewish Arab Relations, 1914–1918* (1973; 2nd edn., New Brunswick, NJ, 1992); Elie Kedourie, 'Sir Herbert Samuel and the Government of Palestine', *MES*, V, 1 (Jan. 1969), pp. 44–68, and *Islam in the Modern World and Other Studies* (London, 1980), chap. 8, pp. 93–170; Wm. Roger Louis and Robert W. Stookey, eds., *The End of the Palestine Mandate* (Austin, Tex., 1986); Elizabeth Monroe, 'Mr Bevin's Arab Policy', in Albert Hourani, ed., *St. Antony's Papers*, XI (London, 1961), pp. 9–48. Moshe Mossek, *Palestine Immigration Policy Under Sir Herbert Samuel: British, Zionist and Arab Attitudes* (London 1978); Ritchie Ovendale, 'The Palestine Policy of the British Labour Government, 1945–1946', *International Affairs*, LV, 3 (July, 1979), pp. 409–31; Ilan Pappé, *Britain and the Arab-Israeli Conflict, 1948–1951* (New York, 1988); G. Sheffer, 'Intentions and Results of British Policy in Palestine: Passfield's White Paper', *MES*, IX, 1 (Jan. 1973), pp. 43–60, and 'British Colonial Policy Making Towards Palestine, 1929–1939', *MES*, XIV, 3 (Oct. 1978), pp. 307–22; Mayir Vereté, 'The Balfour Declaration and Its Makers', *MES*, VI, 3 (Jan. 1970), pp. 48–76; Bernard Wasserstein, *The British in Palestine: The Mandatory Government and the Arab–Jewish Conflict, 1917–1929*, 2nd edn. (Oxford, 1991).

[38] See, for example, Barbara J. Smith, *The Roots of Separatism in Palestine: British Economic Policy, 1920–1929* (London, 1993), and Kenneth W. Stein, *The Land Question in Palestine, 1917–1939* (Chapel Hill, NC, 1984).

[39] Robert Ilbert, *Héliopolis. Le Caire, 1905–1922: Genèse d'une ville* (Paris, 1981) and *Alexandrie, 1830–1930: Histoire d'une communauté citadine*, 2 vols. (Cairo, 1996); M. J. Reimer, 'Les fondements de la ville moderne: un tableau socio-démographique entre 1820 et 1850'; 'Alexandrie entre deux mondes', *Revue de l'Occident Musulman et de la Méditerranée*, XLVI (1987), pp. 110–20; Michael J. Reimer, *Colonial Bridgehead: Government and Spatial Change in Alexandria, 1850–1882* (Boulder, Colo., 1997); May Seikaly, *Haifa: Transformation of a Palestinian Arab Society, 1918–1934* (London, 1995). See also Henry Kendall, *Jerusalem: The City Plan, Preservation and Development During the British Mandate, 1918–1948* (London, 1948).

Paradoxically, therefore, we are in some ways rather better informed about certain aspects of economy and society in, say, Jerusalem and its hinterland under Ottoman rule in the sixteenth century than under British rule in the twentieth.

The contribution of the rise of nationalism to the end of empire has formed the subject of lively debate in writings about imperialism and colonialism. Like the relative weight to be given to strategic or economic considerations in the acquisition of colonial territory in the first place, it probably does not make much sense to come down sharply on one side or the other. From the point of view of the nationalist historian, it is clear that the weight of pressure from his fellow countrymen was the key factor in expelling the British or the French. But it is also the case that the metropolitan countries' priorities changed over time, and it may no longer have been in their interest, or perhaps they could no longer afford, to maintain the relationship in the same fashion. In addition, both Britain and France were eclipsed by the irresistible rise of the United States as the supreme world power, and their roles were redefined to meet the new exigencies of the cold war. In the Middle East, the creation of Israel was an additional and unique factor in the 'decolonization' process. Although his discussion is largely confined to South-East Asia and Africa, D. A. Low has drawn attention to some of the complexities of this topic in a collection of essays entitled *Eclipse of Empire* (Cambridge, 1993).

Simply listing and dating events show what very different processes were involved in the cases of Jordan (for the sake of argument, independent in 1946), Palestine (1948), Egypt (1952), Iraq (1958), Cyprus (1960), South Arabia (1967), and the Gulf States (1971). Even by the standards of the post-1918 peace settlement, Jordan was a remarkable creation, owing its existence to a fortuitous community of interest between Abdullah ibn Husayn and Britain at the end of 1920, and to Abdullah's extraordinary persistence in wishing to increase the extent of the territory he ruled, specifically to include what gradually came to be recognized as 'Arab Palestine'.[40] Due to the circumstances of its origin and the sparseness of its population, a nationalist movement was slow to develop in Jordan; its two principal rulers, Abdullah (1921–51) and Husayn (1953–1999] owe their positions very largely to the support of external 'partners', Britain and indirectly the Zionists for Abdullah, and Britain, the United States, and Israel for Husayn. Naturally, neither was unaffected by the rhetoric of anti-Zionism and Arab nationalism; indeed, it is most probable that Abdullah was assassinated because he did not pay sufficient heed to them. In a sense, decolonization never quite took place in Jordan,

[40] This is discussed in two indispensable books: Mary C. Wilson, *King Abdullah, Britain and the Making of Jordan* (Cambridge, 1987), and Avi Shlaim, *Collusion Across the Jordan* (Oxford, 1988); and an abridged version of the latter, *The Politics of Partition: King Abdullah, the Zionists and Palestine, 1921–1951* was published in 1990.

although of course the British presence diminished and the Commander of the Arab Legion, Sir John Glubb, was unceremoniously dismissed in March 1956.

Palestine, of course, was an entirely different matter. As Bernard Wasserstein says at the end of his book on the period between 1917 and 1929, 'the British mandate in Palestine was doomed from the outset',[41] given the insoluble nature of the conflict between the two principal communities. In addition, the initial partiality shown towards Zionism by such politicians as Balfour, Churchill, and Lloyd George meant that British policy would always be at loggerheads with the aspirations of the Arab population. By the time of the Biltmore Declaration of 1942 it was clear that the Zionists would ultimately be able to rely on the United States; by 1945–46 the British realized that the only policy which the United States would support was partition, which the British first thought might be implemented peacefully, but soon came to realize could not be. One of the many merits of Wm. Roger Louis's meticulous discussion of these events (both in his essay in the collection he and Robert W. Stookey edited on *The End of the Palestine Mandate* and the more detailed treatment in *The British Empire in the Middle East, 1945–1951: Arab Nationalism, the United States and Post-War Imperialism*) is the clear inference that Ernest Bevin's distaste for Zionism derived largely from the negative effect its apparent objectives were having on relations between Britain and the United States, whose partnership he had come to see as the foundation of any post-war world order in which Britain's role was not to be reduced to insignificance. The end of the Mandate cannot, of course, be compared usefully to other colonial transfers of power, but the writings of Louis and his co-authors in *The End of the Palestine Mandate* and Ritchie Ovendale's *Britain, the United States and the End of the Palestine Mandate, 1942–1948* (London, 1989) are of major importance in gaining an understanding of these complex events.

Egypt and Iraq achieved full independence from Britain by the overthrow of regimes which were generally unpopular, but particularly so because of the sense that the local rulers were little more than British stooges. In *Egypt from Independence to Revolution, 1919–1952* (Syracuse, NY, 1991) Selma Botman describes the development of nationalism in Egypt, the creation of forms of imperfect but nevertheless fairly genuine forms of political pluralism, against the background of fast-moving social and political change. The limited independence granted by Britain in 1922 was a chimera because of the weight of the four 'reserved points' which Britain had ruled as being beyond discussion—the Suez Canal, the Sudan, the capitulations, and the defence and foreign policy of Egypt,

[41] Wasserstein, *The British in Palestine*, p. 244.

all of which were reserved for Britain.[42] In addition, the limited democracy inaugurated in the inter-war period became discredited, partly because of the extent of the gerrymandering involved and partly because of the absence of 'genuine' popular participation. As in Iraq, the general sense was that the system, as it was, could neither reform itself nor lead the country to national independence; in both countries, a small group within the military was able to seize power and set up regimes which, however defective, brought the British connection to an end. The work of Israel Gershoni and James Jankowski, *Egypt, Islam, and the Arabs: The Search for Egyptian Nationhood, 1900–1930* (New York, 1986) and *Redefining the Egyptian Nation, 1930–1945* (Cambridge, 1995), though not directly concerned with Anglo-Egyptian relations, describes the political and intellectual processes involved; Jacques Berque's *Egypt: Imperialism and Revolution* (New York, 1972) is a subtle essay in the interpretation of Egypt's socio-economic, political, and cultural history in the nineteenth and twentieth centuries. The Suez expedition of 1956, perhaps the last major assertion of Britain's pretensions as a colonial power, is analysed in a collective volume edited by Wm. Roger Louis and Roger Owen, *Suez 1956: The Crisis and its Consequences* (Oxford, 1989).

In Iraq the abrupt and unilateral termination of the British connection was not exactly a surprise, as many of the contributors to Robert Fernea and Wm. Roger Louis's *The Iraqi Revolution of 1958: The Old Social Classes Revisited* make clear. The economic and social history of the pre-revolutionary period forms the principal topic of Hanna Batatu's *Old Social Classes and the Revolutionary Movements of Iraq* although, as has already been mentioned, the British connection is not Batatu's principal concern. In his chapter in *The Iraqi Revolution of 1958: The Old Social Classes Revisited*, Wm. Roger Louis shows how British officials in both London and Baghdad wondered how long they would be able to rely on Nuri al-Sa'id. It is difficult to see, in their terms, what else they could have done, especially when it became impossible to groom Salih Jabr as an acceptable successor, although Britain's failure to reach out to the genuine and widely shared concerns of opposition politicians and organizations—not only in Iraq but in Egypt and Iran as well—is a constant characteristic of the period. In general, the British wanted to maintain control at a discreet distance; oil production and revenue increased fivefold between 1951 and 1958, and the Iraq Petroleum Company (British, American, French, and Dutch-owned) controlled production and dictated the royalties that the Iraqi government was to receive. Oil nationalization did

[42] For the negotiations leading to the (British) declaration of Egyptian independence in Feb. 1922, see Harold Nicolson, *Curzon: The Last Phase, 1919–1925: A Study in Post-War Diplomacy* (Boston, 1934), chap. 6, and Elie Kedourie, 'Sa'd Zaghlul and the British', in *The Chatham House Version and Other Middle Eastern Studies* (London, 1970), pp. 82–159.

not take place until June 1972, but it was always seen, however mistakenly (as the later history of the oil industry was to prove), as a vital building-block for national independence.

Cyprus exhibits certain parallels with Palestine, in the sense of the profound complications caused by the presence (and the fundamentally irreconcilable aims) of two deeply rooted ethnic-national groups. Britain acquired Cyprus in 1878 as part of the settlement under the Congress of Berlin, and declared it a Crown Colony in 1925, but what turned out to be its rather limited strategic potential was only developed after Egypt became independent in 1952. As early as the 1930s the various parties assumed a number of fundamentally conflicting positions. Until the late 1950s Britain insisted on staying in Cyprus in order to maintain a military presence in the eastern Mediterranean; a number of Greek politicians pressed for the union of Cyprus and Greece (*enosis*), an ideal shared by the overwhelming majority of Greek Cypriots. Turkey, while generally advocating the independence of Cyprus from Britain, would not countenance any steps which appeared to be in the direction of *enosis*, a point of view shared by the entire Turkish Cypriot community, which formed about a fifth of the population. After a violent campaign by Greek Cypriot activists beginning in March 1955, independence from Britain was eventually negotiated; Archbishop Makarios became President of the republic and Turkish Cypriots gained proportional representation in government and the civil service. For its part, Britain retained the right to station Royal Air Force bases on the southern part of the island, which it does to this day.

The political and constitutional arrangements were not strong enough to satisfy the widely divergent aspirations of the Greek and Turkish communities, and collapsed after a Turkish military invasion of northern Cyprus in 1974, which resulted in the creation of a separate 'state' in the north of the island. These events are chronicled by J. A. McHenry, *The Uneasy Partnership on Cyprus, 1919–1939* (New York, 1987), George H. Kelling, *Countdown to Rebellion: British Policy in Cyprus, 1939–1955* (Westport, Conn., 1990), and John Reddaway, *Burdened with Cyprus: The British Connection* (London, 1986), all of which exude an air of bewildered head-shaking in the face of the difficulties encountered in unravelling this particular Gordian knot, but see above all the recent book by Robert F. Holland *Britain and the Revolt in Cyprus, 1954–1959* (Oxford, 1998).

Finally, South Arabia and the Gulf. It is not entirely easy to understand—except perhaps in terms of placating her other friends in the region and safeguarding the oilfields against attempts to take them over—why Britain held on so tenaciously to these last outposts of Empire. In *The End of Empire in the Middle East: Britain's Relinquishment of Power in Her Last Three Arab Dependencies* (Cambridge, 1991),

Glen Balfour-Paul, who was personally involved in the episodes he describes, shows that in the late 1960s the United States was still trying to persuade Britain not to abandon her 'East of Suez' role in the aftermath of the Suez crisis; King Faisal of Saudi Arabia appealed to Britain as late as May 1966 to maintain her 'defence responsibilities' in the Arabian peninsula. Of course, once it had been decided to withdraw from Aden, it followed that the Gulf could no longer be defended. The first chapter of Fred Halliday's *Revolution and Foreign Policy: The Case of South Yemen, 1967–1987* (Cambridge, 1990) provides an interesting account of the decolonization process, how, at the very end of the colonial period, because of personal and ideological splits—the Front for the Liberation of Occupied South Yemen (FLOSY) versus the National Liberation Front (NLF)—it was by no means clear who would take over power when the British left.

In the Gulf the situation was rather different, in that Britain's announcement in 1968 that she would leave at the end of 1971 caused consternation to the rulers of the smaller sheikhdoms (Kuwait became independent of Britain in 1961, and—perhaps paradoxically—Oman moved towards greater independence after the British-engineered removal of Sultan Sa'id in 1970),[43] who actually offered to pay Britain to continue to defend them—fearing some form of takeover by one or other of their powerful neighbours, Iran, Iraq, or Saudi Arabia. A fascinating diatribe against Britain's 'untimely' departure can be found in J. B. Kelly's *Arabia: The Gulf and the West* (New York, 1980), although, in terms its author uses to damn-with-faint-praise another work of which he does not approve, Kelly's account does contain 'a solid layer of information' (p. 139). In fact, after Iran dropped its claim to Bahrain in 1970, and although Bahrain and Qatar decided not to join in, the transition from Trucial States to United Arab Emirates took place with relative ease.

Perhaps because of the nature of the ending of the colonial regime when it came, and probably because (with the exception of Aden) there was nothing comparable to the labour migration between former French North Africa and France, relatively little has survived Britain's 200-year connection with the Middle East. All that remains is the pride of place given to the English language (although this may also reflect American global primacy), some aspects of military organization, an entirely exaggerated sense of the persistent strength of British power and influence, and the scholarship that has formed the subject of this chapter. Given the amount that has been written, a more detailed treatment of the topic is clearly necessary. Much of it is diplomatic and economic history of high quality; what is lacking, as has been mentioned (except perhaps for Palestine and Egypt) are

43 See J. E. Peterson, *Oman in the Twentieth Century: Political Foundations of an Emerging State* (London, 1978), pp. 200–17.

detailed local studies of the machinery of government, the changes brought about in city and countryside when rulers and administrators looked to Jerusalem or Baghdad instead of Istanbul, the effects of the new laws and new forms of economic organization which the British brought with them. It may be that the materials for such studies are not and never will be available, but it is clear that much of the history of this long relationship remains to be written, perhaps, if the materials should happen to exist, by the descendants of those who so long formed the object of British Imperial attentions.

Select Bibliography

ROGER ADELSON, *London and the Invention of the Middle East: Money, Power, and War, 1902–1922* (New Haven, 1995).

JUAN R. I. COLE, *Colonialism and Revolution in the Middle East: Social and Cultural Origins of 'Urabi's Movement* (Princeton, 1993).

M. W. DALY, *Empire on the Nile: The Anglo-Egyptian Sudan, 1898–1934* (Cambridge, 1986).

—— *Imperial Sudan: The Anglo-Egyptian Condominium, 1934–1956* (Cambridge, 1991).

JOHN DARWIN, *Britain, Egypt and the Middle East: Imperial Policy in the Aftermath of War, 1918–1922* (London, 1981).

ROBERT A. FERNEA and WM. ROGER LOUIS, eds., *The Iraqi Revolution of 1958: The Old Social Classes Revisited* (London, 1991).

DAVID GILLARD, *The Struggle for Asia, 1828–1914: A Study in British and Russian Imperialism* (London, 1977).

ELIE KEDOURIE, *England and the Middle East: The Destruction of the Ottoman Empire, 1914–1921* (London, 1956, repr. 1978).

—— *In the Anglo-Arab Labyrinth: The McMahon-Husayn Correspondence and Its Interpretations, 1914–1939* (Cambridge, 1976).

J. B. KELLY, *Britain and the Persian Gulf, 1795–1880* (Oxford, 1968).

MARIAN KENT, *Moguls and Mandarins: Oil, Imperialism and the Middle East in British Foreign Policy, 1900–1940* (London, 1993).

WM. ROGER LOUIS, *Imperialism at Bay: The United States and the Decolonization of the British Empire, 1941–45* (London, 1977).

—— *The British Empire in the Middle East, 1945–1951: Arab Nationalism, the United States and Post-War Imperialism* (Oxford, 1984).

—— and ROBERT W. STOOKEY, eds., *The End of the Palestine Mandate* (Austin, Tex., 1986).

TIMOTHY MITCHELL, *Colonising Egypt*, 2nd edn. (Berkeley, 1991).

ELIZABETH MONROE, *Britain's Moment in the Middle East, 1914–1971*, new and revised edn. (Baltimore, 1981).

ROGER OWEN, *The Middle East in the World Economy, 1800–1914* (London, 1981).

Avi Shlaim, *The Politics of Partition: King Abdullah, the Zionists, and Palestine, 1921–1951* (Oxford, 1990).

Bernard Wasserstein, *The British in Palestine: The Mandatory Government and the Arab–Jewish Conflict, 1917–1929*, 2nd edn. (London, 1991).

Mary C. Wilson, *King Abdullah, Britain and the Making of Jordan* (Cambridge, 1987).

28

Informal Empire in Latin America

RORY MILLER

Although Britain's role in Latin America has remained marginal to most historians of the British Empire,[1] other specialists have produced an impressive volume of publications. Writers in Latin America itself have generally considered British influence fundamental to explaining their countries' evolution during the nineteenth century. The growth of Latin American studies in North American and British universities from the 1960s also stimulated much research from historians in the developed world.

Several features stand out from the resulting literature.[2] An intense confrontation developed between those influenced by the major currents of Latin American political economy (nationalism, Marxism, structuralism, and dependency) and those who preferred a more empirical approach.[3] This was exacerbated by disagreements over what terms like 'imperialism' signified. These difficulties were probably greater in Latin American history than elsewhere, because of the significance of Marxist traditions among academics in the region and the absence of important British colonies. The latter also meant that empirical research concentrated more on the economic and business relationship than on political or social issues.[4]

I am grateful to Raúl García Heras, Robert Greenhill, Paul Henderson, Tony Hopkins, Alan Knight, Walter Little, Roger Louis, and Ricardo Salvatore for comments on earlier drafts.

[1] Important exceptions are John Gallagher and Ronald Robinson, 'The Imperialism of Free Trade', *Economic History Review* (hereafter *EcHR*), Second Series, VI (1953), pp. 1–15; P. J. Cain and A. G. Hopkins, *British Imperialism*, 2 vols. (London, 1993): Vol. I, *Innovation and Expansion, 1688–1914*; Vol. II, *Crisis and Deconstruction, 1914–1990*.

[2] For fuller bibliographies see Rory Miller, *Britain and Latin America in the Nineteenth and Twentieth Centuries* (London, 1993), pp. 261–311, and Christopher Abel and Colin M. Lewis, eds., *Latin America, Economic Imperialism and the State: The Political Economy of the External Connection from Independence to the Present* (London, 1985), pp. 500–12.

[3] Cristóbal Kay, *Latin American Theories of Development and Underdevelopment* (London, 1989), provides a succinct analysis of these concepts.

[4] British Honduras, the Malvinas/Falklands, and British Guiana were marginal both to the Empire and to Latin American historiography.

The Literature Before 1950

Britain's role in Latin America provoked controversy from the time of independence (1810–25). Local politicians complained about the impact of British textile exports on indigenous producers as well as the arrogance of British merchants backed by their Consuls and the Royal Navy. Later in the century more comprehensive critiques began to relate the problems facing individual countries to the British presence. Not surprisingly, questioning of Britain's political and economic influence was greatest at times when economic disappointments were most profound.[5] Yet even at the height of export prosperity, early in the twentieth century, dissenting voices which were critical of the long-term effects of dependence on foreign trade and investment still appeared in Latin America.[6]

The Great Depression stimulated greater doubts. The Roca–Runciman Pact of 1933 and pleas for special treatment from British firms evoked a furious response from nationalist authors in Argentina. Raúl Scalabrini Ortíz, the best-known, published two influential volumes of essays in which he claimed that Britain's policies had been designed to conserve Argentina as an 'immense *estancia* [cattle ranch]', using the railways as the principal instrument of their hegemony.[7] Marxist writers also blamed the British for maintaining Latin American economies in a subordinate and underdeveloped state, whether the agents were merchants (in José Carlos Mariátegui's essays on Peru) or finance capital (as Caio Prâdo Jr. argued in Brazil).[8] Besides criticizing the structural distortions arising from British capitalism, some Marxists alleged that the British had continually interfered in internal political struggles in order to forestall autonomous development.[9]

Changes in the international economy between the two world wars also provoked some North American attempts to explain Britain's historical involvement in Latin America. This resulted in work of lasting value. J. Fred Rippy's studies of investment and Alan K. Manchester's monograph on Britain's relations with Brazil remain essential references.[10] In Britain herself, however, there was little academic

[5] For example, Luís Esteves, *Apuntes para la historia económica del Perú* (Lima, 1882), written at the end of the guano period.

[6] Francisco A. Encina, *Nuestra inferioridad económica: sus causas, sus consecuencias* (Santiago, 1911); Alejandro Bunge, *La economía argentina*, 4 vols. (Buenos Aires, 1928–30).

[7] *Política británica en el Río de la Plata* (Buenos Aires, 1940), and *Historia de los ferrocarriles argentinos* (Buenos Aires, 1940).

[8] José Carlos Mariátegui, *Siete ensayos sobre la realidad peruana* (Lima, 1928), translated as *Seven Interpretive Essays on Peruvian Reality* (Austin, Tex., 1971); Caio Prâdo, *História econômica do Brasil* (São Paulo, 1945).

[9] Hernán Ramírez Necochea, *Historia del imperialismo en Chile* (Santiago, 1960).

[10] J. Fred Rippy, *British Investments in Latin America, 1822–1949: A Case Study in the Operations of Private Enterprise in Retarded Regions* (New York, 1959); Alan K. Manchester, *British Pre-Eminence in Brazil: Its Rise and Decline* (New York, 1933).

interest in relations with Latin America. The first chair of Latin American history was not established until 1948 (at University College, London). Before then the British literature on Latin America consisted principally of travellers' accounts and business propaganda. The exceptions were some semi-official economic surveys and two collections of documents on Britain's role in Latin American independence, both published at the outbreak of the Second World War.[11]

Theories and Concepts

After 1945 Latin Americans played a leading role in the evolution of development economics. Their work inevitably affected interpretations of the region's historical relationship with advanced industrial economies, in particular that with Britain during the nineteenth century. The structuralist theories elaborated by Raúl Prebisch, who headed the United Nations Economic Commission for Latin America, drew on his own experience of negotiating with the British and directing the Argentine Central Bank during the 1930s.[12] Structuralists considered Latin American countries to have suffered from declining terms of trade and from their weaker bargaining positions compared with metropolitan economies. Economic development had been hindered because British investors had retained control of finance and technology, while dependence on primary exports and foreign capital inflows had magnified the impact of metropolitan crises on peripheral countries.[13]

The dependency theorists of the 1960s had even more influence on historians. Two books were particularly significant. André Gunder Frank, a North American working in Chile, blended the arguments of authors such as Encina, Ramírez, and Prâdo with the Marxist political economy of Paul Baran to argue that after independence Britain drained the economic surplus from Latin America, making autonomous development impossible. The mechanism was the greater power of British merchants and investors, aided by élites adopting free-trade policies. Any opposition, Frank claimed, met with armed intervention or British interference in

[11] Royal Institute of International Affairs, *The Problem of International Investment* (London, 1937) and *The Republics of South America* (London, 1937); C. K. Webster, ed., *Britain and the Independence of Latin America, 1812–1830: Select Documents from the Foreign Office Archives* (London, 1938); R. A. Humphreys, *British Consular Reports on the Trade and Politics of Latin America, 1824–1826* (London, 1940).

[12] Raúl Prebisch, 'Argentine Economic Policies Since the 1930s: Recollections', in Guido di Tella and D. C. M. Platt, eds., *The Political Economy of Argentina, 1880–1946* (London, 1986), pp. 133–53; Joseph L. Love, 'Raúl Prebisch and the Origins of the Doctrine of Unequal Exchange', *Latin American Research Review* (hereafter *LARR*), XV, 3 (1980), pp. 45–72.

[13] Celso Furtado, *Economic Development of Latin America: A Survey from Colonial Times to the Cuban Revolution* (Cambridge, 1970), pp. 30–39 and 151–52.

internal politics.[14] Fernando Henrique Cardoso and Enzo Faletto offered a less pessimistic and more complex 'dependency' perspective. While recognizing the constraints imposed by the British presence, they argued that each country's relationship with Britain depended on the ownership of its principal exports and choices made by its élite.[15] Nevertheless, by 1970 the popular view in Latin America was that Britain's exports had crushed local industry, her merchants had dominated overseas trade, her financiers had secured enormous profits, and her officials had intervened frequently on behalf of business. In the words of two eminent North American historians sympathetic to dependency analysis: 'The English had been the major factor in the destruction of Iberian imperialism; on its ruins they erected the informal imperialism of free trade and investment.'[16]

Rather surprisingly, this approach developed largely in isolation from the British literature on the 'Imperialism of Free Trade'. In 1953 John Gallagher and Ronald Robinson deliberately linked the establishment of formal colonies and the promotion of informal empire as parts of the same process. Nineteenth-century Latin America offered them a prime example of informal dominion. Immediately after independence, they claimed, Britain had used force to open the Latin American economies; later this became unnecessary as the élites which benefited from British trade and investment worked 'to preserve the local political conditions needed for it'.[17] The Canadian historian H. S. Ferns also used the phrase 'informal empire' in discussing nineteenth-century Argentina, arguing that the *estanciero* élite's desire for foreign trade and investment created a situation where intervention became superfluous.[18]

Language barriers inhibited the dissemination of these ideas in Latin America itself. In the developed world, meanwhile, it was only during the 1960s, with the growth of institutes of Latin American studies (in the United States in response to the cold war and in Britain to economic anxieties), that historians began to address them seriously. Then, however, as postgraduate and travel grants became available and the major university presses expanded their publishing programmes

[14] André Gunder Frank, *Capitalism and Underdevelopment in Latin America: Historical Studies of Chile and Brazil* (New York, 1967).

[15] Fernando Henrique Cardoso and Enzo Faletto, *Dependencia y desarrollo en América Latina* (Mexico City, 1969), expanded and translated as *Dependency and Development in Latin America* (Berkeley, 1979). The time-lag before publication in English made Cardoso and Faletto less influential than Frank among Anglophone historians during the 1970s.

[16] Stanley J. Stein and Barbara H. Stein, *The Colonial Heritage of Latin America: Essays on Economic Dependence in Historical Perspective* (New York, 1970), p. 155.

[17] Gallagher and Robinson, 'Imperialism of Free Trade', pp. 8–10.

[18] H. S. Ferns, 'Britain's Informal Empire in Argentina, 1806–1914', *Past and Present* (hereafter *P&P*), IV (1953), pp. 60–75.

on Latin America, the volume of empirical research grew.[19] In time, several studies of individual countries appeared bearing the unmistakable intellectual imprint of Gallagher and Robinson.[20]

By then the reaction had already commenced. Other historians using British archives rejected the assumptions that the British deliberately underdeveloped Latin America, constantly intervened in internal politics, and manipulated their commercial and financial superiority to extract huge profits. Ironically, one of the earliest revisionists was Ferns himself. In 1960 he concluded a major study based on Foreign Office documents by arguing that, since the British government had 'never had the power to oblige Argentina to pay a debt, to pay a dividend, or to export or import any commodity whatsoever', the relationship resembled one of mutual advantage rather than informal imperialism.[21]

The most persistent critic was D. C. M. Platt, Professor of Latin American History at Oxford from 1972 until his premature death in 1989. Platt's early work took issue with Gallagher and Robinson over the frequency of forcible British intervention. In contrast, Platt emphasized the gulf between government and the businessman and the reluctance of the Foreign Office to intercede, for example, in disputes between Latin American states and foreign bondholders.[22] He then began to minimize the commercial contacts between Britain and Latin America, especially before 1860, thereby questioning the region's relevance to theories of informal imperialism.[23] This still left open the possibility that businessmen, rather than governments, were the primary agents of imperialism during the half-century before 1914, but research by his students in corporate archives produced little evidence that British companies enjoyed excessive profits or long-term bargaining advantages.[24] These ideas coalesced at the end of the 1970s in Platt's frontal assault

19 The major US journal, *Latin American Research Review*, began publication in 1965. Cambridge University Press initiated its Latin American monograph series in 1967 and launched the *Journal of Latin American Studies* (hereafter *JLAS*) in 1969.

20 Richard Graham, *Britain and the Onset of Modernization in Brazil, 1850–1914* (Cambridge, 1968); Michael Monteón, 'The British in the Atacama Desert: The Cultural Bases of Economic Imperialism', *Journal of Economic History* (hereafter *JEcH*), XXXV (1975), pp. 117–33; Peter Winn, 'Britain's Informal Empire in Uruguay during the Nineteenth Century', *P&P*, LXXIII (1976), pp. 100–26; George E. Carl, *First Among Equals: Great Britain and Venezuela, 1810–1910* (Syracuse, NY, 1980); Roger Gravil, The *Anglo-Argentine Connection, 1900–1939* (Boulder, Colo., 1985).

21 H. S. Ferns, *Britain and Argentina in the Nineteenth Century* (Oxford, 1960), p. 488.

22 D. C. M. Platt, *Finance, Trade, and Politics in British Foreign Policy, 1815–1914* (Oxford, 1968).

23 D. C. M. Platt, *Latin America and British Trade, 1806–1914* (London, 1972) and 'Further Objections to an Imperialism of Free Trade, 1830–1860', *EcHR*, Second Series, XXVI (1973), pp. 77–91.

24 D. C. M. Platt, ed., *Business Imperialism, 1840–1930: An Inquiry Based on British Experience in Latin America* (Oxford, 1977). Rather curiously, this book was dismissed by H. S. Ferns as 'radical chic': review in *History*, LXIII (1978), pp. 435–36.

on the *dependentistas*, which ignited a somewhat intemperate controversy with more radical writers.[25]

Empirical support for Platt's early revisionism came from other historians in Britain. W. M. Mathew undermined earlier beliefs that the London firm of Antony Gibbs & Sons had extracted most of the profits from the Peruvian guano trade and controlled the actions of successive governments in Lima.[26] Harold Blakemore repudiated the view of Ramírez and Frank that British interests seeking to forestall autonomous state-led development had initiated the Chilean Civil War of 1891.[27] Neoclassical economists elsewhere also questioned structuralist and *dependentista* assumptions about movements in the terms of trade, the reasons for underdevelopment, and the degree of autonomy possessed by Latin American states during the nineteenth century.[28]

Research in the 1970s and 1980s

These controversies established the boundaries for much of the research undertaken after 1970. Latin Americans formed in the nationalist and Marxist traditions, radicals in the United States and Britain attracted by ideas of informal imperialism and dependency, and more empirical and theoretically eclectic historians together created an extensive literature. While some historians largely reiterated older views without undertaking primary research, the majority relied on new information obtained from British sources, particularly Foreign Office papers and corporate archives.[29] The growth of area studies programmes, improved international travel, and (more tragically) political exile for many Latin American academics all facilitated access. Much less research was undertaken in Latin America itself, due to the lack of organization of many archives and libraries there and a distaste for the authoritarian regimes of the 1970s.[30] The emphasis was

[25] D. C. M. Platt, 'Dependency in Nineteenth-Century Latin America: An Historian Objects', *LARR*, XV, 1 (1980), pp. 113–30; Stanley J. Stein and Barbara H. Stein, 'D. C. M. Platt: the Anatomy of "Autonomy"', ibid., pp. 131–46.

[26] W. M. Mathew, 'The Imperialism of Free Trade: Peru, 1820–1870', *EcHR*, Second Series, XXI (1968), pp. 562–79, and *The House of Gibbs and the Peruvian Guano Monopoly* (London, 1981).

[27] Harold Blakemore, *British Nitrates and Chilean Politics, 1886–1896: Balmaceda and North* (London, 1974).

[28] Carlos Manuel Peláez, 'The Theory and Reality of Imperialism in the Coffee Economy of Nineteenth-Century Brazil', *EcHR*, Second Series, XXIX (1976), pp. 276–90; Nathaniel H. Leff, *Underdevelopment and Development in Brazil*, 2 vols. (London, 1982).

[29] On the latter see D. C. M. Platt, 'Business Archives', in Peter Walne, ed., *A Guide to Manuscript Sources for the History of Latin America and the Caribbean in the British Isles* (London, 1973), pp. 442–513. Despite undertaking this survey, Platt never conducted any extensive research himself in Latin America.

[30] Since 1980 many national and provincial archives have become much better organized, creating greater opportunities for original research.

very much one of political economy at the 'micro' level. Most historians focused on government and business behaviour, ignoring the broader structural issues. Relatively little was written about the cultural impact of the British, even though the internalization of foreign values by local élites was crucial to both the nationalist and informal imperialist arguments.[31]

Within these constraints books and articles appeared on many important subjects. Perhaps paradoxically, given the extensive use of the Public Record Office, Platt's views on the passive role of British governments remained largely unchallenged. The questioning that did occur concentrated on particular instances of intervention, in Brazil against the slave trade, or in Central America, where Anglo-American rivalries were particularly acute.[32] Attempts to prove British perfidy in episodes such as the Paraguayan War (1865–70), the Pacific War (1879–83), the Chilean Civil War (1891), and the early phase of the Mexican Revolution (1910–13) came to very little.[33] Overall, therefore, Platt's insistence on continuity in British policy, and on the gulf between business and government, remained the orthodox interpretation.[34] This, perhaps, further encouraged historians to concentrate on the economic relationship.

Foreign merchants resident in Latin America provided the most significant business links with Britain immediately after independence. However, since many firms had been temporary partnerships vulnerable to commercial crises, few important archives survived. Despite this difficulty, some detailed local studies of merchants in Argentina, Mexico, and Chile did serve to delineate their role and influence more precisely.[35] Evidence that expatriate British houses were often a

[31] One important exception is British influence on anti-slavery campaigns: see Graham, *Britain and the Modernization*, pp. 160–86; David Eltis, *Economic Growth and the Ending of the Transatlantic Slave Trade* (New York, 1987).

[32] Leslie Bethell, *The Abolition of the Brazilian Slave Trade: Britain, Brazil, and the Slave Trade Question, 1807–1869* (Cambridge, 1970); Mario Rodríguez, *A Palmerstonian Diplomat in Central America: Frederick Chatfield, Esq.* (Tucson, Ariz., 1964); Craig L. Dozier, *Nicaragua's Mosquito Shore: The Years of British and American Presence* (Tucolosa, Ala., 1985).

[33] Diego Abente, 'The War of the Triple Alliance: Three Explanatory Models', *LARR*, XXII, 2 (1987), pp. 47–69; V. G. Kiernan, 'Foreign Interests in the War of the Pacific', *Hispanic American Historical Review* (hereafter *HAHR*), XXXV (1955), pp. 14–36; Thomas F. O'Brien, 'The Antofagasta Company: A Case Study of Peripheral Capitalism', *HAHR*, LX (1980), pp. 1–31; Luis Ortega, 'Nitrates, Chilean Entrepreneurs, and the Origins of the War of the Pacific', *JLAS*, XVI (1984), pp. 337–80; Peter Calvert, *The Mexican Revolution, 1910–1914: The Diplomacy of Anglo-American Conflict* (Cambridge, 1968).

[34] For a dissenting view see Miller, *Britain and Latin America*, pp. 47–69. See also Peter Rivière, *Absent-Minded Imperialism: Britain and the Expansion of Empire in Nineteenth-Century Brazil* (London, 1995); David McLean, *War, Diplomacy, and Informal Empire: Britain and the Republics of La Plata, 1836–1853* (London, 1995).

[35] Vera Blinn Reber, *British Mercantile Houses in Buenos Aires, 1810–1880* (Cambridge, Mass., 1979); Hilarie J. Heath, 'British Merchant Houses in Mexico, 1820–1860: Conforming Business Practice and

minority within the foreign merchant communities suggested limits to their influence, although there were times when their loans were indispensable to impoverished governments, allowing them to procure significant concessions in return.[36] A *dependentista* attempt in 1985 to reassert old ideas that foreign merchants, rather than Latin American élites, bore the primary responsibility for Latin America's problems thus met with sharp rejoinders from both sides of the Atlantic.[37]

The debt crisis of the early 1980s stimulated research on earlier cycles of foreign investment. Studies of government borrowing produced more sophisticated interpretations of the interrelationships between British capitalists and Latin American states.[38] However, it was already clear that in the later nineteenth century much of Britain's investment flowed through limited companies quoted on the Stock Exchange rather than government loans, and research on business imperialism tended to concentrate on these activities.[39] The British-owned railways, the leading destination for new investment after 1880, were intensively studied, interest focusing on finance and company–government relations. These analyses tended to affirm the capacity of governments to take action contrary to the railways' interests and profits, especially after the First World War. Research on the most important cases, Argentina and Brazil, however, suffered greatly from the destruction of company archives following nationalization in the late 1940s.[40]

The balance of research on other activities was rather uneven. Commercial

Ethics', *HAHR*, LXXIII (1993), pp. 261–90; John Mayo, *British Merchants and Chilean Development, 1851–1886* (Boulder, Colo., 1987); Eduardo Cavieres, *Comercio chileno y comerciantes ingleses, 1820–1880: un ciclo de historia económica* (Valparaiso, 1988).

36 Barbara A. Tenenbaum, *The Politics of Penury: Debts and Taxes in Mexico, 1821–1856* (Albuquerque, N. Mex., 1986).

37 Eugene W. Ridings, 'Foreign Predominance among Overseas Traders in Nineteenth-Century Latin America', *LARR*, XX, 2 (1985), pp. 3–27; Carlos Marichal, 'Foreign Predominance among Overseas Traders in Nineteenth-Century Latin America: A Comment', *LARR*, XXI, 3 (1986), pp. 145–50; D. C. M. Platt, 'Wicked Foreign Merchants and Macho Entrepreneurs: Shall We Grow Up Now?', *LARR*, XXI, 3 (1986), pp. 151–53.

38 Carlos Marichal, *A Century of Debt Crises in Latin America: From Independence to the Great Depression, 1820–1930* (Princeton, NJ, 1989); Frank Griffith Dawson, *The First Latin American Debt Crisis: The City of London and the 1822–25 Loan Bubble* (New Haven, 1990).

39 Irving Stone, 'British Long-Term Investment in Latin America, 1865–1913', *Business History Review* (hereafter *BHR*), XLII (1968), pp. 311–39, and 'British Direct and Portfolio Investment in Latin America Before 1914', *JEcH*, XXXVII (1977), pp. 690–722; Peter Svedberg, 'The Portfolio-Direct Composition of Private Investment in 1914 Revisited', *Economic Journal*, LXXXVIII (1978), pp. 763–77.

40 Colin M. Lewis, *British Railways in Argentina, 1857–1914* (London, 1983) and 'The Financing of Railway Development in Latin America, 1850–1914', *Ibero-Amerikanisches Archiv*, IX (1983), pp. 255–78; Paul B. Goodwin, *Los ferrocarriles británicos y la U.C.R., 1916–1930* (Buenos Aires, 1974); Harold Blakemore, *From the Pacific to La Paz: The Antofagasta (Chili) and Bolivia Railway Company, 1888–1988* (London, 1990); Steven Topik, *The Political Economy of the Brazilian State, 1889–1930* (Austin, Tex., 1987).

banking supplied one of the earliest examples of corporate history, a commissioned study of the Bank of London and South America, but relatively little thereafter.[41] The availability of business archives, together with controversies over the nitrate firms' political behaviour, stimulated much research on Chile before the 1891 Civil War, but less on the mature phase of the industry between then and 1914.[42] Studies of the early petroleum industry, in Mexico, Peru, and Venezuela, benefited from extensive government records, due to the industry's strategic importance, as well as the multinationals' archives.[43] Much less, however, appeared on other significant business activities, whether in the primary sector (metals-mining, landowning), or services such as the commodity trades, insurance, shipping, cables, and urban utilities.[44]

Apart from the unbalanced coverage of different sectors and countries, the literature on the nineteenth century suffered from other deficiencies. One serious impasse lay in defining imperialism. For some historians the term implied any asymmetrical relationship between an advanced and less developed economy, but for others imperialism existed only when a substantial infringement of Latin American sovereignty equivalent to quasi-colonial status was evident.[45] Nor did the concept of dependency offer an alternative. Empirical research demonstrated the degree of autonomy of Latin American élites and the limits to British profits and power, undermining the popular but reductionist theses of authors such as Frank. Once dependency theorists were in retreat, early in the 1980s, no strong paradigm remained to orientate research. The focus on foreign business at the

41 David Joslin, *A Century of Banking in Latin America* (London, 1963); Charles Jones, 'Commercial Banks and Mortgage Companies', in Platt, ed., *Business Imperialism*, pp. 17–52.

42 Thomas F. O'Brien, *The Nitrate Industry and Chile's Crucial Transition, 1870–1891* (New York, 1982); Robert G. Greenhill, 'The Nitrate and Iodine Trades, 1880–1914', in Platt, ed., *Business Imperialism*, pp. 231–83; Juan Ricardo Couyoumdjian, *Chile y Gran Bretaña: durante la Primera Guerra Mundial y la posguerra* (Santiago, 1986).

43 Jonathan C. Brown, 'Domestic Politics and Foreign Investment: British Development of Mexican Petroleum, 1889–1911', *BHR*, LXI (1987), pp. 387–416, and 'Why Foreign Oil Companies Shifted their Production from Mexico to Venezuela During the 1920s', *American Historical Review*, XC (1985), pp. 362–85; Rory Miller, 'Small Business in the Peruvian Oil Industry: Lobitos Oilfields Limited before 1934', *BHR*, LVI (1982), pp. 400–23.

44 Exceptions are Eduardo C. Míguez, *Las tierras de los ingleses en la Argentina, 1870–1914* (Buenos Aires, 1985); Robert G. Greenhill, 'Merchants and the Latin American Trades: An Introduction', in Platt, ed., *Business Imperialism*, pp. 159–97; Greenhill, 'The Brazilian Coffee Trade', in ibid., pp. 198–230; Charles Jones, 'Insurance Companies', in ibid., pp. 53–74; Greenhill, 'Shipping', in ibid., pp. 119–55; M. H. J. Finch, 'British Imperialism in Uruguay: The Public Utility Companies and the *batllista* State, 1900–1930', in Abel and Lewis, eds., *Latin America*, pp. 250–66; Raúl García Heras, *Transportes, negocios, y política: la Compañía Anglo-Argentina de Tranvías, 1876–1981* (Buenos Aires, 1994); Carlos Marichal, ed., *Las inversiones extranjeras en América Latina, 1850–1930: nuevos debates y problemas en historia económica comparada* (Mexico City, 1995).

45 Compare the definitions of Finch, 'British Imperialism', p. 250, and Mathew, 'Imperialism of Free Trade', p. 563.

'micro' level, reliance on metropolitan archives, and isolation from mainstream imperial history had all caused horizons to narrow. Few historians attempted to reformulate concepts of informal imperialism or to explore Gramscian concepts of hegemony (surprisingly in the academic context of the time).[46]

In retrospect, it seems that the popularity of dependency theories, especially in the United States, caused specialists to concentrate on Latin America's *external* relationships precisely when the emphasis in Imperial and colonial history moved towards *internal* agents of resistance and change. Once the disjuncture between radical theories and archival realities became evident, historians found themselves in a cul-de-sac. However, several interconnected developments then began to revitalize research. Although dependency perspectives retained some influence, a younger generation of Latin American historians, often those who had studied abroad, produced more-nuanced interpretations of British influence, emphasizing the complex interplay between foreign businessmen and domestic élites.[47] These further developments towards the end of the 1980s instilled new life into the subject. Interest in the period of British decline grew. Research on British trade and investment began to incorporate theoretical insights from the broader field of business history. Trends occurring in social history more generally filtered into the study of Britain's relations with Latin America.

Broadening Horizons

Research on the twentieth century was hindered, until 1967, by the fifty-year closure of British government archives. Even then, many historians, including Platt, remained bound by the conventional watershed of 1914. It thus took time to appreciate, first, that in some countries British influence had remained a reality until after the *Second* World War; secondly, that Foreign Office archives, the conventional starting-point, probably offered less for this period than those of the Treasury and the Bank of England; and thirdly, that Latin American sources could shed considerable light on intergovernmental relations, especially the negotiations over disinvestment. Significantly, the most important research on Britain's active role during the First World War, especially in Mexico where the

[46] Exceptions are Charles Jones, ' "Business Imperialism" and Argentina, 1875–1900: A Theoretical Note', *JLAS*, XII (1980), pp. 437–44, and A. G. Hopkins, 'Informal Imperialism in Argentina: An Alternative View', *JLAS*, XXVI (1994), pp. 469–84.

[47] Examples are Luis Ortega, 'Economic Policy and Growth in Chile from Independence to the War of the Pacific', in Abel and Lewis, eds., *Latin America*, pp. 147–71; Alfonso Quiroz, *Banqueros en conflicto: estructura financiera y economía peruana, 1884–1930* (Lima, 1989).

revolution created enormous problems for the oil companies, was undertaken by historians well outside Platt's sphere of influence.[48]

Initially the literature on Britain's decline and withdrawal concentrated on Argentina, where its substantial investments and commercial interests created major tensions following the Depression. Debate centred on the Roca–Runciman Pact, the behaviour of the transport companies, and Anglo-American conflicts over Argentina during the Second World War and early Peronist period.[49] Much of this research was undertaken by Latin American historians using British government archives, a comment true also of the subsequent work on Brazil.[50] The events leading to the 1938 expropriation of the oil companies in Mexico eventually received attention too.[51] Yet much remained unresearched, especially on Venezuela, Chile, Uruguay, and Peru, and, curiously, most historians ignored company archives for this period. Many questions about the timing, causes, and extent of the decline of British interests thus remained unresolved.[52] However, trends in business history which became apparent in the mid-1990s may help to elucidate these issues. In particular, some of Platt's former research students began

[48] Emily S. Rosenberg, 'Economic Pressures on Anglo-American Diplomacy in Mexico, 1917–1918', *Journal of Inter-American Studies and World Affairs,* XVII (1975), pp. 123–52, and 'Anglo-American Economic Rivalry in Brazil During World War I', *Diplomatic History*, II (1978), pp. 131–52; Friedrich Katz, *The Secret War in Mexico: Europe, the United States, and the Mexican Revolution* (Chicago, 1981); Bill Albert with Paul Henderson, *South America and the First World War: The Impact of War on Brazil, Argentina, Peru, and Chile* (Cambridge, 1988).

[49] Daniel Drosdoff, *El gobierno de las vacas, 1933–1956: tratado Roca–Runciman* (Buenos Aires, 1972); Joseph S. Tulchin, 'Decolonizing an Informal Empire: Argentina, Great Britain, and the United States, 1930–1943', *International Interactions*, I, 3 (1974), pp. 123–40; Roger Gravil and Timothy Rooth, 'A Time of Acute Dependence: Argentina in the 1930s', *Journal of European Economic History*, VII (1978), pp. 337–78; Peter Alhadeff, 'Dependency, Historiography, and Objections to the Roca Pact', in Abel and Lewis, eds., *Latin America*, pp. 367–78; Raúl García Heras, 'World War II and the Frustrated Nationalization of the Argentine British-Owned Railways, 1939–1943', *JLAS*, XVII (1985), pp. 135–55; García Heras, 'Hostage Private Companies under Restraint; British Railways and Transport Coordination in Argentina during the 1930s', *JLAS*, XIX (1987), pp. 41–67; Mario Rapaport, *Gran Bretaña, Estados Unidos, y las clases dirigentes argentinas, 1940–1945* (Buenos Aires, 1981); Jorge Fodor, 'The Origin of Argentina's Sterling Balances, 1939–1943', in di Tella and Platt, eds., *Political Economy*, pp. 154–82; Callum A. MacDonald, 'The United States, Britain, and Argentina in the Years Immediately after the Second World War', in ibid., pp. 183–200.

[50] Winston Fritsch, *External Constraints on Economic Policy in Brazil, 1889–1930* (Basingstoke, 1988); Marcelo de Paiva Abreu, 'Anglo-Brazilian Economic Relations and the Consolidation of American Pre-Eminence in Brazil, 1930–1945', in Abel and Lewis, eds., *Latin America*, pp. 379–93, and 'Brazil as a Creditor: Sterling Balances, 1940–1952', *EcHR*, Second Series, XLIII (1990), pp. 450–69.

[51] Jonathan C. Brown and Alan Knight, eds., *The Mexican Petroleum Industry in the Twentieth Century* (Austin, Tex., 1992); Lorenzo Meyer, *Su Majestad Británica contra la Revolución Mexicana, 1900–1950: el fin de un imperio informal* (Mexico City, 1991).

[52] For different interpretations of British decline, see Platt, *Latin America*, pp. 305–13; Leslie Bethell, 'Britain and Latin America in Historical Perspective', in Victor Bulmer-Thomas, ed., *Britain and Latin America: A Changing Relationship* (Cambridge, 1989), pp. 1–24; Miller, *Britain and Latin America*, pp. 179–238.

to shift their focus from the debates over imperialism towards more mainstream controversies in business history concerned with Britain's apparent backwardness in corporate structure and management compared with the United States.[53]

The other important development, foreshadowed in some earlier work, in particular that of Richard Graham on Brazilian modernization, Winthrop R. Wright on Argentine nationalism, and Alan Knight on the Mexican Revolution, was renewal of interest in the wider political and social impact of British investment.[54] The expansion of labour history in the developed world stimulated research on the relations between British managers and local workers.[55] Interest then broadened to encompass other spheres of economic and social history: the transmission of liberal ideas to Latin American élites; contested ideas of progress pitting Anglophile élites and foreign companies against the urban poor; the role of British firms in company towns and enclaves; and British influence on consumption, working life, and leisure. Association football, after all, was perhaps the most lasting British contribution to Latin American popular culture, adopted first by the expatriate British communities and then quickly appropriated by the Latin American masses.[56] The growth of such research reflects one persistent feature of historical writing on this subject, the interplay between Latin American realities and academic fashions in the developed world.

[53] Robert G. Greenhill, 'Investment Group, Free Standing Company, or Multinational? Brazilian Warrant, 1909–52', *Business History*, XXXVII, 1 (1995), pp. 86–111; Charles Jones, 'Institutional Forms of British Foreign Direct Investment in South America', *Business History*, XXXIX, 2 (1997), pp. 21–41; Rory Miller, 'British Free-Standing Companies on the West Coast of South America', in Mira Wilkins and Harm G. Schröter, eds., *The Free-Standing Company in the World Economy, 1830–1996* (Oxford, 1998) pp. 218–52; Robert Greenhill and Rory Miller, 'British Trading Companies in South America after 1914', in Geoffrey Jones, ed., *The Multinational Traders* (London, 1998), pp. 102–27.

[54] Graham, *Britain and the Modernization*; Winthrop R. Wright, *British-Owned Railways in Argentina: Their Effect on the Growth of Economic Nationalism, 1854–1948* (Austin, Tex., 1974); Alan Knight, 'The Political Economy of Revolutionary Mexico, 1900–1940', in Abel and Lewis, eds., *Latin America*, pp. 288–317.

[55] Manuel A. Fernández, 'British Nitrate Companies and the Emergence of Chile's Proletariat, 1880–1914', in Barry Munslow and Henry Finch, eds., *Proletarianisation in the Third World* (London, 1984), pp. 42–76; Joel Horowitz, 'Occupational Community and the Creation of a Self-Styled Elite: Railroad Workers in Argentina', *The Americas*, XLII (1985), pp. 55–81. Charles Bergquist, *Labor in Latin America: Comparative Essays on Chile, Argentina, Venezuela, and Colombia* (Stanford, Calif., 1986), contains studies of nitrate and oil workers.

[56] Muriel Nazzari, 'Widows as Obstacles to Business: British Objections to Brazilian Marriage and Inheritance Laws', *Comparative Studies in Society and History*, XXXVII (1995), pp. 781–802; Joseph L. Love and Nils Jacobsen, eds., *Guiding the Invisible Hand: Economic Liberalism and the State in Latin American History* (New York, 1988); Anton Rosenthal, 'The Arrival of the Electric Streetcar and the Conflict over Progress in Early 20th Century Montevideo', *JLAS*, XXVII (1995), pp. 319–41; Marshall C. Eakin, *British Enterprise in Brazil: The St John d'El Rey Mining Company and the Morro Velho Gold Mine, 1830–1960* (Durham, NC, 1989); Arnold J. Bauer, 'Industry and the Missing Bourgeoisie: Consumption and Development in Chile, 1850–1960', *HAHR*, LXX (1990), pp. 227–53; Benjamin Orlove, ed., *The Allure of the Foreign Imported Goods in Postcolonial Latin America* (Ann Arbor, 1997); Tony Mason, *Passion of the People? Football in South America* (London, 1995).

Select Bibliography

CHRISTOPHER ABEL and COLIN M. LEWIS, eds., *Latin America, Economic Imperialism and the State: The Political Economy of the External Connection from Independence to the Present* (London, 1985).

BILL ALBERT with PAUL HENDERSON, *South America and the First World War: The Impact of War on Brazil, Argentina, Peru, and Chile* (Cambridge, 1988).

LESLIE BETHELL, *The Abolition of the Brazilian Slave Trade: Britain, Brazil, and the Slave Trade Question, 1807–1869* (Cambridge, 1970).

—— ed., *Cambridge History of Latin America*, 10 vols. (Cambridge, 1984–95).

FERNANDO HENRIQUE CARDOSO and ENZO FALETTO, *Dependency and Development in Latin America* (Berkeley, 1979).

H. S. FERNS, *Britain and Argentina in the Nineteenth Century* (Oxford, 1960).

ANDRÉ GUNDER FRANK, *Capitalism and Underdevelopment in Latin America: Historical Studies of Chile and Brazil* (New York, 1967).

JOHN GALLAGHER and RONALD ROBINSON, 'The Imperialism of Free Trade', *Economic History Review*, Second Series, VI (1953), pp. 1–15.

RICHARD GRAHAM, *Britain and the Onset of Modernization in Brazil, 1850–1914* (Cambridge, 1968).

ROGER GRAVIL, *The Anglo-Argentina Connection, 1900–1939* (Boulder, Colo., 1985).

CRISTÓBAL KAY, *Latin American Theories of Development and Underdevelopment* (London, 1989).

ALAN K. MANCHESTER, *British Pre-Eminence in Brazil: Its Rise and Decline* (New York, 1933).

CARLOS MARICHAL, *A Century of Debt Crises in Latin America: From Independence to the Great Depression, 1820–1930* (Princeton, 1989).

LORENZO MEYER, *Su Majestad Británica contra la Revolución Mexicana, 1900–1950: el fin de un imperio informal* (Mexico City, 1991).

RORY MILLER, *Britain and Latin America in the Nineteenth and Twentieth Centuries* (London, 1993).

D. C. M. PLATT, *Finance, Trade, and Politics in British Foreign Policy, 1815–1914* (Oxford, 1968).

—— *Latin America and British Trade, 1806–1914* (London, 1972).

—— ed., *Business Imperialism, 1840–1930: An Inquiry Based on the British Experience in Latin America* (Oxford, 1977).

J. FRED RIPPY, *British Investments in Latin America, 1822–1949: A Case Study in the Operations of Private Enterprise in Retarded Regions* (New York, 1959).

29

Britain and the Scramble for Africa

JOHN E. FLINT

From the beginning the historiography of the British role in the Scramble for Africa was a controversy between apologists for expansion and their critics, and this remained a profound influence upon most who have written about the Scramble. Each generation reinterpreted in the light of changing concerns—the economic depression at the end of the nineteenth century, the origins of the First World War, Nazism and racist theory, decolonization and African nationalism. Equally important after 1920 was the progressive release of the archives of the British Foreign and Colonial Offices, in fits and starts up to the 1960s, which governed the quantity of academic studies of the Scramble, and their complexity.

The first article of substance was a piece of 'futurism' written in 1877 by W. E. Gladstone, whose government, ironically, would occupy Egypt five years later. Gladstone attacked Edward Dicey's view that Britain should occupy bankrupt Egypt, arguing that this would lead inevitably to the creation of a vast British Empire in Africa:

> our first site in Egypt, be it by larceny or be it by emption, will be the almost certain egg of a North African Empire, that will grow and grow until another Victoria and another Albert, titles of the Lake-sources of the White Nile, come within our borders: and till we finally join hands across the Equator with Natal and Cape Town, to say nothing of the Transvaal and the Orange River on the South, or of Abyssinia or Zanzibar, to be swallowed by way of viaticum on our journey.[1]

Gladstone's argument that Egypt would drag its occupiers deep into tropical Africa would intrigue almost all subsequent historians.

With the onset of annexations and Protectorates in the 1880s, writing about the Scramble was largely polemical. From the first there was moral opposition and arguments that expansion provided careers, or profits, for privileged groups at British taxpayers' cost. Seymour Keay's *Spoiling the Egyptians: A Tale of Shame*,

[1] W. E. Gladstone, 'Aggression on Egypt and Freedom in the East', *Nineteenth Century* (Aug.–Dec. 1877), pp. 149–66.

published in London in 1882, portrayed the Cabinet as pawns to bondholders and financiers; this was another idea with a long history thereafter. Explorers and Proconsular figures responded with reminiscences, and with articles in the gentlemen's magazines which stress the need to forestall competitors or lose trade, and to 'civilize' Africans.

In the 1890s the new British chartered companies produced a number of these early works, and assisted others. They had particular axes to grind. P. L. McDermott's *British East Africa, or IBEA*, published in 1893, stressed the huge costs the Imperial British East Africa Company (IBEA) had incurred in bringing 'civilization' to Uganda and pleaded for Imperial reimbursement should the company go bankrupt. When the Royal Niger Company (RNC) faced an end to its charter, its chairman, Sir George Goldie wrote an eloquent foreword to S. Vandeleur's account of the Company's wars against Nupe and Ilorin, arguing that the RNC's policy of ruling through African authorities was in fact more effective and humane than French practices.[2]

The first attempt at an overall account of the partition, by Sir John Keltie, Secretary of the influential Royal Geographical Society, in 1893,[3] also received help from Sir John Kirk, the former Consul-General in Zanzibar and director of the IBEA, from other officials of that Company, and from Goldie of the RNC as well as from officials of the Colonial Office. Strongly supporting British expansion in Africa, Keltie echoed earlier criticisms that without more determination Britain would lose valuable areas. Nevertheless, Keltie's study, though the Scramble was far from complete, pinpointed themes discussed by most later historians. He described activity before 1875 as slow, often 'unofficial' (later writers would call it 'informal'), and suggested that missionaries and explorers, to him heroic figures, served to create conditions for later annexations. Keltie saw the partition as a sudden profound change in European policies. He dated its beginning at 1875, with the coming together of H. M. Stanley and King Leopold of the Belgians; the Brussels Conference of 1876 was 'epoch-making', and led to the struggle over the Congo mouth. Leopold's international stance 'rapidly degenerated into a national scramble', pushing Britain to secure Protectorates on the West African coast against France, and pulling Germany into the picture. The German entry was a 'natural' result of her unification in 1871, her industrial growth, the search for new markets, and a desire for prestige, coupled with a popular 'fever for colonization'. With Germany in, the Scramble became an inevitable rush to peg out claims for the future.

Little was added to Keltie's overall narrative or interpretation by subsequent

[2] S. Vandeleur, *Campaigning on the Upper Nile and Niger* (London, 1898).

[3] Sir John Scott Keltie, *The Partition of Africa* (London, 1893).

popularizers,[4] former Proconsuls[5] or Colonial Office officials such as Sir Charles Lucas, who carried forward Keltie's general approach to cover the years from 1893 to 1914.[6]

The predominance of semi-official accounts was partly a result of the dearth of archival sources open to those less privileged.[7] Before the 1920s only two governmental series of published documents were open to scholars, the annual reports of colonial governments and Foreign Office Protectorates, and *Parliamentary Papers*. The former said little about territorial acquisition; their main use was for statistics of imports, exports, and revenues. *Parliamentary Papers* were fuller, with selected official correspondence printed for use in Parliament in forthcoming debates, major crises, and international conferences like that in Berlin in 1884–85 on West Africa and the Congo. They were, however, of limited value to scholars. Selected by officials, 'sensitive' documents were omitted, and published papers often lacked crucial passages, had wording and even dates altered, and, though rarely, could contain concocted *ex post facto* documents.

Nevertheless, annual reports and *Parliamentary Papers*, combined with Board of Trade figures and other economic material, were ammunition for critics of expansion in Africa. Such evidence, particularly for South Africa and Egypt, was mined by J. A. Hobson's *Imperialism: A Study*, published in London in 1902. Hobson's book was not, however, about the Scramble for Africa, though it was later often treated as such.[8] Rather, it was a hostile analysis of 'imperialism' by a radical liberal deeply opposed to the Anglo-Boer War of 1899–1902. Hobson argued that the sectional interest of finance capitalism, bankers, Egyptian bondholders, and Transvaal gold companies had usurped control of the state to create secure markets for their investments. Hobson's *Imperialism* was to have a lasting impact on the historiography of the Scramble. By focusing on who benefited from imperialism, Hobson set up a problem which future historians of African partition had to address. Later, with better archival access, it became common sport to demolish Hobson, for financiers were conspicuous by their absence in tropical Africa, before and after the Scramble. For South Africa and Egypt, however, Hobson was not so easy to undermine.

The First World War produced important changes in attitudes towards the

4 See chap. by A. D. Roberts, notes 15 and 16.

5 e.g. Sir Harry H. Johnston, *A History of the Colonization of Africa by Alien Races* (Cambridge, 1889).

6 Sir Charles P. Lucas, *The Partition and Colonisation of Africa* (Oxford, 1922).

7 In 1909 Foreign and Colonial Office archives from 1780 to 1837 were opened.

8 Eric Stokes, 'Late Nineteenth Century Colonial Expansion and the Attack on the Theory of Economic Imperialism: A Case of Mistaken Identity', *Historical Journal*, XII, 2 (1969), pp. 285–301, drew attention to the way Hobson's views, and V. I. Lenin's *Imperialism: The Highest Stage of Capitalism* (Moscow, 1917), had been misunderstood.

Scramble for Africa, and in the historiography. The carnage of the war led to obsessional concerns about its causes and who was 'guilty' of provoking it. There was widespread condemnation of 'secret diplomacy', characteristic of the Scramble and the alliance system in Europe. Further to the left, Lenin's *Imperialism: The Highest Stage of Capitalism* argued that 'imperialism' (seen as the latest stage of monopolistic industrial capitalism) was the cause of the war. Even Sir Charles Lucas could suggest, in his *Partition and Colonisation of Africa* in 1922, that the Scramble and its rivalries 'were among the determining causes of the War of 1914'.[9] The cynicism about diplomacy was simplistically married to Hobson's, and even Lenin's, versions of financial interests as the 'taproot' of imperialism in books like H. N. Brailsford's *The War of Steel and Gold* (London, 1914). Leonard Woolf, a renegade former Colonial Officer in Ceylon, in his *Empire and Commerce in Africa: A Study in Economic Imperialism* (London, 1920, reprinted 1968), focused on the activities of the three British chartered companies in Africa, picturing them as capitalist-imperialists nakedly exposed.

Before 1923 academic historians, lacking access to archives, contributed nothing to the historiography of the Scramble.[10] This changed when the former belligerents began publishing collections of diplomatic documents from their archives of the period from 1870 to 1914. Prompted partly by the new communist government in Russia, which published the details of Tsarist secret agreements, governments now wished to justify their own records in the events which led to 1914. Germany, condemned in the peace settlements as the aggressor and as an unfit colonial trustee, was the first to act, publishing forty volumes of documents between 1922 and 1927.[11] The British began their series in 1927,[12] as did the French two years later.[13] These collections, though selective, were much more valuable than P*arliamentary Papers* and the like. Volume editors in all countries were senior and respected academic historians, concerned to document significant historical trends. They concentrated on high policy, but included much on the rivalry over African partition. Documented studies of the Scramble were now possible, but such sources ensured that the Scramble would be seen as a purely European phenomenon, written by diplomatic historians.

[9] Lucas, *Partition and Colonisation*, p. 105.

[10] The first academic account, essentially narrative, was W. H. Dawson's chap. in Sir A. W. Ward and G. P. Gooch, eds., *The Cambridge History of British Foreign Policy*, Vol. II, *1783–1919* (Cambridge, 1923).

[11] Johannes Lepsius, Albrecht Mendelsohn Bartholdy, and Friedrich Thimme, eds., *Die Grosse Politik der europäischen Kabinette, 1871–1914*, 40 vols. (Berlin, 1922–27).

[12] G. P. Gooch and Harold Temperley, eds., *British Documents on the Origins of the War*, Vol. I (London, 1927), reproduced documents relating to the Scramble.

[13] Ministère des affaires étrangères, *Commission de publication des documents relatifs aux origines de la Guerre de 1914: Documents diplomatiques français, 1871–1914*. 1re serie (Paris, 1929–). The series is still incomplete.

A surprising result was the domination of the field until the late 1930s by historians from the United States.[14] Parker Thomas Moon's *Imperialism in World Politics*[15] was a college textbook of a high order, which made extensive use of the volumes of *Die Grosse Politik* as well as the previous literature. Two hundred and thirty-three pages were devoted to the Scramble for Africa. The book became a standard text, unchanged, for American undergraduates for almost forty years, with its twentieth printing in 1964. Moon emphasized the view that 1870–1914 witnessed a feverish 'new imperialism', in stark contrast to the peaceable, free-trading 'anti-imperialism' of the mid-Victorians. The Scramble was driven by economic and social forces among the 'nation-empires', among whom, rather surprisingly, he included the United States.

It was another American, William L. Langer, who came to dominate the field with his mastery of the newly published documents. In two massive studies[16] he examined the secret diplomacy from 1871 to 1914. His focus was the catastrophe of 1914, but readers were now presented for the first time with detailed accounts of the Scramble for Africa. Langer also contrasted the 'new imperialism' with mid-Victorian times, and characterized Britain as pushing to secure and expand export markets. The partition reflected the forces of the new imperialism and was a watershed in modern history. Langer stressed the role of Egypt in the story, seeing Arabi's movement of 1881–82 as an embryonic nationalism, and the British occupation of Egypt as catalyst of the Scramble.

The British historian A. J. P. Taylor, in a brilliant monograph on Bismarck's decision to acquire colonies,[17] explicitly argued that the Scramble was not a cause of the war. Taylor argued that Bismarck was not pulled into expansion by popular clamour, fear of a Reichstag defeat, or German economic interests. Rather, German colonies were an accidental by-product of Bismarck's wish to build an *entente* with France, by opposing Britain on colonial issues, to complete a German diplomatic system guaranteeing security. Taylor extended this into a broader argument that imperialist expansion reduced the danger of European war by diverting rivalries into peripheral areas. Africa was not worth owning, even less worth fighting for. Taylor saw Egypt and South Africa as the only major

[14] George Louis Beer, the distinguished historian of the 'old colonial system', served as President Wilson's adviser in the Versailles peace settlement. On Beer see Wm. Roger Louis, 'The United States and the African Peace Settlement of 1919: The Pilgrimage of George Louis Beer', *Journal of African History* (hereafter *JAH*), IV (1963), pp. 413–33. The best account of the repartition of Africa after the war is Louis's *Great Britain and Germany's Lost Colonies, 1914–1919* (Oxford, 1967).

[15] Parker Thomas Moon, *Imperialism and World Politics* (New York, 1926).

[16] William L. Langer, *European Alliances and Alignments, 1871–1890* (New York, 1931) and *The Diplomacy of Imperialism, 1890–1902* (New York, 1935).

[17] A. J. P. Taylor, *Germany's First Bid for Colonies, 1848–1884* (London, 1938), published at the height of Nazi Germany's demand for the return of Germany's former African colonies.

British interests, and suggested that new acquisitions were made to protect them.[18]

In 1930 Foreign and Colonial Office documents were opened to 1885.[19] This allowed a number of monograph studies of the early Scramble.[20] Reginald Coupland made use of this material to outline early phases of European rivalry in East Africa.[21] Sybil Eyre Crowe wrote a well-documented study of the Berlin West African Conference of 1884–85,[22] which convincingly demolished many nostrums, in particular the view that the Conference defined rules for effective occupation. Her study of the diplomacy between Germany, France, and Britain during the Conference also appeared to strengthen Taylor's view of Bismarck's motives.

The Second World War and its aftermath produced changes which transformed the historiography of partition. Colonial reforms in British Africa ushered in the era of African nationalism, parties, and elections, and the founding of new universities.[23] If Africa were to be decolonized, the origins of colonial subjection became of general interest. Archival access was transformed in 1948 when the government records for 1885–1902 were opened. Young research students of the post-war generation rushed to stake out their protectorates in an academic scramble. The result was a flood of academic monographs, starting in the mid-1950s, and reaching high levels in the 1960s and 1970s.[24]

Before these could appear, Ronald Robinson and John Gallagher produced in 1953 their famous article on 'The Imperialism of Free Trade', starting their continuing reconceptualization of imperialism, its periodization, and its causation.[25]

18 Ibid., p. 7.

19 More liberal access began in 1919 when the Foreign Office and Colonial Office archives were opened to 1860, and in 1925 this was extended to 1878. Public Record Office, *Records of the Foreign Office, 1782–1939* (London, 1939), p. 93.

20 For examples see chap. by A. D. Roberts, notes 52–54.

21 R. Coupland, *The Exploitation of East Africa, 1856–1890: The Slave Trade and the Scramble* (London, 1939).

22 S. E. Crowe, *The Berlin West African Conference, 1884–1885* (London, 1942).

23 See chap. by Roberts, pp. 474–79 for a discussion of the effects of the new university colleges in Africa. A full study is Apollos Nwauwa, *Imperialism, Academe, and Nationalism: Britain and University Education for Africans, 1860–1960* (London, 1998).

24 Jean Van der Poel, *The Jameson Raid* (Cape Town, 1951), was perhaps the first to use these new sources, exposing evidence linking politicians such as Chamberlain and Rosebery with Rhodes's plans. In several of the years in the 1960s and 1970s more studies were produced in a single year than in the fifty years before 1945.

25 With Hobson, Robinson and Gallagher are the only authors in this field about whom an entire book of critical assessment has appeared. Space prevents a full assessment of their significance here, but this has been achieved with some brilliance in Wm. Roger Louis, ed., *Imperialism: The Robinson and Gallagher Controversy* (New York, 1976), particularly in Louis's own introduction, 'Robinson and Gallagher and Their Critics', pp. 2–51, which outlines their ideas as a developing continuum. This volume also reprints on pp. 53–72, the article 'The Imperialism of Free Trade', originally published in *Economic History Review* (hereafter *EcHR*), Second Series, VI, 1 (1953), pp. 1–15.

The article challenged all previous work by denying that there was a mid-Victorian age of anti-imperialism, reeling off a list of places annexed between 1840 and 1870, and seeing an essential continuity of expansion during the so-called period of 'new imperialism'. They saw annexations as transitions from informal to formal means of control. From this emerged a new definition of imperialism as 'a sufficient political function of integrating new regions into the expanding economy'.[26] For many young researchers this helped to explain the continued reluctance to expand in the supposed age of 'new imperialism', and it provided clues to the puzzle of why so many strange forms of Imperial rule emerged after 1880, chartered companies, Protectorates, protected states, and the like. Finally, it suggested the need to search for local causes of a shift from informal to formal rule; if integrating new regions into an expanding economy was a constant, precipitants of annexation might lie in the collapse of local institutions, or in their resistance to economic penetration.

The large number of monograph studies which began to appear after 1955 were for the most part studies of how particular areas fell under colonial rule, such as those of K. Onwuka Dike, John E. Flint, and C. W. Newbury on West Africa,[27] Alexander John Hanna on British Central Africa,[28] or Roger Anstey on Britain and the Congo.[29] More-senior scholars were also exploiting the newly released archives, generally for themes with a wider geographical import, as in G. N. Sanderson's steady flow of new work on the Nile valley,[30] or the important biographies by Roland Oliver[31] and Margery Perham.[32]

The most original contribution to the field came in 1961 with the publication of Robinson and Gallagher's *Africa and the Victorians*.[33] The book was massively documented from the British official archives, and sought to display the motives leading British officials and politicians to impose formal rule on areas hitherto

[26] Louis, *Imperialism: The Robinson and Gallagher Controversy*, p. 59.

[27] See K. Onwuka Dike, *Trade and Politics in the Niger Delta, 1830–1885. An Introduction to the Economic and Political History of Nigeria* (Oxford, 1956), which argues that the transition from informal to formal rule lay in changed economic conditions behind the delta of the Niger. John E. Flint, *Sir George Goldie and the Making of Nigeria* (London, 1960, repr. 1966) continued Dike's story into a study of the emergence of the chartered Royal Niger Company. C. W. Newbury, *The Western Slave Coast and its Rulers* (Oxford, 1961) encompassed areas partitioned between Britain and France.

[28] Alexander John Hanna, *The Beginnings of Nyasaland and Northern Rhodesia, 1859–95* (Oxford, 1956).

[29] Roger Anstey, *Britain and the Congo in the Nineteenth Century* (Oxford, 1962).

[30] Culminating in G. N. Sanderson, *England, Europe and the Upper Nile, 1882–1899* (Edinburgh, 1965).

[31] Roland Oliver, *Sir Harry Johnston and the Scramble for Africa* (London, 1957).

[32] The first volume of Margery Perham's *Lugard*, subtitled *The Years of Adventure, 1858–1898* (London, 1956) was a study of Lugard's role in the Scramble in eastern, central, and West Africa.

[33] Ronald Robinson and John Gallagher with Alice Denny, *Africa and the Victorians: The Official Mind of Imperialism* (London, 1961; 2nd edn., 1981).

informally controlled, and to extend control into their hinterlands. In this sense it took the concepts of the earlier article into the later period. However, Africa was not seen as an area which now needed a 'sufficient political function' to integrate it into Britain's expanding economy, for Robinson and Gallagher saw Africa as worthless economically, and were not even ready to concede economic motives in Egypt or the new mineral resources of South Africa. The motivation was strategic, to protect the routes to India through the Suez Canal and around the Cape. What prompted the 'sufficient political function' for the occupation of Egypt, and later the war in South Africa, was the challenge of indigenous nationalism, Arabi's movement in Egypt, and the threat that the newly rich Transvaal republic would dominate all South Africa, including the Cape. Of these two nodes, it was the occupation of Egypt in 1882 which touched off the continental partition, for once in Egypt, the protection of its life-blood, the Nile valley, began a domino process which led Britain into Uganda, into Kenya to control coastal access to Uganda, and ultimately to the conquest of the Sudan. France, outraged by the loss of influence in Egypt, was compensated by steady British concessions in West Africa. The British motives in the partition were thus strategic, and a 'gigantic footnote to the history of India'. Economic imperialism in Africa came later, with railway building, settlers in Kenya, and cotton in Uganda, all designed to raise revenues to pay for the new governments. In similar manner, the imperialist political movement was an *ex post facto* rationalization for what had already taken place. The causes of the Scramble lay in Africa, in the emergence of proto-nationalist regimes in Egypt and the Boer Republics.

Criticism of this brilliantly written book now became an academic industry. Reviewers pointed out that scrambling had begun on the Congo as early as 1875, on the upper Niger from 1879, in the Oil Rivers and Lower Niger in 1880, and that France occupied Tunis in 1881, all before the occupation of Egypt.[34] Historians of West Africa challenged the view that partition there was a sideshow provoked by Egypt.[35] Marxists dismissed it as a whitewash over economic imperialism.[36] Others stressed that the book said nothing about the dynamic that drove other European powers into rivalry over Africa, if Britain's position was defensive.[37]

[34] For a fuller discussion of these attacks see Wm. Roger Louis, 'Robinson and Gallagher and Their Critics', in *Imperialism: The Robinson and Gallagher Controversy* (New York, 1976), pp. 2–51, as well as the selected reviews and comments of other authors.

[35] e.g. C. W. Newbury, 'Victorians, Republicans and the Partition of West Africa', *JAH*, III, 3 (1962), pp. 493–501; A. G. Hopkins, 'Economic Imperialism in West Africa: The Case of Lagos, 1880–92', *EcHR*, Second Series, XXI, pp. 580–606; John E. Flint, 'Britain and the Partition of West Africa', in J. E. Flint and G. Williams, eds., *Perspectives of Empire* (London, 1973).

[36] V. G. Kiernan, 'Farewells to Empire', *Socialist Register* (New York, 1964), pp. 259–79.

[37] Geoffrey Barraclough, *An Introduction to Contemporary History* (Harmondsworth, 1967), pp. 56–67.

In 1962, in their chapter on African partition for the *New Cambridge Modern History*, Robinson and Gallagher extended their arguments to the other European partitioners.[38] Proto-nationalisms provoked French intervention in Tunis in 1881, which was strategically motivated to secure France's Mediterranean position. Muslim resistance offered throughout the Sudanic belt, in East Africa, and the Congo basin was similarly seen as proto-nationalist awakenings, luring the European partitioners into the so-called age of imperialism.

These two works were published just as British, French, and Belgian colonies in tropical Africa became independent. African scholars at the new universities were much attracted to the new interpretation, despite its strictures against economic explanations. If there was one thing Africanists hated more than the Eurocentric view that Africa had 'no history', it was the assertion that historical change in Africa was exclusively the work of European agency. Robinson and Gallagher seemed to turn this upside-down, explaining European scrambling in Africa as the result of African initiatives. Moreover these were 'proto-nationalist' and thus appealed to those who were attempting to provide the contemporary nationalisms with historical depth.

In general, African scholars had shown little interest in the processes of European rivalry and scrambling for African territory. They preferred the search for origins in missionary and social history, where could be found the early nationalism of educated élites. The outstanding exception is Godfrey Uzoigwe's well-documented study *Britain and the Conquest of Africa*, published in 1974.[39] Resistance to partition and colonial rule, however, proved to be much more attractive to African scholars, and Robinson and Gallagher's approach helped to stimulate such studies. Even more so the controversial article by T. O. Ranger in 1968,[40] which argued that there was a connected history of nationalism from the primary resistance to European occupation, through secondary rebellions, milleniary movements, élite nationalism of educated elements, up to modern mass nationalism. Much work on Central and Southern African resistance followed, though it appears that West Africans were more sceptical of the thesis.[41] Resistance studies established themselves as a sub-theme of partition history in the 1970s,

[38] 'The Partition of Africa', in F. H. Hinsley, ed., *New Cambridge Modern History*, Vol. XI (Cambridge, 1962).

[39] G. N. Uzoigwe, *Britain and the Conquest of Africa: The Age of Salisbury* (Ann Arbor, 1974).

[40] T. O. Ranger, 'Connexions between "Primary Resistance" Movements and Modern Mass Nationalism in East and Central Africa', *JAH*, IX, 3 (1968), pp. 437–53, and *JAH*, IX, 4, pp. 631–41.

[41] Michael Crowder, ed., *West African Resistance: The Military Response to Colonial Occupation* (London, 1971), suggested in the introduction that these West African case studies would show Ranger's thesis as applicable to West as well as Central Africa, but few of the contributors seemed to share this view.

with a large number of monographs, often by Africans, which argued that patterns of African resistance or collaboration shaped the nature of partition.[42]

By the late 1960s a considerable wealth of regional case studies of the Scramble had been amassed, and co-operative volumes began to emerge. Prosser Gifford and Wm. Roger Louis edited volumes stressing comparative studies of the colonial powers, with material on partition which remains of great value.[43] L. H. Gann and Peter Duignan's first volume of *Colonialism in Africa* contained chapters on the Scramble by European, American, and South African authors.[44]

Detailed studies of local scrambles were virtually completed by the end of the 1970s,[45] including John S. Galbraith's books on the British chartered companies in East and South Africa[46] and Iain R. Smith's on the Emin Pasha relief expedition.[47] The debate about motives and causes continued unabated. D. K. Fieldhouse, in his *Economics and Empire*,[48] extended the Robinson and Gallagher thesis, while rejecting its stress on Egypt and proto-nationalism outside Africa to argue that imperial expansion everywhere after 1880 was caused by simultaneous crises in the periphery, themselves the result of earlier European informal penetration. John Hargreaves began publishing his magisterial work on West African partition in 1974,[49] which reinforced the view that France and Britain had diverse interests to maintain long before the Egyptian occupation.

The 1980s saw attention among scholars shift to South African partition, as South Africa became *the* political issue of the continent. Liberal–Marxist polarization became central to controversies over interpretation, with the left provocatively led

[42] Early examples were R. A. Adeleye, *Power and Diplomacy in Northern Nigeria, 1804–1906* (London, 1971); Francis Agbodeka, *African Politics and British Policy on the Gold Coast, 1868–1900* (London, 1971); and B. O. Oloruntimehin, *The Segu Tukulor Empire* (Ibadan, 1972). Boniface I. Obichere, *West African States and European Expansion: The Dahomey–Niger Hinterland, 1885–1898* (New Haven, 1971), was directly concerned with the way African states helped to shape the partition. See also Obichere's article 'The African Factor in the Establishment of French Authority in West Africa, 1880–1900', in Prosser Gifford and Wm. Roger Louis, eds., *France and Britain in Africa: Imperial Rivalry and Colonial Rule* (New Haven, 1971).

[43] Prosser Gifford and Wm. Roger Louis, eds., *Britain and Germany in Africa: Imperial Rivalry and Colonial Rule* (New Haven, 1967) and *France and Britain in Africa*.

[44] L. H. Gann and Peter Duignan, eds., *Colonialism in Africa, 1870–1960*, Vol. I, *The History and Politics of Colonialism, 1870–1914* (London, 1969).

[45] A full listing of works relating to the Scramble published before 1984 can be found in Roland Oliver and G. N. Sanderson, *The Cambridge History of Africa*, Vol. VI, *From 1870 to 1905* (Cambridge, 1985), pp. 824–91.

[46] John S. Galbraith, *Mackinnon and East Africa, 1878–1895: A Study in the 'New Imperialism'* (Cambridge, 1972) and *Crown and Charter: The Early Years of the British South Africa Company* (Berkeley, 1974).

[47] Iain R. Smith, *The Emin Pasha Relief Expedition, 1886–90* (Oxford, 1972).

[48] D. K. Fieldhouse, *Economics and Empire, 1830–1914* (London, 1973).

[49] John D. Hargreaves, *West Africa Partitioned*, Vol. I, *The Loaded Pause, 1885–89* (London, 1974). Vol. II, *The Elephants and the Grass*, appeared in 1985.

by Shula Marks,[50] triggering responses by Robert V. Kubicek,[51] A. N. Porter,[52] and D. M. Schreuder.[53] A. Keppel-Jones published a massively documented study of the white occupation of Zimbabwe,[54] while Robert I. Rotberg wrote the fullest and best documented biography of Cecil Rhodes yet to appear.[55]

Recent years have seen a shift among historians of the Scramble into studies of decolonization, which many of them see as a 'mirror image' of their earlier work.[56] Consequently, recent co-operative works dealing with the partition tend to be reflective assessments and syntheses. Outstanding among these is Volume VI of the *Cambridge History of Africa*.[57] The volume is dominated by partition themes, with attention to the role of all the European powers from French and Belgian authors, and important contributions from G. N. Sanderson, John D. Hargreaves, Shula Marks, and John Lonsdale, each of whom writes from distinctly individual perspectives. Read in conjunction, the result is the fullest and most recent survey of partition.

The same year, 1985, also saw the publication of Volume VII of the UNESCO *General History of Africa*, entitled *Africa under Colonial Domination*, edited by the Ghanaian historian A. Adu Boahen. All but three of the contributors were Africans, with G. N. Uzoigwe providing an overview chapter discussing previous interpretations of partition and conquest and stressing the need for an 'African dimension'. This theme is set up in T. O. Ranger's chapter on African initiatives and resistance, which forms the framework for all the subsequent regional chapters. The volume is thus more a history of African resistance than of the Scramble itself. Another notable co-operative volume was produced by the scholarly conference in Berlin on the centenary of the Berlin Conference of 1884–85.[58] This brought together many of those who had pioneered the academic study of the Scramble, and included a significant number of African contributors.

While researchers have by now thoroughly mined the main archival collections and major new 'revelations' are unlikely, the field continues to be lively with

[50] See her article 'Scrambling for South Africa', *JAH*, XXIII, 1 (1982), pp. 97–113.

[51] Robert V. Kubicek, *Economic Imperialism in Theory and Practice: The Case of South African Gold Mining Finance, 1886–1914* (Durham, NC, 1979).

[52] A. N. Porter, *The Origin of the South African War: Joseph Chamberlain and the Diplomacy of Imperialism, 1895–1899* (Manchester, 1980).

[53] D. M. Schreuder, *The Scramble for Southern Africa, 1877–1895* (Cambridge, 1980).

[54] A. Keppel-Jones, *Rhodes and Rhodesia: The White Conquest of Zimbabwe, 1884–1902* (Kingston, Ont., 1983).

[55] Robert I. Rotberg, *The Founder: Cecil Rhodes and the Pursuit of Power* (Oxford, 1988).

[56] See chap. by John Darwin.

[57] Oliver and Sanderson, eds., *Cambridge History*, VI.

[58] Stig Förster, Wolfgang J. Mommsen, and Ronald Robinson, eds., *Bismarck, Europe and Africa: The Berlin Africa Conference, 1884–1885, and the Onset of Partition* (Oxford, 1988).

continuous reappraisal. Earlier interpretations re-emerge in a new light, as in the innovative attempt by P. J. Cain and A. G. Hopkins to build a new interpretation of British imperialism as a product of 'gentlemanly capitalism'.[59] Taking Hobson's dictum that 'finance is the governor of the imperial engine', Imperial history is viewed from the City and the partition of Africa reinterpreted away from Robinson and Gallagher's strategic imperatives. The occupation of Egypt was not a conspiracy of bondholders, but it was a matter of restoring public finances there. Similarly, Southern Africa was occupied as a result of British investments and the crucial role of gold for the pound sterling. Even 'useless' tropical colonies provided safe havens for cautious investors in colonial bonds. The debate continues.

[59] P. J. Cain and A. G. Hopkins, *British Imperialism* (London, 1933), Vol. I, *Innovation and Expansion, 1688–1914*; Vol. II, *Crisis and Deconstruction, 1914–1990.*

Select Bibliography

A. ADU BOAHEN, ed., *General History of Africa*, Vol. VII, *Africa Under Colonial Domination, 1880–1935* (UNESCO, London, 1985).

D. K. FIELDHOUSE, *Economics and Empire, 1830–1914* (London, 1973).

JOHN E. FLINT, *Sir George Goldie and the Making of Nigeria* (London, 1960; repr. 1966).

JOHN S. GALBRAITH, *Mackinnon and East Africa, 1878–1895: A Study in the 'New Imperialism'* (Cambridge, 1972).

L. H. GANN and PETER DUIGNAN, eds., *Colonialism in Africa, 1870–1960*, Vol. I, *The History and Politics of Colonialism, 1870–1914* (Cambridge, 1969).

PROSSER GIFFORD and WM. ROGER LOUIS, eds., *Britain and Germany in Africa: Imperial Rivalry and Colonial Rule* (New Haven, 1967).

JOHN D. HARGREAVES, *West Africa Partitioned*, Vol. I, *The Loaded Pause, 1885–1889* (London, 1974); Vol. II, *The Elephants and the Grass* (London, 1985).

J. A. HOBSON, *Imperialism: A Study* (London, 1902).

WILLIAM L. LANGER, *The Diplomacy of Imperialism, 1890–1902*, 2 vols. (New York, 1935; 2nd edn. with supplementary bibliography, 1951).

WM. ROGER LOUIS, ed., *Imperialism: The Robinson and Gallagher Controversy* (New York, 1976).

PARKER THOMAS MOON, *Imperialism and World Politics* (New York, 1926).

COLIN W. NEWBURY, *The Western Slave Coast and its Rulers: European Trade and Administration among the Yoruba and Adja-Speaking Peoples of South-Western Nigeria, Southern Dahomey and Togo* (Oxford, 1961).

ROLAND OLIVER and G. N. SANDERSON, *The Cambridge History of Africa*, Vol. VI, *From 1870 to 1905* (Cambridge, 1985).

MARGERY PERHAM, *Lugard: The Years of Adventure, 1858–1898* (London, 1956).

A. N. PORTER, *The Origins of the South African War: Joseph Chamberlain and the Diplomacy of Imperialism, 1895–1899* (Manchester, 1980).

Ronald Robinson and John Gallagher with Alice Denny, *Africa and the Victorians: The Official Mind of Imperialism* (London, 1961; 2nd edn. 1981).

Robert I. Rotberg, *The Founder: Cecil Rhodes and the Pursuit of Power* (New York, 1988).

G. N. Sanderson, *England, Europe and the Upper Nile, 1882–1899: A Study in the Partition of Africa* (Edinburgh, 1976).

D. M. Schreuder, *The Scramble for Southern Africa, 1877–1895: The Politics of Partition Reappraised* (Cambridge, 1980).

G. N. Uzoigwe, *Britain and the Conquest of Africa: The Age of Salisbury* (Ann Arbor, 1974).

30

The British Empire in Tropical Africa: A Review of the Literature to the 1960s

A. D. ROBERTS

Amateur Beginnings

It was only in the 1890s, when the Scramble was in its last stages, that a literature on the British past in tropical Africa began to emerge. The subject, of course, reached back to the sixteenth century, but formal control by government had been confined to the littoral of Senegambia (1765–83), Sierra Leone (1808–), the Gambia, (1821–), the Gold Coast (1821–27, 1843–), Lagos (1861–), and Mombasa (1824–26), even if by 1860 Zanzibar was firmly in the sphere of the British in Bombay. For most of the nineteenth century British tropical Africa seemed a small subject, and attracted little retrospective consideration. Thomas Clarkson remained the principal authority on the slave trade and its abolition.[1] The genesis of a British presence in West Africa was briefly noted in a compendium of 1835,[2] but the only other relevant works, for many years, were essentially—like Clarkson's—extensions of the personal memoir, whether missionary[3] or military.[4] A growing sense of shared history among the Krio (Creoles) of Sierra Leone

[1] Thomas Clarkson, *The History of the Rise, Progress and Accomplishment of the Abolition of the African Slave Trade by the British Parliament* (London, 1808). Cf. A. P. Newton, *An Introduction to the Study of Colonial History* (London, 1919), p. 35; Judith Blow Williams, *A Guide to the Printed Materials for English Social and Economic History, 1750–1850*, 2 vols. (New York, 1926; repr. 1966), II, p. 416. The first scholarly approach to the subject was W. E. B. Du Bois, *The Suppression of the African Slave Trade to the U.S.A., 1638–1870* (Cambridge, Mass., 1896).

[2] R. M. Martin, *History of the British Colonies*, 4 vols., IV (London, 1835), IV, pp. 535–68.

[3] William Fox, *A Brief History of the Wesleyan Missions on the Coast of Africa* (London, 1851), pp. 203–605 constitute a collective biography of missionaries in Sierra Leone, the Gambia and the Gold Coast from 1792 to 1850; John Leighton Wilson, *Western Africa: Its History, Condition and Prospects* (London, 1856). Henry Seddall, *The Missionary History of Sierra Leone* (London, 1874); this is confined to the Church Missionary Society.

[4] A. A. Gore, *A Contribution to the Medical History of Our West African Campaigns* (London, 1876); this is primarily an account of Asante in 1873.

found expression in books by Horton and Sibthorpe.[5] Then, in the 1890s, the process of partition excited new interest in tropical Africa among various kinds of readers; furthermore, this coincided with developments in historical scholarship which gradually began to impinge on the study of British expansion in Africa.

In the years between 1890 and 1920 several genres may be discerned. There was the territorial narrative, a by-product of service in tropical Africa and addressed chiefly to others with African experience. Sources tended to be cited erratically; they might include *Parliamentary Papers*, and even unpublished materials, but British public records were mostly unavailable.[6] None the less, some serious work was done. For the Gold Coast, note should be made of A. B. Ellis, a British army officer; C. C. Reindorf, an African mission pastor;[7] and especially W. W. Claridge, a medical officer.[8] In Sierra Leone, J. J. Crooks, a senior civil servant, transferred early government records to London and in retirement compiled a history;[9] a more limited study by Claude George, an African official, drew partly on records that have since vanished.[10] Another type of history was the quasi-official *apologia* for Britain's role in partition: P. L. McDermott on the Imperial British East Africa Company (IBEA),[11] R. N. Lyne on Zanzibar,[12] and Flora Lugard on Northern Nigeria.[13] The theme was systematically expounded by John Scott Keltie, editor of the *Geographical Journal*, who was helped by several participants: John Kirk, George Goldie, and officials of the IBEA Company.[14] In a third genre, British activity in Africa was brought to the attention of a wider audience: by Robert

5 J. Africanus Horton, *West African Countries and Peoples* (London, 1868; 2nd edn., Edinburgh, 1969); A. B. C. Sibthorpe, *History of Sierra Leone* (London, 1868; 2nd edn., 1881).

6 In 1868 the open date for Colonial Office records was advanced to 1760; in 1903 that for Foreign Office records was advanced to 1780; from 1909 both archives were open to 1837. P[ublic] R[ecord] O[ffice], *Records of the Foreign Office, 1782–1939* (London, 1969), p. 93; Anne Thurston, *Records of the Colonial Office, Dominions Office, Commonwealth Relations Office and Commonwealth Office* (London, 1995), p. 64.

7 A. B. Ellis, *History of the Gold Coast of West Africa* (London, 1893); C. C. Reindorf, *History of the Gold Coast and Asante, Based on Traditions and Historical Facts . . .* (Basle, 1895).

8 W. W. Claridge, *The History of the Gold Coast and Ashanti*, 2 vols. (London, 1915). See the introduction by W. E. F. Ward to the reprint (London, 1964).

9 J. J. Crooks, *A History of the Colony of Sierra Leone, Western Africa* (Dublin, 1903).

10 Claude George, *The Rise of British West Africa, Comprising the Early History of the Colony of Sierra Leone* (London, 1903). See Christopher Fyfe, *A History of Sierra Leone* (London, 1962), pp. 494–95.

11 P. L. McDermott, *British East Africa Company or, IBEA, A History of the Formation and Work of the Imperial British East Africa Company* (London, 1893; 2nd, enlarged edn., 1895). The author was assistant, and then acting, Secretary to the Company, and drew on its records.

12 R. N. Lyne, *Zanzibar in Contemporary Times: A Short History of the Southern East in the Nineteenth Century* (London, 1905). This was approved by Kirk before publication.

13 Lady Lugard, *A Tropical Dependency* (London, 1905).

14 John Scott Keltie, *The Partition of Africa* (London, 1893). Cf. *British Africa* (London, 1901) by various authors, including Mary Kingsley.

Brown, a veteran popularizer for the publishing firm of Cassell;[15] Edgar Sanderson, a retired headmaster;[16] and Harry Johnston, while Consul at Tunis.[17] Fourth, there was the compendium which purported to combine high academic and official credentials: a medium dominated by C. P. Lucas (later Sir Charles) from the Colonial Office and All Souls, Oxford.[18]

1900–1945

Professional scholarship first addressed the subject by turning away from the nineteenth century and focusing instead on the first British companies to trade in West Africa. This was an outgrowth of two related trends in historiography around 1900. The economic history of Britain was being systematically investigated, while on both sides of the Atlantic research was advancing on the history of mercantilist enterprise overseas.[19] The academic beginnings of the subject are to be found in a dissertation by Edward Day Collins, presented to Yale in 1899, on the Royal African Company.[20] Mysteriously, this considerable work seems to have remained unknown to all subsequent writers on the subject, though it drew on material in the Public Record Office (PRO) which formed the basis of an article in 1902 by a pioneer of business history, W. R. Scott of St Andrews.[21] A few years later these African company records were catalogued and described by Hilary

[15] Robert Brown, MA, Ph.D., *The Story of Africa and its Explorers* (London, 1892–94), 4 vols. Brown (ibid., IV, p. 105 n.) knew J. Africanus Horton, the Sierra Leone doctor and author of *West African Countries and Peoples: British and Native*. See also S. Nowell-Smith, *The House of Cassell, 1848–1954* (London, 1958), p. 104.

[16] Edgar Sanderson, *Africa in the Nineteenth Century* (London, 1898); see also DNB.

[17] H. H. Johnston, *A History of the Colonization of Africa by Alien Races* (Cambridge, 1899; 2nd edn., 1905; 3rd edn., 1913), chaps. 6, 9, 12.

[18] C. P. Lucas, *A Historical Geography of the British Colonies*, Vol. III, *West Africa* (Oxford; 1st edn. with R. L. Antrobus, 1894; 2nd edn. revised by H. E. Egerton; 3rd edn. revised by A. B. Keith, 1913); Vol. IV, *South and East Africa*, part I, *Historical* (Oxford, 1897). In 1913 it was hoped to devote a separate volume to central and East Africa, but this never appeared. *The Oxford Survey of the British Empire* was in a similar mould: cf. Vol. III, *Africa* (Oxford, 1914).

[19] Cf. publications between 1893 and 1908 listed in Godfrey Davies, *Bibliography of British History, 1603–1714* (Oxford, 1928), pp. 186–90.

[20] Edward Day Collins, 'The Royal African Company: A Study of the English Trade to Western Africa under Chartered Companies from 1585 to 1750', unpublished Ph.D. dissertation, Yale, 1899. From this research, Collins (1869–1940) published only a paper on the Company's dealings in the West Indies. He later became President of Middlebury College, Vermont.

[21] William R. Scott, 'The Constitution and Finance of the Royal African Company', *American Historical Review* (hereafter *AHR*), VIII (1902–03), pp. 241–59; see also W. R. Scott, *The Constitution and Finance of English, Scotch and Irish Joint Stock Companies to 1720*, 3 vols., II (Cambridge, 1910), pp. 3–35.

Jenkinson; he reflected on the opportunities and problems facing 'anyone who wishes to write—it has not been done—the history of the African Slave Trade'.[22] The African companies' charters were published by the Selden Society in 1913;[23] Charles Andrews, of Yale, published a list of PRO records relating to these companies;[24] and meanwhile another American scholar, George Zook, had studied the Royal Adventurers of 1662–72.[25]

This was the context in which several theses on early British activities in West Africa were supervised in London by A. P. Newton, of King's College, who in 1921 became Rhodes Professor of Imperial History.[26] One such thesis was published in 1927: Eveline C. Martin's study of the Company of Merchants Trading to Africa (1750–1821). A note of cool detachment is soon struck: 'The annals of the Company . . . provide little material for those in search of the heroic in empire-building, while the villains they provide could be outmatched in almost any London newspaper of the time.'[27] Martin's book is an admirable examination of British officialdom in the Gold Coast, Senegambia, and Sierra Leone, but it is not concerned with traders *per se*, and relations with Africans are noted only incidentally.[28] It was some years before these latter subjects were to be taken up by professional historians of Martin's period. However, much relevant documentation was published between the wars, by J. J. Crooks,[29]

[22] Hilary Jenkinson, 'Records of the English African Companies', *Transactions of the Royal Historical Society* (hereafter *TRHS*), Third Series, VI (1912), p. 206. Jenkinson (1882–1961) became Deputy Keeper of the Records in 1947; see DNB.

[23] C. T. Carr, *Select Charters of Trading Companies, A.D. 1530–1707* (London, 1913), pp. 99–105, 172–81, 186–92.

[24] C. M. Andrews, *Guide to the Materials for American History to 1783, in the Public Record Office of Great Britain*, 2 vols., II (Washington, 1914), pp. 255–59.

[25] G. F. Zook, 'The Royal Adventurers Trading into Africa', Ph.D. dissertation, Cornell, 1914; published as *The Company of Royal Adventurers Trading into Africa* (Lancaster, Pa., 1919). Zook (1885–1951) intended to follow this with a history of the Royal African Company, 1672–1750 (ibid., p. iv), but instead pursued a career in educational administration, see *Dictionary of American Biography*, supplement 5 (1977), pp. 761–62.

[26] Kate M. Eliot, 'The Beginnings of English Trade with Guinea and the East Indies, 1550–1559', unpublished MA thesis, London, 1915 (Eliot was at Westfield College); Thora G. Stone, 'The Struggle for Power on the Senegal and Gambia, 1660–1713', unpublished MA thesis, London, 1921; Eveline C. Martin, 'English Establishments on the Gold Coast in the Second Half of the Eighteenth Century', MA thesis, London, 1921, cf. *TRHS*, Fourth Series, V (1922), pp. 167–208.

[27] Eveline C. Martin, *The British West African Settlements, 1750–1821: A Study in Local Administration* (London, 1927), p. 16. This was a Ph.D. thesis (London, 1926); it is summarized in E. A. Benians and others, eds. *Cambridge History of the British Empire* (hereafter *CHBE*), 9 vols., I (Cambridge, 1929), chap. 15. Eveline Martin (1894–1960) taught at Westfield College from 1923 and was Reader in Imperial History at London, 1932–59. She edited Nicholas Owen, *Journal of a Slave Dealer [1746–57]* (London, 1930).

[28] Martin, *British West African Settlements*, pp. 50–54, 151–61.

[29] John Joseph Crooks, *Records Relating to the Gold Coast Settlements from 1750 to 1874* (Dublin, 1923; repr. London, 1973). J. J. Crooks, *Historical Records of the Royal African Corps* (Dublin, 1925).

Ruth A. Fisher,[30] and Elizabeth Donnan.[31] And in the 1930s another Newton student, J. W. Blake, looked again at the beginnings of European rivalries in West Africa; his thesis was also published,[32] and was followed by a matching selection of documents.[33] Meanwhile, academic research in the PRO was extended to West Africa in the nineteenth century: in 1919 the 'open date' for Foreign Office and Colonial Office records was brought forward to 1860; in 1925 to 1878; and in 1930 to 1885. Early in the 1920s Newton supervised a thesis on the suppression of the slave trade, and himself wrote on the subject.[34] In the 1930s two more of his students focused on British policy in Sierra Leone and the Gold Coast.[35] The growth of 'legitimate trade' in the earlier nineteenth century began to receive attention: in Massachusetts in an unduly neglected article by the eminent bibliographer Judith Blow Williams,[36] and in Birmingham from a pupil of W. K. Hancock.[37] Beyond the academy, valuable work on the Gambia was done by J. M. Gray, a judge there since 1934,[38] while the fourth Baron Leconfield consulted Colonial Office files for his study of slavery and emancipation, though he did not give much prominence to British activities in West Africa.[39]

The British connection with East Africa derived largely from the suppression

30 Ruth A. Fisher, ed., *Extracts from the Records of the African Companies* (Washington, *c.*1930).

31 Elizabeth Donnan, *Documents Illustrative of the History of the Slave Trade to America*, 4 vols. (Washington, 1930–35). Between 1920 and 1938 the PRO published, in 14 vols., the *Journal of the Commissioners for Trade and Plantations* (1704–82), which has much material bearing on West Africa.

32 J. W. Blake, *European Beginnings in West Africa* (London, 1937); this originated in an MA thesis (London, 1935). A 2nd edn. appeared in 1977, with the title *West Africa: Quest for God and Gold, 1454–1578*.

33 J. W. Blake, trans. and ed., *Europeans in West Africa, 1450–1560*, 2 vols., Hakluyt Society (London, 1942).

34 Elsie I. Herrington, 'British Measures for the Suppression of the Slave Trade upon the West Coast of Africa, 1807–33', unpublished MA thesis, London, 1923. A. P. Newton, in A. W. Ward and G. P. Gooch, eds., *Cambridge History of British Foreign Policy*, Vol. II. *1815–66* (Cambridge, 1923), pp. 220–47.

35 P. G. James, 'British Policy in Relation to the Gold Coast, 1815–50', unpublished MA thesis, London, 1935; G. R. Mellor, 'British Policy in Relation to Sierra Leone, 1808–52', unpublished MA thesis, London, 1935. This was the kernel of Mellor's *British Imperial Trusteeship, 1783–1850* (London, 1951).

36 Judith Blow Williams, 'The Development of British Trade with West Africa, 1750 to 1850', *Political Science Quarterly*, L (1935), pp. 194–213. Williams taught at Wellesley College, Mass., as did Elizabeth Donnan.

37 N. H. Stilliard, 'The Rise and Development of Legitimate Trade in Palm Oil with West Africa', unpublished MA thesis, Birmingham, 1938.

38 John Milner Gray, *History of the Gambia* (Cambridge, 1940; new impression, London, 1966).

39 Hugh Archibald Wyndham, *The Atlantic and Slavery* (London, 1935) and *The Atlantic and Emancipation* (London, 1937). Wyndham (1877–1963) had devised a trilogy for the Royal Institute of International Affairs on 'Problems of Imperial Trusteeship', of which the first volume (1933) dealt with colonial education in South-East Asia. His first book was: Hugh Archibald Wyndham [Earl of Leconfield], *The Early History of the Thoroughbred Horse in South Africa* (London, 1924).

of slave trading by others. This cause was most famously associated with the career of David Livingstone, which by the 1920s had inspired many a hagiography but no critical research.[40] However, the campaign against the East African slave trade also owed much to John Kirk, Consul at Zanzibar between 1868 and 1887. Kirk died in 1922; when his son sought a biographer, he turned to Reginald Coupland, Beit Professor of Colonial History at Oxford. Coupland had lately published a biography of Wilberforce; this laid no claim to original research, but it introduced him to the controlling theme of his most important work: the history of British humanitarianism.[41] Coupland soon saw that, with the papers at his disposal, Kirk's experience as botanist and doctor on Livingstone's Zambezi expedition (1858–63) merited a book in its own right. This duly appeared in 1928,[42] and Coupland moved on to study Kirk's career at Zanzibar. He realized, however, that to make sense of this he needed to examine the earlier history of Zanzibar, and this in turn became the subject of a large-scale study. Drawing on records of the Foreign Office and India Office, and archives in Zanzibar, Coupland traced the growth of British interests in the western Indian Ocean from the eighteenth century.[43] By the time his book appeared in 1938 there were also biographies of C. P. Rigby, Political Agent in Zanzibar (1858–62),[44] and Lloyd Mathews, commander of the Sultan's army (1877–1901).[45] Meanwhile, under Newton's supervision in London, Mabel Jackson (a former student of W. M. Macmillan in South Africa) completed an enterprising study of European rivalries further south in the earlier nineteenth century.[46] In 1936–37 Coupland served on the Royal Commission on Palestine; when he finally came to write on Kirk in Zanzibar, he was driven on by his determination both to complete the task before war broke out in Europe and to set out the British record in East Africa at a time

[40] The most careful biography was also among the first: W. G. Blaikie, *The Personal Life of David Livingstone* (London, 1880). On Livingstone see chap. by Robert A. Stafford.

[41] See J. D. Fage, introduction to R. Coupland, *The British Anti-Slavery Movement* (London, 1933; 2nd edn., 1964), pp. ix–xxi; Ronald Robinson, 'Oxford in Imperial Historiography', in A. F. Madden and D. K. Fieldhouse, eds., *Oxford and the Idea of Commonwealth* (London, 1982), pp. 36–38.

[42] R. Coupland, *Kirk on the Zambesi* (Oxford, 1928; repr. 1968).

[43] R. Coupland, *East Africa and its Invaders: From the Earliest Times to the Death of Seyyid Said in 1856* (Oxford, 1938). Coupland travelled in East Africa in 1928.

[44] Mrs C. E. B. Russell (Lilian Rigby), *General Rigby, Zanzibar and the Slave Trade* (London, 1935).

[45] R. N. Lyne, *An Apostle of Empire, Being the Life of Sir Lloyd William Mathews, K.C.M.G.* (London, 1936).

[46] M. V. Jackson, 'International Relations on the South-East Coast of Africa, 1786–1856', Ph.D. thesis, London, 1938; this was published as M. V. Jackson Haight, *European Powers and South-East Africa* (London, 1942; 2nd edn., 1967). Drawing on the work of Jackson and earlier students, Newton contributed 'British Enterprise in Tropical Africa, 1783–1890', in Benians and others, eds., *CHBE*, II (Cambridge, 1940), pp. 633–76.

when it seemed that appeasing Germany might yet involve colonial concessions in Africa.[47] *The Exploitation of East Africa, 1856–1890: The Slave Trade and the Scramble* (London) was completed and published, with remarkable speed, in 1939; what the outbreak of war delayed was a study of Livingstone's last expedition which Coupland had begun some years earlier but put aside: though enriched by materials unavailable to previous writers, it scarcely marked a new approach.[48]

Coupland's *Exploitation*, despite its challenging title, disdained to mention the most substantial attempt so far by a British writer to explain the Scramble, Leonard Woolf's *Empire and Commerce in Africa*, even though this had paid special attention to Zanzibar and East Africa. Woolf, indeed, was far removed from academic discourse on Empire in Oxford or London. His book was written as a report for the research department of the Labour Party; in the aftermath of the First World War, it argued that 'our generation . . . has come to regard the main function of the state as the pursuit of national economic interests by means of organized national power'.[49] Woolf had not read deeply on Africa, nor (more surprisingly) does his discussion of 'economic imperialism' refer either to his friend J. A. Hobson or to Marxist writers, but he raised questions which for long were avoided by professional historians. A less provocative sketch of partition was supplied in 1923 by W. H. Dawson, the veteran historian of imperial Germany.[50] In the United States the subject was addressed in Parker T. Moon's influential textbook, and more extensively investigated by William L. Langer, on the basis of recently published diplomatic documents.[51] By the 1930s British public records bearing on the earlier phases of partition were available, and research students began to turn them to account. In London, Newton supervised a thesis on European rivalries on the West African coast;[52] at the London School of Economics (LSE), Daphne

[47] J. Simmons, introduction to R. Coupland, *The Exploitation of East Africa, 1856–1890: The Slave Trade and the Scramble* (London, 1939; 2nd edn., 1968). Coupland had been much helped by Simmons. *Exploitation* was trenchantly reviewed by Harry Rudin of Yale in the *AHR*, XLV (1939–40), pp. 875–76. Coupland contributed 'The Abolition of the Slave Trade' in Benians and others, eds., *CHBE*, II, pp. 188–216.

[48] R. Coupland, *Livingstone's Last Journey* (London, 1945).

[49] Leonard Woolf, *Empire and Commerce in Africa: A Study in Economic Imperialism* (London, 1920; repr. 1968), p. 6. J. H. Oldham was much impressed: see his review in *International Review of Missions* (hereafter *IRM*), IX (1920), p. 461.

[50] W. H. Dawson, 'Imperial Policy in the Old and the New World', in A. W. Ward and G. P. Gooch, eds., *Cambridge History of British Foreign Policy*, Vol. III, *1866–1919* (Cambridge, 1923), pp. 200–22 and 242–58. See also C. P. Lucas, *The Partition and Colonisation of Africa* (Oxford, 1922).

[51] Parker T. Moon, *Imperialism in World Politics* (New York, 1926); William L. Langer, *The Diplomacy of Imperialism, 1890–1902* (New York, 1935; 2nd edn. 1951). See chap. by John E. Flint.

[52] William H. Scotter, 'International Rivalry in the Bights of Benin and Biafra, 1815–85', unpublished Ph.D. thesis, London, 1933.

Trevor, a former Macmillan student, dilated upon British expansion into Bechuanaland and Rhodesia.[53] As a third German empire loomed in Europe, German ambitions in Africa, and British reactions, were studied in Bedford College, under Lillian Penson;[54] in Manchester by A. J. P. Taylor;[55] and in Cambridge, under Harold Temperley.[56] It was for Cambridge, moreover, that S. E. Crowe wrote what is still the standard work on the Berlin West African conference of 1884–85.[57]

By the Second World War, then, a beginning had been made in the academic study of British expansion in nineteenth-century tropical Africa. The twentieth century was normally beyond the scope of the professional historian. However, access to official archives mattered more to political historians then it did to those (still few in any field) interested in economics. Lilian Knowles, who in 1921 became Professor of Economic History at the LSE, firmly believed that her subject could and should encompass the British Empire, present as well as past.[58] In 1922 she launched Allan McPhee, an economics graduate, on a thesis which became *The Economic Revolution in British West Africa* (London, 1926), focusing on changes since the 1890s though giving them a nineteenth-century context. On the basis of printed sources, McPhee analysed key factors in change so acutely that his work was still a necessary point of departure fifty years later.[59] McPhee's subsequent career diverted him from Imperial history, but the kinds of question he addressed were taken up by other economists. In 1932 Austin Robinson, at Cambridge, was recruited for an enquiry, on behalf of the International Missionary Council, into the social effects of copper mining in Northern Rhodesia: he examined the growth of the industry, its labour demands, and its implications for agriculture. Robinson does not cite McPhee's work, but he came

53 Daphne Trevor, 'Public Opinion and the Acquisition of Bechuanaland and Rhodesia, 1868–1896', unpublished Ph.D. thesis, London, 1936.

54 Margaret A. Adams, 'The British Attitude to German Colonial Development, 1880–85', unpublished MA thesis, London, 1935. Penson also supervised Irene Bains, 'British Policy in Relation to Portuguese Claims in West Africa, 1876–84', unpublished MA thesis, London, 1940. See also O. T. Lewis, 'British Relations with Zanzibar, 1880–86', unpublished MA, thesis, Wales, 1936.

55 A. J. P. Taylor, *Germany's First Bid for Colonies, 1884–1885: A Move in Bismarck's European Policy* (London, 1938).

56 William Osgood Aydelotte, *Bismarck and British Colonial Policy: The Problem of South West Africa, 1883–1885* (Philadelphia, 1937), based on a Cambridge thesis (Ph.D., 1934–35).

57 S. E. Crowe, *The Berlin West African Conference, 1884–1885* (London, 1942), based on a Cambridge thesis (Ph.D., 1939). The Italian invasion of Ethiopia prompted Enid Starkie, in Oxford, to make a pioneering study of Anglo-French rivalry in the Red Sea region, for which she used British sources up to 1890: *Arthur Rimbaud in Abyssinia* (Oxford, 1937).

58 L. C. A. Knowles, *The Economic Development of the British Overseas Empire*, 2 vols., I (London, 1924).

59 A. G. Hopkins, introduction to Allan McPhee, *The Economic Revolution in British West Africa*, 2nd edn. (London, 1971), p. ix.

close to echoing his title, likening economic transition in Northern Rhodesia to the European industrial revolution.[60] In 1934 Robinson joined the team for Malcolm Hailey's African Research Survey, and wrote two long chapters (amounting to a book) on economic development: these were based on work by Charlotte Leubuscher, a refugee scholar from Germany who had made a pioneer study of black workers in South Africa.[61] Robinson's other main source was work by the South African economist S. Herbert Frankel, another Hailey conscript, whose own contribution to the *Survey* soon grew into a bulky separate volume.[62] Much of Frankel's *Capital Investment in Africa* consists of territorial studies, of tropical as well as southern Africa, informed by a historical perspective,[63] backed by statistical series, and by no means uncritical of Imperial management.[64] One official report, also published in 1938, deserves mention: Sir Alan Pim's far-researching financial and economic enquiry in Northern Rhodesia, which reviewed the past two decades in arguing for public investment in African welfare and education.[65] In the same year, Pim gave the Beit Lectures in Oxford, on African economic history: these leaned heavily on McPhee and Frankel.[66]

Meanwhile, two seasoned historians had turned their attention to the recent economic history of tropical Africa. W. M. Macmillan, who had taught Frankel history in Johannesburg but had left South Africa in 1932, also prepared material for Hailey which eventually became a separate book. This was *Africa Emergent: A Survey of Social, Political, and Economic Trends in British Africa* (London, 1938), interrupted but inspired by a study of the West Indies in 1935.[67] The book was a tract, rather than a treatise, but it analysed the economic and social trends and tensions which, in the author's view, justified greater intervention by the state. Macmillan helped to create a new climate of concern with the economics of Empire, in which W. K. Hancock decided, in 1937, to provide a sequel to his study

[60] E. A. G. Robinson, 'The Economic Problem', in J. Merle Davis, ed., *Modern Industry and the African* (London, 1933; 2nd edn. 1967), p. 203; cf. Sir Alec Cairncross, *Austin Robinson: The Life of an Economic Adviser* (Basingstoke, 1993), pp. 51–77.

[61] Lord Hailey, *An African Survey: A Survey of the Problems Arising in Africa South of the Sahara* (London, 1938), pp. 1309 n, 1325 n.

[62] The economic content of *An African Survey* is largely ignored in John W. Cell, *Hailey: A Study in British Imperialism, 1872–1969* (Cambridge, 1992), pp. 222–34.

[63] Cf. S. Herbert Frankel, *Capital Investment in Africa: Its Course and Effects* (London, 1938), pp. 3, 305–06. See also his *An Economist's Testimony: The Autobiography of S. Herbert Frankel* (Oxford, 1992), pp. 128–40.

[64] e.g. *Capital Investment*, pp. 173–91, on the interest burdens incurred by public debt.

[65] *Report of the Commission Appointed to Enquire into the Financial and Economic Position of Northern Rhodesia*, Col. 145 (London, 1938).

[66] Sir Alan Pim, *The Financial and Economic History of the African Tropical Territories* (Oxford, 1940).

[67] See John E. Flint, 'Macmillan as a Critic of Empire', in Hugh Macmillan and Shula Marks, eds., *Africa and Empire: W. M. Macmillan, Historian and Social Critic* (London, 1989), pp. 223–28.

of Commonwealth politics. This culminated in his masterly essay on 'The Evolution of the Traders' Frontier: West Africa', which illuminated the conflicting interests of traders, producers, and governments over more than half a century.[68]

The politics of British colonial Africa did not lack for commentators in the earlier twentieth century, but many were partisan, and it was rare for academic detachment to be combined with historical perspective. Significantly, some of the best work was done by foreigners. In 1911–12 the Belgian jurist Henri Rolin visited Rhodesia and made a searching report on the first decades of company rule and capitalist enterprise.[69] In the 1920s early colonial Kenya was sceptically reviewed by Norman Leys and McGregor Ross, who had both worked there.[70] Three academic studies came from the United States. The first, and most impressive, was the survey of sub-Saharan Africa in 1925–27 by Raymond Leslie Buell, who travelled widely in Africa as well as Europe.[71] The circumstances of this remarkable undertaking remain obscure.[72] It was sponsored by Harvard and Radcliffe, with much the same aims as Hailey's survey ten years later: to examine government responses to the problems arising from 'the impact of primitive peoples with an industrial civilization' (*sic*). Of the 700 pages devoted to British tropical Africa, almost half deal with Kenya (white settlers) and Tanganyika (the Mandate). Buell focused firmly on the allocation of land and labour in early colonial Africa and explored the tensions between vested interests; he was also alert to a variety of African protest movements. However, he left Harvard in 1927 and his interests changed; he had no Africanist students.[73] Meanwhile, A. N. Cook wrote a dissertation on the British in Nigeria, expanded much later for publication,[74] while James Aggrey, Assistant Vice-Principal of Achimota College in the Gold Coast, began a dissertation for

[68] W. K. Hancock, *Survey of British Commonwealth Affairs, 1918–1939*, Vol. II, pt. 2 (London, 1942), pp. 154–298; W. K. Hancock, *Country and Calling* (London, 1954), pp. 147, 167, 170. Cf. D. K. Fieldhouse, 'Keith Hancock and Imperial Economic History', in Madden and Fieldhouse, eds., *Oxford and the Idea of Commonwealth*, pp. 144–63.

[69] Henri Rolin, *Les Lois et l'administration de la Rhodésie* (Brussels, 1913); trans. Deborah Kirkwood, *Rolin's Rhodesia* (Bulawayo, 1978). Cf. also J. W. Fisher, 'The Development of Rhodesia under the British South Africa Company (1890–1914)', unpublished MA thesis, Wales, 1924.

[70] Norman Leys, *Kenya* (London, 1924); William McGregor Ross, *Kenya from Within: A Short Political History* (London, 1927). Less critical histories came from others who had worked in Africa: C. W. Hobley, *Kenya—From Chartered Company to Crown Colony* (London, 1929); W. N. M. Geary, *Nigeria under British Rule* (London, 1927); A. C. Burns, *A History of Nigeria* (London, 1929).

[71] Raymond Leslie Buell, *The Native Problem in Africa*, 2 vols. (New York, 1928). Coupland considered this 'a fair book and a candid book', *International Review of Missions*, XVIII (1929), p. 382.

[72] No light on the matter was shed by my researches in 1988 in the Harvard University archives, and among Buell's papers in the Houghton Library.

[73] From 1927 Buell (1896–1946) worked for the Foreign Policy Association in New York.

74 A. N. Cook, 'Nigeria: A Study in British Imperialism', Ph.D. dissertation, Pennsylvania, 1927; *British Enterprise in Nigeria* (Philadelphia, 1943; repr. New York, 1965).

Columbia University on British rule in West Africa, though he died two months later.[75] Early in the 1930s, on the Pacific coast, Marjorie Dilley made a careful, if library-bound, study of Kenya.[76] This was not known to Hancock when he wrote on Indians in Kenya,[77] but he did draw much upon the recent, admiring, biography of the settler leader Lord Delamere by Elspeth Huxley, who herself grew up in Kenya.[78] By 1941, when Hancock considered South Africa's northern neighbours, he was able to refer to a London thesis critical of segregation in Rhodesia.[79]

The Second World War interrupted production by research students, and to this extent marks a caesura in the subject. At a more advanced level—where knowledge was sought by the powerful—there was a measure of continuity, and some important innovation. The *African Survey* had whetted, rather than sated, the appetite for Imperial self-knowledge; it helped to inspire the Colonial Development and Welfare Act of 1940 which set a new premium on understanding Africa. One project carried out during the war had grown directly from the African Research Survey. In 1935 Hailey asked R. R. Kuczynski of the LSE to make a study of population statistics in Africa; like Frankel's work, this soon acquired a life of its own. In 1939 Kuczynski produced a huge volume on the British Mandates in West Africa,[80] and meanwhile had been engaged by the British government's Population Investigation Committee to make a demographic survey of the Colonial Empire, with a view to improving census procedures. War precluded census-taking, and Kuczynski's work became essentially historical. Two volumes on Africa duly appeared in 1948–49;[81] they are 'monuments of sceptical erudition, which tell us as much about the counters as about the counted: the author himself clearly valued them for the light they throw on colonial administration rather than the elusive facts of birth, migration and death.'[82] Another project which survived the outbreak of war was Leubuscher's study of economic policy in Tanganyika, which she pur-

[75] Edwin Smith, *Aggrey of Africa* (London, 1929), pp. 271–77.

[76] Marjorie, R. Dilley, 'British Policy in East Africa', unpublished Ph.D. dissertation, Washington, 1934; *British Policy in Kenya Colony* (New York, 1937; 2nd edn. 1966).

[77] W. K. Hancock, *Survey of British Commonwealth Affairs*, 2 vols., I (London, 1937), pp. 209–38.

[78] Elspeth Huxley, *White Man's Country*, 2 vols. (London, 1935).

[79] Roy MacGregor, 'Native Segregation in Southern Rhodesia: A Study of Social Policy', unpublished Ph.D. thesis, London, 1940; cf. Hancock, *Survey*, II (1942), pt. 2, p. 113 n. Macgregor, a schoolmaster and friend of A. S. Cripps, belonged in the 1930s to the London Group on African Affairs; in 1939 he joined the BBC and in 1943 went to Freetown for the British Council. Cf. Mona Macmillan, *Champion of Africa: W. M. Macmillan: The Second Phase* (Long Wittenham, 1985), pp. 98–99, 109, 162, 172.

[80] R. R. Kuczynski, *The Cameroons and Togoland: A Demographic Survey* (London, 1939).

[81] R. R. Kuczynski, *A Demographic Survey of the British Colonial Empire*, Vol. I (London, 1948); Vol. II (London, 1949).

[82] A. D. Roberts, 'The Earlier Historiography of Colonial Africa', *History in Africa*, V (1978), p. 160.

sued at Oxford.[83] And it was a new venture at Oxford which gave rise to further studies of British Africa between the wars. True, Coupland had had to abandon plans for a three-volume study of Kenya, on which Leubuscher and Margery Perham might have collaborated.[84] However, the university decided in 1941 to fund a series of projects in colonial research directed by Perham from Nuffield College. These generated studies of Legislative Councils in the Gold Coast, Northern Rhodesia, and Nigeria;[85] economic organization in Nigeria (on which Leubuscher made a contribution);[86] and European commercial firms in East Africa.[87]

1945–1967

After the war various factors combined to stimulate research into the history of tropical Africa. Military service had oriented several British historians towards study of the tropics.[88] New opportunities were created by the expansion of higher education and research within tropical Africa. After a decade of official deliberation, the Inter-University Council for Higher Education Overseas was founded: this facilitated the emergence of university colleges in Africa whose students, and teachers, could receive degrees from the University of London. Between 1946 and 1949 such colleges were established in Nigeria (Ibadan), the Gold Coast, and Uganda (Makerere), as well as in the Sudan and the West Indies. The Rhodesias followed in 1955; Dar es Salaam and Nairobi in 1961. The need for teachers encouraged research focused on Africa. Expatriates turned to local subjects and sources while working for higher degrees and developing courses on African history.[89] Adult education

[83] Charlotte Leubuscher, *Tanganyika Territory: A Study of Economic Policy Under Mandate* (London, 1944). It may be noted here that war did not deter Hancock from visiting West Africa in 1939–40: cf. *Country and Calling*, p. 187.

[84] George Bennett, 'British East Africa', in Robin W. Winks, ed., *The Historiography of the British Empire-Commonwealth: Trends, Interpretations, and Resources* (Durham, NC, 1966), p. 253.

[85] Martin Wight, *The Gold Coast Legislative Council* (London, 1947); J. W. Davidson, *The Northern Rhodesian Legislative Council* (London, 1948); Joan Wheare, *The Nigerian Legislative Council* (London, 1950).

[86] Margery Perham, ed., *Mining, Commerce and Finance in Nigeria* (London, 1948). Another Oxford teacher, John Mars, contributed chapters of some historical depth on foreign businesses, money, and banking. After the war, in Manchester, Leubuscher worked on *The West African Shipping Trade, 1909–59* (London, 1963).

[87] Kathleen Stahl, *The Metropolitan Organisation of British Colonial Trade* (London, 1951), pp. 179–290.

[88] e.g. John D. Fage, John D. Hargreaves, Kenneth Ingham, R. E. Robinson, G. N. Sanderson, and George A. Shepperson. More generally, see John D. Fage, 'British African Studies Since the Second World War: A Personal Account', *African Affairs*, LXXXVIII (1989), pp. 397–413.

[89] Cf. Eric Ashby with Mary Anderson, *Universities: British, Indian, African* (London, 1966), pp. 233, 239–40; Anthony Kirk-Greene, ed., *The Emergence of African History at British Universities: An Autobiographical Approach* (Oxford, 1995).

classes contributed to the demand for (and supply of) new knowledge. Institutes for social research, in East, West, and Central Africa, included history in their schemes. African graduates, mostly from the new colleges, began coming to Britain to do historical research. Amid such stimuli—and the post-war troubles of Empire—there was less and less room for the paternalist belief in Imperial mission which had prevailed in academic circles before the war. A new scepticism was abroad, and a new curiosity about African societies. There was also an important enlargement of material resources for historians of Empire. In 1948 the 'open date' for records of the Foreign Office and Colonial Office was brought forward from 1885 to 1902, which prompted a spate of new research on the partition.

The new special relationships with colleges in Africa reinforced London's position as the main academic centre for the subject, though other universities soon became significant. Within London, King's College, with its Rhodes Chair, remained preponderant. There was some continuity of focus from the pre-war era of A. P. Newton.[90] His successor, Vincent T. Harlow, supervised a thesis on British involvement with east-central Africa in the later nineteenth century;[91] he also took on an African scholar. Kenneth O. Dike, from Nigeria, had come (by way of Fourah Bay College, Sierra Leone) to do an MA at Aberdeen, which enabled him to spend a summer working on Nigerian history in Oxford with Jack Simmons (Beit lecturer, 1943–47).[92] It was Simmons who suggested Dike's subject of research—relations between the British and states of the Niger delta in the nineteenth century.[93] Harlow moved to Oxford in 1949; over the next decade his successor, Gerald S. Graham, supervised a series of theses on tropical Africa in the nineteenth century.[94] Two were by Nigerians, and one of them was Jacob Ajayi, who as an undergraduate at Leicester had been taught by Simmons.[95] At Westfield

[90] By the time he retired in 1938, Newton had supervised at least eight of the fourteen British theses in the field. Interestingly, up to 1940, nine out of seventeen such theses were by women.

[91] A. J. Hanna, *The Beginnings of Nyasaland and North-eastern Rhodesia, 1859–95* (Oxford, 1956), based on a London thesis (Ph.D., 1948).

[92] K. O. Dike, 'The Study of African History: The Present Position', in C. Ifemesia, ed., *Issues in African Studies and National Education* (Awka, Nigeria, 1988), p. 92.

[93] K. Onwuka Dike, *Trade and Politics in the Niger Delta, 1830–1885: An Introduction to the Economic and Political History of Nigeria* (Oxford, 1956), p. vi. The book was based on a London thesis (Ph.D., 1950).

[94] Freda Wolfson, 'British Relations with the Gold Coast, 1843–1880', unpublished Ph.D. thesis, 1951; L. W. Hollingsworth, 'The History of Zanzibar, 1891–1913', unpublished Ph.D. thesis, 1951; J. E. Flint, 'British Policy and Chartered Company Administration in Nigeria, 1879–1900', Ph.D. thesis, 1951—this became *Sir George Goldie and the Making of Nigeria* (London, 1960); C. C. Ifemesia, 'British Enterprise on the Niger, 1830–69', unpublished Ph.D. thesis, 1959.

[95] J. F. Ade Ajayi, *Christian Missions in Nigeria, 1841–1891: The Making of a New Elite* (London, 1965), p. xvi; the book was based on a London thesis (Ph.D., 1958). Simmons himself wrote *Livingstone and Africa* (London, 1955); see also his 'The Opening of Tropical Africa, 1870–1885', in Benians and others, eds., *CHBE*, III (Cambridge, 1959), pp. 65–94.

College, Eveline Martin, who had already supervised the Nigerian J. C. Anene,[96] looked after Graham's students during his Commonwealth tour in 1957–58.[97] By the late 1950s the subject had acquired momentum: at Ibadan Anene taught Emmanuel A. Ayandele, who went on to be supervised at King's by John E. Flint, a former student of Graham's.[98]

In Oxford Nuffield College remained for some years the main centre in the field. Margery Perham was busy with her biography of Lugard,[99] while assisting research on the British Mandate in Tanganyika by an American and an African from Southern Rhodesia,[100] as well as an indulgent study of colonial administrators by another American.[101] Others worked on economic history in East and Central Africa[102] and nineteenth-century West Africa.[103] Elsewhere in Oxford there was research on white settlers in Rhodesia and Kenya.[104] K. G. Davies completed a study of the Royal African Company which had originally been supervised by F. J. Fisher at the LSE.[105] At a tangent from all these endeavours, Thomas Hodgkin struck out on new paths from the Delegacy for Extra-Mural Studies. In 1947–50 he visited the Gold Coast, Nigeria, and the Sudan in order to promote extramural studies; as a result, he was drawn into African

[96] J. C. Anene, 'The Establishment . . . of Imperial Government in Southern Nigeria, 1891–1904', MA thesis, London, 1952; this was revised for publication as *Southern Nigeria in Transition, 1885–1906* (Cambridge, 1966).

[97] In 1953–54 Martin taught at the University College, Ibadan. In 1944 she had served on the Elliot Commission on higher education in West Africa.

[98] Emmanuel A. Ayandele, *The Missionary Impact on Modern Nigeria, 1842–1914* (London, 1966), p. xix; this book was based on a London thesis (Ph.D., 1964).

[99] Margery Perham, *Lugard: The Years of Adventure, 1858–1898* (London, 1956); *Lugard: The Years of Authority, 1898–1945* (London, 1960). Cf. Mary Bull, 'Writing the Biography of Lord Lugard', in Alison Smith and Mary Bull, eds., *Margery Perham and Colonial Rule in Africa* (London, 1991), pp. 117–36.

[100] Margaret L. Bates, 'Tanganyika under British Administration, 1920–1955', unpublished D.Phil. thesis, Oxford, 1959; B. T. G. Chidzero, *Tanganyika and International Trusteeship* (London, 1961), based on a dissertation for McGill (Ph.D., 1958) supervised by Cranford Pratt.

[101] Robert Heussler, *Yesterday's Rulers: The Making of the British Colonial Service* (Syracuse, NY, 1963).

[102] M. D. McWilliam, 'The East African Tea Industry, 1920–56', unpublished B.Litt. thesis, Oxford, 1957; William J. Barber, *The Economy of British Central Africa: A Case Study of Economic Development in a Dualistic Society* (London, 1961), based on an Oxford thesis (D.Phil., 1957).

[103] Cherry Gertzel, 'Imperial Policy towards British Settlements in West Africa, 1860–75', unpublished B.Litt. thesis, Oxford, 1953; 'John Holt: A British Merchant in West Africa in the Era of Imperialism', unpublished D.Phil. thesis, Oxford, 1959.

[104] Colin Leys, *European Politics in Southern Rhodesia* (Oxford, 1959); M. P. K. Sorrenson, *Origins of European Settlement in Kenya* (Nairobi, 1968), based on an Oxford thesis (D. Phil., 1962).

[105] K. G. Davies, *The Royal African Company* (London, 1957). Davies acquired his interest in the slave trade while working for the PRO under Sir Hilary Jenkinson.

political debate and was inspired to write a seminal study of African nationalism.[106]

In Cambridge the study of British tropical Africa was put in train by some of the first post-war research students, relying on their own initiative rather than that of their supervisors. The first lectures on the subject for undergraduates were given in 1948–49 by John Fage, who had studied company rule in Southern Rhodesia,[107] and John Gallagher, who had written on mid-nineteenth-century policy in West Africa.[108] Roland Oliver made a study of missionaries in East Africa, partly indebted to Coupland but leavened by irony.[109] Ronald Robinson appraised the moral dimension in British policy toward Central Africa.[110] Fage went to the Gold Coast, whence in 1959 he moved to the School of Oriental and African Studies (SOAS) in London. Oliver moved directly to SOAS and pioneered the pre-European history of Africa, but he also wrote a biography of Harry Johnston,[111] and supervised theses on British expansion.[112] Gallagher and Robinson remained in Cambridge and embarked on a joint enquiry into the motives for British expansion in Africa. They sought to rescue the subject from teleology, whether of Imperial apologists invoking philanthropy or critics of Empire invoking economics. They challenged J. R. Seeley's conception of Empire as an organism bound by ties of kinship and constitutional dependence; instead, they took up C. R. Fay's term 'informal empire' and looked for the connections between such exercise of influence and the emergence of formal empire. They were impressed by Hancock's focus on the interaction between metropolis and periphery; furthermore, they wrote in the aftermath of Indian independence, and from the perspective of a post-war Europe which itself

[106] Thomas Hodgkin, *Nationalism in Colonial Africa* (London, 1956); cf. his 'Where the Paths Began', in Christopher Fyfe, ed., *African Studies Since 1945: A Tribute to Basil Davidson* (London, 1976), pp. 6–10.

[107] J. D. Fage, 'The Achievement of Self-Government in Southern Rhodesia, 1898–1923', unpublished Ph.D. thesis, Cambridge, 1949; cf. his 'Reflections on the Genesis of Anglophone African History after World War II', *History in Africa*, XX (1993), pp. 15–26.

[108] J. Gallagher, 'Fowell Buxton and the New African Policy', *Cambridge Historical Journal*, X (1950), pp. 36–58; see also his 'Economic Relations with Africa', in J. O. Lindsay, ed., *New Cambridge Modern History*, Vol. VII: *The Old Regime, 1713–63* (Cambridge, 1957), pp. 566–79.

[109] Roland Oliver, *The Missionary Factor in East Africa* (London, 1952), based on a Cambridge thesis (Ph.D., 1951).

[110] R. E. Robinson, 'The Trust in British Central African Policy, 1889–1939', unpublished Ph.D. thesis, Cambridge, 1951; see also his 'Imperial Problems in British Politics, 1880–1895', in Benians and others, eds., *CHBE*, III (1959), pp. 127–80.

[111] Roland Oliver, *Sir Harry Johnston and the Scramble for Africa* (London, 1957).

[112] Marie de Kiewiet, 'The History of the I.B.E.A. Company, 1876–95', unpublished Ph.D. thesis, 1955; A. A. B. Aderibigbe, 'Expansion of the Lagos Protectorate, 1862–1900', unpublished Ph.D. thesis, 1959; A. Adu Boahen, *Britain, the Sahara and the Western Sudan, 1788–1861* (Oxford, 1964), based on a London thesis (Ph.D., 1959).

seemed peripheral within the informal American empire signalled by the Marshall Plan.[113]

Much research in the 1950s was carried out by teachers in the 'special relation' colleges in Africa and by research officers in associated institutes, using local as well as metropolitan archives. In Northern Rhodesia, the social anthropologist J. A. Barnes quarried historical records in studying African submission to colonial rule.[114] At Makerere, D. A. Low and R. C. Pratt investigated Britain's relations with the kingdom of Buganda.[115] The economic history of colonial East Africa was pioneered by P. G. Powesland and C. Ehrlich[116] at Makerere, and by C. C. Wrigley and H. S. Fearn[117] at the East African Institute for Social Research. Powesland had been supervised by Frankel in Oxford; Wrigley had worked with Hancock in London; Ehrlich and Fearn had been supervised by Fisher at the LSE. In Nairobi G. H. Mungeam tackled the early years of British rule in Kenya.[118] In Nigeria Robin Hallett began studying the European exploration of western and northern Africa, focusing on the African Association.[119] In the Gold Coast, Fage, G. E. Metcalfe, and D. S. Coombs worked on British rule in the nineteenth century,[120] William Tordoff on the recent history of Asante,[121] and David Kimble (director of extra-mural studies) on the rise of nationalism in the colony.[122] In Sierra Leone work as an

[113] John Gallagher and Ronald Robinson, 'The Imperialism of Free Trade', *Economic History Review*, Second Series, VI (1953), pp. 1–15; cf. R. E. Robinson and Anil Seal, 'Professor John Gallagher, 1919–1980', *Journal of Imperial and Commonwealth History*, IX (1981), pp. 119–24; Robinson, 'Oxford in Imperial Historiography' (cited in n. 41 above), pp. 42–45.

[114] J. A. Barnes, *Politics in a Changing Society: A Political History of the Fort Jameson Ngoni* (London, 1954), chap. 3; this was based on an Oxford thesis (D.Phil., 1951).

[115] D. A. Low, 'The British and Uganda, 1862–1900', unpublished D.Phil. thesis, Oxford, 1957; D. A. Low and R. C. Pratt, *Buganda and British Overrule* (London, 1960).

[116] Philip Geoffrey Powesland, *Economic Policy and Labour: A Study in Uganda's Economic History* (Kampala, Uganda, 1957). Powesland died in 1954. C. Ehrlich, 'The Marketing of Cotton in Uganda, 1900–50', unpublished Ph.D. thesis, London, 1958.

[117] C. C. Wrigley, *Crops and Wealth in Uganda: A Short Agrarian History* (Kampala, 1959); Hugh Fearn, *An African Economy: A Study of the Economic Development of the Nyanza Province of Kenya, 1903–53* (London, 1961), based on a London thesis (Ph.D., 1957).

[118] G. H. Mungeam, *British Rule in Kenya, 1895–1912* (Oxford, 1966), based on an Oxford thesis (D.Phil., 1965).

[119] Robin Hallett, *The Penetration of Africa to 1815* (London, 1965), and Hallett, ed., *Records of the African Association for Promoting the Discovery of the Interior Parts of Africa, 1788–1831* (London, 1964).

[120] J. D. Fage, 'The Administration of George Maclean on the Gold Coast, 1830–44', *Transactions of the Gold Coast and Togoland Historical Society*, I, 4 (1955), pp. 104–20; George E. Metcalfe, *Maclean of the Gold Coast: The Life and Times of George Maclean* (London, 1962); Douglas Coombs, *The Gold Coast, Britain and the Netherlands, 1850–74* (London, 1963). Fage also began work on a biography of Sir Gordon Guggisberg, Governor of the Gold Coast, 1919–27: Ronald E. Wraith, *Guggisberg* (London, 1967), p. viii.

[121] William Tordoff, *Ashanti under the Prempehs, 1888–1935* (London, 1965), based on a London thesis (Ph.D., 1961).

[122] David Kimble, *A Political History of Ghana (1850–1928)* (Oxford, 1963), based on a London thesis (Ph.D., 1960).

archivist led Christopher Fyfe to undertake an extensive history of the territory up to 1900.[123] At Fourah Bay College N. A. Cox-George made historical studies of public finance in Sierra Leone and the Gold Coast,[124] while John Hargreaves (a former junior colleague of Lewis Namier) wrote the life of an eminent Victorian Sierra Leonean before embarking on a three-volume study of partition in West Africa.[125] Meanwhile, in Khartoum the scramble for the Nile valley was studied by G. N. Sanderson (a former student of Lillian Penson).[126]

Events in Central Africa provided new impulses and opportunities for research. The federation of the Rhodesias and Nyasaland in 1953 increased the responsibility of white settlers for Africans north as well as south of the Zambezi. This put a premium on the study of 'race relations', a subject invented by liberals in pre-war South Africa. In London research in this field was organized at Chatham House, and from 1958 at a separate Institute of Race Relations. The director, Philip Mason (a former civil servant in India), wrote the first and last parts of a trilogy on Central Africa:[127] the most original research, on the period 1918 to 1953, was by Richard Gray.[128] A chair in race relations was established in Oxford in 1953, and the first professor, Kenneth Kirkwood, supervised some research on central Africa.[129] In Southern Rhodesia the Federal Archives employed a historian of their own: this was Lewis Gann, who had been a research officer at the Rhodes–Livingstone Institute in Northern Rhodesia, and had studied that territory under company rule.[130] In due course Gann produced

[123] Christopher Fyfe, *A History of Sierra Leone* (London, 1962).

[124] N. A. Cox-George, *Finance and Development in West Africa: The Sierra Leone Experience* (London, 1961), based on a London thesis (Ph.D., 1954), and *Studies in Finance and Development: The Gold Coast (Ghana) Experience* (London, 1973; datelined 1961). Another Sierra Leonean scholar, Arthur Porter, wrote on the history of Freetown: *Creoledom: A Study of the Development of Freetown Society* (London, 1963), based on a Boston dissertation (Ph.D., 1959).

[125] John D. Hargreaves, *A Life of Sir Samuel Lewis* (London, 1958) and *Prelude to the Partition of West Africa* (London, 1963).

[126] G. Neville Sanderson, *England, Europe and the Upper Nile, 1882–1899: A Study in the Partition of Africa* (Edinburgh, 1965), based on a London thesis (Ph.D., 1959).

[127] Philip Mason, *The Birth of a Dilemma: The Conquest and Settlement of Rhodesia* (London, 1958) and *Year of Decision: Rhodesia and Nyasaland in 1960* (London, 1960).

[128] Richard Gray, *The Two Nations: Aspects of the Development of Race Relations in the Rhodesias and Nyasaland* (London, 1960).

[129] H. A. C. Cairns, *Prelude to Imperialism: British Reactions to Central African Society, 1840–1890* (London, 1965), based on an Oxford thesis (D.Phil., 1963); Robert I. Rotberg, *Christian Missionaries and the Creation of Northern Rhodesia, 1880–1924* (Princeton, 1965), based on an Oxford thesis (D.Phil., 1960).

[130] L. H. Gann, *The Birth of a Plural Society: The Development of Northern Rhodesia under the British South Africa Company, 1894–1914* (Manchester, 1958), based on an Oxford thesis (B.Litt., 1956) supervised by Harlow.

compendious histories of both Rhodesias, which were strongly sympathetic to white settlers.[131]

The 1950s also witnessed the rapid expansion of African studies in the United States. Very little work in the field was based on archival research; as yet, colonial Africa was studied in departments of political science rather than history. None the less, some valuable history was written, notably James Coleman's wide-ranging study of nationalism in Nigeria.[132] And in the course of the decade a distinguished historian of Jamaica turned his attention to Africa: Philip D. Curtin explored the interaction between British experience in West Africa and intellectual history, including the growth of pseudo-scientific racism in the nineteenth century.[133]

By 1960 the subject had been put on a firm academic footing. The history of British tropical Africa was no longer the preserve of a few eccentrics; it was a fast-expanding field of debate and diversification. Moreover, it was coming to be seen as an aspect not only of British but of African history.[134] The advent of independence in much of tropical Africa since 1956 underlined the importance of understanding Africa. An emphasis on African agency in history now came both from African scholars and from others with African experience. To be sure, Africans had been audible in the work of Martin Wight and Joan Wheare on councils, and in some pages by Hancock.[135] But there was now a growing literature in which they were prominent, and sometimes leading, players—whether in confronting British intrusion or coping with British rule. In seeking to transcend the perspectives of their archival sources, historians sought help not only from private papers and oral testimonies but from ethnographers and sociologists. Dike on the Niger delta, Low on Buganda, and Barnes on the Ngoni presented African polities with their own intelligible histories. The social roots of contemporary political movements were illuminated by Hodgkin, by Gray on central Africa, and by Coleman on

[131] L. H. Gann, *A History of Northern Rhodesia: Early Days to 1953* (London, 1964); and *A History of Southern Rhodesia: Early Days to 1934* (London, 1965). Cf. his 'Ex Africa: An Africanist's Intellectual Autobiography', *Journal of Modern African Studies*, XXXI (1993), 477–98.

[132] James S. Coleman, *Nigeria: Background to Nationalism* (Berkeley, 1958), based on a Harvard dissertation (Ph.D., 1953). Cf. F. M. Bourret, *The Gold Coast: A Survey of the Gold Coast and British Togoland . . . 1919–1946* (Stanford, Calif., 1949, revised under other titles, 1952, 1960), based on a Stanford dissertation (Ph.D., 1947); see also Jean Herskovits Kopytoff, *A Preface to Modern Nigeria: The 'Sierra Leoneans' in Yoruba, 1830–1890* (Madison, 1965), based on an Oxford D.Phil. thesis (1961).

[133] Philip D. Curtin, *The Image of Africa: British Ideas and Action, 1780–1850* (Madison, 1964; London, 1965).

[134] Cf. J. D. Fage, *An Introduction to the History of West Africa* (Cambridge, 1955; 2nd edn., 1959); Roland Oliver and J. D. Fage, *A Short History of Africa* (Harmondsworth, 1962). An early manifesto came from an established 'Imperial' historian: J. W. Blake, 'The Study of African History', *TRHS*, Fourth Series, XXXII (1950), pp. 49–69.

[135] See above, notes 85 and 68.

Nigeria. George Shepperson and Thomas Price, in a *tour de force* of research off the beaten track, brought to light the multifarious origins of John Chilembwe's rising in Nyasaland in 1915.[136] Here was history of a kind to gratify the young medical officer in Nyasaland who in 1895 had imagined 'a stupid old historian taking infinite pains to get to the original Foreign Office despatches and thinking that at last he had hit on the truth, the plain and uncontroverted truth'.[137] Yet it was Foreign Office records which in large part supported the other *magnum opus* of this period, Robinson and Gallagher's *Africa and the Victorians*.[138] Here too an Afrocentric emphasis was perceptible; in constructing the first overarching explanation of partition, they argued that Britain's acquisition of African territory was largely a reaction to events within Africa: nationalist movements in South Africa and Egypt. The thesis was brilliantly expounded, but was far from conclusive, and provoked further research over the next decade and more.[139]

In the course of the 1960s the institutional underpinnings of African studies continued to be strengthened. University provision in Britain was markedly increased, following the Hayter Report of 1961: for example, a centre for West African studies was created at Birmingham, to which Fage moved from SOAS.[140] Hayter had been influenced by the recent expansion of area studies in the United States; in the 1960s history departments there attracted numerous research students in the field. In East and West Africa, in 1961–63, 'special relation' colleges became independent universities and centres for graduate research. Outlets for publication multiplied, within as well as outside Africa.[141] Access to British public records was enlarged in 1959 with the institution of a fifty-year closed period, updated annually.[142] Within Africa, it was possible to consult a growing range of colonial records in the archives of most independent states. The main thrust of historical research was now strongly Afrocentric. Much of the best new work focused on rebels, not rulers. Encouraged by Shepperson's example, Terence Ranger in Salisbury (until his deportation in 1963) investigated the African risings

[136] George Shepperson and Thomas Price, *Independent African: John Chilembwe and the Origins, Setting and Significance of the Nyasaland Native Rising of 1915* (Edinburgh, 1958; 2nd edn., 1987).

[137] Wordsworth Poole to his mother, 15 Oct. 1895 (Malawi National Archives), quoted in Cairns, *Prelude*, p. 237.

[138] Ronald Robinson and John Gallagher, with Alice Denny, *Africa and the Victorians: The Official Mind of Imperialism* (London, 1961); R. E. Robinson and J. Gallagher, 'The Partition of Africa', in F. H. Hinsley, ed., *New Cambridge Modern History*, Vol. XI (Cambridge, 1962), pp. 593–640. They acknowledge a debt (*Africa and the Victorians*, p. 43 n) to Robinson's student R. J. Gavin, author of 'Palmerston's Policy towards East and West Africa, 1830–65', unpublished Ph.D. thesis, Cambridge, 1959.

[139] See chap. by John E. Flint.

[140] Fage, 'British African Studies', pp. 406–07.

[141] The *Journal of African History* was founded in 1960.

[142] A major selection was published: C. W. Newbury, *British Policy towards West Africa: Select Documents*, Vol. I, *1786–1874* (Oxford, 1965); Vol. II, *1875–1914* (Oxford, 1971).

of the 1890s in Southern Rhodesia.[143] His work on this subject dominated a lively, if at times oversimplified, debate as to why Africans might choose to resist or collaborate with Europeans. In Nigeria, colonial rule and African reactions were scrutinized by several historians at the University of Ibadan.[144] At the same time, new light was shed on metropolitan dimensions. Kenneth Robinson, who had worked in the Colonial Office during the war, made a pithy appraisal of British colonial policy in the light of the advent of independence in most of tropical Africa.[145] Robert G. Gregory's study of Asian politics in East Africa explored tensions between the Colonial and India Offices.[146] Two especially intrepid projects of the 1960s focused on the African diaspora: from Wisconsin, Curtin made a ground-breaking attempt to compute the volume of the Atlantic slave trade, and in Germany Imanuel Geiss traced the growth of black solidarity within and beyond the British Empire.[147]

Since 1967

In 1967 the normal closed period for British public records was reduced from fifty to thirty years; it thus became possible to study metropolitan files for the inter-war period during which British rule in Africa seemed most entrenched. In 1973 Colonial Office files for 1939–45 were opened to inspection. Historians of tropical Africa focused intensively on both world wars;[148] they also became ever more specialized in terms of time, space, and topic. Many benefited from the creation of a whole new archival resource: the Oxford Colonial Records Project (1963–72)[149]

143 T. O. Ranger, *Revolt in Southern Rhodesia, 1896–97: A Study in African Resistance* (London, 1967).

144 Relevant Ph.D. theses for Ibadan which reached publication were written by A. E. Afigbo (1964/1972), F. Omu (1965/1978), S. A. Akintoye (1966/1971), P. A. Igbafe (1967/1979), J. A. Atanda (1967/1973), O. Ikime (1967/1969). See also J. F. Ade Ajayi and Michael Crowder, eds., *History of West Africa*, 2 vols., II (London, 1974).

145 Kenneth Robinson, *The Dilemmas of Trusteeship: Aspects of British Colonial Policy Between the Wars* (London, 1965).

146 Robert G. Gregory, *India and East Africa: A History of Race Relations Within the British Empire, 1890–1939* (Oxford, 1971).

147 Philip D. Curtin, *The Atlantic Slave Trade: A Census* (Madison, 1969); Imanuel Geiss, *Panafrikanismus: zur Geschichte der Dekolonisation* (Frankfurt-am-Main, 1968), trans. Ann Keep, *The Pan-African Movement: A History of Pan-Africanism in America, Europe, and Africa* (London, 1974).

148 *World War I and Africa*: a special issue of the *Journal of African History*, XIX, 1 (1978); Melvin E. Page, ed., *Africa and the First World War* (London, 1987); David Killingray and Richard Rathbone, eds., *Africa and the Second World War* (London, 1985); *World War II and Africa*, a special issue of the *Journal of African History*, XXVI, 4 (1985).

149 Patricia M. Pugh, 'The Oxford Colonial Records Project and the Oxford Development Records Project', *Journal of the Society of Archivists*, VI, 2 (1978), pp. 76–86. There are published guides to the Africana MSS collections at Rhodes House, by L. B. Frewer (1968, 1971) and W. S. Byrne (1978); See also Clare Brown, *Manuscript Collections in Rhodes House Library: Accessions, 1978–1994* (Oxford, 1996).

assembled a collection of administrators' private papers which nourished a great variety of research projects as well as facilitating the study of administrators themselves.[150]

These new opportunities seemed to devalue two imposing series which began to appear in the 1960s and had been conceived and planned when few twentieth-century records were open to scholars. One was the Oxford *History of East Africa*, originating in a colonial Governors' conference in 1952 and drawing together much research since then, mostly at Oxford and Makerere.[151] The other was *Colonialism in Africa*, edited by Lewis Gann and Peter Duignan from the Hoover Institution, Stanford.[152] There were, however, other reasons why some chapters received less attention than they deserved. Both series embodied broadly liberal assumptions and procedures (including the separation of political from economic history) which were increasingly questioned among Africanists. Once again, contemporary realities impinged upon historians. By the 1970s they were looking back into the African past through perspectives not of widening liberty so much as deepening poverty. Development was commonly reinterpreted as 'underdevelopment'; the problems of modern Africa were traced to its involvement in external trade. Marxist approaches gained a new appeal. In much writing on tropical Africa in the 1970s the controlling theme was neither the achievements of administrators nor the initiatives of Africans but the operations of capital and the growth of social classes. The continuing validity of economic history, rooted in classical economics, as distinct from Marxist 'political economy', was cogently demonstrated in A. G. Hopkins's wide-ranging analysis of West Africa, which acknowledged a debt to Hancock and McPhee.[153]

The last three volumes of the *Cambridge History of Africa*, spanning the century since 1870, appeared in 1984–86. By this time an interest in social history, transcending politics and economics, had gained momentum among historians of Africa, as expatriates who had worked in Africa moved to Europe or North American and mixed with colleagues who studied quite different regions. New attention was paid to the history of bodies and minds: much of the best research since 1980 on British tropical Africa concerned health and disease, famine and conservation; gender relations; law, propaganda, and language use. At the same

[150] L. H. Gann and Peter Duignan, *The Rulers of British Africa, 1870–1914* (Stanford, Calif., 1978); A. H. M. Kirk-Greene, *A Biographical Dictionary of the British Colonial Governor*, Vol. I, *Africa* (Brighton, 1980).

[151] Roland Oliver and others, eds., *History of East Africa*, 3 vols. (Oxford, 1963–76).

[152] L. H. Gann and Peter Duignan, eds., *Colonialism in Africa*, 5 vols. (Cambridge, 1969–75).

[153] A. G. Hopkins, *An Economic History of West Africa* (London, 1973). A. G. Hopkins, 'Imperial Business in Africa', *Journal of African History*, XVII (1976), pp. 29–48, 267–90.

time, soldiers and policemen were rescued from institutional history, while the last years of colonial regimes came under ever closer scrutiny as the 'open date' at the Public Record Office moved towards, and beyond, 1960. These developments may be traced in several thematic chapters, and in the regional chapters which follow.[154]

154 See also bibliographies in A. D. Roberts, ed., *The Colonial Moment in Africa* (Cambridge, 1990).

Select Bibliography

RAYMOND LESLIE BUELL, *The Native Problem in Africa*, 2 vols. (New York, 1928).

Cambridge History of Africa, Vols. VI, VII, VIII (covering the period 1870–1975) (Cambridge, 1984–86).

JAMES S. COLEMAN, *Nigeria: Background to Nationalism* (Berkeley, 1958).

R. COUPLAND, *East Africa and its Invaders: From the Earliest Times to the Death of Seyyid Said in 1856* (Oxford, 1938).

PHILIP D. CURTIN, *The Image of Africa: British Ideas and Action, 1780–1850* (Madison, 1964; London, 1965).

K. G. DAVIES, *The Royal African Company* (London, 1957).

K. ONWUKA DIKE, *Trade and Politics in the Niger Delta, 1830–1885: An Introduction to the Economic and Political History of Nigeria* (Oxford, 1956).

L. H. GANN and PETER DUIGNAN, eds., *Colonialism in Africa*, 5 vols. (Cambridge, 1969–75).

IMANUEL GEISS, *The Pan-African Movement: A History of Pan-Africanism in America, Europe and Africa*, trans. Ann Keep (London, 1974).

RICHARD GRAY, *The Two Nations: Aspects of the Development of Race Relations in the Rhodesias and Nyasaland* (London, 1960).

LORD HAILEY, *An African Survey: A Study of Problems Arising in Africa South of the Sahara* (London, 1938).

W. K. HANCOCK, *Survey of British Commonwealth Affairs, 1918–1939*, Vol. II, *Problems of Economic Policy, 1918–1939*, Part 2 (London, 1942).

ALLAN MCPHEE, *The Economic Revolution in British West Africa* (London, 1926; 2nd edn., with introduction by A. G. Hopkins, London, 1971).

EVELINE C. MARTIN, *The British West African Settlements, 1750–1821: A Study in Local Adminstration* (London, 1927).

ROLAND OLIVER and others eds., [*The*] Oxford *History of East Africa*, 3 vols. (Oxford, 1963–76).

T. O. RANGER, *Revolt in Southern Rhodesia, 1896–97: A Study in African Resistance* (London, 1967).

A. D. ROBERTS, ed., *The Colonial Moment in Africa: Essays on the Movement of Minds and Materials, 1900–1940* (Cambridge, 1990).

KENNETH ROBINSON, *The Dilemmas of Trusteeship: Aspects of British Colonial Policy Between the Wars* (London, 1965).

Ronald Robinson and John Gallagher with Alice Denny, *Africa and the Victorians: The Official Mind of Imperialism* (London, 1961).

George Shepperson and Thomas Price, *Independent African: John Chilembwe and the Origins, Setting and Significance of the Nyasaland Native Rising of 1915* (Edinburgh, 1958; 2nd edn., 1987).

31

West Africa

TOYIN FALOLA

The study of the British Empire in West Africa began before the birth of African history as an academic discipline. There were three major currents. The first was the literature generated by Europeans. For most of the nineteenth century and part of the twentieth, information on Africa was limited, attitudes somewhat condescending and Eurocentric. The popular framework of world history was one in which Africans played no major role. African societies were understood to be either at a standstill (a view expressed by Ranke) or to have no history at all (Hegel). There was a widely held perception that Africa had no sources from which to reconstruct its history, that the society was static or reactionary before colonial contact, and that its people were primitive, deficient both in philosophy and technology. These themes can be traced in exploration writings, early anthropological work, and amateur historical writing. Even when the authors had good intentions, many groups were still presented as savage, or as timeless tribes permanently engaged in conflict and migration. In cases where evidence of 'civilization' was discovered, it was attributed to external agencies.[1]

British rule stimulated an 'academic' interest. To be able to govern, the history and societies of the colonies had to be understood. Administrators and missionaries compiled a series of 'reports' on many societies, and general histories for use in schools that stressed the positive contributions of the British Empire.[2] In academic circles, where Imperial history touched upon West Africa it was often as an aspect of European expansion. Heroes of British rule were more important than

[1] See Augustus Ferryman, *British West Africa: Its Rise and Progress*, 2nd edn. (London, 1990); Walter Fitzgerald, *Africa: A Social, Economic and Political Geography of Its Major Regions* (London, 1934); and Lord Hailey, *An African Survey: A Study of Problems Arising in Africa South of the Sahara* (Oxford, 1938).

[2] See, for example, W. T. Hamlyn, *A Short History of The Gambia* (Bathurst, 1931); T. J. Alldridge, *A Transformed Colony: Sierra Leone: As It Was, and As It Is: Its Progress, Peoples, Native Customs and Undeveloped Wealth* (London, 1910); and W. Walton Claridge, *A History of the Gold Coast and Ashanti: From the Earliest Times to the Commencement of the Twentieth Century*, 2 vols. (1915; London, 1964).

colonial subjects.[3] Most historians were positivists who believed that historical reconstruction was possible only by relying on written documents. Some societies and institutes were created, notably the Royal African Society, established in 1901, and the International African Institute, established in 1926, to provide venues to discuss Africa.[4]

The second current was the literature generated within West Africa, mainly by Arabic chroniclers and local historians such as Carl Reindorf of Ghana and Samuel Johnson of Nigeria.[5] These works belonged to the early historical tradition and contained preliminary comments on British rule. Many expressed the fear that British expansion would destroy indigenous institutions, but some welcomed it for its promise of progress.[6] The third and least known current was the interest in West African history in the United States, due mainly to the activities of pan-Africanist W. E. B. Du Bois. His study on the slave trade is perhaps the most enduring legacy of this period.[7] As early as 1916 the *Journal of Negro History* was established, but it was dominated by African-American history. West Africa was treated as part of a larger 'Negro history', which received attention in the segregated black colleges.[8]

Post-Second World War Scholarship

This chapter is concerned with the work of professional historians, and particularly on work since 1945.[9] The three currents mentioned above led to the foundation for the post-Second World War creation of African history as an academic field. This was an era of reform and change in both politics and academic provision. Decolonization began, universities were created in West Africa, and greater attention was paid to research. In African history there was a revolution: a new

[3] Among exceptions are John W. Blake, *Europeans in West Africa: 1450–1560*, 2 vols. (London, 1941–42), which was widely used in university teaching, and W. K. Hancock, 'Evolution of the Traders' Frontier, West Africa', in his *Survey of British Commonwealth Affairs*, Vol. II, Part 2 (London, 1942), pp. 154–299.

[4] For the major books of this period see chap. by A. D. Roberts.

[5] Carl Christian Reindorf, *History of the Gold Coast and Asante, Based on Traditions and Historical Facts* (Basel, 1889); Samuel Johnson, *The History of the Yorubas: From the Earliest Times to the Beginning of the British Protectorate* (London, 1921).

[6] Toyin Falola, ed., *The Pioneer, Patriot and Patriarch: Samuel Johnson and the Yoruba People* (Madison, 1994).

[7] W. E. B. Du Bois, *The Suppression of the African Slave-Trade to the United States of America, 1638–1870* (New York, 1896).

[8] See George Shepperson, 'Notes on Negro American Influences on the Emergence of African Nationalism', *Journal of African History*, I, 2 (1960) pp. 299–312.

[9] For the early history of British interest in West Africa and comment on historiography see Volume I, chap. by P. E. H. Hair and Robin Law, p. 243, n. 3.

discipline was born and speedily recognized worldwide. The development of this discipline in the West will be considered before turning to West Africa itself.

Colonial history, as part of 'overseas history', flourished after 1945. The orientation was different from the pre-war years: coherent and respectable history became the standard, and the assessment of British rule was more daring. The University of London created a post in African history, occupied by Roland Oliver, who travelled widely in Africa, for research and the teaching of African history.[10] He and a handful of other academics responded creatively to the understanding of African history. Most of these scholars had served in the war, and most were critical of colonial rule. Imperial history would no longer be the same. Decolonization set the stage for the re-examination of the strategic worth and political stability of the colonies; it enabled Africans to assert themselves and vindicate their past. The decline of Europe called into question the Eurocentric approach.

New perspectives were pursued, many gaps in knowledge about Africa were filled, and the public also became interested in the area. The colonial encounter, the institutions of non-Europeans, and the British contribution to world civilizations became popular subjects. In their views on British rule, the early Africanists can be divided into three groups. The first included the radical anti-colonialists: Basil Davidson, Thomas Hodgkin, and others influenced by the ideas, among others, of the British Labour Party. The second included those who ignored or underplayed the colonial period, perhaps because they thought that such a contemporary issue should be left to political scientists, or were simply more interested in the pre-colonial period. The third, and the largest, included scholars who felt that British rule brought many positive things to Africa (for example, Christianity, Western education, and modernization), although they believed that the continent should be in charge of its own destiny.[11]

By 1960 the trends in West African historiography had crystallized. Students had been trained for higher degrees in many universities and sources were available. Various journals and books were devoted to West Africa. A landmark was John Fage's *An Introduction to the History of West Africa*, published in 1955, which demonstrated the availability of sources and long historical heritage.[12] In 1959 Basil Davidson published *Old Africa Rediscovered*,[13] which generated considerable public interest in Britain and validated the new study of African history. Opinions about Africa and its peoples rapidly became positive and widely known, although occasionally a few authors, such as A. J. Hanna and even the leftist Endre Sik,

[10] On these important developments see chap. by A. D. Roberts.

[11] Jan Vansina, *Living With Africa* (Madison, 1994), chap. 3.

[12] Cambridge, 1955. [13] London, 1959.

would repeat the old Eurocentric opinions—only now they were unable to do so unchallenged.[14] Hostility to African history diminished after the publication of the multi-volume *Cambridge History of Africa* in 1978.

Since 1960 British West Africa has continued to feature prominently in non-Western studies, as in the analysis of European expansion and world civilizations. The field created interest in the United States, where the politics of the civil rights movement shaped the anti-colonial orientation of a new generation of Africanists who specialized in nationalist movements and resistance of European rule. Afro-American intellectuals joined in the attack on colonialism, within the framework of the well-known Senegalese writer Cheikh Anta Diop's Afrocentric perception of history which stressed the dominance of Black civilization and its impact on the West.[15] Trends in mainstream history, such as the rise of social and economic history, influenced the study of colonial West Africa. Its frontiers expanded beyond administrative and political accounts to include migration, agriculture, urbanization, and interracial relations. Similarly, Marxist perspectives and a variety of other ideologies were applied to the examination of many aspects of British rule, notably the economy, in the 1960s and 1970s. In the last fifteen years the use of computers has aided such studies as those dealing with the profits of the Empire and the cost of Imperial expansion. Theoretical ideas from anthropology, literary criticism, and subaltern studies[16] are now extensively applied to the interpretation of colonialism.[17]

Yet another major post-Second World War development was the participation of Africans in the reconstruction of their own history. In the post-war period three African university colleges were established in West Africa, two of which were affiliated to the University of London and one, in Sierra Leone, was affiliated to the University of Durham. History was part of the curriculum in these colleges, but courses on Africa were limited. For instance, at the University College, Ibadan, Nigeria, in 1950 there was only one course about Africa, the 'History of European Activities in Africa from the Middle of the 14th Century to the Present Day'. For this course the major text was Harry H. Johnston's *A History of the*

[14] A. J. Hanna, *The Story of the Rhodesias and Nyasaland* (London, 1960), p. 40; and Endre Sik, *The History of Black Africa*, 4 vols. (Budapest, 1966), I, p. 17. See also Margery Perham, 'The British Problem in Africa', *Foreign Affairs*, XXIX, 4 (July 1951), p. 637; Hugh Trevor-Roper, *The Rise of Christian Europe* (London, 1965), p. 9.

[15] See Adelaide Cromwell Hill and Martin Kilson, eds., *Apropos of Africa: Sentiments of Negro American Leaders on Africa from the 1800s to the 1950s* (London, 1969).

[16] Frederick Cooper, 'Conflict and Connection: Rethinking Colonial African History', *American Historical Review*, LXLIX, 5 (Dec. 1994), pp. 1516–45.

[17] This is a concern for the experiences and histories of ordinary people, a move away from élite history, in order to understand the 'voices' that have been suppressed in intellectual discourse. See chap. by D. A. Washbrook.

Colonization of Africa by Alien Races.[18] Furthermore, African history was marginalized in secondary schools, where the major book in use was T. R. Batten's *Tropical Africa in World History*.[19]

The situation was to change dramatically in the 1950s. K. Onwuka Dike of Nigeria led the way, and was followed by others who completed their theses in the 1950s. The relationship between trade and politics in Africa fascinated pioneers such as Dike and it has remained a major area of research as a causative factor of imperialism.[20] Colonialism shaped the orientation of these pioneer historians by way of the subjects they chose, the arguments they pursued, and the conclusions they reached. They responded to the nationalist impulse of the time that insisted on liberation from the intellectual domination of the West, the search for an African identity, and the use of history to establish the continent in the mainstream of world civilization.

The first major statements by African scholars corrected what they regarded as errors in the interpretation of the African past created by the colonial encounter. They attacked the Eurocentric view that Africa had no history before contact with Europe, and that it played no significant role in world history.[21] Consequently, they sought data to broaden the historical span beyond the colonial period and to include a variety of local issues such as inter-group relations, indigenous religion, and state building. They asserted that history had always existed in Africa. The dignity of Africans was to be restored by elaborating on indigenous economic, social, and political institutions. Lord Lugard was no more important than African heroes and state-builders such as Dan Fodio of Sokoto or patriots like Jaja of Opobo who resisted British encroachment. The colonial period was just a short phase in the long history of a dynamic people.[22] As independence approached, the attendant euphoria encouraged excessive condemnation of British rule, as in the case of Ghana where Kwame Nkrumah was idolized,[23] and more generally in pamphlets and books that glorified Africa[24] and made use of history to establish political legitimacy.

[18] 1st edn., Cambridge, 1899.

[19] T. R. Batten, *Tropical Africa in World History*, 4 vols. (Oxford, 1938–40).

[20] See K. Onwuka Dike, *Trade and Politics in the Niger Delta, 1830–1835: An Introduction to the Economic and Political History of Nigeria* (Oxford, 1956). See also works by John E. Flint, and C. W. Newbury.

[21] See K. O. Dike, 'History and Politics', *West Africa*, no. 1879 (28 Feb. 1953), pp. 169–70, 177–78, 225–26, 251.

[22] For the early expressions of these views see, for example, the editorial statements and essays in the *Transactions of the Historical Society of Ghana* founded in 1957 and the *Journal of the Historical Society of Nigeria* established in Ibadan in 1956.

[23] George Padmore, *The Gold Coast Revolution: The Struggle of an African People from Slavery to Freedom* (London, 1953).

[24] See, for example, J. C. de Graft-Johnson, *African Glory: The Story of Vanished Negro Civilizations* (New York, 1954).

Together with other pioneers, African scholars popularized the use of non-written sources to reconstruct history. Such sources are not only valid, they are essential in order to demonstrate that African history is not about the expansion of Europe or British rule, but about African peoples. With respect to written sources, the 1950s witnessed the creation of several archives. In addition, African historians used their role as university teachers to Africanize the curricula, publish handbooks for schoolteachers, and set up academic societies and journals.

An 'African perspective', usually labelled as nationalist historiography, emerged in the course of interpretation of British rule. Not having to negotiate with British authorities or fear Imperial historians in their universities, and still basking in the glory of independence, scholars confronted British hegemony head on. To many African scholars there was no such a thing as a 'balance sheet' of British rule, with positive achievements on one side and negative side-effects on the other. In the 1950s and 1960s the trend was to be distrustful of the European interpretation of African history, castigating it as 'imperialism'. African scholars were not to take their cue from the West, were to avoid writing about awkward issues in their society, and were to relate history to the task of nation-building. The study of resistance to British rule was more important than the activities of pioneer British administrators, and African reactions to colonial rule were more important than colonial policies.

Nationalist historiography has addressed both the causes of the partition of Africa in the late nineteenth century and the consequences of British rule in an anti-imperialist context. Pre-colonial society is presented as stable and orderly, with Africa making considerable progress on the eve of British rule. British imperialism brought destructive change and halted indigenous creativity.[25]

Not all African scholars subscribe to the 'African perspective' as it has been presented. In the 1950s and 1960s, when the first African academics were writing, nationalism aimed at reclaiming a dignity damaged by colonial rule. The historical problem was understood as 'nationalist versus colonialist historiography'. Thus, the African past was highlighted and the colonial factor minimized in the historical process. Ade Ajayi concluded that colonial rule was merely an episode,[26] a thesis that trivialized the colonial experience. His motive was to assert the primacy of pre-colonial history and stress the ability of Africans to initiate changes on their own.

[25] A. Adu Boahen, *African Perspectives on Colonialism* (Baltimore, 1987).

[26] J. F. Ade Ajayi, 'The Continuity of African Institutions under Colonialism', in T. O. Ranger, ed., *Emerging Themes of African History: Proceedings of the International Congress of African Historians* (Dar es Salaam, 1968), and his 'Colonialism: An Episode in African History', in L. H. Gann and Peter Duignan, eds., *Colonialism in Africa*, 5 vols., I, *The History and Politics of Colonialism, 1870–1914* (Cambridge, 1969), pp. 497–509.

At Ahmadu Bello University, Zaria, Nigeria, and some other places, notably Dar es Salaam, nationalism was defined in the 1960s and 1970s as radicalism, a view of history anchored to Marxist historical materialism.[27] African history was thus conceived to mean 'Left versus Right'. Works emanating from such a perspective are highly critical of colonial rule and of the capitalist ideology associated with it. To the left, colonialism was not 'an episode', but rather a 'major epoch' that marked a break with the past. The left was concerned with British exploitation, labour, gender, and class formation in colonial societies.[28]

When the failure of leadership in post-colonial West Africa became obvious, frustration was manifested in historical scholarship. By the early 1970s the nationalists, previously eulogized in heroic terms, were condemned as imperialist collaborators, 'deluded hybrids and windsowers'.[29] Pre-colonial West Africa was being demystified, with charges that the past had been glorified.

More theoretical objections have been raised against 'nationalist historiography' and its characterization of history. The first is that by the time Africans were writing academic history, nationalist historiography had been discredited in Europe because it was amenable to abuse (the case of Hitler's Germany was used by some as an analogy). In the attempt to promote African history, it distorts the colonial era. It emphasizes élitism, focusing principally on African and colonial leaders; it obscures problems in African society; and is unable to account adequately for the social changes of the colonial period.[30]

Four major themes dominate the historiography of British West Africa. The first is Anglo-African relations, including such issues as the origin of British penetration into different areas, commercial relations, missionary activities, geographical expeditions, and partition.[31] Of all these issues, controversy has raged most about

[27] Donald Denoon and Adam Kuper, 'Nationalist Historians in Search of a Nation: The "New Historiography" in Dar es Salaam', *African Affairs*, LXIX (Oct. 1970), pp. 329–49.

[28] Samir Amin, *Neo-Colonialism in West Africa* (New York, 1973); R. Howard, *Colonialism and Underdevelopment in Ghana* (London, 1978); G. B. Kay, *The Political Economy of Colonialism in Ghana* (Cambridge, 1972); B. Magubane, 'Toward a Sociology of National Liberation from Colonialism: Cabral's Legacy', *Contemporary Marxism*, VII, (1983), pp. 5–27.

[29] E. A. Ayandele, T*he Educated Elite in the Nigerian Society* (Ibadan, 1974).

[30] Arnold Temu and Bonaventure Swai, *Historians and Africanist History, A Critique: Post-Colonial Historiography Examined* (London, 1981).

[31] On the period before the partition see, for example, Thomas Clarkson, *The History of the Rise, Progress and Accomplishment of the Abolition of the African Slave Trade by the British Parliament* (London, 1808); Mora Dickson, *The Powerful Bond: Hanna Kilham, 1774–1832* (London, 1980); Harry A. Gailey, Jr., *A History of the Gambia* (London, 1964); C. W. Newbury, *British Policy Towards West Africa: Select Documents, 1786–1874* (Oxford, 1965) and *British Policy Towards West Africa: Select Documents, 1875–1914* (Oxford, 1971); Charlotte A. Quin, *Mandingo Kingdoms of the Senegambia: Traditionalism, Islam, and European Expansion* (Evanston, Ill., 1972).

the motives for partition and for imperialism in general. Against the backdrop of decolonization and the decline of Europe, John Gallagher and Ronald Robinson published a celebrated reinterpretation of British imperialism which emphasized political and strategic considerations, as opposed to the economic thesis.[32] Gallagher and Robinson have few followers in West Africa, where their thesis is fiercely attacked by those who argue that British rule was instigated by the desire for economic exploitation.[33] West African authors seek to validate or modify a number of well-established assumptions associated with the classical theory of capitalist imperialism put forward by J. A. Hobson and its later adaptation by Lenin, or the more complex world system analysis propounded by Immanuel Wallerstein. Hobson, Lenin, and Wallerstein have been severely criticized, but this sort of economic interpretation of British conquest remains the most popular in West Africa.

There are many works on the process of Imperial acquisition. African authors focus on their own countries and usually devote generous space to chronicles of resistance to British conquest.[34] British authors prefer broad issues of expansion.[35] In general, these studies are straightforward history, based on archival sources in Britain or West Africa. They are usually preceded by accounts of Euro-African relations since the fifteenth century. Historians remain deeply divided about how 'dependent' Africans were upon Europeans before 1870, both 'nationalist' and 'Imperial' historians arguing that Europeans were dependent on Africans in the slave trading system.[36] Many historians have shown how white missionaries were dependent on African kings before 1870.[37]

A second theme examines British administration, a 'colonial epoch' that lasted sixty years, roughly from 1900 to 1960. Studies deal with the establishment of British rule, the evolution and nature of the colonial administration,[38] law, order,

[32] Ronald Robinson and John Gallagher with Alice Denny, *Africa and the Victorians: The Official Mind of Imperialism* (London, 1961).

[33] See, for example, Boniface I. Obichere, 'African Critics of Victorian Imperialism: An Analysis', *Journal of African Studies*, IV, 1 (Spring, 1977), pp. 1–20.

[34] See J. F. A. Ajayi and Michael Crowder, eds., *History of West Africa*, 2 vols., II (London, 1974); and Michael Crowder, ed., *West African Resistance: The Military Responses to Colonial Occupation* (New York, 1971); also Michael Crowder, *West Africa under Colonial Rule* (Evanston, Ill., 1968).

[35] John D. Hargreaves, *Prelude to the Partition of West Africa* (London, 1963).

[36] On the slave trade see Volume II, chap. by David Richardson, p. 449.

[37] For missionaries see J. F. Ade Ajayi, *Christian Missions in Nigeria, 1841–1981: The Making of a New Elite* (London, 1965); E. A. Ayandele, *The Missionary Impact on Modern Nigeria, 1842–1914: A Political and Social Analysis* (London, 1966), and chap. by Norman Etherington.

[38] See F. D. Lugard, *The Dual Mandate in British Tropical Africa* (London, 1922); I. F. Nicolson, *The Administration of Nigeria, 1900–1960: Men, Methods and Myths* (Oxford, 1969); and Lord Hailey, *Native Administration in the British African Territories*, 4 vols. (London, 1950–51), III.

and security,[39] new policies and changes in infrastructure, economy, and education, and comparisons between the British and French policies.[40] Many writers have stressed African innovations and reactions to colonial policies. In terms of religion, Africans turned Christianity into an ideology with which to fight colonial rule. Islam spread, thanks to enhanced mobility, an improved infrastructure, and political stability. In the economy, the era brought important changes in transportation, the production of cash crops for export, and international commerce. From the 'African perspective', the literature insists that West Africans carried the burdens of British rule and seized upon every opportunity to protest. Some studies have also pointed to the danger of orienting the economy towards cash crops, and the undermining of indigenous crafts. There are a few works of synthesis.[41] Social structures were affected by changes in slavery, marriage, and family life. Colonialism and cultural identity are interlocked. New European values were introduced, which left Africans with difficult choices between new and indigenous values. Literary works show how Africans dealt with the tensions in culture and identity,[42] and many essays have explored the related issues of élitism, education, class, and ideology. A few studies have gone so far as to 'psychologize' the colonial situation, condemning the acceptance of Western culture.[43]

There is little agreement as to what the impact of these changes was. At one extreme are analysts who overstate the consequences as negative and devastating. This view has been associated with Marxist, radical, and dependency scholarship, which argues that colonialism destroyed the region in many ways: standards of living declined, peasants were marginalized and exploited, and resources were taken for use abroad. At the other extreme are those who overstate the positive impact, especially in such areas as education, infrastructure, health, and the economy. According to these authors, British rule brought development, opened the region to international trade, and transformed it from a 'traditional society' to a modern one.[44] A number of scholars minimize the colonial impact simply

39 See, for example, Kristin Mann and Richard Roberts, eds., *Law in Colonial Africa* (Portsmouth, NH, 1991).

40 See A. I. Asiwaju, *Western Yorubaland under European Rule, 1889–1945: A Comparative Analysis of French and British Colonialism* (London, 1976).

41 A. G. Hopkins, *An Economic History of West Africa* (New York, 1973); R. Olufemi Ekundare, *An Economic History of Nigeria, 1860–1960* (New York, 1973).

42 Chinua Achebe, *Things Fall Apart* (London, 1958); Wole Soyinka, *Myth, Literature and the African World* (Cambridge, 1976).

43 Frantz Fanon, *Les Damnés de la terre* (Paris, 1961; English trans. *The Wretched of the Earth*, New York, 1963); and Chinweizu, *The West and the Rest of Us: White Predators, Black Slavers and the African Elite* (New York, 1975).

44 Flora L. Shaw (Lady Lugard), *A Tropical Dependency: An Outline of the Ancient History of the Western Soudan With an Account of the Modern Settlement of Northern Nigeria* (London, 1905); Alan McPhee, *The Economic Revolution in British West Africa* (London, 1926); Sir Alan Pim, *The Financial*

because it was short in duration, with limited opportunity to create many changes, thus allowing pre-colonial institutions to survive.

A third theme is West African nationalism and independence.[45] Several studies have established a link between resistance to colonial rule and post-Second World War nationalism. Many works have examined the development of national consciousness since the nineteenth century, attributing it to both missionary education and the West African élite's belief that it was denied opportunities by the British. Most accounts divide decolonization into two phases, using the Second World War as the watershed.[46] The focus is on the activities of a small group of nationalists, and from the West African perspective this is always ideological: nationalists were heroes, the people were radicalized, and independence was inevitable. Recent literature includes an examination of different forces (the colonial state and the local and international environment) that combined to bring about independence. The international dimension of nationalism, with respect to issues such as pan-Africanism and the two world wars, has been extensively documented.[47] There are many case studies of individual colonies' routes to independence. Among the leading topics are political mobilization, the formation of political organizations and subsequent rivalries among African leaders, the attitude of colonial officers to West African nationalists, the views of African leaders about their future, the strategies adopted, and the limitations of independence.[48] The concept of nationalism has been criticized in some studies, which suggest the synchronous but mutually antagonistic development of both nationalism and ethnicity. West African nationalists have also been attacked for their élitism and their parochialism, and even accused of intellectual deficiency because of their failure to question the very concept of the nation state.[49]

and Economic History of The African Tropical Territories (Oxford, 1940). Kenneth Blackburne, *Lasting Legacy: A Story of British Colonialism* (London, 1976); J. M. Gray, *A History of the Gambia* (Cambridge, 1966).

[45] For a comprehensive bibliography see A. H. M. Kirk-Greene, 'A Historiographical Perspective on the Transfer of Power in British Colonial Africa: A Bibliographical Essay', in Prosser Gifford and Wm. Roger Louis, eds., *The Transfer of Power in Africa* (New Haven, 1982), pp. 567–602.

[46] Among others, see James S. Coleman, *Nigeria: Background to Nationalism* (Berkeley, 1958); David Kimble, *A Political History of Ghana: The Rise of Gold Coast Nationalism, 1850–1928* (Oxford, 1963); G. E. Metcalfe, *Great Britain and Ghana: Documents of Ghana History, 1807–1957* (London, 1964); and Thomas Hodgkin, *Nationalism in Colonial Africa* (London, 1956).

[47] See J. Ayodele Langley, *Pan-Africanism and Nationalism in West Africa, 1900–1945: A Study in Ideology and Social Classes* (Oxford, 1973); S. K. B. Asante, *Pan-African Protest: West Africa and the Italo-Ethiopian Crisis, 1934–1941* (London, 1977).

[48] John Flint, 'Planned Decolonization and its Failure in British Africa', *Africa Affairs*, LXXXII, 328, (1983), pp. 389–411.

[49] See, for example, Basil Davidson, T*he Black Man's Burden: Africa and the Curse of the Nation State* (New York, 1992).

A final and most controversial theme is the assessment of British rule in the history of West Africa. One premise is that British rule was notable for modern changes. However, the way 'modernity' is sometimes presented is misleading. In this tradition pre-colonial society is characterized as tradition-bound, unchanging, and backward. Thus, British rule put an end to the grip of tradition, and introduced forces that propelled the region to 'modernity'. African authors and many others, however, have queried this interpretation. Indeed, much of the literature on Indirect Rule[50] and economic change suggests that the British did all they could to stifle social change and limit the creation of new classes of educated Africans, and that they practised minimal government on a shoestring budget. One major area central to the European role in Africa is that of the missionary impact. Here African historians Ajayi and Ayandele have made major contributions.[51]

While some works glorify the creation of modern West Africa, others think that the new 'nation states' are chaotic and unstable. British rule has been blamed for many problems, for promoting ethnicity, laying down the foundations for political dictatorship, and influencing political culture. Critics of British rule maintain that it rendered Africa incapable of developing, and its leaders incapable of taking initiatives.[52] The most radical critique of British rule and the nature of decolonization has been expressed within the framework of dependency theory. Popularized in the 1960s by Latin Americanists, dependency theory argues that the economic problems of the Third World result from underdevelopment, a process which allows the West to exploit weaker nations through trade.[53] The impetus for this theory was the failure of the new African states to develop as they had hoped. In seeking an answer, dependency theorists brought the role of the West in global history under greater scrutiny. Dependency theory was applied to African history by many authors, drawing from the widely cited work of Walter Rodney.[54] This theory has been attacked on several grounds. It exaggerates the colonial impact and the damage to society in such areas as technology and crafts, and it denies that Africans had the ability to make decisions.

The historiography of British West Africa over three generations is rich, vibrant and deserves to be celebrated. In the West, colonial rule boosted the expansion of 'overseas history', thus ensuring Africa's place in many history programmes.[55] The

[50] On Indirect Rule see chap by A. D. Roberts, and in Vol. IV esp. chap. by John W. Cell.

[51] On nineteenth-century missions in general see Volume III, chap. 11 by Andrew Porter, and in this Volume that of Norman Etherington.

[52] Toyin Falola, ed., *Nigeria and Britain: Exploitation or Development?* (London, 1987).

[53] See chap. by Rory Miller.

[54] Walter Rodney, *How Europe Underdeveloped Africa* (London, 1972).

[55] See Henk Wesseling, 'Overseas History' in Peter Burke, ed., *New Perspectives On Historical Writing* (University Park, Md., 1991).

need to correct errors about their past spurred African scholars to contribute to the assessment of colonialism. However, the interpretation of British rule has overtones of 'historicism', that is, it interprets the past in terms of contemporary ideology or politics.

While an 'African perspective' is combative and revisionist in many ways, disengagement from Britian has proved impossible. With easier access to education in general and to archival materials in particular, Western historians continue to dominate the field and set the agenda, not with an African audience in mind but rather with a more narrow concern for professionalism. Scholars in Africa are usually one step behind in new research findings. European and American colleges continue to attract large numbers of African students, who become influenced by the dominant epistemologies in the West. Africans travel to British archives to collect data not available locally, and the subjects they choose are suggested by Imperial historians, though less so than previously. The highly productive years in African universities—the 1950s to 1970s—marked by vigour and breadth in scholarship, appear to have reached a watershed. In recent years scholarship has declined, with problems in the universities and the region due to persistent political instability, economic underdevelopment, and the marginalization of Africa in world affairs since the end of the cold war.

There is now an active political side to the study of British rule. For the Africans in diaspora, attempts to exaggerate and eulogize colonial rule have inspired the search for an 'authentic Africa', an Africa where society functioned without contact with the West. In the United States such a search has crystallized in the idea of Afrocentricity which, like pan-Africanism and Negritude before it, is concerned with identity and is critical of the British impact on Africa. To Afrocentrists, European contacts with Africa left nothing but mass destruction. Alternatively, the stress on black contributions to world civilization, including Europe, attempts to minimize the impact of colonial legacy.[56] Here is not the place to critique Afrocentricity, but its construction of the African past, as one universe of coherence that was both pure and orderly, is a false one.

There is yet another side which maintains that the universalist values brought by the West are useful and should be exploited by Africans. In this perspective, Africans should regard themselves as part of a 'global family', stressing less the uniqueness of their continent, but drawing from universal bodies of knowledge to improve themselves.[57] Such a view has recently become widely associated with

[56] See, for example, Molefi K. Asante, *The Afrocentric Idea* (Philadelphia, 1987); also his *Kemet, Afrocentricity and Knowledge* (Trenton, NJ, 1990).

[57] Paulin J. Hountondji, *African Philosophy, Myth and Reality* (first published in French, Paris, 1967; English trans., Bloomington, Ind., 1983).

'post-modernism'.[58] An overlooked study by Abiola Irele argues that the colonial culture is 'engaged in a forced march, in a direction dictated by the requirements of a modern scientific and technological civilization'.[59] Africans must seek to profit from the 'paradigm' but must ignore the 'complexes implanted in us under colonialism, and which are only intensified by cultural nationalism'.[60]

The study of British West Africa requires reinvigoration. From the West African side, it is time to add other topics rather than further to condemn the Empire. Colonial rule has to be contrasted with the post-colonial period in order to reconstruct history over a longer duration and to evaluate regimes and leaders. British rule, too, deserves to be contrasted with Arab cultural and religious imperialism. Islam and Arab imperialism are presented as indigenous to the Gambia, northern Ghana, and Nigeria, as a background to British rule. From this perspective, British rule destroyed Islamic legacies. Because they are understood to be indigenous value systems, Islam and Arab culture offer alternatives to Western perspectives leading to contemporary arguments about the desirability of a secular state; but many of the arguments in support of the ascendancy of Islam and Afro-Arabic culture draw from an inaccurate reading of the past.

There is unevenness in the quality and quantity of the historical literature. There is more information available on political than social history. Histories of agriculture, race relations and commerce, art, material culture, ecology, gender, and technology are inadequate and sometimes unreliable. Nigeria, followed by Ghana, dominates the field. Studies of Sierra Leone are fewer, and the Gambia is generally neglected in works of synthesis. Biographies are few, and most are uncritical. Finally, if the argument about the worth and relevance of universalist Western values in the development of Africa is sustained, it may generate a revisionist history that could interpret British rule in West Africa as the most significant event of the twentieth century.

[58] See, for example, V. Y. Mudimbe, *The Invention of Africa: Gnosis, Philosophy, and the Order of Knowledge* (Bloomington, Ind., 1988).

[59] Abiola Irele, *In Praise of Alienation: An Inaugural Lecture* (Ibadan, 1983).

[60] Ibid., p. 34.

Select Bibliography

ABIOLA IRELE, *In Praise of Alienation: An Inaugural Lecture* (Ibadan, 1983).

A. AFIGBO, 'Anthropology and Colonial Administration in Southeastern Nigeria, 1891–1939', *Journal of the Historical Society of Nigeria*, III, 2 (1965), pp. 295–312.

A. ADU BOAHEN, ed., *General History of Africa*, Vol. VII, *Africa Under Colonial Domination, 1880–1935* (London, 1985).

PETER PALMER EKEH, *Colonialism and Social Structure: An Inaugural Lecture* (Ibadan, 1983).

Toyin Falola, ed., *African Historiography: Essays in Honour of Jacob Ade Ajayi* (London, 1993).

J. D. Fage, *On the Nature of African History* (Birmingham, 1965).

—— 'The Writing of West African History', *African Affairs*, LXX, 280 (1971).

Christopher Fyfe, ed., *African Studies Since 1945: A Tribute to Basil Davidson* (London, 1976).

David S. Newbury and Bogumil Jewsiewicki, eds., *African Historiographies: What History for Which Africa?* (Beverly Hills, Calif., 1986).

R. W. July, *The Origins of Modern African Thought* (London, 1968).

—— *An African Voice: The Role of the Humanities in African Independence* (Durham, NC, 1987).

Ali Al Amin Mazrui, ed., *General History of Africa*, Vol. VIII, *Africa Since 1935* (London, 1993).

Caroline Neale, *Writing 'Independent' History: African Historiography, 1960–1980* (Westport, Conn., 1985).

Kwame Nkrumah, *Neo-Colonialism: The Last Stage of Imperialism* (London, 1966).

Terence O. Ranger, ed., *Emerging Themes of African History: Proceedings of the International Conference of African Historians* (Dar es Salaam, 1968).

A. J. Temu and Bonaventure Swai, *Historians and Africanist History, A Critique: Post-Colonial Historiography Examined* (London, 1981).

Jan Vansina, *Living With Africa* (Madison, 1994).

32

East Africa: Metropolitan Action and Local Initiative

CHARLES AMBLER

The historiography of British East Africa began, in the last years of the nineteenth century, in the attempts of participants and observers to describe, explain, justify, or condemn the actions of British intruders. Led by Frederick Lugard, a parade of aspiring Proconsuls wrote personal and highly detailed accounts of these actions in order to defend their own reputations, to make the case for British expansionism, and not least to cash in on the market for tales of Imperial redemption set among exotic peoples and cultures.[1] Like many of his successors, Lugard concentrated his attention on the complicated politics of Buganda. Here was a state, whose structure and scale invited attention and whose court provided sufficient intrigue and examples of unfamiliar customs to fill many volumes. The religious conflict that wound its way through this history ensured too that missionary writers would quickly provide their own records and interpretations.[2] Thus, the historiography of Buganda's encounter with the British began essentially as a journalistic enterprise. From the 1890s in the pages of *The Times* and sectarian papers, and by 1900 in the Uganda press, the various parties argued policy in part through their interpretations of the establishment of Imperial power in the East African interior.[3] Writing in the 1930s, the early Anglican missionary Albert Cook noted that 'if it be at all true that the interest of a country may be gauged by the amount of literature written about it, then the Protectorate of Uganda must rank very high among our African dependencies'.[4]

[1] Frederick Lugard, *The Rise of Our East African Empire*, 2 vols. (1893; London, 1968). Many of these works are discussed in George Bennett, 'British East Africa', in Robin Winks, ed., *The Historiography of the British Empire-Commonwealth: Trends, Interpretations, Resources* (Durham, NC, 1966).

[2] e.g. Robert Pickering Ashe, *Two Kings of Uganda* (1889; London, 1970); Bishop Alfred Robert Tucker, *Eighteen Years in Uganda and East Africa*, 2 vols. (London, 1908); and Charles F. Hartford-Battersby, *Pilkington of Uganda* (London, 1898).

[3] Albert Cook, 'An Early Newspaper in Uganda and Comments on the News Contained Therein', *Uganda Journal* (hereafter *UJ*), IV (1936), pp. 27–28.

[4] 'The Journey to Buganda in 1896', *UJ*, I (1934), p. 83.

Most readers of *The Times* letters page were unaware, however, that in East Africa itself local people were constructing their own interpretations of the advent and impact of British rule. Nowhere was this more evident, again, than in Buganda. As early as 1901, 'traditional' texts began to appear in print in the Ganda language, most notably under the authorship of Apolo Kaggwa.[5] If the putative topic was usually pre-colonial history, the subject was nevertheless often colonialism. These publications provided important accounts of Ganda dealings with early European visitors, but equally significant was their construction of political and social contexts for the Uganda Agreement of 1900 and the re-establishment of the Buganda state.[6] Oral accounts of British rule evolved in tension with these published versions, sustaining into the post-Second World War period a popular belief that the British had been invited into Uganda by the Buganda monarch.

Across East Africa communities struggled to develop their own histories of British expansion. In the Kenya highlands prophetic traditions of colonial invasion and resistance shaped a larger interpretation of the advent of British rule.[7] Although generally unpublished, these accounts of prophets and their visions—like the Buganda traditions—advanced a radically different understanding of colonialism from that inscribed in the writings of officials, missionaries, and white settlers. Whereas most British writers assumed the inexorability of European expansion and explained British advance in the morally charged vocabulary of slave trade suppression, African accounts portrayed British authority as ephemeral and described instances of resistance and accommodation from the perspective of local history.

After 1900 the debate over white settlement in Kenya overshadowed all others. In the local and metropolitan press and legislatures, and in the testimony provided to a long list of official commissions, the contending parties bitterly contested the history of the colony. The liberal critics Norman Leys and W. McGregor Ross and their allies condemned settlers as parasites whose demands blocked the natural development of an African peasantry, and denounced British policy as a violation of trust.[8] While the settler camp argued that ambitious white pioneers had shaped Kenya's history, both sides shared much the same view of pre-colonial African societies as a 'medley of hostile tribes' transformed by colonialism.[9]

[5] J. A. Rowe, 'Myth, Memoir and Moral Admonition: Luganda Historical Writing, 1893–1969', *UJ*, XXXIII (1969), pp. 17–40, 217–19; also Apolo Kaggwa, *The Kings of Buganda*, trans. and ed. M. S. M. Kiwanuka (Nairobi, 1971).

[6] Michael Twaddle, 'On Ganda Historiography', *History in Africa*, I (1974), pp. 85–100.

[7] See David M. Anderson and Douglas H. Johnson, eds., *Revealing Prophets: Prophecy in Eastern African History* (London, 1995).

[8] See Diana Wylie, 'Norman Leys and McGregor Ross: A Case Study in the Conscience of African Empire, 1900–39', *Journal of Imperial and Commonwealth History* (hereafter *JICH*), V (1977), pp. 294–309.

[9] W. McGregor Ross, *Kenya From Within: A Short Political History*, 2nd edn. (1927; London, 1968), p. 59.

In the 1920s Leys and Ross made the first serious attempt to write colonial history.[10] Ross's polemical book, *Kenya from Within*, was subtitled *A Short Political History* and included a sympathetic account of the rise of Harry Thuku and the East African Association. Nevertheless, it was mainly a study of administration. Raymond Leslie Buell's *The Native Problem in Africa* (Cambridge, Mass., 1928), the influential American survey of colonial rule, displayed a similar hostility to white settler influence in the nearly 400 pages devoted to colonial Kenya, Tanganyika, and Uganda.[11] The author criticized the development of British administration in East Africa from a liberal perspective, but in his narrative Africans emerged mainly, as the work's title suggests, as 'problems'. In the same tradition, Marjorie Dilley's more scholarly *British Policy in Kenya Colony* (New York, 1937) scarcely mentioned Africans at all.[12] By that time Elspeth Huxley had responded to the attacks on white settlement with *White Man's Country*, a record of white settler achievement in Kenya in the guise of a biography.[13] She continued the debate in a published exchange of letters with Margery Perham that dealt substantially with their contending interpretations of the history of Kenyan colonialism.[14]

By the late 1930s Perham had become the chief guardian of the liberal vision of British rule in East Africa. In her view, a powerful settler community's relentless pursuit of self-interest had created bitterness among Africans and thwarted African progress in Kenya. In contrast, 'new men' had emerged in African societies 'who could speak with the sureness and grasp that comes from having been given trust and responsibility'.[15] Perham described colonial history as a social transformation that provided new opportunities for ambitious African men—and women—and she celebrated their efforts to improve their conditions of life.[16] This optimism saturates her *Africans and British Rule*, a brief book for general audiences.[17] She begins with a detailed description of a model of African development: the slow evolution of English society and institutions from tribal roots to capitalism, democratic politics, and women's rights. Although Perham's book was essentially an Imperial apologia, her anti-settler views nevertheless ensured its banning in Kenya.[18]

Many of the women and men who pioneered the scholarly study of colonial

[10] Norman Leys, *Kenya* (London, 1924).

[11] 2nd edn., 2 vols. (London, 1965).

[12] 2nd edn. (London, 1966).

[13] *White Man's Country: Lord Delamere and the Making of Kenya*, 2 vols. (London, 1935; 2nd edn., 1953).

[14] Elspeth Huxley, ed., *Race and Politics in Kenya: A Correspondence between Elspeth Huxley and Margery Perham* (London, 1944; 2nd edn., 1956).

[15] Ibid., p. 137.

[16] See Margery Perham, ed., *Ten Africans* (London, 1936; 2nd edn., 1963).

[17] (London, 1941; rev. edn., 1941).

[18] Michael Twaddle, 'Margery Perham and *Africans and British Rule*: A Wartime Publication', *JICH*, XIX (1991), p. 102.

history—as distinct from the history of Imperial policy—shared the evolutionist assumptions that infused Perham's work. The earliest scholarly works were ethnological compendia that attempted to reconstruct, in often impressive detail, the traditional societies and cultures of particular 'tribes' as they were observed in the years before the First World War.[19] In contrast to some of their successors, these writers were in general sensitive to historical process, as in the administrator Charles Dundas's 1913 study of a Kenya district, a 'History of Kitui', and his later book on the people of the Mount Kilimanjaro region in Tanganyika.[20]

The establishment of learned journals in the region during the inter-war years proved to be a critical stimulus to the growth of serious research. *The Uganda Journal*, founded in 1934, and *Tanganyika Notes and Records*, in 1936, from their inception regularly published historical articles, mainly concerning pre-colonial coastal societies or the larger interior states—notably Buganda. Although influenced by historical scholarship elsewhere, the amateur historians who published in local journals at least attempted to write from the East African perspective.[21] A few of these authors, notably Ham Mukasa, were themselves East Africans.[22]

These same journals engaged the historiography of British East Africa through the publication of articles which examined various aspects of colonial administration. Whether authors discussed Indirect Rule or criminal law, they contributed not only to debates about colonial governance but to interpretations of the motivations and impact of British overrule. Strong partisans of Indirect Rule emphasized the enduring power of local cultures and advocated codification of customary law.[23] Others saw such efforts as misreadings of colonial history. Foreshadowing modernization theory, writers such as Margery Perham, in *Africans and British Rule* (London, 1941), portrayed colonialism as having launched Africans and African societies towards an individualist, capitalist future.

Even if their voices were often not heard beyond their own communities, East Africans contested these interpretations. They sought out public forums, especially

[19] C. W. Hobley, *Ethnology of Akamba and other East African Tribes* (London, 1910; 2nd edn., 1971); Gerhard Lindblom, *The Akamba in British East Africa* (Uppsala, 1920); John Roscoe, *The Baganda* (London, 1911); and W. S. and K. Routledge, *With a Prehistoric People: The Akikuyu of British East Africa* (London, 1910).

[20] *Journal of the Royal Anthropological Institute*, XLIV (1913), pp. 480–549; *Kilimanjaro and its People* (1924; London, 1968).

[21] See the editorial in *Tanganyika Notes and Records*, LIII (1959), pp. 145–47, focusing on the contribution of Sir John Gray to this historiography.

[22] Ham Mukasa, 'Some Notes on the Reign of Mutesa', *UJ*, I (1934), pp. 116–33, in Ganda and English.

[23] See (Governor) Philip Mitchell, 'Indirect Rule', *UJ*, IV (1936), pp. 101–07. See H. R. Home, 'The Natives of Uganda and the Criminal Law', *UJ*, VI (1938), pp. 1–16.

the series of commissions that examined colonial policies in East Africa between the wars. In fact these commissions represented one of the most important arenas for exposing conflicting visions of colonial history. The Buganda government, for example, regularly used such opportunities to articulate versions of Buganda history that resisted romantic antiquarianism.[24] Beginning in the 1920s, the African press in Uganda debated the details of the 1900 Uganda Agreement, addressing in the process the role of the Buganda government with the colonial system and ultimately the legitimacy of Imperial trusteeship.[25] In Kenya, in the pages of *Muigwithania* and in Jomo Kenyatta's *Facing Mount Kenya* (London, 1938), an aggressive ethnic-nationalist critique of colonialism took shape.[26] The struggle to articulate such a perspective on Kenya's colonial history emerges vividly in testimony to the Kenya Land Commission (Nairobi, 1934). But not surprisingly, the first generation of professional historians of Africa, emerging in the 1950s, found very different sources of inspiration.

The academic study of East African history began in the late 1930s with the publication of two books on the nineteenth-century East African coast by Professor Reginald Coupland.[27] These works, which concentrated on British policies and actions, fit within the interpretive tradition of humanitarian imperialism and anti-slavery. Roland Oliver's *Missionary Factor in East Africa* (London, 1952) extended Coupland's concern with British humanitarian activities, but once established at the University of London, Oliver turned to the study of Africans.[28] The developmentalist impulse that accompanied East Africa's post-1945 'second colonial occupation' created the institutional basis in East Africa itself for the rapid expansion of historical research. The founding of a history department at Makerere University in Uganda, together with the expansion of secondary and post-secondary education across East Africa, created a textbook market which in turn inspired the first attempts at regional historical synthesis.

The first general history of East Africa appeared in 1957, the work of two

[24] David Apter, *The Political Kingdom in Uganda: A Study in Bureaucratic Nationalism* (Princeton, 1961), pp. 175–80.

[25] James Scotten, 'The First African Press in East Africa: Protest and Nationalism in Uganda in the 1920s', *International Journal of African Historical Studies*, VI (1973), pp. 211–28.

[26] See John Lonsdale, 'The Moral Economy of Mau Mau: Wealth, Poverty, and Civic Virtue in Kikuyu Political Thought', in Lonsdale and Bruce Berman, *Unhappy Valley: Conflict in Kenya and Africa*, 2 books (London, 1992), esp. II, pp. 322–32. Also D. W. Cohen and E. S. Atieno Odhiambo, *Siaya: The Historical Anthropology of an African Landscape* (London, 1989), pp. 35–40, on the production of history in western Kenya.

[27] *East Africa and its Invaders: From the Earliest Times to the Death of Seyyid Said in 1856* (Oxford, 1938; New York, 1965); and *The Exploitation of East Africa, 1856–1890: The Slave Trade and the Scramble* (London, 1939; Evanston, Ill., 1967).

[28] Roland Oliver, *In the Realms of Gold: Pioneering in African History* (Madison, 1997).

high-school teachers from Kenya.[29] Written with the assistance of Roland Oliver and Margery Perham, it was firmly Eurocentric and committed to a progressive vision of British rule. Nevertheless, the book went through three editions and was widely available into the early 1970s. The one chapter on 'early history' dealt almost exclusively with the coast; most of the rest of the book concerned British expansion, including an entire chapter devoted to Lugard. Brief sections on colonialism largely avoided African politics, with only a passing reference to 'Mau Mau terrorism'. The 1965 edition remained much the same. White settlers continued to play heroic roles, but by now the economic history of Uganda had received attention as a story of 'steadily increasing prosperity'.[30] Kenneth Ingham's *A History of East Africa* (London, 1962) gave substantial coverage of pre-colonial states, but defined colonial history in bureaucratic terms.[31] Pioneer African historians, focusing on pre-colonial history, were slow to contest this preoccupation with administration.[32] As late as 1971, a modern history aimed at secondary school students could still be published that was essentially a record of Europeans 'opening up the interior' and which celebrated the efforts of British officials and missionaries to defend African interests.[33]

In retrospect, it was the founding of the East African Institute for Social Research (EAISR) in Kampala that ensured that the history of the colonial era would receive serious scholarly attention, although in the guise of the social sciences. Well into the 1960s, the most important work on colonial history came from social scientists or from historians whose approaches were interdisciplinary. Once again, much of this work focused on Buganda. In his path-breaking *Crops and Wealth in Uganda: A Short Agrarian History* (Kampala, 1959), C. C. Wrigley described rural economic change from the perspective of African farmers. Similarly, the studies gathered in a volume edited by Audrey Richards, *East African Chiefs: A Study of Political Development in Some Uganda and Tanganyika Tribes* (London, 1960), explored the changing nature of 'traditional' authority in various colonial and 'tribal' contexts. Several works examined neo-traditionalism in colonial Buganda politics, notably D. A. Low and R. C. Pratt, *Buganda and British Overrule: Two Studies* (London, 1960) and David Apter's *The Political Kingdom in*

29 Zoe Marsh and G. W. Kingsnorth, *An Introduction to the History of East Africa* (Cambridge, 1957; 3rd edn., 1965).

30 Ibid. (3rd edn.), pp. 189 and 211.

31 Also Kenneth Ingham, T*he Making of Modern Uganda* (London, 1958); George Bennett, *Kenya, a Political History: The Colonial Period* (London, 1963).

32 On the surprising resilience of Eurocentric imperial history in Kampala and Nairobi see B. A. Ogot, 'Three Decades of Historical Studies in East Africa, 1949–1977', Presidential Address, Historical Association of Kenya (Nairobi, 1977).

33 W. E. F. Ward and L. W. White, *East Africa: A Century of Change, 1870–1970* (London, 1971), p. 74.

Uganda (Princeton, 1961).[34] Similarly, John Taylor's *The Growth of the Church in Buganda* (London, 1958) studied the transformation of faith, rather than the acceptance of external creeds.[35] Drawing extensively on local written and oral sources, these works eschewed the pervasive intellectual dichotomy between modern and traditional and considered the changes associated with colonialism in terms of historical process. The implications of this paradigmatic shift are nowhere more evident than in a comparison between George Bennett's 1963 political history of Kenya and Carl Rosberg's and John Nottingham's *The Myth of 'Mau Mau': Nationalism in Kenya* (New York, 1966).[36] In the former Europeans determined whether Africans were exploited or protected, while in the latter Africans emerge as forceful characters in a dramatic story of their own making.[37]

The publication of the three-volume, officially subsidized, Oxford *History of East Africa* marked this transition.[38] The second volume, appearing in 1965 and covering the period from 1895 to 1945, perpetuated Bennett's narrow conception of politics. Several of the chapters made enduring contributions, but others, including an introduction by Margery Perham, today resemble intellectual artefacts of Empire. By the time this volume appeared, a new group of scholars—including East Africans, Britons, and North Americans—had begun to disengage Imperial history from the study of administration. The new *Journal of African History* had published an article by the Kenyan historian B. A. Ogot analysing political change in colonial western Kenya through local court cases and religious movements, as well as in formal organizations and official policy.[39] John Lonsdale and Terence Ranger followed with influential articles that connected the history of nationalist movements to a wide range of forms of popular resistance.[40] By the mid-1960s

34 Also Lloyd Fallers, ed., *The King's Men: Leadership and Status in Buganda on the Eve of Independence* (London, 1964). Richards was director of the EAISR and Fallers her successor. D. A. Low's influential articles from this period were collected in *Buganda in Modern History* (London, 1971).

35 Also R. B. Welbourn, *East African Rebels* (London, 1961).

36 Bennett's discomfort with the contrast is plain in his review of *Myth of Mau Mau* in the *Journal of African History* (hereafter *JAH*), VIII (1967), pp. 560–63.

37 Other studies of nationalist history include, Michael Lofchie, *Zanzibar: Background to Revolution* (London, 1965); G. Andrew Maguire, *Toward 'Uhuru' in Tanzania: The Politics of Participation* (Cambridge, 1969); and J. Gus Liebenow, *Colonial Rule and Political Development in Tanzania: The Case of the Makonde* (Nairobi, 1971), based on field research conducted in the mid-1950s.

38 Vol. I (Oxford, 1963), eds. Roland Oliver and Gervase Mathew; Vol. II (Oxford 1965), eds. Vincent Harlow and E. M. Chilver; and Vol. III (Oxford, 1976), eds. D. A. Low and Alison Smith. Each of these volumes includes an extensive bibliography.

39 'British Administration in the Central Nyanza District of Kenya, 1900–60', *JAH*, IV (1963), pp. 249–74.

40 John Lonsdale, 'Some Origins of Nationalism in East Africa', *JAH*, IX (1968), pp. 119–46; and Terence Ranger, 'Connexions between "Primary Resistance" Movements and Modern Mass Nationalism in East and Central Africa', *JAH*, IX (1968), pp. 437–54, 631–42.

J. Forbes Munro, Michael Twaddle, Ralph Austen, Marcia Wright, and others had started the process of collecting documentary and oral evidence to build social histories of the colonial experience.[41] Margaret Jean Hay's influential research extended the work of the scholars of the EAISR to explore the economic and social impact of colonial rule from the perspective of farming families and communities.[42]

The Congress of African Historians held in Dar es Salaam in 1965, and hosted by a department then only a year old, articulated a manifesto of decolonized history. In his introduction to the proceedings (written two years after the event), Terence Ranger gave the study of the recent past prominence, arguing that 'much of the so-called history of colonialism in Africa is myth rather than historiography'. At the same time he drew a battle line between the 'radical pessimists', who had come to see independence as 'an episode in a comedy in which the colonial powers handed over to their selected and groomed bourgeois successors', and those scholars—like himself—who emphasized 'African adaptation, African choice, African initiative'.[43]

Evidence of initiative accumulated in numerous studies of resistance, activism in a wide range of spheres, and nationalist politics. The Dar es Salaam history department organized a project to collect oral and written materials related to the Maji Maji rebellion. From 1967 the new Kenya historical society published papers on the colonial period in its annual *Hadith* series, culminating in a volume devoted to nationalism.[44] The key text, however, was the self-consciously nationalist *A History of Tanzania*.[45] In its emphasis on African initiative, this work became the flashpoint for, in retrospect, an exaggerated attack on the entire 'Dar es Salaam school'. The critics charged that the book's contributors romanticized African society and focused on élites. They called once again for emphasis on the transformational impact of imperialism and colonial capitalism.[46] This controversy, in

41 J. Forbes Munro, *Colonial Rule and the Kamba: Social Change in the Kenya Highlands, 1889–1939* (Oxford, 1975); Michael Twaddle, *Kakungulu and the Creation of Uganda, 1868–1928* (London, 1993); Ralph Austen, *Northwest Tanzania Under German and British Rule, 1889–1939* (New Haven, 1968); and Marcia Wright, *German Missions in Tanganyika, 1891–1941* (Oxford, 1971).

42 'Economic Change in Luoland: Kowe, 1890–1945', unpublished Ph.D. dissertation, Wisconsin, 1972.

43 T. O. Ranger, ed., *Emerging Themes in African History* (Nairobi, 1968), pp. xv and xxi.

44 See *Tanzania Zamani*, no. 1 (1967), the newsletter of the History Department, University of Dar es Salaam; and B. A. Ogot, ed., 'Politics and Nationalism in Colonial Kenya', *Hadith*, IV (Nairobi, 1968). Also K. King and A. Salim, eds., *Kenya Historical Biographies* (Nairobi, 1971); and John Iliffe, ed., *Modern Tanzanians: A Volume of Biographies* (Nairobi, 1973).

45 I. N. Kimambo and A. J. Temu, eds. (Nairobi, 1969).

46 Donald Denoon and Adam Kuper, 'Nationalist Historians in Search of a Nation: The "New Historiography" in Dar es Salaam', *African Affairs* (hereafter *AA*), LXIX (1970), pp. 329–49. See also John Saul, 'Nationalism, Socialism, and Tanzanian History', in Lionel Cliffe and John Saul, eds., *Socialism in Tanzania*, 2 vols. (Nairobi, 1972), I, pp. 65–75.

fact, set in motion a dramatic revival of an externally focused British colonial history.

At Dar es Salaam a profound appreciation of the entrenched legacy of colonialism combined with growing political engagement to produce a history that explored the 'processes of underdevelopment and class formation . . . with a view to establishing the degrees of dependence (loss of initiative), differentiation, and selective impoverishment, which resulted from the colonial economic system'.[47] No work was more broadly influential in effecting this redirection than Walter Rodney's *How Europe Underdeveloped Africa* (Dar es Salaam, 1972).[48] The linked concepts of dependency and underdevelopment, articulated in particular in E. A. Brett's comparative study of economic policy in the East African colonies and Colin Leys's analysis of post-colonial Kenya, had a powerful influence on the field during the 1970s.[49] But the longer-term impact of the sudden rise of underdevelopment theory is less than clear. The argument that metropolitan and settler capital shaped colonial policy in fact had a well-established historiographical pedigree in anti-Imperial works such as Ross's *Kenya from Within*.[50] Moreover, the tendency in this new literature to aggregate Africans and to dismiss culture echoed the old Eurocentric narratives.

Historians variously responded to the challenge of underdevelopment theory. For a number of scholars, Marxist categories provided the route away from the determinism of dependency analysis.[51] John Lonsdale and Bruce Berman collaborated in an influential examination of the complex role of the colonial state in Kenya that linked the history of administration to a materialist analysis of conquest and incorporation.[52] Gavin Kitching explored the penetration of the state and the market in rural areas in terms of differentiation and class formation.[53]

47 B. P. Bowles and G. C. K. Gwassa, 'Editorial', *Tanzania Zamani*, no. 14 (Jan. 1974).

48 Rodney was a member of the Dar es Salaam history department, 1966–68 and 1969–74.

49 E. A. Brett, *Colonialism and Underdevelopment in East Africa: The Politics of Economic Change, 1919–1939* (London, 1973); and Colin Leys, *Underdevelopment in Kenya: The Political Economy of Neo-Colonialism, 1964–71* (London, 1975). Some of the important works in this tradition include, M. H. Y. Kaniki, ed., *Tanzania Under Colonial Rule* (London, 1980); Sharon Stichter, *Migrant Labour in Kenya: Capitalism and African Response, 1895–1975* (London, 1982); and I. N. Kimambo, *Penetration and Protest in Tanzania: The Impact of the World Economy on the Pare, 1860–1960* (London, 1991).

50 See also S. and K. Aaronovitch, *Crisis in Kenya* (London, 1947).

51 See Bill Freund, *The Making of Contemporary Africa: The Development of African Society Since 1800* (Bloomington, Ind., 1984). For the Kenya literature see P. Hetherington, 'Explaining the Crisis of Capitalism in Kenya', *AA*, LXXXXII (Jan. 1993), pp. 89–103; and David Anderson, 'The "Crisis of Capitalism" and Kenya's Social History: A Comment', *AA*, XCII (April 1993), pp. 285–90.

52 'Coping with the Contradictions: The Development of the Colonial State in Kenya, 1895–1914', *JAH*, XX (1979), pp. 487–506. This essay and others are reprinted in Lonsdale and Berman, *Unhappy Valley*. Also see Berman, *Control and Crisis in Colonial Kenya: The Dialectic of Domination* (London, 1990).

53 *Class and Economic Change in Kenya: The Making of an African Petite Bourgeoisie, 1905–1970* (New Haven, 1980).

Frederick Cooper's important books on the Kenya coast located analysis of the colonial state and capital within the history of class consciousness and struggle—a perspective that differed sharply from that put forward in studies of underdevelopment.[54] Cooper's emphasis on culture and hegemony is elaborated in Jonathon Glassman's study of popular rebellion in towns along the Tanganyika coast during the late nineteenth century.[55] These works were part, too, of a broadened exploration of the history of imperialism and its impact that focused more on ordinary people, local politics and culture, and the environment.

The publication in 1979 of John Iliffe's *Modern History of Tanganyika* (Cambridge, 1979) demonstrated powerfully the intellectual resilience of the historiography of African initiative. Although sensitive to external economic and political forces, this work investigated the multiple meanings of colonialism from the perspective of Tanganyika's peasants and urban dwellers. Whereas studies of underdevelopment, like earlier Imperial histories, charted the disruption of static and monolithic tribes, Iliffe showed how peoples invented and reshaped identities in colonial contexts.[56] He emphasized the struggles of people to construct systems of belief and cultural forms in rapidly changing circumstances. Iliffe's emphasis on the history of Christianity underscored the absence of serious study of the missionaries and converts who were such central characters in the Imperial story.[57]

Whether radical in perspective or local in orientation, the new discipline of African history almost entirely ignored women, despite women social scientists having pioneered the academic study of British rule in East Africa. Scholars such as Perham, Huxley, and Dilley, as well as Lucy Mair, Audrey Richards, Monica Wilson, Charlotte Leubuscher, and somewhat later Margaret Bates and Cherry Gertzel, gave serious attention to women in their analyses of the impact of British rule. Partly inspired by this scholarship, Jean Hay began in the late 1960s to investigate the differentiated experience and 'initiative' of women in western Kenya; but relatively few scholars—with the notable exceptions of Margaret Strobel and Luise

[54] *From Slaves to Squatters: Plantation Labor and Agriculture in Zanzibar and Coastal Kenya, 1890–1925* (New Haven, 1980) and *On the African Waterfront: Urban Disorder and the Transformation of Work in Colonial Mombasa* (New Haven, 1987).

[55] *Feasts and Riot: Revelry, Rebellion, and Popular Consciousness on the Swahili Coast, 1856–1888* (London, 1995).

[56] This issue is pursued in Charles Ambler, *Kenyan Communities in the Age of Imperialism* (New Haven, 1988), and by Thomas Spear and Richard Waller, eds., *Being Maasai: Ethnicity and Identity in East Africa* (London, 1993).

[57] But note Holger Hansen's magisterial, *Mission, Church, and State in a Colonial Setting: Uganda, 1890–1925* (London, 1984).

White—have attempted to reinterpret the impact of British colonialism in gender terms.[58]

Resistance remained a central theme in historical studies of the East African colonial era, notwithstanding political economy's momentary hegemony.[59] If their colleagues in Dar es Salaam proclaimed that nationalism was a dead topic, Nairobi historians gave it renewed scrutiny, breaking down sharp dichotomies between collaboration and resistance and exploring the legitimacy of the colonial state.[60] During the 1970s intensifying political and economic crises in Uganda and Tanzania accentuated the scholarly concentration on Kenyan history. Studies of the Mau Mau rebellion inexorably drew historians of Kenya to the convergence of Imperial policy, social change, political action, and culture.[61] With the publication in 1960 of the official 'Corfield Report', the initial and often blatantly racist efforts to explain the rebellion and justify its suppression had been succeeded by an interpretation that located the source of Mau Mau in social and psychological dislocations associated with modernization.[62] By the mid-1960s an intensely nationalist memoir literature of guerrilla fighters and political activists challenged this colonialist orthodoxy, sustaining a point of view rooted in some of the earliest efforts of Africans to interpret imperialism.[63] This perspective persisted in the explosion of Mau Mau scholarship in the 1980s.[64]

The culmination of that trend, John Lonsdale's dense reinterpretation of the origins of the rebellion, calls for the study of class consciousness within the frame of a Kikuyu civic discourse.[65] In a sense, his analysis takes the field back to the prophetic texts in which Kikuyu people—and others across East Africa—articu-

[58] Jean Hay, 'Luo Women and Economic Change during the Colonial Period', in Nancy J. Hafkin and Edna Bay, eds., *Women in Africa: Studies in Social and Economic Change* (Stanford, Calif., 1976); Margaret Strobel, *Muslim Women in Mombasa, 1890–1975* (New Haven, 1979); and Luise White, *The Comforts of Home: Prostitution in Colonial Nairobi* (Chicago, 1990).

[59] See e.g. C. Ojwando Abuor, *White Highlands No More* (Nairobi, c.1974), and Maina wa Kinyatti, ed., *Kenya's Freedom Struggle: The Dedan Kimathi Papers* (Nairobi, 1987).

[60] e.g. E. S. Atieno Odhiambo, *The Paradox of Collaboration and Other Essays* (Nairobi, 1974); and Benjamin Kipkorir, ed., *Biographical Essay on Imperialism and Collaboration in Colonial Kenya* (Nairobi, 1980).

[61] Notably David Throup, *Economic and Social Origins of Mau Mau, 1945–53* (London, 1987), and Tabitha Kanogo, *Squatters and the Roots of Mau Mau, 1905–63* (London, 1987). For analysis of a vast literature, see John Lonsdale, 'Mau Maus of the Mind: Making Mau and Remaking Kenya', *JAH*, XXXI (1990), pp. 393–422.

[62] *Historical Survey of the Origins and Growth of Mau Mau*, Cmnd. 1030 (London, 1960).

[63] Among many, note Donald Barnett and Karari Njama, *Mau Mau From Within* (London, 1966); J. M. Kariuki, *Mau Mau Detainee* (London, 1963); Harry Thuku and Kenneth King, *Harry Thuku: An Autobiography* (Nairobi, 1970); Tom Mboya, *Freedom and After*; and Oginga Odinga, *Not Yet Uhuru: An Autobiography* (New York, 1969).

[64] See Wunyabari O. Maloba, *Mau Mau and Kenya: An Analysis of a Peasant Revolt* (Bloomington, Ind., 1993).

[65] 'The Moral Economy of Mau Mau' in Lonsdale and Berman, *Unhappy Valley*.

lated their first interpretations of the arrival of Europeans. Drawing on post-structuralist anthropology, scholars such as Steven Feierman in a study of Tanzania's 'peasant intellectuals' and David Cohen and E. S. Atieno Odhiambo in their book on *Siaya* have grappled with similar kinds of issues in different circumstances.[66] These approaches have challenged the intellectual confidence implicit in works as strikingly different as Iliffe's *History of Tanganyika* or Rodney's *How Europe Underdeveloped Africa*. Their project is not a reconstruction of the evolution of ideas and beliefs within a broader social history or an analysis of class struggle within a global division of labour, but an attempt to make local knowledge systems the moving context within which British Imperialism can be understood.

Does this trend signal the inevitable death of the Imperial historiography of East Africa? Certainly, there are signs enough of decline. Nostalgic studies of white settlers still find publishers, but serious examinations of Imperial institutions and their managers are few.[67] Scholars have largely lost interest in the history of East African questions in British politics.[68] Nevertheless, important books by Dane Kennedy on white settlement and David Throup on British policy suggest the body.[69] And works which explore the realms of local colonial functionaries, whether black or white, are no less Imperial because their main characters have never visited the precincts of Whitehall. Even in the regions of high politics, serious biographies of men such as Jomo Kenyatta and Tom Mboya perhaps prefigure a new kind of history that incorporates the careers of such men, individuals who, after all, were as much commanding actors in the drama of East African imperialism as celebrated Governors or settler-aristocrats.[70]

66 Steven Feierman, *Peasant Intellectuals: Anthropology and History in Tanzania* (Madison, 1990). Cohen and Odhiambo, *Siaya: The Historical Anthropology of an African Landscape*.

67 But see Kipkorir, *Biographical Essays*; Berman, *Control and Crisis*. An earlier example is B. T. G. Chidzero, *Tanganyika and Inter-national Trusteeship* (London, 1961).

68 But see Robert Maxon, *Struggle for Kenya: The Loss and Reassertion of Imperial Initiative, 1912–1923* (Rutherford, NJ, 1993).

69 Dane Kennedy, *Islands of White: Settler Society and Culture in Kenya and Southern Rhodesia, 1890–1939* (Durham, NC, 1987); Throup, *Mau Mau*.

70 Jeremy Murray-Brown, *Kenyatta* (London, 1972); David Goldsworthy, *Tom Mboya: The Man Kenya Wanted to Forget* (London, 1982). Note, for example, Governor Donald Cameron's memoirs, *My Tanganyika Service and Some Nigeria* (London, 1939).

Select Bibliography

CYNTHIA BRANTLEY, *The Giriama and Colonial Resistance in Kenya, 1800–1920* (Berkeley, 1981).

BERNARD CHIDZERO, *Tanganyika and International Trusteeship* (London, 1961).

ANTHONY CLAYTON and DONALD C. SAVAGE, *Government and Labour in Kenya, 1895–1963* (London, 1974).

JOHN S. GALBRAITH, *Mackinnon and East Africa, 1878–1895: A Study in the 'New Imperialism'* (Cambridge, 1972).

JAMES L. GIBLIN, *The Politics of Environmental Control in Northeastern Tanzania, 1840–1940* (Philadelphia, 1992).

ROBERT GREGORY, *Sidney Webb and East Africa* (Berkeley, 1962).

ROBERT HEUSSLER, *British Tanganyika: An Essay and Documents on District Administration* (Durham, NC, 1971).

MARTIN H. Y. KANIKI, ed., *Tanzania under Colonial Rule* (London, 1980).

HELGE KJEKSHUS, *Ecology Control and Economic Development in East Africa History: The Case of Tanganyika, 1850–1950* (Berkeley, 1977).

MICHAEL LOFCHIE, *Zanzibar: Background to Revolution* (Princeton, 1965).

D. A. LOW, *Lion Rampant: Essays in the Study of British Imperialism* (London, 1973).

—— and ALISON SMITH, eds., *History of East Africa*, Vol. III (Oxford, 1976).

DENNIS MICHAEL PATRICK MCCARTHY, *Colonial Bureaucracy and Creating Underdevelopment: Tanganyika, 1919–1940* (Ames, Iowa, 1982).

H. F. MORRIS and JAMES S. READ, *Indirect Rule and the Search for Justice: Essays in East African Legal History* (Oxford, 1972).

GORDON HUDSON MUNGEAM, *British Rule in Kenya, 1895–1912: The Establishment of Administration in the East African Protectorate* (Oxford, 1966).

WILLIAM R. OCHIENG', ed., *A Modern History of Kenya, 1895–1980: In Honour of B. A. Ogot* (Nairobi, 1989).

ABDUL SHERIFF, *Slaves, Spices, and Ivory in Zanzibar: Integration of an East African Commercial Empire into the World Economy, 1770–1873* (London, 1987).

ROBERT W. STRAYER, *The Making of Mission Communities in East Africa: Anglicans and Africans in Colonial Kenya, 1875–1935* (London, 1978).

R. VAN ZWANENBERG, *Colonial Capitalism and Labour in Kenya, 1919–1939* (Kampala, 1975).

GARY WASSERMAN, *Politics of Decolonization: Kenya, Europeans and the Land Issue, 1960–65* (Cambridge, 1976).

33

Southern and Central Africa

WILLIAM H. WORGER

Between the 1860s and the First World War all the indigenous inhabitants of southern and central Africa were brought under British rule. Historical writing on southern Africa, including what later became British Central Africa, began at the same time. In 1869, among the pioneers were Alexander Wilmot and John Chase, who published the first history of the Cape of Good Hope. They argued that their 'narrative of the progress of civilization' focused on the most interesting of all the settlements in the British Empire, but one that had not progressed as well as it might have. For the authors, both colonial civil servants, the problem lay with Imperial government's failure to listen to local settlers. In particular, they asserted that Whitehall officials were too easily convinced by the criticisms made of settler treatment of slaves and other Africans. They suggested that missionaries such as John Philip, and their Manchester and Birmingham textile-manufacturing allies, were drawn together not by concern at the ill-treatment of Africans but by the connection 'between the propagation of Christianity and the market [among Africans] for calicoes'. They concluded with the hope that rumours of 'the existence of vast and rich fields of gold in the interior . . . and the actual discovery of valuable diamonds', would give 'fresh impetus' to the Cape.[1]

George McCall Theal, in his *Compendium of South African History and Geography*, published five years later, reinforced the themes of Wilmot and Chase. By turn a journalist, failed diamond miner, native labour agent, magistrate, and clerk in the Cape Native Affairs Department, Theal was a strong proponent of the benefits of Empire.[2] He argued that the eighteenth-century origins of British rule in southern Africa were strategic, and that the expansion of Empire in the nineteenth century was caused by the need to impose order on a lawless frontier.[3]

[1] *History of the Colony of the Cape of Good Hope from its Discovery to the Year 1819* (Cape Town, 1869), pp. 1, 132, 344–45, 530.

[2] *Progress of South Africa in the Century* (London, 1902).

[3] *Compendium of South African History and Geography* (Cape Town, 1st edn., 1874; 3rd edn., 1877). See also his edited collections of documents, *Records of the Cape Colony*, 36 vols. (Cape Town, 1897–1905) and *Records of South-Eastern Africa*, 9 vols. (Cape Town, 1898–1903).

Wilmot and Theal (Chase died in 1877) published almost one hundred volumes of historical interpretation, edited documents, popular studies, and school texts. The dominant historians of their time, they—Theal in particular—continued to have influence into the twentieth century. Leonard Thompson,[4] of Yale University, noted in the mid-1960s that 'most of the textbooks' used in South African primary and secondary education at that time still derived from Theal, a situation that did not begin to change until the demise of white rule in the 1990s.

The pro-Empire, pro-settler—usually meaning British settler—views of Wilmot, Chase, and Theal were challenged. Indeed, these first histories were consciously repudiated in a lengthy tradition of missionary writing. The missionaries John Philip and Stephen Kay in the 1820s and 1830s had documented the ill-treatment of slaves and indigenous Khoisan peoples, and had, in colonial eyes at least, been largely responsible for Whitehall's unwillingness to back up settler demands for an expansionist frontier policy.[5] In the 1870s Bishop John Colenso of Natal and his daughter Frances condemned the British invasion of Zululand in 1879, and argued that colonial officials, in collusion with British settlers, had provoked the war for reasons that had nothing to do with civilization and everything to do with demands for African land and labour. England, Frances Colenso argued, had interfered in South Africa 'not only unwisely and mistakenly, but cruelly and falsely . . . and will herself some day most grievously reap the whirlwind.'[6] Nor did all settlers favour the British Empire. In 1877 the Revd S. J. du Toit, one of the founders of the Cape Afrikanerbond, published *Die Geskiedenis van Ons Land in die Taal van Ons Volk* ('The History of Our Land in the Language of Our People').[7] Though essentially a compilation and translation of the more favourable references to Dutch settlers drawn from earlier publications by English authors, du Toit's was the first history written in Afrikaans and marked the beginning of a growing settler grievance literature in Dutch and Afrikaans.[8] Thus, while Wilmot, Chase, and Theal reflected what might be termed the dominant view in late-

[4] Leonard M. Thompson, 'South Africa', in Robin W. Winks, ed., *The Historiography of the British Empire-Commonwealth: Trends, Interpretations, Resources* (Durham, NC, 1966), p. 213.

[5] John Philip, *Researches in South Africa: Illustrating the Civil, Moral, and Religious Conditions of the Native Tribes . . .*, 2 vols. (London, 1828); Stephen Kay, *Travels and Researches in Caffraria: Describing the Character, Customs, and Moral Conditions of the Tribes . . .* (London, 1833).

[6] Frances Colenso, *History of the Zulu War and its Origin* (London, 1879) and *The Ruin of Zululand: An Account of the British Doings in Zululand Since the Invasion in 1879*, 2 vols. (London, 1884–85), I, pp. vi–vii quoted. On Bishop Colenso see Jeff Guy, *The Heretic: A Study of the Life of John William Colenso, 1814–1883* (Johannesburg, 1983).

[7] Paarl, 1877. For the pro-settler accounts on which du Toit drew see esp. D. C. F. Moodie, *The Record*, 3 vols. (Cape Town, 1838–41).

[8] See Ken Smith, *The Changing Past: Trends in South African Historical Writing* (Cape Town, 1988), for additional titles.

nineteenth-century scholarship on Empire in southern Africa, strongly dissenting views were also apparent.

Cecil Rhodes, Prime Minister of the Cape, 1891–95, and head of both De Beers Consolidated Mines and the British South Africa Company, appreciated the usefulness of history. He appointed Theal in the 1890s to the honorary position of 'Colonial Historian' and then commissioned him to travel abroad and collect documents which Rhodes hoped would demonstrate that African settlement in the subcontinent was of a relatively recent date.[9] Rhodes and his British South Africa Company also commissioned Alexander Wilmot to investigate the historical origins of Great Zimbabwe, and invested money in a prospecting company run by the novelist H. Rider Haggard's brother (in order to avoid any 'literary campaign against us' with regard to Rhodes's dealings with Lobengula). Perhaps as a result of such investment, Haggard popularized the notion of Phoenician origins while supporting strongly Rhodes's business endeavours in Central Africa.[10] Moreover, as Robert Rotberg has pointed out, Haggard's fictional depiction of Africans so influenced British administrators in London that they drew from his novels in corresponding with Lobengula in a pompous mix of grand allusions and clichéd phrases, language 'believed appropriate for illiterate potentates in far-off lands'.[11]

Another recipient of Rhodes's largesse, Harry Johnston, wrote an enthusiastic and highly influential account of British colonialism north of the Zambezi in which he argued that 'all that is required in Africa south of the Zambesi to convert a State of barren steppes ... into the richest country in the world ... is a large supply of manual labour' recruited from central Africa.[12] Support for the Empire extended also to arguments that Kruger's Transvaal government was irredeemably corrupt and had to be dealt with severely. Before 1899 Haggard wrote of there being room for 'only one paramount power in South Africa', and of the need 'to suppress by arms a small, but sullen and obstinate people', even at the inevitable cost that in 'South Africa new Irelands will arise, and from the dragon's teeth that we are forced to sow the harvest of hate will spring, and spring again'.[13] At the conclusion of the Boer War Johnston celebrated the war aims of the British and their

[9] See Christopher C. Saunders, *Making of the South African Past: Major Historians on Race and Class* (Cape Town, 1988), p. 39.

[10] Alexander Wilmot, *Monomotapa: Its Monuments, and Its History from the Most Ancient Times to the Present Century* [Rhodesia] (London, 1896); quoted passage from Rhodes to Rudd, 17 Dec. 1888, cited in Robert I. Rotberg, with the collaboration of Miles F. Shore, *The Founder: Cecil Rhodes and the Pursuit of Power* (New York, 1988), p. 268; H. Rider Haggard, *Black Heart and White Heart* (London, 1903). See also Norman Etherington, *Rider Haggard* (Boston, 1984).

[11] *The Founder: Cecil Rhodes*, p. 270.

[12] H. H. Johnston, *British Central Africa* (London, 1897) and 'The Native Labour Question in South Africa', *Nineteenth Century and After*, CCCIX (Nov. 1902), pp. 724–31.

[13] *The Last Boer War* (London, 1899), pp. xxiv–xxv.

allies in South Africa in lofty terms: the creation of a Federation of the British Empire which would be 'the most closely knit, the most unassailable, the most wealthy, and the happiest commonwealth that the world has ever known'.[14]

This pro-Empire orthodoxy, supported by the funds of the diamond and gold magnates, did not go unchallenged. Olive Schreiner, who had experienced what it was like to live in the company town of Kimberley under De Beers's rule, denounced Rhodes's treatment of his workers, produced a scathing depiction of atrocities committed by the British South Africa Company in Rhodesia, and campaigned tirelessly against the attempts of Rhodes and his 'monopolists' to foment war against the Boers in order to serve their own business interests.[15] J. C. Smuts, State Attorney of the Transvaal and later Prime Minister of South Africa, wrote in *A Century of Wrong* a fiery critique of British colonial policies towards Dutch settlers since 1815, and concluded that soon 'from the Zambesi to Simon's Bay it will be "Africa for the Afrikander" '.[16] Smuts's case received considerable support in Britain with the publication of Emily Hobhouse's descriptions of the horrendous conditions to which women and children prisoners of war were subjected in the British concentration camps. Her exposés called into question the high moral claims of Empire.[17] J. A. Hobson argued in a series of influential publications that the war, rather than being the product of Boer intransigence or intent, was engineered by British officials, particularly Joseph Chamberlain and Alfred Milner, with the latter serving as the 'easy instrument of political partisans and business men'.[18] Such criticisms accounted in part for the defeat of Chamberlain's Unionist Party in the British general election of 1906 and the triumph of Liberal Party opponents of the war.[19]

The Act of Union in 1910 left many South Africans, white and black, dissatisfied with their place in the self-governing state. The emergence of a distinct Afrikaner nationalist movement, signalled especially by the formation of the National Party in 1913, provided a growing audience for literature that focused

[14] 'Problems of the Empire', *Nineteenth Century and After*, CCCIII (May 1902), pp. 716–31.

[15] See, for example, her *Trooper Peter Halket of Mashonaland* (London, 1897), *An English-South African's View of the Situation* (London, 1899), and, with C. S. Cronwright-Schreiner, *The Political Situation* (London, 1896).

[16] Jan Smuts, *A Century of Wrong* (London, 1900) issued by the State Secretary of the South African Republic, F. W. Reitz.

[17] Emily Hobhouse, *The Brunt of War, and Where It Fell* (London, 1902).

[18] *The War in South Africa: Its Causes and Effects* (London, 1900), *Imperialism: A Study* (London, 1902), and *The Evolution of Modern Capitalism* (London, 1906). Jeffrey Butler has described *Imperialism: A Study* as 'perhaps the most important legacy of the Raid and the war'. See Jeffrey Butler, *The Liberal Party and the Jameson Raid* (Oxford, 1968), p. 17.

[19] Chamberlain had resigned from the Cabinet in 1903 over issues not related specifically to South Africa. On British critics of the war see Stephen Koss, ed., *The Pro-Boers: The Anatomy of an Antiwar Movement* (Chicago, 1973).

specifically on Afrikaners and the historical bases of their political grievances. Gustav Preller, a journalist, from the 1910s onward established for Afrikaners their major lines of historical interpretation, focusing on the heroic struggles of Dutch settlers, the unjustness of British officials, and the treachery of Africans.[20] The formation of the South African Native National Congress in 1912 produced its own account of suffering. Solomon T. Plaatje, Secretary of the SANNC, published (1916) an examination of the historical roots and impact of land shortage that blamed the local administrators rather than London officials for the immiseration of Africans. Denounced in Parliament by the Minister of Lands as being nothing more than 'a scurrilous attack upon the Boers', Plaatje's study was reprinted several times before 1919 and then largely forgotten until reissued in the 1980s.[21]

Professional writing on South African history really began with the passage of legislation in 1916 abolishing the examining University of the Cape of Good Hope (founded 1873) and enabling the establishment as independent universities of Cape Town (founded as the South African College in 1829) and Stellenbosch (founded as a Gymnasium in 1866). Other colleges (Witwatersrand, Pretoria, Natal, Orange Free State, Rhodes, and Potchefstroom) became constituent parts of the concurrently established University of South Africa, until receiving independent charters (in 1920, 1930, 1948, 1949, and 1950—for both Rhodes and Potchefstroom—respectively). The 1916 legislation also provided an annual grant for the separately constituted South African Native College at Fort Hare. The 'white' universities and colleges (black students were not legally excluded until the 1957 Extension of University Education Act, but the numbers permitted to enrol were minuscule, and black teaching staff were not hired) gave instruction in either English or Afrikaans, and the social composition of faculty and students reflected that division. Central Africa did not get its own institution of higher education until the 1959 opening of the multiracial University College of Rhodesia and Nyasaland.[22]

Most English-speaking historians writing in South Africa after the First World War were certain that colonial expansion and white settlement were necessary for the economic uplift and civilizing of Africans, but highly critical of the racial policies being espoused by Afrikaner nationalists. Eric A. Walker, first holder of the King George V Chair in History at the University of Cape Town, wrote about the benefits of British colonialism in publications from the 1910s to the 1960s. In

[20] *Voortrekkermense*, 6 vols. (Cape Town, 1918–38). See also Isabel Hofmeyr, 'Building a Nation From Words: Afrikaans Language, Literature, and Ethnic Identity, 1902–1924', in Shula Marks and Stanley Trapido, eds., *The Politics of Race, Class, and Nationalism in Twentieth Century South Africa* (Harlow, 1987), pp. 95–123.

[21] *Native Life in South Africa* (London, 1916; repr., 1982), quote from p. 9.

[22] See A. J. Hanna, *The Story of the Rhodesias and Nyasaland* (London, 1960; 2nd edn., 1965).

Walker's prose, Africans were 'warlike', 'spare-living alien folk', envious always of the 'high standard of living' of 'Western peoples'.[23] He was the main adviser on the South Africa volume of the *Cambridge History of the British Empire* (1936), a work authored primarily by South African scholars which celebrated the history of the country (including the British High Commission Territories and Rhodesia) as 'a story of bold and progressive development, to which men both of Afrikander and British stock have contributed of their best'.[24] For Walker, the Great Trek was 'the central event in South Africa's history', a movement by 'an isolated and suspicious folk' trying to continue in the interior a 'rigid and circumscribed life' marked by belief in Calvinism, frontier tradition, and racial prejudice. Walker argued that these beliefs continued to 'profoundly influence' South Africa well into the twentieth century.[25]

W. M. Macmillan, Walker's contemporary and Professor of History at the University of the Witwatersrand, was a Fabian socialist and son of a Scottish missionary. Macmillan's first publication was a study of white poverty in South Africa.[26] In the 1920s he wrote two books which examined the ways in which settlers and officials had mistreated Africans at the early Cape, and praised the missionary John Philip for fighting against such inhumanity.[27] Macmillan reflected the paternalism of his time in arguing that most Africans 'must, for many years, remain incapable of independent political thought and action'.[28] Both Walker and Macmillan left South Africa in the 1930s, Walker to take up a chair in Imperial history at Cambridge, Macmillan to experience lengthy periods of unemployment. Neither man wrote anything of significance about South African history after his departure from South Africa.[29]

With the rise of power of J. B. M. Hertzog's National Party in the 1920s, and its

[23] Eric A. Walker, *A History of South Africa* (London, 1928; 2nd edn., London, 1940), republished as *A History of Southern Africa* (London, 1957), p. vi.

[24] (hereafter *CHBE*), p. vi.

[25] See Walker's chap. on 'The Formation of New States, 1835–1854', in *CHBE*, pp. 318–19; *The Great Trek* (London, 1938), and his biographies of two politicians, *Lord de Villiers and His Times: South Africa, 1842–1914* (London, 1925), and *W. P. Schreiner: A South African* (London, 1937). Walker's pro-Empire scholarly contemporaries in the 1920s included Basil Williams with his eulogistic study of *Cecil Rhodes* (London, 1921), and Reginald Coupland, who documented the advance of Empire in Central and East Africa in *Kirk on the Zambesi* (Oxford, 1928), and *East Africa and Its Invaders from the Earliest Times to the Death of Seyyid Said in 1856* (London, 1938).

[26] *The South African Agrarian Problem and Its Historical Development* (Johannesburg, 1919).

[27] *The Cape Colour Question: A Historical Survey* (London, 1927) and *Bantu, Boer, and Briton: The Making of the South African Native Problem* (London, 1929; 2nd revd. and enlarged edn., Oxford, 1963); see also *My South African Years: An Autobiography* (Cape Town, 1975), p. 162.

[28] Quoted in Smith, *The Changing Past*, p. 111.

[29] Macmillan died in 1974, Walker in 1976.

continuation in office in the 1930s (though in combination with J. C. Smuts's South African Party), several scholars sought to explain the historical roots of Afrikaner ethnocentrism. J. S. Marais, himself an Afrikaner brought up to abhor Macmillan's 'heresies' but teaching in the English-medium University of the Witwatersrand and persuaded by the findings of his own research, argued in 1939 in *The Cape Coloured People, 1652–1937* (a work that he considered 'scientific' in contrast to the amateurism of Theal) that South Africa's 'colour problem . . . owes its complexity, first and foremost, to the attitude of mind of the dominant European', particularly that of the Afrikaner who held to a 'philosophy of blood and race . . . with a Nazilike fervour'.[30] I. D. MacCrone, Professor of Psychology at the University of the Witwatersrand, proposed that the roots of this philosophy of blood and race lay in the frontier experiences of Dutch settlers during the eighteenth century when, he argued, they had developed an overwhelming hatred of Africans. His hypothesis was hardly original, but what gave it substance and influence at the time was the social science language in which it was expressed.[31] The argument that Afrikaners adhered to their beliefs because of some backward-looking mentality fitted well with articles appearing in English-medium publications such as the *South African Journal of Science* that linked Afrikaner poverty to low IQs.

Other scholars, fearful of Afrikaner separatism, sought to provide an explanation, and often a justification, for nineteenth-century Imperial policies. The most influential scholar, C. W. de Kiewiet, Dutch-born and a student of Macmillan, wrote that British colonial policy in the latter half of the nineteenth century had been a matter of 'high motives and worthy ends'.[32] De Kiewiet, who left South Africa permanently in 1925 for graduate study in Britain followed by an academic career in the Unites States, argued on the basis of his reading in British archives that there was no substance to the statements made by Afrikaner politicians and historians that Britain had been intent on following an expansionist policy in southern Africa. Rather, he suggested, officials beset by economic and political developments not of their own making, and often beyond their control, 'grop[ed] for some means of ending South African disunity', only to be frustrated in matters such as 1870s' Confederation by the internecine disputes of the various British colonies and Boer states. In the end war was necessary to overthrow 'the *ancien*

30 (Johannesburg, 1939), pp. ix, 282. Marais did feel, though, that Macmillan had 'overstate[d]' the case against the colonists and had failed to address the 'realities' of the 'Colonial situation'. See also his *Maynier and the First Boer Republic* (Cape Town, 1944).

31 *Race Attitudes in South Africa: Historical, Experimental and Psychological Studies* (Johannesburg, 1937).

32 *The Imperial Factor in South Africa: A Study in Politics and Economics* (Cambridge, 1937), p. 5.

régime of separate and conflicting communities' and to usher in a modern nation state.[33]

An Australian-born academic, W. K. Hancock, took up in his *Survey of British Commonwealth Affairs* (1937) the political theme of Empire into Commonwealth. The word 'empire', he noted, had lost its prestige, and people, including 'South African statesmen', subscribed increasingly to the developing theory of the British Commonwealth.[34] Hancock did not consider South Africa a unique society, but compared it to Canada—he described the conquest and incorporation into the Empire of French Canadians and Afrikaners as a parallel process of the 'reciprocal adjustment of cultures'—and Australia. There was, he argued, no difference in impulse behind the cries for a 'White Australia' and a 'White South Africa'. Each society wanted 'to protect their customary economic and social standards'; each saw the danger to those standards coming 'principally from peoples of a different race and colour'. But whereas Australians erected barriers in the form of 'protective tariffs and immigration restriction laws', South Africans saw the problem coming from within and erected 'internal barriers, both political and economic'.[35] While confident that the Commonwealth principle of racial reconciliation could bring together Afrikaners and English-speakers, Hancock wondered whether the principle was 'powerful enough to mould other racial relationships in South Africa', especially given the country's dependence on cheap black labour. He concluded that 'the Europeans of South Africa have the power to decide whether their [Africans'] participation [in 'European civilization'] will be that of a sullen and rebellious proletariat, or of a people learning to collaborate in freedom, friendliness, and hope'.[36]

The growing likelihood that the only future for Africans would indeed be as a disadvantaged proletariat attracted scholars to study the economic underpinnings of racial discrimination. De Kiewiet wrote in the *Cambridge History of the British Empire*, and later in his 1941 social and economic history of South Africa, that the key development of the nineteenth century, occasioned in part by the frontier

[33] *A History of South Africa Social and Economic* (Oxford, 1941), pp. 139–40. See also his *British Colonial Policy and the South African Republics, 1848–1872* (London, 1929). Contemporaneous studies focusing on Imperial policies included Cornelius J. Uys, *In the Era of Shepstone: Being a Study of British Expansion in South Africa, 1842–1877* (Lovedale, Cape Province, 1933); and two books which looked at the interrelation between economics and politics: Jean van der Poel, *Railway and Customs Policies in South Africa, 1885–1910* (London, 1933), and R. I. Lovell, *The Struggle for South Africa, 1875–1899: A Study in Economic Imperialism* (New York, 1934). Favourable images of English settlers were presented in George Cory, *The Rise of South Africa*, 5 vols. (London, 1910–30), and A. F. Hattersley, *Portrait of a Colony: The Story of Natal* (Cambridge, 1940).

[34] 2 vols. (London, 1937, 1942), I, p. 55; II, pt. 2, p. x.

[35] Ibid, I, p. 269; II, pt. 2, pp. 63–64.

[36] Ibid., II, pt. 2, pp. x, 153.

policies of settlers and officials, but owing much more to the industrial revolution of diamonds and gold, was the creation of a landless 'black proletariat, without independence or initiative, and with the growing "resentment of men convinced that there is something false and degrading in the arrangement and justice of their world" '.[37] An economic historian, Sheila van der Horst, noted in a comprehensive work on 'native labour' the considerable costs of such a development, especially as perpetuated by segregationist policies in the 1930s: 'a caste system . . . [that could be] maintained only by the use of force'; the promise of 'racial and social strife'; and reduced 'national productivity' and damage to the 'national income'.[38] Alternatively, S. Herbert Frankel in his *Capital Investment in Africa: Its Causes and Effects* suggested that the incorporation of Africa in general and South Africa in particular into world markets would bring more capital into the subcontinent, lead to improvements in technology, and increase the standard of living of all residents irrespective of race.[39] When African behaviour did not fit with supposed economic laws, the economists tended to suggest that the behaviour was aberrant rather than the 'laws'.[40]

Yet knowledge of how Africans adapted to changing circumstances was limited, since historians in the 1930s by and large left study of their societies to amateur enthusiasts and to members of the newly emerging field of anthropology. At the beginning of the century civil servants such as James Stuart and missionaries such as A. T. Bryant had collected information from African informants, though their published writings tended to focus on the esoteric and the savage.[41] Henri Junod's study of the southern Mozambican Tsonga, with its detailed examination of the economic, political, and religious organization of their society, was a notable exception in this regard.[42] Anthropology developed in the inter-war years

[37] See de Kiewiet's chap. on 'Social and Economic Developments in Native Tribal Life', in *CHBE*, VIII, p. 828, and his *A History of South Africa Social and Economic* (Oxford, 1941). He was quoting J. L. Hammond.

[38] *Native Labour in South Africa* (Oxford, 1942), pp. 324–25. See also the earlier works of Raymond Leslie Buell, *The Native Problem in Africa*, 2 vols. (New York, 1928), and Charlotte Leubuscher, *Der Südafricanische Eingeborene als Industriearbeiter und als Stadtbewohner* (Jena, 1931).

[39] (London, 1938). See also M. J. de Kock, *Selected Subjects in the Economic History of South Africa* (Cape Town, 1924); D. M. Goodfellow, *A Modern Economic History of South Africa* (London, 1931); and C. G. W. Schumann, *Structural Changes and Business Cycles in South Africa, 1806–1936* (London, 1938).

[40] See, for example, Arnold Plant, 'Economic Development,' in *CHBE*, pp. 759–807.

[41] James Stuart, *A History of the Zulu Rebellion* (London, 1913); C. de B. Webb, and J. B. Wright, eds., *The James Stuart Archive of Recorded Oral Evidence Relating to the History of the Zulu and Neighbouring Peoples*, 4 vols. to date (Pietermaritzburg, 1976–); A. T. Bryant, *Oldentimes in Zululand and Natal* (London, 1929). Bryant's study was based primarily on published sources.

[42] *Life of a South African Tribe*, 2 vols. (London, 1912).

with strong links to native administration.[43] Studies, based often on extensive fieldwork in southern and central Africa and still of great value to historians, were written by Max Gluckman, Eileen Krige, Hilda Kuper, Audrey Richards, Isaac Schapera, and Godfrey and Monica Wilson. N. J. van Warmelo, appointed Government ethnologist in the early 1930s, produced a stream of state-funded publications that aimed to document the history and customs of every 'tribe' in South Africa.[44] All of these studies focused not so much on change and adaptation as on decay, and assumed that 'traditional' ways were disappearing and being replaced by 'modern'.

Africans wrote about their economic and political situation, yet had difficulties reaching a wide audience. Authors, such as S. M. Molema and John H. Soga, who produced 'tribal' histories found ready publication with mission and anthropological presses fascinated by the ethnographic detail and appreciative of the stress placed on the benefits of civilization and Christianity.[45] More overtly political accounts were less well received. Clements Kadalie, founder of the Industrial and Commercial Workers Union, published a brief history of the labour movement in 1927, but his much fuller autobiography did not find a publisher until 1970, well after his death.[46] A. T. Nzula, the first black Secretary-General of the South African Communist Party, wrote before van der Horst a study of African 'forced labour'. Nzula, however, published his book in Russian in 1933 while exiled in Moscow, and the English translation was not published until 1979.[47]

With the accession to power in 1948 of Daniel Malan's right wing of the National Party, and the implementation of apartheid and strict censorship, many of the more radical critics (often amateur historians) were forced underground, overseas, or into pseudonyms. Edward Roux, a botanist, published in 1948 *Time Longer than Rope*, a study of black resistance to white oppression, but the book

[43] See Henrika Kuklick, *The Savage Within: The Social History of British Anthropology, 1885–1945* (Cambridge, 1991). See Vol. IV, chap. by John W. Cell.

[44] See, for example, Eileen Krige, *The Social System of the Zulus* (London, 1936) based on published sources; Hilda Kuper, *An African Aristocracy* (London, 1947); Audrey Richards, *Land, Labour, and Diet in Northern Rhodesia* (London, 1939); Isaac Schapera, ed., *The Bantu-Speaking Tribes of South Africa* (London, 1937); Monica Wilson (Hunter), *Reaction to Conquest* (London, 1936); and J. Merle Davis, ed., *Modern Industry and the African* (London, 1933). For an extensive listing of publications see Isaac Schapera, ed., *Select Bibliography of South African Native Life and Problems* (London, 1941, and later supplements).

[45] S. M. Molema, *The Bantu, Past and Present: An Ethnographical and Historical Study of the Native Races of South Africa* (Edinburgh, 1920); John H. Soga, *The South-Eastern Bantu* (Johannesburg, 1930), and *The Ama-Xosa: Life and Customs* (Lovedale, Cape Province, 1932).

[46] *The Relation Between Black and White Workers* (Johannesburg, 1927), and *My Life and the I.C.U.* (London, 1970).

[47] A. T. Nzula and others, *Forced Labour in Colonial Africa* (Moscow, 1933, republished 1979).

was soon banned under the terms of the 1950 Suppression of Communism Act.[48] Hosea Jaffe, an engineering student at the University of Cape Town, using the pseudonym 'Mnguni', parodied Smuts's *Century of Wrong* with his own *Three Hundred Years* of 'conquest, dispossession, enslavement, segregation, and disenfranchisement of the Non-Europeans of South Africa'.[49] Dora Taylor, a political activist writing as 'Nosipho Majeke', described the story of European settlement in southern Africa as 'one of continuous plunder . . . [and] economic enslavement', facilitated by the actions of missionaries.[50] Contemporary political writing, such as that of Moses Kotane, Govan Mbeki, and Albert Luthuli, was almost always banned in South Africa and increasingly had to be published overseas.[51]

The development of separate Afrikaans-medium universities and the close association between academic debate in these institutions and the emergence of Afrikaner nationalist ideology in the 1920s, 1930s, and 1940s provided fertile ground for the continued growth of a distinct historiographical tradition. Afrikaner scholars focused on the two events that they considered formative in the development of a distinct and victimized people divided from English-speakers. Studies of the Great Trek emphasized the heroic qualities of the 'racially pure' Voortrekkers, the chicanery of the British, and the barbarity of Africans (full of 'bestial blood-thirstiness').[52] Histories of the South African War, the other main topic of study, placed responsibility for the war firmly with the British and their mine-magnate allies, much as had been the case at the beginning of the century when, as Smuts had noted, 'It was the rooted conviction of the Boers generally . . . that the war was at bottom a mine-owners' war', a line of interpretation that mirrored that of J. A. Hobson.[53]

[48] *Time Longer Than Rope; A History of the Black Man's Struggle for Freedom in South Africa* (London, 1948; 2nd edn., Madison, 1964).

[49] 2 vols. (Cape Town, 1952).

[50] *The Role of the Missionaries in Conquest* (Alexandra, South Africa, 1952), p. v.

[51] Moses Kotane, *South Africa's Way Forward* (Cape Town, 1954); Govan Mbeki, *South Africa* (Harmondsworth, 1964); Albert Luthuli, *Let My People Go: An Autobiography* (London, 1962). See also H. J. and R. E. Simons, *Class and Colour in South Africa, 1850–1950* (Harmondsworth, 1969).

[52] Smith, *The Changing Past*, p. 72, quotes H. B. Thom's words: H. B. Thom, *Die Lewe van Gert Maritz* (Cape Town, 1947); C. F. J. Muller, *Die Britse Owerheid en die Groot Trek* (Cape Town, 1948).

[53] Quoted in Iain R. Smith, *The Origins of the South African War, 1899–1902* (London, 1996), p. 393. Smuts wrote these words between 1903 and 1906. For the main study in Afrikaans see G. D. Scholtz, *Die Oorsake van die Tweede Vryheidsoorlog, 1899–1902*, 2 vols. (Johannesburg, 1948–49). Outside the general emphasis on Afrikaner suffering at the hands of the British were P. J. van der Merwe's studies of the trekboer frontier, *Die Noordwartse Beweging van die Boere voor die Groot Trek, 1770–1842* (Den Haag, 1937), *Die Trekboer in die Geskiedenis van Kaapkolonie, 1657–1842* (Cape Town, 1938), republished in an English translation by Roger B. Beck as *The Migrant Farmer in the History of the Cape Colony, 1657–1842* (Athens, Oh., 1995), and *Trek: Studies oor die Mobiliteit van die Pioniersbevolking aan die Kaap* (Cape Town, 1945). See in general F. A. van Jaarsveld, *The Afrikaner's Interpretation of History* (Cape Town, 1964).

Most English-speaking critics of Afrikaner nationalism and the emerging apartheid regime had little time for the radicals' blanket condemnation of European colonialism or for the Afrikaners' claims to victimhood. These authors were concerned primarily that South Africa was repudiating the principle of racial reconciliation that scholars such as W. K. Hancock had identified as central to the transition from Empire to Commonwealth. Whereas in the 1920s there had been some sympathy in Britain and the White Dominions for the challenge to the Empire to reform itself in a fashion acceptable to white South African nationalists, by the 1950s the cost of winning that consent was seen by members of an increasingly multiracial Commonwealth as unbearably high.[54] Leonard M. Thompson, Professor of History at the University of Cape Town, argued in his 1959 study of the making of the 1910 Union Constitution that by adopting the Westminster practice of a simple majority rather than the 'better model' of American checks and balances, South Africa's constitution-makers had opened themselves to the possibility that a small majority of voters 'would have the opportunity . . . to obtain control of Parliament'. The tragedy for South Africa was that such a small majority, instead of representing the liberal tradition of the Cape, was composed after the Second World War of Afrikaners with a 'deeply engrained' view of themselves as a 'distinct people', combined in a political party 'nourished by racial fervour', and determined 'to maintain their supremacy at all costs'.[55] Active throughout the 1940s and 1950s in political opposition to National Government policies, Thompson left South Africa for the United States, becoming in 1961, the same year that Hendrik Verwoerd took the newly established Republic out of a hostile Commonwealth, the first Professor of African History at the University of California, Los Angeles.

With the British Empire virtually coming to an end in the 1950s and 1960s, and the transition to a multiracial majority-ruled Commonwealth receiving its greatest challenge in apartheid South Africa and federating Central Africa, Thompson's contemporaries focused on the historical roles of white settlers and Imperial officials in bringing about division when there should have been unity. In a study of the Jameson Raid based on newly available official and private papers, Jean van der Poel, a Cape Town colleague of Thompson, argued that Joseph Chamberlain, British Secretary of State for the Colonies from 1895, was 'deeply implicated' in the Raid and by his actions had 'interrupted the natural growth of unity in South Africa'.[56] Van der Poel's mentor, J. S. Marais, in a 1961 study of the origins of the

[54] Hancock, *Survey*, I, pp. 268–69.

[55] *The Unification of South Africa, 1902–1910* (Oxford, 1959), pp. 480–83.

[56] *The Jameson Raid* (Cape Town, 1951), pp. 259, 261. Van der Poel used the unpublished papers of Sir Graham Bower, Imperial Secretary at the Cape, and those of Sir James Rose Innes, Attorney-General in Rhodes's first Cabinet, but, for Chamberlain, van der Poel relied on the long-available material published in J. L. Garvin, T*he Life of Joseph Chamberlain*, 3 vols. (London, 1932–34); another 3 vols. by Julian Amery, were published, Vol. IV (1950), Vols. V and VI (1969).

South African War, condemned British aims and actions.[57] G. B. Pyrah, on the other hand, argued the post-war British policy stood 'as a monument to what can be achieved by mutual goodwill, good faith, and co-operation' despite the separatist policies of men like Hertzog.[58]

The view that British intervention in nineteenth-century southern Africa was reluctant rather than aggressive dominated Imperial scholarship in the early 1960s. Ronald Robinson and John Gallagher, in *Africa and the Victorians*, argued that 'supremacy' in southern Africa 'seemed indispensable to British statesmen of the 1870s and 1880s for much the same reason as it had for Pitt': to protect the Cape route to India. What drew the British into the subcontinent against their wishes was the rise of a local 'nationalist threat'. The growing antagonism 'between a liberal multi-racial imperialism and a racialist republicanism' resulted in a quixotic quest by Chamberlain and Milner to reassert 'imperial supremacy' as they followed Rhodes and his Rhodesian partners 'over the edge of war' into a bitter conflict that was fought 'for a concept that was finished, for a cause that was lost, for a grand illusion'.[59] A South African student of Gallagher's, D. M. Schreuder, writing in 'the twilight of Empire' about the 1880s, fleshed out themes stressed in *Africa and the Victorians*—especially the attempts of 'Gladstonian Liberals' to maintain 'the imperial connection in the face of local nationalist challenge', and 'to kill the problem of the Afrikaner with kindness'—the result of which, he argued, was that the British had unwittingly given concrete political form to a pan-Afrikaner movement that in the 1880s had been 'perhaps no more than a mirage, a shadow, a spectre'. British rule in southern Africa in the nineteenth century was not, as Smuts had put it, a 'Century of Wrong', but rather, Schreuder suggested, 'a century of vacillation'.[60]

The main scholar of British policy in the 1870s was C. F. Goodfellow, who wrote his dissertation under the supervision of Nicholas Mansergh. Goodfellow disagreed with Robinson and Gallagher's contention that there were not 'any conscious or willing imperialists', arguing to the contrary that British interests were pursued according to a 'long-term imperialist plan' of Lord Carnarvon, that was

[57] *The Fall of Kruger's Republic* (Oxford, 1961). For another view of the South African War that stressed the responsibility of British officials, especially that of Sir Alfred Milner, see G. H. Le May, *British Supremacy in South Africa, 1899–1907* (Oxford, 1965).

[58] *Imperial Policy and South Africa, 1902–10* (Oxford, 1955), p. 236.

[59] *Africa and the Victorians: The Climax of Imperialism in the Dark Continent* (New York edn., 1961), pp. 53, 59, 461, 468. Note the different subtitle from the British edition's *The Official Mind of Imperialism*.

[60] Deryck M. Schreuder, *Gladstone and Kruger: Liberal Government and Colonial 'Home Rule', 1880–85* (London, 1969), pp. vii, xv, 13, 475–76.

based not on humanitarian concern for the sufferings of Africans or on any 'commercial consideration' but was the product of Carnarvon's 'temperament'.[61]

Whatever the disagreements, the overall impression conveyed by early to mid-1960s scholarly work on British imperialism was that southern African policy had been a series of unmitigated disasters. John S. Galbraith's study of early nineteenth-century frontier policy captured well the sense of loss and foreboding felt by scholars of the area as apartheid became entrenched. Emphasizing that in pursuing a policy of 'Reluctant Empire' the 'early Victorians were tinged with humanitarianism and dominated by materialism', Galbraith argued that the result of such a policy—'weak and poverty-stricken [Afrikaner] states' and 'native tribes [subject to] aggression from white settlers' in a disordered interior—was 'disastrous' for South Africa and a 'tragedy'.[62]

The theme of tragedy dominated biographical studies. Alan Paton's unfootnoted study of Jan Hofmeyr, entitled *South African Tragedy* in the American edition, described the defeat of Hofmeyr's United Party in the 1948 election as a defeat for 'every South African . . . who desired to strengthen inter-racial bonds, to deepen inter-racial knowledge . . . to see each other as men and women with a common land and a common destiny', and mourned that with Hofmeyr's death in the same year 'a great light went out in the land'.[63] W. K. Hancock's two-volume *Smuts* described its subject 'as a fighter . . . at times triumphant, but at times [and ultimately] tragic'.[64] Rhodes received similarly sympathetic treatment in J. G. Lockhart and C. M. Woodhouse's officially commissioned life, but most scholars much preferred John E. Flint's biographical essay which described the mining magnate as a man whose 'rape of South Africa . . . [underlaid] the present system of white supremacy and apartheid'.[65] Phyllis Lewsen's biography of J. X. Merriman portrayed the Prime Minister of the Cape as a man who 'fought both jingo imperialism and Afrikaner nationalism', whose 'liberalism . . . was exceptional in his time', and in whom 'Beauty and tragedy . . . [were] both present', and was more in line with the theme of personal tragedy.[66]

[61] C. F. Goodfellow, *Great Britain and South African Confederation, 1871–84* (Cape Town, 1966), pp. 217–19.

[62] John S. Galbraith, *Reluctant Empire: British Policy on the South African Frontier, 1834–1854* (Berkeley, 1963), p. 276.

[63] *South African Tragedy: The Life and Times of Hofmeyr* (New York 1965), abridged, pp. 384, 410. The original and larger (by 100 pages) edition was *Hofmeyr* (London, 1964).

[64] *Smuts*, 2 vols. (Cambridge, 1962–68), comment quoted from the dust-jacket of Vol. II. See also Hancock and Jean van der Poel, eds., *Selections From the Smuts Papers*, 7 vols. (Cambridge, 1966–73).

[65] J. G. Lockhart and C. M. Woodhouse, *Cecil Rhodes: The Colossus of Southern Africa* (New York, 1963); John E. Flint, *Cecil Rhodes* (London, 1976), p. xvi. The most exhaustive biography is now Rotberg's *The Founder.*

[66] *John X. Merriman: Paradoxical South African Statement* (New Haven, 1982), pp. 1, 372.

The growth of white supremacy in central Africa concurrent with that of apartheid in South Africa—the Central African Federation was formed in 1953, the same year that Malan's Nationalists won re-election in South Africa with a greatly increased majority and Verwoerd became Minister of Native Affairs—attracted more attention to the study of the Rhodesias and Nyasaland than had ever before been the case. The establishment of the white-ruled federation—Roy Welensky called it the 'eighth Dominion', while Godfrey Huggins referred to the need to rule through a 'benevolent aristocracy'—despite the overwhelming opposition of Africans (who comprised over 90 per cent of the population) became an issue of considerable importance for an Empire-Commonwealth that was meant to be based on racial reconciliation.[67] A. J. Hanna sought to provide a history of the Federation territories that 'supplement[ed]' the 1897 volume of H. H. Johnston and continued the latter's theme of celebrating the benefits of Empire and settler colonialism. Hanna, however, held out South Africa as an example of the dangers of a policy of racial privilege with the inevitable result of 'widespread disturbances and vicious repression'.[68] Philip Mason, Colin Leys, and Richard Gray, writing at the time of debate about Federation, produced studies critical of the settlers and their plans to impede majority rule.[69] The impending collapse of the Federation, evident by 1959, and the divergent trajectories of its constituent parts (black-ruled independence for Malawi and Zambia in 1964, continued white rule in Southern Rhodesia with Unilateral Declaration of Independence in 1965), produced a divided scholarship. Work on the newly independent states, such as that by Robert I. Rotberg, focused on the origins and development of African nationalism, while studies of Southern Rhodesia, for example, Claire Palley's *The Constitutional History and Law of Southern Rhodesia*, examined the constitutional implications of settler power for Empire and Commonwealth through to UDI.[70]

The rise of apartheid and African nationalism meant the end of any possibility

[67] The references to Welensky and Huggins are from Walker, *History of Southern Africa*, p. 801.

[68] *The Beginnings of Nyasaland and North-Eastern Rhodesia, 1859–95* (Oxford, 1956), and *The Story of the Rhodesias and Nyasaland* (London, 1960), p. 278.

[69] Philip Mason, *The Birth of a Dilemma: The Conquest and Settlement of Rhodesia* (London, 1958); Colin Leys, *European Politics in Southern Rhodesia* (Oxford, 1959); Richard Gray, *The Two Nations: Aspects of the Development of Race Relations in the Rhodesias and Nyasaland* (London, 1960). For more favourable views of settler colonialism see the volumes by Lewis H. Gann, commissioned as an official historian by the National Archives of Rhodesia and Nyasaland, *The Birth of a Plural Society: The Development of Northern Rhodesia under the British South Africa Company, 1894–1914* (Manchester, 1958), *A History of Northern Rhodesia: Early Days to 1954* (London, 1963), and *A History of Southern Rhodesia: Early Days to 1934* (London, 1965).

[70] Robert J. Rotberg, *The Rise of Nationalism in Central Africa: The Making of Malawi and Zambia, 1873–1964* (Cambridge, Mass., 1965), and *Christian Missionaries and the Creation of Northern Rhodesia* (Princeton, 1965); Claire Palley, *The Constitutional History and Law of Southern Rhodesia, 1888–1965* (Oxford, 1966). For pre-UDI Southern Rhodesia see also D. J. Murray, *The Governmental System in*

of the idea of a greater South Africa, even though still promoted by Malan in the 1950s when he boasted that with regard to 'self-government for the Natives . . . England should come to learn from us, not we from England'.[71] Indeed, Anthony Sillery, former Resident Commissioner of the Bechuanaland Protectorate, argued in his 1952 history of the territory—the first written—that Bechuanaland owed its very existence to a combination of British evangelism and 'the conflict of Boer and Briton', and that the main thread in Imperial rule was 'British solicitude for the material and social needs of the [Tswana] people'.[72] With Botswana independent in 1966, Lesotho in the same year, and Swaziland in 1968, it seemed that no one in the Empire-Commonwealth was listening to Malan. Studies written in the aftermath of the breakup of the Federation and the independence of the High Commission Territories examined why South Africa politicians from Smuts to Malan had failed to incorporate the rest of southern and central Africa into their state, and the implications of such failure for the regions, for Britain, and for the Commonwealth.[73]

Despite the failure of Federation and a greater South Africa, scholars noted the continuing influence of white Rhodesians and South Africans on British policy toward the region. Martin Chanock argued that British attempts to use the Federation as a counterweight between Afrikaner nationalism to the south and African to the north essentially continued after UDI, with white Rhodesians acquiring as a result a significance in British policy-making out of all proportion to their numbers.[74] Geoff Berridge suggested that official British claims about the country's interests in South Africa—that it had a strategic interest in the Cape, that it was responsible for the High Commission Territories, that it had general economic connections, and that there were historical ties of 'kith and kin'—paled

Southern Rhodesia (Oxford, 1970). For UDI and its political consequences see Larry Bowman, *Politics in Rhodesia: White Power in an African State* (Cambridge, Mass., 1973); Robert C. Good, *The International Politics of the Rhodesian Rebellion* (Princeton, 1973); Patrick O'Meara, *Rhodesia: Racial Conflict or Co-Existence?* (Ithaca, NY, 1975); and Elaine Windrich, *Britain and the Politics of Rhodesian Independence* (London, 1978).

71 Malan, quoted in Walker, *History of Southern Africa*, p. 853.

72 *The Bechuanaland Protectorate* (Oxford, 1952), pp. 97, 103.

73 See Ronald Hyam, *The Failure of South African Expansion, 1908–48* (London, 1972); Nicholas Mansergh, *Documents and Speeches on British Commonwealth Affairs, 1931–1952* (London, 1953) and *South Africa, 1906–1961: The Price of Magnanimity* (London, 1962); J. D. B. Miller, *Survey of Commonwealth Affairs: Problems of Expansion and Attrition, 1953–1969* (London, 1974); Lord Hailey, *The Republic of South Africa and the High Commission Territories* (Oxford, 1963); James Barber, *South African Foreign Policy, 1945–1970* (Oxford, 1973); and Sam C. Nolutshungu, *South Africa in Africa: A Study in Ideology and Foreign Policy* (Manchester, 1974). On Lesotho see J. E. Spence, *Lesotho: The Politics of Dependence* (London, 1968); and on Swaziland, Christian Potholm, *Swaziland: The Dynamics of Political Modernization* (Berkeley, 1972). On South Africa's claims to Namibia see John Dugard, *The South West Africa/Namibia Dispute* (Berkeley, 1973).

74 *Unconsummated Union: Britain, Rhodesia, and South Africa, 1900–45* (New York, 1977).

in comparison to what he considered, on the basis of research in British official records, were the real attractions, South African gold and uranium.[75]

But a real shift in focus from the long-standing stress on Imperial and settler relations had been prefigured in 1958 by the publication of *Independent African* by George Shepperson and Thomas Price. Their study of John Chilembwe and his attempt in 1915 to throw the British 'oppressors' out of Nyasaland, with its focus on African agency, its careful examination of the transatlantic links evident in Chilembwe's thought and action, and its conscious looking forward to the rise of African nationalism, marked a watershed in the writing of the history of Africa.[76] Thereafter the study of southern and central Africa became primarily the study of Africans and African history rather than the study of white settlers and Imperial history.

The incorporation of 'the forgotten factor' in southern African history dominated scholarly writing on southern and central African history in the 1960s and 1970s.[77] Thompson, planning in California a new history of South Africa to replace the *Cambridge History* (reissued in 1963 under the editorship of Eric Walker and largely unchanged from the 1936 edition), thought an interdisciplinary approach essential and collaborated with a University of Cape Town anthropologist, Monica Wilson, in organizing the projected volumes. Such an approach, they believed, would enable them to refute effectively what they considered misleading assumptions about South African history.[78] At much the same time that Wilson and Thompson were planning their history, John Omer-Cooper, a South African teaching in newly independent Nigeria, published a ground-breaking study of early-nineteenth-century southern and central Africa, *The Zulu Aftermath*. Subtitled A *Nineteenth-Century Revolution in Bantu Africa*, Omer-Cooper's book aimed to show the dynamic nature of political change in pre-colonial Africa and to demonstrate the ability of leaders such as Shaka to create powerful centralized states without European influence, themes that drew explicitly on the author's disapproval of apartheid and his enthusiasm for the development of

[75] Geoff Berridge, *Economic Power in Anglo-South African Diplomacy: Simonstown, Sharpeville and After* (London, 1981), pp. 4, 164. Ritchie Ovendale discusses the South African policy of the Labour and Conservative governments of the 1940s and 1950s in 'The South African Policy of the British Labour Government, 1947–51', *International Affairs* (Winter 1982/83), pp. 41–58, and 'Macmillan and the Wind of Change in Africa, 1957–1960', *Historical Journal*, XXXVIII, 2 (1995), pp. 455–77.

[76] *Independent African: John Chilembwe and the Origins, Setting, and Significance of the Nyasaland Rising of 1915* (Edinburgh, 1958).

[77] Leonard M. Thompson, ed., *African Societies in Southern Africa: Historical Studies* (London, 1969). However, the main Afrikaans university text of this period consigned Africans to a brief appendix. See C. F. J. Muller, ed., *Five Hundred Years: A History of South Africa* (Pretoria, 1967 [Afrikaans], 1969 [English]).

[78] *The Oxford History of South Africa*, 2 vols. (Oxford, 1969–71), I, pp. vii–x.

black rule in the rest of Africa.[79] Terence Ranger, formerly head of the history department at the University College of Rhodesia but expelled in 1963 and writing thereafter at the University of Dar es Salaam and then at UCLA (where he succeeded Thompson, who moved to Yale University), argued in a series of studies that Africans had organized in complex ways to resist conquest and that strong linkages existed between their initial forms of 'primary' resistance and the later rise of nationalist movements (especially those fighting Ian Smith's regime).[80] For South African historiography, the most important work published was Wilson and Thompson's *Oxford History of South Africa* which, appearing in two lengthy volumes in 1969 and 1971, sought to illustrate the editors' 'belief that the central theme of South African history is the interaction between peoples of diverse origins, languages, technologies, ideologies, and social systems, meeting on South African soil'.[81] The contrast with the *Cambridge History* was stark. In place of the latter's emphasis on Imperial policy and settler politics, the *Oxford History* devoted more than half its text to Africans and presented thematic chapters on 'Farming', 'The Growth of Towns', and 'Peasant Communities'. Still, politics was evident in an unexpected direction. Fearing censorship by the South African government and possible repercussions for Monica Wilson, since she still lived in the country, the South African edition was published without the chapter on African nationalism by Leo Kuper. Kuper strongly criticized the editors and the Press for what he considered their 'purely gratuitous act of political repression'.[82]

The *Oxford History* served as a lightning-rod for an increasingly acrimonious debate about southern African history that took place largely in England and the United States. Objections to white supremacy had caused numerous scholars to leave South Africa and Southern Rhodesia, while the Empire-era 'tradition' of students pursuing postgraduate degrees in England continued with most doctoral training (primarily of white South Africans) taking place at Oxford University (under the supervision of Stanley Trapido), the University of London (under the

[79] (London, 1966). A work that dealt with later Zulu resistance to colonial expansion, and inspired by Shepperson and Price, was Shula Marks, *Reluctant Rebellion: The 1906–1908 Disturbances in Natal* (Oxford, 1970).

[80] See esp. his *Revolt in Southern Rhodesia, 1896–7: A Study in African Resistance* (Evanston, Ill., 1967), *The African Voice in Southern Rhodesia, 1898–1930* (London, 1970), and the collection he edited as a 'corrective' to Hanna and others, *Aspects of Central African History* (London, 1968). On Central Africa in general see also E. R. Stokes and R. Brown, eds., *The Zambesian Past* (Manchester, 1966). Ranger's interpretation of the 1896–97 rising was effectively critiqued by Julian Cobbing, 'The Absent Priesthood: Another Look at the Rhodesian Risings of 1896–1897', *Journal of African History* (hereafter *JAH*), XVIII, 1 (1977), pp. 61–84, and David Beach, ' "Chimurenga": The Shona Rising of 1896–97', *JAH*, XX, 3 (1979), pp. 395–420.

[81] *Oxford History*, I, p. v.

[82] See the correspondence printed in Leo Kuper, *Race, Class and Power: Ideology and Revolutionary Change in Plural Societies* (London, 1974), pp. 289–314.

supervision of Shula Marks), and to a lesser extent in the United States, where Leonard Thompson supervised students (mostly American, but also from Canada, New Zealand, and South Africa) at UCLA and then Yale.[83] While admiring the interdisciplinary spirit of the *Oxford History*, many critics complained of the static nature of the anthropological chapters. Others argued that there was too much stress on 'interaction' and too little on 'conflict'. Reactions to the *Oxford History* marked a public divide that extended throughout the 1970s and 1980s between 'liberals' and 'radicals' (terms not necessarily accepted by those so labelled), with the former usually distinguished by an emphasis on the role of ideology (especially Afrikaner racism) in the making of modern southern Africa, and the latter associated with interpretations that stressed the importance of economic causes (linked to British capital) for the development of white supremacy.[84]

To a considerable extent, this divide was a result of Africanist work. In the mid-1960s Martin Legassick, a student of Thompson's at UCLA researching a thesis that focused initially on the African side of frontier relations in the mid-nineteenth-century northern Cape, was struck by the absence rather than presence of race and racism in relations between Africans and Dutch settlers. Legassick decided, like Nzula and others before, that 'race relations are at bottom a class question'.[85] The emphasis on class and industrialization rather than race and Afrikaners also meant that South Africa could, indeed should, be viewed within a larger comparative framework rather than deemed a uniquely aberrant society (a return to a theme pursued by W. K. Hancock thirty years earlier).

Most of the work produced in opposition to the *Oxford History* did aim to place developments in southern and central Africa within a wider, often self-consciously Marxist, theoretical framework that, in place of the unifying theme of Empire, stressed instead mineral extraction and migrant labour as binding together all the societies of the subcontinent. Legassick was strongly influenced by Eugene

[83] Ranger produced few completed doctorates, either during his brief tenure at UCLA or later at Manchester University. Research work in South Africa was largely limited to BA Hons. and MA theses. Smith's UDI-Rhodesia was not hospitable to academic researchers, nor was Hastings Banda's Malawi, while study at the University of Zambia and at the University of Botswana, Lesotho, and Swaziland was limited to the undergraduate level.

[84] Saunders, *The Making of the South African Past*, has a discussion of the reviews. See also Thompson, 'South Africa,' and George Shepperson, 'British Central Africa', in Winks, ed., *The Historiography of the British Empire-Commonwealth*; and Smith, *The Changing Past.* Useful, though often self-serving, discussions of the different camps can be found in Harrison M. Wright, *The Burden of the Present: Liberal–Radical Controversy Over Southern African History* (Cape Town, 1977); Jeffrey Butler, Richard Elphick, and David Welsh, eds., *Democratic Liberalism in South Africa: Its History and Prospect* (Middletown, Conn., 1987); and Belinda Bozzoli and Peter Delius, 'Radical History and South African Society', *Radical History Review*, 46/7 (Winter 1990), pp. 13–45.

[85] See esp. his essay on the frontier in Shula Marks and Anthony Atmore, eds., *Economy and Society in Pre-Industrial South Africa* (London, 1980), pp. 44–79.

Genovese's work on American slavery. Giovanni Arrighi, an Italian sociologist drawing heavily on the underdevelopment ideas of André Gunder Frank, wrote several highly influential analyses of Southern Rhodesia's political economy that placed the region on the periphery of a world capitalizing economy.[86] Frederick A. Johnstone, a Canadian who quoted liberally from Marx, argued in a seminal article that, far from economic growth eliminating racism in South Africa as economists had maintained, the combination of increased profits and greater levels of racial discrimination in the 1960s proved that the South African economy was built fundamentally on a 'racially coercive and exploitative capitalism'.[87] In another influential piece, Colin Bundy suggested along underdevelopment lines that Africans, far from remaining entrapped by traditionalism, had adapted rapidly and successfully to new market opportunities, and it was only through conquest caused by white demands for African labour that people were forced to become the black proletariat remarked upon by de Kiewiet.[88]

The expanding focus on African societies within the context of political economy led some historians to re-examine the old debates about the causes of British imperialism. Why did the British in the late nineteenth century incorporate in their Empire practically all the southern African societies, when for the first half of the century their policy could only be described as 'reluctant'? Was the conquest of the Afrikaner republics related to that of the African communities? Historians from Theal to de Kiewiet to Robinson and Gallagher had argued for the importance of politics, especially strategic concerns related to the Cape sea route to India, and had stressed the role of particular officials and politicians, as in Goodfellow's references to Carnarvon's 'temperament' or Le May's labelling of 'Milner's War'.[89] Shula Marks, however, whose early work had focused on African resistance to British rule in Natal, wrote, much as Hobson had done three-quarters of a century before, that historians should give much greater attention to the salience of economic determinants. In a series of co-authored articles she argued that British colonial officials acted aggressively to protect their country's economic interests: by pursuing confederation in the 1870s; going to war against the Transvaal in 1899; and intervening during the post-war period of reconstruction to establish racially discriminatory labour policies and practices that benefited British capitalists and the British economy. For Marks, the

[86] 'Labour Supplies in Historical Perspectives: A Study of the Proletarianization of the African Peasantry in Rhodesia', *Journal of Development Studies*, VI, 3 (1970), pp. 197–235.

[87] 'White Prosperity and White Supremacy in South Africa Today', *African Affairs*, LXIX (1970), pp. 124–40. See also his *Class, Race and Gold: A Study of Class Relations and Racial Discrimination in South Africa* (London, 1976).

[88] 'The Emergence and Decline of a South African Peasantry', *African Affairs*, LXXI (1972), pp. 369–88.

[89] Le May, *British Supremacy.*

distinctiveness of twentieth-century South Africa was due to the 'imperatives of South Africa's capitalist development'. Marks's articles sparked a renewed debate about the origins of the South African War, with more Imperial-minded historians returning to de Kiewiet's strategic argument (though overlooking the emphasis that he had also placed on gold), and again focusing their research on political issues rather than economic, though unlike their pre-1970s peers only after extensive research in business records as well as in the more conventional sources of official documents and personal papers.[90]

Much of the new work incorporating discussion of economic issues benefited from the opening up of private business archives to scholarly researchers. Though the doors to the South African Chamber of Mines remained firmly closed, researchers were able to circumvent this embargo in part and illuminate the early history of the gold industry through access to the records of some of the leading magnates (especially those of H. Eckstein, Julius Wernher, Alfred Beit, and Lionel Phillips) when Barlow Rand established a professionally organized Archives Department.[91] De Beers Consolidated Mines established an archive, but selectively limited access.[92] Perhaps the most useful of the new archives established—partly because of the richness of its records, more so because of the professionalism of

[90] Shula Marks and Anthony Atmore, 'The Imperial Factor in South Africa in the Nineteenth Century: Towards a Reassessment', *Journal of Imperial and Commonwealth History*, III, 1 (1974), pp. 105–39; Shula Marks and Stanley Trapido, 'Lord Milner and the South African State', *History Workshop*, VIII (1979), pp. 50–80; and, 'Lord Milner and the South African State Reconsidered', in Michael Twaddle, ed., *Imperialism, the State and the Third World* (London, 1992), pp. 80–94; Donald Denoon, *A Grand Illusion: The Failure of Imperial Policy in the Transvaal Colony During the Period of Reconstruction, 1900–1905* (London, 1973); Robert V. Kubicek, *Economic Imperialism in Theory and Practice: The Case of South African Gold Mining Finance, 1886–1914* (Durham, NC, 1979); Peter Warwick, ed., *The South African War: The Anglo-Boer War, 1899–1902* (Harlow, 1980); A. N. Porter, *The Origins of the South African War: Joseph Chamberlain and the Diplomacy of Imperialism, 1895–9* (Manchester, 1980); D. M. Schreuder, *The Scramble for Southern Africa, 1877–1895* (Cambridge, 1980); Russell Ally, *Gold and Empire: The Bank of England and South Africa's Gold Producers, 1886–1929* (Johannesburg, 1994); Smith, *The Origins of the South African War*. Studies which focus on blacks in the war include Peter Warwick, *Black People and the South African War, 1899–1902* (Cambridge, 1983), and Bill Nasson, *Abraham Esau's War: A Black South African War in the Cape, 1899–1902* (Cambridge, 1991). Thomas Pakenham, *The Boer War* (London, 1979), is the fullest account of the military aspects since L. S. Amery, ed., *The Times History of the War in South Africa, 1899–1902*, 7 vols. (London, 1900–09), and Sir John Frederick Maurice and Maurice Howard Grant [Official, War Office], *History of the War in South Africa, 1899–1902*, 4 vols. (London, 1906–10).

[91] See Maryna Fraser and Alan Jeeves, *All That Glittered: Selected Correspondence of Lionel Phillips, 1890–1924* (Cape Town, 1977).

[92] William H. Worger was permitted access in the late 1970s when researching the history of the diamond mining industry, but was denied it in the 1980s: *South Africa's City of Diamonds: Mine Workers and Monopoly Capitalism in Kimberley, 1867–1895* (New Haven, 1987). C. W. Newbury was able to get access to important records in the 1980s for his business-focused study, *The Diamond Ring: Business, Politics, and Precious Stones in South Africa, 1867–1947* (Oxford, 1989).

its archivists, who adhered strictly to policies of rapid accessioning of records and completely open access to all researchers—was that of the Standard Bank.[93] At much the same time that business records became available in South Africa, firms in Britain, particularly shipping companies (Union-Castle Line) and banks (Rothschilds) also made their records available to researchers.[94] Paradoxically, just as formerly embargoed private business records became available, the South African government limited or closed completely access to official records previously open for inspection. The archives for the Prime Minister and for the Governor-General, used by scholars in the 1970s, were placed off-limits in the 1980s, while people using Native Affairs records were subjected to a longer closed period and faced considerable official scrutiny (and often the denial of visas if coming from overseas), particularly during the various states of emergency. In the 1990s, however, access became much less policed, with official records closed for twenty years only, while even the Chamber of Mines had already begun making its archives available to researchers.[95]

Marxist theoretical influences had a considerable impact on study of the relationship between economics and Empire, particularly regarding the conquest of African societies. The dominant trend in 1970s analyses was to view British expansion and conquest in southern and central Africa in the late nineteenth century as propelled by a search for cheap African labour. In this scholarship, much of it done under the supervision of Shula Marks at the University of London with students allocated to research the history of practically every African people in southern Africa, conquest was seen as aggressive rather than reluctant, rational rather than quixotic, and, above all, as the product of the demands of urban British industrialists supported by colonial officials concerned about increasing state revenues, rather than of backcountry Afrikaners. Africans were conquered so that the British could build a modern industrial economy with the labour of men who were forced to migrate to often dangerous urban centres, and had to accept falling real wages from the 1880s to the 1970s.[96] This was a different scenario from that

[93] See Alan Mabin and Barbara Conradie, eds., *The Confidence of the Whole Country: Standard Bank Reports on Economic Conditions in Southern Africa, 1865–1902* (Johannesburg, 1987). Barclays Bank also established an archive but retained far fewer of its records than did the Standard.

[94] See, for example, A. N. Porter, *Victorian Shipping, Business and Imperial Policy: Donald Currie, the Castle Line and Southern Africa* (Woodbridge, 1986); Geoff Berridge, *The Politics of the South Africa Run: European Shipping and Pretoria* (Oxford, 1987); Ally, *Gold and Empire.*

[95] See, for example, Randall M. Packard, *White Plague, Black Labor: Tuberculosis and the Political Economy of Health and Disease in South Africa* (Berkeley, 1989).

[96] See the following studies based on London dissertations, Jeff Guy, *The Destruction of the Zulu Kingdom: The Civil War in Zululand, 1879–1884* (London, 1979); William Beinart, *The Political Economy of Pondoland, 1860 to 1930* (Cambridge, 1982); P. L. Bonner, *Kings, Commoners, and Concessionaires: The Evolution and Dissolution of the Nineteenth-Century Swazi State* (Cambridge, 1983); Peter Delius, *The Land Belongs To Us: The Pedi Polity, the Boers, and the British in the Nineteenth-Century Transvaal*

sketched out in the pages of the *Cambridge History*, where the process of African incorporation into urban labour had been seen primarily as a problem of adaptation and improvement for primitive peoples, or from Robinson and Gallagher's conclusion that 'the movement [of Europeans] into Africa [in the late nineteenth century] remained superficial'.[97]

A focus on African labour and research in corporate records led historians to argue that many of the most distinctive features of twentieth-century society had their origins in the nineteenth-century industrial workplace.[98] Charles van Onselen demonstrated in a study of the Witwatersrand how the industrial practices of British gold magnates created and destroyed classes along racial lines within Johannesburg.[99] William H. Worger examined the connections between business policies and racial discrimination in the diamond industry.[100] For these historians, late-nineteenth-century British imperialism in southern and central Africa was economic in origin and profound in impact.

Greater attention to corporate enterprise, combined with research in southern African as well as metropolitan archives, enabled historians to illuminate in new directions the complicated relationship between business, the colonial state, and metropolitan interests from the late nineteenth century. Theodore Gregory, in his company-commissioned study of Ernest Oppenheimer, analysed the contribution of the Anglo-American Corporation to southern and central Africa. Duncan Innes argued that Oppenheimer's quest for monopoly control of extractive industries intensified the exploitation of African workers and left one company with unprecedented (and unparalleled in Africa and elsewhere) control over the regional economy.[101] Andrew Porter's research in British shipping records and

(Johannesburg, 1983); Kevin Shillington, *The Colonisation of the Southern Tswana, 1870–1900* (Braamfontein, 1985). Paul Maylam, in a Queen's University (Canada) dissertation, dealt with the conquest of the Tswana in a study that 'stress[ed] the role of key individuals', European and African, and that was 'not based on a Marxist analysis'. See his *Rhodes, the Tswana, and the British: Colonialism, Collaboration, and Conflict in the Bechuanaland Protectorate, 1885–1899* (Westport, Conn., 1980), p. 8. On falling real wages, see Francis Wilson, *Labour in the South African Gold Mines, 1911–1969* (Cambridge, 1972).

97 *Africa and the Victorians*, p. 472.

98 See Van Onselen, *Chibaro: African Mine Labour in Southern Rhodesia, 1900–1933* (London, 1976); Charles Perrings, *Black Mineworkers in Central Africa: Industrial Strategies and the Evolution of an African Proletariat in the Copperbelt, 1911–41* (London, 1979). See also Alan Jeeves, *Migrant Labour in South Africa's Mining Economy: The Struggle for the Gold Mine's Labour Supply, 1890–1920* (Kingston, Ontario, 1985); and Elena L. Berger, *Labour, Race, and Colonial Rule: The Copperbelt from 1924 to Independence* (Oxford, 1974).

99 *Studies in the Social and Economic History of the Witwatersrand*, 2 vols. (London, 1982).

100 *South Africa's City of Diamonds.*

101 Theodore Gregory, *Ernest Oppenheimer and the Economic Development of Southern Africa* (Cape Town, 1962), p. 3; Duncan Innes, *Anglo-American and the Rise of Modern South Africa* (New York, 1984). While Gregory had full access to Anglo-American's records, Innes had to rely on published materials only for his analysis. On Anglo-American's diamond interests see also Newbury, *The Diamond Ring.*

South African government archives enabled him to document in more thorough fashion than previous scholars the 'persistent interplay between shipowners' attempts to manipulate government needs' and the desire of politicians to exploit business interests 'in order to secure their imperial aims' during the period 1870–1910.[102] Geoff Berridge, drawing on London business records, argued that after the Second World War the South African government was able to make a 'captive cartel' of British shipping to southern Africa.[103] Nancy Clark, in a study of state intervention in the South African economy set well within the post-1910 national period, concluded that South African politicians and businessmen had to work together in mutual defence against foreign financial interests. Twentieth-century economically based racial discrimination owed much, in this analysis, to the nineteenth-century Imperial foundations of the local economy.[104]

The stress on connections between Imperialism, colonialism, and the search for cheap labour evident in much of the post-1960s scholarship on politics, business, and the urban workplace, appeared also in the writings of historians focusing on rural areas.[105] Later work placed more emphasis on the ability of African societies to adapt constantly to new conditions in ways that led often to fundamental changes in generational and gender roles.[106] The key role of women in agricultural production throughout colonial central Africa has received considerable attention.[107] This work often involved a re-examination and use for historical purposes of early anthropological writings.[108] Patrick Harries used Henri Junod's work in analysing the origins of southern Mozambican migrant labour to South Africa's mines; a far cry from the dual economies (one 'modern', one 'primitive') of the *Cambridge History*.[109] In accounting for the persistence of rural

[102] *Victorian Shipping*, p. 10.

[103] *The Politics of the South Africa Run*, p. 225.

[104] *Manufacturing Apartheid: State Corporations in South Africa* (New Haven, 1994).

[105] Robin Palmer and Neil Parsons, eds., *The Roots of Rural Poverty in Central and Southern Africa* (London, 1977); see also Robin H. Palmer, *Land and Racial Domination in Rhodesia* (London, 1977).

[106] For a criticism of the rise-and-fall paradigm see Kenneth P. Vickery, *Black and White in Southern Zambia: The Tonga Plateau Economy and British Imperialism, 1890–1939* (New York, 1986). See also George Chauncey, 'The Locus of Reproduction: Women's Labour in the Zambian Copperbelt, 1927–1953', *Journal of Southern African Studies* (hereafter *JSAS*), VII, 2 (1981), pp. 135–64.

[107] See Elias Mandala, *Work and Control in a Peasant Economy: A History of the Lower Tchiri Valley in Malawi, 1859–1960* (Madison, 1990); Elizabeth Schmidt, *Peasants, Traders, and Wives: Shona Women in the History of Zimbabwe, 1870–1939* (Portsmouth, NH, 1992); Megan Vaughan, *The Story of an African Famine: Gender and Famine in Twentieth-Century Malawi* (Cambridge, 1987). There is as yet no equivalent scholarship for South Africa. See chap. by Diana Wylie, and in Vol. IV, chap. by Rosalind O'Hanlon.

[108] Megan Vaughan and Henrietta Moore, *Cutting Down Trees: Gender, Nutrition, and Agricultural Change in the Northern Province of Zambia, 1890–1990* (Portsmouth, NH, 1994).

[109] *Work, Culture, and Identity: Migrant Labourers in Mozambique and South Africa, c.1860–1910* (Portsmouth, NH, 1994).

poverty, environmental degradation as a result of Imperial and colonial land-use and land-alienation policies rather than inefficient African farming techniques also captured considerable attention. Leroy Vail's pioneering 1977 article linking 'expanding capitalism . . . colonial administration . . . and ecological catastrophe' in eastern Zambia remains required reading.[110] A special issue of the *Journal of Southern African Studies* in 1989 focused on conflict arising between state and settlers, and officials and African communities, over 'the politics of conservation in southern Africa', and suggested that there might be considerable similarities between 'Ecological practices in African societies . . . [and] modern ecological science'.[111] Emmanuel Krieke researched both colonial land-use policies in southern Angola-northern Namibia and the steps taken by Kwanyama to deal with their changing environment.[112] What distinguished much of this work from the earlier studies of Imperial historians was the emphasis on research in local records rather than metropolitan and, often, the incorporation of African oral testimony.

While many of the studies dealing with the impact of Empire and colonialism on peasant economies were influenced by Marxist or underdevelopment theories, both 'liberal' and 'radical' scholars in the 1970s and after also took an increasingly critical view of nineteenth-century British imperialism, judging it more aggressive than reluctant. David Welsh, a prominent defender of the ideals of Cape liberalism, argued that the segregationist impulses of twentieth-century South Africa had their origins not in the racial desires of Afrikaner frontiersmen nor the economic accounting of British capitalists, but rather in the policies developed by the Natal Secretary for Native Affairs, Theophilus Shepstone, between 1856 and 1876.[113] J. B. Peires claimed, in a study of the Xhosa cattle-killing of the 1850s, that Governor George Grey 'was the true perpetrator . . . of the catastrophe' because of the way in which he 'first encouraged and then capitalized on the movement'.[114] Richard Elphick and Hermann Giliomee, in a key text on pre-industrial South Africa, suggested that while 'the racial order [w]as largely in place by the end of the eighteenth century', British policies in the early nineteenth century hardened

110 'Ecology and History: The Example of Eastern Zambia', *JSAS*, III, 2 (1977), pp. 129–55. Vail's work, like that of later environmental scholars, draws in part from John Ford, *The Role of Trypanosomiases in African Ecology: A Study of the Tsetse Fly Problem* (Oxford, 1971).

111 XV, 2 (1989), p. 146 quoted.

112 'Recreating Eden: Agro-Ecological Change, Food Security and Environmental Diversity in Southern Angola and Northern Namibia', unpublished Ph.D. dissertation, Yale, 1996.

113 David John Welsh, *The Roots of Segregation: Native Policy in Colonial Natal, 1845–1910* (Cape Town, 1971). Welsh's analysis of the creation of nineteenth-century Natal customary law was extended to twentieth-century central Africa by Martin Chanock, *Law, Custom, and Social Order: The Colonial Experience in Malawi and Zambia* (Cambridge, 1985).

114 *The Dead Will Arise: Nongqawuse and the Great Xhosa Cattle-Killing Movement of 1856–7* (Johannesburg, 1989), p. x.

'the ideology of European identity and European supremacy'.[115] This line of interpretation was reinforced by Timothy Keegan's work of synthesis, *Colonial South Africa and the Origins of the Racial Order*, which used the same word, harden, in concluding that 'British influence [in the early nineteenth century had] tended to harden the hierarchies of race rather than dissolve them'.[116] J. Cobbing started an academic firestorm with his contentious argument that the Zulu state-making celebrated by John Omer-Cooper had been set off not by developments internal to African societies (such as population increase) but by the depredations of slave raiders, including among them some of the very same missionaries (especially members of the London Missionary Society such as Robert Moffat) heretofore seen as exponents of British humanitarianism.[117]

Cobbing's critical representation of Moffat seemed something of a caricature compared with work that focused on the interaction of missionaries, Africans, Imperial officials, and Christianity. Leonard Thompson, in his Africanist-phase *magnum opus* on the BaSotho king Moshoeshoe and the Lesotho kingdom, *Survival in Two Worlds*, combined the stress on evangelism evident in Sillery with that on personal triumph and tragedy that ran through Paton's and Hancock's biographies.[118] Landeg White used a detailed case study of the Malawian village of Magomero—in 1861 chosen by David Livingstone as a site for the Universities Mission to Central Africa, in 1915 the main centre of John Chilembwe's uprising, in the 1980s the impoverished home of Malawian migrant workers among whom the author carried out field research—to show how Livingstone's family had applied in practice the nineteenth-century doctrines of Christianity and commerce.[119] Works by Ian Linden and John McCracken followed earlier studies of scholars such as Robert I. Rotberg in demonstrating links between the adoption of Christianity by new African élites and their use of religious ideology in the development of nationalist political movements.[120] South African anthropologists Jean and John Comaroff in the 1990s focused attention on the Tswana and missionaries by looking at what they termed the long conversation between

[115] *The Shaping of South African Society, 1652–1840*, 2nd. edn. (Middletown, Conn., 1988), pp. 522, 560.

[116] (Charlottesville, Va., 1996), pp. 12, 293.

[117] 'The Mfecane as Alibi: Thoughts on Dithakong and Mbolompo,' *JAH*, XXIX, 3 (1988), pp. 487–519. The arguments for and against J. Cobbing are taken up in Carolyn Hamilton, ed., *The Mfecane Aftermath: Reconstructive Debates in Southern African History* (Johannesburg, 1995).

[118] *Survival in Two Worlds: Moshoeshoe of Lesotho, 1786–1870* (Oxford, 1975), pp. vi–vii.

[119] *Magomero: Portrait of an African Village* (Cambridge, 1987). On David Livingstone see also Tim Jeal, *Livingstone* (London, 1973).

[120] Ian Linden and Jane Linden, *Catholics, Peasants, and Chewa Resistance in Nyasaland, 1899–1939* (London, 1974); John McCracken, *Politics and Christianity in Malawi, 1875–1940: The Impact of the Livingstone Mission in the Northern Province* (Cambridge, 1977); Rotberg, *Christian Missionaries and the Creation of Northern Rhodesia.*

European and African.[121] Paul Landau criticized the Comaroffs for providing an analysis that still seemed to suggest that the European missionaries determined the terms on which Christianity would be applied and accepted, and argued instead that Ngwato royalty, clergy (European and Tswana), and Tswana women interacting together created a 'political realm of power' that extended well beyond religion throughout society. Landau's own analysis, however, while stressing the incorporation of new voices, itself fitted well within the interpretative tracks laid down by Sillery and Thompson, with their emphasis on the ways in which Africans made use of missionaries and Christianity to fashion new political structures for themselves within the imposed Imperial and colonial worlds.[122]

The end of colonial rule in the region and the fall of apartheid created a demand for a reassessment of South African history. Future work is likely to focus on the social and economic legacy of colonialism and on the triumph of African protest.[123] For such enduring problems as poverty, ecological degradation, and ethnic division increasing use is being made of African oral testimony and language sources.[124] There is already a greater interest in African political biography evident, for example, in the latest volume of the *Dictionary of South African Biography* which, unlike all the preceding volumes, focused almost without exception on Africans.[125]

New conflict is also likely as to who will set the agenda for post-Empire, post-colonial scholarship. The writing of history has not flourished on campuses in the independent states, and the bulk of work done has been pursued in the universities of Europe and North America. In such circumstances debate about the legacy of Empire will be as intense in the future as it has been in the past.

[121] *Of Revelation and Revolution*, Vol. I, *Christianity, Colonialism, and Consciousness in South Africa* (Chicago, 1991); Vol. II: *The Dialectics of Modernity on a South African Frontier* (Chicago, 1997).

[122] Paul Stuart Landau, *The Realm of the Word: Language, Gender, and Christianity in a Southern African Kingdom* (Portsmouth, NH, 1995).

[123] The changes are evident already in the latest editions of histories of South Africa, T. R. H. Davenport, *South Africa: A Modern History*, 4th edn. (Basingstoke, 1991); Leonard M. Thompson, *A History of South Africa* (London, 1990); Nigel Worden, *The Making of Modern South Africa: Conquest, Segregation and Apartheid* (Oxford, 1994); and William Beinart, *Twentieth-Century South Africa* (Oxford, 1994). Cf. Andrew Roberts, *A History of Zambia* (London, 1976), and David Birmingham and Phyllis M. Martin, eds., *History of Central Africa*, 2 vols. (London, 1983).

[124] Leroy Vail, ed., *The Creation of Tribalism in Southern Africa* (London, 1989); Vail and Landeg White, *Power and the Praise Poem: Southern African Voices in History* (Charlottesville, Va., 1991).

[125] E. J. Verwey, ed., *New Dictionary of South African Biography* (Pretoria, 1995), Vol. 1. See also, T. O. Ranger, *Are We Not Also Men? The Samkange Family and African Politics in Zimbabwe, 1920–64* (Harare, 1995), and Charles van Onselen, *The Seed is Mine: The Life of Kas Maine, a South African Sharecropper, 1894–1985* (New York, 1996).

Select Bibliography

William Beinart, *The Political Economy of Pondoland, 1860 to 1930* (Cambridge, 1982).

Colin Bundy, 'The Emergence and Decline of a South African Peasantry', *African Affairs*, LXXI (1972), pp. 369–88.

Richard Elphick and Hermann Giliomee, eds., *The Shaping of South African Society, 1652–1820* (London, 1979; 2nd. enlarged edn. 1988).

John K. Galbraith, *Reluctant Empire: British Policy on the South African Frontier, 1834–1854* (Berkeley, 1963).

Jeff Guy, *The Destruction of the Zulu Kingdom: The Civil War in Zululand, 1879–1884* (London, 1979).

W. K. Hancock, *Smuts*, 2 vols. (Cambridge, 1962–68).

Frederick Johnstone, 'White Prosperity and White Supremacy in South Africa Today', *African Affairs*, LXIX (1970), pp. 124–40.

C. W. de Kiewiet, *A History of South Africa: Social and Economic* (Oxford, 1941, repr. 1966).

W. M. Macmillan, *Bantu, Boer, and Briton: The Making of the South African Native Problem* (London, 1929).

Shula Marks and Stanley Trapido, 'Lord Milner and the South African State', *History Workshop*, VIII (1979), pp. 50–80.

Charles van Onselen, *Studies in the Social and Economic History of the Witwatersrand*, 2 vols. (London, 1982).

John Philip, *Researches in South Africa*, 2 vols. (London, 1828).

Solomon T. Plaatje, *Native Life in South Africa: Before and Since the European War and the Boer Rebellion* (London, 1916; repr. 1982).

Terence Ranger, *Revolt in Southern Rhodesia, 1869–97: A Study in African Resistance* (Evanston, Ill., 1967).

Edward Roux, *Time Longer Than Rope: A History of the Black Man's Struggle for Freedom in South Africa* (London, 1948; repr. 1964).

George Shepperson and Thomas Price, *Independent African: John Chilembwe and the Origins, Setting, and Significance of the Nyasaland Rising of 1915* (Edinburgh, 1958).

Leonard M. Thompson, *The Unification of South Africa, 1902–1910* (Oxford, 1959).

—— *Survival in Two Worlds: Moshoeshoe of Lesotho, 1786–1870* (Oxford, 1975).

Landeg White, *Magomero: Portrait of an African Village* (Cambridge, 1987).

William H. Worger, *South Africa's City of Diamonds: Mine Workers and Monopoly Capitalism in Kimberley, 1867–1895* (New Haven, 1987).

34

Decolonization and the End of Empire

JOHN DARWIN

Before 1914, although Britain had encountered many Imperial setbacks, there had been no occasion for a general theory of decolonization. The historiography of Imperial decline begins with the crisis of Empire that followed the First World War. Anti-British revolt in Ireland, India, Egypt, and Iraq, and the spread of Bolshevism abroad and unrest at home, revealed to some anxious Imperialists the nightmare vision of an Empire far gone in irreversible decay, brought down by a genetic flaw in the structure of its politics.

The Lost Dominion: The Story of England's Abdication in India (1925) was a brilliant polemic written by a British official in India against the Montagu–Chelmsford reforms scheme with its promise of eventual self-government for the Raj.[1] Political dissidence at home, he argued, had destroyed the ideo-logical coherence and practical autonomy of Britain's enlightened despotism in India. With the decay of British rule, abdication was inevitable. In this bitter cry of the outcast imperialist we can recognize a sophisticated account of the incompatibility between the political processes of the metropole and those of its colony once the colonial regime was no longer carefully insulated from interference by its political masters at home.

At the other end of the political spectrum a similar stress on the inevitability of Imperial disintegration was to be found in the Leninist doctrine which gradually made its way into the mainstream of British political commentary in the 1920s. In *Imperialism: The Highest Stage of Capitalism* (1917), Lenin had prophesied the downfall of empires as the prelude to the destruction of capitalism in the Imperial centre itself. With the onset of global depression, coinciding with the resurgence of political unrest in India, the plausibility of what might be called 'vulgar Leninism'—the inevitability of colonial revolt against imperialist exploitation—increased sharply.[2] When even ardent imperialists agreed that colonial

[1] Al. Carthill, *The Lost Dominion: The Story of England's Abdication in India* (London, 1925).

[2] John Strachey, *The Coming Struggle for Power* (London, 1932). For the spread of Marxist and Hobsonian critiques of Imperialism see Richard Koebner and Helmut Dan Schmidt, *Imperialism: The Story and Significance of a Political Word, 1840–1960* (Cambridge, 1964), pp. 270–79.

nationalism was an unstoppable force to be managed, not resisted, it was not surprising to find predictions of a general 'crumbling of Empire'.[3] But accounts of the death of British imperialism before the Second World War were, at the least, much exaggerated.

Indeed, it might well be wondered whether these two obituarists were discussing the same cadaver. In *The Lost Dominion*, it was the coming end of British *rule* that was lamented. The Leninist thesis, on the other hand, anticipated the destruction of a much wider system of Western domination maintained through what we have come to call 'informal empire' as much as by direct colonial rule. The historian grappling with the causes of British decolonization has to decide what it is that needs explanation: as much as the historian of Imperial expansion, he is 'at the mercy of his own particular concept'.[4]

Four different definitions of decolonization, at least, can be identified in the historical literature. The most conventional and user-friendly is the usage which equates decolonization with the legal-constitutional event of a transfer of sovereignty. When colonial rule is formally terminated and an independent state has been born, decolonization has taken place. The causes of decolonization are, therefore, to be found in the events and circumstances which have led up to this constitutional consummation. This definition has the virtue of precision, but also the defects. Constitutional status may be a pointer to the substantive relationship between two states, but it is not a reliable guide. This is a commonplace of the large literature on informal empire. Historians of British imperialism would also find it difficult to fit Britain's relations with Egypt (declared independent in 1922 but occupied until 1956) or the 'White Dominions' (conceded constitutional equality with Britain in 1931 under the Statute of Westminster) into a definitional straitjacket that seems to have been devised for the experience of a tropical dependency. Yet any account of British decolonization which excludes informal empire, Egypt, and the White Dominions would be merely vacuous.[5]

One solution to this difficulty is to treat decolonization as a mere formality: a piece of constitutional fol-de-rol whose purpose was as often to preserve Imperial influence as to end it. Decolonization could be regarded as the pursuit of a modified imperialism by other means: as an extra twist in the tortuous saga

[3] Moritz J. Bonn, *The Crumbling of Empire: The Disintegration of World Economy* (London, 1938). For a survey of official attitudes in the inter-war years see J. Darwin, 'Imperialism in Decline? Tendencies in British Imperial Policy between the Wars', *Historical Journal*, XXIII, 3 (1980), pp. 657–79.

[4] John Gallagher and Ronald Robinson, 'The Imperialism of Free Trade', *Economic History Review*, Second Series, VI, 1 (1953), p. 1.

[5] Robin W. Winks, 'On Decolonization and Informal Empire', *American Historical Review*, LXXXI, 3 (1976), pp. 540–56.

of collaboration designed to install moderates and pre-empt extremists in the struggle to control the (ex-) colonial state. In this view, independence was no more than a new collaborative bargain. Such a definition certainly has greater utility than that put forward by Frantz Fanon, for whom only the complete extrusion of all foreign influence from the new state was sufficient proof that decolonization had occurred.[6] On such utopian criteria decolonization would still be an aspiration, not an accomplished fact. But to reduce decolonization to a change of form rather than substance creates more problems than it solves. In so far as it implies that the end of *formal* empire left the underlying structures of British, European, or Western imperialism intact, it is plainly wrong. Worse still, if we pin the label of decolonization only to the donkey's tail, we still need a name for the donkey—those changes of substance which *have* taken place in the relations between Britain and her former Imperial system, and more generally between the West and the 'Third World'.

Considerations of this kind might propel us towards a more radical definition of decolonization, whose main advantage is to draw attention to the collapse since 1945 of the global infrastructure which sustained British and other European imperialisms. In this broader view, decolonization is to be seen as the breakdown not just of colonial rule but of a much larger complex which might be called the 'global colonial order'. Although European colonialism had a long history, it was not 'globalized' until the later nineteenth century, when the world was effectively partitioned into spheres of formal and informal domination by the European powers and their two junior partners, the United States and Japan. Underlying this division of the world was a conception of international order which explicitly repudiated self-government for 'backward' societies and tacitly recognized forcible intervention in them, or the assertion of authority over them, in pursuit of the national interest of 'civilized' powers.

In economic terms, the colonial order was founded upon a world economy with a division of labour which allotted the production of commodities to the colonial and semi-colonial world and the functions of banking, investing, and manufacturing to their industrialized masters. This division was maintained by the institution of the 'open economy' accepted by, or imposed upon, colonies and semi-colonies:[7] the denial of protective tariffs, important substitution or self-sufficiency; the easy repatriation of profits; a secure international 'property regime';[8] the acceptance of international (through the gold standard) or Imperial

[6] Frantz Fanon, *The Wretched of the Earth*, paperback edn. (Harmondsworth, 1967), chap. 1.

[7] The term 'open economy' was given currency in A. G. Hopkins's influential book *An Economic History of West Africa* (London, 1973).

[8] Charles Lipson, *Standing Guard: Protecting Foreign Capital in the Nineteenth and Twentieth Centuries* (Berkeley, 1985).

control over local currency; and a programme of economic development mainly through the more intense exploitation of local natural resources. Demographically, the colonial order sanctioned the movement of Afro-Asian labour to accelerate economic development since, except in white settler societies, ethnic diversification was assumed to hold little significance for territories having no 'national' future. The immigration of Europeans into colonial regions was considered desirable for their economic betterment, if not always practicable. Finally, globalized colonialism was sustained by powerful cultural prejudices which viewed most extra-European cultures as so many picturesque cul-de-sacs whose 'low social efficiency'[9] meant that they were incapable of spontaneously generating what the annual reports of the Government of India termed 'moral and material progress'.

In its larger sense, then, decolonization should be defined as the more or less complete overthrow of this structure of institutions and ideas between 1945 and the mid-1960s, and its replacement by a 'post-colonial order' whose first phase ended in 1990. To make full sense of *Britain's* decolonization, it must be located in this larger breakdown: the *virtually* simultaneous collapse of all the European colonial empires is a warning against any explanatory scheme that lays too much weight upon purely British circumstances, or upon the bilateral relations of a particular colony with the Imperial metropole. In short, the end of the British Empire was part of a systemic failure, or change; and theories of British decolonization should depend for their plausibility on how far they can accommodate not merely its constitutional but also its ideological, economic, demographic, and cultural aspects.[10] Without these our understanding of the demolition of Western versions of imperialism would be impoverished. For whatever new forms of international inequality may have emerged during and after decolonization, their distinctive characteristic was precisely their rejection of the classical features of the global colonial order of *c*.1880–*c*.1960.

Two familiar explanations for British decolonization may be dealt with summarily. The first has sentimental charm: the disintegration of the British Empire as a case of 'planned obsolescence'. The British had accepted the burden of colonial administration as a trust to be exercised until such time as their colonial subjects were competent to manage their own affairs. The transfers of power after 1945, almost uniformly voluntary and peaceful, were a triumph of altruistic purpose

[9] Benjamin Kidd, *Social Evolution* (London, 1894), p. 292.

[10] On decolonization see Vol. IV, chap. by Wm. Roger Louis. For the cultural consequences of decolonization see James Clifford, *The Predicament of Culture: Twentieth-Century Ethnography, Literature and Art* (Cambridge, Mass., 1988).

and pragmatic timing. They were not to be seen, insisted Harold Macmillan,[11] as evidence that the British people had lost the will to rule, nor as a defeat for Britain's standing in the world. That had been enhanced by the evident enthusiasm of almost every ex-colonial territory for the retention of a special connection with the former Mother Country through membership of the Commonwealth.

Macmillan's flair for the invention of history would be sufficient ground for scepticism. But there are other reasons for rejecting this account of decolonization apart from its obviously self-serving purpose as a salve to conservative opinion. Before 1939 there was no evidence of British enthusiasm for accelerating *full* self-government in the colonial possessions. Even in India, which had travelled further towards self-government than any other non-Dominion, the 1935 constitution had left their timetable for achieving Dominion Status undefined, while hedging about the promise of future self-government with statutory 'safeguards' giving London ultimate control over defence, external relations, currency questions, and minority rights. Even after 1945 the timetable of political change remained, over much of the colonial Empire, a leisurely one. The rapid accelerations that occurred in India between 1945 and 1947 and in East and Central Africa after 1959, sprang from the calculation that without prompt colonial withdrawal London faced dangerous crises of local control. But perhaps the strongest reason for rejecting this explanation as inadequate is that it is concerned entirely with constitutional status and offers no wider insight into the shift in Britain's relations with her spheres of informal as well as formal influence.

Almost equally unsatisfactory, so far as our present knowledge extends, is the suggestion that the abandonment of colonial rule after 1945—as a key element in the overall process of decolonization—was the result of a change in the structure of international capitalism. This is the 'neo-colonialist' thesis brilliantly sketched by Paul Baran in 1957: that colonial policy was geared to the political requirements of big business which lost interest in maintaining old-style colonial rule. As business became more international in its scope and multinational in organization, it increasingly regarded the perpetuation of colonial government as both an obstacle and a threat, blocking the way to an accommodation with the new nationalist politicians waiting in the wings. Continued political frustration was likely to drive otherwise pliable colonial politicians into anti-foreign and anti-capitalist extremism. By contrast, prompt self-government would install a new ruling class ready to collaborate with international capital and preserve a congenial environment for its operations.[12] For all the superficial appeal of explaining Imperial withdrawal as a conspiracy of commercial interests (in a symmetrical counterpart to Hobsonian

[11] Harold Macmillan, *Pointing the Way, 1959–61* (London, 1972), pp. 116–17.

[12] Paul A. Baran, *The Political Economy of Growth* (New York, 1957). See also Gary Wasserman, *Politics of Decolonization: Kenya Europeans and the Land Issue, 1960–1965* (Cambridge, 1976).

accounts of Imperial expansion), it is confronted by three fundamental objections. The comparative simultaneity of British withdrawal from almost all the dependencies between 1947 and 1964 was clearly not a function of any similarity in the economic character of hugely disparate territories. The nature and significance of external economic interests across the colonial Empire was much too varied for accelerated transfers of power to have been regarded as uniformly desirable, or even, in many cases, of any commercial significance. That would be a less powerful objection if it could be shown that in several key instances the policy of decolonization was shaped decisively by business interests. But the evidence is lacking. On the contrary, detailed investigation of British enterprise in India and West Africa strongly suggests that its influence both locally and in London was extremely limited, and that surprisingly little official account was taken of British commercial interests and opinions in the approach to independence.[13] Such a conspiracy theory rests upon a reductionist view of the 'British' interests which Imperial policymakers sought to preserve or promote. There is, in fact, no warrant for presuming that the commercial interests of private enterprise were elevated over considerations of strategy, diplomacy, or the more modest objective of escaping from a quagmire of unwanted administrative responsibilities.

Partisan explanations may be contrasted with three more 'tough-minded' but essentially monocausal theories which still possess a wide influence. John Strachey's pioneering study argued that the key factor in the British decision to give up a world Empire was the shift in political thinking at home. Empire was not wrenched from Britain's grasp: it had become embarrassing or redundant, and was dropped. There are several strands to this argument, not all readily compatible with each other. Thus, it was once fashionable to maintain that, especially after 1945, British opinion had grown too liberal to be comfortable with the authoritarianism and overt racism inseparable from the exercise of colonial authority. In the age of Butskellite consensus, 'middle opinion' could not stomach the revelations of colonialist brutality that occurred with depressing frequency by the later 1950s. Instead, the pace was set politically by those who demanded the democratization of the Empire and the renunciation of inegalitarian or racist ideologies intolerable to a social democracy.[14]

[13] The response of British business to political change has been examined in two (as yet) unpublished theses: S. Stockwell, 'British Business, Politics and Decolonisation in the Gold Coast, *c.*1945–60', D.Phil. thesis, Oxford, 1995; A. M. Misra, 'Entrepreneurial Decline and the End of Empire: British Business in India, 1919–52', D.Phil. thesis, Oxford, 1992.

[14] John Strachey, T*he End of Empire* (London, 1959), pp. 215–16, for the importance of an anti-imperialist tradition in working-class politics. For the influence of sentimental imperialism, Elie Kedourie, *The Chatham House Version and Other Middle-Eastern Studies* (London, 1970), p. 155; L. H. Gann and Peter Duignan, *The Burden of Empire: An Appraisal of Western Colonialism in Africa South of the Sahara* (New York, 1967), chap. 19.

It was also possible to suggest that the Empire (and by extension a 'world role') became not so much embarrassing as obsolete, a tiresome liability, not an attribute of power. The crucial change in Imperial policy was the realization that British interests had changed fundamentally in the post-war world. The orientation of trade, investment, and strategy was no longer towards the extra-European world with its great archipelago of Imperial territories. Now prosperity depended upon economic partnership with the rich industrialized states in Europe and North America, not half-developed colonial commodity producers.[15] The strategic priority had become the guarding of Europe against Soviet aggression, not the far-flung call of Imperial defence. Investment abroad on the old Imperial scale could not be afforded now that the modernization of the British economy and funding a welfare state demanded the concentration of resources at home. Thus, when colonial territories demanded independence there was no will to resist: quite the contrary. Empire had become an irrelevant burden, an obstacle to the rational allocation of Britain's resources. The turn to Europe in 1960–61 and the repudiation of a strategic role East of Suez in January 1968 thus marked a climacteric in the domestic politics of Britain's external relations.

Underlying these two interpretations of the politics of decolonization are conflicting assumptions about public opinion. The first version sees public opinion as shaped by anti-Imperial values and increasingly hostile to anti-democratic policies abroad. The second treats it as fundamentally indifferent to Empire, but driven to an impatient renunciation when costs were no longer balanced by benefits. Both assumptions are too extreme. There is, in fact, little evidence of any sustained anti-imperialism in British politics after 1945, although there was much criticism on the Left of the *practice* of colonial administration.[16] Usually, enthusiasm for a rapid advance to colonial independence was combined with a naive optimism that the new states would draw ideological inspiration from Britain and remain closely aligned with her internationally. But equally, it is doubtful whether British opinion, or its leaders, drew the brutal conclusion that the shift in Britain's post-war circumstances had made the substance of world power redundant. Certainly, successive British governments up to 1968 made every effort to reassure domestic opinion that, whatever form decolonization took, it was reconcilable with Britain's survival as a great world power: an anaesthetizing rhetoric in which the Commonwealth idea was an indispensable painkiller.[17] Even in the 1980s, as the Falklands crisis revealed, British leaders of both main parties were willing to

[15] Strachey, *Empire*, pp. 189–90.

[16] See Stephen Howe, *Anti-Colonialism in British Politics: The Left and the End of Empire, 1919–1964* (Oxford, 1993).

[17] J. G. Darwin, 'The Fear of Falling: British Politics and Imperial Decline', *Transactions of the Royal Historical Society*, Fifth Series, XXXVI (1986), pp. 27–43.

take huge political risks rather than accept Britain's forcible dispossession of a colony whose remoteness and redundancy might have been thought—indeed were officially regarded as—unarguable.

To a second school of thought this domestic British bickering about Imperial policy was a dispute about the arrangement of the deckchairs. The reality was an international environment that had become so inhospitable after 1945 that the real choice for British leaders was to scuttle first or await the inevitable collision with an iceberg. This argument falls into two connected parts. On the one hand, it represents Britain as fundamentally under-engined for the era of superpowers: incapable of matching the military, economic, and ideological strength of the United States or the Soviet Union, and squeezed between their conflicting ambitions for world domination.[18] On the other, it suggests that, partly as a consequence of superpower rivalries, the post-war climate of international opinion, exemplified by the United Nations Charter, was profoundly hostile to formal colonialism. Empire in its classical form had become internationally illegitimate. The significance of the Suez crisis could thus be seen to lie in its fusion of both these sources of international pressure, revealing that old-style imperialism was no longer acceptable and that Britain was too weak to maintain its influence by other means.

The evidence for Britain's relative decline as an international power is hard to resist. So also is the implicit suggestion that the possession of a colonial Empire was a function of Britain's international strength and not the other way round. The real difficulty with 'internationalist' explanations lies in their tendency to exaggerate Britain's post-war weakness and the strength of the superpowers; and to regard the decline of British power as a continuous process from 1945 to the 1970s. Moreover, many weaker empires than Britain's have survived adverse international conditions for much longer. It is puzzling that British leaders were unable to exploit a period of intense international rivalry to win a longer respite for their embattled Imperial system: after all, as Roger Louis has shown, wartime American antipathy had softened rapidly once the threat of Soviet imperialism had been recognized by 1945.[19] And if tiny, backward, isolated Portugal could cling to its Imperial possessions until 1975, how is the disintegration of the British Empire a decade or more earlier to be explained?

These considerations suggest that even if the international setting played a key role in the breakup of the British Empire, it could only do so in interaction with British thinking about where their international priorities lay. International pressures were

[18] See Stewart C. Easton, *The Twilight of European Colonialism: A Political Analysis* (New York, 1960), p. 31; Paul M. Kennedy, *The Rise and Fall of Great Powers*, paperback edn. (London, 1988), pp. 472–78, 506, 547–49.

[19] Wm. Roger Louis, *Imperialism at Bay: The United States and the Decolonization of the British Empire, 1941–1945* (Oxford, 1977).

mediated by the refusal of British leaders to contemplate a tenacious Portugal-style resistance to colonial liberation. For the third school, however, domestic policy-making and international circumstances were of only marginal relevance to decolonization, whether in its narrow meaning of the transfer of sovereignty or in the larger sense of the collapse of the global colonial system.

For historians, such as Henri Grimal or D. A. Low, the decisive arena of change was in colonial (or semi-colonial) society itself, where once-compliant peoples revolted against foreign rule or domination.[20] Without this movement of resistance and rebellion, neither the impact of international politics nor the influence of domestic reappraisal would have been sufficient to smash the structures of Imperial power. In practice, this assertion of the primacy of colonial politics divides into two different if connected explanations for the breakdown of colonial rule and semi-colonial overlordship. The older view, given classic expression by Immanuel Wallerstein, lays greatest emphasis upon the rise of colonial nationalism as an ideology through which an educated colonial élite progressively mobilized a mass following.[21] Skilfully exploiting the racial exclusiveness of their masters, the pervasive climate of socio-economic discontent, and a curiously ubiquitous supply of charismatic leadership, nationalist movements successfully invented imaginary nations and rallied colonial opinion against an arthritic administrative autocracy. An influential alternative, less perhaps a 'nationalist' theory than a broader-based 'peripheral' theory, was Ronald Robinson's depiction of nationalism more as a symptom than a cause of colonial breakdown. Here it is the reliance of the colonial state (and informal imperialism) upon collaborators which is the critical factor.[22] In its heyday, British imperialism had derived its power chiefly from its ability to win allies and rally support in regions of formal and informal Empire alike. The British had held the initiative in selecting these local collaborators: colonial governance had been the subtle art of checking and balancing rival interests, castes, and communities. But in the age of decolonization the British found that this clockwork politics no longer sufficed: they could no longer rally enough collaborators. Instead, it was their anti-colonial enemies who were able to form larger and larger coalitions against them until eventually they were confronted by the grim alternatives of rule by coercion (impossibly expensive and politically futile) or a final collaborative 'bargain' in which they 'chose' their successors.

[20] Henri Grimal, *Decolonization: The British, French, Dutch and Belgian Empires, 1919–1963* (1965; Eng. trans., London, 1978); D. A. Low, 'The Asian Mirror to Tropical Africa's Independence', in Prosser Gifford and Wm. Roger Louis, eds., *The Transfer of Power in Africa: Decolonization, 1940–1960* (New Haven, 1982), pp. 18, 29.

[21] Immanuel Wallerstein, *Africa: The Politics of Independence* (New York, 1961), chap. 3. See also Thomas Hodgkin, *Nationalism in Colonial Africa* (London, 1956).

[22] See R. E. Robinson, 'The Non-European Foundations of European Imperialism', in Roger Owen and Bob Sutcliffe, eds., *Studies in the Theory of Imperialism* (London, 1972).

The peripheral theory is a salutary reminder of the weakness and fragility of the colonial state, the poverty of its coercive resources and the frequency with which local political unrest punctuated the last phase of British Imperial power. But it also leaves several questions unanswered. Why was it that the British had once found winning collaborators so easy, but now so hard? Why were they unwilling or unable to take the counter-measures against their 'nationalist' opponents which had proved so effective in the past? How had nationalist leaderships been able to overcome the obstacles of social, religious, and regional fragmentation which had frustrated earlier attempts to build nations? And why, in the bewildering variety of colonial and semi-colonial circumstances, was the successful withdrawal of collaboration achieved with such astonishing simultaneity across the colonial and semi-colonial world? It begins to look as if the peripheral theory is as incomplete as its international and domestic counterparts.

The solution may be to find a means of integrating the different arenas of political change to produce a more 'systemic' explanation for the Imperial breakup. In his *Decline, Revival and Fall of the British Empire*[23] John Gallagher had shown with characteristic verve how this approach could illuminate the course of British imperialism between 1900 and 1945. For Gallagher, the key to decline and fall was to be found in the unstable triangular relationship between Great Power diplomacy, domestic politics, and the terms of colonial collaboration. Gallagher's account stopped short of applying this fundamental insight to the last phase of British Imperial history after 1945. But a highly effective and influential example of how it could be developed was advanced by R. F. Holland in his general model of European decolonization.[24] Here stress was laid upon a process of mutual 'disimperialism' in both Imperial core and colonial periphery. At both ends of the Imperial nexus new interests and needs had been identified which rendered the old collaborative bargains obsolete. In Britain, and more generally in Europe, the post-war triumph of social democracy, the transition to a high mass-consumption economy, and the simultaneous appearance of a severe new strategic threat from the East swiftly eroded the will and ability to sustain the burden of colonial Empire and marginalized the adherents of the 'imperial idea'. Among colonials and semi-colonials, the indifference and inadequacy of their former masters, the need to court new international sponsors, and safeguard the political inheritance of the colonial state against new centrifugal forces, made independence not only desirable but necessary. Though frequently disfigured by local violence whose significance was

[23] Cambridge, 1982.

[24] R. F. Holland, *European Decolonization, 1918–1981: An Introductory Survey* (London, 1985).

essentially 'tactical', decolonization was thus a process of voluntary disengagement, once the gravitational pull of the old colonial system had all but vanished.

An alternative approach is to preserve many of the systemic features identified by Holland but to place much less emphasis upon the extent to which decolonization arose from a willing disengagement by both rulers and ruled.[25] At the international level, what was striking was the struggle of the 'Old Colonial Powers' led by Britain to preserve rather than repudiate the main elements of the pre-war colonial order. Their failure was not immediate nor outright but was the cumulative result of the impact of the Pacific War, post-war economic weakness, and the gradual attrition of their spheres of influence by the two superpowers. The effect of this adverse international conjuncture on Britain was to raise steadily the domestic costs (in both resources and ideological legitimacy) of the effort to uphold Great Power status but not to induce any fundamental reappraisal of its necessity. Colonially, the logic of the post-war situation was to balance the more intensive exploitation of economic relationships (made necessary by the new poverty of the metropole) by the promise of political devolution and a new rhetoric of Imperial partnership. This meant moving gradually and selectively away from formal rule towards an imperialism of informal influence. Tactfully disguised, the British Commonwealth was to be a satellite system in all but name.

This last and highest stage of British imperialism imploded not so much because it was disavowed at home but because it collapsed abroad. Informal imperialism was not an easy option for a declining power: that was the real lesson of Suez. Despite persistent official optimism, Britain's economic recovery was too slow and too partial to sustain her pre-war role as the leading market, supplier, and investor for the Imperial system. The transition to a more informal empire required a stronger not a weaker Imperial centre. At the colonial level, it quickly became apparent that managing devolution without the means to exclude foreign influence, apply sustained coercion (as in pre-war India), or invest the resources needed to rally new collaborators was a hopeless task. The 'statesmanship' of Macmillan and Iain Macleod after 1959 lay in their grudging acknowledgement of this unpalatable fact. Thereafter, with unseemly haste, the old timetables were rolled up and new ones proclaimed the unexpectedly early arrival of colonial political maturity. But domestically and internationally, no British government could bring itself to renounce a Great Power role until the devaluation crisis of November 1967 enforced strategic abdication East of Suez in January 1968. By contrast with the 'disimperialism' model, this version suggests that the Second World

25 John Darwin, *Britain and Decolonization: The Retreat from Empire in the Post-War World* (London, 1988).

War set in motion a complex vicious circle from which the British struggled in vain to escape.

Enough has been said to suggest that the history of decolonization requires the careful fusion of three 'sub-historiographies': the domestic politics of 'decline'; the tectonic shifts of relative power, wealth, and legitimacy at the international level; and the colonial (or semi-colonial) politics of locality, province, and nation. The historian, or reader, who wants to take a large view of decolonization depends heavily upon the progress of enquiry in each of these fields. The future of the subject really lies in the systematic exchanges of ideas and information between the three academic provinces into which it has been conventionally divided, as well as upon regional or local studies where the insights of each sub-historiography can be brought to bear.

In fact, in recent years each of the three divisions has been the scene of vigorous activity. Britain's decline is an academic growth area, but historians are now at pains to show that there was no simple correlation between the decay of the British industrial economy and the loss of Empire. In the second volume of their *British Imperialism* (1993), P. J. Cain and A. G. Hopkins drew attention to the prolongation well after 1945 of the British vision of an economic empire.[26] Subsequent studies by Catherine Schenk[27] and Hopkins himself[28] have explored further the argument that it was the financial and currency imperatives in the 1950s that made the retention of a colonial empire (in the formal sense) more and more unattractive, and empire (of any kind) less and less feasible. Stephen Howe's cool assessment of 'anti-imperialism' in Britain[29] revealed that the fire-eating anti-colonial radicals of the Movement for Colonial Freedom could hardly keep pace with the pragmatism of the policy-making establishment, while sharing much of the naïve confidence in the continuity of Britain's post-colonial influence. Two studies of the party-political arena by Miles Kahler[30] and Philip Murphy[31] helped to explain how the Conservative Party was persuaded that the end of Empire was

[26] P. J. Cain and A. G. Hopkins, *British Imperialism: Crisis and Deconstruction, 1914–1990* (London, 1993), pp. 275 ff.

[27] Catherine R. Schenk, *Britain and the Sterling Area: From Devaluation to Convertibility in the 1950s* (London, 1994).

[28] Anthony G. Hopkins, 'Macmillan's Audit of Empire, 1957', in Peter Clarke and Clive Trebilcock, eds., *Understanding Decline: Perceptions and Realities of British Economic Performance* (Cambridge, 1997), pp. 234–60.

[29] Howe, *Anti-Colonialism in British Politics.*

[30] Miles Kahler, *Decolonization in Britain and France: The Domestic Consequences of International Relations* (Princeton, 1984).

[31] See Philip Murphy, *Party Politics and Decolonization: The Conservative Party and British Colonial Policy in Tropical Africa, 1951–1964* (Oxford, 1995).

the logical fulfilment of its deeper purposes—one of the grand delusions of modern political history. Some advance has been made on the hagiographical innocence with which the older biographies treated the main political actors of the decolonization era,[32] although Macleod's reputation as a visionary has enjoyed a perverse immunity from this greater realism.[33]

At the level of international politics and policy, there exists a large and growing literature which reflects the high level of interest in contemporary or near-contemporary international relations. Only very gradually, however, has recognition of the profound importance of decolonization made much impact on a discipline so long obsessed with the minutiae of superpower relations. The response of the policy-making élite—that inner world of politicians, diplomats, and civil servants enigmatically christened the 'official mind' by Gallagher and Robinson—to Britain's kaleidoscopic changes of fortune after 1945 has yet to be charted in full archival detail.

Here and there clearings have been made in the great forest of official records. The difficulty of the task is compounded by the way in which the management of Britain's Imperial interests after 1945 was increasingly caught up in international diplomacy or, as in Egypt and other regions of informal empire, had always been treated as an aspect of foreign policy. Here the historian must unpick the threads of a bilateral colonial or semi-colonial relationship in the larger fabric of regional or global diplomacy, and weigh the strength of local nationalism against the pressures of international competition or alliance politics in an era of emergent superpowers. The major achievement in this field has been Wm. Roger Louis's *Britain's Empire in the Middle East, 1945–1951* (1984).[34] This was a forceful assertion that British experience in the Middle East, predominantly a region of informal empire, was indispensable to understanding the larger story of the end of Empire. It was a careful reconstruction of official thinking, which argued that British policy in a period of acute economic stress had been to adapt the British presence in the region to the new climate of Arab nationalism—though with little success. It built upon the author's earlier work on wartime American attitudes to the European colonial empires,[35] to expose the delicacy of Anglo-American relations and the strains of alliance-building in a region that the cold war had made more strategically vital than ever.

This theme of Anglo-American imperial collaboration was developed much further in the joint article published by Louis and Robinson in 1994. The

[32] Alistair Horne, *Harold Macmillan*, 2 vols. (New York, 1988–89).

[33] But see Robert Shepherd, *Iain Macleod* (London, 1994).

[34] Wm. Roger Louis, *The British Empire in the Middle East, 1945–1951: Arab Nationalism, the United States and Post-War Imperialism* (Oxford, 1984).

[35] Louis, *Imperialism at Bay.*

'Imperialism of Decolonization' argued that the survival of British Imperial power was deliberately prolonged by the infusion of American economic and military aid, while the British themselves acknowledged that the conversion of their Colonial Empire to a community of nation states ('decolonization') was the only means available to retain their influence over them ('imperialism').[36] Meanwhile, the best general introduction to the large-scale changes in international politics, law, and notions of legitimacy—the context of British policy-making—can be found in the collection of essays edited by Hedley Bull and Adam Watson, *The Expansion of International Society* (Oxford, 1984).

The local scene of colonial or semi-colonial politics is simultaneously the most fascinating and the most frustrating. After the early rush of 'nation-building' histories celebrating the achievements of nationalist 'founding fathers', the breakup of the colonial state as an historical topic was overtaken by the fashion for different kinds of 'subaltern' history. In many places the siren-call of fashion was less influential than the fact of archival poverty, neglect, or restriction, or even the collapse of history-writing as a scholarly enterprise. But no account of decolonization which neglects the particularities of local politics, or assumes the uniformity of colonial nationalism, can have much value. Nor should the abstractions of 'policy-making' or diplomacy be permitted to crowd out the real politics of decolonization as they were felt in colonial societies. Herein lies the value of John Hargreaves's *Decolonization in Africa*,[37] where it is the African role in political change and the African experience of colonial freedom which occupies the foreground. Subtle studies of the political, economic, ecological, and cultural transformations which preceded the end of colonial rule can be found in John Iliffe's *A Modern History of Tanganyika*[38] and in *Unhappy Valley*, a collection of essays by John Lonsdale and Bruce Berman on Kenyan history, which offers, among other things, a compelling account of Mau Mau, the most violent anti-colonial explosion in Black Africa.[39] The pervasive myth that in the British Empire, unlike the French, Belgian, Dutch, or Portuguese, the transfer of power was effected over tea in an atmosphere of sweetness and light is confronted in some of the essays to be found in *Emergencies and Disorders in the European Colonial Empires after 1945*.[40] And at long last, the Marxian speculation that the local operations of colonialism

[36] Wm. Roger Louis and Ronald Robinson, 'The Imperialism of Decolonization', *Journal of Imperial and Commonwealth History*, XXII, 3 (1994), pp. 462–511.

[37] J. D. Hargreaves, *Decolonization in Africa* (London, 1988).

[38] Cambridge, 1979.

[39] Bruce Berman and John Lonsdale, *Unhappy Valley: Conflict in Kenya and Africa*, 2 vols. (London, 1992).

[40] R. F. Holland, ed., *Emergencies and Disorders in the European Colonial Empires After 1945* (London, 1994); David Killingray and David Anderson, eds., *Policing and Decolonization: Politics, Nationalism, and the Police, 1917–65* (Manchester, 1992).

in the decolonization era were driven by the changing commercial needs of expatriate business is beginning to be investigated systematically—with results that suggest the Olympian disregard of official policy for commercial interests in the formulation of its political and constitutional programme.[41] By contrast, the colonial authorities displayed a strong but largely ineffectual desire to shape labour politics and policy, an enterprise surveyed in Frederick Cooper's *Decolonization and African Society*.[42] Very gradually the profile of what might be called 'the late colonial state'—a rickety, under-engined vehicle staggering under its burden of local and imperial aspirations—is starting to take shape.

Understanding decolonization requires the connection of three levels of analysis, but it also dictates a comparative approach if the peculiarities of one colonial relationship are not to distort the overall impression. Making comparisons has become easier with the publication of large tranches of official documentation. Nicholas Mansergh's twelve monumental volumes on *The Transfer of Power in India, 1942–7*[43] set the pattern. It was followed by two further volumes on Burma.[44] Now the interested reader can follow the twists and U-turns of official policy in the synoptic volumes of the British Documents on the End of Empire Project[45] and in its series on individual colonies.[46] The metropolitan, or at least governmental, perspective which dominates these volumes can be varied to some extent by inspecting British actions and motives through (official) Canadian and Australian eyes[47] or through those of (unofficial) Indians. But only so far and in some places. The financial resources,

[41] David K. Fieldhouse, *Merchant Capital and Economic Decolonization: The United Africa Company, 1929–1987* (Oxford, 1994); Nicholas J. White, *Business, Government, and the End of Empire: Malaya, 1942–1957* (Oxford, 1996).

[42] Frederick Cooper, *Decolonization and African Society: The Labour Question in French and British Africa* (Cambridge, 1996).

[43] Nicholas Mansergh, ed., *Constitutional Relations between Britain and India: The Transfer of Power*, 12 vols. (London, 1970–83). See chap. by Ian Talbot for full details.

[44] Hugh Tinker, ed., *Constitutional Relations Between Britain and Burma: The Struggle for Independence, 1944–1948*, 2 vols. (London, 1983–84).

[45] S. R. Ashton and S. E. Stockwell, eds., *Imperial Policy and Colonial Practice, 1925–1945*, British Documents on the End of Empire Project (BDEEP), Series A, Vol. I (London, 1996); Ronald Hyam, ed., *The Labour Government and the End of Empire, 1945–1951*, BDEEP, Series A, Vol. II (London, 1992); David Goldsworthy, ed., *The Conservative Government and the End of Empire, 1951–1957*, BDEEP, Series A, Vol. III (London, 1994).

[46] Richard Rathbone, ed., *Ghana*, BDEEP, Series B, Vol. I (London, 1992); K. M. de Silva, ed., *Sri Lanka*, BDEEP, Series B, Vol. II (London, 1997); A. J. Stockwell, ed., *Malaya*, BDEEP, Series B, Vol. III (London, 1995).

[47] For the resentment of Canadian officials at their 'colonial' subordination to Britain in 1939 see J. Munro, ed., *Documents on Canadian External Relations* (Ottawa, 1972), VI, pp. 1247–49. For Australian attitudes see R. G. Neale and others, eds., *Documents on Australian Foreign Policy, 1937–1949*, 9 vols. to date (Canberra, 1975–).

technical expertise, and documentary treasure-trove which such enterprises demand are in short supply: in most ex-colonies, impoverished governments, moribund nationalist movements, derelict party machines—let alone the chaotic multitude of local, unofficial, or private interests—lack the means, the will, or both to publish the documentary evidence on which future historians of late-colonial politics will depend. Nor can the preservation of more than the barest minimum of the archival record be taken for granted.

As a result, the well-intentioned scholarly endeavour which makes accessible the archive of Imperial authority at its last gasp may yield an unintended and unfortunate consequence. It may become progressively harder, in scholarly rather than popular writing, to balance the view of the Imperial centre or of its agencies—richly, efficiently, and accessibly documented—with that of the local, indigenous, colonial periphery—archivally voiceless or disinherited. As so many respectful histories of official policy reveal, archives all too easily turn their readers into captives, and the self-serving official minute is insidiously transformed into historical narrative. This problem is not to be solved by dubious means of 'representing' the 'voiceless', still less by the vacuous sentimentalism of much 'post-modernist' writing, whose intellectual rigour and use of evidence would hardly satisfy an early modern astrologer. The decay of universities and the barriers to independent scholarly inquiry in many post-colonial states add to the difficulty. Yet the advance of decolonization as an academic subject of the widest relevance and importance—what other recent historical experience unites so much of the world's population?—depends upon maintaining the delicate balance between our knowledge of metropolitan, international, and colonial processes, and on our sensitivity to the historical experience of ex-subjects as well as ex-rulers. It would be ironic indeed if the study of decolonization became (as colonial history once was) the intellectual monopoly of those who dwell in 'the ruins of the Capitol'.

Select Bibliography

BRUCE BERMAN and JOHN LONSDALE, *Unhappy Valley: Conflict in Kenya and Africa*, 2 books (London, 1992).

HEDLEY BULL and ADAM WATSON, *The Expansion of International Society* (Oxford, 1984).

P. J. CAIN and A. G. HOPKINS, *British Imperialism*, Vol. II, *Crisis and Deconstruction, 1914–1990* (London, 1993).

JOHN DARWIN, *Britain and Decolonization: The Retreat from Empire in the Post-War World* (London, 1988).

—— 'The Fear of Falling: British Political and Imperial Decline', *Transactions of the Royal Historical Society*, Fifth Series, XXXVI (1986), pp. 27–43.

JOHN A. GALLAGHER, *The Decline, Revival and Fall of the British Empire: The Ford Lectures and Other Essays*, ed. Anil Seal (Cambridge, 1982).

DAVID GOLDSWORTHY, ed., *The Conservative Governments and the End of Empire, 1951–1957*, 3 vols., British Documents on the End of Empire Project (London, 1994).

J. D. HARGREAVES, *Decolonization in Africa* (London, 1988).

R. F. HOLLAND, *European Decolonization, 1918–1981: An Introductory Survey* (London, 1985).

—— ed., *Emergencies and Disorder in the European Empires After 1945* (London, 1994).

STEPHEN HOWE, *Anti-Colonialism in British Politics: The Left and the End of Empire* (Oxford, 1993).

RONALD HYAM, ed., *The Labour Government and the End of Empire, 1945–1951*, 4 vols., British Documents on the End of Empire Project (London, 1992).

MILES, KAHLER, *Decolonization in Britain and France: The Domestic Consequences of International Relations* (Princeton, 1984).

DAVID KILLINGRAY, *Policing and Decolonisation: Politics, Nationalism, and the Police, 1917–1965* (Manchester, 1992).

WM. ROGER LOUIS, *Imperialism at Bay: The United States and the Decolonization of the British Empire, 1941–1945* (Oxford, 1977).

—— *The British Empire in the Middle East, 1945–1951: Arab Nationalism, the United States and Post-War Imperialism* (Oxford, 1984).

—— and RONALD ROBINSON, 'The Imperialism of Decolonization', *Journal of Imperial and Commonwealth History*, XXII, 3 (1994), pp. 462–511.

R. E. ROBINSON, 'The Non-European Foundations of European Imperialism: Sketch For a Theory of Collaboration', in Roger Owen and Bob Sutcliffe, eds., *Studies in the Theory of Imperialism* (London, 1972).

JOHN STRACHEY, *The End of Empire* (London, 1959).

A. P. THORNTON, *The Imperial Idea and its Enemies: A Study of British Power* (London, 1959).

35

The Commonwealth

W. DAVID MCINTYRE

In his welcoming speech to Commonwealth Heads of Government at Edinburgh on 24 October 1997 Tony Blair, the host Prime Minister, defined the word 'Commonwealth' as 'the commonweal; a shared richness; something to be possessed by all'. He had, of course, taken only the first, and earliest, of the five main usages listed in the *Oxford English Dictionary*.[1] The other four are: body politic, or body of people constituting a state; republic, or a state where power is vested in the people; the formal title of specific states (Massachusetts, Pennsylvania, Virginia, and Kentucky, Australia, the Bahamas, and Dominica, and the English regime of 1649–60); and a group of the like-minded, such as 'the commonwealth of letters'. Blair's choice may have been appropriate to his political purpose of 'puffing' New Labour's 'New Britain' of the 1990s, but it did less than justice to the 'elusive' origins of the appellation applied to the contemporary legacy of the Empire.

Fugitive uses of 'Commonwealth' for Empire-as-a-family-of countries had appeared before American independence and again from mid-Victorian times. The full style 'British Commonwealth of Nations' popularized by Alfred Zimmern, Lionel Curtis, and J. C. Smuts at the time of the First World War, was 'consecrated' by its inclusion in the 1921 Irish Treaty,[2] further enshrined in the Balfour definition of 1926, and legalized by the Statute of Westminster in 1931. But it proved relatively short-lived. 'British' was dropped before 'Commonwealth of Nations' on the advice of Whitehall mandarins in 1948, and 'Commonwealth' was the style adopted by the Secretariat in 1965 and in all declarations after 1971.

This confusing saga dictated that excursions into 'nomenclature' became *de rigeur* for writers on the Commonwealth.[3] Their work may be discussed as four

[1] See S. R. Mehrotra, 'On the Use of the Term "Commonwealth" ', *Journal of Commonwealth Political Studies* (hereafter *JCPS*), II, 2 (1963), pp. 1–16.

[2] Alfred Zimmern, *The Third British Empire* (London, 1926), p. 3.

[3] W. K. Hancock, *Survey of British Commonwealth Affairs*, 2 vols., Vol. I, *Problems of Nationality, 1918–1936* (London, 1937), pp. 52–62; P. N. S. Mansergh, *The Name and Nature of the British Commonwealth* (Cambridge, 1955), pp. 1–8; K. C. Wheare, *The Constitutional Structure of the*

overlapping phases, defined roughly as: 'Statute of Westminster Commonwealth', 1930s–40s; 'New Commonwealth', following South Asian independence, 1940s–50s; multilateral international association, following the establishment of the Secretariat, 1960s–80s; and 'People's Commonwealth', 1980s–90s.

The supreme irony of the Statute of Westminster Commonwealth is that it represented the antithesis of the federal ideal espoused by the popularizers of the title. At the general level, Commonwealth was the appellation for an exalted ancient-Greek-derived view of citizenship and self-government held by members of the Round Table movement. More specifically, they identified a particular contemporary problem of the 1910s, namely, that Britain could not afford to defend the Empire without the Dominions' support, yet the Dominions which would furnish that support did not share responsibility for decisions over peace and war. In privately circulated 'Round Table Studies', the history of the Empire was manipulated to present the stark alternatives of independence or organic union, the desirability of the latter, and the need for some Imperial taxation.[4] On this point the movement could not unite, so Lionel Curtis took responsibility for publishing two popular books in 1916. *The Problem of the Commonwealth* (London) asked how British subjects in the Dominions could have equal responsibility with those at home for defence and foreign policy. *The Commonwealth of Nations* (London) suggested that the schism of 1776 could only have been avoided by constitutional changes giving American colonists the same responsibility for Imperial affairs as the people of Britain. Without organic union, ran the argument, the Dominions would go the way of the United States.

Practical statesmen shied away from Curtis's severe logic. Although large-scale wartime voluntary co-operation led the Imperial War Conference of 1917 to resolve to review Imperial constitutional arrangements after the war, and Smuts produced a draft federal proposal before the 1921 Imperial Conference, the issue was avoided. But an Australian, in studying debates in Dominion Parliaments on the Versailles peace, realized that the dilemma highlighted by Curtis was unresolved. If federation was impossible, disintegration was undesirable. In *The British Commonwealth of Nations: A Study of its Past and Future Development*, published

Commonwealth (Oxford, 1960), pp. 1–6; J. D. B. Miller, *The Commonwealth in the World* (London, 1965), pp. 10–15; K. Roberts-Wray, *Commonwealth and Colonial Law* (London, 1966), pp. 2–17; H. Duncan Hall, *Commonwealth: A History of the British Commonwealth of Nations* (London, 1971), pp. 179–98; W. David McIntyre, *The Commonwealth of Nations: Origins and Impact, 1869–1971* (Minneapolis, 1977), pp. 4–6; W. Dale, *The Modern Commonwealth* (London, 1983), pp. 33–34; W. David McIntyre, *The Significance of the Commonwealth, 1965–1990* (London, 1991), pp. 13–16.

[4] J. E. Kendle, *The Round Table Movement and Imperial Union* (Toronto, 1975), pp. 107–20, 181–205.

in London in 1920, Duncan Hall suggested that, to resolve tension between Dominion autonomy and Imperial unity, a general declaration of constitutional right should render obsolete the legal sovereignty of the British Parliament. Similarly, L. S. Amery suggested to Smuts that full independence for the parts could be associated with unity based on common citizenship and allegiance to the Crown. Smuts's draft and Amery's letter were resurrected from the files in Pretoria by General J. B. M. Hertzog as he prepared for the 1926 Imperial Conference. Although minutes were not kept at the celebrated Committee on Inter-Imperial Relations, Amery's memoirs in 1952 made it clear that he had emphasized, at the time, that 'freely associated' in the 'defining sentence' or 'status formula' also meant freedom to dissociate.[5] The same was implied in the preamble to the Statute of Westminster. After 1931 the Dominions were as independent as they wished to be.

The historiographical monuments to the Statute of Westminster Commonwealth are the 'Chatham House Surveys' of Sir Keith Hancock and Nicholas Mansergh. Hancock was asked to undertake the post-1918 study by Arnold Toynbee in 1934. In 1937, the year when his *Nationality* volume was published, Hancock told Lionel Curtis: 'Your thought is throughout the centre of reference, even when the reference is critical.'[6] He would later recall that he welcomed the challenge of studying 'a group of states living in tension between the dangerous pressures of external circumstance and their own domestic habits of law, liberty, persuasion and compromise'. Starting work in the aftermath of the status debates, he found that there was too much 'sweetness and light' in a picture of the Commonwealth which emphasized the Durham Report, Balfour Declaration, and Statute of Westminster and put the colonies 'in a triumphant procession to the finishing post of self-government'. Hancock saw the 'procession was getting rather ragged' in Newfoundland, Malta, Ireland, India, Palestine, and South Africa. Indeed, he started work with the Irish Treaty.[7] Yet in his critical approach to the line preached by Curtis, Zimmern, and others Hancock did not reject their idealism. He saw that the popularizers of the Commonwealth idea 'intended it to signify their faith that liberty, even when it had grown into equality, would not bring disintegration but a deeper unity'. In a 'Perspective View' he saw the post-1918 Commonwealth displaying the outward forms of command and

[5] H. Duncan Hall, *The British Commonwealth of Nations: A Study of its Past and Future Development* (London, 1920), pp. viii, 226, 260, 279; L. S. Amery, *My Political Life*, 2 vols. (London, 1953), II, pp. 390–95; H. Duncan Hall, 'The Genesis of the Balfour Declaration of 1926', *JCPS*, I, 3 (1962), pp. 187–89.

[6] Deborah Lavin, *From Empire to International Commonwealth: A Biography of Lionel Curtis* (Oxford, 1995), p. 256.

[7] W. K. Hancock, *Country and Calling* (London, 1954), pp. 149–51.

subordination but an inner reality of equality and co-operation. The central problem was the reconciliation of *imperium* and *libertas*—the freedom of the parts with the unity of the whole. In his famous aphorism he defined the Commonwealth as 'nothing else than the "nature" of the British Empire defined, in Aristotelian fashion, by its end'. He recognized 'a satisfying intellectual subtlety and finish' in the resolution of the recent status debates, but warned of 'uncertainties and hesitations' outside the White Dominions.[8] In his two-part *Economic Policy* volume (published in 1942) Hancock set out to relate 'intractable economic material to the basic political forces'. He adopted as the threefold conceptual framework Frederick Jackson Turner's frontier thesis—'the advancing fringe of a dynamic society'; classical economic theory and the free trade–protection debate; and fellow Australian Stanley Bruce's growth formula focusing on 'men, money, and markets'. Hancock concluded that there was a 'parallelism between the economic and constitutional evolution of the Commonwealth'.[9]

Mansergh's first survey covered foreign policy issues over a similar time-span to Hancock's but, published as it was in 1952 (followed shortly by companion volumes of documents and speeches covering the same period),[10] it already displayed a post-war, 'New Commonwealth', perspective. Eschewing generalizations about the Dominions collectively, he focused on the emerging policies of the individual Dominions in the difficult pre-war days. The system of consultation and compromise which 'presumed fraternity . . . assured liberty . . . guaranteed equality' was unsuited to quick decisions in the international field. But Mansergh concluded that, although Commonwealth governments made serious errors of judgement before 1939, 'they remained true to the principles which were at once the indisputable foundation of their society of free and equal states and the condition of its future growth. Because they kept faith in the great essentials they were able, when the final crisis came, to astonish the world by their capacity for united and resolute action.'[11]

Wartime co-operation was the subject of Mansergh's second survey, published in 1958, though he presented some of his conclusions at Chatham House in 1953.[12] Mansergh displayed some of the ambiguities being expressed about the 'New

[8] Hancock, *Survey*, I, pp. 1, 24, 53, 61, 487.

[9] Hancock, *Survey*, II, *Problems of Economic Policy, 1918–1939*, pt. 1 (London, 1940), pp. 1, 4, 28, 143, 288.

[10] Nicholas Mansergh, ed., *Documents and Speeches on British Commonwealth Affairs, 1931–1952*, 2 vols. (London, 1953).

[11] Nicholas Mansergh, *Survey of British Commonwealth Affairs: Problems of External Policy, 1931–1939* (London, 1952), pp. 447–49.

[12] Nicholas Mansergh, 'The Commonwealth at the Queen's Accession', *International Affairs*, XXIX, 3 (1953), pp. 277–91.

Commonwealth'. His themes were now: the capacity of the Commonwealth to sustain unity of purpose in wartime; its adaptability to changes in what had been a largely British or white membership; and its ability to preserve coherence and sense of purpose in face of the changed balance of power. In the aftermath of South Asian independence and India's membership as a Republic, he wrote the epitaph on the Statute of Westminster Commonwealth. Being a 'reasonably exact phrase' only for the years 1931–49, it has been characterized by equality of status, free association, and common allegiance. In Coronation year, 1953, wrote Mansergh, 'no such equilibrium' existed; these characteristics, 'once a challenge . . . had become a relic'.

Yet Mansergh clung to the idealism and optimism evident in the Hancock surveys. He saw the 1949 London Declaration permitting India's membership as a republic and the recognition of the King as Head of the Commonwealth as 'signal evidence of the adaptability of the Commonwealth in changing circumstances'. Although he noticed misgivings about continuing cohesion in face of doubts about any capacity to influence events, he was prepared to transpose the 1930s experience to the new age. Ending all vestiges of inequality had removed inhibitions to co-operation. This could extend to Asia. The Commonwealth 'constituted an experiment in international co-operation that was supremely worth undertaking . . . At a time when the liberal democratic world appeared so often on the defensive, the Commonwealth, it seemed, had embarked on an experiment which had about it a quality of greatness.'[13] Mansergh later looked back on the early 1950s as 'brief and, retrospectively, golden years of hope in a multi-racial Commonwealth'.[14]

This 'New Commonwealth' (or the 'Second Commonwealth' in Frank Underhill's phrase) was an eight-member association comprising Australia, Britain, Canada, Ceylon, India, New Zealand, Pakistan, and South Africa. It had a brief period of stability until Ghana and Malaya joined in 1957. Thereafter, in the aftermath of the Suez crisis, Macmillan's 'Wind of Change' accelerated decolonization in Africa, and the whole nature of the Commonwealth changed. Conservative British ministers in the 1950s hoped a 'mezzanine status' might be found to consign certain independent ex-colonies and divert them from full membership. South African leaders deplored the possibility of sitting beside African Prime Ministers. But when it was agreed that Cyprus—with a population of only 500,000—could join in 1961, everyone realized that the precedent had been

[13] Nicholas Mansergh, *Survey of British Commonwealth Affairs: Wartime Co-operation and Post-War Change, 1939–52* (London, 1958), pp. xv, 368–69, 398–99, 418–19, 421.

[14] Nicholas Mansergh, *The Commonwealth Experience* (London, 1969), p. 337.

set for some thirty small states.[15] At the same time South Africa's departure gave the Commonwealth a permanent non-Euro-British majority. By 1965 there were twenty-one members.

While writers such as Mansergh retained an optimistic, idealistic approach, others were puzzled about how to interpret the New Commonwealth. Ivor Jennings, a constitutional authority writing in Ceylon (the 'youngest Dominion') in 1948, admitted that in days of rapid change 'the way of an author is hard'. He saw the Commonwealth as a new sort of entity—'a collection of nations associated for a few purposes but dissociated for most'.[16] Underhill, a Canadian, lecturing at Duke University in 1955, said the experiment of a multiracial association was 'the most audacious adventure' Britain had ever embarked on, and that India's acceptance as a republican member was the 'most spectacular event' in the Commonwealth's evolution. However, he noted British apathy over the end of the Raj ('Not a cock crowed') and detected a hiatus of British leadership in the 1950s, which he dubbed the 'nemesis of creativity'.[17] Paul Knaplund, another Canadian, but based at the University of Wisconsin, writing in 1956 noted the likely tensions between South Africa and future African members and concluded: 'If the Commonwealth falls because it is dedicated to the cause of freedom and human rights, nothing in its history will become it so well as its end.'[18] Patrick Maitland, a member of 'The Expanding Commonwealth Group' of British Conservative MPs, welcomed impending expansion in 1957, but wanted to erect an outer ring of ' "Associated" or Candidate countries on probation'.[19]

These ambiguous interpretations continued into the early 1960s. M. S. Rajan, in an inaugural lecture in New Delhi, highlighted the lasting impact of India's membership both at independence in 1947 and as a republic from 1949. Both had been unexpected, but became 'powerful precedents' for other dependencies. He also noted that the New Commonwealth, not entirely the creation of Britain and the Dominions, seemed to be disowned by the British—'they do not seem to want the preservation and promotion of the Commonwealth'.[20] Similarly, Guy Arnold, in a critical analysis of British foreign policy since the war, said Britain 'appears to have little idea what to do with the new multiracial Commonwealth'.[21] The Australian Lord Casey wrote in 1963, 'the Commonwealth is not going to

[15] See W. David McIntyre, 'The Admission of Small States to the Commonwealth', *Journal of Imperial and Commonwealth History*, XXIV, 2 (1996), pp. 244–77.

[16] Sir Ivor Jennings, *The British Commonwealth of Nations* (London, 1948), p. 77.

[17] Frank H. Underhill, *The British Commonwealth* (Durham, NC, 1956), pp. 66, 79, 90, 94.

[18] Paul Knaplund, *Britain, Commonwealth and Empire, 1901–1955* (London, 1956), p. 320.

[19] Patrick Maitland, *Task For Giants: An Expanding Commonwealth* (London, 1955), p. 10.

[20] M. S. Rajan, *The Post-War Transformation of the Commonwealth* (London, 1963), pp. 6, 49, 50. For the best assessment see R. J. Moore, *Making the New Commonwealth* (Oxford, 1987).

[21] G. Arnold, *Towards Peace and a Multiracial Commonwealth* (London, 1964), p. 24.

breakup, but it may well fade out through inaction'.[22] A Duke University symposium covering the decade after Suez epitomized the ambiguities of the New Commonwealth. W. B. Hamilton, the American editor, saw the Commonwealth as a devolution *from* something, a growth *towards* an association unique in history, but he felt it was too close to say where it all might lead. 'It can just as well be the beginning of something as the end.'[23] Yet, even as the Duke volume went to press, the most critical turning-point had been passed and a new historiography had commenced.

In 1965 the Commonwealth Secretariat was created. The association's co-ordination moved from Whitehall to Marlborough House in Pall Mall, and the Secretary-General took office as the servant of the Heads of Government collectively. In the same year, an Australian scholar, J. D. B. [Bruce] Miller published his *Commonwealth in the World*, which investigated the nature of the Commonwealth as an international entity. Like Hancock and Mansergh, he was impressed by the growth of nationalism in member states, but his concern was the association's role in international affairs. Finding it difficult to put the Commonwealth into any recognized international category, he called it 'a concert of convenience'.[24] In 1971 Margaret Ball saw the Commonwealth's main function as consultation, on the basis of equality, non-interference, and non-discrimination. She called it the 'Open' Commonwealth because it was not exclusive, it welcomed co-operation with other bodies, and members were free to join such bodies.[25]

In the same year the first of new-style consultations called Commonwealth Heads of Government Meetings (Chogms) was held in Singapore. Here thirty-one member states adopted a Declaration of Principles, in which they pledged themselves *in favour* of peace, liberty, and co-operation and *against* racial discrimination, colonial domination, and wide inequalities of wealth.[26] Observing this conference was Bruce Miller, now engaged upon the third Chatham House survey, published in 1974. Subtitled *Problems of Expansion and Attrition, 1953–1969*, Miller's survey tackled five themes: the more complex international environment; the decline in unity; the growth of the machinery of co-operation; Britain's turning to Europe; and the changing concept of what the Commonwealth stood for. He detected disappointment that there had been a retreat from earlier ideals. He

[22] [R. G.] Lord Casey, *The Future of the Commonwealth* (London, 1963), p. 12.

[23] 'The Transfer of Power in Historical Perspective', in *A Decade of the Commonwealth, 1956–1964* (Durham, NC, 1966), p. 35.

[24] Miller, *Commonwealth in the World*, p. 271.

[25] M. Margaret Ball, *The 'Open' Commonwealth* (Durham, NC, 1971), pp. vi, 201.

[26] Text in *The Commonwealth at the Summit* (London, 1987), pp. 156–57.

found a Commonwealth bigger, looser, more diffuse. His muted conclusion was that the Commonwealth was 'something to belong to, to deal with unfinished colonial business . . . and to serve as a link with history'.[27] A similar suspension-of-judgement conclusion was reached by W. David McIntyre in his 1977 contribution to the Minnesota 'Europe and the World in the Age of Expansion' series: 'The mood of romanticism and optimism, of hypocrisy and sentiment, which marked the 1960s appeared to be giving way. A new age of realism had commenced in which the Commonwealth continued, was taken for granted, but did not have too much expected of it.'[28]

By the early 1980s serious analyses of the Commonwealth as an international association were providing modest but mainly positive interpretations. Arnold Smith, the first Secretary-General, published his memoirs in 1981, giving an account of the genesis and establishment of the Secretariat and his battle to establish its independence from Whitehall. He had adopted as Commonwealth motto: 'Consultation is the life-blood.'[29] Denis Judd and Peter Slinn, in a useful textbook in 1982, saw the Commonwealth as the forum for functional co-operation.[30] A. N. Papadopoulos's monograph about multilateral diplomacy in 1982 analysed the institutions and procedures of the Commonwealth.[31] In 1983 Sir William Dale, a former legal adviser to the Commonwealth Office, returned to the legal-constitutional approach. He found three 'cardinal influences'—the adaptability of the Crown, the process of constant discussion, and the influence of the common law. While the 1971 Declaration was 'informal' compared with the United Nations Charter, some of its statements were 'of a constituent nature'.[32] Aspects of Dale's approach were taken up by Stephen Chan, a former Secretariat officer who, in his 1988 monograph, had a section on 'Constitutionalism Revisited'. Testing the Commonwealth against international patterns of co-operation, harmonization, and co-ordination, he concluded that it stood for a 'harmonised liberalism'.[33]

Some less favourable interpretations were made. In a symposium on *The Commonwealth in the 1980s*, published in 1984, the editors took their stand at

[27] J. D. B. Miller, *Survey of Commonwealth Affairs: Problems of Expansion and Attrition, 1953–1969* (London, 1974), pp. 15–18, 517, 519–20, 525.

[28] McIntyre, *Commonwealth of Nations: Origins and Impact*, p. 474.

[29] Arnold Smith, *Stitches in Time: The Commonwealth in World Politics* (London, 1981), p. 14. The phrase was first used in the officials' feasibility report on a secretariat.

[30] Denis Judd and Peter Slinn, *The Evolution of the Modern Commonwealth, 1920–80* (London, 1982), p. 147.

[31] A. N. Papadopoulos, *Multi-lateral Diplomacy Within the Commonwealth: A Decade of Expansion* (The Hague, 1982).

[32] W. Dale, *The Modern Commonwealth* (London, 1983), pp. 3, 42.

[33] Stephen Chan, *The Commonwealth in World Politics: A Study in International Action, 1965–1985* (London, 1988), pp. 47–50.

opposite poles. A. J. R. Groom said that although the Commonwealth could not take decisions, it could clarify issues and create a conventional wisdom, which was 'an undramatic but worthwhile achievement'. But Paul Taylor said the Commonwealth was based on two forgivable hypocrisies—'a hypocrisy of structure, and a hypocrisy of ideology'. A structure based on equality nevertheless had Britain as the main paymaster and generator of the administrative heritage. An ideology of constitutional democracy and anti-racialism was tarnished by one-party states, military rule, and discriminatory practices.[34] A similar critical view appeared in Dennis Austin's *The Commonwealth and Britain* (London, 1988) based on a Chatham House seminar, and probably representing the Foreign and Commonwealth Office viewpoint. Although he professed himself more 'among the believers than the sceptics', Austin found the Commonwealth weak on symbolism, eroded in values, disproportionately representative of small states, with a Secretariat which had multiplied its functions without strengthening its position, and having 'no great directive force or animating principle'. 'Xenophobia rather than fraternity, and the decline of liberal beliefs, are said to be the hallmarks of the modern Commonwealth.' Searching for some cautious words of praise, he concluded: 'For the Commonwealth to have reached a position of "qualified amiability" among a third of the world's nation-states is no small achievement.'[35]

The scepticism of writers in the late 1980s paled into insignificance beside the attitude of the British Prime Minister Margaret Thatcher, who broke Commonwealth consensus over sanctions against South Africa's apartheid and, at the 1987 and 1989 Commonwealth Heads of Government Meetings, insisted on repeated insertions of the phrase 'with the exception of Britain' in the conference communiqués. Thatcher's defiant cry in Kuala Lumpur in 1989 that, 'if it's forty-eight against one, I'm sorry for the forty-eight', marked a nadir in Britain's relations with the Commonwealth. Yet in the same year the first scholarly study of the Secretariat, by Margaret Doxey, was published, in which she asserted that the Commonwealth existed because the members felt the benefits of membership outweighed the costs; the main benefits were 'not political but practical'.[36] She pointed to what would become the chief interest in the 1990s—the positive elements of what was now called the 'People's Commonwealth'.[37]

[34] A. J. R. Groom and Paul Taylor, *The Commonwealth in the 1980s* (London, 1984), pp. 296, 307, 309.

[35] Dennis Austin, *The Commonwealth and Britain* (London, 1988), pp. 8, 13, 17, 48, 64.

[36] Margaret P. Doxey, *The Commonwealth Secretariat and the Contemporary Commonwealth* (London, 1989), p. 11.

[37] 'Towards a People's Commonwealth', Royal Commonwealth Society paper, 22 Aug. 1985.

The chief distinguishing feature of the post-Britannic Commonwealth compared with other international organizations was the unique 'width and breadth' provided by its non-official activities. These had long been recognized but rarely studied. H. Duncan Hall's influential 1920 book had only a brief appendix on Inter-Imperial Voluntary Associations.[38] During the disillusioned early 1960s Patrick Gordon-Walker advanced the novel notion that the Commonwealth was a 'Natural Unit', wrote about 'links of affinity', and saw professional linkages making an 'active cultural community'. In 1962 he called for a Trust or Foundation to foster such unofficial interchanges.[39] Lord Casey's call for re-revitalization in 1963 included a plea for an 'organized system of personal contacts'.[40] During the 1964 Prime Ministers' Meetings, when the proposal for a Secretariat as 'a clearing house' emanated from three New Commonwealth members, a British proposal for a Foundation to foster professional exchanges was also accepted. Although overtaken by the Secretariat, the Commonwealth Foundation began in 1966. Its first director, John Chadwick, wrote a chapter on 'Non-governmental Associations' in the Duke symposium.[41]

In 1971 Margaret Ball used the image of an iceberg, because the Commonwealth's main bulk was invisible. She found the non-governmental networks so extensive 'as to defy description'.[42] J. D. B. Miller's 1974 Chatham House survey also recognized that the Commonwealth was 'an assembly of peoples as well as an association between governments'.[43] Groom and Taylor's *Commonwealth in the 1980s* was the first to provide essays on the youth programme, education, the arts, science, health, and law, as well as trade and political ties. John Chadwick provided a full account of the first fifteen years of the Foundation in 1982.[44] Doxey defined the Commonwealth in 1989 as 'a conglomerate of structured and unstructured official and unofficial relationships of a political, economic and cultural nature'.[45] McIntyre's *Significance of the Commonwealth*, published in 1991, devoted nearly half its length to functioning at the non-political level.

'People's Commonwealth' became the contemporary sobriquet for a myriad of activities usually designed by the labels which defined them, somewhat unfortunately, by what they were *not*—unofficial, or non-governmental. NGOs (Non-Governmental Organizations) became official shorthand for institutions which

38 Hall, *British Commonwealth*, pp. 372–78.

39 Patrick Gordon-Walker, *The Commonwealth* (London, 1962), p. 369.

40 Casey, *Future of the Commonwealth*, p. 114.

41 Hamilton, *Decade of the Commonwealth*, pp. 25–147.

42 Ball, *'Open' Commonwealth*, pp. 78–79.

43 Miller, *Survey*, p. xiii.

44 John Chadwick, *The Unofficial Commonwealth: The Story of the Commonwealth Foundation, 1965–1980* (London, 1982).

45 Doxey, *Secretariat*, p. 12.

D. A. Low preferred to call 'personal, professional and philanthropic'.[46] These might properly be designated 'voluntary, independent, professional, philanthropic, and sporting organizations' (or VIPPSOs)—a designation indicating both their nature (voluntary and independent) and their main functions (professional, philanthropic, and sporting).

The original mission of the Commonwealth Foundation was to foster professional exchanges. These had begun in the heyday of Empire with the Press Union (1909), Parliamentary Association (1911), and Universities Association (1913).[47] These were joined after the Second World War by Commonwealth associations devoted to broadcasting, engineers, government science, the blind and the deaf. From the mid-1960s, however, over thirty new pan-Commonwealth organizations came into being with Foundation help. A brief history of this movement was published in 1993.[48]

The second group were the philanthropic organizations concerned with care and welfare. For them *Guidelines for Good Policy and Practice* was adopted in 1995 which outlined a history and typology of such endeavours.[49] The third and most visible group were the sporting bodies, especially the Commonwealth Games Federation, organizer of the single most popular element of the Commonwealth—the Commonwealth Games, successor of the first Empire Games of 1930. The addition of some team sports in 1998, seven-a-side rugby, one-day cricket, netball, and field hockey, gave belated recognition to the almost universal popularity of some of the sports which had been codified in Victorian England. Their spread, as an adjunct to imperialism, was subject of a pioneer article in 1959 by Charles Tennyson entitled 'They Taught the World to Play'. The role of sport in the emerging national identities of Commonwealth countries had long been evident—especially cricket in Australia, the West Indies, India, and Pakistan, and rugby football in New Zealand and South Africa. Classics, such as C. L. R. James's *Beyond a Boundary* (London, 1963), had related sport to class and race. Richard Holt's *Sport and the British*, in 1989, discussed the role of sport in imperialism and nationalism.[50]

[46] D. A. Low, 'Commonwealth Policy Studies: Is there a Case for a Centre?', *The Round Table* (1988), pp. 308, 369.

[47] See H. Brittain, *Pilgrims and Pioneers* (London, n.d.), chap. 17; I. Grey, *The Parliamentarians* (London, 1986); E. Ashley, *Community of Universities* (Cambridge, 1963); and H. W. Springer, *The Commonwealth of Universities* (London, 1988).

[48] *The Commonwealth Foundation: A Special Report, 1966 to 1993* (London, 1993), pp. 4–17.

[49] *Non-Governmental Organisations: Guidelines for Good Policy and Practice* (London, 1995).

[50] C. Tennyson, 'They Taught the World to Play', *Victorian Studies*, II, 3 (1959), p. 211. See also J. A. Mangan, *The Games Ethic and Imperialism* (London, 1986); R. Cashman and M. McKernan, eds., *Sport in History* (St Lucia, Queensland, 1979); Richard Holt, *Sport and the British* (Oxford, 1989).

By 1997, half-a-century after the end of the Indian Raj had heralded the New Commonwealth, it had become unhistorical to treat official and unofficial elements separately. In 1989, even as Thatcher tried to distance Britain from current Commonwealth concerns, the Heads of Government appointed a High Level Appraisal Group to plan for the Commonwealth in the 1990s. In 1991 the principles of 1971 were reaffirmed in the Harare Declaration, which now specified as 'fundamental values' democracy, human rights, honest governance, the rule of law, gender equality, and educational opportunity. The Commonwealth Foundation organized the first NGO Forum in the same year. Over the next few years the Commonwealth Human Rights Initiative highlighted infringements of rights in several 'errant states'. Nigeria's membership was suspended in 1995, and in 1997 a military regime in Sierra Leone was suspended from official Commonwealth activities.

Fruitful symbiosis between official and unofficial organizations was demonstrated by the way the intra-governmental organs—the Secretariat, the Fund For Technical Co-operation, the Foundation, and the Commonwealth of Learning—co-operated with, and sometimes relied on, the NGOs. In 1995 Katherine West extended the revived appreciation of the Commonwealth by pointing to the economic advantages provided by a 'Commonwealth Business Culture'.[51] These themes were taken up by the House of Commons Foreign Affairs Committee in 1996, which reported that the post-decolonization, post-cold war Commonwealth gave Britain 'both friends and opportunities'.[52]

In 1997, the 'Year of the Commonwealth' in Britain, Doxey's dictum that benefits of membership outweighed costs was attested by the expanding membership. Pakistan had returned after an absence of seventeen years in 1989; South Africa returned in 1994 after thirty-three years. Surprise newcomers in 1995 were Cameroon and Mozambique, and Fiji's ten-year lapse of membership ended in 1997. Applicants in 1997 included Rwanda, Yemen, and the 'Palestinian Authority'. There was even talk of Israel, Somalia, Myanmar, and Ireland. Membership stood at fifty-four in 1997 (with one under suspension). The fifty-one[53] representatives who gathered in Edinburgh matched exactly in total the fifty-one original UN members who attended the first General Assembly in London in 1945. At the same time a week-long Commonwealth Forum enabled over eighty NGOs to organize exhibits, give presentations, and run mini-conferences. The Queen, who as Head of the Commonwealth attended the opening session for the first time, spoke of a

[51] Katherine West, *Economic Opportunities for Britain and the Commonwealth* (London, 1995), pp. 26–31.

[52] *The Future Role of the Commonwealth* (London, 1996), p. lxix.

[53] Two Special Members, Tuvalu and Nauru, are not entitled to attend Heads of Government Meetings.

Commonwealth with 'no centre and no periphery' in which the peoples provided 'the real soul . . . the motor, the drive'. These are all developments which historians can no longer afford to neglect.

Select Bibliography

DENNIS AUSTIN, *The Commonwealth and Britain* (London, 1988).

MARY MARGARET BALL, *The 'Open' Commonwealth* (Durham, NC, 1971).

STEPHEN CHAN, *The Commonwealth in World Politics: A Study of International Action, 1965 to 1985* (London, 1988).

LIONEL CURTIS, *The Problem of the Commonwealth* (London, 1916).

—— *The Commonwealth of Nations* (London, 1916).

MARGARET P. DOXEY, *The Commonwealth Secretariat and the Contemporary Commonwealth* (Basingstoke, 1989).

A. J. R. GROOM and PAUL GRAHAM TAYLOR, eds., *The Commonwealth in the 1980s: Challenges and Opportunities* (London, 1984).

H. DUNCAN HALL, *The British Commonwealth of Nations: A Study of its Past and Future Development* (London, 1920).

WILLIAM BASKERVILLE HAMILTON and others, *A Decade of the Commonwealth, 1955–1964* (Durham, NC, 1966).

W. K. HANCOCK, *Survey of British Commonwealth Affairs* Vol. I, *Problems of Nationality, 1918–1936* (London, 1937); Vol. II, *Problems of Economic Policy, 1918–1939*, pt. 1 (London, 1940), pt. 2 (London, 1942).

PAUL KNAPLUND, *Britain: Commonwealth and Empire, 1901–1955* (London, 1956).

NICHOLAS MANSERGH, *Survey of British Commonwealth Affairs: Problems of External Policy, 1931–1952*, 2 vols. (London, 1952, 1958).

—— *The Commonwealth Experience* (London, 1969).

W. DAVID McINTYRE, *Colonies into Commonwealth*, 3rd edn. (London, 1974).

—— *The Commonwealth of Nations: Origins and Impact, 1869–1971* (Minneapolis, 1977).

—— *The Significance of the Commonwealth, 1965–90* (Basingstoke, 1991).

S. R. MEHROTRA, 'On the Use of the Term "Commonwealth" ', *Journal of Commonwealth Political Studies*, II, 1 (1963), pp. 1–16.

J. D. B. MILLER, *The Commonwealth and the World* (London, 1965).

—— *Survey of Commonwealth Affairs: Problems of Expansion and Attrition, 1953–1969* (London, 1974).

R. J. MOORE, *Making the New Commonwealth* (Oxford, 1987).

ARNOLD SMITH, *Stitches in Time: The Commonwealth in World Politics* (London, 1981).

36

Art and Empire

JEFFREY AUERBACH

The first works of art concerning the British Empire were probably produced by John White, draughtsman on Ralegh's 1585 expedition to America.[1] The study of the art of the British Empire, however, did not begin to develop until the mid-nineteenth century. Although travellers to Africa and the Americas occasionally described the arts or crafts produced by indigenous peoples, and although amateur collectors filled their cabinets with all sorts of 'curiosities' from distant lands during the eighteenth century, these can in no way be considered systematic studies.

Since the mid-nineteenth century scholars from history, art history, anthropology, and cultural studies have produced hundreds of books, articles, and exhibition catalogues about the art of the British Empire, looking not only at British art, but at the art of those lands that were a part of the British Empire, Commonwealth, or sphere of colonial influence. Despite this prodigious scholarly output, synthetic, analytical literature on the art of Empire pales in comparison with that on its other aspects. Moreover, despite the quantity of material that has been produced, and the very high quality of some of it, the history of the art of the British Empire remains to be written.

The historiography of art and the British Empire can be usefully divided into four phases, each capturing a certain need, or function, of the Empire at the time. During the nineteenth century analyses of the art of Empire were concerned with trade and commerce; that is, with fueling Britain's Imperial economy. From the turn of the century until about 1947 there was a nationalist historiography, searching for authenticity and aimed at developing independent states; an interest in so-called 'primitivism', which served to denigrate black African peoples; and, for the first time, an interest in British artists in India (or anywhere in the Empire), as a means of enhancing Britain's Imperial image. After 1947 and through the late-1970s it is possible to trace the impact of decolonization, as scholars began to re-evaluate, often

[1] P. H. Hulton and David B. Quinn, *The American Drawings of John White, 1577–1590*, 2 vols. (London, 1964).

nostalgically, Britain's Imperial legacy. Finally, since 1980 the focus has shifted to reflect the colonized, by looking at the ways British artists represented the colonial 'Other'. In short, the historiography of art and the British Empire has not only paralleled and reflected changes in the Empire, but can be expressed in terms of the Empire's changing needs and functions.

The earliest studies of the art of the British Empire focused on the decorative arts and the twin issues of design and ornamentation that concerned mid-nineteenth-century British art critics such as Owen Jones and John Ruskin. When J. Forbes Royle first brought to the attention of Henry Cole and the other organizers of the Great Exhibition of 1851 the importance of Indian decorative arts in his book *On the Culture and Commerce of Cotton in India* (London, 1851), he characterized India 'as the cradle of one . . . of the nations who earliest practised the arts and cultivated the sciences which characterize civilization'. He was not enamoured of Indian sculpture, however, which he considered 'rude', favouring instead raw materials and manufactured articles, which would benefit British trade.[2] J. Forbes Watson's *The Textile Manufactures and the Costumes of the People of India* (London, 1866), and T. N. Mukharji's *Art Manufactures of India* (Calcutta, 1888), compiled for the Glasgow International Exhibition of 1888, were similarly oriented towards selling British-made goods in India, and introducing Indian products and designs to British manufactures.

Also driving these works was a widespread fear that industrialization had led to a loss of vitality in design, a decline in trade craftsmanship, stylistic confusion, and the misuse of ornamentation. Owen Jones, in *The Grammar of Ornament* (London, 1856), found Indian and Islamic art critically important in his formulation of 'correct' principles of design, and George C. M. Birdwood, in his introduction to the *Handbook to the Indian Court for the Paris International Exhibition of 1878*, pilloried the effects of industrialization and the Indian schools of art for creating 'mongrel articles'.[3] They too were at least implicitly interested in increasing the sale of domestically manufactured goods by using design principles adopted from regions such as India to advance British trade interests with the Empire as well as with more economically developed states. It is worth noting that, with only one obvious exception, this economic phase applied exclusively to India.[4]

[2] J. Forbes Royle, *On the Culture and Commerce of Cotton in India* (London, 1851), p. 586.

[3] George C. M. Birdwood, *Handbook to the Indian Court for the Paris International Exhibition of 1878* (London, 1878), p. 49, and *The Industrial Arts of India* (London, 1880). See also Henry Cole, *Catalogue of the Objects of Indian Art Exhibited in the South Kensington Museum* (London, 1874).

[4] The exception, and in all likelihood the first chronological entry in the historiography of the art of the British Empire, is William Dunlap, *A History of the Rise and Progress of the Arts of Design in the United States*, 2 vols. (New York, 1934; rept. Boston, 1918; New York, 1964).

Art critics did not begin to admire Indian painting and drawing until the beginning of the twentieth century. E. B. Havell's *Indian Sculpture and Painting* (London, 1908) and *The Ideals of Indian Art* (London, 1911) attempted to bring about the aesthetic appreciation of Indian art, in contrast to earlier design critics who had focused on stylistic qualities. It was Havell who first suggested that Indian art needed to be judged 'on the basis of standards of art criticism evolved within the Indian tradition instead of employing European standards which were extraneous to that tradition'.[5]

Havell's work also marked the beginning of a nationalist period in the historiography of the art of Empire. With respect to India, this nationalism was especially apparent in the work of Ananda Coomaraswamy, Keeper of Indian and Muhammaden Art at the Museum of Fine Arts in Boston, who in a succession of books wrote about a distinctive Hindu view of life that informed Indian art. Indian art, he wrote, 'is the statement of a racial experience'.[6] Percy Brown, Principal of the Government School of Art, acknowledged his intellectual debt of Havell and Coomaraswamy, but in *Indian Painting under the Mughals* (Oxford, 1924) he started with Persian and Indian elements, in contrast to Coomaraswamy, who stressed that Rajput painting belonged 'to a pure Indian tradition' and was 'totally unlike Persian art of any period'.[7] Throughout his book Brown emphasized the hybridity of Indian art, which drew on both Hindu (Rajput) and Muslim (Mughal) traditions and was, beginning in the sixteenth century, influenced by European art as well. Nevertheless, as with Coomaraswamy, he portrayed Indian art as sophisticated and elaborate, and asserted that rather than criticizing it for its underdeveloped techniques with perspective, it was better to realize 'that the Oriental had his own system of perspective'.[8] In short, Indian art needed to be judged on its own terms, in its own cultural context, and not always in relation to Western notions of art.

A similar sort of national reclamation project was under way in North America and Australia at approximately the same time, which corresponded with Britain's interest in fostering independent states. The search for something 'Canadian' in painting had actually begun in the late nineteenth century,[9] but the great surge of academic interest came in the 1930s, when the Ryerson Press in Toronto began to publish books devoted to Canadian art. Albert H. Robson, in *Canadian Landscape*

[5] Quoted in Partha Mitter, *Much Maligned Monsters: History of European Reactions of Indian Art* (Oxford, 1977), p. 271.

[6] Ananda K. Coomaraswamy, *Introduction to Indian Art* (Madras, 1923), p. v. See also his *Rajput Painting* (London, 1916) and *History of Indian and Indonesian Art* (London, 1927).

[7] Coomaraswamy, *Introduction to Indian Art*, pp. 121–22.

[8] Percy Brown, *Indian Painting under the Mughals* (Oxford, 1924), p. 135.

[9] See W. A. Sherwood, 'A National Spirit in Art', *Canadian Magazine* (1894).

Painters (Toronto, 1932), wrote unabashedly of the need for 'more artists who will interpret the Canadian landscape through their own eyes'.[10] He and his contemporaries gave only passing mention to the British colonial period, implying that there was little if no 'Canadian' art before there was an independent Canada, and dismissing the contributions of Native Americans as merely decorative.[11]

The study of American and Australian art, at least that produced by the colonists, was also focused on locating an authentic tradition independent from the British. There was a surge of interest in colonial American art in the 1920s and 1930s, most notably Frank Bayley's *Five Colonial Artists of New England* (Boston, 1929) and Louisa Dresser's *Seventeenth Century Painting in New England* (Worcester, Mass., 1935). The first comprehensive survey of Australian art was William Moore's *The Story of Australian Art*, 2 vols. (Sydney, 1934), a book which served as the basis for most subsequent studies, even though at the time, according to Bernard Smith, the leading scholar of Australian art, it 'fell on thin soil and initially aroused little interest'. Smith regarded his own book, *Place, Taste and Tradition: A Study of Australian Art Since 1788* (Sydney, 1945; rev. edn., Melbourne, 1979) as a 'contribution to the war effort', thus acknowledging its nationalistic agenda. *Place, Taste and Tradition* is much more than that, however. It was the first study of the art of the British Empire to highlight the relationship between the course of art in the colonies and the concurrent European tendencies from which that art drew so substantially. Smith also emphasized aesthetics far less than his predecessors, drawing links between art, economic developments, and social change.

Meanwhile, critics were evaluating the art of Africans, Native Americans, and Pacific Islanders in a dramatically different manner. This mode of analysis, which focused on so-called 'primitivism', reflected the British view of non-whites as lacking in national identity and racially inferior. Practised largely by anthropologists, and drawing its inspiration from evolutionary thought, this approach saw art as a reflection of progress in the material culture of mankind as a whole. Some of the earliest work was undertaken by A. C. Hattan, especially his *Decorative Art of British New Guinea* (Dublin, 1894), and by A. H. Lane-Fox Pitt-Rivers, in a series of papers published together as *Evolution of Culture and Other Essays* (Oxford, 1906). Both espoused what can be called the 'degeneration theory', which attempted to demonstrate that copying natural forms without a full comprehension of them led to purely geometric forms. This theory continued the centuries-old

[10] Albert H. Robson, *Canadian Landscape Painters* (Toronto, 1932), p. 13.

[11] M. O. Hammond, *Painting and Sculpture in Canada* (Toronto, 1930); William Colgate, *Canadian Art: Its Origin and Development* (Toronto, 1943); Donald W. Buchanan, ed., *Canadian Painters: From Paul Kane to the Group of Seven* (London, 1945); Graham McInnes, *A Short History of Canadian Art* (Toronto, 1939).

European tradition that viewed painting as the highest art form and the latest to evolve, and led to the designation of African art as 'primitive'.

The study of so-called 'primitive art' underwent a revolution, beginning with the work of Franz Boas, whose *Primitive Art* (Oslo, 1927; Cambridge, Mass., 1928) demolished the degeneration theory by arguing that all 'races' have the same mental processes, and that 'Even the poorest tribes have produced work that gives to them aesthetic pleasure'.[12] Boas dismissed the pretences to objectivity claimed by his anthropological predecessors, as well as their attempts to seek the origin of all decorative art in realism and technical details. He defined art as the attainment of a certain standard of excellence, and suggested that the ornamentation which appeared formal to European observers was to Native American Indians full of complex symbolic meaning.

At the same time, and due largely to the influence of Lord Curzon, Viceroy of India 1899–1905, Anglo-Indian scholars began to show interest in British artists in India, as opposed to indigenous Indian art, largely as a means of boosting Britain's Imperial image. After Queen Victoria became Empress of India in 1878, the British increasingly saw themselves as the successors to the Mughals, although it should be pointed out that this process began as early as the late eighteenth century, as in Sir Joshua Reynold's portrait of Captain John Foote. Curzon's passion for India's past, and for bolstering Britain's presence, encouraged members of the Anglo-Indian community to begin to collect works by British artists who had visited India in the late eighteenth and early nineteenth centuries. Guided by Evan Cotton and William Foster, two prominent art critics, wealthy Bengalis modelled themselves on the British aristocracy, furnishing their houses in European style and building up large collections of paintings by artists such as the Daniells.[13] Cotton, who was honorary editor of *Bengal Past and Present*, wrote two path-breaking articles for that journal in which he began to document the work of British artists in India.[14] Foster, who spent most of his career in the India Office, also published regularly in *Bengal Past and Present*, and contributed a lengthy article to *The Walpole Society* on 'British Artists in India, 1760–1820', in essence a biographical dictionary listing more than sixty artists who worked in India at the turn of the nineteenth century.[15] This early work dating from the 1920s and 1930s, however, was little more than compiling and cataloguing, and it was not until after

[12] Franz Boas, *Primitive Art* (New York, 1955 edn.), p. 9.

[13] See Mildred Archer's Foreward to Maurice Shellim, *Oil Paintings of India and the East by Thomas Daniell R. A. 1749–1840, and William Daniell R. A., 1769–1837* (London, 1979), p. 9.

[14] Evan Cotton, 'The Daniells in India', *Bengal Past and Present*, XXV (1923), pp. 1–70; 'British Artists in India', ibid., XLII (1931), pp. 136–42.

[15] William Foster, 'British Artists in India, 1760–1820', *The Walpole Society*, XIX (1930–31), pp. 1–88. See also his *Descriptive Catalogue of Paintings, Statues, etc. in the India Office* (London, 1902).

the British withdrawal from India in 1947 that scholars began to evaluate British painting in India in a serious manner.

The beginnings of decolonization unleashed a flurry of writings about the art of the British Empire, especially Indian art. Much of this work came from the pen of Mildred Archer, Curator of Prints and Drawings at the India Office Library from 1954 to 1979, and her husband W. G. Archer, a member of the Indian Civil Service from 1931 to 1948 and later Keeper of the Indian Section of the Victoria and Albert Museum.[16] Together they wrote *Indian Painting for the British, 1770–1880* (London, 1955), a landmark (if Whiggish) view of the westernization and modernization of India and Indian art. In an attempt to re-evaluate Britain's presence in India, the Archers traced the process by which Indian artists adopted British techniques and attempted to flatter British taste. In an analysis that at times appears to justify Britain's domination of India, the Archers recounted how the British made up for an absence of Indian patronage, thus providing some relief from 'conditions of economic plight', and how British-inspired painting played a role in fostering democracy by 'habituating the Indian public to democratic themes'. On the other hand, perhaps reflecting ambiguous feelings about the legacy of Britain's Imperial presence, the Archers wrote that although 'Indian painters had inherited highly cultured traditions', Indian painting for the British was disappointing. The British, unlike the Mughals, were unable to spark any sort of creativity in Indian art. In short, the Imperial presence was a failure. Overall, the Archers provided comprehensive and at times sophisticated analyses that looked at stylistic changes, took into account historical events such as the replacement of the East India Company with the Raj after 1858, and were cognizant of 'Victorian assumption[s] of ethical superiority'.[17]

Mildred Archer has been, without a doubt, the leading scholar in the field of Indian art for the British. In addition to her catalogues of the collections in the India Office Library, she has also written and co-authored a number of monographs.[18]

[16] W. G. Archer's works include *Kangra Painting* (London, 1952), *Indian Paintings from Rajasthan* (London, 1957), *Indian Painting* (London, 1959), *Paintings of the Sikhs* (London, 1966), and *Kalighat Paintings* (London, 1971).

[17] Mildred Archer and W. G. Archer, *Indian Painting for the British, 1770–1880* (London, 1955), pp. 15, 100, 108, 113.

[18] Mildred Archer's catalogues include *Natural History Drawings in the India Office Library* (London, 1962), *British Drawings in the India Office Library*, 2 vols. (London, 1969), *Company Drawings in the India Office Library* (London, 1972), and *The India Office Collection of Paintings and Sculpture* (London, 1986). Her more important articles and monographs include 'The East India Company and British Art', *Apollo*, LXXXII (1965), pp. 401–09; *India and British Portraiture, 1770–1825* (London, 1979), and *Early Views of India: The Picturesque Journeys of Thomas and William Daniell, 1786–1794* (London, 1980). See also Mildred Archer and T. Falk, *Thomas and William Prinsep in India* (London, 1982), and Mildred Archer and Ronald Lightbowm, *India Observed: India as Viewed by British Artists, 1760–1960* (London, 1982).

But for all the importance of her contributions, her work, like most recent studies of British art of India, has tended towards narrativity and has been overly concerned with issues of art production at the expense of thematic and critical analysis.[19] She has resisted making links between natural history drawings and the Enlightenment project of systematizing knowledge, and in her focus on the 'cult of the picturesque' she missed an opportunity to point out how the drawings of William Simpson, for instance, reveal much more than crude Orientalism of the sort outlined by Edward W. Said.[20] Nevertheless, Archer's work inspired a generation of scholars to begin to look closely at individual British artists in India. It is now possible to write of two distinct strands in the historiography of the art of India: that of indigenous Indian art, and that of British artists in India, although the latter has been hampered by its authors' occasionally nostalgic enthusiasm for British India.

This trend towards re-evaluation is also evident in the study of the other areas that were once a part of the British Empire. The great surge of interest in African art, at least in the English-speaking world, took place beginning in the late 1950s, just after the onset of decolonization, but since this subject has been dealt with elsewhere it will not be duplicated here.[21] In Canada, a notable shift occurred in the early 1960s when R. H. Hubbard began to emphasize not only Canada's colonial past, but its hybrid, bi-cultural colonial experience as the product of both French and British colonization.[22] Hubbard also analysed the stylistic contributions of the British to Canadian art, just as the Archers were doing with Indian art. This trend received its most sophisticated and historically oriented treatment in Donald Blake Webster's *Georgian Canada: Conflict and Culture, 1745–1820* (Toronto, 1984). The intricacies of how Anglo-American colonial relations were manifested in art received attention in Waldron P. Belknap's *American Colonial Painting: Materials for a History* (Cambridge, Mass., 1959), Jules Prown's *John*

[19] See Shellim, *Oil Paintings of India and the East;* Jagmohan Mahajan, *Picturesque India: Sketches and Travels of Thomas and William Daniell* (New Delhi, 1983) and *The Raj Landscape: British Views of Indian Cities* (South Godstone, Surrey, 1988); Pheroza Godrej and Pauline Rohatgi, *Scenic Splendours: India through the Printed Image* (London, 1989); Vidya Dehijia, *Impossible Picturesqueness: Edward Lear's Indian Watercolours, 1873–1875* (New York, 1989). On the Middle East see Peter A. Clayton, *The Rediscovery of Ancient Egypt: Artists and Travellers in the Nineteenth Century* (London, 1982), and Briony Llewellyn, *The Orient Observed: Images of the Middle East from the Searight Collection* (London, 1989).

[20] Archer, *Natural History Drawings*, p. 2; *Visions of India: The Sketchbooks of William Simpson, 1859–1862* (Oxford, 1986).

[21] *African Art Studies: The State of the Discipline* [Symposium papers, National Museum of African Art, Smithsonian Institution, Sept. 1987] (Washington, 1990).

[22] R. H. Hubbard, *An Anthology of Canadian Art* (Toronto, 1960), *The Development of Canadian Art* (Ottowa, 1963), and, with J. R. Ostiguy, *Three Hundred Years of Canadian Art* (Ottowa, 1967). See also J. Russell Harper, *Painting in Canada: A History* (1966; Toronto, 1977); Dennis Reid, *A Concise History of Canadian Painting* (1973; Toronto, 1988); and Michael Bell, *Painters in a New Land* (Toronto, 1973).

Singleton Copley, 2 vols. (Cambridge, Mass., 1966), and in two collections of essays edited by Ian Quimby, *American Painting to 1776: A Reappraisal* (Charlottesville, Va., 1971) and *Arts of the Anglo-American Community in the Seventeenth Century* (Charlottesville, Va., 1975), which focused on decorative arts.

It was during this period of decolonization that Bernard Smith wrote *European Vision and the South Pacific* (Oxford, 1960; 2nd edn., New Haven, 1985), one of the most important books written on the art of the British Empire. It anticipated many issues that would not be raised fully for another twenty-five years. Smith charted the difficulties experienced by artists in adapting their European training and preconceptions to a new environment, and emphasized that artists look at other humans and the landscape around them through conditioned eyes. He also made the critical distinction between the sketches of the draughtsmen who accompanied Ralegh, Cook, and the other explorers, and the engravings that were later mass-produced, which projected a different sort of image. Part of the importance of *European Vision and the South Pacific* was that it was an attempt at truly interdisciplinary work, in addition to taking the perspective that all perception is culture-bound, although Smith did not go so far as to suggest, as he claimed post-modernists have, that 'Europeans (or for that matter the members of any other ethnic or cultural grouping) are incapable as individuals of seeing what is actually before them'.[23]

Smith's approach prompted a considerable amount of research into European perceptions of non-European peoples and parts of the globe. There are now studies of images of blacks, women, Native American Indians, and the Irish.[24] One example is Hugh Honour's *The European Vision of America* (Cleveland, 1975), written in connection with the American bicentennial, in which Honour documented how the New World was 'revealed: not suddenly with the news of Christopher Columbus's landfall, but very gradually over the course of more than half a century'. In this respect, one can talk about America being 'invented' more than discovered. The primary difference between Smith's and Honour's work is that in the latter there is analysis of images and background and context, but no broader exploration of the relationship between art and Empire. Nevertheless,

[23] Bernard Smith, *European Vision and the South Pacific*, 2nd edn. (New Haven, 1985), p. vii. The culmination of Smith's research on Captain Cook was a four-volume set he co-edited with Rudiger Joppien, *The Art of Captain Cook's Voyages* (New Haven, 1985–88). For a recent critique of Smith see William Eisler, *The Furthest Shore: Images of Terra Australis from the Middle Ages to Captain Cook* (Cambridge, 1995).

[24] L. Perry Curtis, Jr., *Apes and Angels: The Irishman in Victorian Caricature* (Washington, 1971); Ellwood Parry, *The Image of the Indian and the Black Man in American Art, 1590–1900* (New York, 1974); Lynne Thornton, *Women as Portrayed in Orientalist Painting* (Paris, 1985); Hugh Honour, *The Image of the Black in Western Art: From the American Revolution to World War I* (3 vols. to date) IV (Cambridge, Mass., 1989); Jan Nederveen Pieterse, *White on Black: Images of Africa and Blacks in Western Popular Culture* (New Haven, 1992); Mark Gidley, ed., *Representing Others: White Views of Indigenous Peoples* (Exeter, 1992).

what unites the writings in this period is that they are from a British perspective (even when written by non-Britons), and attempt, in cautious ways, to reflect upon the colonial enterprise after its collapse.

The historiography of the art of the British Empire has turned in a radically different direction since the late 1970s. No longer solely a reflection of the British perspective, it has shifted to consider the colonized by focusing on representations of the 'Other'. While it might seem to make sense to date the beginnings of this movement from Edward W. Said's *Orientalism* (New York, 1978) and Linda Nochlin's article in *Art in America* on 'The Imaginary Orient' which effectively applied Said's theories to the world of art, neither of these works deal with art and the British Empire.[25] As noted above, studies of European representations of non-Europeans began with Smith's *European Vision and the South Pacific.* But Said gave the study of the 'Other' a theoretical basis that had an immense impact on subsequent studies, as has Nochlin's argument that Orientalist paintings have to be analysed in terms of imperial ideology, and that art history has to break out of its celebratory mode and abandon its concern for aesthetics.

In some respects, what is most remarkable about Said and Nochlin is how *little* impact they have had on art historian's analyses of the art of the British Empire.[26] In *The Oriental Obsession: Islamic Inspiration in British and American Art and Architecture, 1500–1920* (Cambridge, 1988), John Sweetman called Said's 'an interesting if debatable thesis which in the visual arts . . . is especially worth pondering', but on the whole Sweetman ignored Said. Sweetman also disregarded Nochlin's plea for a new form of art history, writing rather drily about the effects of the motifs of Islamic art.[27] Nor is he an exception. Most art historians concerned with British depictions of 'the East' have remained within the older Orientalist tradition that Said so roundly criticized.[28] One of the few books in this field that has been openly influenced by *Orientalism* is James Thompson's *The East: Imagined, Experienced, Remembered* (Dublin, 1988). Steeped in Said's language, Thompson's catalogue notes how the 'Orient represented an alluring Other to Western eyes', how the Orient is 'essentially a work of *fiction* . . . a hermeneutic', and how Europe's East was a frontier land 'ripe for exploits and exploitation'.[29]

[25] Linda Nochlin, 'The Imaginary Orient', *Art in America*, LXXI (1983), pp. 118–31 ff.

[26] There is, for example, no mention of Said in Godrej and Royatgi, *Scenic Splendours*, Llewellyn, *The Orient Observed*, or Clayton, *The Rediscovery of Ancient Egypt.*

[27] John Sweetman, *The Oriental Obsession: Islamic Inspiration in British and American Art and Architecture, 1500–1920* (Cambridge, 1988), pp. 8–9, 117.

[28] Philippe Jullian, *The Orientalists: European Painters of Eastern Scenes* (Oxford, 1977).

[29] James Thompson, *The East: Imagined, Experienced, Remembered: Orientalist Nineteenth Century Painting* (Dublin, 1988), pp. 4, 6, 30, 34. Bernard Smith has also noted the influence of Said in his most recent book, *Imagining the Pacific: In the Wake of the Cook Voyages* (Melbourne, 1992), p. 10.

In the field of cultural studies, on the other hand, where expressions of attitudes, both conscious and subconscious, have become legitimate as well as essential subjects for deconstruction, the impact of Said and Nochlin has been enormous. Anne McClintock's *Imperial Leather: Race, Gender and Sexuality in the Colonial Contest* (New York, 1995) uses advertisements, newspaper cartoons, and maps to support the author's contention that Victorian imperialism meant racial politics and degradation. McClintock makes clear that the Empire was always about race, gender, and class, subjects which had been for the most part ignored in the historiography until the mid-1970s at the earliest. In her analysis of advertisements she was building on the earlier work of Thomas Richards, whose book *The Commodity Culture of Victorian England: Advertising and Spectacle, 1851–1914* (Stanford, Calif., 1990) explored how exhibitions, advertisements, and Victorian kitsch all served to turn the commodity into 'an instrument of unprecedented violence', an icon of the expanding Empire.[30]

These recent studies that focus on race, gender, and representation have contributed vitally to the field by explicitly focusing on the power relationship inherent between Britain and the Empire, while also offering a more rigorous, less descriptive mode of analysis than that of the art historians discussed above. Missing in so many of these studies, however, is a historical grounding that specifically links the analysis to the Empire, and takes into account fissures, inconsistencies, and changes in Imperial attitudes. In Richards's account, for example, it is the commodity that colonizes. What has happened to the colonizers? In this type of approach there are no longer actors or agency, only representations. In the most trenchant critique yet of cultural studies approaches to art and Empire, John M. MacKenzie emphasized, in his *Orientalism: History, Theory, and the Arts* (Manchester, 1995), the need to guard against 'presentism' and moral condemnation, to consider the relationship between élite and popular culture, to avoid unchallenged notions of Western dominance and binary approaches to alterity, and to consider the contrasting socio-economic circumstances of different Imperial territories.

The importance of the approach begun by Bernard Smith, given theoretical rigour by Said and Nochlin, and carried forward by practitioners of cultural studies, is that it is now a virtual truism that art is ideological, political, and served Imperial purposes. The significance of this trend has been both attitudinal and methodological: scholars can no longer approach the material the way they once did.[31] On the other

[30] Thomas Richards, *The Commodity Culture of Victorian England: Advertising and Spectacle, 1851–1914* (Stanford, 1990), p. 128.

[31] Pratapaditya Pal and Vidya Dehejia, *From Merchants to Emperors: British Artists and India, 1757–1930* (Ithaca, NY, 1986); Edward J. Nygren, *Views and Visions: American Landscape Before 1830* (Washington, 1986); Michael Jacobs, *The Painted Voyage: Art, Travel and Exploration, 1564–1875* (London, 1995); Jane Carruthers and Marion I. Arnold, *The Life and Work of Thomas Baines* (Vlaeberg, 1995).

hand, recent studies have tended to ignore artistic developments altogether. Art can be produced for ideological purposes, but the form it takes can be just as conditioned by prevailing aesthetic sensibilities. The significance of the year 1757 on art, for example, may be less Imperial (the British victory at Plassey) than aesthetic (the publication of Edmund Burke's *Enquiry Concerning the Origin of our Ideas of the Sublime and the Beautiful*). Moreover, in addition to this lack of historical and aesthetic grounding, most studies of art and Empire have failed to gauge the effect of Imperial images on historical events, actions, and attitudes except in the vaguest of terms.[32]

It would be wrong to suggest that recent studies of art and the British Empire have focused solely on issues of power and representation. Since the splintering of Soviet Eastern Europe in 1989, and the emergence of subaltern studies, scholars have returned to issues of nationalism and national identity, emphasizing the 'inventedness' of nations and the complex relationship between art and history. Two critically important works by Indian authors that discuss art and aesthetics from within the framework of colonial politics are Tapati Guha-Thakurta, *The Making of a New 'Indian' Art: Artists, Aesthetics and Nationalism in Bengal, c.1850–1920* (Cambridge, 1992) and Partha Mitter, *Art and Nationalism in Colonial India, 1850–1922* (Cambridge, 1994).[33] With so much having been written about the British influence on Indian politics, culture, and society, these two books redress this imbalance by providing a discussion of the indigenous response to British art-making in the Indian Subcontinent that evolved simultaneously. Similarly, M. Franklin Sirmans's important exhibition catalogue, *Transforming the Crown: African, Asian and Caribbean Artists in Britain, 1966–1996* (New York, 1997), explores how 'non-white' artists in Britain have addressed such issues as home, representations of the body, and the implications of skin colour and ethnicity.

Another burgeoning area of study with close links to issues of identity-formation has focused on museums and international exhibitions, especially as scholars begin to examine the way in which art produced throughout the Empire returned to Britain and triggered responses there as well.[34] Scholars have also begun to

[32] This problem is especially apparent in Carol A. Breckenridge, 'The Aesthetics and Politics of Colonial Collecting: India at World's Fairs', *Comparative Studies in Society and History*, XXXI (1989), pp. 195–216.

[33] See also Jules David Prown and others, *Discovered Lands, Invented Pasts: Transforming Visions of the American West* (New Haven, 1992); Stephen Daniels, *Fields of Vision: Landscape Imagery and National Identity in England and the United States* (Cambridge, 1993).

[34] Paul Greenhalgh, *Ephemeral Vistas* (Manchester, 1988); Brian Durrans, 'The Future of the Other: Changing Cultures on Display in Ethnographic Museums', in *The Museum Time-Machine: Putting Cultures on Display*, ed. Robert Lumley (London, 1988); Annie E. Coombes, *Reinventing Africa: Museums, Material Culture and Popular Imagination in Late Victorian and Edwardian England* (New Haven, 1994); Tony Bennett, *The Birth of the Museum: History, Theory, Politics* (London, 1995).

explore the interactions between art, imperialism, and popular political culture through the vehicle of propaganda.[35] There have been several useful thematic studies, especially on images of the military and of battles, although these have remained in the earlier 'compile and catalogue' mode.[36] And, there have finally begun to appear some studies that break down the binary division between colonizer and colonized, the most sumptuous of which is *The Raj: India and the British, 1600–1947* (London, 1990), edited by C. A. Bayly.[37] To date there has, however, been only one attempt at a synthetic analysis of art and the British Empire.[38]

It should be clear by now that there is much excellent work that has been written on art and the British Empire, produced both by British artists and by indigenous peoples. Ultimately, however, this is a fragmented field, divided by disciplinary training and national focus. To paraphrase an infamous phrase, although the sun has set on the British Empire, it has only just begun to rise on that Empire's art.

[35] John M. MacKenzie, *Propaganda and Empire: The Manipulation of British Public Opinion, 1880–1960* (Manchester, 1984), and his edited collection of essays, *Imperialism and Popular Culture* (Manchester, 1986); Catherine Hughes, 'Imperialism, Illustration and the Daily Mail, 1896–1904', in Michael Harris and Alan Lee, eds., *The Press in English Society from the Seventeenth Century to the Nineteenth Century* (Rutherford, NJ, 1986), pp. 187–200; Stephen Constantine, *Buy & Build: The Advertising Posters of the Empire Marketing Board* (London, 1986).

[36] The most interesting of these is Alan McNairn's *Behold the Hero: General Wolfe and the Arts in the Eighteenth Century* (Montreal, 1997), about the multitude of representations that turned General Wolfe into a hero after his death in the Battle of Quebec in 1759. See also J. M. W. Hichberger, *Images of the Army: The Military in British Art, 1815–1914* (Manchester, 1988); Peter Harrington, *British Artists and War: The Face of Battle in Paintings and Prints, 1700–1914* (London, 1993).

[37] See also John Guy and Deborah Swallow, eds., *Arts of India: 1550–1900* (London, 1990); Barbara Soler Miller, ed., *The Powers of Art: Patronage in Indian Culture* (Delhi, 1992).

[38] John M. MacKenzie, 'Art and the Empire', in P. J. Marshall, ed., *The Cambridge Illustrated History of the British Empire* (Cambridge, 1996), pp. 296–315.

Select Bibliography

MILDRED ARCHER, *Company Paintings: Indian Paintings of the British Period* (London, 1992).

—— and W. G. ARCHER, *Indian Painting for the British, 1770–1880* (London, 1955).

C. A. BAYLY, ed., *The Raj: India and the British, 1600–1947* (London, 1990).

PERCY BROWN, *Indian Painting Under the Mughals* (Oxford, 1924).

JANE CARRUTHERS and MARION I. ARNOLD, *The Life and Work of Thomas Baines* (Vlaeberg, 1995).

ANANDA COOMARASWAMY, *Introduction to Indian Art* (Madras, 1923).

ANNIE E. COOMBES, *Reinventing Africa: Museums, Material Culture and Popular Imagination in Late Victorian and Edwardian England* (New Haven, 1994).

TAPATI GUHA-THAKURTA, *The Making of a New 'Indian' Art: Artists, Aesthetics and Nationalism in Bengal, c.1850–1920* (Cambridge, 1992).

E. B. Havell, *Indian Sculpture and Painting*, 2nd edn. (London, 1928).

P. H. Hulton and David B. Quinn, *The American Drawings of John White, 1577–1590*, 2 vols. (London, 1964).

John M. MacKenzie, *Orientalism: History, Theory, and the Arts* (Manchester, 1995).

Anne McClintock, *Imperial Leather: Race, Gender and Sexuality in the Colonial Contest* (New York, 1995).

Barbara Stoler Miller, ed., *The Powers of Art: Patronage in Indian Culture* (Delhi, 1992).

Partha Mitter, *Much Maligned Monsters: History of European Reactions to Indian Art* (Oxford, 1977).

Linda Nochlin, 'The Imaginary Orient', *Art in America* (1983), pp. 118–31 ff.

Pratapaditaya Pal and Vidya Dehejia, *From Merchants to Emperors: British Artists and India, 1757–1930* (Ithaca, NY, 1986).

M. Franklin Sirmans and Mora J. Beauchamp-Byrd, *Transforming the Crown: African, Asian and Caribbean Artists in Britain, 1966–1996* (New York, 1997).

Bernard Smith, *European Vision and the South Pacific*, 2nd edn. (New Haven, 1985).

James Thompson, *The East: Imagined, Experienced, Remembered: Orientalist Nineteenth-Century Painting* (Dublin, 1988).

Donald Blake Webster, *Georgian Canada: Conflict and Culture, 1745–1820* (Toronto, 1984).

37

Architecture in the British Empire

THOMAS R. METCALF

Any assessment of architecture within the British Empire must take into account both the historic monuments of the colonized territories and colonial architecture. The British had to come to terms with the often imposing structures they encountered from India across the Middle East and even into Africa. For the most part they did so by constructing a history for these territories, and their architecture, that linked that past to Britain's own past while preserving Britain's superiority. As they assessed the buildings they themselves had erected, the British brought to bear upon them canons of taste informed at once by aesthetics, history, and attitudes towards Empire. They judged such architecture too in terms of its likeness or difference from that with which they were familiar. For the most part early expressions of pride gave way over time, first to severe condemnation, and then ultimately to a critical reappraisal mixed with nostalgia.

As British travellers, in the wake of the conquests of the East India Company, began to explore the Indian Subcontinent they found themselves overwhelmed by the 'sublime grandeur' of its ancient cave temples, while the tombs and palaces of the Mughals excited such admiration that the artist William Hodges exclaimed of the Taj Mahal that, 'the fine materials, the beautiful forms, and the symmetry of the whole, with the judicious choice of situation, far surpasses any thing I ever beheld'.[1] This delight in the 'sublime' and the 'picturesque', shaped by the aesthetics of early-nineteenth-century Romanticism, involved, however, no coherent account of the past, or the present, of these structures. The classifying and ordering of India's historic architecture was to be a product of the mid-nineteenth century, above all the work of two men—James Fergusson and Alexander Cunningham—and it went hand in hand with the establishment of the Raj itself on a new basis after 1858.

A one-time indigo planter and self-taught student of architecture, James

[1] William Hodges, *Travels in India During the Years 1780, 1781, 1782, and 1783* (London, 1793), pp. 126–27.

Fergusson set himself the task of bringing India's architectural history 'within the domain of science'. In the process he not only described and catalogued India's historic architecture, above all in his authoritative *History of Indian and Eastern Architecture* (1876), but he also devised the categories by which it was to be understood for the subsequent century. Two fundamental assumptions shaped the study of India's architecture: the theory of decline, and that of the division of India's peoples into the two opposed communities of Hindu and Muslim. Sustaining these assumptions was the conviction that at no time could India, or its architecture, however great its accomplishments, stand comparison with Europe. As Fergusson wrote on the very first page of his *History*: 'It cannot for one moment be contended that India ever reached the intellectual supremacy of Greece, or the moral greatness of Rome.' Hence, inevitably, her historic architecture could 'contain nothing so sublime as the hall at Karnac, nothing so intellectual as the Parthenon, nor so constructively grand as a medieval cathedral'.[2]

The theory of decline complemented the idea of progress which, from the Enlightenment onwards, defined Europe's perception of its own past. Indeed, the notion of a continuous Eastern 'decline' provided the necessary foil against which the triumphalism of Western 'progress' could be measured. Further, scholars such as Fergusson insisted that their aesthetic judgements were not mere prejudice, but rather expressed universal principles valid for all times and cultures. The superiority of the Parthenon over the Taj Mahal, for instance, was confirmed by its rank upon a numerical scale that measured 'the true principles of beauty in art'. In similar fashion, South India's medieval temples were not merely unpleasing, but constructed according to a 'false system of design'. In contravention of the universal principle that structures required a 'tall central object to give dignity to the whole from the outside', the South Indian temple builders had enclosed the sanctuary with a series of towers that decreased, rather then increased, in size as they approached the centre. This, Fergusson argued, 'is a mistake which nothing can redeem'.[3]

The notion of decline at once made possible an appreciation of India's ancient architecture, and yet, as the two cultures diverged ever more dramatically, paved the way for British colonial conquest. Invariably the oldest structures were the finest. This reflected in part the Oriental scholarship of those who, from Warren Hastings's time onwards, had, with Sir William Jones, been drawn to the 'magnificence' of an ancient civilization whose language, and whose texts, they had themselves deciphered. In the early nineteenth century the discoveries of the Ajanta caves and Gandharan art, with the simultaneous recognition of the existence of an

[2] James Fergusson, *History of India and Eastern Architecture*, 2 vols. (London, 1876; 2nd edn., 1910), I, pp. 4, 6.

[3] Ibid., pp. 366, 379; II, p. 284.

extended period of Buddhist predominance, provided a new and attractive way of marking out India's era of ancient greatness. Not only was the Buddhist faith free of Hindu 'superstition', but its art, shaped by aesthetic forms similar to, and in part influenced by, those of classical Greece, could be awarded unstinting praise. Thenceforward, however, as Hinduism displaced Buddhism, the 'backward decline' of India's architecture proceeded unabated. Products of an 'idolatrous and corrupt' society, neither India's medieval temples nor the rulers who erected them deserved much respect.

With the coming of Islam to India in the medieval era, architectural styles related to those of the Middle East found a footing in South Asia. For the British these styles, which incorporated the dome and arch as central elements, were reassuringly familiar. As Lord Napier, Governor of Madras, wrote in 1870, Islamic architecture united 'dignity, elegance, and the picturesque' with 'perfect constructive science'.[4] Labelled 'Saracenic', the buildings erected by Muslim rulers were juxtaposed to, but seen as wholly separate from, contemporaneous 'Hindu' architecture. From the outset the British had taken it for granted that there existed in India distinct 'Hindu' and 'Muslim' communities, and that these differences in religious belief shaped enduring differences in character. To be Hindu or Muslim by itself, that is, explained much of the way Indians acted. Not surprisingly, therefore, India's architecture, as the British sought to classify it, expressed the values of these religiously defined communities. Much in Indian Islamic architecture, along with the other achievements of these conquering warriors, was seen as deserving of praise. Akbar's capital at Fatehpur Sikri, for instance, marked out his 'wisdom, clemency, and justice', while the Taj Mahal was always seen as the 'central jewel' of a 'brilliant and splendid' architecture.[5] Nevertheless, neither this architecture nor its patrons were exempt from the universal law of 'Oriental' decline. By the eighteenth century the architectural 'abominations' and 'vulgarity' of such post-Mughal rulers as the nawabs of Awadh (Oudh) defined a society of such 'utter degradation' that the British conquest was wholly justified.[6]

The study of India's archaeological remains was informed by much the same schema. Like Fergusson, Alexander Cunningham was determined to place the study of archaeology on a 'scientific' basis, and during the 1860s, as India's first archaeological surveyor, he initiated a systematic investigation that produced a list of monuments, classified, labelled, and deemed worthy of restoration and protection. This enterprise gave India a visible past, but one defined by the Imperial regime, and sustained by the assumption that the Indian people had themselves neglected and defiled these monuments. Preserved in a state of picturesque decay,

[4] *Builder*, 10 Sept. 1870, p. 723.

[5] Ibid., 26 Aug. 1876, p. 823.

[6] Fergusson, *History*, II, pp. 320–28.

isolated from the living present, India's archaeological sites testified at once to the country's past greatness, her subsequent decline, and Britain's essential role as custodian of that greatness.

These assumptions shaped all subsequent study of India's historic architecture. The earliest indigenous scholars, men such as Rajendralal Mitra, the author of a two-volume account of the antiquities of Orissa, contested Fergusson's claim that only the British were able authoritatively to define the nature of India's past, and insisted upon the autonomy and originality of design in India's architectural traditions; in return Mitra found himself, together with all 'native knowledge', vilified.[7] Other scholars, such as A. K. Coomaraswamy, seeking ways to assuage the hurt of the colonized, argued for the existence in India's art and culture of a 'spiritual essence' which set India apart from a 'materialistic' West, and whose elements could be discerned, for instance, in the cosmological symbolism of the Hindu temple.

Nevertheless, neither the nationalists nor later European scholars called into question the larger theory of decline or the division of India's peoples, and her architecture, into the two opposed communities of Hindu and Muslim. Fergusson's *History*, reprinted in 1910, continued to be the standard work on India's architecture until the middle of the twentieth century; and such writers as Percy Brown and Benjamin Rowland only further elaborated its fundamental ideas. To be sure, some critics, such as Hermann Goetz, spoke up for the 'rococo' beauty of India's 'decadent' eighteenth-century art, but for the most part India's architectural history, apart from the great Mughal monuments, still came to an end no later than the thirteenth century. Later structures were at best 'overripe'.[8] The struggles that led to the partition of the Subcontinent also, by the logic of historicism, validated the categories of communal affiliation. Inevitably, after 1947 Hindu and Muslim were read back into the past as the defining markers of South Asia's cultural identity.

Only in the last years of the twentieth century have scholars begun to appraise more favourably the architecture of the later medieval kingdoms, and at the same time to call into question the easy association of religion with architectural style. Writers such as Catherine Asher and George Michell identified regional clusters of styles, shared among religious communities, that embody the 'taste' of particular eras. In this scholarship, the Hindu state of Vijayanagara, for instance, and its Muslim neighbour Bijapur, even while they warred against each other, are seen as joined by architectural styles and forms of patronage that

[7] Rajendralal Mitra, *The Antiquities of Orissa*, 2 vols. (Calcutta, 1875, 1880); James Fergusson, *Archaeology in India, With Especial Reference to the Works of Babu Rajendralal Mitra* (London, 1884), esp. pp. vi–vii, 4.

[8] Hermann Goetz, *The Crisis of Indian Civilization in the Eighteenth and Early Nineteenth Centuries* (Calcutta, 1938).

blurred even the distinction between mosque and temple.[9] The ending of the Imperial connection, with the questioning in recent years of the Orientalist certainties that sustained it, have at last opened up a new historiography of India's historic architecture.

Outside India imposing monuments were rare in the areas that comprised the British Empire. Most were located in the Middle East. The massive tombs and other structures of ancient Egypt exerted a powerful attraction for European observers, especially after the Napoleonic expedition in 1798 and the decipherment of the hieroglyphic script. As the oldest surviving structures on earth they possessed a secure hold on Europe's imagination. Middle Eastern Islamic architecture similarly drew admirers from among European scholars and travellers from the early nineteenth century onward. Most compelling, perhaps, was the Alhambra in Granada, Spain. Exotic yet comprehensible, with its fountains and arches, its coloured tiles and intricate stalactite domes, the Alhambra was well situated to appeal to the Romantic imagination. Travellers and artists, from the American visitor Washington Irving to the painter John Frederick Lewis and the architectural designer Owen Jones, all published extensive volumes of illustrations and stories drawn from the Alhambra. But Moorish Spain had long vanished—that, of course, was part of its attraction—and Spain was now an independent Christian land. Nor was Egypt allowed to escape the logic of 'Oriental' decline. Even the sympathetic Richard Burton, travelling through Cairo, described a 'gradual decadence of art through one thousand two hundred years down to the present day'.[10]

For the most part, as tropical Africa, South-East Asia, and the South Pacific came under Imperial dominion, the British regarded their inhabitants as mere savages. The lack of an imposing architecture, indeed, reinforced this presumption. As hunters and gatherers who did not erect permanent shelters for their homes, the Australian Aborigines, in the view of the British colonizers, could make no claim even over the land itself. Hence the newcomers were free to do with it what they wished. In Malaya, as they built their new capital of Kuala Lumpur, with its massive government offices, the British imagined themselves as taming a wilderness 'where man scarce ever trod, and whose only inhabitants were the beasts of the forests'.[11] In tropical Africa, however, one monumental ruin did exist, that of Great Zimbabwe, and its history and meaning was to prove a subject of enduring controversy.

[9] See e.g. Catherine B. Asher, *Architecture of Mughal India* (Cambridge, 1992).

[10] Richard F. Burton, *Personal Narrative of a Pilgrimage to Al-Madinah and Mecca*, 2 vols. (London, 1893; repr. New York, 1964), I, p. 96.

[11] *Selangor Journal* (Kuala Lumpur), V (2 April 1897), p. 233.

As British adventurers and explorers marched into central Africa to claim what became the colony of Southern Rhodesia, they were drawn by reports of an ancient kingdom associated with the legendary King Solomon's mines. The earliest archaeologists, sent by Cecil Rhodes in the 1890s, refused to believe that the indigenous Shona peoples could have constructed the vast and intricate structure of the Zimbabwe ruin. Imbued with the racist assumptions of the late Victorian era, men such as J. Theodore Bent insisted that the builders had to have been a 'former civilized race' for whom the walled structure would have acted as a defensive fortification amidst a conquered people. Such a race could only, in their view, have been of Semitic stock, and probably consisted of Phoenicians from the Middle East drawn by reports of gold.

By the early decades of the twentieth century professional archaeologists had already begun to question these claims alike of antiquity and of alien builders at Zimbabwe. These experts insisted that there were no gold mines, and no alien races, but rather that the ruins had been built in African style by Africans to serve local purposes. White settlers and their apologists, still anxious to claim a place for themselves in central Africa, now asserted that the workmanship was rudimentary, the product of a society in decline, and the builders one among numerous invaders who had swept through the area. Nevertheless, the image of Zimbabwe as ancient and exotic persisted in the popular mind; from time to time it was reanimated by anthropologists, by tourist promoters, and finally by the secessionist white settler regime after 1965 as it sought to legitimate its position. Throughout, the interpretation of the past remained the handmaiden of politics. Nor did the situation change with the rise of African nationalism. For nationalists Zimbabwe was a reminder of the powerful African states whose vanished glories would return with the ending of colonialism. As early as 1961, Rhodesia's African politicians had claimed the name for their own; in 1980, in the wake of independence, they hastened to rename their land after its illustrious predecessor.[12]

As the Empire expanded across the globe, the British themselves, as settlers and as rulers, erected a wide range of structures, in a variety of architectural styles, in the colonies they established. For the most part these buildings were not, until recently, judged of sufficient importance to be worthy of study. Those modelled on European forms, with the exception of the few designed by famous architects such as Edwin Lutyens, were deemed inferior and derivative by English critics; those that sought to incorporate indigenous forms, whether in the domestic bungalow

[12] For a general account, see Henrika Kuklick, 'Contested Monuments: The Politics of Archeology in Southern Africa', in George W. Stocking, Jr., ed., *Colonial Situations* (Madison, 1991), pp. 135–69.

or the monumental 'Saracenic' façades of British Indian cities, were disparaged as exotics. The exceptional occasions when such unfamiliar forms were employed in Britain, as in the Prince Regent's Brighton Pavilion, and in the architecture of seaside resorts and pleasure palaces, only served to confirm their essential quaintness or their inferior quality.

For those who lived or worked in the colonies, however, these buildings served important purposes. Above all, they marked out the power and authority of the British Empire, and so secured favourable notice from contemporary critics. As early as 1781, the painter William Hodges wrote of Madras that its 'long colonnades, with open porticoes and flat roofs', offered to the eye 'an appearance similar to that which we conceive of a Grecian city in the age of Alexander'.[13] In similar fashion Wellesley's Calcutta Government House (1802), modelled on Kedleston Hall, evoked from Lord Valentia an expression of pride that India was now 'to be ruled from a palace, not from a counting-house; with the ideas of a Prince, not with those of a retail dealer in muslins and indigo'.[14] Britain's Empire, so such structures proclaimed, was one with that of Alexander and of Rome.

Architecture that celebrated colonial difference, such as that erected in the 'Saracenic' style in late-nineteenth-century India, was always more troubling to critics. The 'ecclesiologists', for instance, denounced the use of 'heathen' forms in buildings meant for Christian worship. But these forms had their admirers as well. Oriental scholars insisted, with William Emerson, that 'it was impossible for the architecture of the west to be suitable to the natives of the east'.[15] Further, the incorporation of such forms enabled Britain to represent itself as successor to the Moghuls, hence as an 'Indian' Imperial state. Such considerations ensured for the 'Saracenic' style a favourable reception, which included its adoption even in the Malayan capital of Kuala Lumpur, until the Raj itself was forced on to the defensive in the twentieth century.

In settler cities, such as Sydney and Toronto, the familiar forms of classical and, after the mid-nineteenth century, of Gothic architecture reassured their inhabitants that, even though far from 'home', they remained British. Domestic building too, with its half-timbered cottages and stone mansions, from Australia's Ballarat to India's Ootacamund, though often incorporating the distinctively colonial verandah, evoked a remembered, if sentimentalized, England. By the late nineteenth century, however, in the colonies as elsewhere, architectural critics increasingly disdained the work of their predecessors. Pride in Governor Macquarie's 'elegant' structures, erected from 1816 to 1822 in Sydney by the convict architect

[13] Hodges, *Travels in India*, p. 2.

[14] Curzon of Kedleston, *British Government in India*, 2 vols. (London, 1925), I, p. 71.

[15] T. Roger Smith, 'Architectural Art in India', *Journal of the Society of Arts*, XXI (1873), pp. 286–87.

Francis Greenway, was replaced by condemnation of their 'supreme ugliness of design'.[16] Still, in the 1880s and 1890s the burgeoning Arts and Crafts movement, as it spread from England to the colonies, secured the architecture of the early colonial period, together with the work of contemporary artisans in India, a more favourable appraisal.

For men such as John Ruskin and William Morris, although the European Middle Ages enshrined most fully the values of independent craftsmanship they cherished, India, so they conceived, was a 'timeless' land that kept alive 'medieval' values in the modern world. Hence crafts enthusiasts such as George Birdwood and Lockwood Kipling, father of the poet, trained artisans and organized crafts exhibitions; while F. S. Growse, of the Indian Civil Service, employing only local artisans, erected public buildings conceived in the spirit of Ruskin in the towns in which he served. In his writings on India's architecture during the decade before the First World War, E. B. Havell, more sympathetic to Hinduism than his predecessors, singled out for praise as models of Indian craftsmanship both the domestic architecture of princely Rajputana and the temples in the great pilgrimage centres of Benares and Hardwar.[17]

In South Africa the young English architect Herbert Baker, newly arrived in the Cape in 1892, saw in the gabled thatch-roofed houses built by the early-eighteenth-century Dutch and Huguenot settlers, not the inferior work of rustic Boers but a 'simplicity' that corresponded exactly to the ideals of the Arts and Crafts movement.[18] A more favourable appraisal of early colonial architecture also advanced political objectives within settler communities. Above all, by laying claim to these buildings, the colonists could lay claim to a past for themselves separate from that of Britain, and yet one, as Joseph Fowles wrote of Sydney in 1848, able 'boldly to claim a comparison with London itself'.[19] By the end of the century, as the historic preservation movement gained momentum, writers and artists in each colony meticulously detailed the early architecture of its towns and cities. Characteristic, perhaps, was John R. Robertson's six-volume *Landmarks of Toronto: A Collection of Historical Sketches of the Old Town of York from 1792 until 1837, and of Toronto from 1834 to 1914* (Toronto, 1894–1914).

Such celebratory writing, all the same, helped define, and so set boundaries around, the colonial political community. Everywhere, after an initial curiosity about their dwellings and habits, the aboriginal peoples faded from view. Loving

[16] Morton Herman, *The Early Australian Architects and Their Work* (Sydney, 1954), esp. chaps. 6 and 7.

[17] E. B. Havell, *Indian Architecture: Its Psychology, Structure, and History from the First Muhammadan Invasion to the Present Day* (London, 1913), esp. pp. 219–20, 228–29.

[18] Herbert Baker, *Architecture and Personalities* (London, 1944), p. 23.

[19] Bernard Smith, *European Vision and the South Pacific* (2nd edn., New Haven, 1985), pp. 285–86.

descriptions of old homesteads in the Grahamstown region of the Eastern Cape, for instance, emptied the landscape of native peoples. Hence, in a fashion similar to the commemoration of the 1820 settlers by writers such as Sir George Cory, histories of the region's architecture announced the vitality of a proudly English South African community. Colonial architecture could also bring peoples together. The mining magnate Cecil Rhodes in the 1890s patronized the old Dutch crafts, even to the extent of building a house for himself in the Cape Dutch style. Through this shared past, encompassing both white races but excluding the black, Rhodes sought to generate a distinctive sense of Cape identity, and in the process to advance his own political fortunes.

From the First World War on to the 1950s and 1960s colonial architecture sank increasingly into disfavour among critics. Edwin Lutyens alone among colonial builders, with his ambitious design for India's new capital at Delhi, stirred critical enthusiasms. Robert Byron, for instance, described Lutyens's Viceroy's House on its completion as a 'real fusion of national motives into a pure and highly individual style'.[20] In general, however, colonial nationalism and architectural modernism between them ensured that the lavishly ornate architecture of Empire was treated at best with indifference and at worst with contempt. Symptomatic, perhaps, was Jawaharlal Nehru's selection of the uncompromising modernist, Le Corbusier, to design the new Punjab capital at Chandigarh. The new India, this decision announced, was to be a modern nation free of the encumbrances of the colonial past.

As the passions aroused by the end of Empire faded, the structures erected under Imperial auspices began to be seen as historically significant, and so worthy of serious study. At the same time, from the 1970s the rise of post-modernism in design encouraged a more sympathetic judgement of the ornamented style characteristic of so much colonial building. This reassessment, driven forward as well by other larger currents of historical scholarship, has produced a substantial corpus of writing on the architecture of Empire in recent years. Sten Nilsson's path-breaking *European Architecture in India, 1750–1850* (London, 1968) stood alone, but two works of the later 1970s, though from very different perspectives, announced the coming of the new era. One was Anthony King's *Colonial Urban Development: Culture, Social Power and the Environment* (London, 1976); the other, Edward W. Said's *Orientalism* (London, 1978). Robert Irving's *Indian Summer: Lutyens, Baker and Imperial Delhi* (New Haven), the first full-length study of the architecture of a British Imperial site, followed in 1981. Though neither of the first two took architecture as its central concern,

20 Robert Byron, 'The Architecture of the Viceroy's House', *Country Life* (June 1931), pp. 708–16.

together they opened up new interpretive strategies for understanding colonial buildings within the historical context that had produced them.

King worked from within a Marxist framework, and sought to show how 'the power structure inherent in the dominance-dependence relationship of colonialism influenced urban development in the colonial society' (p. xiii). Unlike traditional Marxists, however, King identified the cultural beliefs and assumptions associated with Western imperialism as the element, situated within the social relations of production of the capitalist state, that most powerfully shaped the built form of the colonial city. In the hierarchical encounter between colonizer and colonized King discerned the emergence of a 'colonial third culture'; to this culture he attributed such distinctively colonial institutions as the residential bungalow, the hill station, and the military cantonment. In his subsequent 1984 study *The Bungalow: The Production of a Global Culture* (London), King assessed the cultural role and worldwide diffusion of this uniquely colonial architectural form.

Side by side with Marxist-inspired studies are those that have drawn inspiration from Michel Foucault, especially as his ideas were directed towards study of the colonial encounter by Edward Said. In his *Orientalism*, Said argued that the 'Orient' existed only in Europe's imagination, so that knowledge about it was never disinterested scholarship, but rather served always to advance Europe's imperial objectives. It was, he wrote, 'a Western style for dominating, restructuring, and having authority over the Orient' (p. 3). Said's critical posture gained further authority during the 1980s from the post-modernist literary theory which insisted upon the 'decentring' and 'deconstructing' of texts, and so denied the existence of any authoritative modes of knowing.

When applied to the study of architecture, such an approach inevitably undercut traditional aesthetic and formalist modes of analysis. To be sure, some scholars have resisted the imputation of political motives to all colonial building, and have insisted upon the autonomy of aesthetics and design, while others have pointed to the existence of a widespread 'sympathy' and 'respect' for Oriental architectural forms not connected to a politics of domination.[21] Still, much recent scholarship, not only on British colonial architecture but on French and Italian as well, has sought to demonstrate the ways in which colonial design was subordinated to the politics of imperialism. As the present author has argued in the 1984 article on 'Architecture and the Representation of Empire', and the subsequent *An Imperial Vision: Indian Architecture and Britain's Raj* (Berkeley, 1989), in the colonial environment 'the choice of architectural style, the arrangement of

[21] See G. H. R. Tillotson, *The Tradition of Indian Architecture: Continuity, Controversy, and Change Since 1850* (New Haven, 1989), and John M. MacKenzie, *Orientalism: History, Theory and the Arts* (Manchester, 1995), esp. chap. 4.

space within a building, and the decision to erect a particular structure all testified to a vision of empire'.[22]

In Britain the 1980s saw an outpouring of celebratory writing on the architecture of Empire. No longer inhibited by lingering colonial guilt, and encouraged by the Thatcherite 'revolution', as well as the patriotic enthusiasms unleashed by the 1982 Falklands War, Britons began to look back with an increasing nostalgia upon their Imperial past. Lovingly detailed and often lavishly produced, these books, mostly written by amateur scholars, include the travel writer and historian Jan Morris's *Stones of Empire: The Buildings of the Raj* (Oxford, 1983); Philip Davies, *Splendours of the Raj: British Architecture in India: 1660–1947* (London, 1985); Raymond Head, *The Indian Style* (London, 1986); and *Architecture of the British Empire* (London, 1986), edited by R. Fermor-Hesketh.

In the old settler societies, where the Imperial past had long since been assimilated to a national past, the earlier study of the architecture of the colonial period has continued unabated. Rarely have these works sought to make connections with the larger British Empire, but they have examined a wide variety of regional styles, together with the work of individual architects, so that the architecture of the colonial era is now, for the most part, well documented.[23] For these societies, together with those of colonial America, recent scholarship has increasingly shifted from civic monuments toward the study of vernacular architecture. In a series of studies of what is called 'material culture', combining textual evidence, architecture, and archaeology, scholars have sought to identify the actual uses to which buildings were devoted, and thus the world of the individuals who inhabited them. In the process they have focused upon the ways local landscape and cultural forms shaped the design of even structures derived from European models. Most stimulating, perhaps, has been the work of such scholars as James Deetz, Dell Upton, and their students in the Eastern Cape Historical Archaeology Project.[24]

Elsewhere, coming to terms with the buildings left behind by the departed Imperial ruler has been more difficult. For most of these former colonial societies, preoccupied with more urgent tasks, neither the study nor the preservation of the

[22] Thomas R. Metcalf, 'Architecture and the Representation of Empire: India, 1860–1910', *Representations*, VI (1984), pp. 37–65. See also Gwendolyn Wright, *The Politics of Design in French Colonial Urbanism* (Chicago, 1991); and Nezar Al Sayyad, ed., *Forms of Dominance: On the Architecture and Urbanism of the Colonial Enterprise* (Aldershot, 1992).

[23] Among others see P. Picton-Seymour, *Victorian Buildings in South Africa* (Cape Town, 1977), and Janet B. Wright, *Architecture of the Picturesque in Canada* (Ottawa, 1984).

[24] See e.g. Dell Upton and John Vlach, eds., *Common Places: Readings in American Vernacular Architecture* (Athens, Ga., 1986), and Margot Winer, 'Landscapes of Power: British Material Culture of the Eastern Cape Frontier, South Africa: 1820–1860', unpublished Ph.D. dissertation, University of California, Berkeley, 1994.

colonial architectural heritage has evoked much interest. Still, younger architects and architectural historians in Malaysia, India, and elsewhere have recently begun to reappraise the colonial past, and to fight, through such organizations as the Delhi Conservation Society, for its recognition as a valid part of a national past. As a result, the fabric of the colonial city is now at last being subjected to detailed scrutiny, together with assessment of the ways indigenous peoples themselves actively participated in its creation. The historiography of the architecture of the British Empire, together with that of its art and the larger colonial culture in which both were embedded, is fast being transformed.

Select Bibliography

KUNLE AKINSEMOYIN, *Building Lagos*, 2nd edn. (Jersey, 1977).

JAMES FERGUSSON, *History of Indian and Eastern Architecture* (1876; London, 2nd edn., 1910).

HANS FRANSEN and MARY ALEXANDER COOK, *The Old Buildings of the Cape: A Survey and Description of Old Buildings in the Western Province* (Cape Town, 1980).

ROBERT GRANT IRVING, *Indian Summer: Lutyens, Baker and Imperial Delhi* (New Haven, 1981).

MICHAEL KEATH, *Herbert Baker: Architecture and Idealism, 1892–1913: The South African Years, 1892–1913* (Gibraltar, 1992).

ANTHONY D. KING, *Colonial Urban Development: Culture, Social Power and Environment* (London, 1976).

—— *The Bungalow: The Production of a Global Culture* (London, 1984).

THOMAS R. METCALF, *An Imperial Vision: Indian Architecture and Britain's Raj* (Berkeley, 1989).

STEN AKE NILSSON, *European Architecture in India, 1750–1850* (London, 1968).

JOHN E. SWEETMAN, *The Oriental Obsession: Islamic Inspiration in British and American Art and Architecture, 1500–1920* (Cambridge, 1988).

GRANVILLE WILSON and PETER SANDS, *Building a City: 100 Years of Melbourne Architecture* (Melbourne, 1981).

38

Orients and Occidents: Colonial Discourse Theory and the Historiography of the British Empire

D. A. WASHBROOK

A striking feature of historical writings on the British Empire over the last decade has been the influence of critical theories of 'colonial discourse'. In part, these share much in common with the more generic discourse critiques which have widely affected most fields of historical inquiry in recent times. They seek to contest an Enlightenment epistemology, informing the practice of 'modern' history, which holds that universal and objective truths about the human condition may be 'discovered' through the exercise of Reason, which itself also provides the guide to Freedom. In opposition, they propose that *all* knowledge is necessarily relative—determined by the contingent linguistic forms, cultural assumptions, and power 'positions' of those who 'construct' it—and that the Enlightenment concept of Freedom—based on the formal liberties of the individual subject or citizen—is too narrow to encompass the emancipation of all human aspirations, desires, and appetites.

Critical discourse theory re-interrogates the past with a view, not to establishing 'scientific' truths and narrating stories of progressive emancipation, but to exposing the particular conditions under which various 'knowledges' were produced and authorized; the self-referential ways in which they 'represented' the subjects of their study; and the relations of domination by which their own constructs were imposed on those subjects, at the expense of the latter's 'different' understandings.[1]

Where theories of 'colonial discourse' advance this general purpose is in their attempt to show how the colonial situation gave rise to certain distinctive types of knowledge and relations of domination.[2] Discourse criticism percolated steadily into the historiography of imperialism over a considerable period

I am grateful to Rajnarayan Chandavarkar, Jonathan Spencer, and Rosalind O'Hanlon for their comments on earlier drafts.

[1] For an introduction to critical discourse theory in historical practice see Lynn Hunt and Aletta Biersack, eds., *The New Cultural History* (Berkeley, 1989).

[2] See Francis Barker, Peter Hulme, and Margaret Iversen, eds., *Colonial Discourse, Postcolonial Theory* (Manchester, 1994); also Patrick Williams and Laura Chrisman, eds., *Colonial Discourse and Post-Colonial Theory: A Reader* (New York, 1994).

through interdisciplinary contacts with anthropology, which responded to it first.[3] However, its widest appeal waited upon literary theory and the publication in 1978 of Edward W. Said's dazzling *Orientalism*.[4]

Said scrutinized a range of authoritative texts from European writers proffering knowledges of the 'Oriental' (specifically Islamic) world. Utilizing the techniques of textual deconstruction pioneered by Jacques Derrida, he sought to show how, through rhetorical devices, linguistic conventions, and narrative structures, these texts represented Oriental subjects in arbitrary, demeaning, and inferiorizing ways, while claiming to speak in the name of objective science and universal truth. He then extrapolated his conclusions towards the politico-cultural theses of Michel Foucault, with Derrida perhaps the other leading contributor to discourse theory.

Foucault had argued that the knowledge represented in discourse was the product of a closed system of reasoning, sealed against counter-information and alternative hypothesis by epistemic axiom. Its only reference-points for representing 'Others' were internal to itself. Said looked at a series of European representations of Islam, from the Christian to the modern ages, and noted that they, too, consisted of inverted self-images, defined only by the observation of 'difference'. Foucault also had argued, famously, that knowledge was inextricably linked to power. Said re-situated the Enlightenment in its world-historical context, which was marked by the expansion of European imperialism. He posited an intimate connection between the two: the Enlightenment project was not merely an attempt to transform European society itself, but also and crucially to make Europe dominant over all other cultures and societies of the world.

By taking as his point of reference its relationship to an Oriental 'Other', Said was able to reveal a number of previously 'occluded' features in European culture itself. First, he showed how Europe's aversion to this Other, through successive epochs, reflected deep epistemic continuities across conventional historical periods. Secondly, he demonstrated the ways in which the Enlightenment's approaches to knowledge had the effect of putting Europe at the centre of all resulting 'universal' schemas—as representing the standards by which the rest of the world was to be judged, the markers from which it was to take its own identity. 'The Orient' was 'backward' in relation to Europe: its only meaningful history—its path to Modernization—was to follow Europe's course. Finally, he argued that Europe's propensity to demean Others was crucial to how it identified and evaluated itself. By a circular process of logic, the representations of inferiority which Europe

3 See esp. Bernard S. Cohn, *An Anthropologist Among the Historians and Other Essays* (Delhi, 1987) and *Colonialism and Its Forms of Knowledge: The British in India* (Princeton, 1996).

4 Edward W. Said, *Orientalism* (London, 1978).

imposed on Others were then objectified, reflected back, and held up to Europeans as 'scientific' proof that their norms were, indeed, superior. 'The Orient' constituted a distorting mirror within which Europe defined, justified, and celebrated itself.[5]

Said's withering critique put European culture under indictment and proposed that its hostility towards and drive for domination over its Oriental Other constructed a distinctive 'Orientalist' discursive field. Following in Said's wake, a number of scholars sought to extend his insights to cover Europe's relations with the whole of the non-European world and to develop them as critical tools for examining colonial cultures and societies.[6] They proposed the existence of a distinctive 'colonial' discursive field.

Such extensions, it should be said, have been very various and their relationship to Said's original formulations sometimes very strained, making it difficult to consider them together and as a single genre.[7] Colonial discourse *critique* is inherently anti-theoretical and hence can scarcely be held to constitute a coherent body of *theory* itself. However, it may gain a form of unity from another source. Apparently responding to the belief that knowledge is constructed through scholarly and political partisanship, many of its practitioners are inclined to impose a collective identity on themselves—through 'self-representation' of a common 'position', selective cross-authorization of one-anothers' views, and emphasis on a shared experience in 'rejecting' Enlightenment Europe.[8] Ironically, if appropriately, discourse critique coheres as theory through practices which make it into a species of discourse itself.[9]

[5] For critical appreciations and explorations of Said's ideas see Michael Sprinker, ed., *Edward Said: A Critical Reader* (Oxford, 1992); also John M. MacKenzie, *Orientalism: History, Theory and the Arts* (Manchester, 1995).

[6] For the wider impact and implications of Said's work see Gyan Prakash, 'Writing Post-Orientalist Histories of the Third World: Perspectives from Indian Historiography', *Comparative Studies in Society and History*, XXXII, 2 (1990), pp. 383–408.

[7] Some of these differences are explored in Robert Young, *White Mythologies: Writing Histories and the West* (London, 1990).

[8] Note particularly, the partisanal rhetoric associated with the 'Subaltern Studies' project, which has become a leading vehicle of colonial discourse critique. See Ranajit Guha and Gayatri Chakravorty Spivak, eds., *Selected Subaltern Studies* (New York, 1988), with foreword by Edward W. Said; Gyan Prakash, 'Writing Post-Orientalist Histories' and 'Subaltern Studies as Postcolonial Criticism', *American Historical Review*, LXLIX, 5 (1994–95), pp. 1475–90; Dipesh Chakrabarty, 'Postcoloniality and the Artifice of History: Who Speaks for "Indian" Pasts?', *Representations*, XXXVII (1992), pp. 1–26; Edward W. Said, *Culture and Imperialism* (1st edn., New York, 1993; London, 1993), esp. pp. 300–13; Gayatri Chakravorty Spivak, *In Other Worlds: Essays in Cultural Politics* (New York, 1987), esp. pp. 197–221.

[9] Aijaz Ahmad has related this self-representation of a common position, in spite of manifest internal differences, to the politics of 'place' inside the American academy, where most leading colonial discourse critics are located: Aijaz Ahmad, *In Theory: Classes, Nations and Literatures* (London, 1992), pp. 159–200.

Whatever its status as theory, however, colonial discourse critique certainly inspired a major paradigm-shift in the historiography of imperialism which strongly informed writing in the 1980s. This shift altered the focus of study away from 'social' and towards 'cultural' history. It also promoted critical methods designed to 'deconstruct' the British Imperial record and the artefacts of the colonial experience in order to demonstrate how the knowledges represented by and in them were the functions of culturally relative assumption and exercised power. The shift very much broadened the range of phenomena brought under the scrutiny of history. Besides archival documentary 'texts', imperial historians now were invited to 'read' buildings and paintings, music and novels, street-plans and public rituals. They were also enjoined to read documentary texts in a very different way.

The new approaches made an impact, first, on study of the ways in which Europeans represented themselves in and to the worlds which they conquered. Previous perspectives had assumed the colonizers to be the subjects and agents of imperial history; now they became its objects, posited by the discourse-logic of colonialism itself. Investigations into this logic revealed how the colonialists themselves were reinvented by the 'strategies' necessary to establishing their cultural difference and effecting their domination. In particular, colonial discourse made free and novel use of those other key-markers of 'difference'—gender, generation, and race—to define the colonizers, almost to the point of caricature, as representatives of the manly, the civilized, and the white.[10]

A second point of focus fell on the ways in which colonialists represented and constructed knowledges about their conquered subjects. Here, the whole apparatus of imperial information-gathering—censuses, ethnographies, land-settlement reports, museums—was brought under a scrutiny which exposed the functioning of the Enlightenment episteme. In the name of scientific Rationality, arbitrary forms of categorization were imposed which had little to do with the self-consciousness of the subjects under report and which objectified, 'essentialized', and exoticized their culture.[11] Put under the same scrutiny were key policy-documents, which revealed how strategies of domination had been primary to colonial administration, biasing it much more towards maintaining Imperial authority than serving the welfare of the colonized.[12]

[10] For examples, Antoinette Burton, *Burdens of History: British Feminists, Indian Women and Imperial Culture, 1865–1915* (Chapel Hill, NC, 1994); Anne McClintock, *Imperial Leather: Race, Gender and Sexuality in the Colonial Context* (New York, 1995); Mrinalini Sinha, *Colonial Masculinity: The 'Manly' Englishman and the 'Effeminate' Bengali in the Late Nineteenth Century* (Manchester, 1995).

[11] For examples, Cohn, *An Anthropologist* and *Colonialism and Its Forms of Knowledge.* 'Essentialization' refers to the tendency of European and Enlightenment thought to 'explain' culture by reference to the presumed fixed and unchanging properties, or essences, of a civilization.

[12] For examples, David Arnold, *Famine: Social Crisis and Historical Change* (Oxford, 1988) and *Colonizing the Body: State Medicine and Epidemic Disease in Nineteenth-Century India* (Berkeley, 1993).

The same messages—of imposed Enlightenment science and 'strategized' imperial authority—also were found in the broader literatures of social science and history. Colonial discourse theory suggested that European epistemology had 'invented' images of non-European cultures largely to suit its own disposition. In particular, several of the institutions which conventional sociological theory held virtually to define Asian and African societies now were exposed as colonial constructions. In India, 'caste' and 'Hinduism' and, in Africa, 'tribe' disintegrated at the touch of critique.[13] The Other worlds, on which imperial Europe had cast its intrusive gaze, appeared little more than the products of its own imagination.

Yet this imagination was clearly powerful and had projected itself into the consciousness of some of the colonized. A third area of enquiry—although one which Said himself did not pursue[14]—looked at the influence of colonial epistemology on the culture of the colonized, to the point where many of the latter accepted its representations, even of themselves, as true. Here emphasis was placed on the hegemonic implications of a variety of colonial projects, which drew colonial subjects under subtle forms of domination. One area of investigation was the 'civilizing mission': the dissemination of Christianity, European literature, and 'science'. A variety of studies showed how educational projects, even when taken over by colonial subjects themselves, trapped them in a web of beliefs and values which validated European superiority.[15] This was held to be especially true of projects involving the Enlightenment discourse of Freedom. Aspirations for freedom of belief and even political freedom, when translated through concepts of 'religion' and 'nation' derived from Europe, were seen to have led colonial subjects into imposing on themselves forms of division and domination which were continuous with the strategies of colonialism.[16]

As colonial discourse theory began to approach constructs of emancipation, so

[13] Ronald Inden, *Imagining India* (Oxford, 1990); Terence Ranger, 'The Invention of Tribalism in Zimbabwe', in Eric Hobsbawm and Terence Ranger, eds., *The Invention of Tradition* (Cambridge, 1983).

[14] This marks a key area of difference between the critique of Orientalism and that of colonialism and also between Said and, for example, 'Subaltern Studies'. Said has not broadened his focus beyond European culture to study experiences and strategies of resistance inside the colonies; and he has denounced as 'essentialist' those strategies, based upon the recovery of supposedly indigenous identities, favoured in 'Subaltern Studies'. See Edward W. Said, 'Orientalism Reconsidered', in Francis Barker and others, eds., *Europe and Its Others: Proceedings of the Essex Conference on the Sociology of Literature* (Colchester, 1985). None the less, Said has also continued to endorse 'Subaltern Studies' writings.

[15] For example, Gauri Viswanathan, *Masks of Conquest: Literary Study and British Rule in India* (New York, 1989); Jean and John L. Comaroff, *Of Revelation and Revolution: Christianity, Colonialism and Consciousness in South Africa* (Chicago, 1991).

[16] For examples, Gyanendra Pandey, *The Construction of Communalism in Colonial North India* (Delhi, 1990); Partha Chatterjee, *Nationalist Thought and the Colonial World: A Derivative Discourse?* (London, 1986).

it also opened up a fourth area of inquiry: if not on the basis of colonial discourses, then how else might subject-peoples represent themselves, 'resist' Europe, and seek their own emancipation? At this point, it collided with a variety of other historical projects, which dated back to the 1960s and also aimed at liberating the oppressed. The influence of New Left, civil rights, and feminist movements had exposed the élitism and selectivity of conventional forms of history received from the 1940s and 1950s. In response, radical attempts had begun to draw within the perspectives of 'scholarship' peoples whose pasts had been either ignored or misconstrued: who had been left at the mercy of 'the enormous condescension of posterity'.[17] In the name of 'history from below', the working-classes, women, 'blacks', and 'gays' pressed for recognition of their own places in history. In colonial studies, 'people without history' appeared on the agenda,[18] the peasant 'returned' to the historical stage[19] and, in the early writings of Ranajit Guha's celebrated 'Subaltern Studies' school, attempts were made to restore a broad swathe of generically 'subaltern' orders to scholarly consciousness.[20]

The influence of discourse theory began to raise new questions about how the history of the subaltern orders ought properly to be represented. The emancipation movements of the 1960s had been driven by a zeal to realize the Enlightenment's promises of Reason and Freedom: they had sought to give the excluded and demeaned a full part in a universal history of mankind. But the philosophical premises of discourse theory suggested that this was a chimerical goal, which actually masked objectives of tyranny. It was precisely through theories of the universal and the 'human' that the Enlightenment had imposed its own authoritarian truths.[21]

In response, and to effect greater 'resistance', discourse theory came to insist that subaltern orders must be given the freedom to represent themselves in and through their own separate histories. This inspired, among much else, new approaches to evidence. Ideally, subalterns should speak for themselves and 'privilege' should be accorded to any sources where they did so. However, such sources

[17] E. P. Thompson, *The Making of the English Working Class* (London, 1963), p. 13.

[18] Eric R. Wolf, *Europe and the People Without History* (Berkeley, 1982).

[19] Eric Stokes, 'The Return of the Peasant to South Asian History' in Eric Stokes, *The Peasant and the Raj: Studies in Agrarian Society and Peasant Rebellion in Colonial India* (Cambridge, 1978), pp. 265–90.

[20] Ranajit Guha, 'On Aspects of the Historiography of Colonial India', in Ranajit Guha, *Subaltern Studies I* (Delhi, 1982). The occasional series 'Subaltern Studies' originally started out from a 'history from below' perspective before being drawn towards colonial discourse critique and post-colonial theory. See 'AHR Forum on Subaltern Studies', *American Historical Review*, LXLIX (1994), pp. 1475–545.

[21] For a critique of the early volumes of *Subaltern Studies* from these angles, see Rosalind O'Hanlon, '"Recovering the Subject", Subaltern Studies and Histories of Resistance in Colonial South Asia', *Modern Asia Studies* (hereafter *MAS*), XXII, I (1988), pp. 189–224; Gayatri Chakravorty Spivak, 'Subaltern Studies—Deconstructing Historiography' in Spivak, *Other Worlds*.

were rare and most voices from the past were those of élites. Hence, new ways were proposed of reading élite documents 'against the grain' and to reveal the 'gaps' and 'silences' in their representations. Where even these techniques were unfruitful, empathies born of shared 'positions' of oppression and victimization between historian and historical subject were to be evoked and accorded privilege instead.[22]

In colonial historiography these approaches came to be applied, specifically to blocking out and countering the hegemonic presence of Europe. As—with all their differences—the writings of the members of the 'Subaltern Studies' group developed across the 1980s, for example, they pushed such applications towards increasingly radical conclusions. First, it was doubted whether the universal categories of Enlightenment emancipation—individualism and class—were appropriate to the context of non-European cultures, where such concepts were not 'local'.[23] Then it began to be asked whether colonial subalterns ought to be conceived as having 'histories' at all, or at least as the norms of scholarship decreed. The narrative structures through which history was told privileged hierarchies of significance and teleological forms of reasoning which, besides being inherently oppressive, were also considered distinctive to European thought.[24]

To resist such methods, alternatives were proposed which might 'reinscribe' the past in the light of a different epistemology. Particularly attractive appeared those devices of post-modernism which, for example, represented experience only in 'fragments'—without imposed form or order—or disintegrated the distinction between fact and myth or reconceptualized time to break linear connections between 'beginning' and 'end'. Subaltern history had not only to be written by and for subalterns themselves, but written in ways which would 'subvert' the logic of history itself.[25]

During the 1980s colonial discourse theory enjoyed a remarkable growth and generated a series of legacies, which are likely to be long-lasting. It helped to reveal how far erstwhile separate academic disciplines shared interests and held methodological assumptions in common; and it contributed to the rise of a new field of pedagogy in 'Cultural Studies'. It also disturbed the received meaning(s) of history to make the imperial past more central to understandings of Europe's own character

[22] Ranajit Guha, 'The Prose of Counter-Insurgency', *Subaltern Studies II*; Dipesh Chakrabarty, *Rethinking Working-Class History: Bengal, 1890–1940* (Princeton, 1989); Spivak, 'Can the Subaltern Speak?', *Wedge*, VII–VIII (1985).

[23] Esp. Chakrabarty, *Rethinking Working-Class History.*

[24] Chakrabarty, 'Postcoloniality and the Artifice of History'; Chatterjee, *Nationalist Thought.*

[25] Prakash, 'Writing Post-Orientalist Histories'; Chakrabarty, 'Postcoloniality and the Artifice of History', 'The Difference-Deferral of (a) Colonial Modernity', *History Workshop Journal*, XXXVI (1993), pp. 1–34; Partha Chatterjee, *The Nation and Its Fragments: Colonial and Postcolonial Histories* (Princeton, 1993).

and what it had bequeathed to the world. History, and above all the history of British imperialism, was forced to respond to a different intellectual agenda.

As history has responded to this agenda, however, so it has started to cast critical doubts on the provenance of colonial discourse critique itself. These doubts arise, first, from empirical observation: claims to reveal previously hidden passages in the historical record appear more than matched by tendencies to 'occlude' other, larger passages. A first set of objections concerns the supposition of consistency in European thought towards the colonial 'Other'. Much recent research has shown substantially greater 'difference' in European perception than colonial discourse theory would allow—including many views favourable to non-Europe and hostile to colonialism.[26]

In two particular respects, what such theory overlooks may challenge its grasp on the colonial past. On the one hand, it tends to obscure the contribution of the Romantic movement to European thought, making European culture, at least in the imperial age, virtually synonymous with the Enlightenment's drive for Universalism and Modernity.[27] But Europe launched its own 'Revolts against Reason', which defined the meanings of 'non-Europe' in different and often more sympathetic ways.[28] On the other hand, discourse theory also seems uncomfortable with the 'differences' refracted by time. The paradigmatic qualities imputed to the 'colonial' episteme are most characteristic of the late nineteenth century, when both Enlightenment and Romantic thinking converged on the centrality of race. But colonialism had a pre- and a post-history, and reading such qualities backwards and forwards across the entire colonial (and European) cultural experience leads to anachronism.[29]

A second set of objections focuses on the occlusion of 'difference' in the ways in which the 'localities' of the colonial world were constructed. In colonial discourse this world was by no means represented as all of one piece—the 'essences'

[26] MacKenzie, *Orientalism*; Kate Teltscher, *India Inscribed: European and British Writing on India, 1600–1800* (Oxford, 1995); Norbert Peabody, 'Tod's Rajast' han and the Boundaries of Imperial Rule in Nineteenth-Century India', *MAS*, XXX, 1 (1996), pp. 185–220; C. A. Bayly, *Empire and Information: Intelligence Gathering and Social Communication in India, 1780–1870* (Cambridge, 1996).

[27] This is much truer of critiques of colonial as opposed to Orientalist discourse. For example, Said and Inden recognize the significance of Romanticism although, perhaps because it also had an imperialist dimension, do not emphasize the extent of its 'revolt' against Enlightenment Reason. But most colonial discourse critics, especially in *Subaltern Studies*, associate European culture exclusively with Enlightenment Modernity. Compare Said, *Orientalism*; Inden, *Imagining India*; Chatterjee, *Nationalism*; Chakrabarty, *Rethinking Working-Class History.* Also see Thomas Blom Hansen, 'Inside the Romanticist Episteme' in Signe Arnfred, ed., *Issues of Methodology and Epistemology in Postcolonial Studies* (Roskilde, 1995).

[28] Javed Majeed, *Ungoverned Imaginings: James Mill's The History of British India and Orientalism* (Oxford, 1992).

[29] See the critique of Inden in Peabody, 'Tod's Rajast'han'.

imputed to its various parts were distinct and discrete. Colonial discourse theory insists that all such difference must be explained by reference to Europe alone: as Gyan Prakash has put it, 'Orientalism was a European enterprise from the beginning. The scholars were European, and audience was European; and the [Orientals] appeared as inert objects of knowledge.'[30] But local historians of the colonial world have rarely gained much insight on the basis of this assertion, and what they have found raises questions about how far colonial discourse is intelligible, exclusively, in European terms.

Recent research, for example, has indicated how colonial constructs frequently overlapped with concepts held previously and independently by some, at least, among the colonized—most notably, by those with whom the Europeans had closest contact and on whom they relied for information. The notion of an Indian society centred on 'caste' and 'Hinduism', for example, was informed by representations long embedded in the discourse of Brahmanic élites; that of an African society centred on 'tribe', one reflected in the rhetoric of lineage and household relations.[31] The colonial 'translation' of such concepts, no doubt, altered them significantly. However, it did not simply invent them: if they were products of 'imagination', it was of an imagination shared between colonizers and certain groups, at least, among the colonized.

Moreover, it is not only local relations of knowledge that reveal marks of mutuality but, and inseparably, local relations of power: as Sheldon Pollock has observed of India, 'the pre-existence of a shared ideological base among indigenous and colonial élites may have been one contributing factor to the effectiveness with which England consolidated and maintained its rule'.[32] Colonial rule was often thinly stretched and could scarcely have sustained itself without the 'collaboration' of local power structures, whose relations of conflict and domination became incorporated into its own constructs. Again, such incorporation certainly reconfigured such structures. But it hardly reconstituted them entirely anew, and it had constantly to take into account the imperatives generated by their specific local forms. The power relations of colonialism were inextricably bound up with the power relations *between* colonial subjects themselves.

These empirical points give rise to a broader range of questions which challenge colonial discourse theory's claims to escape either Europe or the Enlightenment, and point to some of its own conceptual confusions. In the first

[30] Prakash, 'Writing Post-Orientalist Histories', p. 384.

[31] Nicholas B. Dirks, 'Castes of Mind', *Representations*, XXXVII (1992), pp. 109–34 and 'Colonial Histories and Native Informants', in Carol A. Breckenridge and Peter van der Veer, eds., *Orientalism and the Postcolonial Predicament: Perspectives on South Asia* (Philadelphia, 1993); Peter van de Veer, 'The Foreign Hand', in ibid., pp. 23–44; Terence Ranger, 'The Invention of Tradition Revisited', in Preben Kaarsholm and Jan Hultin, eds., *Inventions and Boundaries: Historical and Anthropological Approaches to the Study of Ethnicity and Nationalism* (Roskilde, 1994).

[32] Sheldon Pollock, 'Deep Orientalism?', in Breckenridge and van der Veer, *Orientalism*, p. 101.

place, it is difficult to see how 'Europe' is to be rejected on the basis of ideas which are patently European themselves. Colonial discourse theory's occlusion of Romanticism is interesting not least because it draws so heavily on Romantic precepts itself.[33] The philosophical debts of Foucault to Nietzsche and of Derrida to Herder and Heidegger are clear and acknowledged. Rather than escaping Europe, colonial discourse theory merely cites one of its own philosophical traditions against another. In the field of colonial studies, however, the costs of this 'other' tradition may be very high.

As Ronald Inden has shown with regard to India, Romanticism played a role parallel to the Enlightenment in informing colonialist and 'Orientalist' constructions. It, too, represented an Indian culture centred on caste and Hinduism and merely inverted their evaluation, favouring Tradition over Modernity.[34] A disturbing feature of much colonial discourse theory as applied to India is its tendency to accept such Romantic representations as reflective of the truly 'local' or 'indigenous'—indeed, to accept them as the cultural bases on which resistance to 'Europe' may be erected.[35] But the quality of such 'resistance' can be suspected when it is recalled that Romanticism's representations were devised less to emancipate colonial subjects than to enjoin the preservation over them of ascriptive hierarchies and 'traditional' forms of authority.[36] As these hierarchies and forms were also those incorporated into colonialism to secure its own power positions, it has to be asked where, exactly, the Romantically inspired emancipation of contemporary *post*-colonial society is supposed to lead?[37] Problematically, it seems to be back towards constructs of (usually religious or ethnic) 'community' which were formed by, or in relation to, colonial Orientalism itself.

A second issue concerns the status of colonial discourse theory's pivotal concept of 'culture', especially as applied to Europe and 'the West'. Such applications crucially assume European culture to represent a closed epistemic field and to be 'incommensurable' with non-European cultures. However, it is never specified how 'a' culture might be defined or what closes it or how the boundaries between different cultures or epistemes are meant to be drawn. And it would be difficult to derive any such system of classification from the critical writings of Foucault, for whom, for example, the 'epistemic' represented an 'open field of relationships

33 Hansen, 'Inside the Romanticist Episteme'.

34 Inden, *Imagining*.

35 Hansen, 'Inside the Romanticist Episteme'.

36 Majeed, *Ungoverned Imaginings*.

37 Consider the 'Orientalist' representation of caste in Chakrabarty, *Rethinking Working-Class History*; of hierarchical Hinduism in R. Guha, 'Dominance Without Hegemony and its Historiography', in *Subaltern Studies VI*; and of Indian 'spirituality' in Chatterjee, *The Nation and Its Fragments*. See also Vinay Bahl, 'Class Consciousness and Primordial Values in the Shaping of the Indian Working Class', *South Asia Bulletin*, XIII, 1 and 2 (1993), pp. 152–72.

[which are] no doubt indefinitely specifiable';[38] or from Derrida, who rooted culture in language in ways which, for example, would make India and Europe—'Indo-Europe'—part of the same epistemic field.[39]

As a number of critics have seen, colonial discourse theory's usage of a very finite, certain, and objectified concept of culture is indicative of methods which far less 'disperse' Enlightenment meanings than appropriate and invert them. Kenan Malik has noted how the properties which such theory imputes to culture bear an uncomfortably close resemblance to those which many Europeans at the end of the nineteenth century imputed to 'race'.[40] Equally, the dependence of analysis on a concept which is itself never interrogated but whose 'truth' is held to be self-evident also bears a strong resemblance to the axiomatic or 'foundationalist' practices of Enlightenment epistemology which Derrida ridiculed. What we may actually be offered in colonial discourse theory is less the *dis*placement of Enlightenment science than the *re*placement of its preferred foundational categories of 'individual' and 'class' with those of 'culture' or 'race'; and an inverted evaluation of the latter in order to move 'European and white' from the top to the bottom of what is still assumed to be a hierarchy.[41]

Such propensities are clearly evident in Said's own treatment of Europe and the 'Occident'. The reverse side of his 'Orientalism' is an 'Occidentalism' whereby his analysis of 'the West' follows precisely the same Enlightenment malpractices which he criticizes in the latter's approaches to 'the East'. He represents European culture in ways which essentialize, objectify, demean, de-rationalize, and de-historicize it; and he re-evaluates it negatively in the light of its own standards of Reason and Freedom.[42]

Here the problem may be that, *in practice*, critics of colonialism are unwilling to pay the full price which comes with discourse theory's avowed epistemology of extreme cultural relativism: a price which ought to disenfranchise them entirely from the projects of 'truth' and 'freedom'. If, for example, as Said insists, 'any and all representations . . . are embedded first in the language and then in the culture,

[38] Michel Foucault, 'Politics and the Study of Discourse', *Ideology and Consciousness*, III (1978), p. 10.

[39] As in Jacques Derrida, 'White Mythology', in his *Margins of Philosophy* (Chicago, 1982).

[40] Kenan Malik, *The Meaning of Race: Race, History and Culture in Western Society* (Basingstoke, 1996).

[41] For a critique of 'foundationalism' in colonial discourse, see Prakash, 'Writing Post-Orientalist Histories'.

[42] James Clifford, 'On Orientalism', pp. 255–76, in his *The Predicament of Culture: Twentieth-Century Ethnography, Literature and Art* (Cambridge, Mass., 1988); MacKenzie, *Orientalism*; Young, *White Mythologies*, pp. 126–54; Rosalind O'Hanlon and David Washbrook, 'After Orientalism: Culture, Criticism and Politics in the Third World', *Comparative Studies in Society and History*, XXXIV, 1 (1992), pp. 141–67.

institutions and political ambiance of the representer . . . [and are] interwoven with a great many other things besides the "truth", which is itself a representation'[43]—then so must be *that* representation and *that* truth. Said traps himself inside a web of solipsism. Moreover, it is very hard to see how clues to their emancipation might be offered to 'subjects' who theoretically exist outside discourse only in infinite 'dispersal'.[44]

Yet such nihilism is clearly difficult to sustain and, having demolished the epistemological premises of Enlightenment thought, discourse theory then seems drawn to attaching to its own counter-propositions claims to the same status in 'truth' and 'freedom' as Enlightenment theory makes for its own forms of knowledge. Having used Foucault and Derrida to critique Enlightenment epistemology, for example, Said then proceeds to discard their 'politics' in order to return to the Enlightenment-inspired, Marxist-humanism of Antonio Gramsci and Raymond Williams in order to find bases for the expression of his own programmatics.[45] The result is self-contradictory: but a self-contradiction which is deeply revealing. In practice, discourse theory—like the Romanticism which gave rise to it—appears inextricably bound to the Enlightenment which it cannot entirely 'reject' without silencing itself.[46]

But if colonial discourse theory's praxis, then, is 'imbricated' in the Enlightenment project—merely privileging the foundationalist categories of race or culture over those of individual or class—what happens when its own critique of that project is applied back to itself? If Enlightenment knowledge-constructions are meant to be based on 'self-referentialism', what is the nature of the 'self' informing colonial discourse theory's own knowledge-constructions? Moreover, if such constructions reflect the pursuit of 'domination', what species of 'domination' does it pursue? Gyatri Chakravorty Spivak has defended discourse theory's reversion to its own 'essentialist' forms of representation and 'positivist' forms of knowledge, on the grounds that these strategically 'empower' the positions of those whom conventional Enlightenment discourse marginalizes and victimizes.[47] But whose positions, exactly, are represented in its counter-constructions and whom, exactly, does it empower? Such questions are currently the source of very bitter controversy.[48]

[43] Said, *Orientalism*, p. 272.

[44] See O'Hanlon and Washbrook, 'After Orientalism'.

[45] Said, *Orientalism*, pp. 22–28.

[46] See Jorge Larrain, *Ideology and Culture Identity: Modernity and the Third World Presence* (Cambridge, 1994).

[47] Gayatri Chakravorty Spivak, 'Criticism, Feminism and the Institution', *Thesis Eleven*, 10/11 (1984/1985).

[48] For indications of this bitterness, see the responses to Aijiz Ahmad in *Public Culture*, VI, 1 (1993) *passim.*

Reaction has been most sharp from those who would still seek to pursue the historical projects begun in the 1960s, especially from locations inside the ex-colonies themselves. From these locations, the shift to colonial discourse theory—by focusing inquiry, once again, on Europeans or, at best, on the limited stratum of colonial subjects who were most directly involved in relations of cultural domination and resistance with them—occludes the majorities inside colonized societies and represents a reversion back to an élitist historiography.[49] As *Subaltern Studies* has elaborated itself over successive volumes, for example, the oppressions of the peasantry have largely disappeared from its pages—to be replaced by the *angst* of the Calcutta intelligentsia.[50]

In the course of the shift from 'social' to 'cultural' history, too, concepts of class and capital have gone missing and, with them, serious attempts to address issues of material deprivation and poverty.[51] Instead, such concepts have been replaced by those of 'community' and 'hierarchy', which obscure relations of exploitation internal to the colonized and even legitimize certain forms of domination as functions of 'traditional' and 'local' authority.[52] Reaction here has drawn attention, particularly, to the extent to which most colonial discourse theorists themselves come from upper-status or middle-class groups among the once-colonized, who were privileged by colonialism both in its Romantic representations and its co-opted structures of power. Ironically, as Aijaz Ahmad has most forcefully put it, colonialism's most trenchant critics are its chief beneficiaries[53]—and their Revolt against Reason has the effect of seeking to restore forms of authority which, historically, were secured only under colonialism, against the threats posed to them since by the 'progress' of post-colonial Modernity.

Aijaz Ahmad has gone on to point out, also, how far the majority of such theorists are 'located' now, not in the ex-colonies themselves but in the West, especially in the United States, where discourse theory has become pervasive in academic culture. Here, two points are difficult to dismiss. However little the ontological categories of such theory may make sense of the colonial past, they fit perfectly with the political categories of 'multiculturalism' inside present-day Western societies themselves. The rhetoric of racial and ethnic 'victimization' speaks to a

[49] Sumit Sarkar, 'A Marxian Social History Beyond the Foucaultian Turn', *Economic and Political Weekly*, XXX, 30 (1995), pp. 1916–20.

[50] Compare the contents of *Subaltern Studies I* with that of *Subaltern Studies VII*; also see Ramachandra Guha, 'Subaltern and Bhadralok Studies', *Economic and Political Weekly*, XXX, 33 (1995), pp. 2056–59; Bahl, 'Class Consciousness'.

[51] Note Gyan Prakash's argument that even to address the history of capitalism is to become complicit with capitalism itself: Prakash, 'Writing Post-Orientalist Histories'.

[52] See the critique of Chakrabarty in S. Basu, 'Workers' Politics in Bengal, 1890–1929', unpublished Ph.D. thesis, Cambridge, 1994; Sarkar, 'A Marxian'; Bahl, 'Class Consciousness'.

[53] Ahmad, *In Theory, Classes, Nations, Literature*, pp. 159–220.

political agenda most relevant to the contemporary West.[54] And secondly, by occluding 'differences' of class to privilege 'similarities' of ethnicity, such theory also provides means by which members of now multicultural bourgeoisies located in the West can reassert affinities with and claims to authority over the societies which they left behind. In a final irony, colonial discourse theory becomes a new mechanism of imperialism in an age of multicultural, globalized capitalism.[55]

Most recently, concern over the problems thrown up by the critique of colonial discourse has led historical enquiry in a different direction. Here, the principal focus of interest has become, less the simple imposition of European culture on to non-Europeans, than the contributions made by the latter to the melanges of 'hybridity' and 'Creolity' exhibited in and by colonial cultures; and their contributions, no less, to much of the culture which Europeans, especially in the imperial age, claimed to be uniquely their own. In this focus, emphasis has shifted away from the epistemic closures of 'discourse' to the more open-ended interplay of meanings implied by the concept of 'dialogue'.

The application of 'dialogics' is in its early stages, and some tension exists between two different understandings of the concept. On the one hand, some scholars evoke it in a post-modernist, Bakhtinian sense to suggest dissonance in the way that the many 'pieces' of which colonial cultures were comprised fitted together.[56] But on the other hand, other scholars use the term in a more Enlightenment sense to suggest effective syncretisms and cross-cultural rationalizations.[57] The tension between the two usages is, itself, insightful and may reflect the difficulty of handling complex colonial situations in which not just two but many voices, coming from 'positions' marked by finely graded differentials of power, were speaking.[58]

Where the broad concept of 'dialogue' seems at its most incisive, however, is in questioning one representation which was crucial to imperialism's self-imagery but which, curiously, colonial discourse theory merely accepted and reaffirmed:

54 Ahmad, ibid., pp. 159–220; also Arif Dirlik, 'The Postcolonial Aura: Third World Criticism in the Age of Global Capitalism', *Critical Inquiry*, XX, 2 (1994), pp. 328–56.

55 See K. N. Panikkar, 'In Defence of "Old" History', *International Congress on Kerala Studies. Abstracts*, I (Thiruvananthapuram, 1994), pp. 16–21; also Dirkin, 'Postcolonial Aura'.

56 See N. M. Bakhtin, *The Dialogic Imagination* (Austin, Tex., 1981). Homi Babhar applies it in this sense, see his 'Signs Taken for Wonders', in Barker, *Europe*.

57 This seems the sense used in Eugene F. Irschick, *Dialogue and History: Constructing South India, 1795–1895* (Berkeley, 1994).

58 For treatments engaging these complexities, see Megan Vaughan, *The Story of an African Famine: Gender and Famine in Twentieth-Century Malawi* (Cambridge, 1987); John Lonsdale, 'Moral Ethnicity and Tribalism', in Kaarsholm, *Inventions*; Martha Kaplan and John D. Kelly, 'Rethinking Resistance: Dialogics of "Disaffection" in Colonial Fiji', *American Ethnologist*, XXI, 1 (1994), pp. 123–51.

this is the 'image' that the epistemics of science, universalism, liberty, modernity, and progress were self-generated by, and utterly unique to, Europe and the Enlightenment. Here much research (and some of it not very new)[59] has indicated epistemics which were similarly structured—if differently valenced—in a variety of Other cultures and which, historically, can be shown to have informed Europe's own, usually belated, imitations.

Many of the concepts basic to science and capitalism in Europe came, paradoxically, from 'the Orient' in the first place—their genealogies still traceable in language.[60] In religion, philosophy, and even history too, much which 'Europeans' (and the critical theorists of their discourse) have held to reflect a distinctive racial or cultural 'genius' no longer appears so singular: Other cultures had concepts (fore-) shadowing the 'individual', 'nation', 'religion' as well.[61] In shattering Europe's monolithic conceits, dialogics may come to offer a more far-reaching critique of European world-centrality and dominance than discourse theory ever managed. This critique may also, perhaps, more clearly re-authorize the universalist principles of Reason and Freedom, though not necessarily in their specific European forms.

[59] Classically, Joseph Needham, *Science and Civilization in China*, 6 vols. (Cambridge, 1959–84); also Frits Staal, *Universals: Studies in Indian Logic and Linguistics* (Chicago, 1988); Martin Bernal, *Black Athena: The Afroasiatic Roots of Classical Civilization*, 2 vols. (New Brunswick, 1987).

[60] Jack Goody, *The East in the West* (Cambridge, 1996); also Frank Perlin, *The Invisible City: Monetary, Administrative, and Popular Infrastructures in Asia and Europe, 1500–1900* (Aldershot, 1993) and *Unbroken Landscape* (Aldershot, 1994). Both Goody and Perlin, it should be said, are primarily interested in the common properties of a broad 'Eurasian' civilization, not in reversing the focus of a Eurocentric historiography to replace it with an Asiocentric one.

[61] On analogies to and 'pre-histories' of these concepts in the context of South Asian cultures, see C. A. Bayly, *Origins of Nationality of South Asia: Patriotism and Ethical Government in the Making of Modern India* (New Delhi, forthcoming).

Select Bibliography

AIJAZ AHMAD, *In Theory: Classes, Nations and Literatures* (London, 1992).

FRANCIS BARKER, PETER HULME, and MARGARET IRESEN, eds., *Colonial Discourse, Postcolonial Theory* (Manchester, 1994).

C. A. BAYLY, *Origins of Nationality in South Asia: Patriotism and Ethical Government in the Making of Modern India* (Delhi, forthcoming).

CAROL A. BRECKENRIDGE and PETER VAN DER VEER, eds., *Orientalism and the Postcolonial Predicament: Perspectives on South Asia* (Philadelphia, 1993).

DIPESH CHAKRABARTY, *Rethinking Working-Class History: Bengal, 1890–1940* (Princeton, 1989).

PARTHA CHATTERJEE, *The Nation and Its Fragments: Colonial and Postcolonial Histories* (Princeton, 1993).

BERNARD S. COHN, *An Anthropologist Among the Historians and Other Essays* (Delhi, 1987).

JEAN COMAROFF and JOHN L. COMAROFF, *Of Revelation and Revolution: Christianity, Colonialism and Consciousness in South Africa* (Chicago, 1991).

RANAJIT GUHA and GAYATRI CHAKRAVORTY SPIVAK, eds., *Selected Subaltern Studies* (New York, 1988).

RONALD INDEN, *Imagining India* (Oxford, 1990).

PREBEN KAARSHOLM and JAN HULTIN, eds., *Inventions and Boundaries: Historical and Anthropological Approaches to the Study of Ethnicity and Nationalism* (Roskilde, 1994).

JOHN M. MACKENZIE, *Orientalism: History, Theory, and the Arts* (Manchester, 1995).

EDWARD W. SAID, *Orientalism* (London, 1978).

—— *Culture and Imperialism* (London, 1993).

MRINALINI SINHA, *Colonial Masculinity: The 'Manly' Englishman and the 'Effeminate' Bengali in the Late Nineteenth Century* (Manchester, 1995).

GAYATRI CHAKRAVORTY SPIVAK, *In Other Worlds: Essays in Cultural Politics* (New York, 1987).

MICHAEL SPRINKER, ed., *Edward Said: A Critical Reader* (Oxford, 1992).

GAURI VISWANATHAN, *Masks of Conquest: Literary Study and British Rule in India* (New York, 1989).

ROBERT YOUNG, *White Mythologies: Writing Histories and the West* (London, 1990).

39

The Shaping of Imperial History

A. P. THORNTON

Free intercourse is impossible when men cannot dine together.
(Sir Richard Temple (Indian Civil Service), cited in A. J. Herbertson and O. J. R. Howarth, eds., *Oxford Survey of the British Empire*, II Oxford, 1914).

Are we going to make a supreme additional effort to remain a Great Power, or are we going to slide away into what seem to be easier, softer, less strenuous, less harassing courses, with all the tremendous renunciations which that decision implies?
(Winston S. Churchill, House of Commons, 17 November 1938).

The use of the English language meant the propagation of certain principles that are implicit in its vocabulary.
(C. E. Carrington, *An Exposition of Empire*, Cambridge, 1947).

'Sometimes', Herbert Butterfield confided half a century ago on page 1 of his *The Englishman and His History* (Cambridge, 1944) 'we teach and write the kind of history which is appropriate to our organization, congenial to the intellectual climate of our part of the world.' Sometimes, however, sometimes becomes all the time. Simone de Beauvoir's *Memoirs of a Dutiful Daughter* (London, 1959) tells how she learned history 'as unquestionably as I did geography, without ever dreaming there could be more than one view of past events'.[1] And if we accept G. M. Young's gentle reminder that 99/100ths of the things which happen never get into the books at all, a volume on historiography, listing appropriate and congenial books, may not greatly simplify the problem this fact of life presents.[2] We

Thanks to Peter Austin and Alaine Low and Dan McWiggins for checking the references.

[1] (Penguin edn., London, 1963), p. 127; and cf. Len Deighton's novel *Hope* (London, 1996), pp. 17–18: 'Fiona had a devout faith in England, a legacy of her middle-class upbringing. Its rulers and administrators, its history and even its cooking was accepted without question.'

[2] G. M. Young, in R. C. K. Ensor, G. M. Young, and others, *Why We Study History* (Historical Association Publications, No. 131, London, 1944).

fasten when young on whatever images explain the present and promise a comprehensible future. When that arrives and sufficiently astonishes us we face the reverse problem, how to shape a comprehensible past. Where, for example, is that once-upon-a-time, gone-with-the-wind context, the British Empire?

The aura of ceremony still attending archive and atlas affirms the high assurance of British Imperial history in all its authorized versions—even when, ever reclusive, they reserve errors of omission and commission 'for your eyes only'—*you* being someone with access to the powerhouse, someone in the know.

The British people, not granted access, were not in the know. Britannia in pageants and on pennies, the Union Jack on matchboxes and biscuit tins, came as close to folklore as Empire ever reached. In 1921 one veteran, sifting his experience in the First World War's trenches (hell) and in an 'other-ranks' hospital (the workhouse), decided that Englishmen were habituated to the climate of a colonial situation. (As were Scots, Irish, and Welsh: but they at least knew it.) Ex-Sergeant R. H. Tawney saw England's governance as based on inequality, encased in an apparatus of class institutions. This was evident not in income only, but in housing, education, health, manners, 'and indeed the very physical appearance of different classes of Englishmen almost as different from each other as though the minority were alien settlers established amid the rude civilization of a race of impoverished aborigines'.[3] This echoes the Victorian era's best joke: John Bright's definition of Empire as a gigantic scheme of outdoor relief for the upper classes.

The impoverished Aborigines who did the shirtsleeves work at the far end of the emigrant stream had no such choice. Australian and Canadian historians do not often exchange files on sheep and railroads; and the links between points on the colonial circumference were either non-existent or could sag lower than those between Whitehall and Clydebank. Distance lends ignorance, not enchantment. General Sir William Butler, lamenting a lost friend in a worst-case scenario, was certain that if General Gordon had been sent to Ireland instead of to Khartoum he would have known whether it was Irish men, women, and children he had to consider, or an abstract and imaginary Ireland.[4]

Imagery is neither indexed nor filed. Posted 'out there' during the Second World War to devise a prospectus for *Welfare and Planning in the West Indies* (published Oxford, 1946), sociologist T. S. Simey found colonial life 'a backwater from the mainstream of human affairs', a context wherein 'several centuries of social philosophies and moral values mingled together in the wildest confusion'—one compounded by the Colonial Office's 'continually tinkering with political constitutions, regardless of the social realities which condition their

[3] R. H. Tawney, *The Acquisitive Society* (New York, 1920), pp. 71–72.

[4] Sir W. F. Butler, *Charles George Gordon* (1889; London, 1891), p. 84.

operation'.[5] Yet Simey was doing what he was doing only because the realities had indeed been so regarded. *The Royal Commission* [Moyne] *Report on the West Indies*, ready for publication in 1939, was shelved until 1945—to prevent Nazi Germany from making propaganda about the disgraceful conditions that obtained in a property for three centuries in British hands.

Domestic historians can also sense culture-shock. Certainly they avoid one analysis that has no social dimension, suggesting that English history is not about liberty but about power: Sir John Seeley's long-lived *The Expansion of England* (London, 1883), of which Herbert Butterfield observed that the Whiggism in all Englishmen declined to take the imperialistic version to its heart. Still, historians who have a thesis in their training know history is about *something*. G. M. Young, who had not, found in Edward Gibbon (*History of the Decline and Fall of the Roman Empire*, 6 vols. London, 1776–88) what he, Young, found in himself—'an unceasing compulsion to put the historical particulars into a causal pattern, and then lodge the pattern, once achieved, into a context of related patterns'.[6] Gibbon may so have arranged his *Roman Empire*; but British Imperial historians stay uncompelled towards patterns. (Dominance is ageless: it happens.) Narrative lines may reach conclusions easier to state than explain; one Imperial model is Frederick Lugard's two-volume autobiography, flimsily disguised as *The Rise of Our East African Empire* (Edinburgh, 1893). Some narrators identify the American Revolution as a terminus for the 'First British Empire', conveniently housing a departure-platform for a Second, much larger, more diverse, and very different, Empire in the East.[7]

Yet Imperial historians make no claim to 'a sense of the whole society'. Too many of their protagonists were notoriously antisocial egocentrics, and too many goings-on at ground-level of colonial life were better kept dark, as unfit for histories designed to instruct and uplift. Travellers' tales, designed to inform and entertain, provide franker clues to expatriate attitudes towards the faceless, and the nameless, and the astonishing. Wayfarers uncommitted to staying on side do not mind letting it down. In 1880 Isabella Bird remarked on Europeans striking coolies with their canes or umbrellas in a Hong Kong street.[8]

Half the data is what was ordered done. The other half, to this day, is anyone's

[5] (Oxford, 1946), pp. vi–vii.

[6] Sir Herbert Butterfield, *The Englishman and his History* (Cambridge, 1944), chap. 5; G. M. Young, *Gibbon* (Edinburgh, 1932), p. 7.

[7] 'But the Second British Empire began before the First was lost': Frederick Madden with David Fieldhouse, eds., *Select Documents on the Constitutional History of the British Empire and Commonwealth*, Vol. II, *The Classical Period of the First British Empire, 1689 to 1783: The Foundations of a Colonial System of Government* (Westport, Conn., 1985), p. xxxi.

[8] Isabella L. Bird, *Unbeaten Tracks in Japan: An Account of Travels in the Interior Including a Visitor to the Aborigines of Yeto and the Shrines of Nikkô and Isé*, 2 vols. (London, 1880).

guess. The official doings were witnessed, but not recorded, by people who, like those in Tawney's England, shared space but not context. The single purpose in common was self-preservation. So although no society was formed, civil arrangements and communal guidelines were made. Since a soldier could not be posted at every elbow, impact and implosion were muffled by 'collaboration'.

This term is now as loaded as 'imperialism' itself. But where imperialism is routinely stripped, and operated on under halogen lamps, the history of collaboration is still in shadow. How was life lived in Vichy France? Who did *not* join the European Resistance movement, and who behaved less than fearlessly when in it? There are glimmers. In Batavia in the morning Sukarno clerks for the Dutch; goes for lunch; returns to find the Japanese running the office, Djakarta, the future, and himself. So he protects his rice-bowl. He bends with the wind. Imperial historians, cheerfully ignorant of such savage pressures, resort to such self-congratulatory concepts as 'the plural society'—as much a controller's prop as the local police-force. As the zoologists say, it's hard to describe the behaviour of something if you don't know what it is.

From wherever viewed, Imperial images present a surface as flat, false, and useful as Mercator's projection. When in 1898 the radical Wilfrid Blunt told his Tory friend George Wyndham, Under-Secretary of State for War, that the Anglo-French stand-off at Fashoda reminded him of two highwaymen squabbling over a captured purse, Wyndham replied that it was no use drawing distinctions of right and wrong, 'it was a matter entirely of interest'.[9] The interest of the swift was to win the trophy. (Having, of course, entered the race. That same year, explaining the United States's war with Spain, in the Philippines in particular, one fictitious Irish-American said to another that 'twuz not more thin two months since we larned whither they wuz islands or canned goods').[10] For the victors the spoils! the prestige! and the after-dinner speakers!—for who else knew what progress was and how to extol it? And theirs too, the victors were determined, would be the historians: Whigs conscripted to the duty of instructing the future to honour those who had shaped the past.

Yet Imperial historians have a particular problem: whether to camp in comfort inside officialdom's lighted circle or go out into the areas of darkness—bush, outback, jungle, suburb—there to mix with the locals and rummage among what C. A. Bayly calls the records of Dustypore, if the termites haven't got to them first. The decisions reached shape the history we have. So—who has its measure? And where do we stand, to measure them?

[9] Wilfrid Scawen Blunt, *My Diaries: Being a Personal Narrative of Events, 1888–1914*, 2 vols. (London, 1919–20), I, p. 299.

[10] Finlay Peter Dunne, *Mr Dooley in Peace and in War* (Boston, 1898).

There are guides. John Locke confides he reached his conclusions 'by steadily intending his mind in a given direction'. Don't we all? Charles Darwin recalls how fellow-students of geology, instructed *not* to theorize, went earnestly into gravel-pits to count the pebbles and describe the colours. Darwin remarked how odd it was the anyone should not see that all observation must be for or against some view, if it was to be of any service![11] In history's gravel-pit, what colour of pebbles do we prefer? And philosopher John Macmurray begins his book *Reason and Emotion* (London, 1935) with this: Any enquiry must have a motive or it could not be carried on to all, and all motives belong to our emotional life.[12]

I have often fumbled these wisdoms; but they have saved me from making models, and from trafficking in forces, factors, and trends.

Historiography, advises the historian Henri Brunschwig, 'is not the fact of writing history, but the mode of writing it'.[13] The definition has dimensions absent from *The Oxford English Dictionary*'s: 'the writing of history: written history'. The historiographer, it adds, 'is a chronicler, or historian'. A. J. P. Taylor allowed this wraith more substance, though not much: 'the true historian is not a chronicler. He "makes" history. He creates a version that satisfies contemporaries until a better one comes along.'[14]

Modes are ways of proceeding, but what is *à la mode* goes nowhere. When Alasdair MacIntyre reproves philosophers for pronouncing on concepts without reference to the context they came from, he rings the historian's bell.[15] As time-bound to our culture as our protagonists were to theirs, we yet hope the history we make will 'make history', satisfying not contemporaries only but proving as durable as, say, Gray's *Anatomy.* This *Oxford History* views the British Empire from beyond as well as from above and below. But no stance guarantees accuracy. In the last analysis, nobody is out there making a last analysis. Over sixty years ago R. G. Collingwood instructed that in history, as in all serious matters, no achievement is final, since 'history' is contemporary thinking about the past.[16]

The problem here is context, and getting it right. If we do not think to ask, 'Why did they think that?', we know less about the past than we think. A sense of wonder is an asset to the historian. A state of bewilderment is not. Yet Robert

[11] John Higham, *History: Professional Scholarship in America* (Baltimore, 1983).

[12] John Macmurray, *Reason and Emotion* (London, 1935), p. 13.

[13] P. C. Emmer and H. L. Wesseling, eds., *Reappraisals in Overseas History: Essays on Post-War Historiography About European Expansion* (Leiden, 1979), p. 84.

[14] Chris Wrigley, ed., *A. J. P. Taylor: A Complete Annotated Bibliography and Guide to his Historical and Other Writings* (London, 1980), p. 127.

[15] Alasdair MacIntyre, *After Virtue: A Study in Moral Theory*, 2nd edn. (Notre Dame, Ind., 1984), postscript pp. 264 ff.

[16] R. G. Collingwood, *The Idea of History* (Oxford, 1946), p. 248.

Southey's puzzled *Little Peterkin* (London, 1798), asking a clueless grandfather what the Battle of Blenheim (1705) was all about, is our common ancestor. As a member of 'a generation taught to have no heroes', W. J. Reader wonders, in his *'At Duty's Call'*, why, for the 2½ million men who voluntarily 'joined up' between August 1914 and December 1915 (that is, before conscription), 'the Empire, to a degree incomprehensible in the 1980s, was an indispensable element in their confidence in their nation and themselves'. He is right to conclude 'no definitive answer is possible'.[17] Emotions, though never obsolete, evaporate. Files cannot record where fancy's bred, or where love has gone.

Craft, however, can reconstitute how things looked. The way they were, takes art. And possibly gender. Virago's reissue of Gertrude L. Bell's *The Desert and the Sown* (1907; London, 1985) deflates that hot-air balloon-barrage which sheltered the bonded males in their Middle East club: the 'portentous monumentalisms' of Charles Doughty, the 'self-conscious introspections' of T. E. Lawrence. Rebecca West decided that men saw public affairs 'as by moonlight'—the wood, never the trees. But when Bernard Wasserstein asks why British officials so mishandled 'the Jewish problem' throughout the Second World War, his answer *is* definitive. It throws a light more probing than any moon's on every colonial situation in the book. 'The Pall Mall club and the Palestine internment camp were not merely different places; they were different psychological universes, conditioning attitudes and reflexes which rarely found points of contact.'[18] So—alienation comes with the territory. What was 'Viet Nam' but cultural imperialism stamping an American mould?

Three generations are alive at any one time. They share space but not context. Points of contact between psychological universes do not transpose into close encounters. This is a central theme in the novels of Sir Walter Scott: *Waverley*'s subtitle (London, 1815) is *'Tis Sixty Years Since*. But being born earlier, later, or indeed at all does not automatically confer enlightenment on anyone; and Sir Walter, a master both of art and craft, never argued that it did, had, or could.

The global omnipresence of imperialism naturally promoted it to top-billing on banners of protest. 'Self-determination' was sidetracked after the First World War. (Did a colony have a self to determine?) When on 29 May 1919 the German delegation at Versailles complained that in seizing Germany's colonies the victors were also destroying its rightful role in a vital European mission—'for the essence of activity in colonial work does not consist in capitalistic exploitation . . . but in raising backward peoples to a higher civilisation'—the victors rasped back that 'Germany's dereliction in the sphere of colonial civilization has been revealed too

[17] W. J. Reader, *At Duty's Call: A Study in Obsolete Patriotism* (Manchester, 1988), pp, 2, 38.

[18] Bernard Wasserstein, *Britain and the Jews of Europe, 1939–1945* (Oxford, 1979), p. 356.

completely to admit of a second experiment'. But nobody challenged the principle, thought of leaving these territories masterless, of handing them back to their inhabitants. The Germans, in wanting 'to own overseas possessions commensurate with our position', spoke for imperialists everywhere.[19]

Between the world wars renewed 'activity in colonial work' produced positions of weight and assurance. When in the late 1940s I resumed as a student at Glasgow University, books on Empire were the work of men whose links with public life could be guessed at before a glance at *Who's Who* confirmed them; of men who went there and back again by candlelight, like John Buchan's *Greenmantle* (London, 1916)—'the pass on your right as you go over into Ladakh'; of men with plans—Alfred Milner for Egypt and South Africa; George Curzon on his *howdah*, ever aloft from the *Indian Unrest* recorded by Valentine Chirol (London, 1910); Arnold Wilson, Percy Cox, and the RAF, entrenching ground and aerial fiefdoms in Mesopotamia (Iraq); Ronald Storrs, whose elegant *Orientations* (London, 1937)—'in a sense I cannot explain there is no promotion after Jerusalem'—confirm bearings already registered by march-lords in the desert and lodgers in the sown; and the work of men not always clear what their compatriots were doing there, or whom they 'had a word with' before doing it (but most likely Ralph Furse, from 1911 to 1948 the Colonial Service's recruiting officer, seeing himself as *Aucuparius: Recollections of a Recruiting Officer* (London, 1962), a spreader of nets for birds).

The Imperial ethos tolls imperious bells. In *Making Imperial Mentalities* (Manchester, 1990), Janice N. Brownfoot defines the colonial experience in Malaya as masculine: 'ambivalent, contradictory, and dualistic.'[20] This would have surprised Gertrude Bell in February 1919, when taking bearings in Baghdad during that eleventh hour when the Middle East's destiny was becoming manifest as England's sole trophy of victory. No ambivalence or contradiction stopped her from spelling out reality:

> We have been having a rather difficult time here. The East is inclined to lose its head over the promise of settling for itself what is to become of it. It can't settle for itself really—we out here know that very well, because it might hit on something that wouldn't simplify State government—and that we can't allow in the interests of universal peace. But it's not going to be an easy job to hold the balance straight.[21]

How difficult, had already been gauged by Lord Cromer, the Empire's senior Proconsul, retired from twenty-five years in Egypt to revive his long-lost liberalism.

[19] H. W. V. Temperley, ed., *History of the Peace Conference of Paris*, 6 vols. (London, 1920–24), II, p. 257.

[20] Janice N. Brownfoot, 'Sisters Under the Skin: Imperialism and the Emancipation of Women in Malaya, c.1891–1941', in J. A. Mangan, ed., *Making Imperial Mentalities: Socialization and British Imperialism* (Manchester, 1990), p. 46.

[21] Lady F. Bell, ed., *The Letters of Gertrude Bell*, 2 vols. (London, 1927), II, p. 465.

Europe's imperialists believed themselves a permanent fixture, but 'the Englishman, in his dim, slipshod, but characteristically Anglo-Saxon fashion' was chasing two hares at once: good government, meaning he must stay to manage it; and self-government, meaning he must quit. And since it was an Anglo-Saxon characteristic to think all options stayed open, it was the principle of self-government, then, 'which must manifestly constitute the cornerstone of the new edifice'.[22]

Other Imperial barons, planning grander extensions and stronger fortifications for the old edifice, did not think this manifest. Secluded in its anterooms, confidently awaiting a call, were non-Egyptian Egyptian-bondholders, non-African South African millionaires, and non-Persian Persian-oil concessionaires—a fraternity often embarrassingly frank, as in J. C. McCoan's *Egypt As It Is* (London, 1877), Sir Peter Fitzpatrick's *The Transvaal from Within: A Private Record of Public Affairs* (London, 1898), and W. Morgan Shuster's *The Strangling of Persia: A Record of Oriental Diplomacy and Oriental Intrigue* (London, 1912). Diamonds-magnate Alfred Beit, when wined and dined and possibly bemused by imperialist Leo Amery, endowed Oxford's colonial Chair. Freelance crusaders for the Imperial ethos were publicly welcomed 'out there'. A. E. W. Mason's *The Four Feathers* (London, 1902, and still in print), a tale of redemption in the Sudan, attained passport-status. Some Imperial manuals were best-sellers: C. E. Callwell's on *Small Wars* (London, 1906), Victor Murray's on *The School in the Bush* (London, 1929). Reginald Campbell walked and worked the Burma forests as a *Teak Wallah* (London, 1935), with *Poo Lorn of the Elephants* (London, 1929) for company, under a boss whose name really *was* Orwell.

Reports from another psychological universe were filed but not forgotten, including E. M. Forster's *A Passage to India* (London, 1924), Edward Thompson's *The Other Side of the Medal* (London, 1925), and H. J. Simson's Palestine police-sheet, *British Rule, and Rebellion* (London, 1937); plus the annual package of *exposés* by Somerset Maugham of suburban souls and values going to pieces under the casuarina trees. 'Conduct unbecoming' reached astronomical proportions in John Galsworthy's *The Flowering Wilderness* (London, 1932), whose hero, ambushed in the desert, converts to Islam.

Commitment attends success. Empire was a going concern, an achievement minority-operated, majority-approved, a context of reassurance vivid on the map. On any morning in any year from the 1920s through the 1950s you might hear matrons on Princes Street, Edinburgh, or Buchanan Street, Glasgow, exchanging cheerful bulletins: 'Jack's back from Iraq', 'Alison's marrying that nice doctor in Bechuanaland'. They waved no flag, never had one in the house, but no one knew better than they that England's Empire was Scotland's world stage.

[22] Earl of Cromer, *Ancient and Modern Imperialism* (New York, 1910), p. 121.

Meanwhile in the universities, ex-colonels become advisers of studies directed students with the right stuff into the Indian Civil and Colonial Services (no written examination for the latter); students who were G. A. Henty's likely lads one more time, or (just possibly) the descendants of Sir Richard Burton's tent-and-saddle men.

Can a posterity unaware of heroes, schooled in colonial history's 'unpleasant connotations',[23] empathize with Jack, Alison, their companions, and their mothers? Do ancestral voices encourage, or have the effect of Marley's Ghost? The most persuasive exhortations come from historians who, having surveyed the Imperial terrain, made it their spiritual home. Their commitment pervades—indeed it produced—*The Cambridge History of the British Empire.* Volume I, published in 1929, displays a roster of distinguished scholars—among them James A. Williamson, A. P. Newton, Holland Rose, Charles McLean Andrews, and Harold Temperley. For them, things always good were getting better. 'The story of colonization and imperial policy', the preface states, 'is still in the long process of its growth. These volumes, therefore, provide the foundation on which future generations of students may build.'

But Imperial studies now rest upon personal engagement, not public commitment. If those students materialize, on what foundations can they build? Kenneth R. Andrews emphasizes, in his *Trade, Plunder, and Settlement: Maritime Enterprise and the Genesis of the British Empire, 1480–1630* (Cambridge, 1984), that the Empire's disintegration 'has been accompanied by a disintegration of its history'.[24] (Was Seeley right in thinking historians deal only in power? Does the profession ever ask what the Danes, say, were doing in the 1880s?)

In the Introduction to *Cambridge*'s Volume I, C. P. Lucas confirms Edmund Burke's diagnosis: 'England's colonies were formed, grew, and flourished as accidents, the nature of the climate, or the dispositions of men happened to operate.'[25] Lucas's prose can reach O-King-live-forever! heights: he casts Lord Durham in the Canadas as an imperialist in the best sense—unafraid of force, making concessions not because a majority wanted them, 'but only if they were likely to conduce to future greatness . . . to leave behind a legacy of what is permanently sound'.[26] Yet Lucas's comment that the Empire had reacted on Britain 'more by increasing its size than by changing its character' anticipates much modern historico-sociology; and his dismissal of the trader as 'at best a calculating patriot' mines the progressive path

[23] Emmer and Wesseling, *Reappraisals*, p. 4.

[24] p. vii.

[25] pp. 13, 20.

[26] C. P. Lucas, ed., *Lord Durham's Report on the Affairs of British North America*, 3 vols. (Oxford, 1912), I, pp. 119, 317.

of that New Model Army of 'Gentlemanly Capitalists' which Professors Cain and Hopkins have recently deployed over the entire terrain of *British Imperialism*'s two volumes (London, 1993).

Although agreeing with R. H. Tawney that acquisitiveness is a constant, these scholars allocate no central place to Empire in the evolution of British history. Disinclination is non-researchable; but ambitious politicians, as Nicholas Mansergh remarks, knew that Colonial Office business was of first importance neither to the electorate nor in itself;[27] and most historians concur. John M. MacKenzie's *Propaganda and Empire: The Manipulation of British Public Opinion, 1880–1960* (Manchester, 1984) notes how 'a new scholarly generation' (his own) has emerged 'largely uncontaminated by the intellectual influences of the 1920s and 1930s which so often misled their predecessors'.[28] Ah, but not all of them, at least not all the time: and how many durable influences are intellectual?

Even if one is not inhumanely trapped in what Antony Low calls a historiographical time-warp, contamination or a less virulent form of contact is also always with us, seen from whatever angle, acute or obtuse. T. O. Lloyd's *The British Empire, 1588–1983* (Oxford, 1984) suggests that 'moral revulsion is not the best way to understand the path of Empire'; and, possibly bearing in mind Sir Keith Hancock's celebrated but irritating comment in his Marshall Lectures that imperialism is no word for scholars, shuns that word throughout.[29]

English historians, wary of power, readily distinguish between English expansion and European rapacity overseas. John Buchan declared in 1900 that there were a certain number of things in the world to be done and the British had got to do them.[30] For some the Empire was, 'under Providence, the greatest instrument for good the world has seen'.[31] White Papers and Blue Books regularly say amen: for example, the *Royal Commission* [Peel] *Report on Palestine 1936*, written by Reginald Coupland, from 1920 to 1948 Oxford's Beit Professor of Colonial History, insists that 'Your Majesty's Government cannot stand aside and let the Jews and the Arabs fight their quarrel out'. Coupland also told a Cabinet committee in October 1939 that the war just begun was a fine opportunity to set the dependent Empire 'on the same moral footing' as the Dominions.[32] Colonial policy, to justify its claim on trusteeship both to the

[27] *The Commonwealth Experience*, 2 vols. (Toronto, 1983), I, p. 186.

[28] MacKenzie, *Propaganda and Empire*, p. 9.

[29] See W. K. Hancock, *Wealth of Colonies* (Cambridge, 1950), pp. 8 ff.

[30] John Buchan, *The Half-Hearted* (London, 1900), p. 208.

[31] Sir Arnold Wilson, *The Persian Gulf: An Historical Sketch from the Earliest Times to the Beginning of the Twentieth Century* (Oxford, 1928), p. viii.

[32] *Report of the Palestine Royal Commission 1936, Parliamentary Papers*, Cmd. 5479 (London, 1937), p. 147. Wm. Roger Louis, *Imperialism at Bay: The United States and the Decolonization of the British Empire, 1941–1945* (New York, 1978), p. 104.

British left and to world opinion (especially the United States), must get itself a good name.

Academic visions of sunny futures can exasperate politicians beleaguered in the immediate. (Churchill's frequent invocations of 'broad uplands' inferred their annexation.) By January 1942 Viceroy Linlithgow had heard quite enough, thank you, from his eager Oxford visitor about Dominion Status as India's shape of things to come: 'I found Coupland had got his solution in his mind, his ticket for home in his pocket, and his "subjects", I suspect, neatly arranged in his twelve chapters; and that he was not disposed to welcome criticism which was in any degree destructive of those plans!'[33]

Contexts, where they disintegrate, reveal basic assumptions. Adolf Hitler in August 1939, forecasting a thousand-year Reich, and certain that 'the right history for any nation was worth a hundred divisions', assured his assembled generals, poised for *der Tag*, that 'the victor will not be asked later if he has spoken the truth or not!'[34] In 1943 Eric Walker's *The British Empire: Its Structure and Spirit* was sure that the Empire's downfall would trigger universal disaster, even though its history survived to record 'a great human achievement'.[35] Just then, in Japanese–ruled Singapore (Shonan), the Hindu nationalist Subhas Chandra Bose, enemy to both Raj and Congress, was quoting Trotsky: 'Let us make the history, someone else will write it!'—and gleefully predicting that when Japan's army swept into Bengal under 'Asia for the Asians' banners, himself carrying one of them, 'everyone will revolt! Wavell's whole Army will join me!'[36]

For English landlords, property has never been a political problem (hence the 'Irish Question'). Colonies were property: so, once 'good governance' was in being—peace and quiet, metalled roads, honest bookkeeping—their landlords stopped the clock. Fixtures in place (plantations, settlements) should now become fixtures in time. After the Anglo-American Atlantic Charter of August 1941 had liberated four freedoms (only four?!) from Pandora's box in August 1941, Harold Macmillan was sent over to the Colonial Office to check its policy-statements on file. He found them 'scrappy, obscure, and jejune';[37] a verdict much like medical-missionary Mary Kingsley's in 1897 (long treasured in official circles) that colonial policy was 'a coma, accompanied by fits'.[38]

33 Linlithgow to Amery, 7 Jan. 1942, in Nicholas Mansergh and Penderel Moon, eds., *Constitutional Relations Between Great Britain and India: The Transfer of Power, 1942–7* (London, 1970), I, p. 58.

34 D. Cameron Watt, *How War Came: The Immediate Origins of the Second World War* (London, 1989), p. 485.

35 Oxford, 1943, p. 4.

36 Louis Allen, *Burma: The Longest War, 1941–45* (London, 1984), p. 169.

37 Louis, *Imperialism at Bay*, p. 132.

38 Mary H. Kingsley, *West African Studies* (London, 1899; 2nd edn., 1901), p. 310.

Some District Officers' diaries emphasize the harmony that could grow between controller and controlled. But this, unsupported by social or fiscal capital, was cross-purposed, fundamentally bogus. The single honest but unthinkable policy was to abolish collaboration, and the dependent Empire with it—which was Gandhi's sole practical nostrum, 'We have only to say no'. In Egypt, Lord Cromer ranked as Diplomatic Agent and Consul-General; but as Ronald Storrs remarks, 'the Agency's status amounted, for foreigners as well as Egyptians, to that of Ten Downing Street multiplied by Buckingham Palace'. Reviewing Cromer's two-volume report on *Modern Egypt* (London, 1908), Wilfrid Blunt reckoned it also bogus: 'As a diagnosis of the land he lived in for so many years without really seeing it—for his mornings were spent at his desk and his evenings in the European society of Cairo—his final judgments are fallacious through ignorance, the work of a stranger to Egypt rather than of one for so long resident there.'[39] Clearly, John M. MacKenzie's categorization of imperialism as atavism combined with cultural self-satisfaction and technical advance is not eighty but light-years distant from the legacy which Cromer and all his Proconsular kin designed for their posterity.

A legacy warrants the care of a trustee. Constitutional historians have regularly signed on for this duty. Following separate trails, they agree that law, not militance, second thoughts, not first, ultimately shaped and justified England's expansion. Berriedale Keith's dry prose kindles when telling how jurisprudence and the common law nurtured not just England and her Empire, but the cause of civilization with it. Legal ties, 'sinews of the body politic', were literally inescapable. Emigrants' baggage contained the right to the protection of English law and the obligation to obey it. From 1578 onwards Humphrey Gilbert's land-grants in Ireland and America say so. The East India Company's incorporating charter of 1600 says so. Virginia charters from 1608 through to 1612 say so. The statement, Keith insists, 'is universal throughout colonial history'.[40] English emigrants were not outlaws in Sherwood Forest, or displaced persons in Alsatia, riff-raff living behind God's back; they were Crown subjects (Calvin's case, 1608). 'Let an Englishman go where he will,' legal counsel advised in 1720, 'he carries as much of law and liberty as the nature of things will bear.'[41] But who judges nature, and what it will bear? Westminster had a short way with petitions for 'the rights of Englishmen', as Scotsmen and Irishmen, and John Wilkes and Tom Paine, found out. But Englishmen in America, free to take broad views after being imperially liberated from French encroachment, thought themselves entitled to select whatever English

39 Storrs, *Orientations* (London, 1937), p. 52; W. S. Blunt, *Gordon at Khartoum: Being a Personal Narrative of Events* (London, 1911), p. 61.

40 A. Berriedale Keith, *Constitutional History of the First British Empire* (Oxford, 1930), p. 1.

41 Madden and Fieldhouse, *Classical Period*, II, p. 192.

laws and rights they wanted. Maybe 'the liberty of the subject' included the liberty not to *be* a subject?

When the answer was no, they claimed a status other than what their history had allotted them—what Adam Smith called the paltry raffle of colonial faction—and drew the sword in defence of their own importance. Their successful defection shaped Imperial history thereafter. 'Responsible government', Home Rule, has always been a colonial and not an imperial trophy. Subsequent administrations in London realized they could not simultaneously control the external defence and arrange the internal affairs of distant properties peopled by their own kin. They accordingly loosened their grasp, liberalized their outlook, or did both. The process became statutory in 1850 when colonists in Australia, after only minimal attention at Westminster, peaceably attained that democratic Home Rule which seventy-four years previously had been denied, amid shots heard round the world, to colonists in America. As Radical John Bright told his diary, 'Should like to move the Bill be extended to cover Great Britain and Ireland'. The hundred years dividing King George III's Declaratory Act (1766) from Queen Victoria's Colonial Laws Validity Act (1865) surely mark this getting of wisdom. Decrees the one: 'The said colonies and plantations in America have been, are, and of right ought to be subordinate unto and dependent upon the Imperial Crown and Parliament of Great Britain.' But murmurs the other: 'Every law made by a colonial legislature is valid for the colony except insofar as it is repugnant to an Act of Parliament extending to the colony'.[42]

Protection of peaceful trading being essential, the Empire's rulers after 1850 adopted Free Trade—a doctrine, as Engels noted, based on 'pure delusion . . . that England was to be the one great manufacturing centre of an agricultural world'. British power was thereafter subsumed under the name of British interests, beneficial towards all. A symbol of this self-confidence survives. In the 1840s the English invented the postage-stamp, an official document that did not identify country of origin, date of issue, or the person portrayed. It assumed everyone would know where the document came from and who that was. Everyone did: still does.

Time passed, but not the assumptions. In the 1920s the Empire, harassed by nationalist 'unrest' in places so disparate as Ireland and Egypt, but reassured by the amount of emotional capital invested in it by the 'Great War', was still functioning, unabashed. In some mythic manner Queen Victoria yet presided over what seemed more like a geological formation than an evolving institution. In gratitude for wartime valour a new Dominions Office (1925) granted to colonial

[42] G. M. Trevelyan, *Life of John Bright* (London, 1914), p. 176; Keith, *First British Empire*, pp. 181–82, 351 ff.

whites the sought-after concept of 'Dominion Status', making it statutory in 1931. South Africa's J. C. Smuts, principal beneficiary of the century's first devolution (1910), publicized a new name for Empire, 'the British Commonwealth of Nations'. Outside of official print and establishment editorials it never caught on. The Colonial Office grimaced at it for the next forty years. Winston Churchill stuttered when he pronounced it, which was not often. It altered no British habits, in Washington's eyes. It got nowhere, naturally, in Eire (Southern Ireland). It had its best welcome in *The Round Table*, Empire's in-house journal from 1910, which had become sanctuary for Lionel Curtis and latter-day Milnerites. Only after 1947 would Dominion Status graduate to utility, and Commonwealth membership present colonial nationalist leaders with a ticket-of-leave into the world and a passport-at-large when there. Exhumed from the textbooks by Attlee and Mountbatten, these concepts gave equal though not fraternal dignity to Hindu India and Muslim Pakistan travelling towards republican freedom, pathfinders for Asian and African aspirants on the same quest.

No scenario for this was on file. Because the Statute of Westminster of 1931 gave status but not stature to the Dominions, the Commonwealth, as J. D. B. Miller reports in *Britain and the Old Dominions* (Oxford, 1966), 'remained wrapped in a cocoon of theory, from which would emerge from time to time the formidable voice of Berriedale Keith'.[43] (Keith's works are still mandatory reading for junior jurists in Barbados, Malaysia, and points east and west.) Concluding his survey of *The Constitution, Administration, and Laws of the Empire* (London, 1924), Keith asked himself, would Imperial Unity be preserved in the future? He trod dubiously around the problem: 'In some measure, it is certain, the Empire may be expected to endure, unless influences at present unsuspected arise to destroy it.' And would India eventually settle for autonomy within the Empire? 'The strongest force telling against the possibility of such satisfaction is the impossibility of the grant by the Dominions of freedom of entrance to Indians.'[44] But, to stay racially pure, the Dominions must so refuse.

Good government was on the face of it so much better than self-government that the matter was scarcely discussed. British rule, H. J. Simson wrote, 'was neither harsh nor selfish, but a new form of rule leading to free co-operation by unequals'.[45] Lord Lugard assessed European control of the tropics as another necessary white man's burden. The French lapsed moodily into early *franglais* to accommodate *le Lugardisme*, although French logic insisted that *le self-gouvernement* was not only a contradiction in terms, but a nonsense in Africa. The terms

43 London, 1966, p. 105.

44 London, 1924, pp. 8, 120–22, 311.

45 Simson, *British Rule, and Rebellion*, p. 29.

themselves were sometimes insupportable; forced labour in the Congo, as Keith noted, illuminated the dangers of leaving human life at the mercy of exploitation by commercial interests.

Looming dangers and unsuspected influences never fazed elder statesman Arthur, Lord Balfour. Describing his 1917 Declaration for 'a National Home for the Jews' in Palestine as 'an adventure', he teased his fellow-peers in 1922, 'Are we never to have adventures?' Prefacing an Oxford 'World's Classics' edition of Walter Bagehot's *The English Constitution* (first published London, 1867), he reflected blandly that 'England has given the world an example of ordered freedom and reasonable statesmanship which nations not of English race have never found it easy to equal'. Those nations must surely have already found this out for themselves. Clearly, constitutions were easily copied. Obviously, temperaments were not. Attitudes were not circulating currency. And *noblesse oblige* could operate only where *noblesse* existed:

> If a people have no natural inclination to liberty and no natural respect for law; if they lack good humour and tolerate foul play; if they know not how to compromise, or when; if they have not that distrust of extreme conclusions which is sometimes misdescribed as want of logic; if corruption does not repel them; and if their divisions tend to be either too numerous or too profound—the successful working of British institutions may be difficult or impossible.[46]

So much for the blessings which, twenty years later, an adventurous Colonial Office, in headlong zeal to get itself Professor Coupland's 'good name', attempted to launch, even while still reeling from the global hammer-blows of the Second World War, a policy of genuine development, welfare, and partnership, fuelled by real money. The goal was to export to all and sundry this admirable scheme under the name of the 'Westminster model'!

At her Diamond Jubilee Queen Victoria celebrated an Empire on which the sun never set. (That dauntless missionary Dr Henry Lansdell had already been cross-examined on this one evening in Bokhara: 'Surely, it must set for a *few* hours?')[47] But now the sun is certifiably down, how do we see ourselves? As pathologists, dissecting a body-politic in the dark? Cartographers, overlaying new traces on an old topography? Historiographers, trimming *à la mode*? Our guild condemns bias, but is irretrievably addicted to *order*. William James warned us about systems—'all-inclusive, yet simple: noble, clean, luminous, stable, vigorous, true; what more

[46] W. K. Hancock, *Survey of British Commonwealth Affairs: Problems of Nationality: 1918–1936* (Oxford, 1937), I, p. 429.

[47] Henry Lansdell, *Through Central Asia: With a Map and Appendix on the Diplomacy and Delimitation of the Russo-Afghan Frontier* (London, 1887), pp. 352, 383. The author appears on p. 213, shouldering an axe and clad in a Khokand suit of mail.

ideal refuge could there be?'; but historians, even before travelling thereto, must dispel that 'contemporaneous chaos' James called the real order of the world. How? Why, says he: 'We break that real order; we break it into histories, and we break it into arts, and we break it into sciences; and then we begin to feel at home.'[48]

Empire's home included many mansions. For Hugh Egerton, inaugurating himself in 1910 as Oxford's first Beit Professor, every school building was a citadel of Empire, 'every teacher its sentinel'.[49] *Making Imperial Mentalities* cites pre-1914 Canada, where 'the text-books were in practice the curriculum', reflecting the 'dominant ideas of the people at the time they were written'—one of which was the Empire itself, 'a moral enterprise for the benefit of subject-peoples'. Receiving the freedom of the city in London's Guildhall on 29 July 1915, Canada's Prime Minister, Sir Robert Borden, declared that when future historians analysed the Empire's wartime solidarity, they would see 'how there must have been some over-mastering impulse contributing to this wonderful result'.[50]

A good classroom lesson, like a good stage-play, has a shape. History when rescued from chronology can be shaped to produce interpretations which publishers hail as powerful correctives. One such has reconstituted an entire Imperial landscape. *Was* the scrambling partition of Africa 'driven from start to finish by the persistent crisis in Egypt'? *Was* there 'a broad imperative' to secure the route to the East? These were among the findings of the 1961 *Africa and the Victorians: The Official Mind of Imperialism.* Reviewing this, I prophesied, correctly, that 'Robinson and Gallagher', as this model is known, could look forward to a long and honourable career. Yet Africa as India's bulwark is a notion that would have seriously astonished five generations of Great Gamesmen whose own long and honourable careers were passed concentrating on or swanning above and beyond India's North-West Frontier.[51]

A show-stopping model is tagged *prêt-à-porter* and made to everyone's measure. Literature, Northrop Frye tells us, belongs to a world that man constructs, not to the world he sees. Is history, then, another girder in that same structure? Was the young Simone de Beauvoir right in believing that views of the past depended on status in the present, the luck of the draw? Certainly we should

[48] William James, *The Varieties of Religious Experience: A Study in Human Nature* (London, 1903), pp. 433–4; 'Reflex Action and Theism', in R. B. Perry, ed., *Essays on Faith and Morals* (New York, 1943), p. 119.

[49] Richard Symonds, *Oxford and Empire: The Last Lost Cause?* (London, 1986), p. 53.

[50] Mangan, ed., *Making Imperial Mentalities*, p. 148; Sir Max Aitken, MP, *Canada in Flanders*, 3 vols. (London, 1916), I, p. 215.

[51] A. P. Thornton, 'The Partition of Africa', first published in *International Journal* (Spring, 1962), reprinted in Thornton, *For the File on Empire: Essays and Reviews* (London, 1968), pp. 252–57.

remember this century's luckless, a legion that includes those five historians, successive Rectors of Kiev University between 1921 and 1939, murdered by the State. Did Soviet Chairman Nikita Khrushchev do so in 1956 when denouncing historians as a menace, since they alone could turn the past, and consequently the present, upside down?[52] It is that possibility, perhaps, that has made our Western academy reject all authority, even one so mild as G. M. Trevelyan's, who was sure history's prime purpose lay in its 'didactic public function'.[53]

Still, oracles are no loss, and nobody has yet died from a coarsening of the culture. 'No man who was correctly informed about the past,' states Macaulay, 'is likely to take a morose and desponding view of the present.'[54] ('History never happens as it should,' Mark Twain remarks, 'historians exist to put it right.') Winston Churchill—easy to criticize, impossible to reduce—tests both these attitudes. In *Churchill and the Jews* (London, 1985) Michael J. Cohen, born in 1940, traces England's early drift towards the Arab position in Palestine, and emphasizes that Churchill and England should have known better. Ah, if everyone always knew better, how serene humanity's past, how pleasing its prospects would be! One reviewer of Ronald Hyam's volumes in the British Documents on the End of Empire Project series (London, 1992) complains 'there is little material here to build alternative histories of imperial policy and practice [other] than that current in the mind of contemporaries'.[55] Are contemporaries expendable? How, without becoming romantic novelists, do we record an alternative history? Men and women make do with the lights they have: shall we sell them a new, improved set? If we think them wrong we can say so, but since they cannot hear us saying so, we must be saying it for our own satisfaction. Should not we say that, too?

Do we really need to ask, for instance, why Churchill's government ignored the social problems posed by the presence of black American troops?—'not the only occasion in World War II', declares David Reynolds, listing others more urgent, 'where the government ignored what *we* should *now call fundamental moral principles*'.[56] That approach is better suited to a cure of souls, and explains why English philosophers allocate English history no philosophical base. W. H. Walsh in his *Philosophy of History* (London, 1951) challenges the historian's ability to reconstruct the past.

[52] Robert Conquest, *The Great Terror: A Reassessment* (New York, 1990), p. 293.

[53] David Cannadine, *G. M. Trevelyan: A Life in History* (London, 1992), p. 183.

[54] T. B. Macaulay, *History of England From the Accession of James II*, ed. C. H. Firth (London, 1913), I, p. 2.

[55] B. R. Tomlinson in *International History Review*, XVI, 3 (1994), p. 630.

[56] 'The Churchill Government and the Black American Troops in Britain During World War II', *Transactions of the Royal Historical Society*, Fifth Series, XXXV (London, 1985), pp. 113 ff. Emphasis added.

The Middle East, that principal pillar, provides cases in point.[57] Walter Laqueur's *A History of Zionism* (London, 1972) admits that an impartial account of that subject 'will be written, if ever, only when it has ceased to be of topical interest'. Those claiming detachment and objectivity 'may be no nearer to truth and justice than are the self-avowed partisans'.[58] Christopher Sykes's *Crossroads to Israel* (London, 1965), indeed, vowed that, from wherever that story was viewed, emotion must prevail; for 'if there is an approach decidedly more dislikeable and much more of a hindrance to an understanding of these movements and their consequences, which tore the hearts of men, it is that which tries to reject emotion in favour of a fraudulent god's-eye view'.[59]

Tension also pulsates through the record of British India as presented by its veterans, aware that the shape of their Raj was, as in a kaleidoscope, momentary only. Since nothing was what it seemed or should have been, 'politics' was another name for subversion, 'policy' for fantasy. It was his recognition of this ingrained pessimism that implanted in Mohandas Gandhi, back from South Africa in December 1915, a continuing contempt for these fraudulent alien gods who did nothing, wanted to do nothing, and constantly pretended otherwise.

Thirty years on, in March 1943, Bengal's Governor, R. G. Casey, was more disillusioned even than Gandhi—who was just then confined to a 'Detention Camp' (one of the Aga Khan's palaces) by a Raj needlessly fearful he might there starve himself to death. Casey launched a raking Australian barrage at the Viceroy: The Empire has cause for shame in the fact that in Bengal at least, after a century and a half of British rule, we can point to no achievement in any direction.'[60] And although Wavell sent no answer, he may well have agreed, since his own proposals for India's post-war status had already been rejected by the War Cabinet's India Committee, its chairman Clement Attlee as indignant as everyone else, as 'abject surrender'.[61]

In fact the Raj's attitudes had not changed much down the years. In May 1906 Viceroy Lord Minto, suspecting that the incoming Secretary of State in London, that old Victorian radical John Morley, had brought his old Victorian radicalism into office with him, referred him to an act the Raj had passed in 1898 defining 'disaffection' as 'disloyalty, and all feelings of enmity'. Ever a stockaded community, British India had daily to deal with these and with other 'factors of an inflammability unknown to the western world, unsuited to western forms of government'.

[57] 'The real British "Empire" ', according to both Alfred Milner and Ernest Bevin; Wm. Roger Louis, *The British Empire in the Middle East, 1945–1951: Arab Nationalism, the United States and Postwar Imperialism* (Oxford, 1984), p. 47.

[58] p. xvi.

[59] p. xii.

[60] Mansergh and Moon, *Transfer of Power*, V, p. 638.

[61] Ibid., p. 276.

So, therefore, 'we must be physically strong or go to the wall. We were, after all, *the ruling race*.' Yes, Morley said, but what were we in India *for*? 'Surely, in order to implant—slowly, prudently, judiciously—those ideas of law, justice, and humanity which are the foundation of our own civilization.'[62]

This, though within the military's comprehension, was well beyond its patience. In Madras in 1824 the civilian Sir Thomas Munro, had doubted 'whether good intentions could make everything as English as possible in a country which resembles England in nothing'.[63] Lord Roberts spent forty-one years in India quite certain that he would not, because 'we were not there with the will of the people, and nothing we can do for them will ever make them wish us to remain'.[64] Soldiers 'saving' Burma for the Empire in the 1940s readily confirmed this as they watched the local subjects of the Crown providing their Japanese invaders or liberators not only 'with information of our every movement, but guides, rafts, ponies, elephants, and all the things we couldn't get for love and only with great difficulty for money!'[65]

For Minto's inflammable factors had survived his era, to intensify in ways that absorbed one housemasterly agency of the Home Office, the British Board of Film Censors. This refused to certify for distribution any film depicting 'negative attitudes', such as disrespect to the Crown, its institutions, its officers, and its uniforms, together with such 'conduct unbecoming' as corruption and 'going native'—i.e. over-identifying with the surrounding environment. It was anyway simpler to impound cans of celluloid at entry than to proscribe investigative journalists and ideas of natural right. In the 1930s American movies made major profits in the European market and its satellites overseas. Frank Capra's single box-office failure of that decade was *The Bitter Tea of General Yen* (1933: 'thirty years before its time!', he says), whose story-line conjoined a native rising with a liaison between a female missionary and a Chinese warlord (this role played by a Swede). It was banned—as were *Gunga Din* (1939) and *White Cargo* (1942)—throughout the Empire. Alexander Korda's *The Drum* (1938), depicting uproar on the North-West Frontier (played by Wales), triggered Hindu–Muslim riots in Bombay and Madras. One of Pandora's boxes is a camera.

To summarize. Emigrants took ship to better their prospects. A migrant minority took ship in order to take charge at the far end. Transients only, their

[62] M. N. Das, *India under Morley and Minto* (London, 1964), p. 66.

[63] Madden and Fieldhouse, eds., *Select Documents on the Constitutional History of the British Empire and Commonwealth*, Vol. III, *Imperial Reconstruction, 1763–1840, The Evolution of Alternative Systems of Colonial Government, 1689 to 1783: The Foundations of a Colonial System of Government* (Westport, Conn., 1987), p. 241.

[64] Stanley A. Wolpert, *Morley and India, 1906–1910* (Berkeley, 1967), p. 148.

[65] Louis Allen, *Burma: The Longest War*, p. 28.

baggage and outlook stayed intact. Their historians have followed them closely, presenting Empire as an administrative construct, surfacing the social depths. The Victorian jurist Fitzjames Stephen, seared by his experiences on the Indian circuit, shocked his colleagues by probing these depths and spelling it out: constitutional questions are matters not of law but of power.[66] (In this he was in agreement with John Locke, Adam Smith, and Friedrich Engels: laws are necessary only because most people own nothing.) But the Imperial implications and dimensions of this same problem became incalculable—or perhaps were never calculated; for even as corrosion ate into the foundations of the India Office and the Colonial Office, their underlings and mandarins did not confer. Professionals, they played out their roles of authority and acceptance: the Malays, for example, were conscientiously tutored in nationalism. V. S. Naipaul's *An Area of Darkness* (London, 1964) stresses this element of utility. In Trinidad, 'every child knew we were only a dot on the map of the world, and that it was therefore important to be British: that at least anchored us within a wider system'.

The system's masters were well able to distinguish between the strategies of Gandhi and Nehru and the Indian Congress, and the tactics, say, of Kwame Nkrumah—who claimed no moral authority when starting out—and his cheering peasants in the Gold Coast (Ghana). India's quest for identity and recognition was *not* treated as just one more item in the global politics of complaint. The British knew they had not *invented* India in the same fashion as they had shaped the Gold Coast and some four dozen other random pieces of geography, properly postage-stamped. Even when structured into a steel-framed State, India was what India had ever been: an unalterable culture and civilization. No such context housed British Guiana or North Borneo. Like previous acts under Company and Crown, those of 1919 and 1935 were preambled, 'for the better government of India'. But the governance of colonial dependencies, which attracted attention only in emergency, did not need bettering: it was assumed to be good enough as it was.

To his tally of accident, climate, and disposition as lures taking Englishmen overseas, Edmund Burke might have added war and trade; for these had signally helped keep them there. Those different psychological universes had not yet been sighted, yet the wildest of colonial boys off to wherever in the morning knew a 'New World' was waiting. Seeley's comment on 'absence of mind' referred not to what was done by 'men-on-the-spot' but to his homekeeping countrymen's parochial ignorance. Let 'Foul-Weather Jack' Byron speak for his populous kind—naval officers who were the youngest sons of younger brothers. Ever solicitous of their Lordships' instructions, officers could rarely find them relevant to the situation.

[66] See J. F. Stephen, *Liberty, Equality, Fraternity*, ed. R. J. White (Cambridge, 1967), p. 166.

In the true English pattern, situation and status were linked. Status still decrees whose history is recorded and whose is not: white indentured servants and black slaves in the Caribbean occupy one category, their masters, the 'Gentlemen-Planters', another. The latter in Barbados in 1689 had as spokesman Edward Littleton, whose *The Groans of the Plantations* denounces a reinforcement of the ever-abominated Navigation Acts.[67] A pioneering calculating patriot, Littleton was merchant, planter, slave-holder, rum-runner, devotee of market-forces, and founder of an Imperial dynasty. Very rich, he groaned because he could have been so very much richer.

Some calculations were less self-serving. Norway's Fridtjof Nansen, extolling Polar exploration, quotes a saga singing of 'Man's eternal desire for fame, gain, and knowledge'.[68] But it was not for fame and gain (though not entirely for altruism, either) that from 1815 onwards My Lords of the Admiralty commissioned the sounding and charting of as many of the world's shores, channels, and harbours as their captains of frigates could reach. Britain's Royal Navy was neighbour to every country with a coastline, and its arriving white ensign testified to the persuasive ubiquity of the doctrine of 'the freedom of the seas'. With no enemy fleet in being, the Navy when not sending a gunboat or harrying the oceanic slave-trade made cold war on misinformation—a wickedness fit only for deservedly unsuccessful foreigners. For the Portuguese had once littered Europe with mendacious maps to hoodwink first the Spaniards, then the Dutch; the Dutch had tricked the English likewise; while the imperious Spaniards, the magnificence of their monopoly masked beyond the western haze, published nothing at all. But there is one unique legacy still free for the use of a skipper of whatever nationality on the bridge of whichever ship wherever registered: Britain's Admiralty Charts.

These illustrate a combination of labour, hazard, and industry unburdened by ideology; updating them is one historical exercise uncontaminated by egotism. By a chart originating in 1861 the United States's navy worked a passage in 1942 through the Solomon Islands—only to find the Imperial Japanese navy, thumbing a translation, already there. Manuals make for memorabilia more durable than does the scattered colossus of Ozymandias, King of Kings, or life-size Lord Roberts on horseback, dominating Glasgow's Kelvingrove; and they surely warrant better remembrance than do the tyrants who now lie piled, one prone bronze upon another, in Moscow's Gorky Park.

Romanitas, they say, died for want of a people to appreciate it. That process recurs. The future is like the past, another country where 'they do things differently', but

67 Edward Littleton, *The Groans of the Plantations* (London, 1689).

68 Fridtjof Nansen, *In Northern Mists: Arctic Exploration in Early Times* (London, 1911), cited in John Buchan, *The Last Secrets: The Final Mysteries of Exploration* (London, 1923), pp. 86–87.

where the things done will also be different. Seniors, already suspicious of their juniors, do not suppose that a posterity confined within its own psychological universe, cherishing an impoverished culture on a narrower stage, will get things right either. In 1859 John Stuart Mill's *On Liberty* thought that too: 'Individually small, we only appear capable of anything great by combining . . . But it was men of another stamp that made England what it has been; and men of another stamp will be needed to prevent its decline.'[69]

Still, a monumental aura traditionally encloses a serried *Oxford History.* Harold Temperley, editor of Oxford's six volumes on *A History of the Peace Conference of Paris* (1920–24), knew that the opinions they expressed 'would not be those of posterity'.[70] No indeed—but which posterity will notarize its last analysis as final, and carve it in stone? (Still, France's Premier Georges Clemenceau, who did not believe history would instruct that Belgians invaded Germany in August 1914, has yet to be contradicted.)

Doris Lessing, in her autobiography *Walking in the Shade* (London, 1997), writes that 'facts are easy', but the atmospheres that made them possible are elusive. Facts become both difficult and equally elusive, however, when merged in patterns, and their atmospheres even hazier when infiltrated by that same imagination which exercises itself in colonizing a fantasy future. The twentieth-century empires all ended with long casualty-lists; but it is only the British who are constructing memorials both nostalgic and concrete. So—allowing that no achievement is permanently sound, can the tales about it that these volumes have told (an achievement in itself!) prove sound enough for long enough—to borrow one more time from C. P. Lucas's thinking—'to conduce to future greatness'?

69 Isaiah Berlin, citing Mill's *On Liberty*, in *Four Essays on Liberty* (Oxford, 1969), p. 194.

70 Temperley, *Peace Conference*, p. vi.

Select Bibliography

CARL L. BECKER, *Detachment and the Writing of History: Essays and Letters* (Ithaca, NY, 1958).

HERBERT BUTTERFIELD, *The Whig Interpretation of History* (London, 1931).

—— *The Englishman and His History* (Cambridge, 1944).

—— *Man on His Past* (Cambridge, 1955).

R. G. COLLINGWOOD, *The Idea of History* (Oxford, 1946).

G. T. ELTON, *The Practice of History* (New York, 1967).

R. C. K. ENSOR, G. M. YOUNG, and others, *Why We Study History* (Historical Association Publications, No. 131, London, 1944).

PATRICK GARDINER, *The Nature of Historical Explanation* (Oxford, 1952).

Pieter Geyl, *Debates with Historians* (The Hague, 1954).

W. K. Hancock, *Country and Calling* (London, 1954).

J. H. Hexter, *Reappraisals in History* (London, 1961).

—— *On Historians* (Cambridge, Mass., 1979).

Michael Kammen, ed., *What is the Good of History?: Selected Letters of Carl L. Becker, 1900–1945* (Ithaca, NY, 1973).

John Kenyon, *The History Men: The Historical Profession in England Since the Renaissance*, 2nd edn. (London, 1993).

S. C. Roberts, *Adventures with Authors* (Cambridge, 1966).

40

Development and the Utopian Ideal, 1960–1999

A. G. HOPKINS

Historiography is retrospective by definition and classificatory by common practice. Its value lies in identifying contours and boundaries, and in enabling observers to view the landscape as a whole. If we cannot situate ourselves in relation to the scholarship of our predecessors and contemporaries, we cannot begin to find a place for our own individuality, limited though it may be. Moreover, we now live in a world of buzzwords and sound-bites. As yesterday's news is unread today, so the scholarship of a previous generation can easily be left on the shelf. Where the principle of short-termism operates, students have no accessible means of knowing how they have arrived at the present. Even if the latest is also the best, as we are inclined to suppose, we cannot understand our own genius without relating it to the efforts of those who went before us. Nor can we envisage the possibility that current priorities and approaches may change, as they have done in the past. Yet it is the prospect of change that offers the chance of originality, and it is originality, not merely professionalism, that keeps the subject alive.

Like all forms of historical enquiry, historiography has pitfalls as well as advantages. The construction of categories courts injustice by omitting work that does not fit the chosen headings and by compressing the variety of that which does, while the creation of sequences can easily suggest that one phase or style replaces another by an evolutionary process leading to our own higher form of wisdom. The categorization in this chapter will indeed be schematic and selective. Fortunately, the fuller assessments of regions and periods given in previous chapters attest to the richness and diversity of the literature and provide a corrective to any classificatory excesses that may be encountered here.

The evolution of historical studies is the result of a combination of two related forces: the momentum built up within the scholarly body to find solutions to specific intellectual problems, and the response of scholars to the external influences that have a bearing on their lives. These forces determine what subjects are selected and how they are studied. Although scholars are inclined to suppose that they conduct themselves in a way that is removed from mundane considerations, the evidence suggests that studies of imperialism, Empire, and the post-colonial order are especially responsive to changes in the world at large. All scholars try to solve puzzles, and in doing so they strive to be objective. But the puzzles they select and the solutions they adopt reflect changes in the world about them. War and peace, depression and prosperity, pessimism and optimism all leave their imprint. Some scholars may not be aware that their research is coloured by contemporary events; a few may escape its influence altogether. Generally speaking, however, studies of Imperial history have had a purpose, whether to justify Empire, to condemn alien domination or to understand post-colonial discontents. Imperial history began as a complement to Empire; post-colonial studies are driven by the need to understand its legacy.

Purposive history can be the inspiration for work that is illuminating, meticulous, even monumental. It can also produce instant history, quickly brewed for the needs of the moment, which supports the hypothesis of the day by deploying simple verificatory procedures and by turning a blind eye to alternative possibilities. Such studies, the unconvincing products of conviction, become the tombstones of their time, memorials to those who did not know where they were going because they could not see from whence they came. The balance between the inspirational and the routine is tilted towards the latter by the weight of orthodoxy. In the past, historians of Empire tended to write either in an approving style or at least in a way that was not critical of their subject. Today, very few scholars would attempt to mount a defence of imperialism and Empire. The danger is rather that they may mute criticism of the countries, peoples, and classes they wish to see liberated, while subordinating them to a succession of Western models, methods, and aspirations. If future historians are made aware of the pressures towards conformity, they should be better placed to see that, while all history is of its time, not all of it has to be for its time.

The year 1960 is an appropriate starting-point for this survey because it marks, as well as any single year can, the end of Empire and the beginning of the era of independence. India had already attained independence in 1947, but that event caused the Empire to be repositioned rather than dismantled. The 'second colonial occupation'[1] that followed the Second World War saw a strengthening of Imperial ties with Malaya, Africa and the Middle East, and it was not until the late 1950s that the revived colonial mission was abandoned. Thereafter, the retreat from Empire was rapid: by 1970 the flag flew not over continents but over islands, which by then were small in size and few in number.[2]

[1] The phrase derives from D. A. Low and J. M. Lonsdale, 'Towards the New Order, 1945–63', in D. A. Low and Alison Smith, eds., The Oxford *History of East Africa*, 3 vols. (Oxford, 1976), III, pp. 12–16.

[2] The most recent guide is W. David McIntyre, *British Decolonization, 1946–1997* (London, 1998).

Before 1960 Imperial history was studied mainly from the centre, principally from a political perspective, and largely from the top. This tradition is identified with Seeley in 1883, when the subject first acquired a professional form, and it reached a high-point of orthodoxy in the inter-war years, when Cambridge launched a weighty, multi-handed series on the history of the British Empire.[3] After 1960 the perspective and the style went out of fashion, as did the Empire. The shift of emphasis was marked and rapid: authors of doctoral dissertations with titles beginning 'British Policy Towards . . .' were left high and dry; in their place came a new generation of researchers who were determined, in the first instance, to write indigenous history, preferably of the pre-colonial era. As new states gained their independence, historians helped to liberate them from subjection to Imperial history by decolonizing the presentation of their past. Gallagher and Robinson's justly celebrated study *Africa and the Victorians*, published in 1961, marks the transition particularly well.[4] As an analysis of the 'official mind' of imperialism, the book was a Eurocentric account of high policy; but it also pointed the way towards a different perspective by incorporating the role of 'proto-nationalists' on the frontier, where European agents engaged with indigenous societies. There followed a veritable knowledge revolution: centres, programmes, journals, and monograph series were established; the subject was reconceptualized as Third World studies or simply area studies; a new generation of young researchers arose to put right historical wrongs and to set free minds that had long been kept in subjection.

This is not to say that Imperial history came to an end: the evidence of this volume makes it clear that it did not. But it was no longer seen to be on the side of the future, and even less so on the side of the angels. It lost status and visibility. Ultimately, it had to be reinvented, through a process that is still under way, first by engaging with the new research on indigenous history and then, after a sufficient lapse of time, by revisiting subjects that had become unfashionable after 1960.[5] The results of this refurbishment now span a range of development issues, and their treatment is gradually being disentangled from questions of morality. There has been a large-scale attempt to reinterpret the causes of British imperialism by rethinking the metropolitan basis of modernization.[6] An equally ambitious project

[3] See the chap. by Wm. Roger Louis, pp. 10–12.

[4] Ronald Robinson and John Gallagher with Alice Denny, *Africa and the Victorians: The Official Mind of Imperialism*, 2nd edn. (1961; London, 1981).

[5] For further discussion see chap. by Robin W. Winks.

[6] P. J. Cain and A. G. Hopkins, *British Imperialism: Expansion and Innovation, 1688–1914* (London, 1993) and *British Imperialism: Crisis and Deconstruction, 1914–1990* (London, 1993), and the discussion of the argument of this work in Raymond E. Dumett, ed., *Gentlemanly Capitalism and British Imperialism: The New Debate on Empire* (London, 1999).

has revisited the controversy over the costs and benefits of Empire.[7] Between cause and consequence stand a variety of new studies of expatriate and indigenous enterprise, and of the links between them.[8]

As historians rearranged the files on Empire, they also adjusted to changes of a professional and institutional kind. The study of Imperial history, like other branches of history, has become highly specialized in the course of the last forty years, as the preceding contributions to this volume again bear witness. The proliferation of local studies and the need to take account of the 'indigenous point of view' were imperatives that led historians of Empire to become country and regional specialists. The grand sweep over continents and centuries has become correspondingly more difficult, and therefore increasingly hazardous. A parallel trend caused the subject to lose ground in the syllabus, surrendering territory to area studies and to new thematic approaches that sought to express the voices of peasants, proletarians, and, after a struggle, women.

Institutionally, the most important development—well known but little discussed—has been the shift in the geographical basis of the subject, as it became colonized by scholars from the ex-colonial states. This has been an uneven process. Scholarship in Canada, Australia, and New Zealand is well established and relatively well funded; historians in India have made an indispensable contribution from a less favourable starting-point; those in Africa have suffered particularly from lack of funds. The influence of the greatest ex-colony of them all, the United States, has been especially marked as a result of its post-war role as a superpower, its immense resources, and its several thousand universities. As the United States began to exercise considerable influence over the old Imperial centre, so too it took on and reshaped traditional approaches to writing Imperial history.

The multi-centred and increasingly independent character of the subject has had an invigorating effect: it has encouraged an influx of new recruits, and introduced new themes and fresh ideas. In contrast to the ideology that accompanied the old-style Imperial history, work undertaken since the 1960s has also been associated, generally speaking, with opposition to imperialism and Empire. The influence of the United States has been especially marked in this respect. The quest for

[7] Lance E. Davis and Robert A. Huttenback with the assistance of Susan Gray Davis, *Mammon and the Pursuit of Empire: The Political Economy of British Imperialism, 1860–1912* (Cambridge, 1987).

[8] See, for example, D. K. Fieldhouse, *Unilever Overseas* (London, 1980) and *Merchant Capital and Economic Development: The United Africa Company, 1929–1989* (Oxford, 1994). Research on the history of indigenous enterprise has moved some way beyond early formulations showing that 'traditional' societies could act rationally and could even engage in profit-seeking activities, and now seeks to place economic decisions in the broader context of institutions and values. For a recent example of this approach (and for further references) see John Harriss, Janet Hunter, and Colin M. Lewis, eds., *The New Institutional Economics and Third World Development* (London, 1995).

liberation, democracy, and development that has inspired some of the best (and some of the worst) scholarship in the field is by no means confined to scholars in the United States, but it is they who have given it momentum and direction. The sincerity of anti-colonial sentiment is evident, as is the well-intentioned concern for the welfare of underprivileged people. Less explicit is the way in which these sentiments project abroad a preoccupation with the American soul and the American destiny, just as British preoccupations, expressed in concepts such as trusteeship and the 'civilizing mission', left their mark on the style of history written during the heyday of Empire. In both cases, research priorities and conclusions cannot be fully understood without also understanding the moral impetus behind the production of knowledge.

This proposition can be illustrated by looking at the rise and fall of the major influences on post-Imperial studies of Imperial history, especially the body of work concerned with the central theme of development and its complement, liberation. It is not possible in the space available to do more than insert direction signs to the truly immense literature on this subject. Nevertheless, even this limited exercise has its value. As noted at the outset, the prevalence of short-termism means that new graduate students are often unaware that their starting-point in the present has long historiographical roots. Teachers can be relied upon to advertise their own achievements; their youthful intellectual indiscretions may receive less emphasis.

This inconsistency raises some awkward questions. Why should yesterday's truth, once fervently pursued and proclaimed, become today's error? Why should today's truth be courted and embraced with monogamous intent, when the 'lessons' of historiography suggest that the likely outcome is disillusion and divorce? Are we condemned to adopt simple solutions to a complex world by the well-intentioned search for ways of reconciling our own, often fortunate circumstances with the poverty that afflicts so much of the human race? If so, is our quest doomed to disappointment, like the hopes of members of a cargo cult who vainly await the arrival of airborne deliverance? Do we deliberately burn our intellectual possessions, as they dispose of their material goods, to prepare for redemption—thus making matters worse rather than better? Such questions, so readily asked, admit of no easy answers. But if they cause new entrants to the subject to pause before accepting the beguiling proposition that the latest is not only the best but also beyond ascertainable improvement, they will at least begin by having some means of preserving their individuality and be encouraged to pursue unfashionable as well as fashionable approaches to the subject.

In the beginning, that is, in the 1950s and 1960s, there was modernization theory.[9] The basic assumption of the theory was that development was a process

[9] For a guide to the literature see Allan A. Spitz, *Developmental Change: An Annotated Bibliography* (Lexington, Ky, 1969).

that involved the transformation of traditional societies into modern ones. The qualities required for modernity were first specified and then contrasted with what were held to be typical features of the non-modern world. The resulting discrepancies provided an agenda for a programme of social engineering that spanned the whole of the social sciences and spilled over into the humanities. Talcott Parsons, the most famous sociologist of the day, identified the 'pattern variables' that characterized modern and traditional societies.[10] Anthropologists showed how the structures of the latter differed from those of the West.[11] Economists emphasized the transforming power of capital and technology and debated strategies for effecting the transition from agriculture to industry.[12] Political scientists showed that democratic systems were uniquely placed to promote economic development, and that the polity itself could be analysed scientifically, as if it were an electrical system with positive and negative leads, junctions, and fuses.[13] Psychologists devised ingenious measures of the 'need for achievement' and devoted considerable thought to the problem of raising the competitive ethos in societies whose scores fell below the required threshold.[14] All of this was taken very seriously: indeed, it was more influential in its time than post-modernism is today.

This particular house of cards collapsed in the late 1960s and early 1970s.[15] Its ideology was the product of the need to win the peace after 1945, especially the contest with the Soviet Union for the 'hearts and minds of men'—at that stage (and for some time after) women did not count. Belief in the superiority of the Free World was demonstrated, to the satisfaction of its advocates, by the rapidity of the post-war recovery and by the increasing affluence that accompanied it. The country that had produced Spam, Bakelite, and the atomic bomb seemed to have the world almost literally at its feet. Two events upset these sanguine expectations. By 1968 the political and moral consequences of the Vietnam War within the

[10] A recent introduction is Roland Robertson and Bryan S. Turner, eds., *Talcott Parsons: Theorist of Modernity* (London, 1991).

[11] The influence of the (ahistorical) structural-functionalist school was still marked at this time.

[12] It should be remembered that development economics was only just beginning to emerge as a recognized area of study in the 1950s. W. A. Lewis's *Theory of Economic Growth* (London, 1955) was one of the first texts in the field.

[13] David Easton, *A Framework for Political Analysis* (Englewood Cliffs, NJ, 1965).

[14] David C. McClelland, *The Achieving Society* (London, 1961); Everett E. Hagen, *On the Theory of Social Change: How Economic Growth Begins* (Homewood, Ill., 1962).

[15] Among a host of criticisms see Dean C. Tipps, 'Modernisation Theory and the Study of National Development', *Comparative Studies in Society and History*, XV (1973), pp. 199–226, and E. Wayne Nafziger, 'A Critique of Development Economics in the USA', *Journal of Development Studies*, XIII (1976), pp. 18–34. See also Colin Leys, *The Rise and Fall of Development Theory* (London, 1996), chap. 1.

United States could no longer be contained; by 1973 the economic costs of the war, combined with the sudden, sharp rise in the price of petroleum, shattered confidence in the international economic order that the United States had rebuilt and promoted. As disillusion set in, the dark side of the previously sunlit landscape was revealed: towns, once regarded as the summit of modernity, were now seen to reveal depths of ugliness, decay, and danger. There was much talk of private affluence and public squalor, and of the need to rediscover older verities—including 'traditional' ways of life. Urban man fled the inner cities—if he could afford to do so. Country values gained approval and status. Flower power expressed itself in popular culture; the study of medieval history enjoyed an unexpected revival.

History had contributed little to modernization theory, though it was itself greatly influenced by the trend towards quantification that marked the highest stage of the new learning in the 1960s. The past was irrelevant: the men in white coats could deduce all they needed to know about traditional societies from the axioms of modernization theory. History, however, took revenge for its neglect. The rise of colonial nationalism and the achievement of independence stimulated intense interest in the political antecedents of the new nation states; issues of poverty and development attracted the attention of economic historians. By the early 1970s there was a widening gap between the stereotype of the traditional society shorn of agency and bereft of initiative, and the evidence of new research. Indigenous polities, from the Mughals of northern India to the Asante of central Ghana, were shown to have developed bureaucratic structures, military resources, legal systems, and the tax regimes needed to pay for them.[16] It became apparent that 'traditional' societies were neither simple nor static, but complex and evolving. The evidence, from Africa to Indonesia via India, showed that, while subsistence economics could be indeed found, so too could markets, exchange, specialization, money, and dynamic entrepreneurs.[17] The European presence ceased to be synonymous with the history of the Empire: colonial rule had to be fitted into the story of evolving indigenous societies;[18] decolonization, when it came, was the product not just of high policy, but of local agency too.

In the light of this research, it became clear that the concept of a 'traditional society' was simply the antonym of an assumed modernity. The ex-colonial world was more diverse than had been thought, and it had an unsuspected capacity for

[16] Irfan Habib, *The Agrarian System of Mughal India (1556–1707)* (Bombay, 1963), and the further references given there to the author's other pioneering work on the Mughal economy; Ivor Wilks, *Asante in the Nineteenth Century: The Structure and Evolution of a Political Order* (Cambridge, 1975).

[17] See, for example, A. G. Hopkins, *An Economic History of West Africa* (London, 1973).

[18] A widely influential statement stressing the continuities between colonial rule and the indigenous past was Eric Stokes, 'The First Century of British Rule in India: Social Revolution or Social Stagnation?', *Past and Present*, LVIII (1973), pp. 136–60.

innovation. Equally unsettling was the growing awareness that the concept of modernity itself was a revealed truth rather than a scientific one. On close inspection, the idea turned out to be merely a description of ourselves (that is, the favoured parts of the Western world) decked out with footnotes and quantification. Becoming modern meant no more than becoming like us—or rather, like an ideal version of ourselves, because in reality we fell some way short of pure modernity and in some respects were even rather traditional. As the theory was unravelled, the emperor was shown to have no clothes.

A new suit was provided without delay. Although much of the criticism of modernization theory had used principles of orthodox economics (notably rationality and profit-seeking) to reinterpret the behaviour of supposedly traditional societies, widespread disillusion with capitalism led to the adoption of radical alternatives that offered fresh hope for improving the world.[19] In the 1970s history, the discarded background to the present, became the passport to the future. Social scientists who had distanced themselves from the study of the past now rushed to embrace it. The scales were removed: capitalism did not promote development; it caused underdevelopment. André Gunder Frank crystallized the mood of the moment by popularizing the notion of the 'development of underdevelopment';[20] Immanuel Wallerstein's weighty tomes explored the origins of the 'modern world system' by tracing the relationship between the capitalist core and its various peripheries.[21] Doctoral students explored, in the phrase of the day, the 'roots of underdevelopment';[22] works of synthesis showed how *Europe Underdeveloped Africa*—and other parts of the world.[23] In this way, pulled through a hedge backwards, Imperial history made its reappearance. Capitalism triumphant became capitalism demonic. Indigenous achievements stood proud, but European forces, which were taken to be synonymous with capitalism, had stunted their growth and deflected them from

[19] For an anticipation of the coming trend see A. G. Hopkins, 'Clio-Antics: A Horoscope for African Economic History', in Christopher Fyfe, ed., *African Studies Since 1945: A Tribute to Basil Davidson* (London, 1976), pp. 31–48. Mainstream economic theory continued to be applied to African history, especially in analyses of the mechanics of export growth and the costs and benefits of international trade, but it lacked the impetus and popularity attached to the alternative schools of thought discussed here.

[20] See especially his *Latin American: Underdevelopment or Revolution?* (New York, 1969), and numerous other publications down to *Dependent Accumulation and Underdevelopment* (London, 1978).

[21] Immanuel Wallerstein, *The Modern World System: Capitalist Agriculture and the Origins of the European World Economy in the Sixteenth Century* (London, 1974) and *The Modern World System, III: The Second Era of Great Expansion of the Capitalist World Economy, 1730–1840* (San Diego, Calif. 1989).

[22] Edward A. Alpers, 'Re-Thinking African Economic History: A Contribution to the Roots of Underdevelopment', *Ufahamu*, III (1973), pp. 97–129, was one of several influential contributions at that time.

[23] Walter Rodney, *How Europe Underdeveloped Africa* (London, 1972); Philip C. C. Huang, ed., *The Development of Underdevelopment in China* (White Plains, NY, 1978).

what was held to be the 'normal' course of development. The message from the past rang clear: if capitalism was underdeveloping the Third World, there was no point in co-operating with its contemporary agents, the bourgeoisie, while awaiting (with growing impatience) the rise of a proletariat; the bourgeoisie, in its nationalist guise, needed to be overthrown at once. The political programme had its counterpart in economic policy: if ties with the West produced underdevelopment, then what was needed was autarky. The great states that historians had found in the distant past were seen to be the progenitors of the strong states of the present. Central authority received new scholarly justification. Big was beautiful.

It was again bliss to be alive—especially if you lived in the developed world. The past could be reconciled with the present; disillusion with the West could be transformed into a plan of action for changing the global order. The 'dependency thesis', as it became known, brought external influences and economic history to the centre of the stage. It became possible both to reintroduce a discussion of colonial rule and also to criticize indigenous 'collaborators' who had helped in the exploitation of their own people. This was a significant advance: a new facet of the past was revealed, and it could be viewed without risking the charge of racism that had previously encouraged a degree of self-censorship in the treatment of indigenous history. At the same time, the dependency thesis was something of a catch-all concept. Much of its appeal lay in its seemingly comprehensive scope, but the explanatory formula itself rested on some notably ill-defined terms. Moreover, in emphasizing the role of external factors, advocates of the dependency thesis were obliged to adopt the view that indigenous societies had only a limited ability to shape their own history. This meant, in turn, that they were presented as victims rather than as agents.

As these difficulties appeared, the dependency thesis was overtaken and absorbed by a more thoroughgoing and—so it was claimed—more authentic radicialism that derived directly from Marx.[24] For a decade from about the mid-1970s Marxist influences created a new academic frontier for students of imperialism and Empire. The emphasis on economic forces was retained but relocated. Instead of concentrating on the 'sphere of exchange', historians shifted their interests to production. This move made it possible, in principle, to specify the terms of the analysis more closely and to harmonize it with new research on indigenous societies, thus overcoming two of the most troublesome weaknesses of the dependency thesis. Specification took the form of an examination of modes of production and relations of production. Once the resulting structures had been revealed, their trajectories could be traced by tracking the emergence of social classes and by identifying the ensuing

[24] Samir Amin was one of several widely influential commentators who sought to apply Marxist economics to the Third World at this time. See, for example, *Marxist Theory and Contemporary Capitalism*, 2 vols. (London, 1974).

'contradictions' that their antagonism promoted. This new wave of enthusiasm not only carried historians further inland away from the connection formed by external trade, but also prompted them to plumb the depths of indigenous societies. The result was a new 'history from below' that extended the study of *The Making of the English Working Class* abroad,[25] and gave a welcome prominence to social history. Eagle-eyed investigators sought to pinpoint the appearance of social classes in the pre-colonial era; a flurry of fresh research carried the subject forward to the period of colonial rule, when wage-earners and proletarians could be found in greater abundance and therefore with more confidence. A significant variation on this theme drew on the teachings of Chairman Mao to identify the rural component of the forthcoming revolution. Backing proletarians *and* peasants was more than an each-way bet: it was a certainty.

These powerful insights succumbed, in turn, to their own 'internal contradictions' and 'inner logic'.[26] Modes of production multiplied like rabbits in the spring: to Marx's Asiatic mode was added an African mode of production and numerous subsidiaries, including slave, cattle, and lineage modes of production; Indianists contributed a generic colonial mode of production, which also had its branch offices.[27] Theological disputes—a reliable index of increasing theoretical difficulties—multiplied. There was a continuing wrangle between dependency theorists and Marxists, a dispute between Marxist-Leninists and Maoists about who carried the flame of truth, and further debates (which were strictly for the cognoscenti) about the relative merits of early and late Marx, and of historical and structural Marxism. These formidable problems were complicated by the fact that few scholars in the United States had received any formal training in Marxist thought, the land of the free having gone some way towards proscribing communist influences.[28] Accordingly, several of the main sources of inspiration and information came from outside the United States, and especially from France, which was the principal custodian of left-wing thinking in the West. The work of French intellectuals reached the Anglo-Saxon world not only in translation but also severed from the socio-cultural setting that alone made it fully comprehensible.[29] None of this

[25] E. P. Thompson's celebrated study (London, 1963).

[26] A valuable assessment is Anthony Brewer, *Marxist Theories of Imperialism*, 2nd edn. (London, 1990).

[27] Two rather different surveys of the literature are David Seddon, ed., *Relations of Production: Marxist Approaches to Economic Anthropology* (London, 1978), and John G. Taylor, *From Modernisation to Modes of Production* (London, 1979). See also Stephen P. Dunn, *The Fall and Rise of the Asiatic Mode of Production* (London, 1982), and the still optimistic forecast offered on p. 124.

[28] There was, of course, an American radical tradition, on which see the fine study by John P. Diggins, *The Rise and Fall of the American Left*, 2nd edn. (New York, 1992).

[29] The best introduction (in English) is Tony Judt, *Marxism and the French Left: Studies in Labour and Politics in France, 1830–1891* (Oxford, 1981) and *Past Imperfect: French Intellectuals, 1944–1956* (Berkeley, 1992).

halted the operation of market principles in the distribution of knowledge. Demand created its own supply: theoreticians such as Althusser and Poulantzas (whose work was difficult in any language), and the clutch of anthropologists headed by Godelier, Meillassoux, Terray, and Rey, were names to conjure with and became mandatory citations, backed by Marx and Engels, in the scholarly work of the time.[30]

The increasing complexity of Marxist and *marxisant* doctrine caused it to crumble before the Berlin Wall collapsed in 1989, though it was only then that the proletarians, peasants, and bandits who had roamed the pages of learned journals since the mid-1970s packed their tents and silently stole away. The multiplicity of modes of production became confusing and ultimately self-defeating: if every investigation turned up a mode of production, the result was a lengthening list of particular cases rather than a neat taxonomy of pre-industrial societies. Not for the first time, concepts devised in the West broke on rocks exposed by the jagged diversity of the rest of the world. Similarly, the relentless emphasis on conflict presupposed a greater degree of class solidarity than, in the end, could be found—except by defining terms such as 'peasant' so broadly as to include the greater part of the population, in which case the analysis produced not a solution but a tautology. Accordingly, it became apparent that the reaction against the consensual model of 'traditional' societies espoused by modernization theorists and structural-functionalists had gone too far. In casting about for alternative lines of enquiry that were consistent with one of the approved brands of Marxism, scholars found themselves in an impasse: the state was a superstructure; culture, a heady opium when smoked, nevertheless remained an epiphenomenon. Modes might indeed be fashions, but it was still unclear as to what was to take their place.

During this momentary hiatus the survivors of shipwrecked nostrums began to swim towards the only raft in sight. This was the time when the influence of the *Annales* school, and of its greatest representative, Fernand Braudel, sprang to prominence in the Anglo-Saxon world.[31] The *annalistes* gave due weight to capitalist forces, but did not allow their analysis to be subordinated to a class-based dialectic or to be driven by iron laws of capital accumulation. Their distinction between underlying, long-term forces and surface events was attractive because it held out the prospect of identifying determinants that were not themselves deterministic, and of acknowledging voluntarism without conceding too much to chance, contingency, or extreme individualism. Man made his own history, but he did not make it exactly as he pleased. There was even a place for women too. Consonant with the French academic tradition, the *annalistes* linked history with

[30] Guides include Bob Jessop, *Nicos Poulantzas: Marxist Theory and Political Sociology* (London, 1985), and Steven B. Smith, *Reading Althusser: An Essay in Structural Marxism* (Ithaca, NY, 1984). On the French anthropologists see Seddon, *Relations of Production.*

[31] Traian Stoianovich, *French Historical Method: The Annales School* (London, 1976).

demography, geography, and the law; belatedly, the profession staffed predominantly by men began to recognize, through population studies and social history, the 50 per cent of the human race that belonged to the opposite gender.[32] Opening these new avenues of historical enquiry enabled elements of the radical tradition to be re-routed after they had reached the impassable cul-de-sac formed by Marxist attempts to encompass the Third World.

The popularity of the *annalistes* was also closely related to events in the wider world beyond academe. Interest in gender studies (first known as women's studies) reflected the progress and continuing aspirations of the liberation movement from the 1960s, and was, of course, much stronger in the West than elsewhere. Interest in the environment, ecology, and conservation similarly expressed Western anxieties about the adverse consequences of economic development, though in this case it also reflected a growing concern with demographic issues, drought, and desertification in parts of the Third World. The result was the appearance of studies of climate, disease, and population which began in the 1970s (when they ran parallel to Marxist enquiries), and increased in prominence in the 1980s, as the Marxist inspiration began to flag.[33]

The *annalistes* added an important new dimension to historical studies, but their approach lacked predictive power. Modernization theorists, the dependency school, and the Marxists were compelling because they offered a programme for the future: the *annalistes* aspired merely to understand the past. When Marxism hit the wall in 1989 a huge gap was opened up between descriptive and normative possibilities. The dilemma was acute; the urgency was pressing. Already there was loose talk about the 'end of ideology' and its associate, the 'end of history'. The oppressed needed not just a new voice but new hope. Unless the call was answered, the trumpets would sound a discordant note: that of capitalist triumphalism. Unbridled market forces would run rampant; the law of the jungle would operate; the strong would continue to prevail over the weak.

To the extent that the call was answered, it took the form of post-modernism, which has been the most important single new influence on Imperial history during the past decade.[34] It would be easy to devote considerable space to this school of thought because it is topical and much discussed. The brevity of the assessment offered here is not intended to diminish the significance of post-modernism but to keep it in proportion: so far at least, it has been predominant for about the

[32] Guides to the literature include Margaret Strobel, *European Women and the Second British Empire* (Bloomington, Ind., 1991) and *Gender, Sex and Empire* (Washington, 1993).

[33] The trend is well represented in the titles of articles published in specialist journals, such as the *Journal of African History* and *Modern Asian Studies* during this period.

[34] See the more extended discussion in chap. by D. A. Washbrook.

same length of time as its predecessors, some of which are now forgotten, and its influence has extended across a broadly similar range of disciplines.

Post-modernists define themselves with reference to modernism, which in this context refers to forms of rational and scientific enquiry that are said to characterize Western views of the world since the Enlightenment. The basic argument, put here in the most summary form, is that these views, while purporting to be objective (and bolstered by impressive footnotes), have in reality been prejudicial to the societies they purport to describe. Under the guise of scholarship, the dominant West has produced derogatory stereotypes of other, typically subordinated, societies. These images—or 'representations', in the language of the day—have been embedded by repetition and are now taken as facts—or at least as honorary facts. Their importance lies not just in the past but in the foundations they have laid for contemporary attitudes and policies affecting other ethnic groups and minorities. The task (or 'project') of engaged scholarship is to penetrate (or 'deconstruct') Western texts so that false images of non-Western societies can be unmasked and new truths revealed, especially by enabling the voice of the oppressed to be heard above the noise created by alien intermediaries and translators. The post-modern world, which has given a particular cast to post-colonial studies, is one that will eventually be cleansed of the errors of modernity.

While the political implications of this programme are neither as manifest nor as policy-oriented as those associated with modernization theory, the dependency thesis, and Marxism, they clearly reflect present discontents and also carry a message for those seeking to remedy them. This claim can be understood by considering the combination of internal and external influences that has brought post-modernism to prominence. Intellectually, as we have seen, the demise of Marxism left a vacancy for utopian thought. The economic basis of opposition to capitalism had slid into the sea; a political substitute did not lie readily to hand. The lifeline was provided by the epiphenomenon that had been noted but neglected by Marxist thought: culture. Continuity with the radical tradition was provided by the work of the Italian communist Antonio Gramsci, whose concept of 'ideas as a material force' and related notion of moral hegemony provided authorization for the new emphasis.[35] Other more or less associated streams of thought flowed in the same direction: Edward W. Said's celebrated study, *Orientalism*, revealed the prejudice that lay behind scholarship;[36] Michel Foucault's stress on modes of discourse turned attention to construction of texts and to knowledge as a form of oppression.[37] These intellectual

[35] See Paul Ransome, *Antonio Gramsci: A New Introduction* (London, 1992).

[36] Edward W. Said, *Orientalism* (New York, 1978).

[37] J. G. Merquior, *Foucault*, 2nd edn. (London, 1991), and A. W. McHoul and Wendy Grace, *A Foucault Primer: Discourse, Power and the Subject* (London, 1993). Some recent historical examples are referred to in A. G. Hopkins, *The Future of the Imperial Past* (Cambridge, 1997).

trends were spurred on by a growing concern with developments in what was once referred to, confidently, as the real world. Questions of identity attracted increasing attention as political structures fractured in former colonial states, including those released from the Soviet Union, and as minority rights became a major issue among many of the survivors, especially in the United States but also in Canada, Australia, and New Zealand, where the claims of First Nations (those present before the arrival of white settlers) became increasingly vociferous.[38] If false images could be expunged, underprivileged groups could begin to believe in themselves and seek justice with greater confidence.

The effect of post-modernist influences on Imperial history is well known, but it should nevertheless be recorded in case it slips from future minds, as many earlier influences have been lost to those of the present. The principal outcome has been to elevate cultural history to be the pre-eminent branch of the subject, rising above even social history and displacing older and seemingly dated specializations in political and economic history.[39] Perhaps the most notable feature of this development, in terms of the volume of output, has been the mass conversion of newcomers from literary studies.[40] Re-examinations of established novelists, from Austen to Conrad, exposed their colonialist assumptions; a fresh trawl of explorers, missionaries, and anthropologists revealed the racial prejudice that underlay claims to objectivity. Historians themselves turned increasingly to studies of education, science, and propaganda, and showed how symbols of dominance were enshrined in sport, art, architecture, and museums. Flora and fauna were brought under control by conservation and hunting; in scaling the heights, mountaineers represented the peak of Western dominance.[41] When the summit of Everest was reached in 1953, it was Hillary,

[38] There is now a considerable (and still rapidly expanding) literature on the history of the Maori, the Aborigines, the Canadian Indians, and the Inuit that is beginning to transform conventional approaches to the history of what used to be called the 'white' Empire.

[39] It is important to note that, while post-modernism extended cultural history, it did not create it. Among the alternative sources of inspiration particular credit should be given to Professor John M. MacKenzie and to the excellent series Studies in Imperialism published under his editorial direction by Manchester University Press.

[40] Gayatri Chakravorty Spivak symbolizes the general eminence now accorded to literary critics by historians. Her own work, which is strongly influenced by the French philosopher-critic Jacques Derrida, can now be approached via Donna Landry and Gerald MacLean, eds., *The Spivak Reader* (London, 1996). The editors' contribution bears out the truth of their opening sentence, which states: 'If you have been reading Spivak, you will know that writing an introduction to her work is no easy task.'

[41] Among many possible examples see John M. MacKenzie, *The Empire of Nature: Hunting, Conservation and British Imperialism* (Manchester, 1988), and Peter Hansen, 'Vertical Boundaries, National Identities: British Mountaineering on the Frontiers of Europe and the Empire, 1868–1914', *Journal of Imperial and Commonwealth History*, XXIV (1996), pp. 48–71.

the New Zealander and Greater Briton, who led the way, and Tenzing, his Sherpa subordinate, who followed.[42]

Post-modernism, like its predecessors, has helped to open up new lines of enquiry and to inspire work of considerable merit. Like its predecessors, it has also beguiled unwary travellers by promising more than it can deliver. Its fundamental premise, modernism, is itself a caricature that fails to reproduce accurately the voice (or rather voices) of the Western world. Post-modernism champions the underprivileged, but its methodology of emancipation merely pits one set of European intellectuals against another.[43] In doing so, moreover, its exponents are inclined to read into texts rather than out of them, and to suppose that, in discovering racism, they are contributing more to knowledge than they are to their own awareness of long-established findings. Post-modernism seeks to liberate the oppressed, but it has little to say about politics and nothing at all to say about economics. It is hard to imagine that such a pronounced bias can remain uncorrected should political troubles and economic depression return to the Western world. Indeed, it is even possible that the whole approach may be seen, at a future date, to be an indulgence of affluence. Meanwhile, post-modernism, like the previous schools of thought surveyed here, advertises its originality by promoting a distinctive cult of the obscure that first invents terms of art and then protects their uncertain meaning with inverted commas. The emperor's clothes are always edged with high-quality embroidery.

By focusing on previous scholarship, historiographical surveys can easily convey the impression that mature subjects like Imperial history have been studied so well and for so long that nothing new can be envisaged beyond the latest fashion, whatever that may be. Evidently, if we did not believe that the latest was also the best, we would not adopt it. Yet the 'lessons' of history, or more precisely of historiography, show that the most recent approach is invariably updated in ways that are considered to be even better. It is not the purpose of this short chapter to produce a new programme of research for the next generation of historians—nor is it within the capacity of the author to do so. However, since this chapter has made

[42] The symbolism of this episode is discussed by Gordon P. Stewart, 'Tenzing's Two Wrist Watches: The Conquest of Everest and Late Imperial Culture in Britain, 1921–1953', *Past and Present*, CXLIX (1995), pp. 170–97, and in the ensuing debate with Peter H. Hanson in *Past and Present*, CLVII (1997), pp. 159–90.

[43] In seeking to make contact with the underprivileged, post-modernists such as Spivak have championed the school of Subaltern Studies headed by Ranajit Guha. This group of Indianists has indeed made a valuable contribution to non-élite history, but it is itself an extension of a well-known and long-established endeavour—that of writing history 'from below'. The fact that Subalterns are now being sighted by historians in many other parts of the world seems to be a tribute to the power of words rather than to the power of insight.

a case for keeping an open mind, no matter how persuasive and all-encompassing the latest trend appears to be, there is also an obligation to show how it might be filled in future.

The first step to be taken is to recognize that the greater part of the historiography of imperialism since the nineteenth century derives from the presence of Empire, and consists of a more or less scholarly commentary on its rise, management, and decline. Today, fifty years after India achieved independence, there is reason to doubt the wisdom of carrying the battles of yesteryear into the new century. Values will always enter into the study of history, both to inspire and to delude, but the one hundred years' war between left and right was fought to attack and defend an Empire that no longer exists. The fact that we now inhabit a post-Imperial world makes it necessary to consider new ways of looking at the Imperial past.

Two large possibilities, both manifestations of the emerging post-Imperial order, can be suggested here by way of illustration.[44] The first concerns the uncertainty surrounding the future of Western political institutions—at home and abroad. The nation state, once thought to be the natural successor to Empire, now appears to be an unreliable and possibly even an inappropriate vehicle for delivering political stability and economic progress. The post-Imperial era has seen the disintegration of new states, from Yugoslavia to Rwanda, and has exposed the fragility of many of the survivors—including mature states like Britain, where devolution is not only on the agenda but also becoming a reality. Even the world's remaining superpower, and largest ex-colony, the United States faces a problematic future, being caught between orthodox assimilationist assumptions and the emerging reality of a multicultural society that exhibits centrifugal tendencies. The second issue to compel attention is the continuing problem of world economic development and its relationship to the forces now known as 'globalism'. Current discussion of this question focuses on the extent to which the world is becoming a 'global village' united by transnational economic forces and by a common set of values—the future 'global civil society'—and how far existing institutions are being undermined by problems, such as pollution, that are beyond their control, by new regional economic groupings, and by the relentless and seemingly rootless expansion of international finance, which offers development for some and instability for all—including those it bypasses.

Consideration of these issues ought to prompt some fresh thoughts about the history of the Empire. The continuities with the present are evident: the British Empire operated at levels that were primarily infra-national and supra-national;

[44] The thoughts that follow are drawn from the more extended argument in A. G. Hopkins, 'Back to the Future: From National History to Imperial History, *Past and Present*, CLXIV (Aug. 1999).

as we have seen, the most striking problems of the post-Imperial world fall into the same categories. The Empire was a multi-ethnic conglomerate that straddled different peoples, eliminating some but preserving and even reinforcing others. It reshaped old states and founded new ones, but only rarely created viable nations. Even the Greater Britons in Canada, Australia, and New Zealand remain unsure of their identities, despite long experience of increasing degrees of independence. The British Empire also inaugurated the first age of globalism by penetrating and integrating other parts of the world far more effectively than any of its predecessors had been able to do. This outcome was the result of a comprehensive development plan, the first of its kind, involving the export of political institutions, the growth of multilateral trade connections based on international specialization, and the spread of cultural influences, notably the English language, gentlemanly values, and Christianity.[45]

Conversely, by rethinking Imperial history it becomes possible to illuminate large problems in the post-Imperial era that have yet to be connected to their antecedents. It is at this juncture that the contrasts with the Imperial past come to the fore. The expansion of Empire was bound up with the creation of the nation state at home. Crossing the frontiers of others promoted a sense of 'Britishness' and strengthened social and political institutions that helped to unite the kingdom. Similarly, the first age of globalism expressed and reinforced an emerging British economy; British liberalism and free trade shaped the 'rules of the game' governing the international economy; the English language was a means of promoting British interests. The legacy of Empire, however, was a world of fragile states, not sturdy nations, and it has permitted (where it has not encouraged) the assertion of provincialism and sub-national ethnicities. The new globalism has reinforced these loyalties by revealing the weakness of the nation state in the face of transnational forces, and by promoting alternative regional units, such as the European Union and the North American Free Trade Agreement. Today the global economy is multi-centred, even rootless. The English language, like so much else, has passed out of British control and has become the medium of a cosmopolitan world.

The research possibilities arising from these issues are vast and enticing. They encompass development issues but extend beyond them to include the revival of constitutional history, the most neglected sub-branch of the subject, the reconsideration of the economic ingredients of state-building and sovereignty, and the incorporation of recent work in cultural history. The aim here must surely be, not to pit these specialisms against one another in pursuit of sectional supremacy, but

[45] This argument is developed in Cain and Hopkins, *British Imperialism: Innovation and Expansion, 1688–1914*.

to seek to integrate them without also slipping into commonplace claims about historical truth being an unspecified mixture of a complex totality. The comparison and contrast with the present also suggest ways of effecting an overdue junction between metropolitan and overseas history, and of overcoming the orthodoxy that divides the subject into separate centuries, each patrolled by distinct groups of specialists. Finally, the Imperial perspective reveals the limitations of studying the national epic in any century without giving appropriate weight to the infra-national and supra-national forces that shaped its achievements and determined their extent. It is at this point, in the post-Imperial era, that the importance and relevance of a revitalized history of the Empire becomes apparent. Looking ahead to the twenty-first century, it seems reasonable to predict that Imperial history has a future and not just a past.

Select Bibliography

David Becker, Jeff Frieden, Sayre P. Schatz, and Richard Sklar, *Postimperialism* (London, 1987).

Anthony Brewer, *Marxist Theories of Imperialism*, 2nd edn. (London, 1990).

Harold Brookfield, *Interdependent Development* (London, 1975).

John P. Diggins, *The Rise and Fall of the American Left*, 2nd edn. (New York, 1992).

P. C. Emmer and H. L. Wesseling, eds., *Reappraisals in Overseas History* (Leiden, 1979).

Christopher Fyfe, ed., *African Studies Since 1945: A Tribute to Basil Davidson* (London, 1976).

A. G. Hopkins, *The Future of the Imperial Past* (Cambridge, 1997).

Colin Leys, *The Rise and Fall of Development Theory* (London, 1996).

John M. MacKenzie, *Orientalism: History, Theory and the Arts* (Manchester, 1995).

Traian Stoianovich, *French Historical Method: The Annales School* (London, 1976).

41

The Future of Imperial History

ROBIN W. WINKS

The study of the British Empire, whether by methods of the historian, anthropologist, economist, or another, is embedded in an ever-changing culture, largely but not exclusively academic, and trends and expectations in the field naturally reflect the larger environment. There is no point in the historiography of the British Empire at which development differed in any sustained and significant way from general trends in the development of historical studies broadly, though of course specific lines of inquiry also reflected the more nation-, class- or time-specific cultures from which they came. Nationalism played the most important role in the selection of subjects for study, whether in recently former colonies or in Imperial dependencies long self-governing. The degree to which nationalism influenced conclusions, interpretations, or the selection of evidence differed, in part because of cultural assumptions about what history is or the role of the historian should be, and also (amongst many factors) because of the presumed urgency and relevance to current social and economic problems to be found in the scholar's conclusions. It has ever been thus, and there is nothing fresh or startling in the admission that the development of historical studies will reflect—however much the professional historian may or may not resist the presentist pressures of the public, of politics, or of the market-place—the state of the society that, to varying degrees, sustains those studies.

As Wm. Roger Louis makes clear in his Introduction to this volume, the historiographical revolution of the 1960s, with which he concludes his survey, was a product of the times. The work of the scholars who shaped that revolution was, in part, a response to the dislocations of the Second World War, altered power relationships, and the unleashing of those forces that created the cold war or to which the cold war was itself a response. The civil rights movement obviously influenced the study of slavery or of state-supported oppression, just as the organizing principles associated with the post-war development of area studies grew in part from a perception of the world as divided into operational sectors by Second World War intelligence agencies and the US State Department. Louis has brought this story to the 1960s; A. G. Hopkins has looked specifically at development; here I seek to point towards the future.

Much that was once viewed as Imperial history became the history of a national identity: while history as written in colonial North America was an important contribution to an understanding of the British (and French) Empire, some of that work is now seen as 'American colonial' rather than 'British Imperial' history. Books that would have been discussed as significant to the history of the Empire in, say, 1960, would by the 1990s be reclassified as Canadian or Australian or African history, and many of those books have not appeared in the chapters in this volume. History is the telling of a story, or was before the cliometricians rose to prominence, and the story told was generally meant to engender pride and to explain why things are as they are—and to show that they ought either to be different or precisely as they had become.

We can scarcely be surprised, therefore, to find that the history of the British Empire reflects the changes in the years since the Second World War. Up to that time British scholars had often taken up academic posts in the Dominions or colonies, and the first professor of history at virtually every new post-war colonial university was usually an expatriate scholar. The second or third holder of the chair, however, was usually a scholar from the colony itself, trained in Britain and returning 'home' to launch histories of the Empire, and of the colony itself, from what began to be called 'the periphery'. This had the natural effect of fragmenting the study of Empire. Studies of national reconciliation vied with studies of decolonization and separation, with the latter generally in the ascendancy. With more and more former colonials (including Americans) trained in British universities and, from the 1960s on, more and more British scholars taking positions in the United States, the impact of these cultures upon one another intensified, ultimately to the growing weight of American methodologies in Britain. By the 1990s the social and political desire for diversity of views in the United States, the centripetal tendencies of the modern state, especially after the 'end' of the cold war, and the deeply felt resurgence of more focused identities in 'modern Britain' changed the language of historical debate. Perhaps there never had been a *British* Empire after all? Or perhaps Britain existed only at the water's edge?

The rise of area studies, at first in the United States and then in Britain, seemed to mark a decline in Imperial studies by the mid-1960s, and in 1966 this writer called for new works of syntheses on the history of Empire.[1] This call has been met in abundance; and yet there is no agreement on such basic questions as: what was the prime engine behind the imperialist thrust? Did the Empire oil the wheels of the industrial revolution? What is the balance sheet on Empire? This in spite of

[1] In *Historiography of the British Empire-Commonwealth: Trends, Interpretations, and Resources* (Durham, NC). See also 'Problem Child of British History: The British-Empire Commonwealth', in Richard Schlatter, ed., *Recent Views of British History: Essays on Historical Writing Since 1966* (New Brunswick, NJ, 1984), pp. 451–92.

much work on the economics of Imperial decline, or the publication of such key books as Lance E. Davis and Robert A. Huttenback's *Mammon and the Pursuit of Empire: The Political Economy of British Imperialism, 1860–1912* (New York, 1986) and a wide range of area-specific books and articles.[2]

In the 1960s, in part in resistance to area studies, there was a notable trend towards embedding the history of the British Empire, and of the Commonwealth (which many scholars viewed as a species of decolonization), into the comparative history of imperialism. Comparative history enjoyed something of a vogue in the United States, as American scholars sought to break away from the 'exceptionalist' interpretations which had taken American historiography out of the Western mainstream, and it was inevitable that some students of American imperialism (especially as war in Vietnam escalated) would seek to compare their insights with those of British and Continental scholars. While much that passed for comparative history proved, upon examination, to consist of parallel case studies of annexation, economic exploitation, or overseas settlement, some was genuinely comparative in drawing conclusions that could not have been reached in another context.

The search for areas of useful comparison led, for example, to a substantial growth in studies of slavery. This topic had always encompassed three areas of study: the slave trade; variants within slave systems in specific colonies; and the movement to abolish first the trade and then slavery itself. All three subjects invited comparisons with the history of the United States in particular. It became increasingly apparent that the history of slavery shared, in many ways, the problems of intellectual rather than institutional history. Increasingly, publications shifted from questions about how slave systems worked to enquiries concerning slavery's profitability, the nature of competing sources of labour supply, the problems of economies which required predictive capacity over that supply, and studies of societies which were not slave-owning.[3] Often the effect of these showed the gap between Marxist and non-Marxist interpretations of history, and revealed ever more clearly that questions about profitability and alternative labour systems were, at base, questions in intellectual history, since prevailing opinions of what constituted sufficient profit, just price, or available options were embedded in value systems. More recently, and to excellent effect, attention has shifted from slave systems to the slaves themselves, to the slave family and to their forms of resistance.

Studies of slavery have revealed more clearly than any other cluster of literature the major trends in the field, notably the impact of current political and social

[2] See Vol. III, chap. by Avner Offer and Vol. IV, chap. by D. K. Fieldhouse.

[3] See chap. by Gad Heuman in this volume and see chaps. in Vol. III on this issue.

controversies on the researcher's choice of subject; the need to incorporate the findings and sometimes the methodologies of anthropology, when much of the evidence is inaccessible to traditional historical methods; and the infiltration of new language and new debates based on that language, especially since the publication of Edward W. Said's *Orientalism* (New York) in 1978. Another clear change is towards studies of modes of cultural perception, of the making of stereotypes and their impact upon societies.

Intellectual history is notoriously difficult to define, and perhaps its dimensions within British Imperial studies are best indicated by an indicative census. Five works were especially influential prior to the publication of *Orientalism.* At the highest level of generalization was Henri Baudet's *Paradise on Earth: Some Thoughts on European Images of Non-European Man* (New Haven, 1965). Seldom cited, one discovers this lovely little book lurking in the hedgerows of much scholarship-by-non-attribution. Pushing in the same direction more blatantly, Frantz Fanon's *The Wretched of the Earth* (Paris, 1961; English translation, New York, 1965), with the imprimatur of Jean-Paul Sartre, and O. Mannoni's *Prospero and Caliban: The Psychology of Colonization* (Paris, 1950; English translation, London, 1956) were standard fare for generations of French, British, and American undergraduates. The great service of these two books was to draw attention to the psychological-intellectual problems of understanding the colonial experience from within, from 'below'. Their disservice was to enhance two counter-prevailing stereotypes: if read carelessly, both could be taken as saying that all Western Europeans and Americans were imperialists and all non-whites were victims, thus adding in subtle ways to the notion that indigenous societies had few dynamics of their own other than the dynamics of response and counter-response. Read with care, however, both books showed that Western powers also were victimized by the process of colonialism; but such a message still left many readers with the conclusion that Imperial history was a receptacle for grievance-collecting, and that the ill powerfully outweighed the good. 'Resistance studies', most closely identified with Terence O. Ranger, were a natural response to this thrust, demonstrating clearly the vitality and complexity of indigenous dynamics.[4]

Counter to these works there also arose a literature that found the British Empire, in particular, more easily open to honourable defence than any other. Not so much a defence of empire, as a wry examination of the nostalgia with which we covet an ordered world, James Morris's trilogy, begun with *Pax Britannica: The Climax of Empire* (London, 1968), was rich in anecdote and

[4] See in particular his *Revolt in Southern Rhodesia, 1896–97: A Study in African Resistance* (Evanston, Ill., 1967), on the Ndebele insurrection, *African Voice in Southern Rhodesia, 1898–1930* (London, 1970), and *Peasant Consciousness and Guerilla War in Zimbabwe: A Comparative Study* (London, 1985).

insight. With the addition of *Heaven's Command: An Imperial Progress* (London, 1973) and *Farewell the Trumpets: An Imperial Retreat* (London, 1978), Morris's impressionistic evocation was widely popular. Coming at a time when many younger British scholars appeared to be writing from a sense of shame—and collective shame is no better tool for analysis than assumptions of collective guilt or collective pride—Morris's expansive and beautifully written series of set pieces was, like Fanon and Mannoni, a necessary corrective.

Another approach to intellectual history is through biography. While several Proconsuls of Empire have received new biographical treatment, the happiest development is the essay-length enquiry into figures who illumine new facets of 'the vision of empires'. A. P. Thornton, long one of the most productive students of British imperialism, perhaps did his best service for the cause in a work ostensibly about Britain herself, *The Imperial Idea and its Enemies: A Study in British Power* (London, 1959), a contribution to the then popular debate over 'deference' which, to Imperial historians, has seemed oddly sterile when the Imperial dimension had been lacking. Bernard Semmel's provocative chapters in *Imperialism and Social Reform: English Social-Imperial Thought, 1985–1914* (Cambridge, Mass., 1960) may be said to have launched the sub-genre, with chapters on Chamberlain, Benjamin Kidd, Karl Pearson, William Cunningham, Sir William Ashley, and Sir Halford Mackinder, among others. As more collections of private papers were moved into libraries and archives—especially to Rhodes House, Oxford—postgraduate students were drawn to them for dissertations and articles. There was a substantial increase in the number of biographies, and many major figures were revisited in the light of new theories (including a short but intense vogue for psycho-history) as well as new sources. This was not entirely to the good: a study initiated merely because a body of inert paper exists and may be explored is not invariably enlightening. Still, studies of key figures—Curzon, Gordon, Hailey, Mountbatten, Younghusband, and dozens, indeed hundreds, more—provided rich new insights, their lives used to weave threads through the general Imperial fabric. Perhaps even more important were studies of leaders in the former dependencies. At first hagiographic, then at times critical, these studies have often enriched our understanding of the interplay of forces. One thinks of the work of Judith M. Brown in her four studies of Gandhi, particularly *Gandhi: Prisoner of Hope* (New Haven, 1989), and of Ayesha Jalal's *The Sole Spokesman: Jinnah, the Muslim League, and the Demand for Pakistan* (Cambridge, 1985).

As Hazlitt knew, literature and intellectual history bisect, especially so when one seeks to understand how generations at home came to receive their conventional wisdom about their Empire abroad. Two approaches dominated until the 1980s: the one, straightforward examinations of how 'serious' authors (novelists, poets, and scholars) dealt with non-Western cultures; the other, social-psychological inquiries—much influenced by Philippe Ariés's *Centuries of Childhood* (Paris, 1960; English translation, London, 1962) and contributors to the *Annales* school—into how children's fiction of empire gave rise to attitudes that support imperial expansion. These kinds of inquiry may be said to have been launched by a single book, Alan Sandison's *The Wheel of Empire: A Study of the Imperial Idea in Some Late Nineteenth and Early Twentieth-Century Fiction* (London, 1967), which included studies on Rider Haggard and John Buchan. Such writers generally remained out of fashion, though, and subsequent investigations tended to parallel the prevalent area-studies approach, focusing on the culture of some specific location. The journey towards such influential works as Sara Suleri's *The Rhetoric of English India* (Chicago, 1992), *Decolonising Fictions* (Sydney, 1993) by Diana Brydon and Helen Tiffin, or cultural studies such as Anne McClintock's *Imperial Leather: Race, Gender, and Sexuality in the Colonial Conquest* (London, 1995) led to an ever-less-accessible vocabulary, behind which lay a range of substantial insights little noted by many historians, repelled, one suspects, by talk of 'hegemonic discourse' and 'representations'.

Among the studies of children's literature there was an odd and somewhat repetitive burst of work on the Boy Scouts (at least six books and many articles within ten years), treating the scouting movement as *The Character Factory*—the primary title of Michael Rosenthal's study of *Baden-Powell and the Origins of the Boy Scout Movement* (New York, 1984)—and exploring how young men were led into believing in patriotism, obedience, and duty to God, country, and the Empire. Studies of 'manliness' easily segued into sports history, a subject of substantial importance which, despite the occasional illuminating book, has yet to receive due recognition.[5] But such work did not enter the mainstream, and there was no development of 'men's studies' to parallel 'women's studies'.

The anthropological thrust into British Imperial history was initially felt in African or Asian studies (and to a lesser extent in work on the Pacific Islands), where Western scholars could not gain access to the indigenous story without the use of oral tradition. A sub-literature developed on the problems of research in Africa in particular; and many historical studies of Fulani, Hausa, or Nandi responses to British rule benefited from the insights of the social sciences, especially anthropology and linguistics. Many historians of Africa, though writing about the interaction between indigenous cultures and the British, insisted that they were *African*, not *Imperial* historians, and this distinction is perhaps clearest in the way that anthropology was used in shaping the study. But anthropologists themselves have been accused of being covert supporters of imperialism, and for

[5] See Vol. IV, chap. by John M. MacKenzie; also J. A. Mangan, *The Games Ethic and Imperialism: Aspects of the Diffusion of an Ideal* (Harmondsworth, 1985).

three decades their work has seemed mired in a series of accusations about the role it has played in increasing dependency relationships. This internecine warfare among anthropologists has driven many historians away from the discipline, so that its impact is less evident in the 1990s than in previous decades, but an example of the vitality and the complexity of the debate for historians can be found in a testy exchange between anthropologists Marshall Sahlins and G. A. Obeyesekere over the use of oral tradition and our understanding of the death of Captain Cook.[6]

Cultural studies, with its blend of literary, anthropological, sociological, and psychological methodologies, also suffered from precisely the compartmentalization of which cultural-studies advocates complained. Foucault, Barthes, Gramsci, Derrida, and Lacan became commonplace names, and their insights informed much that was relevant to an understanding of Imperial issues, but it quickly became apparent that the scholars who drew their inspiration from these writers often knew little hard history and had little stomach for rooting about in archives. To be sure, the reverse remained true, and the more fiercely empirical historians refused to find anything of value in Foucault and company. The result was to give the impression of two bodies of scholarship existing in mutual isolation, yet appealing to the same audience, or professing to do so. Certainly there was a trend back towards asking fact-based questions about what 'actually happened', using conventional, even traditional evidence, and not being embarrassed to pursue what G. M. Young's one clerk said to another clerk. These scholars generally worked from either the metropole or the periphery, seldom from both, although the publications of three individuals in particular sought to demonstrate that such a dichotomy was unworkable. In the 1950s and early 1960s British Imperial historiography had been driven towards the periphery, rejecting the view of Whiggish constitutional and legal historians that history was essentially about the rise of the nation state, and that British Imperial history was about the preparation for national independence. Yet history centred on Cape Town, Lagos, or Singapore proved insufficient in itself to an understanding of either the Empire or its units.[7] Bridging the gap between periphery and metropole, though in quite different ways, the work of D. K. Fieldhouse, Ronald Robinson, and John Gallagher set the agendas for the majority of scholars who labelled themselves Imperial rather than area historians from the 1950s until at least the 1980s.

Fieldhouse focused on 'the business of empire' and never lost sight of the fact that economics—real markets, real needs, real exports and imports—and beliefs

[6] See Marshall David Sahlins, *How 'Natives' Think: About Captain Cook, For Example* (Chicago, 1995), which is, in part, a riposte to Gananath Obeyesekere, *The Apotheosis of James Cook: European Mythmaking in the Pacific* (Princeton, 1992), which attacked Sahlins among others.

[7] See chap. by Wm. Roger Louis.

about the components of economics and business were at the root of Imperial understanding. In a much-quoted article, 'Imperialism: An Historiographical Revision', in the *Economic History Review* in 1961,[8] in a collection of extracts from key quasi-theoreticians of Empire, *The Theory of Capitalist Imperialism* (London, 1967), and subsequently in *Economics and Empire, 1830–1914* (London, 1975), which significantly recast his earlier argument, Fieldhouse laid out an agenda for scholars who were moving back towards the metropolitan centres.[9]

As noted in Wm. Roger Louis's Introduction, Fieldhouse's work followed closely on the widely heralded book by Ronald Robinson and John Gallagher, who with Alice Denny published *Africa and the Victorians* in 1961 (London). The book came in the wake of the most widely quoted article ever published in the *Economic History Review*, an article that launched what may well have been the most influential debate in the field for four decades, 'The Imperialism of Free Trade', to which Fieldhouse's article was in some measure a response. The ensuing debate helped ensure that Imperial history stayed relevant for a range of other fields in which issues of free and fair trade, or of 'collaborators' and 'formal' and 'informal empire', provided explanatory force for change.

The 'official view' from the centre was not, of course, truly centric, for one quickly learned that there was the Treasury view and the Foreign Office view and the Admiralty view. These various centres, shifting in significance as they vied for influence, became the focus of several studies. Nor did the centre end with the bureaucracy, and studies continued to appear on how Imperial questions reverberated in British politics. In particular Bernard Porter, in *Critics of Empire: British Radical Attitudes Towards Colonialism in Africa, 1895–1914* (London, 1968), examined the entire body of radical thought about British colonialism from the Boer War to 1914. His work was an acute analysis of what lay behind the notion of 'Indirect Rule'. He also took on the dogma of 'capitalist imperialism', as did Hugh Stretton in a book too little known, *The Political Sciences: General Principles of Selection in Social Science and History* (London, 1969), which contained one of the most interesting statements on what 'caused' imperialism then written.

One suspects that in future the most influential work will be by scholars who explore common themes comparatively in diverse environments. Certainly, the stimulating and original commentaries and studies in D. A. Low's *Lion Rampant: Essays in the Study of British Imperialism* (London, 1973) have given rise to dozens of books on 'social engineering', political authority, and sequence in the demission of power. Low has worked to equal depth on Africa (largely Buganda) and Asia

[8] XIV (1961), pp. 187–209.

[9] For a not-uncritical appreciation of Fieldhouse's work, see a special issue of essays in his honour in *Journal of Imperial and Commonwealth History*, XXVI (May, 1998).

(largely India), and his edited volume *Soundings in Modern South Asian History* (Berkeley, 1968), and his essays in *Eclipse of Empire: Commonwealth and Decolonisation* (Cambridge, 1990) and *The Egalitarian Moment: Asia and Africa, 1950–1980* (Cambridge, 1996), will resonate for years to come.

Economic questions remain fundamental to an understanding of any empire. Possibly the most influential book on this subject to appear in the 1970s was not, at first glance, about the British Empire at all: A. G. Hopkins's *An Economic History of West Africa* (London, 1973).[10] Seeking a balance between the conventional view at the end of the Second World War—that Europe made African economic growth possible by injecting European technology and substituting a market for a subsistence economy—and the Marxist view that pre-capitalist economies were static until replaced by exploitative capitalism; and also refuting the romantic notion, argued by some African nationalist historians, that pre-colonial West Africa had been expansive and healthy prior to its disruption by Europeans, Hopkins sought to analyse a complex interaction of internal and external forces, achieving for economic history a position akin to that taken by Robinson and Gallagher in political history.

Hopkins would, with P. J. Cain, return to the fray in 1993 with a two-volume study of *British Imperialism* (London), which further defined the contested ground. Their argument, known as the 'gentlemanly concept of capitalism', claims that the British landed aristocracy, with its dislike of trade, was imitated by the rising new wealth in finance, industry, and services, who viewed the world of work as demeaning. This view deeply influenced attitudes towards class, race, labour in the colonies, the colonies themselves, and ultimately the decline of the British Empire. They returned, or sought to return, the analysis of British imperialism to the metropolitan economy, reversing the analysis of Robinson and Gallagher which had found so much significance in the actions (and in particular the instabilities) of the periphery. Equally important, Cain and Hopkins maintained that all forms of the exercise of power, and especially economic power, over others must be included in a study of imperialism, giving added stimulus to those scholars who had developed the concept of 'informal empire'. What will centre the debate in economic history at the end of the century and into the next? Perhaps a brilliantly contentious book such as David S. Landes's *The Wealth and Poverty of Nations*, with its clear invocation of Adam Smith, and its brash subtitle, *Why Some Are So Rich and Some So Poor* (New York, 1998).

The developments sketched here represent a further trend when read collectively: there are now not one (the Imperial) or two (the pro- and anti-Imperial or the metropolitan and peripheral) historiographies, but several overlapping, each

[10] See chap. by A. G. Hopkins.

essential yet distinct. The field is the richer for its several historiographies which break along both the traditional geographical or national planes, and along less traditional planes determined by problems rather than boundaries. The two may meet, as they did in Geoffrey Blainey's *The Tyranny of Distance* (Melbourne, 1966), which interpreted the whole of the Australian experience in terms of location in relation to supply and demand, settlement, and defence, in a manner that was at once enormously attractive and badly flawed (flaws which Blainey took into account in a revised edition in 1982). The title has entered our language, used by people who have little idea what Blainey actually meant by it. Some may argue that little of Blainey remains intact today, and yet, with the American Frederick Jackson Turner, their work forms the necessary starting-point of much debate for younger scholars who may have little idea that they are still engaged in an argument from earlier academic generations.

There are now perhaps fifty academic journals which the historian of Empire ought to keep abreast with; one knows this cannot be done, yet one must try, for this is where the work of the next generation is likely to appear first. The *Journal of Imperial and Commonwealth History*, founded in 1972 under the editorship of Trevor Reese of the Institute of Commonwealth Studies and David Harkness, then at the University of Kent, has greatly enriched all students of Empire. But those students must also give thought to the many geographic-specific journals, often launched in the 1960s, for example, the *Journal of African History* (1960–), the *Journal of Pacific History* (1966–), and *Modern Asian Studies* (1967–), not to mention far more specialized venues. If journals reveal the cutting-edge of a field, then, as library budgets shrink and subscription lists are cut back, one might expect less awareness of where historiographical trends are leading us. This risk is somewhat offset by the realities of the computer age. On-line communications broaden and deepen the flow of knowledge, speed the production of scholarship, and ease the burdens of composition and correction. They also mislead, draw facile minds towards facile questions, make the sifting of vast quantities of data an end in itself, and virtually eliminate the popular reader, further cutting the historian, the teller of stories, off from a lay public.

Literary criticism, colonial discourse theory, and the Subaltern School of Indian scholars have all had their major impact in the last decade and a half, and are dealt with in individual chapters in this volume.[11] In December 1994 the *American Historical Review* devoted the better part of an issue to the relevance outside their point of origin of *Subaltern Studies*, and Gyan Prakash set out for the journal's readers the issues and methods of 'Subaltern Studies as Postcolonial Criticism'. Here the time-lag between initial publication and recognition of relevance was far

[11] See, in particular, chap. by D. A. Washbrook.

briefer than in the case of Robinson and Gallagher's work in the 1950s and 1960s. Six years before, in 1988, Ranajit Guha and Gayatri Chakravorty Spivak had drawn together *Selected Subaltern Studies* (New York) so that students might sample the range of research and argument. Guha's own *Dominance Without Hegemony: History of Power in Colonial India* (Cambridge, Mass., 1997) well illustrates the staying power of subalternity. Read against and with a collection of chapters destined to have substantial impact—Dagmar Engels and Shula Marks's *Contesting Colonial Hegemony: State and Society in Africa and India* (London, 1994)—these works have entered the mainstream and convinced many historians who had initially declined to explore these and similar bodies of literature.[12]

Not the subjects of separate chapters here, but noted *seriatim* throughout by the majority of authors in this volume, are three other developments: women's studies, environmental studies, and aboriginal or indigenous studies.[13] The last draws much of its inspiration from Eric R. Wolf's *Europe and the People Without History* (Berkeley, 1982), written by an anthropologist who wanted to 'discover history'. Defining victims and silent witnesses to the rise of a formal 'European history', Wolf derived some of his insights from the school of Immanuel Wallerstein, the world-systems analyst who detected broad structural explanations by which the expansion of Europe might best be explained. Some historians went so far as to refer to colonial or Imperial historiography as 'the historiography of no history'—this was A. E. Afigbo of Nigeria[14]—though most refocused more traditional categories on to the people with no history to discover that, in fact, they had a great deal of it. Several were into the field ahead of Wolf, whose essential concern was Europe, but perhaps Henry Reynolds's book *The Other Side of the Frontier: An Interpretation of the Aboriginal Response to the Invasion and Settlement of Australia* (Townsville, NSW, 1981) most clearly marked this transition, though limited to Australia. The work of M. P. K. Sorrenson, Judith Binney, and James Belich mark this shift with respect to the Maori in New Zealand.[15]

[12] There have been numerous historiographical articles and extended reviews in the second half of the 1990s that attest to the vitality of the field. Of particular note within their respective areas are Frederick Cooper, 'Conflict and Connection: Rethinking Colonial African History', *American Historical Review*, XCIX (Dec. 1994), pp. 1516–45, and Florencia E. Mallon, 'The Promise and Dilemma of Subaltern Studies: Perspectives from Latin American History', ibid., pp. 1491–515. See also the thoughtful remarks of Dane Kennedy in 'The Imperial Kaleidoscope', *Journal of British Studies*, XXXVII (October, 1998), pp. 460–67.

[13] These issues are considered in a number of chaps. in the chronological volumes—see esp. Vol. I, chap. by Peter Mancall; Vol. II, chaps. by Daniel R. Ritcher and Richard Drayton; Vol. III, chaps. by T. M. McCaskie and Susan Bayly; Vol. IV, chap. by Rosalind O'Hanlon.

[14] In Toyin Falola, ed., *African Historiography: Essays in Honour of Jacob Ade Ajayi* (London, 1993).

[15] See the chap. by James Belich; also Judith Binney, *Redemption Songs: The Life of Te Kooti Arikirangi Te Turuki* (Auckland, 1995).

Oddly, environmental history, a field that was one of the greatest growth areas in American universities in the 1980s and early 1990s, has not sustained that growth and has, as yet, had relatively little impact on Imperial studies in general. Perhaps this is because there is so much else to do in either the Imperial or the environmental framework, or, as some scholars have suggested, because early American dominance in the field has led scholars to conceive of environmental history as a sub-aspect of frontier studies. To many the latter claim seems true, for much environmental history as written in the United States (and especially under the influence of Donald Worster, William Cronon, and Richard White) has tended to be the history of the American West, and though environmental history is a growing field in Canada and Australia in particular, few of the contributions from those sources (with the notable exception of Sir (William) Keith Hancock's *Discovering Monaro: A Study of Man's Impact on His Environment*, Cambridge 1972) have had much impact in Imperial terms.

We have a good beginning, however, in Alfred W. Crosby's *Ecological Imperialism: The Biological Expansion of Europe, 900–1900* (New York, 1986). Tracing the effects of the diffusion of plants, animals, diseases, and environmental thought (or the lack of it) on native flora and fauna, limiting himself largely to North America, Australia, and New Zealand, Crosby may be said to have defined a field. Environmentalists, as distinct from historians, have dealt somewhat roughly with his analysis, which invariably sees the impact of exotic invaders in terms of human disasters and gives relatively little thought to more purely scientific issues, but his work has unquestionably encouraged several environmentally concerned scholars to work on African and Asian subjects that have long been neglected. In 1995 Richard Grove's *Green Imperialism: Colonial Expansion, Tropical Island Edens and the Origins of Environmentalism, 1600–1860* (Cambridge) examined environmental degradation in the tropical world of Empire, and Madhav Gadgil and Ramchandra Guha have written of *The Fissured Land: An Ecological History of India* (Delhi, 1993).

A sub-field of environmental history, the study of the 'management' and exploitation of nature, especially through reserves, and of the way in which the creation of such reserves reflects social and political power, is beginning to appear. John M. MacKenzie has staked out the ground in two studies, *The Empire of Nature: Hunting, Conservation, and British Imperialism* (Manchester, 1988) and *Imperialism and the Natural World* (Manchester, 1990); and, provided that its relatively obscure publication admits of wider impact, *Ecology and Empire: Environmental History of Settler Societies*, edited by Tom Griffiths and Libby Robin (Edinburgh for the Keele University Press, 1997), gives promise of much that will be significant and fresh to come.[16] It is instructive to note that the

[16] MacKenzie contributed 'Empire and the Ecological Apocalypse: The Historiography of the Imperial Environment' to Griffiths and Robin, eds., pp. 215–28.

American journal *Environmental History* (1995–), which when launched was focused largely on American topics, had by 1998 a preponderance of non-American content.

The impact of women's studies on British Imperial history has not yet transformed the broader field, for the debates appear to be taking place in a side arena, as though the issues had been marginalized; but, given its intense interaction with literary theory and to debates about Said's 'Other', and the quantity of work being produced in this area, its influence is bound to grow. Not all of women's history is radical by any means—indeed, Antoinette Burton's *Burdens of History: British Feminists, Indian Women, and Imperial Culture, 1865–1915* (Chapel Hill, NC, 1994) suggests that a 'feminist view' of India need not differ significantly from a 'masculine view', while Benita Perry's earlier *Delusions and Discoveries: Studies on India in the British Imagination, 1880–1930* (London, 1972) does little more than express disillusionment at British women who failed to be in advance of their time. Susan F. Bailey's *Women and the British Empire: An Annotated Guide to Sources* (New York, 1983) helped to set goals, while Helen Callaway's *Gender, Culture, and Empire: European Women in Colonial Nigeria* (Urbana, Ill., 1987) set agendas. Kenneth Ballhatchet's *Race, Sex, and Class Under the Raj: Imperial Attitudes and Policies and Their Critics, 1793–1905* (London, 1980) was among the early books to introduce the 'iron triangle' of ethnicity, gender, and class analysis. In *Empire and Sexuality: The British Experience* (Manchester, 1990), Ronald Hyam explored the sexual practices of the guardians of Empire and framed points for debate with an honesty that was startling to many readers, but his work undoubtedly will give rise to much more. At this point Margaret Strobel is making the running, with her succinct tour of the horizon, *European Women and the Second British Empire* (Bloomington, Ind., 1991), and with Nupur Chaudhuri she has edited *Western Women and Imperialism: Complicity and Resistance* (Bloomington, Ind., 1992); while Mrinalini Sinha appears to have stirred the deepest reactions, in support and attack, in *Colonial Masculinity: The 'Manly Englishman' and the 'Effeminate Bengali' in the Late Nineteenth Century* (Manchester, 1995), which takes on stereotypes of the 'manly Englishman' and the 'effeminate Bengali'. Sinha has validated gender studies in a nuanced set of four case examples which are certain to be influential in overlapping areas of concern—women's history, gender theory, 'image studies', and colonial discourse inquiry—for years to come.

All three of these growing fields have in common the notion of Edward W. Said's 'Other' as a catalyst, for they focus on people who stood outside the mainstream, outside the traditional documentation generated by bureaucracies, companies, and armies, outside the matrix of 'decision-makers'. As the common progenitor, Said remains widely read and, despite less careful and more shrill recent work, most influential. While there have been attacks on his conceptualization of the issues, there have been few constructive responses to it. Only one, John M. MacKenzie's *Orientalism: History, Theory and the Arts* (Manchester, 1995), has as yet swayed the debate for those standing on the sidelines. There is some risk that scholars will conclude that 'the Other', by virtue of that designation, need not be further studied, especially given the current tendency to redirect Imperial history back from the periphery to the metropolitan economy and bureaucracies as exemplified in the work of Cain and Hopkins.

One obvious sign that interest in the British Empire is resurgent is the appearance of broad-survey histories, finding aids, atlases, and dictionaries on the subject. In 1996 Bernard Porter's *The Lion's Share: A Short History of British Imperialism, 1850–1995* (London) reached its third edition and became the most widely used text of Imperial history in the dwindling number of universities that use a text at all. First published in 1975, this lively work has marched forward largely in tune with the changing historiography, and while it is not very friendly to colonial discourse theory and generally accepts Cain and Hopkins as the currently enthroned wisdom, it displays a welcome diversity of interest and breadth of range. The same may be said of A. N. Porter's *European Imperialism, 1860–1914* (London, 1994), which looks to Europe more widely and is considerably more friendly to the Orientalist debate, while opening the doors to a host of subjects he shows to be worthy of more analysis. The appearance in 1996 of Alan Palmer's *Dictionary of the British Empire and Commonwealth* (London) and James S. Olson's *Historical Dictionary of the British Empire*, 2 vols. (Westport, Conn.), almost simultaneously with P. J. Marshall's *Cambridge Illustrated History of the British Empire* (Cambridge), and of A. N. Porter's earlier *Atlas of British Overseas Expansion* (London, 1991), suggests a field reaching out to a broader audience.[17]

Where, then, do we stand now, and which of these or other trends is most likely to continue or to dominate the Imperial debate for the next generation? An empirical historian will fear the worst: that more and more books and articles will

[17] For some years there was no general history of the British Empire in print for use in the classroom, until Bernard Porter's book appeared. Now there are several, including Denis Judd, *Empire: The British Imperial Experience from 1765 to the Present* (London, 1996), and T. O. Lloyd, *The British Empire, 1558–1995*, 2nd edn. (New York, 1996).

There also are good collections of critical commentary on the most influential contributions to debate which clearly reflect anticipated student interest. Just as Wm. Roger Louis edited *Imperialism: The Robinson and Gallagher Controversy* (New York, 1976), Raymond E. Dumett has edited *Gentlemanly Capitalism and British Imperialism: The New Debate on Empire* (London, 1999), and Gilbert M. Joseph, Catherine C. Legrand, and Ricardo D. Salvatore have edited *Close Encounters of Empire: Writing the Cultural History of US–Latin American Relations* (Durham, NC, 1998), which will surely introduce a generation of students to reformulated and more sophisticated dependency theory.

lack a firm foundation in primary sources. A practitioner of cultural studies is less likely to fear an outpouring of new biographies or science-based environmental history (both badly needed, and in fact likely trends among the empiricists), because 'the culture'—any culture—is constantly changing, and the methods of cultural studies are, by their very nature, rooted in those changes. One can hope, however, that in the future each camp will need to read the work of the other, if not for intellectual then at least for practical reasons, as the factors external to the life of the university shrink student enrolments in history, require specialists to teach more broadly, and lead to smaller faculties.

It is an indisputable fact that when the last multi-volume history of the British Empire, the *CHBE* or *Cambridge History*, was completed in 1959 there still was an Empire, though much diminished, and that when the last extensive historiographical survey was attempted, there were still numerous colonies. The fifty-year rule on archival access at the Public Record Office, generally copied by archives throughout the Empire, still prevented researchers from using the primary documentation of the inter-war years, Second World War, or the beginning of the cold war. It is equally indisputable that the Empire is now almost entirely of the past—despite bits and pieces here and there, surely no one would date the end of the Empire later than the transfer of Hong Kong to the People's Republic of China in 1997—and that thirty-year rules in many archives make it possible for historians to write authoritatively on events close to us. These two simple realities have changed the historiographical ground-rules.

The *CHBE*, in its coverage and its omissions, helped to set the agenda for future historians, and despite the transformation of public attitudes towards Empire, especially after the Suez crisis, and the quick and often decisive emergence of nationalist schools of history in the former colonies, some at least of that agenda was pursued. The present publication, the *OHBE* or *Oxford History*, will no doubt have a similar impact in revealing areas of enquiry in need of further exploration and in suggesting new areas for research, though how deep that impact will be will depend on the degree of stability in world affairs, in the former units of Empire, and in higher education. Certainly hundreds of students will quarry from these five volumes subjects for papers, theses, and dissertations. Trends already clearly established are likely to continue, though an innovative new book or article can always give a trend, an adjusted direction, method, or point-of-view. These volumes will become, indeed already are, self-referential with respect to broad themes, as well as specific topics.

In the future, writing about the history of the British Empire is likely to require more collaborative ventures such as this one. Practical realities will promote such efforts. Books based on conferences with thematic focus will increase. There will continue to be good one-volume histories that attempt synthesis, based on an economic perception or a political or social purpose, revealed or unrevealed, and those that already exist will be revised intelligently in the light of new approaches, such as the work of the Subaltern School, or the post-modernist critique of how scholarship has privileged certain vantage-points. Co-operative endeavours will be increasingly necessary: co-operation between libraries and archives, between universities, between publishers, between individual scholars.

There was, between the late fifteenth century and the 1960s, an Imperial revolution fully as transformative as those other revolutions accorded textbook canonization—the industrial, the commercial, the intellectual, the scientific—and this revolution, first explored from a position of pride and from the metropole, then by the 1960s often explored in and from the so-called periphery, sometimes with loathing and anger, sometimes with pride in resistance and reconstruction—will continue to fascinate and demand attention. There was an enormous outpouring of significant, original, and interesting work in the 1970s and 1980s, remarked upon in the many chapters in this volume—at times taking the work of the 1950s and 1960s as a baseline, at times reaching further back, at times launched from a running start with little regard for work that had gone before. The books of those decades, and of the 1990s, will—in conjunction with the myriad influences that always shape scholarship—become the basis for the evolving future of Imperial history.

It is surely safe to make one other prediction. There will be more study of the interaction between the metropole and the periphery, more enquiry into the nature of exploitation, of resistance, and of the development of identities. Some of this work will be objective, 'scholarly', based on sources; some will be didactic, blinkered by secularist or religious perceptions that do not admit to alternative questions, let alone alternative conclusions. Once upon a time historians wrote at length about how Empire followed the growth of trade, about how early settlers traded with 'native peoples'. Yet trade is a two-way street—not necessarily or even often, between people with equal bargaining chips, but two-way still. This trade was not, until relatively recently, studied so much in terms of the economies of those 'native peoples' as in terms of the impact it made on them through disease, firearms, and the dislocation of pre-industrial social and political forms. In the future, though, there will be more studies from the perspective of the 'receiving' society; indeed, we already recognize that both societies in any interchange 'received', and this recognition will further alter our line of sight. There will be more studies of 'popular culture'. Historians in Africa, Asia, and Latin America have already been engaged in this, and where necessary their work will receive wider translation. Multilingual scholarship will increase. Scholars of aboriginal, Maori, and multi-'Other' origins will themselves bring radically different points of view to bear. One would like to think that in time the concept of 'Other' will have only a historiographical utility.

CHRONOLOGY

Year	Scholarship, Education, and Culture	Archives and Documents	Historical Publications
1516	Sir Thomas More, *Utopia*		Peter Martyr, *De Orbe Novo Decades*
1555			Publication of accounts of English voyages to the Guinea coast Richard Eden, *Decades of the Newe World or West India*
1577			John Dee, *General and Rare Memorials . . . of Navigation*
1582			Stephen Parmenius, *De Navigatione*
1584			Richard Hakluyt, *A Particular Discourse*
1588 SPANISH ARMADA DEFEATED			
1588			Thomas Hariot, *A Briefe and True Report of the New Found Land of Virginia*
1589			Hakluyt, *Principal Navigations*
1592	Trinity College, Dublin		
1596			Edmund Spenser, *A View of the Present State of Ireland* Walter Ralegh, *The Discoverie of the Large, Rich and Bewtiful Empire of Guiana* George Chapman, *De Guiana, Carmen Epicum*

Year	Scholarship, Education, and Culture	Archives and Documents	Historical Publications
		1600 ENGLISH EAST INDIA COMPANY CHARTER	
1606			Michael Drayton, *To the Virginia Voyage*
1611	William Shakespeare, *The Tempest*		
1619		Records of Secretaries of State, hitherto kept in Palace of Whitehall, moved to what became known as State Paper Office at Holbein Gate	
1620	Francis Bacon, *Instauratio Magna*		
1625			Samuel Purchas, *Hakluytus Posthumous or Purchas His Pilgrims*
1628			Sir Francis Drake, *The World Encompassed*
		1642 –1647 ENGLISH CIVIL WAR 1652–1674 ERA OF ANGLO-DUTCH WARS	
1659			William Davenant, *The History of Sir Francis Drake*
1662	Royal Society for the Improvement of Natural Knowledge		
		1689 GLORIOUS REVOLUTION (ACCESSION OF WILLIAM III AND MARY)	
1697			William Dampier, *New Voyage Round the World*
1698			William Molyneux, *Case of Ireland*
1701	Society for the Propagation of the Gospel in Foreign Parts		

Year	Scholarship, Education, and Culture	Archives and Documents	Historical Publications
1705			Robert Beverley, *The History and Present State of Virginia*
1726	Jonathan Swift, *Gulliver's Travels*		
1743	American Philosophical Society		
1748			George Anson, *A Voyage Round the World*
1756–1763 SEVEN YEARS WAR ('FRENCH AND INDIAN WAR')			
1759		State Paper Office at Holbein Gate demolished; records dispersed among other buildings in Whitehall	
1769	Appointment of first Historiographer to the East India Company		
1770	Benjamin West painting, *The Death of General Wolfe*		
1771		Appointment of Keeper of East India Company records	
1774			Edward Long, *History of Jamaica*, 3 vols.
1776	Adam Smith, *Wealth of Nations*		Edward Gibbon, *Decline and Fall of the Roman Empire* (to 1788)
	Tom Paine, *Common Sense*		
1775–1783 WAR OF AMERICAN INDEPENDENCE			
1782	Royal Irish Academy		
1784	Asiatic Society of Bengal		
1787	Society for the Abolition of the Slave Trade		

Year	Scholarship, Education, and Culture	Archives and Documents	Historical Publications
1792	Massachusetts Historical Society; publication of first volume of Society's *Collections*		
1789–1815 ERA OF FRENCH REVOLUTION AND NAPOLEONIC WARS			
1795	London Missionary Society		
1802	Wellesley's Government House, Calcutta		
1805	Arthur William Devis painting, *Death of Nelson*		
1809	Historical Society of New York; publication of first volume of Society's *Collections*		
1812–1814 WAR OF 1812			
1815			P. Colquhoun, *Resources of the British Empire*
1823	Royal Asiatic Society of London		
1825		State Paper Commission established to print and publish state papers	
1826	Historical Society of Pennsylvania; publication of first volume of Society's *Publications*		
1828			John Philip, *Researches in South Africa*, 2 vols.
1829			Edward Gibbon Wakefield, *A Letter from Sydney, the Principal Town of Australasia, Together with the Outline of a System of Colonisation*

Year	Scholarship, Education, and Culture	Archives and Documents	Historical Publications
1830	Royal Geographical Society		
1832	The *Chinese Repository Journal*, Canton		
1833 EMANCIPATION OF ALL SLAVES IN BRITISH EMPIRE			
1834		New repository for State Paper Office built near Green Park	George Bancroft, *A History of the United States From the Discovery of the American Continent*, 10 vols. (to 1875)
1837			James Macarthur, *New South Wales: Its Present State and Future Prospects*
1838		Public Records Act authorizes creation of single Public Record Office and transfers responsibility for British public records to Master of the Rolls	
1839 DURHAM REPORT			
1846	Hakluyt Society		
1847	Publication of first volume of Hakluyt Society's *Publications* Asiatic Society of China (Hong Kong), affiliate of Royal Asiatic Society		
1848		Custody of many records in State Paper Office, including Colonial Office records, transferred to Master of the Rolls	

Year	Scholarship, Education, and Culture	Archives and Documents	Historical Publications
1849			Edward Gibbon Wakefield, ed., *A View of the Art of Colonization, with Present Reference to the British Empire* Thomas Babington Macaulay, *History of England*
1851	Great Exhibition at Crystal Palace		
1852	Publication of first volume of *Pennsylvania Archives*		
1854	Authorization for establishment of first Indian universities at Bombay, Calcutta, and Madras	State Paper Office finally absorbed into Public Record Office	
1856		Records moved to new Public Record Office building in Chancery Lane (last records from Green Park, including Colonial Office records, moved to Chancery Lane in 1862)	
1857–1858 INDIAN MUTINY			
1857			David Livingstone, *Missionary Travels and Researches in South Africa* Heinrich Barth, *Travels and Discoveries in North and Central Africa*

Year	Scholarship, Education, and Culture	Archives and Documents	Historical Publications
1858		Unrestricted public access granted to pre-1688 records in Public Record Office East India Company records transferred to new India Office	
1859	*Historische Zeitschrift*		Sir James Emerson Tennent, *Ceylon*, 2 vols. (to 1860)
	Charles Darwin, *On the Origin of Species by Means of Natural Selection*		
1860	Charles Dickens, *Great Expectations*	Publication of first volume of *Calendar of State Papers Colonial since 1574 (America and West Indies* added to succeeding volumes in series)	
1861	Henry Maine, *Ancient Law*	Creation of Government of India Records Committee	
1862		Publication of *Calendar of State Papers Colonial, East Indies, China and Japan*, 5 vols. (to 1892)	
1867	New Zealand Institute		
1868	Royal Colonial Institute, London	Colonial Office Records opened to 1760	C. W. Dilke, *Greater Britain*
1869	University of Otago, New Zealand *Transactions and Proceedings* of New Zealand Institute		

Year	Scholarship, Education, and Culture	Archives and Documents	Historical Publications
1869 OPENING OF SUEZ CANAL			
1870			Isaac Butt, *Home Government for Ireland, Irish Federalism: Its Meaning, its Objects and its Hopes*
1872		Establishment of Canadian Public Archives	
1876	*Revue Historique*		James Fergusson, *History of Indian and Eastern Architecture*
1878	Gilbert and Sullivan, *HMS Pinafore*		
1879	Gilbert and Sullivan, *Pirates of Penzance* Institute of Jamaica		
1880	Establishment of weekly *Bulletin*, radical nationalist publication in New South Wales		
1881			James Anthony Froude, *The English in Ireland in the Eighteenth Century*
1882		Establishment of Archives, Cape Colony, South Africa	
1883	Olive Schreiner, *The Story of an African Farm*		J. R. Seeley, *Expansion of England*
1884		Creation of Registry and Records Department in India Office	Francis Parkman, *Montcalm and Wolfe*, 2 vols.
1885	H. Rider Haggard, *King Solomon's Mines* Gilbert and Sullivan, *The Mikado*		

Year	Scholarship, Education, and Culture	Archives and Documents	Historical Publications
1886	Colonial and Indian Exhibition *English Historical Review*		Introduction of first Irish Home Rule Bill contributes to intensification of public debate over Imperial federalism; numerous articles by Gavan Duffy, McCarthy, Goldwin Smith, Chamberlain, Lord Salisbury, and Gladstone
1887	George Joy painting, *Death of Gordon* H. Rider Haggard, *She* and *Allan Quatermain*	Auckland Public Library	
1888	Rudyard Kipling, *Plain Tales from the Hills, Soldiers Three, Wee Willie Winkie*	Opening of record room by Government of Bombay	John Strachey, *India*
1891		Imperial Record Department established at Calcutta	
1892	Herbert Baker designs Cape Dutch style mansion, Groote Schuur, for Cecil Rhodes Rudyard Kipling, *Barrack-Room Ballads* Colonial Society of Massachusetts Polynesian Society and *Journal* *William and Mary Quarterly*		Sir Charles Dilke and Spencer Wilkinson, *Imperial Defence* Alfred Milner, *England in Egypt*
1893			John Scott Keltie, *The Partition of Africa*

Year	Scholarship, Education, and Culture	Archives and Documents	Historical Publications
1897	Rudyard Kipling, *Captains Courageous*	Publication of *Records of the Cape Colony*, ed. George Theal, 36 vols. (to 1905)	Hugh Egerton, *A Short History of British Colonial Policy*
1898			W. P. Reeves, *The Long White Cloud, Ao Tea Roa*
1899–1902 SOUTH AFRICAN WAR ('BOER WAR')			
1899		Keeper of Dutch Records established by Government of Ceylon	Mary Kingsley, *West African Studies* W. S. Churchill, *The River War*
1900	Joseph Conrad, *Lord Jim*		John Hobson, *The War in South Africa: Its Causes and Effects*
1901 DEATH OF QUEEN VICTORIA			
1901	Rudyard Kipling, *Kim* Edward Elgar composes first of the *Pomp and Circumstance* marches (1901–07, 1930); later used as musical setting for A. L. Benson's lyrics, 'Land of Hope and Glory' Victoria League founded Formation of Royal Australian Historical Society in New South Wales, followed by Royal Historical Society of Victoria in 1909, and other state historical societies in Australia Lord Curzon commissions Victoria Memorial in Calcutta		Dadabhai Naoroji, *Poverty and Un-British Rule in India*

Year	Scholarship, Education, and Culture	Archives and Documents	Historical Publications
1902	Joseph Conrad, *Youth* (including 'Heart of Darkness') A. E. W. Mason, *The Four Feathers*		J. A. Hobson, *Imperialism: A Study*
1903		Foreign Office Records opened to 1780	
1904	Joseph Conrad, *Nostromo*		
1905	Beit Chair of Colonial History, Oxford University		Richard Jebb, *Studies in Colonial Nationalism*
1906		State Library of New South Wales acquires major collection of Australiana from David Scott Mitchell, creates Mitchell Library	Publication of *English Factories in India* series (to 1955)
1907	First publication of Champlain Society Calcutta Historical Society *Bengal Past and Present*		
1908	Boy Scouts founded		H. B. Morse, *Trade and Administration of the Chinese Empire* George L. Beer, *The Origins of the British Colonial System, 1578–1660* Earl of Cromer, *Modern Egypt*, 2 vols.
1909	Baker wins commission for Union Buildings, Pretoria, South Africa Chichele Chair in Military Studies, All Souls College, Oxford	Foreign Office and Colonial Office records opened to 1837	
1910	John Buchan, *Prester John*		Sir Valentine Chirol, *Indian Unrest*

Year	Scholarship, Education, and Culture	Archives and Documents	Historical Publications
1910	*Round Table*		Pacificus (F. S. Oliver), *Federalism and Home Rule* H. B. Morse, *The International Relations of the Chinese Empire*, 3 vols. (to 1918)
1911	University of Hong Kong		Erskine Childers, *The Framework of Home Rule* Julian S. Corbett, *Some Principles of Maritime Strategy*
1912	Edwin Lutyens appointed to design New Delhi, new capital of India		Arthur Berriedale Keith, *Responsible Government in the Dominions*, 3 vols.
	1914–1918 FIRST WORLD WAR		
1914	Imperial Studies Committee, University of London Walter Burley Griffin appointed to design new Australian capital, Canberra South African Native College at Fort Hare	Publication of *Historical Records of Australia* (to 1925)	Adam Shortt and Arthur Doughty, eds., *Canada and Its Provinces*, 23 vols. (to 1917)
1916	Separate English-language (Cape Town, Witwatersrand, Natal, Rhodes) and Afrikaans-language (Stellenbosch, Pretoria, Orange Free State, Potchefstroom) universities in South Africa established		Lionel Curtis, *The Commonwealth of Nations* Ernest Scott, *A Short History of Australia* Solomon T. Plaatje, *Native Life in South Africa: Before and Since the European War and the Boer Rebellion*
1917			V. I. Lenin, *Imperialism the Highest Stage of Capitalism*

Year	Scholarship, Education, and Culture	Archives and Documents	Historical Publications
1918			Joseph Schumpeter, 'Zur Soziologie der Imperialismen', subsequently translated as *Imperialism and Social Classes*
1919	Vere Harmsworth Chair of Imperial and Naval History, Cambridge University Rhodes Professorship, University of London *Sudan Notes and Records*	Foreign and Colonial Offices records opened to 1860 Creation of Indian Historical Records Commission	Vincent A. Smith, *Oxford History of India* (later revised by Perceval Spear) Leonard Woolf, *Empire and Commerce in Africa: A Study in Economic Imperialsim*
1920	*Canadian Historical Review*		H. Duncan Hall, *The British Commonwealth of Nations*
1921			Sir Charles Lucas, ed., *The Empire at War* (to 1926) C. E. W. Bean, ed. *Australia in the War*, 14 vols. (to 1942)
1922			Wilfrid Scawen Blunt, *Secret History of the English Occupation of Egypt* F. D. Lugard, *The Dual Mandate in British Tropical Africa*
1924	British Empire Exhibition at Wembley (to 1925) E. M. Forster, *A Passage to India*		R. Coupland, *Wilberforce* L. C. A. Knowles, *Economic Development of the British Overseas Empire*, 3 vols.
1925	Institute of Pacific Relations	Foreign and Colonial Offices records opened to 1878	E. G. Malherbe, *Education* in *South Africa (1652–1922)*

Year	Scholarship, Education, and Culture	Archives and Documents	Historical Publications
1926	Capital of Australia moves from Melbourne to Canberra	Australian Commonwealth Parliamentary Library renamed Commonwealth National Library after move of capital to Canberra	H. B. Morse, *The Chronicles of the East India Company Trading to China*, 5 vols. (to 1929)
			T. E. Lawrence, *Revolt in the Desert*
		Government of India Record Office opened in Delhi on site of present National Archives of India	
1927			M. K. Gandhi, *An Autobiography: The Story of My Experiments With Truth*, 2 vols. (to 1929)
			W. M. Macmillan, *The Cape Colour Question: A Historical Survey*
			R. L. Buell, *The Native Problem in Africa*, 2 vols.
1928			Lowell J. Ragatz, *The Fall of the Planter Class in the British Caribbean, 1763–1833*
1929			*Cambridge History of the British Empire*, 9 vols. (to 1959)
			Arthur Berriedale Keith, *The Sovereignty of the British Dominions*
			W. M. Macmillan, *Bantu, Boer, and Briton: The Making of the South African Native Problem*

Year	Scholarship, Education, and Culture	Archives and Documents	Historical Publications
1930		Foreign and Colonial Offices records opened to 1885 Wei-hai-wei official archive transferred to London	W. K. Hancock, *Australia* H. A. Innis, *The Fur Trade in Canada: An Introduction to Canadian Economic History* W. P. Morrell, *British Colonial Policy in the Age of Peel and Russell* Lewis B. Namier, *England in the Age of the American Revolution*
1931	New Delhi inaugurated		
1931 STATUTE OF WESTMINSTER			
1932			John Strachey, *The Coming Struggle for Power*
1933	National Maritime Museum, Greenwich		L. A. Mills, *Ceylon Under British Rule, 1795–1932* Reginald Coupland, *The British Anti-Slavery Movement* Lord Lloyd, *Egypt Since Cromer*, 2 vols. (to 1934)
1934	George Orwell, *Burmese Days* *Uganda Journal*		Charles M. Andrews, *The Colonial Period of American History*, 4 vols. (to 1938) J. C. Beaglehole, *The Exploration of the Pacific* Edward Thompson and G. T. Garratt, *Rise and Fulfilment of British Rule in India*
1935	Alexander Korda film, *Sanders of the River*		Elspeth Huxley, *White Man's Country: Lord Delamere and the Making of Kenya*, 2 vols.

Year	Scholarship, Education, and Culture	Archives and Documents	Historical Publications
1935			William L. Langer, *The Diplomacy of Imperialism 1890–1902*, 2 vols. T. E. Lawrence, *Seven Pillars of Wisdom*
1936	*Tanganyika Notes and Records*		Lawrence Henry Gipson, *The British Empire before the American Revolution*, 15 vols. (to 1970) J. C. Beaglehole, *New Zealand: A Short History* W. M. Macmillan, *Warning From the West Indies* Jawaharlal Nehru, *An Autobiography* Richard Pares, *War and Trade in the West Indies, 1739–1763* George Padmore, *How Britain Rules Africa*
1937	First publication of the Hudson's Bay Record Society	New Zealand Historical Publications Department	W. K. Hancock, *Survey of British Commonwealth Affairs*, 2 vols. (to 1942) Donald G. Creighton, *The Commercial Empire of the St. Lawrence, 1760–1850* Rupert Emerson, *Malaysia: A Study in Direct and Indirect Rule* Arthur Berriedale Keith, *A Constitutional History of India, 1600–1935* Margery Perham, *Native Administration in Nigeria*

Year	Scholarship, Education, and Culture	Archives and Documents	Historical Publications
1938			George Antonius, *The Arab Awakening* Sally Herbert Frankel, *Capital Investment in Africa: Its Course and Effects* Jomo Kenyatta, *Facing Mt. Kenya* K. C. Wheare, *The Statute of Westminster and Dominion Status* R. Coupland, *East Africa and Its Invaders*
	1939–1945 SECOND WORLD WAR		
1939	Joyce Cary, *Mister Johnson* Alexander Korda film version of A. E. W. Mason's *The Four Feathers*		K. S. Latourette, *History of the Expansion of Christianity*, 7 vols. (to 1958) Brian Fitzpatrick, *British Imperialism in Australia, 1788–1833* C. L. R. James, *The Black Jacobins* Lord Hailey, *An African Survey* Sir Donald Cameron, *My Tanganyika Service and Some Nigeria* R. Coupland, *The Exploitation of East Africa*
1940	Establishment of *Historical Studies Australia and New Zealand* New Zealand *Dictionary of National Biography*		Arthur J. Marder, *The Anatomy of British Sea Power: A History of British Naval Policy in the Pre-Dreadnought Era, 1880–1905* (British edn. published in 1941 under the title *British Naval Policy 1880–1905: The Anatomy of British Sea Power)*

Year	Scholarship, Education, and Culture	Archives and Documents	Historical Publications
1940			Harold and Margaret Sprout, *Toward a New Order of Sea Power*
1941	Nuffield College Colonial Research Project, Oxford University (to 1947)		C. W. de Kiewiet, *A History of South Africa: Social and Economic*
1942			S. E. Crowe, *The Berlin West African Conference, 1884–1885*
1943			W. K. Hancock, *Argument of Empire* Eric A. Walker, *The British Empire: Its Structure and Spirit*
1944	African Dance Festivals New York (1944–46)	Archives Office established in Commonwealth National Library in Australia	Leonard Barnes, *Soviet Light on the Colonies* Eric Williams, *Capitalism and Slavery*
1945			J. B. Brebner, *The Atlantic Triangle: The Interplay of Canada, the United States and Great Britain* R. L. Schuyler, *The Fall of the Old Colonial System; A Study in British Free Trade, 1770–1870*
1946	University colleges in Sudan, Nigeria, Gold Coast, Uganda (to 1949)		
1947 INDEPENDENCE AND PARTITION OF INDIA			
1948	Lectureship in African History, University of London Alan Paton, *Cry the Beloved Country*	Foreign and Colonial Offices records opened to 1902	J. S. Furnivall, *Colonial Policy and Practice: A Comparative Study of Burma and Netherlands India*

Year	Scholarship, Education, and Culture	Archives and Documents	Historical Publications
1949	University College of the West Indies begins teaching History Raffles Professorship of History, University of Malaya Professor of Pacific History, Australian National University Professor of South-East Asian History, University of London Institute of Commonwealth Studies, University of London		
1950	East African Institute of Social Research, Uganda First lectureship in history, Makerere University College, Uganda		
1952	Smuts Chair of Commonwealth History, Cambridge University		Beginning of publication of Australian official history of the Second World War with Paul Hasluck's *The Government and the People*, Vol. I, *1939–1941* Vincent T. Harlow, *The Founding of the Second British Empire*, 2 vols. (to 1964) Nicholas Mansergh, *Survey of British Commonwealth Affairs, 1931–1952*, 2 vols. (to 1958) L. S. Sutherland, *The East India Company in Eighteenth-Century Politics*

Year	Scholarship, Education, and Culture	Archives and Documents	Historical Publications
1952			Roland Oliver, *The Missionary Factor in East Africa*
1953		A. F. Madden, *British Colonial Developments, 1774–1834: Select Documents*	John K. Fairbank, *Trade and Diplomacy on the China Coast: The Opening of the Treaty Ports, 1842–1854* John Gallagher and Ronald Robinson, 'The Imperialism of Free Trade', *Economic History Review* Paul Knaplund, *James Stephen and the British Colonial System, 1813–1847*
1954	John Masters, *Bhowani Junction*		Philip Woodruff (Mason), *The Men Who Ruled India: The Guardians* L. H. Gipson, *The Coming of the Revolution, 1763–1775* S. Y. Teng and J. K. Fairbank, *China's Response to the West: A Documentary Survey, 1839–1923*
1955	The University College of Rhodesia and Nysasaland		J. C. Beaglehole, *The Journals of Captain James Cook on His Voyages of Discovery*, 4 vols. (to 1974) David B. Quinn, ed., *The Roanoke Voyages, 1584–1590*, 2 vols.
	1956 SUEZ CRISIS		
1956	W. S. Churchill, *History of the English-Speaking Peoples* Jorn Utzon designs Sydney Opera House		Elsa Goveia, *A Study on the Historiography of the British West Indies to the End of the Nineteenth Century*

Year	Scholarship, Education, and Culture	Archives and Documents	Historical Publications
1956			Kenneth Onwuka Dike, *Trade and Politics in the Niger Delta, 1830–1855: An Introduction to the Economic and Political History of Nigeria* Thomas Hodgkin, *Nationalism in Colonial Africa* Paul Knaplund, *Britain: Commonwealth and Empire, 1901–1955* Elie Kedourie, *England and the Middle East: The Destruction of the Ottoman Empire, 1914–1921* Margery Perham, *Lugard: The Years of Adventure*
1957		New Zealand National Archives	Keith Sinclair, *The Origins of the Maori Wars*
1958		Public Records Act establishes fifty-year rule for release of public records in Britain	Beginning of publication of New Zealand official history of Second World War with F. L. W. Wood, *The New Zealand People at War* [Historical Publications Branch of the Department of Internal Affairs] J. S. Coleman, *Nigeria: Background to Nationalism*

Year	Scholarship, Education, and Culture	Archives and Documents	Historical Publications
1958			George Shepperson and Thomas Price, *Independent African: John Chilembwe and the Origins, Setting, and Significance of the Nyasaland Rising of 1915*
1959	Chinua Achebe, *Things Fall Apart*	Chinese-language archives of British Embassy in Peking deposited in Public Record Office, London Under fifty-year rule, British public records opened through 1908	Roland Oliver, *Sir Harry Johnston and the Scramble for Africa* John Strachey, *The End of Empire* Leonard M. Thompson, *The Unification of South Africa, 1902–1910* A. P. Thornton, *The Imperial Idea and Its Enemies* Eric Stokes, *The English Utilitarians and India*
1960 MACMILLAN'S 'WIND OF CHANGE' SPEECH			
1960	Hong Kong branch of Royal Asiatic Society revived Trinidad College begins teaching history *Journal of Southeast Asian History* *Journal of African History*		H. S. Ferns, *Britain and Argentina in the Nineteenth Century* Margery Perham, *Lugard: The Years of Authority* W. P. Morrell, *Britain in the Pacific Islands*
1961	*Journal of Commonwealth Political Studies* University colleges, Tanganyika and Kenya		Richard Koebner, *Empire* Arthur J. Marder, *From the Dreadnought to Scapa Flow: The Royal Navy in the Fisher Era, 1904–1913*, 3 vols. (to 1970) Ronald Robinson and John Gallagher with Alice Denny, *Africa and the Victorians*

Year	Scholarship, Education, and Culture	Archives and Documents	Historical Publications
1962	University College of the West Indies becomes University of the West Indies		C. M. H. Clark, *A History of Australia*, 6 vols. Margery Perham, *The Colonial Reckoning: The End of Imperial Rule in Africa in the Light of British Experience* R. E. Robinson and John Gallagher, 'The Partition of Africa', in *The New Cambridge Modern History*, Vol. XI, *Material Progress and World-Wide Problems, 1870–1898* Patrick Gordon Walker, *The Commonwealth* W. K. Hancock, *Smuts: The Sanguine Years, 1870–1919*
1963	Centre of West African Studies, University of Birmingham	Oxford Colonial Records Project (to 1972)	Oxford *History of East Africa*, 3 vols. (to 1976) Elizabeth Monroe, *Britain's Moment in the Middle East* Roland Oliver and J. D. Fage, *A Short History of Africa* John K. Galbraith, *Reluctant Empire: British Policy on the South African Frontier, 1834–1854* John D. Hargreaves, *Prelude to the Partition of West Africa* Robert Heussler, *Yesterday's Rulers: The Making of the British Colonial Service*

Year	Scholarship, Education, and Culture	Archives and Documents	Historical Publications
1964			Philip D. Curtin, *The Image of Africa: British Ideas and Actions, 1780–1850* Thomas R. Metcalf, *The Aftermath of Revolt: India, 1857–1880*
1965	Commonwealth Secretariat created International Congress of African Historians Dar es Salaam *Latin American Research Review*		James George Eayrs, *In Defence of Canada*, 4 vols. (to 1985) R. E. Frykenberg, *Guntur District, 1788–1848: A History of Local Influence and Central Authority in South India* John Shy, *Toward Lexington: The Role of the British Army in the Coming of the American Revolution* J. D. B. Miller, *The Commonwealth and the World* Kenneth Robinson, *The Dilemmas of Trusteeship: Aspects of British Colonial Policy Between the Wars*
1966	New Zealand Historical Association First volume of *Dictionary of Canadian Biography* First publication of *Australian Dictionary of Biography* *Journal of Pacific History* Paul Scott, *The Raj Quartet*, 4 vols. (to 1975)		Eric Ashby (with Mary Anderson), *Universities: British, Indian, African* W. David McIntrye, *Colonies into Commonwealth* Robin Winks, ed., *The Historiography of the Empire and Commonwealth* Carl Rosberg and John Nottingham, *The Myth of Mau Mau*

Year	Scholarship, Education, and Culture	Archives and Documents	Historical Publications
1967 ANNOUNCEMENT OF WITHDRAWAL FROM 'EAST OF SUEZ'			
1967	Publication of first volume of *Hadith* by Kenya Historical Association *New Zealand Journal of History*	Act amending Public Records Act of 1958 reduces archival closure to thirty years	J. W. Davidson, *Somoa mo Samoa: The Emergence of the Independent State of Western Samoa* Terence Ranger, *Revolt in Southern Rhodesia: A Study in African Resistance* André Gunder Frank, *Capitalism and Underdevelopment in Latin America* Bernard Bailyn, *The Ideological Origins of the American Revolution* Gerald S. Graham, *Great Britain in the Indian Ocean: A Study of Maritime Enterprise, 1810–1850* Francis G. Hutchins, *The Illusion of Permanence: British Imperialism in India* Kenneth Bourne, *Britain and the Balance of Power in North America, 1815–1908*
1968	Beginning of publication of *Dictionary of South African Biography* (6 vols. to date) Association of Caribbean Historians		W. K. Hancock, *Smuts, The Fields of Force, 1919–1950* J. B. Kelly, *Britain and the Persian Gulf, 1795–1880* James Morris, *Pax Britannica*, 3 vols. (to 1978) D. C. M. Platt, *Finance, Trade, and Politics in British Foreign Policy, 1815–1914*

Year	Scholarship, Education, and Culture	Archives and Documents	Historical Publications
1969	*Journal of Latin American Studies*		Anil Seal, *The Emergence of Indian Nationalism: Competition and Collaboration in the Later Nineteenth Century* Max Beloff, *Imperial Sunset*, 2 vols. (to 1989) L. H. Gann and Peter Duignan, eds., *Colonialism in Africa*, 5 vols. (to 1975) D. W. Harkness, *The Restless Dominion: The Irish Free State and the British Commonwealth of Nations* H. V. Hodson, *The Great Divide: Britain–India–Pakistan* Nicholas Mansergh, *The Commonwealth Experience* Monica Wilson and Leonard Thompson, *Oxford History of South Africa*, 2 vols.
1970	University of Guyana begins teaching History *Modern Ceylon Studies*	Nicholas Mansergh E. W. R. Lumby, P. Moon, eds., *Constitutional Relations Between Britain and India: The Transfer of Power, 1942–7*, 12 vols. (to 1983)	Carl Berger, *Sense of Power*
1971			Christine Bolt, *Victorian Attitudes to Race*

Year	Scholarship, Education, and Culture	Archives and Documents	Historical Publications
1972	*Journal of Imperial and Commonwealth History* Centre for Maori Studies, Waikato University	Publication of official Canadian documents (to 1973): *Documents on Canadian External Relations* Phyllis Mander-Jones, *Manuscripts in the British Isles Relating to Australia, New Zealand and the Pacific*	Michael Howard's Ford Lectures published: *The Continental Commitment: The Dilemma of British Defence Policy in the Era of Two World Wars* D. C. M. Platt, *Latin America and British Trade, 1806–1914* Ronald Robinson, 'The Non-European Foundations of European Imperialism: Sketch for a Theory of Collaboration', in Roger Owen and Bob Sutcliffe, eds., *Studies in the Theory of Imperialism* Richard S. Dunn, *Sugar and Slaves: The Rise of the Planter Class in the English West Indies, 1624–1713* Walter Rodney, *How Europe Underdeveloped Africa*
1973 BRITAIN JOINS EUROPEAN COMMUNITY			
1973			Phillip Darby, *British Defence Policy East of Suez*
1974	Publications Act passed in South Africa, used to censor publications, films, and entertainment		J. C. Beaglehole, *Life of Cook* J. D. B. Miller, *Survey of Commonwealth Affairs: Problems of Expansion and Attrition, 1953–1969*

Year	Scholarship, Education, and Culture	Archives and Documents	Historical Publications
1975		R. G. Neale, ed., *Documents on Australian Foreign Policy, 1937–49*, Vols. I and II	J. D. Fage and Roland Oliver, eds., *The Cambridge History of Africa*, 8 vols. S. Gopal, *Jawaharlal Nehru*, 3 vols (to 1984) Partha Sarathi Gupta, *Imperialism and the British Labour Movement, 1914–1964* Edmund S. Morgan, *American Slavery: American Freedom: The Ordeal of Colonial Virginia* Ritchie Ovendale, *'Appeasement' and the English Speaking World: Britain, the United States, the Dominions and the Policy of 'Appeasement', 1937–1939* Bernard Porter, *The Lion's Share: A Short History of British Imperialism, 1850–1970*
1976			Ronald Hyam, *Britain's Imperial Century, 1815–1914: A Study of Empire and Expansion* Paul Kennedy, *The Rise and Fall of British Naval Mastery*
1977		Oxford Development Records Project begins New Public Record Office opens at Kew with transfer of 'modern' government department documents from Chancery Lane	T. R. H. Davenport, *South Africa: A Modern History* Wm. Roger Louis, *Imperialism at Bay: The United States and the Decolonization of the British Empire, 1941–1945*

Year	Scholarship, Education, and Culture	Archives and Documents	Historical Publications
1978			*The Cambridge History of China*, Vols. X–XIII (to 1986) Norman Etherington *Preachers, Peasants and Politics in Southeast Africa* Edward W. Said, *Orientalism* K. N. Chaudhuri, *The Trading World of Asia and the English East India Company, 1600–1760*
1979			B. R. Tomlinson, *The Political Economy of the Raj, 1914–47: The Economics of Decolonization in India* Stephen Saunders Webb, *The Governors General: The English Army and the Definition of Empire*
1981			R. F. Holland, *Britain and the Commonwealth Alliance, 1918–1939* W. H. Oliver, ed., *The Oxford History of New Zealand* Roger Owen, *The Middle East in the World Economy, 1800–1914*
1982 FALKLANDS WAR			
1982			Publication of John Gallagher's Ford Lectures, *The Decline, Revival and Fall of the British Empire* First volume of *Subaltern Studies* published in Delhi

Year	Scholarship, Education, and Culture	Archives and Documents	Historical Publications
1982			R. J. Moore, *Escape from Empire: The Attlee Government and the Indian Problem*
1983		Hugh Tinker, ed., *Burma, the Struggle for Independence, 1944–1948: Documents from Official and Private Sources*, 2 vols. (to 1984)	
1984	Granada Television production of Paul Scott's *Raj Quartet*		Wm. Roger Louis, *The British Empire in the Middle East, 1945–1951: Arab Nationalism, the United States and Post-War Imperialism* Jack P. Greene and J. R. Pole, eds., *Colonial British America: Essays in the New History of the Early Modern Era*
1985		Frederick Madden, ed., *Select Documents on the Constitutional History of the British Empire and Commonwealth*	Ayesha Jalal, *The Sole Spokesman: Jinnah, the Muslim League and the Demand for Pakistan*
1986			UNESCO's General History of the Caribbean Project launched Ian K. Steele, *The English Atlantic, 1675–1740: An Exploration of Communication and Community*
1987			*New Cambridge History of India*, launched

Year	Scholarship, Education, and Culture	Archives and Documents	Historical Publications
1988			Dennis Austin, *The Commonwealth and Britain*
			Stephen Chan, *The Commonwealth in World Politics*
			John Darwin, *Britain and Decolonization: The Retreat From Empire in the Post-War World*
			Paul Kennedy, *The Rise and Fall of the Great Powers*
			John Sweetman, *The Oriental Obsession: Islamic Inspiration in British and American Art and Architecture, 1500–1920*
			Nicholas Canny, *Kingdom and Colony: Ireland and the Atlantic World, 1566–1800*
			John Eddy and Deryck Schreuder, eds., *The Rise of Colonial Nationalism: Australia, New Zealand, Canada, and South Africa First Assert their Nationalities, 1880–1914*
1989			Judith M. Brown, *Gandhi: Prisoner of Hope*
			C. A. Bayly, *Imperial Meridian: The British Empire and the World, 1780–1830*
			J. E. Kendle, *Ireland and the Federal Solution: The Debate over the United Kingdom Constitution, 1870–1922*

Year	Scholarship, Education, and Culture	Archives and Documents	Historical Publications
1990	Beginning of publication of *Dictionary of New Zealand Biography*		*UNESCO History of Africa*, Vol. VII, *Africa Under Colonial Domination, 1880–1935*, A. Adu Boahen, ed.
1991			Keith Kyle, *Suez* M. Strobel, *European Women and the Second British Empire*
1992		British Documents on the End of Empire series begins, D. J. Murray and S. R. Ashton, general eds.	Linda Colley, *Britons: Forging the Nation*
1993		Beginning of publication of the Jinnah Papers series	P. J. Cain and A. G. Hopkins, *British Imperialism*, 2 vols.
1994			Crawford Young, *The African Colonial State in Comparative Perspective*
1995		Final transfer of documents from Public Record Office in Chancery Lane to Kew (transfer completed and Chancery Lane building closed in 1996)	Mrinalini Sinha, *Colonial Masculinity: The 'Manly Englishman' and the 'Effeminate Bengali' in the Late Nineteenth Century*
1996	The British Empire and Commonwealth Museum opens in Bristol		
1997 HONG KONG REVERTS TO CHINA			
1997	The 'Year of the Commonwealth' in Britain		
1998			*Oxford History of the British Empire*, 5 vols. (to 1999)

INDEX

The index lists all authors and titles of published works. It does not list articles or unpublished theses (both of which are indexed under their author). Footnotes are indexed by author only, when there is significant information which is additional to the text.

Abreu, Marcelo de Paiva 447 n.
Abu-Lughod, Janet 251
Abeyasinghe, T. B. H. 247
Account of a Voyage to Establish a Colony at Port Philip (Tuckey) 164–5
Achebe, Chinua 494 n.
Acton, Lord 6–7 n., 8, 10–11
Adair, Douglass G. 106
Adams, John 106
Adeleye, R. A. 459 n.
Admiralty Chart, The (Ritchie) 337
Admiralty Hydrographic Service, The (Day) 337
Adshead, S. A. M. 397
Afigbo, A. E. 663
Africa and the Victorians (Robinson and Gallagher) 39–40, 347, 456, 481, 525, 627, 637, 660
Africa Emergent (Macmillan) 471
Africa under Colonial Domination (Boahen) 460
African Ideas of God (Smith) 306
African Poor, The (Iliffe) 283
African Survey, An (Hailey) 31, 471, 473
Africans and British Rule (Perham) 502, 503
After its Own Image (Talib) 414
Against Home Rule (Rosenbaum) 123
Agbodeka, Francis 459 n.
Aggrey, James 472–3
Agha Khan 256
Ah Ku and Karayuki-San (Warren) 414
Ahmad, Aijaz 598 n., 608
Ahmat, Sharom 414
Ahmed, Akbar S. 261
Air Power and Colonial Control (Omissi) 419
Airlie, Shiona M. 392–3
Aitchison, C. U. 197
Ajayi, J. F. A. 307, 475, 491, 496
Albert, Bill 447 n.
Albion, Robert G. 329
Albion's Seed (Fischer) 87
Alcock, Sir Rutherford 380
Alexander, Frederick 170, 171 n.
Alhadeff, Peter 447 n.
Allan, J., Haig, Wolseley T., and Dodwell, H. H. 198 n.
Allen, David Grayson 87 n.
Allen, J. de V. 412
Allies of a Kind (Thorne) 412
American Colonial Painting (Belknap) 577
American Historical Review (journal) 662
American Influences on Canadian Government (Munro) 154
American Painting to 1776 (Quimby) 578
American Slavery, American Freedom (Morgan) 84
Americans, The (Boorstin) 268
Amery, L. S. 15, 123, 234, 342–3, 560
Amin, Samir 643 n.
Amin, Shahid 225
Amos, Keith 118
Analytical History of India, . . . (Sewell) 198
Anatomy of African Misery (Olivier) 20
Anatomy of British Sea Power, The (Marder) 330
Ancient Inscriptions of Ceylon (Muller) 244
Anderson, David M., and Killingray, David 350 n.
Anderson, Frederick 79 n.
Anderson, M. S. 417 n.
Anderson, Robin 367
Andrews, Charles M. 49, 50, 74–9, 82, 92, 103, 466, 620
Andrews, E. M. 356, 357–8
Andrews, K. R. 50, 91 n., 620
Anene, J. C. 476
Angell, Norman 17
Angels of War (film) 374
Anglo-American Political Relations (Olson and Brown) 49
Anglo-American Steamship Rivalry in China, 1862–1874 (Kwang-ching) 397
Anglo-Chinese Commerce and Diplomacy (Sargent) 380
Anglo-Chinese Relations, 1839–1860 (Wong) 388
Anglo-Chinese Relations during the Seventeenth and Eighteenth Centuries (Pritchard) 384
Anglo-Dutch Rivalry in the Malay World, 1780–1824 (Tarling) 410
Anglo-Egyptian Relations, 1800–1953 (Marlowe) 427
Anglo-Indian Attitudes (Dewey) 215
Annexation of Upper Burma, The (Singhal) 410
Ansari, Sarah F. D. 259
Anstey, Roger 24 n., 66, 323, 456
Antiquities of Orissa, The (Mitra)
Antonius, George 25

'Appeasement' and the English Speaking World . . . (Ovendale) 357
Appleby, Joyce 109
Apter, David 505
Arab Awakening, The (Antonius) 25
Arab Nationalism and British Imperialism (Marlowe) 427
Arabia (Kelly) 434
Arasaratnam, Sinnappah 247, 250–1
Archer, Mildred 576–7
Archer, W. G. 576
Architecture of the British Empire (Fermor-Hesketh) 594
Area of Darkness, An (Naipaul) 631
Argument of Empire (Hancock) 33
Ariés, Philippe 658
Arnold, David 70 n., 216, 273, 280, 350 n.
Ar'n't I a Woman? (White) 322
Arrighi, Giovanni 532
Art Manufactures of India (Mukharji) 572
Art and Nationalism in Colonial India, 1850–1922 (Mitter) 226, 581
Arts of the Anglo-American Community in the Seventeenth Century (Quimby) 578
Asar-us-Sanadid (Sayyid Ahmad Khan) 196
Asher, Catherine 587
Ashton, S. R. 233
Ashton, S. R. and Stockwell, S. E. 555 n.
Asquith, H. H. 122
Asiatic Society of Bengal 197
At Duty's Call (Reader) 617
At the Going Down of the Sun (Lindsay) 394
Atlantic Slave Trade, The (Curtin) 142, 316
Atlas of British Overseas Expansion (Porter) 666
Attlee, Clement 240, 241, 629
Attwell, Pamela 392
Aubrey-Maturin novels 339
Aucuparius (Furse) 618
Augier, F. R., Gordon, S. C., Hall, D. G., Reckord, M. 139 n.
Austen, Ralph 507
Austin, Dennis 566
Australia (Crawford) 175
Australia (Greenwood) 172
Australia (Hancock) 29
Australia: The Quiet Continent (Pike) 175
Australia and Imperial Defence, 1918–39 (McCarthy) 346
Australia, New Zealand, and the United States (Reese) 360
Australia Station, The (Bach) 334
Australian Colonists, The (Inglis) 177
Australian Dictionary of Biography 174
Australian Legend, The (Ward) 173
Australia's Colonial Culture (Nadel) 176
Axtell, James 90 n., 311
Ayandele, Emmanuel A. 307, 312 n., 476, 496
Azad, M. A. K. 256

BAAG: Hong Kong Resistance, 1942–1945 (Ride) 394
Bach, John 334
Background to the ANZUS Pact (McIntyre) 339
Baden-Powell, B. H. 197
Bagehot, Walter 626
Bailey, Susan F. 665
Bailyn, Bernard 70, 82, 83 n., 87, 89, 94 n., 95, 98, 107, 268
Bailyn, Bernard and Morgan, Philip D. 90 n.
Baines, Thomas 295
Baker, Christopher J. 218
Baker, Herbert 591
Baker, J. N. L. 294
Balabushevitch, V. V., and Dayakov, A. M. 219
Baldwin, Robert 150
Balfour, A. J. 345, 626
Balfour-Paul, Glen 434
Ball, Margaret 564, 567
Ballard, George A. 329
Ballhatchet, Kenneth 210, 665
Bampfylde, C. A. 406
Bancroft, George 75, 80, 82
Bandaranaike, S. W. R. D. 248
Banks, Sir Joseph 61, 293, 295, 296
Banno, Masatake 398
Bantu, Boer, and Britain. . . (Macmillan) 25
Bantu Prophets in South Africa (Sundkler) 308–9
Banyan Tree, The (Tinker) 249
Baraclough, Geoffrey 457 n.
Baran, Paul 545
Barat, Amiya 201
Baring-Gould, S. 406
Barnes, J. A. 478
Barnes, Leonard 20, 22 n.
Barnes, Viola *see* Dickerson
Barnett, Correlli 3, 339
Barnett, L. D. 245
Barrett, David 309
Barron, T. J. 251
Barrow, Sir John 298
Barrow, Thomas C. 82 n.
Barton, Edmund 168
Bassala, George 269
Bastin, John 404, 408–9
Batutu, Hanna 428, 432
Batten, T. R. 490
Baudet, Henri 656
Baugh, Daniel A. 49, 85 n., 338
Bauss, Rudy 336
Bayfield, Henry 337
Bayley, Frank 574
Bayly, C. A. 36 n. 51, 206, 222, 228–9, 257, 274, 582, 603 n., 615

Bayly, Susan 57 n., 209, 222
Beaglehole, J. C. 33, 34, 185, 294, 298 n., 335–8, 296, 298, 369, 372
Beaglehole, Timothy 203
Beale, Edgar 298
Bean, C. E. W. 176
Beasley, W. G. 389
Beaufort, Sir Francis 298
Beaumont, Christopher 262
Beauvoir, Simone de 612, 627
Becke, Louis, and Jeffrey, Walter 169
Beckles, Hilary McD. 142 n., 318, 322
Beer, George Louis 14, 43, 46, 50, 74–6, 454 n.
Beginning and End of the Management . . . 386
Beginnings of the Egyptian Question . . ., The (Ghorbal) 427
Beinart, William 69 n., 539 n.
Beinin, Joel, and Lockman, Zachary 428
Belknap, Waldron P. 577
Belich, James 663
Bell, Gertrude L. 617, 618
Bell, H. C. P. 244
Beloff, Max 343, 355, 356
Benda, Henry J. (Harry) 409
Bengal Divided (Chatterji) 240
Bengal Native Infantry, The (Barat) 201
Benians, E. A. 11, 52 n.
Benjamin Franklin's Experiments (Cohen) 268
Bennett, George 506
Bennett, Tony 581 n.
Bent, J. Theodore 589
Berger, Carl 146, 160
Berlin, Ira 322
Berlin, Ira, and Morgan, Philip D. 321
Bernal, Martin 610 n.
Berman, Bruce, and Lonsdale, John 554
Berque, Jacques 432
Berridge, Geoff 528, 536
Bethell, Nicholas 428 n.
Between Crown and Swastika (Furlong) 359
Beveridge, Lord 220
Beyond a Boundary (James) 568
Beyond the Tin Mines (Loh Kok Wah) 414
Bibliography on CD-ROM: The History of Britain, Ireland and the British Overseas (RHS) 131–2
Big Business in China (Cochran) 397
Binney, Judith 663
Birch, Alan, and Endacott, George B. 394
Bird, Isabella 614
Birdwood, George C. M. 572, 591
Birmingham, D., and Martin, Phyllis, M. 539 n.
Bitter Tea of General Yen, The (film) 630
Black, Ian 414
Black, R. D. Collison 121 n.
Blackburn, Robin 315 n., 324 n.
Blaikie, W. G. 468 n.
Blainey, Geoffrey 179, 662
Blake, J. W. 467, 487 n.
Blakemore, Harold 442, 444 n.
Blaze, L. E. 245
Bliss, Robert M. 85 n.
Blunt, Wilfred Scawen 615
Blythe, Wilfred 411
Boahen, A. Adu 460
Boas, Franz 575
Bodelsen, C. A. 63 n., 385
Bolitho, Hector 257
Bolland, Nigel 143
Bolton, G. C. 177
Bond, Brian 348
Bonney, Rollins 408
Boorstin, Daniel 268
Borden, Sir Robert 151–2, 627
Borchardt, D. H., and Crittenden, Victor 163 n.
Bose, Sugata 260
Bothwell, Robert 158 *see also* Granatstein
Botman, Selma 431
Boucher, Jonathan 94 n.
Bounty, The (Dening) 336
Bourassa, Henri 149
Bourinot, John George 148
Bourke, E. M. 184
Bourne, Kenneth 346
Bourne, Ruth M. 329
Bourret, F. M. 361
Boustany, S. 56 n.
Boxer, C. R. 251
Brailsford, H. N. 17, 453
Brasted, Howard 121 n.
Brathwaite, Edward (Kamau) 141, 319
Braudel, Fernand 645
Bravo, Michael T. 274
Brebner, John Bartlett 81, 154–5, 294 *see also* Hansen
Breckenridge, Carol A. 212, 581 n.
Breen, T. H. 79 n., 102, 110
Breen, T. H., and Innes, Stephen 317
Brent, Peter 297
Brett, E. A. 508
Brewer, John 98
Bridenbaugh, Carl 80, 83, 87 n.
Bridenbaugh, Carl and Roberta 318
Bridge, Carl 233, 358, 360–1
Bridge, Cyprian 328
Briggs, John 196
Britain and Decolonisation (Darwin) 236, 350
Britain and the Commonwealth Alliance, 1918–1939 (Holland) 363
Britain and the Conquest of Africa (Uzoigwe) 458
Britain and the Old Dominions (Miller) 360, 625
Britain and the Persian Gulf, 1795–1880 (Kelly) 334, 425

Britain and the Revolt in Cyprus (Holland) 433
Britain, China and the Anti-Missionary Riots, 1891–1900 (Wehrle) 398
Britain, the Brookes and Brunei (Tarling) 409
Britain, the United States, and the End of the Palestine Mandate (Ovendale) 362, 431
Britain's Annexation of Labuan in 1846 (Ingleson) 408
Britain's Encounter with Revolutionary China, (Tuck-hong Tang) 395
Britain's Imperial Century, 1815–1914 (Hyam) 355
Britain's Moment in the Middle East (1914–1971) (Monroe) 418
Britannia at Bay (Haggie) 412
Britischer Imperialismus im Fernen Ost . . . (Osterhammel) 399–400
British Baptist Missionaries in India (Potts) 208, 209
British Commonwealth of Nations, The (Hall) 125, 559–60
British Conquest and Dominion of India, The (Moon) 202, 215
British Defence Policy East of Suez, 1947–68 (Darby) 339
British Diplomacy and Finance in China, 1895–1914 (Edwards) 391
British Diplomacy in China, 1880–1885 (Kiernan) 386
British Discovery of Hinduism in the Eighteenth Century (Marshall) 206
British East Africa, or IBEA (McDermott) 451
British Empire, The (Walker) 32–33, 622
British Empire, 1558–1983, The (Lloyd) 356, 621
British Empire before the American Revolution, The (Gipson) 75, 95
British Empire in Australia, The (Fitzpatrick) 173
British Empire in the Middle East, The (Louis) 236, 351, 431, 553
British Historians and the West Indies (Williams) 136
British Imperial Policy and Decolonisation, 1938–64 (Porter and Stockwell) 412
British Imperialism (Cain and Hopkins) 17, 66–7, 400, 552, 661
British Imperialism in Australia, 1788–1833 (Fitzpatrick) 172–3
British in Malaya, 1880–1941, The (Butcher) 414
British Isles, The (Kearney) 131
British Mandarins and Chinese Reformers (Attwell) 392
British Naval Documents, 1204–1960 (Hattendorf) 339
British Navy in Adversity, The (James) 329
British Opium Policy in China and India (Owen) 384
British Orientalism and the Bengal Renaissance (Kopf) 206
British Policy and Malay Politics . . . (Stockwell) 412
British Policy in China, 1895–1902 (Young) 389
British Policy in Kenya Colony (Dilley) 502
British Policy in the Malay Peninsula Archipelago, 1824–71 (Tarling) 408
British Policy in the Malay Peninsula, 1880–1910 (Thio) 408
British Policy Towards the Indian States, 1905–1939 (Ashton) 233
British Rule and Rebellion (Simson) 619
British Seapower and Procurement Between the Wars (Gordon) 338
British Slave Emancipation and Apprenticeship in the British West Indies (Mathieson) 139
British Strategy in the Far East, 1919–1939 (Louis) 391
British Trade and the Opening of China, 1800–42 (Greenberg) 388
Britons (Colley) 131
Brock, Peggy 311
Brockway, Lucille 272
Broomfield, J. H. 222
Brougham, Henry 56
Broughton, Ruka 188
Brown, Donald E. 409
Brown, Jonathan C. 445 n.
Brown, Jonathan. C., and Knight, Alan 447 n.
Brown, Judith M. 217, 218, 657
Brown, Judith M., and Foot, Rosemary 395
Brown, Percy 573, 587
Brown, Robert 464–5
Brownfoot, Janice 285 n., 618
Bruce, James 290
Brunei (Brown) 409
Brunschwig, Henri 616
Bryant A. T. 521
Bryce, James 2, 34
Brydon, Diana, and Tiffin, Helen 658
Buchan, John 618, 621, 658
Buckingham, James Silk 56
Buddhism in Sinhalese Society, 1750–1900 (Malalgoda) 247
Buell, Raymond Leslie 21 n., 472, 502
Buganda and British Overrule (Low and Pratt) 505
Buick, T. Lindsay 186
Bull, Hedley, and Watson, Adam 554
Bulletin (weekly) 167–8
Bullion, John L. 82 n., 92 n.
Bulmer-Thomas, Victor 447 n.
Bundy, Colin 532
Bungalow, The (King) 593
Bunting, Brian 359
Burdened with Cyprus (Reddaway) 433
Burdens of History (Burton) 228, 665
Burke, Edmund 581

Burma (Tinker) 362, 413
Burmese Days (Orwell) 18
Burn, Richard 214
Burn, W. L. 139
Burney, James 366, 367 n., 368
Burns, Sir Alan 138
Burroughs, Peter 158
Burt, A. L. 154
Burt, Ben 375
Burton, Antoinette 228, 285 n., 665
Bush, Barbara 321
Bushman, Richard L. 86 n., 95 n.
Busteed, H. E. 198 n.
Butcher, John 414
Butler, Jeffrey 516 n.
Butler, Jon 110 n.
Butler, Sir William 613
Butlin, Noel 176
Butt, Isaac 118–19
Butterfield, Herbert 612, 614
Buxton, C. R. 21
Byron, Robert 592

Cady, John F. 411
Cain, P. J., and Hopkins, A. G. 17, 66–7, 68, 274, 400, 403 n., 422, 461, 552, 621, 661
Cairns, H. A. C. 479 n.
Callander, John 368
Callaway, Helen 665
Callwell, Colonel C. E. 330, 619
Cambridge History of Africa 460, 483, 489, 529, 530
Cambridge History of China 399
Cambridge History of India 198, 214, 245
Cambridge History of Southeast Asia 405
Cambridge History of the British Empire 10, 11–12, 25, 43, 46, 47, 50, 51, 52, 151, 171–2, 173, 185–6, 264, 265, 294, 295, 306 n., 343, 354–5, 518, 520, 620, 667
Cambridge Illustrated History of the British Empire 666
Cambridge Modern History 10–11
Cambridge Shorter History of India 198
Campbell, Mavis 321
Campbell, Reginald 619
Campbell-Johnson, Alan 255
Canada and Its Provinces (series) 150, 151
Canada and the Age of Conflict (Stacey) 358
Canada, the United States and Great Britain (Burt) 154
Canada under British Rule, 1760–1905 (Bourinot) 148
Canada's First Century (Creighton) 156
Canadian Landscape Painters (Robson) 573–4
Canny, Nicholas, and Pagden, Anthony 88 n.
Cape Colour Question, The (Macmillan) 25
Cape Coloured People, 1652–1937, The (Marais) 519
Capital Investment in Africa (Frankel) 471, 521
Capital of the Tycoon, The (Alcock) 380
Capitalism and Slavery (Williams) 24, 139, 323
Capra, Frank 630
Cardoso, F. H., and Faletto, E. 440
Carey, Peter 56 n.
Carey, William 208
Carter, Harold 299
Carter, Paul 299
Carthill, Al. 541 n.
Cartier, George E. 150
Casada, James 300
Casey, Lord 563–4, 567
Cassells, N. G. 211
Caste Conflict and Élite Formation (Roberts) 247
Cavieres, Eduardo 444 n.
Cell, John W. 20 n., 220, 316 n., 471 n.
Centuries of Childhood (Ariés) 658
Century of Wrong, A (Smuts) 516, 523
Ceylon (Jeffries) 249
Ceylon (Pakeman) 248
Ceylon: An Export Economy (Snodgrass) 247–8
Ceylon (Tennent) 244
Ceylon Historical Journal 250
Ceylon Journal of Historical and Social Studies 250
Ceylon Under British Rule, 1795–1932 (Mills) 245
Ceylon Under the British (Mendis) 246
Ceylon Under the British Occupation, 1795–1833 (de Silva) 246
Chadwick, John 567
Chakrabarty, D. 605 n.
Challenging Colonialism (Davis) 428
Chan, Ming K. 395
Chan, Stephen 565
Chang Hsin-paa 388
Channing, Edward 75
Channock, Martin 528
Character Factory, The (Rosenthal) 658
Charles Grant and British Rule in India (Embree) 208
Charters, David A. 428 n.
Charts and Surveys in Peace and War (Morris) 337
Chase, John 513
Chatterji, Joya 240, 260, 605 n.
Chaudhuri, K. N. 46, 251
Chaudhuri, Muhammad Ali 256
Chaudhuri, Napur 665
Chaudhuri, Nirad C. 218
Cheong, Yong Mun 413
Chesneaux, Jean 389
Chew, Daniel 414
Chew, Ernest, and Lee, Edwin 414
Childers, Erskine 122–3

Childs, John 85 n.
Chilembwe, John 309, 529, 538
Chi-ming, Hou 397
China and Christianity (Cohen) 398
China and England (Soothill) 382
China and Great Britain (Dean) 398
China and the West, 1858–1861 (Banno) 397–8
China, Britain and Hong Kong, 1895–1945 (Lau Kit-ching) 394
China Consuls, The (Coates) 392
China Quest for Railway Autonomy, 1904–1911 (Lee) 397
China Station, The (Graham) 334, 391
China to Me (Hahn) 393
China's Early Industrialization (Feuerwerker) 396
China's Entrance into the Family of Nations (Hsü) 396
China's Response to the West (Fairbank) 395
China's Struggle for Tariff Autonomy (Wright) 384
Chinese Account of the Opium War (Wei Yuan) 381
Chinese in Malaya, The (Purcell) 406
Chinese in South East Asia, The (Purcell) 406
Chinese Leadership and Power in Colonial Singapore (Yong) 414
Chinese Pioneers on the Sarawak Frontier (Chew) 414
Chinese Politics in Malaysia (Heng Pek Koon) 414
Chinese Railways and British Interests, 1898–1911 (Zen) 396
Chinese Repository 379, 381
Chinese Secret Societies in Malaya (Comber) 411
Chinese Thought and Institutions (Fairbank) 396
Chinese War, The (Ouchterlang) 388
Chirol, Sir Valentine 217, 618
Chomondeley, Thomas 183
Ch'ou Pan Yi Wu Shih Mo (Reign of Tao-Kuang) 386
Christian Missions and the Creation of Northern Rhodesia (Rotberg) 307
Christian Missions in Nigeria, 1841–1891 (Ajayi) 307
Christianity in Ceylon (Tennent) 244
Christianity in India (Kaye) 208
Christie, Ian R. 96, 97 n.
Christie, Ian R., and Labaree, Benjamin W. 49, 97 n.
Chronicles of the East India Company Trading to China, 1635–1834, The (Morse) 381, 384–5
Churchill, Cripps and India, 1939–1945 (Moore) 234
Churchill and the Jews (Cohen) 628
Cippola, Carlo, M. 272
Claridge, W. W. 464
Clark, Christopher 108 n.
Clark, C. M. H. (Manning) 68, 174–5
Clark, J. C. D. 89, 110
Clark, John 274
Clark, Nancy 536
Clarke, Dora Mae 82 n.
Clarkson, Thomas 463
Classical Period of the First British Empire, 1689–1783, The (Madden) 43
Clayton, Anthony 349
Clifford, Nicholas R. 390–1
Clive, John 268
Clowes, William Laird 330
Coad, Jonathan 338
Coates, P. D. 392
Cobbing, J. 538
Cochran, S. 397
Codrington, H. W. 245
Coghlan, Sir Timothy 167
Cohen, David, and Odhiambo, Atieno E. S. 511
Cohen, I. B. 268
Cohen, Michael J. 428 n., 429, 628
Cohen, Paul 398
Cohn, Bernard S. 207, 221, 222
Cole, Henry 572
Cole, Juan 424
Colebrooke-Cameron Papers (Mendis) 248
Coleman, James 480
Colenso, Frances 514
Colgate, H. A. 334
Collection and Disposal of the Maritime and Customs Revenue . . . , The (Wright) 384
Collection of Treaties, Engagements and Sunnuds . . . (Aitchison) 197
Colley, Linda 71, 131
Collingwood, R. G. 5 n., 616
Collins, Edward Day 465
Collis, Maurice 395
Colomb, Admiral P. H. 328
Colonial Background of the American Revolution, The (Andrews) 76
Colonial Masculinity (Sinha) 223, 665
Colonial Period of American History, The (Andrews) 76
Colonial Policy and Practice (Furnivall) 26
Colonial Self-Government (Hart) 74
Colonial South Africa . . . (Keegan) 538
Colonial Urban Development (King) 592
Colonialism and Christian Missions (Neill) 307
Colonialism and Iban Warfare (Wagner) 410
Colonialism in Africa (Gann and Duignan) 459, 483
Colonialism's Culture (Thomas) 377
Colquhoun, P. 55 n.
Colvin, Auckland 424–5

Comaroff, Jean 309
Comaroff, John and Jean 313 n., 538
Comber, Leon 411
Comerford, R. V. 117
Commercial Empire of the St Lawrence, 1760–1850, The (Creighton) 153
Commercial Revolution in Nineteenth Century China, The (Hao) 397
Commissioner Lin and the Opium War (Chang Hsin-pao) 388
Commitment to Empire (Ingram) 333
Commodity Culture of Victorian England, The (Richards) 580
Commonsense on Pakistan (Sufi) 255
Commonwealth and Britain, The (Austin) 566
Commonwealth in the 1980s (Groom and Taylor) 567
Commonwealth in the World, The (Miller) 357, 564
Commonwealth of Nations, The (Curtis) 559
Commonwealth of Nations, The (McIntyre) 355
Communal Politics under the Donoughmore Constitution, 1931–1947 (Russell) 249
Community and Consensus in Islam (Shaikh) 258
Compendium of South African History and Geography (Theal) 513
Comprador in Nineteenth Century China, The (Hao Yen-p'ing) 397
Condliffe, J. B. 185
Coney, Sandra 189 n.
Congress and the Raj (Low) 219, 232, 234
Conlon, Frank 205
Connolly, Bob 367
Constantine, Stephen 582 n.
Constitution, Administration, and Laws of the Empire, The (Keith) 625
Constitutional History and Law of Southern Rhodesia, The (Palley) 527
Constitutional History of India, 1600–1935, A (Keith) 28
Constitutional History of the First British Empire (Keith) 28
Consul in Paradise (Wood) 383
Contemporary History of India, A (Balabushevitch and Dayakov) 219
Contemporary Review (journal) 120
Contemporary South Asia (journal) 241
Contest for North Sumatra, The (Reid) 410
Contesting Colonial Hegemony (Engels and Marks) 663
Convict Settlers of Australia, The (Robson) 175
Convict Society and Its Enemies (Hirst) 175
Convict Workers (Nicholas) 175
Convicts and Empire (MacKay) 335–6
Convicts and the Colonies (Shaw) 175
Cook, A. N. 472
Cook, Albert 500
Cooley, W. D. 290
Coolidge, Martha Henderson 382 *see also* Fairbank
Coomaraswamy, A. K. 573, 587
Coombes, Annie E. 581 n.
Coombs, D. S. 478
Cooper, Frederick 509, 555, 663
Copland, Ian 221 n., 233, 241 n.
Coppell, W. G., and Stratigos, S. 369 n.
Corbett, Julian 328–9, 330
Corbett, Percy 154
Cordier, Henri 380
Corris, Peter 375
Cory, Sir George 592
Costello, John A. 130
Costin, W. C. 385–6
Cotton, Evan 575
Cotton and the Egyptian Economy (Owen) 427
Countdown to Rebellion (Kelling) 433
Country and Calling (Hancock) 173
Countryman, Edward 104
Coupland, Sir Reginald 7, 23–4, 52, 58 n., 217, 232–3, 238–40, 295, 307, 322, 455, 468–9, 474, 504, 518 n., 621–2
Couyoumdjian, J. R. 445 n.
Cowan, C. D. 38 n., 408
Cowan, James 186
Cowman, Ian 331 n.
Cox, Edward 322
Cox, Percy 618
Cox-George, N. A. 479
Crackle of Thorns, A (Kirkbride) 426
Crais, C. *see* Worden 316
Cranborne, Lord 129
Cranefield, Paul F. 279 n.
Craton, Michael 139 n., 320, 321
Crawford, Michael J. 88 n.
Crawford, R. M. 173–4, 175
Crawford, W. Sharman 118
Creighton, Donald Grant 153–4, 156, 333
Creighton, Mandell (Bishop of London) 7 n.
Crimean War, The (Lambert) 333
Cripps, Sir Stafford 234
Cripps Mission, The (Mansergh and Lumby) 234
Crisis of Indian Unity, The, 1917–40 (Moore) 224, 233
Critical Study of the First Anglo-Chinese War . . ., A (Kuo) 386
Critics of Empire (Porter) 660
Crittenden, Victor *see* Borchardt
Cromer, Earl of 13, 425, 618–19, 623
Cronon, William 664
Crooks, J. J. 464, 466
Crops and Wealth in Uganda (Wrigley) 505
Crosby, Alfred W. 69 n., 279, 664
Cross, Colin 361

Crossroads to Israel (Sykes) 629
Crowder, Michael 458 n.
Crowe, S. E. 455, 470
Crowley, Frank 175
Crowns of Glory, Tears of Blood (da Costa) 320
Crucial Years of Early Anglo-Chinese Relations, The (Pritchard) 384
Crystal, Jill 426 n.
Culture and Imperialism (Said) 207, 425
Cunneen, Chris 177
Curing their Ills (Vaughan) 280
Curtin, John 360, 361
Curtin, Philip D. 142, 279, 316, 480, 482
Curtis, L. Perry 7, 14–15, 29, 559, 578 n., 625
Curzon, George N. 13, 292 n., 424, 617

da Costa, Emilia Viotti 320
Dafoe, J. W. 153
Dalhousie, Lord 407
Dallas, K. M. 336
Dalrymple, Alexander 290
Daly, Martin 428
Dalziel, Raewyn 189 n.
Dangerfield, George 17
Darby, Philip 339
Darwin, Charles 616
Darwin, John 19 n., 28, 236, 348, 349, 350
Datta, V. N. 211
Davenport, R. *see* Elphick
Davenport, T. R. H. 539 n.
Davidson, Allen K. 313 n.
Davidson, Basil 488
Davidson, J. W. 34, 370–1, 372
Davies, C. C. 202
Davies, K. G. 46, 476
Davies, Philip 594
Davis, David Brion 324
Davis, Eric 428
Davis, Lance E., and Huttenback, Robert E. 351, 638 n., 655
Davis, Thomas 117
Daws, Gavan 372
Dawson, Frank Griffith 444 n.
Dawson, L. S. 337
Dawson, W. H. 453 n., 469
Day, Sir Archibald 337
Dayakov, A. *see* Balabushevitch
de Kiewiet, Cornelius 25, 519, 520, 532, 533
de Silva, Colvin R. 246, 247
de Silva, K. M. 247, 248, 249
de Silva, K. M., and Wriggins, Howard 250
de Valera, Eamon 125, 128, 129
Deadly Dreams (Wong) 388
Deakin, Alfred 168, 169
Dean, Britten 398–9
Death by Migration (Curtin) 279
Decline and Fall of the Roman Empire (Gibbon) 3
Decline, Revival and Fall of the British Empire (Gallagher) 550
Decolonising Fictions (Brydon and Tiffin) 658
Decolonization in Africa (Hargreaves) 554
Decolonization and African Society (Cooper) 555
Decorative Art of British New Guinea (Hattan) 574
Deeds that Won the Empire (Fitchett) 170
Deetz, James 594
Degler, Carl 317
Deighton, Len 612 n.
Delusions and Discoveries (Perry) 665
Democracy Shelved (Yui-sang Tsang) 394
Demos, John 83 n.
Dening, Greg 336–7, 372, 376
Denison, George T. 160
Denny, Alice 39 n., 637 n., 660
Denoon, Donald *see* MacLeod, R.
Deraniyagala, S. U. 250
Derrida, Jacques 597, 606, 648 n.
Desai, A. R. 216
Desai, W. S. 407
Desert and the Sown, The (Bell) 617
Development of Extraterritoriality in China, The (Keeton) 383
Development of the British West Indies, 1700–1763, The (Pitman) 139
Dewaraja, L. S. 247
Dewey, Clive 215
Dharmadasa, K. N. O. 249
Dhiravegin, Likhit 410
Diaries in Ceylon (Woolf) 250
Dicey, Albert Venn 119–20, 123
Dicey, Edward 450
Dickerson, Oliver M. 82 n.
Dickerson, Oliver M., and Barnes, Viola 76
Dictionary of the British Empire and Commonwealth (Palmer) 666
Dictionary of South African Biography 539
Die Geskiedenis van Ons Land in die Taal van Ons Volk (du Toit) 514
Diggins, John Patrick 109
Dike, Kenneth Onwuka 456, 475, 490
Dilke, Charles 8, 167, 342
Dilley, Marjorie 473, 502
Dillon, Peter 372
Dingman, Roger 331 n.
Diop, Cheikh Anta 489
Dipavamsa (Geiger) 245
Diplomacy and Enterprise (Endicott) 391
Diplomacy of Imperial Retreat, The (Fung) 394–5
Diplomacy of Imperialism, 1890–1902, The (Langer) 385, 389

Diplomatic History of Ireland, 1948–49, A (McCabe) 130
Dirks, Nicholas 205, 211
Disastrous Twilight (Hamid) 256
Discovering Monaro (Hancock) 664
Discovery of Australia, The (Wood) 293
Distant Dominion (Gough) 335
District Officer in India, 1930–1947, The (Hunt and Harrison) 220
Divide and Quit (Moon) 255
Dixson, Miriam 178 n.
Dobb, Maurice 65 n.
Documents of the Ceylon National Congress . . . (Roberts) 248
Documents on Australian Foreign Policy (Neale) 357
Documents on Canadian External Relations 358
Dodwell, H. H. 198, 214
d'Ombrain, Nicholas 345
Dominance Without Hegemony (Guha) 663
Donaldson, A. G. 127
Donnan, Elizabeth 467
Donohue, Hector 339
Doughty, Charles 617
Douin, George 427
Doxey, Margaret 566, 567, 569
Dragon and the Iron Horse, The (Huenemann) 397
Draper, Theodore 100
Drayton, Richard 274
Drescher, Seymour 323–4
Dresser, Louise 574
Drosdoff, Daniel 447 n.
Drum, The (film) 630
Drummond, Ian M. 30 n.
Du Bois, W. E. B. 487
du Toit, S. J. 514
Dual Mandate in Tropical Africa, The (Lugard) 21–2
Dubois, Abbé J. A. 196 n.
Dubos, René and Jean 279
Duignan, Peter *see* Gann
Duff, Charles 124
Duff, James Grant 194
Duffy, Charles Gavan 118, 120
Dundas, Charles 503
Dunlap, William 572 n.
Dunn, Peter 413
Dunn, Richard S. 44, 139 n., 317, 318
Dunraven, Lord 123
Durham, Lord 15, 58, 62, 150
Durrani, F. K. 255
Durrans, Brian 581 n.
Dutch Power in Ceylon (Arasaratnam) 247
Dutt, Romesh C. 225, 282
Dutt, R. Palme 216
Early History of Ceylon (Mendis) 246
East, The (Thompson) 579
East African Chiefs (Richards) 505
East India Company, 1784–1813, The (Philips) 202
East India Company in Eighteenth-Century Politics, The (Sutherland) 35, 202
Eclipse of Empire (Low) 430, 661
Ecological Imperialism (Crosby) 664
Ecology and Empire (Griffiths and Robin) 664
Econocide (Drescher) 323
Economic Development (Knowles) 470
Economic History of West Africa, An (Hopkins) 661
Economic Revolution in British West Africa, The (McPhee) 470
Economics and Empire, 1830–1914 (Fieldhouse) 390, 459, 660
Economy of Modern India, 1860–1970, The (Tomlinson) 241
Edney, Matthew 274
Edwards, Bryan 55
Edwards, E. W. 391
Egerton, Hugh 12–13, 14, 627
Egnal, Marc 101
Egypt and Cromer (Sayyid [Marsot]) 427
Egypt As It Is (McCoan) 619
Egypt from Independence to Revolution, 1919–1952 (Botman) 431
Egypt in the Reign of Muhammad Ali (Marsot) 428
Egypt: Imperialism and Revolution (Berque) 432
Egypt, Islam, and the Arabs (Gershoni and Jankowski) 432
Egypt since Cromer (Lloyd) 426
Egypt's Liberal Experiment, 1922–1936 (Marsot) 427–428
Ehrlich, C. 478
Eitel, E. J. 393
Elder, J. R. 186 n.
Elementary Aspects of Peasant Insurgency in Colonial India (Guha) 224
Ellis, A. B. 464
Elphick, R., and Davenport, R. 313 n.
Elphick, R., and Giliomee, Herman 537
Elphinstone, Mountstuart 54, 194, 202 n.
Eltis, David 316–17, 323–4
Elton, G. R, 6 n.
Emancipation and Apprenticeship in the British West Indies (Burn) 139
Emberson-Bain, Atu 372
Embree, Ainslie T. 208
Emergence of Pakistan, The (Chaudhri) 256
Emergencies and Disorders . . . (Holland) 554
Emerson, Rupert 26, 406
Emerson, William 590
Eminent Churchillians (Roberts) 240, 262

Eminent Victorians (Strachey) 18 n., 297
Emmer, P. C., and Mörner, M. 70 n.
Empire and Commerce in Africa (Woolf) 20, 453, 469
Empire and Commonwealth (Martin) 152
Empire and Sexuality (Hyam) 285, 665
Empire at War, The (Lucas) 343
Empire of Nature, The (MacKenzie) 664
Empire of the North Atlantic (Graham) 333
Empire of the St Lawrence (Creighton) 153
Empires of the Monsoon (Hall) 251
End of Empire in the Middle East, The (Balfour-Paul) 433
End of the Palestine Mandate, The (Louis and Stookey) 429
Endacott, George B. *see* Birch
Endicott, Stephen Lyon 391
Endgames of Empire (Moore) 233
End of the Palestine Mandate (Louis) 431
Engage the Enemy More Closely (Barnett) 339
Engels, Dagmar, and Marks, Shula 663
Engels, Friedrich 117, 624
Engerman, Stanley L. *see* Solow
England in Egypt (Milner) 13, 425
England in the Mediterranean (Corbett) 328
England's Case against Home Rule (Dicey) 120
English Constitution, The (Bagehot) 626
English Historical Review (journal) 2, 8, 23, 34–5, 272
English Utilitarians and India, The (Stokes) 203
Englishman and His History, The (Butterfield) 612
Enhan, Lee 397
Enquiry Concerning the Origin of our Ideas of the Sublime and the Beautiful (Burke) 581
Entangled Objects (Thomas) 377
Environmental History (journal) 665
Erikson, Erik 223
Ernst, Joseph A. 101
Errington, Frederick 375
Errington, Jane 160
Escape from Empire (Moore) 125, 237, 260
Etherington, Norman 17 n.
Europe and the People Without History (Wolf) 663
Europe in China (Eitel) 393
European Architecture in India, 1750–1850 (Nilsson) 592
European Imperialism, 1860–1914 (Porter) 666
European Vision and the South Pacific (Smith) 578, 579
European Vision of America, The (Honour) 578
European Woman and the Second British Empire (Strobel) 665
Evatt, H. V. 172
Evolution of Culture (Pitt-Rivers) 574
Ewing, T. T. 167 *see* Coghlan
Expansion of England (Seeley) 3, 8, 10, 13, 43, 57, 59, 385, 614
Expansion of International Society, The (Bull and Watson) 554
Expedient Utopian, The (Manor) 249
Experiment with Freedom: India and Pakistan, 1947 (Tinker) 257
Exploitation of East Africa, 1856–1890, The (Coupland) 295 n., 469
Extraterritoriality in Japan (Jones) 383

Facing Mount Kenya (Kenyatta) 504
Fagan, Brian 282 n.
Fage, John 38–9, 477, 478, 488
Fairbank, John King 395–6, 399
Fairbank, John King; Coolidge, Martha Henderson; Smith, Richard J. 382
Fall of the British Empire, 1918–1968, The (Cross) 361
Fall of Imperial Britain in South East Asia, The (Tarling) 414
Fall of the Planter Class in the British Carribbean, 1763–1833, The (Ragatz) 139, 323
Fallers, Lloyd 506 n.
Famine in Zimbabwe (Iliffe) 283
Fanon, Frantz 273, 543, 494 n., 656
Fanning, Ronan 129
Far East in World Politics, The (Hudson) 385
Far Eastern International Relations (Morse and MacNair) 382
Farewell the Trumpets (Morris) 657
Farley, John 278 n.
Fatal History of Portuguese Ceylon, The (Winius) 247
Faletto, E. *see* Cardoso
Father and Daughter (Shahnawaz) 256
Favenc, Ernest 169
Fay, C. R. 477
Fay, Peter Ward 388
Fear God and Dread Nought (Marder) 331
Feierman, Steven 278 n., 511
Fellowes, Robert 243
Fenians and Canada, The (Senior) 118
Fenians in Australia, The (Amos) 118
Fergusson, James 584–5, 587
Ferishta, Muhammad Kasim Hindu 196
Fermor-Hesketh 594
Fernea, Robert, and Louis, Wm. Roger 432
Ferns, H. S. 440
Feuerwerker, Albert 396, 399
Field, Barron 165
Fieldhouse, D. K. 16, 28, 38, 60 n., 390, 399, 459, 659–60
Finance, Trade, and Politics in British Foreign Policy (Platt) 380 n., 390
Finch, M. H. J. 445 n.

Findlay, G. G., and Holdsworth, W. W. 304–5 n.
First A. I. F., The (Robson) 176
First Contact (film) 367
First Decade of the Australian Commonwealth, The (Turner) 167
First Vietnam War, The (Dunn) 413
Fischer, David H. 87
Fisher, Robin 310 n.
Fisher, Ruth A. 467
Fisher and Cunningham (Ollard) 332
Fisk, Robert 129
Fissured Land, The (Gadgil) 664
Fitchett, W. H. 170
Fitzhardinge, L. F. 177 n.
Fitzpatrick, Brian 172, 176
Fitzpatrick, Peter 373, 619
Five Colonial Artists of New England (Bayley) 574
Fleming, Donald 268, 269
Fletcher, Robert 376
Flight and Rebellion (Mullin) 320
Flinders, Matthew 169, 293
Flint, John E. 31 n., 38, 456, 457 n., 476, 526
Flowering Wilderness, The (Galsworthy) 619
Fodor, Jorge 447 n.
Fogel, R. W., and Engerman, S. L. 315 n.
Foner, Eric 104 n.
Foot, Rosemary *see* Brown
Ford, John 279 n., 537 n.
Foreign Diplomacy in China, 1894–1900 (Joseph) 385
Foreign Investment and Economic Development in China (Chi-ming) 397
Foreign Investments in China (Remer) 383
Foreign Relations of the United States 234
Foreign Rights and Interests in China (Willoughby) 382
Foreign Trade in China (Remer) 383
Forests and Sea Power (Albion) 329
Forman, Charles W. 311 n., 313 n.
Forrest, Denys 251
Forster, E. M. 18, 217, 619
Forster, J. R. 368
Förster, S., Mommsen, W. J., and Robinson, R. 460 n.
Foster, Stephen 268
Foster, William 575
Foucault, Michel 68, 273, 277, 279, 280, 593, 597, 647, 659
Foundation of Dutch Power in Ceylon (Goonewardena) 247
Founding of the Second British Empire, The (Harlow) 36, 336
Four Feathers, The (Mason) 619
Fourth Anglo-Burmese War, The (Tarling) 413
Fox, William 463 n.
Framework of Home Rule, The (Childers) 122
France, Peter 371
Frank, André Gunder 439, 532, 642
Frankel, S. Herbert 471, 521
Franklin, Sir John 291, 337
Fraser, T. G. 125
Frazier, E. Franklin 318
Fredrickson, George M. 316 n.
Freedom and Independence for the Golden Hands of Australia (Lang) 166
Freud, Sigmund 287
Friedberg, Aaron 348
Friedman, Isaiah 429 n.
Fritsch, Winston 447 n.
From Deserts the Prophets Come (Serle) 176
From Empire Defence to the Long Haul (Donohue) 339
From Memory (Noon) 256
From Rebellion to Revolution (Genovese) 320
From the Dreadnought to Scapa Flow (Marder) 331
Fromkin, David 356
Frost, Alan 335–6, 372
Froude, J. A. 8, 120, 167
Fowles, Joseph 591
Fry, Howard T. 336
Frye, Northrop 627
Frykenberg, Robert E. 204, 209, 210
Fung, Edmund S. K. 394–5
Furber, Holden 202
Furlong, Patrick J. 359
Furnivall, B. R. 407, 411
Furnivall, J. S. 26, 141
Fyfe, Christopher 479

Gadgil, M., and Guha, Ramchandra 664
Galbraith, John S. 66 n., 334, 459, 526
Galenson, David W. 318
Gallagher, John (Jack) 4, 32, 343–4, 363, 477, 550
Gallagher, John, and Robinson, Ronald 38, 389, 413, 423–4, 437 n., 440–1, 455, 456–7, 458, 481, 493, 525, 535, 553, 627, 637, 659, 660, 661
Gallagher, J., Johnson, G., and Seal, A. 231, 258 n.
Galloway, Joseph 94 n.
Galsworthy, John 619
Gambling Style of Government, A (Black) 414
Gandhi (Brown) 217
Gann, Lewis 479–80
Gann, L. (Lewis) G., and Duignan, Peter 285, 459, 483
Garrett, John 313 n.
Gascoigne, John 61 n.
Gaspar, David Barry 320
Geiger, Wilhelm 245
Geiss, Imanuel 482
Gelfand, Michael 278, 282
Gellner, Ernest 207, 212 n.

Georgian Canada (Webster) 577
Geography of the Surrounding Oceans (Hsü) 381
Gender, Culture and Empire (Callaway) 665
General History of the Caribbean (UNESCO) 137
Genovese, Eugene D. 315 n., 320, 531–2
Geographical Journal 464
George, Claude 464
Gershoni, Israel, and Jankowski, James 432
Geertz, Clifford 106
Gewertz, Deborah 375
Ghana (Bourret) 361
Gholan Hossain Khan, Saiyid 56, 194, 196
Ghorbal, S. 427
Ghosh, K. K. 414
Gibbon, Edward 1, 3–5, 8, 614
Gibbons, Peter 187
Gibbs, N. H. 344
Gidley, Mark 578 n.
Gifford, Prosser 459
Gilbert, Martin 220
Giliomee, H. *see* Elphick
Gilje, Paul A. 105
Gilks, John *see* Orr
Gillard, D. R. 348
Gilley, Sheridan 131
Gillion, K. L. 371
Gilmartin, David 259
Gipson, Lawrence Henry 49, 74, 79, 95–6
Gittens, Jean 393
Gittings, John 395
Gladstone, W. E. 120–1, 450
Glassman, Jonathon 509
Glazebrook, George 155
Glendevon, John 233
Glubb, Sir John Bagot 426, 431
Gluckman, Max 522
Goetz, Herman 587
Goldberg, Ellis 428
Goldie, Sir George 451, 464
Gollan, Robin 173
Gooch, G. P., and Temperley, Harold 453 n.
Gooch, John 346, 348
Goodfellow, C. F. 525–6
Goodwin, Paul B. 444 n.
Goody, Jack 610 n.
Goonatilake, Susantha 271
Goonewardena, K. W. 247
Gopal, Sarvepalli 240
Gopinath, Aruna 414
Gordon, D. C. 346
Gordon, G. A. H. 338
Gordon, S. C. *see* Augier
Gordon-Walker, Patrick 567
Gore, A. A. 463 n.
Gough, Barry M. 334–5
Gould, Rupert 294
Goveia, Elsa V. 135–6, 141, 319
Government and Politics of Hong Kong, The (Miners) 394
Government and the People, The (Hasluck) 357
Government by Committee (Wheare) 28
Government of Northern Ireland, The (Mansergh) 129
Governors General, The (Webb) 84
Graham, Gerald S. 37–8, 58 n., 272, 327, 332–4, 391–2, 340, 475
Graham, Richard 448
Grammar of Ornament, The (Jones) 572
Gramsci, Antonio 68, 224, 277, 279, 607, 647
Granatstein, J. L. 158
Granatstein, J. L., and Bothwell, Robert 358
Grant, Charles 208
Grant, George P. 156
Grant, John W. 313
Gravil, R., and Rooth, T. 447 n.
Gray, J. M. 467
Gray, Richard 309, 479, 527
Great Britain and China, 1833–1860 (Costin) 385–6
Great Britain and the Opening of Japan, 1834–1858 (Beasley) 389
Great Britain in the Indian Ocean (Graham) 334, 391
Great Britain's Woodyard (Lower) 329
Great Divide, The (Hodson) 240, 255
Great Illusion, The (Angell) 17
Green, William 143
Green Imperialism . . . (Grove) 251, 664
Greenberg, Michael 388
Greene, Jack P. 73 n., 78, 79 n., 88 n., 89, 96, 98, 95
Greenhalgh, Paul 581 n.
Greenhill, Robert G. 445 n., 448 n.
Greenhill, R., and Miller, Rory 448 n.
Greenmantle (Buchan) 618
Greenway, Francis 590–1
Greenwood, Gordon 172
Gregory, Robert G. 482
Gregory, Theodore 535
Greven Jnr., Philip J. 83 n.
Grey, George (Governor) 182–3
Grimal, Henri 549
Griffiths, Tom, and Robin, Libby 664
Groans of the Plantations, The (Littleton) 632
Groom, A. J. R. 566
Groom, A. J. R. and Taylor, Paul 567
Gross, Robert 104, 106
Grove, Eric 339
Grove, Richard H. 69 n., 251, 274, 664
Growing (Woolf) 250
Growing Up in British India (Walsh) 223
Growse, F. S. 591
Growth of Empire, The (Jose) 170

Growth of the Church in Buganda, The (Taylor) 506
Guha, Ramchandra 69 n., 224 n., *see also* Gadgil
Guha, Ranajit 203, 207, 224, 601, 605 n., 649 n., 663
Guha-Thakurta, Tapati 226, 581
Gullick, John 409
Gunawardhana, R. A. L. H. 250
Gunboat Frontier (Gough) 335
Gunga Din (film) 630
Gunson, Niel 371
Guntur District, 1788–1848 (Frykenberg) 204
Gupta, Amit Kumar 232, 235
Gupta, C. 203 n.
Gupta, Partha Sarathi 235
Gutman, Herbert 321
Guy, Jeff 308 n.

H. J. van Mook and Indonesian Independence (Cheong) 413
Haas, Ernest 199 n.
Hacker, Louis M. 100–1
Hadith (series) 507
Haggard, Rider J. 515, 658
Haggie, Ian Paul 331 n., 412
Hahn, Emily 393
Hailey, Malcolm 31–2, 471, 473
Hailey (Cell) 220
Hakluyt Handbook, The (Quinn)
Hakluyt, Richard 290
Half a Century of Australasian Progress (Westgarth) 167
Half a Century of Conflict (Parkman) 147
Haliburton, Gordon M. 309 n.
Hall, D. G. *see* Augier
Hall, D. G. E. 407–8
Hall, Douglas 142 n., 143 n., 321
Hall, H. Duncan 125, 559–60, 567
Hall, Richard 251
Hallett, Robin 478
Halliday, Frederick 434
Hamid, Shahid 256
Hamill, Ian 331 n.
Hamilton, W. B. 564
Hancock, David 87 n.
Hancock, W. K. 7, 28–30, 33, 127, 128, 170, 173, 174, 359–60, 467, 471–2, 473, 474 n., 487 n., 520, 524, 526, 560–1, 664
Handbook to the Indian Court . . . (Birdwood) 572
Handler, Jerome S. 322
Handlin, Oscar, and Mary F. 317
Hankey: Man of Secrets (Roskill) 332
Hanna, A. J. 456, 488, 517 n., 527
Hansen, M. L., and Brebner, J. B. 154
Hao Yen-p'ing 397
Hardy, Peter 206, 257
Hargreaves, John D. 38, 460, 479, 554
Harkness, David W. 128 n., 662
Harling, Philip, and Mandler, Peter 92 n.
Harlow, Vincent T. 32, 35–7, 44, 51, 52, 60–1, 62, 65, 115, 136, 336, 475
Harries, John W. 313
Harries, Patrick 536
Harris, Kenneth 241 n.
Harris, M., and Lee, A. 582 n.
Harris, William Wade 309
Harrison, Henry 129
Harrison, John *see* Hunt
Harrison, Mark 273
Harrop, A. J. 186
Hart, A. B. 74
Hart and the Chinese Customs (Wright) 384
Hartwig, Gerald W., and Patterson, K. David 70 n., 278 n.
Harvey, G. E. 407
Hasan, Mushirul 232, 237, 239, 241
Hasluck, Paul 357
Hastings, Adrian 313 n.
Hattan, A. C. 574
Hattendorf, John B. 339
Havell, E. B. 573, 591
Hawkesworth, John 368
Hay, Jean 509
Hay, Margaret John 507
Hayes, James 394
Head, Raymond 594
Headrick, Daniel R. 272
Hearts and Minds in Guerilla Warfare (Stubbs) 412
Heath, Hilarie J. 443 n.
Heathcote T. A. 349 n.
Heaven's Command (Morris) 657
Henderson, G. C. 369
Henderson, Paul *see* Albert
Hendrickson, David C. *see* Tucker
Heng Pek Koon 414
Henretta, James A. 82 n., 103
Henshaw, Peter James 340
Henty, G. A. 620
Heras, R. G. 445 n., 447 n.
Herbert, Christopher 377
Herodotus 1
Herschel 265
Herskovits, Melville 318
Heuman, Gad 320, 322
Heuston, Robert F. V. 130
Higman, B. W. 319–20, 321
Hill, J. R. 338
Hill, Richard 186 n.
Hindle, Brooke 268 n.
Hirst, J. B. 175
Histoire de l'Egypte moderne . . . (Sammarco) 427

Histoire du règne du Khédive Ismaïl (Douin) 427
Historical and Statistical Account of New South Wales, An (Lang) 164
Historical Dictionary of the British Empire (Olson) 666
Historical Records of Australia (Watson) 169
Historical Relations of the Island Ceylon (Knox) 243
Historical Sketches of the South of India (Wilks) 194
Historical Studies: Australia and New Zealand (journal) 174
History and Culture of the Indian People, The (Mazumdar) 216
History, Civil and Commercial of the British Colonies in the West Indies, The (Edwards) 55
History of Australia (Clark) 174–5
History of Australia (Rusden) 167
History of Australian Exploration from 1788–1888, The (Favenc) 169
History of Barbados (Harlow) 136
History of Britain, Ireland . . . 131–2
History of British India, The (Mill) 194–5
History of British India . . . (Roberts) 198
History of Burma (Hall) 407
History of Canada (Kingsford) 148–9
History of Ceylon . . ., The (Fellowes) 243
History of Ceylon . . ., The (Knighton) 243
History of Ceylon (Paranavitana) 246–7
History of Christian Missions in China, A (Latourette) 383
History of Christianity in India (Hough) 208, 304
History of East Africa, A (Ingham) 505
History of England (1849–55) (Macaulay) 3
History of Freedom Movement in India (Mazumdar) 216
History of Hong Kong, A (Endacott) 394
History of Hong Kong, A (Welsh) 395
History of Indian and Eastern Architecture (Fergusson) 585, 587
History of Modern Sabah, A (Tregonning) 408
History of Serampore and its Missions, The (Potts) 209
History of Singapore, The (Chew and Lee) 414
History of Singapore, A (Turnbull) 414
History of Sri Lanka, A (de Silva) 248, 249
History of Tanganyika (Iliffe) 511
History of Tanzania, A (Kimambo and Temu) 507
History of Tasmania (West) 166
History of the Australian Colonies . . . (Jenks) 170
History of the British West Indies (Burns) 138
History of the Colonization of Africa . . ., A (Johnston) 489–90
History of the Colony of Victoria, A (Turner) 167
History of the Decline and Fall of the Roman Empire (Gibbon) 614
History of the Expansion of Christianity (Latourette) 305
History of the Freedom Movement (Tara Chand) 216
History of the Hong Kong and Shanghai Banking Corporation (King) 395
History of the Laws and Courts of Hong Kong (Norton-Kyshe) 393
History of the Military Transactions of the British Nation in Indostan, A (Orme) 194
History of the National Congress (Sitaramayya) 216
History of New Zealand (Sinclair) 187
History of the Peace Conference of Paris (Temperley) 633
History of the Rise of Mohomedan Power in India (Ferishta) 196
History of the United States, A (Bancroft) 75
History of the Upcountry Tamil People, A (Nadesan) 249
History of Zionism, A (Laqueur) 629
History's Anthropology (Dening) 336–7
Hobhouse, Emily 516
Hobley, C. W. 503 n.
Hobsbawm, Eric 69, 70
Hobson, J. A. 16–17, 22 n., 351, 379–80, 452, 461, 493, 516
Hocken, T. M. 186 n.
Hodges, William 584, 590
Hodgkin, Thomas 476–7, 488
Hodson, H. V. 240, 255
Hofmeyr, Jan 526
Hogarth Press 21
Holdich, Thomas 292
Holding India to the Empire (Bridge) 233
Holdsworth, W. W. *see* Findlay
Holland, Robert F. 363, 433, 550–1
Hollow Crown, The (Dirks) 211
Holt, Richard 568
Home Government for Ireland (Butt) 119
Hong Kong (Sayer) 393
Hong Kong Eclipse (Birch and Endacott) 394
Hong Kong Region, 1850–1911, The (Hayes) 394
Hong Kong Stability and Change (Lethbridge) 394
Hong Kong's Transitions, 1842–1997 (Brown and Foot) 395
Honour, Hugh 578
Hoogenhout, C. P. *see* Toit
Hoover, James W. 201 n.
Hopkins, A. G. 424, 446 n., 457 n., 483, 494 n., 543 n., 653, 661 *see also* Cain
Horn, James 87 n.
Horned Moon (Stephens) 261

Horsfield, John 331 n.
Horton, J. Africanus 464
Horton, Robin 310
Hough, James 208, 304
How Europe Underdeveloped Africa (Rodney) 508, 511, 642
Howard, Michael 343
Howell, Raymond 338
Hsü Chi-yu 381
Hsü, Immanuel C. Y. 396
Hu Sheng 387
Hubbard, R. H. 577
Hudson, G. F. 385
Hudson, W. J. 177 n.
Hudson's Bay Company, . . ., The (Galbraith) 334
Huggins, Godfrey 527
Hughes, Catherine 582 n.
Huenemann, Ralph William 397
Hulugalle, H. A. J. 249
Hume, David 106
Humphreys, R. A. 439 n.
Hunt, Roland, and Harrison, John 220
Hunter, W. W. 198 n.
Hursthouse, Charles 182
Hutchins, Francis G. 223
Huttenback *see* Davis
Huxley, Elspeth 265, 298, 502
Hyam, Ronald 64, 66 n., 236, 285, 355, 555 n., 628, 665
Hyam, Ronald, and Martin, Ged 61 n.
Hydri, Karam 259

I was at Stanley (Gittens) 393
In Defence of Naval Supremacy (Sumida) 332
Idea of History, The (Collingwood) 5 n.
Ideals of Indian Art, The (Havell) 573
Ideological Origins of the American Revolution, The (Bailyn) 107
Ideologies of the Raj (Metcalf) 215
Ikram, S. M. 206
Ilbert, Courtenay 199 n.
Ilbert, Robert 429
Iliffe, John 283, 509, 511, 554
Illusions of Permanence, The (Hutchins) 223
Illustrated Treatise on the Sea Kingdoms (Wei Yuan) 381
Immigrant Labour and the Development of Malaya (Jackson) 411
Impact of Chinese Secret Societies in Malaya, The (Blythe) 411
Imperial Benevolence (Samson) 377
Imperial Defence (Wilkinson and Dilke) 342
Imperial Idea and Its Enemies, The (Thornton) 657
Imperial Leather (McClintock) 287, 580, 658
Imperial Sunset (Beloff) 355, 356
Imperial Vision, An (Metcalf) 227, 593
Imperialism (Hobson) 16, 17, 351, 379, 452
Imperialism (Lenin) 386, 453, 541
Imperialism and After (Mommsen and Osterhammel) 400
Imperialism and Chinese Politics, 1840–1925 (Hu Sheng) 387
Imperialism and Civilization (Woolf) 21
Imperialism and Social Reform (Semmel) 657
Imperialism and the Natural World (MacKenzie) 664
Imperialism at Bay (Louis) 362, 412
Imperialism in World Politics (Moon) 20 n., 454
In Defence of Naval Supremacy (Sumida) 332
In Jeopardy (Murfett) 339
In Search of a Maritime Strategy (Stevens) 339
In Search of Modern China (Spence) 400
In the Anglo-Arab Labyrinth (Kedourie) 425
'In the Name of God, Go!' (Louis) 234
In the Wake of Cook (McKay) 335
In Time of War (Fisk) 129
Inayat Jung 197
Inden, Ronald 603 n., 605
Independent African (Shepperson and Price) 529
Independent Ireland (Fanning) 129
India and the Indian Ocean (Panikkar) 334
India Called Them (Beveridge) 220
India Office, 1880–1910, The (Kaminsky) 215
India, Pakistan or Pakhtunistan? (Jansson) 259
India To-day (Dutt) 216
India Wins Freedom (Azad) 256
Indian Journal of the History of Science 271
Indian Painting for the British, 1770–1880 (Archer) 576
Indian Painting under the Mughals (Brown) 573
Indian Sculpture and Painting (Havell) 573
Indian Style, The (Head) 594
Indian Summer (Irving) 592
Indian Unrest (Chirol) 618
Indians in Malaya (Sandhu) 411
India's Partition (Hasan) 232, 237, 239
India's Political Administrators, 1919–1983 (Potter) 215
Indigenous Political Systems of Western Malaya (Gullick) 409
Indo-British Review (journal) 232
Indrapala, K. 248
Industrial Conflict in Malaya (Stenson) 412
Influence of Sea Power on History (Mahan) 327
Ingham, Kenneth 211, 505
Ingleson, John 408
Inglis, K. S. 176, 177
Ingram, Edward 333, 416 n., 425
Inheritance of Empire (Wainwright) 235
Innes, Harold 156, 333
Innes, Stephen *see* Breen
International Affairs (journal) 130

International Relations of the Chinese Empire, The (Morse) 381
International Review of Missions 305, 307–8
Introduction to the History of West Africa, An (Fage) 488
Introduction to the Political Economy of Burma, An (Furnivall) 26
Inventing Australia (White) 178–9
Inventing the People (Morgan) 89
Invention of Tradition, The (Hobsbawn and Ranger) 70
Iraq (Ireland) 427
Iraq, 1900–1950 (Longrigg) 424
Iraqi Revolution of 1958, The (Fernea and Louis) 432
Ireland, Philip Willard 427
Ireland and the British Empire, 1937 (Harrison) 129
Ireland and the Crown (Sexton) 128
Ireland and the Federal Solution (Kendle) 120
'*Irish Empire?, An*' (Jeffrey) 132
Irish Free State (Mansergh) 129
Irish Historical Studies (journal) 130
Irish People (newspaper) 117
Irish Statesman, The (newspaper) 124
Irschick, Eugene F. 212, 609 n.
Irving, Robert 592
Irving, Washington 588
Irwin, G. 408
Isaac, Rhys 105
Isichei, Elizabeth 313 n.
Isolationism and Appeasement . . . (Andrews) 357–8
Ispahani, M. A. H. 256

Jackson, Mabel 468
Jackson, R. N. 411
Jacobs, Michael 300
Jacobsen, Mark 331 n.
Ja'far Sharif 196
Jaffe, Hosea 523
Jaggi, O. P. 270
Jail Journal (Mitchell) 117
Jalal, Ayesha 238, 239, 241, 260–1, 657
James, C. L. R. 568
James, William R. 329, 626–7
James Barry Munnik Hertzog (Pirow) 359
Jansson, Erland 259
Jankowski, James *see* Gershoni
Jawaharlal Nehru (Gopal) 240
Jayawardena, V. K. 247
J. R. Jayewardene of Sri Lanka (de Silva and Wriggins) 250
Jeal, Tim 297
Jebb, Richard 15–16
Jeffrey, Keith 132, 349
Jeffrey, Walter *see* Becke
Jenkinson, Hilary 465–6
Jenks, Edward 170
Jennings, Francis 90 n.
Jennings, Ivor 563
Jinnah, Mohammad Ali 237–9, 260–1
Jinnah (Bolitho) 257
Jinnah of Pakistan (Wolpert) 238
Jinnah, Pakistan and Islamic Identity (Ahmed) 261
Jinnah Reinterpreted (Khairi) 259
John A. Macdonald (Creighton) 153
John Company at Work (Furber) 202
John Singleton Copley (Prown) 577–8
Johnson, Gordon *see* Gallagher and Seal
Johnson, Richard R. 74 n., 85 n., 86, 100
Johnson, Samuel 487
Johnston, Franklyn 345
Johnston, H. H. (Sir Harry) 19, 292, 465, 489, 515, 527
Johnston, Reginald F. 392
Johnstone, Frederick A. 532
Jolly, Margaret 376
Jones, Charles 445 n., 446 n., 448 n.
Jones, F. C. 383, 387
Jones, Owen 572, 588
Joppien, Rudiger 578 n.
Jordan, Winthrop 317
Jose, Arthur W. 170
Joseph, Philip 385, 388
Joslin, David 445 n.
Journal of African History 38, 282, 662
Journal of Pacific History 662
Journal of Imperial and Commonwealth History 246, 273, 662
Journal of Military History 338
Journal of Modern History 332
Journal of South East Asian History 408
Journal of South East Asian Studies 408
Journal of Southern African Studies 537
Journal of the Malayan Branch of the Royal Asiatic Society (JMBRAS) 406, 408
Joyce, R. B. 373 n.
Joyner, Charles 319
Judd, Denis, and Slinn, Peter 565
Junod, Henri 521, 536

Kadalie, Clements 522
Kaggwa, Apolo 501
Kahler, Miles 552
Kakar, Sudhir 223
Kaminsky, A. P. 215
Kammen, Michael G. 82 n.
Kandyan Kingdom of Ceylon, The (Dewaraja) 247
Kaniki, M. H. Y. 508 n.
Kaplan, Martha 376

Kashmir (Lamb) 241
Katz, Friedrich 447 n.
Kay, Stephen 514
Kaye, John W. 55, 195 n., 202 n., 208
Kearney, Hugh 131
Keay, Seymour 450
Kedah (Ahmat) 414
Kedah, 1771–1821 (Bonney) 408
Kedourie, Elie 425, 429 n.
Keegan, Timothy 538
Keene, H. G. 198 n.
Keesing, Roger 375, 376
Keeton, C. L. 411
Keeton, G. W. 383
Keith, Sir Arthur Berriedale 27–8, 127, 199 n., 623, 625
Kelling, George H. 433
Kelly, J. B. 334, 425, 434
Kelly, J. D. 376
Keltie, J. S. 292, 451–2, 464
Kendle, J. E. 120
Kennedy, Dane 511
Kennedy, Paul M. 5, 272, 327, 333
Kent, John 351
Kent, Marian 420 n.
Kenya from Within (Ross) 502, 508
Kenyatta, Jomo 504, 511
Keppel-Jones, A. 460
Khairi, Saeed R. 259
Khaliquzzaman, Choudry 256
Khoo Kay Kim 408
Khuda Bhaksh 197
Kickham, Charles 117
Kiernan, Victor G. 386, 457 n.
Killingley, D. 211
Killingray, David *see* Anderson
Killingray, David, and Rathbone, Richard 482 n.
Kimambo, I. N. 508 n.
Kimbangu, Simon 309
Kimble, David 478
King, Anthony 592, 593
King, Frank H. H. 395
King Thebaw and the Ecological Rape of Burma (Keeton) 411
Kingdom of Canada, The (Morton) 157
Kingdom of Jaffna, The (Pathmanathan) 248
Kings' Men (Cunneen) 177
Kingsford, William 148–9
Kingsley, Mary H. 30 n., 294, 300, 622
Kipling, Lockwood 591
Kipling, Rudyard 163, 287
Kirby, S. W. 412
Kirk, Sir John 451, 464, 468
Kirk on the Zambesi (Coupland) 468
Kirkbride, Sir Alec 426
Kirkwood, Kenneth 479
Kitching, Gavin 508
Klein, Herbert S. 316
Kloosterboer, W. 315 n.
Kloppenberg, James T. 110
Knaplund, Paul 345, 563
Knapman, Claudia 285 n., 376 n.
Knight, Alan 447 n., 448 *see also* Brown
Knighton, William 243
Knocknagow (Kickham) 117
Knowles, L. C. A. (Lilian) 470
Knox, Robert 243
Kolff, Dirk H. A. 201 n.
Kopf, David 206, 212
Korda, Alexander 630
Kotane, Moses 523
Kotenev, Anatol M. 383
Kothari, Rajni 223
Kozlowski, Gregory 206
Kramnick, Isaac 109
Kraus, Michael 88
Krieke, Emmanuel 537
Krige, Eileen 522
Krüger, D. W. 359
Kubicek, Robert V. 460
Kuczynski, R. R. 473
Kuhn, Thomas 106, 267, 279
Kumar, Deepak 270–1
Kumar, Dharma 203
Kuo, P. C. 386
Kuper, Hilda 522
Kuper, Leo 530
Kwang-ching, Lui 397
Kylie, Edward 150

La Nauze, J. A. 177 n.
Labaree, Benjamin, W. and Christie, Ian R. 49, 97 n.
Labour Government and the End of Empire, The (Hyam) 237
Labour in Power, 1945–1951 (Morgan) 236
Lafontaine, Louis 150
Laird, M. A. 209
Lal, Brij 372, 373 n.
Lamb, Alastair 241, 261–2, 410
Lambert, Andrew D. 333
Lambert, Frank 88 n.
Lambert, Nicholas A. 332
Landlords and Tenants in Ireland (Vaughan) 121
Land Question and the Irish Economy, The (Solow) 121
Landes, David S. 661
Landau, Paul 539
Landmarks of Toronto (Robertson) 591
Lane-Poole, Stanley and Dickens, F. V. 380
Lang, John Duncan 55 n.
Lang, John Dunmore 165

Langer, William L. 16, 20 n., 380, 385, 389, 396, 454, 469
Language, Religion and Ethnic Assertiveness (Dharmadasa) 249
Lanternari, Vittorio 308
Laqueur, Walter 629
Laracy, Hugh 374
Last Journals of David Livingstone, The (Waller) 291
Lasting Honour, The (Lindsay) 394
Latin American Research Review (journal) 441 n.
Latourette, Kenneth Scott 305, 383
Lau, Albert 412
Lau Kit-ching, Chan 394
Laughton, Sir John Knox 328
Lavin, Deborah 560 n.
Law of the Constitution (Dicey) 120
Lawrence, T. E. 18, 426, 617
Lawrey, John 373
Lawson, Philip 158 n.
Le Caire (Raymond) 429
Le Devoir (Bourassa) 149
Le Monde Malais (Robequain) 406
League and Abyssinia, The (Woolf) 21
Lean, David 285
Leap in the Dark, A (Dicey) 123
Leckie, G. F. 54
Lecky, W. E. H. 116, 120
Lectures on Colonization and Colonies (Merivale) 143
Lee, Edwin *see* Chew
Lee, Oey Hong 413
Legacy of a Divided Nation (Hasan) 241
Legassick, Martin 531–2
Legge, J. D. 373, 405
Lenin, V. I. 123, 386, 452 n., 453, 493, 541
Leonard, Daniel 94 n.
Leonard, J. K. 56 n.
Leonard, Karen 205
Lepsius, Johannes, Bartholdy, A. M., and Thimme, F. 453 n.
Lessing, Doris 633
Lethbridge, James Henry 394
Leubuscher, Charlotte 471, 473–4
Lewis, Bernard 207
Lewis, Colin M. 444 n.
Lewis, George Cornewall 43, 48
Lewis, John Frederick 588
Lewis, W. A. 640 n.
Lewsen, Phyllis 526
Leys, Colin 476 n., 508, 527
Leys, Norman 20, 472, 501
Life and Times of Don Stephen Senanayake, The (Hulugalle) 249
Life of Henry Burney, A (Hall) 407
Life of Lord Curzon (Ronaldshay) 220
Life of Matthew Flinders, RN (Scott) 169
Life of Sir Harry Parkes, The (Lane-Poole and Dickens) 380
Limits of British Influence, The (Singh) 241
Lindblom, Gerhard 503 n.
Linden, Ian 538
Lindley, David 306
Lindsay, Oliver 394
Lineham, Walter 406
Linlithgow and India (Rizvi) 234
Lion and Dragon in Northern China (Johnston) 392
Lion and the Kangeroo, The (Souter) 177
Lion Rampant (Low) 660
Lion's Share, The (Porter) 666
Little History of New Zealand (Bourke) 184
Little Peterkin (Southey) 617
Littlefield, Daniel 319
Littleton, Edward 632
Livingstone (Jeal) 538 n.
Livingstone, David 291
Livingstone the Doctor (Gelford) 278 n.
Livingstone's River (Martell) 297 n.
Llewellyn-James, R. 205
Lloyd, Christopher 338
Lloyd, Lord 426
Lloyd, T. O. 356, 621
Locality, Province and Nation (Gallagher, Johnson, and Seal) 231
Locke, John 106, 109, 616
Lockhart, J. G., and Woodhouse, C. M. 526
Lockhart, James Haldane Stewart 392–3
Lockman, Zachary *see* Beinin
Lockridge, Kenneth A. 83 n., 103
Loh Kok Wah, Francis 414
Long, Gavin 176–7
Longmore, Paul K. 103 n.
Longrigg, S. H. 424
Lonn, Ella 82 n.
Lonsdale, John 460, 506, 510–11 *see also* Berman *and* Low
Lost Dominion, The (Carthill) 541, 542
Louis, Wm. Roger 234, 236, 237, 331 n., 351, 362, 374 n., 391, 412, 421 n., 459, 548, 553, 653
Louis, Wm. Roger, and Owen, Roger 432
Louis, Wm. Roger, and Robinson, Ronald 237, 553
Louis, Wm. Roger, and Stookey, Robert W. 429, 431
Love, H. D. 198 n.
Lovejoy, David S. 85 n.
Lovejoy, Paul E. 316 n.
Lovett, Richard 304 n.
Lovett, Verney 216
Low, D. A. (Anthony) 37, 219, 232, 234, 239, 262, 430, 478, 549, 567–8, 660
Low, D. A., and Lonsdale, J. M. 636 n.

Low, D. A., and Pratt, R. C. 505
Lower, Arthur R. M. 329
Loyalties (Wilson) 424
Lucas, C. P. 15, 19 n., 50, 51, 343, 453, 465, 620, 633
Lucas, George 150
Ludden, David 205
Ludowyk, E. F. C. 248
Lugard, Flora 464
Lugard, Sir Frederick 21–2, 500, 614
Lumby, E. W. R. 231 *see also* Mansergh
Lumley, Robert 581 n.
Luthuli, Albert 523
Lutyens, Edwin 589, 592
Lynn, Kenneth 103 n.
Lyne, R. N. 464

McArthur, Duncan 148
Macarthur, James 165–6
McCarthy, J. 331 n.
Macaulay, T. B. 3, 5–6, 7 n., 8, 195, 196 n., 210, 628
McBride, Sean 130
McCabe, Ian 130
McCarthy, John 346
McCarthy, Justin 120
McClintock, Anne 287, 580, 658
McClymont, W. G. 295
McCoan, J. C. 619
McCoy, Drew R. 108
McCracken, John 538
MacCrone, I. D. 519
McDermott, P. L. 451, 464
MacDonagh, Oliver, and Mandle, Bill 132 n.
Macdonald, Barrie 371
MacDonald, Callum A. 447 n.
Macdonald, John A. 150, 153, 154
MacDonald, Roderick A. 142, 321
McEvoy, Frederick 130
McGee, Thomas D'Arcy 118
McGibbon, Ian 331 n.
MacGregor, Roy 473 n.
McHenry, J. A. 433
McIntyre, W. David 331 n., 339, 355, 373, 412, 565, 567, 636 n.
McIntyre, Kenneth 298
Mackay, David 274, 335
MacKenzie, Colin 197
MacKenzie, John M. 69 n., 580, 582 n., 603 n., 621, 623, 648 n., 664, 666
MacKenzie, Robert 6 n.
McKenzie, Ruth 337
McKeown, Thomas 279
Mackinder, Sir Halford 300, 333, 657
McLane, John R. 205
MacLeod, Roy 270, 273 n.
MacLeod, R. M., and Denoon, Donald 273
McMahon, Deirdre 128
Macmillan, Harold 545
Macmillan, Hugh and Marks, Shula 25 n.
Macmillan, W. M. 25, 35, 59, 307, 471, 518
Macmurray, John 616
McNab, Robert 186 n.
MacNair, Harley Farnsworth *see* Morse
McNairn, Alan 582 n.
McNeill, William 279
McPhee, Allan 470
McQueen, Humphrey 178
Madden, Frederick 24 n., 27, 28, 52, 60 n., 614 n.
Madgwick, R. B. 171 n.
Mahajan, Sucheta 236
Mahan, Alfred Thayer 327, 328
Mahavamsa (chronicle) 243, 245
Maier, Pauline 105
Maitland, Frederic 8
Maitland, Patrick 563
Majed, Abdul 204
Making Imperial Mentalities (Mangan) 618, 627
Making of a New 'Indian' Art (Guha-Thakurta) 226, 581
Making of Modern Egypt, The (Colvin) 425
Making of Pakistan, The (Symonds) 255
Making of the English Working Class, The (Thompson) 644
Making of the West Indies, The (Augier *et al*) 138
Making the New Commonwealth (Moore) 241
Malalgoda, K. 247
Malayan Union, The (Allen) 412
Malayan Union Controversy, The (Lau) 412
Malaysia (Emerson) 26, 406
Malcolm, John 55, 194
Malherbe, Gideon *see* Toit
Malik, Kenan 606
Mammon and the Pursuit of Empire (Davis and Huttenback) 351, 655
Manchester, Alan K. 438
Mandarin Enterprise (Feuerwerker) 396
Mandarin Road to Old Hué, The (Lamb) 410
Mander-Jones, Phyllis 177
Mandle, Bill, *see* MacDonagh
Mandler, Peter 92 n.
Mangan, J. A. 618, 627
Mann, Bruce H. 103
Manning, Helen Taft 158
Mannoni, O. 656
Manor, James 249
Mansergh, Nicholas 7, 26 n., 127, 128, 129, 130–1, 231, 356–7, 360, 362, 555, 561–2
Mansergh, Nicholas, and Lumby, E. W. R. 257
Mansergh, Nicholas, Moon, Penderel, and Lumby, E. W. R. 257
Manual of Land Revenue Systems . . . (Baden-Powell) 197
Manuscripts in the British Isles . . . (Mander-Jones) 177

Marais, J. S. 59, 519, 524–5
March of Folly (Tuchman) 96
Marder, Arthur Jacob 327, 328, 330–2, 340
Mariátegui, José Carlos 438
Marichal, Carlos 444 n., 445 n.
Markham, Clements 291, 293
Marks, Shula 460, 530 n., 532–3, 534 *see also* Engels; Macmillan
Marlowe, John 427
Maroons of Jamaica, The (Campbell) 321
Mars, John 474 n.
Marshall, P. J. 38, 61 n., 201, 203, 206, 666
Marsot, Afaf Lutfi al-Sayyid 427–8
Martel, Gordon 351 n.
Martell, George 297 n.
Martin, A. W. 177 n.
Martin, Chester 146, 147, 152, 157
Martin, Eveline C. 466, 476
Martin, Ged 158 *see also* Hyam
Martin, Marie-Louise 309 n.
Martin, Montgomery 55
Martin, Phyllis M. *see* Birmingham
Marx, Karl 117, 196 n., 386
Masks of Conquest (Vishwanath) 211
Mason, A. E. W. 619
Mason, Philip 201, 215, 349, 479, 527
Massey, Vincent 155 n.
Mathew, W. M. 442
Mathieson, William Law 139
Matson, Cathy *see* Onuf
Matter of Honour, A (Mason) 201
Matthews, Lloyd 468
Maude, H. E. 371
Maugham, Somerset 285, 619
Mayo, John 444 n.
Mazumdar, Ramesh C. 216, 229
Mbeki, Govan 523
Mboya, Tom 511
Meaning of Pakistan, The (Durrani) 255
Melbourne, A. C. V. 171 n.
Meleisea, Malama 372
Melvoin, Richard I. 91 n.
Memoir . . . of . . . Christian Frederick Swartz (Pearson) 208
Memoirs of Agha Khan (Agha Khan) 256
Memoirs of a Dutiful Daughter (Beauvoir) 612
Memoirs of a Malayan Official, The (Purcell) 411
Men who Ruled India, The (Mason) 215
Menard, Russell R. 318
Mendis, G. C. 245, 246, 248
Mercenaries and Mandarins (Smith) 398
Merivale, Herman 43, 46, 143
Merrell, James H. 90 n.
Merriman, J. X. 526
Metcalf, Barbara Daly 206
Metcalf, Thomas R. 204, 215, 227, 593–4
Metcalfe, G. E. 478
Meyer, Eric 251
Meyer, Lorenzo 447 n.
Middle East in the World Economy, 1800–1914, The (Owen) 428
Middle Passage, The (Klein) 316
Middlekauff, Robert 97 n.
Middleton, Dorothy 296
Midgley, Clare 324
Mighty Empire, A (Egnal) 101
Míguez, Eduardo C. 445 n.
Military Operations and Maritime Preponderance (Callwell) 330
Mill, Hugh 294
Mill, James 6 n., 194, 197, 203
Mill, John Stuart 10, 121 n., 633
Millat Ka Pasban (Hydri) 259
Miller, Joseph 315 n.
Miller, J. D. B. (Bruce) 38, 178, 357, 360, 177, 564–5, 567, 625
Miller, Perry 80
Miller, Rory 445 n., 447 n. *see also* Greenhill
Mills, David 160
Mills, Lennox A. 245, 406
Mills, Richard Charles 171 n.
Milner, Alfred 13–14, 425
Miners, Norman 394
Mingling of the Canadian and American Peoples, The (Hansen and Brebner) 154
Mintz, Sidney W. and Hall, Douglas 142 n., 321
Mintz, Sidney W. and Price, Richard 318
Minutemen and their World, The (Gross) 104
Mission with Mountbatten (Campbell-Johnson) 255
Missionaries and Education in Bengal (Laird) 209
Missionary Factor in East Africa, The (Oliver) 307, 504
Missionary Impact on Modern Nigeria, The (Ayandele) 307
Mitchel, John 117
Mitchell, David Scott 169
Mitchell, George 587
Mitchell, Timothy 422 n.
Mitra Rajendralal 587
Mitter, Partha 226, 581
Modern Asian Studies (journal) 236, 662
Modern Egypt (Earl of Cromer) 13, 425, 623
Modern History of Ceylon, The (Ludowyk) 248
Modern History of Tanganyika (Iliffe) 509, 554
Modernization of the Chinese Salt Administration, The (Adshead) 397
Molema, S. M. 522
Mommsen, Wolfgang J., and Osterhammel, Jürgen 400 *see also* Förster
Mond, Sir Alfred 123

Monroe, Elizabeth 418, 422, 429 n.
Moodie, T. Dunbar 59 n.
Moody, T. W. 117
Moon, Parker Thomas 20 n., 454, 469
Moon, Penderel 202, 215, 231, 234, 255, 257 n. *see also* Mansergh
Moon of Wintertime (Grant) 313
Moore, Clive 373 n.
Moore, Clive, Munro, Doug, and Leckie, Jacqui 373 n.
Moore, Henrietta, and Vaughan, Megan 283–4, 536 n.
Moore, R. J. 125, 223–4, 233, 234, 241, 260
Moorehead, Alan 296
Morgan, Edmund S. 80, 82–3, 84, 89, 95, 317
Morgan, Edmund S., and Morgan, Helen 83 n., 97
Morgan, J. H. 123
Morgan, Kenneth O. 236
Morgan, Philip D. *see* Bailyn; Berlin
Morison, J. L. 151
Morison, Samuel Eliot 80, 81
Morley, John 629–30
Morner, Magnus *see* Emmer
Morrell, W. P. 185, 372
Morrill, John 132
Morris, James (Jan) 594, 656–7
Morris, Rear Admiral Roger 337
Morris, William 591
Morrissey, Marietta 321–2
H. B. Morse, Customs Commissioner (Fairbank, Coolidge, and Smith) 382
Morse, Hosea Balbu 381–2
Morton, W. L. 156–7
Moss, F. J. 184–5
Mossek, Moshe 429 n.
Mountbatten (Ziegler) 240
Mountbatten Viceroyalty (Transfer of Power, XII) 258
Mr Bligh's Bad Language (Dening) 376
Mukasa, Ham 503
Mukherjee, Nilmani 203 n., 205
Mukherjee, Rudrangshu 65 n.
Mukherjee, S. N. 206
Muller, Eduard 244
Müller, Max 305–6
Mullin, Gerald W. 320
Munich to Vietnam (Bridge) 360
Munro, J. B. 154
Munro, J. Forbes 507
Munro, Thomas 203, 630
Munz, Peter 189
Murdock, Kenneth B. 80
Murfett, Malcolm 331 n., 339
Murphy, Philip 552
Murray, Victor 619
Murrin, John M. 86, 96
Muslims and Missionaries in Pre-Mutiny India (Powell) 209
Muslims of British India, The (Hardy) 257
Myth and Reality (Gupta) 232, 235, 236
Myth of 'Mau Mau', The (Rosberg and Nottingham) 506

Nabobs, The (Spear) 203–4
Nadel, George 176
Nadesan, S. 249
Naipaul, V. S. 631
Name of Brooke, The (Reece) 413
Namier, Lewis 14
Nandy, Ashish 223
Nansen, Fridtjof 632
Naoroji, Dadabhai 225
Napier, Lord 586
Nash, Gary B. 104
Natarajan, S. 63 n.
National Geographic Atlas 92
National Review (journal) 120
Native Administration in Nigeria (Perham) 22
Native Problem in Africa, The (Buell) 502
Naval Operations (Corbett and Newbolt) 329
Naval Pioneers of Australia, The (Becke and Jeffrey) 169
Navy, the Company, and Richard King, The (Wallace) 337
Navy and the Slave Trade, The (Lloyd) 338
Navy in India, The (Richmond) 329
Navy in the War of 1739–48, The (Richmond) 329
Neale, R. G. 357
Needham, Joseph 610 n.
Neidpath, James 331 n., 347, 412
Neill, Stephen 307, 313 n.
Nelson, Paul David 97 n.
Neumann, Klaus 377
Neutrality of Ireland, The (Harrison) 129
New Boer War (Barnes) 20
New Britannia, A (McQueen) 178
New Cambridge Modern History 458
New England's Outpost (Brebner) 80–1
New Guinea Villager, The (Rowley) 373
New History of Australia, A (Crowley) 175
New Irish Constitution, The (Morgan) 123
New South Wales (Macarthur) 165
New World of the South, The (Fitchett) 170
New Zealand (Morrell) 185
New Zealand: A Short History (Beaglehole) 185
New Zealand in the Making (Condliffe) 185
New Zealand Journal of History 190
New Zealand or Zealandia (Hursthouse) 182
New Zealand People at War (Wood) 359
Newbolt, Sir Henry 329
Newbury, C. W. (Colin) 38, 456, 457 n., 533 n.
Newton, A. P. 11, 35, 44, 466–7, 469, 475, 620

Ngata, Apirana 188
Nicholas, Stephen 175
Nightingale, Pamela 65
Nilsson, Sten 592
1911 Revolution, The (Ho Sheng) 387
Nineteenth Century (journal) 120
Nineteenth-Century Borneo (Irwin) 408
Nineteenth-Century Britain (Robbins) 131
Nineteenth-Century Malaya (Cowan) 408
Nochlin, Linda 579
Noon, Firoz Khan 256
North Atlantic Triangle, The (Brebner) 154–5
Northern Whig (journal) 118
Norton-Kysche, James William 393
Notestein, Wallace 87 n.
Nottingham, J. *see* Rosberg
Numnonda, Thamsook 410
Nwauwa, Apollos 455 n.
Nzula, A. T. 522

Obeyesekere, G. A. 659
Obichere, Boniface 459 n.
O'Brien, John B. 130
O'Brien, Patrick K. 92 n., 339, 351–2
O'Brien, R. Barry 123
O'Brien, Thomas F. 445 n.
O'Connell, Daniel 114
O'Connor, Daniel 308 n.
Oddie, G. A. 63 n., 311 n.
Odiambo, Atieno E. S. 511
Of Islands and Men (Maude) 371
Offer, Avner 352
Official History of New Zealand in World War Two 186
Ogot, B. A. 506
O'Higgins, Kevin 126 n., 127–8
Old Africa Rediscovered (Davidson) 488
Old China Hands and the Foreign Office (Pelcovits) 388
Old Friends, New Enemies (Marder) 331
Old Roads New Highways (Schofield) 262
Old Social Classes and the Revolutionary Movements of Iraq, The (Batutu) 428, 432
Oliver, Douglas 374–5
Oliver, F. S. (Pacificus) 122, 124
Oliver, Roland 307, 456, 477, 488, 504–5
Oliver, Roland, and Fage, J. 38
Oliver, W. H. 187
Oliver, W. H., and Orange, Claudia 186 n.
Olivier, Sydney 20
Ollard, Richard 332
Oloruntimehin, B. O. 459 n.
Olson, Alison Gilbert 49, 85 n., 86
Olson, James E. 666
Olunsanya, G. O. 361
O'Malley, L. S. S. 199 n.
Omer-Cooper, John 529, 538
Omissi, David E. 215, 349 n., 419
On Liberty (Mill) 633
On the Culture and Commerce of Cotton In India (Royle) 572
One Blood (Harris) 313
One Hundred Days (Woodward) 339
Onuf, Peter, and Matson, Cathy 109, 110 n.
Onuf, Peter, and Onuf, Nicholas 111 n.
Opium and Empire (Trocki) 414
Opium War, 1840–1842, The (Fay) 388
Opium War through Chinese Eyes, The (Waley) 388
Orange, Claudia *see* Oliver
Order and Discipline in China (Stephens) 392
O'Regan, Tipene 188
Oriental Obsession, The (Sweetman) 579
Orientalism (MacKenzie) 580, 666
Orientalism (Said) 70, 207, 224 n., 272, 425, 579, 592, 593, 597, 647, 656
Orientalism and the Postcolonial Predicament (Breckenridge and Van der Veer) 212
Orientations (Storrs) 618
Origins of American Politics, The (Bailyn) 89
Origins of British Borneo, The (Wright) 410
Origins of the Maori Wars (Sinclair) 187
Origins of the Partition of India, The (Singh) 234, 260
Orme, Robert 194
Orr, John Boyd 281–2
Ortega, Luis 446 n.
Ortíz, Raúl Scalabrini 438
Orwell, George 18
Osgood, Herbert 74–6
Osterhammel, Jürgen 399–400 *see also* Mommsen
Other Side of the Frontier, The (Reynold) 663
Other Side of the Medal, The (Thompson) 619
O'Tuathaigh, M. A. G. 131
Ouchterlong, John 388
Our Earliest Colonial Settlements (Andrews) 76
Our Heritage series (Mendis) 246
Our Nation's Story (Moss) 185
Out of the House of Bondage (Heuman) 320
Ovendale, Ritchie 357, 362, 421 n., 429, 431
Owen, David Edward 384–5
Owen, E. R. J. (Roger) J. 427–8 *see also* Louis
Owen, John H. 329
Owen, Nicholas 361–2
Owens, John 187
(Oxford) History of East Africa 483, 506
Oxford History of India 198, 214
Oxford History of South Africa 530
Oxford History of New Zealand 187, 190
Oxford Illustrated History of the Royal Navy (Hill) 338

Pacific Islands (Davidson) 370

Pacific Since Magellan, The (Spate) 372
'Pacificus' *see* Oliver, F. S.
Packard, Randall M. 273, 278 n., 279 n.
Pagden, Anthony 56 n. *see also* Canny
Page, Melvin E. 482 n.
Pahang (Gopinath) 414
Pakeman, S. A. 248
Palley, Claire 527
Palmer, A. 666
Palmer, R., and Parsons, N. 536 n.
Pandey, Gyanendra 220, 253 n.
Panikkar, K. M. 21 n., 334
Papadopoulos, A. N. 565
Pappé, Ilan 429
Paradise on Earth (Baudet) 656
Paranavitana, S. 246–7
Parekh, Bhikhu 223
Pares, Richard 32, 34–5, 36
Park, Mungo 290
Parker, Edward H. 381
Parkinson, Cyril 38
Parkman, Francis 147–8
Parliamentary Papers 338, 380, 452, 464
Parry, Ellwood 578 n.
Parry, John H. 138, 296
Parsons, Neil *see* Palmer
Parsons, Talcott 640
Parsonson, Ann 187
Partition and Colonisation of Africa (Lucas) 453
Partition in Ireland, India, and Palestine (Fraser) 125
Partition of India, The (Philips and Wainwright) 231
Partition of India, The (Tinker) 232
Pascoe, C. F. 304 n.
Passage to India, A (Forster) 18, 217, 619
Pathmanathan, S. 248
Paton, Alan 526
Patterson, K. David *see* Hartwig
Patterson, Orlando 141, 319
Pax Britannica (Morris) 656
Peabody, Norbert 603 n.
Peace to End All Peace, A (Fromkin) 356
Peacocks, Pagodas and Professor Hall (Sarkisyanz) 407
Pearce, R. D. 361
Pearn, B. R. 407
Pearson, Edward 320
Pearson, H. N. 208
Pedersen, Susan 288 n.
Peebles, Patrick 251
Peires, J. B. 537
Pelcovits, Nathan A. 388
Pencak, William 79 n.
Penson, Lillian 470
People in Revolution, A (Countryman) 104
Percival and the Tragedy of Singapore (Smyth) 412
Perera, Fr S. G. 245
Perfidious Albion (Marlowe) 427
Perham, Margery 21–3, 28, 32, 456, 474, 476, 502, 503, 505
Peripheries and Center (Bailyn) 89
Perlin, Frank 610 n.
Perry, Benita 665
Personalities and Policies (Watt) 357
Phayre, Sir Arthur 407
Philby, St John 426
Philip, Dr John 307, 513, 514
Philips, C. H. 202
Philips, C. H., and Wainwright, Mary Doreen 231
Phillip, Arthur 164
Phillips, A. A. 175 n.
Phillipson, Nicholas 88 n.
Philosophy of History (Walsh) 628
Pieris, Sir Paulus 245, 246
Pieris, Ralph 247
Pike, Douglas 175
Pilgrims (Purchas) 290
Pim, Sir Alan 471
Piracy and Politics in the Malay World (Tarling) 410
Piracy, Paramountcy and Protectorates (Rubin) 410
Pirate Wind, The (Rutter) 409
Pirouet, M. Louise 312 n.
Pirow, Oswald 359
Pitman, Frank 139
Pitt-Rivers, A. H. Lane-Fox 574
Plaatje, Solomon T. 517
Place, Taste and Tradition (Smith) 574
Platt, D. C. M. 390, 441–2, 443, 446–8
Pocock, J. G. A. 107
Pole, J. R. 88
Police Power and Colonial Rule (Arnold) 216
Political Economy of the Raj, 1914–47, The (Tomlinson) 236
Political Inheritance of Pakistan, The (Low) 239, 262
Political Kingdom in Uganda, The (Apter) 505–6
Political Representation in England . . . (Pole) 88
Political Sciences, The (Stretton) 660
Politics of Decentralisation, The (Wah) 414
Politics of Naval Supremacy, The (Graham) 333
Pollock, Sheldon 604
Polynesian Mythology (Grey) 183
Poo Lorn of the Elephants (Campbell) 619
Porter, A. N. (Andrew) 132, 460, 535–6, 666
Porter, A. N., and Stockwell, A. J. 412
Porter, Bernard 363, 660, 666
Portrait of an Admiral (Marder) 331

Portuguese in Ceylon, 1617–1638, The (de Silva) 247
Portuguese Rule in Ceylon, 1594–1612 (Abeyasinghe) 247
Potter, D. (David) C. 215, 236
Potter, Janice 94 n.
Potts, E. Daniel 208–9
Powell, Avril Ann 209
Powesland, P. G. 478
Prâdo, Caio 438
Prakash, Gyan 604, 608 n., 662
Pratt, Sir John 387
Pratt, R. C. 478 *see also* Low
Prebisch, Raúl 439
Precarious Balance (Chan) 395
Pre-history of Sri Lanka (Deraniyagala) 250
Preller, Gustav 517
Preston, Richard A. 158, 346
Price, Pamela G. 205
Price, Richard *see* Mintz
Primitive Art (Boas) 575
Principal Navigations (Hakluyt) 290
Pringle, Robert M. 411
Prins, Gwyn 278
Prinsep, Henry T. 194 n.
Prince of Pirates (Trocki) 410
Princes of India in the Endgame of Empire, The (Coupland) 233
Pritchard, Earl H. 384
Problem of Asia, The (Mahan) 327
Problem of the Commonwealth, The (Curtis) 559
Problems of Empire (Marshall) 203
Problems of the Far East (Curzon) 13
Propaganda and Empire (MacKenzie) 621
Progress of Australasia . . . , The (Coghlan and Ewing) 167
Prospero and Caliban (Mannoni) 656
Protected Malay States, The (Sadka) 408
Prown, Jules 577–8
Pugh, Patricia M. 482 n.
Pugh, R. B. 355
Punjab Crisis and Cure (Rajput) 255
Purcell, Victor 406, 410, 411
Purchas, Samuel 290
Pyrah, G. B. 525

Qanun-I-Islam (Sharif) 196
Quaid-e-Azam Jinnah as I Knew Him (Ispahani) 256
Queen Anne's Navy in the West Indies (Bourne) 329
Quest for Power, The (Greene) 78
Quest for Security in New Zealand, 1840–1966, The (Sutch) 360
Quimby, Ian 578
Quinn, D. B. 45, 50, 298
Quiroz, Alfonso 446 n.
Qureshi, I. H. 206, 257

Rabb, Theodore K. 91 n.
Rabitoy, Neil 203 n.
Raboteau, Albert J. 321
Race Problem in Africa (Buxton) 21
Race Problem in Canada, The (Siegfried) 58
Race, Sex, and Class under the Raj (Callaway) 665
Radicalism of the American Revolution, The (Wood) 109
Raffles, Lady Sophia 55 n.
Ragatz, Lowell 24 n., 39, 323
Ragsdale, Bruce A. 102
Rahman, S. 255
Raj, The (Bayly) 582
Raja Rammohan Ray (Robertson) 211
Rajahs and Rebels (Pringle) 411
Rajan, M. S. 563
Rajput, A. B. 255
Rakove, Jack N. 99
Ramuasubbin, R. 273
Rammohum Roy in Hindu and Christian Tradition (Killingley) 211
Rand, Barlow 533
Ranger, T. (Terence) O. 70, 458, 460, 481–2, 506, 530, 531 n., 656
Rapaport, Mario 447 n.
Rathbone, Richard 555 n. *see also* Killingray
Rawlinson, H. G. 198 n.
Rawson, J. O. 348
Ray, H. C. 246
Raymond, André 429
Reader, W. J. 617
Reason and Emotion (Macmurray) 616
Reber, A. L. 410
Reber, Vera Blinn 443 n.
Reckord, M. *see* Augier
Reddaway, John 433
Redefining the Egyptian Nation (Gershoni) 432
Reece, R. H. W. 413
Reed, A. H. 185, 186
Reed, S. W. 369
Rees, J. F. 47
Reese, Trevor R. 360, 662
Reeves, William Pember 185
Reformers in India (Ingham) 211
Reid, Anthony 405, 410
Reid, John Phillip 98
Reimer, Michael J. 429
Reindorf, C. C. 464, 487
Relations de la Chine . . . (Cordier) 380
Religion and the Pilgrim Tax . . . (Cassells) 211
Religions of the Oppressed (Lanternari) 308
Remer, Charles F. 383–4
Report on the Constitutional Problem in India (Coupland) 232–3

Republicans and Imperialists (McMahon) 128
Responsible Government in the Dominions (Keith) 27–8
Restless Dominion (Harkness) 128
Retreat from China (Clifford) 390
Revolution and Foreign Policy (Halliday) 434
Reynolds, David 628
Reynolds, Henry 180, 663
Rhetoric of English India, The (Suleri) 658
Rice and Slaves (Littlefield) 319
Richardson, David 316 n.
Richards, Audrey 281–2, 505, 522
Richards, Thomas 580
Richmond, Herbert 329
Richter, Daniel K. 90 n., 91 n.
Rickshaw Coolie (Warren) 414
Ride, Edwin 394
Rigby, C. P. 468
Rippy, J. Fred 438
Rise and Fall of British Naval Mastery, The (Kennedy) 327, 333
Rise and Fall of the Great Powers, The (Kennedy) 5
Rise and Fall of the Singapore Naval Base, The (McIntyre) 412
Rise and Fulfilment of British Rule in India (Thompson and Garratt) 25–6, 214
Rise of Our East African Empire, The (Lugard) 614
Rise of the Labor Movement in Ceylon, The (Jayawardena) 247
Ritchie, George S. 337
Rizvi, Gowher 233–4
Road to Peace and Pakistan Freedom, The (Suleri) 255
Robbins, Caroline 106
Robbins, Keith 131
Robe and Plough (Gunawardhana) 250
Robequain, Charles 406
Roberts, Andrew 240, 262
Roberts, A. D. (Andrew) 539 n.
Roberts, Michael 247, 248
Roberts, P. E. 198
Roberts, S. H. 170, 171 n.
Robertson, Bruce Carlisle 211
Robertson, John R. 591
Robin, L. *see* Griffiths
Robinson, Austin 471–2
Robinson, Francis 258
Robinson, Kenneth 37 n., 482
Robinson, Portia 175
Robinson, R. (Ronald) E. 32–3, 67, 237, 477, 549
Robinson, Ronald, and Gallagher, John 39–41, 67, 347 *see also* Gallagher and Robinson *and* Louis
Robson, Albert H. 573–4
Robson, L. L. 175, 176
Rodger, N. A. M. 338
Rodney, Walter 496, 508, 642
Roebuck, J. A. 56
Rogers, John 251
Rolin, Henri 472
Ronaldshay, Lord 220
Roots of Nationalism, The (Wickremeratne) 250
Rosberg, C., and Nottingham, J. 506
Rose, Deborah Bird *see* Swain
Rose, J. Holland 11, 265, 620
Rosenbaum, R. 123 n.
Rosenberg, Emily S. 447 n.
Rosenthal, Michael 658
Roskill, Stephen W. 331, 332, 339
Ross, Angus 373
Ross, James Clark 299
Ross, William McGregor 472, 501–2, 508
Rostow, W. W. 269
Rotberg, Robert I. 297, 307, 460, 479 n., 515, 527, 538
Rothenberg, Winfred Barr 108 n.
Round Table (journal) 130
Routledge, W. S., and Routledge, K. 503 n.
Roux, Edward 522
Rowland, Benjamin 587
Rowley, C. D. 373
Roy, Asim 237–8
Roy, Ram Mohan 195
Royal African Company (Davies) 46
Royal Australian Navy in World War II, The (Stevens) 339
Royal Dockyards, 1690–1850, The (Coad) 338
Royal Historical Society 131–2
Royal Navy, The (Clowes) 330
Royal Navy and the Northwest Coast of North America, 1810–1914, The (Gough) 334
Royal Navy and the Slave Trade, The (Howell) 338
Royle, J. Forbes 572
Rubin, A. P. 410
Rulers of India (series) 198
Rulers of the Indian Ocean (Ballard) 329
Runciman, Sir Steven 409
Rusden, G. W. 167
Ruskin, John 572, 591
Russell, Jane 249
Ruthnaswamy, M. 200 n.
Rutter, Owen 409

Sadka, Emily 408
Safeguard of the Sea (Rodger) 338
Sahlins, Marshall 375, 659
Said, Edward W. 70, 197, 207, 211, 224 n., 227, 272, 277, 280, 425, 577, 579, 592, 593, 597, 600, 606, 647, 656, 665
Saints, Goddesses and Kings (Bayly) 209
Salar, Jung 197

Salmond, Anne 189
Salutary Neglect (Henretta) 82
Sammarco, Angelo 427
Samoa mo Samoa (Davidson) 34
Samson, J. 377
Samuel, Horace Barnett 21
Sandison, Alan 658
Sanderson, G. N. 460, 479
Sangwan, Satpal 271
Sandhu, K. S. 411
Sanneh, Lamin 312–13
Sargent, Arthur John 380
Sargent, John 208 n.
Sarkar, Sumit 218, 220
Sarkisyanz, Emil 407
Sartre, Jean-Paul 656
Sati (Datta) 211
Saunders, Christopher, and Smith, Iain R. 57 n.
Savarkar, V. D. 58 n.
Sayer, Geoffrey Robley 393
Sayyid, Ahmad Khan 196
Scarr, Deryck 373
Schapera, Isaac 522
Schenk, Catherine 552
Schism and Renewal in Africa (Barrett) 309
Schmidt, Leigh Eric 88 n.
Schofield, Victoria 262
Schölch, Alexander 424
Scholefield, Guy 369
School History of New Zealand (Moss) 184–5
School in the Bush, The (Murray) 619
Schreiner, Olive 516
Schreuder, D. M. 460, 525
Schröter, Harm G. *see* Wilkins
Schumpeter, Joseph 16
Schultz, Benjamin 209
Schutz, John A. 81 n.
Schuyler, Robert Livingston 63
Scott, Ernest 169, 170, 171–2, 173, 293
Scott, Joan Wallach 284
Scott of the Antarctic (Seaver) 295
Scott, Robert Falcon 292, 293, 298
Scott, Sir Walter 617
Scott, W. R. 465
Seal, Anil 38 *see also* Gallagher
Seaver, George 295
Second World War and Politics in Nigeria, The (Olusanya) 361
Seddall, Henry 463 n.
Seeley, John Robert 3, 8–10, 13, 43, 57, 59, 304, 385, 477, 614, 631
Seikaly, May 429
Select Documents on the Constitutional History of the British Empire . . . (Madden, Fieldhouse, Darwin) 28
Semmel, Bernard 657
Sen, Amartya 69 n., 283
Sender, Henny 205
Senior, Hereward 118
Separate and Unequal (Tinker) 249
Separatism Among Indian Muslims (Robinson) 258
Sepoy and the Raj, The (Omissi) 215
Serle, A. G. 176
Servant of India (Gilbert) 220
Seven Pillars of Wisdom (Lawrence) 426
Seventeenth Century Painting in New England (Dresser) 574
Sewell, Robert 198
Sexton, Brendan 128
Shahnawaz, Jahan Ara 256
Shaikh, Farzana 258
Shalhope, Robert 110
Shammas, Carole 91 n.
Shanghai (Wei) 398
Shanghai and Tientsin . . . (Jones) 387
Shanghai, Its Mixed Court and Council (Kotenev) 382
Shann, Edward 171, 176
Shaw, A. G. L. 175
Sheffer, Gabriel 429
Shelburne, Lord 65
Shell, Robert C.-H. 316 n.
Shepherd, Robert 553 n.
Sheppard, M. C. 406
Shepperson, George, and Price, Thomas 309 n., 481, 529
Sheridan, Richard B. 139 n., 319
Sherlock, Philip 138
Shineberg, Dorothy 371
Shlaim, Avi 430 n.
Short, Anthony 412
Short History of Australia, A (Clark) 175
Short History of Australia (Scott) 170
Short History of Australasia, A (Jose) 170
Short History of British Colonial Policy, A (Egerton) 12–13
Short History of the West Indies, A (Sherlock) 138
Shuster, W. Morgan 619
Shy, John 82 n., 92 n., 95, 97
Siam under Rama III (Vella) 410
Siaya (Cohen) 511
Sibthorpe, A. B. C. 464
Siddiqui, Asiya 203 n.
Siegfried, André 58
Significance of the Commonwealth (McIntyre) 567
Sik, Endre 488–9
Sillery, Anthony 528, 538, 539
Simey, T. S. 613–14
Simmons, J. 469 n., 475
Simpson, William 577
Simson, H. J. 619, 625

Sinclair, Keith 38, 187, 191
Singapore (Kirby) 412
Singapore Naval Base . . . , The (Neidpath) 412
Singh, Anita Inder 234, 237, 241, 260
Singhal, D. P. 410
Sinha, Mrinalini 223, 665
Sinhalé and the Patriots, 1817–1818 (Pieris) 246
Sinhalese Monastic Architecture (Bandaranaike) 248
Sinhalese Social Organisation (Pieris) 247
Sio, Arnold 322
Sir William Jones (Mukherjee) 206
Sirman, M. Franklin 581
Sitaramayya, P. 216
Six Days to Shake an Empire (Duff) 124
Skelton, O. D. 153, 160
Sketch of the History of India from 1858–1918, A (Dodwell) 214
Slave Women in Caribbean Society (Bush) 321
Slaves and Missionaries (Turner) 320
Slinn, Peter *see* Judd
Smail, John 409
Small Wars (Callwell) 619
Smith, Adam 4, 7, 46, 47, 624
Smith, Bernard 372, 376, 574, 578, 579 n.
Smith, Crosbie, and Wise, Norton 274
Smith, Edwin William 306
Smith, Goldwin 120
Smith, Iain R. 459 *see also* Saunders
Smith, Ken 59 n.
Smith, M. G. 141
Smith, Richard J. 382, 398 *see also* Fairbank
Smith, Stephenson Percy 184
Smith, V. A. 198, 214
Smith, W. H. Saumarez 220
Smuts, J. C. 58, 125, 358–9, 516, 523, 560, 625
Smuts: The Fields of Force (Hancock) 359
Smuts: The Sanguine Years (Hancock) 388–9
Smyth, Sir J. 412
Snodgrass, Donald R. 247
Sobel, Mechal 90 n., 319 n.
Social Background of Indian Nationalism (Desai) 216
Social Change in Nineteenth Century Ceylon (Peebles) 251
Social Policy and Missionary Organizations in Ceylon (de Silva) 247
Society for Promoting Christian Knowledge 208
Sociology of Slavery, The (Patterson) 319
Soga, John H. 522
Sole Spokesman (Jalal) 238, 260–1, 657
Solow, Barbara L. 121
Solow, Barbara L., and Engerman, Stanley L. 324
Some Aspects of Irish Law (Donaldson) 127
Soothill, W. E. 382
Sorrenson, M. P. K. 188, 476 n., 663
Sosin, Jack M. 82 n., 85 n., 86
Soundings in Modern South Asian History (Low) 219, 661
Souter, Gavin 177
South African Journal of Science 519
South African Tragedy (Paton) 526
Southey, Robert 616–17
Soyinka, Wole 494 n.
Spate, O. H. K. 366, 372
Spear, Percival 203–4, 210
Speck, W. A. 85 n.
Spence, Jonathan D. 398, 400
Spivak, Gayatri 207, 280, 607, 648 n., 649 n., 663
Splendours of the Raj (Davies) 594
Spoiling the Egyptians (Marlowe) 427
Spoiling the Egyptians: A Tale of Shame (Keay) 450–1
Sport and British Society (Holt) 568
Srinivas, M. N. 222
Staal, Frits 610 n.
Stacey, C. P. 158, 346, 358
Stafford, Robert A. 274, 299 n.
Starkie, Enid 470 n.
State of Martial Rule, The (Jalal) 241
Statesmen and Sea Power (Richmond) 329
Statistical, Historical and Political Description of the Colony of New South Wales . . . (Wentworth) 165
Statute of Westminster, The (Wheare) 28, 127
Statute of Westminster and Dominion Status, The (Wheare) 28
Stearns, Raymond Phineas 268 n.
Steele, Ian K. 82 n., 86 n., 87
Stein, Burton 206
Stenson, Michael 412
Stephen, Fitzjames 631
Stephens, Ian 261
Stephens, Thomas B. 392
Stevens, David 339
Stichter, Sharon 508 n.
Stock, Eugene 304 n.
Stockwell, A. J. 555 n. *see also* Porter
Stokes, Eric 6, 38, 62 n., 203, 204, 452 n., 641 n.
Stone, Lawrence 85 n.
Stones of Empire (Morris) 594
Stookey *see* Louis
Storrs, Ronald 618, 623
Story of Anzac, The (Bean) 176
Story of Australia, A (Shaw) 175
Story of New Zealand, The (Olivier) 187
Story of New Zealand (Reed) 185, 186
Story of Sri Lanka (Ludowyk) 248
Strachan, Hew 344
Strachey, Sir John 216, 546
Strachey, Lytton 18, 297
Straits Settlements, The (Turnbull) 414

Strange Death of Liberal England, The (Dangerfield) 17
Strangers at the Gate (Wakeman) 398
Strangling of Persia, The (Shuster) 619
Stratigos, S. *see* Coppell
Stretton, Hugh 660
Strobel, Margaret 509, 665
Strong, William E. 305 n.
Structure of Scientific Revolutions, The (Kuhn) 267
Stuart, James 521
Stubbs, Richard 412
Stubbs, William 7 n., 8, 34
Studies in Colonial Nationalism (Jebb) 15
Studies in Mid-Victorian Imperialism (Bodelsen) 385
Study on the Historiography of the British West Indies . . . , A (Goveia) 135–6
Subaltern Studies (Guha) 222, 224–5, 229, 286, 376, 598 n., 600 n., 601–2, 603 n., 608, 649 n., 662–3
Suez 1956 (Louis and Owen) 432
Sufi, Ghulam Muhayyaddin 255
Sugar and Slavery (Sheridan) 319
Suleri, Sara 658
Sureri, Zia-ud-din-Ahmad 255
Sulte, Benjamin 150
Sulu and Sabah (Tarling) 410
Sulu Zone, The (Warren) 414
Sumida, Jon Tetsuro 332, 338
Summers, Anne 178 n.
Sun Yat-sen 386–7
Sundkler, Bengt 308–9
Supple, Barry 4
Survey of British Commonwealth Affairs (Hancock/Mansergh) 29, 30, 33, 127, 173, 356–7, 360, 520, 560, 561
Survival in Two Worlds (Thompson) 538
Sutch, W. B. 187, 360
Sutherland, Lucy 32, 34–5, 202
Swain, Tony, and Rose, Deborah Bird 313
Sweetman, John 579
Swettenham, Sir Frank 406
Swift, Roger 131
Sykes, Christopher 629
Sykes, Sir Percy 294
Symonds, Richard 255, 256

Talib, Sharahil 414
Talbot, Ian 239 n.
Tanganyika Notes and Records (journal) 503
Tara Chand 216
Tarling, Nicholas 408, 409, 410, 413, 414
Tasie, G. O. M. 312 n.
Tate, Thad W. 83 n.
Tawney, R. H. 613, 621
Taylor, A. J. P. 4, 363–4, 454, 470, 616
Taylor, Elizabeth 293
Taylor, Dora 523
Taylor, John 506
Taylor, Paul 566
Taylor, Robert H. 411
Te Rangi Hiroa (Sir Peter Buck) 188
Tea for the British (Forrest) 251
Teak Wallah (Campbell) 619
Telscher, Kate 603 n.
Temperley, Harold 470, 620, 633 *see also* Gooch
Temperley, Howard 324, 453 n.
Tennent, Sir James Emerson 243–4
Tennyson, Charles 568
Testing the Chains (Craton) 320
Textile Manufacturers . . . , The (Watson) 572
Theal, G. M. 58, 513–14, 515
Thistle and Bamboo (Airlie) 392–3
Thimme, F. *see* Lepsius
Thio, Eunice 408
Thomas, G. C. Rajiv 241
Thom, H. B. 523 n.
Thomas, Nicholas 377
Thomas, P. D. G. 82 n., 97
Thomas, Sir Shenton 26 n.
Thompson, Edward 619
Thompson, Edward, and Garratt, G. T. 25–6, 59, 198–9 n., 214
Thompson, E. P. 69
Thompson, Joseph 292
Thompson, Leonard 38, 514, 524, 529, 530–1, 538, 539 *see also* Wilson
Thompson, Roger 373
Thomson, David 298
Thorne, Christopher 412
Thornton, A. P. 38, 44, 657
Thornton, Lynne 578 n.
Thornton, Richard 296
Three Hundred Years (Jaffe) 523
Three White Rajas, The (Runciman) 409
Throup, David 511
Tides of Empire (Graham) 333
Tiffin, Helen *see* Brydon
Tikao Talks 184
Time Longer than Rope (Roux) 522
Times, The 13, 23, 28, 122, 393, 500–1
Tinker, Hugh 62 n., 232, 235, 249, 257, 362, 411, 413, 555 n.
Tinker, Tailor, Textile Worker (Goldberg) 428
To Change China (Spence) 398
Todd, John 270
Toit du, Revd., Hoogenhout, C. P., and Malherbe, Gideon 58 n.
Tomlinson, B. R. 236, 241
Tordoff, William 478
Toynbee, Arnold 29, 560
Trade and Administration of the Chinese Empire, The (Morse) 381

Trade and Diplomacy on the China Coast (Fairbank) 395–6
Trade, Plunder, and Settlement (Andrews) 620
Trading World of Asia . . . , The (Chaudhuri) 46
Transactions of the Royal Historical Society (journal) 131
Transfer of Power, 1942–7, The (Mansergh; Lumby; Moon) 231, 234, 237, 257, 362, 413, 555
Transformation of Virginia, 1740–1790, The (Isaac) 105
Transforming the Crown (Sirman) 581
Translation of the Seir-ul Mutagherin, A (Golham Hossein Khan Tabatabai) 196
Transvaal from Within, The (Fitzpatrick) 619
Tregonning, K. G. 408
Trevelyan, G. O. 210
Trevelyan, G. M. 628
Trevor, Daphne 469–70
Trevor-Roper, Hugh (Lord Dacre) 38
Trocki, Carl 410, 414
Trollope, Anthony 167
Tropical Africa in World History (Batten) 490
Tsang, Steve Yui-sang 394
Tsiang, T. F. 396
Tuchman, Barbara W. 96, 97
Tuck-hong Tang, James 395
Tucker, Robert W., and Hendrickson, David C. 99, 100 n.
Tuckey, J. H. 164–5
Tuker, Sir Francis 255, 256
Tulchin, Joseph S. 447 n.
Tully, Alan 105
Tunstall, W. C. B. 343
Turnbull, C. M. (Mary) 414
Turner, Frank 267
Turner, Frederick Jackson 662
Turner, Harold 309 n.
Turner, Henry Gyles 167
Turner, Mary 320, 321
Turning Point in Africa, The (Pearce) 361
Turnour, George 243
Turshen, Meredeth 278 n.
Tuma, A. D. Tom 312 n.
Twaddle, Michael 507
Twain, Mark 628
Twentieth Century Malaysia (Ghosh) 414
Twilight of the Mughals (Spear) 204
Twomey, Paul 358
Tyranny of Distance, The (Blainey) 662

Uganda Journal, The 503
Underhill, Frank 14, 153
Uneasy Partnership on Cyprus, The (McHenry) 433
Unequal Treaty, 1898–1997 (Wesley-Smith) 394
UNESCO General History of the Caribbean 137, 460
UNESCO see *Africa Under Colonial Domination* 460
Unhappy Valley (Berman and Londsale) 554
Universal Suffrage, 1931–1981 (de Silva) 249
Unresolved Question, The (Mansergh) 131
Upton, Dell 594
Usner, Daniel H. 90 n.
Uzoigwe, Godfrey 458, 460

Vail, Leroy 537, 539 n.
Valentine, D. B. 413
van der Horst, Sheila 521, 522
van der Merwe, P. J. 523
Van der Poel, Jean 455 n., 524
Van der Veer, Peter 212
van Leur, J. C. 404, 409
van Onselen, Charles 535
van Warmelo, N. J. 522
Vandeleur, S. 451
Vanguard to Trident (Grove) 339
Vatcher Jr., W. H. 359
Vaughan, Megan 273, 280 *see also* Moore, H.
Vaughan, W. E. 121
Vella, W. F. 410
Vereté, Mayir 429 n.
Verwey, E. J. 539 n.
Viceroy at Bay, The (Glendevon) 233
Vishwanath, Gauri 211
Voigt, Johannes H. 234
von Ranke, Leopold 2, 8
Vovage of the Endeavour, The (Frost) 336
Voyages (Hawkesworth) 368
Voyages to the West (Bailyn) 70, 87

Wadell, D. A. G. 134–5
Wagner, Ulla 410
Wah, Yeo Kim 414
Waiko, John 371–2
Wainwright, A. Martin 235–6
Wainwright, Mary Doreen *see* Philips
Wakeman Jr., Frederic 398
Waley, Arthur 388
Walker, Eric A. 32, 517–18, 622
Walker, Ranginui 188
Walking in the Shade (Lessing) 633
Wallace, Hugh 337
Wallestein, Immanuel 251, 493, 549, 642
Wallis, J. P. R. 295
Walsh, Judith 223
Walsh, W. H. 628
Walvin, James 300, 324
Waverley (Scott) 617
War and Diplomacy in Indonesia (Lee) 413
War and Politics in China (Pratt) 387
War and Trade in the West Indies (Pares) 32, 35

War at Sea, The (Roskill) 332, 339
War at Sea Under Queen Anne, 1702–1708 (Owen) 329
War in the Desert (Glubb) 426
War of Steel and Gold, The (Brailsford) 17, 453
Ward, J. M. 177, 366
Ward, J. R. 319, 324
Ward, Russell 173
Warning from the West Indies (Macmillan) 25
Warren, James 414
Washbrook, D. A. 218
Wasserstein, Bernard 429, 431, 617
Watson, A. *see* Bull
Watson, Don 179
Watson, J. Forbes 572
Watson, Dr Frederick 169
Watt, D. C. 346, 357
Wavell: The Viceroy's Journal (Moon) 234
Waverley (Scott) 617
Wayfoong (Collis) 395
Wealth and Poverty of Nations, The (Landes) 661
Wealth of Nations, The (Smith) 46
Weary Titan, The (Friedberg) 348
Webb, Stephen Saunders 49, 84–5
Webster, C. K. 439 n.
Webster, Donald Blake 577
Wehrle, Edmund S. 398
Wei Peh-T'i, Betty 398
Wei Yuan 381
Welfare and Planning in the West Indies (Simey) 613
Welsh, David 537
Welsh, Frank 395
Welsh and Scottish Nationalism (Coupland) 24
Wentworth, William 165
Wesley-Smith, Peter 394
West, Francis 373 n.
West, John 166
West, Katherine 569
West, Rebecca 617
Westerkamp, Marilyn J. 88 n.
Western Malay States, 1850–1873 (Kho Kay Kim) 408
Western Women and Imperialism (Strobel and Chaudhuri) 665
Westgarth, William 167
Wheare, Joan 480
Wheare, Sir Kenneth 27, 28, 127
Wheel of Empire, The (Sandison) 658
Wheeler, J. Talboys 198 n.
While Memory Serves (Tuker) 255
White, Deborah Gray 322
White, John 571
White, Landeg 278 n., 538, 539 n.
White, Luise 509–10
White, Richard 90 n., 178–9, 664
White Cargo (film) 630
White Ensign, The (Roskill) 332
White Man's Country (Huxley) 502
Why Pakistan? (Rahman) 255
Wickremeratne, Ananda 250
Wickwire, Franklin B. 82 n.
Wight, Martin 480
Wigley, Philip G. 158
Wilkins, Mira, and Schröter, Harm G. 448 n.
Wilkinson, Spenser 342
Wilks, Mark 194
Willard, Myra 171 n.
Williams, Basil 518 n.
Williams, Eric 23, 24, 136, 139, 323–5
Williams, Glyndwr 38
Williams, Judith Blow 467
Williams, Raymond 607
Williams, Rhodri 345 n.
Williamson, J. A. 294, 335 n., 620
Willoughby, Westel W. 382
Wilmot, Alexander 513, 514, 515
Wilson, Sir Arnold 424, 618
Wilson, Godfrey 522
Wilson, John L. 463 n.
Wilson, Mary C. 430 n.
Wilson, Monica 529, 530
Wilson, Monica and Thompson, Leonard M. 530
Windstedt, Sir Richard 406
Winius, George Davison 247
Wiremu Maihi Te Rangikaheke 183
Wise, Norton 274
Wise, S. F. 160
Wolf, Eric R. 663
Wolpert, Stanley 238
Women and the British Empire (Bailey) 665
Women Against Slavery (Midgley) 324
Women of Botany Bay, The (Robinson) 175
Wong, John Y. 67 n., 388
Wood, George Arnold 170, 293
Wood, Gordon 107, 109
Wood, Peter 319, 320
Wood, W. A. R. 383
Woods, F. L. W. 359
Woodward, Llewellyn 3 n.
Woodward, Sandy 339
Woolf, Leonard 20, 21, 250, 453, 469
Woolf, Virginia 469
Worboys, Michael 273, 283
Worden, Nigel 316 n., 539 n.
Worden, Nigel, and Crais, C. 316 n.
Worger, William H. 533 n., 535
Workers on the Nile (Beinin and Lockman) 428
Wormell, Deborah 8 n.
Worster, Donald 664
Wretched of the Earth, The (Fanon) 656
Wriggens, Howard *see* de Silva
Wright, Harrison 188

Wright, L. R. 410
Wright, Marcia 507
Wright, Stanley F. 384
Wright, Winthrop R. 448
Wrigley, C. C. 478, 505
Writing on the Wall, The (Andrews) 357
Wrong, George M. 147, 150, 153
Wyndham, Hugh Archibald 467 n.

Yapp, M. E. 417 n.
Yong, C. F. 414
Young, Alfred F. 104, 109
Young, G. M. 612, 614, 659
Young, Leonard K. 389
Young, Michael 376
Young Man's Country, A (Saumarez Smith) 220

Zen, Sun E-tu 396
Ziegler, Philip 240, 241
Zook, George 466
Zuckerman, Michael 83 n., 88 n., 111
Zulu Aftermath, The (Omer-Cooper) 529